Canadian Tax Paper No. 85

SO-AXM-204

A FISCAL HISTORY OF CANADA— THE POSTWAR YEARS

J. Harvey Perry

Canadian Tax Foundation
L'Association Canadienne
d'Études Fiscales

Canadian Cataloguing in Publication Data

Perry, J. Harvey, 1912-
   A fiscal history of Canada

Bibliography: p.
Includes index.
ISBN 0-88808-038-7

1. Fiscal policy - Canada - 20th century.
2. Canada - Economic policy 1945-
I. Canadian Tax Foundation.   II. Title.

HJ793.P47   1989   336.71   C89-094398-2

Preface

Of several large writing projects I have undertaken from time to time in my career this turned out to be the most formidable, giving me frequent cause to ask myself why I had undertaken it. Put it down to an inability to resist the lure of a phenomenon as challenging as the massive growth of government in the postwar period, one of the fascinating features of the twentieth century. I had traced the main Canadian fiscal developments to the end of World War II in *Taxes, Tariffs, and Subsidies* and had been more than a bystander to events of the following four decades. The rest of the story remained to be told, and offered an irresistible challenge.

Not that it had been neglected by any means; in the last quarter-century the output of Canadian writing on fiscal and economic issues has been monumental. But what appeared to me to be lacking was a consistent overview of the whole period, one of the most complex and significant in Canadian history.

Inevitably the centrepiece was the federal government, in view of its dominant influence. The momentum it had gathered from its role in World War II was augmented by its postwar adoption of centralized economic management in the Keynesian model; its efforts to contain endemic inflation and cope with almost chronic unemployment; its initiation of massive social programs of universal application; its fiscal manoeuvres to harmonize taxes, equate revenue yields among all governments, and periodically reform the tax system; its active support of policies to encourage international trade, and its initiatives in many other areas. And of course in the end its massive deficit was the shocking and historic landmark of the Canadian financial scene. But as part of the mosaic the provinces could by no means be neglected. To give them fair treatment would have required another book as large as this one, but they receive enough attention to portray their key role in the governmental system.

My main objective has been simply to record the principal events of the period. This has meant organizing a mass of complicated concepts and data to produce an informative, reasonably understandable and readable narrative, a greater challenge than may appear. For one, the paucity of the fiscal vocabulary was a constant handicap; even the thesaurus gives little help. By contrast, the rapid and unpredictable changes in the context was a daily challenge to exposition. In the five years since writing started these have included free trade, tax reform, defence renewal, collapsed oil prices, massive federal deficits, etc. etc., none in evidence at the beginning. What has been equally troublesome is that nearly every important data series I was using as a base for much of the analysis was changed in mid-stream by revisions of Statistics Canada and the Department of Finance. These are the hazards in any writing in the field of government and must be dealt with as one best can. But they do not make a difficult job any easier.

While there are occasional observations throughout the book on individual developments it seems fair to question whether the author has not formed some general views after five years of close study of the period. The following are offered as purely personal and subjective observations.

The central issue of the times—the peacetime role of government—was by no means unique, but for several reasons took on special meaning at this particular juncture in history. At the conclusion of World War II governments everywhere, rather than reverting to their prewar roles, retained a large element of the control they had assumed during the conflict. There were several reasons for this. For one, the cold war period meant continuing with a major defence program. Defence was the largest expenditure of government in Canada during the fifties. Another was the fear of a repetition of the Great Depression of the thirties. The solution was to be the interventionist role for the state proposed by the brilliant English economist J.M. Keynes, whose ideas were more influential than those of almost any economist since Adam Smith. There was also the general feeling that the brutal depression and war were the product of a system that fell far short of the ideal. Changes had to be made.

It appears in retrospect that there are few absolutes in this area; the past four decades reveal mainly pragmatic changes motivated by practical experience. Initially economists of Keynesian persuasion had an astonishing influence on Canadian governmental economic policy. But in the end Keynes turned out to be fallible, and no single economist or school of economics emerged to replace him. And the devastating effects of inflation and unemployment ultimately led to disillusionment with interventionist policies. Combined with the massive deficits that accompanied the later years of the period the trend has been towards a reduced role for government. But it must be quickly added, not to broad rejection of all government action. For many purposes the general Canadian public appears to have as strong an appetite for it as ever.

This appetite is most apparent in social programs. Canada finally abandoned its eighteenth century austerity in social policy and roughly caught up with most of the rest of the world, and there are few areas now without a program. As a result the crucial decision to be faced in the 1990s is what share of hard-pressed budgets should go to these programs and—even more contentious—how the competing demands of different interests are to be reconciled. All this is overshadowed by the fatal flaw of the welfare state— the firm conviction among its beneficiaries that all increases should be at the expense of others; "others" of course being taxpayers now devoting an inordinate effort to minimizing their tax liabilities. This confrontation, along with the general conviction that any reduction in lifestyle would be intolerable, presents a grim prospect for further deficit reduction.

And then there is the plague of inflation. The Canadian experience, mild as it was compared to many other countries, clearly nominates it as the most devastating of the social enemies. Its effects are enduring and inescapable. Inflation was largely responsible for the chaos of government finances over the last decade and we will continue to bear its cost for many years.

On the subject of authorship; while I personally carried out most of the research and writing for this book (thanks to my word-processor) my indebtedness to others is very heavy. I have drawn extensively on the work of the growing number of tax practitioners, academics, journalists and others now concerned with governmental financial and economic issues, and gratefully acknowledge my obligation to them. I have also made heavy use of publications of several research organizations, of official sources and the many excellent studies produced by the Canadian Tax Foundation.

Helpful assistance has been given by the Foundation staff. The Director has followed the project with interest, the library staff has assisted in various ways, and members of the research staff, in particular David Perry and Mary Gurney, have been unfailing in their assistance, the latter having undertaken the onerous task of editing and checking the final manuscript. I would also thank an unnamed reader for his valuable comments.

As my wife looked forward to years of travel and the usual occupations of retirement and has been forced to defer these hopes while I wrestled with this monster I must thank her for her patience and understanding.

Readers of *Unfinished Business*, my last previous publication, will appreciate that the chapters on defence and trade it contained have been updated and embodied in the current publication. This treatment has resulted in some loss of editorial nicety, but this has not detracted seriously from the narrative. Finally, in order to stem the flow at a convenient period for last-minute updating and rewriting a general deadline of mid-1988 was imposed, but where crucial subsequent events have transpired, such as the fall federal election, these have been briefly noted.

J. Harvey Perry

Prologue

New Role of the State

The state as an identifiable political entity is probably no more than three thousand years old (or thereabouts), a short span in the history of humanity. But in that time it has supplanted nearly all other institutions as the dominant influence on the life and times of its people. And this has seldom been more evident than in the twentieth century. In postwar Canada government has assumed a role radically different in its relations with individual citizens than in any previous time.

The origins of this development are not entirely clear. Certainly the active role forced upon government during two world wars and the massive depression of the thirties not only created a new and more receptive environment toward governmental intervention but as well provided a demonstration of goal accomplishment through this means. Wars and human tragedy also appear to leave a heritage of compassion, which no doubt played a large role in the adoption of humanitarian programs since mid-century. Philosophically of course there was also the emergence of the Marxian ethic, always a challenge to a capitalist based society. The author can recall the genuine concern of people of his generation, following the harrowing experiences of the Great Depression, that the Canadian social and political structure, always fragile at best, might not survive a repetition of this experience. In a frame of mind that was as much pragmatic as philosophical, a generation that had keen and painful memories of the previous two decades, faced an uncertain world in 1945 with a strong determination that these devastating experiences should not be allowed to recur. This view was shared by leaders in many countries. This objective would have to be a primary responsibility of government, aided and supported by whatever other organizations were required to implement it. Action would be necessary at both the international and individual country levels. For the former, world organizations would have to be established to foster international peace, enhance world trade, and promote economic growth and the relief of human distress. For the latter it would be necessary for the governments of individual countries to adopt programs with the same general objectives. The so-called "welfare state" was the embodiment of these programs, and "Keynesian economics" the guiding spirit for economic growth.

International

In the international sphere permanent organizations were established under the United Nations and other auspices which have made substantial contributions in their own areas. These included the International Monetary Fund, the World Bank, and the General Agreement on Tariffs and Trade (GATT). Apart from their actions of substance these and similar organizations provide a regular channel for communication, consultation, and compromise. As a result, in economic matters such as trade, foreign indebtedness and currency problems, there is today a much stronger compulsion to find constructive solutions by cooperation than half a century ago. The most devastating shortfall in expectations has been the international tension in the postwar years, with its constant threat of massive armed conflict. For Canada, in view of its exposed position between the two contending world powers, the achievement of an appropriate role has been a perpetual dilemma and has required the maintenance of a peacetime military establishment, an unhappy experience for this peaceable country.

National

Canada adopted the new role for government without reservation, and admittedly with mixed results. On the positive side the postwar period included some of the best years in Canadian peacetime history. Population doubled, there were several years of nearly full employment, cities and towns were renewed and revitalized, new homes, hospitals, universities, schools, super-highways and airports were built, resources were developed, Canadian products were exported in volume to the rest of the world, Canadian culture was strengthened, living standards rose markedly (two-car families, radio, TV, travel, advanced education, etc.). A range of social measures was introduced which gave the country a well rounded program as a complement to activist government measures designed to maintain economic growth.

On the negative side there were serious shortfalls. The "welfare state" has been the source of almost continuous controversy. Its implementation has been criticized as being either excessive or inadequate, and on either account many problems have been laid at its door. The management of the economy has also failed to meet expectations. Inflation has been almost chronic since the end of World War II and there have been frequent lapses in economic performance with higher levels of inflation and unemployment accompanying each recurrence, all culminating in the dismal combination of the unemployment and inflation of the last decade. To this distasteful brew there lately has been added unprecedented government deficits, an outcome that has definitely lessened convictions regarding the merits of the interventionist role of government; in this area, a re-examination is underway.

We will be reviewing much of the record of the failures and achievements of the new approach in the following pages. The main purpose is to provide an uncluttered view of what has happened, with fairly detailed but non-technical descriptions of the main developments in taxation and fiscal policy, social welfare, tariffs and trade, intergovernmental finances, defence, and education. But first there will be some introductory chapters for general background before launching into this detailed examination.

The Canadian People

Between 1946 and 1986 the population of Canada more than doubled, rising from 12.3 million to 25.4 million. In Canadian history this was a population leap, second only to that of 1900-15, when the west was opening. In total in the 1946-85 period 15.5 million babies were born and there were 5.8 million deaths of all ages, giving a net natural increase of 9.7 million; in addition, as is common with Canada, 5.3 million immigrants arrived and 2.2 million emigrants left, giving a net increase from abroad of 3.1 million. The net total increase was (1946-85) 12.8 million, 75 percent home-grown and 25 percent imported. Much of the domestic increase took place in the 1946-62 years, when the birth rate remained above 25 per thousand of population (in several years exceeding 28), one of the highest rates among industrialized countries. The immigration rate also was high during the fifties and, unlike several previous periods, an unprecedented proportion of the arrivals came to Canada to stay, attracted by the buoyant economy of that period.

High natural growth and heavy net gains from immigration gave a population growth rate of 2.7 percent between 1951 and 1961, compared to 1.4 percent before the war. Growth peaked in the early sixties. In 1963 the annual birth rate fell below 25 per thousand, and has been falling ever since, reaching 15 per thousand in the early eighties. The fertility rate (the number of children per female) dropped from the high level of 3.9 in 1959 to below 2.0 in the seventies. The replacement level that will maintain the total population is 2.1 children per woman; the actual rate fell below this figure in 1971, and has remained there since. As well, immigration has fallen to half that of the mid-fifties. As a result population growth has declined from the 2.7 percent per annum level in the fifties to 1.0 to 1.2 percent in recent years.

Declining population growth is evident from the following figures of increase over recent decades: 1951-60, 4.2 million; 1961-70, 3.4 million; 1971-80, 2.3 million. These are, respectively, average annual increases of 420,000, 340,000 and 230,000. The 1986 increase was 237,000, or less than 1 percent.

The Youth Bulge. The high birth rate of the fifties produced the well-known "baby boom." The addition of 6¼ million babies born after 1945 meant that over 40 percent of the population was under 20 years of age by 1960; over one-third was under 15 by that year. The forward passage of this "wave" through the social structure has already had profound effects, first on housing requirements, then on the educational system, later on the economy, and ultimately it will have an impact on health and retirement measures.

The consequences for the educational system were most acute. Elementary and secondary full-time school enrolment rose from 2.6 million in 1951 to a peak of 5.9 million in 1970, and has declined in each year since; it is now estimated at 4.9 million for 1987. However, post-secondary enrolment climbed steadily from 91,000 in 1951 to an estimated 795,000 in 1987, as older age students reached this level. Along with social services and health, education has been one of the most expensive outlays of government. From $393 million in 1950 total government outlays rose to $35 billion in 1987, accounting for about 12 percent of total government expenditure.

The effect of the wave on the employment market is apparent in the increased number of people of working age (20-64). The proportion rose from 50.6 percent of the population in 1961 to 55.4 percent in 1976 and will be an estimated 60 percent or more by the end of the century. Although growth in the labour force has been slowing in recent years this population pattern poses a challenge for future job creation, an acute one in view of the 1987 unemployment rate of about 8 percent.

As a result of a declining birth rate it is forecast that the youth bulge will have been reduced to 30 percent or less of the population by the end of the century. The succeeding bulge by then will be in grandfathers and grandmothers, but especially in grandmothers. In the last decade the female population for the first time in Canadian history has passed the male, and women are outliving men by seven years or more.

The Age Bulge. The proportion of the population aged 65 and over has been consistently growing, not just in recent years but since the beginning of the century. From 5 percent in 1901 the proportion rose to 8.7 percent in 1976; it is expected to reach 11-12 percent by the end of the century. Statistics Canada gave the following explanation for this phenomenon: "Three main reasons account for this relatively high growth. First, the early 1900s were marked by high birth rates of about 36.0 per 1,000 population. Since then there has been an over-all decline in birth rates, with ups and downs in its trends, reaching a low of 15.7 in 1976. The aging of persons born at the turn of the century has resulted in an increase in the proportion of 65+ to the total population. Second, between 1911 and 1931, 2.6 million immigrants arrived in this country. Their age on arrival generally ranged from 20 to 35 years. By now, most of these people are 65 and over. Third, medical advances, combined with significant improvements in the over-all standard of living, have increased average life expectancy by over 10 years (from 61 to about 73 years) between 1931 and 1971. This increase has contributed to the growing number of the elderly." One of the main contributing causes for the longer general life expectancy has been the dramatic fall in the death rate for females. Between 1921 and 1976, for example, in age groups 65-69 and 70-74 the death rate for men changed very little, but for females it dropped by at least half in both categories.

The growing proportion of aged in the population has already been reflected in the rising cost of pensions and medical and retirement facilities for the elderly. This rise will continue as the "baby-boom" generation moves into the higher ages in the early decades of the new century. By 2006 the 65+ proportion of the population is estimated to be 14.7 percent compared with 9.7 percent in 1981, and as a proportion of the elderly (over 65), those 85+ are projected at 11.8 percent compared to 8.2 percent in 1981.

Changing Character of Immigration. In the postwar decade the origin of immigrants coming to Canada underwent a radical change. Traditional European immigration declined to less than half its former role, and was replaced by arrivals of African, Indian, Oriental, Central and South American and Caribbean origin. Between 1956 and 1977 immigrants from the United Kingdom and Europe dropped from 88 to 35 percent of the total, while Indian and other Asian nationals rose from 2 percent to 27 percent, Caribbean from 1 percent to 10 percent, Central and South American from 1 percent to 8 percent and African from 0.4 percent to 5.5 percent. This statement will hardly be news for the older residents of some of the larger Canadian cities, where the presence of the new arrivals is quite evident. The impact on communities and educational systems has been acute, but the major adjustments appear to have been made by the early eighties.

Urban Living. In the postwar period Canada has become highly urbanized. More than three-quarters of Canadians now live in urban centres. Over half the population lives in centres of 100,000 or more; over one-quarter lives in three large metropolitan areas—Toronto, Montreal, and Vancouver. Toronto and Montreal are now at the 3 million level, and Vancouver is at 1¼ million. This growth has created many problems for local government, particularly in the provision of community facilities such as water, sanitation, education, and transportation.

Movement Between Provinces. In general there has been a western shift in population between provinces. Ontario has been the favourite for migrants leaving Quebec and the Eastern Provinces, while British Columbia and Alberta have both gained from inter-provincial movement, the former being the goal of many migrants from the prairies.

Economic Overview

It would be an exercise far beyond present purposes to give a detailed account of the postwar Canadian economy. It has a few features however that are essential background for this book.

In the four postwar decades there were years of intense—even spectacular—economic growth, but there were also recurrent slumps, the last and worst being that of the early eighties. Rapid population and income growth and high levels of investment alternated with bouts of inflation and unemployment, both finally culminating in stagflation, from which Canada was still recovering in the mid-eighties. Foreign trade remained a vital element in the Canadian economy, and was heavily influenced by the GATT tariff agreements and increasingly close ties with the United States. The labour market attempted with moderate success to cope with one of the heaviest population increases in the industrial world combined with a rapid rise in female participation, but had lost ground in the eighties, when unemployment still remained above normal levels. Furthermore, the economy had shown rigidities in adapting to rapidly changing international industrial developments. Some of these challenged past Canadian positions of resource superiority; others simply demonstrated that Canada had been slow in adopting new technologies.

Governments played a growing role in the economy in keeping with Keynesian precepts, but abnormally heavy deficits that accumulated as the period moved forward forced it to the sidelines where its efforts were limited largely to achieving fiscal respectability. We return to government policies later.

Basic data on key aspects of the economy are given in table 1, with data on growth rates in table 2, and on capital expenditure in table 3. See also tables in the appendix to this chapter.

On a superficial view statistics for the four decades seem to present a picture of continuous growth. From 1947 to 1987 the nominal gross national product increased in every year and rose from $13.5 billion to $537 billion, a forty-fold increase. The value of exports rose forty-seven-fold and capital expenditures forty-eight-fold, all seemingly indicative of a rapidly growing and prosperous country. Growth there was to be sure, but all was not well with the economy. Much of the apparent progress was the product of inflation, which we now examine.

Inflation

With two minor exceptions, since 1947 the Consumer Price Index has risen in every year above the previous year. Periods of particularly marked increase, when prices rose by 10, 20, or 30 percent, were 1945-48, 1951-53, 1967-70, and 1974-82, the last period far out-pacing all previous peacetime price records. Period by period there were causative factors. The removal of price ceilings and the return of boom economic conditions in the immediate postwar period, the effect of Korean war defence expenditures, the pressure of demand on resources during the intense period of prosperity in the sixties, the increase in petroleum and agricultural prices in the seventies and expansionary budget and monetary policies are listed among contributing factors, although the relative share of each is not agreed upon among economists.

Government took steps to cope with the worst situations—the Prices and Incomes Commission (1969-72), the Anti-Inflation Board (1975-78) and the voluntary 6 and 5 program of the June 1982 budget—but in the end it required a very severe dose of economic stringency to squeeze the water out of the price system.

Real Economic Change

The "real" facts on the postwar economy emerge only after removing the effects of inflation, and when this is done a remarkably different picture emerges. In table 4 the results are given at five-year intervals for the consumer price index and the implicit GNP price index; as well the table gives GNP and GNP per capita on both a current dollar and 1947 base.

While the above admittedly has some shortcomings as a precise statistical calculation, it is sufficient for present purposes; and its results are astonishing. The effect of deflating GNP for the nearly six-fold increase in prices between 1947 and 1985 is to reduce the nominal $462 billion figure for 1985 to $69 billion, a shrinkage of about 85 percent. Compared to $13.5 billion in 1947 this of course is still a quite remarkable five-fold rise in real GNP, but is a far remove from the unadjusted increase. A substantial growth in population in four decades further waters down the per capita real GNP, but even so the 150 percent rise in this figure over the same period is still quite substantial.

The deflation of current dollar GNP to approximately 15 percent of its nominal value is a dramatic revelation of the effect of price rises continued over a long period. However, a word of caution. It has become the fashion to label all price rises as inflation, without regard to the changing quality of the goods and services available. In truth, the food, clothing, automobiles, household appliances, etc. of 1987 are vastly different—and generally vastly improved—over those of 40 years ago, and this is reflected in higher prices. There were also "price shocks" during the seventies, such as the drastic petroleum price increases of 1973 and 1979, which would not qualify as inflation under some definitions.

While these observations are of some interest, they do not in any way diminish the fact that prices have risen dramatically over the last four decades. The result has been to create an almost constant problem for government in maintaining a stable economy free of the turmoil of unstable prices. Furthermore, the effect has been to distort all money values and create an inflationary illusion far removed from the "real" facts of the economy.

This inflation illusion can be offset by re-calculating the basic economic data to remove the price effect. Until recently this was done by freezing prices at 1971 levels, but the base for most series has now been moved forward to 1981. We will use such "constant dollar" figures shortly, but with the base retained at 1971 in order not to lose the impact of the inflation of the seventies. See table 5 for a comparison of nominal GNP and GNP at 1971 prices for the postwar period.

Economic Cycles

The general dilemma posed for government by inflation was aggravated by recurring booms and recessions in the economy. The booms were usually marked by shortages of men and materials and rapid price and wage rises. The worst of the declines were accompanied by calamitous unemployment, offering a severe challenge to the newly adopted role of economic management, especially as the effective instruments were national and the problems were frequently regional.

A brief introduction to the economic changes of the last four decades will assist in understanding postwar policy issues. For this purpose we will use mainly Gross National Product and its components in constant dollars, as this, rather than the Gross Domestic Product, now favoured, was the accepted measure over the last four decades. This is not a serious disadvantage, as differences between the two are not as great as was expected by commentators. Table 6 compares the results of the two bases. Tables 7 and 9 later give data on trends for the whole postwar period for the main economic indicators in 1971 values.

Table 1 Principal Economic Indicators, Current Dollars, 1947-87, Dollar Figures in Millions

Year[a]	Gross national product	Expenditure Goods and services			Capital as a % of GNP	Merchandise exports	Merchandise trade balance	Consumer price index 1981=100	Unemployment rate
		Personal	Government	Capital					
	$	$	$	$	%	$	$	$	%
1947	13.5	9.4	1.3	2.4	17.4	2.7	0.2	20.8	2.2
1948	15.5	10.4	1.5	3.1	19.7	3.0	0.4	23.8	2.3
1949	16.8	11.4	1.7	3.4	20.5	3.0	0.3	24.5	2.9
1950	18.5	12.5	1.9	3.9	20.9	3.1	—	25.2	3.6
1951	21.6	13.9	2.8	4.4	20.4	3.9	-0.2	27.8	2.4
1952	24.6	15.2	3.6	5.1	20.7	4.3	0.5	28.5	2.9
1953	25.8	16.2	3.8	5.7	22.2	4.2	-0.1	28.3	3.0
1954	25.9	16.9	3.8	5.7	22.0	3.9	—	28.4	4.6
1955	28.5	18.4	4.0	6.4	22.5	4.3	-0.2	28.5	4.4
1956	32.1	20.1	4.4	8.0	24.9	4.8	-0.7	28.9	3.4
1957	33.5	21.5	4.6	8.7	25.9	4.9	-0.6	29.8	4.6
1958	34.8	22.8	4.9	8.5	24.5	4.9	-0.2	30.6	7.1
1959	36.8	24.4	5.0	8.6	23.5	5.2	-0.4	31.0	6.0
1960	38.4	25.5	5.3	8.5	22.1	5.4	-0.1	31.4	7.0
1961	39.6	25.9	6.2	8.4	21.2	5.9	0.2	31.6	7.1
1962	42.9	27.5	6.6	8.9	20.7	6.4	0.2	32.0	5.9
1963	46.0	29.2	7.0	9.6	20.8	7.1	0.5	32.6	5.5
1964	50.3	31.4	7.6	11.2	22.3	8.2	0.7	33.2	4.7
1965	55.4	33.9	8.4	13.2	23.8	8.7	0.1	34.0	3.9
1966	61.8	36.9	9.7	15.4	24.8	10.3	0.3	35.2	3.6
1967	67.8	41.1	11.1	16.2	24.0	11.3	0.6	36.5	4.1
1968	74.2	44.8	12.7	16.5	22.2	13.7	1.5	38.0	4.8
1969	81.8	49.1	14.2	18.1	22.2	15.0	0.9	39.7	4.7

Cycles: 1946-1988

1946-49. The economy responded much more rapidly under peacetime conditions than had been anticipated. Heavy capital investment for industrial conversion and the spending of military severance pay and cashed-in wartime savings gave an immediate stimulus to the economy. Initial shortages in Canada were met mainly by imports from the United States, causing an outflow of U.S. dollars which, along with substantial lending to Great Britain, created a balance of payments problem. Quotas and taxes on U.S. imports had to be imposed in 1947 to cope with this situation.

Prices were erratic. Shortages and removal of the wartime price ceilings created a brief but damaging period of inflation in 1946-48, which substantially raised costs to the detriment of export trade. With completion of the conversion of Canadian plants to peacetime production prices and employment stabilized; unemployment averaged only 2.5 percent in 1947-49. This period henceforth remained a standard for potential levels of operation for the economy, but was never again achieved. The balance of payments was a problem of this era, and persisted for the whole of the postwar period.

1950-56. The period was one of relatively high growth, spurred by high personal expenditure and exceptional capital investment in resource development, (oil and minerals), housing, government outlays on defence (the Korean War), offices, schools, hospitals, highways, etc. As a percentage of GNP capital expenditure rose from 17.4 in 1947 to 24.9 in 1956, an increase of 43 percent and one of the highest rates in the four postwar decades. Korean War shortages precipitated a 10.3 percent inflation rate in 1951, but the index was then relatively stable, and even declined for two years, an exceptional phenomenon. Merchandise exports moved up strongly, rising by about two-thirds in 1950-56. Two weak years—1953 and 1954—fell below the average growth of the period, but were followed by an upsurge in 1955 and 1956. Employment showed growth, but not enough to avoid an increase to an average unemployment rate of 3.6 percent in 1950-56, 44 percent higher than the 1946-49 period. Prices resumed their rise, and by 1956 the CPI was 39 percent above 1947.

1957-61. There was a definite slowing up during this period. Despite a modest expansion in 1958-59 growth rates were one-third to one-half those of the early fifties. Capital expenditures were temporarily buoyant in 1957, reaching 25.9 percent of GNP, the highest postwar year, but declined sharply to 21 percent in 1961. Unemployment was severe. In three of the five years it exceeded 7 percent and averaged 6.4 percent, a rate 78 percent higher than the previous period. Such levels were not to be seen again until the seventies and eighties, and were blamed partly on the very high immigration of the fifties, which had temporarily overloaded the labour market in a declining economy. Exports were sluggish, a state attributed to a decline in the U.S. economy, the level of Canadian costs, including high interest rates, and an over-priced Canadian dollar. The Consumer Price Index continued its upward rise.

1962-66. In a dramatic rebound from the stagnant late fifties Canada entered what was almost a golden age for the economy. Increases in real

GNP exceeded 6½ percent in all years but one; personal expenditure rose rapidly with higher incomes and capital expenditures reached very high levels. Unemployment declined to a low of 3.6 percent in 1966, making this one of the best postwar years. But the Consumer Price Index continued to rise; by 1966 it was up 70 percent from 1947.

1967-73. Except for the onset of serious inflation this period might well be regarded as a continuation of the previous very prosperous years. Real growth was in the 5-7 percent range, except for below average performances in 1967 and 1970. Although capital expenditures were relatively stable the increases in 1971 and 1973 were exceptional. The negative feature was the beginning of the price inflation that was to plague the economy during the seventies, accompanied by rising unemployment. The inflation rate was over 4 percent in four years, and reached 7.6 percent in 1973. Unemployment exceeded 6 percent in 1971 and 1972. The period closed with the first petroleum price increase.

1974-81. Energy, inflation, and unemployment were the unhappy themes of the late seventies and early eighties, and absorbed most of the attention of governments. Inflation of unprecedented severity resisted all efforts to combat it. Starting from 10.9 percent in 1974 the Anti-Inflation Board and other measures succeeded in reducing the level to 7.5 to 8 percent, but this was temporary. The upward trend soon reappeared, and, further stimulated by the 1979 oil price increase, rose to a peak of 12.5 percent in 1981. Meantime, unemployment had also been rising, exceeding 8 percent in 1977 and 1978, but dropping moderately to 7.5 percent in 1981. The calamitous climax of the period was the recession of 1981, when for the first time in the postwar years the GNP actually declined in real terms—by 4.4 percent. The economy was virtually brought to its knees by interest rates in the twenties and severe money supply restrictions designed to crush inflation. The goal was achieved, but at severe cost.

One of the oddities of the seventies was a spectacular housing boom. In 1976 housing starts reached an unprecedented level (273,000) followed by two further robust years (1977, 246,000; 1978, 228,000), a little light in an otherwise dismal period. There will be more to say about it later.

1982-85. Recovery from this bruising experience took the next two or three years. The first encouraging signs were a modest real growth of 3.3 percent in 1982 and a decline in inflation to 5.8 percent. Healthy increases in GNP of 5.0 percent in 1984 and 4.4 percent in 1985 followed, and inflation dropped to the 4-5 percent level. Exports had been buoyant, particularly in the 1983-85 period.

But there were other less welcome signs. Unemployment rose sharply from 7.5 percent in 1981 to 11 percent in 1982; then to 11.9 percent in 1983, followed by 11.4 percent in 1984. 1985 was slightly better at 10.5 percent. As a result of a drastic drop in housing starts and business outlays, capital expenditure reached a postwar low of 19.6 percent of GNP in 1984.

1986-88. Increases in real GNP (now GDP) were 3.3 percent in 1986 and 3.8 percent in 1987, with 2.8 percent forecast by the Department of Finance for 1988. These were greater increases than were being experienced by any other country of the Group of Seven. Investment expenditure was expected to be a buoyant element, with heavy housing starts and, according to a mid-1988 survey, a rise of 20 percent in business investment. Employment increased by a remarkable 955,000 between 1984 and 1987, dropping the unemployment rate from 11.3 percent to 8.9 percent for 1987, with a further decline below 8 percent in early 1988. Nonetheless in 1988 there were still over one million persons on unemployment insurance rolls.

The inflation rate was 4.4 percent in 1987 but was expected to be 4.0 percent in 1988. But the threat of renewed price rises, with the U.S. economy approaching full capacity, was dictating a cautious monetary policy in both Canada and the U.S., with interest rates being held at levels above those of recent years. There were marked differences in regional recovery. The Ontario economy, and to a lesser degree the Quebec, were undergoing a boom, with unemployment in the Toronto area in the 4-5 percent range. But the western provinces were facing drought and declining grain prices and Alberta and Saskatchewan were suffering from the low and precarious state of oil prices. All depressed regions were complaining of the discouraging effect of high interest rates required to cope with economic pressures in the buoyant parts of the economy, an age old complaint, to which the central bank can only give its age old response that it is impossible to have regional monetary policies. And always in the background is the concern over the general state of government budgets, all with high deficits, and the unknown effects of free trade, still very much in the air at mid-1988.

International Trade

In view of their central role in Canada's economy international influences call for some special comment.

Growing Role of Trade. The increasing share of Canadian activity originating in international trade was a central feature of the postwar period. As a ratio of GNP it rose from 16-18 percent in 1950-65 to over 20 percent in 1967 and to a range of 22 to 26 percent ever since, with all years exceeding 26 percent from 1982 on. Increased trade in autos and parts following the 1965 Auto Pact accounted for some of this, and the decline of the Canadian dollar assisted many other exports, particularly of manufactured products.

Table 10 gives U.S.-Canadian dollar values for 1947-87. In the 1948-51 period the range was: 1949, 97 cents; 1950, 92 cents; 1951, 95 cents. From 1952 to 1960 it was in the $1.02 to $1.04 area, dropped to 99 cents in 1961, and following action taken by the government was held at approximately 93 cents from 1962 to 1970. It rose to 96 cents in 1970 and to 99 cents in 1971, following which it held close to par until 1976. In 1977 it commenced a decline that carried it to a historic low point of 71 cents in January, 1986. From this bottom the value has moved up, accelerating in 1987 and 1988 to a level of 80-82 cents in mid-1988.

Table 7　Principal Economic Indicators, 1971 Dollars, 1947-85

Year[a]	GNP	Expenditure					Consumer price index		Unemployment rate
		Goods and services							
		Personal	Government	Capital	Export of goods and services	Import of goods and services	1981 base[b]	1971 base[c]	
		billions of dollars							%
1947	29.5	18.6	4.7	5.3	6.2	−6.4	20.8	49.3	2.2
1948	30.2	18.1	4.5	6.1	6.4	−5.8	23.8	56.4	2.3
1949	31.4	19.1	5.0	6.6	6.0	−5.9	24.5	58.0	2.9
1950	33.8	20.4	5.4	7.0	6.0	−6.5	25.2	59.7	3.6
1951	35.5	20.5	7.0	7.1	6.5	−7.3	27.8	65.9	2.4
1952	38.6	22.0	8.6	7.9	7.3	−7.5	28.5	67.5	2.9
1953	40.6	23.5	8.9	8.9	7.2	−8.2	28.3	67.0	3.0
1954	40.1	24.4	8.5	8.9	6.9	−7.8	28.4	67.3	4.6
1955	43.9	26.5	8.7	9.7	7.4	−8.8	28.5	67.5	4.4
1956	47.6	28.4	9.0	11.4	8.0	−10.2	28.9	68.5	3.4
1957	48.7	29.5	8.8	12.3	8.1	−10.1	29.8	70.6	4.6
1958	49.8	30.6	9.1	12.1	8.0	−9.4	30.6	72.5	7.1
1959	51.7	32.3	9.0	12.2	8.4	−10.4	31.0	73.5	6.0
1960	53.2	33.4	9.2	11.8	8.7	−10.3	31.4	74.4	7.0
1961	54.7	33.8	10.5	11.7	9.4	−10.6	31.6	74.9	7.1
1962	58.5	35.3	10.9	12.3	9.7	−10.8	32.0	75.8	5.9
1963	61.5	37.0	11.1	12.8	10.6	−11.1	32.6	77.2	5.5
1964	65.6	39.2	11.6	14.5	12.1	−12.6	33.2	78.6	4.7
1965	70.0	41.6	12.3	16.3	12.6	−14.1	34.0	80.5	3.9
1966	73.8	43.8	13.4	18.0	14.3	−16.0	35.2	83.5	3.6
1967	77.3	45.9	14.3	17.9	15.8	−16.8	36.5	86.5	4.1
1968	81.9	48.1	15.4	18.0	17.7	−18.3	38.0	90.0	4.8
1969	86.2	50.4	16.0	18.9	19.5	−20.7	39.7	94.1	4.7

Year									
1970	88.4	51.5	17.7	18.9	21.2	−20.6	41.0	97.2	5.9
1971	94.5	55.6	18.4	20.8	22.2	−22.0	42.2	100.0	6.4
1972	100.2	59.8	18.9	22.0	23.7	−24.5	44.2	104.8	6.2
1973	107.8	63.9	19.8	24.4	26.2	−27.8	47.6	112.8	5.5
1974	111.7	67.2	20.6	25.7	25.6	−30.5	52.8	125.0	5.3
1975	113.0	70.6	21.4	26.7	24.0	−29.7	58.5	138.5	6.9
1976	119.6	75.2	21.6	27.7	26.3	−32.3	62.9	148.9	7.1
1977	122.0	77.0	22.3	27.6	28.2	−32.8	67.9	160.8	8.1
1978	126.3	79.0	22.7	27.6	31.2	−34.3	73.9	175.1	8.3
1979	130.4	80.6	22.8	29.4	32.1	−36.7	80.7	191.2	7.4
1980	131.7	81.4	22.9	30.6	32.8	−35.9	88.9	210.7	7.5
1981	136.1	83.0	23.1	32.6	33.7	−37.3	100.0	237.0	7.5
1982	130.1	81.2	23.2	28.8	33.2	−33.1	110.8	262.6	11.0
1983	134.4	83.7	23.7	27.6	35.3	−35.9	117.2	277.8	11.9
1984	141.1	86.8	24.4	27.8	42.2	−41.0	122.3	289.9	11.3
1985	147.4	91.3	24.9	29.7	44.1	−43.7	127.2	301.5	10.5

Note: National Accounts figures on revised basis for 1981-85. 1985 is the last year for official figures on 1971 price base. [a]Calendar year. [b]1981 = 100. [c]1947 to 1960 and 1980 to 1985 obtained by conversion of 1981 base series.

Sources: Canada, Department of Finance, *Economic Review* April 1985; Statistics Canada, *National Income and Expenditure Accounts*, Fourth Quarter, 1986; Bank of Canada *Monthly Review: Historical Statistics of Canada.*

Table 8   Annual Rates of Change in Principal Economic Indicators, 1971 Dollars, 1948-85

Year	GNP	Goods and services Personal	Goods and services Government	Capital	Export of goods and services	Import of goods and services	Consumer price index 1981 base	Consumer price index 1971 base	Unemployment rate
		percent change							*point change*
1948	2.5	-2.4	-5.1	14.8	3.3	-9.8	14.4	14.4	0.1
1949	3.8	5.7	10.6	7.4	-5.9	2.7	2.9	2.8	0.6
1950	7.6	6.6	7.7	7.5	-0.7	8.9	2.9	2.9	0.7
1951	5.0	0.8	30.4	0.4	9.4	12.5	10.3	10.4	-1.2
1952	8.9	7.0	23.2	11.7	11.5	3.4	2.5	2.4	0.5
1953	5.2	7.0	3.1	12.3	-1.0	8.3	-0.7	-1.0	0.1
1954	-1.2	3.7	-3.8	—	-3.7	-4.8	0.4	0.4	1.6
1955	9.4	8.5	2.2	9.3	7.6	13.4	0.3	0.3	-0.2
1956	8.5	7.5	2.5	18.3	7.5	16.1	1.4	1.5	1.0
1957	2.4	3.7	-1.7	7.1	0.9	-1.2	3.1	3.1	1.2
1958	2.3	3.6	3.0	-1.1	-0.4	-7.0	2.7	2.7	2.5
1959	3.8	5.6	-0.8	0.5	3.9	10.4	1.3	1.4	-1.1
1960	2.9	3.5	2.4	-3.3	4.3	-0.1	1.3	1.2	1.0
1961	2.8	1.1	13.8	-0.4	7.5	2.1	0.6	0.7	0.1
1962	6.8	4.5	4.0	4.5	4.0	2.0	1.3	1.2	-1.2
1963	5.2	4.9	1.5	4.6	9.1	3.3	1.9	1.8	-0.4
1964	6.7	6.0	5.1	13.3	13.4	13.2	1.8	1.8	-0.8
1965	6.7	6.1	5.3	11.8	4.5	12.3	2.5	2.4	-0.6
1966	7.0	5.2	9.3	10.8	13.6	13.1	3.5	3.7	-0.3
1967	3.3	4.8	7.1	-0.4	10.2	5.1	3.6	3.6	0.8
1968	5.8	5.0	7.6	0.1	12.4	8.8	4.0	4.0	0.4
1969	5.3	4.6	3.7	4.9	9.8	13.4	4.5	4.5	-0.1

1970	2.5	2.3	10.4	0.3	9.1	−0.7	3.4	3.3	1.2
1971	6.9	7.9	4.1	10.0	4.5	6.9	2.8	2.9	0.5
1972	6.1	7.6	3.1	5.6	6.7	11.2	4.8	4.8	−0.2
1973	7.6	6.8	4.6	11.1	10.6	13.6	7.6	7.6	−0.7
1974	3.6	5.1	4.0	5.4	−2.1	−2.1	10.9	10.8	−0.2
1975	1.2	5.2	4.0	3.8	−6.3	−2.8	10.8	10.8	0.6
1976	5.9	6.4	0.9	4.0	9.6	8.7	7.5	7.5	0.2
1977	2.0	2.4	3.3	−0.5	7.2	1.6	8.0	8.0	1.0
1978	3.6	2.6	1.7	−0.1	10.6	4.1	8.9	8.9	0.2
1979	3.2	2.0	0.4	6.8	2.9	6.9	9.2	9.2	−0.9
1980	1.0	1.0	0.8	3.9	2.2	−2.2	10.2	10.2	0.1
1981	3.4	1.9	0.5	6.5	2.7	3.9	12.5	12.5	—
1982	−4.4	−2.1	0.1	−11.7	−1.5	−11.3	10.8	10.8	3.5
1983	3.3	3.1	2.1	−4.2	6.3	8.5	5.8	5.8	0.9
1984	5.0	3.7	2.9	0.1	19.5	14.2	4.3	4.3	−0.6
1985	4.4	5.2	2.0	6.8	4.5	6.6	4.0	4.0	−0.8

Based on Table 7.

Table 9 Capital Expenditures, National Accounts Basis, 1971 Dollars, 1947-85

Year[a]	Government	Business	Housing	Total
		billions of dollars		
1947...	0.6	3.6	1.1	5.3
1948...	0.8	4.0	1.3	6.1
1949...	0.8	4.2	1.6	6.6
1950...	0.9	4.4	1.8	7.0
1951...	0.9	4.9	1.4	7.1
1952...	1.1	5.4	1.5	7.9
1953...	1.2	5.8	2.0	8.9
1954...	1.3	5.4	2.2	8.9
1955...	1.3	5.6	2.8	9.7
1956...	1.4	7.3	2.8	11.4
1957...	1.8	8.1	2.5	12.3
1958...	1.9	7.1	3.1	12.1
1959...	2.1	6.9	3.2	12.2
1960...	2.1	7.0	2.6	11.8
1961...	2.4	6.8	2.6	11.7
1962...	2.7	6.9	2.7	12.3
1963...	2.7	7.4	2.8	12.8
1964...	2.7	8.6	3.3	14.5
1965...	3.0	9.8	3.4	16.3
1966...	3.3	11.5	3.2	18.0
1967...	3.4	11.3	3.2	17.9
1968...	3.4	10.8	3.7	18.0
1969...	3.4	11.3	4.2	18.9
1970...	3.3	11.9	3.7	18.9
1971...	3.8	12.2	4.8	20.8
1972...	3.8	12.8	5.4	22.0
1973...	3.8	14.7	6.0	24.4
1974...	4.0	15.8	5.9	25.7
1975...	4.1	17.0	5.5	26.7
1976...	3.9	17.2	6.6	27.7
1977...	3.9	17.4	6.2	27.6
1978...	3.9	17.6	6.1	27.6
1979...	3.6	19.8	6.0	29.4
1980...	3.7	21.3	5.5	30.5
1981...	3.8	22.9	5.7	32.4
1982...	3.9	20.8	4.5	29.3
1983...	3.8	18.1	5.6	27.6
1984...	4.1	18.3	5.4	27.8
1985...	4.2	19.2	6.4	29.7

Note: 1981-85 figures on 1981 revised National Accounts basis. 1985 is the last year for official figures on 1971 price basis.

[a] Calendar year.

Sources: Canada, Department of Finance, *Economic Review*, April 1985; Statistics Canada, *National Income and Expenditure Accounts*, Fourth Quarter, 1986.

Table 10   Canada-U.S. Dollar Values, 1949-87

Year[a]	Canadian dollar in U.S. funds[b]	U.S. dollar in Canadian funds[b]
1949	0.970	1.031
1950	0.918	1.089
1951	0.950	1.053
1952	1.020	0.979
1953	1.020	0.983
1954	1.030	0.973
1955	1.014	0.986
1956	1.016	0.984
1957	1.043	0.959
1958	1.030	0.971
1959	1.043	0.959
1060	1.031	0.970
1061	0.987	1.013
1962	0.935	1.069
1963	0.927	1.079
1964	0.927	1.079
1965	0.927	1.078
1966	0.927	1.077
1967	0.927	1.079
1968	0.929	1.077
1969	0.929	1.077
1970	0.958	1.044
1971	0.989	1.011
1972	1.009	0.991
1973	1.000	1.000
1974	1.022	0.978
1975	0.983	1.017
1976	1.014	0.986
1977	0.940	1.063
1978	0.877	1.141
1979	0.854	1.171
1980	0.855	1.169
1981	0.834	1.199
1982	0.810	1.234
1983	0.811	1.232
1984	0.772	1.295
1985	0.732	1.365
1986	0.720	1.389
1987	0.754	1.326

[a]Calendar year. [b]Average of noon rates.

Source: Bank of Canada *Review*.

Among other influences this bargain price value gave a dramatic stimulus to exports and in the eighties produced unprecedented favourable trade balances, as follows: 1982, $18.0 billion; 1983, $17.7 billion; 1984, $20.6 billion; 1985, $17.4 billion. However this did not last. In 1986 the balance dropped off to $10.8 billion, and remained at that level in 1987.

U.S. Trade. There has been a marked shift in Canada's export trade from traditional European markets to the United States. In the late 1930s the balance was about even—36 percent to U.S. and 40 percent to the United Kingdom. In the immediate postwar years the ratio began to swing markedly towards the U.S. and by the mid-eighties had reached 78 percent, with only 3 percent going to U.K. and 5 percent to other EEC countries.

Balance of Payments Problem. As will be described later, while Canada participated in all the GATT rounds and made substantial headway with international trade, it was plagued with balance of payment problems for most of the postwar period. Immediately following the war for some years it was forced to impose quotas and additional taxes on imports to conserve U.S. dollars under the Emergency Foreign Exchange Conservation Act. The varying relationship of the Canadian dollar to the U.S. dollar was a problem throughout, calling for government or central bank intervention on several occasions. Overall the Canadian dollar has been at a discount in U.S. terms for a substantial part of the last quarter-century, a situation now almost taken for granted as normal.

Changing Nature of Exports. There has been a marked shift away from exports of foods and raw materials toward manufactured goods in the last two decades. This is illustrated by the following comparisons of main categories for 1967 and 1987. The notable change was in the manufactured category, which increased from 28 percent to 43 percent. Of the latter figure about 59 percent was in the automotive category, but there were also substantial exports of other machinery and equipment.

Employment and Unemployment

After the very encouraging experience of the immediate postwar years, when unemployment averaged 2.5 percent, the record has been disappointing. As the Economic Council of Canada pointed out in its *First Annual Review*, the unemployment rate in Canada had been below the U.S. rate in all but one year of the first postwar decade, but in the following seven years the rate had been higher in six. It is indicative of the expectations of the time (1964) that the Council set a target rate of 3 percent for 1970. In fact the rate remained above this level and accelerated with each recession. Postwar averages by period were: 1946-53, 2.8 percent; 1954-57, 4.3 percent, and 1958-62, 6.7 percent. For 1963-69 the average dropped to 4.5 percent (though still higher than 1946-53) but then rose for 1970-75 to 6 percent and for 1976-86 to 9.1 percent. The 1986 Canadian rate was again substantially higher than the U.S. rate, and remained so in 1987. Unemployment was also common in Europe. The record was a far cry from the great expectations for postwar economic policy, and governments faced a chronic problem in

Table 11   Main Categories of Canadian Exports, 1967 and 1987

Category	1967	1987
	percent	
Food, beverages, and tobacco	14	8
Inedible crude materials	19	14
Inedible fabricated materials	38	33
Manufactured goods	28	43
Other	1	2
Total	100	100

Sources: Statistics Canada, *Canada Year Book* and *Canadian Economic Observer*.

coping with this unsatisfactory situation, particularly in view of substantial regional differences. The Atlantic region consistently had the worst record of any, but Quebec and British Columbia were also above the national average in most years. By contrast, Ontario and the Prairie region were consistently below the national average. To illustrate, for 1987, with a national average rate of 8.9 percent, the following were the regional rates: Atlantic, 14.1 percent; Quebec, 10.3 percent; Ontario, 6.1 percent; Prairies, 8.7 percent and British Columbia, 12.0 percent.

Participation Rates. A principal cause of the high unemployment ratios was the surge of the population in the fifties and sixties which outran economic growth. In addition, an increasing share of the higher population was looking for jobs. The participation rate (the percentage of population in the labour force) grew from 55 percent in 1946 to 66 percent in 1987. The rate for men dropped from 85 percent to 77 percent, with the biggest decline in the 65+ age group. But the most marked change (enter the liberated female!) was in the rate for women, which went from 25 percent in 1946 to 56 percent in 1987, with all age groups showing an increase. It is one of the ironies of history that this otherwise welcome development has happened to coincide with a general reduction in the role of humans in the economic processes, as body-replacing technology makes rapid inroads.

Employment in Service Sector. In the last two decades employment has been increasingly shifting to the services side of the economy. In 1961 some 28 percent of non-agricultural employment was in manufacturing; by 1982 the ratio had dropped to 19 percent. Between 1980 and 1987 employment in goods production actually declined by 0.5 percent; in the same period the service sector rose by 18 percent, public and social services by 20 percent, business and financial services by 16 percent and consumer and personal services by 19 percent. The largest historical shift was out of agriculture. With technological advances labour needs dropped sharply after the war, and employment in this sector fell from 25 percent of the total in 1946 to 4.4 percent in 1981.

The foregoing is intended as no more than a brief glance at the economy of the postwar period in Canada, but serves to give an impression of the background of the governmental fiscal developments that are the main subject of this book.

Fiscal Overview

The new role of the state, the rising expectations of a growing population and the attempts of politicians to meet those expectations had massive fiscal implications. In 1947 total government expenditure in Canada was just over $3 billion. In 1987 it was almost $250 billion. This rise of nearly eighty times is much of the content of this book. We will go about studying it in several ways and in considerable detail.

Expenditure by Level of Government

What levels of government have been responsible? A partial answer to this question is given in tables 12 and 13.

An obvious and well-worn comment is that government has absorbed an ever growing share of GNP, about doubling its take from one-quarter in 1947 to nearly one-half in 1987. And the pace has accelerated. The growth in the last 16 years was approximately equal to that of the previous 24, a reflection not only of higher outlays but of the accelerating rate of inflation and government spending. In 1950 and 1960 federal and provincial/local expenditures were about even. In 1970 and 1980 the emphasis had moved to provincial/local (from over 50 percent to about 40 percent federal). This was a return to the historic pattern. But between 1980 and 1987 federal expenditure rose so rapidly that the provincial/local share dropped below 50 percent and the federal rose above 40. These ratios exclude hospital expenditures, largely a provincial function; their inclusion would more than restore the traditional balance.

The Principal Outlays

On what was this massive amount of money spent? Another source gives expenditure data for familiar governmental functions which are quite revealing. See tables 14 and 15.

Obviously in the last four decades there have been some drastic changes in the pattern of government expenditures. The three "social" expenditures —health, social services and education—in the immediate postwar era represented about one-third of the total. By 1987 they were nearly one-half. (Social services in 1987 were almost one-quarter and health and education shared the other quarter about equally). The aspect of government which most impresses the public—General services, the largest item being salaries —after about doubling by 1970, has been fairly flat ever since, and is one of the smallest of the main categories. With rising debt and higher interest costs debt charges have become a new and growing burden in the last decade, having increased from 7.9 percent in 1975 to 15.2 percent in 1987, a rise of 92 percent. The share of some major categories has declined over the period, notably defence and transportation and communications. The years selected fail to reveal the dominant position of defence in the 1950s. This category reached 29 percent in 1953 and was still 25 percent in 1955. It gradually declined from that level to 4 percent or less in the 1980s. The "Other"

Table 12   Expenditure by Level of Government, Selected Years, 1947-87

	1947	1950	1960	1970	1980	1986	1987
	billions of dollars						
Federal...............	1.9	2.1	5.8	11.9	48.5	94.9	100.1
Provincial	0.7	1.1	2.8	8.8	40.3	76.2	81.0
Local	0.6	0.9	2.8	7.9	24.9	39.4	42.3
Hospitals............	—	—	—	2.4	8.6	15.6	16.9
CPP and QPP........	—	—	—	0.1	2.7	7.6	9.5
Total	3.2	4.1	11.4	31.1	124.9	233.9	249.7
% of GNP	23.7	22.1	29.7	35.4	41.4	47.4	46.5

Note: National Accounts basis.

Table 13   Expenditure by Level of Government, Percentage Distribution, Selected Years, 1947-87

	1947	1950	1960	1970	1980	1986	1987
	percent						
Federal...............	59.4	51.2	50.9	38.3	38.8	40.6	40.1
Provincial	21.9	26.8	24.6	28.3	32.3	32.6	32.4
Local	18.7	22.0	24.5	25.4	19.9	16.8	16.9
Hospitals............	—	—	—	7.7	6.9	6.7	6.8
CPP and QPP........	—	—	—	0.3	2.1	3.3	3.8
Total	100.0	100.0	100.0	100.0	100.0	100.0	100.0

Based on Table 12.

Table 14   All Governments: Expenditure by Principal Outlays, Selected Years, 1947-87

Function	1947	1950	1960	1970	1980	1987
	billions of dollars					
General services.............	0.1	0.2	0.5	2.0	8.3	15.6
Social welfare..............	0.8	0.8	1.9	5.8	29.4	59.1
Health....................	0.1	0.2	0.8	4.3	15.7	32.1
Education..................	0.3	0.4	1.6	6.0	18.1	30.2
Transportation	0.3	0.5	1.4	3.2	10.9	12.1
Defence...................	0.2	0.5	1.5	1.7	4.9	10.1
Debt charges	0.5	0.5	0.8	2.6	14.8	37.0
All other..................	0.8	1.0	2.3	5.9	30.4	47.9
Total.....................	3.1	4.1	10.8	31.5	132.5	244.1

Source: Statistics Canada, *Consolidated Government Finance*, and CANSIM.

Table 15   All Governments: Expenditure by Principal Outlays,
Percentage Distribution, Selected Years, 1947-87

Function	1947	1950	1960	1970	1980	1987
			percent			
General services.............	3.2	4.9	4.6	6.3	6.2	6.4
Social welfare...............	25.8	19.5	17.6	18.4	22.2	24.2
Health.....................	3.2	4.9	7.4	13.6	11.9	13.1
Education..................	9.7	9.8	14.8	19.0	13.7	12.4
Transportation	9.7	12.2	13.9	10.2	8.2	5.0
Defence....................	6.4	12.2	13.9	5.4	3.7	4.1
Debt charges	16.1	12.2	7.4	8.2	11.2	15.2
All other..................	25.9	24.3	20.4	18.9	22.9	19.6
Total.....................	100.0	100.0	100.0	100.0	100.0	100.0

Based on Table 14.

category is a mixed bag, in which national energy program expenses have been significant in the 1980s. However, historically this category is generally in the 15-20 percent range and, at 20 percent in 1987, is about normal.

The main explanation of expenditure growth is the explosion in the three categories—health, education and social services—and more recently the growing cost of debt; and a very important cause of the ballooning of figures in the last two decades has been inflation.

How Was This Growth Paid For?

Governments obtain their revenues from taxation, from non-tax sources, and from borrowing. Of these taxation is by far the most important, and some major changes have taken place in this source. Tables 16 and 17 show revenues and the overall deficits of governments in dollars and on a percentage basis.

Personal and corporate income taxes were the major source, and with remarkable consistency together provided 35-40 percent of revenues throughout. However, there was a substantial internal shift between the two sides as the period developed, with revenue from the personal tax growing and the corporate declining. In 1947 the division was even, but in the following years it gradually changed to favour personal income tax by 55-45 in 1960, 74-26 in 1970, 75-25 in 1980, and by 83-17 in 1987. By 1987 in fact the corporate income tax had been surpassed by every other major category of revenue. We will be examining this phenomenon in some detail later. Among the traditional sources, customs duties have dropped to a nominal 2 percent, but the shares of most of the others have remained fairly stable, including general sales taxes and the property tax. Health and social insurance premiums, which include unemployment insurance and hospital and medicare premiums, now account for one dollar in ten of the total.

Of the non-tax sources, return on investments is the most prominent, now representing 9 percent of total revenues.

Table 16 All Governments: Revenue from Main Sources, and Deficits, Selected Years, 1947-87

Source	1947	1950	1960	1970	1980	1987
			billions of dollars			
Personal income tax	0.7	0.7	2.0	9.1	34.5	72.3
Corporate income tax	0.7	1.0	1.6	3.2	11.7	14.7
General sales tax	0.4	0.6	1.3	4.1	11.6	26.3
Property tax	0.3	0.4	1.3	3.5	9.8	17.9
Customs duties	0.3	0.3	0.5	0.8	3.2	4.3
Health and social insurance levies	—	—	—	2.7	10.5	24.0
Other taxes	0.7	0.8	1.6	3.2	10.0	16.1
Total taxes	3.1	3.8	8.3	26.6	91.4	175.6
Non-tax revenue	0.7	0.6	1.4	5.6	31.5	40.6
Total revenue	3.8	4.4	9.7	32.2	122.9	216.2
Deficit or surplus	0.7	0.3	− 1.1	0.7	− 9.6	− 27.9

Source: Same as Table 14.

Table 17 All Governments: Revenues from Main Sources, Percentage Distribution, Selected Years, 1947-87

Source	1947	1950	1960	1970	1980	1987
			percent			
Personal income tax	18.4	15.9	20.6	28.3	28.1	33.4
Corporate income tax	18.4	22.7	16.5	10.0	9.5	6.8
General sales tax	10.5	13.6	13.4	12.8	9.5	12.2
Customs duties	7.9	6.9	5.1	2.5	2.6	2.0
Property tax	7.9	9.1	13.4	10.9	8.0	8.3
Health and social insurance levies	—	—	—	8.4	8.5	11.1
Other taxes	18.4	18.1	16.5	9.8	8.2	7.4
Total taxes	81.5	86.3	85.5	82.7	74.4	81.2
Non-tax revenue	18.5	13.7	14.5	17.3	25.6	18.8
Total revenue	100.00	100.0	100.0	100.0	100.0	100.0

Based on Table 16.

Government Deficits: Pre-1970

Deficits are by no means the exclusive concern of the present age. In the 23 years 1947 to 1970 deficits were experienced in roughly one-half the years on the consolidated finances basis of accounting (using the Financial Management analysis established by Statistics Canada). These were not large by recent standards and were substantially offset by surpluses in other years. Only a relatively small group expressed much concern about them—chiefly ministers of finance, provincial treasurers, businessmen, economists (some of whom as we will see wanted them larger and more frequent), some editorial writers, and probably a few members of the public. To a degree they were the inevitable result of the increases in expenditures just outlined. At the federal level they reflected the commitment of that government to adopt broad welfare programs and maintain a fully employed economy. The former emboldened it to adopt new and expensive programs with only secondary concern for fiscal consequences. The latter called for alternating surpluses and deficits to counterbalance activity in the economy, and turned out to be easier to implement on the deficit side than on the surplus.

However, none of the effects of this relatively relaxed approach to budgeting were very significant until the 1970s. Net federal debt increased from about $12.7 billion in 1946 to $18.5 billion in 1970, but in relation to GNP declined from 107 percent to 21.6 percent, nearly the lowest ratio of the postwar period. The annual cost of the debt rose from 2.8 percent to 5.1 percent (gross) or from 3.2 percent to 4.6 percent (net). Even with this increase public debt charges were only 5.7 percent of budgetary expenditures in 1970, a ratio about one-third of 1946, and lower than that of most interventing years. In short, until the seventies federal government deficits were a difficulty, but not a serious one. Nor were provincial-local deficits of much consequence, although some provinces were less fortunate than others.

Government Deficits: Post-1970

All this began to unravel as the seventies progressed. Drastic measures taken toward the end of the sixties improved a worsening budget position, but the effect was temporary. The early seventies brought a see-saw between deficits and surpluses, but the bottom fell out in 1976. Deficits rose to the $6 to $9 billion range, but got completely out of hand when they soared to $27 billion in 1982, reached $38 billion in 1984, and dropped to about $28 billion in 1987. As a result, federal gross debt increased from $37 billion in 1970 to $303 billion in 1986; net debt rose from $18.5 billion to $264 billion. The latter was an increase in the crucial relationship to GNP from 20.6 percent to 51.8 percent. In the same period provincial-local-hospital debt rose from $8.7 billion to $43.6 billion.

All aspects of government finance will receive much more detailed analysis later. An essential prelude to that exercise, and a crucial element in understanding the fiscal history of the postwar period, will be a review of the major annual fiscal event—the federal budget. Thirteen different ministers of finance have striven in the last four decades to use this powerful weapon to achieve a vast variety of results, all of which will be appraised. We will begin by simply describing their actions; appraisal will come later. But first, a word on the politics of the period.

Political Overview

The second half of the twentieth century has been the age of the politician. In earlier times public figures were kings, warriors, religious prophets, philosophers, writers, scientists, sports heroes, even movie stars, but today politicians are pre-eminent. Their hold on public regard is tenuous and their fortunes can take sudden tumbles, but as a breed they dominate the scene. And private citizens normally remote from politics now turn first to the political processes to achieve their own goals. Even the apparent state of decline of political figures and the recent conservative trend has made little impact on this philosophy in Canada. Government is still looked to for an answer to most problems. This is the inevitable result of four generations of hopeful promises and assurances from government leaders that all is well or, if not, will be made well. Politicians then have had much to do with the policies and programs we will be reviewing in this book.

For reasons that no doubt have been the subject of much reflection and must tell something profound about the Canadian ethos the Liberal party dominated the national political scene for decades. Of the 65 years since it became a strongly organized party in 1921 it has been in power for 41. Three periods of Conservative rule broke this regime, that of R.B. Bennett (1930-35), John G. Diefenbaker (1957-63), and the government of Brian Mulroney elected in 1984. There were also very brief spells of Conservative power—in 1926 (Arthur Meighen) and in 1979-80 (Joe Clark). With these exceptions the Liberals have governed for the rest of the time. The longest serving Liberal leader was W.L. Mackenzie King (1921-48), who was followed by Louis St. Laurent (1948-57), Lester B. Pearson (1963-68), Pierre Trudeau (1968-84), and John Turner, (1984). Equally relevant to this study are the ministers who served in key Cabinet posts in the Liberal and Conservative governments of the postwar period. These are given in table 18.

The last four decades have been marked by constant stress and turmoil in Canadian politics. This is not unusual in federations such as the Canadian. A federation begins as a compromise between conflicting racial, cultural, and regional interests, and the compromise must be continually renewed as these differences inevitably persist. Canada has dedicated itself to maintaining the distinct characteristics of its peoples, and the need for new adjustments is therefore constant. During the sixties and seventies drastic steps became essential just to preserve the federation, as one of its members, Quebec, moved toward withdrawal.

Normal strains were exacerbated by the new role the national government was determined to play in the everyday life of the citizen. On the cessation of hostilities in 1945 the main provinces wished only to resume the roles they had traditionally played, and reacted strongly against the announced intention of the federal government to shoulder its way into their territory. The initial repulse of this effort, as we will see, only temporarily upset the federal program. Its efforts over the postwar period, particularly in social, economic and inter-regional matters, have been a constant source of friction. In this struggle political scientists identify periods of trends to centralization and the reverse. Much of course has depended on the nature of the issues, some of which have been beyond provincial constitutional powers. Recent examples of these have been the international energy crisis and trade and tariff negotiations. Both have required national leadership, but have directly involved provincial governments as well, and in practice have required close consultation. There are dozens of other issues in the ordinary run of government on which differences, although less acute, arise from time to time.

This constant state of stress is reflected in the fragmentation of Canadian political allegiances. Gone is the simple 19th century division between two parties—Liberal and Conservative. Break-away parties began to appear in the federal House in the twenties under labels such as the United Farmers, Liberal Progressive, Progressive, and Labour. With the election of 17 members from the Social Credit party and 7 from the new Cooperative Commonwealth Federation (CCF) in 1935 a four-party system emerged which persisted until the mid-seventies. In several sessions the smaller parties held 10 percent or more of the seats. The Ralliement creditiste appeared briefly from Quebec between 1965 and 1972, and then disappeared. The Social Credit party had a small but diminishing representation until the early 1980s. Since then there has been basically a three-party system in the federal Parliament—Liberal, Conservative and the New Democratic Party (NDP).

The federal parties, however, do not reflect the full political spectrum of the country. In Quebec the Union nationale and the Parti-Quebecois have been strong political organizations, as is the Social Credit party in British Columbia, all having formed provincial governments.

This political fragmentation spelled the end of the system under which the federal government in power had been elected with a substantial majority and governed more or less without challenge. Of 14 governments elected in the postwar period 7 have served with either a minority standing or a very slim majority. This included the following elections: (percentage of seats shown in brackets) Conservatives—1957 (42) and 1962 (44); Liberals—1945 (51), 1963 (48), 1965 (49), 1972 (42), and 1974 (53). The electorate in fact seemed for some time to prefer minority governments, for reasons on which one can only speculate. However, as the experience of several recent majority governments has demonstrated, aggressive opposition tactics have ended the serenity with which a majority government once went about its task. There is today no peace in Parliament.

It would be difficult to establish the exact effect of this political instability on government programs of the recent past. At the same time it would be unreasonable to assume that it had had no effect at all. The NDP, as the party closely affiliated with the Canadian labour union movement, has pressed throughout for more and better social legislation, and it would be naive to assume that a minority government which relied on its support to continue in power would be totally indifferent to its appeals. A striking instance of the influence of even a single dedicated opposition member is the role played by Stanley Knowles of the NDP in the furtherance of federal pensions for the elderly, a role recognized by the whole House in the granting of honorary status for him as a member after his retirement. This is an outstanding instance but no doubt the program of social legislation in particular was given strong momentum through the dependence of minority governments on third parties for support.

Table 18 The Changing Political Spectrum

Party	Term	Prime Minister	Finance	Defence	Minister of National Health and Welfare
Liberal	1945-48	King		Abbott Gibson Claxton	Claxton
Liberal	1949-57	St. Laurent	Abbott Harris	Claxton	Martin
Conservative	1957-63	Diefenbaker	Fleming Nowlan	Pearkes Harkness Churchill	Montieth
Liberal	1963-68	Pearson	Gordon Sharp	Hellyer Cardin Cadieux	LaMarsh MacEachen
Liberal	1968-72	Trudeau	Benson	Macdonald Cadieux	Munro
Liberal	1972-74	Trudeau	Turner	Richardson	Lalonde
Liberal	1974-79	Trudeau	Turner Macdonald Chrétien	Richardson Danson	Lalonde Bégin
Conservative	1979-80	Clark	Crosbie	McKinnon	Crombie
Liberal	1980-84	Trudeau	MacEachen LaLonde	Lamontagne	Bégin
Liberal	1984	Turner	Lalonde	Blais	Bégin
Conservative	1984-	Mulroney	Wilson	Coates Neilsen André Beattie	Epp

A Digression on Government Financial Statistics

Statistics on government finance are scattered throughout this work, and there are some fundamentals about them that should be understood. This might all be conveniently left for an appendix, and any reader may feel free to pass on to other subjects. But there are aspects that are essential for full understanding of much that follows.

The main data of course deals with government revenues, expenditures, deficits, and debt, all basic to the citizen's understanding of how the government is conducting its affairs. At the present juncture it can be said that if governments had the design of utterly confusing the average citizen on the state of the nation's finances, which seems hardly likely, they could not have been more successful. The following explanation will describe the situation, unfortunately without making it any less bizarre.

Basic Sources

Most information on government finance is contained in official documents usually known as the Public Accounts or Financial Statements, and, for the future, as the Estimates. These official documents are usually designed more to meet requirements of legislation passed by Parliament or provincial legislatures than of the interest of the general public in the affairs of government. For this general use they need a good deal of reworking, particularly if information from several levels of government is to be combined on a uniform basis.

Budgetary Basis

The most common analysis of the basic information is that presented annually with the government's budget. In general this is based directly on the public accounts, but with sufficient revision to support or illustrate the main message of the budget presentation. The principal shortcoming of this data is that it is seldom on a basis comparable to that of any other government. It is also subject to frequent revision, sometimes from year to year and usually retroactively, as new methods of presenting the basic accounts are adopted. This destroys comparability for historical writing, as an event such as a major tax change must be viewed in the light of the financial data as it existed at the time, not as it was revised 25 years later.

The Cash Requirement

Recent changes in the federal accounts are typical of the revisions. They have mainly involved bringing into the budget various funds and accounts, such as the old age security fund, the unemployment insurance fund, and others previously excluded. Annual figures have been revised for 25 years, and these are relevant for today's purposes. But they are not the figures on which the budgets of earlier times were based.

One saving feature of the older accounts is the data for the "cash requirement." This in effect is a bottom line figure for the government's overall operations, and indicates the amount that will have to be borrowed for the coming year. It includes revenues and outlays that are not part of the usual accounts, and therefore is a more accurate picture of the financial situation than the deficit as normally calculated. As non-budgetary revenues frequently exceed the normal revenues, the result is often a cash need that is less than the deficit. And of course, as the final bottom line figure, is more or less consistent over a period of time.

Some authorities favour this concept as giving a more comprehensive statement of the government's position, and certainly ministers of finance and provincial treasurers take considerable comfort from its usually lower figure than the deficit. For the fiscal year 1987-88, for example, the federal deficit was forecast to be over $29 billion, whereas the anticipated cash requirement was just over $21 billion. However, while this data is always given in the budget, and no doubt is highly relevant for some purposes, such as an indication of future demands on the financial markets, it is a figure that emerges from transient factors of the year and gives little guidance as to fundamental trends in government revenues and expenditures.

Financial Management System

To overcome some of the problems in the budgetary figures and achieve uniformity between governments Statistics Canada prepares a series of reports on a comparable basis known as the Financial Management Series. A most useful series under this system is Consolidated Government Finance, which gives a combined presentation for the three levels of government for revenues by source and expenditures by function. The analysis of expenditures on a functional basis (health, education, defence, transportation, etc.) is particularly useful and is only available in the Consolidated Series.

The National Accounts

Statistics Canada also compiles data on government finance as part of its annual series known as the National Accounts. Compiled for 1926 and later years, like the Consolidated Government Finance Series, from the beginning it has been broader in its scope than the budgetary data, and in general includes all aspects of government having economic and financial implications. The series has the advantage of being on a reasonably consistent basis for over half a century and of course is essential for the often repeated calculation of the ratio of government expenditure to Gross National Product. However, for governmental financial analysis it suffers from lack of detail in either expenditures or revenues, and now—unfortunately for historical writing—the GNP concept has been discarded for Gross Domestic Product, a change which we have been forced to disregard. Just before publication revisions in National Accounts data from 1926 to 1986 became available but except in a few tables these have been implemented only for years since 1981. This has created some lack of uniformity but it has not been catastrophic for government data.

Intergovernmental Transfers

In presenting data for all levels of government on a common basis a problem arises because of the massive transfers between governments. If the figures for say, health, were included in both the federal health grants to provinces and the actual expenditures of the provinces and municipalities on health, there would be enormous double counting. This duplication can be removed by eliminating the overlapping expenditure; different treatments have been used for this purpose in the Consolidated Government Finance series. Under concepts in effect since 1970, grants from another government for a designated function are recorded as expenditure of the government that actually administers the function. For any other purpose than a consolidation of all levels of government this of course is misleading. For each government looked at individually, grants from other governments must be included as revenues and grants to other governments as expenditures.

A complication is that in the National Accounts treatment a different method is used. In a consolidation of all governments, transfers are treated as expenditures of the originating government. However, sufficient detail is available under either system that intergovernmental payments can be identified and treated separately.

Specific Use

Historical writing has enough hazards without the addition of quavering and unreliable statistics, and the author has simply done his best with what is available, in the assurance that no one will be seriously mislead by the results. All sources have been drawn on, and employed as best suited the text. For the review of annual federal budgets it has of course been necessary to retain the financial figures used at the time. For longer periods recent revisions of federal figures dating from 1961 and published in the 1986 and 1987 budgets have been used, supplemented for earlier years (1947-61) with data from *Historical Statistics of Canada*. Inconsistencies in the two bases are negligible, and in any event largely disappear in the presentation of most figures in billions of dollars, the only basis that makes sense for current use. Either the Consolidated Government Finance or National Accounts series are used where they best contribute to the presentation. As explained, they vary both from each other and from the budgetary basis, and must be used with this knowledge. The difference between fiscal and calendar years has been largely eliminated by the commonly used practice of bringing all fiscal years nearest to the calendar year that they most extensively overlap; i.e. the preceding calendar year.

A Final Word

This book is heavily laden with statistical tables of many kinds, some provided simply for further study if the reader so wishes. But it was not prepared primarily as a statistical source, although a great deal of time and effort went into this aspect of it. The purpose of the statistics is mainly to provide an index of the direction in which events were moving rather than a fully accurate and detailed audit of the last four decades of government finance in Canada. If the tables are useful to this end they will have served their purpose.

Part 1

The Federal Fiscal Performance

1
Peacetime Transition; Korea Renews Defence; Welfare State Progresses (1947-56)

During the war the main powers of government had been assumed by the national authority. A military force of over a million had been created, strategic industries had been taken over, manpower had been regulated, prices had been controlled, and many goods had been rationed. The federal government had achieved exclusive use of the main direct taxes under the Wartime Tax Agreements, and incomes and corporate profits had been taxed at unprecedented rates. A federal death tax was introduced and other areas hitherto strictly provincial had been invaded.

With the end of hostilities this massive structure had to be unwound. The military forces were rapidly demobilized and controls and rationing ended. The task of conversion to peacetime production was aided by capital assistance and accelerated depreciation in the 1944-48 period. As a prelude to assuming a more active role in the economy the federal government had attempted to persuade the provinces to allow it to continue exclusive use of the main direct taxes. At conferences in 1945 and 1946 it failed to reach this goal, and had been forced to work out compromise arrangements with seven of the nine provinces which would also accommodate the two non-agreeing provinces, Ontario and Quebec. These arrangements created at least a tolerable situation that, with many shifts and changes, have served as the basis for most federal-provincial developments of the postwar years.

The end of hostilities was marked by budgets in 1945 which made substantial tax reductions, beginning a process that went on for the next five years. Room had to be made for resumed provincial taxation, the economy had to be assisted and a war-weary public had to be given the relief it legitimately expected.

The government had also promised social legislation of great public appeal. It had sponsored the establishment of unemployment insurance in 1940 and had introduced family allowances in 1945. Its proposals included a new universal plan of pensions for the elderly and medical and hospital insurance; political pressure and public interest kept these plans alive. But all these programs were fated to unfold slowly; many hazards stood in the way, including a return to war.

Ilsley Unwinds from War

May 1945: Ilsley. In May, immediately after the end of European Hostilities, the federal Minister of Finance announced the reduction or removal of heavy consumer goods taxes to assist in conversion to peacetime conditions. Heavy taxes on automobiles, cameras, films, radios and phonographs were reduced to 10 percent; special taxes on electrical and gas appliances were removed entirely.

By far the most significant step taken in this otherwise relatively light tax program was the exemption for the first time of building materials from the federal sales tax. This exemption was later to have a chequered career, with a variety of treatments.

October 1945: Ilsley. Changes in an October budget were broader. By this time government departments had been able to get some fix on their peacetime requirements and a first conference had been held with the provinces. The future was beginning to be somewhat less obscure. The personal income tax was reduced by 4 percent for 1945 and 16 percent for 1946. The excess profits tax was retained but with reduced rates. The War Exchange Tax, which had applied at 10 percent to all imports except those under British Preferential rates (or their equivalent) was repealed. Significant tax proposals of a royal commission were made relating to pension plans, annuities, and closely held corporations.

Again one of the most lasting changes related to the sales tax, in the exemption, for the first time, of apparatus and machinery used in manufacturing and production. This exemption, except for a short period in the mid-sixties, has lasted throughout the postwar period.

The Minister forecast that his tax changes would reduce an expected revenue of $2,265 million by $100 million. He forecast a deficit of $2,250 million, which in fact turned out to be $2,123 million.

June 1946: Ilsley. By 1946 the possibility of a general agreement with all the provinces had faded, and a proposal was put forward that a province could accept or not at its option; results would have to await further negotiation. The main accomplishment of this budget was to simplify the complex structure of income tax that had developed during the war—with a national defence tax, a compulsory savings portion, etc. The new structure had higher exemptions and lower rates. The minimum excess profits tax rate was embodied in the normal corporate rate structure to raise the corporate rate from 18 to 30 percent, and the rate applying to excess profits was reduced. Other changes related to taxation of cooperatives, authors and artists, income averaging of farmers and fishermen, expense allowances for elected members, oil and mineral expenses, etc. For new mines the rate of tax was reduced to one-half after January 1, 1947. The federal succession duties rates were doubled, with an allowance up to half for provincial duties on the same estate, as part of federal-provincial arrangements. Minor other revisions were made. A significant move was the announcement of the establishment of the Income Tax Appeal Board, now the Tax Court of Canada. The Minister estimated that his tax changes would reduce the 1946-47 expected revenue of $2,510 million by $35 million, and that the deficit for the year would be $300 million. In actuality it turned out to be a surplus of $374 million.

$20,000 and 47 percent on the excess (both excluding the old age security tax, to be discussed presently). All in all a happy occasion for taxpayers, and one seldom enjoyed since. Despite this there was still a budget surplus of $46 million, or 1.1 percent of expenditure.

April 1954: Abbott. By 1954 the Minister could hold out no further goodies for the taxpayers. The economy was in a minor slump, the first in the postwar period. Defence expenditures still predominated, and the $2½ billion budget level foreseen three years before had now become $4⅓ billion, with no prospect of reduction. Social security commitments already undertaken were beginning to have budgetary implications, although financed largely outside the budget. The surpluses of earlier years had ended, and prospects were for an approximate balance. The budget made only minor tax changes, and those all in the commodity tax area. Some excises were repealed, the rate on others was reduced from 15 percent to 10 percent, and some additional items were exempted from sales tax; all in all a tidying up affair, costing no more than 1 percent of tax revenues.

Harris Holds the Line

April 1955: Harris. 1954 had turned out to be a slower year than anticipated in the spring budget. The GNP had been almost flat and unemployment at 4.6 percent had been a postwar peak. A new Minister of Finance decided therefore that a modest deficit would be appropriate as a fiscal stimulus. Tax reductions amounting to 5 percent of tax yields were made to produce an expected deficit of about $200 million, the first in the postwar period. These took the form of a 2 point reduction from July 1 in personal income tax rates, a reduction from 47 to 45 percent in the general corporate tax rate from January 1, 1955, a reduction in the automobile tax from 15 percent to 10 percent, and exemption of additional goods from sales tax.

March 1956: Harris. The economy in 1955 appeared to have responded to the budget stimulus with a substantial rise in the GNP. There had been a modest deficit of about $150 million in a budget of $4.3 billion in the previous year, and a further minor deficit was forecast. The prospects were for a moderately good year, and the Minister concluded that no dramatic moves were required. His budget was very much of the stand-pat variety. Under the sales tax a long list of further items, mainly related to the exemption for building materials and manufacturing and production equipment, was exempted. (The tax system frequently gives forecasts of coming events. Interestingly, in view of recent "new" public awareness of the subject, thirty years ago one of the items in this list of goods to be exempted from the sales tax was "electric freezing machines and parts and materials used exclusively for their manufacture for use in the processing and storing of frozen semen at extreme temperatures"). A new proposal was a tax at 20 percent on gross advertising revenues of special editions of non-Canadian periodicals, effective January 1, 1957. This tax had a short life, being repealed by the Conservatives 18 months later. Nevertheless it began a cross-border battle that was to rage for some years before a compromise was reached.

March 1957: Harris. Although chronologically it belongs in the following period we will deal here with what was to be the last of the Liberal budgets for six years. With signs of growing inflationary pressure from a buoyant 1956 economy (7 percent real growth) the Minister presented a "hold the line" budget, contrary to usual practice before an election. There were fears that the economy would not be able to cope with the heavy demands on it for consumer and capital expenditure and for exports, and the government should not contribute to this pressure through either tax reductions or increased expenditure. However, some moderate changes were made.

Family allowances were simplified (two age groups were substituted for the existing four) and increased slightly. Old Age Security and related payments were increased from $40 to $46 per month, and veterans' pensions and allowances were raised. Among the tax changes were introduction of what was to become everyman's tax shelter, the registered retirement savings plan (a budget sleeper if there ever was one!). Along with this came the $100 standard deduction, now repealed. A long list of goods, including many foods, were added to the sales tax exemption list, and excises were removed from a long list of commodities, some imposed for the Korean war program.

The expenditure changes were expected to cost $98 million and the revenue $55 million in the 1957-58 fiscal year. (The cost of the RRSP provision was included in this $55 million. In 1985 the cost for that year was estimated at $3.4 billion). Total expenditures were expected to be $5,018 million and revenues $5,170 million, leaving a surplus of $152 million. Actual results for the year were altered by an interim December 1958 mini-budget of the new government, to which we will return later.

Other Developments

We will briefly leave this chronicle at 1956. The succeeding six years were a time of testing, with quite a different economic climate, almost continuous deficits, and a different government in charge. As the Liberal government had been able to realize some elements of its social security program, one of the most significant aspects of the period for the future, it will be appropriate to mention these briefly here before going on.

Social Security Moves Ahead

In 1952 the federal government, in the midst of mounting defence expenditures and drastically increased taxation, introduced what in time was to become one of its most expensive single programs—old age security. It had promised the provinces in its 1945 proposals to replace the existing joint means-tested program with a universal plan for which it would be solely responsible, and this had been generally acceptable. The government also felt justified in proceeding with the plan on the basis that it would be self-sustaining, following the model established for unemployment insurance in 1940. This suited the "pay as you go" mood of the treasury in the early

1950s, aimed at limiting the government's commitment to old age pensions by keeping financing in a separate fund outside the regular budget with its own clearly identified revenue sources. If increased pensions were wanted, higher taxes would have to be levied.

At the outset it encountered what seemed at the time to be an insurmountable problem. The setting of an actuarially sound premium could have been mastered, as this was required of insurance companies regularly. The real problem was the collection of such a premium. The government had insisted that all persons 70 and over would be eligible, but it was unable to develop a collection system that would not miss large groups in the community—self-employed farming, professional and business persons, low income families, the elderly, the very young, and so on.

Failing in this it had to fall back on levying special ear-marked additions to existing taxes, the revenue from which would go into a special fund. The fund would be kept out of the regular budget, which would serve the government's basic objective of protecting itself from constant pressure for increases. This objective was so deeply rooted in the Department of Finance that even after the special taxes were repealed as such in 1972, the operations of the fund continued to be calculated on a hypothetical basis. This lasted until 1976, when the struggle for fiscal probity was finally given up.

The Old Age Security pension commenced on January 1, 1952, at $40 per month to all persons 70 or over meeting a residence test. The ear-marked taxes started out as the 2-2-2 formula—2 percent of the 10 percent sales tax rate, an extra 2 percent on the corporate income tax rate, and 2 percent on taxable personal income, with a ceiling of $60 for the latter. The first two charges came into effect on January 1, 1952, but the latter was held to July 1, so that for 1952 the effective tax rate was 1 percent, with a ceiling of $30. Revenue from these sources gradually rose from $224 million in the first full year (1953) to $372 million in 1957, and expenditures rose from $323 million to $379 million in the same years. After an initial deficit of $100 million in 1953 the annual shortfall averaged about $50 million a year. These deficits, amounting to about $350 million in the first six years, were either written off against the value of assets or charged against the general accounts.

To achieve a better balance all three rates were increased to 3 percent in 1959, and from fiscal 1961 onward the fund showed a surplus. The addition of the Guaranteed Income Supplement in 1967, the lowering of the age of eligibility from 70 to 65, which began in one-year steps from 1967 on, and frequent changes in the amount of the regular pension, were thenceforth offset by raising the personal income tax element of the formula. The rate was increased to 4 percent (maximum $120) in 1964 and in 1967 the maximum was raised to $240, without change in rate. These revenue changes brought the fund into surplus until fiscal 1971, and by then produced a cumulative balance of over $700 million. For 1972 the fund was wound up and the taxes were embodied in the regular rates. As mentioned, a calculation was made of the position that the fund would have maintained until 1976, which showed that there would have been a deficit from 1972 onward. No doubt substantially increased charges would have been necessary to keep it in balance during the seventies and eighties. (Further details on Old Age Security are given later.)

Other Related Social Programs

Concurrently with the enactment of the Old Age Security Act the federal government obtained legislation authorizing it to enter into agreements with the provinces for joint programs in related fields. These were the Old Age Assistance Act and the Blind Persons Act. Later, in 1954, it enacted the Disabled Persons Act and, in 1956, legislation under which it shared half the cost of unemployment relief in excess of normal unemployment (taken as 0.45 percent of the provincial population). The payments under these arrangements were charged directly to the budget and, while not large in total, represented a final and substantial commitment by the federal government to participation in social programs at all levels of government.

Family Allowances and Health Grants. Two further substantial features of the social measures program were family allowance and health grants. The former, introduced under the Family Allowances Act in 1946, provided a straight monthly payment per child under the age of 16. Costs were assumed entirely by the federal government, and went rapidly from $172 million in the first partial year to nearly $500 million by fiscal 1960. The number of children covered rose from 3.3 million to 6.2 million in 1960, and rose as high as 6.9 million in 1968. There have been several revisions in the plan, each designed to give it a more prominent role in the federal income security program. (See later chapter). As an item exceeding half a billion dollars in costs annually it was clearly a substantial burden in the federal budget of the fifties.

The Health Grants were part of a National Health Program announced in 1948 by the Prime Minister as a prelude to the ultimate introduction of health insurance. The 1948 program included grants for health surveys, hospital construction, general public health, and grants for aid with tuberculosis, venereal disease, mental health, crippled children, cancer, and research and training. While not a substantial budgetary expenditure, over the 22 years from 1948 to 1971 some $867 million was granted the provinces under the legislation. Of this the largest amount went for hospital construction.

Finally, after long consultation with the provinces in 1957, just prior to the election in which it was defeated, the Liberal government passed the Hospital insurance and Diagnostic Services Act to provide for joint federal-provincial hospital insurance. Under this Act five provinces signed agreements by July 1, 1958, and the balance came under it in the next two years.

The 1947-56 Period in Perspective

Tables 1.2 to 1.5 give summary data on fiscal developments of the period.

Table 1.2 Federal Government: Revenue, Expenditure, and Deficit or Surplus, Budgetary and National Accounts Bases, 1947-56

Year[a]	Revenue		Expenditure		Deficit or Surplus	
	Budgetary	National accounts	Budgetary	National accounts	Budgetary	National accounts
	billions of dollars					
1947.....	2.9	2.8	2.2	2.1	0.7	0.7
1948.....	2.8	2.7	2.2	2.0	0.6	0.8
1949.....	2.6	2.7	2.4	2.2	0.2	0.5
1950.....	3.1	3.0	2.9	2.4	0.2	0.6
1951.....	4.0	4.2	3.8	3.2	0.4	1.0
1952.....	4.6	4.7	4.6	4.5	—	0.2
1953.....	4.7	4.8	4.7	4.7	—	0.1
1954.....	4.4	4.6	4.7	4.7	− 0.3	− 0.1
1955.....	4.7	5.0	4.8	4.8	− 0.1	0.2
1956.....	5.6	5.7	5.3	5.1	0.3	0.6

[a] Fiscal years ending nearest December 31 of year named.

Source: *Historical Statistics of Canada*; Department of Finance *Economic Review*, April 1985.

Table 1.3 Federal Government: Revenue by Principal Source, Budgetary Accounts Basis, 1947-56

Year[a]	Personal income tax	Corporate income taxes	Sales and excise taxes[b]	Other tax revenue	Non-tax revenue	Total[c]
	billions of dollars					
1947.....	0.7	0.6	1.1	0.1	0.4	2.9
1948.....	0.8	0.5	1.1	0.1	0.3	2.8
1949.....	0.6	0.6	1.0	0.1	0.3	2.6
1950.....	0.7	0.8	1.2	0.1	0.3	3.1
1951.....	1.0	1.1	1.5	0.1	0.3	4.0
1952.....	1.2	1.3	1.5	0.1	0.4	4.6
1953.....	1.3	1.2	1.5	0.1	0.4	4.7
1954.....	1.3	1.1	1.5	0.1	0.4	4.4
1955.....	1.3	1.1	1.6	0.2	0.4	4.7
1956.....	1.5	1.3	1.8	0.4	0.5	5.5

[a] Fiscal year ending nearest December 31 of year named. [b] Includes excise duties and customs duties. [c] Excludes unemployment insurance contributions.

Source: *Historical Statistics of Canada*.

Table 1.4 Federal Government: Expenditure by Major Outlay, Budgetary Accounts Basis, 1947-56

Year[a]	Major transfers to persons	Major transfers to governments	National defence	Other	Total program expenditure	Public debt charges	Total
	billions of dollars						
1947.....	0.4	0.2	0.2	0.9	1.7	0.5	2.2
1948.....	0.4	0.1	0.3	0.9	1.7	0.5	2.2
1949.....	0.5	0.1	0.4	0.9	1.9	0.5	2.4
1950.....	0.5	0.1	0.8	1.1	2.5	0.4	2.9
1951.....	0.6	0.1	1.4	1.2	3.3	0.5	3.8
1952.....	0.8	0.3	2.0	1.0	4.1	0.5	4.6
1953.....	0.9	0.3	1.9	1.1	4.2	0.5	4.7
1954.....	0.9	0.4	1.8	1.1	4.2	0.5	4.7
1955.....	1.0	0.4	1.8	1.0	4.2	0.5	4.8
1956.....	1.0	0.4	1.8	1.5	4.7	0.5	5.2

[a]Fiscal year ending nearest December 31 of year named.

Source: Based on *Historical Statistics of Canada*.

Table 1.5 Federal Government: Main Categories of Expenditure, National Accounts Basis, 1947-56

Year	Goods and services	Transfers to persons	Interest on debt	Subsidies and capital assistance	Capital formation	Transfers to other governments	Total
	billions of dollars						
1947.....	0.7	0.6	0.5	0.2	—	0.2	2.1
1948.....	0.6	0.6	0.5	0.1	—	0.2	2.0
1949.....	0.8	0.6	0.5	0.1	0.2	0.2	2.2
1950.....	0.9	0.6	0.4	0.1	0.1	0.3	2.4
1951.....	1.6	0.6	0.5	0.1	0.1	0.3	3.2
1952.....	2.3	1.0	0.5	0.1	0.2	0.4	4.5
1953.....	2.5	1.1	0.5	0.1	0.1	0.4	4.7
1954.....	2.3	1.2	0.5	0.1	0.2	0.4	4.7
1955.....	2.4	1.2	0.5	0.1	0.2	0.4	4.8
1956.....	2.5	1.2	0.5	0.2	0.2	0.5	5.1

Source: Department of Finance, *Economic Review*, April 1985.

excise on automobiles for personal use was repealed, reductions were made in excises on radios, cigarette lighters, various types of radio and TV tubes, etc. Many other non-revenue changes were made; for example, corporations incorporated in Canada and carrying on business here were to be deemed to be resident in Canada.

It was projected that there would be a deficit of $650 million for the year, on expenditures of about $6.4 billion, or about 10 percent, the highest of the postwar era. In the event, it reached nearly $800 million as a result of declines in revenue and increases in expenditure. The Minister's dream two years before of a balanced budget had eluded him entirely. (As we will see, fiscal policy during this period was the subject of great controversy among Canadian economists, many of whom would have prescribed much more vigorous fiscal action, and most of whom disagreed violently with Governor Coyne).

April 1962: Fleming. 1961 had shown some encouraging economic movements—higher exports, a favourable trade balance, a peaking of unemployment at 7.8 percent in February 1961, to drop to 6 percent by February 1962, and a very slight rise in prices—but the budget took the view that stimulation continued to be required. At it turned out, the proposals of the April 1962 budget were doomed not to be implemented for some time. A general election was held in September before the supporting legislation was passed, and it was some time after that before the budget proposals were given final approval. However, in the nature of the Canadian parliamentary process it can be taken for granted that they were effective from the budget date.

In fact the tax changes were not substantial. Deductions for dependants under the income tax were increased. A new incentive scheme was introduced under which lower taxes would be granted on profits attributable to increased sales—a 50 percent reduction on the first $50,000 and a 25 percent reduction on the balance. A further stimulus was given for increased capital and current expenditure on scientific research—a deduction of 150 percent of the increase over a pre-budget base, to be applicable for the next five years. The double depreciation plan for high unemployment regions was extended for a further period. A long list of incentive measures for mining, oil and gas exploration and development was also introduced. Further exemptions from the sales tax were granted. Minor amendments were made to the estate tax.

The final result for this budget was another substantial deficit—$692 million on expenditures of about $6.6 billion, or about 9½ percent.

Foreign Exchange Crisis

May 1962: Fleming. *Foreign Exchange Changes.* Within three weeks of his budget the Minister of Finance was deeply involved in measures to stabilize the value of the Canadian dollar at 92.5 U.S. cents. The International Monetary Fund had pressured Canada to adopt a fixed value for over a decade, and Canada finally responded by setting the 92.5 cents value as from May 2, 1962.

To support this program a series of emergency measures was announced on June 24. These measures included a reduction in government expenditures of $250 million in a full year, temporary surcharges ranging from 5 to 15 percent on about half of Canada's imports, a reduction in the duty-free import allowance for returning travellers, the establishment of lines of credit for foreign borrowing with the IMF and the Export Import Bank, the fixing of the bank rate at 6 percent. The combined revenue from the import surcharges and the reduction in expenditures was expected to reduce the government deficit, then forecast to be $745 million, by $450 million in a full year. This expectation was hardly realized. In announcing actual budget cuts in October 1962 a revised deficit of $570 million had been forecast for the year ending March 31; in fact it exceeded that estimate by $122 million. Expenditures reached $6.6 billion, so that on a budgetary basis the deficit remained in the 10 percent range, the level of recent years.

As will become evident later, Prime Minister Diefenbaker started the ball rolling on the next main element in the health program by the appointment in 1961 of a Royal Commission under Mr. Justice Hall to enquire into the subject. His report favoured the introduction of a prepaid government operated plan of health insurance which, like several other reports (Glassco Commission on Government Organization, Carter Commission on Taxation, the Clark study which led to the Canada Pension Plan, etc.), was left to the Liberals to implement.

Gordon Budgets in Prosperity

June 1963: Gordon. The government changed after a spring election so a new Liberal Minister of Finance presented the 1963 budget. Since the last budget the economy had taken on a bright new look. In real terms the GNP had increased by nearly 7 percent over 1961, capital expenditure had risen by over 4 percent, exports were growing, and for the second year there had been a favourable trade balance. Unemployment had fallen below 6 percent. Prices were rising, but slowly—for example, between 1959 and 1962 the index had gone up only from 31 to 32, (1981-100)—a slower rate than in the previous three years. Despite these improvements the Minister declared that his priorities were much those of the previous government—economic growth, reduced unemployment, and a balanced budget. However among the proposals in his budget were measures directed toward reducing foreign investment in Canada, one of the principal being a 30 percent tax on foreign takeovers of Canadian firms. This proposal created such a stir in the business community that it was withdrawn.

The balance of the budget was not without interest however. The principal revenue measures (most of which were designed for impact in the following fiscal year) were the extension of the federal sales tax to processing material, building material, and production equipment (all exemptions of long standing), the acceleration of corporate tax instalments, and the with-

Table 2.4 Federal Government: Main Categories of Expenditure, National Accounts Basis, 1957-65

Year[a]	Goods and services	Transfers to persons	Interest on debt	Subsidies and capital assistance	Capital formation	Transfers to other governments	Other	Total
				billions of dollars				
1957.....	2.5	1.5	0.5	0.1	0.2	0.5	0.1	5.4
1958.....	2.5	1.9	0.6	0.1	0.3	0.7	0.1	6.2
1959.....	2.4	1.8	0.7	0.2	0.4	0.9	0.1	6.5
1960.....	2.4	2.0	0.8	0.3	0.2	1.0	0.1	6.7
1961.....	2.6	2.0	0.8	0.3	0.3	1.1	0.1	7.2
1962.....	2.7	2.1	0.9	0.3	0.3	1.1	0.1	7.5
1963.....	2.6	2.1	0.9	0.5	0.2	1.2	0.1	7.6
1964.....	2.8	2.2	1.0	0.5	0.2	1.3	0.1	8.0
1965.....	2.8	2.3	1.1	0.5	0.4	1.4	0.1	8.6

[a]Calendar year.

Source: Department of Finance, *Economic Review*, April 1985.

3
Tougher Budgets to Beat Inflation (1966-74)

By 1966 the economy was beginning to show the effects of four years of accelerating growth. In the previous year GNP, capital expenditure, and exports had all increased substantially, and unemployment had declined to a 3.9 percent average for the year (3.5 percent at year-end), lower than any year in the last eight. More ominously, the consumer price index had risen by 2.4 percent, well in excess of any recent increase.

Sharp Faces Inflation

March 1966: Sharp. The prospect for 1966 was for even further growth. Where real GNP had risen by 6½ percent in 1965 the forecast was for a slackening to 5 percent in real terms, but with an expectation of a 4 percent price rise. (In the event this forecast turned out to be modest; real growth was nearer 7 percent). In the Minister's view "most sectors of the economy today and most regions of the country are working at or close to capacity. Shortages of skilled labour have become widespread, shortages of other labour have appeared, and unit labour costs have been rising . . . We have been successful . . . in stimulating the economy until it is now operating close to capacity."[3.1]

His main concern for the future was with the high levels of capital expenditure, the "investment boom." Governments were spending heavily on schools, universities, hospitals, and super-highways; forecasts of business investment were pointing to continuing high levels. There were signs that prices would also rise further as workers spent incomes bolstered by full employment.

In these conditions the approach was to dampen rather than fan the flames. As a general anti-inflation measure the Minister withdrew most of the income tax reduction given in the previous year. For corporations he proposed to reduce liquidity by a 5 percent refundable tax on "cash profits" in excess of $30,000, and reduced capital cost allowances on a range of assets if acquired in the 18 months following the budget. Another change, although in the reverse direction, was the return of the sales tax exemption for production machinery and equipment withdrawn by his predecessor, to be staged in two steps—reduction to 6 percent on April 1, 1967 and to zero on April 1, 1968.

Among several other tax amendments was one to exempt from withholding tax interest paid on government bonds issued abroad after April 15,

---

[3.1] Canada, Department of Finance, Budget Speech, March 29, 1966, 3.

1966. This exemption was extended to corporate bonds over the intervening years and is still in effect.

The Minister had originally estimated the deficit for the 1966-67 year to be $150 million; this was later revised to $300 million following increases in expenditures (a pay rise for the armed forces mainly). In September the Minister announced to the House of Commons the postponement of the introduction of medicare from July 1, 1967 to a year later and several other reductions or postponements in outlays to reduce the inflationary impact of the projected deficit. Even this move had little effect; some increases in expenditure had to be faced and far from the happy fate of his predecessor (with his $39 million deficit) the Minister ended with an actual deficit for fiscal year 1966-67 of $420 million, some $120 million above his revised forecast and $300 million above his original forecast. By this point federal expenditures had reached $8.8 billion and revenues $8.4 billion.

June 1967: Sharp. 1967 promised to be a difficult year. There was little chance that the boom conditions of 1966 would continue. The 7 percent increase in real GNP had been the largest in a decade, capital expenditure had reached nearly 25 percent of GNP, one of the highest rates among industrial countries, exports had risen phenomenally and unemployment had dropped to 3.6 percent—all in all a record-breaking year. The one threatening note (and a harbinger of troubles over the next two decades) was an increase of 3.5 percent in the CPI. The acceleration in costs had been reflected in a decline in productivity—the relationship of cost of input to the value of unit output.

By the time of the June budget a lower profile for 1967 was becoming apparent. An increase in real GNP of less than 4 percent was then forecast, and declines in capital expenditure for both business and housing were emerging. Prices were continuing to rise, and unemployment was also moving up for the first time in six years.

In March 1967 collection of the refundable tax was dropped and the reductions in capital cost allowances announced in the 1966 budget were terminated. The budget in June was "mildly stimulative" but contained no major tax changes. The Report of the Royal Commission on Taxation had been made public and the Minister proposed that major changes be postponed until he had received reactions to it. However, he proposed that the removal of the remaining sales tax from production machinery and equipment be moved forward from April 1, 1968 to June 1967. Quite important reductions in federal revenues would also result from an increase in the abatement for provincial personal income tax from 24 to 28 percent and from a raise in the federal credit for provincial corporate tax from 9 percent to 10 percent. A notable feature of this budget was attention to drug prices. As part of a "major government attack on higher drug prices" drugs were exempted from sales tax and tariff changes were also made. Continuing study of the problem was promised.

In a December 1966 mini-budget, to provide some offsetting revenues, the rate of federal sales tax had been increased, effective January 1, 1967, from 11 percent to 12 percent.

The Minister was deeply concerned with the rising tide of wage and salary increases and the effect of this on productivity. "The chief obstacle I see to our attaining stable growth in the next few years is the danger of excessive increases in prices and costs . . . Wages and salaries have been increasing at rates several times the overall increase in our productivity per man . . . If unchecked, such increases in costs and prices must lead to increasing inequity and dissension in the country and to a worsening of our competitive position vis-a-vis the United States."[3.2] He mentioned the programs of the federal government designed to increase productivity—education, adult training programs and increased emphasis on scientific and technical research, and urged that both business and labour devote more attention to this aspect of the economy.

1967-1970: The Sharp-Benson Blitz. In November 1967, five months following his June budget, Sharp introduced a round of stiff tax increases aimed at the coming rather than the current year. Inflation had now taken centre stage as the great threat, and prospects for 1968 were disturbing. Both the Consumer Price Index and the unemployment rate had been rising in 1967, and the expectation of further inflation was casting a pall over the whole economy, with effects (now familiar) on interest rates, capital expenditures, and the cost of living. The government was to conclude that some external influence would have to be exerted over prices as a means of stabilizing the economy, and was to appoint the Prices and Incomes Commission in May 1969 for this purpose. But this would only be supplementary to an attack launched by ministers of finance using more orthodox methods. In his November 1967 mini-budget, Sharp introduced rigorous measures designed, in keeping with accepted economic doctrine of the day, to crush inflationary pressures by reducing the government deficit and wiping up purchasing power. This action was sustained by a succeeding minister, Benson, with dramatic results. By fiscal 1970 the budget was showing the first surplus in a decade, and a surprisingly substantial one.

The Sharp mini-budget in November 1967 began the blitz with tax changes designed to bring in half a billion dollars of new revenue for the following fiscal year (1968-69). The first version of the program involved a 5 percent surtax on personal income tax for 1968, increases in liquor and tobacco taxes (the hard-pressed treasurer's constant friend), and acceleration of corporate tax instalment payments, which previously had lagged behind the year of taxation by some months. The latter, involving a speed-up of two months, brought in at least half the expected additional revenue, was politically neutral, and had the great advantage of being repeatable, as this move did not close the gap.

The program had an uncertain life. It suffered a series of political accidents which need not concern us here, and the amendments to the Income Tax Act to implement it were not finally passed until the following March. As ultimately enacted, the 5 percent personal income surtax had been reduced to 3 percent (with a $200 exemption) and a 3 percent surtax had

---

[3.2] Canada, Department of Finance, Budget Speech, June 1, 1967, 12.

been applied to corporations (in addition to acceleration of their instalment payments). The increases were enacted for both 1968 and 1969. Allowing for the repayments of the earlier special refundable corporate tax of $105 million, the final estimate of the additional yield for 1968-69 was $485 million, as follows: personal income tax, $105 million; liquor and tobacco, $95 million, and corporation tax, $285 million. In addition to these revenue increases "austerity" measures were applied to expenditures, with a freeze on public service employment. As the main part of this program was directed to affect the following year it had a hardly perceptible influence on the deficit for 1967-68, which reached the unprecedented budgetary figure of $795 million. At this point budgetary revenues were $9.0 billion and expenditures $9.8 billion; the $10 billion cross-over lay just ahead.

Benson Attacks Inflation

October 1968: Benson. Because of the delay in enacting the changes of the Sharp late 1967 mini-budget, there was no spring budget in 1968; it became the responsibility of the new Minister of Finance to take the next and crucial step in the blitz. He did so in a budget of October 1968.

1967 had been a backward year economically; the increase in real GNP had been about 3.3 percent, there had been a marked decline in capital expenditures and exports, and both prices and unemployment had risen. 1968 was showing more encouraging signs; real GNP was moving ahead and the strain on the capital markets had lessened. On the other hand both prices and unemployment were continuing to move upward.

Despite efforts at pruning, the expenditure Estimates for 1968-69 totalled $10.8 billion, an increase of $0.9 billion from the previous year. With revenues forecast at $10.1 billion, a deficit of $730 million was in prospect. The government took the decision that along with the continued threat of inflation, a deficit of this magnitude could not be tolerated. Furthermore the expenditure projections for the coming fiscal year, with which the Minister would soon have to deal, indicated another rise of nearly a billion dollars to $11.7 billion—with the potential for another substantial deficit.

The Minister's budget met this situation head-on. Tax increases were proposed and adopted that not only balanced the budget for 1969-70 but produced a surplus of nearly $0.4 billion, a turn-around from the deficit of the previous year of just short of a billion dollars.

The main ingredients of this potent tax packet, imposed for 1969 in addition to the tax increases in the Sharp November 1968 budget, and their expected yields in 1969-70 totalling $845 million, were as follows:

1. A Social Development Tax of 2 percent on taxable incomes of all taxpayers, with a maximum of $120; expected yield—$440 million.

2. Taxation of life insurance companies; expected yield—$75 million.

3. Reduction in reserves of financial institutions; expected yield—$45 million.

4. Further acceleration of corporate tax instalments; expected yield—$275 million.

5. Other changes; expected yield—$10 million.

Again the above reckoning allowed for further repayments of $139 million of the earlier refundable tax. (As nearly $400 million of the new tax program was to come from corporations some corporate treasurers must have caught only a brief glimpse of this refund on its way back to the federal government).

As this was the period when some of the proposals of the Royal Commission were being implemented there were many other tax changes. One of significance was a revision of the gift tax to put it on a cumulative basis and to relate it more directly to the estate tax payable on death. This was a misleading indication of future use of the tax by the federal government because it was repealed completely for 1972. The non-resident withholding tax was also extended in its scope to royalty payments to non-residents for the use of various forms of patents, know-how, and equipment.

The effect of the tax increases was to reduce the deficit for 1968-69 to $576 million, some $218 million lower than the previous year. Their full impact was to come in the following year, with the remarkable phenomenon of a sizable surplus.

Benson's Budget Surplus

June 1969: Benson. Inflation continued to threaten. Consumer prices had risen by over 4 percent in 1968 and were continuing to accelerate in 1969. Consumer expenditure was strong and capital expenditure was reviving. Unemployment was too high (4.7 percent) but the economy was comparatively strong, and an increase of 5 percent in real GNP was forecast. But the overriding concern was the threat of further inflation.

Anti-inflationary action was taken through both the tax and expenditure sides of the budget. The 3 percent surtaxes on both personal and corporate income taxes were extended for another year (1970). The 2 percent Social Development tax, introduced without an expiry date, was left in force. An air travel tax was announced, to yield $20 million in its first year of operation. Customs tariff reductions under the Kennedy Round, slated to become fully effective by January 1, 1972, were brought into effect on June 4, 1969, as a means of reducing costs in Canadian industry.

Once again a deferral of capital cost allowances was used as a means of discouraging capital investment deemed excessive by the government, in this instance commercial building. No write-off would be granted for two years on commercial buildings put in place up to the end of 1970 in major centres in Ontario, Alberta, and British Columbia. This included "buildings for wholesale and retail trade and services, office structures, banks, financial institutions and other commercial facilities such as hotels, theatres, and service stations." (This was an impressive degree of interference with town planning from the remote confines of Ottawa)! At any rate it seemed to have the desired effect, as it was extended the next year to catch some expenditures that would otherwise have escaped.

Other revenue-neutral changes were increases in the duty-free allowance for returning travellers; the changes forecast in the previous year in the integration of gift and estate taxes were implemented in legislation which came into effect in 1969. It was in this budget that the Minister was able to forecast with greater certainty the cumulative effect of the recent tax increases, most of which had been enacted in the previous two budgets. In June 1969, the current fiscal year, 1969-70, was forecast to end with a surplus of $375 million, based on revenues of $12 billion and expenditures of $11.7 billion.

As it turned out, the actual surplus was somewhat larger, at $393 million. This was quite a remarkable performance. Compared with a deficit of $576 million in the previous year this represented a turn-around of $969 million from one fiscal year to the next. Some of this was a dividend from the corporate sector—which was non-recurring—but a dividend it was, and a very welcome one. The fiscal year 1969-70 stands like a beacon in a long gray trail of deficits. But the Sharp-Benson blitz had run its course; it was back to deficits in the next year.

March 1970: Benson. In 1970 the economy began to show the effect of the restraints. Although 1969 had shown a real increase in GNP of over 5 percent, growth had been slowing as the year progressed. Export growth had declined, the balance of trade had fallen, business capital expenditures were being postponed, and corporation profits were in decline. There were weak spots in the economy which meant that unemployment remained high. And prices had risen more than any time since immediately after the war—4.5 percent.

Ironically the minister expected a growth in real GNP of 3 to 3.5 percent in 1970, higher unemployment, lower profits, but further inflation. In the choice between a weakening economy and rising prices the government chose to continue its anti-inflationary policies. The budget, which would govern for the 1970-71 fiscal year, was planned to produce another surplus, expected to be $250 million. To produce this result expenditures were to be held at $12.9 billion; revenues were expected to be $13.2 billion. (This was an expenditure increase of $1 billion, or over 8 percent, said to be the result of an austerity program. Obviously the government was having real problems in getting expenditures under control).

The budget made no important proposals for taxation. The surtaxes would expire at the end of 1970, unless renewed, a possibility the Minister hinted at. The capital cost deferral for commercial buildings was extended for an additional year to catch construction costs being incurred before 1972 on buildings started in the balance of 1970. A list of technical amendments was implemented, but generally tax changes were being held up for inclusion in the major tax reform then in progress. The government had issued its own White Paper in November 1969, and committees of the House and Senate had held public hearings and issued reports in September and October of 1970. These were being studied by the government.

Benson Tackles Unemployment

December 1970: Benson. By late 1970 it began to appear that unemployment had become the problem of greatest urgency. Inflationary pressures had eased with a slowing of price rises, but unemployment had climbed, reaching nearly 6 percent for the year. In the view of the government the situation therefore called for a policy which it was hoped would be stimulative without starting prices moving upward again.

This was to be accomplished mainly through a series of expenditure programs. These would include new funds for housing, for federal capital projects, a loan fund for provincial capital projects, extension of incentive benefits to parts of Ontario and Quebec, and enlargement of benefits available to the Atlantic provinces. Unemployment insurance benefits would be increased by 10 percent from January 1971.

On the tax side the 3 percent surtaxes, slated to expire at the end of 1970, were extended for a further year. To encourage capital expenditure in manufacturing, assets installed between December 1970 and March 1972 would be valued at 115 percent of their actual value for purposes of capital cost allowances.

The effect of these proposals on the balance of the budget was almost as dramatic as the performance of the previous year, although in the opposite direction. In place of the surplus of $250 million planned in June, a deficit of $320 million was now expected—a turn-around of $570 million within the year and of $695 million from the previous year. In fact the final budgetary deficit reached $379 million, $59 million more than had been forecast. Budgetary expenditures by this time had reached $13.2 billion, so that the deficit amounted to about 3½ percent of expenditures.

Benson Shepherds Tax Reform

June 1971: Benson. This budget was double-barrelled; it served both the normal purpose of setting the fiscal climate but as well it presented the government's proposals for tax reform. Both were dealt with at some length. The astonishing aspect of the budget was the need to adapt to an entirely changed economic climate. In the first part of the previous year the economy had been sluggish—2.2 percent growth in real GNP, 0.9 percent growth in consumer expenditure—but the pace had quickened in the fall and was remaining high in 1971. Housing expenditure was rising rapidly, to reach a new peak in 1973. Inflation was declining, but very temporarily, as the following months were to prove. The negative factors were flat business capital expenditures, excess inventories, and growing unemployment (1971 was to have the highest rate of the previous decade).

The formula for dealing with this situation was one adopted many times in previous years. Taxes were reduced: the 3 percent surtax on individuals was cut to 1.5 percent, the social development tax was reduced to the lesser of 2 percent of taxable income or $20, rates on low incomes were reduced, the 3 percent corporate surtax was repealed, the 25 percent excise on radios, hi-fi's and television sets was repealed, and minor other changes were made.

Massive further changes were proposed in this budget for the tax reform then in process. These will be outlined briefly in relation to 1972, when they first came into effect, but in more detail under the later discussion of tax reform.

October 1971—a quasi-budget: Benson. By October the government had concluded that more needed to be done to support the economy. In August the United States had taken drastic steps to relieve a balance of payments problem which were bound to affect Canadian exports. Many aspects of the Canadian economy had improved, but not unemployment. Along with the flood of immigration and the baby boom generation there was now the phenomenon of rising female participation—not unwelcome, but a labour market problem nonetheless.

The Minister, in a special emergency debate in October, announced a program which he hoped, along with the tax changes of his June budget, would help in relieving the situation. The program consisted mainly of additional expenditure initiatives, but some further tax changes were added. New monies were made available for local initiatives by community organizations or municipal governments, for on-the-job training, municipal and provincial capital projects, federal capital projects, and for housing. These various programs were estimated to represent outlays of $338 million.

Under the further tax reductions, federal personal income tax for the 18 months from July 1, 1971 to December 1972 was reduced by 3 percent. For corporations, tax for the same period was reduced by 7 percent. Corporations would also be allowed to write off 150 percent of costs for on-the-job training or, alternatively, to receive the equivalent as a payment.

The combined June budget tax reductions and the October expenditure increases and tax reductions were estimated to produce a deficit of $1 billion, the gap between revenues of $13.6 billion and expenditures of $14.6 billion. In fact the deficit, as a result mainly of better revenues than were expected, turned out to be considerably less—$581 million.

Turner Faces Growing Stagflation

May 1972: Turner. A new Liberal Minister of Finance, the third in five years, John Turner, presented the next budget. 1971, as with many of the troublesome years of the seventies, had shown mixed results. Under the stimulus of fiscal and monetary expansion there had been a substantial increase in GNP and capital expenditure, with housing starts a major contributor. The double bogies of the seventies were haunting the scene however: prices began to rise in late 1971 and early 1972; unemployment was on the rise. The Minister therefore foresaw the need for continued expansion, a need which had become even more pressing for Canada's international position because of the imminent entry of Great Britain into the EEC and the U.S. drive to rectify its balance of payments—including the dollar devaluation and the adoption of the DISC incentive for U.S. exports. It was assumed that Canada would require continued stimulus for monetary and fiscal policy to remain active in a general slowing up of world trade.

While most of the changes in this budget related to tax reform the few that were made for fiscal and economic purposes were significant. Among these was the reduction in the corporate tax rate from 49 percent to 40 percent on manufacturing and processing profits earned after January 1, 1973. A corresponding reduction from 25 percent to 20 percent was made in the small business rate.

A two-year rate of depreciation (50 percent per year) was granted for all machinery and equipment purchased after May 8, 1972, for use in manufacturing and processing. This would replace the previous allowance of valuation at 115 percent of cost for depreciation purposes. A previously granted special write-off for air and water pollution control equipment was to be extended for another year.

Under the personal income tax, the additional exemption granted the elderly, the blind, and persons confined to a bed or wheelchair was increased from $650 to $1,000, a new deduction of $50 per month was given for full-time students at certain educational institutions, and new medical expenses were to be allowed, including full-time attendants and long-distance transportation costs.

Although tax reform changes will be dealt with later it is relevant to the fiscal side of the budget that for 1972 and later years the federal government introduced a capital gains tax and repealed its estate tax.

The fate of the May budget fiscal changes was much like those of a previous budget of Finance Minister Sharp. They had not been implemented by legislation when the House was dissolved for an election in September. However they were enacted (relatively unchanged) following the return of a minority Liberal government, in the following year.

By this time federal expenditures had passed the $16 billion mark. Revenues in recent years had been following at a distance of about half a billion dollars, but with a buoyant economy it was expected that revenues would more than close the gap; with final revenues at $16.6 billion and expenditures at $16.2 billion a surplus of $481 million emerged for the 1972-73 fiscal year.

Turner Introduces Indexation

February 1973: Turner. The economic inheritance from 1972 was a good increase in real GNP (over 6 percent), a high rate of capital expenditure, a substantial increase in exports (but not enough to offset an even greater increase in imports), and a restoration of more normal profit levels. But the slowing in the rate of inflation that had been so painfully achieved in 1970 and 1971 was slipping away; consumer prices had risen by nearly 5 percent. The other member of the bad news team was also being difficult. Although there had been a slight decrease in unemployment it remained at the high level of 6.2 percent for the year 1972.

In these conditions the minister relied on the usual devices of tax and expenditure changes, aimed primarily in this case at easing pressures that were thought to be causing inflation. As an interim measure relief under the personal income tax was granted by the increase in all the personal exemptions for 1973 and a reduction of 5 percent in the personal income tax payable (minimum $100; maximum $500) from January 1, 1973. But the main step was the introduction of a permanent system of indexation to commence January 1, 1974 to apply to both personal exemptions and tax brackets, an historic move in Canadian taxation annals. The exemption list under the sales tax was also extended, the principal new item being children's clothing and footwear; an excise tax on cosmetics and toilet articles was repealed and less expensive clocks and watches were exempted from an excise tax. An interesting new venture was a one year reduction in tariffs on various imported consumer goods ranging from 2½ percent to 10 percent (averaging 5 percent) as a means of reducing the price of heavily taxed, scarce, or non-available goods.

The government gave an undertaking at this time to study the results of the reduced rate on manufacturing profits and the two-year write-off for manufacturing and production equipment and report to the House in 1974. It was a provision of the legislation that at the request of 60 or more members Parliament would review these incentives and if it so decided would repeal them in whole or in part. The government declared its intention, in any event, of reviewing the whole of the capital cost allowance system by the end of 1974 with a view to modernizing it. Unlike its predecessor, the fiscal year ending in March 1974 was expected to show a substantial deficit as a result of a $4 billion increase in expenditures and recent substantial tax reductions. The original estimates were for revenues of $18.6 billion and expenditures of $19.4 billion, with a deficit of $789 million. The final reckoning was: expenditures, $20.1 billion; revenues, $19.4 billion; deficit, $673 million, or about 3 percent of expenditures.

These figures are modest by standards of the 1980s, but they reveal nonetheless that in the six years since 1969 expenditures had nearly doubled.

Turner: RHOSP and Other Innovations

May-November 1974: Turner. Once again the political instability of minority government affected the budgeting process. In May the Minister presented a budget that was defeated in the Commons. An election followed in which the Liberals were returned with a majority, and in November a new budget was introduced that basically implemented the earlier version.

The economy had been astonishingly healthy in 1973. There had been some remarkable signs of growth. Real GNP had risen by an almost record breaking 7.6 percent, capital expenditure in all categories reached new high levels, and exports and the balance of trade had improved dramatically. Unemployment fell from 6.2 to 5.5 percent, and appeared to be continuing to fall, and corporate profits were rising. It seemed therefore that the economy might be on the eve of a further period of growth. The bad news however was shocking. The world economy had been given a body-blow with the combined effect of the first oil price shock and a rise in food prices as a result of crop failures. Canada was in a more fortunate position than most countries in absorbing these calamitous events, but could not shield

	1968-69
	$ millions
Payment of training allowances	114
Capital assistance to the provinces for providing training facilities	80
Payments to provinces for the Trans-Canada highway	45
Loss in the operations of the Agricultural Commodities Stabilization Board	144
Selected defence development programs	32
Capital subsidies for ship construction	32
Employment incentives for slow growth areas	34
Subsidies to carriers for transporting wheat	96
CNR deficit	39
Atlantic Development Fund	33
Incentives to industry for scientific research	31
Grants in aid of medical research	27
Scholarships and grants in aid of research	59
Canada Council	20
International Food Aid	69

One can at least express some wonderment that despite the expenditure of these not minor outlays nearly two decades ago on training and research, (the equivalent in 1987 dollars of at least four times the above amounts) and continuing substantial programs since, why the common cry in the mid-1980s is for programs of training and research. What went wrong?

from bad weather. Capital expenditures in all categories had actually declined, unusual in the postwar period, but reflective of the prevailing business uncertainty, both about the U.S. economy and the future of the AIB in Canada.

Retail sales and industrial production were sluggish. The Canadian dollar sank to 94 cents in relation to the U.S. dollar, and began the decline that would bring it to 69-70 cents in early 1985. The only upward movements were in unemployment and inflation; the former reached 8.1 percent, a postwar high, and the latter, as registered by the CPI, rose 7.9 percent over 1976.

In these alarming conditions the new Minister of Finance, Jean Chrétien, decided that some further government action was called for. In an Economic and Fiscal Statement (less formal than a full budget) he cleared up some of the uncertainty regarding the AIB by announcing that it would be gradually phased out starting April 14, 1978. He also pledged the government to expenditure restraint and support of the Bank of Canada's stringent monetary policy.

On the tax side he announced a reduction of personal income tax for lower incomes and tax credits for increased employment in private businesses, along with other minor changes. The only new expenditure was an increase in the funds available for work projects with a high employment content.

Following these changes the forecasts for the year-end position were revised downward from $34.7 billion to $33.1 billion for revenue and upward from $41.9 billion to $42.3 billion for expenditure; the deficit was also revised upward from $7.2 billion to $9.2 billion. This in fact was overly optimistic. The final balance for the year exceeded $10 billion as a result of both a further decline in revenue and an increase in expenditure.

Chrétien: Luring the Private Economy

April and November 1978: Chrétien: Budgeting was becoming a twice-a-year process for the Minister of Finance. There were to be two formal budgets in 1978, and a good deal of public exhortation as well. With the withdrawal of the government's anti-inflation vehicle imminent, the politicians appear to have felt that they could continue a moderating influence by public exhortation. All the leading federal ministers, including the Prime Minister, made a concerted effort in various ways to retain the progress that had been made under the AIB regime. This was to be a year, in the vernacular of the day, of "jawboning" the economy into submission. The process started at a First Ministers Conference in February. Here the heads of all governments united in a declaration that expenditure increases would be kept within the limits of GNP growth and that staff salary levels would follow, not lead, private sector increases.

Budget preparation for 1977-78 went forward in even more uncertainty than usual; 1977 had turned out to be an even worse year than had been expected in the October economic statement. Real growth of GNP of 2 percent was the lowest (except for one year, 1954) in the postwar period. All the main elements of the economy had either been sluggish or had declined. Even consumer expenditure, which had remained a stable and buoyant factor in most postwar years (in the 5-8 percent range), had only grown by 2.4 percent. By contrast the increases of 7.9 percent in inflation and an unemployment rate of 8.1 percent were ominous signs for the future.

The April 1978 budget settled two background policy issues—the government approved of the Bank of Canada's tight monetary policy, by this time a very contentious issue because of the high level of unemployment, and allowed the Canadian dollar to continue within limits to find its own value. It continued to fall and averaged about 88 cents for 1978.

In detail, the fiscal plan was based on the assumption of a GNP rise of 11 percent; 5 percent real growth, more than double that of the previous year, and 6 percent in prices. CPI would rise 7 percent, and unemployment would remain heavy, particularly in some regions.

There was particular concern about consumer spending, in view of the 1977 increase of only 2.4 percent, nearly the lowest rate of the postwar period. The main budget proposal was designed to offset this trend. In a complex deal with provinces levying a sales tax the budget speech offered compensation for a reduction in provincial retail sales tax rates. For the Atlantic provinces it offered full compensation for a 3 point reduction for six months. For the other provinces it offered two-thirds compensation, the provinces to have the option of a 3 point reduction for six months or a 2 point reduction for nine months. The Atlantic provinces, Ontario and Manitoba opted for the 3 point-six months reduction; Saskatchewan and British Columbia for the 2 point-nine months alternative. Quebec accepted neither alternative but completely exempted from tax a selected list of items. No settlement was reached with that province on a form of compensation, but in the final device for settlement (a tax rebate against 1977 federal income tax liability), Quebec taxpayers in effect were included for the federal reduction. On the assumption that all provinces would accept the sales tax proposal the budget estimated its cost at $800 million. Actual outlays, with Quebec abstaining, turned out to be about $600 million. The remaining tax changes related to research and development expenditure, railway capital investment, and tax incentives for heavy oil and oil sands projects. All increased existing provisions.

No new expenditure programs were envisaged in the budget speech; in fact the figure used was lower than that provided in the Main Estimates for the year already tabled in Parliament. Revenues were expected to increase by 10 percent and, despite the absence of new programs, expenditures were forecast to rise by 9 percent; the deficit would be $10.9 billion.

In the months following the budget speech hoped-for signs of recovery failed to appear. By August GNP real growth had been trimmed to 3 to 4 percent, capital expenditure had declined further, consumer expenditure, after a brief flurry, was little above 1977, inflation and unemployment were moving ahead relentlessly, and the international situation was causing grave concern. The value of the Canadian dollar was continuing to drop, and Canada's international reserves were having to be replenished with foreign borrowing. Although there had been a favourable balance of trade for nearly two decades, a substantial unfavourable balance on current account had emerged in 1975 ($4.8 billion) and had persisted in later years at about this level. While official monetary movements had shown a net inflow in most postwar years, they turned sharply to a net outflow in 1977 ($1.4 billion) and a further outflow of more than twice that amount in 1978. In a game that has since become familiar to most Canadians the Bank of Canada was nudging interest rates upward to attract foreign funds; the three-month treasury bill rate rose from 7⅓ percent to 8⅔ percent from 1977 to 1978, and then to 11½ percent in 1979, the highest rate up to that time.

The August 1978 Program

Clearly Canada had lost its attraction as one of the garden spots of the world for international investors. Whether this was a temporary or permanent problem was not clear at this stage, further complicating a deeply troubling experience. With all aspects of the economy deteriorating, the government determined that a drastic change in approach was needed. In a television appearance on August 1 the Prime Minister announced that the main emphasis would be given in government policy to encouraging private sector development and to relieving inflationary pressures.

The first stage of this program concentrated on expenditure cuts. Later in August a detailed statement was issued of individual reductions approved up to that time, which totalled $1.5 billion, with more to come. About the same time provincial premiers were warned that the federal government would be taking a tougher stance on federal-provincial payments. Increases in oil prices were postponed, and the special gasoline tax was reduced from 10 cents per gallon to 7 cents.

Massive changes were announced at this time in various aspects of "people payments." An addition to the Guaranteed Income Supplement would be made. The family allowance, already taxable, would be reduced to $20 a month and supplemented with a refundable tax credit, which would be taxable above a specified income level. The $50 tax credit per child granted in 1977 would be withdrawn. Major revisions were to be made in unemployment insurance, including tighter restrictions on eligibility and taxation of the benefit above a specified income level. A release in September gave details of the whole program of expenditure reductions, then amounting to $500 million for 1978-79 and $2.0 billion for 1979-80.

November 1978: Chrétien. Following this flurry of changes a new budget was required to put them in perspective and to make other adjustments. The economic environment in 1978 had changed with lower real growth in GNP and higher unemployment and consumer prices than expected. The problem now was to provide a climate for 1979 in which the government's program might have some hope of take-off, a challenge that was to be considerably complicated by a sudden doubling of oil prices in December 1978, a development which one assumes was unknown to the Minister in November. The hope for a more lively economy was based on recovery of investment expenditure, personal consumption expenditure, and exports. For 1979 the GNP forecast was 4 to 4½ percent for real growth and 6½ percent for prices, giving the more or less standard expectation of 11 percent. (These forecasts for real growth were generally too optimistic, as indicated by the following: 1978—budget forecast, 5 percent; actual, 3.6 percent; 1979—budget forecast, 4 to 4½ percent; actual, 3.2 percent).

As a bonus from the proposed expenditure reductions and a further stimulus for the economy some substantial tax reductions were presented in the November budget. The largest of these was a reduction in the sales tax rate from 12 percent to 9 percent, except for alcoholic beverages and tobacco. In addition the employment expense deduction was increased from $250 to $500. The basic investment tax credit rate was increased to 7 percent, the rates for slow growth regions raised to 10 and 20 percent, and extended indefinitely for the future. Other relaxations related to research expenditure and resource, pulp and paper, and housing companies.

The total bill on complete adoption of the three phases of this 1978 program was estimated at $3.6 billion in a full year. The elements were costed at $900 million for the April budget; $870 million for the August announcements, and $1.9 billion for the November budget. Their effects would fall between 1978 and 1979, and the final forecasts for each year reflected this division. For 1978-79 the budgetary forecast was $35.2 billion for revenue and $47.3 billion for expenditure, leaving a deficit of $12.1 billion. The actual position for the year was very close to this: $35.2 billion for revenue, $47.4 billion for expenditure, and $12.2 billion for the deficit.

Crosbie: The Aborted 1979 Budget

December 1979: Crosbie. 1979 is memorable for a budget that brought down a newly elected Conservative government. Parliament had been dissolved in March on the calling of an election by the Liberal government, a Conservative government had been elected, and after some delay it presented a budget on December 11. On December 13 the House rejected this budget, following which the government resigned and an election was called for February, when the Liberals were returned to power.

This Conservative budget, though not passed, deserves some attention. Naturally the new Minister of Finance had no way of escaping the grip of that gruesome pair, inflation and unemployment, both of which were threatening catastrophe, and these came in for considerable attention. However, the main features of his budget were the proposals of the new government in the growingly complex area of energy policy. The OPEC announcement of a doubling of oil prices in late 1978 had brought new stresses to the informal Canadian arrangements and more formal measures were becoming inevitable to cope with the situation. Without going into full detail, the budget proposed a schedule of future price increases, of revenue sharing between federal and provincial governments, and of taxation of both the industry and the public to finance the plan. Along with these energy taxes, increased taxes on tobacco and alcohol, a surtax on corporate profits, and a new sharing of the costs of unemployment insurance were proposed.

For economic stimulus the emphasis was placed on the private sector, and several proposals were made to this end. Plans were also made for reducing the deficit by strict control over expenditures.

The unexpected fate of the Conservative government meant that for all intents and purposes there was no budget in 1979. Legislation to implement one of the government's major election promises, the Mortgage Interest and Homeowner Property Tax Credit died a-borning. Some tax increases had been in effect for two days and the revenue was refunded. Otherwise the prevailing tax structure governed for the year.

Notwithstanding this result, some notable changes had taken place under the Conservatives in other aspects of the national finances. One of these was the adoption of the envelope system of expenditure management, which was later followed by the Liberal government (which indeed claimed it as its own invention). The other was the publication of an official estimate prepared by the Department of Finance of the cost of "tax expenditures"— basically the revenue loss from concessions granted under federal taxes. A third and more technical measure, the Adjustment of Accounts Act, wiped out dozens of special accounts and revolving funds, which henceforth would appear directly in the revenue or expenditure accounts. (The bane of historical writing: from this time forward earlier years are no longer comparable)!

As a closing comment on this short-lived government, it is interesting that there were no great expectations of an easy life over future years. By this time budgets were giving a five-year economic and fiscal projection, and the Conservatives were being quite realistic about what lay ahead. No more than a 1 percent real growth in GNP was expected for 1980 (which in fact turned out to be right on the nose) and 3.5 percent for 1981 (which also turned out to be accurate). The forecast for inflation (as measured by the CPI) was equally realistic at 11.0 for 1980 and 11.4 for the following year, the former slightly high and the latter low, but the average was again accurate. Expenditures were forecast to rise from $52 billion in fiscal 1980 to $57 billion in 1981 and $63 billion in 1982 (in considerable part due to the energy program), but revenues were expected to rise at a slightly faster rate, so that the deficit would gradually drop from $11.2 billion in 1980 to $10.5 billion in 1981 and $9.8 billion in 1982. But the Rubicon was not for recrossing; the election and the recession of 1982 were to change all that.

For the record the actual out-turn in this budgetless fiscal year ending March 31, 1980, was $40.1 billion for revenue and $51.5 billion for expenditure, leaving a deficit of $11.5 billion.

Tax Expenditures and Other Reductions

There is some interesting financial information that gives a bearing on the state of the revenue system in 1979. One source, the *Tax Expenditure*

Estimates, has been mentioned; the other was an estimate of the cost in 1979 of indexation of the personal income tax, which appeared a year later in the Department of Finance annual *Economic Review*. Of particular interest in the tax expenditure calculations was the cost of the incentives offered with abandon by nearly every minister over a long period to entice the economy into energetic activity. The cost of some of the more prominent of these in 1979 was listed as $625 million for the investment tax credit; $400 million for the reduced rate of corporate tax on manufacturing and processing profits; $1 billion for the reduced corporate rate for small business; $325 million for the inventory value adjustment; $395 million for the reduced rate of sales tax on building materials; $1.2 billion for the cost of capital cost allowance claims in excess of book value; $600 million for the resource allowance for natural resource industries, and many other allowances and credits costing lesser amounts. Although these sums are not necessarily additive and there are arguments as to what constitutes something special under the income tax, an amount of $4 billion or more can be attributed to corporate tax incentives for 1979.

Equally interesting are the values in 1979 of the actual tax reductions introduced since 1972. The most spectacular of these was the cost of indexation—$6 billion. In 1979 the personal income tax was producing $6 billion less than it would have without indexation. This dimension seems never to have registered with the public or even with some authors who wrote on the subject. Thus with the annual cost to the federal government rising by several hundred million each year ($900 million in 1979) the total accumulated cost by 1979 could easily have exceeded $20 billion. In addition, excluding the reductions covered in the tax expenditure study already mentioned, another $7 billion of reductions (in all categories of taxation) can be identified. Without being too precise on the matter it is clear that by 1979, as the result of a long period of running an economically motivated and socially oriented tax system, the revenue base had been seriously undermined and, with continuing full indexation of the personal income tax for inflation, would continue to be undermined. This is not to deny that some recognition for inflation would have been desirable; it is simply to assert that the actual method chosen was quite an expensive one.

MacEachen: Prelude to Shock

April and October 1980: MacEachen. Minister of Finance MacEachen, of the re-elected Liberal government, faced a situation in which no budget had been adopted for a year and a half and plans formulated by another government had been rejected both by Parliament and the electorate. Economic conditions had worsened in the meantime with the second oil shock, and prospects for 1980 were not bright. Abroad most countries had attempted to snuff out the inflationary potential of higher oil prices with severely restrictive fiscal and monetary policies, and economies would suffer as a result. There was no momentum from 1979. Real GNP had increased by only 3.2 percent and the rise of 3.0 percent in exports of goods and services had been among the lowest in the postwar years. Capital expen-

5
The Deficit Enigma; Strong Measures Needed (1982-87)

The enigma of the closing period is the emergence of deficits of $27.8 billion in 1982 and $32.4 billion in 1983, in place of the $10.5 and the $9.6 billion forecast for those years. But add to this the succeeding deficits of $38.3 billion in 1984, $34.4 billion in 1985 and $32.0 billion in 1986 and the enigma begins to appear as a catastrophe.

Arithmetically of course there is no enigma. Deficits arise when expenditure exceeds revenue. But it was unexpected, and probably unpredictable, that the growth of one would so far exceed the growth of the other. Why did this happen?

The Limping Economy

Clearly the economy had been limping badly for some time. This shows most forcefully in the three main signs of health—real GNP, unemployment, and inflation. In only one year since 1974 had there been real growth in GNP at all comparable to the sixties. In 1976 there had been an isolated rise of 5.9 percent, but all other years had been in the range of 1 to 3½ percent. Unemployment had been in the 7 to 8½ percent range, and inflation between 7½ and 12½ percent, with the years 1978 to 1981 averaging 10 percent. While many countries were suffering a worse fate, and occasionally Canada had a better record than even the United States, the economy was indisputably a long way from full health in the late seventies and early eighties.

1979 was a year that seemed to hold some promise. With a modest increase in real GNP, a rise in capital expenditure, and a reduction in unemployment, it offered some hope for the following year. What might have developed had there not been a sharp second increase in oil prices is difficult to say. Certainly the response of governments to this rise was not designed to be of much help to a lagging economy. Whereas governments and their central banks had taken steps to cushion the inflationary effects of the first oil price rise in 1973 there was a world-wide determination to prevent the second round from setting off further inflation. Monetary policy became the main instrument for this purpose. The Bank of Canada began a process in 1979 of tightening money supply and increasing interest rates to match developments in U.S. and elsewhere. Money supply growth fell to 6.9 percent in 1979, 6.4 percent in 1980, 3.6 percent in 1981 and 0.1 percent in 1982. The Bank of Canada discount rate, the bell-wether rate generally followed by the market, had never in its history exceeded 7½ percent until 1978, but between January 1978 and August 1981, by frequent increases, it was raised to 21 percent. These changes were of course reflected in other interest rates. The chartered bank prime rate, usually in the 5 to 7½ percent area, rose from 8.25 percent in January 1978 to a peak of 22.75 percent in September 1981. Residential mortgages followed a similar path, although at levels 1 to 2 percent higher.

Much of this action followed classical money supply and interest rate prescriptions for combating inflation, but was also required to support the value of the Canadian dollar, which had fallen during this period from 88 cents in 1978 to 81 cents in 1982.

Whether or not the severity of this treatment was justified was hotly debated at the time, and some authorities have since argued that inter-national action on the scale then experienced brought on a recession from which the world is still recovering. Interest rates of 20 percent or more, (though they are remembered with nostalgia by savers) accompanied by a rapidly declining money supply, are not prescriptions for inducing the birth of a lively economy.

Whatever the cause, certainly there was a recession in Canada of notable proportions, capped in 1983 by the first actual fall in real GNP in the post-war period. The data for many of the basic elements of the economy are given in table 5.1 for the three years 1981 to 1983 and demonstrate the scope and magnitude of the collapse.

Implications for Budget-Making

One need only consider the minus signs in this table to grasp the effect of the tightening economic policy, and particularly its financial aspects. Any phase of the economy that relied heavily on borrowed funds—housing and business capital investment in particular—was almost immediately seriously curtailed, and tight money spread its effect throughout the economy. Exports, crucial for the Canadian economy, although sluggish, were no doubt sustained by the depreciating value of the Canadian dollar. Further-more, a substantial decline in imports produced the largest trade surplus of the postwar period ($17.8 billion)—indeed, produced the first favourable current account balance of any consequence in the same period, a no doubt welcome bonus from the restraint program. But of course the current pre-vailing economic conditions—inflation in the 10-12.5 percent range and unemployment of about the same magnitude—were less encouraging. What could a Minister of Finance do in his budget that would be suitable for this climate, given that the state of the economy had become a prime political issue and nearly every trick in the fiscal bag had already been tried?

MacEachen's 6-and-5 Formula; Spending for Revival

June 1982: MacEachen. Perhaps the most notable contribution of the Minister at this critical juncture was the so-called 6-and-5 formula, a simple and understandable appeal that wage and price increases be limited to 6 per-cent after July 1982 and to 5 percent in the following year. This formula was to be applied by the federal government in its own salary and other pro-grams, and was urged on other governments and the private sector for

Table 5.1 Principal Economic Data, 1981-83
(percentage change unless otherwise indicated)

	1981	1982	1983
Real GNP growth	3.3	3.4	-4.4
Unemployment rate (actual)	7.5	11.0	11.9
Inflation rate	12.5	11.1	5.8
Consumer expenditure	1.7	-2.0	3.1
Total capital expenditure	6.5	-11.7	-3.9
Residential construction	3.9	-21.0	24.4
Housing starts	12.0	-29.3	29.2
Mortgage lending ($ billion)	7.6	3.3	12.1
Business investment	7.7	-9.1	-12.4
Exports	3.1	-1.6	6.4
Imports	4.5	-11.2	8.1
Canadian dollar (actual U.S. $)	83.4	81.2	81.2
Unit labour costs	11.8	11.9	2.1
Profits before tax	-13.4	-35.3	54.8
Labour income	15.6	7.0	5.5
Real personal disposable income	4.6	-1.1	-0.3
Personal savings rate (actual)	14.2	15.2	13.3
Consumer credit	6.1	-2.7	3.7
Chartered bank business loans ($ billion)	38.3	2.7	-9.4
Total business borrowing ($ billion)	45.1	15.0	1.3
90 day commercial paper (interest rate)	18.3	14.2	9.5

Source: Department of Finance, *Economic Review*, April 1985.

adoption. Along with the cruel but effective medicine that had been administered through monetary policy and a toughening attitude toward wage and cost increases, inflation came down to 5.8 percent in 1983 and 4.3 percent in 1984. Monetary policy had been relaxed somewhat in 1983, when money supply rose by 10.2 percent to restore some life to the economy, but the anti-inflationary regime had been restored in 1984 with an increase of only 3.2 percent, followed by only a 4.1 percent increase in 1985.

Whatever the main reason for the end of galloping inflation it ceased to be a major concern of budgets from 1983 forward, although of course experience shows that it is an ever-present threat, and can never be dismissed entirely from public policy. The energy program continued to hold attention but, with the collapse of the OPEC oil prices and production restrictions, the problem changed to how best to deal with all the projects started in the expectation of $25-30 a barrel petroleum that had become uneconomic. This called for some financial rescue operations by the federal government; but with abandonment of the National Energy Program by the Mulroney government energy had ceased to be a prime issue in Canada, although a shortage of fossil fuels seems inevitable at some time in the future. The central concerns of budget-makers from 1982 onward were two: reduction of the unemployment rate, stuck in the 10-11 percent area, and controlling the rapidly growing federal deficit.

To return to the budget of June 1982. The evidence that the 1982 economy was far from exuberant need not be repeated. The previous budget had forecast a modest increase of real GNP of 2.2 percent for that year, and by mid-1982 that had been revised downward to a decrease of 2 percent. Even this figure was based on general expectation of an imminent recovery in the United States, which did not materialize. Economic revival, including programs for both inflation and unemployment, therefore remained a top priority. We have seen what steps were taken for inflation—the 6-and-5 formula, along with a continued commitment to keep expenditures within the growth rate of nominal GNP. What was to be done for unemployment?

One of the Minister's main programs was a series of measures designed to create direct employment. This took the form of an addition of $200 million to the Canada Community Development Program and $300 million over a two-year period to promote industrial innovation and adjustment under the Enterprise Development Program, the Defence Industry Productivity Program, and the Labour Adjustment Program. Housing was also given a stimulus through several programs. A grant of $3,000 would be given toward the first-time purchase of a new house (with some restrictions). A plan of interest-free loans for home renovation, announced in March 1982, was enriched. The annual interest-free loan allocation for nonprofit housing was increased, and the Canada Mortgage Renewal Plan, under which the federal government offered assistance with excessive mortgage interest, was extended.

This brief introduction of employment assistance programs, so frequently mentioned in connection with previous budgets, serves as an opportunity to at least list those in effect in 1982. As at October 27, including those already mentioned, the list, and amounts appropriated under each item, was as follows:

	$ million
Canada Community Development Program	194.0
Canada Community Services Projects	11.2
Local Economic Development Assistance	2.7
New Technology Employment Program	3.6
Local Employment Assistance Program	61.0
Outreach	16.7
Program for Employment of the Disadvantaged	55.0
Summer Youth Employment	120.0
Canada Manpower Assistance Program	40.6
Agricultural Manpower Assistance Program	6.5
Special Employment Program	19.9
Job Creation Programs Funded by Unemployment Insurance	
Work Sharing	200.0
Job Creation	85.0
Housing Programs	480.0
(including first-time home-buyers grant (275), home renovation plan (55), and Canada rental supply plan (150))	
Canadian Industrial Renewal Board	30.0
Adult Occupational Training	463.4
Industrial Training Program	121.3
(including critical trade skills training, non-traditional training for women, and native opportunities training)	
Training Allowances	88.1

Further measures proposed in the June budget included a plan to encourage investment in securities by excluding gains from inflation, to be considered by the public and a special committee appointed for the purpose. Lower income families were aided by an increase in the child tax credit, and GIS recipients by retention of full indexation for their payments.

And what of the deficit? Here calamity was beginning to surface. The budget of November in the previous year had forecast 1982-83 revenues at $65 billion and expenditures at $75.5 billion, leaving a deficit of $10.5 billion, somewhat better than the $12 to $13 billion of recent years. But in the budget under review, that of June 1982, the forecasts for the same year had been revised drastically. Revenue had been reduced by 10 percent to $58.6 billion and expenditure raised by 3½ percent to $78.1 billion. As a result the forecast deficit had increased to $19.6 billion, or close to double the previous expectation. None of the changes proposed in the June budget would have produced an increase of this order.

Lalonde: Revival Programs; Growing Deficits

October 1982: Lalonde. By October a new Minister of Finance was facing a situation that in every way had deteriorated from June expectations. Real GNP, then expected to decline by 2 percent, was now forecast to drop by 4.4 percent (the exact final decline), unemployment was rising, and inflation was moderating only slightly. In these conditions the Minister confirmed his support for the 6-and-5 formula, continued restraint on government expenditure, and principal reliance on the private sector for economic stimulus. His main effort was concentrated on further development of the job creation programs outlined previously. To these he proposed to add another substantial sum—$500 million in further job creating programs, $200 million for jobs in the housing industry, and $400 million for modernization of railways in western Canada. Along with $9.1 billion of expenditures from the Unemployment Insurance Account it was estimated that in 1982-83 $10.9 billion would be spent on employment creation or on training and support for the unemployed.

On the tax side the Minister had before him a proposal that the federal sales tax be changed from the manufacturers' to the wholesale level; he postponed a decision for further consideration. A special committee to consider one of the previous minister's more contentious proposals—that the deduction for interest costs related to investment be limited to the return on that investment—reported against the proposal and it was dropped, with some limitations. The Minister also accepted the recommendation of the Lortie Committee that capital gains on security investments arising from inflation be excluded through use of a new measure, the Registered Shareholder Investment Plan.

In a total budget now in the neighbourhood of $79 billion the revenue implications of these changes were nominal. The greater was the shock, therefore, when the Minister announced that far from the deficit of $19.6 billion forecast in the June budget the outlook was now for a deficit of

Table 5.2   Major Revenue Sources, 1981-83

	1981	1982	1983	Increase or decrease 1981-82	Increase or decrease 1982-83
		billions of dollars			
Personal income tax	19.8	24.0	26.3	4.2	2.3
Corporation income tax	8.2	8.1	7.1	−0.1	−1.0
Sales tax	5.4	6.2	5.9	0.8	−0.3
Customs duties	3.2	3.4	2.8	0.2	−0.6
General taxes	36.6	41.7	42.1	5.1	0.4
Petroleum and gas revenue tax	—	0.9	2.0	0.9	1.1
Gas and gas liquids tax	0.2	1.0	1.3	0.8	0.3
Oil export charge...................	0.8	0.5	0.4	−0.3	
Special petroleum compensation charge	—	0.5	—	−0.5	−0.5
Gasoline tax.......................	0.5	0.4	0.4	−0.1	—
Energy taxes and charges	1.5	3.3	4.1	1.8	0.8
Total taxes	40.7	48.0	49.3	7.3	1.3
Total revenue......................	46.5	54.6	55.1	8.1	0.5

$23.6 billion, $4 billion higher than the June forecast and $13 billion higher than the $10.5 billion forecast a year before. The forecast of 11 months before, given the unpredictable nature of 1982, is hardly a fair base, but does at least indicate the roots of the problem.

Revenue Trends, 1981-83

Actual changes, as compared to forecasts, are a more accurate reflection of the trauma of this crucial period. Table 5.2 gives details of the major revenue sources between 1982 and 1983, and between 1981 and 1982 as well for comparison.

Obviously the minor increase in total revenue of $0.5 billion in fiscal 1983 fell far short of the $8 billion increase the year before, which in turn had been preceded by fairly substantial increases in prior years. A drop of $1 billion in corporation income tax with sagging profits and a similar drop in energy taxes were the largest negative entries. The sales tax decline reflected the reduction in rate to 9 percent, as well as sluggish sales, and customs revenue dropped with drastically reduced imports. Personal income tax revenue was no doubt reflecting the drag of indexation, which for 1982 amounted to a reduction of an additional $11.4 billion in personal income tax revenue. It is astonishing under these conditions that personal income tax revenue was not actually declining. In 1983 the post office ceased to be a budget item with its establishment as a Crown corporation, and from that time on only its deficit appeared. This meant no appreciable change in the net budgetary position.

Expenditure Trends, 1981-83

Actual expenditure changes were also revealing, as table 5.3 shows.

Table 5.3   Major Expenditure Changes, 1981-83

	1981	1982	1983	Increase or decrease 1981-82	Increase or decrease 1982-83
		billions of dollars			
Old age security	7.4	8.6	9.6	1.2	1.0
Family allowances	1.9	2.0	2.2	0.1	0.2
Canada assistance plan	1.9	2.4	2.9	0.5	0.5
Public debt charges	10.8	15.2	18.6	4.4	3.4
Defence	5.0	6.0	7.0	1.0	1.0
General purpose payments to other governments	3.8	4.5	5.4	0.7	0.9
Unemployment insurance contribution	2.5	1.0	2.1	− 1.5	1.1
Energy	3.2	4.2	4.8	1.0	0.6
Transport	2.5	2.3	2.9	− 0.2	0.5
Total expenditure	62.4	67.5	78.3	5.1	10.8

The high interest rates of the period raised public debt charges by nearly $8 billion between 1981 and 1983, which accounted for half the total increase of $16 billion. Although declining, the increase of $3.4 billion was also the largest factor in the rise between 1982 and 1983. In addition there were increases of $1 billion or thereabouts in each of defence, the federal contribution to unemployment insurance, and general purpose payments to other governments. Substantial increases in family allowances, the Canada Assistance Plan, energy, and transport and smaller rises in a myriad of other categories accounted for the balance. The only large categories showing declines in 1983 were federal grants for hospital and health insurance. This resulted from recent tougher federal bargaining with the provinces (but in fact the declines were quite temporary and offset only a small part of the increases).

To round out the full reckoning for the year, the final revenue was $55.1 billion and expenditure $79.8 billion, giving an actual deficit of $24.7 billion. The increase of $11 billion over 1982 was a new record for peacetime, and exceeded anything seen before or since. But $25 billion was not to be the end; a second Rubicon beckoned to be passed at $30 billion, and passed it was in the next year.

Lalonde: More Steps for Private Revival

April 1983: Lalonde. Canada was recovering from the recession, but at a slower pace than expected. From the 4.4 percent decline in real GNP in 1982 an increase of 2.3 percent was forecast for 1983, a turnaround of 6.7 percent (actual real growth was 3.3 percent, a rise of 7.7 percent). Capital expenditure was lagging but exports were beginning to recover, and inflation was no longer the dread dragon that it had been. Consumer savings had been exceptionally high (thousands of families had become first-time investors in deposit certificates and other instruments at 20 percent return or greater) and it was hoped that lower interest rates would disgorge some of this money. The most discouraging feature of the economy was the high level of unemployment. Inflation had been defeated at the cost of bringing the economy to its knees, and the challenge faced by the Minister of Finance was to make a worthwhile contribution to job creation.

The formula produced by the Minister in his April 1983 budget was a four-year program of combined public and private measures. The federal government would accelerate projects planned for the next four years ($690 million) and would add another $1.5 billion in new projects. About half the total of $2.2 billion was to go for transportation facilities and vessel procurement, and the balance would be spent on research and training facilities, high technological procurement, resource development, land and tourism development, and miscellaneous other programs. Of the total, $1.4 billion represented direct employment creation, of which about half would be spent in the current year.

For the private sector there were some major incentives for enterprise and investment. These included an extension of the carry-back and carry-forward periods for business losses; removal of any limit on deduction of the investment tax credit and cash refunding of the credit for new investment in the following three years if it was not possible for the taxpayer to make use of them; a share-purchase tax credit at 25 percent of the value of new shares first issued between July 1, 1983 and the end of 1986. Following proposals made in a budget discussion paper—*Research and Development Tax Policies*—the 50 percent additional income deduction for incremental R and D expenditures was replaced by an increase in the tax credit for all R and D expenditures. The rate of the general tax credit was raised from 10 to 20 percent and higher rates were enacted for the Atlantic Region and for small businesses. In addition, all corporations would be allowed to flow-through their R and D tax credits to shareholders providing funds for this purpose at a rate of 50 percent of the funds advanced, an innocent sounding proposal that later would result in the loss of a great deal of revenue through spurious "quick flip" transactions.

In addition to the tax measures a special recovery investment fund of $300 million was provided to support private investment over a two-year period as well as an amount of $180 million for additional export financing by the Export Development Corporation. An extra $300 million was also provided for support of the housing industry, largely by expanding existing programs.

Even this is only part of the details of this complex budget. Several significant income tax changes were also made. The Indexed Security Investment Plan would begin in October; persons purchasing a newly constructed home before December 1984, would be allowed an income deduction equal to $10,000 less their previous RHOSP deductions, and RHOSP money could be withdrawn free of tax in 1983 for the purchase of home furnishings and appliances; the employment expense deduction was increased to 20 percent of income from 3 percent, the maximum remaining at $500; the child tax credit was increased but the threshold for the recovery tax left unchanged; the maximum deduction for child care expenses was increased from $4,000 to $8,000; the optional standard deduction was removed; the federal tax credit began to be phased out for higher incomes; the overseas employment deduction was increased, and a telecommunications service tax of 6 percent was introduced (cable rental, pay TV, etc.). Finally, as a means of financing some of the recovery program expenditures, in October 1984, nearly a year and a half ahead, the sales tax rate would be increased by 1 percent for a period of four years. As one point of the sales tax would annually yield $1 billion or more its imposition for four years in the future would provide revenue to pay for the $4.6 billion special recovery program, in the hope that by then its effects would have been realized.

From this tangle of special recovery program measures, investment tax concessions, regular tax changes, and special appropriations it is difficult to determine net financial results. Expenditures and tax incentives were to cost approximately an extra $1 billion under the recovery program in 1983-84. The general tax changes in 1983-84 represented a revenue loss of possibly $800-900 million, including the energy taxes. Both sides of the budget therefore added substantially to the deficit.

The final results for the year were much in the previous pattern: sluggish revenues and rapidly rising expenditures. Revenues rose by little more than one billion dollars (from $55.1 billion to $56.2 billion); expenditures rose by nearly nine billion (from $80.0 billion to $88.9 billion). Of the main tax sources only the sales tax and customs duties showed modest increases; some of the energy taxes were declining, but the basic problem lay with the personal income tax, the source of half the revenue, which rose by only 2.4 percent (less than the increase in real GNP) over 1983. Of the expenditure increases, social security payments accounted for about $3 billion, employment and job creation programs for $1.3 billion, public debt charges for about $1 billion, and defence for $1 billion. Dozens of other programs showed lesser increases. The year wound up with a deficit of $32.6 billion, $7.7 billion above the year before. Once again it had become amply clear that the federal budget was seriously under-financed.

February 1984: Lalonde. As this last Liberal budget was to be overtaken before passage by the election of a Conservative government in September it need only be mentioned to complete the record. Real growth in GNP was expected to reach 4.9 percent in 1984, inflation was continuing to decline, and employment was expected to drop to 10.9 percent. Actual real growth for the year was 5.0 percent, but unemployment only declined to 11.9 percent. The surprising turn of the year was in exports, which increased by nearly 20 percent; no doubt a further decline in the Canadian dollar and a reviving U.S. economy were responsible for this pleasant development.

Some announcements of this period are significant. The 6-and-5 program would end on January 1, 1985, and social security and income tax indexation would reflect full inflation thenceforth; the federal sales tax would not be transferred to the wholesale level, except for highway motor vehicles, to be effective on March 1, 1985. A variety of personal and corporate income tax changes was proposed, but of course not enacted. Budget papers dealing with the tax treatment of various forms of pension plans were tabled, which were part of the review of pensions then in progress at all levels of government.

In this budget the deficit for 1984-85 was expected to drop to $29.6 billion from the $32.4 billion level of the previous year. It actually ended up at 38.3 billion, a fact which fell to a new Conservative Minister of Finance to report.

Wilson Launches Agenda to Balance Budget

November 1984: Wilson. Two months following the election of the Conservative government the Minister of Finance presented a broad review of the government's financial and economic plans in two documents—the *Economic and Fiscal Statement* and *A New Direction for Canada*, the latter described as An Agenda for Economic Renewal. The emphasis in both was on the need to reduce the deficit. Of four objectives given in the *Economic and Fiscal Statement* the first was "to put our own fiscal house in order so that we can limit, and ultimately reverse, the massive build-up in public debt and the damaging impact this has on confidence and growth." The success of the government's economic policies would depend on its ability to achieve this objective.

In reviewing the fiscal position it said:

In each of the past ten years the expenditures of the federal government have exceeded its revenues. These continuing deficits have led to enormous growth in the burden of debt and the costs of servicing that debt. Moreover, unless we begin now to put our fiscal house in order, the burden of debt will continue to mount rapidly in the future. We are on a very dangerous treadmill.[5.1]

Furthermore, the position was bleaker than had been expected, as the February forecast for the deficits of the current and following year had worsened. The deficit of $29.6 billion for 1984-85 forecast in the previous government's last budget had been revised upward to $34.5 billion, and the deficit for 1985-86, forecast to fall to $28 billion, instead was now expected to rise to $37 billion.

What did the Minister propose as a remedy for this dire situation?

Our immediate goal is to reduce the deficit through expenditure reductions and not through major tax increases. We have begun a searching examination of our own operations and of government programs . . . As a result of this review, I am able to announce that more than $4.2 billion of expenditure reductions and revenue recovery measures will be implemented in 1985-86, the first full fiscal year of our mandate

---

[5.1] Canada, Department of Finance, Budget Papers, *Economic and Fiscal Statement*, November 8, 1984, 3-4.

... About $700 million of the total expenditure reductions I am announcing tonight comes from overhead reductions and general restraint measures . . . I want to stress that we went as far as we could in the short time available. We do not believe that the job is finished. Further action will be required. A committee under the chairmanship of the Deputy Prime Minister is continuing its review of federal programs and regulations, with a view to consolidation, simplification, ending duplication and improving service to the public . . . In the coming months we will have to examine all government programs . . . We will review a number of major programs including our economic development and foreign aid programs, unemployment insurance, housing and transfer payments to individuals and provinces . . . Our goal is to reduce the projected level of annual expenditures by 1990 by $10 to $15 billion, inclusive of the measures I am announcing tonight.[5.2]

The Minister clarified the status of several outstanding tax matters; the last income tax bill released by the Liberal government in August would be proceeded with; proposals by the Task Force on Revenue Canada would be implemented; the sales tax would be increased by 1 point on October 1, as the Liberals had proposed; the customs and excise changes of the February budget would also be adopted, and changes in pension and profit-sharing legislation would receive further study. The Minister announced changes in resource and petroleum taxation, and stated that further study would be given to both. Among other tax issues for future consideration he listed a minimum income tax, the budgetary process, and the custom of collecting taxes before legislation had been passed.

In other areas he announced that the increase in the unemployment fund charge would be kept to the minimum, that the spouses allowance would be extended to all widows and widowers aged 60 to 64, and that $1 billion would be committed in 1985-86 "to help Canadians to acquire new skills and to find jobs in the private and public sectors."

The Minister summed up the financial effect of these proposals as follows:

The total cost of the new expenditure and tax initiatives I have announced tonight will be $1.5 billion in 1985-86. In addition, the government previously announced an allocation of $200 million to the Canada Works program, for direct employment creation in 1985-86. The expenditure reduction and revenue recovery measures I announced earlier will more than offset the cost of these measures. Indeed the deficit we inherited for 1985-86 will be brought down from $37.1 billion to $34.9 billion and our inherited financial requirements will be reduced even further, from $32 billion to $29.2 billion.[5.3]

[5.2] Ibid., at 6-7.

[5.3] Ibid., at 14.

The $34.9 billion deficit forecast for 1985-86 reflected expenditures of $105 billion and revenues of $70.1 billion. The federal budget had thus passed the $100 billion mark.

Wilson Moves to Job Creation

May 1985: Wilson. In his first official budget speech the Minister was able to report that the economy in 1984 had been stronger than forecast. Real growth was 4.7 percent, the highest since 1976, inflation had fallen to 4.4 percent and interest rates had declined. Employment was up, but the effect on the unemployment rate had been nominal. Unfortunately it appeared from the figures then available that the deficit would be higher even than forecast. In place of the $34.6 billion it now appeared that it would be just under $36 billion. (In fact, as recorded later, on the existing accounting basis it turned out to be $36.9 billion). It now appeared that had no action been taken the deficit for the following year would not have been $37 billion as originally thought but $40 billion. The government's target for that year was $32.7 billion.

With some apparent shifting of priorities from the deficit—"Our priority goal is jobs for Canadians"—the minister delivered what he obviously regarded as a dramatic solution that would help "individual Canadians to pick winners within a tax framework that rewards success." This was a lifetime exemption of $500,000 in capital gains, to be phased in over six years. The net cost of this change (several capital gains tax reliefs were repealed at the same time) was estimated to be $700 million in 1986.

Other major tax moves were directed to increasing revenue, however. In future brackets and exemptions for personal income tax would be indexed only to the extent that inflation exceeded 3 percent. There would be surtaxes on personal income tax of 5 percent on the excess over $6,000 and a further 5 percent on the excess over $15,000. The $50 federal income tax reduction would be withdrawn. No further deductions would be allowed for RHOSPs (although the amount accumulated could be withdrawn and used for any purpose). It was estimated that these four changes would increase revenue by $1.9 billion in 1986. In addition corporations would pay a 5 percent surtax, there would be a special 1 percent capital tax on banks and trust companies and the scientific research tax credit would be terminated. The sales tax would be increased from 11 to 12 percent on January 1, 1986, a 2 cents per litre excise tax would be levied on gasoline, and a substantial increase would be made in tobacco taxes. The levies on alcohol would also be increased by 2 percent and the sales tax would be extended to candy and confectionary, soft drinks, pet food, health goods, and surgical and dental instruments and minor other items.

These increases, totalling over $5 billion, appeared to reflect a marked departure from the government's rejection of massive tax increases only eight months before. And there was more. On the tax reduction side the most costly changes were the various measures that unwound the National Energy Program, implemented the Western Energy Accord, and gave other reliefs to the petroleum industry. In total these were estimated to amount to $1.9 billion for 1986. There was also another $280 million for higher tax deductions for pension contributions, increases in the child tax credit, and miscellaneous other changes under the personal income tax and a net amount of about $150 million for several changes under the corporate income tax.

The net revenue increase from this program was a negligible $200 million for the 1985-86 year but was a more impressive $1.8 billion for the following year. The Minister projected a deficit of $33.8 billion for 1985-86 and $32.7 billion for 1986-87. For the future he would only say that the deficit for the end of the decade would be $20 billion lower than it would have been without the changes introduced since November 1984. The by now familiar five-year projection was omitted.

On the tax side further changes included the enactment of a minimum personal income tax for 1986, curtailment of tax shelters relating to yachts, etc., and substantial revisions in the terms for participation in pension plans and RRSPs. There were also significant new incentives for research and development and for scientific research, and enriched incentives for investment in Cape Breton. Proposals relating to the corporate income tax were put forward in the form of Discussion Papers. One of these, *The Corporate Income Tax System*, proposed the abandonment of certain concessions accompanied by a substantial reduction in rate. The second, *A Corporate Loss Transfer System*, proposed a method for regularizing the transfer of losses between related corporations to replace the various devices being resorted to for this purpose.

On the expenditure side further progress by the Ministerial Task Force (Nielsen Task Force) was lauded and its first report tabled. Attention was being paid to the cost of tax expenditures, and the Minister promised submission of a revised compilation in the near future. Several specific expenditure reductions for the coming year were listed—reduced expenditures on transportation, reduced grants and subsidies, $900 million in savings through phasing out the Petroleum Incentive Program, abandonment of the heavy water plants in Nova Scotia, and sale of various Crown companies. The Minister also warned provincial authorities that he would be attempting to save $2 billion in transfers to the provinces by the end of the decade.

In the social area a significant change was an increase in the child tax credit. This was popular enough, but at the other end of the age spectrum the Minister stirred a hornet's nest. Following a solemn assertion that an expected actual decline of $1 billion in non-statutory program expenditures, excluding defence and foreign aid, would not be enough progress towards deficit reduction, the Minister appealed for broader sharing of the load and dared to intrude on the sacred realm of transfer payments to the elderly. He said: "With total spending that now exceeds $100 billion, we cannot make significant savings without examining transfer programs . . . Accordingly, I propose to modify indexation for old age security payments and family allowances. Beginning January 1, 1986, these payments will be indexed only for the annual increase in the consumer price index greater than 3 percent.

No payment will be reduced as a result of this measure. Any increase in inflation above 3 percent will be fully compensated."[5.4]

If the Minister was not aware before of the political clout of the geriatric community he was soon to learn. Their organizations literally stormed the government in Ottawa, hurling charges of broken promises and crass indifference to the aged, with the emotional support of all branches of the media. Never has the unwritten covenant of the welfare state been so starkly revealed. After a futile attempt to defend its position the government gave way; old age security payments would continue to be fully indexed (but not family allowances); an additional gasoline tax was imposed to pay the cost. Obviously the Minister had failed to persuade at least one potent element in the community that reducing the deficit was a matter of prime and presumably general concern.

A mass of information was provided in separate documents with this budget. For further details on the progress of the expenditure review see *New Management Initiatives*, Initial Results from the Ministerial Task Force on Program Review; for further details on the budget outlook see *The Fiscal Plan*; the customary *Budget Papers* document contains much significant information, as does *Canada's Economic Prospects*; unfortunately there is a great deal of repetition in these documents—a knowledgeable editor could reduce them to one or at the most two publications; the discussion papers have already been mentioned: *A Minimum Tax for Canada*, *The Corporate Income Tax System*, and *A Corporate Loss Transfer System for Canada*. One other has yet to be mentioned—*The Canadian Budgetary Process: Proposals for Improvement*. And of course there is the Budget speech itself. (When Robert Bryce and I first produced a brief collection of fiscal and economic data in an appendix to the budget of April 1939, to relieve the Minister of reciting it in his budget speech, we had no idea of what would ultimately emerge from this humble beginning.)

February 1986: Wilson. The Minister of Finance reported with satisfaction that expenditures for 1985-86 would be $1 billion less than the $105 billion forecast and that the deficit target of $33.8 billion would be met. He further predicted that the current budget would reduce the deficit for the new fiscal year to $29.8 billion.

A recitation of steps taken to control expenditures listed several moves, some of them previously reported, including reductions in the federal staff, elimination of programs, reduction in grants and subsidies, sale of Crown corporations and winding up of others, all adding up to savings of $5.8 billion. Program spending would be limited to $86.6 billion, lower than in the previous year. In this process the Ministerial Task Force on Program Review had been very helpful. The report of all the study teams would shortly be released. (A summary of the more significant reports is given in the Appendix to this chapter).

[5.4]Canada, Department of Finance, Budget Papers, *Securing Economic Renewal*, The Budget Speech, May 23, 1985, 17.

The economy had also been stronger than forecast. Growth, spurred by business investment, housing starts, and consumer expenditure, had been stronger than in most European countries, twice as great as in the United States and equal to that of Japan. Unemployment had fallen from 11.7 percent in September 1984 to 9.8 percent as a result of creation of 580,000 new jobs.

New expenditure constraints announced in the budget included no salary increases for senior executive staff and a 2 percent ceiling for other staff, further sale or closing of Crown businesses, a reduction of $850 million resulting from lower operating costs and rearrangement of functions in federal departments, elimination of the Post Office deficit by fiscal 1987-88, and reduction in foreign aid spending and in the rate of increase of defence spending. The cumulative effect of the expenditure cuts since November 1984 would reduce increases in program expenditure below the rate of inflation over the next five years; there would be virtually no growth in spending on non-statutory programs over the next two years.

In the social programs the government reformed family benefits, extended the spouses' allowance, entered into new arrangements with the provinces for the Canada Pension Plan and was moving to revise the terms of employer-employee pension plans and equalize access to employee and self-employed pensions. The report of the Forget Commission on Unemployment Insurance would provide suggestions for further change. The recommendations of the Macdonald Commission were also being examined. The Minister restated the government's policy in revising the social programs as: "Such measures must respect several basic principles. They must maintain universal access. They must direct more resources to those most in need. They must improve the opportunities for individuals to become self-reliant. And they must reduce the after-tax value of the benefits going to higher-income Canadians who do not need assistance."[5.4a]

As immediate further assistance the Minister announced prepayment of $300 of the child tax credit in November, a new sales tax refundable tax credit of $50 per adult and $25 per child for incomes below $15,000 for 1986; an additional $100 million per year for three years to help social assistance recipients find employment, and an increase in the disability deduction. Further assistance would also be provided for farmers having financial problems under the Farm Financial Assistance Policy.

Other Programs

In the economic area the budget promised funding of $300 million for the three leading research fund granting councils over the balance of the decade and matching grants for private contributions to the same organizations; an allocation of $800 million to job training and employment under the Canadian Job Strategy program in the new fiscal year, and $125 million for fund-

---

[5.4a] Canada, Department of Finance, Budget Papers, *Securing Economic Renewal*, The Budget Speech, February 26, 1986, 12.

ing a new program for Older Worker Adjustment. For small businesses various tax proposals would be of assistance (see later) and in addition the amount of guaranteed loans under the Small Business Loans Act would be doubled. For the Atlantic region under a new Atlantic Enterprise Program private enterprise loans totalling up to $1 billion would be guaranteed to a substantial extent by the federal government. Tax incentives for Cape Breton would be retained and expanded. Concessions for Northern Development and Indian Affairs were also announced. Finally, $75 million would be provided in the new year for assistance to a number of specific cultural activities.

Tax Program

The budget announced the first steps towards implementing the restructuring of the corporate income tax proposed in the discussion paper of the previous year. These included elimination of the 3 percent inventory allowance; withdrawal of the general investment tax credit; retention of the Cape Breton investment tax credit at 60 percent, the Atlantic Canada and Gaspé credit at 20 percent and the special credit for manufacturing investment in designated areas at a reduced rate of 40 percent.

Commencing July 1, 1987, the general corporate tax rate would be reduced in stages from 36 percent to 33 percent by 1989, the rate on manufacturing profits from 30 percent to 26 percent, the small business general rate from 15 percent to 13 percent, and the small business manufacturing rate from 10 percent to 8 percent. In addition, effective January 1, 1987, the 12½ percent dividend distribution tax for small business would be repealed. A further instalment of proposals would be issued with the next budget. In the meantime some charges were proposed to "tighten the system and to prevent erosion of the tax base."

For additional revenue further measures were proposed. A 3 percent surtax would be imposed on both personal and corporate income taxes on expiry of the existing surtaxes. The general rate of federal sales tax would be increased by 1 percentage point to 12 percent on April 1, the rate having just been increased to 11 percent on January 1 under the previous budget. The other rates of sales tax would be raised accordingly; excise taxes and duties on alcohol and tobacco were raised by 4 percent and 6 percent respectively. All the above tax measures were expected to raise $1.5 billion in 1986-87 and $2.4 billion in the following year.

For dividend income an important change in this budget was the reduction in the dividend tax credit from one-half to one-third of the cash dividend, or from 22⅔ to 16⅔ percent of the grossed-up dividend. This was associated with the repeal of the 12½ percent dividend distributions tax payable by small business, but was applied to all dividends.

In this budget the Minister began to use the term "tax reform," and specifically named the federal sales tax as in need of revision. A value-added tax was being studied.

Table 5.5 The Federal Deficit: Comparison of Budget Forecasts With Actual Results, 1980-81 to 1986-87 (Budgetary Basis)

	Revenue			Expenditure			Deficit		
	Forecast	Actual	Difference	Forecast	Actual	Difference	Forecast	Actual	Difference
					$ billion				
1980-81	45.2	45.4	0.2	59.4	58.4	-1.0	14.2	13.0	-1.2
1981-82	52.9	54.9	2.0	66.6	69.4	2.0	13.7	13.6	-0.1
1982-83	65.0	56.0	-9.0	75.5	80.0	4.5	10.5	24.9	14.8
1983-84	74.5	57.1	-17.4	84.1	88.9	4.8	9.6	32.6	23.0
1984-85	82.7	64.1	-18.6	92.6	99.9	7.3	10.0	34.5	24.5
1985-86	91.7	71.2[a]	-20.5	103.0	105.0[a]	2.0	10.2	33.8[a]	23.6
1986-87	80.4	77.2[a]	-3.2	106.0	109.9[a]	3.9	25.6	32.7[a]	7.1

Note: This data gives only a rough indication. An attempt has been made to achieve comparability by using figures that exclude the effect of the 1986-87 accounting changes, but this is only approximate. The minus signs represent shortfalls below forecast.

[a] Estimates excluding 1986-87 accounting changes.

Source: Forecasts for 1980-81 and 1981-82, *The Budget*, October 1980; 1982-83 to 1985-86 *Budget Speech*, November 1981; for 1986-87, *The Fiscal Plan*, Budget Papers, April 1983. Actual figures from later budgets.

had been forecast at $10.0 billion, was more than three times that figure. Obviously these results were completely unexpected, and had an explosive effect on the deficit. The forecasts were revised as soon as the situation became apparent, but by then it was too late; the damage had been done.

The Cost of the Debt

One element that would have been inescapable in any event was the effect of the sharp rise in interest rates. This was part of an anti-inflationary program of world scale, and Canada suffered with other countries. Table 5.6 summarizes the results. A debt that rose from $67 billion in 1976 to $269 billion in 1986 would alone have been a crushing burden on the budget, but its effect was compounded by an accompanying spiral of nearly 60 percent in debt costs. Between 1976 and 1981 90-day treasury bill rates rose from 9.87 percent to 17.72 percent and the rate on ten-year bonds from 9.18 percent to 15.22 percent, with the result that the overall cost of debt rose from 7.0 percent to 11.0 percent. And the decline from this peak was slow—in 1985 the average cost was still 9.5 percent, but declined to 8.8 percent in 1986. As a result of the combined impact of rising debt and soaring interest rates debt costs rose from 11.6 percent of the budget in 1976 to 20.2 percent in 1981, or an increase of nearly 75 percent. And of course with deficits since accelerating to two and one-half times their 1981 level the drain has continued to grow. By 1986 it had risen to 25.9 percent, with little prospect that it would decline materially in the near future; in fact trends in interest rates were threatening the reverse.

The Effect of Transfer Payments

The very substantial amounts of money that swell the federal expenditure budget in the form of transfers to other governments, mainly provincial, also contributed to the deficit of recent years. Table 5.7 shows that stripped of these amounts the federal deficits would have been half or less the actual reported figures.

Must of the above has been covered in previous pages, but bears repetition. Indeed so baffling is the deficit enigma that we return to it again later in a different context.

The 1982-87 Period in Perspective

Tables 5.8 to 5.11 give summary data on fiscal developments of the period.

Table 5.6 Federal Government: The Cost of the Debt, 1976 to 1986[a] Budgetary Accounts Basis

Year[b]	Gross national product	Deficit	Ratio of deficit to GNP	Gross public debt	Ratio of gross debt to GNP	Gross public debt costs		
						Total	Ratio to debt	Ratio to budgetary expenditures
	$	$	%	$	%	$	%	%
1976......	194.4	6.3	3.2	67.3	34.6	4.7	7.0	11.6
1977......	213.3	10.4	4.9	79.9	37.5	5.5	6.9	12.3
1978......	235.7	12.6	5.3	97.0	41.2	7.0	7.3	14.2
1979......	268.9	11.5	4.3	104.3	39.0	8.5	8.1	13.9
1980......	302.1	13.5	4.5	120.4	39.9	10.7	8.9	17.1
1981......	344.7	14.9	4.3	137.5	39.9	15.1	11.0	20.2
1982......	361.8	27.8	7.7	166.2	45.9	16.9	10.2	19.1
1983......	394.1	32.4	8.2	199.5	50.6	18.1	9.1	18.7
1984......	432.1	38.3	8.9	237.1	54.9	22.5	9.5	20.6
1985......	465.1	34.4	7.4	269.3	57.9	25.4	9.5	22.9
1986......	493.0	31.0	6.3	302.9	61.4	26.7	8.8	22.5

[a] Dollar figures in billions. [b] Fiscal year nearest December 31 of year named.

Sources: Department of Finance, Budget Papers, February 10, 1988; Statistics Canada, National Accounts.

Table 5.7   Federal Government: Budget Deficit Before Major Transfer Payments to Other Governments, 1979-86

Year[a]		Before transfers to other governments		Actual deficit
	Revenue	Expenditure	Deficit	
	billions of dollars			
1979................	41.9	42.6	− 0.7	− 11.5
1980................	48.8	50.3	− 1.5	− 13.4
1981................	60.0	61.0	− 1.0	− 14.9
1982................	60.7	73.8	− 13.1	− 27.8
1983................	64.2	78.9	− 14.7	− 32.4
1984................	70.9	89.9	− 19.0	− 38.3
1985................	76.8	91.7	− 14.9	− 34.4
1986................	85.8	96.6	− 10.8	− 30.6

[a] Fiscal year nearest December 31 of year named.

Source: Department of Finance, Budget Papers, February 1987 and 1988.

Table 5.8   Federal Government: Revenue, Expenditure, and Deficit or Surplus, Budgetary and National Accounts Bases, 1982-86

Year[a]	Revenue		Expenditure		Deficit	
	Budgetary	National accounts	Budgetary	National accounts	Budgetary	National accounts
	billions of dollars					
1982.....	60.7	66.1	88.5	86.4	− 27.8	− 20.3
1983.....	64.2	69.6	96.6	94.6	− 32.4	− 25.0
1984.....	70.9	76.7	109.2	107.1	− 38.3	− 30.4
1985.....	76.8	83.7	111.2	115.7	− 34.4	− 32.0
1986.....	85.8	91.2	116.4	116.0	− 32.0	− 24.8

[a] Fiscal year ending nearest December 31 of year named.

Source: Budget Papers, February 1988 and Statistics Canada, *National Income and Expenditure Accounts*, 1926-1986.

Table 5.9   Federal Government: Revenue by Principal Source, Budgetary Accounts Basis, 1982-86

Year[a]	Personal income tax	Corporate income tax	Sales and excise taxes[b]	Unemployment insurance contributions	Other	Non-tax revenue	Total
	billions of dollars						
1982.....	26.3	7.1	10.6	4.9	6.3	5.4	60.7
1983.....	27.0	7.3	12.0	7.3	5.2	5.5	64.2
1984.....	29.3	9.4	13.7	7.6	5.6	5.4	70.9
1985.....	33.0	9.2	16.1	8.7	4.5	5.2	76.8
1986.....	37.9	9.9	19.0	9.6	3.5	5.9	85.8

[a] Fiscal year ending nearest December 31 of the year named. [b] Includes excise duties and customs duties.

Source: Budget Papers, February 1988.

Table 5.10 Federal Government: Expenditure by Major Outlay, Budgetary Accounts Basis, 1982-86

Year[a]	Major transfers to persons	Major transfers to governments	National defence	Other	Total program expenditure	Public debt charges	Total
	billions of dollars						
1982.....	22.7	14.6	6.9	27.4	71.6	16.9	88.5
1983.....	23.6	17.5	7.8	29.6	78.5	18.1	96.6
1984.....	25.0	19.1	8.8	33.9	86.8	22.5	109.2
1985.....	26.3	19.3	9.1	31.2	85.8	25.4	111.2
1986.....	27.7	19.8	10.0	32.2	89.7	26.7	116.4

[a] Fiscal year nearest to December 31 of the year named.

Source: Department of Finance, Budget Papers, February 10, 1988; Public Accounts.

Table 5.11 Federal Government: Main Categories of Expenditure, National Accounts Basis, 1982-86

Year[a]	Goods and services	Transfers to persons	Interest on debt	Subsidies and capital assistance	Capital formation	Transfers to other governments	Other	Total
	billions of dollars							
1982.....	18.9	24.1	16.7	8.3	1.3	15.8	1.0	86.4
1983.....	19.6	28.1	17.4	9.3	1.5	17.6	1.2	94.6
1984.....	21.4	29.6	21.3	10.8	2.5	19.9	1.6	107.1
1985.....	23.8	31.7	25.3	9.4	2.1	21.7	1.7	115.7
1986.....	24.1	33.2	26.4	7.3	2.2	21.1	1.6	116.0

[a] Calendar year.

Source: Statistics Canada, *National Income and Expenditure Accounts*, 1926-86.

Bibliography, chapters 1 to 5

Abbott, D.C. "Federal Budget Policy." in *Report of the Tax 1948 Tax Conference*. Toronto: Canadian Tax Foundation, 1949.

Bird, Richard M. *The Growth of Government Spending in Canada*. Canadian Tax Paper no. 51. Toronto: Canadian Tax Foundation, 1970.

_____. *Financing Canadian Government: A Quantitative Overview*. Financing Canadian Federation no. 1. Toronto: Canadian Tax Foundation, 1979.

Canada. Department of Finance. Budgets and Budget Papers, 1947-88. Ottawa: the Department.

_____. Department of Reconstruction. *Employment and Income, with Special Reference to the Initial Period of Reconstruction*. Ottawa: 1945.

_____. Dominion-Provincial Conference (1945). Dominion and Provincial Submissions and Plenary Conference Discussions. Ottawa: 1946.

_____. Dominion Provincial Conference (1945). *Proposals of the Government of Canada*, August, 1945. Ottawa: 1945.

Canadian Tax Foundation, *The National Finances*. annual. Toronto: the Foundation.

Clark, W.C. "Canada's Post-War Finance." Paper presented to the annual meeting of the American Economic Association, Chicago, December, 1952. (January-February 1953) 1 *Canadian Tax Journal*, 6-12, 100-11.

Daly, D.J. *Federal Tax Revenues at Potential Output, 1960 and 1970*. Staff Study. Ottawa: Economic Council of Canada 1969.

Perry, J. Harvey. *Taxes, Tariffs and Subsidies. A History of Canadian Fiscal Development*. Toronto: University of Toronto Press, 1955.

Appendix 1
Four Decades of Federal Revenues, Expenditures, and Taxes

Table A.1   Federal Government: Revenue, Expenditure, and Budget Balances, Budgetary Accounts Basis, 1947-86

Year[a]	Revenue		Expenditure		Surplus or deficit	
	billions of dollars					
1947	2.9		2.2		0.7	
1948	2.8		2.2		0.6	
1949	2.6		2.4		0.2	
1950	3.1		2.9		0.2	
1951	4.0		3.8		0.2	
1952	4.6		4.6		—	
1953	4.7		4.7		—	
1954	4.4		4.7		− 0.3	
1955	4.7		4.8		− 0.1	
1956	5.5		5.2		0.3	
1957	5.4		5.5		− 0.3	
1958	5.1		6.0		− 0.9	
1959	5.8		6.3		− 0.5	
1960	6.2		6.6		− 0.4	
1961	6.5		7.4		− 0.9	
1962	6.7		7.5		− 0.8	
1963	7.1		8.3		− 1.2	
1964	8.2		8.5		− 0.3	
1965	9.0		8.7		0.3	
1966	9.7		9.9		− 0.2	
1967	10.6		11.3		− 0.7	
1968	11.9		12.3		− 0.4	
1969	14.3		14.0		0.3	
1970	14.9		15.7		− 0.8	
1971	16.5		18.1		− 1.5	
1972	19.1		20.8		− 1.7	
1973	22.3		24.3		− 2.0	
1974	29.1		31.2		− 2.0	
1975	31.5		37.3		− 5.7	
1976	34.3		40.6		− 6.3	
1977	34.5		44.9		− 10.4	
1978	36.9		49.5		− 12.6	
1979	41.9		53.4		− 11.5	
1980	48.8	(45.4)	62.1	(58.4)	− 13.4	(− 13.0)
1981	60.0	(54.9)	74.9	(69.4)	− 14.9	(− 14.6)
1982	60.7	(56.0)	88.5	(80.0)	− 27.8	(− 24.0)
1983	64.2	(57.1)	96.6	(88.9)	− 32.4	(− 31.8)

Continued on next page.

Table A.1   Continued

Year[a]	Revenue		Expenditure		Surplus or deficit	
	billions of dollars					
1984	70.9	(64.2)	109.2	(101.1)	− 38.3	(− 36.9)
1985	76.8	(71.2)	111.2	(105.0)	− 34.4	(− 33.8)
1986	85.8	—	116.4	—	− 30.6	—

[a] Fiscal year ending nearest to December 31 of year named.

Note: Bracketed figures exclude forecast effects of accounting changes implemented in 1986 budget.

Sources: *Historical Statistics of Canada*; Canada, Department of Finance, Budget Papers, *The Fiscal Plan*, February 1986; Budget Papers 1987; *Economic and Fiscal Outlook*, June 1987; and *The Fiscal Plan*, February 1988.

**Table A.2 Federal Government: Revenue by Principal
Source, Budgetary Accounts Basis, 1947-86**

Year[a]	Personal income tax	Corporate income tax	Sales and excise taxes[b]	Unemployment insurance contributions	Other	Non-tax revenue	Total
			billions of dollars				
1947.....	0.7	0.6	1.1	—	0.1	0.4	2.9
1948.....	0.8	0.5	1.1	—	0.1	0.3	2.8
1949.....	0.6	0.6	1.0	—	0.1	0.3	2.6
1950.....	0.7	0.8	1.2	—	0.1	0.3	3.1
1951.....	1.0	1.1	1.5	—	0.1	0.3	4.0
1952.....	1.2	1.3	1.6	—	0.1	0.4	4.6
1953.....	1.3	1.2	1.7	—	0.1	0.4	4.7
1954.....	1.3	1.1	1.6	—	0.1	0.4	4.4
1955.....	1.3	1.1	1.7	—	0.2	0.4	4.7
1956.....	1.5	1.3	1.8	—	0.4	0.5	5.5
1957.....	1.6	1.3	1.8	—	0.3	0.4	5.4
1958.....	1.5	1.1	1.7	—	0.3	0.5	5.1
1959.....	1.8	1.2	1.9	—	0.4	0.5	5.8
1960.....	1.9	1.4	1.9	—	0.4	0.6	6.2
1961.....	2.1	1.3	2.2	0.3	0.2	0.4	6.5
1962.....	2.0	1.3	2.4	0.3	0.2	0.5	6.7
1963.....	2.2	1.4	2.5	0.3	0.2	0.5	7.1
1964.....	2.5	1.7	2.9	0.3	0.2	0.6	8.2
1965.....	2.6	1.8	3.3	0.3	0.3	0.6	9.0
1966.....	3.1	1.7	3.6	0.3	0.3	0.7	9.8
1967.....	3.6	1.8	3.7	0.3	0.3	0.8	10.6
1968.....	4.3	2.2	3.7	0.4	0.3	0.9	11.9
1969.....	5.6	2.8	4.0	0.5	0.3	1.0	14.3
1970.....	6.4	2.4	4.1	0.5	0.4	1.1	14.9
1971.....	7.2	2.4	4.6	0.6	0.4	1.3	16.5
1972.....	8.4	2.9	5.3	0.7	0.4	1.4	19.1
1973.....	9.2	3.7	6.1	1.0	0.6	1.7	22.3
1974.....	11.7	4.8	6.8	1.6	2.1	2.1	29.1
1975.....	12.7	5.7	6.7	2.0	2.0	2.4	31.5
1976.....	14.6	5.4	7.4	2.5	1.8	2.7	34.3
1977.....	14.6	5.3	8.1	2.5	1.6	3.0	34.5
1978.....	14.7	5.7	8.9	2.8	1.5	3.4	36.9
1979.....	16.8	7.0	9.1	2.8	2.1	4.2	41.9
1980.....	19.8	8.1	10.2	3.3	2.5	4.8	48.8
1981.....	24.0	8.1	11.3	4.8	5.7	6.1	60.0
1982.....	26.3	7.1	10.6	4.9	6.3	5.4	60.7
1983.....	27.0	7.3	12.0	7.3	5.2	5.5	64.2
1984.....	29.3	9.4	13.7	7.6	5.6	5.4	70.9
1985.....	33.0	9.2	16.2	8.7	4.5	5.3	76.8
1986.....	37.9	9.9	19.0	9.6	3.5	5.9	85.8

[a]Fiscal year ending nearest December 31 of year named. [b]Sales tax, excise taxes, excise duties, and customs duties. [c]Excludes unemployment insurance contribution to 1960.

Source: Based on *Historical Statistics of Canada*; Budget Papers, February 1987; *Economic and Financial Outlook*, June 1987; and *The Fiscal Plan*, February 1988.

Table A.3 Federal Government: Revenue by Principal Source as a Percent of Total Revenue, Budgetary Accounts Basis, 1961-86

Year[a]	Personal income tax	Corporate income tax	Sales and excise taxes[b]	Unemployment insurance contributions	Other	Non-tax revenue	Total
				percent			
1961	31.7	20.1	34.1	4.3	3.0	6.8	100.0
1962	30.3	19.5	36.0	4.3	3.2	6.8	100.0
1963	30.5	19.4	35.6	4.2	3.0	7.3	100.0
1964	30.8	20.3	35.2	3.8	2.8	7.1	100.0
1965	29.4	19.6	37.3	3.7	3.1	6.8	100.0
1966	31.3	17.9	37.2	3.5	3.1	7.0	100.0
1967	34.3	17.1	35.0	3.3	3.0	7.3	100.0
1968	36.3	18.5	31.4	3.6	2.7	7.5	100.0
1969	39.1	19.9	28.1	3.4	2.4	7.1	100.0
1970	43.0	16.3	27.3	3.3	2.5	7.5	100.0
1971	43.8	14.5	28.1	3.4	2.8	7.6	100.0
1972	43.9	15.3	27.6	3.9	1.8	7.5	100.0
1973	41.3	16.6	27.2	4.5	2.8	7.6	100.0
1974	40.2	16.6	23.5	5.4	7.2	7.1	100.0
1975	40.3	18.2	21.1	6.5	6.3	7.7	100.0
1976	42.7	15.6	21.5	7.2	5.2	7.8	100.0
1977	40.5	15.3	23.4	7.3	4.6	8.8	100.0
1978	39.8	15.3	24.0	7.5	4.0	9.3	100.0
1979	40.1	16.6	21.7	6.6	4.9	10.1	100.0
1980	40.7	16.6	21.0	6.8	5.1	9.9	100.0
1981	40.1	13.5	18.9	7.9	9.4	10.2	100.0
1982	43.4	11.8	17.5	8.1	10.3	8.9	100.0
1983	42.0	11.3	18.8	11.3	8.1	8.5	100.0
1984	41.3	13.2	19.3	10.7	7.9	7.6	100.0
1985	43.0	12.0	21.1	11.3	5.9	6.9	100.0
1986	44.2	11.5	22.2	11.1	4.1	6.9	100.0

Based on Table A.2.

Table A.4 Federal Government: Expenditure by Major Outlay, Budgetary Accounts Basis[a] 1947-86

Year[b]	Major transfers to persons	Major transfers to governments	National defence	Other	Total program expenditure	Public debt charges	Total
			billions of dollars				
1947.....	0.4	0.2	0.2	0.9	1.7	0.5	2.2
1948.....	0.4	0.1	0.3	0.9	1.7	0.5	2.2
1949.....	0.5	0.1	0.4	0.9	1.9	0.5	2.4
1950.....	0.5	0.1	0.8	1.1	2.5	0.4	2.9
1951.....	0.6	0.1	1.4	1.2	3.3	0.5	3.8
1952.....	0.8	0.3	2.0	1.0	4.1	0.5	4.6
1953.....	0.9	0.3	1.9	1.1	4.2	0.5	4.7
1954.....	0.9	0.4	1.8	1.1	4.2	0.5	4.7
1955.....	1.0	0.4	1.8	1.0	4.2	0.5	4.8
1956.....	1.0	.0.4	1.8	1.5	4.7	0.5	5.2
1957.....	1.2	0.4	1.7	1.6	4.9	0.6	5.5
1958.....	1.3	0.5	1.7	1.9	5.4	0.6	6.0
1959.....	1.5	0.5	1.5	2.0	5.5	0.8	6.3
1960.....	1.6	0.6	1.5	2.1	5.8	0.8	6.6
1961.....	1.9	0.7	1.6	2.4	6.6	0.8	7.4
1962.....	1.9	0.8	1.6	2.3	6.6	0.9	7.5
1963.....	2.0	0.8	1.7	2.8	7.3	1.0	8.3
1964.....	2.1	1.0	1.5	2.9	7.5	1.1	8.5
1965.....	2.1	0.9	1.5	3.0	7.5	1.1	8.7
1966.....	2.3	1.1	1.6	3.8	8.8	1.2	9.9
1967.....	2.7	1.5	1.8	4.1	10.1	1.3	11.3
1968.....	2.9	1.9	1.8	4.3	10.9	1.5	12.3
1969.....	3.2	2.3	1.8	5.0	12.3	1.7	14.0
1970.....	3.6	3.0	1.8	5.3	13.8	1.9	15.7
1971.....	4.3	3.7	1.9	6.2	15.9	2.1	18.1
1972.....	5.5	4.2	1.9	6.8	18.5	2.3	20.8
1973.....	6.5	4.7	2.2	8.4	21.8	2.6	24.3
1974.....	8.1	6.0	2.5	11.3	27.9	3.2	31.2
1975.....	9.8	7.0	3.0	13.6	33.3	4.0	37.3
1976.....	10.5	8.5	3.4	13.6	35.9	4.7	40.6
1977.....	11.7	8.6	3.8	15.3	39.4	5.5	44.9
1978.....	12.7	9.7	4.1	15.9	42.5	7.0	49.5
1979.....	12.7	10.8	4.4	17.0	44.9	8.5	53.4
1980.....	14.6	11.8	5.1	20.0	51.5	10.7	62.1
1981.....	17.0	13.8	6.0	23.0	59.8	15.1	74.9
1982.....	22.7	14.6	6.9	27.4	71.6	16.9	88.5
1983.....	23.6	17.5	7.8	29.6	78.5	18.1	96.6
1984.....	25.0	19.1	8.8	33.9	86.7	22.5	109.2
1985.....	26.3	19.3	9.1	31.2	85.8	25.4	111.2
1986.....	27.7	19.8	10.0	32.2	89.7	26.7	116.4

[a] Includes accounting changes in 1985 to 1987. [b] Fiscal year ending nearest December 31 of the year named.

Sources: 1947-60, approximate equivalent categories drived from *Historical Statistics of Canada*; 1961-87, Department of Finance, Budget Papers, February 18, 1987; *Economic and Financial Outlook*, June 1987, *The Fiscal Plan*, February 1988.

Table A.5   Federal Government: Expenditure by Major Outlay as a Percentage of the Total, Budgetary Accounts Basis, 1961-86

Year[a]	Major transfers to persons	Major transfers to govern- ments	National defence	Other	Total program expendi- ture	Public debt charges	Total
				per cent			
1961	25.1	9.0	21.9	32.8	88.8	11.2	100.0
1962	25.8	10.2	21.0	30.8	87.8	12.2	100.0
1963	23.9	10.0	20.4	33.7	88.0	12.0	100.0
1964	24.3	11.2	18.0	34.2	87.7	12.3	100.0
1965	24.5	10.1	17.9	34.6	87.2	12.8	100.0
1966	23.1	10.6	16.5	38.0	88.1	11.9	100.0
1967	23.8	13.3	15.5	36.2	88.7	11.3	100.0
1968	23.8	15.0	14.3	35.0	88.1	11.9	100.0
1969	23.0	16.4	12.8	35.7	87.8	12.1	100.0
1970	23.0	19.2	11.6	34.2	87.9	12.1	100.0
1971	23.6	20.3	10.3	34.1	88.3	11.7	100.0
1972	26.4	20.2	9.3	33.0	88.9	11.1	100.0
1973	26.5	19.1	9.1	34.6	89.5	10.5	100.0
1974	26.0	19.1	8.1	36.4	89.6	10.4	100.0
1975	26.2	18.6	8.0	36.6	89.4	10.6	100.0
1976	25.8	20.9	8.3	33.4	88.4	11.6	100.0
1977	26.1	19.2	8.4	34.0	87.7	12.3	100.0
1978	25.7	19.6	8.3	32.2	85.8	14.2	100.0
1979	23.8	20.3	8.2	31.8	84.1	15.9	100.0
1980	23.5	19.0	8.1	32.2	82.8	17.1	100.0
1981	22.6	18.5	8.0	30.7	79.8	20.2	100.0
1982	25.7	16.5	7.8	30.9	80.9	19.1	100.0
1983	24.4	18.1	8.1	30.6	81.3	18.7	100.0
1984	22.9	17.5	8.0	31.0	79.4	20.6	100.0
1985	23.6	17.3	8.2	28.0	77.1	22.9	100.0
1986	23.8	17.0	8.6	27.7	77.1	22.9	100.0

Based on Table A.4.

Table A.6   Federal Government: Revenue, Expenditure, and Balance,
National Accounts Basis, 1947-86

Year[a]	Revenue ($ bill.)	Revenue as a per cent of GNP	Expenditure[b] ($ bill.)	Expenditure as a per cent of GNP	Surplus or deficit		
					($ bill.)	as a per cent of GNP	excluding transfers ($ bill.)
		%		%		%	
1947	2.8	22.2	2.1	15.5	0.7	5.1	0.9
1948	2.7	17.5	2.0	12.6	0.8	4.9	0.9
1949	2.7	16.1	2.2	13.2	0.5	2.9	0.7
1950	3.0	16.3	2.4	12.8	0.6	3.5	0.9
1951	4.2	19.2	3.2	14.8	1.0	4.5	1.3
1952	4.7	19.1	4.5	18.3	0.2	0.8	0.6
1953	4.8	18.6	4.7	18.0	0.1	0.6	0.6
1954	4.6	17.8	4.7	18.0	−0.1	−0.2	0.6
1955	5.0	17.6	4.8	16.8	0.2	0.7	0.7
1956	5.7	17.8	5.1	15.9	0.6	1.9	1.1
1957	5.7	16.9	5.4	16.2	0.3	0.7	0.8
1958	5.4	15.5	6.2	17.8	−0.8	−2.2	−0.1
1959	6.1	16.7	6.5	17.6	−0.4	−0.9	0.5
1960	6.5	17.0	6.7	17.6	−0.2	−0.6	0.8
1961	6.8	17.1	7.2	18.1	−0.4	−1.0	0.7
1962	7.0	16.3	7.5	17.4	−0.5	−1.2	0.6
1963	7.3	15.9	7.6	16.5	−0.3	−0.6	0.9
1964	8.4	16.6	8.0	15.9	0.4	0.7	1.4
1965	9.1	16.4	8.6	15.4	0.5	1.0	2.0
1966	10.0	16.1	9.8	15.8	0.2	0.4	1.9
1967	10.9	16.4	11.0	16.5	−0.1	−0.1	1.9
1968	12.2	16.8	12.2	16.8	—	—	2.4
1969	14.5	18.2	13.5	16.9	1.0	1.3	3.7
1970	15.5	18.1	15.3	17.8	0.3	0.3	3.7
1971	17.2	18.3	17.4	18.4	−0.2	−0.2	4.2
1972	19.6	18.6	20.1	19.1	−0.5	−0.5	4.0
1973	22.8	18.5	22.4	18.1	0.4	0.3	5.2
1974	30.0	20.3	28.9	19.6	1.1	0.8	7.3
1975	31.7	19.2	35.5	21.5	−3.8	−2.3	3.9
1976	35.3	18.4	38.7	20.2	−3.4	−1.8	5.1
1977	36.5	17.4	43.8	20.8	−7.3	−3.5	2.7
1978	38.4	16.5	49.0	21.1	−10.6	−4.6	0.3
1979	43.6	16.5	52.7	19.9	−9.1	−3.5	2.6
1980	50.7	16.5	61.3	20.3	−10.7	−3.5	2.4
1981	65.0	18.6	72.3	21.0	−7.3	−2.1	6.8
1982	66.1	18.0	86.4	23.9	−20.3	−5.6	−4.6
1983	69.6	17.7	94.6	24.0	−25.0	−6.3	−7.4
1984	76.7	17.8	107.1	24.8	−30.4	−7.0	−10.5
1985	83.7	18.0	115.7	24.9	−32.0	−6.9	−10.2
1986	91.2	18.5	116.0	23.5	−24.8	−5.3	−3.7

[a]Calendar year. [b]Including transfers.

Source: Canada, Department of Finance; *Economic Review*, April 1985; Statistics Canada, *National Income and Expenditure Accounts*, 1926-1986.

Table A.7 Federal Government: Revenue by Major Source,
National Accounts Basis, 1947-86

Year[a]	Direct taxes on persons	Direct taxes on corporations	Withholding taxes	Indirect taxes	Investment income	Capital consumption allowances	Total
			billions of dollars				
1947.....	0.8	0.6	—	1.2	0.1	0.1	2.8
1948.....	0.9	0.6	—	1.1	0.1	0.1	2.7
1949.....	0.8	0.6	—	1.0	0.1	0.1	2.7
1950.....	0.8	0.8	0.1	1.1	0.1	0.1	3.0
1951.....	1.2	1.2	0.1	1.5	0.1	0.1	4.2
1952.....	1.4	1.3	0.1	1.6	0.2	0.1	4.7
1953.....	1.6	1.2	0.1	1.7	0.2	0.1	4.8
1954.....	1.6	1.1	0.1	1.6	0.2	0.1	4.6
1955.....	1.6	1.3	0.1	1.7	0.2	0.1	5.0
1956.....	1.9	1.4	0.1	2.0	0.3	0.1	5.7
1957.....	2.1	1.2	0.1	2.0	0.2	0.1	5.7
1958.....	2.0	1.1	—	1.9	0.3	0.1	5.4
1959.....	2.2	1.3	0.1	2.1	0.3	0.1	6.1
1960.....	2.5	1.3	0.1	2.2	0.3	0.1	6.5
1961.....	2.6	1.3	0.1	2.2	0.4	0.1	6.8
1962.....	2.6	1.3	0.1	2.4	0.4	0.1	7.0
1963.....	2.7	1.4	0.1	2.4	0.5	0.1	7.3
1964.....	3.1	1.6	0.1	2.8	0.5	0.1	8.4
1965.....	3.3	1.7	0.2	3.2	0.5	0.2	9.1
1966.....	3.6	1.8	0.2	3.6	0.6	0.2	10.0
1967.....	4.3	1.8	0.2	3.7	0.7	0.2	10.9
1968.....	5.1	2.1	0.2	3.8	0.8	0.2	12.2
1969.....	6.5	2.4	0.2	4.0	1.1	0.2	14.5
1970.....	7.4	2.3	0.3	4.0	1.3	0.2	15.5
1971.....	8.3	2.5	0.3	4.5	1.5	0.2	17.2
1972.....	9.3	2.9	0.3	5.1	1.7	0.3	19.6
1973.....	10.9	3.6	0.3	5.8	1.8	0.3	22.8
1974.....	13.5	5.0	0.4	8.5	2.1	0.4	30.0
1975.....	15.2	5.4	0.5	7.9	2.3	0.4	31.7
1976.....	18.0	5.0	0.5	8.6	2.6	0.5	35.3
1977.....	18.0	5.2	0.5	9.1	3.1	0.6	36.5
1978.....	17.7	5.8	0.6	9.8	3.9	0.6	38.4
1979.....	20.3	7.0	0.9	10.7	4.2	0.7	43.6
1980.....	23.5	8.4	1.0	12.3	4.7	0.8	50.6
1981.....	29.2	9.3	1.1	19.0	5.4	0.9	65.0
1982.....	32.1	9.2	1.2	17.6	5.0	1.0	66.1
1983.....	35.5	9.5	1.0	16.3	6.2	1.1	69.6
1984.....	37.5	11.3	1.1	18.1	7.5	1.1	76.7
1985.....	42.7	11.5	1.1	18.9	8.3	1.3	83.7
1986.....	49.0	9.7	1.7	20.7	8.8	1.3	91.4

Note: 1981-86 figures on 1981 revised National Accounts basis.

[a] Calendar year.

Sources: Canada, Department of Finance, *Economic Review*, April 1985; Statistics *Canada, National Income and Expenditure Accounts*, 1926-86.

Table A.8   Federal Government: Revenue by Major Source as a Percentage of the Total, National Accounts Basis, Selected Years, 1947-86

Year	Direct taxes on persons	Direct taxes on corpora- tions	With- holding taxes	Indirect taxes	Investment income	Capital consump- tion allowances	Total
				percent			
1947	28.6	21.4	—	42.8	3.6	3.6	100.0
1950	26.7	26.7	3.3	36.7	3.3	3.3	100.0
1953	33.3	25.0	—	35.4	4.2	2.1	100.0
1955	32.0	26.0	2.0	34.0	4.0	2.0	100.0
1960	38.5	20.0	1.5	33.9	4.6	1.5	100.0
1965	36.3	18.7	2.1	35.2	5.5	2.2	100.0
1970	47.7	14.8	1.8	25.8	8.4	1.3	100.0
1975	47.9	17.0	1.7	24.9	7.2	1.3	100.0
1977	49.3	14.2	1.5	24.9	8.5	1.6	100.0
1979	46.4	16.0	1.9	24.5	9.6	1.6	100.0
1980	46.3	17.0	1.9	23.9	9.3	1.6	100.0
1981	44.9	14.3	1.8	29.3	8.3	1.4	100.0
1982	48.6	13.9	1.8	26.7	7.4	1.6	100.0
1983	51.0	13.6	1.4	23.4	8.9	1.7	100.0
1984	48.9	14.7	1.4	23.6	9.8	1.6	100.0
1985	50.7	13.9	1.3	22.6	9.9	1.6	100.0
1986	53.7	10.6	1.9	22.6	9.7	1.5	100.0

Source: Based on Table A.7.

Table A.9 Federal Government: Expenditure by Major Category, and Surplus or Deficit, National Accounts Basis, 1947-86

Calendar year	Goods and services	Defence[b]	Transfers to persons	Interest on debt	Subsidies	Capital assistance	Capital formation	Transfers to non-residents	Total expend. excluding grants	Surplus or deficit	Transfers to other governments	Total expend. including grants	Surplus or deficit
					billions of dollars								
1947	0.7	0.2	0.6	0.5	0.2	—	—	—	1.9	0.9	0.2	2.1	0.7
1948	0.6	0.2	0.6	0.5	0.1	—	—	—	1.8	0.9	0.2	2.0	0.8
1949	0.8	0.4	0.6	0.5	0.1	—	0.2	—	2.0	0.7	0.2	2.2	0.5
1950	0.9	0.5	0.6	0.4	0.1	—	0.1	—	2.1	0.9	0.3	2.4	0.7
1951	1.6	1.2	0.6	0.5	0.1	—	0.1	—	2.9	1.2	0.3	3.2	1.0
1952	2.3	1.8	1.0	0.5	0.1	—	0.2	—	4.1	0.6	0.4	4.5	0.2
1953	2.5	1.9	1.1	0.5	0.1	—	0.1	—	4.3	0.6	0.4	4.7	0.2
1954	2.3	1.7	1.2	0.5	0.1	—	0.2	—	4.3	0.4	0.4	4.7	—
1955	2.4	1.8	1.2	0.5	0.1	—	0.2	—	4.3	0.7	0.5	4.8	0.2
1956	2.5	1.8	1.2	0.5	0.1	—	0.2	—	4.6	1.1	0.5	5.1	0.6
1957	2.5	1.8	1.5	0.5	0.1	—	0.2	—	4.9	0.8	0.5	5.4	0.3
1958	2.5	1.7	1.9	0.6	0.1	—	0.3	0.1	5.5	-0.1	0.7	6.2	-0.8
1959	2.4	1.6	1.8	0.7	0.2	—	0.4	0.1	5.6	0.5	0.9	6.5	-0.3
1960	2.4	1.5	2.0	0.8	0.3	—	0.2	0.1	5.7	0.8	1.0	6.7	-0.2
1961	2.6	1.6	2.0	0.8	0.3	—	0.3	0.1	6.1	0.7	1.1	7.2	-0.4
1962	2.7	1.7	2.1	0.9	0.3	—	0.3	0.1	6.4	0.6	1.1	7.5	-0.5
1963	2.6	1.6	2.1	0.9	0.4	0.1	0.2	0.1	6.4	0.9	1.2	7.6	-0.3
1964	2.8	1.6	2.2	1.0	0.4	0.1	0.2	0.1	6.7	1.6	1.3	8.0	0.3
1965	2.8	1.6	2.3	1.1	0.4	0.1	0.4	0.1	7.2	2.0	1.4	8.6	0.5
1966	3.3	1.7	2.5	1.2	0.5	0.1	0.4	0.2	8.1	1.9	1.7	9.8	0.2
1967	3.6	1.8	2.9	1.2	0.5	0.1	0.5	0.2	9.0	1.9	2.0	11.0	-0.1
1968	3.9	1.8	3.3	1.4	0.5	0.1	0.5	0.2	9.9	2.4	2.4	12.2	—
1969	4.2	1.8	3.6	1.6	0.6	0.1	0.5	0.2	10.7	3.7	2.7	13.5	1.0
1970	4.6	1.9	4.1	1.9	0.6	0.1	0.5	0.2	11.9	3.7	3.4	15.3	0.3
1971	5.0	1.9	4.7	2.0	0.5	0.2	0.5	0.2	13.1	4.2	4.3	17.4	-0.2

Year													
1972	5.5	2.0	6.2	2.3	0.6	0.2	0.6	0.3	15.5	4.0	4.6	20.1	−0.6
1973	6.1	2.2	7.0	2.5	0.7	0.2	0.7	0.3	17.6	5.2	4.8	22.4	0.4
1974	7.4	2.5	8.7	3.0	2.1	0.2	1.0	0.4	22.7	7.3	6.2	28.9	1.1
1975	8.3	2.8	10.6	3.7	3.2	0.3	1.1	0.6	27.8	3.9	7.7	35.5	−3.8
1976	9.7	3.2	11.5	4.5	2.4	0.4	1.2	0.5	30.2	5.1	8.5	38.7	−3.4
1977	11.1	3.7	13.1	5.1	2.2	0.5	1.2	0.6	33.8	2.6	10.0	43.8	−7.3
1978	12.0	4.1	14.6	6.4	2.3	0.6	1.2	1.0	38.2	0.3	10.9	49.0	−10.6
1979	12.8	4.2	14.7	8.1	3.2	0.5	0.9	0.8	40.9	2.6	11.8	52.7	−9.1
1980	13.9	4.8	16.5	9.9	5.6	0.8	1.0	0.8	48.2	2.4	12.8	61.3	−10.4
1981	16.5	5.5	18.7	13.7	6.6	0.9	0.9	0.9	58.2	6.7	14.1	72.3	−7.3
1982	18.9	6.7	24.4	16.7	5.8	2.6	1.3	1.0	70.6	−3.1	15.8	86.4	−20.3
1983	19.6	7.1	28.1	17.4	5.7	3.6	1.5	1.2	77.0	−6.7	17.6	94.6	−25.0
1984	21.4	8.1	29.6	21.3	7.5	3.4	2.5	1.5	87.3	−10.0	19.9	107.1	−30.4
1985	23.8	9.5	31.7	25.3	6.4	3.0	2.1	1.6	94.0	−10.0	21.7	115.7	−32.0
1986	24.1	9.4	33.2	26.4	4.8	2.5	2.2	1.8	94.9	−3.0	21.1	116.0	−24.8

[a] Calendar year. [b] Included in goods and services.

Note: 1980-86 figures on 1981 revised National Accounts basis.

Sources: Canada, Department of Finance, *Economic Review*, April 1985; Statistics Canada, *National Income and Expenditure Accounts, 1926-86*.

Table A.10   Federal Government: Expenditure by Major Category as a Percentage of the Total, National Accounts Basis, Selected Years 1947-86

Calendar year	Goods and services	Transfers to persons	Interest on debt	Transfers to other governments	Other	Total
			percent			
1947.....	33.3	28.6	23.8	9.5	4.8	100.0
1953.....	53.2	23.4	10.7	8.6	4.1	100.0
1955.....	49.9	24.9	10.4	10.4	4.4	100.0
1960.....	35.8	29.8	11.9	14.9	7.6	100.0
1965.....	32.5	26.7	12.8	16.2	11.8	100.0
1970.....	30.0	26.8	12.4	22.2	8.6	100.0
1975.....	23.4	29.9	10.4	21.7	14.6	100.0
1977.....	25.3	29.9	11.6	22.8	10.4	100.0
1979.....	24.3	28.2	15.4	22.4	9.7	100.0
1980.....	22.6	17.1	16.2	21.0	13.1	100.0
1981.....	22.8	25.9	18.9	19.5	12.9	100.0
1982.....	21.9	28.2	19.3	18.3	12.3	100.0
1983.....	20.6	29.7	18.4	18.6	12.7	100.0
1984.....	20.1	27.4	19.9	18.6	13.8	100.0
1985.....	20.5	27.4	21.8	18.7	11.6	100.0
1986.....	20.5	28.9	22.7	18.2	9.9	100.0

Based on table A.9.

Table A.11 Federal Government: Expenditure by Major Function, Intergovernmental Transfers Included and Excluded, Consolidated Finance Basis, 1952-86

Year[a]	General govt.	National defence	Resource and ind. develop.	Trans. and comm.	Health	Social serv.	Education	Debt costs	Other	Total excl. general transfers	General transfers to other govts.	Total
						billions of dollars						
1952	0.2	1.9	0.2	0.1	—	1.0	—	0.4	0.4	4.2	0.3	4.5
1953	0.2	1.8	0.2	0.2	—	1.0	—	0.4	0.4	4.2	0.3	4.5
1954	0.2	1.7	0.3	0.2	0.1	1.0	—	0.4	0.3	4.2	0.4	4.6
1955	0.3	1.8	0.2	0.2	0.1	1.1	—	0.4	0.2	4.3	0.4	4.7
1956	0.3	1.8	0.2	0.2	0.1	1.2	—	0.5	0.5	4.8	0.4	5.2
1957	0.3	1.7	0.2	0.3	0.1	1.3	0.1	0.5	0.6	5.1	0.4	5.5
1958	0.3	1.7	0.3	0.3	0.1	1.5	0.1	0.5	0.6	5.4	0.4	5.9
1959	0.3	1.5	0.3	0.4	0.2	1.6	0.1	0.7	0.5	5.6	0.6	6.2
1960	0.3	1.5	0.4	0.4	0.3	1.6	0.1	0.7	0.6	5.9	0.5	6.4
1961	0.3	1.7	0.4	0.4	0.4	1.8	0.1	0.7	0.7	6.5	0.5	7.0
1962	0.3	1.6	0.4	0.4	0.4	1.9	0.3	0.8	0.8	6.9	0.3	7.2
1963	0.4	1.7	0.4	0.4	0.5	2.2	0.2	0.8	0.7	7.3	0.3	7.6
1964	0.5	1.6	0.4	0.5	0.5	2.3	0.2	0.8	0.7	7.5	0.4	7.9
1965	0.4	1.5	0.2	0.9	0.5	2.5	0.3	0.8	0.8	8.3	0.4	8.7
1966	0.4	1.5	0.2	1.0	0.5	2.7	0.4	0.8	1.7	9.2	0.6	9.8
1967	0.5	1.6	0.3	1.0	0.6	3.1	0.6	0.9	1.8	10.4	0.8	11.2
1968	0.7	1.6	0.3	1.0	0.8	3.5	0.3	1.1	2.3	11.6	0.9	12.5
1969	0.7	1.6	0.3	1.1	1.0	3.8	0.8	1.2	2.4	12.9	1.0	13.9
1970	1.0	1.7	0.3	1.0	1.3	4.5	0.9	1.2	2.5	14.4	1.3	15.7
1971	1.1	1.9	0.3	1.2	1.6	5.4	0.9	1.4	2.9	16.7	1.5	18.2
1972	1.3	1.9	0.3	1.4	1.8	6.9	0.8	1.5	3.4	19.3	1.6	20.9
1973	1.4	2.1	0.6	1.8	2.0	8.1	0.9	1.7	3.8	22.4	1.9	24.3
1974	1.7	2.3	1.6	2.2	2.3	10.1	1.0	2.3	4.7	28.2	2.7	30.9

Continued on next page.

Table A.11 Continued

Year[a]	General govt.	National defence	Resource and ind. develop.	Trans. and comm.	Health	Social serv.	Education	Debt costs	Other	Total excl. general transfers	General transfers to other govts.	Total
						billions of dollars						
1975	1.9	2.6	3.9	2.5	2.8	12.4	1.2	2.8	4.0	34.1	2.7	36.8
1976	2.3	3.2	3.5	2.7	3.3	14.0	1.4	3.4	4.5	38.3	3.4	41.7
1977	2.6	3.6	3.6	3.0	3.1	15.6	1.9	3.5	5.6	42.5	3.5	46.0
1978	2.8	4.1	3.4	3.3	3.8	17.1	2.2	4.7	5.8	47.2	3.4	50.6
1979	2.9	4.4	5.3	3.3	4.2	18.3	2.4	5.9	6.5	53.2	4.1	57.3
1980	3.5	4.9	7.2	4.3	4.4	21.5	2.5	8.0	7.8	64.1	4.4	68.5
1981	4.0	5.8	8.5	4.2	4.7	24.3	2.7	11.3	8.6	74.1	5.3	79.4
1982	4.4	6.8	9.7	2.8	4.6	31.2	2.9	12.3	11.5	86.2	6.2	92.4
1983	4.9	7.7	8.8	3.2	6.2	35.3	3.6	13.1	12.6	95.4	6.6	102.0
1984	5.3	8.5	10.9	3.7	7.1	37.3	3.9	16.8	13.7	107.2	6.8	114.0
1985	5.7	8.7	9.2	3.7	7.3	40.0	3.9	18.3	15.2	112.0	7.0	119.0
1986	6.7	9.5	8.2	4.3	7.6	41.3	4.0	20.0	14.5	116.0	7.2	123.3

[a] Fiscal year nearest December 31 of the year named.

Note: Federal grants in aid of a specific function are included in the amounts shown for that function. Years before and after 1965 are not exactly comparable.

Sources: Statistics Canada, *Historical Review, Financial Statistics of Governments of Canada, 1952-62*; CANSIM, *Historical Statistics of Canada*.

Appendix 2
Ministerial Task Force on Program Review

The Ministerial Task Force on Program Review was created by the newly elected Conservative government in September 1984 and put under the general direction of the Deputy Prime Minister, Eric Nielsen. It was given two broad assignments—to improve federal government services for the public and achieve better management within government. Work teams were appointed to conduct studies for individual areas composed of specialists from federal, provincial and municipal governments and from the private sector. The latter included representatives of national business, labour and professional organizations. In all there were 21 volumes in the final report.

Each study team was given three months to complete their reports. They were asked specifically to identify areas of duplication between federal and provincial programs, to suggest programs that could be eliminated, reduced, or consolidated with other programs, and propose improvements in remaining programs. They were also asked to provide summary changes to the legislation and an estimate of the savings in both money and staff that would result from their proposals.

In the process they reviewed any past evaluations of performance, consulted with persons and organizations familiar with the function, including beneficiaries and interested persons in the private sector. For beneficiaries, particular attention was paid to the appropriateness of the original program, the degree to which its operation had been changed in practice, the nature of beneficiaries of federal and provincial programs of the same type, and the extent to which the program met current demographic and geographic requirements. Attention was also directed to overlapping of programs—cases where recipients were receiving benefits under several measures (federal, provincial and municipal); programs that supplemented each other or worked at cross purposes or involved duplication and overlapping; programs that could be delivered more effectively by other levels of government or by private organizations. The efficiency of program delivery was also studied—undue delay, paper work that was confusing and troublesome, offices that were poorly located, etc. The team reports were reviewed by independent specialists, and, after consideration by the main committee, were published. They had no official status, but many resulted in changes both in the content of programs and their management within the government.

The following selection of summaries, part of a more extensive review made by the Canadian Tax Foundation, deals mainly with reports in the area of the economy and the social services.

The Economy

1. Services and Subsidies to Business

This study group carried out 140 program reviews covering 218 distinct federal or federal-provincial programs costing a total of $16.4 billion in 1984-85, and involving 68,000 person years of employment. The task force proposed an examination of the stacking of government incentive programs; under the current system a private investor could invest as little as 10 percent in a project by qualifying for programs from several departments and the three levels of government.

Other proposals affecting trade and industry were as follows: direction of the defence industry productivity program back to its original purpose of aiding defence-related industries; termination of assistance to the shipbuilding industry under the shipbuilding industry assistance program when current contracts run out; simplification of the machinery duty remission program and development of procedures to reduce delays; termination of the credit reinsurance program; merger of the assistance program for small business to demonstrate new technology in an operational setting with the unsolicited proposals fund; coordination of the trade development activities of the department of Agriculture, Fisheries and Oceans, and External Affairs; consolidation of the programs for export market development and promotional products; amalgamation of the industrial cooperation program of CIDA and the cost recoverable technical assistance program of the Department of External Affairs; elimination of duplication in programs competing for communications technology markets; privatization of the National Design Council; integration of the three import review bodies, the Canadian Import Tribunal, the Tariff Board, and the Textile and Clothing Board; new and revised legislation to update the Canada Business Corporations Act, the Trade Mark Act, and the Industrial Design Act; amendment of the Patent Act to allow Canada to accede to the Patent Cooperation Treaty; new subsidiary economic and regional development agreements (ERDAs) dealing with tourism to be funded by the provinces or the private sector unless federal funding is justified by regional disparity considerations.

2. Education and Research

This study team was asked to review all "federal government programs which offer or support formal education and research and development taking place in, or in association with educational institutions." In 1984-85 there were 109 programs that involved direct federal government support of about $1.8 billion; transfers to the provinces and territories relating to education of $4.2 billion for post-secondary education and $207 million for the official languages program. The value of tax exemptions related to tuition fees and other educational items was about $195 million. The study team grouped the programs into seven general categories, as follows:

Support for post-secondary education through established programs financing ($4,524 million in one program);

Support for university research ($631 million and 27 programs);

Support for native education ($570 million and six programs);

Direct education services ($116 million and five programs);

Federal involvement in school programs ($225 million and four programs);

Student aid ($278 million and two programs);

International programs ($42 million and eight programs); and

Miscellaneous ($213 million and five programs).

The study team commented explicitly on the first two areas because the issues are much larger and more fundamental, as well as the joint nature of the programs, and the amount of money involved.

There had never been any serious objection to federal government involvement in support for research but federal support for post-secondary education has always been a source of federal-provincial friction. The provinces insist that the federal role be limited to funding. The study team pointed out that advanced education and research are joint products, carrying with them cost allocation problems. The team found that support for post-secondary education through the Established Programs Financing (EPF) arrangements has several disadvantages: the objectives of the program are not clearly specified and no national standards have been established; the arrangement does not specify that the revenue from the tax point transfer is earmarked for the support of education, and the provinces do not regard this revenue as federal funding but simply as provincial revenue from taxes.

Several options to the present program were presented but the study team recommended that the task force consider continuing the present arrangements but amending the Act to establish an individual ratio for each province of its post-secondary education/health split. Abandonment of the present EPF arrangements would entail a complete separation of the health and education components, and providing transfers through individual arrangements under an amended Act, each setting out federal purposes, conditions, or criteria. Another suggestion was that a completely separate Act could provide a new formula basis for determining education transfers to the provinces and allow the federal government to establish the objectives of its role in post-secondary education financing. As the Constitution does not explicitly allocate any responsibility to the federal government for post-secondary education, there is justification for its total withdrawal from this field; this would not mean the termination of its support for research.

Recommendations for other Education Programs

Native education. Management of Indian education should become the mandate of an Indian education council reporting through a minister but operating independently of the department's bureaucracy; a formula should be established to base expenditures on objective criteria; Indian post-secondary students should be eligible for financial support on the same basis as other students; a sustained emphasis should be placed on encouraging Indians who have left school to acquire basic literacy and job skills.

Educational services to inmates of federal correctional institutions. The process of moving to contracted teaching services should be accelerated and the services should be sustained at an adequate level to ensure that motivated inmates can benefit from them.

Department of National Defence university education programs. The department should shift some of its emphasis to recruitment of those with appropriate university education.

Canadian military colleges. Salaries should not be paid to college students during the academic year. They should be paid for summer training, which is non-academic.

Education in Official Languages. The government should move to separate funding for official language minority schooling and phase out funding for the second official language schooling program. The multiculturalism programs should continue with formal consultation and agreements with the provinces for matching funding. The Canadian studies program should be disbanded.

Student aid. Student aid should be left entirely to the provinces and territories; grants should be provided to the provinces for support of their student aid programs.

Tax expenditures. The only change recommended in this area was the elimination of the registered education savings plan.

3. Research Funding

The three granting councils (Medical Research Council, Natural Sciences and Engineering Research Council, and the Social Sciences and Humanities Research Council) provided $415 million of the 1984-85 total federal government support for university research and development; 23 federal departments awarded $55 million for research and development grants, contributions, and research fellowships; federal departments and agencies let $36 million worth of contracts to universities. All the councils claim a need for more money and also request funding to cover the indirect costs of research.

Federal government support for industrial research and development is provided through contracts, grants and contributions, and tax incentives. The federal government has adopted a policy of encouraging the contracting out of government research and development. The study team concluded that when departmental budgets are reduced, contracting-out projects are the first to suffer; there may be a tendency to by-pass the impartial bidding process; Crown ownership of the developed intellectual property is viewed negatively by researchers.

The study team proposed that the federal government give a more specific policy direction to the three granting councils during approval of their multi-year plans. Long-term commitments for funding by the government could be based on 1984-85 allocations, with increments subject to policy direction. The three granting councils would remain as separate entities but report to one minister; most of the departmental grants, contributions, and scholarships (university and industrial) be administered by the appropriate granting council; a steering committee composed of representatives of the universities, federal and provincial governments, and the private sector be set up to advise on policy and other matters; funding provided to the granting councils be allocated in the same proportions as prevailed in 1979; administrative expenses of the three councils be shared; the councils be encouraged to devote a portion of their budget to first-time applicants.

4. Job Creation, Training, and Employment Services

This study team reviewed 65 job creation, training, and employment services programs that involved an estimated $2.7 billion in direct government expenditure in 1984-85. Training programs, (accounting for 51 percent of program expenditure), job creation, (about 39 percent), and employment programs (10 percent), were carried out by the following departments and agencies:

Program	Department or Agency
7 training	Canada Employment and Immigration
6 job creation	
37 employment	
1 youth training	National Defence
1 youth training and employment, Quebec	National Health and Welfare
1 training program each	Medical Research Council
	Natural Sciences and Engineering Research Council
	Social Sciences and Humanities Research Council
1 labour adjustment benefits	Labour
1 youth program	Secretary of State
8 training and job creation	Public Service Commission

The study team recommended substantial reduction in the funding for the institutional training program and the critical skills training component of the institutional training program, and complete termination of the skills growth fund. The team found that a high proportion of the courses provided training in occupations for which no jobs existed, there was a lack of private sector consultation in course selection and design, and training for the sake of training was undesirable. It also recommended the complete phasing out of the basic academic skills education component of the institutional training program. The team recommended that existing training and job creation programs that were meeting the needs of Canadians be consolidated—Career Access, Job Corps, and General Industrial Training.

The federal government should continue in the job creation field until the unemployment rate is much lower but the study team recommended long-term federal-provincial agreements combining job creation and training rather than the uncoordinated makework projects of Canada Works. There should be a strong input from business and labour in designing programs and more emphasis should be placed on training for the small business and the service sectors. The study team concluded that Katimavik was not beneficial to the unemployed and suggested that it and the Local Employment Assistance and Development program be terminated.

Among other recommendations were: the National Defence department's youth training and employment program be continued but be funded out of the defence envelope; consideration be given to the option of consolidating the research grants and scholarships programs of the three granting councils to increase the supply of qualified research labour; the work-sharing program be evaluated to cut down on the paper burden for employers, remove the adverse effect on employee pensions, reduce unemployment insurance costs associated with the deletion of the two-week waiting period, and re-examine the two-year waiting period for new businesses.

The study team urged the government to take steps over two years to improve the existing placement service or withdraw completely from it. Suggestions for improvement were: better screening of applicants; greater targetting of services to areas where no private services exist, more emphasis on expertise in small- and medium-size business placement; speeding up of services; use of automation; consolidation into one program of the three industrial adjustment programs. Counselling services should be limited to clients with special needs and the counsellors should be better trained.

The study team noted that it had heard a number of complaints about the unemployment insurance program, especially in connection with the sharp escalation of premiums and the use of unemployment insurance funds for employment, work-sharing, and job creation programs and the replacement in some cases of training allowances by unemployment insurance benefits. The unemployment insurance program was outside the mandate of the study team.

5. Agriculture

The study team examined 42 programs that involved $2.7 billion in direct spending and $400 million in tax expenditures carried out by Agriculture Canada and its agencies and five other departments.

Research. The study team recommended that the research branch be reorganized in consultation with industry. It should use part of its budget for pure, basic research and develop or improve products that can be grown in the Atlantic provinces or in areas cultivated by native people. It should also strive to improve marketing of other products, and develop improved methods of slaughtering livestock.

Supply Management Programs. These programs should be redesigned to alleviate the current fragmentation in various branches. The study team considered supply management programs to be an intrusion into the free market system that served neither the consumer nor the producer well. Assurances of a market at a fixed price encouraged inefficiencies. Quotas take on a commercial value that becomes a major portion of the farm business value. The team recommended disbandonment of the dairy subsidies. The Canadian Dairy Commission should become a producer-marketing agency under the supervision of the National Farm Products Marketing Council.

Commissioners of the Canadian Wheat Board should be reorganized along specific lines of accountability for decisions. Leadership should encourage innovation, and be open to criticisms and suggestions.

Inspection. Inspection programs should be reorganized to eliminate duplication of effort at various levels. Provincial inspectors might take over responsibility wherever possible. An advisory committee made up of government experts, private sector citizens, business and consumers should set up acceptable risk factors for revised programs.

Other Recommendations. The study team felt that although farmers face a number of risks uncommon to other businesses, improved actuarial data collection has made it possible to establish many insurance and stabilization programs. Producers and the two senior levels of government could contribute to these schemes on a tripartite basis. A producer should be allowed to take out additional insurance at his own expense if desired. Other risks would still have to be taken care of on an ad hoc basis, and the costs of such programs be shared by the provincial and federal governments.

Farmers should no longer be allowed to use cash rather than accrual accounting for taxation purposes.

6. Natural Resources

The study team reviewed 60 programs that cost $1.4 billion in spending outlays and $2.3 billion in tax expenditures in 1984-85, and involved 2,547 person years of employment in six departments. As the provinces generally own and control the natural resources within their borders, the federal government has responsibility only for common property—fisheries, national parks, Crown lands in the north, Indian reserves, and uranium mining. The federal government's role in mining and forestry is primarily a responsibility for trade. Strong federal leadership is necessary to integrate efforts into a national export-directed initiative. Specialists are spread too thinly across too many departments. The study team proposed the development of national sectoral policies for mining and fisheries, based on sound data, national policy directives, and definition of the role of governments in relation to the industry. Domestic and international marketing strategies must be developed based on solid market information.

The study team recommended: (1) strengthening the input of industries into federal research programs; (2) developing effective technology-diffusion and staff exchange programs between industry and university; (3) increasing industry involvement in the selection of projects under future ERDA sub-agreements; (4) strengthening industry responsibility for conservation, protection of natural resources, and self-regulation.

Responsibility for the social aspects of programs now included in the sectoral departments should be transferred to the Department of Employment and Immigration. A review must be made of the effects of the Unemployment Insurance program on the natural resource sector.

Fisheries: the task force proposed that the fisheries department concentrate on its primary mandate—responsibility for protecting the fisheries resource and maintaining a viable fishing industry. It was not intended to be a department of social welfare or employment. To quote the report: "only the fish, efficiently harvested and processed, can create jobs and wealth; government activities, beyond the primary mandate . . . are largely wasted." The two government-owned fishing enterprises, which were acquired as a result of nationalizing floundering private companies, are viewed as major disincentives to private sector investment in the Atlantic fishing industry. The team found that the government cannot claim to be a protector and allocator of the resource, a regulator of the industry, and at the same time own all or part of fisheries businesses.

The Department has done a good job of protecting and enhancing the resource but the study team felt that outlays of the fisheries management program of $237 million per year to manage a fishery with a landed value of $887 million could not be justified. It meant a ratio of one fisheries management person year for every 10 in the industry. The task force recommended consolidation of the Department's research activities, reduction in the number of research vessels, and increased use of chartered vessels; involving the fishing industry in the resource assessment process, and directing research to important stocks where knowledge was deficient. In the area of small craft harbours it recommended imposing uniform fees for all users, limiting the program to commercial harbours, and withdrawing from the provision of recreational facilities. It also recommended that the regulation of foreign fishing fleets be increased and rules against over-fishing be enforced. The Department of Fisheries should enlist the support of the defence department and the Canadian Coast Guard to raise the profile of Canadian enforcement.

Inspection activities should focus on health, safety, and fairness. The Department must co-operate with the Department of Health with respect to the achievement of common standards. Industry must assume the responsibility as well as the cost of quality control.

Forestry: forest management and renewal must become a continuing and essential part of Canadian forestry. The federal government must continue to make its support conditional on long-term reforestation responsibilities. Marketing potentialities of various trees must be critically examined and a forest products marketing strategy be developed with the private sector and the provinces. The Canadian Forestry Service should play a lead role in coordinating research related to the development of the forestry industry.

Mining: the study team identified a need for national minerals policy to clearly define the roles of the federal and provincial governments, identify national objectives, set priorities for allocating government resources, and consult with industry with regard to the selection of mineral development projects. It suggested that responsibility for northern mining development be transferred to the territories from the Department of Indian Affairs and Northern Development and the Department's mandate then focus solely on its responsibility for native peoples.

7. Transportation

The study team reviewed 126 federal government programs involving net expenditures in 1985-86 of $2.9 billion and 20,544 person years of employment. The basic principles guiding the team were: (1) equitable treatment should be accorded competing modes of transportation with respect to subsidies, degree of cost-recovery to be achieved, and level of service provided or supported by the federal government; (2) subsidies provided should not adversely affect unsubsidized competing private services; (3) the least-cost mode of transportation should be provided in areas where the federal government is required to provide or subsidize transportation services.

The study team concluded that proposals for the elimination or downsizing of some existing programs and entities would lead to public opposition unless they were accompanied by the publication of information dealing with the true costs of such services, revenues and charges, subsidies paid, and data on the users of such services. Their main recommendations were as follows:

1. Elimination of public subsidization of rail passenger services. Higher user charges to reflect the true cost of the service provided. Rail service in remote areas should be provided only where alternative air or bus service cannot be provided at lower public cost.

2. The federal government should, where possible, divest itself of involvement in airports and in other cases impose higher and additional user charges to recover the true cost of providing the service.

3. The provision of subsidies for water transportation in certain areas, particularly in Atlantic Canada, should be reduced by realistic user charges and the substitution of lower cost alternatives where possible, such as air transportation.

4. A grain distribution and handling system based on commercial decision-making should be instituted. Subsidies to farmers for grain transportation should be paid directly to farmers as opposed to being paid to the railways so that producers could choose the mode of transportation most favourable to them.

5. The federal government should try to reduce or eliminate its involvement in a number of other programs, including bridges, dams, highways in the Territories, the Trans-Canada highway, and ferry services. Where possible negotiations should be carried out to have the provinces or territories take over these services.

6. The regulatory burden should be reduced wherever possible, while maintaining necessary safeguards to protect the public.

Social Services

1. Health

The study team reviewed 25 programs that cost an estimated $12.3 billion in spending and tax transfers in 1985-86 and three tax expenditure programs with an estimated value of $205 million; the programs involved seven departments or agencies and 5,850 person years of employment. The major payments were for health insurance and extended health care services through fiscal arrangements with the provinces, estimated at $6.7 billion in cash payments and $4.6 billion in tax transfers.

The team found that the Canada Health Act limited the provinces' flexibility to respond to pressures within their health systems and added irritants to federal-provincial relationships. It felt that the Act should be amended to allow the federal government to monitor adherence to the five standard principles of the health systems and also to remove some provisions that may cause irritation between the two levels of government. The provinces have not yet been able to implement cost control measures.

The study team recommended that payments for health care currently paid through the Established Programs Financing arrangements eventually become unconditional in form, unrelated to health and post-secondary education, and that the cash portion of the EPF package be converted into additional tax room. Interprovincial equity must continue to be protected. Discussions should be held to redefine intergovernmental fiscal arrangements to better align the fundamental issues of responsibility, authority, and accountability.

Federal-provincial discussions related to health for the period 1987-92 should consider: (1) elimination of the split in EPF between health and post-secondary education, or, failing that, calculation of the split on a more realistic basis; (2) setting a five-year period for the modified EPF arrangements; (3) development of a flexible approach to deal with problems encountered under the Canada Health Act.

The study team recommended that health programs should emphasize personal responsibility for one's own health rather than the present reliance on illness-treatment programs.

Proposals of the team for other health programs included: responsibility for Indian and northern health services be transferred to the provinces and territories; fees be charged for pre-market testing of new drugs and appliances; civil aviation and immigration medical programs be transferred to other federal government departments, along with the institution of cost-recovery programs; health care and information statistics be discontinued; the sport program be phased down over a 10-15 year period; a study be made of the causes of the rapid growth in costs of the public service health program.

2. Canada Assistance Plan

The study group on CAP was asked to provide the task force with an understanding of the Plan, a description of how it fits into the context of related federal and provincial/territorial social programs, to identify any suitable alternatives to the program, and ascertain its current fiscal implications. The review covered the period March 10 to June 10, 1985.

"CAP is a complex program, operating over a vast territory with varying conditions of unemployment, demography and population. Thirteen separate governmental jurisdictions . . . plus thousands of service delivery organizations" are involved. The study team found that recent caseloads are distinguished from those of the earlier years mainly in the great rise of "employables." Provincial caseloads now consist of from 30 percent to 70 percent "employables." The team found that there was a certain degree of contention between the levels of government and non-governmental organizations in dealing with the program but felt that some degree of strain was inevitable. Most parties supported continuance of the present system.

The team found no evidence of illegal or unwarranted payments to individuals on an alarming scale. The provinces exert control on overpayments.

3. Housing

This study team reviewed 24 programs that cost the government an estimated $2.0 billion in direct spending and $4.1 billion in tax expenditures in 1984-85, and involved six departments or agencies. They suggested that a reassessment be made of the desired objectives of housing programs, and that a balance be achieved between social and market objectives and between new housing and rehabilitation of existing housing. Past programs tended to benefit Canadians at all income levels. The study team recommended that future programs be directed to people most in need. Past programs have concentrated on the supply of new housing units which, while obviously filling a pressing need, tend to be very costly. A shift toward rental supplements and renovation programs was suggested.

The study team noted that some provinces have tended to reduce their spending on social housing in recent years and federal expenditures have been used to correct distortions in rental markets created by provincial rent controls. A precise delineation of the respective roles was recommended for both the delivery of housing programs and research priorities as well as a consolidation of the present fragmented research and development programs.

The team recommended the increased use of rent supplements, a new community housing program combining the best features of non-profit and public housing, and the institution of a revised residential rehabilitation program to provide assistance to home owners most in need and restricting repairs to those essential to health and safety.

A province agreeing to share housing program costs on a 50-50 basis with the federal government should be given the lead role in administration. The agency providing the higher financial contribution should generally take the lead role in administration and a province providing no money should be allowed no responsibility for delivering programs.

Programs directed to rural, native, and remote housing should continue to receive special allocation but the study team recommended a separate program for remote areas. The CMHC and Department of Indian Affairs and Northern Development programs for on-reserve housing should be consolidated. CMHC would continue to make unsubsidized insured and direct loans available to Indian bands.

To reduce the level of subsidies or to improve the targetting of the existing stock of social housing, the study team recommended that a new federal graduated rent scale be phased in over a three-year period, to apply to all income-tested households in non-profit and cooperative housing, rural and native housing, and to those receiving rent supplements. Negotiations should be carried out to encourage the charging of market rents to all households living in subsidized housing.

Reviewing CMHC's four major functions—housing subsidies, research and technical services, direct lending, and mortgage loan insurance—the team proposed a variety of possible options for change. The preferred option recommended was investigation of the transfer of all CMHC functions to a departmental structure (from a Crown corporation) providing that the direct lending and mortgage insurance functions could be accommodated.

Tax Expenditures. Included in the review of various programs was a proposed option that the exemption for capital gains on owner-occupied homes be included in the $500,000 maximum lifetime exemption. The team recommended that the government maintain the exemption for capital gains on homes and that a tax on imputed rent not be levied because the concept was too difficult to understand or measure.

Research, development, and demonstration. The study team recommended that responsibility for residential building research, development and demonstration be consolidated under the CMHC and non-residential building under the National Research Council; a research committee be established to coordinate federal, provincial, and industry involvement in housing research; and the National Housing Act be amended to permit CMHC to expand its inspection services.

Management of Government—Real Property

The annual operating and capital cost of managing the federal government's real property holdings (valued at between $40 and $60 billion) is about $6.0 billion annually. This study team reviewed 62 programs directed in whole or in part to real property management in 18 different departments and agencies, involving some 35,000 person years of employment annually.

The study team found that real property has been used to distribute benefits across the country, make the federal government's presence known, for development programs, and to provide local employment. Properties have been acquired by federal departments that could have been better managed at the provincial or local level. The cumulative effect of property acquisition is "a real property system that is bloated with inventory, under-managed, and over-staffed." The team urged that the government initiate a program to divest itself of many of its property holdings by transferring the ownership and management of federal airports to local authorities; selling surplus federal property; transferring to local governments and/or selling federal urban development projects in Quebec, Montreal, and Toronto; reassessing the base and station infrastructure of the Department of National Defence; reassessing the land and property holdings of the National Capital Commission; transferring federal responsibility for canals, dams, bridges, and highways to the appropriate level of government; and rationalizing Transport Canada's public ports and Fisheries and Ocean's small craft harbours by closing inactive harbours, transferring them to local authorities, or selling them to private interests.

The role of the Public Works Department should be revised so it is responsible for the management of general purpose properties and, at the option of its clients, the provision of design, contracting, and operation and maintenance services. In the national capital region, the appropriate departments should be responsible for special purpose buildings and the National Capital Commission responsible for designated properties of national interest. Ouside the capital area, the custody responsibility would continue to be split between Public Works and the program departments. There should be an increased contracting out of engineering, architectural, and operational and maintenance services.

Other recommendations of the study team were: the establishment of a real property unit to carry out central management functions; transfer of responsibility for through-park highways and roads from Parks Canada to provincial jurisdiction; new and higher rental rates for leasehold properties in national parks; residents of Banff and Jasper should pay a higher proportion of the costs of municipal services; a detailed review be made of the privatization of housing provided for federal employees in remote areas of the country; and a reduction in the public service staff involved in property management.

Part 2
The Search for a Policy

6
Canada Adopts Keynesian Approach: The First Two Decades

The foregoing review of postwar federal budgets clearly demonstrates that ministers of finance were eons away from their prewar counterparts in their objectives. From 1945 on the annual budget, once devoted largely to an accounting of the position of the treasury, became as much an economic as a fiscal document. The state of the economy and the government's efforts to exert a direct influence on it became the primary focus of attention. This reflected the assumption by government of responsibility for maintaining a high level of employment, reasonable price stability, and a rising standard of living, objectives which were to be achieved by using government taxes, expenditures, and related programs to influence trends in the economy—the Keynesian approach.

Few aspects of the latter half of the 20th century—perhaps nuclear and technological developments excepted—have had more direct influence on the lives of people than the adoption of this role. Among the western industrial nations its influence was at one time almost universal, but in recent years enthusiasm has cooled and, in some countries, it has been abandoned in a "conservative" reaction. While Canadian governments profess lessened faith in the interventionist role, it is still strongly evident in their actions and programs, and neither their past nor current performance could be understood without exploration of this profoundly important philosophical basis. We trace its introduction and evolution in the following chapters.

It all started with the federal government's unilateral (and in retrospect, dramatic) announcement at the very end of the war; was continued with varying degrees of conviction by ministers of finance in framing their annual budget programs over four decades; and in time became the subject of examination and appraisal by royal commissions, parliamentary committees, research organizations, business groups, economists, and others.

This arduous search for a policy ended in the frustration of the disastrous federal deficits of the eighties, which left little room for anything but fiscal retrenchment.

Policy Development in Canada

The federal government adopted this new role without reservation immediately at the end of European hostilities in 1945. Its commitment was given in the White Paper on Employment and Income, of which more later. Three crucial influences played a part in this action: memories of the Great Depression and fears that it would return; the successful experience of run-

151

ning a wartime economy, and finally the approach of the British economist, John Maynard Keynes.

The Great Depression. The grim years of the thirties left a lasting impression—one still very acute for survivors. The almost complete collapse of the economy, the abject poverty of a quarter or more of the population and its total dependence on niggardly "relief," and the seeming inability of governments to cope with the situation were a searing memory in the minds of many. Wartime demands quickly created conditions of full employment, but many leaders feared that this condition was related to war and that the economy would slump with peace. Another depression like that of the thirties could have tragic and disastrous consequences for society as it was then known. This concern was sufficiently real that even at the height of hostilities new policies were being studied to avoid such a calamity.

The need for a new role for government in the economy had been a strong message of the Report of the Royal Commission on Dominion-Provincial Relations in 1940, and the Prime Minister had promised renewed consideration of that document when peace returned. Ministers and officials at all levels of government also recalled the nightmare of attempting to deal with the massive distress of the depression within the policy and administrative limitations of the times, and were ready for a change.

The Wartime Experience. The successful management of the wartime economy by a group of inexperienced politicians and officials was a particularly significant educational process. The war brought severe hardship in many ways, but it at least demonstrated that under stimulus provided by the state an economy could be brought to life. The management of this process meant that for politicians the use of economic and social measures by government in peacetime came quite naturally; in truth may not have happened without this experience.

The Keynesian Approach. The Keynesian influence became dominant immediately after the war and in some degree has been present throughout the postwar period. Keynes, a brilliant Cambridge don and an influential advisor to British governments through much of his life, published two economic studies in the thirties which provided a theoretical basis for a more active and interventionist role for government.

While the main Keynesian policy prescriptions do not seem to be appropriate for current economic problems his approach to broad economic analysis (macro-economics) is still largely followed by economists.[6.1] Most

---

6.1 Paul A. Samuelson and Anthony Scott, *Economics* (Canadian Edition) (Toronto: McGraw-Hill Ryerson, 1980; Blomquist/Wonnacott/Wonnacott, *Economics*, 2nd Canadian edition (Toronto: McGraw-Hill Ryerson, 1983); Bellan, R.C., *Principles of Economics and the Canadian Economy* (Toronto: McGraw Hill Company of Canada Limited, 1960); Richard Lipsey and Peter Steiner, *Economics* (New York: Harper & Row, 1966); Campbell R. McConnell and William Pope, *Economics, Principles, Problems and Policies*, 2nd Canadian edition (Toronto: McGraw-Hill Ryerson Limited, 1981); Warren J. Blackman, *The Canadian Financial System* (Toronto: McGraw-Hill Ryerson, 1980); and D.E. Bond and R.A. Shearer, *The Economics of the Canadian Financial System: Theory, Policy and Institutions* (Scarborough: Prentice-Hall of Canada, 1972).

of his concepts were derived from traditional economics; his great contribution was in seeing them in a new light. Income was the result of business and personal expenditure, but economic growth was related closely to investment, which for Keynes meant expenditure on real assets. Capital investment was in turn dependent on the rate of savings, and the relationship between savings and investment was crucial for economic growth. The rate of savings could be adequate but if the savings were not being invested an economy could be in a stable position and still have unemployment. Without some outside intervention to change the relationship unemployment would persist. The central role of capital expenditure, linked with the concept of the multiplier effect of expenditure on economic growth (the first expenditure ripples out in other expenditures by persons and businesses) represented the main break with traditional economics, which had assumed that all adjustments required to maintain a free-market economy would automatically occur. Keynes disagreed; there would be conditions which could only be rectified by outside intervention. Governments would have to assume that role.

As Keynes was developing his analysis in the midst of the Great Depression his main concern was with the expansionary role that governments could play, and following his untimely death in 1946 it was this aspect of his approach that survived. His likely thoughts on chronic inflation and the phenomenon of stagflation have been the subject of much speculation, largely unproductive. Keynesian policy prescriptions of half a century ago are not in vogue today but, among the many able economists of recent vintage, none have achieved his influence.

Keynes in Practice

The strong emphasis in Keynes on the demand side of the economy (income and expenditure as contrasted with supply—i.e., factors of production) became generalized in operational terms as "demand management." Translated into its simplest form, if demand was maintained at a sufficiently high level and encouragement was given for capital expenditure, all else would follow in the economy. For long-term demand various forms of income maintenance programs—family allowances, old age pensions, unemployment insurance, etc.—could be introduced. These would respond automatically to changes in the economy. Some forms of taxation, such as the personal income tax, would act in the same way. Lower rates would automatically come into effect with reduced incomes. These were labelled "non-discretionary" or "automatic" programs. And governments could also offset economic activity that was either inadequate or excessive by appropriate "discretionary" changes from year to year in their taxation measures and budget balances. A sluggish economy could be stimulated by adding to demand through reduced taxation or increased expenditure to achieve a budget deficit; and for an economy that was over-active the reverse treatment could be applied to withdraw excess demand. In the language of the day this was labelled "contra-cyclical budgeting." Governments could also affect various forms of economic activity by the use of taxation devices—special depreciation to encourage capital expenditures, for example.

While Keynesian thinking was becoming familiar to Canadian economists in the late thirties it had a particular impact on the federal Department of Finance following the arrival of Robert Bryce, in 1938, but lately returned from studies under Keynes at Cambridge. Bryce was later to go on to a brilliant career in the federal public service. Governments were forced to manage the economy during the World War II period for very urgent and practical reasons and as previously mentioned the political leaders of government were conditioned by that experience into adopting a vastly more aggressive role in the economy.

Policy Commitment

As stated, the formal commitment to a new policy was given to Parliament in April 1945, in the government's *White Paper on Employment and Income*, presented by the Minister of Reconstruction, the Hon. C.D. Howe. The White Paper expressed the government's intention

> to accomplish a smooth, orderly transition from the economic conditions of war to those of peace and to maintain a high and stable level of employment and income. The Government adopts this as a primary object of policy. [Under the heading of Government Finance, the traditional peacetime approach to the budget was abandoned and a new one installed in its place.] . . . The Government will be prepared, in periods when unemployment threatens, to incur the deficits and increases in the national debt resulting from its employment and income policy, whether that policy in the circumstances is best applied through increased expenditures or reduced taxation. In periods of buoyant employment and income, budget plans will call for surpluses. The Government's policy will be to keep the national debt within manageable proportions, and maintain a proper balance in its budget over a period longer than a single year. [The last sentence is significant; the long-run objective would be a balanced budget, not one almost always in deficit. Tribute to the wartime experience was given for this policy]: Fiscal policy during the war has necessarily been based on economic as much as purely financial considerations. It is proposed to extend that practice into the post-war years and apply war experience to the problems of peace.[6.2]

The Keynesian influence is clearly apparent in the proposals to encourage capital expenditure: "The Government recognizes that wartime taxation, both in its form and rates, is discouraging to new investment . . . The Government proposes not only to reduce taxation as rapidly as possible but to develop its fiscal policy so as to encourage the increase of private investment

---

6.2 Canadian Trade Committee, *Canadian Economic Policy Since the War* (series of six public lectures September-November 1965), Appendix: Extracts from "The White Paper on Employment and Income. ed. S.F. Kaliski (Ottawa: Carleton University, 1965), 135-52.

to a high and stable level."[6.3] As a means to this end it would also keep interest rates as low as possible, and to add to the support of government investment, a shelf of projects would be created to be drawn on as necessary.

Four months later, at the Dominion-Provincial Conference on Reconstruction in August 1945, a more elaborate presentation covering both fiscal and social measures was made to the provinces. The main objective of the federal government was to maintain the control over the direct tax sources it had held during the war to enable it to carry out its peacetime economic policies. It projected the adoption of both new fiscal and social programs if the provinces would agree, and it made its case for the new fiscal policy as follows:

> The great growth in government revenues and expenditures made necessary by the war makes a responsible policy of this sort an obligation, and at the same time, with our increased knowledge of fiscal techniques, makes it a practical policy in the sense that it can have a really significant effect on the business cycle. The modern government budget must be the balance wheel of the economy; its very size to-day is such that if it were allowed to fluctuate up and down *with* the rest of the economy instead of deliberately *counter* to the business swings it would so exaggerate booms and depressions as to be disastrous . . . [As for capital expenditure]: The creation of conditions under which the initiative and skill of private enterprises will result in new investment on a scale far exceeding pre-war levels is one of the principal problems of reconstruction policy.[6.4]

Government policy, including the maintenance of low interest rates, would be directed to encouraging this objective. This, incidentally, was the only mention of any possible role for monetary policy in the future. Reliance would be placed almost exclusively on fiscal policy. This omission was soon to be corrected as it became evident that tax policy and contra-cyclical budgeting alone were inadequate for the job to be done.

As an aside, while Keynesian ideas were no doubt the immediate origin of Canadian contra-cyclical budgetary policy, it is interesting to speculate on the possible influence of distinguished Queen's University economists in its adoption. The trail begins in 1909, when Dr. O.D. Skelton, then of the political science faculty at Queen's and later Under-Secretary of State, wrote in the Queen's *Quarterly* as follows:

> The proper policy of government expenditure, it may be maintained, is exactly the contrary of that currently accepted. Government expenditure should serve as a flywheel to regulate the speed of the industrial mechanism. In times of prosperity, when the calls of private enterprise are draining the labour market, straining credit to the utmost, and sending prices of materials skyrocketing, government should as far as

---

[6.3] Ibid., at 143.

[6.4] Dominion-Provincial Conference on Reconstruction, *Proposals of the Government of Canada* (Ottawa: King's Printer, 1945).

possible refrain from accelerating the speed. In times of depression, when private enterprise halts, when men and funds lie idle and prices fall, government should push permanent work with all haste.[6.4a]

Moving forward to the 1940s we find that the secretary of the Royal Commission on Dominion-Provincial Relations was Sandy Skelton, a son of O.D., a prominent member of the Commission staff was John Deutsch, a member of the Queen's economics staff and later the Principal of Queen's, the author of the 1945 White Paper W.A. Mackintosh, was also an economics professor and also later the Principal of Queen's, and the federal Deputy Minister of Finance whose task it was to implement the White Paper, W.C. Clark, was a former Queen's professor. If this is not irrefutable proof of a Queen's conception, at least it is strong evidence of the influence once exerted over national affairs by that university.

Ministerial Declarations; Changing Times, Changing Prescriptions

The following pages will trace the fate of the new fiscal policy as it developed in the hands of the dozen or so ministers of finance whose task it was to clothe it with reality. Much of this has already emerged incidental to the fiscal review in the section on Fiscal Performance, but because of the central role assumed by the new policy it is essential to follow its evolution and ultimate standing over the forty year period. Following this review the critics will be allowed to have their say in a later section.

As a general introduction, it will be obvious from the earlier review of budget speeches that much of the effort of ministers of finance was devoted to bringing to heel the dread dual threat of inflation and unemployment. This had not been anticipated by the authors of the White Paper, and indeed was an onerous fate for which few of these gentlemen were prepared by profession, most of them being lawyers. In general they were arguing a case of which they had no inborn conviction, and if put to it would probably far rather have been supporting the merits of a balanced budget. If nothing else this was a demonstration of the hazards of political life, and in particular of the risks entailed in being Minister of Finance.

We follow the subject through 1946 to 1987 with excerpts from budget speeches. Here we will concentrate on the use of government policy instruments for economic management as far as it can be extracted from the usual entanglement of issues in the average budget. Where relevant, actual quotations will be used, thus putting ourselves in the same position as entrail-readers of the time, intent on discerning from the Minister's words any new trends in government thinking.

The First Two Decades

In this chapter we deal with experience in the first two postwar decades, a period showing every variety of experience.

[6.4a] O.D. Skelton, *Queen's Quarterly*, vol. XVI (July 1908-Apr. 1909) 376.

June 1946: Ilsley. Mr. Ilsley made a brief bow in the direction of the new policy in linking it with the need for central control of the main direct tax sources, as follows:

> The government attached great importance to the benefits which would be available through a single administration of these important tax fields . . . from the means it would have available through appropriate changes in policy to help offset fluctuations in the business cycle.[6.5]

April 1947: Abbott.

> We must expect, I believe, that at times when our employment, production and incomes are below satisfactory levels, our revenues will fall short of expenditures. Indeed, at such times it will probably be necessary to incur expenditures of various kinds to assist in restoring better levels of employment and income. It is a necessary corollary of this that we should aim at a surplus in times of prosperity and very high levels of income and employment, such as we have at the present time.[6.6]

May 1948: Abbott.

> We view the national budget now as an integral part of the nation's business, influenced by and having an influence upon the state of employment, income and prices . . . We should deliberately budget, as a matter of policy, for substantial surpluses in times like these. Only that way can we hold inflationary forces in check . . . Parliament and the government have a wider responsibility than before the war, particularly in the field of economic affairs . . . We know that to attain these great purposes, we must frame our policies and direct our efforts towards achieving and maintaining a high and expanding level of employment and income.[6.7]

March 1949: Abbott. Following three years of substantial surpluses the Minister offered major tax reductions, with the following revealing comment:

> . . . we must recognize that most Canadians, like other people in recent years, have shown that they prefer to pay taxes in other forms than high income taxes. I think most of us believe the income tax on individuals is the fairest and best tax we have. The trouble is we don't like it, or at least we don't like much of it . . . Consequently we must plan on retaining as normal sources of revenue substantial taxes on goods and services and taxes on corporate profits.[6.8]

[6.5] Canada, Department of Finance, Budget Speech, June 27, 1946, 10.

[6.6] Canada, Department of Finance, Budget Speech, April 29, 1947, 11.

[6.7] Canada, Department of Finance, Budget Speech, May 18, 1948, 10-19.

[6.8] Canada, Department of Finance, Budget Speech, March 22, 1949, 11.

October 1949: Abbott. The Minister's March budget failed to be passed by the intervention of an election, and in re-introducing it in the fall he gave a length review of the international currency crises that had produced a devaluation of most of the world's main currencies in terms of the U.S. dollar. He outlined his budgetary policy as follows:

> Our four preceding post-war budgets—those of 1945, 1946, 1947 and 1948—were all brought down at times when shortages of commodities, materials and men were either acute or serious, and when the fundamental economic conditions called for anti-inflationary policies. The 1949 prospects were different. Production, employment and incomes were at very high levels—indeed at record levels—but over most sectors of our economy production and demand had come into better balance and the post-war price inflation had passed its peak . . . Under these conditions, it was appropriate that we should modify our fiscal policy by moderating its anti-inflationary aspects and aiming at a closer balance in over-all revenues and expenditures.[6.9]

March 1950: Abbott.

> We must have a tax system that will at least balance the budget in good years, in those times when private expenditures and exports will sustain our employment and incomes at high levels; for otherwise we should slide quickly into inflation at such times and pile up our national debt more quickly than we add to the economic and financial capacity of the nation to carry it . . . Given the conditions I have outlined . . . the wise and prudent fiscal policy calls for a balanced budget . . .[6.10]

April 1951: Abbott. The Korean war having broken out, the Minister's attention turned to two issues, the pursuit of peace and the control of inflation.

> The government can exercise careful control over its own expenditures; we can follow a fully pay-as-we-go policy; we can restrain the expansion of credit; and we can apply direct controls either to particular conditions, or if necessary, more generally. In Canada we have done all of these and we shall continue to develop and apply these policies. [A direct Keynesian touch emerged regarding investment]: There is, I think, a growing realization throughout the country that at a time of full employment the level of investment cannot exceed the current level of new saving by the community without having an inflationary influence. In such circumstances extension of credit requires particularly careful scrutiny . . . The important thing is to achieve an increase in aggregate saving up to a level at least equal to the new capital investment which we shall have to make this year.[6.11]

[6.9] Canada, Department of Finance, Budget Speech, October 20, 1949, 6.

[6.10] Canada, Department of Finance, Budget Speech, March 28, 1950, 11.

[6.11] Canada, Department of Finance, Budget Speech, April 10, 1951, 6-7.

The Minister rejected both price controls and an excess profits tax, for which there was public pressure, as unnecessary for the times.

April 1952: Abbott. The Minister, who by this time had occupied his onerous post for five years, some of them very difficult years, could no longer restrain his frustrations with an Opposition that in his view had been wholly unreasonable in their attitude toward his fiscal policy, being equally critical of either a deficit or a surplus. (In this the Opposition generally reflected the views of the public, for whom contra-cyclical budgeting was largely a black mystery. The lack of general understanding was indeed a major problem in its implementation). The Minister said:

> We have heard a good deal from some quarters in recent months about bad budgeting. Year by year my Conservative friends opposite have charged me with being too optimistic. The hon. member for Greenwood (Mr. Macdonnell) not so long ago, when I was budgeting for a $20 million surplus, gravely rebuked me for being reckless. Only a moderate worsening of conditions, he warned me, would plunge the national treasury into deficit. But year after year as we approach the end of our fiscal period these same hon. members join in quite a different chorus—we have overtaxed the Canadian people! Let me say quite plainly, Mr. Speaker, that so long as we have such years of rising prosperity as we have experienced while I have been Minister of Finance I am not going to apologize for having a surplus and making some reductions in the deadweight of our huge national debt.[6.12]

Obviously if the Minister had ever felt any personal fervour for contra-cyclical budgeting as set forth in the 1945 White Paper it had cooled perceptibly by 1952, and the constant political haggling was no doubt largely responsible. At most he was prepared only to defend it as a means of reducing the federal debt.

February 1953: Abbott. In this post-Korean war budget the Minister expressed satisfaction with the economic record of the war period and proposed a tax reduction to use up a small surplus that was anticipated in the budget. He described this as a "social dividend" that the Canadian people had earned through "greater productivity, increased efficiency and a willingness to work hard and vigorously for good wages, salaries and profits—these are the things that power our country today and make possible this surplus for tax relief."[6.13] Not very Keynesian, but the great economist would no doubt have approved a reward for good effort.

April 1954: Abbott. In this, his last budget before becoming a member of the Supreme Court, the Minister reaffirmed his approach to fiscal policy:

> My general philosophy with respect to taxation has always been that in good, prosperous years we should balance the budget with a bit over for the reduction of debt. When we have had exceptional years, and

---

[6.12] Canada, Department of Finance, Budget Speech, April 8, 1952, 4.

[6.13] Canada, Department of Finance, Budget Speech, February 19, 1953, 11.

especially under conditions of inflationary pressures, I have never apologized for having a substantial surplus for debt reduction. I am also convinced that whatever merit there may be in large scale deficit financing under severe conditions, those conditions neither exist nor are in prospect. On the other hand, I do not think one should be unduly cautious and refuse to consider desirable tax reductions just because conditions might deteriorate and we might have a small deficit.[6.14]

While considerably short of the full devotion to contra-cyclical policy expected by the economists (as we shall see later) this was the compromise of an able and working politician with the political realities of his time.

April 1955: Harris. In declaring his own approach to fiscal policy the Minister said:

I think there will also be general agreement that, under boom conditions when abnormal demands are putting undue strain on our resources and inflationary pressures are building up, fiscal policy should play its part, along with other appropriate policies, in placing some restraint on boom conditions. Conversely, when the rate of economic advance slackens, and the economy as a whole is not fully employed, a moderate budgetary deficit should be no cause for alarm.

Let me add at once that I do not think that fiscal policy is the only means of promoting economic stability and expansion. Fiscal policy is just one of several means to that end. Monetary policy, trade policy and policies relating to resource development and basic income maintenance are equally important, and in certain contexts may have considerably greater influence.[6.15]

(To this one can hear the author of the White Paper saying: "But of course, of course!").

March 1956: Harris. The Minister gave further commitment to stabilization policy and the mixed fiscal and monetary roles in the following words:

The blessings of an economy operating at a high level are pleasant indeed to a minister of finance but they bring with them new responsibilities for all of us. The objective should be to maintain a steady growth in economic activity without the process of expansion giving rise to inflation and instability. Consequently, in times like the present when private expenditures are expected to rise still further, the federal government itself has a special responsibility to see that its fiscal policies continue to be directed towards economic stability. The use of the flexible instruments of monetary policy is also being directed towards this objective. But careful judgment and wise spending policies are not solely matters of concern to public authorities. They

---

6.14 Canada, Department of Finance, Budget Speech, April 6, 1954, 9.

6.15 Canada, Department of Finance, Budget Speech, April 5, 1955, 10.

are the normal responsibility of each one of us, regardless of his role in the economy.[6.16]

March 1957. Harris: The Minister gave the following explanation for a hold-the-line budget. An election was in the offing, and some justification was needed for this unusual posture.

I have already explained my reasons for believing that the severe inflationary pressures, which we have resisted so far with a high degree of success, are still with us to a considerable extent. There are signs that these pressures are beginning to moderate, but it would not be wise to let down our guards of fiscal and monetary policy at this juncture. Too hasty action would imperil the success we have achieved so far, and an inflationary rise in prices could take away from our people far more in rising costs than they would benefit from even large reductions in tax rates.[6.17]

Change of Government

Fiscal propriety can have its political cost. After being in power for some twenty years the Liberal government was defeated in the following election, an outcome that was attributed by some observers to the lack of sweeteners in this budget.

June 1958: Fleming. A new Minister of Finance from the Conservative party encountered the phenomenon of stagflation in his first budget.

To go still further into deficit financing at this time could create conditions in which overt inflation of a degree very difficult to control might re-emerge. Indeed, even now we have the somewhat paradoxical situation of simultaneous symptoms of both recession and inflation. If we go too far in the measures we take to combat what is, after all, a fairly mild recession, we might find that we had planted an inflationary time bomb which might later go off with a dangerous explosive effect. Admittedly, it is not an easy matter to judge just the right degree or balance in these matters; but in the present circumstances, it seems to me we have, for the time being at least, a fairly sensible balance of fiscal policy, investment policy and income maintenance policies.[6.18]

April 1959: Fleming. The Minister gave a more detailed exposition of fiscal policy than had been presented in some time.

Government policies relating to taxation and expenditures should be kept flexible. In an earlier generation when government revenues and expenditures were only a very small fraction of the gross national product the broad economic effects of government finance were not of great significance. But in this modern age where the government

---

[6.16]Canada, Department of Finance, Budget Speech, March 20, 1956, 5.

[6.17]Canada, Department of Finance, Budget Speech, March 14, 1957, 11.

[6.18]Canada, Department of Finance, Budget Speech, June 17, 1958, 16.

expenditures constitute 18 to 20 per cent of the gross national product —and in many countries the percentage is much higher than in Canada—the financial policies of government—the amount spent, how it is spent, how the revenues are raised, and the balance between revenue and expenditure—all exert a very direct influence on the health of the private sector of the economy.

As economic conditions change, the government's budget policy needs to change also. It must be flexible; it should be adapted to the shifting economic climate. There are times when a substantial deficit is clearly the right policy; there are times when the budget should be in balance; there are times when some provision should be made for the orderly retirement of debt; and within these ranges there is always the question of degree. The problem of timing the adjustments in budgetary policy is not an easy one, and yet good timing is often of crucial importance . . . Budgetary changes cannot be lightly undertaken or introduced without the most careful consideration. Moreover, it would be very upsetting and confusing to business if changes in taxation were made too frequently or at unusual times.[6.19]

In these paragraphs the Minister touched on some of the key issues; the mere size of government meant that it could no longer be neutral in the economy; the desirable degree of flexibility in policy, some observers holding that policies should be fixed for the longer term rather than on an annual basis, and the upsetting effects on business of frequent and rapid changes in taxes.

March 1960: Fleming. In the midst of heavy capital inflows, foreign exchange problems and a continuing inflationary threat, the Minister introduced some supply-side considerations, generally lacking or low-keyed in previous budgets.

Canadians can increase their own domestic capital and make this country financially more self-reliant if they are prepared to practise increased efficiency, productivity and thrift. This responsibility falls on all levels of government, private business and individuals.

We must place emphasis on greater productivity and efficiency rather than on sheer size, on cost control rather than price increases, on greater saving rather than on excessive consumption . . . Saving— voluntary, purposeful, constructive saving—is essential in an economic system dedicated to freedom and progress . . . If all of us, working and saving together, will increase the total amount of capital available for sound investment in Canada, we can reduce our reliance on foreign resources. In short, we have at our disposal the means to achieve in a positive way, the objectives, which negative courses of action cannot hope to accomplish.[6.20]

6.19 Canada, Department of Finance, Budget Speech, April 9, 1959, 13-14.

6.20 Canada, Department of Finance, Budget Speech, March 31, 1960, 7.

As this statement reflected very much the views of James Coyne, the Governor of the Bank of Canada, with whom the government subsequently had a confrontation leading to the Governor's resignation, its place in the sequence of events is rather confusing. But these themes were not unique; they would re-appear in declamations of later ministers of finance.

1960: Fleming. (Supplementary Budget). This mini-budget represented a reaction to continuing unemployment and a decline in capital expenditure. The emphasis was again on self-help. (The government by this time had established a productivity council and grants for technical education facilities). To encourage capital investment double depreciation was introduced for one year for new investments in areas of high unemployment, a throw-back to wartime and transition period policies.

June 1961: Fleming. Following the Coyne resignation this speech was largely devoted to justifying the government's position. In the area of fiscal policy the Minister, in enumerating his differences with Mr. Coyne, said:

> Fourth, the government believes that, in times like the present, a substantial budget deficit can promote economic expansion, with more jobs and better living standards for many thousands of Canadians; and such a fiscal policy will be more effective if it is accompanied by appropriate flexibility of interest rates and exchange rates. Mr. Coyne, on the other hand, has been preaching all across the country a far more austere and rigid doctrine. Government fiscal policies in general, and government deficits in particular, have received more of his broadside attacks than any other element in our economy . . . Accordingly, rather than allow Mr. Coyne to continue to stand in the way of constructive and expansionist measures of a kind which he had publicly opposed, the government asked him to resign. This budget and Mr. Coyne were simply not compatible.[6.21]

Whatever this statement proves or disproves about the Fleming-Coyne relationship at least it leaves no doubt on where this Minister stood on the issue of contra-cyclical budgeting. His expectations were high. He saw his budget as a measure "to impart an impetus to the economy, to enlarge production, to employ unused productive capacity, to stimulate growth, to increase trade, and thus to expand employment opportunities for our people,"[6.22] objectives fully worthy of any post-Keynesian budget.

April 1962: Fleming. The up-turn of the sixties was just commencing, but the budget still was in deficit. The Minister gave the following justification:

> Employment has been rising rapidly and unemployment falling, but we still have more unemployment than is consistent with our national objectives. Capital investment is picking up sharply, but we need still more. It is important, therefore, not to apply any fiscal brakes at this time by abruptly closing the gap between revenues and expenditures . . . at the present time, with a good deal of surplus

---

[6.21] Canada, Department of Finance, Budget Speech, June 20, 1961, 31.
[6.22] Ibid., at 32.

capacity still in our economy and increasingly keen competition in both domestic and external markets, there appears to be little current risk of inflation. It seems to me, therefore, that the deficit I am presently forecasting will provide a strong degree of economic stimulus and at the same time will not endanger the price level during the coming year.[6.23]

June 1963: Gordon. In a general election the Liberals were returned to power and a new Minister of Finance assumed the role of budget-making. He saw the previous five years as a period of

economic stagnation . . . Our rate of growth over the past six years as a whole has been quite inadequate. We have had a falling rate of new investment. We have had chronic deficits in our international balance of payments. And most important, we have chronic unemployment . . . The prevalence of unemployment is a wrong that must be righted. Any Canadian, young or old, who wants a job must be able to find one.[6.24]

He mentioned several supply-side measures the government proposed to adopt, including "a number of measures to promote new capital investment by providing special financial incentives in the private sector of the economy." He urged the need for more attention to merchandise trade, for "fullest participation in the world around us in an economic sense as in every other sense" and for increasing efficiency and productivity. On fiscal policy as such he said:

I do not propose, Mr. Speaker, to enter into a detailed discussion of the pros and cons of deficit financing. Government deficits can be justified in periods of depression or recession when the resources of the nation are underemployed, provided the expenditures and revenues are so designed as to stimulate the economy and provide more jobs. Unfortunately the budgetary deficits of recent years were not planned in this way. [In his view it was important that] we begin to move toward balancing our federal budget under conditions of high employment. We must take the first steps in this direction now.[6.25]

March 1964: Gordon. On general budget policy the Minister stated

Our present economic problems, such as the persistence of abnormal unemployment in the Atlantic provinces and eastern Quebec and in the less well trained types of male labour, are not such as can effectively be met by a general tax cut. More selective and long term measures are needed, such as the better education and technical training of our young people and the promotion of industrial development in the Atlantic provinces and eastern Quebec. Secondly, in Canada we have been experiencing considerably larger budget deficits, when

---

6.23 Canada, Department of Finance, Budget Speech, April 10, 1962, 18.

6.24 Canada, Department of Finance, Budget Speech, June 13, 1963, 3-4.

6.25 Ibid., at 6.

provincial as well as federal budgets are taken into account, than the United States has been having in proportion to its size.[6.26]

General tax changes were again postponed pending receipt of the Carter Report, but some supply side changes affecting research expenditures, educational expenditures, and capital cost allowances were made.

April 1965: Gordon.

Looking ahead we foresee a further advance this year over 1964. However, we must plan to accommodate a rapid increase in our labour force this summer and in the next several years. We need to assure the market demand to put it to work productively . . . For this new fiscal year our budgetary accounts will not be quite so close to a balance . . . In terms of our national economic accounts, however, the federal budget will be a restraining influence this year unless we make some further changes. Accordingly, after weighing up these considerations and the advice I have received from many quarters—including business men, trade unions, academic circles and the Review of the Economic Council—I believe this budget should be an expansionary one. To achieve this effect we should reduce moderately the weight of taxation.[6.27]

[6.26] Canada, Department of Finance, Budget Speech, March 16, 1964, 10.

[6.27] Canada, Department of Finance, Budget Speech, April 26, 1965, 16.

7
Inflation Becomes the Target

March 1966: Sharp. A new Liberal Minister of Finance was in charge of the 1966 budget. There was beginning to be concern about the inflationary impact of heavy capital expenditure and, where for some years efforts had been directed to encouragement, this budget took the opposite approach.

In its last report the Economic Council of Canada pointed out that the recent rate of expansion of investment spending is clearly not sustainable on a long-term basis. Our economy will grow more if the rate of expansion of investment keeps broadly in line with our longer-term potential requirements instead of fluctuating on the basis of the short-term outlook . . . I find myself generally in agreement with the substance of much that the Council has said in both its First and Second Reviews.[7.1]

He proposed steps, such as deferred depreciation, to slow up the capital investment boom. On policy implementation, however, he had differences with the Council.

I have taken to heart the concern that it expresses and implies about the way time lags can impair the effectiveness of fiscal measures and its concern that we must not lose sight of our longer-term goals in dealing with our immediate problems. On the other hand I consider unduly pessimistic its opinion that fiscal measures should not be used to deal with what it calls "shorter term cyclical instability" and I do not share its view that fiscal policy can and should be reduced to an arithmetical formula.[7.2]

(Sharp is one of the few Ministers of Finance with economic training; the others, most of whom have been lawyers, with a sprinkling of accountants, did not attempt to exchange views with the Economic Council on techniques of fiscal policy). In his judgment,

While our present situation clearly calls for restraint on the increases in spending, rather than stimulus, this could change fairly quickly. Our objective is a steady and sustained rate of growth. Our intention is to keep our fiscal policies flexible, and readily adaptable to changing circumstances.[7.3]

June 1967: Sharp (Main budget). As on some other occasions when the economy failed to perform as expected and government efforts seemed to

---

[7.1] Canada, Department of Finance, Budget Speech, March 29, 1966, 6-7.

[7.2] Ibid., at 7.

[7.3] Ibid.

have been frustrated, the principal villain in the piece has been found to be the great unwashed, economically ignorant, public.

Whatever the complex causes, it is evident that we in Canada had not learned to pace ourselves; too many Canadians were anxious to exploit the situation quickly—to get while the getting was good—and in doing so they overloaded the economy with excessive demands. Higher prices were the result. We Canadians have not taken to heart the obvious point that increases in our incomes must be founded upon increases in our productivity if we are to avoid self-defeating and inflationary efforts to profit at one-another's expense. In 1966 our productivity in industry and trade increased very little, apart from a phenomenal grain crop and consequently there was little indeed to support an increase of the magnitude that occurred in average money incomes.

As time goes on we can expect to improve the skill and mobility of our labour force, the state of our technology, the efficiency of our management and the competitiveness of our industry. Such improvements should enable us to increase our productivity and get more real return for our work. In addition these improvements should enable the economy to operate with a lower proportion of unemployment without running into inflationary and unstable conditions, and thus should enable us to achieve the 3 per cent unemployment rate which the Economic Council proposed several years ago as a goal for 1970. If this is to come about, our immediate objective must be to combine growth with stability.[7.4]

The Minister later discussed programs for increasing productivity and an incomes policy to contain inflation, but put his trust finally in attempting to create a public opinion that would

persuade management, labour and government to follow practices that will lead to a dampening down of the upward sweep in consumer prices that has been taking place in the past twleve months. This budget statement and the other economic statements that may follow from time to time should serve at least as contributions to the discussion of our possibilities and limitations, that will help develop not only more understanding but some form of that consensus so necessary for success.[7.5]

Brave words, but the following decade was to show how remote was the realization of this hope.

November 1967: Sharp (Supplementary Budget). Largely reflecting concern with a continuing slide toward inflation the Minister announced a sweeping review of government expenditure and a tax increase in an effort to balance the budget. He said:

[7.4]Canada, Department of Finance, Budget Speech, June 1, 1967, 9.

[7.5]Ibid., at 7.

[T]he federal government cannot by itself control inflation. What this government can do—and is determined to do—with the support of parliament—is to keep its own finances in order, take action to steady the economy and give leadership to other governments in Canada and to the country at large. This task is difficult and involves some tough decisions. But, as I remarked earlier, an ounce of prevention now is far preferable to a pound of cure later.[7.6]

October 1968: Benson. A new Liberal Minister of Finance continued the struggle against inflation.

Needless to say, we shall continue to work toward all the broad goals which are widely accepted in the western industrial countries—full employment, economic growth, price stability, balance in external payments, and an equitable sharing of rising incomes . . . In the broad fields of economic policy the most urgent need now is to check further the continuing increase in prices and living costs. There appears to have been some easing of inflationary pressure in recent months. But there is little evidence that the damaging upward spiral of prices and costs has been effectively broken. Further, unless our policies are firmly set to resist inflation, there is great danger that continued prosperity in 1969 will cause pressures that will set in train a new round of price and cost increases. [The Minister, after a detailed explanation of the unhappy results that would follow from further inflation, stated]: In deciding on over-all fiscal strategy for 1968 and '69 we must take into account both the financial prospects I have described and the broad economic situation I have outlined. After doing so we have reached the conclusion that we must raise substantially more revenues in order to bring the budget into balance in 1969-70.[7.7]

The Minister then proposed tax increases, which, along with other changes made by Sharp, produced a substantial surplus in the accounts for the following fiscal year (1969-70), one of the few in the postwar years. At the time this was regarded as one of the most stringent measures taken by a western industrial country.

June 1969: Benson. Inflation continued to be the main concern.

. . . the vigor of the current economic expansion and the persistence of strong inflationary tides necessitate a re-assessment of our position. They lead in turn to further important decisions on the course of fiscal policy for the period ahead . . . There can be no question that the number one priority in economic policy today must be to deploy all available forces—public and private—more aggressively than ever in the battle against inflation in Canada. . . . In this regard, I am confident that the establishment of the Prices and Incomes Commission recently announced by my colleague, the Minister of Consumer and

---

[7.6] Canada, Department of Finance, Budget Speech, November 30, 1967, 13.

[7.7] Canada, Department of Finance, Budget Speech, October 22, 1968, 7-8.

Corporate Affairs, represents an important step forward. In too many cases not enough is known as to why the prices we have to pay have risen. Still less is known as to what can be done about the problem, fairly and effectively, in a free market economy which we have in this country . . . [The Minister referred to the success of his surplus seeking efforts]: Taken together with the deficit of $566 million experienced in the last fiscal year, the swing amounts to a total of nearly one billion dollars, considerably more than one per cent of the G.N.P. It can be regarded as a very substantial budgetary restraint upon the growth of total demand in the economy, and provides a powerful general check upon inflationary forces pushing up prices and costs in the economy.[7.8]

Indeed, so pleased was the Minister with this result that he proposed to leave in force the temporary increases that had produced it.

For these reasons I have given no consideration to a reduction in taxes, attractive as such a prospect might be. On the contrary, so important is it not to relax the fiscal brakes exerted by the present structure of income taxes upon inflationary forces in the economy, that I have concluded they should be maintained in full force for the period ahead.[7.9]

An interesting fiscal step designed to increase competition was to announce that Kennedy Round tariff changes, which were not slated to come into full effect for another two and one-half years, would come into operation immediately. The Minister also announced the third use of deferral of depreciation on selected new structures to dampen investment spending.

March 1970: Benson.

With the pace of economic activity now somewhat reduced, I expect that the economy will continue to move upward in 1970, but at a lower rate than in 1969 . . . It is the policy of the government to restrain the growth of total spending in the economy, for that is a necessary condition for achieving our primary economic objective. We shall continue to support the work of the Prices and Incomes Commission which is striving to engage business, labour, consumers and governments in a united resistance against inflation . . . We have also been encouraged in our efforts to check the inflationary rise of costs and prices by the co-operative approach of the provincial governments . . . However, there has been no slowing down in the rate of increase of prices and wages and other incomes. Costs continue to push prices up. Slower real growth has not yet reduced inflation . . . It is evident that the federal government's fiscal position as a whole in 1970-71 will be exerting somewhat less restraint on the economy than in this year . . . In these circumstances, I feel some additional specific restraints upon

---

[7.8] Canada, Department of Finance, Budget Speech, June 3, 1969, 1-4.

[7.9] Ibid., at 4.

the economy are necessary to maintain the pressure against the price and cost increases.[7.10]

The Minister, no doubt, with a smile on his face, then announced: "I am not proposing any tax increases in this budget." The inevitable explosive reaction of the Members was recorded by the Hansard reporter in the hallowed use of "Some hon. Members: Hear, hear!" and "Some hon. Members: Oh, oh!" which generally indicate a state of bedlam in the House. The "non-increasing" measures the Minister proposed were to extend the deferral of depreciation so that it would apply to construction undertaken over a period of one year and nine months rather than just the original nine months, and controls over the terms of consumer credit, which in fact were not implemented.

June 1971: Benson. In this budget speech primary attention was devoted to a long and elaborate introduction of the government's proposals for tax reform to come into effect on January 1, 1972. General economic policy was now in a rapid state of reverse. 1970, as revealed in his Supplementary December budget, had turned out to be a far different year than the Minister had forecast, and the government had been scrambling to offset a marked decline in real GNP, a slump in capital investment, and an increase in unemployment. Monetary policy had been eased from mid-1970 onward, and various new programs for increased expenditure had been launched. The Minister described these as increased assistance for the provinces, major initiatives in the field of social security and measures for strengthening the structure of the national economy. He said:

All of these measures—each a major step in itself—contribute in a real and selective way to the same goals of equity and justice which we have sought to achieve in tax reform. They build in, as well, stronger safeguards against periodic slowdowns in the growth of the total volume of demand, and thus add new dimensions to the automatic stabilization of the economy. In the area of measures for strengthening the structure of the national economy, we have been concerned to integrate the short-term stimulus in spending with longer-term structural needs. A major point of emphasis has been to increase the attractions to industry to make investments in the slow-growth regions.[7.11]

The Minister described economic policy during this period (later to become a matter of some contention as the possible source of the inflation during the seventies) as follows:

The government is determined to do what governments can do to ensure that the expansion in real income and employment now under way shall be vigorous and broadly based. The building up of such an expansion depends ultimately on the decisions of the millions of persons and of the thousands of businesses that make up the private

---

[7.10] Canada, Department of Finance, Budget Speech, March 12, 1970, 3-4.

[7.11] Canada, Department of Finance, Budget Speech, June 18, 1971, 31-2.

sector of the economy. To achieve the results we seek, these decisions of investors and consumers cannot be defensive and protective; they must be bold and confident decisions. The principal measures I have to propose are designed to encourage this kind of confident spending in the private sector of the economy.[7.12]

Under the government's stimulative program the hoped-for economic recovery had taken place handsomely. However the Minister obviously had no premonition of what lay ahead in the next decade—nor did anyone else, for that matter.

October 1971: Benson. (Quasi-budget). Despite many encouraging economic indications (declining inflation, a housing boom, and others) the Minister, in the prevailing faith in fine-tuning, introduced tax reductions and grants for local winter programs to combat expected higher unemployment following drastic restrictive measures taken by the United States in August 1971 to cope with a balance of payments crisis.

May 1972: Turner. Again a new Liberal Minister of Finance propounded his views on economic policy in a budget speech. Having stated that his first priority was "jobs," he went on to elaborate:

I am hoping to achieve industrial growth at a pace that will not aggravate the inflationary impulses in the economy and escalate the cost of living. This government is committed to reasonable price stability . . . I said once before to this House that a Minister of Finance is not an economic czar. It is true that through its fiscal policies the federal government can and must play a central role in guiding the course of the economy. It is important to understand, however, that there are some very real constraints on the ability of the federal government alone to ensure that the economy remains precisely on course at all times.[7.13]

The Minister mentioned the difficulties that arose from conflicting policies and programs of the provincial and municipal governments, from the free market economy, and from forces abroad, and observed:

The difficulty of anticipating and responding to the impact on the economy of all these forces is further compounded by the universal limitation of economic information. For all these reasons, it makes good sense for the government to stand ready to make periodic adjustments in its fiscal policies as the need for them becomes evident. [1971 had been a year of rapid recovery, and] The overall fiscal policy of the government has continued to be expansionary. In this it is supported by monetary policy. This policy last year created credit conditions conducive to economic expansion and relief of upward pressures on the value of the Canadian dollar. There was a large expansion of the money supply . . . Summing up, the Canadian economy is expanding

---

7.12 Ibid., at 33.

7.13 Canada, Department of Finance, Budget Speech, May 8, 1972, 1-2.

firmly and steadily . . . We must continue to press for lower levels of unemployment. Price increases must be kept in check. But there is no question that the economy is advancing and gaining strength.[7.14]

February 1973: Turner. The Minister's main priorities were stated to be "to bring about a substantial reduction in unemployment . . . reducing inflationary pressures in Canada" and "offsetting the effects of past inflation." To help manufacturing he announced a review of the whole system of capital cost allowances, and welcomed the growth in business investment that had followed his previous measures. As for inflation he rejected the pressure for direct controls.

Controls would demand a far wider public consensus and more evidence of an emergency situation than is now the case. Our approach is to increase the supply of goods and services, to increase personal disposal income, to relieve the pressure on those hurt, to restrict the government's own demands upon the economy and, above all, to trust Canadians, in their own self-interest—businessmen, working men and women, professionals, farmers—to exercise restraint in their demands for higher income. If that self-interest is not reflected in good judgment, then there will be a self-defeating escalation of costs and prices.[7.15]

(It was only a decade later, after the bruising experience of a bout of extreme inflation, that this message would be very generally understood). The most spectacular step taken in this budget was the announcement of full indexation of the income tax exemptions and rate brackets commencing in 1974, described as a "lasting solution to this problem should inflation continue." It did continue, and this modest change turned out to be one of the most expensive concessions ever to be granted to taxpayers by any government in Canada.

November 1974: Turner. The continuing struggle was with inflation. The Minister rejected any extreme measures, and gave seven elements in his own approach.

The first essential is action to sustain demand . . . This is imperative if we are to achieve a rate of growth of production and employment that more closely approaches potential . . . Second, the fiscal stimulus should come primarily from a further cut in taxes, rather than an additional increase in expenditure . . . Third, we must do all we can in these circumstances to restrain growth of governmental expenditures . . . Fourth, we should apply stimulus selectively where we can help to buttress weak points in the economy . . . Fifth, we must ensure that private investment remains strong . . . Sixth, continued attention must be given to mitigating the effects of inflation on the more vulnerable members of our society . . . The final element in our over-all

---

[7.14] Ibid., at 4.

[7.15] Canada, Department of Finance, Budget Speech, February 19, 1973, 8.

approach is a comprehensive series of consultations with all sectors of the economy.[7.16]

On the psychology of inflation the Minister had some hard things to say:

> Given the inflation which has occurred, no one group is willing to exercise restraint unless it knows that others will also exercise restraint. Rather each group feels compelled to seek protection against the highest rate of inflation which it thinks might occur. The hard truth remains, however, that in this struggle the sum total of all the claims on the nation's resources—however justified they may seem to be—clearly exceeds what is in fact available to be shared.[7.17]

In justification for some tax reductions which leaned to the supply side he admitted that this was now the direction of his thinking.

> Through our taxation system, and in other ways, we are encouraging the private sector to maintain a healthy level of activity now and to build new capacity to increase the supply of goods and services for the future. I am more persuaded now than ever that this is a prerequisite for moderating prices in a lasting way. The taxation measures I have announced tonight . . . have been designed with this goal in mind.[7.18]

Did supply-side economics live for a brief period in Canada in 1974 before emerging in the United States with the Reagan administration?

June 1975: Turner. By this time the country was deep in the problems caused by the energy crisis, and this became a third primary element in budgets.

> Faced with these conflicting requirements in dealing with inflation, unemployment and energy, I have had to strike a careful balance in the choice of policies . . . Dealing with this inflation problem without adversely affecting our immediate employment prospects constitutes the heart of this budget . . . The major cause of this increase in costs has been the accelerating rise of wages and salaries . . . what is surprising and disturbing is the size of recent increases in Canadian wages and salaries and their continuing acceleration in a period of slow growth and high unemployment . . . Wage and salary increases are now running well above the increase in the cost of living. [This degree of inflation] undermines the effectiveness of the traditional instruments of demand management policy to keep the economy on course. When inflation reaches a certain point, the stimulation of spending may simply lead to higher prices rather than more goods and more jobs; in the longer run, it actually makes unemployment worse.[7.19]

With this statement Keynesian demand management is conclusively dropped as a guide to economic policy under conditions of inflation. (Of

---

7.16 Canada, Department of Finance, Budget Speech, November 18, 1974, 8-9.

7.17 Ibid., at 9-10.

7.18 Ibid., at 31.

7.19 Canada, Department of Finance, Budget Speech, June 23, 1975, 2-10.

course it had been considerably diluted over many past years with a variety of other policies). But the Minister also rejected the solution that in fact was ultimately adopted.

Among the various policy options open to us, there is one which this government has rejected, and rejects again, in the most categorical manner. This is the policy of deliberately creating, by severe measures of fiscal and monetary restraint, whatever level of unemployment is required to bring inflation to an abrupt halt. Such a course of action would be completely at odds with my own instincts. The cost would be too high. The hard-won sense of security in our society would be replaced by a sense of fear and anxiety . . .[7.20]

(All too true, as is now clear from the perspective of 1988. Even worse—the process of slowing inflation was not "abrupt," as the Minister visualized, but long drawn out and painful).

In the confusion of choices the Minister elected to retain current tax arrangements but to impose severe restraints on growth of government expenditures.

December 1975: Chretien announcement. As a supplement to the Budget and the program of the Anti-Inflation Board the President of the Treasury Board issued a statement in December announcing expenditure cuts of $1.5 billion in the following fiscal year, including dropping indexation of family allowances, and freezing of remuneration of members of Parliament and senior civil servants.

[7.20] Ibid., at 11.

8
A Time of Testing; Seventies and Eighties

From the mid-1970s the annual budgets dealt with an entanglement of increasingly complex economic issues. The energy crisis demanded growing attention and, following the announcement of the National Energy Policy, long sections were devoted exclusively to it. The government had been engaged in a running battle with the provinces over prior rights to taxation of natural resources, and this had taken up substantial space. The effects of monetary policy in raising interest rates, finally to historic highs, had to be explained and justified. Canada's international payments position and the external value of the Canadian dollar required analysis and explanation. The aftermath of tax reform had repercussions on every budget for some years. And of course there was the chronic problem of inflation, only to be subdued finally by extreme measures of repression. Unemployment, always a postwar concern became even more acute in 1979 and later years. Occasionally the annually accelerating budget deficit received some passing attention. Measures to control government expenditure were severe and gradually curbed the previous excessive rates of growth, but tax reductions and the effects of the recession on revenues hurtled the government forward into deficits that were only in 1986 beginning to decline and were still high in 1988.

Ironically the stern messages for economy and control were delivered each year in increasingly numerous, elaborate, and expensive budget publications, now weighing in total each year more than a strong man would wish to carry more than a few blocks.

All this is by way of saying that for the most part all budgets of the last decade have been predominantly economic in their thrust. To do full justice to each would require much more elaborate treatment than can be afforded here. We must settle therefore for continuing to track the rhetorical trail, as this is an essential exercise. With no dependable theory of fiscal policy we are in bad trouble indeed. We must understand this mandate for prodding, restraining, or otherwise bashing the economy—and budgets are the key.

May 1976: Macdonald. In reviewing the recent course of events the minister said:

> During the course of 1974, fiscal and monetary policies became more expansionary. Federal policies, including further major tax reductions, were strongly reinforced by provincial governments. Automatic stabilizers in the economy such as unemployment insurance also played their role, helping to soften the impact of unemployment and buoying up the economy as a whole.
>
> Given these circumstances and deliberate policy decisions, the fiscal position at all levels of government swung heavily into deficit last

year. I would re-emphasize the point that if these expansionary policies had not been adopted, the Canadian economy would have experienced a much more severe recession than in fact it did . . . Over a period of many months, the crucial national need has been to gear down the rate of inflation without impeding economic recovery. To this end, over a year ago the government sought to develop a consensus, particularly with labour and business, in support of a program of voluntary restraint on prices and incomes. Unfortunately, as we all know, that effort was not successful.[8.1]

The Minister then went on to describe the establishment of the AIB and some of the results of its activities.

On capital expenditure:

Many measures have already been put in place to stimulate capital investment. I am thinking particularly of the manufacturing incentives, the investment tax credit introduced in the last budget and the various programs by which the government provides financing directly . . . these measures have helped to sustain high levels of business investment in Canada . . .[8.2]

On the venture capital problem:

Clearly what is needed is a tax regime which will help to do the job effectively but efficiently. I have already instructed my officials to study this matter on a priority basis.[8.3]

On fiscal and monetary policy he said:

The monetary policy of the Bank of Canada has been set out by the Governor in his 1975 Annual Report and recent speeches. It carries my full support. Last autumn the Bank announced an initial target for the growth of the narrowly-defined money supply in the range from 10 to less than 15 per cent and the rate of increase since the second quarter of 1975 is now at the lower end of the range . . . This monetary policy, in its refusal to underwrite continuing high rates of inflation, is helping to destroy expectations that they will continue . . . The goal of fiscal policy is the same as that of monetary policy—to manage the increase in demand in a way which is consistent with moderate real growth and a decline in the rate of inflation. In the present circumstances, this can best be achieved by maintaining close control over the rise in government spending. As I have stressed, our expenditure targets over the next two years involve a commitment to keep growth of expenditure below the growth of the GNP. However, our revenues will grow more rapidly than GNP because of the very nature of the tax system. The financial requirements will therefore decline.[8.4]

[8.1] Canada, Department of Finance, Budget Speech, May 25, 1976, 8-9.

[8.2] Ibid., at 17.

[8.3] Ibid., at 18.

[8.4] Ibid., at 23.

(In making the last statement someone appears to have overlooked the fact that the indexation of the personal income tax had substantially neutralized the acceleration rate of that tax).

March 1977: Macdonald.

Over the last 18 months the government has directed much of its effort in economic policy to countering inflation . . . The rise of costs and prices disrupted many aspects of our economic life, and continues to do so. We must persist in our efforts to control it . . . One of the worst effects of inflation from which we continue to suffer is high unemployment. There never was any doubt that inflation would bring this result in its train . . . Nor was there any doubt that the after-effects of inflation would be prolonged. We must not forget that fact now. Apart from all its adverse social results, inflation weakens the ability of our producers to compete at home and abroad. It also erodes the confidence so essential to the conduct of business and to investment in business capital . . . One hazard of all this is that we will over-react and administer a shock of stimulus that is too strong to be absorbed without regenerating inflationary forces . . . Another hazard is that we will succumb to the temptation to become more protectionist in the face of our impaired competitive position . . . the right policy over the longer run is to regain our competitive position by ensuring that our inflation is brought under control and to seek removal of barriers against our exports . . . [an interesting preview of the free-trade recommendation in the mid-eighties by the Royal Commission of which the Minister was Chairman; politicians are not noted for such consistency]. In developing a budget under these circumstances, two important constraints have had to be observed. The restraint of growth in the government's spending has been an integral part of our anti-inflationary policies . . . The second constraint is the limit upon our ability to reduce taxes that is imposed by the need to restrict our demands upon the capital markets . . .

The essential task of both monetary and fiscal policy in present circumstances is to encourage a growth of demand consistent with the expansion of employment and winding down of inflation . . . For some time, our policy has entailed a sizable deficit. As the slack in the economy is taken up, the deficit will be reduced. However, to attempt to cut deficits too soon would threaten the recovery. Indeed, with present levels of unemployment, further stimulus is required.[8.5]

The Minister went on to propose tax changes designed, in his words, "to increase the total demand for goods and services, expand direct job creation, encourage investment and risk-taking on a national basis, and strengthen regional growth."[8.6]

[8.5]Canada, Department of Finance, Budget Speech, March 31, 1977, 1-10.

[8.6]Ibid., at 19.

April 1978: Chretien. Another new Liberal Minister assumed the Finance post (the exactions of this portfolio led to rapid turn-over). The Minister gave a candid review of previous years.

It is now clear that many of our current difficulties have their roots in the period of extraordinary growth Canada experienced between the mid-1960s and the mid-1970s. With the great advantage of hindsight, we can see that we did not always use our good fortune wisely . . . we all came to expect too much of the economy. Governments increased their spending too quickly. The money supply was increased too fast. Too much was asked and given at the wage bargaining table. Other forms of income rose too rapidly. Too little attention was paid to the long-run efficiency of the Canadian economy, and its ability to compete.[8.7]

(The Minister might have added that the task of coping with the political stresses that had arisen from the Quebec separatist movement and the National Energy Plan had distracted the attention of all governments from the fundamental problems of the economy). But some progress was being made with inflation.

Wage increases have returned to more realistic levels. New settlements came down from 17 per cent in 1975 to 10 per cent in 1976 and under 8 per cent in 1977. They are now down to the guideline of 6 per cent. The underlying rate of inflation has also been reduced . . . The controls program has played a key role in these developments.[8.8]

Time lost in strikes had also been greatly reduced. But the economy was still lagging. Employment was rising and confidence improving:

The question now is whether the gradual recovery that has been established should be given an additional push from policy. I have decided it should . . . Any further stimulus should obviously be fast-acting. It should encourage consumer spending, not more spending by government . . . A reduction in retail sales tax fits these requirements best . . .[8.9]

The Minister went on to propose to compensate the provincial governments for their loss of revenue from a six-months' reduction in their retail sales taxes. In general this program, the first large-scale cooperative action by the two levels of government in the use of fiscal policy for economic objectives, was successfully implemented, although with some friction in the case of Quebec. Aspects of budgets occurring with increasing frequency were measures designed for "structural changes," changes not just in the environment in which the economy operated but in the economy itself. Examples appeared in the Turner, Macdonald, Chrétien and later budgets. Of course the tariff had been a vehicle for this type of measure for a century, and the

---

8.7 Canada, Department of Finance, Budget Speech, April 10, 1978, 5.

8.8 Ibid., at 6.

8.9 Ibid., at 13.

National Energy Program leaned heavily on them. About this time talk began to be heard of a national industrial policy, talk which met a chill reception from the business community.

November 1978: Chrétien. This was the second budget of 1978. The economy had worsened and was in deep trouble and some additional attention was felt to be necessary. The Minister pointed out positive accomplishments:

> . . . Canada has made great progress since the introduction of the Anti-Inflation Program in 1975 . . . In the last three years the Bank of Canada has gradually reduced the rate of growth of the money supply . . . Expenditures by all levels of government have been brought under tight control.[8.10]

For further progress the Minister had faith in the process of "consultation between business, labour and government," and expressed himself as being skeptical about the search for

> a single grand industrial strategy in a competitive market system . . . Our most immediate challenge, however, is to hold onto the gains we have been making in our competitive position, as we come to the end of mandatory controls over prices and incomes. [On fiscal policy generally he was conservative]: I have been urged to cut taxes massively in order to stimulate the economy. Given the expansionary forces which are already at work, I do not think this would be wise, particularly when our cash requirements are so high.[8.11]

He proposed some quite substantial tax measures, including reduction of the manufacturers' sales tax from 12 percent to 9 percent, an expensive gesture designed to reduce the consumer price index by one-half of one percent. We have examined the fiscal record of this period earlier, and clearly the annual tax reductions amounting to 5 to 10 percent of revenues, along with the continuing erosion of revenues through indexation, were laying the basis for the massive deficits of the 1980s.

December 1979: Crosbie. In an election in May 1979, the 17-year regime of the Liberal party was ended and for approximately 10 months the Conservative party was in power. Its Minister of Finance produced a budget in December 1979, on which the government was defeated and an election was called. This budget was not enacted and is therefore not relevant to this record. However, as the Minister of Finance remarked, it was "the first Progressive Conservative Government budget in 17 years." It therefore deserves at least a brief note. His views on the past policies were as follows:

> The need for a new approach is apparent from our experience during the 1970s. In broad terms, the performance of the economy has been about half as good on average as during the 1960s. Our rates of price inflation and unemployment have been roughly twice as high and our

---

8.10 Canada, Department of Finance, Budget Speech, November 16, 1978, 6.

8.11 Ibid., at 7-10.

rate of productivity growth has fallen by half. Over the past five years, productivity growth, the essential source for increases in the living standards of Canadians, has approximated zero . . .

Our recent experience proves again that simply printing money and increasing government expenditures and the deficit does not help. Such actions only make our difficulties worse. A disciplined and realistic fiscal and monetary framework is essential. It is evident that a system of incentives in both the private and public spheres is critical. Individual choice in response to positive incentives is much more effective than attempts by governments to persuade, dictate and direct. A major priority in this and our subsequent budgets will be to create a system of incentives that will encourage Canadians to work, to save, to invest, to take risks in Canada, to become more efficient in production and to conserve energy and other scarce resources.[8.12]

Very extensive changes were proposed in the energy area, not to be considered here. These, it turned out, were the cause of the defeat of the budget. But in the end the message was the same as that of budgets for many years past.

Our major challenge is to bring down the rate of inflation. This government fully endorses the Bank of Canada's policy of gradually reducing money supply growth. The government's overall fiscal plan, and the tax measures I am presenting tonight, indicate our determination to reduce our deficit. Fiscal policy will now share in the task of reducing inflation and so provide a better balanced restraint than is the case when monetary policy is left to attempt to do the job alone.[8.13]

Extensive tax changes were proposed, but these were defeated with the rest of the budget.

October 1980: MacEachen. Following the return of the Liberals to power in an election in February 1980, some months went by before a new budget was presented in October. The new Minister, one of the few economists to ever hold the post, is best remembered by his second budget, a year later, which made a general onslaught on taxpayers, the first since the Benson and Sharp budgets of 1968-69, and one for which the Minister was not lightly forgiven by taxpayers softened up by years of tax reductions.

The economist's approach is evident in the Minister's general appraisal of the situation at the end of 1980.

In this environment the tasks of economic policy present a great challenge. Within industrial countries, we have all learned that we cannot achieve full employment, stable prices and other economic goals simply by influencing the demands for goods and services by cutting taxes or by increasing government expenditure—or alternatively by raising taxes and cutting spending. The problems are

---

8.12Canada, Department of Finance, Budget Speech, December 11, 1979, 2-3.

8.13Ibid., at 7.

obviously deeper and more complex, and they relate to our basic ability to produce . . . the amount of goods and services which each worker produces on average is not growing as fast as it was, because we are not investing enough . . . to keep up the pace of technological improvement. Shortages of resources and slower productivity growth mean that costs go up faster and this makes the problem of inflation more intractable . . . We have experienced falling output this year. Productivity has dropped quite sharply and the inflation rate has moved back up to 10 per cent. It is time that we moved to realize our great potential. We are more likely to do so if we understand that the problem is not a simple matter of ensuring an appropriate demand for goods and services but is more deep-seated. There are no quick solutions, so we need to be patient and plan in a longer-term framework. There are no single solutions either, so we need to combine structural, industrial and regional policies with the right setting of fiscal and monetary policy. But we can then feel confident that we are dealing with the fundamental issues and embarking on the new directions which can secure the future of the country.[8.14]

And what were the Minister's prescriptions for this goal? Many of them were familiar.

The maintenance of government expenditures within the rate of growth of the economy . . . a steady reduction in the government deficit and financial requirements . . . the avoidance, insofar as possible, of personal and corporate tax increases . . . to support the Bank of Canada in its pursuit of monetary policies that will not accommodate inflation . . . expand our assistance to the developing world . . . sustain social and economic assistance to those . . . most in need.[8.15]

A different note (although in all the views expressed over the four decades it would be difficult to find something completely new) was struck in the following:

. . . within the commitment to expenditure restraint, the need nonetheless to provide for major new expenditures in energy, economic development, industrial adjustment and manpower training; . . . a resolve to see the competitive forces in our economy strengthened and the weight of government regulation reduced.[8.16]

The Minister for the first time discussed the expenditure program in terms of the envelope system, the foundations for which he said had been laid under the previous Liberal government, with important further advances made under the Conservatives. He emphasized that one of the largest increases was in the economic development envelope, which would allow the Economic Development Committee

---

[8.14]Canada, Department of Finance, Budget Speech, October 28, 1980, 1-3.

[8.15]Ibid., at 3.

[8.16]Ibid.

to expand existing programs and launch new initiatives in support of research and development, industrial expansion and export development. These programs which are now under intensive development will contribute to the renewed gains in productivity and to the high levels of business investment on which we depend for our prosperity in the years ahead.[8.17]

A particular program he announced in the budget was a special allocation of $350 million over four years "to promote industrial restructuring and manpower retraining and mobility in areas of particular need." These programs would be in addition to previous efforts to promote technical education, regional economic development, industry R and D expenditures, capital investment, exports, etc. which in total represented a considerable overlay of direct measures to nudge the economy in directions conceived by the government. There was some irony, therefore, in the Minister's comment that

> we now have a tax system characterized by higher tax rates relieved by a complex network of incentives and tax preferences. One questions whether the economy might not be better served by a tax system with lower rates but with fewer and more selective incentives.[8.18]

He was looking at the whole area of "tax expenditures," and would have a revised version of the one study already issued available in a short time.

November 1981: MacEachen. This budget, delivered in the context of the highest postwar rate of inflation, but with other signs that were more encouraging, was concerned, in the Minister's words, with "restraint, equity and renewal." The restraint element related to the deficit:

> I believe we must reduce our deficit and our borrowing requirements substantially—even more than I proposed a year ago. . . . The control of the money supply by the Bank of Canada is an essential element in our strategy to fight inflation, but it has to be supported by greater fiscal restraint . . . I have had to seek additional revenues from the personal and corporate tax . . . Most fundamentally, we are committed to restraining the growth of our spending over the next few years . . . the second theme of the budget is equity. I dedicate myself and this government in this and succeeding years to maintaining a fundamental sense of fairness in our society. As evidence of that dedication, I am proposing a major overhaul of the personal tax system . . . the third theme must be renewal . . . I will be tabling this evening a major policy document on economic development for Canada in the 1980s . . .[8.19]

The five main policy areas were to be industrial development, resource development, transportation, export promotion, and human resources. (The policy document laid emphasis on mega-projects in several areas;

8.17 Ibid., at 13.

8.18 Ibid., at 15.

8.19 Canada, Department of Finance, Budget Speech, November 12, 1981, 1-3.

although it was seldom referred to, its influence could be seen in some later programs, such as the doubling of the western railway tracks.)

Much of this budget was devoted to detailed revision of several features of the personal income tax, which attracted by far the greatest attention of any budget in a decade. These will be reviewed later in connection with tax reform. The general theme regarding economic policy was the oft repeated adjuration for patience, refusal to consider income and price controls, and assurances that conditions were gradually improving. For greater details a collection of six budget documents was made available.

June 1982: MacEachen. 1982 was one of the darkest years in recent history. For only the second time in the entire postwar period the GNP actually declined. Inflation was still above 11 percent and the unemployment rate had increased by 47 percent over the previous year.

This budget, the last by Mr. MacEachen, attacked the economy on several fronts. Preceded by slightly new appeals for a "tougher, more resilient society . . . greater discipline in our income demands and other inflationary behaviour . . . a dynamic, confident business sector . . ." the Minister proposed several measures to buoy the economy in this year of deep recession, "despite the very limited room for manoeuvre imposed by the deficit." The economic setting was one of

> persistence of the U.S. recession and high interest rates . . . We are now doing much worse on inflation than our key trading partners. Our productivity performance has also been very disappointing . . . Our wage settlements are . . . running about 5 percentage points higher than the trend in the United States. [After reviewing fiscal demands of the past year he said]: The result is that the projected budgetary deficit for the current year is very much higher than that forecast in the November budget: $19.6 billion, compared to the $10.5 billion initially projected . . . Our financial requirements are now projected at $17.1 billion, instead of the November budget forecast of $6.6 billion.[8.20]

This situation was the logical result of the fiscal system.

> These increases reflect mainly the automatic response of our tax and expenditure systems to the recession. These automatic stabilizers must be allowed to operate to avoid making the recession worse. This is not the time to do away with these stabilizers, not the time to cut unemployment insurance or slash expenditures that provide income to Canadians . . . I am introducing new tax and expenditure initiatives to respond to pressing needs, but I am not adding further to the deficit already facing us in 1982-83 . . . We have rejected massive fiscal stimulus and the abandonment of monetary restraint because this would only worsen inflation and aggravate unemployment . . . Controls would merely postpone the basic shift in economic behaviour

---

[8.20]Canada, Department of Finance, Budget Speech, June 28, 1982, 2-3.

that is needed—a shift to discipline and restraint, self-willed and self-imposed. It is to that basic change, rather than to massive government intervention, that the government has decided to devote its energies.[8.21]

The Minister's single and simple proposal for inflation became known as the "6-and-5" formula—that all wage increases be limited to 6 percent in the 12 months ending in July 1983 and 5 percent in the following 12 months. This rule would apply for all government payrolls, including ministers and Members of Parliament, and, except for GIS and veterans' pensions, would also apply to all indexation, including that for personal income tax. Several measures were proposed to stimulate investment, both domestic and foreign, and to assist payers of interest, many suffering from recent levels that had exceeded 20 percent. Other measures included the Small Business Development Bond, grants to assist with housing purchases, several programs for direct employment, and relief from some of the onerous tax proposals of the previous year. Overall the Minister was not expecting an increase in the deficit as a result of his proposals.

October 1982: Lalonde. A new Liberal Minister of Finance felt it necessary to present a second statement for 1982 in late October as this gloomy year moved to its close. Like his predecessor he was prepared to place greater reliance on the private sector than would have been true a decade previously. (In truth the government had about used up its bag of tricks, and its budget was being strangled under the burden of interest on its growing debt).

He made the customary commitment of the government to fiscal responsibility, and care for the victims of the recession, but gave strong emphasis to reliance

primarily on the dynamism and creativity of the private sector as the engine of growth in Canada. The government will be seeking areas where it can act in close cooperation with business and labour to improve the financial health of the private sector as well as its ability to expand and prosper. I intend to foster the certainty and stability that are basic preconditions for a favourable economic climate . . . we must continue to develop effective mechanisms for consultation so that the broadest range of organizations and institutions, as well as provincial governments, may participate in the continuing revision and improvement of our economic policies . . . it is my intention to appoint a panel of economic advisers made up of outstanding Canadian economists to advise me . . . most importantly, we must build on the spirit of the 6 and 5 program to devise and implement an effective strategy for national recovery and economic development. [Of the challenges ahead he said]: Our productivity performance continues to lag. New production techniques must be developed and implemented. This requires development of our technological base, increased invest-

---

[8.21] Ibid., at 3.

ment, and new and innovative approaches to organizing work and labour-management relations.[8.22]

(As these are still frequently mentioned goals in editorial and other comment in 1988 it is clear that something has been lost in the intervening years).

The Minister pleaded once again the limitations on action imposed by the budget deficit but, in recognition of the number of employees who would have exhausted their unemployment insurance, announced a program known as the new Employment Expansion and Development Program. The main elements of this were continued housing assistance, western rail expansion, and re-allocation of some $1 billion of existing expenditures to projects under Official Development Assistance that would have more immediate impact on employment. The Minister made a revealing comment on the limitations of this type of action:

> This reallocation exercise has been very difficult. One billion dollars may not seem much in a context of total outlays of $80 billion. But roughly 75 percent of total government outlays is made up of transfers to persons, provinces and other countries, grants or capital assistance to industry, subsidies, loans, and interest on the public debt. Of the 25 per cent or $20 billion remaining, which accounts for the operating expenditures of the federal government inclusive of defence, some $11 billion is made up of wages, salaries, and other personnel costs, which have already been restrained by the 6 and 5 program.[8.23]

Other economically-oriented programs included easing of the necessary increase in unemployment insurance premiums and promised action on the Registered Shareholder Investment Plan proposed by the Advisory Committee on Inflation and the Taxation of Personal Investment Income (the Lortie Committee). One of the main purposes of the budget was to clear up confusion regarding the status of Mr. MacEachen's tax reform proposals, which had not yet been passed. Most were adopted, with some softening of application; one or two major ones were dropped. Meanwhile the budget deficit for the current fiscal year, 1982-83, originally forecast at $19.5 billion, was now expected to be $23.6 billion.

April 1983: Lalonde. By this time inflation had begun to subside, but at the cost of virtually strangling the economy. GNP was beginning to rise, but unemployment reached its highest rate since the Great Depression. This was reflected in the 1983 budget speech. The Minister said:

> My dominant concern in preparing this budget has been to help the more than one and a half million Canadians who want to work but cannot find jobs. Economic recovery is under way in Canada . . . Yet the pace, scope, stability and duration of the recovery remain highly uncertain . . . This recovery budget, therefore, has two central and

---

[8.22] Canada, Department of Finance, Statement on the Economic Outlook and the Financial Position of the Government of Canada, October 27, 1982, 3-4.

[8.23] Ibid., at 12.

inseparable goals. The first is to make sure that recent stirrings of growth pervade the whole economy as quickly as possible. The second is to make the recovery a durable one by beginning immediately to create the conditions required for sustained growth and development during the rest of the eighties . . . The pursuit of these twin goals calls for actions that take hold immediately but that are also geared to the medium term. But the second goal would be unattainable without decisive action now to reduce the deficit in future years. Expenditure restraint will therefore continue, and measures will be introduced to raise more revenue as the recovery buoys up income and employment.[8.24]

On inflation:

Canadians have supported the 6 & 5 program introduced in last June's budget. The government remains committed to this program. We have come a long way together in reducing inflation. It is essential that this progress continue as we recover . . . But it also demands continued responsibility in the exercise of monetary and fiscal policies.[8.25]

On economic recovery:

I am relying primarily on the dynamism and creativity of the private sector to bring about durable recovery. My budget is outward-looking and avoids protectionist measures, in recognition of the fact that recovery in one country at the expense of others is neither feasible nor desirable.[8.26]

The main economic proposal of the budget was a Special Recovery Program, involving investment expenditure of $4.6 billion designed to ensure "that Canada has the capital equipment, productive facilities, skills and knowledge we need to meet the competitive challenge that will arise from world-wide recovery." One part of the program was a collection of over 100 federal government projects costing $2.2 billion that would be launched within six months. Another $2.4 billion would be made available to the private sector over four years through assistance for exports, investment spending (tax credits), refundable tax credits, share purchase tax credits, and R and D expenditures. Particular attention was given the latter in a discussion paper entitled *Research and Development Tax Policies*. It proposed mainly the substitution of increased tax credits for the current income deductions, with the right of the company to "flow through" the tax credit to the investor. The abuse of the "flow through" privilege through the so-called "quick flip" under the final legislation passed in early 1984 scandalized many taxpayers and did much to discredit the growing use of tax credits for specific objectives.

An accompanying change designed to encourage investment in equities by substantially nullifying the effects of inflation in increasing security

---

8.24 Canada, Department of Finance, Budget Speech, April 19, 1983, 1.

8.25 Ibid., at 2.

8.26 Ibid.

values was the Indexed Securities Investment Plan. Other measures were designed to broaden the loss carry-over provisions, assist small business and farming, and encourage housing.

Under the National Training Act of 1982 and the Student Loans Act the government would continue to assist in raising the level of education; technical research would be encouraged by the establishment of new federal research facilities across Canada; grants would continue to be given science and technology, and productivity would be encouraged by the establishment of a National Centre for Productivity and Employment Growth. Several reliefs were given under the personal income tax. There were some penalties for this program; the federal sales tax would be raised from 9 to 10 percent, but not for nearly a year and a half—on October 1, 1984. The federal personal income tax credit would also be reduced for 1984.

On expenditures:

> In 1975, this government made the commitment that, over the medium term, expenditures would grow no more quickly than the trend growth in GNP . . . This commitment was met until the recession last year. I am reaffirming this commitment tonight.[8.27]

On the deficit:

> The fact that the deficit has reached such a high level means that it will inevitably take time to bring it down. Indeed, as I have indicated previously, because recovery will be moderate, because unemployment will remain high, and because oil prices have fallen abroad and will fall in Canada, the deficit would have been higher this year than last year even without the actions I have announced in this budget. The direct impact of these actions will increase the deficit by $1.8 billion and bring it to $31.2 billion for the current year.[8.28]

February 1984: Lalonde. As the government was defeated in an election before its 1984 budget was implemented its contents are of academic interest only. However it is significant as the final word of a Liberal approach to activist policy.

With inflation moderating (although still at levels that would have caused consternation in the sixties) the main concern continued to be unemployment, still in excess of 11 percent. The central theme of the budget was

> creating jobs through partnership. The private sector must be the main creator of jobs. But the government can help—by providing assistance where desirable, by lightening the burden of administration where feasible and by leading directly where necessary . . . Securing growth and jobs depends on our success in four basic areas: reducing and controlling inflation; increasing investment; reducing the government's deficit and improving our competitiveness and productivity.[8.29]

[8.27] Ibid., at 20-21.

[8.28] Ibid., at 19.

[8.29] Canada, Department of Finance, Budget Speech, February 15, 1984, 1-2.

Inflation would be contained after termination of the 6-and-5 program by the example of continued "wage and price restraint" by the federal government; capital investment would be aided by the federal Special Recovery Projects program and the tax incentives of the 1983 budget; the then estimated deficit of $31.5 billion was expected to fall to $29.6 billion in the following year; employment would be aided by the Special Recovery Program and by the new Youth Opportunity Fund.

But we must all recognize that there are limits to what government alone can do. The jobs Canadians seek—good jobs and permanent jobs—must come from a healthy and growing economy, led by a strong and vigorous private sector.[8.30]

Measures directed to improved productivity were the establishment of a Canadian Labour Market and Productivity Centre, tax incentives for profit-sharing plans, financial assistance for Canadian firms operating in developing countries and a tax concession for small businesses.

November 1984: Wilson. *A New Direction for Canada; An Agenda for Economic Recovery.* As earlier indicated, the economic priorities of the new Conservative government were based on reducing the deficit, which was accepted as a major hindrance to economic development. While this was to be the first priority, the Minister had given three others in his Economic and Financial Statement, indicative of the growing disillusionment with the interventionist state; these were "to redefine the role of government so that it provides a better framework for growth and job creation . . . to foster higher investment, greater innovation, increased international competitiveness and a positive climate for the birth of new enterprise . . . to bring about these changes in a way that is fair, open and consistent with the basic sense of compassion, tolerance and justice that is characteristic of Canadian society".[8.31]

According to the economic forecast these large changes would have to be implemented in an unfavourable economic climate. The Agenda assumed an average real growth in GNE of 3.4 percent in 1986-90, with an employment increase of 2.7 percent, giving an average unemployment rate of 8.9 percent, declining to just over 7 percent in 1990. Furthermore, without strong corrective action the budget deficit was forecast to remain in the neighbourhood of $35-37 billion to 1990-91. Sluggish revenues would be mainly responsible, but high debt charges would also contribute. In these conditions there was no easy way to "buy" growth. "The government's current and prospective fiscal situations are a serious constraint on its ability to use the major levers of fiscal policy to stabilize the economy in traditional ways."[8.32]

8.30 Ibid., at 6.

8.31 Canada, Department of Finance, Economic and Fiscal Statement, November 8, 1984, 2-3.

8.32 Canada, Department of Finance, *A New Direction for Canada*, An Agenda for Economic Renewal, November 8, 1984, 14.

The key to real economic growth would therefore have to be the private economy. Essential to its revitalization would be lower interest rates, for which a reduced deficit would make a crucial contribution. But there would also have to be a reduction of government's direct interference with the economy.

> Government has become too big. It intrudes too much into the marketplace and inhibits or distorts the entrepreneurial process. Some industries are over-regulated. Others are over-protected, not just from imports but also from domestic competition. Some programs designed to facilitate investment have the perverse effect of distorting investment decisions. Other programs carry on long after the need for them has passed, and are only a fiscal drain.[8.33]

The Agenda reviewed the status of R&D innovation and technological diffusion; export markets and financing; private sector investment; and labour markets and human resources. It also discussed economic regulation and intervention, and energy policy. The Agenda concluded:

> The preceding review of opportunities for promoting growth in the private sector amply shows that a substantial element of current federal spending on economic development may be doing more to hinder than to promote private sector growth. Cutting back in some of these areas can provide greater scope for private sector initiative and growth, and either permit reduced federal spending or free up funds for redeployment in more productive areas. We cannot seriously consider further financial support to even the most attractive measures for spurring private sector growth, until we are confident that there is a source of funds from savings elsewhere, from both economic and other programs.[8.34]

In the end implementation of the Agenda had:

> two closely related major thrusts. First, government policies and programs must be changed to ensure that Canada's private sector can become the driving force of economic renewal in an increasingly competitive world marketplace. To foster growth in the private sector, Canadians must begin a process of change towards a new environment that encourages entrepreneurship and facilitates adaptation to new market realities . . . Second, the federal deficit must be reduced to limit the steadily rising federal debt burden and its serious consequences for interest rates, private investment and the government's room to manoeuvre.[8.35]

It is tempting to seek in the words of the Agenda, presumably conceived in the space of two months, the seeds of later long-term policy developments. The effort is not without reward, as the following quotations indicate:

[8.33] Ibid., at 23.

[8.34] Ibid., at 69.

[8.35] Ibid., at 83-84.

On free trade with the United States:

> Canada and the U.S. have been considering whether there are sectors where new bilateral arrangements could be negotiated. This initiative has generated public interest in exploring broadly-based bilateral arrangements with the U.S. [A question raised in this regard was even more pertinent]: How would Canadian firms and regions adjust to the changed trade flows in a Canada/U.S. free trade arrangement?[8.36]

On tax reform:

> The government will continue to examine its tax system, not only from a revenue standpoint, but in terms of its impact on growth, equity and simplicity . . . In this context, some have suggested that Canada adopt a "value added" tax, possibly as a replacement for the current federal sales tax . . . Close consultations between governments, the private sector and other affected groups would be necessary before deciding whether to proceed with such a tax.[8.37]

On universality in social programs:

> Social responsibility dictates that wherever possible, and to a greater extent than is the case today, scarce resources should be diverted first to those in greatest need.[8.38]

Obviously a considerable amount of signalling was going on in this Conservative Magna Carta.

May 1985: Wilson. In the budget speech and papers the Minister of Finance referred to the *Agenda for Economic Renewal* as the source of the principles being followed by the government. The Minister related the Agenda commitment to the accord reached at a recent Bonn Summit, as being "to free up the entrepreneurial spirit of our citizens, to remove obstacles to productive growth, to lower barriers to international trade, to control and reduce high deficits, and to let the dynamism of our renewed economies produce jobs and opportunities for all."[8.39] He cited the occasions on which the government had consistently carried this message to the provincial First Ministers at the Regina Conference in February; to the National Economic Conference; to President Reagan at the Quebec Summit in March, and to the Bonn Economic Summit.

In support of the government's efforts to implement the Agenda he cited new programs for employment and training, the establishment of Investment Canada in place of the Foreign Investment Review Agency, the energy accords with Newfoundland and the western producing provinces, the efforts to gain greater access to trade with foreign markets and comprehensive new rules for governing financial institutions in Canada.

8.36 Ibid., at 33.

8.37 Ibid., at 67.

8.38 Ibid., at 71.

8.39 Canada, Department of Finance, The Budget Speech, Securing Economic Renewal, May 23, 1985, 1.

The major economic change in the 1985 budget was the introduction of the lifetime $500,000 capital gains exemption, which for many taxpayers effectively repealed the capital gains tax. Ancillary to this were moves to facilitate access to finances for small business and to encourage research and development through tax credits. A review of unemployment insurance, reform of some aspects of corporate taxation, and removal of some of the tax expenditures also fulfilled the Agenda program.

February 1986: Wilson. The Minister continued to adhere fairly closely to the spirit of the Agenda, although this did not involve complete abandonment of the intercession role for the federal government. This was evident in the tax increases announced in the 1985 and 1986 budgets. For most citizens the primary intrusion of the government is in its desire to share part of his or her income, and the share Mr. Wilson was demanding was higher each year. This however was inevitable, as the long course of tax reductions in the 1970s had left the federal budget seriously under-financed. There were of course renewals or revivals of ideas long since tried by other governments, such as programs to assist development in the Atlantic provinces, to encourage small business, to stimulate employment, to encourage research, etc. etc. But the biggest gambles were still ahead, particularly in the negotiation of free trade with the United States and in a major program of tax reform just beginning to appear on the horizon. The accomplishment of these almost simultaneously would represent more intervention in the affairs of Canadian society than any attempted by any government in decades.

As for the economy, the outlook was beginning to improve. Inflation was remaining around 4 percent, although this was acceptable mainly in comparison to the 12 percent of a few years before. Interest rates were declining, and with the help of a depreciated dollar and heavy automobile-related exports there was a substantial surplus in the trade balance. Real growth in GNP had averaged 3½ percent per year since 1984, and was forecast at 3.3 percent for 1986. However, weak signs in the economy were unemployment in excess of 9 percent, lagging capital expenditures, and serious problems in the petroleum industry and agriculture. Both were in deep difficulty with debt burdens and declining markets and prices, as the Minister was to learn before his next budget.

In concluding his budget address the Minister again expressed his commitment to the general objectives of the 1984 Agenda:

This government has demonstrated its resolve to restore fiscal responsibility to Canada.

We are doing this in a way that is consistent with the commitment we made to Canadians in November of 1984. Our objective, then and now, is to solve the problems of the past in order to create jobs today and into the future.

We are reducing the crushing burden of interest payments that has accompanied a decade of uncontrolled growth in our debt. Just as Canadians seek to pay down their personal debt to use the savings for better things, we are doing the same in government, creating room to respond to the nation's needs.

Cutting the deficit is not an end in itself. It is the means to an end. It is the means to achieve lower interest rates, higher growth and more jobs.

The actions we have taken reflect the priorities we set out in November 1984 and acted on in May 1985:

- to release the creative spirit of individuals from the heavy hand of government;
- to enhance our capacity to compete by promoting trade, investment and technology;
- to play a constructive role in the global community;
- to assist individuals to adjust to a changing world;
- to help Canadians who need assistance.

This is what we promised. This is what we are delivering. We will continue to act with consistency and determination. Canadians can look to the future with confidence.[8.40]

February 1987: Wilson. Obviously the view of the role of government in the economy had undergone a considerable revision under the Conservatives. The government had an important role to play, but one less interventionist than that foreseen in the 1945 White Paper. The ideology was summed up again in the preface to *The Agenda for Economic Renewal: Principles and Progress*, a paper that accompanied the 1987 budget.

In November 1984, the Government of Canada published *An Agenda for Economic Renewal*, a document that laid out the government's course for restoring health to the flagging Canadian economy . . . It stressed the need to encourage private sector initiative, the need to make the government less obstructive and more efficient, and the imperative of restoring good fiscal management . . . Our principal objective [a little uncertainty about the principal objective, which seemed to vary from statement to statement] has been to improve the competitive position of Canadian business, at home and abroad, so that the country will grow and thrive and its people prosper in a caring and open society. The objective underlies each of many initiatives we have taken—in restoring fiscal order, in reforming regulation, in encouraging investment and initiative, in everything we have done . . . More remains to be done. The tax system will be reformed. A national child care strategy will be put in place. The deficit will be reduced further. Deregulation will continue. Science and technology will be promoted. The development of resource industries demands our close attention, as does the challenge of enhancing regional development. The government is committed to these efforts. We are undertaking

---

[8.40]Canada, Department of Finance, Budget Speech, February 26, 1986, 23.

them in the spirit—and the directions—established in the first half of our mandate.[8.41]

February 1988: Wilson. The continuing commitment to the current "conservative" philosophy is apparent in the last budget speech before the coming election. In it the Minister of Finance stated:

This government brought to office a vision for a stronger, more prosperous Canada, now and into the next century.

Our vision is rooted in the belief that the source of real, lasting jobs and economic strength is the creative energy of Canadians themselves—their capacity to innovate and produce, their desire to excel, their determination to build greater opportunities for the future.

To make this vision a reality, we set out a long-term plan—our Agenda for Economic Renewal—to transform the economy so that it can meet the challenges of a more competitive world.

Step by step, we have been putting in place a wide-ranging series of actions. These actions complement one another. Together they strengthen Canada's economic and social fabric and reinforce our place among the leading nations of the world.

- We have revitalized the private sector and positioned Canada's economy to meet the challenge of international competition in the 1990s.

- We have restored fiscal responsibility by reducing the deficit and cutting the growth of the national debt.

- We have implemented priority programs, and we have helped regions and sectors hurt by unexpected developments in the world economy.[8.42]

Perspective—A Personal View

This review has clearly demonstrated through the annual budget statements, so crucial to government policy, that the federal government has exercised economic initiatives in the last four decades of unprecedented scale and effect. Where budget speeches at one time were limited mainly to reviewing the financial status of the public treasury in the last four decades they have become far ranging surveys of an endless array of social and economic issues, accompanied by frequent announcements of programs and actions to influence those issues. Our interest here is primarily in the consequences of the adoption of the Keynesian inspired White Paper in 1945. How did it fare in practice?

[8.41] Canada, Department of Finance, Budget Papers, The Agenda for Economic Renewal: Principles and Progress, February 18, 1987, Preface.

[8.42] Canada, Department of Finance, The Budget Speech, Securing Economic Renewal, February 10, 1988, 1-2.

1. Clearly most of the ministers of finance were warriors (not always happy, granted) in attacking the problems of the economy. Most appear to have held a strong conviction that government should play a prominent role in influencing the economy, in the earlier decades by direct intervention and more recently by removing intervention. Many of the ideas on which these policies were based originated with economists, and as few of the ministers were of this profession they were forced to accept a good deal on faith, particularly as they were untried ideas that were generally incapable of proof. This was particularly true of the first three decades of the period.

2. The almost constant concerns with inflation and unemployment were perplexing and unhappy conditions that complicated the application of the interventionist philosophy, cast doubts on its legitimacy and ultimately undermined its acceptance. Politically there never was a convincing answer as to whether the interventionist approach was in itself contributing to the dilemma or was simply not capable of coping with it. Certainly the experience showed that much more knowledge was needed on the response of the economy to measures of stimulus or retrenchment for their use with any confidence. There was always the view, of course, held by many economists outside government, that the policy was simply not administered with the single-minded concentration and skill that would have been required to make it a success. We consider these views in the next section.

3. The interventionist program went through a variety of phases, each reflecting the perceived needs of the period. Starting with the simple objectives of contra-cyclical budgeting and stimulation of capital investment, mainly designed for stabilization purposes, during the sixties the "growth" objective became popular, and at the same time concern with shortcomings of the economy began to appear. This took the form of attempts to remedy structural problems, programs to balance regional development, to stimulate research, facilitate technological change, to further job training and technological education, to finance federally sponsored mega-projects, etc. The tax system was also used in a variety of ways (stimulation of consumption by tax reductions, encouragement or discouragement of capital expenditure, enhancement of a vast array of industrial developments through special tax provisions, etc.). And along with all this it was deemed necessary to resort to at least three income and price programs—that of the Incomes Commission (1968-70), of the AIB (1976-78), and of the 6-and-5 program (1983-84)—of varying severity and success.

The result of this process was an almost constant state of discontinuity. Programs were adopted and dropped with dizzying speed, with expectations of almost immediate results. Some persistence with longer term objectives has come only in the battle against inflation and the deficit in recent years.

4. The struggle against growing expenditures was a constant theme of Ministers of Finance, but in the end this objective slipped away from them and massive deficits ensued. The landslide that began in 1975 with an increase to $5.7 billion from $2.0 billion the year before, gathered sufficient momentum to reach $15 billion in 1981 and sped on for the next three years to reach $38 billion in 1984. We have already examined this phenomenon in

some detail in the previous section; its effect undoubtedly has been to undermine confidence both nationally and internationally in the economic management of the federal government. This led to rejection of the programs that had produced this result and the election of a government dedicated to the reduction of the deficit as its first and highest priority.

5. Politically the unhappy emergence of combined inflation and unemployment in the last decade has cast serious doubt on the interventionist role of the state. There is little evidence of enthusiastic support for it in the economic realm in recent years. On the contrary most governments of western industrial countries have now rejected it, the most prominent being the United States under the influence of President Reagan. In Canada its waning influence first appeared most dramatically in the MacEachen budgets with the rejection of easy short-term cures for the 1981-82 recession, a trend further evidenced in the Lalonde budgets and finally adopted without reservation in the Wilson economic statements. A cynic might say that these recent conversions were the result of lack of money rather than of ideas for spending it. One cannot underestimate the political pressure for new programs and the rarity of politicians dedicated to reducing the budget. In any event it will be many years before the federal finances will offer much room for extravagance; the federal finances will only recover health by long and persistent attention.

APPENDIX
Tax Measures for Economic Impact
(excluding natural resource and energy allowances)

Date	Type of Measure
1944	Double depreciation for assets for postwar production
1944	Specific deduction for scientific research expenditures, to be fully deductible in year incurred
1945	Building materials exempted from sales tax
	Machinery and apparatus used in manufacturing and production exempted from sales tax
1949	Reduced rate for small corporations, 10 percent dividend tax credit and depreciation at double existing rates on declining balance method introduced; loss carry-over extended from three years to five
1951	Special depreciation established for assets used for defence production for Korean War
	Depreciation on new less-essential assets deferred for four years; terminated prior to full term
1961	Initial allowance: firms allowed to deduct double the amount for capital costs in the first year in respect of manufacturing and processing equipment (i.e., 40 percent instead of 20 percent)
	Only assets acquired (a) in areas of chronic unemployment; (b) for investment in the further processing of Canadian resources; (c) for the manufacture of new products were eligible
	Initial allowance: firms allowed to deduct 150 percent of the amount for capital costs in the first year in respect of manufacturing and processing equipment intended for re-equipment and modernization, (i.e., 30 percent instead of 20 percent.) Only assets in excess of those purchased during recent base period were eligible
1962	Production Incentive Plan in the form of a tax credit to a specified percentage of increased sales volume over and above that of a base period; tax reduced by 50 percent on first $50,000 of profits due to sales increase and 25 percent on remainder.
	Additional 50 percent deduction allowed for scientific research expenditure on excess over base year
1963	Two-year write-off: firms allowed to deduct entire cost of manufacturing and processing equipment within two years, at a rate of 50 percent per annum. Only applicable to firms having a min-

imum 25 percent beneficial Canadian ownership and a proportionate number of Canadian directors

Three-year tax-holiday for firms establishing manufacturing and processing facilities in designated areas of slower economic growth; no Canadian ownership requirement

Two-year write-off: as above, except that it was intended for assets acquired by firms in designated areas of slower economic growth; no Canadian ownership requirement

Five-year write-off: firms allowed to deduct entire cost of manufacturing and processing buildings and structures in five years instead of twenty and ten. Only assets acquired by firms in designated areas of slower economic growth were eligible; no Canadian ownership requirement

Sales tax exemption for production equipment and processing material withdrawn; building materials made taxable but not at full rate

1965   Grant equal to 25 percent of current year capital expenditure on research and development on excess over average of preceding three years

Regional tax incentives replaced by cash grants under Area Development Incentives Act

1966   Depreciation on new investments in period March 1966 to October 1967 deferred for three years ·

Exemption of producer's equipment and processing materials to be restored in 1967 and 1968 in two stages. Building materials remain taxable at reduced rate

1969   Depreciation on commercial buildings constructed between June 1969 and December 31, 1970, in urban centres over 50,000 in B.C., Alberta, and Ontario deferred for two years

1970   Investment allowance: firms allowed to value 115 percent of the cost of manufacturing equipment and structures for depreciation purposes. Only firms deriving over two-thirds of revenue from goods manufactured and processed in Canada were eligible

1972   Two-year write-off: firms allowed to deduct entire cost of manufacturing and processing equipment within two years; no Canadian ownership requirement

1973   Manufacturing and processing profits deduction; corporate income tax rate reduced to 40 percent from 49 percent for profits earned by manufacturing and processing firms; no Canadian ownership requirement

1974   Two-year write-off for new machinery and equipment for manufacturing and processing extended indefinitely.

MURB allowance introduced for multi-unit residential buildings constructed between November 1974 and December 1975

1975   5 percent investment tax credit granted for new buildings or machinery and equipment in manufacturing and processing industry and some resource sectors

100 percent write-off of certified feature films introduced

1976   Following a review of the capital cost allowance rates some increases were granted

Two year write-off granted for certain energy efficient equipment

1977   MURBs provision extended to 1978

Investment tax credit rate raised to 7½ percent in DREE designated areas and 10 percent in Atlantic provinces and Gaspé. Otherwise 5 percent

3 percent inventory allowance introduced

1978   An additional 50 percent deduction for excess of qualified current and capital expenditure on scientific research over such expenditure in previous three-year period

General rate of investment tax credit raised to 7 percent and to 10 percent in DREE designated regions and 20 percent in Atlantic provinces and the Gaspé; extended indefinitely

MURB provision extended to 1979

Employment tax credit enacted to subsidize wages in high unemployment areas to March 1981

Certain current and capital scientific expenditures made after November 16, 1978 were made eligible for enriched investment tax credit of 10 percent, 20 percent in Atlantic Provinces and the Gaspé, and 25 percent for Canadian controlled private corporations eligible for small business deduction

Two-year write-off for anti-pollution equipment extended indefinitely

1980   50 percent tax credit granted for new investment in manufacturing plant and equipment between 1980 and 1986 in selected incentive areas as defined in the Regional Development Act

MURB provisions re-introduced to apply to new construction between October 1980 and before 1982

Employment tax credit extended to March 1982

Small Business Development Bond introduced to finance expansion. Lender exempt from tax on interest

1981   Capital cost allowance reduced in the first year a property is acquired to one-half the normal rate

1982   Small Business Development Bond extended to individuals and partnerships, but limited to cases of financial difficulty. Interest exemption restricted

1983   Carryback and carryforward of unused tax credits extended to three years and seven years. Future unused portions of tax credits earned between April 1983 and April 1986 to be refunded directly

A share purchase tax credit introduced under which corporations would be able to give their future investment tax credits to new share owners to the extent of 25 percent of the purchase value of the shares

Business losses, previously allowed to be carried back one year and forward five years granted a three-year carryback and a seven year carryforward

The budget for April 1983 presented a paper on Research and Development Tax Policies proposing changing from grants and deductions to refundable tax credits for investment in research and development and a 50 percent "flow-through" to investors on purchase of shares or debt of the corporation. An Income Tax Amending bill introduced late in 1983 contained measures to implement these provisions

1984   Under legislation passed in the new year tax credits for R and D became available for investment after September, 1983

In October a new Minister of Finance announced a moratorium on tax credits for investment in R and D due to abuses through "quick flips"—the issuance and immediate redemption of shares or debt to convey the tax credit to investors

1985   Scientific research tax credit terminated due to abuses

Investment tax credit on $2 million of R & D expenditure of small companies made refundable at 35 percent rate

50 percent investment tax credit extended for one year

60 percent tax credit granted for approved projects on Cape Breton Island

Small business bond extended

1986   3 percent inventory allowance dropped

Withdrawal of 7 percent general investment tax credit begins, to 5 percent in 1987, 3 percent in 1988, and 0 in 1989; 10 percent rate also being phased out

50 percent special investment tax credit reduced to 40 percent

20 percent investment tax credit retained for Atlantic Region

Tax credit rates for research and development retained at 20 percent and 30 percent

1987-88   Various further changes were made under Tax Reform. See Chapter 14.

Bibliography, chapters 6 to 8

Bladen, V.W. *From Adam Smith to Maynard Keynes: The Heritage of Political Economy*. Toronto: University of Toronto Press, 1974.

Bryce, Robert B. *Maturing in Hard Times. Canada's Department of Finance Through the Great Depression*. Institute of Public Administration of Canada. Kingston and Montreal: McGill-Queen's University Press, 1986.

Harris, W.B., Weldon, J.C., and Hartle, Douglas G. "Role of Government in the Economy." *Report of Proceedings of the Twenty-Eighth Tax Conference*, 1976 Conference Report. Toronto: Canadian Tax Foundation, 1977.

Harrod, R.F. *Life of John Maynard Keynes*. London: MacMillan, 1951.

Horn, M. ed. *The Dirty Thirties: Canadians in the Great Depression*. Toronto: Copp, Clark, 1972.

Plumptre, A.F.W. *Three Decades of Decision*. Toronto: McClelland and Stewart, 1977, (Chapter 1).

Popkins, John W. *Government and the Economy—Stabilization Policies*. Toronto: Canadian Foundation for Economic Education, 1977.

Raynauld, Andre. Chairman. "Fiscal Policy for Growth and Stability." In *Report of Proceedings of the Twenty-Second Tax Conference*, 1970 Conference Report, Toronto: Canadian Tax Foundation, 1971.

Safarian, A.E. *The Canadian Economy in the Great Depression*. Carleton Library Series. Toronto: McClelland and Stewart, 1970.

Samuelson, Paul A., and Scott, Anthony. *Economics*. (Canadian Edition). Toronto: McGrawHill Ryerson, 1980.

Economists Appraise Performance

9
General Discontent

Economists have been vocal in expressing their views on the management of the economy over the four decades since the White Paper was issued. Much of their comment has been critical, and has mainly reflected the exacting judgments that arise from evaluating results in terms of mathematical models which presuppose exact cause-effect relationships and from which many of the troublesome conflicting elements (now labelled exogenous) are excluded. There were great expectations in the immediate postwar years that a combination of fiscal and monetary policies could be devised that would ensure price stability with reasonable levels of employment, and there was great frustration with what appeared to many, despite the record we have just reviewed, of a weak effort on the part of government to apply the new policies.

The principal measure of success was the extent of use of "discretionary" contra-cyclical budget measures combined with appropriate monetary policies. Under this test balanced budgets counted generally as zero, even though the few of them that emerged were accomplished in the face of constant public pressure for tax reductions and urgent demands from the provinces for the transfer of more tax sources. Similar harsh judgments were reserved for budgets in which a surplus was said to be due only to the effects of inflation, even though in the circumstances a surplus was the right medicine. Even harsher judgment was reserved for early budgets in which the actual surplus that resulted turned out to be far in excess of the moderate surplus forecast, a result known by some people to be the outcome of a conspiratorial agreement between the Minister and his officials to persuade the public into doing the right thing. Nor was much credit given by the pure theorists for the many initiatives taken over the years by direct action on incomes policies, efforts to stimulate capital expenditure, technological innovation and education, regional development, exports, etc. For many economists these were simply distractions from the true purpose of applying aggregate economic policies with sufficient skill and vigour to achieve the desired results, and as such were thought likely to produce as much harm as benefit.

Recent attention has focused heavily on the implications of the federal deficit. In this regard some old truths are re-emerging; budgets should be kept reasonably in balance over the cycle and should not be allowed to stay substantially and increasingly in deficit.

Without further comment the following are a selection of quotations from papers, books, speeches, and other sources on postwar fiscal and economic policy.

1958, McIvor.

Concerning the fiscal policy of the earliest postwar years, it appears reasonable to conclude that at least the magnitude, and on occasion the mere existence, of budgetary surpluses was fortuitous, for there were repeated warnings of a recession which in fact did not develop. If this conclusion is correct, then there was no serious conflict at this time between the monetary and fiscal *policies* of the government, although these policies were conditioned by what in retrospect proved to be essentially false premises. At the time of the 1948 Budget Speech, the continuing insistent inflationary pressures rendered non-restrictive policies much less justifiable, and a fair inference from the Speech is that the continuation of budgetary surpluses was regarded as a feasible means of overcoming the inflationary consequences of the relatively easy-money policy which the government was extremely reluctant to terminate. . . .

During the post-War II decade, Canada had shifted its emphasis in combating inflation from an almost exclusive reliance upon fiscal measures in the early years to a comparable dependence upon monetary techniques after mid-1955. The inherent limitations of the latter approach, as revealed by Canadian experience . . . emphasize the shortcomings of an anti-inflationary policy which has shifted from one "extreme" to another, in the sense that fiscal and monetary instruments have been utilized mainly as alternative rather than complementary techniques of control.

The rejection of fiscal policy as the prime approach to economic stabilization appears to have rested upon several grounds . . . the problem of educating the public as to the objectives and implications of counter-cyclical budgets is difficult . . . The existence of a budget surplus leads, *ipso facto*, to charges of over-taxation, and also encourages wasteful and excessive government expenditures. Particular fiscal measures designed to affect resource allocation in the economy, being in some sense discriminatory, arouse violent and, from the viewpoint of the sectors affected, legitimate complaints . . . there is the very real problem in Canada of maintaining its effectiveness in the face of possibly conflicting fiscal measures adopted by the provincial and municipal governments . . . the Canadian recession of 1953-54 . . . revealed clearly the difficulties of applying fiscal measures to what were highly selective weak spots rather than parts of a general economic recession . . . the lags which are inevitable in the democratic process of government render such policy insufficiently adaptable for tactical use . . . many technical problems remain to be solved . . . there is a great need for further study of the particular reactions of given economic units to specific fiscal measures . . . Moreover, effective action requires not only a knowledge of what to do but when to do it, and the problem of timing is one of crucial importance.[9.1]

[9.1] R. Craig McIvor, *Canadian Monetary, Banking and Fiscal Development* (Toronto: The Macmillan Company of Canada Limited, 1958), 211-41.

1962, Johnson. The late Harry Johnson, one of Canada's uniquely distinguished economists, in his Allan B. Plaunt Memorial Lecture at Carleton University in 1962, spoke of the unemployment and inflation of the previous three years as "a direct consequence of Canadian government policy (or lack of policy) and specifically of the policy of the central bank." His recommendations were for a less independent role for the central bank and the adoption of "some simple rule of monetary management, for example to increase the money supply at a constant rate corresponding to the long-run rate of growth." The latter was the monetarist view of Milton Friedman at the University of Chicago where Johnson was a faculty member.[9.2]

1963, Report of the Royal Commission on Banking and Finance.

On balance, it is difficult to avoid the conclusion that financial policies in the post-war period have not made the contribution that they might to the attainment of major economic goals. Quite apart from the inherent limitations of such policies and the difficulties of accurately predicting economic developments, there have been occasions when the instruments of policy seemed to be working against each other or when bolder measures could have been taken in the light of the evidence then in hand. Recessions in the post-war period in Canada as elsewhere have indeed been shorter and milder than those of earlier days, in part because of a lesser dependence on agricultural production but mainly because of the powerful role played by the automatic stabilizers and of more deliberate government policies.[9.3]

1964, First Review of the Economic Council of Canada. In its first report the Council, in comparing Canada's record with the basic objectives of "high employment, sustained economic growth, reasonable price stability, a viable balance of payments position, and balanced regional development" concluded that Canada's past record had

clearly been mixed. Outstanding successes in some respects have been marred by conspicuous shortfalls in others. Periods of consistently high standards of performance have been rare and short-lived. In the two decades since the war, there have been few periods when all five basic economic objectives were being simultaneously attained with reasonable degrees of success. For example, there have been periods of full employment accompanied by sharp increases in prices and costs; periods of price stability with high unemployment and slow economic growth; periods of critical strain in the balance of payments, both with and without price stability and high employment; and

---

9.2 Harry Johnson, *Canada in a Changing World Economy*. Alan B. Plaunt Memorial Lectures, Carleton University, February 15, 17, 1962 (Toronto: University of Toronto Press, 1962).

9.3 Canada, Report of the Royal Commission on Banking and Finance (Ottawa: Queen's Printer, 1965), 416.

periods of accentuation of the longer term weaknesses of some regions.[9.4]

The Council set as its objectives for 1970 the achievement of a 3 percent unemployment level:

> *An appropriate combination of strong expansionary policies is therefore required to generate adequate levels of demand both at home and in export markets in support of rapidly expanding employment. . . .*
> There must also be strong emphasis on increased efficiency . . . It is this combination of sustained high employment and sustained advances in productivity which together provide the basis for sustained economic growth.[9.5]

There would also have to be a "considerably improved performance regarding price and cost constraints," although it was conceded that this "could be very difficult to attain under conditions of high employment and vigorous growth." And the government would have to lengthen its time horizon for fiscal policy, and reduce its concern for short-term stabilization.

> [W]hile we recognize that it may well be necessary under certain conditions to adapt fiscal policy to shorter term objectives and special needs, such as those of moderating cyclical instability, we believe that the consistent shaping of fiscal policy to longer term economic objectives and potentials will contribute to a pattern of smoother and steadier growth in which the risks of cyclical instability would be reduced.[9.6]

The same prescription was offered for monetary policy.

1965, Carleton University Conference. The Twentieth anniversary of the White Paper on Employment and Income was signalled by a series of six public lectures at Carleton University. The first of these was by W.A. Mackintosh, who explained its origins and identified himself as its principal author, and the last was a summing up by John J. Deutsch. The intervening four papers, by H. Scott Gordon, Ronald Bodkin, John W.L. Winder, and David W. Slater dealt with its implementation in some detail, and were a mixture of sober appraisal of the difficulties of implementing the new policy and unexpectedly harsh criticism of the government's inability to carry out the neat game plan that the economists set forth for it.

> Gordon: "Mr. Ilsley's two post-war budgets and Mr. Abbott's budget of 1947, taken together, reduced the burden of personal income taxes by more than half . . . Mr. Abbott's last three budget speeches as Minister of Finance also show this strong adherence to the principle of budget balancing, both in their texts and in the actual policies proposed . . . it is clear that the era in our fiscal history over which Mr.

9.4 Economic Council of Canada, *Economic Goals for Canada to 1970* First Annual Review (Ottawa: Queen's Printer, 1964), 7.

9.5 Ibid., at 186.

9.6 Ibid., at 198.

Abbott presided as Minister of Finance was one of pure Gladstonianism in fiscal policy . . . Keynesian statements were confined to the abstract plane of discourse; they were not connected with actual policy.[9.7]

Several of the budgets of the fifties are given good marks as Keynesian, but Mr. Fleming's special budget of December 1960, along with Mr. Abbott's of 1947, "represent the crucial turning points in Canada's fiscal history since the White Paper of 1945." The Fleming budget marked "the official rejection of Keynesian-type expansionary fiscal policies, designed to increase aggregate demand, as inappropriate to Canada." Gordon's reason for this conclusion was the adoption of structural measures to cope with the unemployment problem.

Thus the decision was made to attack the unemployment problem by measures of a non-budgetary character . . . This remained the dominant characteristic of economic policy during the remainder of Mr. Fleming's tenure of office . . . The treasury ran substantial deficits, but these were of the passive variety and reflected the effect of the recession itself, rather than positive efforts to combat it.[9.8]

His successor, Walter Gordon, exacerbated this apostasy by not only retaining the structural measures but as well attempting to balance the budget. In view of these comments Gordon's concluding appraisal will come as no surprise:

Three decades have gone since Keynes' *General Theory of Employment, Interest and Money* was first published, and two since our own White Paper on policy; and it must be confessed that Keynesian economics has made virtually no impact on the Canadian public mind or on the business community. It has made little headway in advancing the analytical work in the bureaucracy that underlies the formulation of employment and other economic policies; and despite some brief period of favour, it does not appear to have won its way to any appreciable acceptance as a sound principle of fiscal policy.[9.9]

Thus spoke a Keynesian purist.

Winder: A more balanced view was taken by Winder.

The Royal Commission on Banking and Finance concluded that financial policies could have played a stronger role in support of the built-in stabilizers which alone seem to account for the relative improvement in our economic performance during these years . . . The work on lags shows clearly that lags are variable, and that, on the average, a long time expires between the need for a change and

---

9.7 H. Scott Gordon, "A Twenty Year Perspective: Some Reflections on the Keynesian Revolution in Canada," in S.F. Kaliski, ed., *Canadian Economic Policy Since the War* (Montreal: Canadian Trade Committee, 1966), 23-46, at 36-38.

9.8 Ibid., at 40.

9.9 Ibid., at 46.

the time that policy action has its effect. Under these circumstances, it is quite conceivable that the net effect of intentionally stabilizing monetary (or fiscal) policy could be to increase rather than diminish instability. It is, therefore, sometimes argued that monetary policy, at least, should be directed toward longer-run trends of upward growth of the economy rather than be subjected to discretionary management in the ill-advised . . . pursuit of greater short-run stability . . . We need better tools to adequately assess the performance of our policy-makers; and they would surely do a better job if economists could provide more reliable specification of the economic mechanisms and the relevant measurements.[9.10]

Slater.

. . . the Canadian economic experience in the 1970s was mediocre, equivalent on an academic scale to probably a C + or at best a B − ; but if the whole of the last 8½ years are considered, from the business cycle peak in the first quarter of 1957 to the present, the grade on Canadian economic performance is even lower . . . A fairly good case can be made for the view that the Canadian economy is still operating below reasonably attainable full-capacity output levels . . . Fiscal policy was decidedly wrong much of the time, e.g., the increases in tax rates in 1959, but might have been made more sensible if the country had followed a very aggressive easy-money policy. However, the monetary and debt management policies of the federal government were extremely tight and have earned near universal scorn for their biases toward deflation amid high unemployment, and towards importing foreign capital amid surfeits of savings . . . I believe that the best that can be said for Canada's new economic policies in 1963 to 1965 has been that they have been neutral in their impact on the economic expansion. The harmful policies have been just about balanced out by the beneficial ones, and many highly touted elements of policy had only a minor effect, for good or ill.[9.11]

Slater's main criticisms appeared to be that the wrong policies were followed for some conditions and that when right policies were used they were not exploited with sufficient vigour, a common complaint among economists.

Deutsch. In rounding up the papers, John Deutsch, then President of the Economic Council, attributed policy failures to three main causes:

First, the problems of social and economic policy have proved to be much more complex than was thought during the first flush of the Keynesian revolution after the war. It has now been shown that the Keynesian doctrine has provided only a partial answer to the questions

---

9.10 John W.L. Winder, "Some Policy Implications of Recent Empirical Work," *supra* footnote 9.7, 79-97, at 95-96.

9.11 David W. Slater, "Canadian Economic Policy in the 1960s," *supra* footnote 9.7, 99-121, at 100-04.

of policy in the present-day world. Secondly, the maintenance of reasonable stability in the rate of economic activity seems to depend more on the strong automatic stabilizers which now have been built into our government expenditure and revenue system than on the short-term manipulation of the monetary and financial levers . . . Thirdly, there is an urgent need for much more empirical research in order to improve our understanding of the complex interrelationships in the economy and our understanding of how the policy instruments work. I believe it was Professor Winder who remarked on ". . . the appalling distance which still separates the theorists among us from the practitioners of economic policy." I would hope that more empirical analysis would help to shorten this distance.[9.12]

The irony of these comments was that they were being made in the midst of one of the best economic decades that Canada has ever enjoyed.

1965, Smith. This appeared to be a time for reflection on economic policy. In an article in *The Canadian Banker*, of which he was pro tem editor at the time, Prof. David Smith wrote of "Full Employment Policy: A new force or a hollow slogan?"

From post-war economic literature a number of distinctive features of a full employment policy program have emerged . . . The experience of North America during the past decade has cast some doubt, however, on whether the economists' model for full employment policy has been of much use or has received much attention in actual policy decisions . . . One of the . . . features of post-war thinking on employment policy is the principle of governmental responsibility for full employment . . . The popularity of such acknowledgements of governmental respnsibility in this area was high, but the methods, outlined by economists, through which this responsibility should be exercised have always been greeted more suspiciously . . . One particular aspect of this prescription, however, has caused difficulties for public acceptance. It is that levels of government expenditures and tax rates should be determined by reference to general demand conditions and not by the principle of balancing the budget. Economic reasoning has clearly established that there is no economic defence of an annually balanced budget . . . Nevertheless, the persistence of what seems to be at times little more than a public mythology on the need to balance exactly or approximately has weakened the exercise of governmental responsibility for employment levels.[9.13]

Other features of postwar employment policy have been the trend to setting targets in terms that can be measured and the realization of possible conflicts between the goal of full employment and other goals, such as price stability.

[9.12] John J. Deutsch, "Canadian Economic Policy 1945-65—A Summing Up," supra footnote 9.7, 123-33, at 131-32.

[9.13] David C. Smith, "Full Employment Policy: A New Force or a Hollow Slogan?" (Autumn 1965) *The Canadian Banker* 5-17, at 5-8.

The possibility of "trade-offs" among economic goals and the importance of the particular combination of economic policies for trying to achieve more than one goal have focussed more interest on the coordination of the decisions of policy-makers than there used to be.[9.14]

This interest had centred on "concern about the rate of price increases that have been associated with low unemployment rates" and on "discussions of economic growth . . . Finally, there has been recognition of particularly large and stubborn adjustment problems which market mechanisms may have difficulty in handling smoothly." He mentioned as an example the flood of "baby-boom" young people seeking employment. Research appeared to have established a relationship between high levels of employment and inflation. "[T]here is evidence from past experience that, as the unemployment rate is pushed lower, particularly below the four percent level, increased price pressures build up . . ." (an observation that to survivors of recent combined 12 percent inflation and 11 percent unemployment has a certain element of fantasy).

The dissatisfaction that had arisen reflected the fact that

actual employment policies in Canada have not been closely related to this body of reasoning. As a result, economists, disenchanted with the apparent ineptness of the policy maker, have continued undaunted to build further refinements to their theory, occasionally pausing to scold at the lack of public appreciation of the beauties of their work. Those engaged in the study or practice of political decisions have dismissed these activities as naive but largely harmless . . .[9.15]

Some of the problems that appear to have caused a gap between theory and practice were that

the theory has frequently assumed an availability of information to the policy maker which is unlikely to occur in a highly uncertain world . . . the motives governing the decisions of policy makers are likely to be somewhat different than the ones which economists tend to assume . . . more emphasis will be placed on policy measures, the benefits of which can be directly identified by the public . . . the organizational structure for decision making in the government may be weak for applying a co-ordinated, consistent employment policy. Economic analysis has demonstrated the importance of co-ordination of major types of government policies . . . the growth in complexity of government has forced increased attention to a myriad of small problems with perhaps inadequate attention to the problem of co-ordination of broad lines of government policy. Canada is also faced with particular difficulties in achieving co-ordination of policies because of the federal structure and the country's vulnerability to decisions of foreign governments . . . This factor indicates that the scope for manoeuverability of policy measures is likely to be more limited than

---

[9.14] Ibid., at 9.

[9.15] Ibid., at 13.

is often assumed by economists . . . Finally, there is the problem of the economic information available for a public evaluation of employment policies . . . The most promising development would appear to be a greatly expanded program of independent economic research in Canada . . . much of the divergence between theory and practice on employment policy can be expected to disappear with more economic research and, in particular, more informed and critical public discussion of national economic matters.[9.16]

1965, Economic Council of Canada, Second Annual Review. The Annual Review was expanded to cover a broader sphere of interest, much of which will have to be left unexplored. On the subject of fiscal policy, however, it repeated its previous plea for a longer time horizon, as time lags vitiated much of the effectiveness of short-term fiscal measures:

. . . it appears that the total of recognition, action, administrative and outside lags may be too great for either tax reductions or expenditure increases to be very effective in reversing recessions, considering their typical length in the post-war period . . . In the light of post-war experience, the principal discretionary instruments of stabilization policy have turned out in practice to be rather clumsy tools for flexible and timely countering of short-term cyclical instability . . . A shift in the emphasis of such policies towards the promotion of sustained annual growth appears to be required, focusing attention on actual growth in relation to potential growth. This does not mean that fiscal and monetary policies will have any less effective role to play. Indeed, the primary thrust of this conclusion is that these policies should be given wider scope to play the role which they can most effectively play, and that they should not be narrowly confined in the field of short-term cyclical stabilization where, in any event, their adaptability and usefulness has proved to be subject to important limitations, at least under post-war Canadian conditions.[9.17]

On use of the tax structure for economic purposes it stressed that

under current conditions, policies having a productivity-stimulating effect should be given increasing relative priority. To facilitate stable and sustained high levels of employment and growth, many aspects of expenditures at all levels of government, for example, should now be more carefully scrutinized in terms of their ultimate effects for promoting the growth of productive capacity and of real output and living standards . . . Elements of the present tax structure also warrant closer appraisal in similar terms.[9.18]

1966, Royal Commission on Taxation. The Commission's *Report* echoed the current dissatisfaction with fiscal policy performance.

9.16 Ibid., at 14-17.

9.17 Economic Council of Canada, *Towards Sustained and Balanced Economic Growth* Second Annual Review (Ottawa: Queen's Printer, 1965), 162-64.

9.18 Ibid., at 190.

There is no single explanation of past policy failures. Mistaken diagnosis of the underlying causes of unemployment certainly played an important part in the late 1950's and early 1960's. [Also]: Just as there is no single explanation of past failures, there is no single change that would solve all of Canada's problems. There are, however, many specific actions that could be taken to improve future performance. Although a few new instruments for stabilization purposes are available, what is mainly required is a better understanding of when and how to use existing policy tools and more boldness and steadfastness in pursuing stabilization goals.[9.19]

The Commission thereby shared the view that fiscal tools, for a variety of reasons but especially because of problems of timing, were unreliable for short-term influence. The objective should be to adopt a longer-term stance and change it only when required for longer-term objectives.

Taxation Commission Study: *Canadian Fiscal Policy Policy 1945-63*. A Commission study by Robert W. Will reviewed postwar fiscal performance in detail. On the plan for a shelf of public works projects that could be expedited or delayed to suit economic conditions as forecast in the White Paper he noted that

this experiment with a public works shelf proved to be singularly unsuccessful . . . One of the obstacles to the advanced planning of public works during this period was the critical shortage of technical staff . . . Departments, with their staffs overworked completing plans for projects included in the current year's construction programme, were unable to plan additional projects for the shelf . . . By early 1949 it was generally recognized that the public works shelf would be of dubious usefulness in the event of an economic downturn . . . the shelf was officially abandoned in December 1949 . . . virtually no advanced planning of public works projects was undertaken specifically for stabilization purposes after 1949.[9.20]

Probably a more significant contribution to capital expenditure performance was the initiation by the Department of Reconstruction and Supply of the Survey of Investment Intentions, still prepared each year and still serving as an important indicator of economic conditions in Canada.

Will examined the record of fiscal performance for the five main phases of the two decades following World War II. These were:

(1) the immediate postwar period of inflationary pressure that resulted in a 29 percent increase in consumer prices between June 1946 and December 1948; (2) the second period of postwar inflationary pressure that begain with the outbreak of the Korean War in the summer of 1950 and ended early in 1952; (3) the recession of 1953-54;

[9.19] Canada, Report of the Royal Commission on Taxation (Ottawa: Queen's Printer, 1966),

[9.20] Robert M. Will, *Canadian Fiscal Policy 1945-63*, Study for the Royal Commission on Taxation no. 17 (Ottawa: Queen's Printer, 1967), 9-10.

(4) the period from mid-1955 to the economic downturn of 1957 when upward pressures on prices were again experienced; and (5) the period from the 1957 downturn until the end of 1963, the terminal date of the study.[9.21]

In measuring changes in fiscal performance from year to year during this period Will used the concept of the "full employment surplus." Under this concept an annual calculation is made of the budgetary balance that would emerge under the given tax and expenditure measures of the year if the economy were operating at full employment (taken for this study at 96.5 percent employment of the labour force). Will's use of the concept was to identify from year to year the effect of discretionary budgetary changes. Equally interesting were the data for the differences between actual GNP for the year and the GNP that would have resulted under conditions of full employment. A table in the Appendix to the Will study showed that for the seven years 1947-1953 the economy performed beyond its potential, with minor shortfalls in 1954-1957. But from 1958 to 1963 performance was consistently below potential. This was particularly marked following the first quarter of 1960, when shortfalls were continuously in the range of 8 to 9 percent, with a peak of 10.9 percent in the first quarter of 1961. It was this gap, among other deficiencies, that accounted for the heated comment by some Canadian economists during this period.

Of performance during the 1946-49 period Will said:

It was more or less taken for granted that the pervading influence on economic conditions in the postwar period, as in the decade prior to World War II, would be deflationary.[9.22]

But in fact inflation became the main threat. The government ran surpluses but they were inadequate for the inflation being encountered.

These surpluses were sufficient to satisfy most people—the public and policymakers alike—that fiscal policy was appropriately anti-inflationary. The tendency existed to identify anti-inflationary fiscal policy with budgetary surpluses and anti-deflationary policy with deficits, and to pay little, if any, attention to the appropriate size of the surpluses or deficits needed to attain a given stabilization goal, or to the manner in which these surpluses or deficits are to be achieved. It would be accurate to say that there was a lack of appreciation on the part of all concerned of the difference between surpluses (and deficits) that are attributable to the working of the fiscal system's built-in stabilizers and those that are the direct result of the discretionary changes in tax and expenditure policy.[9.23]

The Korean Inflation. Regarding the feasibility of tax increases sufficient to counter Korean war inflation in the budget for 1951-52:

[9.21] Ibid., at 5-6.

[9.22] ibid., at 13.

[9.23] Ibid., at 22.

Tax increases of this magnitude . . . must surely be regarded as being in excess of the limit placed on annual tax increases by political considerations, especially when over half of the revenue derived from higher taxes would have been for the purpose of building up a surplus . . . [Furthermore, the government had other views]: First, the government appears to have actually believed that a pay-as-you-go fiscal policy that left the budget essentially in balance was capable of "going to the root of the inflationary problem", and secondly, the government was inhibited from raising taxes by more than it did out of fear of what higher taxes would do to incentives and the economy's ability to produce . . . what was not seen was that a sizable surplus was needed just to offset the inflationary impact of a higher level of government spending. Very high rates of taxation, it was felt, rather than curbing inflation, could actually contribute to rising prices by discouraging production and inflating costs through encouraging extravagant expenditure by businesses.[9.24]

The 1953-54 Recession:

The feeling was widespread, after nearly eight years of uninterrupted prosperity, that the inherent danger facing the postwar economy was not depression, as first thought, but inflation. The need for a flexible policy to combat depression was, accordingly, judged to be of less and less importance.[9.25]

This condition made government less alert to signs of a downturn, and the one-year (1953-54) recession came as a surprise. It demonstrated the need for up-to-date information on the economy and talent in the government to interpret that information.

1955-57 Inflation: Rising capital expenditures were countered mainly by monetary constraints. Government expenditures were kept under restrictions and tax reduction were limited. The government contended that its "modest surpluses" were contributing to lessening inflation.

1957-63: Persistent Unemployment.

The period from roughly mid-1957 to mid-1963, although encompassing three swings of the business cycle and part of a fourth, was a period of generally unsatisfactory economic performance characterized throughout by high unemployment, and during the downswing of 1957-58, by a continuation of fairly strong inflationary pressures. It was the persistence and chronic nature of unemployment between 1957 and 1963, however, that provide focus for the present discussion and give special significance to the period for the study of both the nature of economic instability and stabilization policy.

It will be argued below that had federal economic policy during the early part of this period been appropriate, a quick return to full em-

---

[9.24] Ibid., at 35-36.

[9.25] Ibid., at 45.

ployment following the 1957-58 recession might have been achieved. As events turned out, recovery from the recession was slow and incomplete . . .[9.26]

A detailed review of the period is given, but the general observation is that unemployment was the result of inadequate aggregate demand and that the government refrained from taking the necessary stimulative contra-cyclical action because its "preoccupation with inflation and its control bordered on being an obsession." Fiscal changes were designed mainly to remove structural obstacles, with emphasis on supply side improvements rather than demand stimulation. The period saw one use of a special fiscal measure during the foreign exchange crisis of 1962. Following devaluation of the Canadian dollar a 15 percent surcharge was imposed on imports to divert demand from imports to domestic production.

General Conclusions. As a result of the review of the total postwar period Will came to the general conclusion that

Federal fiscal policy contributed without question to the stability of the Canadian economy in the period 1945-63. Instability would have been greater than it was had a strict policy of balancing the budget at all times been pursued, or had the government placed sole reliance on the fiscal system's automatic stabilizers to help achieve the primary goals of full employment and price stability. Discretionary changes in fiscal policy proved to be an imperfect regulator of the economy but not so imperfect a regulator as to support the view that discretionary fiscal policy, on account of its alleged inflexibility, it likely to be on balance destabilizing rather than stabilizing. With a few exceptions such as the period of fiscal restraint of 1959-60 when economic conditions called clearly for an expansionary budgetary policy, the direction of the budget's over-all impact has been appropriate for economic stabilization, although the magnitude and exact timing of changes in impact have not always been appropriate.[9.27]

Factors that have militated against more effective policy had been:

First, was the tendency on the part of policymakers and the public to view countercyclical fiscal policy in terms of budgetary surpluses and deficits rather than in terms of the discretionary changes in fiscal policy, e.g., tax changes and changes in government spending, needed to achieve economic stability . . . [T]his habit of associating budgetary surpluses with an anti-inflationary fiscal policy and deficits with the opposite type of policy stood in the way of a more vigorous anti-inflationary policy during the 1955-57 inflation . . .

Secondly, political considerations placed real limitations on use of the budget for economic stabilization, and would have made pursuit of a more vigorous countercyclical policy difficult even had the

---

[9.26] Ibid., at 61.

[9.27] Ibid., at 90.

authorities perceived the need for it. Fiscal policy, of necessity, had to be geared to political reality, and for this reason was almost always a compromise between what policymakers would have liked it to be and the dictates of practical politics. The public's acceptance of the principle of countercyclical budgeting was severely qualified by its refusal to accept tax increases at a time when the budget was already in surplus, and also by the warnings of a small but influential minority who believed that deficit financing spelled fiscal irresponsibility and inflation . . .

A third factor impairing the efficiency of countercyclical fiscal policy was a lack of budgetary flexibility . . . Variations in government spending, whether on public works or not, is likely to remain a fairly inflexible weapon of countercyclical control, better suited to determining the broad impact of budgetary policy than to atuning the budget's impact to changes in the short-term economic outlook. The contribution that expenditure control can make to economic stability appears to be greatest during periods of inflationary pressure when increases in government capital spending can be kept to a minimum . . .

Lastly, fiscal policy as an arm of stabilization policy could have been improved with improvements in economic forecasting and analysis of the current economic situation.[9.28]

While the Will study was a landmark document as a detailed postwar review, it failed to carry full weight with the Commissioners, who in their report showed markedly less enthusiasm than Will for discretionary fiscal manoeuvres. The Will approach was adopted by the authors of a study of more recent fiscal policy done for the Macdonald Royal Commission.[9.29]

1966. Economic Council of Canada, Third Annual Review. The Council had been requested by the federal government "to launch a broad examination into prices, costs, incomes, and productivity, and their relationship to sustained economic growth." The Council saw as the objective of this reference, "not merely how to get reasonable stability in the cost of living and the general level of prices in Canada, but how to do so within a framework of other important economic goals." In reviewing experience to that time it said:

The most pervasive and recurrent goal-conflict of modern industrial economies has proved to be that between full employment and reasonable stability of prices . . . while the average Canadian and U.S. price performance through much of the 1950's and the early 1960's was better than that of most countries and was widely commended for this

---

[9.28] Ibid., at 90-92.

[9.29] Douglas D. Purvis and Constance Smith, "Fiscal Policy in Canada: 1963-84," in John Sargent, research coordinator, *Fiscal and Monetary Policy*, Collected Research Studies of the Royal Commission on the Economic Union and Development Prospects for Canada, vol. 26 (Toronto: University of Toronto Press, 1986), 1-41, at 37.

reason, a good deal of it occurred in a context of slow growth and high unemployment . . . there has been a growing appreciation of the importance of total supply and demand within economies, and the role of the "big levers" of fiscal and monetary policy in affecting these aggregates . . . Regardless of the nature or size of the problems being experienced by the Canadian economy, they must always be related to what is happening to total supply and demand, and the setting of the main policy levers. Thus, the correct management of the supply of money in relation to the over-all state of the economy is at all times a matter of central importance. There is no substitute for it, and it remains *par excellence* the classic defence against severe inflation. Similarly, there is no substitute for broad fiscal policy, defined as the management of total government revenues and expenditures with a view to influencing aggregate demand in the economy. There are no other policies which can take the place of a well co-ordinated use of these two instruments; their proper setting is always of basic significance. We shall, in due course, be advocating certain *complementary* policies, but these are to be seen as allies and auxiliaries rather than as substitutes.[9.30]

On the specific problem of reconciling high employment with reasonable price stability, which has been common to many countries, the question is why has use of these two main instruments not been effective?

Particularly in the early post-war period, and again at the onset of the Korean War, when relatively severe outbreaks of inflation took place, the big levers were not generally used with all the vigour that the situation warranted. Subsequently, too, there have been cases of inadequate response by monetary and fiscal policy to seriously overstrained economies—cases where a more stringent restraint of demand growth would have produced better price performance without any important sacrifice of employment and growth goals. [On the other hand], it seems clear that monetary and fiscal management cannot reasonably be asked to shoulder the whole blame. Some quite considerable price increases have occurred in economies which were running well below full employment and growing potential output. A problem of conflict between policy objectives has unmistakenly emerged.[9.31]

The Council's prescriptions for "maintaining reasonable price stability at high levels of employment" ran to 12 parts; the following are the most relevant for present purposes.

(2) A first and indispensable part of an effective programme to meet the problem is a well co-ordinated and otherwise appropriate use of the broader instruments of economic policy, including fiscal and monetary policy, exchange rate policy, and commercial policy. If

---

[9.30] Economic Council of Canada, *Prices, Productivity and Employment* Third Annual Review (Ottawa: Queen's Printer, 1966), 35-37.

[9.31] Ibid., at 37.

these policies are not being properly operated there is little that other policies can do to bring about a better reconciliation of price and employment goals . . .

(3) To achieve a more satisfactory reconciliation of economic goals, the main policy "levers" must be complemented by policies whose primary focus is the *supply* rather than the *demand* side of the economy . . .

(7) Programmes for productivity improvement and adequate measures for dealing with the manpower problems arising from technological and other change should be pressed ahead with all possible speed . . .

(10) Much more basic economic research needs to be done on problems relating to prices, costs, incomes and productivity in the Canadian economy.[9.32]

It is apparent that the Council had retained much of the immediate postwar faith in the major policies and the "big levers," but was also willing to propose almost anything that had a chance of success. However, it rejected income policies: "A formal incomes policy would not be an effective way of meeting the problem in Canada, except possibly under rare emergency conditions and then only on a temporary basis."

1967, Economic Council of Canada, Fourth Annual Review. The Council continued to express its reservations on the government's use of monetary and fiscal policies for short-term stabilization (a reservation which it will be recalled brought a sharp difference of view from the then current Minister of Finance). The Council said:

If monetary and fiscal policies are aimed primarily at moderating shorter-term fluctuations in the Canadian economy rather than, as we have suggested, at sustaining stable longer-term growth of final demand, there is a serious danger that policy adjustments may overdo the needed corrections or have highly uneven, belated or untimely impacts. In other words, policies designed largely by way of reaction to emerging short-term instabilities may well contribute to an unfortunate "stop-go" pattern of development, and may even accentuate the instabilities . . . it appears on various occasions in the past, the major impact of fiscal and monetary policy changes on output and demand was experienced after the results of such changes were no longer appropriate. [Over the next few years] a very large rise in total demand must take place in the Canadian economy . . . Economic policies must assure that such an expansion of demand can be realized . . . In the absence of international instabilities . . . the underlying concerns of monetary and fiscal policy . . . should be these:

(1) to facilitate a monetary expansion that avoids sudden and large surges of new money creation; and

---

9.32 Ibid., at 190-93.

(2) to prevent the increase in over-all government expenditures from outpacing the revenue gains (at whatever tax levels are considered to be appropriate) that can be realized when the economy is expanding at its potential rate of growth.[9.33]

The Council retained its objective for a 97 percent employment rate, but now moved its target date forward to the mid-1970s. The Council's many proposals for action on the supply side may have had more influence than the above recommendations. They included

measures for promoting greater efficiency, competition, manpower mobility, training and education, and more ready adjustments to technological and other change; intensified efforts to develop and apply new technology; effective means and incentives to stimulate industrial research and development, including research into the specific factors affecting the productivity of the individual firm.[9.34]

For direct budget policy, concern was expressed that

the accelerated increase in government spending in 1966 and 1967 is outpacing the growth of government revenues at existing tax levels . . . These developments have led to a growing uneasiness in Canada about the current pace of the over-all advance in government spending. [This resulted in some greater attention to economy in government]. However, this has not been matched by comparable advances in the development of procedures and machinery for dealing with much larger questions: for *consistent and comprehensive determination of objectives and priorities; for continuing evaluation of the impact and effectiveness of the growing range and diversity of government programmes in relation to their cost*; and *for increased coordination between governments in relation to these matters.*[9.35]

1969, Economic Council of Canada, Sixth Annual Review. This review set objectives for 1975. As for the goal of 97 percent employment by the mid-seventies it said:

We believe that this goal, having regard to the various aspects mentioned above, is still valid. This is not, of course, an ultimate goal, satisfactory for all time to come. We continue to hope that with sustained improvement in our economic performance, an even better employment performance may ultimately be a realistic aim. [The hopes that were possible in the late sixties! The price stability goal was to keep the] average rates of change in prices and costs over the medium-term future within the limits of the movements over the decade 1953 to 1963 . . . To put it another way, we believe that a satisfactory price performance would involve reducing the rates of increase in the

---

9.33 Economic Council of Canada, *The Canadian Economy from the 1960's to the 1970's* Fourth Annual Review (Ottawa: Queen's Printer, 1967), 256-57.

9.34 Ibid., at 258.

9.35 Ibid., at 261.

general price indexes as soon as possible to less than 2 percent per year . . .[9.36]

(Again-what hopes!). The Council renewed its faith in the big levers, but asserted that a good deal more was needed for economic growth, the increasing concern of the period.

During the past year, considerable controversy has arisen in North America about the influence and effectiveness of monetary and fiscal policies as instruments of demand management. We have no doubts about the ultimate power and effectiveness of these policies when properly used. At the same time, we believe strongly that they are necessary, *but by themselves insufficient*, for achieving and maintaining high standards of performance in our economy.[9.37]

And again the Council emphasized its view that the "proper" use of monetary and fiscal measures was for longer term objectives.

1979, W.I. Gillespie. This is probably as good a place as any to introduce an appraisal by Professor Irwin Gillespie of the stabilization effects of all budgets introduced in the period 1945-75. In this he calls on the score-keeping of Professors Gordon and Will, already reviewed, Professor Auld, not yet mentioned, The Economic Council of Canada, and his own evaluations. The results were as follows:

Gordon (1945-63). Fiscal policy was adequate four years, inadequate seven years and perverse eight years.

Will (1945-63). Fiscal policy was adequate six years, inadequate five years, perverse seven years, and ambiguous one year.

Auld (1957-62 and 1965-67). Fiscal policy was adequate one year, inadequate five years, and perverse three years.

Economic Council (1965-73). Fiscal policy was adequate three years, inadequate in four years, and perverse in two years.

Gillespie (1960-75). Perverse in one year, inadequate in thirteen, and ambiguous in one.

Gillespie's reflections on this performance were:

While it is clear from the foregoing critical assessment that contracyclical economic budgeting failed, it is less obvious why it failed so persistently. It is unlikely that contracyclical economic budgeting failed owing to . . . a lack of flexibility in the timing of budgets . . . It is unlikely that the failure occurred because of errors and inadequacies in analysis of the current economic environment and forecasting of the immediate future . . . it is unlikely that the failure occurred because of low tax and/or expenditure multipliers or the lag in fiscal

---

[9.36] Economic Council of Canada, *Perspective 1975* Sixth Annual Review (Ottawa: Queen's Printer, 1969), 7-8.

[9.37] Ibid., at 159-60.

policy . . . it is also unlikely that the limited scope for federal discretionary changes on the expenditure side of the budget, or the decreasing relative share of federal spending among all three levels of government could have seriously impaired a federal government's determined attempt to carry out a vigorous contracyclical stabilization policy.[9.38]

Gillespie concludes that the federal government failed because it was not really trying:

Stabilization policy failed because the goal of stabilization of incomes has not been the sole goal, or even the most important among several goals, or (possibly) even *one* of the goals which the federal government has actively attempted to achieve. [He gives a hint of his own view of the problem as follows]: If the federal government responds to these voter concerns, the room to manoeuvre away from a balanced budget would be limited to a range that is trivial in terms of contracyclical stabilization policy. A policy instrument which can be used when recessions and inflations are minor but cannot be utilized when recessions and inflationary periods are major is not going to score high on a measure of fiscal performance for stabilization purposes.[9.39]

He was working on a model that would explain federal government budgetary behaviour, presumably based on his views of the forces that motivated politicians.

[9.38] W. Irwin Gillespie, "Postwar Canadian Fiscal Policy Revisited, 1945-1975" (May-June 1979), 26 *Canadian Tax Journal* 265-76, at 274-75.

[9.39] Ibid., at 275-76.

Table 9.1 Evaluations of Federal Fiscal Policy Performance: Summary of Results, 1945-1975

Evaluation study:	Royal Commission on Taxation	Will	Gordon	Auld	Economic Council of Canada	Gillespie	Curtis and Kitchen
Years examined:	(1954-63)	(1945-63)	(1957-67)	(1965-74)	(1960-75)	(1953-71)	
	(number of years)						
Adequate	2	6	4	1	3	0	7
Inadequate	5	5	7	5	4	13	4
Perverse	3	7	8	3	2	1	8
Ambiguous	—	1	—	—	—	1	—
Total observations	10	19	19	9	9	15	19
	(percentage of observations)						
Adequate	20	31	21	11	33	0	37
Inadequate	50	26	36	56	45	86	21
Perverse	30	36	42	33	22	7	42
Ambiguous	—	7	—	—	—	7	—
Total	100	100	100	100	100	100	100

Source: W.I. Gillespie, "Postwar Canadian Fiscal Policy Revisited 1945-1975" (May-June 1979), 27 *Canadian Tax Journal*, 266.

10
Policy Challenges for the Seventies and Eighties

As the sixties closed inflation, unfortunately an inescapable and repetitious subject in this book, gathered momentum and became the centre of concern. The government was forced to apply stronger measures than any before used in peacetime, primarily through the budget but also by direct means of influence. In the early part of the decade prices had been relatively stable by most measures. Until 1965 the annual increase in consumer prices had been less than 2 percent. However in that year the index moved up to 2.4 percent, and rose to 4.5 percent in 1969, an increase of 150 percent. In 1970 the rate declined to 3.3 percent and in 1971 to 2.9 percent. This was a temporary relief, however, and the subsequent inflation is still familiar to most people—11 per cent in 1975, 8-9 percent in 1977-79, 10 percent in 1980, 12.5 percent in 1981, and 11 percent in 1982. We have described elsewhere the drastic measures that eventually brought the inflation rate to its current 4 percent level; for the present we will review briefly the record of the late sixties and early seventies, a period that was essentially a prelude to more drastic experience to come.

Concern with Mounting Inflation

As we have seen, through its budget policy the government began an anti-inflationary "austerity" program in November 1967, with heavy tax increases, and followed this with another round of heavy increases in the 1968 budget. These were accompanied by expenditure controls and staff reductions. The results were eventually to produce the first budgetary surplus in many years in fiscal 1971. However, in the meantime prices had continued to rise, and the government reluctantly decided that further more direct forms of persuasion were required.

1969-72: The Prices and Incomes Commission

In 1969 he federal government appointed a Commission "to inquire into and report upon the causes, processes and consequences of inflation and to inform those making current price and income decisions, the general public and the Government on how price stability may best be achieved." The government itself had issued a preparatory White Paper in 1968 on Policies for Price Stability, in which it concluded that "stagflation" was beyond the reach of the normal fiscal and economic instruments.

The Commission strove for three years to achieve a degree of agreement on a price and restraint program through meetings, consultations, studies, a National Conference on Price Stability, and the launch of a six percent wage and salary target. The Commission had no power to set prices or ceilings, and as its influence was entirely persuasive it was a rather thankless task, although during the life of the Commission the rate of inflation did decline temporarily. However, this was probably attributable as much to the harsh mauling the ministers of finance had given the economy in their 1967-69 budgets, and which was achieved at the cost of an increase in unemployment from 4.4 percent in 1969 to 6.2 percent in 1971.

The Commission's Views

The following extracts from the Summary of its Report give the Commission's principal conclusions:

> The main factor which initiated the relatively rapid inflation of prices and costs in Canada in the mid-1960s was a build-up of unusually strong demand pressure on the economy's productive capacity and manpower resources . . . much of the demand stimulus resulted from the re-pegging of the Canadian dollar exchange rate in 1962 at a substantially reduced level, and from expansionary fiscal and monetary policies in Canada. In modern societies national governments are responsible for the overall management of the economy. In this sense, if an overshoot of demand is allowed to occur, the responsibility must lie with the government . . . It was not until 1970 that demand pressure clearly ceased to be a factor in the more buoyant regions of the country and unemployment rose to relatively high levels . . . In our view, the degree to which inflation has persisted under recent conditions of slack demand pressure and abnormally high unemployment can be explained largely in terms of lags in the response of costs and prices to short-run changes in demand, together with the existence of strongly held "inflationary expectations" formed on the basis of experience during the prolonged inflationary expansion of the 1960s . . . In effect an "inflation factor" appears to be incorporated, implicitly if not explicitly, in the setting of wages and prices and in the level of interest rates.[10.1]

Alternatives for the future included living with a substantial degree of inflation as the price for lower unemployment and/or relying on other policies, such as manpower, regional economic expansion, selective demand, tariff and competition policy. The former is rejected on the grounds that it "cannot be counted on to enable the Canadian economy to operate . . . at average rates of national unemployment much lower than those experienced since the mid-1950s." The latter programs may work in some limited conditions, but are not sufficient to cope with a large-scale national problem.

If we reject more rapid inflation as only a temporary postponement of our difficulties and recognize that supply and selective demand

---

[10.1] Canada, Prices and Incomes Commission, *Summary Report: Inflation, Unemployment and Incomes Policy* (Ottawa: Information Canada, 1972), 2-3.

policies have considerable limitations, we are left with two policy instruments for dealing with the problem, general demand management and incomes policy. Demand management must play a central role, but can it do the job alone? A case can be made that if the growth of demand could be kept sufficiently steady, this would go a long way toward meeting the problem. This is more easily said than done. There are many sources of economic instability and there are serious difficulties both of a technical and political nature which make it unlikely that periodic undershoots or overshoots of demand can be avoided . . . In conjunction with policies aimed at creating and maintaining a more stable demand environment, temporary resort to controls offers a means of bringing cost and price increases more promptly and reliably into line with the change in demand conditions . . . It may be that before long the march of events will bring Canadians to the view that serious consideration should be given to a temporary program of controls.[10.2]

This was either a self-fulfilling prophesy or the Commission was gifted with rare visionary powers; in another four years the government had resorted to a stronger control program through the Anti-Inflation Board.

1971: Report of the Senate Committee on National Finance on Growth, Employment and Price Stability

Standing committees, when authorized by the Senate, have frequently conducted extremely interesting inquiries. This happened to be one of the most productive in the area of economic policy. Witnesses representing some of the most enlightened economic thought of the day were summoned before it. The papers it received were directed to the crucial theme of "methods by which fiscal and monetary policy in Canada may be exercised to achieve full potential growth and employment without inflation." It would be fascinating to explore these in detail, but we must settle for the following brief summary of the Committee's recommendations in its report:

General:

Even though the Canadian economy is very open to the influences of the world economy there is still significant room for the purposeful management of national economic stabilization policies in Canada . . . There is no simple solution to the problem of economic management, but government does possess powerful policy tools for stabilizing the growth of the economy and important improvements can be made in the use of these tools . . . While new forces are obviously at work in our society, the main problems of economic stabilization are still economic in nature . . .[10.3]

10.2 Ibid., at 7.

10.3 Canada, Standing Senate Committee on National Finance, *Report on Growth, Employment and Price Stability* (Ottawa: Information Canada, 1971), ix-x.

On levers:

> The three big levers of monetary, fiscal and exchange rate policies remain central and indispensable in stabilizing the Canadian economy . . . Co-ordination of fiscal and monetary policies and close cooperation between the Department of Finance and the Bank of Canada in the exercise of these policies are essential.[10.4]

On fiscal policy:

> The use of fiscal policy should lean more to adjustments in taxes than adjustments in government expenditures. Despite "tax shifting", (the treating of taxes as transferable costs) tax changes remain a highly effective means of stabilizing the economy . . . In containing a boom, increases in direct taxes (income taxes, etc.) are more effective than increases of indirect taxes (sales taxes, etc.). But in stimulating a weak economy that is still suffering from lagged price increases, decreases of indirect taxes are more effective than decreases of direct taxes. Account should be taken of this in deciding which particular taxes to change for stabilization purposes . . . As a broad but valuable discipline and protection for sound fiscal policy the Federal Government should adopt the concept of high-employment budgeting, at least to the extent of always estimating in budget presentations what the budgetary position would be at high employment and of analyzing reasons for changes in the estimated figures since the previous presentation.[10.5]

On lags:

> Recognition of these time lags is of fundamental importance in the successful operation of monetary, fiscal and exchange rate policies . . . Lags make nonsense out of attempts to "fine-tune" the economy with these blunt instruments . . . Recent research indicates that these lags are even longer and more variable than was previously thought. Canadian economic policy has not taken adequate account of lags, nor are the existence and significance of lags sufficiently known to Parliament and the general public.[10.6]

On trade-offs:

> Although our goal must be full employment, effective policy making in the context of a trade-off problem requires the setting of realistic interim operational goals for the Canadian economy. The Federal Government should commit itself to moving the economy, over some reasonable time period, from the present position where unemployment is in the neighbourhood of 6% to 7% of the labour force (seasonally adjusted) to a position where unemployment is no more than a range of 4% to 4½% of the labour force.[10.7]

[10.4] Ibid., at x.

[10.5] Ibid., at x-xii.

[10.6] Ibid., at xi.

[10.7] Ibid., at xiii.

On incomes policies:

> . . . we are in general deeply skeptical about most varieties of controls, guidelines and income policies. Their historical record of effectiveness against inflation is poor, and they pose important threats to personal freedom and economic dynamism. They also tend to divert attention from more effective anti-inflationary policies . . . no substantial or long-term reliance should be placed on such a policy.[10.8]

On supplementary measures:

> The three big levers of monetary, fiscal and exchange rate policies primarily focus on the demand side of the economy. They must be complemented by supply and structural policies (such as manpower and competition policies) which encourage growth in the supply of goods and services and which channel resources into their best use. Since these policies act to improve trade-off over the longer term, they should receive heavy emphasis in our economic stabilization strategy.[10.9] [Finally:] We believe that a new openness should be brought to the process of economic policy making in Canada. This means that the direction of important government policies and the impact they have on the Canadian economy should be systematically estimated before and after the event. It means too that Parliament and the public should be told more about these policy evaluations and about the processes of economic decision-making.[10.10]

Reuber and Bodkin

Although many briefs to the Comittee could be quoted we will refer only to one, that of Professors Reuber and Bodkin. In reviewing monetary and fiscal policy of the 1960s a later edited and published version of this brief had the following to say:

> Over the period 1963 to 1968, the federal government can scarcely be said to have followed very active monetary and fiscal policies to combat inflation . . . On the fiscal side, a surplus of $625 million gradually became a deficit of $256 million in 1967 and $165 million in 1968. A substantial surplus in 1969 was followed in 1970 by a small deficit . . .
>
> Turning to money supply, one finds not only a very rapid increase during the period since 1965 but also wide fluctuations in the rate of increase, ranging from over 20 per cent per year in mid-1968 to a net reduction in the third quarter of 1969. During the period of rapidly rising prices from 1965 to 1969, the money supply increased almost 55 per cent compared with a 19 per cent increase in real output. Thus $2.87 of new money was created per $1.00 of additional real output.

[10.8] Ibid., at xiv.

[10.9] Ibid.

[10.10] Ibid., at xvi.

In 1969 the increase in money supply matched the increase in real output, but in 1970—when inflation had been a major preoccupation—the rate of change in the money supply again accelerated (10.0 versus 5.6 per cent).

From 1969 to 1971, as the unemployment rate rose from about 4.5 per cent to almost 7 per cent, both monetary and fiscal policy were much tighter than from 1965 to 1968, when unemployment was generally below 5 per cent.

This picture scarcely conforms with prevailing conventional notions of appropriate monetary and fiscal policy. During much of this period one might have expected changes in the money supply at least not to exceed significantly the changes in real output. And, on the fiscal side, one would have expected to find large and growing federal surpluses deliberately designed to reduce inflationary pressure. Thus, the indictment of conventional monetary and fiscal policy can hardly be that it was tried but didn't work. Indeed, during much of this period these conventional levers appear to have been moved in the wrong direction; and to the extent they were effective, the policies followed tended to enhance the upward pressures on prices rather than decrease them. [The reasons for this result were several]: In part, it reflected political pressures, in part a series of events beyond the control of the authorities, and in part inadequate analysis and understanding, within government as well as without, of the unfolding economic scene and the degree to which policies being followed were inconsistent with the requirements of stabilization policy.[10.11]

1971: Province of Ontario

Through its Department of Treasury and Economics the Province of Ontario was taking a more active role in national economic policy discussions. In November 1971, the current Minister presented a paper to a meeting of Ministers of Finance on the Reconstruction of Economic and Fiscal Policy in Canada. The tone of this paper reflected the enormous advantage a provincial government enjoys in the greater certainty it can bring to a much narrower range of objectives than the national government—which is always attempting to bring some order out of dozens of issues, including the interests of ten almost sovereign provincial governments. On fiscal policy it said:

In the past two years, the federal government's fiscal policy has swung dramatically from fiscal and monetary constraint to belated expansion. It has introduced broad new measures of regional differentiation, and implemented programs to modify seasonal unemployment. Unfortunately, in terms of results, these federal policies have failed. We have high levels of unemployment, continuing inflation, and an

[10.11] Grant L. Reuber, *Canada's Political Economy, Current Issues* (Toronto: McGraw-Hill Ryerson Limited, 1980), 260-61.

external value for our dollar that prevents the maximum penetration of foreign markets. Throughout this period of volatile economic policy, the Ontario government has stated repeatedly that fiscal policy has been "handed down" to the provinces rather than developed in a harmonized manner through these meetings.

We warned in early 1970 about excessive federal tax drag in Ontario, but the federal government was apparently not prepared to listen. It persisted with the view that inflation was to be cured by slowing down the growth of new job opportunities in Ontario and other high-growth regions. That policy failed and had to be abandoned. Similarly, we warned the federal government at the end of 1970 that the business community was in a cash-flow squeeze and that action would be required to head off a decline in private investment in production facilities. Events proved this judgment to be correct, but it was not until October of this year that substantive fiscal actions were taken by the federal government to use its tax flexibility to shore up the business and consumer sectors . . . Because of the deficiencies in the performance of federal fiscal policies, the Ontario Government was obliged to assume a major role in reinforcing the Ontario economy . . .

Considering the scale of the fiscal and monetary resources available to the federal government, the Ontario Government's independent actions in economic stabilization policy in 1971-72 are comparatively and significantly larger than those of the federal budgets of June and October 1971.

It is quite appropriate that provincial governments play an active role in stabilization policies in co-operation with the federal government. However, in this instance, Ontario was obliged to implement expansionary economic policies to offset the effects of contractionary federal fiscal policies which we opposed and had no part in designing. This dramatically underscores our main point, concerning the absence of fiscal policy co-ordination in Canada.[10.12]

The provinces also had objections to the sporadic nature of and delays in employment programs in which they were expected to play a leading role. To cope with these and other problems the province had four proposals:

First, we need to define more carefully the appropriate intergovernmental division of responsibilities in stabilization policy . . . Second . . . we urge the federal government to take immediate action to improve the quality and scope of both the labour force survey and the investment survey . . . Third . . . we need more rigorous estimates of the revenue-generating capacity of the federal tax system at different levels of economic activity . . . Finally . . . the First Ministers should

---

[10.12] Ontario, Department of Treasury and Economics, *The Reconstruction of Economic and Fiscal Policy in Canada*. Statement to the Meeting of the Ministers of Finance, Ottawa, November 1-2, 1971. (Toronto: the Department, 1971), 4-7.

form a national Joint Economic Committee composed of the Ministers of Finance as their representatives. We envision that our terms of
reference should require us to set short- and long-term economic and
social goals, and to examine regularly our progress in realizing these
goals.[10.13]

C.D. Howe Research Institute

In 1974 a new voice began to be heard in the policy debate—HRI, the C.D.
Howe Research Institute. Although its constituents had periodically issued
many studies on economic matters, in 1974 the Institute began to publish an
Annual Policy Review and Outlook, from which the following quotations
have been taken. Although HRI had business, labour, academic, and
professional members on its Board these statements were issued as staff
papers without endorsement.

1974: In many respects the key to fighting both inflation and
unemployment in Canada (and a basic factor in Canada's contribution to the international effort to curb inflation) will be to ensure that
new investment in industrial capacity takes place to the extent required
to meet future consumption requirements. In other words, Canada
must mobilize a program to increase the share of current output going
into capital formation.[10.14]

1975: Cost push inflation cannot be treated effectively by manoeu-
vering fiscal and monetary policies. *Government, business, and
labour should therefore jointly participate in a program of cooperative restraint for one year or perhaps two.* This program would
require a major but temporary market intervention in order to override the misleading incentives being created by inflation. It would
involve a combination of indexing and price and wage restraints.
*Governments should provide the underpinning for this program by
introducing spending cuts to ease supply bottlenecks and tax reductions to protect the purchasing power of each sector of society.
Business and labour should provide the basic fabric of the program:
Labour should agree to forego increases in real incomes, and business
should agree to raise selling prices only to cover increases in operating
costs* . . . Although specific spending and tax reductions are required
. . . this is not a time for a dramatic shift in the big policy levers of
fiscal and monetary policies . . . *governments should use tax reductions rather than spending increases to stimulate demand and should
bias their policies towards reductions in spending when they are trying
to restrain demand . . . Governments should . . . consider tax and
other incentives that will support saving and stimulate investment.*[10.15]

10.13 Ibid., at 10-12.

10.14 Judith Maxwell and Carl Beigie, *Policy Review and Outlook, 1974: The Disappearance
of the Status Quo* (Montreal: C.D. Howe Research Institute, 1974), 91.

10.15 Judith Maxwell, ed., *Policy Review and Outlook, 1975: Restructuring the Incentive
System* (Montreal: C.D. Howe Research Institute, 1975), 155-56.

It is interesting that this Review contained the suggestion for five-year budget forecasts, since adopted by the federal and some of the provincial governments.

1976: There are no simple, easy ways out of the current situation. The economy is seriously out of balance, and many of the built-in stabilizing forces have been disrupted by double-digit inflation and by the deterioration in the sense of common purpose that makes our economic process work . . . The sources of imbalances are diverse. Some are *international,* such as the abrupt shift in oil prices; some are *institutional,* such as the sudden introduction of collective bargaining into the public service . . . some are *cumulative,* such as the build-up in government spending that has taken place . . . some are the results of *inflation* itself, such as the distortions to investment decisions . . . some are *political,* such as the loss of confidence in the ability of governments to act in the national interest . . . The first priority must be to abandon the search for a culprit and to alter the tone of the public debate . . . The second priority must be to make the price and income controls work fairly . . . The third priority must be to ensure that economic growth proceeds at a pace somewhat higher than the long-term potential of the economy . . . the country should not settle for less than a 5 to 5½ per cent increase in real GNP in 1976 . . . Work should begin on a long-range plan to control the growth in spending at both the federal and provincial levels of government . . . the size of the federal and provincial deficits must be constrained so that they do not create stresses in the capital market that would divert the Bank of Canada from its announced objective of pursuing a gradual reduction in the growth in the money supply . . . 1976 will not be the year that the solutions will emerge, but we hope it will be the year when the problems are attacked.[10.16]

1977: The stabilization questions plaguing Canada are common to all industrial countries, for the combination of inflation and unemployment in recent years has challenged the social and political fabric of a number of democracies. Even the United States, which appears to have shed the excesses of the mid-1970s with some success, is still grappling with the problem of setting economic policies that can deal simultaneously with inflation and unemployment. Economic experts in nearly all the industrial countries are therefore attempting to adapt the well-established tools of monetary and fiscal policies to a turbulent period of economic history. It was the economic predicament of the 1930s that inspired the Keynesian revolution in economic thinking, and the current period certainly presents an opportunity for another breakthrough in the policy applications of economic theory. In the meantime, there is no reason why Canada should expect to sort out these problems on its own, and there are good reasons to expect

---

[10.16] Judith Maxwell, *Policy Review and Outlook, 1976: Challenges to Complacency* (Montreal: C.D. Howe Research Institute, 1976), 165-68.

that Canadians can learn a lot from the experience of other countries over the next few years.[10.17] [For Canada the] government can no longer be preoccupied solely with inflation. The emphasis must be on two targets—employment (which means growth and productivity, as well) and inflation. The key will be to introduce packages of policy measures that will optimize the country's performance on growth and price stability. The general direction for policy in the next year will be to stimulate economic growth as a means of achieving progress on both fronts—unemployment and inflation . . .

The transition from controls [AIB] would be eased if the federal and provincial governments introduced a tax reduction as soon as budgets can be prepared. The most effective tax change would be a reduction in the provincial retail sales tax . . . Since the federal government has the responsibility for stabilizing the economy, it should consider reimbursing the provinces for revenues lost as a result of the tax cut . . . [This step incidentally was taken, as earlier recounted]. The federal government should also consider tax concessions to business as part of a fiscal package, in order to speed up the timing of the response to better market prospects . . . There should continue to be strict control on the growth of government spending; thus the stimulus to economic growth should come from tax reductions rather than from spending increases . . . The combination of tax reductions and spending controls will mean another large deficit in the government sector in 1977-78. Such a deficit is not only appropriate but necessary at this time because the economy needs stimulus in order to restore a rate of economic growth that will generate productivity gains, more employment, and a better profit performance.[10.18]

1978: The chief weakness in the current policy of gradual reduction in inflation through restraints on fiscal and monetary policies is that prices and wages respond only a little to gradualism while production and employment respond a lot. As a result, Canada has made significant progress in curbing the rise in prices and costs since 1975, but it has done so at the cost of both high unemployment and rates of economic growth well below the long-term average . . . In the past couple of years, federal and provincial budgets have consistently overestimated the growth momentum of the economy and have therefore failed to inject the proper stimulus to keep the recovery going . . . The target for macro-economic policy should be to sustain economic growth at a rate above 4½ per cent, on the grounds that further slack in the economy is unlikely to reduce inflation and will add seriously to unemployment . . . To achieve this target the combined effect of monetary and fiscal policies should be moderately stimulative . . . The appropriate form of fiscal stimulus should be permanent tax reduc-

---

10.17 Judith Maxwell, *Policy Review and Outlook, 1977: An Agenda for Change* (Montreal: C.D. Howe Research Institute, 1977), 113-14.

10.18 Ibid., at 117-19.

tions . . . The tax reductions should be focused on sales taxes . . . Structural policies to supplement these macro policies should be designed to promote efficiency and to work through a system of incentives.[10.19]

1979: If one were to survey leaders in the private and public sectors as to their worry about Canadian policy, they would probably mention either the size of the federal deficit or the slide in the value of the Canadian dollar. In both cases their concern reflects a sense that "things are out of control" and that some crisis was on the horizon. Unfortunately, the public debate on these "big worries" has failed to focus on the most important aspects of the problem . . . Indexing of the personal income tax now accounts for an accumulated revenue loss of $6 billion a year, equal to one-half of the 1978-79 borrowing requirement. Other permanent tax cuts in the past three years amount to another $3 billion . . . The concern expressed by many Canadians about the federal deficit is misplaced. The problem is not the present size of the deficit in relation to that of the United States or to the gross national product, but the ability of the federal government to eliminate that deficit when and as the credit needs of the private sector begin to grow during an economic recovery . . . The indexing of the personal income tax, combined with the uncontrollable increases in many expenditure programs, mean that, during a period of weak economic activity, deficits tend to mount and to endure for an extended period of time. Nevertheless, the federal government, in particular, tends to introduce "busy" budgets which implement a wide range of tax reductions and other concessions that reduce revenue growth. One is left with the feeling that . . . the deliberate increases in the federal deficit . . . do not reflect . . . a sufficient respect for the challenge that will arise in reducing the deficit in the 1980s. [It was only about this time that the prospects for the deficit began to register with organizations that had hitherto shown little concern for it].

The decline in the Canadian dollar in 1977 and 1978 was a delayed reaction to the problems that emerged in the mid-1970s . . . Such a depreciation, properly handled, can provide the basis for stronger economic growth in the 1980s, provided that the immediate increases in costs are absorbed by those buying imported goods . . . the response to the depreciation to date suggests that Canada has been handling the adjustment problem in a way that will help to build a competitive industrial base for the future . . .

On fiscal policy, the present size of the deficit and its tendency to increase in response to rising prices (which add to the cost of indexed programs) and to sluggish growth (which reduces revenue growth) give the federal government little room to stimulate economic activity. The purpose of the strategy of gradualism and the restraint on expenditure

[10.19] Judith Maxwell, ed., *Policy Review and Outlook, 1978: A Time for Realism* (Montreal: C.D. Howe Research Institute, 1978), 155-56.

growth has been to give the federal government greater flexibility in controlling the size of the deficit. However, three years of expenditure restraint have not provided Cabinet with clear managerial control over the federal expenditure process, despite internal political struggles that have taken place. The effort to gain control over expenditures must be sustained.[10.20]

1980: In the prospects for the 1980s there were serious problems. These problems, in summary, were:

A federal deficit that will persist and grow worse . . . A deficit in international transactions in goods and services that is being financed only through major additions to international indebtedness . . . An oil-pricing structure that is out of line with the costs of developing new supplies . . . The fact that Canada's productivity performance . . . has slipped in comparison with earlier years. [As a result of these developments] an increasing number of Canadians are beginning to realize that they have entered a period that calls for toughness in dealing with economic problems . . . The legacy for the late 1980s and beyond can be considerably improved if energy prices are increased to reflect current domestic replacement costs, if taxpayers begin to finance a greater portion of the federal government's current outlays, and if firms and individuals increase their investment in competitive new production facilities. [Achievement of these objectives would be complicated by several adverse conditions]: First, borrowing from the future has created major internal imbalances that limit the policy options from which Canada can choose. Structural imbalances in federal finances and in international payments mean that many types of stimulative policies will yield perverse results. Most efforts to stimulate growth tend to encourage imports and thus to augment the current-account deficit; this weakens the Canadian dollar, which in turn aggravates inflation. Stimulus also increases the fiscal deficit, which undermines confidence in the capital and foreign exchange markets. Lack of confidence can affect growth prospects adversely. The importance of these perverse results is compounded by the fact that changes in the structure of the economy have reduced the amount of stimulus derived from a given tax or expenditure measure.[10.21]

Among the reasons given for this are the rise in the personal savings rate and increased import dependency, which have widened leakages from the spending stream and dampened the effect of stimulus.

Second, Canada's exposure to external shocks has increased at a time when these are becoming larger, more intense, and more frequent. [But all is not lost]. This loss of policy independence does not mean

[10.20] C.D. Howe Research Institute, *Policy Review and Outlook, 1979: Anticipating the Unexpected* (Montreal: The Institute, 1979), 171-77.

[10.21] C.D. Howe Research Institute, *Policy Review and Outlook, 1980: Investing in Our Own Future* (Montreal: The Institute, 1980), 61-64.

that government should stand idly by while the country is swamped by waves of inflation and unemployment, but it does mean that Canada must attack the fundamental sources of the imbalances that have given rise to these constraints on policy. Measures intended to cushion the effects of external shocks must therefore be designed so that they do not aggravate the basic imbalances we have described. This can be done only if Canadians are willing to invest a greater proportion of their current income in their own future.[10.22]

February 1983, The C.D. Howe Institute, *Commentary*. The C.D. Howe Institute gave the following perceptive summary of the seventies:

Our economy was relatively strong until the mid-1970s. Since then it has . . . become one of the worst in the OECD region. It was plagued by inflation and unemployment that were among the highest, a recession that was among the sharpest and most severe, and an absence of any improvement in productivity growth . . . Those difficulties had a combination of causes, some of which affected other countries as well, and some that were peculiar to Canada. Like most market economies, Canada experienced changes in economic processes and relationships in the 1970s that have reduced the ability of monetary and fiscal policy to maintain high employment and stable prices. The fine-tuning of demand-management policies—which lowered unemployment by expanding aggregate demand and raising inflation—were less successful than they had been in the 1960s. The flexibility in economic behavior that was essential to the success of those policies declined as various groups in society adapted to changes by protecting themselves against them . . .

The serious dilemma for the makers of macroeconomic policy intensified in the inflationary aftermath of the 1979-80 oil-price shocks. In 1980 the U.S. Federal Reserve Board severely restricted the growth of U.S. monetary aggregates in an effort to reduce aggregate demand. This policy subsequently clashed with President Reagan's expansionary fiscal policies and resulted in real interest rates of unprecedented levels and in serious world-wide recession. Canadians suffered both severe inflation and a recession.[10.23]

For Canada the problems of the seventies had been exacerbated by a belief that its rich natural resources would maintain economic growth, by concentration of government on policies to redistribute income rather than to ensure economic efficiency, on the delay in facing up to the pricing of oil, and on distracting internal federal-provincial disputes.

Federal-provincial rivalry and the desire for equity among regions have, in recent years, tended to relegate economic efficiency to secondary place. We have luxuriated in our quarrels, paying little or no

---

[10.22] Ibid., at 64.

[10.23] C.D. Howe Institute, *Commentary: Taking Stock* (Toronto: The Institute, February 1983), 1-2.

attention to their rising economic cost. Canada's collective bargaining system is another factor that has contributed to economic rigidity . . . The failure of management and labor to communicate their concerns to each other have strained Canada's industrial relations and have contributed to militancy in collective bargaining and to inflexibility in wages.[10.24]

Economic Council of Canada

1970, ECC Seventh Annual Review. At the outset of the seventies the Council turned its attention to a detailed appraisal of the Canadian economy.

The analysis is directed mainly at clarifying the basic elements in growth—labour and capital, and the efficiency with which these have been used—in major groups of industries over the past two decades. [It found that] some sectors have achieved strong advances in their efficiency of use of labour and capital; others have apparently lagged or been unable to make substantial productivity gains . . . All of this confirms that economic growth is a highly uneven process reflecting differing combinations of forces and conditions in various parts of the economic system.[10.25]

Education and commercial policy were stressed as government instruments that would foster growth. (Obviously a long distance had been travelled from the simple White Paper approach based largely on the Keynesian assumption that high demand and heavy capital expenditure would ensure growth throughout the economy.)

1971, ECC Eighth Annual Review. This review dealt primarily with the processes of government decision-making. Government was now such a large element in the economy that its efficient management was crucial. New approaches, such as the Planning, Programming, Budgeting System (PPBS) were being introduced. The Review emphasized the importance of systematic policy analysis and decision-making, of establishment of goals, of public information on policy goals, the founding of an institute for systematic policy analysis (later to appear as the Institute for Research in Public Policy) and the strengthening of academic and private initiatives in research on governmental questions.

1971, ECC Special Study—*Performance in Perspective, 1971.* The Council from time to time had calculated the shortfall of the Canadian economy below potential. For years following 1967 it had found a "gap" averaging 3 to 4 percent below the GNP that would have emerged with reasonably full use of Canada's labour force and other resources. This represented an annual shortfall of some $3 billion. And this had been

---

10.24 Ibid., at 2-3.

10.25 Economic Council of Canada, *Patterns of Growth* Seventh Annual Review (Ottawa: Queen's Printer, 1970), 3-4.

recalculated at the Council's new target for unemployment of 3.8 percent for 1975 (as compared with the original goal of 3 percent for 1970). To reach potential growth by 1975 would require annual growth rates in personal consumption, housing, business plant and equipment well above recent rates. There would also have to be a readjustment of costs and profits, which had turned markedly unfavourable to industry in the 1965-70 period, when "Wages and Salaries per Unit of Output" increased 34 percent while "Profits per Unit of Output" declined 9.8 percent. The study remarked that this situation "provides an environment in which the possibility of further relatively large price increases is quite high.[10.26]

External trade had been a buoyant element in the sixties. The decade had been described as one of "export-led growth," prompted by the 13 percent depreciation of the Canadian dollar and the effects of the automobile agreement with the United States. For the first time since 1952 the foreign accounts in 1970 had shown not only a trade surplus but as well a surplus on current account. On the challenge ahead:

> Canada faces a major task of job creation over the next few years . . .
> By far the largest increase in employment requirements will occur in the 25-34 age group, and it will be especially great for males where the rate of employment growth will need to be *more than double* that of the last half of the 1960s.[10.27]

On prices:

> . . . we believe that inflation will continue to remain a major problem for policy in the 1970's . . . There are many reasons for this assessment. First are the changes in psychological and sociological attitudes relating to job security, greater militancy, and rising demands for public goods . . . Second is the fact that the growth potential of the industrialized countries is very large in the 1970's—larger than in the 1960's—and that the commitment by governments to try to attain these potentials is likely to keep employment high and demand pressures strong. Third is the squeeze on profit margins . . . given the international linkages through which price pressures are transmitted from country to country, Canada cannot expect to be able to cope with inflation occurring on an international scale through unilateral action.[10.28]

1972, EEC Ninth Annual Review. Forecasts in this Review were derived from the Council's new CANDIDE econometric model, named to reflect the participation of six federal institutions in its construction. CANDIDE had been preceded by other models developed at the University of Toronto and the Bank of Canada. CANDIDE appeared to have performed in a satisfac-

---

10.26 Economic Council of Canada, *Performance in Perspective, 1971* (Ottawa: Information Canada), 1970, 36.

10.27 Ibid., at 51.

10.28 Ibid., at 55-56.

tory way in retrospects of the 1955-1970 period, but its projections for the next decade were advanced with some caution. The projections were based on a main scenario of strong external and government forces and on alternative less optimistic scenarios. For the economy as a whole the "strong" projection was for

> a rapid rate of growth in output and employment over the decade to 1980. For output, an average annual rate of growth of 5.6 per cent is projected for the economy as a whole, compared with 5.4 per cent in the 1960s, and reflects a small improvement in the rate of growth of output per person employed because of an unchanged employment rate.[10.29]

For government the "strong" forecast was that revenues would increase so rapidly at existing rates of tax that heavy surpluses would emerge in the last part of the decade. These would create a "fiscal drag," bringing unemployment of 6 percent with price rises reduced to 2 percent a year. It was assumed that this situation would be avoided either by reduced taxation or increased expenditure. In the choice of "Alternative Patterns" of change allowance was made for less favourable external conditions. It could hardly have been foreseen however that in the following year OPEC would throw world oil markets and supplies into disarray and crop failures in many countries would send food prices spiralling upward. The 1980 results fell far short of the CANDIDE forecasts for these and other reasons.

The Review contained some pertinent reflections on the size and role of government in the economy, particularly in relation to inflation.

> In Canada, the share of all levels of government as a percentage of the Gross National Product increased from 26 to 36 per cent from 1955 to 1970 . . . the share of governments is expected to increase during the 1970s to 39.2 per cent by 1980. [It actually turned out to be 41.8 percent]. The economic and social impact of such structural change will certainly take on considerable importance . . . Another source of concern is the belief that an increasing role of government may result in an inflationary bias in the economy. In our opinion, this danger originates in the adjustments in nominal incomes induced by tax increases . . . This is evidenced by the criteria used to support claims for income increases. For example, price increases are now generally accepted as justification for higher wages . . . Another criterion is net disposable income ("take home pay"), which is of course reduced by increases in income tax and contributions to social security plans . . . In short, people want to obtain increases in nominal incomes that will be sufficient to compensate them for both increases in price and increases in taxes, and so protect their real disposable incomes . . . We do believe that present conditions call for a slower and more regular rate of increase in the government share of GNP.[10.30]

[10.29]Economic Council of Canada, *The Years to 1980* Ninth Annual Review (Ottawa: Information Canada, 1972), 35.

[10.30]Ibid., at 100-01.

In this comment the Council was joining a growing volume of economic opinion, which of course amounted to a rejection of the classically prescribed use of tax increases for anti-inflationary purposes.

1976, EEC Thirteenth Annual Review. Devoted entirely to causes and consequences of inflation, this issue is a mine of information to which scant justice can be done here. The origins of the mid-seventies' inflation were summed as:

. . . the recent inflation experience reflected an initial international surge of industrial output and trade, followed by unanticipated rounds of increases in food and industrial commodity prices, and by the OPEC energy shock. The consequence was a dramatic increase in the cost of living in almost all western countries, an accommodating monetary policy, and a continuous realignment of foreign exchange rates, all occurring sequentially and thus reinforcing cost and price pressures. Attempts by workers to catch up and to achieve real income gains brought about substantial wage increases. Employers, too, secured higher prices and profits. As a result, the increase in total unit costs in Canada accelerated from 3.7 per cent in 1971 to 12.3 per cent in 1975—a development that, if maintained, could well jeopardize our ability to compete in international trade markets. [10.31]

The AIB program was supported:

The lowering of public expectations and the relearning by all parties of the virtues of self-restraint also take time. It is for this reason that the Council supports the continued vigorous application of the anti-inflation program . . . [10.32]

For the future after removal of the AIB restraints the CANDIDE gave an ominous and, as it turned out, accurate warning of continuing dangers.

For, even if the controls program were 100 per cent successful during its years of operation, our projections show that, under circumstances in which unemployment would decline to 5 per cent or lower by the early 1980s, partly because of slower labour force growth, the cost of living could rise to disturbing levels once again. Continuing restraint on all fronts will be necessary if we are to escape new rounds of inflationary pressures and wage catch-up demands. At the same time, such restraint will need to be balanced by initiatives that will maintain the nation's economic recovery and growth. A critical issue will be our competitiveness compared with that of the United States. If our productivity levels continue to lag behind those of other industrial countries, and if domestic inflation rates run ahead of those of our major trading partners, we will almost certainly be faced again with severe economic difficulties and a further depreciation of the Canadian

[10.31] Economic Council of Canada, *The Inflation Dilemma* Thirteenth Annual Review (Ottawa: Supply and Services, 1976), 99.

[10.32] Ibid., at 160.

dollar.[10.33] [Ten years later this seems to have been a remarkably accurate forecast].

1977, ECC Fourteenth Annual Review. This Review confirmed the cheerless outlook of the previous year. It considered several possible combinations of policies, and reported:

> In appraising these alternative policy scenarios, it appears that—if our extrapolations and assumptions are correct—there is little hope of achieving simultaneously a low unemployment rate, a low inflation rate and a sound equilibrium of the current account balance over the next five years. [But all is not lost]. It is possible, however, to gauge the trade-offs and to measure the relative gains and losses of different policies with respect to growth, unemployment, inflation and balance of payments.
>
> Our simulations indicate that the recourse to stimulative policies may improve the medium-term performance of the economy in some areas but that, in other fields, additional initiatives will be required. This in turn suggests that structural problems cannot be solved by the sole use of stabilization instruments, although a healthier economic environment may facilitate the achievement of needed structural adjustments.[10.34]

In the latter area it proposed the development of joint federal-provincial industrial strategies, encouragement of increased foreign equity investment in Canadian businesses, specific incentives for the Canadian tourist industry and export-oriented or import-competing enterprises, and further direct job-creating programs, such as the winter work program and the employment tax credit. It also proposed that the federal government establish an advisory and consultative mechanism to examine long-term structural issues. For monetary polity it recommended firm control over the growth of the money supply; for fiscal policy it proposed cuts in income tax to increase disposable incomes of consumers and a reduction in provincial sales taxes by at least one percentage point.

But the final note was still not very encouraging:

> Even with the initiatives that we are suggesting, unemployment rates will probably not fall below 7 per cent until after 1980. Inflation will persist roughly in line with the inflation rates of Canada's major trading partners. Without improvement in this country's capacity to control costs and improve productivity, we face the prospect of persistent overall government deficits, no improvement in current account balances, and rising foreign indebtedness. Neither federal nor provincial governments will have much flexibility for new expenditure

---

[10.33] Ibid., at 161-62.

[10.34] Economic Council of Canada, *Into the 1980s* Fourteenth Annual Review (Ottawa: Supply and Services, 1977), 75.

programs. A concerted effort to improve the structure of the Canadian economy over the medium term is obviously needed.[10.35]

We leave the Council here; in retrospect its forecasts seems to have been painfully accurate.

Additional Economic Views

Canadian Tax Foundation Study

Fiscal Dimensions of Canadian Federalism, 1980. In a collection of conference papers, edited by Richard Bird, dealing with various aspects of fiscal issues in a federal system three Canadian economists expressed views on "The Scope for Short-Run Fiscal Stabilization Policy Within Confederation." Their views on the use of short-run policies are of interest in the background of this chapter.

D.A.L. Auld

In the context of our discussion fiscal stabilization policy is defined as a *temporary* change in one or more fiscal instruments for the purpose of altering the time path of aggregate demand and/or wholesale or retail prices to mitigate fluctuations in unemployment and inflation . . . A fiscal stabilization policy is considered to be meaningful if it has enough leverage to make a correct and appreciable impact on the time profile of the target variable . . . If total personal income tax revenue is 20 per cent of GNP and it is entirely under the jurisdiction of the federal government, an increase/decrease of 4 percentage points will have considerable leverage on GNP. This is not the case if the federal government's share of the tax is only one-third. In this case, it would take a 12 percentage point change in the rate to exert the same leverage . . . [Furthermore, as econometric studies have revealed, the impact of tax changes over the postwar period has been declining]; . . . the "leverage" effect of tax changes is probably slightly less than it was two-and-a-half decades ago.

On the expenditure side of the federal budget, it is not clear what expenditures legitimately can be considered to have potential fiscal leverage. Lacroix and Rabeau have argued that 96 per cent of federal spending is not available as a fiscal stabilization instrument. They reach this conclusion by considering all noncapital expenditure (including transfers to persons, business and government) as recurrent and hence *inflexible* . . .

The difficulty with the Lacroix-Rabeau analysis is that they *assume* current spending is inflexible, because there appears to be a legislative commitment to a certain "output" goal. The actual level of spending in a given fiscal year . . . does not preclude the use of such expenditure

---

[10.35] Ibid., at 91.

as a short-term stabilization instrument, because the rate of spending on such projects can be controlled . . . It comes down to the age-old problem of the lengths of time lags involved. Evidence on the outside lags of fiscal policy suggests that given an increase in public expenditure on goods and services, there is a considerable impact on the economy in the first six to nine months . . . The critical fact is the speed with which a policy can be enacted.[10.36]

Following a review of some of the recent academic debate over the role of fiscal policy Auld confirms his own belief in the value of short-term changes, given certain conditions:

The policies chosen should be ones which can be introduced quickly and have, as one of their characteristics, a substantial multiplier effect in the short run . . . The fear that short-run stimulative fiscal policy will "crowd out" private investment and completely offset fiscal policy is not empirically justifiable. The evidence on this point suggests that "crowding out" in a period of recession is small . . . As a means of stimulating demand within a short period or as a means of reducing the price level, the retail sales tax is the most effective instrument . . . it can . . . be used as a joint policy instrument by the federal and provincial governments, as was the case in 1978. The apparent growing reluctance to employ short-run national fiscal policy is partly the result of the present size of the federal deficit and the belief that if a deficit this large can't produce full employment, fiscal policy is of little value in smoothing short-run cycles. Such a view oversimplifies the story as to how the federal budget deficit became too large and completely ignores the method by which this deficit has been financed. Furthermore, the absolute size of the deficit is an inappropriate measure of fiscal stimulation; the *change* in the deficit is much more relevant. It would be inappropriate, then, to discount fiscal policy as an instrument of stabilization based on the size of the deficit over the last few years.[10.37]

C.L. Barber. In general agreeing with the Auld viewpoint, Barber expressed some supplementary thoughts:

Recently, an increasing number of economists have begun to argue that our enterprise system can be depended upon to generate automatically, if not high employment, what they view as the natural rate of unemployment. I seriously question the validity of this view. . . . the sustained prosperity the developed world experienced for 25 years after World War II should not be viewed as the norm. It reflected in some degree the momentum and backlogs built up during fifteen years of depression and war . . . I would strongly urge our policy-makers to

---

[10.36] D.A.L. Auld, "The Scope for Short-Run Stabilization Policy Within Confederation," in *Fiscal Dimensions of Canadian Federalism*, ed. by Richard M. Bird, (Toronto: Canadian Tax Foundation, 1980), 91-109, at 91-94.

[10.37] Ibid., at 108.

pay more attention to the maintenance of the longer-run growth and strength of the economy . . . There is also a need to reassess the importance of achieving an appropriate mix of monetary and fiscal policy . . . it seems to me that over much of the past four years our policy mix has been almost exactly wrong.

[On regional economic development]: . . . I have long been an advocate of a role for provincial fiscal policy. However, except for the largest provinces, such as Ontario and Quebec, the leakages from any policy measures taken at the provincial level may well be so great that they inhibit even an economically well informed provincial Premier. What may be needed are more federal initiatives such as conditional grants for provincial public works when unemployment in a region exceeds a certain level, or even a repetition of the federal subsidization of sales tax reductions, perhaps this time on a longer-term basis with each province free to choose areas of tax reduction.

[On regional economic development]: The problem is complicated by the recurrent conflict which occurs in Canada between the pull of resource development and the claims of our secondary manufacturing industries. Strong resource development booms usually produce an inflow of capital funds, which causes an appreciation of the Canadian dollar; this in turn results in a deterioration in the competitive position of our secondary manufacturing industries. When the resource boom ebbs, the dollar may in time depreciate, leading to an improved status for secondary manufacturing . . . All these factors suggest that appropriateness of regional fiscal policy measures is partly conditioned by exchange rate policy as well as monetary policy. . . .

Finally, I think we should take note of the fact that fiscal policy at all levels of government is being unnecessarily restricted today by a confusion as to the size of current deficits. If some two-thirds of the debt interest payments were removed from the current budgets of our government and treated, as it should be, as a capital amount needed to keep the real value of the bondholders' assets intact, we would find that the size of government deficits would decline quite dramatically. In this case it is what we don't know and appreciate that is hurting us.[10.38]

T.A. Wilson. Choosing first to examine further the issue of crowding out, Wilson did so in the taxonomy of transactions crowding out via interest rate effects; portfolio crowding out via wealth effects; and inflation crowding out via price level effects. On the latter effect he said: "I am not as sanguine as previous speakers who have argued that because the unemployment rate is above 7 per cent, we can go ahead with an expansionary fiscal policy and not worry about price-level effects. Because we are also dangerously close to double digit inflation again—that is, when *both*

[10.38]Clarence L. Barber, Comment in "The Scope for Short-Run Stabilization Policy Within Confederation," supra, footnote 10.36, 110-12.

inflation and unemployment have accelerated to unacceptable levels—I think we cannot neglect possible price-level effects . . . Another important aspect of fiscal policy which is neglected in Doug Auld's paper is the possible supply side effects of fiscal policy, that is, the impact of increases in tax rates on the available supplies of labour, capital and entrepreneurial activities. I think these effects may be significant. I won't go to the extreme of Laffer in arguing that an increase in tax rates actually reduces tax revenues, but I do think that increased marginal tax rates have significant effects in diverting socially productive activities . . . to activities which one can argue are socially less productive than the highly taxed activities . . . Let me now comment on one other general issue . . . the issue of fine tuning. It is all too frequently argued that we should not fine tune because of forecasting errors. There are two sources of errors we have to bear in mind here: one is the accuracy of forecasts of the course of the economy in the absence of policy changes and the other is the accuracy of forecasts of the *impacts* of policy changes. I think there is general agreement that neither type of forecast is very accurate. However, they are not totally inaccurate either. What does the economic analysis of lags, forecasting errors and policy errors suggest? . . . as long as you have any forecasting accuracy at all, that is, as long as your forecasts are better than random guesses, some stabilization policy should be undertaken. Secondly, if the forecasts are better in the short term than they are in the long term, which appears to be the case, then any activity which reduces the "inside lags" of fiscal policy will improve the effectiveness of fiscal policy. Finally, even in the absence of forecasting accuracy, it may be desirable to improve the built-in stability system."[10.39]

[10.39]Thomas A. Wilson, Comment in "The Scope for Short-Run Stabilization Policy Within Confederation," supra, footnote 10.36, 112-17, at 112-14.

11
Economic Consequences of the Federal Deficit

We have already dwelt at some length on the circumstances that led to the federal deficits of the mid-eighties and will return to the subject again later. Undoubtedly the rise from a ratio of 1.8 percent of GNP to 7 percent in 1984 and 1985 was a traumatic experience for many, and there continues to be deep concern with the slowness in overcoming the shortfall compared to the speed with which it arrived. However before going further into the issue, let the economists have their say on the subject. It has been dealt with in a great many studies and reports, of which it will only be possible to use a few here. Table 11.1 gives some up-to-date figures on the relationship of deficits to GNP.

The Departmental View

A Budget Paper, *The Federal Deficit in Perspective* presented in April 1983, gave a thorough examination of the deficit and its consequences as seen at the official level. On the question of crowding out it said:

> Evidence on this issue from simulations with macroeconomic models suggests that crowding out is not a significant problem in the short run. That is, in the absence of any change in monetary policy, a bond-financed increase in government spending will cause a rise in economic

Table 11.1   Government Deficits, National Accounts Basis, 1976-86

							All Governments
		Federal Government					
	Revenue		Expenditure		Deficit		Deficits
Year	($ billion)	As a per-cent of GNP	($ billion)	As a per-cent of GNP	($ billion)	As a per-cent of GNP	($ billion)	As a per-cent of GNP
1976.....	35.3	18.4	38.7	20.2	− 3.4	− 1.8	− 3.2	− 1.0
1977.....	36.5	17.4	43.8	20.8	− 7.3	− 3.5	− 5.0	− 1.0
1978.....	38.4	16.5	49.0	21.1	− 10.6	− 4.6	− 7.3	− 1.0
1979.....	43.6	16.5	52.7	19.9	− 9.1	− 3.5	− 4.6	− 1.0
1980.....	50.6	17.0	61.0	20.5	− 10.4	− 3.5	− 8.1	− 1.0
1981.....	65.0	18.9	72.3	21.0	− 7.3	− 2.1	− 5.2	− 1.5
1982.....	66.0	18.2	86.4	23.9	− 20.4	− 5.6	− 21.5	− 5.9
1983.....	69.6	17.7	94.5	24.1	− 25.1	− 6.2	− 26.6	− 6.8
1984.....	76.7	17.9	107.2	35.0	− 30.5	− 7.1	− 29.1	− 6.8
1985.....	83.7	18.1	115.9	25.1	− 32.3	− 7.0	− 31.3	− 6.8
1986.....	91.4	18.7	116.2	23.8	− 24.8	− 5.1	− 27.3	− 5.6

Sources: Department of Finance, *Economic Review*, April 1985 and Statistics Canada, - *National Income and Expenditure Accounts*, Fourth Quarter, 1986.

activity that is generally thought to be equal to or greater than the original stimulus.[11.1]

On the use of deficits as a fiscal policy device the paper had the following to say:

> Although fiscal policy can be used to stimulate the economy in the short run, its effectiveness may diminish over time, even in situations of less than full employment. Continuing large bond-financed deficits mean that individuals and firms must be induced to hold a growing share of government debt in their financial portfolios. This may require rising interest rates on government bonds, which will tend to put upward pressure on yields of all financial assets.
>
> The possible existence of what is often called portfolio crowding out would be signalled by a rise in the ratio of government debt to wealth or to GNP, since the two are likely to be highly correlated. It is worth repeating that since Canada represents a small part of a large integrated capital market, yields on Canadian financial assets may not be greatly affected by an increase in the supply of government debt . . . A more fundamental issue is whether the budget position is consistent with high employment and no additional pressure on prices. Clearly, the sum of private and public demands cannot exceed the productive capacity of the economy; a budget stance that creates excess demand will cause some combination of price and interest rate increases that will effect the transfer of resources from the private to the public sector . . . To the extent that private investment falls as a result of the budgetary imbalance, there will tend to be a reduction in the high employment level of output, although this effect may be offset to the extent that the fiscal stimulus involves investment in capital or human resources that will increase future productivity.[11.2]
>
> [The document then asks]: Given that fiscal policy has a role to play in diminishing cyclical fluctuations in the economy, what is the appropriate level for the federal deficit on average over a complete cycle? There is no simple answer to this question since it depends on savings and investment flows in the economy, the extent that the economy is self-equilibrating in the medium term and the level of government investment . . . If the economy is expected to fluctuate around the "trend" growth path, then a reasonable budgetary norm for the medium term might be that government savings (on an inflation-adjusted basis), average zero over the cycle; private savings would then equal private investment at the high employment level of output, which is assumed to be attained on average over the cycle.[11.3]

[11.1] Canada, Department of Finance, *The Federal Deficit in Perspective*, Budget Papers, April 1983, 68.

[11.2] Ibid., at 68-69.

[11.3] Ibid., at 70-71.

The paper, after reviewing available data, concludes:

The review of the evidence on the effects of government deficits on private investment suggests that crowding out has not been a major issue during this recent period of relatively large government deficits. Private investment was an above average share of GNP over the last cycle and there is little direct evidence of a conflict between public and private sector credit demands, partly because of accessibility of foreign capital markets. [11.4]

(In 1983 of course the deficit had not reached the high level of later years). A notable feature of this document was the use of the concepts of the "cyclically" and "inflation" adjusted deficits. The former is defined as the "balance that would prevail under the existing revenue and expenditure structure if the economy were operating in any given year at an average level of activity. [11.5] This is the obvious successor to the former full-employment budget. The inflation adjustment is somewhat more obscure. It is explained as follows:

As indicated in the text, inflation adjustment of government balances is oriented to changes in real indebtedness of governments . . . for the purposes of inflation adjustment, it is necessary to obtain an estimate of net liabilities having a fixed nominal redemption value. [11.6]

Table 11.2 illustrates the results of these adjusments as calculated by the Department of Finance in 1983 with additional years to 1988 estimated by Bruce and Purvis[11.7] for a Macdonald Commission study. They are for illustration only, as more up-to-date calculations are given later.

The budget paper gives a caution as to the reliability of these adjustments:

As such the cyclically-adjusted budget balance provides some help in identifying structural as opposed to cyclical factors in the deficit. However, due to the uncertainty associated with any estimates of adjusted output level and the static nature of the adjustments to revenues and expenditures, any calculated level of the cyclically-adjusted balance must be treated with considerable caution . . . Rather than concentrating on levels, therefore, attention is more often focussed on the *change* in the cyclically-adjusted budget balance. [11.8]

This is approximately the same caution that was given for the earlier full-employment budget balance.

[11.4] Ibid., at 77.

[11.5] Ibid., at 57.

[11.6] Ibid., at 63.

[11.7] See footnote 11.16.

[11.8] Supra, footnote 11.1, at 57-58.

Table 11.2   Federal Government Structural Deficits[a]

	Inflation-adjusted NIA Deficit (1)	Cyclical Adjustment (CA) (2)	Structural Deficit (SD) (3)	SD as % of CA GNP (4)
	($ billion current)			
1970...................	− 0.9	− 0.3	− 1.2	− 1.4
1971...................	− 0.3	− 0.1	− 0.4	− 0.4
1972...................	− 0.2	0.1	− 0.1	− 0.1
1973...................	− 1.5	1.0	− 0.5	− 0.4
1974...................	− 2.6	1.6	− 1.0	− 0.7
1975...................	2.3	0.0	2.3	1.4
1976...................	1.8	0.7	2.5	1.3
1977...................	5.4	− 0.5	4.9	2.3
1978...................	8.1	− 0.8	7.3	3.1
1979...................	5.7	− 0.4	5.3	2.0
1980...................	5.1	− 2.0	3.1	1.0
1981...................	− 0.1	− 1.8	− 1.9	− 0.6
1982...................	13.2	− 9.4	3.7	2.0
1983...................	18.8	− 10.6	8.2	2.0
1984[b]................	20.8	− 8.5	12.3	2.7
1985[b]................	15.6	− 7.4	8.2	1.7
1986[b]................	10.1	− 5.7	4.4	0.8
1987[b]................	9.9	− 3.5	6.4	1.1
1988[b]................	9.1	− 0.9	8.2	1.4

[a] A minus sign indicates a surplus. [b] Projected (using Department of Finance low-trend productivity).

Source: Neil Bruce and Douglas D. Purvis, "Consequences of Government Budget Deficits," in John Sargent, research coordinator, *Fiscal and Monetary Policy*, Collected Research Studies of the Royal Commission on Economic Union and Development Prospects for Canada, vol. 26 (Toronto: University of Toronto Press, 1986), 71.

The C.D. Howe Institute View

The C.D. Howe Institute also gave the deficit intensive study from 1984. Its conclusions reflected its current views on the state of the economy, which are therefore relevant.

1983. Taking Stock, February 1983. Given the delicate economic problems created by the 1982 recession and the continued high unemployment and inflation, what programs should be adopted for 1983? The Institute recommended further lowering of the inflation rate, reduction of unemployment through labour-market policies aimed at target groups and restoration of productivity growth. It also advised that attempts be made to achieve more flexible income and price arrangements to avoid continued resort to income rules such as the "6 and 5" on every occasion of price rises. On the issue of the deficit, the Institute was opposed to short-term efforts to stimulate the economy in the pattern of many past budgets. It might only have the result of increasing the deficit without achieving economic gains. Some temporary stimulus might be given by reducing commodity taxes, but this should be very limited. With the end of money-supply targeting the

Bank of Canada had been concentrating on reducing interest rates from their extremely high levels, which meant closer ties to interest rate levels in the United States. As U.S. rates were being reduced the Bank would have a delicate path to follow if it was to avoid rekindling inflation in Canada.

1984. By 1984 the authors of the Institute's *Policy Review and Outlook* felt that progress was being made in the right direction with more realistic attitudes toward wage and price increases, more modest budget expectations, and repairs to the financial structure with lower interest rates. For the future

the most important challenge facing policymakers in 1984 is to restore jobs as quickly as possible, while ensuring that conditions exist for the sustained growth needed to create new jobs. [The policy priorities for this included]: Maintaining the momentum for recovery . . . Improving the climate for investment . . . reducing the federal deficit as the recovery proceeds . . . Increasing the flexibility of labor markets . . . Reducing the rate of increases in costs and prices . . . Cushioning, rather than shielding against, change . . . Reducing vulnerability to external shocks and increasing access to international markets.[11.9]

The statement prescribed against raising taxes to reduce the federal deficit at this point as possibly undermining confidence. It preferred reductions in outlays, particularly in limitations on growth of transfers to provinces and individuals. To achieve a sufficient reduction in the total deficit a 3 percent cap could be imposed to succeed the "6 and 5" ceiling that was due to expire in 1984.

1986. In surveying the recent past the 1986 *Policy Review and Outlook* expressed guarded satisfaction with Canadian economic performance, which since mid-1984 had been better than every other industrial country except Japan. The main shortfalls had been consumer expenditure on nondurables and private investment, the latter being ascribed to

depressed commodity prices in world markets, excess capacity in several industries, and stiff competition from low-wage developing countries that makes investment unprofitable in Canada.[11.10]

Two important signs of problems indicated that further remedial steps needed to be taken in Canada: one was the continuation of levels of unemployment considerably higher than in the United States, and the other was the imbalance in growth between regions of the country.

The *Review* presented some long-range targets, which should form the basis of future policy. These included

a tax and transfer system that promotes adjustment; an internationally competitive industrial sector; an efficient and flexible private

---

11.9C.D. Howe Research Institute, *Policy Review and Outlook, 1984: Beyond Recovery Adjusting to the Future* (Toronto: The Institute, 1984), 61.

11.10Edward A. Carmichael, *Policy Review and Outlook, 1986: Reorienting the Canadian Economy* (Toronto: C.D. Howe Research Institute, 1986), 4-5.

sector; an efficient public sector; and secure access to the large U.S. market.[11.11]

In these contexts it had specific proposals for forthcoming Canada-U.S. trade negotiations, for reducing the federal deficit, and for reform of the tax and transfer system, all matters discussed elsewhere in this publication.

C.D. Howe Specifics for the Deficit

In 1984 the Institute published two studies dealing specifically with the deficit—*Evaluating the Deficit* and *Tackling the Federal Deficit*. The former, by Professors Bruce and Purvis, emphasized the concept of a "prudent fiscal plan," defined as "one that neither causes government debt to rise without limit relative to nominal GNP, nor results in a debt-to-GNP ratio that rises to an unacceptably high level before levelling off."[11.12] The authors chose the 1979 debt-to-GNP ratio as the target.

> This value is approximately equal to the average of the period 1969-84. It also precedes the sharp rise in the debt-to-GNP ratio that occurred during the recession. Thus, we set the target ratio of net fixed-value liabilities to trend GNP at 15.1 percent for the federal government and at 17.9 percent for consolidated governments. [Calculations based on these data] indicate that the federal fiscal plan is imprudent. To establish fiscal prudence, the projected federal deficit must be reduced by $11 billion between now and 1988. This would ensure that, if the economy operates "normally" on average after 1988 and the target inflation rate is achieved, the target debt-to-GNP ratio will be reached.
>
> [How to reach this objective]? First, we believe that some, if not all, of the cuts should come from government spending . . . The rate of growth of nominal expenditure would have to fall to 4.5 percent from the presently projected 6.9 percent for each of the next four fiscal years . . . A more difficult issue is that of tax revenues Politically, some tax increase may be necessary to meet the expenditure cuts "halfway." But we are not comfortable with this political compromise . . . If tax revenue were to be increased, we would favor the use of revenue-enhancing tax reform rather than simple increases in tax rates. But even revenue-enhancing tax reform worries us somewhat, given the track record governments have shown in their ability to spend their revenue.[11.13]

The second paper, *Tackling the Federal Deficit*, by a staff member, E.A. Carmichael, said:

[11.11]Ibid., at 74.

[11.12]Neil Bruce and Douglas D. Purvis, *Evaluating the Deficit: The Case for Budget Cuts*, Policy Commentary no. 4 (Toronto: C.D. Howe Institute, 1984), 11.

[11.13]Ibid., at 22-29.

Eventual action to reduce deficits is inevitable. The continuing increase of federal debt relative to GNP is an inherently unstable situation. Rising interest rates associated with heavy debt financing could touch off another recession in the mid-1980s. In that event, deficits and the debt could spiral, forcing severe fiscal austerity. Alternatively, monetization of deficits to keep interest rates from rising could reignite inflationary expectations and force another severe, policy-induced recession.

[The paper suggested several possible strategies:] The first alternative reflects the judgment of those who believe that the existing size and role of government spending programs is about right. This group would oppose cuts in government services and favor increased government efficiency and increased revenues as the appropriate method of cutting the deficit. The second alternative reflects the judgment that, while the level of federal services is about right, substantial savings could be achieved by more careful targeting of the $50 billion spent each year on social programs. This group would support the redesign of social transfer programs to begin the task of deficit reduction and some tax increases to get the job done. The third alternative is based on the view that taxes are already too high and that government programs are often ineffective, or even counterproductive, in achieving their objectives. The best approach to deficit reduction, according to this view, would be to cut back government spending selectively, based on a tough evaluation of each program's effectiveness. If sufficient spending cuts cannot be found to achieve the deficit reduction target, then some tax increases—perhaps designed to reduce distortions in the tax system—should be implemented.[11.14]

The paper appears to accept that universality of social benefits must be preserved, that transfers to business have been over-generous and should be reduced, that a relaxed monetary policy can be employed to offset a tightened fiscal regime; but above all it insists that there must be broad public understanding of the need to reduce the deficit, adoption by the government of a course of action and persistence in that course, and transitional assistance for those are hurt by the program.

1984. Symposium on the Deficit: C.D. Howe and Institute for Policy Analysis. A press release issued following this symposium speaks in terms now familiar. On the deficit it said:

Of the federal budget deficit currently estimated at $30 billion, less than one-third ($7-10 billion) would exist even if the economy's resources were fully employed and inflation had been eliminated. This component is often called the "structural" deficit . . . In the longer term, the persistence of the structural deficit, if it leads to a continual increase in the ratio of public debt to GNP, is a cause for concern. The

---

[11.14]Edward A. Carmichael, *Tackling the Federal Deficit*, Observation No. 26 (Toronto: C.D. Howe Institute, 1984), 63-68.

higher the ratio of public debt to GNP the higher will be a number of longer-term economic costs, such as a higher tax burden to service the public debt, lower investment, and increased foreign debt. To limit these costs, longer-term fiscal planning must aim to stabilize the ratio of debt to GNP at an acceptable level . . .

[As to policy for the future]: Canada should now adopt a more desirable "policy mix" by tightening fiscal policy (reducing the deficit), accompanied by an offsetting easing of monetary policy. The contractionary effect of tighter fiscal policy could be offset by an easing of monetary policy that may lower the value of the Canadian dollar (thereby increasing exports), and temporarily reduce interest rates . . . An essential first step in reducing the federal deficit would be to hold the average growth of federal expenditures—including interest payments on the national debt—below the average growth of GNP. This will generate a steady, gradual reduction in the deficit which would gradually stabilize the debt-to-GNP ratio even with the existing tax structure (including already-scheduled tax increases).

There is no necessity at this time for further increases in tax rates. If, in the future, stimulative fiscal policies are deemed necessary, they should be clearly temporary and targeted to areas that have maximum impact on economic growth and employment.

Co-ordination of monetary and fiscal policy will be critical to the success of this deficit reduction strategy. In our view, a *quid pro quo* will be necessary; the Bank of Canada must be prepared to ease monetary policy in response to action by the federal government to bring down the structural deficit.[11.15]

This statement was signed by ten economists, representing mainly the two sponsoring organizations.

Macdonald Commission Papers

The Macdonald Commission. A series of studies prepared for the Macdonald Commission dealt extensively with the special subject of Fiscal and Monetary Policy. In this publication two contributions are from the authors of the Howe study previously cited, Professors Bruce and Purvis, and another by Professor Bossons.

The Bruce and Purvis Study

For Bruce and Purvis the ultimate test of the budget is its "fiscal prudence;" to quote:

. . . a fiscal plan is prudent if, given some realistic estimates of economic performance and inflation targets over the medium term,

11.15 C.D. Howe Research Institute, *Economists Agree on Federal Deficit's Significance.* Press Release (Toronto: The Institute, June 13, 1984), 1-3.

the ratio of stock of interest-bearing government debt to nominal GNP will not remain permanently above some target value.[11.16]

For these calculations, as previously explained, the data used are the values for the GNP and the National Accounts deficit figures adjusted both for structural and inflationary effect, the resulting figure being now referred to as the "structural" deficit. The result of the analysis is the same as that of the Howe paper—the current fiscal plan of the federal government (1984) is imprudent and will require a reduction of over $11 billion by 1988. This does not represent "a need for a drastic fiscal cut-back; rather the action called for is systematic and concerted, but gradual."

In contrast to the view of economists four decades previously that the only marks earned by governments in fiscal performance were for discretionary actions, Bruce and Purvis now advance just the opposite rating system.

Not only do discretionary changes run the risk of being perverse because of administrative lags and misreadings of economic signals, they are also difficult, if not impossible, to combine with fiscal prudence. In contrast, automatic stabilizers (or, more generally, fiscal rules) can exploit the potential for stabilization while maintaining credibility that any deficits created are consistent with fiscal prudence. Fiscal prudence relies on an essential symmetry between expansionary and contractive fiscal actions; automatic stabilizers are by their very nature symmetrical while the political process imparts a distinct asymmetry (and imprudence) to discretionary fiscal policies.[11.17]

Economists appear to be constantly at odds with politicians, although in this instance the cause of discontent has made a full turn over the postwar cycle.

The Bossons Study

The delightful aspect of the adjustment process is that if enough steps are introduced the deficit can be made to vanish. This is illustrated in a study by Bossons in the form of a comment on the Bruce and Purvis paper, previously mentioned. By bringing into the calculation for 1984 some additional transient factors Bossons in fact produced a deficit of only $0.6 billion, about one-tenth of the unadjusted deficit of $6.3 billion for that year. However, Bossons is unwilling to accept the obvious inference that on this basis nothing need be done about the deficit. He said:

However, the fact that the deficit is widely perceived to be a structural problem imposes constraints on government policy makers, regardless of whether such perceptions are valid. At a minimum, it is necessary

---

[11.16] Neil Bruce and Douglas D. Purvis, "Consequences of Government Budget Deficits," in John Sargent, research coordinator, *Fiscal and Monetary Policy*, Collected Research Studies of the Royal Commission on the Economic Union and Development Prospects for Canada, vol. 26 (Toronto: University of Toronto Press, 1986), 43-117, at 73.

[11.17] Ibid., at 77.

on political grounds to appear to be undertaking action to reduce government borrowing requirements . . . Apart from the perceptual problem, two other considerations lead to the conclusion that the appropriate long-run target for fiscal policy is not structural balance, but structural surplus. First, as noted earlier, public debt imposes costs on society. As a result, social welfare is increased by reductions in the debt-to-GNP ratio, so that optimal long-run fiscal policy almost certainly implies that government fiscal policy should on average yield a structural surplus . . . Second, as was also noted, the future deficits (or surpluses) implied by any fixed set of government tax and expenditure programs are influenced by chance factors and hence are not predictable . . . it is appropriate to set a structural surplus as a long-run fiscal target in order to provide a reserve to reduce the social costs of unpredicted future shocks that increase the debt-to-GNP ratio . . .

Given all these considerations, the policy implications of this paper are that a moderate degree of fiscal restraint is appropriate from a long-term perspective. Current fiscal policy should thus be consistent with the attainment of a longer-run target of a structural surplus averaging perhaps one or two percent of GNP. However, it should be strongly emphasized that this does not imply that fiscal policy should be made more restrictive now. What it implies is that there should be a credible medium-term fiscal plan which is consistent with the longer-run target of a structural surplus.[11.18]

(To clear up the point, the structural surplus is one adjusted for both structural and inflationary factors; in effect it is the surplus that would prevail under "normal" conditions in the economy, i.e. absence of unusual price rises and unusual unemployment).

Wilson and MacGregor 1986 Budget Appraisal

Wilson and MacGregor in an article on the macroeconomic effects of the 1986 budget in the May-June 1986 *Canadian Tax Journal* concluded: "Our results suggest that the short-term negative impacts of the budget should be small, particularly if firms accept the government's program of announced corporate tax changes and bring investment plans forward in anticipation of future changes. Over the medium term, the budget will have adverse effects on investment and real output, unless monetary policy is eased (or some other expansionary policy adopted) to encourage investors and traders to make up the aggregate demand room vacated by the budget. Such a coordinated monetary-fiscal program would have the added bonus of achieving sharper declines in the debt-to-GNP ratio.[11.19]

The article has the added value of presenting an update, based on Department of Finance calculations, of the structural deficit projections to

---

[11.18] John Bossons, "Comments I: Issues in Analysis of Government Deficits," in *Fiscal and Monetary Policy*, supra footnote 11.16, 85-112, at 106-07.

[11.19] Thomas A. Wilson and Mary E. MacGregor, "The Macroeconomic Effects of the 1986 Budget" (May-June 1986), 34 *Canadian Tax Journal* 563-87, at 584.

Table 11.3 Federal Budget Deficits

Calendar year	National income account deficit	Inflation adjustment term	Cyclical adjustment term	Structural deficit	Structural deficit as % of adjusted GNP
	$ billion				
1979	9.1	4.5	0.3	4.3	1.8
1980	10.4	5.1	1.7	3.6	1.3
1981	7.4	6.2	1.5	− 0.4	− 0.1
1982	18.9	5.5	9.5	3.9	1.1
1983	24.1	2.8	11.3	10.1	2.5
1984	29.7	3.3	9.1	17.3	4.0
1985	29.7	4.8	7.5	17.3	3.8
1986	23.7	7.3	6.0	10.3	2.2
1987	20.0	8.4	5.6	6.0	1.2
1988	17.9	8.9	5.0	4.0	0.7
1989	16.3	9.7	4.5	2.2	0.4
1990	13.5	8.4	4.0	1.0	0.2
1991	11.1	6.8	3.6	0.7	0.1

Source: Department of Finance Worksheets, February 21, 1986.

1991. These were before the Minister of Finance's announcement in September 1986 of a projected shortfall but were the most recent available at the time this was written.

Macdonald Commission Report

The Commissioners, as Commissioners are wont to do, although borrowing much of the language of the day, had different views than the studies on the main causes of the deficit. They attributed it mainly to reduced capital expenditures:

A review of the historical record suggests that the primary cause of the growth of government-sector deficits since about 1975 has been a private sector weakness in capital spending in relation to savings rates . . . This view of the cause of larger government sector deficits is supported by data on the behaviour of gross capital formation in the OECD countries. From 1960 to 1973, real gross capital spending increased at an average of 6.3 percent per year. Over the following eight years, this growth rate fell sharply to a mere 0.3 percent; in other words, capital spending levelled out almost completely after 1973. For the European members of OECD, the decline was even sharper: from 5.5 percent for 1960-73 to − 0.7 percent for 1973-81 . . . Canada experienced no downward shift in the investment share of GNP until after 1981, although our savings have tended to be relatively high since 1973 . . . From 1982 to 1984, private sector capital spending averaged about 16.5 percent of GNP, that is, about 3.5 percentage points below the average that prevailed during the 1947-81 period. To return to an average 20 percent level would require an increase in private capital spending of the order of $14 billion (based on the GNP expected by mid-1985) . . . to enable the government to bring its budget back to a balanced position would require an increase in private sector spending of some $26 billion.[11.20]

On the question of reducing the deficit the Commissioners made the following recommendations:

Commissioners share the widespread concern about the size of the federal government's deficit. We recognize that if the government does not reduce the current structural deficit, it will have to increase taxes just to pay interest costs and will find its flexibility seriously constrained. Commissioners recommend a strategy of gradual deficit reduction, given the current outlook of slow recovery. To stabilize or decrease the debt/GNP ratio, the government will need to reduce the deficit by about 1.5 percent of GNP, which would be equivalent to $10 billion by 1990-91. The practice of laying out an explicit medium-term fiscal plan, introduced in the December 1979 budget and continued since, is useful. We favour using a combination of tax increases and rather broad expenditure reductions to reduce the deficit.[11.21]

For the latter the Commissioners recommended a reduction in the indexation factor where used.

On the future mix of policies it said:

Under present circumstances of high unemployment, a shift to a less expansionary fiscal stance, so as to reduce the deficit, should be matched by a temporary shift to a less restrictive monetary stance. A moderate increase in the projected growth of demand, which might significantly reduce unemployment and strengthen investment, should still be consistent with a further reduction in inflation.[11.22]

Departmental View, 1988

The Department of Finance appears to have settled on two alternative variations of the basic deficit. In the budget paper, "The Fiscal Plan," it described one of these as the primary budget balance, and the other as the structural budget balance. The primary balance was described as the "budget balance excluding interest payments," and the structural balance as "a measure which attempts to remove the influence of cyclical economic factors on the budget."[11.23] The primary deficit was projected to be eliminated in 1989-90, moving from a deficit of $20 billion in 1984-85 to a surplus of $11 billion in 1992-93. No data are given for the structural or adjusted balance, but it is estimated that of an expected 4.1 decline in the deficit as a percentage of GDP between 1984-85 and 1989-90, 70 percent will

---

[11.20]Canada, *Report of the Royal Commission on the Economic Union and Development Prospects for Canada*, vol. 2 (Ottawa: Department of Supply and Services, 1985), 299-300.

[11.21]Ibid., vol. 3, at 433.

[11.22]Ibid.

[11.23]Canada, Department of Finance, Budget Papers, The Fiscal Plan, February 10, 1988, 77.

be due to structural factors. Small wonder that Ministers of Finance speak so fervently of the blessings of the buoyant economy.

Whatever comfort the Minister of Finance derives from these exercises in juggling the data may also be fortified by the reflections of Professor Douglas Hartle, one of Canada's most knowledgeable students of the expenditure control processes. At the conclusion of this second and most comprehensive examination of this aspect of the federal government he modified some of his former skepticism in the following words:

> When confronted with an apparent contradiction in successive judgments, an English jurist is reported to have said, "It does not appear to me now as it appears to have appeared to me then." I look with the same equanimity upon any inconsistencies between this and my earlier study of the federal expenditure budget process. Certainly one aspect of the two studies has not altered: neither is infused with overwhelming optimism concerning the likelihood of fundamental "reform." One thing is different, however: I am now more sanguine about it.[11.24]

Not the Final Word

Obviously these brief comments are not the final word on the federal deficit. Financial experts, economists, business organizations, policy think-tanks and other governments have continued to press for more vigorous action in reducing its level, and the Minister of Finance has continued to state that this is one of his highest priorities. There appears to be some general public concern over it, but this seems to be reflected more in a cynical view that the whole thing is the result of government waste and profligacy rather than the outcome of policies, such as indexation of the personal income tax on the revenue side, that had full approval at the time they were introduced. As the government moved to an election in the fall of 1988 clearly deficit reduction had been abandoned as a saleable political article and new expenditure programs were the order of the day, no doubt to the dismay of the Minister of Finance. By the time this is being read the results of this ploy will be known; in mid-1988 they were impossible to predict.

[11.24] Douglas G. Hartle, *The Expenditure Budget Process of the Government of Canada: A Public Choice—Rent-Seeking Perspective*, Canadian Tax Paper no. 81 (Toronto: Canadian Tax Foundation, 1988), 288.

12
Appraisal

In the End—How to Assess It All?

Only the crucial importance of economic policy in the arena of government action makes this overlong exploration excusable. In the everyday welfare of the citizen it has far greater relevance for example than the dreaded nuclear warfare—a vague fear about a future that is not by any means pre-ordained. By contrast the consequences of economic performance, as we have seen, are here and now; the lives of two generations of Canadians have been profoundly altered by the ebb and flow of the economy. Governments in the last four decades have acted on the advice of economists that policies could be adopted to lessen the cycles of good and bad times, and we have followed through the implementation of this proposition in some detail. What has been learned in the course of this experience?

Maturing Economic Research

Although much still remains uncertain, there has been considerable progress in economic knowledge beyond the simple Keynesian model adopted in the 1945 White Paper. During the 1950s and 1960s there was recognition that policies for economic growth might be quite different from those that might be suitable for stabilization purposes. The role of fiscal and monetary policies became more clearly delineated. It appears to have been a postulate of immediate postwar Keynesian thought that if demand were sustained economic growth would follow, the role of capital expenditure in that process being particularly emphasized. (At least according to the main-line interpretations of Keynes; there seem to have been as many versions as there are rock groups today). Disappointed in their expectations for growth in the sixties economists pointed out that economic growth depended not just on maintaining an active economy but on allocating resources to those uses that would create jobs and incomes. This normally meant increasing the productive capacity of the country and the skill and industry of its workers: it was argued that attention to aggregate demand policies should not be lessened but the policies needed to be supplemented with other more specific measures addressed to these objectives. Canada's rate of capital investment in the postwar period in relation to GNP in some years was among the highest in the world but it has not recently provided adequate growth and furthermore has generally been extremely erratic and destabilizing. In the 1980s it has been one of the least active features of the economy.

A major forward step was the concept that employment and inflation were closely linked; or put another way, unemployment and inflation tended to move in opposite directions. As unemployment rose prices tended to decline; a lowering of unemployment was frequently accompanied by a rise in prices. This led an English economist to devise what became known as the Phillips curve, which attracted attention as a means of demonstrating that there could be a "trade off" between tolerable degrees of the two evils. Much subsequent experience has undermined the idea of a precise trade-off concept but the basic idea of the Phillips curve is still accepted. Much was also learned too about lags in the effects of fiscal and monetary policy. Research done for royal commissions of the period demonstrated that timing was far more crucial than had been thought; and as has been seen, much of the non-governmental comment was to the effect that because of uncertainties as to the timing of their impacts—for that matter uncertainty as to the general results of policy changes—their use for short-term adjustments should be curtailed.

In Canada increasing attention has been paid to income distribution, with increasing knowledge of both distribution by class and region, as well as other regional differences (employment, investment, etc.). In the view of many economists these appear to be beyond the reach of aggregate economic measures, and call for special programs. The federal government has devoted much effort to alleviating these conditions; unfortunately, although there has been some improvement, major differences remain.

As economic issues became more omplex in the seventies and eighties a reaction against intervention developed in many countries, and particularly in the United States. This grew from dissatisfaction with the performance of the economy—the continued and growing levels of inflation and unemployment—and increasing skepticism over the past attempts of government to maintain stability.

Monetarism

The most persistent of the non-interventionist philosophies was monetarism. Not by any means an idea of the 20th century (the so-called "quantity theory of money" was at least a century old) it was given active and, to many people, convincing demonstration by Milton Friedman of the University of Chicago and his colleagues there, including the late Canadian economist, Harry G. Johnson. If the key to a stable economy for the Keynesians was demand, for the monetarists it is money supply. Friedman's basic thesis, which he had advocated for over a quarter-century, is that "inflation is always and everywhere a monetary phenomenon." If the monetary authorities do not validate pressures for price increases by raising the money supply they simply will not take place. If they do increase the money supply and the goods are not available the result will be simply to drive up prices. Furthermore attempts to achieve short-term gains by varying the money supply will do more harm than good. The inflationary effect of monetary increases will be perpetuated long after their introduction, despite later efforts to retract the initial step, and may be destabilizing under altered conditions. Money supply should be the primary concern of the central bank, with matters such as interest rates and the foreign exchange value of the currency taking secondary places. (Some monetarists would have it that the latter should flow from whatever happens when the money supply is proper). Above all the central banks should stop tinkering with the money supply. It should be set at the lowest possible level consistent with activity in the economy and allowed to grow only at the same rate as the economy.

While monetarism is essentially a prescription for central bank policy it also represents a rejection of Keynesian interventionism. Its counterpart approach for fiscal policy was a balanced or nearly balanced budget, with the minimum of other interventionist governmental activities. (However, as will be seen later, Friedman was also a strong advocate of a negative income tax for transfer payment purposes, long regarded by some conservatives as the ultimate step toward the welfare state).

In Canada there are several adherents of the monetarist school. Particularly prominent are academics, then members of the Economics Faculty of the University of Western Ontario (D. Laidler and T.E. Courchene) and members of the Fraser Institute of Vancouver, B.C. whose board has at one time or another in recent years included Friedman, Courchene, Laidler and Johnson, all committed monetarists). Professor Courchene has subjected Bank of Canada policy of the period 1969 to 1981 to two lengthy analyses published by the C.D. Howe Institute. These find execution, judged by monetarist standards, to be wanting. It was in fact the conclusion of one study that the anti-recession increases in money supply in the early 1970s (five years in the 10 to 15 percent annual range) were the breeding ground for much of the inflation that characterized the next decade.

What of the Canadian experience? The monetarist solution was adopted by the Bank of Canada in the targeting of money supply growth from September 1975 to 1982. This appears to have succeeded in reducing inflation to tolerable limits, although (along with other negative developments) at the expense of severe unemployment and for a time extremely high interest rates. Since that time a more "eclectic" policy has been adopted, and money supply growth has periodically exceeded economic activity, as it did in 1983 and the last two quarters of 1985. It can also fall below the rate of economic growth, as it did throughout much of 1986.

The monetarist experience left much unproven, and won few friends in Canada. It failed to satisfy the monetarists, as the execution was thought to be sullied by over-attention to such issues as the level of interest rates and the external value of the dollar. It was held that there should have been more concentration simply on the monetary base of the chartered banks. Furthermore other conditions, such as the growing federal deficit, the oil price shocks, and the issue of the proper concept of money supply were also felt to have worked against a fair trial.

Among the unconvinced, monetarism was an extremely contentious matter. It bore the full brunt of the anger and frustration of politicians, businessmen, labour union leaders, homeowners and others who were suffering the effects of tight credit and high interest rates on loans and mortgages. Many Canadians, accustomed to decades of promises from politicians that "help was on its way," felt that the government had abandoned them to a heartless central bank. Many economists were unwilling to accept the monetarist thesis that most other economic policies should be abandoned, and argued strenuously for the retention of fiscal and other devices. The experiment had undoubtedly given the Bank of Canada, which had previously relied largely on credit conditions as a guide to policy—in which interest rates played a large role—a broadened spectrum of concerns. But in the end it proved to be an insufficient guide for all purposes, and its abandonment was regretted by few.

Supply Side Economics

One of the new policies that emerged in the seventies, primarily in the United States, was labelled Supply Side Economics, and was new mainly in degree, rather than in substance. As is frequently mentioned in the review of Canadian developments, many of the measures adopted were directed to bolstering supply conditions—as contrasted with demand—in the economy. Supply side economics placed full stress on improving all aspects of supply, and in particular the incentive aspects. As applied in the United States, for example, a prominent feature of the Reagan-Stockman supply side program was a substantial reduction in income taxes as an incentive to additional work effort. The resulting huge deficits that have emerged in the U.S. budget have somewhat tarnished this approach.

The Role of Expectations

The most important development in recent policy analysis has been the prominence given to expectations. In particular, *expectations* of the future degree of inflation have been integrated into models of the economy as a governing element. The level of interest rates, for example, will be influenced by the inflationary expectation, as investors will look to the "real" expected return after allowing for expected inflation. But, more disastrously, the process will be self-perpetuating and cumulative. The Macdonald Royal Commission Report explained it as follows:

> If inflation continues for some time, people begin to expect it to continue, and they adjust their behaviour accordingly. If the rate of wage increase starts to rise as unemployment drops below a certain point and labour markets tighten, it is presumably because workers are in a position to earn higher *real* wages. Once the higher rate of wage increase is reflected in costs, however, prices also start to rise more quickly, with the result that workers do not obtain expected increases in *real* wages. If labour markets remain tight, the nominal wage rates demanded and obtained will increase again, to offset the higher rate of price increase. In short, the inflation spiral will continue as long as labour markets are tight.[12.1]

[12.1] Supra footnote 11.20, at 275.

The NAIRU

While reference to an "inflationary spiral" has a familiar ring, the conclusions drawn from the Phillips curve earlier mentioned are new, and ominous. To quote the Macdonald report again:

> The short-run Phillips curve might appear to offer a trade-off between inflation and unemployment. It is critically important, however, to recognize that the position of this curve is fixed only for the rate of inflation *expected* by most participants in the economy. If demand-management policy attempts to take advantage of this apparent short-run trade-off by trying to reduce unemployment below the so-called "normal" unemployment rate for any significant period of time, the expected and actual rates of inflation will progressively shift upward. As the expected rate of inflation increases, as it will if unemployment falls enough to add upward pressure, the short-run Phillips curve and the actual rate of inflation will tend to ratchet progressively upward . . .
>
> The longer the period of time under consideration, the steeper is the trade-off curve. Ultimately, there is no trade-off between sustainable levels of unemployment and the rate of inflation. Associated with this "no long-run trade-off" principle is the notion that there is a critical level of unemployment rate that tends to prevail, on average, over the longer run. This critical unemployment rate has been variously called the "natural," "normal" or "full employment" rate, or, more neutrally, "the non-accelerating inflation rate of unemployment" (NAIRU). When unemployment stands above this rate, inflation will tend to decrease continuously. When unemployment stands below this rate, inflation will tend to increase continuously . . .
>
> The NAIRU is a critically important concept . . . The "no long-run trade-off" principle implies that the NAIRU sets a lower limit to the level of unemployment that expansionary demand-management policy can achieve on a sustained basis. Demand management may still have an important potential function: in general, to stabilize the economy within the range of the NAIRU. Nevertheless, the notion that demand-management policy could achieve even lower rates of unemployment if society were willing to tolerate higher *but stable* rates of inflation evaporated with the general acceptance of the "no long-run trade-off" view. Another key corollary is that the chief way to achieve lower average rates of unemployment over the longer run is to reduce the NAIRU through policies supplementary to demand management policies.[12.2]

The Commission later proposes a range of such policies. It added:

> The proposition that there is no long-run trade-off between inflation and unemployment is consistent with one contention of the monetarist

---

12.2 Ibid., at 275-76.

school: that an increase in the rate of growth of the money supply, beyond the increase required to accommodate the sustainable increase in real output, will eventually result only in higher prices, and not in greater expansion of output and employment. This proposition has now gained wide, though not universal, acceptance. [12.3]

Rational Expectations School

Another evidence of the "expectations" phenomenon is the "Rational Expectations" school of thought. Put briefly, this approach holds that

individuals and businesses base their expectations on a "rational analysis" of the future effects of current and prospective economic policy and other circumstances. In particular, participants in the economy may anticipate the ultimate inflationary impact of any expansionary policy measures. This foresight leads them to boost inflation immediately by demanding higher prices, wages and nominal interest rates in order to avoid being left behind . . . Behaviour based on such rational expectations, combined with very flexible prices and wages, can dissipate, virtually from the start, any real expansionary thrust of macro-economic measures . . . The theory of rational expectations may suggest that demand management can have no impact on real variables such as output and employment. Yet most policy makers would agree that this conclusion goes beyond what happens in the real world . . . Nonetheless, the rational expectations analysis at least reminds us of the common-sense tenet that expectations have a critical influence on economic behaviour. [12.4]

Open Economy Problems

Most relevant for Canada is increased attention to the problems of economic management in an open economy. The Mundell-Fleming model held that

a country with fixed exchange rates could use fiscal policy but not monetary policy, to pursue domestic income and employment goals. Flexible exchange rates reversed the possibilities. [This model was later found wanting, but it had at least] yielded two insights of lasting importance for macro-economic theory. First, it stressed, as earlier analysis had not, that the balance of payments consists of more than the trade balance; it also includes the balance of capital flows, to which economists and policy makers must pay attention in devising economic policy in an open economy. Secondly, the analysis clearly demonstrated the fact that in an open economy, the manner in which domestic policy impinges on purely domestic goals, let alone on the balance of payments and exchange rate targets, depends on the nature of the country's exchange rate regime. [12.5]

12.3 Ibid., at 276-77.

12.4 Ibid., at 278-79.

12.5 Ibid., at 291.

Later analysis led to different conclusions.

Modern analysis makes it abundantly clear that, contrary to the Mundell-Fleming model, adopting a flexible exchange rate does not turn an open economy into one that for the purposes of conducting policy may be treated as if it were closed. Flexible rates do give an open economy latitude in choosing its own long-run inflation rate, but they do not insulate it from the short-run, but often severe, effects of monetary turbulence abroad . . . Above all, this theory increasingly stresses that the pursuit of domestic policy goals is interdependent with actions affecting the balance of payments and exchange rates . . .

These conclusions are very different from those formed by macro-economists of the early post-war period, which seemed to suggest that the authorities of a country such as Canada had broad scope to fine-tune the performance of their domestic economies. Views on these matters have shifted for two reasons. First, understanding of the way in which the economy works has changed. To some extent, the current, more pessimistic view of the possibilities of fine-tuning the economy are based on analyses of interactions that have long been at work in the world, but that earlier analyses failed to take into account. However, the second reason—one that encourages Commissioners to take those views seriously—is the changed nature of the world. The international economy is much more integrated now than it was 20 or 30 years ago. In particular, the world capital market has been transformed beyond recognition, both in size and efficiency, reducing the latitude available to the government of an open economy to pursue autonomous macro-economic policies.[12.6]

Continuing Research

There is continuing attention in economic research to the emergence of stagflation, the ultimate contradiction in economic theory. The tenor and content of much of this process has already been indicated. Much exploratory research has continued through computer engineered econometric models on unemployment, inflation, energy price shocks and shortages, and the relationship of money supply, exchange and interest rate levels, social attitudes, and government programs to these phenomenon. The flavour of some of this research is given, for example, in the Supplement to *Canadian Public Policy* of April 1981, on "The Challenge of Inflation and Unemployment," and "Has Monetarism Failed?" Numerous other sources could be cited.

The Macdonald Commission on Economic Policy

The Macdonald Commission Report had some relevant thoughts on the status of fiscal and monetary policy. In a review of the performance, after

---

[12.6] Ibid., at 293-94.

outlining some of the advances in economic knowledge over the recent period (lags, trade-offs, expectations, etc., with much emphasis on the NAIRU concept) the report sums up the present position of economists as follows:

> The majority of to-day's macro-economists still use an expanded version of the analytical framework that evolved out of Keynes' theories. They think that both monetary and, at least in the shorter run, fiscal policy can influence nominal aggregate demand, and that changes in nominal demand have at least some short-run effects on real demand, output and employment. Generally, they believe that what can be broadly termed "Keynesian policies" have contributed significantly to making economic fluctuations substantially less severe in the post-war period than they were in the preceding hundred years. Finally, many still accept that periodic severe shortfalls of total demand which the operation of "normal" market forces does not solve quickly— the basic Keynesian problem—are a continuing danger and create an important function for active monetary and fiscal policy.

> To-day's economists do, however, generally stress short- and long-run effects on prices more than did the original Keynesian analysts. Furthermore, the majority now accept the view that there is little or no possibility of using expansionary demand policy to achieve sustained reductions in unemployment that will reduce that factor below the NAIRU, and they are unwilling to tolerate the inflation that would accompany such policy. Although they do not view the work of establishing a satisfactory analytical framework as complete, they sometimes think back wistfully to the "good old days", when it seemed unnecessary for economic analysis to concern itself with such a variable human element as expectations, when the profession's reputation for forecasting . . . was higher, and when the policy advice it offered tended to be more palatable and more welcome.

> These general propositions appear to command the support of a sufficient number of to-day's macro-economists to be considered as the mainstream view. [However, on important issues of degree there are differences. On inflation]: Neither is there consensus as to whether attempting to achieve further reductions in inflation (say, going all the way to a zero rate) would be worthwhile, given the economic and social costs of postponing full recovery that such a course would probably involve. Nor is there any agreement about whether inflation should be addressed solely through non-inflationary demand management, which relates, primarily, to monetary policy, or by supplementing such policy with some form of incomes policy . . . A smaller number claim that a permanent incomes policy would make it possible to achieve permanently lower rates of unemployment, without touching off another inflationary spiral: that is, that such a policy would lower the NAIRU. Finally, there is no consensus as to whether monetary and fiscal policy are best conducted according to fixed, relatively simple, publicly stated rules, or whether it is useful to take

discretionary action in response to the evolving course of, and outlook for, the economy.[12.7]

These variations largely involve quantitative measurements and judgements as to crucial turning points, and are of great importance.

These differences, which reflect considerable uncertainty about the effectiveness of various policy options and the nature of the trade-offs among them, are important because they underlie the difficulties we Canadians face as we consider means of improving macro-economic performance.[12.8]

The Commissioners themselves had some penetrating observations to make on past and future economic management.

Commissioners conclude that the difficulties to which fine-tuning is so clearly subject and the potential contribution to stable expectations that governments can make by following steady policies oriented to the medium term provide a strong case for rejecting short-term adjustments of monetary and fiscal policy as long as departures from a non-inflationary growth path are moderate. Granting this, however, we note that the current state of economic analysis falls considerably short of offering clear guidance for developing satisfactory medium-term guidelines for setting policy. For this reason, we think it worth considering an approach based on targeting monetary and fiscal policy in relation to non-inflationary growth of nominal GNP. Furthermore, while we support a medium-term rather than a "fine-tuning" approach, we do not exclude the possibility of supplementing automatic stabilization with discretionary action in times of wide and protracted departures from satisfactory levels of nominal demand. The existing high levels of unemployment and the prospects for their slow reduction suggest that the current situation may constitute the kind of exceptional case just described.[12.9]

This admonition, while based on latest economic thought, has somewhat of a familiar ring.

[12.7] Ibid., at 279-81.

[12.8] Ibid.

[12.9] Ibid., at 313.

Bibliography,
chapters 9 to 12

Auld, D.A.L. "The Scope for Short-Run Stabilization Policy Within Confederation." In *Fiscal Dimensions of Canadian Federalism*. ed. Richard M. Bird. Toronto: Canadian Tax Foundation, 1980.

Barber, Clarence L. Comment. "The Scope for Short-Run Stabilization Policy Within Confederation. In *Fiscal Dimensions of Canadian Federalism*. ed. Richard Bird. Toronto: Canadian Tax Foundation, 1980.

Beigie, Carl E. *Inflation is a Social Malady*. British-North American Committee. Montreal: C.D. Howe Institute, 1979.

Bossons, John. "Comments I: Issues in Analysis of Government Deficits." In *Fiscal and Monetary Policy*. Collected Research Studies of the Royal Commission on the Economic Union and Development Prospects for Canada, vol. 26. Toronto: University of Toronto Press, 1986.

Bouey, Gerald. *Monetary Policy—Finding a Place to Stand*. 1982 Per Jacobsson Lecture. Toronto: September 5, 1982.

Bruce, Neil, and Purvis, Douglas D. "Evaluating the Deficit: The Case for Budget Cuts." *Policy Commentary no. 4*. Toronto: C.D. Howe Institue, 1984.

———. "Consequences of Government Budget Deficits." In John Sargent, research coordinator, *Fiscal and Monetary Policy*. Collected Research Studies of the Royal Commission on the Economic Union and Development Prospects for Canada, vol. 26. Toronto: University of Toronto Press, 1986.

Canada. Department of Finance. *The Federal Deficit in Perspective*. Budget Papers. Ottawa: 1983.

———. Prices and Incomes Commission. *Summary Report: Inflation, Unemployment and Economic Policy*. Ottawa: 1972.

———. *Report of the Royal Commission on Banking and Finance*. Ottawa: 1965.

———. *Report of the Royal Commission on the Economic Union and Development Prospects for Canada*, vol. 2. Ottawa: 1985.

———. *Report of the Royal Commission on Taxation*. Ottawa: 1966.

———. Standing Senate Finance Committee on National Finances. Report. *Growth, Employment and Price Stability*. Ottawa: 1971.

Canadian Institute for Economic Policy. *Out of Joint with the Times*. Ottawa: The Institute, 1979.

Carmichael, Edward A. "Tackling the Federal Deficit." *Observation no. 26*. Toronto: C.D. Howe Institute, 1984.

C.D. Howe Research Institute. *Policy Review and Outlook, 1974-80*. Montreal: the Institute, 1974.

Courchene, Thomas J. *Money, Inflation and the Bank of Canada*. An Analysis of Canadian Monetary Policy from 1970 to early 1975. Montreal: C.D. Howe Research Institute, 1976.

———. *Money, Inflation, and the Bank of Canada, Volume II*. An Analysis of Monetary Gradualism, 1975-80. Montreal: C.D. Howe Institute, 1981.

———. *No Place to Stand? Abandoning Monetary Targets: An Evaluation*. Montreal: C.D. Howe Institute, 1983.

Donner, Arthur W., and Peters, Douglas D. *The Monetarist Counter-Revolution*. Toronto: Canadian Institute for Economic Policy, James Lorimer, 1979.

Economic Council of Canada. *Review, 1964-1988*. Ottawa: annual.

Gibson, J. Douglas. "Government Spending as an Engine of Inflation." Editorial. (March-April 1975), 82 *The Canadian Banker and ICB Review*.

Gillespie, W. Irwin. "Postwar Canadian Fiscal Policy Revisited, 1945-1975." (May-June 1979) 26 *Canadian Tax Journal*, 265-76.

Gordon, H. Scott, Winder, John W.L., Slater, David W., and Deutsch, John J. In Kaliski, S.F. ed. *Canadian Economic Policy Since the War*. Montreal: Canadian Trade Committee, 1966.

Gordon, H. Scott. *The Economists versus The Bank of Canada:* Why twenty-nine economics professors signed a letter to the Minister of Finance calling for a drastic reorganization of the Bank of Canada. Toronto: Ryerson Press, 1961.

Johnson, Harry. *Canada in a Changing World*. Alan B. Plaunt Memorial Lectures, Carleton University, 1962. Toronto: University of Toronto Press, 1962.

McIvor, Craig R. *Canadian Monetary, Banking and Fiscal Development*. Toronto: The MacMillan Company of Canada Limited, 1958.

Ontario. Department of Treasury and Economics. *The Reconstruction of Economic and Fiscal Policy in Canada*. Toronto: the Department, 1971.

Ontario. Economic Council. *Policies for Stagflation: Focus on Supply* vols. 1 and 2. Toronto: the Council, 1981.

Perry, J. Harvey. "Some Aspects of Recent Fiscal Policy." Paper presented at Annual Meeting of the Canadian Political Science Association. Ottawa, 1957. (July-August 1957) 5 *Canadian Tax Journal*, 285-98.

Purvis, Douglas, D. and Smith, Constance. "Fiscal Policy in Canada: 1963-84." In John Sargent, research coordinator, *Fiscal and Monetary Policy*. Collected Research Studies of the Royal Commission on the Economic Union and Development Prospects for Canada, vol. 26. Toronto: University of Toronto Press, 1986.

Shoyama, T. "The Economics of Gradual Improvement." (March-April 1982) 3 *Policy Options*, 6-11.

Smith, David C. "Full Employment Policy: A New Force or a Hollow Slogan?" (Autumn 1975) *The Canadian Banker*, 5-17.

_____. *Economic Policy Advising in Canada*. Essays in Honour of John Deutsch. Montreal: C.D. Howe Institute, 1981.

Reuber, Grant L. *Canada's Political Economy, Current Issues*. Toronto: McGraw-Hill Ryerson Limited, 1980.

University of Guelph. "The Challenge of Inflation and Unemployment." *Has Monetarism Failed?* Special Number *Canadian Public Policy*, 1981.

Will, Robert M. *Canadian Fiscal Policy 1945-63*. Study for the Royal Commission on Taxation, no. 17. Ottawa: Queen's Printer, 1967.

Wilson, Thomas A. "The Scope for Short-Run Stabilization Policy within Confederation." Comment. In *Fiscal Dimensions of Canadian Federalism*. Ed. Richard M. Bird. Toronto: Canadian Tax Foundation, 1980.

Part 3
Tax Reform

13
Reform by Royal Commission

From the survey we have conducted so far it is obvious that taxes are in a constant state of change. No other aspect of government annually produces more than a small fraction of the legislation, frequently running to hundreds of pages of provisions of baffling complexity, required for the income tax alone. However, as though to stem the tide and examine the flood in situ, governments periodically conduct a process known as "tax reform." For the general public the only reform that would be of relevance would be a reduction in the tax burden, and this is such an unlikely outcome that the process is regarded with a certain skepticism. Lately this expectation has been completely aborted by "revenue-neutral" reforms, an objective that leaves much to the imagination and introduces a certain teasing element to the quest.

For government officials and tax professionals reform offers an opportunity to clear up anomalies that have arisen in the process of making annual amendments under pressure. More important is the opportunity provided for the public, legislators, tax specialists, economists, and others to see the tax system as a whole. This includes an appraisal of the general state of individual taxes, the relationship of these to each other and the extent to which the system overall is promoting some larger objectives, such as economic growth, industrial development, equity, income distribution, frequently expected that all of them, and others as well, will be simultaneously achieved. The process of overall revision is therefore a delicate one. As the British government discovered in its tax policies for the American colonies, the results of ineptitude can be explosive. Citizens and businesses that have made long-term plans on the basis of existing tax provisions do not take at all kindly to having these provisions drastically revised or even withdrawn. For this reason alone the scope for major changes is rather limited, unless by an unusual combination of circumstances and political skill the public is persuaded to accept some drastic alterations. This appears to have been the situation in the United States in 1986, when a very substantial reform package was passed by the Congress with only limited public protest.

Canadian Experience

There have been only three revisions of sufficient scope to qualify as "tax reform" in Canada, that of the Royal Commission on Taxation (1967-71), the November 1981 budget (MacEachen) and the reforms proposed in the Reform White Paper of June 1987 (Wilson). We will turn to these in a moment. There are several lesser developments that may be mentioned, however.[13.1] The tariff, of course, since adoption of the National Policy in 1879 has been subjected to periodic reforms; later developments under the GATT agreements and other arrangements are described in chapters 30 to 35.

The Report of the Royal Commission on Dominion-Provincial Relations (1940) made proposals for extensive changes in the Canadian tax system, which, although World War II prevented adoption of many specific proposals, nonetheless provided the philosophical basis for much postwar development. Two royal commissions reported in 1945 on vexing issues—the Royal Commission on Taxation of Annuities and Family Corporations and the Royal Commission on Co-operatives, their findings being substantially implemented. A clean-up and overhaul of the Income Tax Act took place after World War II, as explained in the following:

Immediately after the war there was pressure from the business and professional community for a review of all the federal tax laws and their administration. Many of the hastily introduced wartime emergency measures had cluttered up the statutes with provisions that badly needed revision. There was also growing impatience with the lack of official and published rules for the guidance of taxpayers. In many important areas the administration had been given authority to make a decision with no right of appeal for the taxpayer—the so-called ministerial discretion. This system had been acceptable before the war when income tax affected only 300,000 taxpayers at most and was a game played largely by professionals. But the war changed all that; by 1945 it had become a mass phenomenon affecting millions of Canadians. A wholly new approach was called for.

This pressure for reform resulted in the enactment of a completely revised Income Tax Act that came into effect in 1949. Extensive public hearings by a Special Committee of the Senate in 1945 and 1946 (Counsel Mr. Heward Stikeman) produced a catalogue of complaints which was useful to the process of revision. In addition to some clarification of its basic principles, the main features of the new statute were: the replacement of nearly all areas of ministerial discretion with written law; the establishment of a Tax Appeal Board as an informal tribunal for the average taxpayer; the adoption of a new basis of depreciation, known as the capital cost allowance system, with regulations which established schedules of rates for categories of capital expenditures; and the incorporation of the 10 percent dividend tax credit, introduced in the budget of 1949, as a permanent feature of the tax system.[13.2]

The adoption of the dividend tax credit and the granting of a reduced rate for small corporations represented a marked shift in principle under the income tax, one that has persisted in some form until today.

[13.1] In view of the author's extensive writing on tax reform in other publications and in the interests of economy of time and effort, he will be quoting liberally from those sources in the following pages.

[13.2] J. Harvey Perry, *Background of Current Fiscal Problems*, Canadian Tax Paper no. 68 (Toronto: Canadian Tax Foundation, July 1982), 77.

One of the first of many reviews of the federal manufacturers' sales tax was made by a small committee in 1956 under the chairmanship of Kenneth Carter; the sales tax still stands largely unrevised over 30 years later, despite general agreement on the need.

The conversion of the federal death tax from a succession duty to an estate form of tax in 1959 was a significant change, although not nearly as important as the complete abandonment of the federal estate tax in 1972.

The Royal Commission on Taxation, 1962-67

The author, a member of the commission, explained its origin and work in the following paper to a Conference on its Twentieth Anniversary held in March 1987.

The Background

The Commission was appointed by the Diefenbaker government during a period rather reminiscent of our own. The economy was ailing, there was heavy unemployment, inflation was a constant threat, and the budget was in deficit. After the end of World War II there had been a decade of almost unbroken prosperity, but this had begun to unravel in the mid-fifties. The break had come in 1957, when real growth in GNP dropped from 8½ percent in the previous year to 2½ percent, and then averaged 3 percent over the next four years. Unemployment, after being in the 2-4 percent range for a decade, went to 7 percent in 1958 and stayed in that region for another four years. Capital expenditure had declined and there were serious balance of payments problems.

These conditions were in shocking contrast to the previous decade, and represented the first serious test of the government's Keynesian full-employment policies adopted in 1945. In keeping with the general prescription for deficits to counterbalance an economic slump the budget had gone into the red in 1958 and stayed there for the following five years.

Various direct tax incentives and employment measures had been adopted, but with negligible results. Economists were later to say that the effort had been too weak, and that more aggressive action should have been taken. However, then, as now, the business community was seriously concerned about deficits for which there appeared to be no end. These deficits were moderate compared to current experience, but brought heavy pressure on the Minister of Finance, Donald Fleming, to get control of the situation. In a dilemma that most postwar Ministers of Finance have faced, he tried to serve the dual purposes of economic stimulation and deficit reduction, without notable success with either. For the latter he relied mainly on tax increases, particularly in the 1959 and 1960 budgets. As a result the federal-Ontario corporation tax rate rose from 49 percent in 1958 to 52 percent in 1960, almost the highest postwar rate. The top marginal rate of personal income tax was 80 percent, quite high compared to our present 50-plus top combined tax. Many commodity tax rates had also been raised. But deficits had persisted, due partly to a sluggish economy but also to a 50 percent rise in expenditures between 1956 and 1962. The government had inherited from the Liberals the beginnings of the social security program—unemployment insurance, family allowances, old age security, the hospital insurance plan —and these outlays, along with larger payments to the provinces, were mainly responsible for the expenditure increase.

The Tax Side

Obviously there were grounds for concern in these conditions, and they no doubt were part of the reason for the appointment of the Commission. But there were problems more directly related to taxation which needed attention.

The Canadian federal tax structure of 1962 was the product of half a century of improvisation, and this process had left its mark. Except for the tariff, its main elements—the corporate income tax, the personal income tax, and the manufacturers' sales tax—had been thrown together in the five years 1916 to 1921 during and following World War I, and an inheritance tax had been hastily added in World War II. In short, most of the main taxes had been imposed under conditions of grave emergency, with no time for planning and study. The wording of the income tax statute had been borrowed largely from the United States, and as it had to be interpreted in the light of British jurisprudence, the results were frequently chaotic.

Worse still, a myth had been perpetuated for provincial consumption that possibly these taxes were temporary and would someday be repealed, a myth given some substance by the low level to which they were reduced in the late twenties. A corollary of this myth was the retention of the word "War" in the two main statutes for 30 years after they were first enacted. They were only removed in 1949, by which time it had become fairly clear that the feds had moved in to stay.

Despite the tentative status of the federal taxes their nurture from year to year was about the same as that of other countries—they were modified, amended, raised, lowered, and otherwise adapted to whatever was the immediate need, be it a war, a boom, a depression, an election, a federal-provincial agreement, or whatever. On the whole our taxes were neither markedly worse nor better than those of other countries. But they had never been subjected to any thorough examination as a whole system to determine whether the various components were in best order, and whether there was any logical relationship between them—known in current language as the tax mix.

The Royal Commission on Dominion-Provincial Relations in its 1940 report had come close to such a study, and there had been attention to some of the main components, such as the revision of the Income Tax Act in 1949, and studies of selected features by commissions and committees. Beginnings had been made in some areas, such as the dividend tax credit introduced in 1949, but these had not been pursued to their logical conclusion. In short, changes were pretty much the result of an annual process of improvisation to meet the latest acute problem without a firm base to guide decisions. This pragmatism was thought by many to be a thing of beauty, and of course there is much to be said for the incremental process, as long as the basic objectives are clear. But having observed some 25 years or so of improvisation, both from inside and outside of government, by 1962 I found it amateurish, unprofessional, and in the end disastrous. It was like a football or hockey game for which no rules had been devised. All sorts of important decisions were being made by annual changes frequently having no sounder base than that taxpayers wanted them. Measures were being introduced to provide a temporary answer for situations that should have been dealt with years ago in accordance with some general principles.

Some Instances

For example, one of the issues that was acute at the time was the tax status of so-called capital gains, a subject on which obfuscation has probably achieved its finest hour. The courts had been struggling with this question and the results were almost complete chaos, in general because of the need to apply British jurisprudence to law basically American in origin. There were mixed views as to how long this process should be allowed to continue, but as the issue became more and more confused there were increasing demands for certainty, some argued even at the price of a tax—a small tax, that is. But if there ever was an instance of the need for very solid grounds in principle to end a confused situation this was it. The courts were trying to decide whether an adventure in the nature of trade was being carried out, but no one was trying to decide what income was and why we were trying to tax it.

Another vexing issue of the day, in which the administration and the taxpayers had fought to a draw, was the matter of surplus stripping. Distributions from corporate surpluses were taxable at the prevailing high rates and whereas, with a public company, the surplus could in effect be liquidated by selling shares on the market, in the case of a closely held company the only alternative was to liquidate by selling out. Surplus stripping avoided this undesirable choice, and generally could be easily achieved by a series of bookkeeping stratagems. As a result the government had adopted increasingly severe and arbitrary legislation to neutralize these practices. There had been several studies and attempts at solutions, but no permanent answer had been found. Again the wrong approach was being taken; the questions that should have been asked, and were not, were: where does the corporation fit into the tax constellation? should it be taxed? if so, how? and how should that tax fit into the rest of the tax system?

One could list dozens of similar issues where lack of a conceptual basis resulted in constant confusion and improvisation. It may sound like pie in the sky, but the tax commission started out to find answers not just to some of these questions, but to all of them. And it did find answers; the fact that they frightened many of the good citizens in the country half to death was perhaps not surprising, as they departed very materially from previous answers.

The Commission is Appointed

The exact motives of the Diefenbaker government in appointing the commission are slightly obscure. Obviously the Prime Minister would not have been deeply concerned with these rather technical tax issues. In fact the terms of reference were said to have been drawn up by three senior officials, one of whom I suspect is on the platform this morning. It has been said that Mr. Diefenbaker acted with an eye to political advantage, not an unreasonable objective for a politician, as the proposal of an inquiry had been advanced by politically influential persons and organizations. However, it seems equally possible that Mr. Diefenbaker simply liked royal commissions. Certainly he appointed enough of them—there was the Glassco Commission on Government Organization, the O'Leary Commission on Canadian Magazines and Other Periodicals, the Porter Commission on Banking and Finance, The Gill Committee on Unemployment Insurance, the Carter Commission on Taxation, and the Hall Commission on Health Services, among others. Whatever his motives in this approach he gave heavy hostage to political fortune—and time ran out. His government was defeated in 1963 and the reports of most of his commissions were left for the Liberals to implement or not, as they wished. This inevitably meant that the Report of the Royal Commission on Taxation was not embraced with as much ardour as one would have expected had the Commission been a Liberal appointment; but I have never personally felt that this was a major factor in its consideration. In the end the Liberals were not prepared to go to bat for the full report, but their White Paper was a pretty good try, and it was factors beyond government control that determined the final outcome.

The appointment of the commission and its six members was announced by September 1962. The Chairman, Kenneth Carter, was a prominent Canadian accountant who had headed several organizations, including the Canadian Tax Foundation, and had been chairman of a small committee appointed by the Liberals in 1955 to consider problems under the manufacturers' sales tax. I had known him for many years as a liberal-minded and able person having no identifiable political leanings.

The other two members with a fairly extensive background in taxation were myself and Emile Beauvais. I had been in the Taxation Division of the Department of Finance for 16 years when it was composed largely of Kenneth Eaton and myself; the Canadian Tax Foundation had published my *Taxation in Canada* while I was still in government. In 1952 I left Ottawa to become Director of the Tax Foundation, where for eight years I was in close contact with the best tax professionals in the country. I had undertaken missions to two African countries on fiscal matters, and by frequent visits to Washington and Europe had kept closely in touch with major international tax developments. In short I was reasonably well equipped for the commission assignment. Emile Beauvais, with extensive professional and business experience, was to serve the dual role of tax professional and regional representative for Quebec.

The three other members were largely appointed on a regional basis: Charlie Walls, an agricultural association executive in British Columbia;

Mrs. Eleanor Milne, the prairies' representative with connections with The National Council of Women, who also assisted her husband in his accounting practice; and Donald Grant, of Halifax, Nova Scotia, Director and General Manager of the Nova Scotia Trust Co., who had other business connections.

The Terms of Reference

In mid-September 1962, the commission's terms of reference were published. They included almost every significant aspect of taxation, except for the tax transfer system, now so important, federal-provincial relations, and the tariff. There is not time to read them in full here, but the following will give a notion of their breadth. We were to inquire into: the incidence and effects of taxation, the operation of the national economy, the conduct of business, the organization of industry, and the position of individuals. Also we were to consider specifically: the distribution of the burdens among taxpayers; exemptions, reliefs and allowances provided in the personal and corporate income tax; the effects of the tax system on employment, living standards, savings and investment, industrial productivity, and economic stability and growth; anomalies or inequities; action to close loopholes; encouragement of Canadian ownership; greater clarity, simplicity and effectiveness, and generally anything else the commission felt was relevant to its study. Obviously the government wanted a very broad inquiry.

Carter and Perry Meet

With terms of reference in hand Carter and I agreed on an early meeting to consider strategy. As we enjoyed a close personal relationship based on a long friendship there were no communication problems between us and we agreed fairly quickly and easily on a general approach. We agreed that the work of the commission would be based on thorough research into all the known principles and practices of taxation, with input from the three main professions concerned—the legal, the accounting, and the economic. We would pay little attention to specific problems until some principles had been developed and tested. Carter had a favourite saying that we were all to hear many times—"There is no good practice that is not based on a sound theory"—and this became an answer to all doubters about the direction of our research. I didn't need any inspiration to stimulate me; I had been disillusioned with band-aid tax-making for some time, and was ready to seek a different approach.

Carter and I had both developed short lists of areas to cover and at his request I developed these into a much more detailed compilation. After substantial revisions and additions by the research staff this became the basis of what has been described as the most ambitious program of tax research ever undertaken to that time.

I must summarize the actual operations of the commission as briefly as possible in the interests of getting to our report. The planned research program called for a delicate process of coordinating the efforts of three disciplines not noted for their mutual warm regard—lawyers, accountants, and economists. This task was carried out with supreme skill and unstinting application by Professor Douglas Hartle, of the Department of Political Economy of the University of Toronto, as Director of Research. Although the staff numbered over 100 at its peak we seemed always to be delayed by the difficulty of obtaining economists, the other royal commissions having depleted the supply. Nonetheless we had some excellent people from all three disciplines; studies were also prepared for us by outside experts.

At the outset the chairman visited all provinces to explain our role and to suggest the launching of similar provincial studies. Most provinces responded, and as we progressed there were meetings between both commission members and staffs and exchange of research materials, although obviously not of conclusions. We held private sessions with distinguished fiscal experts from abroad, and the chairman, sometimes accompanied by myself, visited fiscal experts and officials both in Europe and the United States. Commissioner Walls went to Australia to study their sales tax, which we thought might hold some lessons for our federal tax.

The commission of course met its expected public responsibilities; hearings were held all over Canada, and in all 300 briefs were received. The research approach was extended to these briefs, and commissioners were required not only to study the original presentation but as well a staff analysis that was sometimes longer than the original—altogether a tiring business. It was further complicated by the simultaneous production by the research staff of papers based on the agreed research program, which seldom had anything in common with the material that was originating from our hearings. In fact the gap between the unlimited vistas the commissioners were privately viewing and the particular subjects our witnesses regarded as important put considerable strain on our ability to maintain public aplomb. I suppose in the trauma-prone atmosphere of Washington this would have qualified as some sort of a cover-up—probably a Cartergate—but I assure you that no witness had any cause to feel that his or her representation had not been fully and patiently considered. In this we were greatly aided by our counsel, Jack Stewart, Stanley Edwards, and later Jack Coyne. Perhaps in the end we were too accommodating to our witnesses. They quite properly assumed from the careful attention they received that it was their problems and their suggested solutions that formed the substance of the inquiry, and were shocked and angered to find when the report appeared that the commission had developed a mind of its own of which there had been no previous indication whatever. This appears to be a problem with all public inquiries, where the decisions as to recommendations must of necessity be made in private; otherwise they would probably never be made. Perhaps Donald Macdonald broke new ground in signalling the free trade recommendation of his commission very early on, and this certainly opened the subject for debate before his report was broadly circulated. At the same time I doubt if free trade had the immediate, personal and painful impact of a suggestion to tax capital gains in full.

The Report

The following is a very simplified presentation of the commission's main conclusions and the manner in which it recommended that they be implemented. I will treat these as general views, acknowledging that two members disagreed with some of them. I paraphrase here to save time, and will by no means be able to cover everything in this massive document.

The Economic Analysis

First, a brief comment on the extensive economic analysis that appeared mainly in Volume 2. The attention of economists of the day had focused on the fiscal and monetary performance of the 1957-62 period, and there was general disillusionment with what was regarded as the ineptness of the government in applying the new programs for economic stabilization. The commission's economists were no exception, agreeing with the general conclusion that the problem had been a shortfall in aggregate demand, which the government could have overcome with more aggressive action. However, the report expressed continued confidence in the value of the revenue-expenditure system for stability and growth, employing in its analysis concepts that were then in vogue, such as overcoming the fiscal drag, measuring the success of fiscal policy by the full employment surplus, being mindful of the limitations implied by the post-Keynesian Phillips curve, etc. For short-term stabilization the personal income tax was superior; for long-term growth, general tax measures to stimulate saving and capital expenditure were suitable. But shifts in policy should be less drastic and less frequent. Those of the past caused confusion and because of lags were often counterproductive. There should be longer term objectives, and a steadier course for achieving them.

One statement I observed in a quick rereading of the economic document was a warning against employing a formula for automatic full indexation for inflation. As in my own view inflation's effects could have been alleviated without bringing the budget to its present shambles, I found this most gratifying. As a further expression of personal view I must say that the implementation of postwar fiscal policy has left my loyalties about equally divided between the economists and the politicians. Ministers of Finance, most of whom were lawyers—present company excepted—were being asked to apply policies that were generally contrary to all public expectations, were incapable of being tested, and the limitations of which have become more apparent with growing economic sophistication. Who, twenty years ago, had even heard of NAIRU, the expectations adjusted Phillips curve, or the cyclically and inflation adjusted deficit, or even the tax expenditure concept? But here I will stop, mindful that I am on a platform with Bob Bryce, Canada's original and most distinguished Keynesian scholar, and Ben Benson, the deficit giant-killer of all time—see his 1968 to 1970 budgets.

The Tax Side

Turning to the taxation side, the following are the basic propositions of the report, from which almost everything else followed:

1. Taxes are levied mainly to provide revenues for the conduct of government.

2. Taxes are paid by people. They are not paid by corporations, partnerships, gifts, bequests, estates, trusts, sales, transfers, investments, savings, property, consumer expenditures, or any of the long list of things we usually list as subjects of taxation. Taxes imposed on these subjects are only a means of taxing people.

3. As taxes are paid by people, the first rule in imposing them is that they must be fair. To demonstrate—one simple method of financing government might be just to divide the total government expenditure of, let us say, $200 billion by the total population, of, say, 25 million, and levy a per capita tax of $8,000, leaving it to each individual to find that amount of money as best he or she could. Single wealthy millionaires would pay $8,000 and poor families with four children would pay $48,000. The immediate reaction of everyone, except perhaps wealthy single millionaires, would be that this would be an extremely unfair method of taxation. A fairness concept in taxation implies that the burden must be commensurate with the economic position of the taxpayer.

4. A progressive tax system best reflects this concept of fairness. As surplus income above needs increases, it is fair to tax a larger proportion of that surplus.

5. It also follows from the fairness test that distinctions between taxpayers in similar circumstances should be kept to the minimum. While the imposition of taxes cannot escape having economic effects these should not be deliberately introduced into the system, as they result in differences in tax burden. Taxes should therefore be kept as neutral as possible.

6. The tax that is most capable of fairly reflecting taxable capacity is the personal income tax, as it can directly take account of the economic status, family obligations, and other non-discretionary commitments of the taxpayer.

7. Using the personal income tax as the sole source of revenue would require rates so high that there would be unpredictable consequences for incentives, savings, and investment. Furthermore, other proposals the commission was making required that the top personal rate should not exceed 50 percent. Therefore to provide sufficient revenue without exceeding this rate, taxes on businesses, corporations, personal consumption, and property would have to be continued. But they should be kept to a minimum and wherever possible should be integrated with the personal income tax.

8. As a means of removing the discriminatory effect of double taxation of corporate income, the corporation income tax should be allowed in full as a credit against personal income tax. This would be achieved through a gross-up-and-credit procedure, since known as integration.

9. Fairness required that the concept of income should be made as broad as possible. The term the commission used, one familiar in tax literature, was "comprehensive tax base." It was described technically as the increment in command over economic resources in the year by individuals and families. Technically all increments, whether realized or not, should be included, but the Commission did not push the concept that far. Nor could all benefits, such as the rental value of a home, be included for reasons of practical administration. For most taxpayers, with only wage and salary income, the effect would be minimal, mainly involving inclusion of some forms of employee benefits not previously taxed, but with an offsetting allowance for employment expenses. For others the effect would be a substantial addition to income, arising principally from the full inclusion of capital gains, gifts, bequests, and some but no all forms of accruing income. These inclusions would be offset by deductions such as the full amount of capital losses, provision for retirement pensions, and other forms of saving and averaging devices to smooth lifetime personal income.

10. In its approach to accruing and untaxed income the Commission took the position that a tax deferred was a tax minimized or possibly a tax escaped entirely. The full application of this rule would have required taxing all income as earned—for example, treating corporations in the same way as partnerships—which of course was recognized as unreal. However, as often as possible the commission favoured the removal of tax deferral opportunities, such as that offered by foreign non-business income.

11. The family should be the basic economic unit for personal income tax. This would end tax minimization by intra-family transactions and give a fairer measure of ability to pay.

The Theories in Practice

It would require several hours to spell out the way in which the commission visualized the application of these basic propositions. They were illustrated with great diligence—those who were to suffer would say with masochistic tenacity—in the five volumes of the report and its accompanying 27 studies. Again I will have to merely sketch, without details.

The Personal Income Tax

The personal income tax would be the centrepiece, with a top rate of 50 percent. Capital gains would be taxed in full, capital losses would be allowed in full, and gifts and bequests would be included as income, thereby allowing repeal of the gift and death taxes. The existing dividend tax credit would be replaced by a tax credit of 50 percent of the grossed up dividend from Canadian companies, with a refund for any amount of tax not offset. Some forms of income would be newly taxed, such as patronage dividends, benefits accruing for the taxpayer in various ways, such as interest on insurance policies, and several previously untaxed casual receipts and employment benefits.

Capital gains would be taxed without distinction for holding periods or type of property, except for a $25,000 lifetime allowance on the sale of a principal residence. Dividends, whether in cash or the equivalent, would be taxable, with full credit for corporation tax. As the prevailing economic unit, family income would be pooled for tax purposes. Personal exemptions would be converted to tax credits. The tax base, broadened as outlined, would permit a substantial reduction in personal income tax rates, particularly for the lower incomes. The net result would be a considerable redistribution of tax burden, which the commission had found was far from progressive.

Corporate Income Tax

The corporation is one of the miracles of the 20th century. Whether small or large or privately or publicly owned it has been the vehicle for much of our economic growth. But the corporate income tax gave the commission endless problems. The more it studied the tax the more it regretted that it had ever been conceived. The corporation is an intermediary, having no life apart from the humans who own it, manage it, and deal with it, and as a subject for taxation presents a tangle of problems. Its effects and incidence are unpredictable and its revenue yields uncertain. It creates tax complexities out of all proportion to its low contribution to the revenues, about 7 percent at present in Canada.

There were so many arguments against and so few for the tax that our mood was to recommend that it be entirely abandoned. No business representative ever made this suggestion, but the commissioners would have had a job containing their enthusiasm if anyone had. Complete repeal of course would be naive and unacceptable politically, even though the "corporate bum" label had yet to make its appearance. The source of much of the national income and the holder of much of the national wealth could not, politically, be excused from taxation. Only the commission members could enjoy the luxury of imagining a world without the corporation profits tax.

In the end the commissioners saw, as the strongest practical argument for the tax, the fact that it represented a wholly justifiable levy on the many large foreign-owned companies that operated in Canada. To give it up would simply be handing several hundred million dollars to foreign treasuries in tax credits they would no longer have to grant. Some penalty was also justified to compensate for the great advantage of almost indefinite deferral of income tax on accumulated income offered by the corporation. In the end as close as we could come to abandonment was to propose the allowance of the tax as a credit against personal income tax, to be achieved through the gross-up and crediting device. But more important, along with the capital gains tax, this proposal dealt effectively with both the capital gains and surplus stripping problems. The confusion about whether capital gains were taxable would be ended—they would be. The credit for a 50 percent corporate income tax against a maximum personal income tax of 50 percent would remove the double tax penalty for distributions from surplus, as it did for current distributions. We thought this was a pretty neat answer.

Ironically, it was on the corporation tax—the tax that it would have been most pleased to see repealed—that the commission's proposals ran into most difficulty. The allowances for the mining and oil industries failed to meet our neutrality test, and it was recommended that the depletion allowance and the three-year exemption for new mines be repealed, but with full deduction for exploration and development expenses. The reduced corporate rate for small business broke the symmetry of the integration for a 50 percent corporate rate; it was viewed as quite inadequate as a help for small business and the source of endless complications in the Income Tax Act, so we recommended that it be withdrawn, to be replaced by a generous allowance for capital expenditures. Insurance companies had been practically exempt from corporate profits tax, and we recommended that they be made more fully taxable. In order to ensure that the federal government had control over the main elements of the commission's proposals, we recommended that, in return for compensation, it take over exclusive use of the corporate income tax and also that the provinces repeal their death taxes, which of course the provinces opposed, along with several other features of the report.

The full taxation of capital gains raised little warmth in any breasts, and the family unit tax proposal ran head on into the burgeoning female rights movement as I discovered in a very personal way. In attempting to justify this proposal to a meeting of Laura Sabia's militant feminists, I was told in no uncertain terms that far from accepting the idea of pooling their income with their husbands' for tax purposes it was intolerable that their husbands even know what they were earning, where they were earning it, or even what they were doing. After that harrowing experience I knew the family income proposal was dead. I have since thought that these women must have suffered considerable trauma when faced with the opportunity of spousal RRSPs, a venture in financial consanguinity for which they were emotionally unprepared.

International Taxation

The commission in general accepted the test of residence as the basis of liability for full tax, but acknowledged a right of taxation for the country of origin, with a responsibility for relief of double tax in some form in the country of destination. Much of its interest was centred on the status of income earned abroad through direct investment. This had previously been totally exempt from tax in Canada when received from a subsidiary more than 25 percent owned by Canadians under section 28(1)(d) of the Income Tax Act. This had turned Canada into a major tax haven for all kinds of companies through the simple device of having over 25 percent of ownership located in Canada, and the commission had decided that it had to go. But this left the problem of an alternative treatment to provide for income earned through Canadian direct investment abroad. The Commission recommended that the test of ownership be reduced to 10 percent from over 25 percent, and its main proposal, to quote the report was as follows:

Canadian taxpayers having foreign direct investments should report annually the foreign income earned and the foreign income taxes paid in each foreign jurisdiction. If foreign income taxes were paid at a rate of at least 30 percent, no further Canadian tax would be payable unless or until the foreign income was received by a Canadian individual. If foreign income taxes paid on this current income were less than 30 percent of the foreign income earned, the difference should be paid to Canada as a special tax. This procedure would ensure that all foreign source direct investment income would immediately become subject to income taxes of at least 30 percent on an accrual basis . . . [And further]: Dividends or other income (net of withholding taxes) received from a foreign direct investment should be deemed to have been subject to foreign tax at a rate of 30 percent. The Canadian taxpayer (individual or corporate) should be required to bring into income the grossed-up equivalent of the dividend or other income . . . Where the Canadian taxpayer was a corporation receiving income from foreign direct investment, no further tax would be payable at the time of receipt. On the distribution or allocation of the income to Canadian shareholders of that corporation, credit would be granted on the grossed-up amount of the dividend or allocation for the 30 percent foreign tax deemed to have been paid.[13.3]

The same treatment would be granted to any individual receiving a dividend directly from a foreign direct investment of which he was a shareholder.

It will be apparent that this system, with no distinction between passive and active income, was a long way from FAPI, the Foreign Affiliate and the Controlled Foreign Affiliate concepts that later emerged. However, it should be said for the commission that it saw its 30 percent proposal as a rough interim measure, and foresaw the ultimate development of some sort of business test to distinguish legitimate foreign business activity from simple tax deferral or avoidance. I think this was one of the areas where we simply ran out of time—or perhaps of energy.

For income leaving Canada the Commission recommended that the withholding tax rate be retained at 15 percent for dividends, in order not to discourage foreign investment, but for most other payments to be raised to 30 percent, largely as a means of strengthening Canada's bargaining position in negotiating treaties with other countries.

Tax Administration

The commission argued for a much more open process for tax formulation, administration, and adjudication. Some of these proposals resulted in immediate developments while others are still to be adopted. We did recom-

---

[13.3] Canada, Report of the Royal Commission on Taxation, vol. 4 (Ottawa: Queen's Printer, 1966), 572-74.

mend the granting of advance rulings, one proposal that was implemented fairly early. Undoubtedly the whole taxing process is becoming more open and accessible, but there is a way to go yet, particularly in the exposure of details of plans for future changes.

Commodity Taxation

Finally, partly because of its relevance to current tax reform proposals, the federal sales tax. The commission accepted the necessity for commodity taxation, but found little good to say about the manufacturers' sales tax. For reasons that are becoming familiar today it urged that it be abandoned. Its preferred alternative was a tax imposed at the retail level to be collected jointly with the provincial taxes. However, it made the reservation that the combined federal-provincial retail sales tax rate should not exceed 14 percent, as this was the level beyond which it felt that evasion attempts would become serious. If this were to be the situation it offered an alternative, which in view of the current level of rates, which are at or very close to the line, would today be the effective proposal. And a very interesting one it is indeed—it is a form of value-added tax. In discussing the types of that tax it distinguished between the "tax to tax" and the "base to base." It preferred the former as being more accurate and possibly more self-enforcing, although administratively more complex. The latter would be acceptable as a second choice, because it would employ information already generally available to businesses and accomplish much the same purpose as the "tax to tax" method.

Whichever method was followed, or even if the existing sales tax were to be continued, the scope of taxation should gradually be extended to include services, and the commission listed those that should be brought in, and in what order. Only a very limited number of services should be exempted, the principal being medical services. It also recommended that all consumption goods be taxed, with the exception of food products, fuel, and electricity, medical or health related expenditures and magazines, books, and newspapers. For the lower incomes the additional burden resulting from the extension of the tax base could be alleviated by the system of cash payments.

In case this all sounds recent and familiar I commend a reading of pages 46 to 80 of volume 5 of the report. As I read it—and I admit to some difficulty in becoming an expert on the Business Transfer Tax—the "base to base" method appears to have anticipated it by some 20 years, as they seem almost identical. I find the business transfer tax label quite meaningless and therefore confusing. I would favour calling it what it is—a value added tax. Or perhaps I should say what it appears to be about to become, since we are still in suspense.

On other aspects of the sales tax the commission recommended restoration of the exemption for producers' machinery and equipment, which had been removed by a Liberal government during the commission's life. This proposal was implemented by a different Liberal Minister of Finance almost as soon as the report was issued. The exemption of building materials had also been removed, and it was proposed that it be restored, but at the government's discretion as to timing.

The main proposals for the sales tax obviously were not taken up, although the government stated that they would be in time. There have of course been periodic attempts to come to grips with its several problems, and some of its worst features have been softened. But one can't help but be impressed that the passage of nearly two decades has brought us back in 1987 substantially to where we were in 1967 at the time of the filing of the commission's report.

Reception of the Report

To avoid an anti-climactic and morose retrospection over the reception of the report I have hinted earlier at some of its hazards and I don't want to get into it any further here. I will only say that in presenting a document that touched so many interests, strong opposition could be expected, but at least there was the hope that its main intent would be read and respected. This happened only outside Canada; for example, there was a course in the Carter report at Harvard University, and I know from participating in a panel on European developments in Amsterdam that it had an influence there. But opposition in Canada on a few aspects was so unremitting that the general philosophy of the report was completely overwhelmed.

Perhaps in the end, however, it has been vindicated. Anyone at all familier with the course of Canadian tax developments in the last two decades would agree that at least the agenda, if not the actual performance, has been strongly influenced by the concepts and analyses presented by the commission. Furthermore, I have been surprised and pleased that the general tone of the briefs on current tax reform that I have been able to read follows very closely on that of the report—the need for fairness, neutrality, broadening the base, and so on. This was particularly notable in the restrained and well reasoned brief of the Business Council on National Issues. The Minister's own list of basic principles also suggests an approach that would in principle be very familiar to a reader of the report or for that matter of the government's 1969 White Paper. Perhaps this is a reaction from the over-indulgence in tax unneutralities of the last 15 years, most of them ineffectual, but it might just be that the report and the White Paper are finally being given the study in Canada they failed to receive at their inception.[13.4]

Reform in Practice—the Seventies

Opposition to the Commission's main proposals was intense, and implementation in most cases was partial or non-existent. The government made no commitment to reform until the White Paper was issued in November

---

[13.4] J. Harvey Perry, "Background and Main Recommendations of the Royal Commission on Taxation, in W. Neil Brooks ed., *The Quest for Tax Reform: The Royal Commission on Taxation Twenty Years Later*, (Toronto: Carswell, 1988), 23-42, at 23-34.

1969, nearly two years after the report had been submitted, and no final action was taken for another two years when legislation was passed late in 1971 to apply to 1972. Much of this four-year period was devoted to acrimonious public debate over proposals for a capital gains tax, the change in taxation of some Canadian industries, and sundry other proposals; the final outcome represented a multitude of compromises with the original report. Nonetheless, as the following summary of the progress of reform indicates, the federal tax system was substantially changed in 1972 and later years from the tax system of 1967.

The steps in this process are set out in a table in the Appendix. The author has described the substance of the changes, some of which carried on through most of the seventies, in his *Background of Current Fiscal Problems,*[13.5] from which the following text is drawn. This traces developments through to the eve of the 1981 budget, when another lesser round of tax reform was launched. In addition a steady stream of official papers was issued by the Department of Finance on such subjects as the treatment of charitable institutions, capital cost allowances, retirement income, capital gains taxation, consumption taxes, the integration of taxes and social security measures, and other subjects, all of value in understanding the nature of the 1970s reform process.

The reader will be aware of course that some of the tax developments have already been described, although in general matters relating to reform had been put aside for this section.

Pre-Reform Budgets

While the major event in tax reform was the Tax Reform Bill of 1972, several steps had been taken in prior budgets which either grew out of the Carter commission's report or were related to tax reform. Some of these may have been mentioned earlier, but as part of the reform record they are listed here.

Budget, June 1967: Comprehensive tax base—pensions from old age security and Canada Pension Plan were made taxable.

Budget, November 1967: Corporate tax instalments were partially accelerated as recommended by the commission.

Budget, October 1968: Life insurance companies were made taxable, bank reserve allowances were reduced, and further steps were taken in accelerating corporate tax instalments as recommended by the commission. Gift and estate taxes were integrated, a move which was logical but not related to any particular aspect of tax reform.

Budget, June 1971: This budget was a major one in implementation of tax reform and set the principal changes that would commence in 1972. Some necessary tidying up was also done. In place of a jumble of surtaxes, special taxes, and taxes for old age security, there was substituted a single corporate

---

[13.5] Perry, supra footnote 13.2, at 95-113.

profits tax at 50 percent, with concessionary allowance for Canadian-controlled private corporations, and a personal income tax with slightly increased exemptions and a single rate schedule. The special taxes for old age security and other additional income taxes were embodied in the normal tax structure.

Income tax changes included a reduction of 1 percent each year in the corporate rate to reach a rate of 46 percent in 1976; for the personal income tax a schedule was adopted with a top rate of 47 percent in place of the previous 80 percent; however, when combined with provincial rates the total was 60 percent. (The commission had hoped that this rate could be 50 percent; clearly the divergence in rates that would exist by 1976—46 percent corporate and 60 percent personal—would put the commission's proposal for full offsetting of these taxes out of the question.)

As part of the same budget the allowable deductions for contributions to registered pensions and registered retirement savings plans were considerably increased, a forerunner of the great popularity of these forms of savings at a later period.

Another and quite unexpected move at this time was the repeal of federal estate and gift taxes as of December 31, 1971. Apparently this was motivated by the fact that the federal government was receiving only 25 percent of the revenues from these sources under current federal-provincial arrangements and did not feel that this small gain was worth the bother of collecting a very troublesome form of tax.

Personal Income Tax Reforms

The White Paper

Comprehensive Tax Base

Income would recognize full capital gains and full capital losses, except that residences and farms were to be virtually exempt. Capital gains would be measured from a common valuation day. Gains on shares of closely held corporations would be taxable in full and losses deductible in full; for widely held corporations, one-half gains on shares would be taxable and one-half losses deductible. As a trade-off for this preferential treatment a deemed disposition of such shares would be required every few years. Fellowships, scholarships, and bursaries were to be taxable, but not gifts, bequests, or windfall gains. Unemployment insurance benefits would be taxable and contributions deductible. Many aspects of so-called expense-account living would either be non-deductible or would create taxable income. Allowances would be made for moving expenses, child care expenses, employment expenses (the latter as a 3 percent deduction from gross income, with a maximum). Medical expenses and charitable donations would continue to be deductible, along with pension and RRSP contributions. A general income averaging formula would be available to all taxpayers in any year in which income exceeded by more than one-third the average income of the preceding four years.

Tax Unit and Rates

The family basis was not adopted (small wonder—this was about the time the nuclear family was beginning to break up and women, whether married or not, were seeking liberation from all possible restrictions of their independence and freedom of action). Personal exemptions were to be retained in the form of deductions rather than credits, with one rate schedule applying to taxable income. Credit would be given in full for corporate taxes paid to Canadian shareholders receiving dividends from Canadian corporations.

The Tax Reform Act, 1971

Comprehensive Tax Base

Capital gains: in place of full taxation of capital gains only one-half of gains was made taxable. One-half of losses would be deductible against gains, but not more than $1,000 per year would be deductible from other income; losses could be carried back or forward against capital gains in other years. A principal residence would be exempt. Accrued gains on property left at death would be taxable and a taxpayer giving up Canadian residence would be taxed as though he had realized gains on his property at the time of departure. A deemed disposition of shares of widely held corporations every five years proposed in the White Paper was dropped.

Other Income

Other amounts to be included in income were payments received under an income protection plan where the employer had made contributions; certain allowances under government training programs; scholarships, fellowships, and bursaries to the extent that they exceeded $500; research grants (with deduction for costs); contributions by an employer on behalf of an employee to a public medical care program; unemployment insurance benefits; a value fixed by formula for the use of an employer's automobile. No deduction would be allowed to commission salesmen or self-employed persons for membership fees or dues at a recreational, dining, or sporting club, nor the cost to a business of maintaining a yacht, hunting or fishing lodge, or a golf course for business entertainment. Strike pay, gambling winnings, casual gains, and windfalls would not be included, nor would an allowance paid by an employer to employees at special work-sites. (Inclusion of some items must have been argued to the end; the bill contained a side heading for strike pay, but the clause itself had been dropped.)

Among new deductions were: a general allowance for employment expenses of 3 percent of gross income (maximum $150 per year) and for moving expenses; unemployment insurance contributions; and child care expenses. Deductions for charitable donations, medical expenses, and union dues were continued, in some cases at substantially increased levels (although a 10 percent limit for foreign investments was established for pension and profit-sharing plans). Expenses for conventions held in a location appropriate for the organization would continue to be deductible.

A general averaging provision was introduced where income of the year exceeds the average of the previous four years by 20 percent or more, or the income of the preceding year by 10 percent or more, to be applied automatically by the administration on the taxpayer's behalf. In addition the legislation provided for an income averaging annuity, purchase of which allowed deferment of tax on certain forms of income. Several forms of averaging under the old law would eventually disappear, but were allowed to be used at the option of the taxpayer for a limited time.

Shareholder's depletion allowance on natural resource dividends was dropped, as proposed by the commission.

Credit for a part of corporate taxes paid was allowed to shareholders. This was achieved through a procedure which started with a gross-up of 33.3 percent and produced a dividend tax credit of 20 percent of the "grossed-up" dividends on the tax return. The steps in arriving at this result were as follows. The dividend received by the taxpayer was grossed-up by 33.3 percent to restore it in part to pre-tax amount in the corporation. Since this gross-up is the amount for which credit is to be allowed, the credit can properly be described as one for 33.3 percent. However, expressed in terms of the grossed-up dividend it is a lesser credit, in the present case only 25 percent. Since the provinces impose their own personal income taxes based on the federal income tax, it was established from the beginning that they would assume a share of the credit. Room for this provincial share was provided by reducing the federal credit by one-fifth, a reduction which produced the figure of 20 percent which appeared on the tax return.

The provincial credit was not allowed for in the same manner as the federal, because the provinces apply their surtaxes to the federal tax base *after* deduction of the federal credit. In practice this results in somewhat higher provincial credit than would be produced by a separate provincial calculation, an over-allowance that was reduced by a change in the November 1981 budget.

For the regime in effect since 1976 the federal credit is 50 percent, derived from a gross-up of that amount. As a percentage of the "grossed-up" dividend, the credit drops to 33.3 percent which, after being reduced by one-quarter to allow for the provincial share of the credit, comes to the 25 percent that appears on the tax return. It is now general practice to refer to the credit in terms of the gross-up, and this will be followed here.

The extent of integration achieved by the credit depends of course on the marginal rates of the individual taxpayer. It provides full integration for marginal rates equal to or less than the effective combined tax credit, and is partial for higher marginal rates.

Tax Unit and Rates

No further steps were taken towards the family unit as the tax base. In place of several rates of tax a new single schedule was introduced at a lower level to accommodate the new system under which provincial taxes would be an "add-on" rather than a credit. Rates under this schedule ran from 17 percent to 47 percent. With a provincial rate of 30 percent the new combined top rate of tax was about 60 percent compared with a previous top rate of 80 percent.

Reform Developments

In the ten years after the Tax Reform Act was passed there were hundreds of amendments affecting the income tax, and there is space to mention only those related to the main subjects of reform already discussed. As such this is a very selective list, as it omits many important changes that do not fall within these limits. (Later sections of the book describe more recent developments.)

Comprehensive Tax Base

Capital gains: A principal feature of capital gains tax developments after 1971 has been the increasing number of rollovers. A rollover is a deferral granted where a gain arises from a transfer or exchange of assets in a specified situation. At the outset rollovers included transfers to a spouse, either directly by gift or will, or indirectly through a trust; transfers of property on incorporation of a sole proprietorship or partnership; transfers of property to an 80 percent owned corporation; transfers on winding up of a wholly owned subsidiary or on statutory amalgamation of corporations; on replacement of expropriated or destroyed property; on exchange of property for shares in specified capital reorganizations; or on the conversion of convertible securities.

To these there were later added a rollover for family farms passing at death to a child or children who continue to operate the farm; transfers of depreciable property by inter-vivos gifts between farmer and child; gains on sale of business assets if the proceeds were reinvested before the end of the following year; transfers of shares of an incorporated farm, interest in a farm partnership, or inter-vivos transfers of agricultural quotas or other eligible property.

A package of rollover provisions for small business was provided in 1978. These included rollovers of transfers at death or by gift to a child or grandchild of shares in a Canadian-controlled private corporation engaged in a qualifying active business, up to a maximum of $200,000 in capital gains. A special concession was given where a deemed realization at death was taxable, by extending the period for payment of the tax from six to ten years. Capital losses on investment after 1977 in shares or debts of Canadian-controlled private companies would be deductible without limit against other income, and any undeducted part may be carried back one year or forward five years by the taxpayer. Losses on shares of bankrupt companies would be fully deductible in the year of bankruptcy.

Other capital gains tax developments since 1971 include the elective use of a "tax-free" zone by individuals; a right to make a one-time election under which gains would be treated permanently as capital gains (or losses); the inclusion as a principal residence of a home ordinarily inhabited by the spouse; the eligibility of capital gains under the $1,000 exemption for investment income, and the increase from $1,000 to $2,000 in the amount of capital loss that could be offset against other income. Numerous other changes, some of them of crucial importance in narrowly defined situations, have also been made almost annually.

A review of the Canadian experience with capital gains taxation was issued by the Minister of Finance in November 1980. In general this supported the existing system, but elicited public discussion of specific aspects, including the effect of inflation on the measurement of capital gains, the allowance of capital losses, lock-in effect, bunching of gains, and exemptions.

Other Income

There has been increasing insistence on the inclusion of fringe benefits arising from employment. The use of an employer's automobile for personal purposes is becoming a favourite target of the administration. Since 1979, with certain exceptions, the benefit of low-interest or non-interest-bearing loans made by a corporation to employees or shareholders has been taxed. Revenue Canada also announced that from January 1, 1978, it would no longer consider a travel pass as a non-taxable employee benefit, but this does not appear to have been pursued. (In the same context, unemployment insurance, previously subject only to normal income tax rates, is now subject to special recovery over specified income amounts under the Unemployment Insurance Act.)

In contrast to these rather minor inclusions, several new or increased deductions have been introduced. In 1974 the Registered Home Ownership Plan was initiated, granting exemption for up to $1,000 a year set aside in a type of savings account leading to home ownership, up to a total of $10,000. At the same time exemptions for the first $1,000 of private pension income and the first $1,000 of interest and/or dividend income were introduced. The employment expense deduction was increased from $150 to $250 in 1977 and to $500 in 1979, the 3 percent of income limit remaining.

Amounts for contributions to Registered Pension Plans and Registered Retirement Savings Plans have also been increased. In 1976 the allowance for the former, where the taxpayer is a member of a pension plan, was increased by $1,000 to $3,500 per year. For the latter, where the taxpayer is not a member of a pension plan, the increase was $1,500 to a total of $5,500. The type of plan that would qualify as an RRSP has also been liberalized over the years. In addition to the former allowance for use of funds in an RRSP to purchase an annuity for life not later than age 71, taxpayers were allowed two further options: purchase of a fixed term annuity with benefits to age 90; and rollover into a new vehicle, the Registered Retirement Income Fund, under which the taxpayer may manage his own fund as in a self-administered RRSP. Transfers must occur between age 60 and 70.

Tax Unit

While the basic unit of taxation is still the individual, various minor changes have affected taxation of the family. The unexpected repeal of the gift tax left the way open after 1971 for splitting of investments between husband and wife without payment of this tax, although the rule that income continues to be that of the donor was retained and is a substantial deterrent. A less exotic measure was the new treatment of family allowances for 1978 and later years. The cash allowance was reduced, and supplemented with a refundable tax credit payable to all mothers, whether they were taxable or not. This tax credit is reduced by a special arrangement under which it gradually declines to zero as *family* income exceeds a specified amount. For this purpose a statement of *family* income must be filed with the authorities. This is the most visible use yet of the family income concept, and appears to have been accepted with little protest. Another move was the right to transfer between spouses any unused portion of the exemptions for interest and dividends, capital gains, retirement pensions, the student living allowance, and the over age 65 allowances.

A deduction of $50 a month for a student living allowance, to be taken either by the student or a supporting parent, is another example of a tax feature in the "family" category.

Also in this category is the allowance for child care expenses of working wives and single fathers which was increased from $500 to $1,000 per child to a maximum of $4,000 per family. Another instance is the right given to a spouse to use his or her RRSP entitlement to set up an RRSP for the other spouse, and to deduct contributions made for that purpose. Finally, a recent move in the same area is the right of a spouse to deduct salary paid to a spouse employed in an unincorporated business, a right formerly limited to an incorporated business.

Other Changes

Probably the most significant change in the personal income tax during the period is the indexation for inflation of both exemptions and rate brackets instituted in 1974. While a major change, it falls somewhat outside the reform agenda being examined here. Within that agenda a significant revision was the move to closer integration in 1977, applicable to 1978, with the increase in the dividend tax credit from 33.3 percent to 50 percent. Several major areas of taxation have been clarified by special studies along the way, one of the more significant being the conditions for operation of charitable organizations and the status of donations thereto, and area badly in need of review.

A proposal that came to nought during the period was that of the 1979 Conservative government for a deduction from income tax of mortgage interest and real property tax. This was part of a budget introduced in December 1979, which was defeated two days later. It was not reintroduced by the successor Liberal regime.

Again it should be emphasized that the preceding is a review of only some of the major changes during the seventies more or less related to the reform process. Many later changes are dealt with under other chapter headings.

Corporate Income Tax Reforms

The White Paper

The White Paper accepted the concept of integration, with the important exception that the allowance would be limited to one-half the corporate tax for widely held corporations. It also accepted the partnership proposal for closely held companies. It was more precise about the status of intercorporate dividends, requiring that a receiving public corporation take a dividend from another corporation into income at a reduced tax rate of 33.3 percent and claim credit against that tax for tax paid by the paying corporation. The White Paper proposed that a 15 percent tax could be levied to clear up past undistributed surpluses on commencement of the new system of integration. It also proposed that the reduced corporate rate for small businesses be eliminated gradually over a period of five years.

The Tax Reform Act 1971 and Changes to 1981

Integration: Public hearings on the White Paper produced a storm of protest against even the modified version of integration it proposed. Corporations feared that the lure of dividend distributions which brought tax refunds for their shareholders would be so strong that they would have to strip their treasuries to meet shareholder demands. Provincial governments protested against granting such a credit for the corporate tax on many theoretical grounds, although their subsequent actions indicated that they much preferred that credit be given for some of their own taxes (sales and real property). Withdrawal of the reduced rate for small corporations aroused such protest that an organization was even created to defend its perpetuation.

As a result of the public opposition the integration proposal appeared in an emasculated form in the final legislation. For the ordinary shareholder the credit for tax on a dividend was substantially reduced (where the White Paper would have given a credit of 50 percent, the Act gave 33.3 percent), and no refunds would be given where the credit exceeded the tax payable. However, a measure of liberalization was introduced in the legislation: whereas under the commission proposals and the White Paper the credit would have been limited to tax actually paid by the corporation, it now applied to any dividend from any taxable Canadian corporation, irrespective of the tax it had paid. As already indicated, for 1978 the rate was increased from 33.3 percent to 50 percent.

Private Corporations: A new entity, the Canadian-controlled private corporation, was created, with several special tax features. In part, this replaced the former personal corporation; but it was also a vehicle for coping with the constant problem of eligibility for the reduced corporate rate.

Where the personal corporation was essentially a tax-free funnel for income from family investments, the new entity was just the reverse, as it carried penalties for such use. From 1972 onwards, a Canadian-controlled private corporation (generally one whose shares are not publicly listed) would alone qualify for the concessionary small business rate. This was to take the form of a credit against tax, in 1972 sufficient to reduce the rate on the first $50,000 of "active business income" to 25 percent. It would cease to be eligible for the reduced rate when active business income after 1971 totalled more than $400,000. Since dividend distributions could be deducted in determining this amount, the limitation had much of the character of an undistributed income ceiling.

To discourage use of the private corporation for postponing tax on investment and other non-business income interest, rental, royalty, capital gains, and similar income was taxed under Part IV at 50 percent, and dividends from another taxable corporation at 33.3 percent. A refund of 25 percent of the non-active business income and all of the 33.3 percent rate would be given on distribution of dividends to shareholders of the corporation. Combined with the gross-up and dividend credit, this would put shareholders in approximately the same position as if they had received this income and active business income directly.

Active business income reinvested in "ineligible" non-active assets was also to carry a tax penalty; these amounts were to be subject to tax at the full corporate rate of 50 percent. However, this feature, because of its complexity, was dropped within two years retroactively to January 1, 1972.

To round out later developments for the private corporation: following the increase in the dividend tax credit in 1977 the Part IV tax on portfolio dividend income was reduced from 33.3 percent to 25 percent and in 1978 dividends received from another corporation owned in excess of 10 percent were exempted from that tax. For investment income the 25 percent refundable amount was reduced to 16.66 percent. The most significant changes over the decade have been the gradual increase in the annual amount eligible for the lower rate from $50,000 in 1972, to $100,000 in 1974, and $150,000 in 1976. At the same time the eligible accumulated total was raised from the original $400,000 to $500,000 in 1974 and to $750,000 in 1976.

The change in 1978 to eliminate the use of the small business deduction for personal and professional service corporations, for which a new effective rate of 33.3 percent was established, was also a major move. This rate preserves the integration concept: that is, when the 66.6 percent of after-tax income is paid out as dividends and grossed-up by 50 percent, the shareholder is taxed on 100 percent as though the earnings had been directly received.

Business deductions: Several changes were made affecting the general corporation income computation. One of these was a concession to long-standing requests to allow a deduction for interest on borrowing to acquire the shares of another corporation—a key element in almost any merger or takeover. A limited allowance was also granted for discount on issue of an interest-bearing obligation. A modest allowance was granted for goodwill and other "nothings" in a form which amounted to a 5 percent annual deduction for their cost, with one-half the proceeds of any sales includable in income. The limit on deductibility of charitable donations was increased from 10 percent of income to 20 percent.

Capital cost allowances: The capital cost allowance system was retained, but with a review promised for later. However, a significant change was made for immediate effect. Under the pre-1972 arrangements, individuals and companies not in a real estate business had been acquiring rental properties and offsetting capital cost allowances in excess of rental income against other income. This practice was stopped by changes which, for rental buildings costing $50,000 or more, in effect restricted the allowance to income from the property for which it was claimed (except for individuals and corporations whose main business was ownership and rental of real estate). This rule has been retained, with an exception being made only for multiple unit residential buildings (MURBs). This provision was in effect from 1974 to 1979, and lapsed at the end of the latter year, but was renewed for construction started after October 28, 1980 and before 1982.

Following an intensive review between 1973 and 1976 the Minister of Finance announced changes in the capital cost allowance system. He stated that "the present system is basically sound in generally providing a legislative system of allowances, with a relatively small number of classes, and the diminishing balance method of calculation." Rates had been reviewed, however, and were changed in several classes, both upward and downward. The system has been frequently used for economic incentives by granting special treatment of manufacturing, processing, research, anti-pollution, and other investments, which are described elsewhere.

Capital gains: Like individuals, corporations since 1972 pay tax on one-half their capital gains, unless they are deemed to be in the business of making such gains, in which case they are taxed in full. Rollover relief between corporations and between corporations and their shareholders has ameliorated many of the effects of the capital gains tax on such transactions by postponing the tax.

Undistributed income: With a gap between the dividend tax credit rate and combined federal-provincial top marginal rates of 60 percent or more, there remained considerable advantage in completely avoiding personal income tax on corporate accumulations, although this was somewhat reduced by the taxation of capital gains. As a result the 1971 Act returned to the fray with renewed fury. In order to get old surplus out of the way and start afresh with new rules it provided that pre-1950 undistributed surplus could be distributed free of further tax and that 1950-1971 surplus could also be so distributed after payment of 15 percent thereon (although with reduction in the shareholder's cost base for purposes of capital gains tax). As a precaution in moving forward, both the old concept of designated surplus and the Minister's arbitrary right to deem a taxable dividend to have been created by a transaction were retained.

A completely new approach to the tax status of distributions was made under the law. Under the pre-1972 statute any distribution by way, for example, of a share reduction, was deemed to create a taxable dividend to the extent that there was undistributed income on hand. Under the 1972 Act, tax-free redemption of paid-up capital and pre-reform capital surplus was allowed, even though there was undistributed income in the corporation. The complex statutory provisions by which this result was achieved almost defied understanding. They involved such historic monstrosities as corporate "tax equity," "1971 capital surplus on hand," "paid-up capital deficiency," "paid-up capital limit," and several other concepts now fortunately buried in obscurity.

In time these statutory provisions simply fell of their own weight. In 1977 the elaborate legal structure was abandoned, following nearly annual amendments of increasing complexity, many of them made necessary to limit the distributions from pre-1972 surplus, the amount of which and the means for creating it having been seriously underestimated. This move may also have reflected a sense that some relaxation was justified following an increase in the dividend tax credit in the same year.

In essence, after 1977 the principle of allowing withdrawal of paid-up capital was retained, but in place of the complicated statutory provisions and regulations that had been developed the relevant corporate law would henceforth apply. The designated surplus concept was repealed, and with it the 25 percent tax that had been levied on distributions from such surplus. The right to pay the 15 percent tax on 1971 undistributed income was also repealed, effective December 31, 1978.

This action led taxpayers to anticipate post-1978 conditions through the immediate issue of instruments that would qualify during the remaining time available but would require no cash distribution until later. The favourite was the stock dividend, and this move was blocked by an amendment which declared that stock dividends were not dividends, but were made subject to capital gains treatment. Another device produced the rather anomalous provision that a reduction of capital—i.e., the return of some paid-up capital, other than by redemption or cancellation of a share—was to be treated as a dividend.

Pre-1981 budget events: A recent development is the "capital gains strip." This in general consists of trying to turn taxable capital gains into taxable dividends through a series of manoeuvres, though dividends are not usually taxable when moving between Canadian corporations. Legislation designed to counter the new "strips" now deem certain deemed dividends to be capital gains. The savings within the corporate structure of tax on one-half the gain at the corporate rate is attractive enough to make this an appealing transaction, and produced a voluminous blocking amendment in the 1981 Act. Old hands at the "stripping" game can only look back with nostalgia to the swashbuckling days of the 1950s when the prize was complete avoidance of an 80 percent or higher personal income tax rate on accumulated corporate surplus.

A late episode in the saga of corporate taxation was the extensive use of term preferred shares and income debentures as a form of financing in the 1970s. Under this form of financing, payments by a corporation to a lending institution were not deductible to that corporation and were not taxable to the lender. This had been made possible by the allowance of a deduction for interest paid as part of a transaction to acquire the shares of another corporation. This arrangement was ideal for a low-income or loss corporation and was so favourable for the lender that rates were negotiated at levels well below the market. However, the popularity of these instruments was resulting in such a substantial loss of revenue that this treatment was discontinued for new debentures having a term of ten years or less issued after November 1978.

It must be reiterated that this brief review is not intended as a complete listing of corporate changes of the reform period. Several of these are dealt with elsewhere under other headings. Others would include the long and contentious record of non-deductibility of advertising costs in foreign publications and on across-the-border radio and television stations; the pseudo-tax approach under the Anti-Inflation Board, with its threatened (but dropped) 100 percent tax on export profits; the ramifications of the taxation of life insurance companies; and the many adjustments required to accommodate the autonomous Quebec tax system. Later changes are described in other chapters.

International Taxation

The Carter Commission approved of the system of taxing foreign-source income in Canada, with allowance of a credit for taxes paid abroad. However, in its view a provision of the existing law allowing tax-free receipt of dividends from a foreign subsidiary has been used for tax avoidance through offshore tax havens. Originally intended as an incentive for business activities abroad, it was being used to shelter non-business, or "passive" income. The commission recommended a system under which foreign "business" income would pay an annual tax of at least 30 percent, either to Canada or to the foreign country, and the adoption of measures to frustrate tax avoidance. The essence of its proposals for this purpose was that investment and similar "non-business" income of the subsidiary be deemed to be received by the Canadian shareholders as it accrued, whether distributed or not.

Tax reform legislation made proposals much along these lines. A new element, however, was the placing of heavy emphasis on the network of tax treaties with other countries. As in the past, dividends from a foreign affiliate would continue to be exempt from Canadian tax until 1975, but then would only be exempt if received from a treaty country. From 1973, Canadians would be deemed to receive their share of non-business income of a foreign affiliate (foreign-accrued property income, or FAPI) annually and be taxable thereon immediately. As matters developed, the FAPI provisions did not come into effect until 1975, and then applied only to shareholders of controlled foreign affiliates. Foreign business corporations, a special Canadian concept, ceased to exist after 1972.

Although the basic system is relatively simple in form, it has become immensely complicated by the need to distinguish the tax status of dividends between their origin in pre-acquisition surplus, exempt surplus, and taxable surplus. The rules for these calculations are so long and complex that they are contained in a regulation rather than in the statute. In general, dividends from a foreign company located in a country with which Canada has entered into a tax treaty, and which is owned 10 percent or more by Canadian shareholders, are received free of tax by a Canadian corporation. Otherwise a tax credit (or in some cases an income deduction) may be claimed.

The treaty negotiation process went on apace. By March 1982, treaties had been signed and were in force with 32 countries, were signed but not yet in force with 3 countries, and were under negotiation or renegotiation with 32 countries.

For dividends, interest, and similar amounts leaving the country, Canada has retained a 25 percent withholding tax. Most treaties reduce this to 15 percent, and in some cases to lower amounts for specified types of income. Important exemptions have also been introduced for interest on long-term securities. Interest on government bonds issued between 1966 and December 31, 1982, has been exempted from withholding tax, and interest on corporate bonds issued at arm's length to non-residents with a term of five years or more between June 25, 1975, and December 31, 1982, has also been exempted.

Commodity Taxes

The Commission Proposals

The commission examined several forms of commodity taxes, including the value-added tax, and concluded that none were more efficient than the retail sales tax. It found many serious shortcomings in the existing federal tax collected at the manufacturers' level, and proposed that they be overcome by changing the tax base to retail sales, with the provinces acting as collector for the federal government.

The White Paper

The White Paper dealt exclusively with the income tax, and the Minister announced that further study was being given to commodity taxation. No action ensued until 1975, when a discussion paper entitled *Federal Sales and Excise Taxation*, prepared by the Commodity Tax Review Group, a committee of officials, was tabled with the budget. It reviewed various alternative bases for the tax, but favoured the wholesale level, and invited public discussion on this proposal. Following this a report from the group was submitted to the House in June 1977, and referred to the House of Commons Standing Committee on Finance, Trade and Economic Affairs. No report appears to have been issued by this committee on the subject. However, the Minister of Finance stated in his October 1980 budget speech that he hoped to announce a final decision in his next budget; he did so in November 1981, and opted for a switch to the wholesale level.

It should not be assumed that activity has been entirely lacking in this area; there have been almost constant changes, the most substantial being the reduction in the sales tax rate from 12 percent to 9 percent in 1978. Rates of several other taxes have been amended in recent years. There have also been administrative changes. Compliance requirements have been eased through the exclusion of small taxpayers. For the previous exclusion from licensing of general manufacturers with sales volumes of $3,000 or less and lumber manufacturers of $5,000 or less, there was substituted a general exclusion for sales volumes of $10,000 or less from April 1, 1977. In the following year this amount was increased to $50,000. At the same time, small manufacturers were granted authority to import production machinery and apparatus tax free. Further concessions enacted permit taxable small manufacturers to pay quarterly or semi-annually, depending on their tax liability. However, in a move in the opposite direction from January 1, 1981, licensing for sales tax was extended to persons performing marginal manufacturing activities such as assembling, cutting to size, blending, mixing, and packaging.

In a move to simplify alcoholic beverage taxes, the former "proof spirit" and other bases were abandoned for absolute alcohol content by volume for all spirits, including beer and wine. The specific taxes on liquor and tobacco were to be revised upward on a quarterly basis as retail prices increased, the first adjustment being made on April 1, 1981. In the course of passage, later adjustments were changed to an annual basis, the first change being made on September 1, 1981.

This very superficial review is not intended as a comprehensive listing of all the many commodity tax changes of the last decade. The main issue for tax reform was the tax base, and it remained unsettled until 1988; see later chapters.

Tax Administration

The Carter Commission proposed a more open, communicative, and less centralized administration of taxes. To a great extent this objective has been achieved. For income tax there are now several series of information publications, advance rulings are given, district offices have much greater autonomy than formerly, and computerized handling of records has increased efficiency. Appeal procedures have been improved as well.

Only nominal progress has been made in opening up the consideration of policy issues in the conception and enactment of budget proposals, the result of which is apparent in the reception of the 1981 budget as previously discussed. It is granted that the Minister and his officials are accessible, and in recent years have shown greater receptivity to proposals for amendments to new legislation, much of it now very complex. The fact remains, however, that these steps are entirely within the discretion of the Minister, and represent the departmental conception of what response needs to be given. There is no opportunity, as there is with much other legislation, for a public examination before a parliamentary committee to permit all interests to be heard. No doubt this degree of public participation would slow up the passage of legislation (although it has not been noticeably expeditious in recent years), but it would remove much of the present stigma of secrecy in the budgetary process, an objective which has been urged in connection with tax reform as an essential step.

Overview, 1982

The reform process to 1981 achieved a somewhat broader base for personal income tax by the inclusion of a portion of capital gains and some previously untaxed employment benefits, a specific recognition of employment expenses, a fairly generous treatment of income deferred through pension savings plans, better provisions for averaging, some concessions to the family or inter-spousal basis of tax, and a closer integration of personal and corporate income tax. Indexation, not a part of the original reform package, had a predominant influence on the impact of the personal income tax from 1974. The overall effect of these and other changes has been to enhance the role of the personal income tax in the total tax system, a central objective of the reform process.

For the corporate income tax, reform steps include a more consistent recognition of the corporation as an intermediary in the taxing process, more rigorous and somewhat more logical terms for giving the reduced rate, the recognition of some deductions previously disallowed, some reduction of tax deferral possibilities, particularly for foreign investment income, possibly a more rational treatment of inter-corporate and corporate-to-shareholder distributions (although views would differ on this), and a more logical basis for incentives for the resource industries.

Administrative procedures for the federal taxes have been greatly improved. Steps include the provision of much more information, advance rulings, improved appeal procedures, greater decentralization, and in nearly all respects a system much more accessible and responsive to the taxpayer.

Tax policy formation has been opened to some extent through the publication of discussion papers, but public participation is still limited by close budget secrecy.

The role and form of consumption taxes in the federal structure was not yet decided in late 1981, a long-delayed aspect of the reform process.

This is the record as it appeared in 1981 before the fall federal budget. Obviously it stood a long way from the objective of a decade earlier. Full of compromises and half measures, it was the result of the most thorough review given to the taxes of any country. Any further efforts at change therefore would have to start from this base.

Bibliography, chapter 13

Bird, Richard M. "The Tax Kaleidoscope: Perspectives on Tax Reform in Canada." (September-October 1970) 18 *Canadian Tax Journal*, 444-73.

_____. *Taxing Corporations*. Montreal: The Institute for Reseach on Public Policy, 1980.

Brooks, W. Neil, ed. *The Quest for Tax Reform: The Royal Commission on Taxation Twenty Years Later*. Toronto: Carswell, 1988.

Brown, James R. "Tax Reform-Six Years Later." In *Report of Proceedings of the TwentyNinth Tax Conference*, 1977 Conference Report. Toronto: Canadian Tax Foundation, 1978.

Bucovetsky, Meyer, and Bird, Richard M. "Tax Reform in Canada: A Progress Report." (March 1972) 35 *National Tax Journal*, 15-42.

Canada. *Report of the Royal Commission on Taxation*. Ottawa: Queen's Printer, 1966.

_____. Department of Finance. Budget Speech. June 1, 1967.

_____. Budget Speech. November 30, 1967.

_____. Budget Speech. October 22, 1968.

_____. Budget Speech. June 3, 1969.

_____. Budget Speech. March 12, 1970.

_____. Budget Speech. June 18, 1971.

_____. Discussion Paper. *Federal Sales and Excise Taxation*. 1975.

_____. Budget Paper C. *Capital Costs Allowances*. 1976.

_____. Budget Paper D. *Charities Under the Income Tax Act*. 1976.

_____. *A Review of the Taxation of Capital Gains in Canada*. 1980.

_____. Proposals for Tax Reform (White Paper), 1969.

_____. *Summary of 1971 Tax Reform Legislation*. 1971.

_____. House of Commons. Eighteenth Report of the Standing Committee on Finance, Trade and Economic Affairs. *Respecting the White Paper on Tax Reform*. Ottawa: 1970.

_____. Senate Standing Committee on Banking, Trade and Commerce. *Report on the White Paper on Tax Reform Presented to the Senate of Canada*. Ottawa: 1970.

_____. *Report on Bill C-259*. Ottawa: 1970.

Canadian Institute of Chartered Accountants. *Tomorrow's Taxes*. Toronto: the Institute; 1971.

_____. *Spotlight on Reform*. The Institute, 1972.

Canadian Tax Foundation. *Proceedings of the April Conference on the Report of the Royal Commission on Taxation*. Toronto: the Foundation, 1967.

_____. *Report of Proceedings of the Nineteenth Tax Conference*, 1967 Conference Report. Toronto: the Foundation, 1968.

_____. *Report of Proceedings of the Twentieth Tax Conference*, 1968 Conference Report. Toronto: the Foundation, 1969.

_____. *Report of Proceedings of the Twenty-First Tax Conference*, 1969 Conference Report. Toronto: the Foundation 1970.

_____. *Report of Proceedings of the Twenty-Second Tax Conference*, 1970 Conference Report. Toronto: the Foundation, 1971.

_____. *Report of Proceedings of the Twenty-Third Tax Conference*, 1971 Conference Report. Toronto: the Foundation, 1972.

_____. *Report of Proceedings of Twenty-Fourth Tax Conference*, 1972 Conference Report. Toronto: the Foundation, 1973.

_____. *The Royal Commission on Taxation: Key Proposals*. Tax Memo no. 42. Toronto: the Foundation, 1967.

_____. *White Paper on Tax Reform*. Tax Memo no. 49. Toronto: the Foundation, 1969.

_____. *Summary of Committee Proposals*. Tax Memo no. 51. Toronto: the Foundation, 1970.

CCH Canadian Limited. *Royal Commission on Taxation, Summary of Public Hearings 1963-64*. Toronto: CCH Canadian, 1964.

_____. *Analysis of White Paper on Tax Reform*. Toronto: CCH Canadian, 1969.

Due, John F. "The Dilemma of Canadian Federal Sales Tax Reform." In *Report of Proceedings of the Twenty-Seventh Tax Conference*, 1975 Conference Report. Toronto: Canadian Tax Foundation, 1976, 188.

_____. *The General Manufacturers Sales Tax in Canada*. Toronto: Canadian Tax Foundation, 1951.

Gillespie, W.I., and Johnson, J.A. "Sales Tax Reform: A Critique of the Federal Government's Proposals." (Autumn 1976) 11 *Canadian Public Policy*, 638-44.

Gillespie, W. Irwin. "The 1981 Federal Budget: Muddling Through or Purposeful Tax Reform?" (November-December 1983) 31 *Canadian Tax Journal*, 975-1002.

Hartle, Douglas G. and others. *A Separate Personal Income Tax for Ontario. An Economic Analysis*. Toronto: Ontario Economic Council, 1983.

Kierans, Eric, Saltsman, Max, McDonnell, T.E., Evans, Linda, and Surrey, Stanley S. "The Tax Reform Process." (Winter 1979) 1 *Canadian Taxation*, 22.

Maslove, Allan. *The Pattern of Taxation in Canada*. Ottawa: Economic Council of Canada, 1972.

Perry, J. Harvey. *Anatomy of a Tax System and the Carter Report*. Toronto: CCH Canadian, 1967.

_____. "Reform in Income Tax Administration." (March 16, 1981) 1.22 *Canadian Business Management Developments*. Toronto: CCH Canadian, 1981.

Petrie, J. Richards. *The Taxation of Corporate Income in Canada*. Toronto: University of Toronto Press, 1952.

Private Planning Association of Canada. *The White Paper on Taxation*. (A series of six studies). Montreal: the Association, 1971.

Ross, Howard. *Our Taxes: Lessons from Carter and Benson*. Montreal: the Private Planning Association of Canada, 1971.

Salyzyn, V. *Canadian Income Tax Policy*. Don Mills: CCH Canadian, 1974.

Simon, Henry. *Federal Tax Reform*. Chicago: University of Chicago Press, 1950.

Scace, A.R.A. "Ontario Proposals on Tax Reform" (July-August 1970) 18 *Canadian Tax Journal*, 310.

Sherbaniuk J. Douglas. *Report of the Director*. Twenty-Sixth Annual Meeting. Toronto: Canadian Tax Foundation, 1972.

_____. "Budget Secrecy." (May-June 1976) 24 *Canadian Tax Journal*, 223-310.

Special Symposium. Papers Delivered at a Conference on the Royal Commission on Taxation Report. 26 *Osgoode Hall Law Journal*, 1988.

"Symposium on the Report of the Royal Commission on Taxation (Canada 1966)— The Carter Commission." (March 1969) 22 *National Tax Journal*, 1-177.

14
Ministry Reform: MacEachen and Wilson

November 1981; the MacEachen Budget

Attention in the budgets of the late 1970s had been directed mainly to the National Energy Program, and tax reform in the broad sense had been played down. Nonetheless there were some indications of coming events. The Department of Finance had published its first study of tax expenditures, and there had been extensive public comment based on it. In his 1980 budget the Minister had signalled his own dissatisfaction with some features of the tax system. He had said then:

> I have a special responsibility to ensure that our tax system is fair and that it contributes to the achievement of our economic and social objectives . . . I am particularly concerned to ensure that the tax system is fair and seen to be fair. Three areas of the tax system are worth examining from this point of view.

> First, tax expenditures. Honourable Members will be familiar with the concept, which was described in a paper tabled by my predecessor last year. Within a short period of time I intend to table an updated tax expenditure account.

> The incentives and preferences identified in the tax expenditure analysis raise important issues. They are expensive and it is incumbent on government to ensure that the incentives are effective and that their cost is justified.

> Tax incentives tend to pyramid with the result that a number of profitable corporations or wealthy individuals pay little or no tax. Other countries have responded to this by introducing minimum taxes or special levies on tax preferences. While this approach may be an answer to the problem, perhaps a fundamentally different one would be preferable. We now have a tax system characterized by higher tax rates relieved by a complex network of incentives and tax preferences. One questions whether the economy might not be better served by a tax system with lower rates but with fewer and more selective incentives.

> Second, Madam Speaker, let me say a few words about the commodity tax structure. Because the federal sales tax is levied at the manufacturing level, it falls unequally on commodities wherever there are differences in the degree of value added by wholesalers and retailers. It is particularly worrisome that the tax generally falls more heavily on goods produced and sold in Canada than on competing goods imported from abroad. A recent study by my officials showed that for many goods the rate of tax on imports is two to three percentage

points, or effectively 20-35 percent, lower than on a comparable product made in Canada. Ad hoc measures have been taken to address some issues, but the problem arises out of the basic structure of the tax. I would hope to be in a position to make a final decision in this fairly important issue in the next budget.

Third, I will be releasing shortly a discussion paper on the taxation of capital gains. It shows that Canada's system of taxing gains is favourable to taxpayers. As well, the taxes on inheritances and wealth in Canada are the lowest among 21 OECD countries surveyed. The paper notes that, while the system has imperfections, the taxation of capital gains is an important source of government revenue, has important tax structure implications and is essential for the equity and fairness of the system. I look forward to the discussion of the important issues raised in the paper.[14.1]

For taxpayers with sensitivity dulled by the relatively "soft" budgets of the mid and late 1970s this message obviously did not register. However, it was implemented not only in words but in deeds in the 1981 budget. In stronger language than had been heard from any Minister of Finance in some time he said:

Many Canadians find our tax system unfair, and I agree with them. They realize that taxes are necessary to pay for important government services, but they feel that rates of tax are too high. They sense that others, the well-advised or the wealthy, very often pay less than their share.

A study of selective tax preferences available to individual taxpayers, which I am tabling tonight, shows that the revenues lost through these selective write-offs, exemptions and deferrals, are massive. Over \$47 billion of personal income escaped tax in 1979. If these preferences were eliminated, rates of tax could be halved without reducing federal revenues. Some higher-income individuals are able to reduce their tax to well below that paid by lower-income Canadians. Some can escape paying tax entirely. This is unacceptable.

A cutback of tax preferences will permit a lowering of tax rates. Madam Speaker, the simple truth is that if only half of income is taxed the rates have to be twice as high to yield the same revenue. Lower rates will improve the incentives to work, save and invest. These incentives will be direct, easy to understand and available to all. Lower tax rates will also reduce the tendency for taxpayers to devote wasteful effort and money in finding artful ways of avoiding tax. For these reasons I propose to end a number of special tax preferences, to restrict others, and to lower marginal rates.[14.2]

[14.1] Canada, Department of Finance, The Budget, October 28, 1980, 14-16.

[14.2] Canada, Department of Finance, Budget Speech, November 12, 1981, 3.

Personal Income Tax

The main changes in revenue terms proposed by the Minister affecting individuals were withdrawal of the income averaging annuities—revenue gains or losses are shown in brackets—($895 million); restriction of general averaging under a new provision ($250 million); restriction of interest cost deduction to income from investments ($190 million); repeal of reserves for capital gains ($50 million); reduced dividend tax credit ($140 million); reduced first year capital cost allowance to one-half ($100 million); broadened taxation of employee benefits ($175 million). Several other less significant revenue changes were proposed, including limitation of residential capital gains exemption to one residence; capitalization of soft costs on real estate investment; heavier taxation of benefits from low-interest employee loans; taxation of work in progress for professionals; reduced exemptions for some forms of pension transfers, and miscellaneous other minor items. The revenue increase from these personal tax changes was estimated at $2.1 billion for a whole year.

Offsetting these deductions was a very marked reduction in the rate schedule, including establishment of a top federal rate of 34 percent, (giving a combined top rate of about 50 percent in most provinces) for a revenue loss of $1.3 billion, leaving a net increase of $0.8 billion. With later changes not all of this gain was realized. The principal of these was the withdrawal of the restriction of the deduction for interest costs, and the exclusion from the first year capital cost reduction of projects under contract or construction at the date of the budget. Lesser changes were also made to alleviate the effect of some of the other provisions, most particularly those related to the capital gains reserve and the taxation of employee benefits. But the main personal income tax change, the withdrawal of the income averaging annuity, remained unchanged.

Corporate Tax Changes

In the corporate income tax by far the most significant change was the reduction by 50 percent in the capital cost allowance for the first year of a new asset. This came into effect immediately, and was estimated to yield $1.1 billion in 1982-83 and $840 million in 1983-84. (This expectation would be reduced by the exclusion of construction and contracts "in progress" at the date of the budget).

The corporate surtax was extended to 1982 and 1983 at 5 percent and 2½ percent to yield $720 million in all. In order to remove an advantage enjoyed by companies eligible for the reduced rate a tax of 12½ percent was levied on their distributions, to yield $110 million in 1983-84. The reserve allowed for capital gains in sales of property was cancelled, along with more than a dozen other changes of considerable importance. Two relieving measures increased the amount of income qualifying for the small business concession and extended the small business bond provision for another year for corporations in financial difficulty. As with some of the personal income tax changes, later concessions alleviated the impact of these measures, usually by postponing their effective date or by excluding transactions in process at the time of the budget. One or two changes were held over for further consideration. In total the corporate changes were expected to yield a net $1.7 billion in 1982-83 and $1.2 billion in 1983-84.

The total program, including the personal income tax changes, was estimated to produce $1.4 billion in 1982-83 and $2.1 billion in 1983-84. All these estimates were subject to reduction for concessions granted. In addition, as we have seen earlier, the recession of this period had disastrous consequences for government revenues, and it would be almost impossible, without a great deal of highly speculative research, to say in the end what had been the budget impact of the 1981 changes.

Not the least interesting aspect of this mini-reform budget is that, although the Minister achieved 90 percent of his objective, it has since been referred to as an abortive effort that was stopped in its tracks by public protest. Although the Minister involved won no great public esteem for his performance—despite his signals in 1980 everyone was taken by surprise—it is a rare political accomplishment to have achieved most of one's objective and at the same time leave protesters convinced that they were the winners.

The Looming 1987 Reform Package

Almost from his first public statements Michael Wilson, the Minister of Finance under the Conservative government, had appeared to favour tax reform. His intentions were clearly evident in budget papers presented in November 1984, only two months after the government was elected. The most sweeping commitment appeared in the Agenda for Economic Renewal, as follows:

> The government's focus must be on reducing the growth of federal expenditures. Tax increases cannot be ruled out, but they must be avoided if at all possible. The government will continue to examine its tax system, not only from a revenue standpoint, but in terms of its impact on growth, equity, and simplicity. As already noted, there is need to examine closely the incentives provided to business investment. It may be that some investments are no longer appropriate, in terms of current economic needs and the burden of the federal deficit.
>
> There also may be merit in other changes to the tax system, which should be made on an evolutionary basis. In this context, some have suggested that Canada adopt a "value-added" tax, possibly as a replacement for the current federal sales tax. The implications of such a major change would require careful study, which has begun. It would have important federal-provincial implications. Close consultations between governments, the private sector and other affected groups would be necessary before deciding to proceed with such a tax.[14.3]

[14.3] Canada, Department of Finance, Budget Papers, "A New Direction for Economic Renewal," November 8, 1984, 67.

He also raised questions on specific uses of taxation at other points in the Agenda. On investment incentives:

> . . . governments must consider the degree to which tax incentives and grants overlap, resulting in unduly generous government support. Should not tax and grant policies be reviewed to ensure that the combined level of incentives is not so high that it negates market signals? If so, could a reduction in the level of certain incentives contribute not only to enhancing the efficient allocation of resources but also to reducing the federal deficit? [On small business taxation]: The tax system is overly complex . . . The small business tax simplification package that will be tabled in Parliament illustrates how complexity can be reduced. Yet more simplification is possible, and this will be a high priority with the government.[14.4]

In the social security area many possibilities for change were raised. In the Economic and Financial Statement—the actual speech given by the Minister to the House—emphasis turned to another potential subject of tax reform. The Minister said there:

> We are concerned about the few high income tax filers who are paying little or no personal income tax because of the combined effect of tax credits and deductions. We are considering the introduction of a tax designed to ensure that the effective tax rate for high income individuals does not fall below a minimum level. In this issue, as in so many tax issues, the challenge is to make the system more equitable without undermining incentives for Canadian investment. We must also take care not to complicate the tax system unduly for the many Canadians not directly affected but who would face a more complex tax return. The government will undertake a thorough review of the situation commencing with a discussion paper to provide background information on a minimum tax.[14.5]

Obviously with this much on his plate within two months of taking office the new Minister had a busy schedule ahead of him on tax reform alone. But these were just the opening items, and more were to follow.

Budget, May 1985

The Minister's first official budget was bristling with tax reform ideas, the product of only nine months in office. By far the most significant—and unexpected—proposal was the lifetime exemption of $500,000 of taxable capital gains. Thus was virtually removed from the scene the tax change that even in its final emasculated form had been one of the main features of the 1967-71 tax reform. The Minister's explanation for the proposal was as follows:

[14.4] Ibid., at 41.

[14.5] Canada, Department of Finance, Budget Papers, "Economic and Fiscal Statement," November 8, 1984, 12.

This measure will encourage more Canadians to invest in small and large businesses. It will help Canadian companies to accelerate their return to a healthy financial position by attracting new equity investment. It will assist smaller businesses in raising capital to pursue new ideas and new directions. It will help raise capital for research and development.

Most important, this is a broadly-based incentive that allows individual Canadians to decide where to put their money and how to create wealth, economic activity and jobs. This is central to our philosophy. The decisions should and will be made by individuals across Canada, not by politicians or public servants here in Ottawa. This is a measure designed to unleash the full entrepreneurial dynamism of individual Canadians.[14.6]

On tax fairness he made the following comment, with accompanying proposals:

Many Canadians have questioned the fairness of the tax system and of tax administration. This is a matter the government views with great concern. Our tax system rests on a foundation of self-assessment and voluntary compliance. If Canadians feel that the system is unfair, this foundation will erode.

The greatest source of concern is the ability of some high-income individuals to take advantage of existing tax incentives to shelter virtually all of their income. There is no question that such tax planning is legitimate, and that the incentives serve valid objectives. Canadians nevertheless feel frustrated when some high-income individuals pay little or no tax. I share this frustration.

I will therefore be introducing a minimum personal income tax, beginning in 1986, to ensure that high-income Canadians pay their fair share. I am tabling today a paper that explores three alternative ways of imposing a minimum tax. I will use this consultation process to encourage the provinces to adopt the same system in order to maintain uniformity and consistency across the country.

In addition, I am moving to curtail the tax-shelter financing of certain types of property, including yachts, recreational vehicles and hotels when used in certain circumstances. I am also proposing to end the tax advantages of splitting income through interest-free or low-interest loans among family members. Transitional rules will ensure that the new rules are introduced fairly.

Building on the significant initiatives introduced by the Minister of National Revenue, I am proposing a number of further measures to achieve fairer tax administration consistent with the Charter of rights and Freedoms. Additional protection will be provided for taxpayers in the area of search and seizure, audits and examinations, and demands for tax information.

[14.6]Canada, Department of Finance, The Budget Speech, May 23, 1985, 6.

We will continue to move forward with necessary and effective change in the tax system in a responsible, moderate way. This approach is reflected in our commitment to a minimum tax for Canada and in the discussion paper on the corporate income tax. But I have deliberately not launched a process of massive tax reform as a solution to the problem of tax fairness or any other problem. We must not and we will not risk creating the kind of uncertainty and instability that could undermine the effort to get Canadians investing strongly in opportunities that will lead to growth and jobs.[14.7]

These proposals were amplified in discussion papers submitted with the budget—The Corporate Income Tax System; A Corporate Loss Transfer System and A Minimum Tax for Canada.

The Corporation Income Tax

The corporate income tax paper reviewed the effect of various incentives and allowances under the corporate income tax by sector, by average tax rates, by different activities and regions, and by economic growth, and touched on the problem of unused deductions, the subject of the other corporate paper. The results of this study were summarized as follows:

> The analysis demonstrates that the current corporate tax system creates substantial variation in tax rates across firms in different sectors and types of business. The present corporate tax incentives not only favour certain sectors but favour certain types of investment activity such as machinery over others such as buildings.

> The various tax incentives to industries have tended to have an offsetting impact across sectors. While certain sectors are favoured relative to others, each sector has special deductions and credits. Could the number of specific incentives be reduced without affecting the total taxes paid by corporations? Such a change might simplify the tax system by reducing the number of specific deductions and credits without significantly affecting the level of corporate investment.

> At the same time, the paper suggests that the current pattern of tax rates among sectors could be altered to reduce the degree of variation. The tax system would be less distorting of market-driven business decisions. This could lead to a more efficient allocation of resources and enhanced prospects for economic growth and employment creation. Analysis of the existing system also shows that many firms are unable to use the incentives they have earned . . . Firms have naturally tried to make use of these accumulated tax benefits by, for example, transferring them to taxpaying firms through a variety of mechanisms . . .[14.8]

[14.7] Ibid., at 14-15.

[14.8] Canada, Department of Finance, Budget Papers, "The Corporate Income Tax System: A Direction for Change," May 1985, 1-2.

The cure proposed for consideration involved a "significant reduction in statutory tax rates for all corporations. This is coupled with reductions in the most rapid rates of write-off and elimination of the investment tax credit. The purpose of the changes is to make the corporate tax system more sensitive to the needs of the economy, not to increase government revenues. Thus, the proposal is designed to leave the level of corporate taxes unchanged."[14.9]

It will be seen that in the following budget this was substantially the proposal adopted for the future, and represents a very fundamental change in the federal corporation profits tax made in advance of the general reform movement.

The Minimum Tax

The Minimum Tax paper reviewed the statistics of high-income low-tax filers. Based on 1982 data some 3,995 filers with adjusted gross incomes of $50,000 or more paid no tax, and 26,983 paid 10 percent or less. In total 30,983 filers with incomes of $50,000 or more, or 7.6 percent of total filers, paid little or no federal tax. By category these were mainly farmers, fishermen, business proprietors, property owners and investors; few were employees or professionals. This situation was explained as follows:

In general, the major reductions in taxes result either from the manner in which investment income is taxed or from incentives to encourage investment. Business losses are also a significant cause of reduced taxes, but these can arise both from real business losses and from the use of tax incentives such as accelerated capital cost allowances. . . . one of the main sources of tax reduction was the dividend tax credit; both its frequency of use and the average amount of credit claimed were high . . . The second most important item is the tax exemption for half of realized capital gains . . . Carrying charges (mainly interest expenses) in excess of investment income are the third most significant source of low average tax rates for high-income earners . . . The general investment tax credit, as well as the specific tax incentives to encourage certain types of investment such as multiple unit residential buildings (MURBs), Canadian films and petroleum exploration ventures also led to significant reductions in the taxes paid by high-income earners . . . Social policy deductions, such as those related to pensions, charitable donations, alimony, medical expenses and gifts to the Crown, are less important . . .[14.10]

The paper cited that the United States had enacted a minimum tax in 1969, and had revised it in 1983. It explained the three main forms of tax as the Alternative Minimum Tax, The Add-on Minimum Tax, and the Limit on Tax Preferences, but at this stage expressed no preference among these

---

[14.9] Ibid., at 2.

[14.10] Canada, Department of Finance, Budget Papers, "A Minimum Tax for Canada: Executive Summary," May 1985, 5-7.

choices. A tax was adopted in the following year to apply to 1986, of such complexity that it will have to be passed over in this limited survey.

Corporate Loss Transfer System

The paper was introduced as putting forward for discussion "a proposal that would allow the transfer of losses within a commonly-owned group of corporations. Such a system would recognize that under current rules the corporate structure of commonly-owned groups can affect their tax position.[14.11] The document recognized that the common methods for using losses in a group were amalgamations and wind-ups, but conceded that there were "important factors that make this approach undesirable or impossible, including the need to maintain management independence, financial considerations, limiting of liability, effects of regulation and the existence of minority shareholders. The review of the existing ability to use losses in commonly-owned groups indicates there is a broad range of circumstances where losses cannot be used, as well as considerable variation in the means by which corporations are able to use losses."[14.12] The study stated that the U.S. federal tax provided for tax consolidation while the U.K. tax allowed loss transfers, and many other countries had similar provisions.

The specific proposal (for which draft legislation was provided) was that "loss transfers would be allowed between a subsidiary corporation and its parent or between subsidiaries within a group. A subsidiary corporation would be defined as a taxable Canadian corporation . . . where 95 per cent of the outstanding shares of each class of the subsidiary's capital stock (other than fixed asset preference shares) are held by the parent or other subsidiary."[14.13] The proposal was later implemented by legislation.

1986-87: Tax Reform is Launched

In the Budget Speech of February 1986 (now the agreed month for this event) the Minister proposed further steps in his reform agenda, and later in the year officially announced that he would proceed with a complete and comprehensive program in the near future. As usual with the supersensitive subject of tax reform this prospect aroused both extravagant expectations and alarming fears, neither of which were justified by actual hard information. There were rumours and leaks as to what would actually be proposed, and differences in Cabinet were hinted at, but very little solid information was available. Ultimately time dragged on far beyond the period most observers had expected, two or three deadlines were passed, and the Minister had nearly exhausted public patience when he announced, in May 1987, that the reform package would be issued on June 18.

[14.11] Canada, Department of Finance, Budget Papers, "A Corporate Loss Transfer System for Canada," May 1985, iii.

[14.12] Ibid., at 1-2.

[14.13] Ibid., at 13.

The February 1986 Budget

The 1986 budget is interesting for the major step taken in what the Minister called "the first phase of corporate tax reform." The features of this program, as listed in the budget speech, were as follows:

- The 3-percent inventory allowance will be eliminated effective today.

- The general investment tax credit will be phased out starting next year.

- The 20-percent investment tax credit will remain to encourage investment in Atlantic Canada and the Gaspé Peninsula. This credit will be extended to include investments in adjacent offshore areas.

- The Cape Breton investment tax credit will remain at 60 percent and will be improved. Smaller investments will qualify and the rate of refundability will be increased, as recommended by the Cape Breton Advisory Committee.

- The special investment tax credit for manufacturing investments in designated areas will be extended past its termination date at the end of this year at a reduced rate of 40 percent.

- Corporate tax rates will be reduced over a three-year period beginning July 1, 1987. By 1989, the basic federal corporate rate will have been reduced from 36 percent to 33 percent of taxable income.

- Manufacturing companies will continue to have a lower tax rate, falling from 30 percent to 26 percent by 1989.

- The federal tax rate for small business will fall from 15 percent to 13 percent.

The effect of all these measures will be to generate an additional $765 million of net revenue during the period of transition to 1988-89. As a result of these changes, there will be an increase in the number of profitable corporations that pay tax.

These actions are the first phase of corporate tax reform. I will release a new discussion paper later this year. It will propose further reductions in tax preferences and further tax rate reductions, consistent with the principles set out in the May 1985 budget paper.[14.14]

In this budget the Minister cast his tax reform net further to include the sales tax. He said:

Let me now address the question of federal sales tax reform. Like the debate on pensions, discussions on a better sales tax system have been going on for a long time. The problems with the current system are well known. It results in serious inequities among competing business firms. It puts Canadian manufacturers at a competitive disadvantage relative to importers. It results in hidden taxes on exports. Canada is

---

[14.14] Canada, Department of Finance, Budget Speech, February 26, 1986, 13.

now the only industrialized country in the world that still imposes a sales tax at the manufacturers' level.

It is time to act on this issue, to bring our sales tax system into line with today's realities.

My officials have for some months been examining the value-added tax. They are also looking at alternative systems, including a business transfer tax, which involve less administrative complexity and paper burden.

I expect to complete a review of the options in the very near future and put foward a paper with a concrete proposal for public discussion at an early date. Our intention is to move to a new system that will encourage growth, improve equity, and yield revenues sufficient to replace the federal sales tax, to end the surtaxes I have announced today and to provide adequate offsets for low-income Canadians.[14.15]

The reference to the business transfer tax caused alarm bells to start ringing, as few people had any notion of what it involved and no country appeared to have imposed such a tax. Nor did the Minister, despite promises of a discussion paper, take steps to relieve their ignorance during the following months. It was not until the final release of a document dealing with the sales tax, in June 1987, that its full nature was explained.

The announcement of a "refundable sales tax credit" established an advance bulwark against those who would oppose an increase in consumption taxes as being inequitable to lower income groups. It would be paid, from 1986 onward, at $50 per adult and $25 per child to families and individuals having less than $15,000 of income, with a recapture equal to 5 percent of income above $15,000—which reduces the payment to zero at $18,000. While basically a social welfare measure, the allowance was closely related to the forthcoming revision of the federal sales tax, and was one of the more innovative steps taken in advance of the revision. It was forecast to cost $330 million in a full year, the equivalent of about 3 percent of the current sales tax revenue.

The July 18 Press Interview

In an interview at the National Press Building in Ottawa on July 18, 1986, the Minister issued the following statement:

I am announcing today that the government intends to proceed with a review of options for comprehensive tax reform.

During the past two years, we have made important progress in restructuring the corporate income tax, introducing a minimum tax and eliminating many tax expenditures. A principal objective in these changes to date is to broaden the tax base in order to get tax rates down. We must also restore a healthier balance among the personal,

---

[14.15] Ibid., at 16.

corporate and sales tax and, specifically, reverse the trend which has resulted in greater reliance on personal income taxes.

In considering the work that has been done on a business transfer tax, we have concluded that further consideration needs to be given to the linkages between the three major elements of the federal tax system and the overall thrust of tax reform in Canada. The balance among personal, corporate and sales taxes in funding government programs needs to be assessed together with structural reform to each system.

Moreover, since my budget in February, the pace of comprehensive tax reform in the United States has accelerated. While the final shape of changes to the U.S. tax system is not yet clear, what is clear is that the changes will be extensive and will come into effect at an early date. These developments bear a close relationship to the tax issues we are facing in Canada and we must ensure that Canada maintains a tax system that is competitive with that of the United States. This means looking even more carefully at all the elements of the federal tax system.

I have therefore instructed my officials to examine broader options for a more comprehensive reform of the federal tax system, including a business transfer tax as a replacement for the federal sales tax, and to report back to me in the autumn.

Continued reform of the tax system is both a major challenge and opportunity for Canadians. The government is determined to move forward in a careful and co-ordinated way to ensure that the tax system is made less complex wherever possible and is structured so that the burdens are shared in an equitable manner. In developing our options for reform, we must also ensure that our tax system provides a strong and positive framework for economic growth and the expansion of job opportunities for Canadians.[14.16]

In reply to questioning he stated that two papers were now being prepared, one on the Business Transfer Tax (BTT) and the other on Phase II of corporate tax reform, which would be released in due course (neither were); the direction that would be followed in all taxes would be to broaden the base and if possible reduce the rates; he would aim to reduce the emphasis on personal income tax in the Canadian structure; the U.S. reforms would influence the Canadian changes to some extent but there was a basically different tax philosophy in the two countries which would be retained.

The October 23, 1986 Parliamentary Statement

The Minister made further speeches about his plans, such as the one given to the American Council for Capital Formation in Washington on September 5, in which sales tax reform—the business transfer tax—was promi-

---

[14.16] Canada, Department of Finance, Release no. 86-129, "Opening Remarks by the Honourable Michael Wilson, Minister of Finance, at a News Conference," July 18, 1986.

nently featured. On October 23 he made his most definite commitment in a speech to the House of Commons, stating that he was now prepared to have consultations on tax reform with all concerned preparatory to making an announcement in his next budget. At this time he set forth the guidelines that would be followed in the reform. These were: "First, fairness . . . The second guideline is simplification . . . Third, balance . . . Fourth, revenue stability . . . Fifth, international competitiveness . . . Sixth, economic growth . . . A reformed tax system must also recognize distinctly Canadian priorities and values . . . Eighth, measured transition . . . A final important guideline is consultation." [14.17]

A detailed paper, "Guidelines for Tax Reform in Canada," elaborated each of these, and stated that The House of Commons Committee on Finance, Trade and Economic Affairs would be asked "to review these guidelines and make recommendations on how the government's goals for tax reform can best be achieved, while maintaining a system that suits Canada's needs."

Budget Speech, February 18, 1987

It had been anticipated that the government would announce its tax reform plans in the 1987 budget, but this was not to be. The message was: "From the standpoint of new initiatives, this budget represents a breathing space prior to the presentation of major proposals for tax reform." [14.18] The Minister did hint at some of his objectives, however. For the personal income tax they were: lower tax rates, significantly fewer brackets, conversion of exemptions to tax credits and building on the refundable sales tax credit; for the corporation income tax: lower rates, reduced corporate preferences, and control over tax loss trading; for the sales tax: removal of the discrimination against domestic as compared with imported goods, broadening the base, and making the tax fairer and more efficient. No mention was made of the business transfer tax. Only minor tax changes were made in this interim budget, which have already been recorded.

This budget left a vacuum in which the government's intentions were subject to wide and not always flattering speculation. With the Minister's assurance that a comprehensive reform package would be presented in the spring, betting turned on the date of June 21, the end of the spring equinox. This was confirmed by a statement by the Minister on May 7 that the full program would be issued on June 18. The Minister revealed that the new personal income tax would have only three brackets, some exemptions would be withdrawn, and others replaced by tax credits, and the sales tax, whatever form it was to take, would apply to both goods and services and might be collected jointly with the provinces—the Minister spoke of a "national sales tax."

14.17 Canada, Department of Finance, Release no. 86-177, "Notes for an address by the Honourable Michael Wilson, Minister of Finance, to the House of Commons; Pre-budget Consultations, Tax Reform," October 23, 1986, 6-8.

14.18 Canada, Department of Finance, Budget Speech, February 18, 1987, 13.

Members of Parliament were only slightly appeased by this announcement, and dogged the Minister for days as to whether or not food would be subject to tax under the new regime, a possibility that some officials had been careless enough to hint at earlier.

Other Developments Related to Tax Reform

Tax Simplification

In June 1986, the Standing Committee on Finance and Economic Affairs issued a report on tax simplification. In dealing with the personal income tax it urged the government to pay more attention to the complexity of its tax proposals, recommended that the tax system be used for economic purposes only if no simpler and cheaper method was available, the federal act be redrafted along the lines of the Quebec statute, and the Department experiment with a questionnaire tax form. The committee listed the tax changes over the previous ten years which had complicated the form, an impressive list indeed.

Tax Incentives

The effect of economic tax incentives has come under increasing review in recent years. Studies issued by the Canadian Tax Foundation alone represent a substantial contribution. In 1979 it published *Tax Expenditures in Canada* by Roger S. Smith, a landmark event.[14.19] In 1980 in Richard Bird's survey of tax incentives for investment, his own reflections and his review of the existing studies brought him to the following conclusion:

> In summary, then, the major result of investment incentives is apparently to channel investment to some degree into some favoured sectors. Whether the benefits achieved from doing this are worth the costs incurred is not at all clear, however, since the benefits have never been clearly specified and the real costs have never been studied at all. The disappointing result of all the studies that have been carried out to date is thus that while incentives apparently do have some such channelling effect on investment, we have no idea whether the exercise is worthwhile or not . . . It is frustrating to thus conclude that we know so little, and can know so little, about such an important subject as tax incentives for investment, but, on the evidence available, no other conclusion seems possible.[14.20]

Another study, *Canadian R & D Incentives: Their Adequacy and Impact*, by Donald G. McFetridge and Jacek P. Warda, concluded that Canada's incentive programs for R & D had been among the most generous

---

14.19 Roger S. Smith, *Tax Expenditures: An Examination of Tax Incentives and Tax Preferences in the Canadian Federal Income Tax System*, Canadian Tax Paper no. 61 (Toronto: Canadian Tax Foundation, 1979).

14.20 Richard M. Bird, *Tax Incentives for Investment: The State of the Art*, Canadian Tax Paper no. 64 (Toronto: Canadian Tax Foundation, November 1980), 55.

in the world. It made the following interesting observations in relation to comparisons with other countries and, in particular, Japan:

Two questions arise. First, conventional wisdom has it that the Japanese government provides powerful assistance to Japanese firms, especially in the high technology field. Yet, in terms of its B-index either narrowly or broadly defined, Japan ranks well behind Canada. What does this say? It says that, in terms of formal tax measures, R & D subsidies, and contracts, Japan does not provide a great deal of support for domestic R & D by international standards. Unless we have missed some of the relevant programs, Japanese government support for domestic high technology firms must, to the extent that it exists, be conveyed to the latter by other means such as tariff and purchasing policy and through the capital market. It appears that in the Japanese, the German, and, to a certain extent, the French cases, if domestic firms are receiving a high level of support, it is not coming through the channels examined in this study.

Second, if Canada has been an innovator in the past as far as its policies toward R & D are concerned, why should it not be an innovator in the future? Canada should not be held back from providing more government support for industrial R & D by the mere fact that it is already providing more support than most, if not all, countries.

In response, it must be conceded that the R & D incentives of all countries, not excluding Canada, may be inadequate. We have investigated this possibility and have come to the conclusion that the R & D incentives presently in place are sufficient to offset an R & D externality of something over 40 per cent. Very little information exists on the magnitude of the R & D externality, but what information there is indicates that the R & D externality may be as high as 77 per cent. This would imply that the R & D incentives of Canada and all the other countries examined are not sufficient to offset the R & D externality.[14.21]

Articles in the *Canadian Tax Journal* on incentives included "The Federal Corporate Income Tax: Tax Expenditures and Tax Discrimination in the Canadian Manufacturing Industry 1972-1981,"[14.22] "Towards a Neutral Capital Income Tax System,"[14.23] and "The Taxation of Income from Capital in Canada; An International Comparison."[14.24] On reform

---

[14.21] Donald G. McFetridge and Jacek P. Warda, *Canadian R & D Incentives: Their Adequacy and Impact*, Canadian Tax Paper no. 70 (Toronto: Canadian Tax Foundation, February 1983), 90-91.

[14.22] Andre Blais and Francois Vaillancourt, "The Federal Corporate Income Tax: Tax Expenditures and Tax Discrimination in the Canadian Manufacturing Industry, 1972-1981" (September-October 1986), 34 *Canadian Tax Journal* 1122-39.

[14.23] Michael J. Daly, Jack Jung, and Thomas Schweitzer, "Toward a Neutral Capital Income Tax System" (November-December 1986), 34 *Canadian Tax Journal* 1131-76.

[14.24] Michael J. Daly, Jack Jung, Pierre Mercier, and Thomas Schweitzer, "The Taxation of Income from Capital in Canada: An International Comparison: (January-February 1987), 35 *Canadian Tax Journal* 88-117.

more generally articles included "A Call for Fundamental Tax Reform from the U.S. Treasury: Some Implications for Canada,"[14.25] and "The Recent Corporate Income Tax Reform Proposals in Canada and the United States."[14.26] Panels at both the 1985 and 1986 conferences of the Canadian Tax Foundation discussed tax reform possibilities, both in general and specific terms.

International Trends

For some reason that is not at all clear tax reform appears periodically as an international phenomenon. No doubt the closer integration of the world economy requires greater regard for international tax rates and other features affecting trade and investment, but these are seldom the primary motivation for a domestic reform movement. Despite the close ties between Canada and the United States in neither country was the recent tax reform trend directly inspired by actions in the other country, although some minor features were common to both revisions.

If there is any discernible trend in the recent international movement it is one toward base broadening and rate reduction. This has been characteristic of all the three main sources—personal income tax, corporate income tax, and consumption taxes. There has also been some shift away from direct taxes on persons through the personal income tax toward greater emphasis on taxes on corporate profits and consumption. The shift to the latter base was not sufficiently strong to reflect the advocacy in some quarters for taxation based almost exclusively on consumption, as represented in Canada for example by the Macdonald Commission *Report*.[14.27]

The specifics of the reforms in other countries need not concern us here in detail, as they have been described frequently elsewhere. It might be desirable, however, to dispel one of the most enduring of the tax myths—the alleged affinity between the Canadian and U.S. federal tax systems. The two systems have never been very closely related and except in superficial ways will have no closer similarity after the Canadian tax reform than before. The U.S. income tax has applied to capital gains from its beginning in 1913; Canada only began taxing them in 1972. Under the 1986 U.S. tax reform package concessions on capital gains taxation were abandoned so that capital gains became taxable in full; in Canada a lifetime exemption of $500,000 given in 1985, (later reduced to $100,000) awarded substantial relief for capital gains. Canada has provided recognition for double taxation of corporate income through the dividend tax credit since 1949, and retains it today; the U.S. gave only a token recognition and withdrew even

14.25 Gordon Bale, "A Call for Fundamental Tax Reform from the U.S. Treasury: Some Implications for Canada" (March-April 1985), 33 *Canadian Tax Journal* 269-99.

14.26 Patrick Grady, "The Recent Corporate Income Tax Reform Proposals in Canada and the United States" (January-February 1986), 34 *Canadian Tax Journal* 111-28.

14.27 Canada, *Report of the Royal Commission on the Economic Union and Development Prospects for Canada*, vol. 2 (Ottawa: Department of Supply and Services, 1985), 206-09.

that in 1986. Canada has levied a substantial sales tax at the manufacturers' level—the source of an important revenue—for many years; the U.S. federal government has no comparable tax. Estate and death taxes are levied in the U.S.; there are no such taxes in Canada. There are other differences, but the above are sufficient to establish that each country has developed its federal tax system almost independently of the other, and no doubt will continue to do so in the future regardless of tax reforms.

The Case of the Sales Tax

Few aspects of the federal tax structure have suffered more study, and been found to be more in need of revision, than the federal sales tax. And no aspect has so obdurately remained almost unchanged. Despite its hybrid origin in a grab-bag of excise taxes levied immediately after World War I and a subsequent turnover tax that was imposed for four years, it has survived for over sixty years as a major revenue source since its introduction in its present form in 1924. Needless to say the manufacturers on whom it was imposed did not appreciate this distinction, and raised such determined opposition that in 1927 the government declared its intention of gradually withdrawing the tax. This would have happened following 1930, when the rate had been reduced to 1 percent, had the need for revenue during the Great Depression not required its retention. Instead the rate was increased to 4 percent in 1931, to 6 percent in 1932, and to 8 percent in 1936, where it remained until 1951, when it was raised to 10 percent. Although a portion of the rate was labelled for old age security from 1952 to 1971 (at first 2 percent, later 3 percent), for taxpayers the rates were the inclusive total. Table 14.1 gives the rates for selected years in the period 1952 to 1987, including the special rates for certain products.

Role as a Revenue Source

As a source of revenue the sales tax has gradually declined in importance in the federal budget. From providing as much as 15-20 percent of the total in earlier times (the late thirties and 1950-70) its contribution has dropped to the 10-12 percent level in recent years. This is due in part to the increase in other forms of tax, particularly for social security and energy, but is probably mainly attributable to the growing list of exemptions (food, clothing, services, etc.) leaving dependence on only a few products (some already heavily taxed—automobiles, alcohol, tobacco and fuel)—for over half the revenue. It is also no doubt partly the result of the shift in spending to the service side of the economy—services not being taxed under the federal levy.

Nature and Problems of the Tax

In economic terms consumption taxes are regarded as acceptable provided they rest with reasonably equal weight on all products on which consumers spend their money. Ideally there would be no exemptions from such a tax in order to remain as "neutral" as possible in its effect on consumer choices, and consumer services would be taxed along with goods. Furthermore the

Table 14.1   Federal Sales Tax Rates, Selected Years, 1951-88

Year	General rate	Articles made by disabled	Building materials	Motor fuels[a]	Alcohol and tobacco	Telecommunications Programming services	Tax
				percent			
1951-59	10	5	—	—	10	—	—
1959-63	11	5½	—	—	11	—	—
1963-64	11	5½	4	—	11	—	—
1964.............	11	5½	8	—	11	—	—
1965-66	11	5½	8	—	11	—	—
1967 (part)	12	6	11	—	12	—	—
1967-72	12	6	11	—	12	—	—
1972-73	12	—	11	—	12	—	—
1973-74	12	—	11	—	12	—	—
1974-76	12	—	5	—	12	—	—
1976-77	12	—	5	—	12	—	—
1977-78	12	—	5	—	12	—	—
1978-80	9	—	5	*per gal.*	12	—	—
1980.............	9	—	5	9	12	—	—
1983.............	9	—	5	9	12	6	—
1984-85	10	—	6	10	13	6	—
1986 (Jan.)	11	—	7	11	14	7	—
1986 (Apr.).......	12	—	8	12	15	8	—
1988 (Jan.)	12	—	8	12	18	10	10

[a]Motor fuel taxes are levied on a per litre basis, at 1.5 cents for 1983 and 1984, at 3.5 cents for 1985 and 1986, and 4.5 cents for 1987 and 1988.

Source: *The National Finances.*

tax would be levied on the retail price to the final purchaser to eliminate as far as possible any distortions arising from differences in production, distribution, and other costs. The Canadian federal sales tax is about as far away from this ideal tax prescription as can be imagined. In legal form it is imposed on the sale price of all goods manufactured or produced in Canada or imported into Canada unless specifically exempt from tax. Apart from the fact that there are massive exemptions from the tax its base is as far removed from the price to the final consumer as one can get.

The main, and largely inescapable, defect of a tax imposed on the manufacturer's price is that, unlike the retailer, a manufacturer will sell the same product at a variety of prices, depending on the customer, with a resulting wide diversity of tax incidence for the final consumer. At the one extreme a manufacturer may have his own retail outlets and sell to final purchasers at competitive retail prices. More commonly he will sell to retailers for resale to final consumers (now estimated with changing marketing practices to be the major type of sale) at a lower price to compensate for the costs now incurred by the retailer. He may manufacture "private brand" goods for retailers, possibly at a different price again. He may also sell to independent wholesalers at a price different from any of the above, and he may also sell goods for export, for which the tax base will be different again. If his product is one that might be embodied in a product being manufactured by another producer his price might again be different from any of the above. Further, in any of these situations the price charged could vary where the transaction is between two or more affiliated companies not dealing at arm's length.

There is no reason why manufacturers should sell their products at a uniform price, and different circumstances call for different pricing, the principal differences being in distribution systems. The resulting allocation of costs between elements in the system will call for legitimate differences in prices between those elements.

In the absence of any single price that could be accepted as a base for tax the administration has been forced to establish a price described as a "notional value." This price has frequently been negotiated with the industry involved, and has tended to reflect the price at which the largest volume of goods is sold. Because of the heavy volume of sales to retailers the mechanism for establishing the tax base has frequently taken the form of a discount from the price for costs the manufacturer would not incur on a simple sale at his factory door. These "notional values," however determined (and there have been several methods), have been secret in the past, and have been a tribute to the skill and integrity of the officials administering the tax. Over a long period they have made a tax work that had nearly every imaginable defect and that in general the politicians did not want to hear about, except when it became possible to add a new exemption—which by and large was every year.

A particular defect of the tax lies in the advantage it gives to imports over domestically produced goods. The import sales tax base is the value for duty of the good plus the duty thereon, a figure which excludes many costs incurred after importation, such as transportation, advertising, etc. which are usually included in the value for sales tax of domestically manufactured goods. Recently this discrimination has been lessened for some products by a shift to the wholesale level for selected imported goods, a level which would include many of these costs. Equally significant is the element of taxation in Canadian exports under the present regime, an element that could be excluded under the VAT formula. A further problem inherent in a tax levied at the farthest remove from the final customer is the likelihood that tax will be applied to tax as the goods move through the production and distribution stream, resulting in multiple taxation of the same article.

To illustrate with an extreme example: if no steps were taken to prevent it a tax could be levied on all the equipment used to manufacture a product, on all the ingredients in the product, and then on the finished product as well. In practice this is avoided or reduced by specific exemption of manufacturing machinery and equipment and by licensing manufacturers to buy materials and other ingredients without tax. Sales between licensed manufacturers are tax-free to avoid duplication, and tax applies only when the purchaser is unlicensed. Despite this procedure it is apparent from available data that a substantial share of the revenue comes from businesses.

One might well ask why a tax fraught with such problems would have survived for six decades. The official explanation has been the efficiencies of administration obtained in dealing with the much smaller number of manufacturers than, for example, wholesalers or retailers. Whether this has compensated for the multitude of additional problems involved in the manufacturers' base is open to question.

Efforts at Reform

This attenuated explanation of the complexities of the manufacturers' sales tax is sufficient to serve as background for a brief discussion of reform proposals. The tax has been a happy hunting ground for academics and official inquiries for many years, and much of the resulting material is easily accessible. For those wishing to pursue the matter further a brief but competent history of the origins and problems of the tax from its beginning may be found in an article by Malcolm Gillis in the *Canadian Tax Journal* of January-Feburary 1985.[14.28] For greater depth there are official discussion papers, committee recommendations and the Report of the Royal Commission on Taxation, along with studies and conference panels of the Tax Foundation, and articles by academics and others.

What in general have been the proposals for reform in the postwar period when some of the defects of the tax began to be taken seriously?

The Due Study, 1951

Much credit belongs to Professor John Due for his pioneering 1951 study of the federal sales tax sponsored by the Canadian Tax Foundation.[14.29] His painstaking and detailed analysis revealed most of the shortcomings that have been outlined in the previous pages, and set the pattern for most subsequent studies. Professor Due made further studies of the Canadian consumption taxes, including the provincial sales tax, for the Foundation and spoke frequently at Foundation conferences. He has also examined at first hand the consumption taxes of nearly every country; as a result he has become one of the world's leading authorities, if not the leading authority, on this subject. Professor Due's writings are an essential element in any examination of the Canadian federal sales tax and are largely responsible for stimulating interest in it.

Sales Tax Committee Report, 1956

As a result of representations from the Foundation the federal government in 1955 appointed a committee of three—K.LeM. Carter, M. Raymond Dupuis, and A.E. McGilvray—to study four aspects of the sales tax: (1) the tax base; (2) appeals from administrative decisions; (3) import versus

---

14.28 Malcolm Gillis, "Federal Sales Taxation: A Survey of Six Decades of Experience, Critiques, and Reform Proposals" (January-February 1985), 33 *Canadian Tax Journal* 68-98.

14.29 John F. Due, *The General Manufacturers Sales Tax in Canada*. Canadian Tax Paper no. 3 (Toronto: Canadian Tax Foundation, 1951).

domestic burdens, and (4) exemptions based on use. On the issue of tax base
the committee favoured switching to the wholesale price, with a definition
in the statute; recommended that a process for appeals be established; for
the export-domestic problem, the transfer to the wholesale level to provide
substantial relief; and the restrictions of exemptions dependent on end-use
be somewhat relaxed. No substantial action was taken by the government
on the basis of this report, but the notion of transferring the base to the
wholesale level was to re-appear later. [14.30]

The Royal Commission on Taxation Report, 1967

The Royal Commission in its report deplored the by-now familiar shortcomings of the manufacturers' type of sales tax, and as its first option
proposed that it be abandoned and replaced by a tax at the retail level, to be
administered under some form of joint arrangement with the provincial
governments. As an alternative it proposed that, if the combined federal-
provincial rate of tax were to exceed 14 percent, which would encourage
evasion, the federal tax should take the form of a value-added tax. This is
the proposal that would probably be effective today, although it would
hardly be possible to adopt it independently of the provinces if it were
carried through to the retail level. In any event the government, as was mentioned earlier, postponed action on the sales tax, and neither proposal was
adopted.

1975 Discussion Paper

With the 1975 budget the Minister of Finance tabled a Discussion Paper,
Federal Sales and Excise Taxation. Although the paper examined the main
alternative bases for the sales tax it favoured the wholesale level—in effect,
the retailers' purchasing price. It supported this proposal on the ground that
a growing share of sales were already made directly from manufacturer to
retailer, and the need for establishing notional and artificial values for
tax would be correspondingly reduced. A discounting procedure would be
required only where manufacturers did not sell directly to retailers, a
diminishing share of the total. The higher base that would result from
moving to the wholesale level would give adequate revenue with a 10 percent
rate if domestic transportation costs were included; if they were excluded
10.5 percent would be required.

The paper had been prepared by an official committee—the Commodity
Tax Review Group—and comments on its proposals were requested.

Report of the Commodity Tax Review Group, 1977

Following study of some 200 briefs received in response to the 1975 Discussion Paper, the Review Group renewed its support for a switch to the
wholesale base for the sales tax. In support of this position it cited the

---

14.30For a more detailed review of the report, see John F. Due, "Report of the Sales Tax
Committee: One Year in Retrospect" (March-April 1957), *Canadian Tax Journal* 98-105.

results of a survey which showed that 44 percent of taxable goods were sold directly by manufacturers to retailers and 5 percent to individual users, a total approaching one-half of all taxable sales. It discussed and discarded as politically non-acceptable the idea of a joint federal-provincial retail sales tax, and gave only brief consideration to the idea of a federal value-added tax before dismissing it.

November 1981 Budget

Following a further prolonged period of gestation the federal Minister of Finance, then Allan J. MacEachen, made the following announcement in a budget paper accompanying his fall 1981 budget: "After an extensive review of a range of options, the government has concluded that the imposition of the tax at the last trade level prior to the retail level, that is the wholesale level, would be the most direct method of correcting the defects of the present system. The necessary legislation to effect this change will be introduced early in 1982. In order to allow adequate time for business firms to familiarize themselves with the new system, its actual implementation will be delayed until July 1, 1982 . . . A move to the wholesale level will permit a lowering of the general tax rate, while yielding the same revenues. The general rate will be reduced from 9 per cent to 8 per cent. The reduction will, however, be delayed by six months, until January 1, 1983, in order to offset a one-time revenue loss resulting from refunds of tax on wholesalers' inventories."[14.31]

April 1982 Postponement

On April 30, 1982, the Minister of Finance tabled two documents in the House of Commons relating to revision of the Excise Tax Act. One of these was a background paper on the proposed shift in the sales tax base which had been opposed by the majority of taxpayers and tax specialists, *Proposal to Shift the Federal Sales Tax to the Wholesale Trade Level*; the other was a draft amendment to the Excise Tax Act to accomplish this and other purposes. This was accompanied by a six months' postponement of the effective date of the change to January 1, 1983.

The Paper on the Proposal advanced the following arguments for it:

Introduction of a wholesale tax will:

- remove the present bias against domestically produced goods;
- achieve a more uniform tax burden on competing domestic manufacturers marketing their goods in different ways in Canada;
- cause the tax to be calculated on the actual sale price in most instances, thereby obviating many of the discretionary adjustments in taxable values now made by Revenue Canada;
- permit the introduction of an effective appeal mechanism;

[14.31] Canada, Department of Finance, *The Budget in More Detail*, November 12, 1981, 48-49.

- facilitate the administration by eliminating many refund claims from wholesalers (and retailers) who have made sales of tax-paid goods to customers entitled to exemption;

- allow wholesalers to obtain their inventories exempt of tax and thus reduce their cost of inventories by an estimated $400 million; and

- permit a lowering of the general rate from 9 per cent to 8 per cent.[14.32]

The paper also pointed out that steps had already been taken to move certain taxpayers to the wholesale level, including marginal manufacturers and producers of cosmetics and motor vehicle fuels, (and since then has been extended to other goods, including automobiles and motorcycles from Europe and Asia, pet foods, snack foods, candy and confectionery, microwave ovens, televisions, and VCRs). But it was argued that this item-by-item approach could not cope with the total problem—the system should be generalized. Ancillary proposals were to retain unchanged the range of goods that were taxable or exempt, and to reduce some excises then at a 10 percent rate to 8 percent, the projected new rate for the sales tax. In order to maintain a balance between the position of large and small retailers the former would be subject to an additional tax on their purchases of 1.2 percent. There would be provision under the revised act for a formal tax assessment system and a formal appeal mechanism very similar to the Income Tax Act.

Economic Statement, October 1982

In this general review of the state of the economy and the budget, the Minister took the opportunity to announce that in view of continuing debate over the proposed shift it would be delayed beyond the January 1 date announced in April.

The Federal Sales Tax Committee, 1983

In February 1983, a new Minister of Finance, Mark Lalonde, announced the appointment of a well-rounded committee drawn from the private sector with broad terms of reference to examine "structural problems in the manufacturer's tax system," to recommend optional solutions, to evaluate the wholesale tax draft legislation and report to the Minister by May 15th, or roughly within three months. The committee, composed of 17 members representative of nearly every element among the business, professional, and consumer groups, under the chairmanship of Wolfe Goodman, held 19 meetings, considered over 70 briefs and submitted a detailed report in May as requested. As the last comprehensive review in the steps leading up to the 1987 revision it deserves more attention than can be given here. In general it examined the shortcomings of the manufacturers' sales tax and discussed the merits of various alternatives in overcoming them. It rejected the shift to the wholesale level: "It is the opinion of the Committee that the marginal

---

[14.32] Canada, Department of Finance, Budget Papers, "Proposal to Shift the Federal Sales Tax to the Wholesale Trade Level," April 1982, 5.

improvements which shifting the tax to the wholesale level would produce do not justify the disruption which it would cause in an already functioning system." As an alternative, and apparently as an interim measure, it recommended some revisions of the manufacturers' sales tax, including, among seven broad proposals, that "certain importers be deemed to be manufacturers for sales tax purposes," that "established and determined values be given a statutory basis, subject to appeal" and that "a full and proper system of assessment, objection and appeal be enacted."

Clearly this step was a second best compromise for the Committee, its final proposal was that the Minister of Finance "immediately undertake intensive and serious study, in consultation with the provinces, with regard to shifting the federal sales tax at the earliest possible date to the level at which consumers purchase goods in Canada." In its detailed discussion of alternatives (Chapter VIII, A New Direction for Canadian Sales Tax) it indifferently examined the possibility of a joint federal-provincial retail sales tax and of an independent federal retail sales tax, with some impartiality as to advantages and disadvantages. However, its real preference emerged more clearly when it examined the value-added tax. In testing such a tax for neutrality, tax relief for producer inputs, reduction in the tax content of exports, and improvement in government cash flow, it awards the value-added tax of the tax-against-tax type high marks on every count. The disadvantages were found to be additional administrative complexity from the greatly increased number of taxpayers, and the probable need of a constitutional amendment to allow the provinces to impose an indirect sales tax if they agreed to join with the federal government in a federal-provincial arrangement for this type of tax. These considerations led to the recommendation "That special attention be given to studying the merit of introducing a federal value-added tax up to the level at which taxable goods and selected services are sold to final consumers and that the provinces be encouraged to join in the administration of such a tax."[14.33]

Budget, February 1984

The Budget Papers accompanying the Budget Speech of February 15, 1984 contained the following statement regarding the Committee's report:

Sales Tax Measures

The federal manufacturer's sales tax has been studied extensively over the past 30 years. All the studies have concluded that the majority of difficulties with the present system stem from the trade level at which the tax is imposed. These difficulties could be eased by changing the level at which the sales tax is levied either to the retail or wholesale levels. Given the difficulties in seeking a federal and provincial agreement on a common system for a retail sales tax, the government decided to examine the option of shifting the sales tax to the wholesale level.

[14.33] Federal Sales Tax Review Committee, Report of the Committee submitted to the Hon. Marc Lalonde, Minister of Finance, May 1983 (Wolfe D. Goodman, Chairman), 58.

On February 10, 1983, the government appointed the Federal Sales Tax Review Committee to allow a further opportunity for consultation and re-examination of the sales tax issues. The committee concluded that a shift in the tax to the wholesale trade level would produce only marginal improvements in the system and that these would not justify the disruption that it would cause.

The government accepts the basic recommendation of the committee not to proceed with the wholesale tax legislation. The tax will continue to apply at the manufacturer's level for most goods. Rather than changing the general application of tax, the government will review any identified inequities in the application of tax on a sector-by-sector basis and make appropriate changes in the trade level at which the tax is imposed in the given sector or for specific goods.

The government is proceeding with the committee's recommendation that a full and proper system of assessment, objection and appeal be enacted. The committee's recommendations to provide a refund of tax on sales that become bad debts, to credit interest on overdue tax refunds, and to correct other technical and administrative deficiencies in the Excise Tax Act are also being implemented.

A further issue that has received considerable discussion is the codification of current valuation rules in the Excise Tax Act. Given the complexity involved, the government does not propose to proceed with the codification of valuation rules in legislation at this time. Revenue Canada will continue its current practice of allowing taxpayers to base their sales tax liability on "established" and "determined" values where they make sales to retailers or consumers. Although this system does not have legal sanction, manufacturers are familiar with it and have found it satisfactory. It allows adequate flexibility to accommodate a wide variety of pricing practices.[14.34]

The budget at the same time proposed the step of transferring the tax base for imported vehicles to the wholesale level (i.e. the retailer's buying price) in order to remove the advantage enjoyed by vehicles imported from Europe and Asia through taxation on the duty-paid value. The assessment and appeal procedure to be introduced for sales tax was explained in some detail in the Budget Papers.

The legislation for this budget had not been passed when an election was called for the fall of the year, but the new Conservative government, elected in September 1984, ultimately re-introduced most of it unchanged and it then became law.

The Effect of the New Appeal Procedure

The appeal procedure promised in the February 1984 budget became law in early 1985. Its result has been to allow manufacturers with grievances

---

[14.34] Canada, Department of Finance, *Budget Papers*, February 15, 1984, 9-10.

against some of the arbitrary decisions made under the present inadequate sales tax law to challenge these in court. The success rate for these cases has been very high, and it is indicated that refunds in the millions have had to be granted. This was hinted at by Minister of Finance Wilson in his 1987 budget, when he stated that the present inadequate basic sales tax law was costing the treasury substantial sums.

This review brings the sales tax up to the ideas of the new Conservative government, including the business transfer tax, discussed in previous pages. The sales tax aspect of the tax reform process will fall into place in the following review of the June 1987 proposals.

A Personal View on Tax Reform, 1987

The York University panel on the Carter Royal Commission Report included, in addition to the author, the Hon. Edgar Benson, Robert B. Bryce and Ronald Robertson—all closely associated with the 1967-71 reform process. Each expressed some views on the current reform outlook, and these may be found in the volume of papers issued by Osgoode Hall following the conference. The author may be excused for using this opportunity to reproduce his closing statement on this subject. These remarks of course related to expectations in the Spring of 1987.[14.35]

Just to close with a few remarks about the future. We will apparently soon have some concrete information on the government's proposals. It would appear that a basic objective will be a re-shuffling of the tax mix— more commodity and corporate income tax and less personal income tax. This appears to be an inevitable goal at the moment, as the real issue is to create a federal tax structure that will withstand the pressure required to reduce the massive federal deficit. Certainly the manufacturers' sales tax, with its revenue base now narrowed by the exclusion of services and a constantly lengthening list of exemptions, is not a viable revenue base in its present form. Its scope must be extended, and a value-added tax seems to be the favoured vehicle. The success of such a venture to my mind will depend on meeting three conditions: (1) making satisfactory arrangements with the provinces so that the tax can be pushed through to the retail level and be compatible with the provincial retail sales taxes; (2) maintaining an exemption for food; and (3) beefing up the transfer system so that lower income taxpayers will not suffer as a result of the change.

In the latter connection I am reassured by the Minister's proposal to pay refundable tax credits. I would register a strongly negative vote against pushing the system any farther in the direction of an expenditure tax. To my mind such a tax flies in the face of all tax precepts. Apart from accepting a base that is the test of poverty in most countries—that is, the degree to which income is spent on consumption—in actual operation its effect is to

---

[14.35] Perry, supra footnote 13.4, at 34-36.

make all forms of savings and investment tax deductible. This would be creating the ultimate in tax shelters at a time when efforts are directed to reducing shelters.

In my view the last thing we need in this savings-prone country—where the savings rate is normally twice that of United States and even I, who am long past eligibility, annually receive at least 50 pounds of RRSP promotional literature—is more encouragement for saving. I have nothing against the RRSP; in fact looking back to the early fifties it is very likely that I was present at its creation. I simply do not feel that we need the tremendous savings stimulus that would result from a personal expenditure tax, under which all the tax expenditures we are now so painfully deleting from the system (and many more) would again become deductible, as not being personal expenditures.

As for the corporation income tax, I am no happier with it than I was twenty years ago. It always seems to be producing situations in which some of our best tax brains, both inside and outside government, are locked in sterile confrontation—the only justification for which is the high money stakes involved. It would be a troublesome enough tax if it fell on only one great corporation, but the opportunities offered by interlocking chains of other corporations make its care a constant and time-consuming occupation. We have moved from surplus-stripping to capital-gains-stripping, to unused tax losses and credits stripping, and there will undoubtedly be a new form of this activity in the future. Furthermore, if there are major distortions in the tax system they stem mainly from preoccupation with tax deductibility, where a dollar of tax saved is as important as a dollar of income earned. This seems to be particularly true of the corporation profits tax. Replacing this attitude with more objective criteria would be very healthy. This prognosis was confirmed by one business man, who, when I confronted him with the thought of abolishing the corporate profits tax, immediately said: "No! that would spoil half the game!" So there we are.

The widely disparate incidence of the tax, as revealed in studies over the last five years, has resulted in increasing attention to corporate tax reform. The government has made its own proposals, which seem to be going ahead relatively unchanged. The two-pronged approach of reducing deductions on the one hand and the tax rate on the other seems to be a withdrawal to a more neutral position, and therefore commendable. However it does raise doubts about abandoning the one hardy feature of postwar tax policy that has been retained by all previous governments—the encouragement of capital expenditure through accelerated depreciation. This follows the Keynesian dictum that investment is the key to economic growth. Research may have outmoded this dictum to give emphasis to other factors, but as capital expenditure is still the most conspicuously lagging element of the economy at present, the timing may not be too felicitous. The changes now in progress are described as revenue-neutral. To obtain more revenue from the corporation tax it is obvious that, apart from raising rates (which does not seem to be in the picture), some pretty severe medicine would have to be applied. The overhang of undeducted amounts will apparently wipe out the tax of many corporations for years to come. The Minister of Finance is welcome to deal with that little problem.

Finally, for the personal income tax—sure, let's have a little reduction. It will probably do neither much harm nor good. Anyway it is one of the traditional pre-election rituals, and is therefore inevitable.

I hope, however, that we will not be overly influenced by the rate structure the United States has enacted for next year. The situations in the two countries are now so completely different that it is difficult to visualize any brain drain resulting from it. We have a $500,000 lifetime exemption which for all intents and purposes has repealed taxation of capital gains. The United States has just made capital gains fully taxable. The current dividend tax credit reduces the top marginal federal personal income tax rate on dividends from Canadian companies to approximately 13 percent. The United States has never given more than a token recognition to double taxation of corporate income, and in the tax reform process it withdrew even that token. We are in the process of liberalizing the tax treatment of pension contributions—the United States has just restricted its treatment. The Canadian treatment of these key aspects of initiative and enterprise is so favourable that I see no strong compulsion to drive our top federal rate of approximately 36 percent down to the 28 percent U.S. top rate for 1988. No one would be more willing to be convinced that such a move would be the key to restoring momentum to our economy, but I am skeptical. That would make it all too simple, and our present economic problems are far more complex than that.

A final word; the federal fiscal scene will present unprecedented challenges in the next two to three years. We are now talking only of tax reform at this meeting, but in this same time span we will be making a crucial decision on free trade with the United States and we must also continue to make progress in reducing our enormous federal deficit. These are assignments enough for any two years and will call for all the skill and cool judgment we can muster. May we find that by 1990 we have made the right decisions on all these momentous issues.

Tax Reform Arrives

Overview

We left the Minister earlier having announced to the House of Commons on October 23, 1986 that a tax reform program was now on the government's official agenda—not a particular surprise in view of his previous indications. His statement set forth the guidelines that would be followed, and he asked for advice and consultation from all concerned. In the following months he saw several delegations and received many briefs, some of which were made public at the time. This activity raised expectations of a specific program in the February 1987 budget, but the Minister was not yet ready.

The full reform program was presented in a White Paper on June 18, 1987, which brought together the changes for personal and corporate income tax as Stage One of reform; changes for the sales tax would follow later as Stage Two.

Hearings on the White Paper were held during the fall by the House of Commons Committee on Finance and Economic Affairs and the Senate Banking, Trade and Commerce Committee and reports were submitted by both committees. Based on these reports and other representations the Minister almost duplicated his previous documentation in submitting to Parliament in December a further version of his proposals as none of the changes were of great substance. This was followed by the release of draft legislation in April 1988, and submission of a Ways and Means Motion on June 13, 1988 (basically the proposed bill). Although the stage had been well and truly set for tax reform by mid-1988, and indeed much of the program was in effect, Parliament had not yet acted on it. The tax reform under discussion therefore was one of which at mid-1988 many of the provisions were in operation but not yet authorized by statute, a situation not unusual for tax legislation.

Some Reflections on 1987 Reforms

The reform of the seventies began with sweeping changes proposed by the Royal Commission on Taxation reflecting an approach that many viewed as alarmingly radical; by contrast, the reform of the eighties, while substantial, has been much more pragmatic, involving marginal rather than fundamental changes. These produced a shift in balance between existing taxes rather than a basic alteration in their character and relationship. The main departure from the past was the reduced role foreseen for the personal income tax, which had been the cornerstone of the seventies. The changes here were intended not only to reduce the total tax burden but as well to reduce the load on lower income taxpayers. By contrast the corporate profits tax was to have a more prominent place, mainly through base broadening and loophole closing—in some cases by withdrawal of concessions adopted for economic stimulus by previous governments, some of long standing. These had produced widely disparate tax loads among corporations, and had left the general impression that corporations were not pulling their weight. While details of the sales tax revision were not yet known at mid-1988 their main purpose would be to broaden the base and increase revenues. As the previous review has indicated sales tax reform has been a long sought objective for administrative reasons, but no doubt it also reflected the view of some economists that a tax on one's consumption expenditures had much lower economic disincentive effects than a tax, such as the income tax, on the results of one's labours.

Changes by Increment

While the 1971 reforms were long delayed by controversy over principles, major elements of the 1987 reforms were introduced before any general commitment to reform or indication of its basic objectives had been given. Some parts of the program therefore anticipated the White Paper introduced in 1987, a process that was by no means covert, as the Minister explained his actions on numerous occasions and expressed his appreciation for the advice and consultation he had received. It is clear, in fact, that an incremental process of base-broadening had really begun with the MacEachen budget of 1982, from which experience it was also evident that a great deal of ground-breaking consultation would be necessary to overcome natural resistance.

However, for one of his first actions in 1984 after election the new Minister had neither opportunity nor need for ground-breaking; this was the suspension of the flow-through for research expenditures that some unscrupulous taxpayers were using to swindle the government of hundreds of millions of dollars. As it turned out this was just the beginning of a war by the Minister on corporate tax practices that he considered unacceptable, and many of his early budget changes were addressed to these practices or to the features of the tax that made them possible. These changes were too urgent to wait until 1987, but later proposals were preceded by extensive explanations and consultation.

The personal income tax changes were not as prone to the incremental reform treatment, although there were some fairly significant changes in pre-White Paper budgets.

Personal Income Tax

Pre-White Paper Changes

Several significant changes made prior to the White Paper probably should be included in the reform category. In the May 1985 budget there was the announcement of the $500,000 lifetime capital gains tax exemption and in the same budget the end of the flow-through tax credit for individuals contributing to scientific research. Various new measures were introduced to encourage R&D investment, particularly in small and medium sized companies. Steps were taken to curtail tax abuse of yachts, recreational vehicles and hotels, income from trusts and income splitting between members of a family. These moves were capped with the announcement of a minimum personal income tax for 1986, for which a budget paper gave alternative options.

In 1986 a significant anticipatory change was the introduction of the refundable sales tax credit. The rate of the sales tax had increased from 9 percent to 12 percent between 1983 and 1986. Along with heavy increases in tobacco and liquor taxes there was therefore a substantial increase in consumption taxes even before tax reform. The reduction in the dividend tax credit from one-half to one-third of the cash dividend, although related to a change in small business taxation, was also an augur of things to come later for dividend recipients. In the same budget the RHOSP was withdrawn.

The February 1987 budget made no further moves toward personal income tax reform, although the Minister again discussed his objectives and even the means he was likely to use in achieving them. The White Paper appeared in June.

The White Paper Reforms

The revised personal income tax is summarized in table 14.2. Reductions granted in the overall tax for most taxpayers were the combined result of a new three rate tax schedule in place of the existing ten rates and conversion of most exemptions and deductions to a tax credit at a general rate of 17 percent. No substantial changes were made in the income concept for individuals, although many upper income taxpayers would be affected by a reduction in the dividend tax credit, a less generous allowance for investment expenses, and an increase in the taxable portion of a capital gain from one-half to two-thirds for 1988 and 1989 and to three-quarters for 1990 and after. (The lifetime exemption of $500,000 had already been reduced to $100,000, except for farms and small businesses). For lower incomes there would be losses from dropping the general deduction in lieu of employment expenses (maximum $500) and the deduction for the first $1,000 of interest and dividend income. Increases in the income tax deductions for contributions made to a pension plan or an RRSP promised earlier would proceed, although at a slower pace than originally expected. The new system would not now come into effect until 1989.

The revision took aim at business expense deductions. There would be stricter rules for business meals and entertainment, home office, and automobile expenses. New tests would be introduced for farm losses and MURB deductions would be eliminated in two stages. Capital cost allowances for Canadian films would be reduced from 100 percent to 30 percent, but the half-rate limitation in the first year would be removed and investors would be allowed to offset all their income from films by future investments. The minimum tax was retained and a general anti-avoidance rule introduced.

An ancillary change announced by the Minister of National Health and Welfare increased child care income tax deductions from $2,000 to $4,000 for children under six and for all children requiring special care. For others not having receipted child care expenses a supplement to the child tax credit would be paid.

Although the revised personal income tax was enacted for 1988 it did not affect deductions from salary and wages, etc. until July. At mid-1988 therefore most taxpayers had yet to see the effects of the new tax in their take-home pay.

Effects of Personal Income Tax Reform

The "Summary for Taxpayers, Tax Reform 1987" presents the following information.

General Impact

- Income taxes will be reduced for 9.7 million households, over 85 percent of all households, by an average of $490.
- About 850,000 lower-income Canadians will have their income tax reduced to zero or receive refundable credits.

Table 14.2   Summary of Revised Personal Income Tax, 1988

Income: generally the same as in the past, except for increased capital gains and reduced deductions and exemptions (employment expenses and interest and dividend income and stricter rules for business expenses).

Tax Credits: nearly all former allowances against income (married status, dependants, charitable donations, medical expenses, etc.) were converted to tax credits, generally at a 17 percent rate.

Tax Rates: On the first $27,500—17 percent;
on the next $27,500—$4,675 plus 26 percent;
on the excess over $55,000—$11,825 plus 29 percent.
Plus 3 percent surtax on total tax.

Tax credits: to be deducted from the tax as calculated under the above rates

Basic credit.....................................	$1,020
Married..	850
Total married..................................	1,870

Married credit is reduced by 17 percent of spouse's income in excess of $5,000; credit wiped out at $5,500 of spouse's income.

Transfer of unused credits is continued, but with reduction of 17 percent of transferor's income over $6,000.

Dependants (18 and over, if infirm) .... Reduced by 17 percent of dependant's income over $2,500.	$250
Children under 18	$65
Third and subsequent children under 19...........	$130
Refundable child tax credit .... Reduced by 5 percent of family income over $24,000.	$559
Education credit, per month	$10
Age 65 and older	$550
Disability	$550
Sales tax credit, per adult	$70
per dependent child	$35

Reduced by 5 percent of family income over $16,000.

Pension income deduction: 17 percent, maximum $170.

Medical expenses: 17 percent of expenses in excess of $1,500 or 3 percent of income, whichever is lesser.

Charitable donations: 17 percent of first $250 and 29 percent of balance.

Tuition fees: 17 percent.

Unemployment insurance premiums: 17 percent.

CPP and QPP employee contributions: 17 percent.

Capital gains liftime exemption: $100,000
     66⅔ percent of gains taxable in 1988;
     75 percent in 1990. Exemption for principal residence retained.

Dividend tax credit: reduced to 13⅓ percent of dividend grossed up by one-quarter.

Eliminated: $1,000 exemption for interest and dividends
           $500 employment expense deduction
           Forward averaging and block averaging
           MURB allowances in 1988 for some; 1993 for others.

Reduced: Business expenses for meals and entertainment, home office, and automobiles.

Farm losses to be tested more severely.

- Income taxes will be cut for about 1.3 million of the 1.4 million households with at least one person aged 65 and over. About 250,000 elderly Canadians will have their income tax reduced to zero.

- Personal income taxes will be lower for all ranges of income.

- Most taxpayers whose income consists primarily of salary or wages, family allowance, or standard pension and retirement revenue will receive tax reductions.

- Net personal income tax revenues to the federal government will be reduced by about $12 billion over the next five years.[14.36]

Impact on Individual Taxpayers

Table 14.3   Personal Income Tax, Single Earner Under 65

Income level		Tax payable 1988		Tax cut as a percent of tax
	Pre-reform	Post-reform	Tax cut	
$	$	$	$	%
10,000	1,045	970	75	7.2
15,000	2,430	2,260	170	7.0
20,000	3,880	3,540	340	8.8
25,000	5,415	4,825	590	10.9
30,000	7,180	6,485	695	9.7
40,000	11,125	10,590	535	4.8
50,000	15,605	14,700	905	5.8
60,000	20,345	19,045	1,300	6.4
75,000	27,770	25,915	1,855	6.7

Source: Canada, Department of Finance, "Summary for Taxpayers," Tax Reform 1987, December 1987, 20.

Table 14.4   Personal Income Tax, Couple With One Earner, Two Children 18 and Under

Income level		Tax payable 1988		Tax cut as a percent of tax
	Pre-reform	Post-reform	Tax cut	
$	$	$	$	%
10,000	−1,015[1]	−1,120	105	[2]
15,000	85	−400	485	570.6
20,000	1,470	885	585	39.8
25,000	2,925	2,215	710	24.3
30,000	4,705	4,115	590	12.5
40,000	9,010	8,725	285	3.2
50,000	13,465	13,150	315	2.3
60,000	18,205	17,495	710	3.9
75,000	25,350	24,370	980	3.9

[1]Negative amounts represent refunds from the tax system due to the refundable child tax credit. [2]Taxfilers receive an increase in their tax refund.

Source: Canada, Department of Finance, "Summary for Taxpayers," Tax Reform 1987, December 1987, 21.

[14.36]Canada, Department of Finance, Tax Reform 1987, "A Summary for Taxpayers," December 1987, 16.

Table 14.5 Personal Income Tax, Couple, Both Earning Income, Two Children, 18 or Under

Income level	Pre-reform	Tax payable 1988			Tax cut as a percent of tax
		Post-reform	Tax cut		
$	$	$	$		%
10,000	− 1,050[1]	− 1,120	70		2
15,000	− 455	− 735	280		2
20,000	415	170	245		59.0
25,000	1,415	1,110	305		21.6
30,000	2,510	2,225	285		11.4
40,000	5,815	5,295	520		8.9
50,000	9,460	8,725	735		7.8
60,000	13,065	12,235	830		6.4
75,000	18,595	17,495	1,100		5.9

[1] Negative amounts represent refunds from the tax system due to the refundable child tax credit. [2] Taxfilers receive an increase in their tax refund.

Source: Canada, Department of Finance, "Summary for Taxpayers," Tax Reform 1987, December 1987, 22.

Corporate Tax Reform

Pre-White Paper Changes

The reform process for corporation taxation began earlier than for personal taxation and much of it had been introduced before the 1987 White Paper made reform official. Most of the early changes have already been mentioned, but as part of a continuing process will be listed again. There will be one omission. To spare the reader the details of some of the most complex provisions ever to be enacted in the Income Tax Act we will not review the several anti-avoidance measures introduced in recent years. For the most part these dealt with schemes entered into between corporations to take advantage of the tax saving opportunities of unused losses or tax credits through transactions that were not illegal but were costing the federal government substantial amounts of tax revenue. The measures taken formed a major element in the Minister's avowed goal of base-broadening to permit a reduction in rate sufficient to remove the attraction for such devices. These measures are described in government tax reform documents and other sources, to which the reader is referred for further details.

As already mentioned, the 1985 budget gave the final demise to the much abused flow-through tax credit for scientific expenditures. But other measures were to follow related to much less exotic aspects of the corporate income tax that were part of the base broadening rate reduction objective. The Minister presented the main objectives of his corporate reforms in a 1985 budget paper, and in the 1986 budget introduced a fairly comprehensive program of pre-reform proposals based on these objectives. Described as the first phase of corporate tax reform, they began a process that led to further developments in the 1987 White Paper. As described, these changes included withdrawal of the inventory allowance, the general investment tax credit, and reduction of the special tax credit for manufacturing investment in designated areas. Special tax credits for investment in Atlantic Canada, the Gaspé, and Cape Breton were retained. Corporate tax rates were to be reduced over a three-year period beginning July 1, 1987. The general federal rate would be reduced from 36 to 33 percent, the rate on manufacturing profits from 30 to 26 percent, and the small business rate from 15 to 13 percent. The effect of these changes would be an increase of $765 million in revenue over the three years. They were accompanied by removal of a 12½ percent tax on dividend distributions of small companies.

The White Paper Reforms

The main changes in the corporate tax structure proposed in the White Paper of June 1987 were summarized as follows:

- Capital Cost Allowance (CCA) rates will be lowered to bring them more into line with economic depreciation. CCA rates will still provide incentives for investment in key manufacturing and resource sectors.

- The proposals will ensure that the finance, insurance and real estate industries bear their fair share of tax. A tax on the capital of large banks and trust companies will be imposed.

- The 33⅓ percent depletion deduction will be phased out and eliminated as of December 31, 1989.

- The portion of capital gains realized by corporations that is taxed will be increased from 50 percent to 66⅔ percent in 1988 and to 75 percent in 1990.

- Business expenses for entertainment and meals will be restricted to 80 percent of actual costs.

- A general anti-avoidance rule will be introduced to prevent misuse or abuse of the provisions of the *Income Tax Act*.

- After-tax financing advantages available to non-taxpaying companies through the use of preferred shares will be reduced.

- The use of investment tax credits will be restricted to three-quarters of tax otherwise payable to ensure that profitable corporations cannot use them to completely eliminate their tax liability.

Starting in July 1988, corporate tax rates will be reduced:

- The general federal rate will drop to 28 percent.

- The rate for manufacturing will drop to 23 percent by 1991.

- The small business rate will drop to 12 percent.[14.37]

Capital Cost Allowances

The capital cost allowance changes were detailed in the White Paper document as follows:

[14.37] Ibid., at 33.

Table 14.6 Major Changes in CCA Rates After Full Implementation

	Current CCA rate	Proposed CCA rate
Manufacturing machinery and equipment	three-year straight line[1]	25% declining balance
Manufacturing retooling	immediate write-off	subject to half-year rule
Resource extraction assets	30% declining balance plus immediate write-off up to income from new mine)	25% declining balance (plus immediate write-off up to income from new mine)
Drillships and offshore platforms	30% declining balance	25% declining balance
Earth-moving equipment	50% declining balance	30% declining balance
Buildings	5% declining balance	4% declining balance
Satellites	40% declining balance	30% declining balance
Outdoor advertising signs	35% declining balance	20% declining balance
Certified Canadian films	100%	30% declining balance (plus immediate write-off up to film income)
Public utility property	6% declining balance	4% declining balance

[1] Taking account of the half-year rule.

Source: Canada, Department of Finance, "Income Tax Reform", June 18, 1987, 102.

An important change in the timing of the allowance was the abandonment of the time of acquisition for the time of use of the asset.

Other Measures

Tax on Financial, Insurance and Real Estate Companies

These changes were explained as follows:

> The reform proposals will reduce the deductions now allowed to financial institutions for doubtful debt reserves. Tax treatment of reserves for all types of financial institutions will be comparable. The tax treatment of bank reserves will no longer be directly linked to the prudential requirements for reserves.

> These measures, applicable to the finance and insurance companies, will contribute 28 percent of the total corporate tax base broadening over the next five years.

> Real estate companies and other land developers will be required to capitalize costs of carrying vacant land for development and unused land held in the course of a business, and to capitalize "soft costs," as is now generally required for financial accounting purposes and as is applied to other taxpayers.[14.38]

[14.38] Canada, Department of Finance, "The White Paper on Tax Reform," June 18, 1987, 49.

A tax at 15 percent on the investment income of insurance companies was part of this financial package.

The Depletion Allowance

This change was explained as follows: "Earned depletion, which provides for the generation of tax deductions that exceed amounts actually spent for certain exploration and resource development expenditures, will be phased out. The rate at which depletion can be earned will be reduced from 33⅓ percent to 16⅔ percent of eligible expenditures on July 1, 1988, and eliminated as of July 1, 1989. The phase out of the 33⅓ percent of depletion provision will apply to tar sands and enhanced oil recovery investments."[14.39]

Higher Capital Gains Inclusion

As with personal income tax, the proportion of capital gains to be included in income will be increased from one-half to two-thirds in 1988 and 1989 and to three-quarters in 1990.

Business Expenses for Meals and Entertainment

As with personal income tax, the deduction will be reduced to 80 percent of the expenditure.

General Anti-Avoidance Rule and After-Tax Financing

The revision included a general anti-avoidance provision and limitations on the use of dividends on preferred shares as a means of transferring after-tax benefits (accumulated losses, tax credits, etc.) between corporations.

Limit on Use of Investment Tax Credits

There was at first to be a limit of 50 percent on the tax otherwise payable that could be offset with tax credits. This was later increased to 75 percent. No such limit had been imposed in the past.

Reduced Tax Rates

The following table gives the tax rates that will be in effect for the years 1988 to 1991 and thereafter.

Features Retained

The research and development tax credits would be retained with regional differentials; but building costs will not be eligible. The rates of tax credits were to be as follows:

The deduction for a farm loss was increased from $5,000 to $15,000 but a more rigorous test based on share of gross revenue was introduced for part-

---

14.39 Ibid., at 48.

Table 14.7 Federal Corporate Income Tax Rates

	Current statutory rates	New statutory rates effective July 1 each year			
		1988	1989	1990	1991 and subsequent years
		(percent)			
General business	36	28	28	28	28
Manufacturing business	30	26	25	24	23
General small business	15	12	12	12	12
Small manufacturing business	10				

Note: These changes will not affect the tax rate reductions scheduled to take effect on July 1, 1987. All the rates are after the 10-per-cent provincial abatement.

Source: Canada, Department of Finance, "Income Tax Reform", June 1987, 98.

Table 14.8 Proposed Investment Tax Credit Rates, 1987-89

	1987	1988	1989
	(percent of eligible investment)		
Current 5-per-cent rate[a]...........................	5	3	0
Current 7-per-cent rate[a]...........................	7	3	0
Special regional rate for manufacturing in .... specified areas	40	40	30
Research and development	unchanged from current rates of 20, 30 and 35 depending on location and size of firm		
Atlantic region	20	20	15
Cape Breton	60	60	45
High-cost exploration	unchanged from current rate of 25		

[a]The phase-out of general rates of ITC as announced in February 26, 1986 budget.

Source: Canada, Department of Finance, "Income Tax Reform", June 1987, 110.

time farmers. Flow-through shares were retained but with much stricter rules for eligibility based on a degree of risk for the shareholder.

Subsequent Changes: December 1987

In presenting his Ways and Means Motion on December 16, 1987, the Minister released documents very similar to those issued with his White Paper in June. There were detailed reviews of comments and suggestions on the White Paper proposals, most of which it turned out had been rejected by the Minister. Among those accepted were an increase to 75 percent in the corporate tax that could be offset by tax credits, the farm losses provision was held over for further consultation, the phase-out of the depletion allowance was extended for six months to July 1, 1989, the capital tax on deposit-taking institutions was increased, and minor other changes were made. Some further revisions appeared in the draft bill released in April 1988 but there were none that affected the basic framework of the reform. To all intents and purposes therefore the corporate reform changes were as described above.

Corporate Tax Reform: The Overall Impact

Increasing Corporate Income Tax Share of Current Revenues

Tax reform will result in corporations making a significantly higher contribution to the total tax revenues collected by the federal government . . . the share of corporate tax revenues will rise from 15.6 percent currently to 17.2 percent by 1992. Federal revenues will increase by $470 million in 1988, and the increase will grow to about $1.6 billion in 1992, as the measures are fully phased in. Over the period, corporate taxes will increase by over $5 billion in total. These increases in corporate taxation will help to fund the personal income tax rate reductions.

Corporate Base Broadening to Fund Tax Rate Cuts

Substantial corporate tax base broadening allows a significant reduction in corporate tax rates, while at the same time helping to fund personal tax rate cuts. Over all, the percentage of financial statement income for profitable firms that is subject to tax will increase from its current level of 72 percent to over 84 percent.

All sectors of the economy contribute to base broadening. . . . The base broadening is concentrated in sectors that now have relatively low proportions of their income subject to tax and relatively more profitable firms that do not pay tax.[14.40]

Stage 2: Sales Tax Reform

The Minister's objectives for the main sales tax reform became fairly clear as the reform process developed. Interim measures included the extension of the tax to goods that the Minister was persuaded should be taxed (base broadening) and some major changes in its legal basis. The 1985 budget implemented changes of both kinds. New taxable goods included candy and confectionery, soft drinks, pet foods, beauty and health goods, and some goods related to energy efficiency. The differential basis between on-site and off-site construction materials was removed. The legal changes were much more fundamental, however. As the Budget Paper of May 23, 1985 explained, "The Excise Tax Act now contains no provisions for assessing a person's liability for sales and excise taxes levied under the Act, and provides a relatively limited system for taxpayers to appeal tax disputes to independent adjudicators. This budget proposes the introduction of a comprehensive system of assessments and appeals, modelled after the income tax system and incorporating the concept of not requiring the payment of taxes in dispute that was recently proposed for income tax purposes."[14.41] The

[14.40] Ibid., at 50.

[14.41] Canada, Department of Finance, Budget Papers, "Securing Economic Renewal," May 23, 1985, 65.

amendments that followed this proposal gave taxpayers the right to bring their grievances over the labyrinthian minutiae of the sales tax before the Tariff Board and the Federal Court-Trial Division, with apparently quite expensive results for the fisc, as refunds were common.

In his 1986 budget the Minister mentioned his continuing concern over the sales tax, and stated that his officials were examining the value-added tax and alternative systems, including a business transfer tax, the latter a completely foreign and disturbing concept to the business community. However, apart from promising release of a paper on the subject in the near future no further attention was given the subject. Much the same could be said of the February 1987 budget. There were some base-broadening extensions of tax to include so-called snack foods, some further exemptions for health goods—the recent favoured category—and a promise of a plan for a revised sales tax to come; but no details were given at this stage. These were to come in the White Paper proposals in June, which we will leave for the moment to continue with the course of actual changes in the tax, which were quite substantial.

The "Sales Tax Reform" volume of the Tax Reform 1987 series proposed, as an interim measure pending the final decision on the basic form of the tax, changes in the present tax "to correct some of the most serious inequities in the existing system and to stem the erosion of the tax base through the use of tax avoidance mechanisms."[14.42]

The changes proposed for this purpose were (1) application of the sales tax to sales by marketing companies related to a manufacturer and (2) for a range of products shifting the sales tax base from the manufacturers' to the wholesale level. Both these moves of course were designed to broaden the base to which the tax applied by bringing in costs that otherwise escaped through the marketing arrangements for the goods. In particular the changes were aimed at manufacturers which had set up marketing companies to which goods were sold at a price that was lower than if the marketing costs had been incurred by the manufacturer. The Paper explained as follows:

> To address these problems, the government is proposing that where a manufacturer sells goods primarily through a related person, that person will be deemed to be the manufacturer of all such goods sold by him and will be liable for tax on his sale price. This will remove the incentive for manufacturers to establish marketing companies to reduce the tax otherwise payable on their sales. The tax on sales through related marketing companies would be the same as on direct sales by manufacturers to independent distributors. This measure will apply to both domestic and imported goods. It will thus ensure greater fairness in the application of tax between domestic and imported goods.[14.43]

14.42 Canada, Department of Finance, Tax Reform 1987, "Sales Tax Reform," June 18, 1987, 153.

14.43 Ibid., at 154.

A basic accompanying amendment would modify the current fair price provisions of the Excise Tax Act "so that in other cases of non-arm's-length sales where the manufacturer is making substantial sales to independent persons, the tax will apply to the fair market value of the goods. Fair market value will be readily determinable in such cases by reference to prices charged to independent persons. This will obviate the need for Ministerial determination of the value for tax.[14.44]

The list of goods to be taxed on wholesale value, for reasons previously explained, were household soaps, cleaning and similar materials; pet litter; games, toys and sporting goods; and records, tapes and discs.

Papers released in December 1987, "Supplementary Information Relating to Tax Reform Measures," reaffirmed the government's decision to proceed with these proposals (page 113). The Act would be amended eventually to introduce a concept of "fair market value" for non-arm's-length sales from January 1, 1988, and taxpayers were advised in the meantime to be guided by international transfer pricing rules.

But this whole proposal met an interesting fate in the 1988 budget. It was dropped in favour of a quite different and much more imaginative approach. This was explained in the Budget Papers for February 10, 1988, as follows:

In the June 1987 White Paper on tax reform, the government brought forward proposals to deal with some of these problems. Implementation of two of the proposals—the application of tax to sales by marketing companies related to a manufacturer, and the shifting of the tax to the wholesale level for a range of products—was delayed pending further consultation to ensure that they could achieve the intended purposes in an effective manner.

These consultations have resulted in a revised proposal. The government will proceed, effective November 1, 1988, with amendments to the Excise Tax Act to deal with the tax treatment of marketing and distribution expenses and related distortions. The effect of the new proposal will be to tax all those goods presently taxable at the basic 12-percent rate at the manufacturer's trade level on their manufacturing cost plus profit.

This will be accomplished by allowing the deduction from the manufacturer's selling price of either actual marketing and distribution costs or standard deductions. Since these deductions would otherwise substantially reduce the value subject to tax, the resulting value, net of deductions, will be adjusted upward by 25 percent. This tax base, when subject to the 12-percent tax rate, will produce revenues to ensure that sales tax revenues are maintained at the level forecast last June when the initial proposals were announced. The system of standard deductions will afford significant relief for taxpayers with annual

---

[14.44] Ibid., at 155.

taxable sales of less than $250,000 (representing about two-thirds of all federal sales tax payers).

Under the revised method of calculating the tax, domestic manufacturers currently paying tax on their selling price, including all marketing and distribution costs, will now pay tax at a level more in line with that for goods imported or channeled through marketing companies. This will significantly reduce many of the existing tax inequities between competing goods. As a result, it will be unnecessary to proceed with the June proposals to shift the sales tax to the wholesale level for household chemicals, games, toys, sporting goods and equipment, and records and tapes. In addition, the wholesale tax on pet foods, snack foods, candy and confectionery, microwave ovens, televisions and video recorders and players will be shifted back to the manufacturer's trade level, effective November 1, 1988.

Notwithstanding this new approach to the treatment of marketing and distribution costs, the fundamental problems of the current federal sales tax remain. The only adequate solution is to replace the tax. This will occur in the second stage of tax reform.

To assist taxpayers and their advisers and to receive input on the design of the measure, the government asked professional organizations to hold information seminars in a number of cities. Written submissions to the Department of Finance before March 15, 1988 were to be taken into consideration in developing final legislation to implement the proposal.

The measure was described in detail in the accompanying technical notes, *Sales Tax: Measure Relating to the Treatment of Marketing and Distribution Costs* under separate cover.[14.45]

One is tempted to suggest that, while many problems would remain unsolved in the sales tax, this sensible, simple, and crude device would neatly bring a rough order of justice to the worst of them, the sale price. The proposal of course took a battering before a legislative hearing from those wedded to the present arrangements, and was rejected in a report from those hearings. Nonetheless the Minister declared his intention to proceed, but in order to give the proposal further study postponed its effective date from November 1, 1988 to April 1989. At mid-1988 one can only speculate on its ultimate fate—and for that matter on the fate of the whole sales tax revision program.

Basic Reform: The White Paper

It was not surprising, in view of earlier comments by the Minister, that the final Sales Tax Reform proposals favoured a value-added tax, or a multistage tax as it is now known (a definite improvement over the business

---

14.45 Canada, Department of Finance, Budget Papers, "Securing Economic Renewal," February 10, 1988, 19-20.

transfer tax label). What is considerably more surprising is that under 1988 tax rates this would have been the choice of the Carter Commission, as put forward in its report of two decades before. Nothing has been more durable in the Canadian fiscal system than this ancient monster that has survived substantially unchanged for over 60 years, despite growing discontent among both taxpayers and governments.

The flaws have been well documented and need not be detailed again here. The tax proposed as a replacement was to be "a broadly based multi-stage sales tax that extends to the retail level. This multi-stage tax would be a form of value-added tax. It would be levied on and collected from all businesses, in stages, as goods move from primary producers and processors to wholesalers, retailers, and finally consumers. Under this multi-stage tax, businesses will pay tax on their sales and claim a credit for any tax paid on their purchases."[14.46] Such a tax was said to have the following advantages:

- eliminate tax on business inputs, thereby ensuring there are no hidden taxes on consumer products;
- treat all business firms uniformly, regardless of how they manufacture and distribute their products;
- apply tax in a fair way to consumers purchasing different goods and services and, by broadening the base of the tax, make possible a lower rate of tax for consumers;
- ensure uniform effective rates of tax on the final sale price of products and, in the process, remove difficult and administratively cumbersome valuation problems;
- treat imports in the same manner as domestically produced goods;
- remove completely the hidden taxes from Canadian exports.[14.47]

Three options were put forward for implementation of such a tax. Option 1 is a national sales tax, basically a multi-stage tax collected by one administration on behalf of the provinces and the federal government. There would be a common tax base, but there could be differences in the tax rate between provinces. Options 2 and 3 would be two variations of a federal-only multiple-stage tax, both carried through to the retail level.

Option 2 would be a Goods and Services Tax, a levy applied at a uniform rate to virtually all goods and services in Canada. With a minimum of exemptions and special categories a system could be developed under which businesses would calculate the tax on their total sales and a tax at the same rate on their total taxed purchases and in effect pay the difference. Such a tax of broad application would require an enrichment of the sales tax credit in order not to penalize lower incomes. It was pointed out that the main disadvantage of this approach is that it does not allow exemption of particular goods and services (e.g. food, medical services, etc.).

[14.46] Supra footnote 14.42, at 25.
[14.47] Ibid.

The third option, the Value-Added Tax, would be basically the same as the previous option except that tax would be imposed on an item by item basis and exemptions and special categories could be established. (A reservation over the high cost of exempting food and clothing in this explanation set the alarm bells ringing and the Minister was ultimately forced to state in Parliament that it was not the government's intention to abandon the long-standing exemption for food under the sales tax). The main disadvantage of this option was the additional paper work and compliance costs for businesses; in fact it was conceded that at the retail level the task of collecting tax for both federal and provincial governments, with different rates and exemptions, would be well nigh impossible.

Status at Mid-1988

It is understood that there have been discussions between federal and provincial governments on this vexing question—another of the many instances in which the interests of both are deeply involved. The root problem is that there is little to be gained if a multi-stage tax is not pushed through to the retail level, and the provinces now occupy that level with their own taxes at very substantial rates.

At mid-1988 there was no indication of what had resulted from the federal-provincial exchange, nor was the federal government making any move toward replacement of the sales tax. Future developments are therefore somewhat obscure. And the federal-provincial connection was not the only block in the way of a goods and services tax. Experience of some of the American states has demonstrated that the taxation of services is a particularly sensitive area. Florida tried it, but was forced by taxpayer rebellion to give up after a few months.

The Public Reception

In retrospect by mid-1988 it was clear that tax reform had been over-long on the public agenda. Public indifference became general once it was clear that the federal government was not plotting to obtain massive additional revenues to liquidate its deficit and that food would not be included under the revised sales tax.

Indifference of course was not true of political, business, social, and other interests having a broader concern for its implications. The volume of literature produced on the subject is probably not even indexed adequately, and even a partial review would take us far beyond our present scope. Much of this of course reflected expectations for revolutionary changes that were far beyond the intentions of the government; many in fact urged an interventionist role for a government that, like many other governments, was increasingly assuming a non-interventionist posture.

The main protests of course came from taxpayers and their organizations whose prospects were being dimmed by the base-broadening process. Business organizations were generally opposed to the reduction in capital cost allowances, the closer limits on research and development expenditure, the increase in the taxable share of capital gains, and of course the measure to limit the tax advantages of inter-corporate transfers. The film industry protested the narrowing of the tax advantages that had drawn film producers to Canada, and the mining industry had to be compensated with a special fund of $200 million to offset possible losses of financing through flow-through share financing. Financial institutions of course were not at all pleased with the reduction in their loss provisions at a time when possible losses for developing country loans were still in the billions.

The Sales Tax

In a sense the changes in the federal income taxes were a turning back of the clock to past positions and objectives. But this could not be said of the sales tax, the proposals for which could properly carry the label of reform. If revised as proposed, the sales tax will be a quite different, and much improved, measure than the 65-year-old manufacturers' sales tax. But the obstacles are enormous. A revision based on the cooperation of all nine provinces now imposing taxes at the retail level would be a triumph of federal-provincial negotiation equal to the original Confederation settlement. As we have said, at mid-1988 there was no certainty that this miracle would take place.

Provincial Budget Reactions

While the sales tax change was still in the future, the provinces had a more immediate interest in the budgetary effects of tax reform as the joint occupant of the principal tax field involved. The reform effects on their share of approximately one-third of the personal income tax yield would be immediate, and with a lower level of tax would be restrictive. In several provinces rates were raised to recoup some of the lost revenue. Provincial taxes based on the federal tax were increased as follows: Ontario, from 50 percent in 1987 to 51 percent in 1988 and 52 percent in 1989, with an increase in the provincial surtax to 10 percent on tax over $10,000; Prince Edward Island, from 55 percent in 1987 to 57 percent in 1988, plus a new 10 percent surtax on taxes in excess of $12,500; New Brunswick, from 58 percent in 1987 to 60 percent in 1988; Saskatchewan, flat rate tax raised from 1.5 percent to 2 percent for 1988. The other provinces made no increases in personal income tax; Alberta reduced its flat rate from 1 percent to 0.5 percent. In other areas there were the usual raises in gasoline and tobacco taxes; the most notable commodity tax increase was the raise in the Ontario sales tax from 7 to 8 percent.

On the whole given the pressure on the provinces for additional revenues these were not radical responses; many of the changes would probably have been made regardless of the federal reforms. (For further details see "Provincial Budget Roundup, 1988, Part I," (May/June 1988), 36 *Canadian Tax Journal*, 615-54).

Bibliography, chapter 14

Aaron, Henry J. ed. *The Value-Added Tax Lessons from Europe*. Studies of Government Finance. Washington, D.C.: The Brookings Institution. 1981.

Aaron, Henry J., and Galper, Harvy. *Assessing Tax Reform*. Washington: The Brookings Institution, 1985.

Ballantyne, Janet. "The Impact of Tax Reform on Personal Income." (July-August 1987) 35 *Canadian Tax Journal*, 1050-58.

Bale, Gordon. "A Call for Fundamental Tax Reform from the U.S. Treasury: Some Implications for Canada." (March-April 1985) 33 *Canadian Tax Journal*, 269-99.

Bird, Richard M. "Federal Sales Tax: The End of the Tale?" (March-April 1982) 30 *Canadian Tax Journal*, 214-18.

_____. *Tax Incentives for Investment: The State of the Art*. Canadian Tax Paper no. 64. Toronto: Canadian Tax Foundation, 1980.

_____. "What Should We Tax: Income or Consumption?" In *Report of Proceedings of the Thirtieth Tax Conference*, 1978 Conference Report. Toronto: Canadian Tax Foundation, 1980.

Blais, Andre, and Vaillancourt, Francois. "The Federal Corporate Income Tax: Tax Expenditures and Tax Discrimination in the Canadian Manufacturing Industry, 1972-81." (September-October 1986) 34 *Canadian Tax Journal*, 1122-39.

Boadway, Robin, and Kitchen, Harry M. *Canadian Tax Policy*. Canadian Tax Paper no. 63. Toronto: Canadian Tax Foundation, 1980.

Boadway, Robin W., Bruce, Neil, and Mintz, Jack M. *Taxes on Capital Income in Canada: Analysis and Policy*. Canadian Tax Paper no. 80. Toronto: Canadian Tax Foundation, 1987.

Boadway, Robin and Bruce, Neil. "Theoretical Issues in Tax Reform." In David Laidler, research coordinator, *Approaches to Economic Well-Being*. Collected Research Studies of the Royal Commission on the Economic Union and Development Prospects for Canada, vol. 36. Toronto: University of Toronto Press, 1985.

Bossons, J. "The Potential Role of a Value-Added Tax in Canada." In *Report of Proceedings of the Twenty-Fourth Tax Conference*, 1972 Conference Report. Toronto: Foundation, 1973.

Broadhurst, David G. "Tax Reform: Raising the Cost of Capital." (July-August 1987) 35 *Canadian Tax Journal*, 980-86.

Brown, Joseph B. "Commodity Tax Update." In *Report of Proceedings of the Thirty-Second Tax Conference*, 1980 Conference Report. Toronto: Canadian Tax Foundation, 1981.

Burtless, Gary, and Haveman, Robert. "Taxes, Transfers and Economic Distortions: Evaluating the New View." (March-April 1987) *Challenge*, 45-51.

Business Council on National Issues. *Taxation Policy Reform in Canada*. Ottawa: the Council, 1986.

C.D. Howe Institute. *Tax Reform in a New Light*. Commentary no. 13 Toronto: the Institute, January 1987.

"Commons Finance Committee Rejects Proposed Measure to Reform Sales Tax." *The Globe and Mail*, July 14, 1988.

"Federal Finance Department Revising Sales Tax Measures." *The Globe and Mail*, July 16, 1988.

_____. Canada. Department of Finance. Budget Paper. *Analysis of Federal Tax Expenditures by Individuals*. November 12, 1981.

_____. Budget Speech. April 29, 1947.

_____. Budget Speech. May 18, 1947.

_____. Budget Speech. March 22, 1949.

_____. Budget Speech. October 20, 1949.

_____. Budget Speech. March 28, 1950.

_____. Budget Speech. October 28, 1980.

_____. Budget Speech. November 12, 1981.

_____. Budget Speech. May 23, 1985.

_____. Budget Speech. February 26, 1986.

_____. Budget Speech. February 18, 1987.

_____. Budget Papers. *A New Direction for Economic Renewal: Economic and Fiscal Statement*. Ottawa: 1984.

_____. Budget Papers. *The Corporate Income Tax System: A Direction for Change*. Ottawa: 1985.

_____. Budget Papers. *A Minimum Tax for Canada: Executive Summary*. Ottawa: 1985.

_____. Budget Papers. *A Corporate Loss Transfer System for Canada*. Ottawa: 1985.

_____. Budget Papers. *Securing Economic Renewal*. Ottawa: 1985.

_____. Budget Papers. *Securing Economic Renewal*. Ottawa: 1988.

_____. Commodity Tax Review Group. *Report*. Ottawa: 1977.

_____. Discussion Paper. *Federal Sales and Excise Taxation*. Ottawa: 1975.

_____. Federal Sales Tax Review Committee. *Report*. Ottawa: 1983.

_____. *Proposal to Shift the Federal Sales Tax to the Wholesale Trade Level*. Ottawa: 1982.

_____. *Questions and Answers on Tax Reform*. With the Canadian Institute of Chartered Accountants and The Canadian Bar Association. Ottawa: 1987.

_____. Sales Tax Committee. *Report to the Minister of Finance*. Ottawa: 1956.

_____. *The Budget Process*: A paper on budget secrecy and proposals for broader consultation. Ottawa: 1982.

_____. *Tax Reform, 1987*. Speech Delivered in the House of Commons by the Honourable Michael H. Wilson, Minister of Finance, June 1987. Ottawa: 1987.

_____. The White Paper. *Tax Reform 1987*. Ottawa: June 1987.

_____. *Tax Reform 1987. Income Tax Reform*. Ottawa: June 1987.

_____. *Tax Reform 1987. Sales Tax Reform*. Ottawa: June 1987.

_____. *Tax Reform, 1987. Ecomonic and Fiscal Outlook*. Ottawa: June 1987.

_____. *Tax Reform, 1987*. Speech by the Honourable Michael H. Wilson on

Tabling of a Notice of Ways and Means Motion to Amend the Income Tax Act, December 1987. Ottawa: 1987.

———. *Tax Reform, 1987.* Notice of Ways and Means Motion to Amend the Income Tax Act. Ottawa: December 1987.

———. *Tax Reform, 1987. Tax Treatment of Farm Losses.* Ottawa: December 1987.

———. Draft Income Tax Regulations, Legislation and Explanatory Notes. Ottawa: December 1987.

———. Supplementary Information Relating to Tax Reform Measures. Ottawa: December 1987.

———. *The Budget Process.* A paper on budget secrecy and proposals for broader consultation. Ottawa: April 1982,

———. House of Commons. Bill C-139 (Income Tax Act and Related Acts); first reading, June 30, 1988; passed, August 29, 1988. After passage by Senate, Royal Assent given September 13, 1988.

———. Standing Committee on Finance and Economic Affairs, Minutes of Proceedings and Evidence Respecting White Paper on Tax Reform and Other Related Documents, issues no. 70, 71, 73 to 77, 78 to 125. Ottawa: 1987.

———. *Report on the White Paper on Tax Reform (Stage 1).* Ottawa: 1987.

———. *Report on the White Paper on Tax Reform—Stage II (Sales Tax).* Ottawa: March 24, 1988.

———. *Report of the Royal Commission on the Economic Union and Development Prospects for Canada.* Ottawa: 1985.

———. Senate. Standing Committee on Banking, Trade and Commerce. *Twentieth Report* (Interim) December 1987. Ottawa: 1987.

Canadian Council on Social Development. "Tax Reform?" (November-December 1987) 11 *Perception*, 11-28.

Canadian Institute of Chartered Accountants. *1982 Commodity Tax Symposium.* Toronto: the Institute, 1982.

Canadian Tax Foundation. "Background of Current Federal Tax Reform." *The National Finances, 1986-87*, 1:1-1:10. Toronto: the Foundation, 1987.

———. *1982 Federal Sales Tax Conference. Report of Proceedings*, June 1982. Toronto: the Foundation, 1982.

———. *On Opening Up the Budget Process.* A Report to the Honourable Allan J. MacEachen, Minister of Finance. From a Committee formed under the auspices of the Foundation. Toronto: 1982.

———. *Report of Proceedings of the Thirty-Fifth Tax Conference*, 1983 Conference Report. Toronto: the Foundation, 1984.

———. *Report of Proceedings of the Thirty-Sixth Tax Conference*, 1984 Conference Report. Toronto: the Foundation, 1985.

———. *Report of Proceedings of the Thirty-Seventh Tax Conference*, 1985 Conference Report. Toronto: the Foundation, 1986.

———. *Report of Proceedings of the Thirty-Eighth Tax Conference*, 1986 Conference Report. Toronto: the Foundation, 1987.

———. *Report of Proceedings of the Thirty-Ninth Tax Conference*, 1987 Conference Report. Toronto: the Foundtion, 1988.

———. *The Economic Impacts of Tax Reform.* Monograph of Papers presented at a conference held in Toronto on October 8-9, 1987. Sponsored by the Foundation, the John Deutsch Institute for the Study of Economic Policy, Queen's University and the Department of Economics, University of Western Ontario. Toronto: the Foundation, 1988.

――――. *Tax Policy Options in the 1980's*. (Eleven papers delivered at a conference). Toronto: the Foundation, 1981.

Couzin, Robert. "The Process of Simplification." (May-June 1984) 32 *Canadian Tax Journal*, 487-500.

Cnossen, Sijbren. "VAT and RST: A Comparison." (May-June 1987) 35 *Canadian Tax Journal*, 559-615.

Daly, Michael J., Jung, Jack, and Schweitzer, Thomas. "Towards a Neutral Capital Income System. (November-December 1986) 34 *Canadian Tax Journal*, 1331-76.

Daly, Michael J., Jung, Jack, Mercier, Pierce, and Schweitzer, Thomas. "The Taxation of Income from Capital in Canada: An International Comparison." (January-February 1987) 35 *Canadian Tax Journal*, 88-117.

Daly, Michael J. and Mercier, Pierre. "The Impact of Tax Reform on the Taxation of Income from Investment in the Corporate Sector." (March-April 1988) 36 *Canadian Tax Journal*, 345-68.

Dodge, David A. "A New and Coherent Approach to Tax Avoidance." (January-February 1988) 36 *Canadian Tax Journal*, 1-22.

Due, John F. "The Wholesale Sales Tax in Australia and New Zealand." (March-April 1983) 31 *Canadian Tax Journal*, 207-27.

――――. "The New Zealand Goods and Services (Value-Added) Tax—A Model for Other Countries." (January-February 1988) 36 *Canadian Tax Journal*, 125-44.

Dungan, Peter, and Wilson, Thomas. "Macroeconomic Effects of Tax Reform in Canada." (January-February 1988) 36 *Canadian Tax Journal*, 110-24.

Economic Council of Canada. *Road Map to Tax Reform: The Taxation of Savings and Investment*. A Statement by the Economic Council of Canada. Ottawa: the Council, 1987.

Gillis, Malcolm. "Federal Sales Taxation: A Survey of Six Decades of Experience, Critiques, and Reform Proposals." (January-February 1985) 33 *Canadian Tax Journal*, 68-98.

Grady, Patrick. "The Recent Corporate Income Tax Reform Proposals in Canada and the United States." (January-February 1986) 34 *Canadian Tax Journal*, 111-28.

Goodman, Millie. "Federal White Paper on Tax Reform." (July-August 1987) 35 *Canadian Tax Journal*, 1069-86.

Hartle, D.G. *The Revenue Budget Process of the Government of Canada*. Canadian Tax Paper no. 67. Toronto: Canadian Tax Foundation, 1982.

――――. *The Expenditure Budget Process of the Government of Canada: A Public Choice—Rent-Seeking Perspective*. Canadian Tax Paper no. 81. Toronto: Canadian Tax Foundation, 1988.

Krever, Richard. "Tax Reform in Australia: Base Broadening Down Under." (March-April 1986) 34 *Canadian Tax Journal*, 346-94.

Kuo, Chun-Yan, McGirr, Thomas C., and Poddar, Satya N. "Measuring Non-Neutralities of Sales and Excise Taxes in Canada." (May-June 1988) 36 *Canadian Tax Journal*, 655-70.

Loveland, Norman C. "Scientific Research Tax Credit and Share Purchase Tax Credit Investment—A Legal Perspective." (July-August 1984) 32 *Canadian Tax Journal*, 706-26.

McFetridge, Donald G., and Warda, Jacek P. *Canadian R & D Incentives: Their Adequacy and Impact*. Canadian Tax Paper no. 70. Toronto: Canadian Tax Foundation, 1983.

McQuaig, Linda. *Behind Closed Doors: How the Rich Won Control of Canada's Tax System*. Toronto: Viking, 1987.

National Westminster Bank. "Tax Reform: An International Perspective." (May 1987) *Quarterly Review*, 2-13.

Ort. Deborah L. *Tax Reform 1987*. Tax Memo no. 73. Toronto: Canadian Tax Foundation, 1988.

Pechman, Joseph A. ed. *What Should be Taxed: Income or Expenditure?* Washington: The Brookings Institution, 1981.

Perry, J. Harvey. *Background of Current Fiscal Problems*. Canadian Tax Paper no. 68. Toronto: Canadian Tax Foundation, 1982.

Pocklington, Peter. *Reforming Canada's Tax System: A Blueprint for Change*. Fraser Forum. Vancouver: Fraser Institute, 1987.

Robinson, A.J. *The Retail Sales Tax in Canada*. Canadian Tax Paper no. 77. Toronto: Canadian Tax Foundation, 1986.

Shinder, Bernard. "The Taxation of Small Business: An Historical and Technical Overview." (January-February 1984) 32 *Canadian Tax Journal*, 1-53.

Smith, Roger S. "Base Broadening and Rate Changes: A Look at The Canadian Federal Income Tax." (March-April 1984) 32 *Canadian Tax Journal*, 277-93.

————. "Rates of Personal Income Tax: The Carter Commission Revisited." (September-October 1987) 35 *Canadian Tax Journal*, 1226-1248.

————. *Tax Expenditures: An Examination of the Tax Incentives and Tax Preferences in the Canadian Income Tax System*. Canadian Tax Paper no. 61. Toronto: Canadian Tax Foundation, 1979.

Thirsk, Wayne R. "The Value-Added Tax in Canada: Saviour or Siren Song? (September 1987) 13 *Canadian Public Policy*, 259-83.

Thirsk, Wayne R., and Whalley, John. *Tax Policy Options in the 1980s*. Canadian Tax Paper no. 66. Toronto: Canadian Tax Foundation, 1982.

Appendix 1

Tax Reform 1962-71: The Process

Royal Commission appointed . . . . September, 1962

Royal Commission reported . . . . December, 1966

Report released by Government . . . . January, 1967

Minister of Finance called for comments . . . . April, 1967

Government White Paper issued . . . . November, 1969

White Paper referred to House of Commons
  Standing Committee on Finance, Trade
  and Economic Affairs for hearings . . . . December, 1969

Senate Standing Committee on Banking, Trade
  and Commerce also held hearings during
  1970 and issued report . . . . September, 1970

House Committee issued report . . . . October, 1970

1971 budget gave Government's main
  proposals in Appendix . . . . June, 1971

Amending legislation, Bill C 259, introduced
  for first reading . . . . June 30, 1971

Bill C 259 Second reading debate . . . . September 13 to
  October 12, 1971

Bill C 259 Third reading debate and passage . . . . October 13 to
  December 17, 1971

Senate Committee Hearings and Reports
First Report . . . . November 4, 1971

Second Report . . . . November 30, 1971

Final Report . . . . December 13, 1971

Senate passed Bill 259 . . . . December, 1971

Legislation became effective . . . . January 1, 1972

Appendix 2

Tax Reform 1985-88: The Process

The 1987 steps included budget speeches, a White Paper, ministerial statements, committee hearings and reports, ways and means motions, and draft legislation. The following is a brief record of events.

Budget Speeches: the budget speeches of May 23, 1985, February 26, 1986, February 18, 1987, and February 10, 1988 all contain some reference to tax reform or give word of changes in taxes related to it.

White Paper on Tax Reform, June 18, 1987. The White Paper was a set of four heavy documents, including Tax Reform, 1987; Income Tax Reform; Sales Tax Reform; and Economic and Fiscal Outlook. It was presented to Parliament in an explanatory speech by the Minister of Finance.

House Committee Hearings: hearings on the White Paper by the Commons Finance and Economic Affairs Committee began in Ottawa on August 31, and were held throughout Canada over the following month. The Committee reported its views on November 16, 1987, making several recommendations for changes.

Senate Committee Hearings: hearings on the White Paper were also held by the Senate Committee on Banking, Trade and Commerce. The Committee issued a report on December 1, 1987.

Department of Finance clarifications: during the fall months the department issued several clarifications of the White Paper.

Notice of Ways and Means Motion, December 16, 1987: the Motion (a preliminary to introduction of legislation) was introduced in the Commons to set forth the tax reform proposals the government proposed to adopt in the light of public review of the White Paper. Some minor changes were proposed, mainly as a result of the committee hearings. The motion was presented in a further speech by the Minister, accompanied by more explanatory documents, including Draft Income Tax Regulations and Tax Treatment of Farm Losses.

Draft legislation: on April 13, 1988, draft legislation based on the December 16 Ways and Means Motion was issued by the Department of Finance, followed by explanatory notes on April 21.

Ways and Means Motion: June 13, 1988: a revised Ways and Means Motion was presented by the Minister, the December 1987 motion not having been acted upon.

House Committee Hearings, March 1988. The House Committee on Finance and Economic Affairs reported on March 15 on its study of the

Goods and Services Tax and on March 23 on its study of a multi-stage sales tax. (Fifteenth and Sixteenth Reports); The former favoured a tax along the lines of the New Zealand goods and services tax, with few exemptions; the latter declared that until more was known of the future of the new tax in Canada the committee would hold no further hearings.

Implementation; At mid-1988, although many of the tax changes had come into effect on January 1, 1988, as earlier mentioned, legislation for the bulk of them had not yet been passed by Parliament.

Final legislation: the final act and a massive explanatory statement were given to Parliament on June 30. The legislation was passed by both House and Senate before the November election announcement.

Part 4
Governments in the Large

15
General Fiscal Arrangements

It is time now to widen the scope of our inquiry to include the whole network of government in Canada, attention having been concentrated hitherto mainly on national affairs. This concentration is justified by the scale of postwar issues and the crucial role of the federal government in dealing with them. There are also ten other senior governments and some 4,500 local units, and it is the policies and actions of all together that constitute the government of Canada.

The Federal System

We need not dwell at length on the federal form of the Canadian constitution. Almost all its aspects, and in particular the financial arrangements, have been the subject of a flood of constitutional writings. Furthermore we have almost daily reminders of its problems—witness the Meech Lake Accord.

Briefly, as we have said earlier, the basic characteristic of federalism is an agreed sharing of powers and responsibilities between a central body and separate regional jurisdictions—in Canada's case, the provinces. By no means a recent invention, this form of constitution has been the vehicle in the last two centuries for achieving a common structure of government for peoples divided by conflicting regional, cultural, and economic interests. Examples in this period, distinguished particularly by the large land masses involved, are the United States, Canada, and Australia. No form of government is free of defects, and least of all the federal. Its unique characteristic is the establishment of a delicate balance of governmental power through consultation and compromise; and if the federation is to retain its vitality, compromise must continue throughout its history.

It is recognized that the political leaders who joined in creating the new nation of Canada in 1867 were fully aware of the potential for disagreement in the structure they were creating. The need for unity had arisen from existing deep internal divisions, and these were not likely to disappear of their own accord. Given these troubled origins it is agreed that the Fathers of Confederation wrought extremely well in devising rules for the governance of the new nation. The members of the Rowell-Sirois Commission, following an intensive examination, in their 1940 report paid the following tribute: "In the course of our work we have come to appreciate as never before the achievements of the Fathers of Confederation . . . they devise[d] an instrument of government which has successfully withstood the test of seventy years of rapid and in large part quite unpredictable change . . . By their achievements they laid the foundations of national unity and of the federal system."[15.1] The document which implemented these high purposes was known as the British North America Act, a title singularly barren of appeal as the fundamental and, to some, sacred testament of Canada's creation. Canada was rescued from this ignominy only in 1982, when the BNA statute was replaced by the Constitution Act.

Financial Arrangements

The main interest in the constitution for present purposes is the financial consequence of the allocation of powers and responsibilities between the two principal levels of government. These are listed in sections 91 and 92 of the Constitution Act. Couched in the language of 120 years ago, one may look in vain for mention of two of the main present outlays of government —social security and health programs. The third expensive function, education, is prominently there, a reflection of the concern of the provinces to retain exclusive control over this sensitive area.

Section 91 deals with powers of the national government. In addition to general authority to enact laws for the "Peace, Order and Good Government of Canada," it was given exclusive jurisdiction over the postal services, census and statistics, defence, navigation and shipping, money and banking, criminal law, and several other areas. Taxing powers were heavily weighted in its favour; it was empowered to raise money "by any Mode or System of Taxation."

In section 92 the provinces are given rights to the "Management and Sale of Public Lands belonging to the Province and of the Timber and Wood thereon" (the basis of provincial control over natural resources); the establishment and management of public hospitals, asylums, charities and eleemosynary institutions in the province, municipal government, local works and undertakings, "Property and Civil Rights in the Province" and other matters. Section 93 dealt in detail with provincial rights in the field of education, obviously a delicate area. Under section 94, agriculture and immigration, both levels of government were given authority. For taxation, in contrast to the unlimited powers given the national government, the provinces were restricted to "Direct Taxation within the Province in order to the raising of a Revenue for Provincial Purposes."

Effect of Judicial Decisions

These various powers were gradually clarified by appeals to the higher courts. The fact that until 1949 the final court for Canadian cases was the Privy Council in England, which gave some of the crucial precedent-setting early decisions, undoubtedly had a profound effect on the course of government in Canada. Its decisions leaned heavily toward the provinces, particularly in the interpretation of the so-called residual clauses—those that gave

---

[15.1] Parliamentary Task Force on Federal-Provincial Fiscal Arrangements, *Fiscal Federalism in Canada* (Ottawa: Supply and Services, 1981), 25-26.

broad undefined powers. The full details are complex; briefly, the Privy Council held, in the Local Prohibition case in 1896, that broad powers given the federal government "for the Peace, Order and Good Government of Canada" were secondary to powers over "property and civil rights" given the provinces. The federal power for the "regulation of trade and commerce" was later given such restrictive interpretation as to render it almost meaningless for use in any but emergency conditions.

The most profound implication of the province-leaning judgments was in allocating responsibility for social legislation. Following earlier cases, and in particular the decisions on the Bennett government's social legislation in 1937, the provincial governments have been held to have almost exclusive powers in this area. As a result the provinces have become responsible for enormous and expensive functions, the cost of which far exceeded their revenue resources. Furthermore many of the other provincial functions, such as education and highways, have turned out to be very costly. Such an outcome could hardly have been foreseen by the Fathers of Confederation.

There had been grants from the federal government to the provinces long before 1947, but none had been a major element in the financial budgets of either level. The most ambitious of the programs was the jointly financed means-tested old age pension started in 1927, although there had been earlier experiments. The most serious dilemma arose in introducing the social programs characteristic world-wide of the postwar period. One way of solving this problem was to have the provinces turn over to the federal govjernment their authority to enact specific programs by an amendment to the constitution; this was done for the introduction of unemployment insurance in 1940 and old age security in 1952. But this answer was of limited application. The provinces, and most particularly Quebec, were unwilling to pursue it to possible final transfer of all their social authority to the federal government, and the federal government was equally unwilling to become the sole financial support of all social programs.

The compromise was to share sponsorship and financing, but of course the dilemma remained that provincial financial resources were much more restricted than the federal. To overcome this problem ways have had to be devised for transferring funds in substantial amounts from the national government to the provincial treasuries, and these have taken a variety of forms. Most prominent was a grant toward a program meeting specified federal requirements to be administered by the province; to this recently there has been added the transfer of tax sources for designated objectives. In this process the long-recognized fact that provinces vary greatly in resources has been given vastly increased recognition through the equalization process.

There has been some provincial unrest over the conditional grant, particularly in the role of initiator of social programs it appeared to give the federal government. Quebec has been the strongest opponent, as it claims full autonomy over its social programs. The Meech Lake Accord reflects this discontent, and it gives the provinces the right to receive the equivalent of payments under a specific federal program which does not attract it—as long as it can demonstrate that it is using the funds for an alternative approved purpose.

Taxing Powers

The sharing of overlapping taxing powers has also been a source of conflict. Problems were avoided in the first half century by federal abstention from direct taxation, while the provinces introduced death taxes, corporation taxes and, in some cases, personal income taxes. During World War I however the need for funds forced the national government to impose corporate and personal income taxes, and of course it has levied such taxes ever since. But Canada has coped with these conflicts more successfully than most federations through temporary intergovernmental agreements and similar devices. In general it has followed a "middle of the road" path, avoiding either the rigid constitutional compartmentalization of taxes found in some countries or the open "tax jungle" characteristic of others. Questions in this area are by no means fully settled, however. Academic discussion tends to span a range between consternation with any departure from complete and neat uniformity throughout and the view that differences in pattern are inevitable and are the sign of a healthy vitality in a federal system.[15.2]

The most recent issue calling for some new thinking is the federal government's 1987 tax reform proposal to move its existing manufacturers' sales tax to a new base. Both of its proposals—for a tax at the retail level or a multi-stage tax carried through to the retail level—called for provincial cooperation, as all provinces but one have already occupied the retail sales tax area. The outcome of this issue was still unknown at the time of writing.

More of this later; for the moment the main point is that the management of the nation's finances under the federal form of government is a considerably more complex matter than it would be in a unitary state. It has been said indeed that "federalism is finance," and while this may be a modest exaggeration, the validity of the statement will become clearer as the influence of the federal-provincial fiscal arrangements emerges in the following review of general government finances, revenues and expenditures, over the postwar period.

Summary Overview: The Postwar Period

Revenue: All Governments

Government revenues rose from approximately $4 billion in 1947 to approximately $224 billion in 1987 (national accounts basis). From 1949 to 1959 they ranged in the area of 25-27 percent of GNP, but passed 30 percent in 1965. From that level they climbed steadily to over 39 percent in 1974, a quantum leap in a decade. They declined to slightly below this mark until

---

[15.2]Richard M. Bird, *Federal Finance in Comparative Perspective*, Financing Canadian Federation no. 6 (Toronto: Canadian Tax Foundation, 1986), ch. 7-8.

1981, when they rose to 41.1 percent, to climb from there to 42.0 percent in 1986 and 1987.

Expenditure: All Governments

Expenditures followed the same general pattern, but with a sharper slope, rising from $3.2 billion in 1947 to $249 billion in 1987. In the years immediately following the war they were lower than revenues at 22-24 percent of GNP, but with the Korean defence program they went quickly to 27 percent in 1954 and continued to rise to approximately 30 percent in 1965. The increase in the next decade was less than for revenues, reaching about 38 percent of GNP in 1974. However a jolt came in 1975 in an abrupt rise to almost 41 percent, a level which held to 1981, when there was a further jump to 42.6 percent. This was followed by a quantum leap to 48.0 percent in 1982, and a peak in 1983 and 1985 of 48.2 percent, just short of one-half of GNP; 1986 and 1987 were just below this level.

Deficits: All Governments

In terms of overall surplus or deficit, the results were surpluses from 1947 to 1953, deficits for most years to 1963, surpluses from 1964 to 1974, and deficits ever since. Even the highest deficits in most earlier years were 2-4 percent of GNP, but in the period since 1983 they reached the historic high levels of 6-7 percent, with a slight downward trend in 1986 and 1987. (Table 15.1 gives annual data for the 1947-86 period).

Debt: All Governments

Because governments borrow from one another authoritative data on total government debt is not easily obtained. On the basis of such information as is available an approximation is that net government debt (gross debt less assets) rose from $20.8 billion in 1947 to around $300 billion in 1986. Of the latter figure about 88 percent is federal debt, a ratio that reflected the drastic increase to $264 billion in 1986 from $38 billion a decade before.

(See chapter 17 for more detailed data).

Revenues: The Basic Structure

We will examine the evolution of revenues in more detail in the next chapter. What follows is an introduction.

Personal Income Tax

As shown in tables 15.2 and 15.3, the principal source of revenue for the postwar period was the personal income tax. Its yield rose from $0.7 billion in 1947 to $62.1 billion in 1986; its contribution to revenues rose at the same time from 18 percent of the total to 31 percent in 1986. Table 15.4 gives a measure of the general weight of the personal income tax over the postwar period measured as a percent of personal income. The climb has been a steady one from a low of 4.5 percent in 1949 to 14.5 percent in 1986.

Table 15.1 All Governments: Revenue, Expenditure, and Balance,
National Accounts Basis, 1947-87

Year[a]	Revenue[b]		Expenditure[b]		Surplus or Deficit[b]	
	$ billion	% of GNP	$ billion	% of GNP	$ billion	% of GNP
1947..........	4.0	29.6	3.2	23.7	0.8	5.9
1948..........	4.1	26.4	3.4	21.9	0.7	3.5
1949..........	4.2	25.0	3.8	22.6	0.3	1.8
1950..........	4.6	25.1	4.1	22.1	0.6	3.3
1951..........	6.1	28.2	5.2	24.1	0.8	3.7
1952..........	6.7	27.2	6.6	26.8	0.1	0.4
1953..........	6.9	26.7	6.8	26.4	0.1	0.4
1954..........	6.8	26.3	7.1	27.4	−0.3	−5.0
1955..........	7.5	26.1	7.5	26.3	—	—
1956..........	8.5	26.5	8.2	28.8	0.3	0.3
1957..........	8.9	26.6	8.9	27.7	—	—
1958..........	8.9	25.6	9.9	28.4	−1.1	−3.2
1959..........	10.0	27.2	10.6	28.8	−0.6	−1.6
1960..........	10.7	27.9	11.4	29.7	−0.7	−1.8
1961..........	11.4	28.8	12.2	30.8	−0.8	−2.0
1962..........	12.5	29.1	13.2	33.3	−0.7	−1.6
1963..........	13.3	28.9	13.9	32.4	−0.6	−1.3
1964..........	15.0	29.8	14.9	29.6	0.1	0.2
1965..........	16.8	30.3	16.6	29.9	0.2	0.4
1966..........	19.5	31.6	19.1	30.9	0.4	0.7
1967..........	22.0	33.1	21.8	32.9	0.1	0.2
1968..........	25.0	34.4	24.5	33.7	0.5	0.7
1969..........	29.1	36.5	27.2	34.1	1.9	2.3
1970..........	32.0	37.3	31.1	36.4	0.8	0.9
1971..........	35.3	37.4	35.2	37.3	0.1	0.1
1972..........	39.8	37.8	39.7	37.8	0.1	0.1
1973..........	46.3	37.5	45.0	36.5	1.3	1.1
1974..........	58.8	39.7	56.0	37.9	2.8	1.9
1975..........	64.2	38.0	68.5	40.5	−4.3	−2.5
1976..........	73.4	37.8	77.0	39.6	−3.5	−1.8
1977..........	81.4	38.2	86.9	40.7	−5.5	−2.6
1978..........	89.3	37.9	96.9	38.6	−7.6	−3.2
1979..........	101.5	37.7	107.0	39.8	−5.5	−2.1
1980..........	116.3	38.5	124.9	41.4	−8.6	−2.9
1981..........	141.6	41.1	146.9	42.6	−5.2	−1.5
1982..........	151.3	41.8	173.5	48.0	−22.2	−6.1
1983..........	162.1	41.1	190.2	48.2	−28.0	−7.1
1984..........	177.9	41.3	206.7	48.0	−28.8	−6.7
1985..........	190.6	41.0	224.1	48.2	−33.5	−7.2
1986..........	205.9	42.0	233.3	47.6	−27.4	−5.6
1987..........	223.9	42.0	249.0	46.7	−25.1	−4.7

Note: All figures for 1981-86 are 1981 revised national accounts basis.

[a]Calendar year. [b]Excludes intergovernmental transfers.

Sources: Department of Finance, *Economic Review*, April 1985; and *Quarterly Economic Review*, June 1988.

However, contrary to popular belief that there has been a sharp recent rise, the overall weight has been relatively unchanged for the last 15 years. The new feature, however, is the imposition of additional direct personal charges, mainly for social and health insurance purposes. These have tripled from about 2 percent of personal income in the early fifties to over 5 percent today. With these charges added the combined ratio has been 18-18.5 percent in the eighties. Again, however, even this combined ratio has changed very little in the last fifteen years. Table 15.5, relating solely to the federal income tax, shows a relatively stable level since 1970.

Corporation Taxes

By contrast with the growing dependence on personal income tax, revenue from corporation taxes, long a staple element for all governments, dropped from the same share as the personal income tax in 1947 (18.4 percent) to a low of 6.2 in 1982, rising to 7.6 percent in 1986.

An overall measure of the weight of corporation taxes is given in a national accounts compilation of direct taxes on corporations as a percent of profits before tax. (See table 15.6). Most years are in the 35-40 percent range, or about what one would expect, given the reduced rate for small corporations and other concessions. The infrequent years above this norm are explained by exceptional rate increases, as in 1951 and 1952 (Korean War) or else sharp declines in profits, as in 1982 (recession). The gradual, and by no means even, decline from 40 percent in 1970 to 30 percent in 1979 marks not only decreasing rates but a narrowing tax base with broadening exemptions. A further consideration is that in common with experience in many other countries corporate profits have remained relatively unchanged in relation to GNP. By decades they were 10.9 percent in the fifties, 10.6 percent in the sixties, and 11.3 percent in the seventies, a very narrow range of change.

Consumption Taxes

Despite increases in all provincial sales tax rates over the period and a rise in revenue from $0.5 billion just after the war to nearly $24 billion in 1986, consumption taxes have contributed a lower share of total revenue in the last decade than in the previous three. Now accounting for 11-12 percent, they fall considerably short of the share in the mid-sixties, when they reached nearly 16 percent. A long-standing federal source, the customs tariff, declined from nearly 8 percent in 1947 to only 2 percent in 1986.

Table 15.7 shows the weight of consumption taxes (including other taxes along with general sales taxes) expressed as a percent of consumer expenditure. Most years have been in the 12-15 percent range. The highest level prevailed from the mid-sixties to the mid-seventies. There was a fairly steady decline thereafter from a peak of 15.3 percent in 1973 to a low of 11.3 percent in 1982, a drop of 23 percent, certainly confirmation that the impact of consumption taxes on the consumer has been greatly reduced in recent years.

Table 15.2　All Governments: Revenue by Major Source, Consolidated Finance Basis, 1947-86

Year[a]	Income tax Per-sonal	Income tax Corpo-ration	General sales tax	Customs duties	Prop-erty taxes	Health and social insurance levies	Other taxes	Total taxes	Natural resource levies	Sale of goods and services[b]	Return on invest-ment[c]	Other	Total
							billions of dollars						
1947	0.7	0.7	0.4	0.3	0.3	—	0.7	3.1	—	—	—	0.7	3.8
1948	0.8	0.6	0.4	0.2	0.3	—	0.9	3.2	0.1	—	—	0.5	3.8
1949	0.6	0.7	0.5	0.2	0.4	—	0.8	3.2	0.1	—	—	0.5	3.8
1950	0.7	1.0	0.6	0.3	0.4	—	0.8	3.8	0.1	—	—	0.5	4.4
1951	1.0	1.3	0.7	0.3	0.5	—	1.0	4.8	—	—	—	0.7	5.5
1952	1.2	1.3	0.8	0.4	0.6	—	1.0	5.3	—	—	—	0.9	6.2
1953	1.3	1.3	0.9	0.4	0.7	—	0.9	5.5	0.2	—	—	0.8	6.5
1954	1.3	1.1	0.9	0.4	0.7	—	1.0	5.4	0.2	—	—	0.7	6.3
1955	1.3	1.1	1.0	0.5	0.8	—	1.1	5.8	0.3	—	—	0.8	6.9
1956	1.6	1.4	1.1	0.5	0.9	—	1.2	6.7	0.3	—	—	0.9	7.9
1957	1.7	1.5	1.1	0.5	1.0	—	1.2	7.0	0.3	—	—	0.9	8.2
1958	1.5	1.3	1.1	0.5	1.1	—	1.3	6.8	0.3	—	—	1.0	8.1
1959	1.8	1.4	1.3	0.5	1.2	—	1.5	7.7	0.3	—	—	1.1	9.1
1960	2.0	1.6	1.3	0.5	1.3	—	1.6	8.3	0.3	—	—	1.1	9.7
1961	2.1	1.6	1.5	0.5	1.4	—	1.7	8.8	0.3	—	—	1.2	10.3
1962	2.4	1.7	1.7	0.6	1.6	—	1.7	9.7	0.3	—	—	1.2	11.2
1963	2.6	1.7	1.8	0.6	1.7	—	1.9	10.3	0.4	—	—	1.4	12.1
1964	3.0	2.1	2.3	0.6	1.8	—	2.1	11.9	0.4	—	—	1.6	13.9
1965	3.5	2.3	2.7	0.7	1.8	0.7	2.4	14.1	0.5	—	0.9	1.5	17.0
1966	4.2	2.3	3.1	0.8	2.3	1.4	2.5	16.4	0.5	—	1.1	1.6	19.6
1967	5.1	2.4	3.4	0.7	2.7	1.5	2.6	18.4	0.5	—	1.2	1.9	22.1
1968	6.1	2.9	3.5	0.8	2.5	1.7	3.3	20.8	0.6	—	1.5	2.3	25.2
1969	7.7	3.7	4.0	0.8	3.0	1.8	3.8	24.8	0.6	—	1.8	2.5	29.8

Year												
1970	9.1	3.2	4.1	0.8	3.5	2.7	3.2	26.6	0.6	1.2	2.3	1.5	32.2
1971	10.2	3.2	4.7	1.0	3.7	2.9	3.3	29.0	0.6	1.3	2.7	1.8	35.4
1972	12.0	3.9	5.4	1.2	4.1	3.2	3.4	33.2	0.8	1.6	3.0	2.0	40.6
1973	13.6	4.9	6.6	1.4	4.3	3.7	4.1	38.6	1.3	2.0	3.5	2.3	47.7
1974	17.3	6.7	7.5	1.8	4.8	4.8	5.8	48.7	2.4	2.1	4.4	2.5	60.1
1975	19.1	7.8	7.2	1.9	5.7	5.7	5.8	53.2	2.6	2.3	5.4	2.8	66.3
1976	22.3	7.6	8.5	2.1	6.6	7.2	6.4	60.6	3.0	3.5	6.2	2.7	76.1
1977	22.9	7.9	9.4	2.3	7.4	7.8	6.6	64.3	4.4	3.9	7.1	3.1	82.8
1978	25.0	8.8	9.3	2.7	8.1	8.8	6.8	69.5	5.5	5.0	8.5	3.9	92.4
1979	29.4	10.0	10.5	3.0	8.5	9.3	8.2	78.9	6.8	5.8	10.0	4.6	106.1
1980	34.5	11.7	11.6	3.2	9.8	10.5	10.0	91.4	7.4	6.5	12.6	5.1	122.9
1981	41.5	11.8	13.2	3.4	11.1	13.9	17.1	112.1	6.8	7.4	14.6	6.4	147.2
1982	46.1	9.5	13.6	2.8	12.2	14.7	18.1	117.1	6.9	6.4	15.7	6.5	152.5
1983	48.1	10.3	15.7	3.4	14.0	17.9	16.5	125.9	7.8	7.1	16.6	6.7	164.2
1984	50.6	13.1	17.9	3.8	15.0	18.8	18.0	137.3	8.4	7.2	17.4	7.3	177.5
1985	57.7	13.5	21.1	4.0	15.7	20.5	16.8	149.2	7.7	7.6	19.2	7.3	191.1
1986	62.1	15.2	23.8	4.2	16.9	21.9	15.5	159.6	5.7	7.7	20.5	7.8	201.3

Note: Years prior to 1965 not exactly comparable with later years.

aFiscal years ended nearest December 31 of the year named. bIncluded in Other Revenue to 1970. cIncluded in Other Revenue to 1965.

Source: Statistics Canada, *Historical Statistics of Canada* and CANSIM.

Table 15.3 All Governments: Revenue by Major Source, as a Percentage of the Total, Consolidated Finance Basis, 1947-86

Year[a]	Income tax		General sales tax	Customs duties	Property taxes	Health and social insurance levies	Other taxes	Total taxes	Natural resource levies	Sale of goods and services[b]	Return on investment[c]	Other	Total
	Personal	Corporation											
							percent						
1947	18.4	18.4	10.5	7.9	7.9	—	18.4	81.5	—	—	—	18.5	100.0
1950	15.9	22.7	13.6	6.9	9.1	—	18.1	86.3	2.2	—	—	11.5	100.0
1953	20.0	20.0	13.9	6.2	10.8	—	13.9	84.7	3.1	—	—	12.2	100.0
1955	18.9	15.9	14.5	7.2	11.6	—	16.0	84.1	4.3	—	—	11.6	100.0
1960	20.6	16.5	13.4	5.1	13.4	—	16.5	85.5	3.1	—	—	11.4	100.0
1965	20.6	13.5	15.9	4.1	10.6	4.1	14.1	82.9	2.9	3.7	5.3	8.9	100.0
1970	28.3	10.0	12.8	2.5	10.9	8.4	9.8	82.7	1.9	3.5	7.2	4.5	100.0
1975	28.8	11.8	10.9	2.9	8.6	8.6	8.7	80.3	3.9	4.7	8.2	4.1	100.0
1977	27.7	9.6	8.9	2.8	8.9	9.4	8.0	77.8	5.3	5.5	8.6	3.6	100.0
1979	27.7	9.9	8.0	2.8	8.0	8.8	7.8	74.4	6.4	5.3	9.4	4.3	100.0
1980	28.1	9.5	9.5	2.6	8.0	8.5	8.2	74.4	6.0	5.3	10.3	4.0	100.0
1981	28.2	8.0	9.0	2.3	7.5	9.4	11.7	76.1	4.6	5.0	9.9	4.4	100.0
1982	30.2	6.2	8.9	1.8	8.0	9.6	12.0	76.7	4.5	4.2	10.3	4.3	100.0
1983	29.2	6.3	8.5	2.1	8.5	10.9	10.1	76.7	4.8	4.4	10.1	4.0	100.0
1984	28.5	7.4	8.4	2.1	8.4	10.6	10.1	77.2	4.7	4.1	9.0	4.2	100.0
1985	30.2	7.1	11.0	2.1	8.2	10.7	8.7	78.0	4.0	4.0	10.0	4.0	100.0
1986	30.8	7.6	11.8	2.1	8.4	10.9	7.7	79.3	2.8	3.8	10.2	3.9	100.0

Based on table 15.2.

Table 15.4 All Governments: Revenue from Personal Direct Taxes and
Charges as a Percentage of Personal Income, National Accounts Basis, 1947-86

Yeara	(1) Personal income	(2) Personal income taxes	(2) as a % of (1)	(3) Other personal direct changes	(3) as a % of (1)	Combined taxes and charges as a % of personal income
	$ billion		%	$ billion	%	%
1947	10.9	0.7	8.1	0.3	2.7	10.8
1948	12.6	0.8	6.3	0.2	1.6	7.9
1949	13.4	0.6	4.5	0.3	2.2	6.7
1950	14.3	0.7	4.9	0.3	2.1	7.0
1951	16.8	1.0	5.9	0.3	1.8	7.7
1952	18.6	1.2	6.4	0.4	2.1	8.5
1953	19.6	1.3	6.6	0.4	2.1	8.6
1954	19.7	1.3	6.6	0.5	2.5	9.1
1955	21.3	1.3	6.1	0.6	2.8	8.9
1956	23.5	1.6	6.8	0.6	2.6	9.5
1957	25.2	1.7	6.8	0.7	2.8	9.8
1958	26.7	1.5	5.6	0.8	3.1	8.8
1959	28.1	1.8	6.4	0.9	3.2	9.5
1960	29.6	2.0	6.8	1.0	3.4	10.2
1961	30.1	2.1	7.0	1.1	3.7	10.6
1962	32.8	2.4	7.3	1.0	3.0	10.5
1963	34.8	2.6	7.5	1.1	3.2	10.5
1964	37.3	3.0	8.0	1.2	3.2	11.4
1965	41.1	3.4	8.3	1.4	3.4	11.7
1966	46.1	4.2	9.1	2.0	4.3	13.4
1967	50.6	5.1	10.1	2.4	4.7	14.7
1968	55.7	6.1	11.0	2.8	5.0	15.9
1969	61.8	7.7	12.5	3.2	5.2	17.6
1970	66.6	9.1	13.7	3.5	5.3	18.9
1971	74.1	10.2	13.8	3.9	5.3	19.1
1972	83.8	12.0	14.3	3.7	4.4	18.7
1973	97.8	13.6	13.9	4.5	4.6	18.5
1974	116.9	17.3	14.8	5.0	4.3	19.1
1975	136.2	19.1	14.0	6.1	4.5	18.5
1976	155.1	22.3	14.4	7.5	4.8	19.2
1977	171.5	22.9	13.3	10.3	6.0	19.4
1978	191.5	25.0	13.0	10.4	5.4	18.5
1979	215.4	29.0	13.4	10.4	4.8	18.3
1980	244.7	34.5	14.1	10.4	4.2	18.4
1981	293.2	39.1	13.3	13.6	4.6	17.9
1982	324.8	43.9	13.5	14.9	4.6	18.1
1983	342.8	46.4	13.5	17.1	5.0	18.5
1984	371.9	49.6	13.3	18.8	5.1	18.4
1985	402.0	54.2	13.5	20.7	5.1	18.6
1986	429.8	62.2	14.5	22.8	5.3	19.8

Note: Figures for 1981-86 on 1981 revised national accounts basis.

aCalendar year.

Source: Canada, Department of Finance, *Economic Review*, April 1985; Statistics Canada, *National Income and Expenditure Accounts*, Fourth Quarter, 1986; CANSIM; *Historical Statistics of Canada*.

**Table 15.5   Federal Government; Revenue from Personal Direct Taxes
Related to Personal Income, National Accounts Basis, 1947-86**

Year[a]	Personal income	Personal direct taxes	Ratio of taxes to income
	$ billion	*$ billion*	*%*
1947..........................	10.9	0.8	7.3
1950..........................	14.3	0.8	5.6
1955..........................	21.3	1.6	7.5
1960..........................	29.6	2.4	8.1
1965..........................	41.1	3.3	8.0
1970..........................	66.6	7.4	11.1
1975..........................	136.2	15.2	11.1
1980..........................	244.7	23.5	9.6
1981..........................	293.2	27.2	10.0
1982..........................	324.8	31.9	9.8
1983..........................	342.8	35.5	10.9
1984..........................	371.9	37.5	10.1
1985..........................	402.0	42.4	10.5
1986..........................	429.8	49.0	11.4

[a] Calendar year.

Sources: Canada, Department of Finance, Economic Review, April 1985; Statistics Canada, National Income and Expenditure Accounts, Fourth Quarter, 1986.

Table 15.6 All Governments: Revenue from Corporation Taxes as a Percentage of Corporate Profits, National Accounts Basis, 1947-86

Year[a]	Corporation profits before tax	Direct corporation taxes	Taxes as a % of corporation profits
	billions of dollars		*percent*
1947	1.9	0.7	36.8
1948	2.0	0.7	35.0
1949	2.0	0.7	35.0
1950	2.6	1.0	38.5
1951	3.1	1.4	45.2
1952	3.1	1.4	45.1
1953	3.0	1.2	40.0
1954	2.8	1.1	39.3
1955	3.5	1.3	37.1
1956	3.9	1.4	35.9
1957	3.6	1.4	38.9
1958	3.7	1.4	37.8
1959	4.0	1.6	40.0
1960	3.9	1.6	41.0
1961	4.1	1.6	39.0
1962	4.5	1.8	40.0
1963	4.9	1.9	38.8
1964	5.8	2.1	36.2
1965	6.3	2.2	34.9
1966	6.7	2.4	35.8
1967	6.8	2.4	35.2
1968	7.7	2.9	37.7
1969	8.3	3.2	38.6
1970	7.7	3.1	40.3
1971	8.7	3.3	37.9
1972	10.8	3.9	36.1
1973	15.4	5.1	33.1
1974	20.1	7.1	35.3
1975	19.7	7.5	38.0
1976	20.0	7.1	35.5
1977	20.9	7.3	34.9
1978	25.7	8.3	32.2
1979	34.0	10.2	30.0
1980	37.7	12.2	32.4
1981	37.7	12.6	33.4
1982	26.5	11.5	43.4
1983	36.7	12.1	33.0
1984	45.4	14.8	32.6
1985	47.5	15.3	32.2
1986	45.2	13.2	29.2

Note: Figures for 1981-86 on 1981 revised national accounts basis.

[a] Calendar year.

Sources: Department of Finance, *Economic Review*, April 1985; Statistics Canada, *National Income and Expenditure Accounts*, Fourth Quarter, 1986.

Table 15.7   All Governments: Consumption Taxes as a Percentage of Consumer Expenditure, National Accounts Basis, 1947-86

Year[a]	Consumer expenditure	Consumption taxes	Consumption taxes as a % of consumer expenditure
	billions of dollars		*percent*
1947	9.4	1.3	13.8
1948	10.4	1.3	12.5
1949	11.4	1.3	11.4
1950	12.5	1.5	12.0
1951	13.9	1.8	12.9
1952	15.2	2.0	13.2
1953	16.2	2.1	13.0
1954	16.9	2.0	11.8
1955	18.4	2.3	12.5
1956	20.1	2.6	12.9
1957	21.5	2.6	12.1
1958	22.8	2.6	12.1
1959	24.4	2.9	11.9
1960	25.5	2.9	11.4
1961	25.9	3.2	12.4
1962	27.5	3.6	13.1
1963	29.2	3.8	13.0
1964	31.4	4.3	13.7
1965	33.9	5.0	14.7
1966	36.9	5.5	14.9
1967	40.0	6.0	15.0
1968	43.7	6.3	14.4
1969	47.5	7.0	14.7
1970	50.3	7.3	14.5
1971	55.6	8.2	14.7
1972	62.2	9.3	15.0
1973	71.3	10.9	15.3
1974	83.4	12.4	15.0
1975	97.0	12.8	13.2
1976	111.7	14.9	13.3
1977	123.6	16.2	13.1
1978	136.5	16.6	12.2
1979	152.1	18.3	12.0
1980	170.2	20.2	11.9
1981	196.2	23.1	11.8
1982	212.5	23.7	11.2
1983	232.5	27.1	11.7
1984	251.4	30.1	12.0
1985	274.7	34.7	12.6
1986	297.3	38.5	12.9

Note: Figures for 1981-86 on 1981 revised national accounts basis.

[a] Calendar year.

Sources: Department of Finance, *Economic Review*, April 1985 and Statistics Canada, - *National Income and Expenditure Accounts*, Fourth Quarter, 1986; CANSIM.

Property Taxes

Property tax revenues show great vitality for a source that is commonly assumed to be worked out. Although lower than in some earlier years, the property tax has maintained a steady share of total revenues in the 8-9 percent range. As a share of municipal revenue it contributes just under half, most of the balance coming in grants from provincial governments.

Social Insurance Taxes

An element of growing importance on the tax scene, as mentioned earlier, are the various levies for health and social insurance—unemployment insurance, health insurance and hospitalization, workers' compensation, Canada and Quebec Pension Plans, etc. Starting from a modest 4 percent in 1965 these accounted for nearly 11 percent in 1986. (Obviously, this new revenue has reduced the relative importance of older sources in recent years).

Other Tax Revenues

A miscellany of other levies—death taxes, energy taxes, etc.—make up the remainder. The swelling share of the "other" category from 1981 to 1984 largely reflects the heavy energy taxes imposed during this period.

Non-tax Revenues

In the non-tax category, one of the oddities of Canadian governmental finances, particularly at the provincial level, is the relatively minor share originating from natural resources. In 1986 only 2.8 percent came from this source, and the highest postwar level was only 6.4 percent in 1979. This of course represents only direct charges; the mining, forestry, petroleum and other corporations are also subject to the general corporation taxes, so that some natural resource revenue, although probably not a great amount, is included under that heading.

Return on investments has become a major non-tax source in recent years, accounting for over 10 percent in 1986. Higher return on invested funds and increased governmental investment in separate enterprises accounts for this rise. One of the main items is profits from liquor boards which, along with liquor regulation, account for 1½ to 2 percent of total government revenues. Substantial other revenues from liquor are collected through federal taxes.

The Overall Sharing

Table 15.8 gives a perspective on the sharing of the main tax sources between the federal and provincial-municipal levels of government in the postwar period. In all categories the pattern is similar: a steady withdrawal by the national government from the dominant position it reached during World War II as the provinces and municipalities assumed greater and more costly responsibilities.

Transfers

Transfers between governments are now a major source of provincial and municipal revenues. These may be treated as revenues of some governments or expenditures of others, but not as both, as this would involve double counting. We look at these in detail later.

Table 15.8   Federal and Provincial-Municipal Share of Revenue from Main Tax Sources, Consolidated Accounts Basis, Selected Years, 1952-86

Year[a]	Personal income tax		Corporation income tax		Consumption taxes	
	Federal	Prov./Mun.	Federal	Prov./Mun.	Federal	Prov./Mun.
			percent			
1952...........	98	2	93	7	85	15
1958...........	94	6	85	15	76	24
1961...........	95	5	81	19	71	29
1962...........	83	17	76	24	69	31
1966...........	74	26	74	26	65	35
1967...........	67	33	75	25	63	37
1976...........	66	34	71	29	54	46
1977...........	59	41	73	27	53	47
1982...........	59	41	76	24	48	52
1984...........	61	39	72	28	48	52
1986...........	62	38	70	30	50	50

[a] Fiscal year ended nearest December 31 of year named.

Source: Based on Statistics Canada, *Historical Review, Financial Statistics of Governments in Canada*, 1952-62; *Consolidated Finances*, and CANSIM.

16
Revenues: The Postwar Evolution

The Personal Income Tax

The personal income tax became the main weapon in the government arsenal in meeting the crucial need for revenues in World War II, and it has remained so ever since. Formerly regarded as affecting only a few well-to-do citizens, it now reaches almost everyone receiving an income. Although exemptions have been increased and rates reduced through indexation, a large proportion of the work-force comes under it, with tax deducted from their pay before they receive it. To a degree seldom encountered with any other tax the personal income tax is now the daily concern of millions of Canadians.

The universality of its coverage is borne out by some elementary data. In 1938, of a total population of 11 million, only 250,000, or 2.3 percent, filed returns. By 1955 15 times that number, or 3.6 million, (24 percent of the population) were taxable. By 1985 the number had risen to 11.2 million, or 45 percent of the population. In addition another 4.6 million non-taxable persons filed returns in 1985 to claim refunds, child tax credits, guaranteed annual income, and provincial tax relief and assistance programs.

The wartime experience also had other effects; from it emerged the design that has profoundly influenced the course of federal-provincial tax-sharing in the last four decades. To follow the development of the personal income tax in this period an understanding of the intergovernmental tax arrangements is essential.

The Tax Rental Agreements; 1947-61

Under the Wartime Tax Agreements in order to give the federal government free rein for its revenue measures the provincial governments withdrew all personal and corporate taxes in return for compensation. The federal government proposed that this arrangement, with the addition of death taxes, be continued in peacetime, but when some provinces rejected this proposal a revision was necessary to allow provinces to accept or reject as they wished. Under modified proposals seven provinces accepted the offer, and this rose to eight after Newfoundland joined Canada in 1949. In return for compensation, (to be explained more fully later) the eight provinces "rented" their personal and corporation income taxes and death taxes; in effect they undertook to refrain from levying such taxes for five years— the period of the first agreements. Neither Ontario nor Quebec entered the arrangement in 1947, and in order to accommodate their position the federal government allowed a credit against its taxes for the personal and corporate income taxes they imposed. The credit for personal income tax was at first 5 percent of the federal tax, increased to 10 percent in 1954 and to 13 percent in 1958. Ontario entered into an agreement in 1952 for its personal income tax, which has since been administered by the federal administration. Quebec levied its own corporation tax from 1947 and introduced a personal income tax in 1954; although separate from the federal tax both were fairly close to the federal base.

Tax Collection Agreements; 1962-76

The tax rental approach lasted to 1961, and was abandoned in the following year. In place of a system under which provinces were compensated for not imposing taxes the federal government reversed its position and proposed to reduce its taxes and leave it to the provinces to obtain their revenues by enacting their own legislation. If this legislation were uniform with the federal act the federal government would collect the tax for the province. In effect the provinces were forced to assume responsibility for imposing their own taxes in two main areas, but with federal collection.

This was the beginning of a trend toward increased provincial fiscal responsibility, which is still in process. To accommodate the new provincial taxes the existing federal tax abatement of 13 percent was raised in 1962 to 16 percent, and the federal government undertook that an additional 1 percent would be added in each year to reach 20 percent in 1966. In fact for 1965 and 1966 a further 2 percent was given, so that the share reached 21 percent for 1965 and 24 percent for 1966. The former "agreeing" provinces, including Ontario after 1951, levied personal income taxes at these rates under statutes identical with the federal act and had their taxes collected for them by the federal government. (They also received equalization amounts which will be explained later). Quebec continued to levy and collect its own taxes.

Opting Out

A new feature, which was to play a major role in later developments, was the substitution of additional tax room for cash payments under federal programs. The option was first introduced in 1960 when the yield of 1 percentage point of the corporation income tax was given to Quebec in lieu of cash university grants. Under increased pressure for fiscal autonomy from Quebec in 1964 further tax room was given in the form of an additional 3 percentage point abatement of personal income tax in lieu of federal grants for 16- and 17-year-olds (an offer made to all provinces but accepted only by Quebec). In the following year, under the Established Programs Financing Act, an offer was extended to all governments for a range of programs. The credits were for personal income tax, as follows: 14 percentage points in exchange for cash payments for hospital insurance, 4 percent for payments under the Canada Assistance Act, and 1 percent each for vocational training and health grants. Quebec opted for all these alternatives, so that in 1965 the Quebec abatement was 44 percent compared to 21 percent for the other provinces (which of course were continuing to receive direct grants for the same programs). With the additional 3 points promised by the federal government and increases in 1965, the standard abatement became 32 percent; and for an opting out province (Quebec), a doubling in 1966 of the two 1 point abatements to 2 points apiece raised the Quebec abatement to 49 percent. Under arrangements renewed in 1967 the federal standard personal income tax abatement was raised 4 points to 28 percent; with this addition the Quebec abatement became 52 percent (a one-point vocational training program had expired in 1967). A further step was taken in the 1971 renewal, in the transfer of 4 points to all governments for post-secondary education, raising the standard abatement to 32 percent, with a special additional abatement then totalling 24 percent for Quebec, or 56 percent in all.

It should be mentioned that these are the totals of all tax room concessions for the provinces under the postwar intergovernmental arrangements. Later much lower figures relate only to abatements and reductions under Established Programs Financing, as explained.

Tax Transfers: 1976-87

In the 1976 renewal further steps were taken through the tax abatement device. An additional 9.143 points of personal income tax were abated (for Established Programs Financing) to bring the total to nearly 40 percent. The federal government also made tax reductions at this time to provide further tax room for the provinces. In the 1982-86 arrangements more emphasis was given to cash payments, and no further tax changes were made.

Significance for the Personal Income Tax

The cumulative effect of the tax credits and tax abatements has been to increase the provincial share of personal income tax revenue very substantially in the postwar years. During the period since 1962, when provincial taxes first began to be levied separately, the provincial share rose from about 17 percent of the total in 1962 to 38-40 percent in recent years. For 1987 the provincial rates for individual provinces (as a percentage of the federal tax) were as follows: Newfoundland, 60.0 percent; Prince Edward Island, 50.0 percent; New Brunswick, 56.5 percent; Nova Scotia, 58.0 percent; Ontario, 50.0 percent; Manitoba, 54.0 percent; Saskatchewan, 50.0 percent; Alberta, 56.5 percent; British Columbia, 51.5 percent. For rates in earlier years, see Table 16.4.

Tax Credits

As the basic statute was out of bounds for changes, the provinces had developed a variety of credits against the final tax for social and economic purposes, with the agreement of the federal tax authorities. This technique has been used mainly to exempt low income taxpayers, but there have been credits for older citizens, political contributions, property tax and sales tax, dependent children, renters, investment in venture capital corporations, and so on. Many of these are "vanishing" credits, which expire with higher incomes. On the other hand, the reverse approach of surtaxes has been used to raise additional revenues. Although purists regard these variations as a blemish on the "harmonization" of the national tax structure, they do allow a necessary degree of flexibility for provincial aspirations, and in fact have been much less questionable than similar devices under the corporation income tax.

Appraisal

While there is occasional dissatisfaction among the provinces with the lock-in effect of the required adherence to the federal statute the joint use of the personal income tax has survived forty turbulent years of federal-provincial relations, a remarkable record. The arrangement lived through a major tax reform, that of 1967-71, which brought drastic changes in the tax base, including the introduction of a capital gains tax, by no means popular in all provinces. Equally upsetting to the provinces was the introduction of full indexation of rates and allowances in the basic federal tax in 1973, at considerable cost in provincial revenues. And in the last half of the 1980s another tax reform was undertaken, which appears likely to survive.

Although a far remove from the sole use of the personal income tax the federal government thought indispensable for postwar fiscal policy, the outcome has not been as debilitating as would have been expected in 1945. Certainly there is nothing in the experience of other countries that would guide Canada to a more acceptable result, as patterns vary widely. In the United States, for example, preliminary figures for 1986 indicate that the federal share of the personal income tax was about 82 percent, as compared with less than 60 percent in Canada. Our closest neighbours, therefore, have their unique approach—as does Canada. The keynote of the Canadian solution has been flexibility, which has allowed for constant adaptation to changing conditions.

Quebec

Quebec of course has continued since 1954 to levy its own personal income tax. Under it taxpayers file a separate return to the Quebec government at rates and exemptions different from those in all other provinces. In addition, in filing their return to the federal government they were in 1987 entitled to a tax abatement of 16.5 percent, as provided under the Established Programs Financing system previously explained. The general features of the Quebec tax have been similar to the federal tax, but substantial changes were made in 1986 in a tax reform process which developed from a White Paper on the *Personal Tax and Transfer Systems* issued in 1985. Many of the changes are being phased in over the 1986-88 period. The principal are a reduction in marginal rates; revision of exemptions, with some extensions but greater emphasis on dollar for dollar reduction for income received, defined in future to include most forms of welfare or social payments; an increase in the employment expenses deduction; a reduction to $500 in the $1,000 interest and dividend deduction, except for retired persons, but with a reduction in their case for employment or business income; substantial revision of the treatment of family allowance payments; introduction of a new consumer tax credit, and revision of the existing property tax credit. Other features that are retained include income deductions for purchase of shares of Quebec companies under terms similar to the federal RPP/RRSP plans, a dividend tax credit, tax credits for political contributions, research and development and venture capital outlays, and special credits for taxi firm operators and woodlot owners.

Tables 16.1 to 16.5 give further details of personal income taxes.

Indexation of Federal Personal Income Tax

From 1974 onward an inflation adjustment was made in the exemptions and schedule brackets of the federal personal income tax. From 1974 through 1982 this adjustment was based on the average inflation in the 12 months ending in October of the previous year. This was modified in 1983 and 1984 to 6 percent and 5 percent respectively. 1985 reverted to the original basis, but for 1986 and later years the adjustment was only for the extent to which inflation exceeded 3 percent.

The indexing factors from 1974 onward were as follows:

percent

1974	6.6	1981	9.8
1975	10.1	1982	12.2
1976	11.3	1983	6.0
1977	8.6	1984	5.0
1978	7.2	1985	4.0
1979	9.0	1986	0.8
1980	8.9	1987	1.1

Federal Dividend Tax Credit History

1949 introduced as 10 percent of cash dividend received (no gross-up)

1953—increased to 20 percent of cash dividend received (no gross-up)

1972—calculated as 20 percent of dividend grossed up by 33⅓ percent

1978—calculated as 25 percent of dividend grossed up by 50 percent

1981—calculated as 22⅔ percent of dividend grossed up by 50 percent

1987—calculated as 16⅔ percent of dividend grossed up by 33½ percent

1988—calculated as 16⅔ percent of dividend grossed up by 25 percent.

Other Allowances

1957—RRSP and $100 standard deduction introduced.

1966—old age deduction extended to age 65-69 not receiving OAS.

1972—students' education deduction of $50 per month introduced.

—employment expense deduction at 3 percent, maximum $150.

—charitable donations deduction increased from 10 percent to 20 percent.

—child care allowance introduced; $500 per child, maximum $2,000 per family.

—unused spouse deductions allowed to be transferred to other spouse.

1974—most allowances indexed for inflation in previous year.

1976—child care expense allowance doubled to $1,000, maximum $4,000.

1982—employment expense deduction increased from 3 percent to 20 percent; maximum remains at $500.

1983—child care allowance doubled to $2,000, maximum $8,000.

1984—optional standard deduction repealed.

1988—exemptions changed to tax credits.

Corporation Taxes

The intergovernmental agreements also influenced the course of taxation for corporations. The general terms were the same—rental to the federal government until 1961 and thereafter federal collection of provincially enacted taxes; but where only Quebec remained outside the five-year arrangements for personal income tax, three provinces—Quebec from 1947, Ontario from 1957, and Alberta from 1981—have levied and administered their own corporate income taxes.

Tax Agreements

In the tax rental phase the federal government levied a tax on all corporations, compensating the "renting" provinces for not imposing a tax and allowing a tax credit for taxes collected by Ontario and Quebec up to 5 percent of profits. As the provincial rates were 7 percent, there was some overlapping. To give room for these provincial taxes the agreeing provinces were asked to levy a 5 percent tax, revenue from which was deducted from federal payments to them. This tax was repealed in 1952.

Under the 1952 renewal Ontario dropped its tax (temporarily, as it turned out), and Quebec continued to impose a 7 percent levy. In 1953 the federal credit was increased to 7 percent and in 1957, when the federal credit was raised to 9 percent, Ontario re-introduced its own tax at 11 percent. Quebec continued its tax at 9 percent for four years, but in 1961 went to 12 percent. Ontario held at 11 percent until 1967, when it also went to 12 percent; for the following decade the two provinces had identical rates. For much of the time since 1978 the Ontario rate was one or two points higher than the Quebec rate, but both have risen to the 14-15 percent region in recent years. Meanwhile the standard federal credit has remained at 10 percent, leaving considerable overlapping of tax on Ontario and Quebec income.

As with the personal income tax in 1962 the other provinces were obliged to pass legislation identical with the federal in order to tap this field with federal collection. All eight did so, with rates at 9 percent, except for

Table 16.1 Federal Government: Personal Income Tax Exemptions and Credits, For Selected Years, 1949-88

Year	Single	Married	Wife's tax-free income	Dependent child	Other dependant	Child tax credit	Allowances Interest and dividends	Pensions	Employment expenses	Old age
					dollars					
1949-57	1,000	2,000	250	150	400	—	—	—	—	500
1958-61	1,000	2,000	250	250	500	—	—	—	—	500
1962-71	1,000	2,000	250	300	550	—	—	—	—	500
1972	1,500	2,850	250	300	550	—	—	—	150	1,000
1973	1,600	3,000	300	300	550	—	—	—	150	1,000
1974	1,706	3,198	314	320	586	—	—	—	150	1,066
1975	1,978	3,522	334	352	646	—	—	—	150	1,174
1976	2,090	3,920	370	390	720	—	—	—	150	1,310
1977	2,270	4,260	400	420	780	—	1,000	—	250	1,420
1978	2,430	4,560	430	460	840	200	1,000	1,000	250	1,520
1979	2,650	4,970	440	500	910	218	1,000	1,000	500	1,660
1980	2,890	5,420	460	540	990	238	1,000	1,000	500	1,810
1981	3,170	5,950	490	590	1,090	261	1,000	1,000	500	1,980
1982	3,560	6,670	550	670	1,220	343	1,000	1,000	500	2,220
1983	3,770	7,070	570	710	1,300	343	1,000	1,000	500	2,360
1984	3,960	7,430	490	710	1,360	367	1,000	1,000	500	2,480
1985	4,140	7,770	510	710	1,420	384	1,000	1,000	500	2,590
1986	4,180	7,840	520	710	1,420	454	1,000	1,000	500	2,610
1987	4,220	7,920	520	560	1,200	489	1,000	1,000	500	2,640
1988a	1,020	1,870	500	65/130	—	559	—	170b	—	550

a Tax credits under 1987 tax reform for 1988. b Maximum allowance.

Table 16.2 Federal and Provincial Governments: Combined Personal Income Taxes[a]—Single Taxpayer Without Dependants, By Assessed Income Range, For Selected Years, 1943-86

Year	1,000	1,500	2,500	5,000	7,500	10,000	15,000	20,000	30,000	50,000	100,000	200,000
							dollars					
1943	92	247	626	1,728	3,023	4,312	7,579	11,029	18,396	34,903	80,337	178,304
1949	—	75	235	700	1,270	1,960	3,760	5,960	10,660	21,814	53,714	126,414
1952[b]	—	88	274	820	1,487	2,301	4,406	6,951	12,371	25,192	61,960	145,880
1955[b]	—	70	220	660	1,205	1,870	3,620	5,770	10,370	21,324	52,724	124,424
1958[b]	—	44	166	573	1,110	1,722	3,412	5,507	10,002	20,747	51,637	122,332
1966	—	53	203	675	1,239	1,874	3,593	5,700	10,388	20,833	50,723	119,418
1967	—	51	202	727	1,374	2,060	3,850	6,045	10,740	21,185	51,075	119,770
1971	—	—	206	802	1,491	2,177	3,967	6,178	10,857	21,302	51,192	119,887
1972	—	—	167	754	1,430	2,204	4,012	6,199	10,874	21,283	50,640	110,565
1973	—	—	37	630	1,318	2,103	3,888	6,035	10,628	21,201	51,243	112,578
1976	—	—	3	301	943	1,634	3,223	5,097	9,370	20,010	51,078	117,113
1978	—	—	—	—	695	1,350	2,862	4,609	8,768	18,581	46,446	108,366
1980	—	—	—	—	648	1,270	2,624	4,144	7,831	17,206	44,234	105,448
1981	—	—	—	53	549	1,154	2,457	3,937	7,410	16,502	43,106	103,685
1982	—	—	—	29	450	1,053	2,345	3,767	7,289	15,811	40,192	90,172
1983	—	—	—	13	306	913	2,225	3,618	7,032	15,254	39,555	89,535
1984	—	—	—	10	273	875	2,182	3,556	6,873	15,160	37,628	89,264
1985	—	—	—	5	319	918	2,212	3,575	6,780	14,931	39,570	91,250
1986	—	—	—	14	413	1,107	2,322	3,697	6,888	15,089	46,621	94,511

[a]Combined federal and provincial taxes as approximated for provinces which imposed taxes at or below the federal abatement to 1971; thereafter provincial tax calculated at 30.5 percent of federal tax from 1972 to 1977; at 44 percent 1978 to 1983, and at 47 percent thereafter. [b]Excludes old age security taxes.

Table 16.3 Net Federal Personal Income Tax Rates, Selected Marginal Rates on Taxable Income, After Provincial Credit or Abatement, For Selected Years, 1943-87

Year	$1,001	$2,001	$5,001	$10,001	$20,001	$50,001	$100,001	$200,001	$500,001
					percent				
1943	36	41	51	64	74	88	98	98	98
1949	16.2	18.1	20.9	33.2	42.8	56.1	65.5	70.3	79.8
1952	19.7	22.2	24.4	38.9	49.4	66.0	76.5	91.2	90.2
1955	14.4	16.2	18.9	30.6	39.6	52.2	61.2	65.7	74.7
1966	13.2	15.4	16.0	25.5	34.2	41.8	49.4	53.2	60.8
1967	13.0	15.1	18.8	25.2	32.4	39.6	46.8	50.4	57.6
1969	14.4	16.9	20.7	25.9	33.4	40.8	48.2	51.8	59.0
1972	18.6	19.6	22.6	26.5	34.3	42.2	46.0	46.0	46.0
1973	19.1	20.1	23.1	27.1	33.8	43.2	47.0	47.0	47.0
1975	18.0	19.0	21.0	25.0	35.0	43.0	47.0	47.0	47.0
1977	16.0	17.0	19.0	23.0	32.0	36.0	43.0	43.0	43.0
1980	16.0	17.0	18.0	21.0	28.0	36.0	39.0	43.0	43.0
1982	6.0	16.0	18.0	19.0	23.0	30.0	34.0	34.0	34.0
1986	6.0	16.0	17.0	19.0	23.0	30.0	34.0	34.0	34.0
1987	6.0	16.0	17.0	19.0	23.0	30.0	34.0	34.0	34.0

Note: Federal rate is exclusive of surtaxes.

Source: Canadian Tax Foundation, *The National Finances*.

Table 16.4   Provincial Governments: Personal Income Tax Rates as a Percentage of Federal Rate, Selected Years, 1949-88

Year	Nfld.	PEI.	N.B.	N.S.	Que.	Ont.	Man.	Sask.	Alta.	B.C.
					percent					
1949[a]	5.0	5.0	5.0	5.0	5.0	5.0	5.0	5.0	5.0	5.0
1954[a]	10.0	10.0	10.0	10.0	10.0	10.0	10.0	10.0	10.0	10.0
1958[a]	13.0	13.0	13.0	13.0	13.0	13.0	13.0	13.0	13.0	13.0
1961[a]	13.0	13.0	13.0	13.0	13.0	13.0	13.0	13.0	13.0	13.0
1962	16.0	16.0	16.0	16.0	[b]	16.0	22.0	22.0	16.0	16.0
1966	24.0	24.0	24.0	24.0	[b]	24.0	29.0	29.0	24.0	24.0
1971	33.0	33.0	28.0	38.0	[b]	28.0	39.0	34.0	33.0	28.0
1976	41.0	36.0	38.5	40.7	[b]	30.5	42.5	40.0	26.0	31.5
1979	58.0	50.0	52.5	52.4	[b]	44.0	54.0	53.0	38.5	45.0
1980	58.0	51.2	52.5	52.4	[b]	44.0	54.0	53.0	38.5	44.0
1981	58.0	52.5	52.5	52.4	[b]	46.0	54.0	52.0	38.5	44.0
1982	59.0	52.5	56.5	55.5	[b]	48.0	54.0	51.0	38.5	44.0
1983	60.0	52.5	56.5	58.0	[b]	49.2	54.0	51.0	43.5	44.0
1984	60.0	52.5	56.5	58.0	[b]	50.4	54.0	51.0	43.5	45.8
1985	60.0	52.5	56.5	58.0	[b]	48.0	54.0	50.5	43.5	47.5
1986	60.0	52.5	56.5	58.0	[b]	50.0	54.0	50.0	43.5	47.5
1987	60.0	55.0	56.5	58.0	[b]	50.0	54.0	50.0	46.5	51.5
1988	60.0	56.0	56.5	60.0	[b]	51.0	54.0	50.0	46.5	51.5

[a] Rates allotted the provinces under the tax rental agreements or allowed as a credit for non-agreeing provinces. [b] A separate schedule was imposed by Quebec.

Note: Rates do not include surtaxes in effect at various times over the period.

Table 16.5 Federal-Provincial Governments: Combined Personal Income Tax Marginal Rates,[a] by Income Ranges, Selected Years, 1943-88

Year	$1,001	$2,001	$5,001	$10,001	$15,001	$20,001	$50,001	$100,001	500,001
					percent				
1943[b]	36.0	41.0	51.0	64.0	69.0	74.0	88.0	98.0	98.0
1949	17.0	19.0	22.0	35.0	45.0	45.0	59.0	69.0	84.0
1952	20.7	23.4	25.7	41.0	52.2	52.0	69.5	80.5	95.0
1955	18.0	20.0	21.0	34.0	44.0	44.0	58.0	68.0	83.0
1966	17.4	20.3	21.1	33.6	43.2	43.2	55.0	65.0	80.0
1967	18.0	21.5	26.0	35.0	45.0	45.0	55.0	65.0	80.0
1969-70	20.0	23.5	28.7	36.0	46.4	46.4	56.6	66.9	82.4
1971	21.8	24.0	28.0	35.0	45.0	45.0	55.0	65.0	80.0
1972	24.2	25.5	29.3	34.4	44.6	44.6	54.8	60.0	60.0
1973	24.8	26.1	30.0	35.2	43.9	43.4	56.1	61.3	61.3
1974	5.5	24.8	27.4	35.2	43.9	43.9	56.1	61.3	61.3
1975	5.5	24.8	27.2	32.6	40.5	44.0	56.1	61.3	61.3
1976	5.5	5.8	27.4	32.6	38.0	42.9	54.8	66.0	66.0
1977	5.5	5.8	27.4	32.6	33.8	42.9	50.9	61.3	61.3
1978	7.0	7.5	27.4	30.2	36.0	37.8	51.8	61.9	61.9
1979	7.0	7.5	27.4	30.2	36.0	33.1	51.8	61.9	61.9
1980	7.0	7.5	27.4	30.2	36.0	33.1	51.8	56.2	61.9
1981	7.0	24.5	25.9	30.2	31.1	33.1	51.8	56.2	61.9
1982	2.6	24.5	25.9	27.4	28.8	33.8	43.2	49.0	49.0
1983	2.8	7.5	26.5	27.9	29.4	33.8	44.1	50.0	50.0
1984	2.8	7.5	26.5	27.9	29.4	33.8	44.1	50.0	50.0
1985	2.8	7.5	25.0	27.9	29.4	33.8	44.8	51.7	51.7
1986	8.9	23.8	25.3	28.2	29.7	34.2	46.1	53.9	53.9
1987	9.0	24.0	25.5	28.5	30.0	34.5	45.0	51.0	51.0
1988	1 to 27,500: 26.01;			27,501 to 5,000: 39.78;			over 55,001: 44.37		

Note: Provincial rates assumed to be equal to tax credit or tax abatement in 1947 to 1972 and thereafter at nominal supertaxes on federal tax of 30.5 percent 1972 to 1977, at 44 percent 1978 to 1983 and 47 percent thereafter.

aIncludes old age security tax where applicable.   bExcludes refundable tax.

Sources: Canadian Tax Foundation, The National Finances and Canadian Fiscal Facts.

Manitoba and Saskatchewan, which went to 10 percent. Increases since then have brought most provinces to the 15-16 percent area. Manitoba and Saskatchewan reached 17 percent in 1986 and 1987, while even Prince Edward Island and Alberta, where rates had been respectively 10 and 11 percent, went to 15 percent; all these increases were signs of the tight state of provincial budgets.

Concessions for Small Business

Although the federal government introduced a reduced rate for small corporations in 1949 the provinces did not follow until 1975, when British Columbia took the first step. Other provinces joined in gradually, with rates 5 to 10 points below the standard rate, generally following eligibility rules for the federal small business rate or the manufacturing and processing rate, or both. The latest trend in several provinces is to give lower rates or even complete exemption for small corporations meeting special conditions.

Economic Incentives

Provincial governments use their corporation taxes in various ways for economic stimulus, and freedom to do so is no doubt one of the reasons for independent taxes in Quebec, Ontario and, since 1981, Alberta. Many of the incentives offered take the form of tax credits. In 1986 these included credits for research and development, manufacturing investment, royalty payments, venture capital investment, livestock and livestock facilities, logging taxes, certain forms of interest receipts, small business venture capital and employment, mining exploration expenditures, and political contributions.

Tax Room in Lieu of Cash

The substitution of tax points for cash has been very limited under the corporation income tax. In 1960 Quebec opted for 1 point of corporate income tax in lieu of federal university grants. None of the tax room provided under the 1976 Established Programs Financing Arrangements involved the corporation tax, nor did any of the changes made in later years.

Other Corporate Taxes

Several provinces have restored corporate taxes other than those on profits. The most common of these is the so-called "capital tax," with higher rates for banks and similar organizations.

Quebec

Quebec throughout has imposed a separate tax on corporations. Differences of base have been minimized, however, by annual amendments which followed fairly closely those to the federal act. As in most provinces rates have been raised well beyond the limits of the federal 10 percent abatement, although the Quebec special rates for small corporations are below the general level. Quebec's basic structure is three-tiered: 3 percent for businesses qualifying for the federal small business tax credit, 5.5 percent for "eligible" income (a long list covering nearly all goods-producing industries), and a general rate of 13 percent. From May 1, 1986 a 7.25 percent surtax was enacted, to raise these rates for 1986 to 3.15 percent, 5.77 percent and 13.63 percent. For 1987 the full annual effect of the surtax produced rates of 3.22 percent, 5.90 percent, and 13.94 percent. Exemption is granted for three years for small corporations incorporated after May 1, 1986. Various tax credits are also allowed, including a credit for logging taxes, for salaries of scientific research employees, and flow-through tax deductions and tax credits for investors in various types of Quebec controlled private investment companies directing funds to specified businesses.

Appraisal

The taxation of corporation profits on a regional basis is a much different matter than regional taxation of personal income. The latter can be reasonably accomplished by taxing on the basis of residence at year-end, as this is an almost universally accepted test of liability for personal income tax and generally presents few problems. However, corporate income, particularly that of a large corporation, is likely to be earned in several domestic and foreign jurisdictions, and although a corporation undoubtedly has a legal residence, provincial authorities would refuse to accept a system which awarded all the tax receipts from that corporation to the province of residence. Corporation income must therefore be allocated by some reasonable method to each of the jurisdictions in which it does business. The most marked progress in developing rules for making this allocation has been in the international sphere, where conflicts could be a serious deterrent to international trade and investment (see chapters 41-43). But for internal divisions progress has been slower. In a country like United States, where potentially 50 state jurisdictions could be involved, argument has been going on for decades.

In Canada, a set of rules drawn up in 1947 under a uniform corporation tax act to be used as a model for provincial governments has since been accepted by all provinces, including those levying their own taxes, as the basis for liability under current tax laws. However, this has hardly been the result of a goodwill gesture towards either the federal government or the other provinces; strong compulsion lies in the fact that the same rules have been followed by the federal government in determining the amount of provincial tax that would be recognized for its tax credit, and for a province not to follow them would create severe problems for its taxpayers. But whatever the reason a set of rules based largely on international principles and involving some fairly arbitrary ratios for allocating special forms of income for forty years have smoothed the rocky road of taxing regional corporate profits in Canada. This is probably not a situation that will last in perpetuity, as it is another instance of the lock-in effect of present arrangements, against which, given the probable lifespan of sensible ideas, there no doubt will be pressure for release in the future. But for the moment it is not a top priority, as the provinces are more concerned about changes in the federal corporation tax that will result from tax reform.

Tables 16.6 to 16.11 give further details of corporation taxation.

Death Taxes

Although estate and inheritance taxes are no longer levied in Canada by any jurisdiction and were never an important source of revenue, they formed part of the postwar intergovernmental arrangements and may best be dealt with here before going on to other forms of taxation. As postwar develop-

Table 16.6   Federal Government: Corporation Income Tax Rates by Type, 1949-88[a]

Year	Small business reduced rate[b]	General rate[c]	Manufacturing or processing profits		Abatement for provincial tax
			Small business[c]	Other[c]	
			percent		
1947-48	30%	30.0	30.0	30.0	0
1949.	10% on first $10,000	33.0	22.0	33.0	0
1952.	22% on first $10,000	52.0	22.0	52.0	5
1953-4	20% on first $10,000	49.0	20.0	49.0	7
1955-6	20% on first $10,000	47.0	20.0	47.0	7
1957.	20% on first $10,000	47.0	20.0	47.0	9
1958.	20% on first $10,000	47.0	20.0	47.0	9
1959-60	21% on first $10,000	50.0	21.0	50.0	9
1961.	21% on first $35,000	50.0	21.0	50.0	9
1962-6	21% on first $35,000	50.0	21.0	50.0	9
(plus 5% refundable tax on cash profits from May, 1966 to March, 1967)					
1967.	21% on first $35,000	50.0	21.0	50.0	10
1968-71	21.54% on first $35,000	51.41	21.54	52.41	10
1971 (from July).	19.74% on first $35,000	46.71	19.74	46.71	10
1972.	23.25% on first $50,000	46.5	23.25	46.5	10
1973.	25% on first $50,000	49.0	20.0	40.0	10
1974.	25% on first $100,000	50.6	20.0	40.0	10
1975.	25% on first $100,000	48.2	20.0	40.0	10
1976.	25% on first $150,000	46.0	20.0	40.0	10
1977-9	25% on first $150,000	46.0	20.0	40.0	10
1980-81	25.75% on first $150,000	47.8	20.5	41.5	10
1982.	25% on first $200,000	47.8	20.0	41.5	10
1983.	25% on first $200,000	46.9	20.0	40.0	10
1984.	25% on first $200,000	46.0	20.0	40.0	10
1985.	25% on first $200,000	46.9	20.0	40.75	10
1986.	25% on first $200,000	47.8	20.0	41.5	10
1987.	24.94% on first $200,000	46.57	19.27	39.87	10
1988.	23.39% on first $200,000	42.45	20.3	37.81	10

[a] Includes Old Age Security tax to 1971. [b] Reduced rate limited to 1972 and later years to qualifying income of a Canadian private company. [c] Before provincial abatement.

Source: Canadian Tax Foundation, *The National Finances* and *Canadian Fiscal Facts*.

Table 16.7 Federal Government: Effective Corporation Income Tax Rates (After Credit for Provincial Tax), Selected Years, 1948-71

Year	$10.000	$15,000	$25,000	$50,000	$100,000	$500,000	$1,000,000
				percent			
1948.......	30.0	30.0	30.0	30.0	30.0	30.0	30.0
1949.......	10.0	17.7	23.8	28.4	30.7	32.5	32.8
1952.......	21.0	30.5	38.1	43.8	46.7	48.9	49.7
1953-54....	18.7	18.7	24.1	34.9	40.3	44.6	45.2
1958.......	18.4	18.4	18.4	30.7	36.9	41.8	42.3
1959-60....	19.4	19.4	19.4	32.6	39.2	44.5	45.3
1961.......	19.4	19.4	19.4	27.3	36.6	44.0	45.0
1962-6.....	12.0	12.0	12.0	20.7	30.9	39.0	40.0
1967.......	11.0	11.0	11.0	19.7	29.9	38.0	39.0
1968-71.... June 30	11.54	11.54	11.54	20.49	30.95	39.32	40.36
1971.......	9.74	9.74	9.74	17.83	27.27	34.82	35.77

Notes: The variety of rates under the corporation income tax in later years does not lend them to this type of analysis. Credits or abatements for provincial taxes were 5 percent in 1952; 7 percent in 1953-54; 9 percent in 1958 to 1966 and 10 percent thereafter. Includes Old Age Security Tax.

ments related to no particular period the following calendar will serve to plot the path they followed.

1941—A federal death tax was introduced under the Dominion Succession Duties Act for the first time with rates at about the same level as under the existing provincial statutes, most of which had been enacted before World War I. This was simply an additional tax, without credit for provincial taxes.

1947—As part of the federal offer to the provinces, federal rates were to be doubled and the provinces given the option of repealing their duties and receiving compensation from the federal government or else of continuing their duties with a credit allowed their residents up to one-half the federal duty, the value of the credit to be deducted from other payments due them. All provinces but Ontario, Quebec, and British Columbia repealed their laws under the offer. These three provinces continued to levy their own taxes.

1959—The federal tax was changed from a succession duty to an estate tax, with no change in the provincial sharing.

1964—The federal sharing of the estate tax revenue was increased from 50 percent to 75 percent for "agreeing" provinces, and the abatement for the three provinces levying their own taxes was also increased to 75 percent.

1967—Alberta began to refund to its citizens the revenue it received from the federal government in respect of death duties.

1968—The federal gift and estate taxes were integrated, with substantial changes in the gift tax.

Table 16.8 Provincial Governments: General Corporation Taxes, Selected Years, 1949-88

Year	Nfld.	P.E.I.	N.S.	N.B.	Que.	Ont.	Man.	Sask.	Alta.	B.C.
					percent					
1949	5	5	5	5	7	7	5	5	5	5
1952	0	0	0	0	7	0	0	0	0	0
1953-54	0	0	0	0	7	0	0	0	0	0
1955-56	0	0	0	0	7	0	0	0	0	0
1957	0	0	0	0	9	11	0	0	0	0
1958	0	0	0	0	9	11	0	0	0	0
1959-60	0	0	0	0	9-10	11	0	0	0	0
1961	0	0	0	0	12	11	0	0	0	0
1962-66	9	9	9	9	12	11	10	10	9	9
1967	11	10	10	10	12	12	11	11	10	10
1968	12	10	10	10	12	12	11	11	10	10
1969	13	10	10	10	12	12	11	11	11	10
1970	13	10	10	10	12	12	13	11	11	10
1972	13	10	10	10	12	12	13	11	11	10
1975	13	10	10	10	12	12	13	12	11	13
1976	14	10	12	10	12	12	15	12	11	15
1977	14	10	12	12	12	12	15	14	11	15
1978	14	10	12	12	12	13	15	14	11	15
1979	14	10	12	12	13	14	15	14	11	15
1980	15	10	13	12	13	14	15	14	11	16
1981	15	10	13	14	13	14	15	14	11	16
1982	16	10	15	14	13	14	15	14	11	16
1983	16	10	15	14	13	15	16	14	11	16
1984	16	10	15	15	13	15	16	16	11	16
1985	16	10	15	15	13	15	16	16	11	16
1986	16	10	15	15	13.9	15.5	17	17	11	16
1987	16	15	15	15	13.9	15.5	17	17	15	15
1988	16	15	15	16	13.9	15.5	17	17	15	14

Note: These rates do not include surtaxes in effect at various times over the period.

Source: Canadian Tax Foundation, *Provincial Finances* and *Provincial and Municipal Finances*.

Table 16.9 Provincial Governments: Reduced Rates for Small Corporations, 1975-88

Year	Nfld.	P.E.I.	N.S.	N.B.	Que.	Ont.	Man.	Sask.	Alta.	B.C.
					percent					
1975	—	—	—	—	—	—	—	—	—	10
1976	—	—	—	9	—	9	13	—	—	12
1977	12	—	—	9	—	9	13	12	—	12
1978	12	—	—	9	—	10	11	11	—	12
1979	12	—	10	9	—	10	11	11	5	12
1980	12	—	10	9	12	10	11	10	5	10
1981	12	—	10	9	3	0	10	10	5	8
1982	12	—	10	9	3	0	10	10	5	8
1983	12	—	10	9	3	0	10	10	5	8
1984	12	—	10	9	3	0	10	10	5	8
1985	10	—	10	9	3	10	10	10	5	8
1986	0/10	10	0/10	5/9	3.2/5.9	10	10	0/10	0/5	8
1987	0/10	10	0/10	5/9	0/3.2	10	10	0/10	0/5	11
1988	0/10	10	0/10	5/9	0/3.2	10	10	0/10	0/5	10

Note: (—) means no reduction was given.

Sources: Canadian Tax Foundation, *Provincial and Municipal Finances.*

Table 16.10 Federal and Provincial Governments: Combined General Corporation Tax Rates, 1949-88

Year	Nfld.	P.E.I.	N.S.	N.B.	Que.	Ont.	Man.	Sask.	Alta.	B.C.
					percent					
1949	38	38	38	38	40	40	38	38	38	38
1952	52	52	52	52	54	52	52	52	52	52
1953-4	49	49	49	49	49	49	49	49	49	49
1955-6	47	47	47	47	47	47	47	47	47	47
1957-8	47	47	47	47	47	49	47	47	47	47
1959-60	50	50	50	50	50	52	50	50	50	50
1961	50	50	50	50	52	52	50	50	50	50
1962-6	50	50	50	50	52	52	51	50	50	50
1967	51	50	50	50	52	52	51	51	50	50
1968	53.4	51.4	51.4	51.4	53.4	53.4	52.4	52.4	51.4	51.4
1969	54.4	51.4	51.4	51.4	53.4	53.4	52.4	52.4	52.4	51.4
1970	54.4	51.4	51.4	51.4	53.4	53.4	54.4	52.4	52.4	51.4
1972	49.5	46.5	46.5	46.5	48.5	48.5	49.5	47.5	47.5	46.5
1973	52.0	49.0	49.0	49.0	51.0	51.0	52.0	51.0	50.0	51.0
1974	53.6	50.6	50.6	50.6	52.6	52.6	53.6	52.6	51.6	52.6
1975	51.2	48.2	48.2	48.2	50.2	50.2	51.2	50.2	49.2	51.2
1976	50.0	46.0	48.0	46.0	48.0	48.0	51.0	48.0	47.0	51.0
1977	50.0	46.0	48.0	48.0	48.0	48.0	51.0	50.0	47.0	51.0
1978	50.0	46.0	48.0	48.0	48.0	49.0	51.0	50.0	47.0	51.0
1979	50.0	46.0	48.0	48.0	48.0	50.0	51.0	50.0	47.0	51.0
1980	52.8	47.8	50.8	49.2	50.8	51.8	52.8	51.8	48.8	52.8
1981	52.8	47.8	50.8	51.8	50.8	51.8	52.8	51.8	48.8	53.8
1982	53.8	47.8	52.8	51.8	50.8	51.8	52.8	51.8	48.8	53.8
1983	52.9	46.9	51.9	50.9	49.9	51.9	52.9	40.9	47.9	52.9
1984	52.0	46.0	51.0	51.0	49.0	51.0	52.0	52.0	47.0	52.0
1985	52.9	46.9	51.9	51.9	49.9	51.9	52.9	52.9	47.9	52.9
1986	53.8	47.8	52.8	52.8	51.4	53.3	54.8	54.8	48.8	53.8
1987	52.57	51.57	51.57	51.57	50.51	52.07	53.57	53.57	50.58	51.57
1988	48.45	47.45	47.45	48.45	46.39	47.95	49.45	49.45	47.45	46.45

Note: Federal rate includes old age security taxes to 1971.

Sources: Canadian Tax Foundation, *Canadian Fiscal Facts*, *The National Finances*, and *Provincial and Municipal Finances*.

Table 16.11 Federal, Ontario, and Quebec: Combined Corporation Income Tax Rates, 1972-88

Year	Manufacturing and processing profits eligible for small business deduction		Non-manufacturing and non-processing profits not eligible for small business deduction		Manufacturing and processing profits not eligible for small business deduction		Other	
	Ont.	Que.	Ont.	Que.	Ont.	Que.	Ont.	Que.
				percent				
1972	25.25	25.25	25.25	25.25	48.5	48.5	48.5	48.5
1973	22.0	22.0	27.0	27.0	42.0	42.0	51.0	51.0
1974	22.0	22.0	27.0	27.0	42.0	42.0	52.6	52.6
1975	22.0	22.0	27.0	27.0	42.0	42.0	50.2	50.2
1976	19.0	22.0	24.0	27.0	42.0	42.0	48.0	48.0
1977	19.0	22.0	24.0	27.0	42.0	42.0	48.0	48.0
1978	20.0	22.0	25.0	27.0	43.0	42.0	49.0	48.0
1979	20.0	22.0	25.0	27.0	43.0	42.0	50.0	48.0
1980	20.5	22.5	25.75	27.75	44.5	44.5	51.8	50.8
1981	20.5	13.5	25.75	18.75	44.5	44.5	51.8	50.8
1982	10.0	13.0	15.0	18.0	44.5	36.3	51.8	50.8
1983	10.0	13.0	15.0	18.0	44.75	36.25	51.9	49.9
1984	10.0	13.0	15.0	18.0	44.0	35.5	51.0	49.0
1985	20.0	13.0	25.0	18.0	44.75	36.25	51.0	49.9
1986	20.0	13.0	25.0	18.15	46.0	37.27	53.3	51.43
1987	19.27	12.49	24.94	18.16	44.37	35.77	52.07	50.51
1988	20.3	13.22	23.39	16.61	42.31	33.71	47.95	46.39

Source: Canadian Tax Foundation, *The National Finances* and *Provincial and Municipal Finances*.

1969—Quebec reduced its death tax rates and increased exemptions; Saskatchewan followed Alberta and refunded to its citizens the revenue it received from the federal government for its suspended death duties.

1972—The federal estate and gift taxes were repealed; the federal government offered to administer taxes levied by any province for three years. All provinces but Alberta and Saskatchewan imposed gift and death taxes.

1975—All provinces but Quebec, Ontario, Manitoba, and British Columbia withdrew their taxes on termination of administration by the federal government.

1977—British Columbia and Manitoba repealed both their gift and death taxes.

1978—Quebec reformed its base to a straight succession duty, with exemption for inter-spousal bequests.

1979—Ontario repealed both its gift and death taxes.

1983—Quebec further increased exemptions and relaxed other aspects of its tax.

1985—the Quebec budget of April 23 announced repeal of gift and death taxes. The implementing legislation first made the effective date December 31, 1985, but this was later changed to May 27, 1986.

Table 16.12 gives an outline of the main features of the federal death and gift taxes; table 16.13 gives figures for federal and provincial revenue from death taxes in the postwar period. At their highest yield—$278 million in 1971—they amounted to less than one percent of total revenues, but in the eyes of some were a useful corrective against the accumulation of massive wealth. Their demise was related to the taxation of a deemed capital gain on property left at death, a feature which was hardly comparable. The move was popular; the author does not recall any evidence of regret in the last decade over their passing.

Consumption Taxes

General Sales Taxes

Provincial taxes on sales of goods at retail are largely a product of the postwar period, although there were some levies prior to 1940. From initial rates of 2-4 percent, levels had climbed to 6-12 percent in 1987. The highest rates are imposed in the Atlantic provinces, and decline as one moves west. Alberta still has no tax. Along with a federal manufacturers' sales tax of 12 percent, which translates to the neighbourhood of 8 percent at the retail level, combined rates of general sales taxes would be 16 percent in Ontario, 17 percent in Quebec, and 19 percent in Newfoundland. These rates are somewhat deceptive, however, as neither the federal nor provincial taxes are as "general" as their name implies.

As mentioned earlier, much of the revenue from the federal tax is now derived from half a dozen sources, many of them already subject to other

Table 16.12 Federal Government: Succession Duties, Estate Tax, and Gift Tax Exemptions and Rates, Selected Years, 1941-71

Succession Duty and Estate Tax[a]

Year	General exemption	Deductions		Lowest and highest rates
		Spouse	Dependants	
	dollars			*percent*
1941	5,000			
1948	50,000	20,000	5,000	Initial rate—3% at $50,000; 20% at $5 million and over; additional rates: 2.5% depending on class; 34% on all classes over $5 million.
1959	50,000	60,000	10,000	10% at $5,000; 54% on excess over $2 million.
1968	50,000	exempt	10,000	15% at $20,000; 50% on excess over $300,000
1971	tax repealed in respect of deaths occuring after Dec. 31, 1971.			

Gift Tax[b]

Year	General exemption	Individual gifts	Other exemptions	Rates
	dollars			*percent*
1947	4,000	—	—	
1958	4,000	1,000	10,000 for transfer of interest in a home or a farm	10% to 28%
1968	none	gifts between spouses exempt	2,000	Rates to apply to cumulative total of gifts after October 1968, 12% at $15,000 to 75% over $200,000
1971	Tax repealed for gifts made after December 31, 1971.			

Note: A credit up to 50 percent was allowed for death duties imposed by a province; after March 1964, this was increased to 75%.

[a] Dominion Succession Duty in effect from 1941 to 1958, when replaced by Estate Tax Act effective from January 1, 1959. [b] First introduced in 1934, and last imposed under Part IV of Income Tax Act.

heavy taxes, and the same is probably true of the provincial taxes. The bases of all these taxes have been constantly narrowed over the postwar period by the regular announcement of additional exemptions in the annual budget. With such major consumer purchases as, for example, food, clothing and footwear now being totally or partially exempt in most jurisdictions, along with many other consumer items, the base of all these taxes is therefore far from "general." A main objective of the federal tax reforms, as we have seen, was addressed to broadening the base for consumer taxation. Table 16.14 gives further details for the postwar period.

Table 16.13 Federal and Provincial Governments: Death Tax Revenue, 1947-87

Fiscal year ending March 31	Federal	Provincial	Total
	millions of dollars		
1947.........................	23.6	34.1	57.7
1948.........................	30.8	31.1	61.9
1949.........................	25.5	29.1	54.6
1950.........................	29.9	29.2	59.1
1951.........................	33.6	31.2	64.8
1952.........................	38.2	34.2	72.4
1953.........................	38.2	32.7	70.9
1954.........................	39.1	31.1	70.2
1955.........................	44.8	40.7	85.5
1956.........................	66.6	72.0	138.6
1957.........................	79.6	64.6	144.2
1958.........................	71.6	53.0	124.6
1959.........................	72.6	55.8	128.4
1960.........................	88.4	56.0	144.4
1961.........................	84.9	60.5	145.4
1962.........................	84.6	66.0	150.6
1963.........................	87.1	72.0	159.1
1964.........................	90.6	85.7	176.3
1965.........................	88.6	92.2	180.8
1966.........................	108.4	107.9	216.3
1967.........................	101.1	118.0	219.1
1968.........................	102.2	109.3	211.5
1969.........................	112.4	121.9	234.3
1970.........................	100.6	140.5	241.1
1971.........................	119.8	158.1	277.9
1972.........................	132.0	137.9	269.9
1973.........................	60.9	151.3	212.2
1974.........................	14.4	185.0	199.4
1975.........................	7.1	167.4	174.5
1976.........................	11.0	143.5	154.5
1977.........................	—	143.9	143.9
1978[a].........................	—	24.6	24.6
1979.........................	—	24.9	24.9
1980.........................	—	41.9	41.9
1981.........................	—	39.8	39.8
1982.........................	—	37.8	37.8
1983.........................	—	45.0	45.0
1984.........................	—	46.7	46.7
1985.........................	—	45.1	45.1
1986.........................	—	30.5	30.5
1987[b].........................	—	7.0	7.0

[a] 1978 and after Quebec only. [b] Estimate.

Table 16.14 Provincial Governments: Rates of Sales Tax, Selected Years, 1949-88

Year	Nfld.[a]	P.E.I.[b]	N.S.[c]	N.B.[d]	Que.[e]	Ont.[f]	Man.[g]	Sask.[h]	Alta.[i]	B.C.[j]
					percent					
1949	—	—	—	—	2 prov. / 2 mun.	—	—	2	—	2
1951	3	—	—	4	2 prov. / 2 mun.	—	—	3	—	3
1955	3	—	—	4	2 prov. / 2 mun.	—	—	3	—	5
1961	5	4	5	3	2 prov. / 2 mun.	3	—	3	—	5
1966	6	5	5	6	8 prov.	5	—	5	—	5
1971	7	8	7	11	8	5	5	5	—	5
1976	10	8	8	8	8	7	5	5	—	7
1979	11	8	8	8	8	7	5	5	—	4
1980	11	9	8	8	8	7	5	5	—	4
1981	11	10	10	8	8	7	5	5	—	6
1982	11	10	10	8	9	7	5	5	—	6
1983	12	10	10	10	9	7	6	5	—	7
1984	12	10	10	10	9	7	6	5	—	7
1985	12	10	10	11	9	7	6	5	—	7
1986	12	10	10	11	9	7	6	5	—	7
1987	12	10	10	11	9	7	7	7	—	6
1988	12	10	10	11	9	8	7	7	—	6

[a] Introduced in 1950 at 2%. [b] Introduced in 1950 at 2%. [c] Introduced in 1959 at 2%. [d] Introduced in 1950 at 4%. [e] Introduced by the City of Montreal in 1935 and by the province in 1940. [f] Introduced in 1940. [g] Introduced in 1961. [h] Introduced in 1967. [i] Alberta has no sales tax. [j] Introduced in 1948 at 2%.

Sources: Canadian Tax Foundation, *Provincial Finances and Provincial and Municipal Finances.*

Gasoline Taxes

The provincial gasoline taxes are of much longer standing, most having been first imposed during the twenties to pay for roads for the burgeoning numbers of automobiles. In general these taxes have tripled or quadrupled since 1947, as indicated in table 16.18. In gallonage terms 1987 rates ranged from a low of 20 cents (Alberta) to a high of 65 cents (Quebec). Most provinces were in the 35-40 cent range, as compared to 9-13 cents in 1949.

Cigarettes

Special provincial taxes on cigarettes, in addition to the already substantial federal taxes, have appeared in the last 20 years. Starting at 2-5 cents per pack of 20 in the early sixties, by 1987 they ranged from 78 to 95 cents, a twenty- to forty-fold increase in most instances. Combined with a federal tax of 58 cents on the same package, as well as provincial retail sales tax on their purchase at the counter, the total taxes in the highest provinces are in the $1.60-1.70 range; for a 25 cigarette package the total would be over $2.00. All of this explains why smokers were paying at least $2.50 for a pack in 1987, and with further increases even more in 1988.

Liquor

In addition to very heavy taxes imposed by the federal government the provinces derive substantial revenue from the sale of liquor through government-owned outlets. Otherwise these revenues would have to be derived through taxes, as they are for example in many of the American states. In actual fact only one province, Prince Edward Island, imposes a special tax on liquor, payable at the time of purchase through a government liquor store. As a result of the special attention given alcohol by governments the bulk of the cost of liquor, as with cigarettes, is now tax.

Fiscal Contribution of Drinkers, Smokers, and Drivers

As a measure of the importance of some of the current high charges just described for tobacco and alcohol the author has attempted, in table 16.15, to assess the share of revenues of all governments derived over a period of three decades under these headings, in the case of the latter including all provincial profits and revenues from liquor sale and consumption. The contribution of the automobile driver includes all revenues identifiably related to the purchase, ownership, or use of an automobile. The interesting result of this compilation is that in general these much used sources, with rates at unprecedented levels in recent years, now provide in all cases less than one-half the share of thirty years ago. This largely reflects the declining role of the consumption type of tax in relation to other taxes, and in some part to reductions in actual consumption, particularly for tobacco, rather than a decline in the affection of government officials for this long-suffering element of the population. Tables 16.16 to 16.18 provide further details of rates of the main consumer taxes.

Table 16.15   Federal and Provincial Governments: Revenue Contribution
of Tobacco, Alcohol and Automobiles, Federal and Provincial Charges
Combined, As a Percentage of Total Revenue, Selected Years, 1950-82

Year	Tobacco	Alcohol	Automobile[a]	Total
		percent		
1950...................	2.2	4.5	6.8	13.5
1955...................	2.9	4.3	5.8	13.0
1960...................	3.1	4.2	6.2	13.5
1965...................	2.9	3.5	5.3	11.7
1970...................	2.2	3.1	4.7	10.0
1975...................	1.5	2.3	3.8	7.6
1980...................	1.3	1.9	2.8	6.0
1982...................	1.4	2.0	3.1	6.5

[a] Includes fuel taxes.

Social Security and Related Charges

The fact that taxes for financing social security programs now account for
over 10 percent of government revenues has been noted. This compares,
for example, with 2 percent from the much revered customs tariff, the subject of so much contention in the free trade negotiations. Details of these
charges are given later in the sections on the social security programs.

Natural Resource Taxes

As contrasted with the cooperative arrangements for other areas, natural
resource taxation has been marked by federal-provincial conflict and
competition, particularly in the last decade.

Mining

Provincial revenues from mining resources come from two main sources—
Crown-owned resources and privately-owned resources, the former pre-
dominating. Where the resources are Crown-owned, as they substantially
are in all but the Atlantic provinces, the charges have taken three main
forms: (1) charges for exclusive access to the resource; (2) charges for the
right to explore the resource; and (3) a charge as a share of production,
usually described as a royalty. For non-Crown-owned property, a special
form of income tax was devised, which seeks to tax income from the mine as
such, as contrasted with a general tax on the income of the corporation.
With evolution of thought on resource taxation this special form of income
tax has become the favoured form of levy for all types of ownership in most
provinces. While there had been some modest intergovernmental tax problems in this field in the past, these became acute after the mid-sixties. At
that time the provinces began a series of rate increases which, by the mid-
seventies, in most instances had raised rates to double or triple their starting
level. The inducement for this action was the allowance of provincial taxes
as a deduction from income subject to federal tax, which considerably offset the heavier provincial burden on the companies. It also considerably

Table 16.16 Federal Government: Rates of Main Consumption Taxes, 1947-87

Year	Sales tax		Cigarettes[b]	Alcohol			Autos[f]	Gasoline	
	Gen.	Bldg. Mat.	pack of 20	liquor[bc]	beer[d]	wine[e]		per gal.	per litre
	%	%	cents	$	cents	cents	%	cents	cents
					per gallon				
1947	8	0[e]	20	11	16	50	25	3	0.6
1948	8	0	20	11	16	50	10	—	—
1949	8	0	20	11	16	25	10	—	—
1950	8	0	20	12	21	25	15	—	—
1951	10	0	23	12	21	25	25	—	—
1952	10	0	16	12	21	25	15	—	—
1953	10	0	16	12	21	25	15	—	—
1954	10	0	16	12	38	25	15	—	—
1955	10	0	16	12	38	25	15	—	—
1956	10	0	16	12	38	25	10	—	—
1957	10	0	16	12	38	25	7.5	—	—
1958	11	0	16	12	38	25	7.5	—	—
1959	11	0	18	13	38	25	7.5	—	—
1960	11	0	18	13	38	25	7.5	—	—
1961	11	0	18	13	38	25	—	—	—
1962	11	0	18	13	38	25	—	—	—
1963	11	4	18	13	38	25	—	—	—
1964	11	8	18	13	38	25	—	—	—
1965	11	11	18	13	38	25	—	—	—
1966	11	11	18	13	38	25	—	—	—
1967	12	11	18	13	38	25	—	—	—
1968	12	11	20	14	42	25	—	—	—
1969	12	11	20	14	42	25	—	—	—
1970	12	11	20	14	42	25	—	—	—
1971	12	11	20	14	42	27.5	—	—	—
1972	12	11	20	14	42	27.5	—	—	—

Year									
1973	12	11	20	14	42	27.5	—	—	—
1974	12	5	22	16	42	27.5	—	—	—
1975	12	5	22	16	42	27.5	—	10	2.2
1976	12	5	22	16	42	27.5	—	10	2.2
1977	12	5	22	16	42	27.5	—	10	2.2
1978	9	5	22	16	42	27.5	—	7	1.5
1979	9	5	22	16	42	27.5	—	7	1.5
1980	9	5	24	17	54	60.0	—	7	1.5
1981	9	5	25	17.70	57	61.0	—	7	1.5
1982	9	5	27	19.20	61	67.0	—	7	1.5
1983	9	5	31	22.13	70	77.0	—	7	1.5
1984	10	6	36	25	80	87	—	7	1.5
1985	10	6	58	26	84	91	—	7	1.5
1986	11	7	61	27	85	93	—	16	3.5
Jan. 1986	11	7	65	28	85	93	—	16	3.5
Feb. 1986	12	8	65	28	85	93	—	16	3.5
Apr. 1987	12	8	68	28	85	93	—	20	4.5

a Includes old age security tax 1952 to 1971. b Beginning from 1981 excise taxes on tobacco products and wines were indexed annually on September 1 for inflation. The rates given are those that applied in the year for the period up to September 1. The last increase on this basis was made in 1984; later increases dated mainly from the budget date. c Shown as dollars per proof gallon; actual basis was changed in 1981 to charge per litre of absolute alcohol. d Per pound of malt to 1954; per gallon of beer thereafter; actual basis was changed in 1981 to a charge per litre of beer. e Per gallon of medium wine; actual basis was changed to charge per litre in 1981. (Changes in the tobacco and alcohol rates in the early eighties resulted mainly from indexation). f Automobiles were free of special taxation from 1961 to 1974, when a tax based on the weight of the vehicle was imposed under the energy conservation program, which was still in effect in 1987.

Sources: Canadian Tax Foundation, *Canadian Fiscal Facts* and *The National Finances*.

Table 16.17   Provincial Governments: Cigarette Taxes, Selected Years, 1963-88

cents per pack of twenty[a]

Year	Nfld.	P.E.I.	N.S.	N.B.	Que.	Ont.	Man.	Sask.	Alta.	B.C.
1963	—	4	2	4	4	—	—	—	—	—
1965	5	4	2	4	4	—	8	—	—	—
1967	5	4	2	4	5	2	8	4	—	—
1969	10	8	8	8	8	8	8	6	6	6
1971	10	8	8	8	8	8	8	6	6	6
1973	20	8	8	8	8	10	12	7	6	6
1975	20	16	8	8	8	10	12	7	6	6
1978	27	16	12	14	22	22	20	19	6	19
1979	32	20	20	20	22	24	20	22	6	19
1980	40	20	20	20	24	24	24	24	6	19
1981	50	20	20	27	32	29	28	26	6	27
1982	64	28	28	34	37	37	36	30	6	30
1983	90	30	28	57	41	49	42	42	30	40
1984	96	40	28	60	50	53	52	54	30	47
1985	96	30	48	74	72	53	62	62	30	54
1986	96	30	70	80	90	54	82	82	30	69
1987	96	70	90	85	90	57	92	94	80	76
1988	96	94	90	90	90	77	92	114	80	90

Note: Taxes are rounded to closest whole number; in addition cigarettes are also subject to provincial sales taxes on purchase in 1987 in Newfoundland, Ontario, and Manitoba.

[a] As cigarettes are also sold in packages of 25 the equivalent tax would be 25 percent higher.

Sources: Canadian Tax Foundation, *Provincial Finances* and *Provincial and Municipal Finances*.

Table 16.18   Provincial Governments: Gasoline Taxes, Selected Years, 1949-88

cents per litre

Year	Nfld.	P.E.I.	N.S.	N.B.	Que.	Ont.	Man.	Sask.	Alta.	B.C.
1949	3.1	2.9	2.9	2.9	2.4	2.4	2.0	2.2	2.0	2.2
1956	3.8	2.9	3.8	3.3	2.9	2.4	2.4	2.4	2.2	2.2
1961	4.2	3.6	4.2	4.0	2.9	2.9	3.1	3.1	2.7	2.9
1966	4.2	4.0	4.2	4.0	3.6	3.6	3.8	3.3	2.7	2.9
1971	5.6	4.7	4.7	4.4	4.2	4.0	3.8	4.2	5.6	3.3
1976	6.0	4.7	4.7	4.4	4.2	4.2	4.0	3.3	2.2	3.8
1979	6.0	4.7	4.7	4.4	4.2	4.7	4.0	4.2	—	3.8
1980	6.0	5.0	4.7	4.4	20%	4.7	20%	4.2	—	3.8
1981	7.1	7.3	4.7	4.4	20%	5.4	5.7	5.6	—	5.3
1982	8.5	8.9	7.8	5.8	13.0	6.6	6.4	—	—	6.2
1983	9.6	9.7	8.8	8.1	15.8	7.6	7.5	—	—	6.5
1984	10.1	10.0	9.6	8.7	11.9	8.4	7.5	—	—	7.7
1985	10.7	9.7	9.8	8.9	12.9	8.0	8.9	—	—	8.4
1986	9.9	8.7	8.3	9.7	13.6	8.3	8.9	—	—	8.5
1987	9.8	8.9	8.3	7.8	14.4	8.3	8.9	7.0	5.0	9.5
1988	9.8	8.7	8.6	8.5	14.4	9.3	8.0	7.0	5.0	8.08

Note: from 1949 to 1978 per litre figures are the approximate equivalent of gallonage charges actually imposed; in several instances the charges shown are the per litre rate equivalent of an ad valorem charge.

Sources: Canadian Tax Foundation, *Provincial Finances* and *Provincial and Municipal Finances.*

reduced the federal government's revenue from the resource sector, to which it took strong exception. It responded to this "raid" on its revenues with a series of stratagems. Following a general and particularly heavy round of provincial increases in 1975, the federal government cancelled all deductions for provincial taxes. In their place there was substituted a "resource allowance"—an exemption of 25 percent of mining income from federal taxation, thus limiting the area to be exploited by the province at federal expense. This had no immediate effect on existing high provincial rates, but with declining mining activity and closer accord between mining officials of the federal and provincial governments the provinces reduced their rates in the eighties. (See table 16.19). The federal "resource allowance" at last report was still in effect. For a more detailed description of this period see the author's *Background of Current Fiscal Problems*,[16.1] Chapter 7.

Petroleum

There is not space here to follow the turbulent course of petroleum concerns of the seventies and eighties; the management of the energy crisis was in itself a prodigious undertaking, but its financial aspects were equally challenging. The spectacular rise in prices in 1973 and 1979 attracted the attention of all governments as a new source of revenue, and vigorous steps were taken to share in the gain both in Ottawa and in the producing provinces. Over the 1973-85 period the federal government enacted a confusing variety of new taxes to tap this exciting new source, both for general revenues and for programs under its energy conservation and oil production stimulation programs—ultimately brought together as the National Energy Program (NEP). At the same time the provinces were making drastic revisions of their own charges for the same general purposes.

The longest-lived of the federal taxes were the oil export charge, the first to be imposed (1973) and only withdrawn in 1985, and the federal gasoline tax (first imposed in 1975 and still levied). Other charges related more specifically to the NEP were the petroleum levy (1979-81), the natural gas and gas liquids tax (1980-83), petroleum compensation charges (1981 to 1985), and the petroleum and gas revenue tax (1980 to 1986). The last was one of the most contentious of the NEP levies, as it applied on a gross basis. Its similarity to a royalty deeply offended the oil provinces, and a newly elected Conservative government repealed it.

The details of higher provincial charges, designed mainly to capture a part of the additional return producers were receiving from higher prices, are too complex to be given here. In any event, the situation changed radically following the virtual withdrawal of the federal government from the petroleum area with the abandonment of the NEP by the Conservative government, including the repeal of the offending petroleum and gas

---

[16.1] J. Harvey Perry, *Background of Current Fiscal Problems*, Canadian Tax Paper no. 68 (Toronto: Canadian Tax Foundation, 1982), ch. 7.

revenue tax in 1986. Even more drastic were the repercussions of the collapse of international oil prices in the last two years, calling for a complete reversal of approach by the provinces, with relief for over-extended oil companies being the main concern.

For the federal government the energy episode is now almost a closed book. Revenues from the federal charges were substantial (see table 16.20) and their virtual disappearance had a shattering effect on the long-range revenue forecast. For the 1985-86 fiscal year the original forecast was $15.1 billion; the actual revenue was $2.4 billion. Expenditures under the energy envelope were expected to be $4.8 billion in that year, and even their decline to around $1 billion hardly compensated for the $12 billion-plus drop in expected revenues. In addition to winding up the National Energy Program and repealing most of the energy related taxes the Conservative government concluded Offshore Petroleum Accords with newly potential provinces— Newfoundland and Nova Scotia. What lies ahead for these provinces, as well as the older producing provinces, will depend very much on oil prices, which, though stabilizing somewhat in the 1987, were far too wobbly to give much assurance for the future. The significance of oil prices for the producing provinces is clear from a statement of an Alberta minister to the effect that each dollar of increase in price per barrel of oil is worth $150 million to that province.

Table 16.19 Provincial Governments: Mining Taxes in Selected Provinces, Selected Years, 1962-87

Year	Profits Taxes				Royalties on Output		
					Sask.		
	Que.	Ont.	Man.	B.C.	Gen.	Potash	Alta.
	percent				*percent*		*percent*
1962...........	4-7	6-12	8	10	12.5	4.25-9	—
1964...........	4-7	6-12	6-11	10	12.5	4.25-9	—
1966...........	9-15	6-12	6-11	10	12.5	4.25-9	12.5
1969...........	9-15	15	6-11	15	12.5	4.25-9	12.5
1971...........	9-15	15	15	15	12.5	4.25-9	12.5
1973...........	9-15	15	15	15	12.5	4.25-9	12.5
1975...........	15-30	15-40	23[a]	15	12.5	4.25-9	12.5
1977...........	15-30	15-40	23[a]	17.5	12.5	4.25-9	12.5
1979...........	15-30	15-30	23[a]	17.5	12.5	4.25-9	12.5
1981...........	15-30	15-30	18	17.5	12.5	4.25-9	12.5
1983...........	15-30	15-30	18	17.5	12.5	4.25-9	12.5
1985...........	18	15-30	18	17.5	12.5	4.25-9	12.5
1986...........	18	20[a]	18	17.5	12.5	4.25-9	12
1987...........	18	20[a]	18	17.5	12.5	4.25-9	12

[a]Effective March 31, 1986 rate of 20 percent levied only on profits over $500,000.

Table 16.20 Federal Government: Energy Tax Revenue, 1973-86

Year[a]	Gasoline tax	Oil export charge	Petroleum levy	Natural gas and gas liquids taxes	Petroleum compensation charges	Petroleum and gas revenue tax	Total
			millions of dollars				
1973	—	286	—	—	—	—	286
1974	—	1,669	—	—	—	—	1,669
1975	425	1,063	—	—	—	—	1,488
1976	600	661	—	—	—	—	1,261
1977	598	432	—	—	—	—	1,030
1978	516	328	—	—	—	—	844
1979	420	750	400	—	—	—	1,570
1980	454	842	1,393	187	—	27	2,903
1981	436	963	3,792	998	473	811	7,473
1982	407	625	—	1,264	3,059	1,857	7,212
1983	386	346	—	524	1,750	1,944	4,950
1984	405	677	—	—	2,208	2,421	4,711
1985	725	326	—	—	1,093	1,849	3,993
1986	1,297	—	—	—	—	1,130	2,427

[a] Fiscal year ending nearest December 31 of the year named.

Source: Statistics Canada, *Federal Government Finance*, CANSIM data, October 9, 1986.

17
All Governments: Expenditure Programs

A detailed study of the major expenditure programs of government (social security, health, pensions, defence, education, etc.) forms a large part of the rest of this book. As well, the shape and trend of federal outlays have already been covered in some detail and provincial and municipal expenditures have by no means been neglected. Furthermore, as the reference lists will attest, library shelves are already heavily laden with lengthy studies of government expenditures and programs, recent and past. We will therefore concentrate here on a general review of the main postwar trends, leaving more detailed attention to the main programs for later.

The Bird Studies

One of Canada's best known fiscal experts, Richard Bird, has traversed this territory in studies for the Canadian Tax Foundation, and his historical writings give helpful leads for further review. Most useful for present purposes is *Financing Canadian Government: A Quantitive Overview*.[17.1] It covers developments of the 1947-77 period, and therefore deals with a substantial part of the period of the present book.

Growth in Relation to Gross National Expenditure

Bird: Government expenditure as a percentage of gross national expenditure (a different concept than GNP but the same total figure) rose from an average of 22.9 percent in 1947-51 to an average of 39.4 percent in 1973-77; the ratio in 1977 was 41.1 percent. Bird makes the point that government expenditure over the period 1947 to 1977 rose 71 percent faster than GNE.[17.2]

Post-1977. Between 1977 and 1986 GNE increased by 123 percent, while total government expenditure rose by 168 percent, 36 percent faster than GNE. As a result government expenditure rose beyond the 41.1 percent level of 1977 to a peak of 48.2 percent in 1984 and 1985, dropping off modestly to 47.5 percent in 1986. These later years reflect as much the sluggishness of the economy as they do the growth of government activity. The break point came in 1982, the year of the recession, when nominal GNE rose by only 4.9 percent (real GNE actually declined by over 4 percent) and government expenditure grew by 18 percent. The result was an almost unprecedented rise of 5 full percentage points in the ratio of government expenditure to GNE—from 42.6 percent in 1981 to 47.7 percent in 1982—a level which has persisted nearly ever since.

[17.1] Richard M. Bird, *Financing Canadian Government, A Quantitative Overview* Financing Canadian Federation no. 1 (Toronto: Canadian Tax Foundation, 1979).

[17.2] Ibid., at 8.

Exhaustive Expenditures v. Transfers

Bird: Over the 1947-77 period 71 percent of expansion in government expenditure in relation to GNE was in goods and services ("exhaustive" expenditures in Professor Bird's nomenclature) and 29 percent was in growth of transfer payments. Fastest growth was in the early fifties and the 1968-77 decade, but with distinct differences in the two periods. In the first, with the revival of defence expenditure for the Korean War, nearly all the growth was in goods and services. In the second, only 32 percent was in goods and services and 68 percent was in transfer payments. Professor Bird saw this as a significant shift in the role of government expenditure. Direct purchase of goods and services by government removes labour, materials, and equipment from the private economy (without judging whether for better or worse) while transfer payments shift money from one individual to another, leaving expenditure decisions to the recipients.

Post 1977. The shift from goods and services to transfer payments accelerated to the point that between 1977 and 1986 the ratio of the former to GNE actually declined from 23.9 percent to 22.8 percent, a drop of 5 percent. As table 17.1 shows, the drop in government capital expenditure contributed heavily to this decline. By contrast, transfer payments increased from 17.2 percent of GNE in 1977 to 24.7 percent in 1986, a rise of 14.3 percent. This increase contributed to a rise in the total ratio of 6.4 percent.

Here a precaution must be entered, as this result could easily be misinterpreted. Transfer payments are commonly thought of as related solely to the social programs—old age security, family allowances, etc.—and for some groups in the community represent the sink-hole that is largely responsible for the federal deficit. But the concept employed by Professor Bird is substantially broader than this. It in fact embraces all national accounts categories of expenditure other than goods and services; along with transfers to persons it includes interest on the public debt, subsidies and capital assistance to industry, and payments to non-residents. And in fact it was not the personal but the non-personal transfers that were largely responsible for the 1977-86 increase in government expenditure. In this period transfers to persons increased from 10.6 percent of GNE to 12.8 percent, a rise of 21 percent, but interest on debt has risen from 4.4 percent to 8.6 percent, a jump of 95 percent, and subsidies and capital assistance from 1.9 percent to 2.8 percent, a growth of 47 percent. In fact since 1982 the combined ratios of interest on debt, capital assistance, and subsidies has been equal to or greater than that of transfers to persons.

Table 17.1 brings together for the period 1977-86 several of the expenditure elements just discussed as percentages of GNE.

Public Employment

Data from national accounts and a special study by Richard Bird, in collaboration with Meyer Bucovetsky and David Foot, showed that the main cause of the postwar increase in public expenditure on goods and services (1947-77) was the growth in the wage bill for civilian employees. This was

Table 17.1 All Governments: Expenditure on Goods and Services and
Transfer Payments, as a Percentage of Gross National Expenditure, 1977-86

	Expenditure			Transfer Payments				
Year[a]	On goods and services[b]	On capital	Total	To persons	Interest on debt	Subsidies and capital assistance	Total[c]	Grand total
				percent				
1977.....	20.7	3.2	23.9	10.6	4.4	1.9	17.2	41.1
1978.....	20.6	3.1	23.7	10.8	4.2	1.8	18.0	41.7
1979.....	19.8	2.8	22.6	10.0	5.2	2.1	17.6	40.2
1980.....	19.9	2.8	22.7	10.3	5.6	2.8	19.1	41.8
1981.....	20.0	2.6	22.6	10.1	6.5	3.1	20.0	42.6
1982.....	21.5	2.9	24.4	12.0	7.5	3.5	23.3	47.7
1983.....	21.1	2.6	23.7	12.7	10.0	4.1	24.2	47.9
1984.....	20.8	2.6	23.4	12.5	8.1	4.2	24.8	48.2
1985.....	20.6	2.5	23.1	12.6	8.7	3.4	25.1	48.2
1986.....	20.4	2.4	22.8	12.8	8.6	2.8	24.7	47.5

[a] Calendar year. [b] Includes defence expenditure. [c] Excludes minor amounts for transfers to non-residents

Sources: Canada, Department of Finance, *Economic Review*, April 1985; Statistics Canada, National Income and Expenditure Accounts, Fourth Quarter, 1986.

the combined result of larger staffs and wage rates which rose faster than in private business (primarily because they were rising from a lower base). Following this increase, which took place in the 1950s, wage trends in government employment paralleled closely those in the private sector. As a share of government expenditure civilian wages rose from 21.0 percent in 1947 to 33.2 percent in 1969, and with minor variations remained at that level to 1977. Professor Bird's conclusion on the latest period was: "To a considerable extent, then, the growth of the government wage bill in recent years appears to be a reflection of general economic trends rather than an independent factor explaining the growth of government expenditures."[17.3]

Post-1977. While there have been improvements in the data on public employment in the last decade it is still not possible to provide figures as comprehensive as those presented in the Bird study. Obviously with an actual decline in the goods and services share of expenditures, the main element of which is civilian salaries and wages, it would appear that the main momentum for increase in government expenditure is not in this area. There are some indicators of numbers of government employees, although with frequent revisions of base these are not reliable for anything but very general impressions. The best official figures are presented in table 17.2 from which it would appear that about 12 percent of the total labour force is now employed in government or government-related activities. But there are major exclusions in this compilation, including half a million teachers and several hundred thousand employees of public utilities.

[17.3] Richard M. Bird, *The Growth of Public Employment in Canada* (Richard M. Bird in collaboration with Meyer W. Bucovetsky and David K. Foot) Public Sector Employment in Canada vol. 3 (Toronto: Institute for Research on Public Policy, 1979), 14.

Table 17.2 All Governments: Employees (Including Government Enterprise Employees) at December 31, 1947-87

Year	Government employees				Total labour force	Government employees as a percentage of labour force
	Federal	Provinciala	Local	Totalb		
	thousands					percent
1947........	125c	—	—	—	4,954	
1948........	118c	—	—	—	5,035	
1949........	124c	—	—	—	5,092	
1950........	127c	—	—	—	5,198	
1951........	125c	—	—	—	5,236	
1952........	132c	—	—	—	5,344	
1953........	165c	—	—	—	5,386	
1954........	171	—	—	—	5,476	
1955........	182	—	—	—	5,585	
1956........	183	—	—	—	5,738	
1957........	179	—	—	—	5,970	
1958........	197	—	—	—	6,120	
1959........	337	122d	—	—	6,186	
1960........	336	168d	—	—	6,411	
1961........	337	170d	141	648	6,521	9.9
1962........	330	172d	145	647	6,615	9.8
1963........	334	183d	150	667	6,748	9.9
1964........	338	192d	154	684	6,933	9.9
1965........	345	268	160	773	7,141	10.8
1966........	364	289	166	819	7,493	10.9
1967........	369	307	174	850	7,747	11.0
1968........	369	326	178	873	7,951	11.0
1969........	370	338	188	896	8,194	10.9
1970........	379	357	201	937	8,395	11.2
1971........	401	393	205	999	8,639	11.6
1972........	413	394	210	1,017	8,897	11.4
1973........	434	427	225	1,088	9,276	11.7
1974........	451	441	237	1,129	9,639	11.7
1975........	459	465	247	1,171	9,974	11.7
1976........	576	475	254	1,305	10,203	12.8
1977........	589	494	268	1,351	10,500	12.9
1978........	584	502	267	1,351	10,895	12.4
1979........	577	539	267	1,383	11,231	12.3
1980........	584	553	274	1,411	11,573	12.2
1981........	590	557	277	1,424	11,904	12.0
1982........	584	569	287	1,440	11,958	12.0
1983........	581	558	288	1,427	12,183	11.7
1984........	583	560	291	1,434	12,399	11.6
1985........	588	633	290	1,511	12,639	12.0
1986........	571	638	293	1,502	12,870	11.7
1987........	572e	670f	310e	1,552	13,121	11.8

aExcludes provincial employees of British Columbia until 1979 when general government employees are included. bExcludes transit, hydro, gas, and telephone systems, school authorities, and municipal hospitals. cAs at March 31. dExcludes Quebec and British Columbia employees. eAs at September 30. fAs at June 30.

Sources: *Historical Statistics of Canada*; Statistics Canada: *Federal Government Employment, Provincial and Territorial Government Employment*, and *Local Government Employment* and earlier compilations: *Bank of Canada Review*.

Expenditure by Level of Government

Bird: On the National Accounts basis, under which expenditures are allocated to the government carrying on the activity, no matter where the funds so spent originate, to 1977 the provinces accounted for the largest share of the growth in total in relation to GNE—41 percent, as compared with 26 percent for local government and 12 percent for federal. Bird acknowledged however that this was a somewhat misleading presentation as it concealed the major role the federal government had played in stimulating provincial expenditure through transfer payments.

Post-1977. In the period 1977 to 1986 there was a reversal of roles. Of a 6.4 point rise (from 41.1 percent to 47.5 percent) in total government expenditure in relation to GNE, the federal growth of 3.4 points (from 16.1 percent to 19.5 percent) accounted for 53 percent. On the same measure, the rise of 3.0 points in provincial expenditure (from 12.5 percent to 15.5 percent) accounted for 47 percent. A drop of 0.8 points in municipal on the other hand was a decline of 12 percent in the ratio for that level. (The resulting gap was offset by rises in hospitals and pension funds). See tables 17.3 and 17.4 for data on expenditures by level of government for the period 1947-86.

Expenditure by Function

Bird: Social expenditures—health, education and welfare—accounted for the greater part of the rise in government expenditure between 1947 and 1977. From 1965 to 1976 the three together accounted for 68 percent of the total growth and by 1976 accounted for over 21 percent of GNE—half of total government spending. Only welfare grew consistently from 1965 on. Education peaked in 1970 and declined in later years. Health accounted for 27 percent of the 1965-70 rise, but for only 5 percent from 1970 to 1976. Welfare however accounted for 20 percent of the total growth in 1965-70 and went up to 51 percent in 1970-76.

Data comparable to that used by Professor Bird is continued for the 1976-86 period in table 17.5. Its distinctive features are the predominance of debt charges and welfare in the total rise from 42.2 percent of GNE in 1976 to 48.4 percent in 1986. Of this growth the former accounted for 61 percent and the latter for 34 percent. Health also ranked high, at 13 percent, followed by general government and other at 10 percent and protection at 5 percent. These increases were offset by declines of 16 percent each for transportation and communication and education.

Professor Bird's observation that in general provincial and local governments accounted for most education expenditure, provincial governments for most health expenditure, and the federal for most welfare expenditure remains valid today, except that the federal proportion of welfare is probably even higher now than it was in 1977.

It should be noted that the term "welfare" as used here embraces much more than the usual concept of aid to those in poverty, as it includes all the

Table 17.3 All Governments: Expenditure by Level of Government, Excluding Intergovernmental Transfers, National Accounts Basis, 1947-86

Year[a]	Federal	Provincial	Local	Hospitals	Pension plans[b]	Total
			billions of dollars			
1947..............	1.9	0.7	0.6	—	—	3.2
1948..............	1.8	0.9	0.7	—	—	3.4
1949..............	2.0	1.0	0.8	—	—	3.8
1950..............	2.1	1.1	0.9	—	—	4.1
1951..............	2.9	1.2	1.1	—	—	5.2
1952..............	4.1	1.2	1.3	—	—	6.6
1953..............	4.2	1.2	1.4	—	—	6.8
1954..............	4.2	1.4	1.5	—	—	7.1
1955..............	4.4	1.5	1.7	—	—	7.5
1956..............	4.6	1.8	1.9	—	—	8.2
1957..............	4.9	1.9	2.1	—	—	8.9
1958..............	5.5	2.1	2.3	—	—	9.9
1959..............	5.6	2.5	2.6	—	—	10.6
1960..............	5.8	2.8	2.8	—	—	11.4
1961..............	6.1	2.4	2.9	0.8	—	12.2
1962..............	6.4	2.6	3.4	0.8	—	13.2
1963..............	6.4	2.9	3.7	0.9	—	13.9
1964..............	6.8	3.2	3.8	1.1	—	14.9
1965..............	7.1	3.8	4.5	1.2	—	16.6
1966..............	8.1	4.5	5.1	1.4	—	19.1
1967..............	9.0	5.5	5.7	1.6	—	21.8
1968..............	9.9	6.3	6.4	1.9	—	24.5
1969..............	10.7	7.2	7.1	2.1	0.1	27.2
1970..............	11.9	8.7	8.0	2.4	0.1	31.1
1971..............	13.1	10.5	8.8	2.7	0.2	35.2
1972..............	15.6	11.6	9.4	2.9	0.3	39.2
1973..............	17.6	13.2	10.5	3.3	0.4	45.0
1974..............	22.7	16.3	12.3	4.1	0.5	56.0
1975..............	27.8	20.2	14.5	4.9	0.8	68.3
1976..............	30.2	23.1	16.7	5.6	1.1	76.7
1977..............	33.8	26.3	18.8	6.0	1.4	86.3
1978..............	38.1	29.8	20.4	6.6	1.8	96.8
1979..............	41.0	34.1	21.9	7.2	2.2	106.3
1980..............	48.2	40.2	24.8	8.5	2.7	124.4
1981..............	58.2	47.1	28.2	10.1	3.3	146.8
1982..............	70.6	55.0	31.7	11.5	4.0	172.8
1983..............	77.0	61.4	33.1	12.4	4.9	188.8
1984..............	87.3	66.0	34.8	13.1	5.7	206.9
1985..............	94.2	71.3	36.6	13.7	6.7	222.4
1986..............	95.1	75.9	38.6	14.6	7.6	231.8

Note: Figures for 1981-86 on 1981 revised national accounts basis.

[a] Calendar year. [b] Canada and Quebec Pension Plans.

Sources: Canadian Tax Foundation, *The National Finances*; Statistics Canada, *National Income and Expenditure Accounts*, Fourth Quarter, 1986.

Table 17.4 All Governments: Expenditure by Level of Government,
Excluding Intergovernmental Transfers, as a Percentage of Total Expenditure,
National Accounts Basis, Selected Years, 1947-86

Year	Federal	Provincial	Local	Hospitals	Canada and Quebec Pension Plans	Total
			percent			
1947..............	59.3	21.9	18.8	—	—	100.0
1950..............	51.2	26.8	22.0	—	—	100.0
1953..............	62.6	17.9	19.4	—	—	100.0
1955..............	58.0	19.7	22.3	—	—	100.0
1960..............	50.9	24.6	24.5	—	—	100.0
1965..............	42.8	22.9	27.1	7.2	—	100.0
1970..............	38.3	28.0	25.7	7.7	0.3	100.0
1975..............	40.8	29.6	21.2	7.2	1.2	100.0
1977..............	39.2	30.5	21.7	7.0	1.6	100.0
1979..............	38.5	32.0	20.6	6.8	2.1	100.0
1980..............	38.7	32.3	20.0	6.8	2.2	100.0
1981..............	39.6	32.1	19.2	6.9	2.2	100.0
1982..............	40.9	31.8	18.3	6.7	2.3	100.0
1983..............	40.8	32.5	17.5	6.6	2.6	100.0
1984..............	42.2	31.9	16.8	6.3	2.8	100.0
1985..............	42.3	32.0	16.5	6.2	3.0	100.0
1986..............	41.0	32.7	16.7	6.3	3.3	100.0

Based on table 17.3.

demogrant and income maintenance payments of all governments—family allowances, old age security, guaranteed annual income, social assistance, unemployment insurance, etc.

An explanatory word should also be given regarding the appearance of "Health" as a major government expenditure in the postwar period. There have always been some governmental expenditures under this heading, but with the introduction of state hospital insurance in the late fifties there was an exponential growth resulting from the shift to the public sector of millions of dollars of "health" expenditure which formerly was part of the household budget. In the national accounts data this was first recognized in 1961 by the introduction of a separate "Hospitals" heading, at that time representing 2 percent of Gross National Expenditure. By the mid-seventies this had risen to 3 percent, and has changed very little since. This was only one part, although a significant one, of the total effect of the shift, which was completed in the late sixties with the introduction of medical insurance. Between 1960 and 1975 the public share of total health costs rose from 43 percent to 75 percent, representing in the latter years 5.3 percent of GNE, a ratio which by 1986 had grown to 6 percent. We explore this very significant phenomenon in detail later.

Table 17.5 All Governments: Expenditure by Main Function, as a Percentage of Gross National Expenditure, 1976-86

Year[a]	General government	Protection[b]	Transportation and communications	Health	Social welfare	Education	Debt costs	Other	Total[c]
					percent				
1976	2.6	3.6	3.7	5.3	9.6	6.6	3.5	7.3	42.2
1977	2.9	3.6	3.8	5.2	9.9	6.6	3.7	7.5	43.2
1978	2.9	3.6	3.7	5.2	9.8	6.5	4.2	7.3	43.2
1979	2.8	3.4	3.4	5.1	9.4	6.2	4.4	7.6	42.3
1980	2.8	3.5	3.7	5.3	9.9	6.1	5.0	8.2	44.5
1981	2.7	3.5	3.3	5.5	9.6	6.0	5.6	8.3	44.5
1982	3.1	3.8	3.0	6.0	11.6	6.4	6.2	9.4	49.5
1983	3.0	3.9	2.8	6.1	12.1	6.5	6.2	8.8	49.4
1984	3.0	3.9	2.7	6.1	11.7	6.0	6.9	8.9	49.2
1985	3.1	4.0	2.7	6.0	11.8	6.0	7.1	8.2	48.9
1986	3.2	3.9	2.7	6.1	11.7	5.6	7.3	7.9	48.4

Note: Excludes intergovernmental transfers.

[a] Fiscal years ending nearest December 31 of year named. [b] Includes defence.

Sources: Statistics Canada, *Consolidated Government Finance* and CANSIM.

Government as a Distributor of Income

Bird: 31 percent of total personal income received by Canadians in 1977 appears to have come directly from government, compared with 19 percent in 1947. Counting in the wages and salaries of persons employed in supplying goods and services purchased by government the total probably reached 38 percent. "Thus it seems not unreasonable to estimate that perhaps 40% of personal income came from government by the mid-1970s, and that probably close to half the adult population of Canada was dependent on government for a significant proportion of its income . . ."[17.4] It seems unlikely that this proportion would have declined in the next decade; on the contrary with heavier unemployment it has much more probably increased.

Deficits and Debt

Writing in 1977 Professor Bird was able to take a fairly relaxed view of the then current deficits, particularly those of the federal government, and the resulting increase in debt. The debt-to-GNE ratio, dominated by the federal position, had been declining steadily for 30 years, and there appeared to be no cause for alarm in the federal deficits of 1975-77. He did hedge his position, however: ". . . it is far from clear that the exceptional circumstances of the last few years indicate a permanent turning point in the long downward decline of the debt ratio in the postwar period. Should future experience suggest that deficits (and debt growth) have indeed become endemic, this conclusion will of course have to be re-evaluated."[17.5] We have seen enough of the federal deficit experience of the following decade that no further comment is needed.

Individual Governments

While this review gives a perspective on broad developments of the postwar period it tells little about the standing of individual governments. The federal government has been well covered, but provincial and municipal governments deserve further attention. We will return to this aspect later; in the meantime the overwhelmingly important subject of transfer payments calls for discussion before leaving the general area.

Transfer Payments

Clearly transfer payments have assumed a commanding position in government finances in Canada. On the broadest interpretation of the term in 1986 they exceeded all other expenditures of government—$120 billion against the balance, $111.5 billion for goods and services and capital. In that year they were 24.7 percent of GNE, a rise of 45 percent over the 17.2 percent of a decade before. As previously noted, this broad concept includes all payments for interest on debt. In what follows we will be dealing mainly with

---

[17.4]Supra, footnote 17.1, at 22.

[17.5]Ibid., at 55.

direct transfers to persons under various social programs and transfers between levels of government.

The Shift in Financing

One of the most dramatic results of the combination of new transfer payments for persons and new intergovernmental transfers has been a remarkable shift in financial responsibility for government services in Canada. In the case of health the notable change is in the emergence of the federal government and the decline of the municipal; in education the largest shift has been from municipal to provincial governments, with the federal government entering as a new element; under social services, although the federal government has remained the dominant factor, the provinces have accounted for an increasing share over the three decades. The municipal role in social services, at one time dominant, is now negligible.

Transfers: The Main Categories

Transfers fall into two main categories, transfers to persons and transfers between governments. The distinction is somewhat confusing as transfers between governments are frequently related to an ultimate program of payments to persons. However the distinction is a valid one as the two types of programs involve quite different considerations for governments.

Transfers to Persons

Table 17.6 gives the breakdown of transfers to persons by level of government. In 1986, 54 percent originated with the federal government, 33 percent with the provincial governments, and 12 percent were through the Canada and Quebec Pension Plans. Municipal transfers were negligible.

Federal Government: Transfers to Persons

Heaviest federal expenditures were for payments to seniors under the old age security group of measures (old age security, guaranteed income supplement, and spouse's allowance) and amounted to $13.1 billion in 1986, or 39.5 percent of federal transfers to persons. The next largest category was unemployment insurance, at $10.4 billion or 31 percent; family allowances were third, at $2.5 billion, or 7.5 percent. Although not covered in the compilation there should be included with the latter the value of the child tax credit, estimated at $1.3 billion in 1986. War veterans' pensions and allowances were $1.3 billion, or 3.9 percent. Canada Pension Plan payments, not included as a federal program in this compilation, amounted to $5.3 billion in 1986. See table 17.7 for transfers under these programs for the years 1947-86.

Provincial Governments: Transfers to Persons

Provincial transfers to persons in the postwar period began with programs of assistance for old age, unemployment, blindness, disability, and poverty

**Table 17.6 All Governments: Transfers to Persons,
National Accounts Basis, 1947-86**

Year[a]	Total	Federal	Provincial	Local	Canada and Quebec Pension Plans
			billions on dollars		
1947........	0.8	0.6	0.2	—	—
1948........	0.9	0.6	0.3	—	—
1949........	0.9	0.6	0.3	—	—
1950........	1.0	0.6	0.4	—	—
1951........	1.0	0.6	0.4	—	—
1952........	1.3	1.0	0.3	—	—
1953........	1.4	1.0	0.4	—	—
1954........	1.6	1.2	0.4	—	—
1955........	1.7	1.2	0.5	—	—
1956........	1.7	1.2	0.5	—	—
1957........	2.0	1.5	0.5	—	—
1958........	2.6	1.9	0.7	0.1	—
1959........	2.7	1.8	0.9	0.1	—
1960........	3.1	2.0	1.1	0.1	—
1961........	2.7	2.0	0.6	0.1	—
1962........	2.9	2.1	0.7	0.1	—
1963........	3.0	2.1	0.8	0.1	—
1964........	3.2	2.3	0.8	0.1	—
1965........	3.4	2.3	1.0	0.1	—
1966........	3.8	2.5	1.2	0.1	—
1967........	4.7	2.9	1.6	0.1	—
1968........	5.5	3.3	2.0	0.1	—
1969........	6.2	3.6	2.4	0.1	0.1
1970........	7.0	4.1	2.6	0.2	0.1
1971........	8.3	4.7	3.2	0.3	0.2
1972........	9.9	6.2	3.2	0.2	0.3
1973........	11.2	7.0	3.6	0.3	0.4
1974........	13.9	8.7	4.5	0.2	0.5
1975........	17.1	10.6	5.5	0.3	0.8
1976........	19.5	11.5	6.6	0.3	1.1
1977........	22.2	13.1	7.5	0.3	1.4
1978........	25.0	14.6	8.4	0.3	1.8
1979........	26.5	14.7	9.4	0.3	2.2
1980........	30.8	16.5	11.4	0.4	2.6
1981........	35.0	18.7	12.6	0.5	3.2
1982........	43.7	24.4	14.8	0.6	4.0
1983........	50.0	28.1	16.4	0.7	4.8
1984........	53.6	29.6	17.5	0.8	5.8
1985........	58.3	31.6	19.1	0.9	6.7
1986........	62.0	33.6	20.4	0.9	7.5

Note: 1981-86 figures on 1981 revised national accounts basis.

[a]Calendar year.

Sources: Canada, Department of Finance, *Economic Review* April 1985; Statistics Canada, *National Income and Expenditure Accounts*, Fourth Quarter, 1986.

Table 17.7 Federal Government: Transfers to Persons, Main Programs, National Accounts Basis, 1947-86

Year[a]	Old age security[b]	War veterans pensions and allowances	Family and youth allow- ances[c]	Unem- ployment insurance	Other[d]	Total	CPP[e]
			billions of dollars				
1947	—	0.3	0.3	—	—	0.6	—
1948	—	0.2	0.3	0.1	—	0.6	—
1949	—	0.2	0.3	0.1	—	0.6	—
1950	—	0.2	0.3	0.1	—	0.6	—
1951	—	0.2	0.3	0.1	—	0.6	—
1952	0.3	0.2	0.3	0.1	—	1.0	—
1953	0.3	0.2	0.3	0.2	—	1.0	—
1954	0.4	0.2	0.4	0.2	—	1.2	—
1955	0.4	0.2	0.4	0.2	—	1.2	—
1956	0.4	0.2	0.4	0.2	—	1.2	—
1957	0.4	0.2	0.4	0.3	—	1.5	—
1958	0.6	0.2	0.5	0.5	0.2	1.8	—
1959	0.6	0.2	0.5	0.4	0.1	1.8	—
1960	0.6	0.2	0.5	0.5	0.1	2.0	—
1961	0.6	0.2	0.5	0.5	0.2	2.0	—
1962	0.7	0.2	0.5	0.4	0.2	2.1	—
1963	0.8	0.2	0.5	0.4	0.3	2.1	—
1964	0.9	0.3	0.5	0.3	0.2	2.3	—
1965	0.3	0.3	0.6	0.3	0.2	2.3	—
1966	1.0	0.3	0.6	0.3	0.2	2.5	—
1967	1.3	0.3	0.6	0.4	0.3	2.9	—
1968	1.5	0.3	0.6	0.5	0.4	3.3	—
1969	1.7	0.3	0.6	0.7	0.3	3.6	—
1970	1.9	0.3	0.6	0.7	0.6	4.1	0.1
1971	2.1	0.3	0.6	0.9	0.8	4.7	0.1
1972	2.4	0.3	0.5	1.9	1.4	6.2	0.2
1973	2.8	0.4	0.7	2.0	1.1	7.0	0.3
1974	3.3	0.4	1.8	2.1	1.1	8.7	0.4
1975	3.8	0.5	2.0	3.2	1.1	10.6	0.5
1976	4.3	0.6	1.9	3.3	1.4	11.5	0.8
1977	4.7	0.6	2.1	3.9	1.8	13.1	1.0
1978	5.2	0.6	2.2	4.5	2.1	14.6	1.3
1979	6.1	0.7	1.7	4.0	2.2	14.7	1.5
1980	7.0	0.7	1.8	4.8	2.7	16.5	1.9
1981	8.2	0.8	2.0	8.5	2.9	18.7	2.3
1982	9.3	0.9	2.2	10.1	3.5	24.4	2.9
1983	10.1	1.0	2.3	10.1	4.7	28.2	3.5
1984	11.0	1.1	2.4	9.9	5.3	29.7	4.0
1985	12.2	1.2	2.5	10.1	5.6	31.6	4.7
1986	13.1	1.3	2.5	10.4	5.9	33.2	5.3

[a]Calendar year. [b]Includes Guaranteed Income Supplement and spouse's allowance. [c]Youth allowances and Quebec schooling allowances commenced in 1965 and terminated in 1973. [d]Includes Canada manpower allowances, aid to refugee immigrants and payments to registered Indians. [e]For comparison only; not included as a federal government transfer.

Source: Statistics Canada, *National Income and Expenditure Accounts*.

under joint programs with the federal government. One of the oldest of these was the means-tested old age pension, started in 1927, which was replaced in 1952 by the federally financed Old Age Security Plan. There are remnants of these programs in some provinces, but most have been withdrawn or are used as modest supplements to other payments. Of growing importance in the social service area are direct provincial relief payments, amounting in 1986 to $5.1 billion or 25 percent of the total.

Other long-standing provincial programs were mothers' allowances and workmen's compensation, the former dropped since 1965 but the latter still a prominent element of government, particularly in the industrial provinces. The four joint supplementary social schemes enacted in the early fifties were replaced by the Canada Assistance Plan after 1966, and were repealed as separate programs. Since 1984 grants to benevolent organizations (non-governmental organizations carrying on social and other activities) have more than doubled as governments have moved to "privatization" of some functions; in 1986 they accounted for $4.2 billion or 20 percent of the total.

As shown in table 17.8, the national accounts compilation of provincial transfers to persons included hospital grants until 1960 and throughout has included grants for post-secondary education. The former have been excluded since 1960 but the latter are still included in this category. For purposes of the current presentation these grants are explained in detail in the following section on intergovernmental transfers.

Municipal Governments: Transfers to Persons

The dramatic upward shift in responsibility for social assistance is evident in current nominal municipal transfers to persons. In 1986 of $62.4 billion paid directly to persons by all governments municipalities contributed $894 million, or 1.4 percent. This was all in the form of direct relief.

Intergovernmental Transfers

In 1986, 20 percent of provincial revenues came from the federal government, and 48 percent of funds spent by municipalities came from the provinces. Put another way—18 percent of federal expenditure went to the provinces and 30 percent of provincial expenditure to the municipalities. (See table 17.9 for total federal and provincial transfers to other governments and their standing as a percentage of expenditures from 1960 to 1986). Transfers have risen each year, but somewhat lower recent ratios reflect the growth of other expenditure categories, the increased use of tax transfers by the federal government, and the growing trend toward independent provincial revenue sources. But transfers remain a crucial element in federal finances, and are vital for the continuation of essential national programs and indeed for the financial survival of certain provinces.

Two Categories of Transfers

There are two main classes of intergovernmental transfers—General Purpose and Specific Purpose. The distinction is not absolute, as some trans-

Table 17.8   Provincial Governments: Transfers to Persons, Main Programs,
National Accounts Basis, 1947-86

Year[a]	Direct relief	Work-men's compen-sation	Grants to hospitals[b]	Post-secondary education	Benevolent organiza-tions	Other[c]	Total
			millions of dollars				
1947	6	35	37	16	6	104	204
1948	11	38	55	23	14	129	266
1949	12	40	87	18	15	165	336
1950	22	41	93	25	19	104	384
1951	17	45	108	27	23	196	416
1952	11	53	121	23	27	99	334
1953	11	57	127	35	29	180	368
1954	14	58	150	38	40	137	417
1955	17	62	160	47	41	122	449
1956	20	70	156	53	55	131	485
1957	18	76	177	53	60	163	547
1958	14	80	221	80	64	199	658
1959	17	85	427	81	59	205	874
1960	24	92	502	111	93	222	1,044
1961	34	94	—	139	134	224	625
1962	39	104	—	165	145	265	718
1963	49	111	—	179	154	266	759
1964	59	116	—	214	147	305	849
1965	73	142	—	264	202	343	1,024
1966	143	156	—	323	201	350	1,173
1967	257	162	—	580	241	407	1,647
1968	381	177	—	662	327	483	2,023
1969	454	203	—	817	354	541	2,369
1970	535	230	—	889	432	525	2,611
1971	712	238	—	1,107	459	623	3,139
1972	751	280	—	1,194	570	443	3,139
1973	829	335	—	1,232	664	515	3,574
1974	1,014	415	—	1,431	881	723	4,464
1975	1,200	546	—	1,721	1,122	893	5,482
1976	1,392	701	—	2,136	1,418	995	6,642
1977	1,611	750	—	2,308	1,718	1,125	7,507
1978	1,762	891	—	2,524	1,888	1,303	8,368
1979	1,941	959	—	2,766	2,183	1,588	9,437
1980	2,414	1,192	—	3,049	1,052	2,251	11,414
1981	2,617	1,425	—	3,480	1,140	2,124	12,832
1982	3,164	1,726	—	3,778	1,358	2,813	14,600
1983	3,651	2,136	—	4,128	1,462	3,043	16,242
1984	4,133	2,461	—	4,498	1,338	3,100	17.773
1985	4,924	2,261	—	4,718	4,093	3,448	19,444
1986	5,144	2,439	—	5,009	4,197	3,603	20,392

[a] Calendar year. [b] Grants to hospitals were removed from this category and shown separately after 1960. [c] Includes old age and blind pensions and mothers' and disabled persons' allowances paid by some provinces.

Source: Statistics Canada, *National Income and Expenditure Accounts*.

Table 17.9 Federal and Provincial Governments: Transfers to Other Governments, National Accounts Basis, 1960-86

Year[a]	Federal government			Provincial governments		
	Total expenditure including transfers	Transfers to other governments	Transfers as percent of expenditure	Total expenditure including transfers	Transfers to other governments[b]	Transfers as percent of expenditure
	$ billion		*%*	*$ billion*		*%*
1960........	6.7	1.0	14.9	3.5	0.7	20.0
1961........	7.2	1.1	15.3	3.9	1.5	38.5
1962........	7.5	1.1	14.7	4.5	1.8	40.0
1963........	7.6	1.2	15.8	4.9	2.0	40.8
1964........	8.0	1.2	15.0	5.5	2.2	40.0
1965........	8.6	1.5	17.4	6.3	2.5	40.0
1966........	9.8	1.7	17.3	7.5	3.0	40.0
1967........	11.0	2.0	18.2	9.1	3.6	39.6
1968........	12.2	2.3	19.0	10.3	4.0	38.8
1969........	13.5	2.8	20.7	11.7	4.5	38.5
1970........	15.3	3.4	22.2	14.1	5.4	38.3
1971........	17.4	4.3	24.7	16.5	6.0	36.4
1972........	20.1	4.5	22.4	18.4	6.8	37.0
1973........	22.4	4.8	21.5	20.7	7.5	36.2
1974........	28.9	6.2	21.4	25.4	9.1	35.8
1975........	35.5	7.7	21.7	31.6	11.3	35.8
1976........	38.7	8.5	22.0	35.9	12.8	35.7
1977........	43.8	10.0	22.8	41.5	15.2	36.6
1978........	49.0	10.9	22.2	45.5	15.7	34.5
1979........	52.7	11.7	22.2	52.4	18.4	35.1
1980........	61.0	12.8	21.0	59.5	19.3	32.4
1981........	72.3	14.1	19.6	69.6	22.5	32.3
1982........	86.4	15.8	18.3	81.5	26.6	32.6
1983........	94.7	17.1	18.7	89.9	28.4	31.6
1984........	107.2	19.9	18.6	96.0	30.0	31.3
1985........	115.9	21.8	18.9	103.6	32.2	31.1
1986........	116.2	21.1	18.2	109.3	33.4	30.6

Note: Figures for 1981-86 on 1981 revised national accounts basis.

[a]Calendar year. [b]Includes transfers to hospitals.

Source: Canada, Department of Finance, *Economic Review*, April 1985 and Statistics Canada, *National Income and Expenditure Accounts*, Fourth Quarter, 1986.

fers are borderline. The growing complexity of the formulas for their calculation also somewhat obscures distinctions between them. However, it is clear that the latter are related to a specific objective or program, while the former are to be spent for the general purposes of the receiving government. Details of federal transfers in the period 1947 to 1976 are given in table 17.10. While this gives a comprehensive picture of federal payments to 1976, program changes since that time necessitate more detailed later information and this is provided in text and tables. Broad headings of provincial transfers to municipalities are given in table 17.11 and 17.12 with more details in later tables.

Table 17.10 Federal Transfers to the Provinces and Municipalities, 1947 to 1975-76

Fiscal year	Statutory subsidies	Equalization	Revenue guarantee	Reciprocal taxation	PUITTA	Municipal grants	Hospital insurance	Medicare	Extended health care	Vocational training	University grants
						millions of dollars					
1947-48	17.1	—	—	—	2.9	—	—	—	—	—	—
1948-49	17.1	—	—	—	3.7	—	—	—	—	—	—
1949-50	25.7	—	—	—	1.4	.4	—	—	—	4.7	—
1950-51	25.2	—	—	—	4.6	1.4	—	—	—	4.1	—
1951-52	26.6	—	—	—	3.7	2.0	—	—	—	4.2	7.0
1952-53	25.8	—	—	—	4.4	2.5	—	—	—	4.9	5.1
1953-54	24.9	—	—	—	6.8	3.4	—	—	—	4.4	5.2
1954-55	24.3	—	—	—	7.3	3.4	—	—	—	4.4	5.4
1955-56	23.4	—	—	—	7.9	7.2	—	—	—	4.3	5.5
1956-57	22.8	—	—	—	6.6	9.7	—	—	—	4.7	16.0
1957-58	22.0	136.0	—	—	7.4	17.5	—	—	—	4.8	16.6
1958-59	35.2	168.4	—	—	8.7	21.9	54.7	—	—	8.1	25.5
1959-60	28.7	208.0	—	—	4.8	22.6	150.6	—	—	8.4	26.1
1960-61	28.7	214.0	—	—	4.2	24.6	188.9	—	—	8.7	19.0
1961-62	31.5	189.7	—	—	6.4	24.9	283.2	—	—	35.9	19.4
1962-63	31.5	211.6	—	—	10.0	29.4	335.8	—	—	207.5	26.3
1963-64	31.6	202.4	—	—	9.9	31.7	391.3	—	—	136.5	26.8
1964-65	31.6	261.6	—	—	9.7	36.2	433.0	—	—	97.2	27.3
1965-66	31.6	310.0	—	—	6.4	37.1	354.5	—	—	158.9	27.7
1966-67	31.6	370.5	—	—	6.0	38.4	383.7	—	—	232.3	70.9
1967-68	31.7	547.6	—	—	6.7	40.8	435.1	—	—	193.1	—
1968-69	31.7	566.1	—	—	20.8	44.3	550.3	33.0	—	—	—
1969-70	31.8	683.3	—	—	23.6	49.5	624.9	181.0	—	—	—
1970-71	31.8	899.2	—	—	23.9	52.2	688.1	400.5	—	—	—
1971-72	33.8	1,049.0	—	—	24.3	55.4	823.5	575.5	—	—	—
1972-73	33.7	1,176.8	—	—	80.0	61.8	1,019.5	629.2	—	—	—
1973-74	33.8	1,500.1	42.6	—	25.9	62.7	1,073.2	676.2	—	—	—
1974-75	33.8	1,795.0	475.2	—	26.7	68.2	1,360.3	760.8	—	—	—
1975-76	33.8	1,956.5	460.5	—	31.8	76.0	1,754.7	793.8	—	—	—

(Continued) Table 17.10 Federal Transfers to the Provinces and Municipalities, 1947 to 1975-76

millions of dollars

Fiscal year	Cash payments				Tax transfers				Total cash plus tax financing	Tax rental payments
	Post secondary education	Welfare including CAP	Other cash payments	Total cash payments	Contracting out	Post secondary education	Established programs financing	Total tax transfers		
1947-48	—	59.1	11.3	90.4	—	—	—	—	90.4	112.5
1948-49	—	66.8	22.0	109.6	—	—	—	—	109.6	84.4
1949-50	—	90.8	20.2	143.2	—	—	—	—	143.2	76.9
1950-51	—	103.6	41.8	180.7	—	—	—	—	180.7	94.1
1951-52	—	84.5	40.9	168.9	—	—	—	—	168.9	96.9
1952-53	—	22.2	43.9	108.7	—	—	—	—	108.7	308.6
1953-54	—	23.2	47.6	115.5	—	—	—	—	115.5	309.2
1954-55	—	24.1	54.5	123.5	—	—	—	—	123.5	327.4
1955-56	—	29.5	55.3	133.1	—	—	—	—	133.1	319.6
1956-57	—	38.4	68.0	166.2	—	—	—	—	166.2	365.9
1957-58	—	48.1	95.4	347.8	—	—	—	—	347.8	213.9
1958-59	—	74.1	117.2	513.8	—	—	—	—	513.8	249.0
1959-60	—	90.9	130.6	670.7	—	—	—	—	670.7	279.7
1960-61	—	102.8	137.4	728.3	7.7	—	—	7.7	736.0	288.7
1961-62	—	143.5	147.0	881.5	7.9	—	—	7.9	889.4	312.6
1962-63	—	159.5	139.8	1,151.4	10.7	—	—	10.7	1,162.1	25.7
1963-64	—	172.2	160.7	1,163.1	10.9	—	—	10.9	1,174.0	10.5
1964-65	—	182.4	229.3	1,308.3	11.1	—	—	11.1	1,319.4	40.9
1965-66	—	153.4	271.5	1,351.1	224.0	—	—	224.0	1,575.1	43.7
1966-67	—	189.7	317.4	1,640.5	294.9	—	—	294.9	1,935.4	54.0
1967-68	108.0	342.6	283.2	1,988.8	333.6	227.6	—	561.2	2,550.0	55.4
1968-69	276.6	382.8	324.1	2,229.7	336.9	247.0	—	583.9	2,813.6	59.7
1969-70	301.4	395.6	293.2	2,584.3	400.4	307.0	—	707.4	3,291.7	59.9
1970-71	388.3	518.7	458.9	3,461.6	473.3	341.3	—	814.6	4,276.2	63.5
1971-72	450.5	624.3	544.5	4,181.4	531.7	398.5	—	930.2	5,111.6	65.9
1972-73	481.1	677.6	275.5	4,435.2	442.3	468.9	—	911.2	5,346.4	12.4
1973-74	485.1	717.6	454.5	5,071.7	543.4	581.1	—	1,124.5	6,196.2	.1
1974-75	503.6	976.3	488.3	6,488.2	742.5	708.2	—	1,450.7	7,938.9	3.7
1975-76	535.0	1,279.2	461.7	7,383.0	913.5	955.4	—	1,768.9	9,151.9	1.1

Source: Public Accounts of Canada.

Table 17.11 Provincial Governments: General Purpose and Specific Purpose Grants to Municipalities, 1967-86

Year[a]	General purpose grants	General purpose as a percent total grants	Specific purpose grants	Specific purpose as a percent total grants	Total grants	Total grants as a percent of	
						Provincial expenditure	Local revenue
	$ million	%	$ million	%	$ million	%	%
1967	259	11.5	1,909	88.5	2,167	24.1	40.6
1968	289	10.7	2,013	89.2	2,302	22.4	38.5
1969	324	9.1	2,321	90.9	2,645	21.8	39.4
1970	326	9.3	2,806	90.7	3,132	21.1	41.5
1971	350	8.9	3,366	91.1	3,716	21.5	42.1
1972	415	9.2	3,550	90.8	3,965	20.8	41.5
1973	608	14.0	3,935	86.0	4,543	20.6	43.3
1974	732	13.9	4,753	86.1	5,485	19.6	44.7
1975	893	14.4	5,766	85.6	6,659	19.4	45.2
1976	1,067	14.8	6,415	85.2	7,482	19.2	43.9
1977	1,114	14.3	7,549	85.7	8,663	20.0	44.1
1978	1,382	14.9	7,878	85.1	9,260	19.1	43.0
1979	2,517	17.5	8,649	82.5	11,166	20.3	45.4
1980	1,231	13.0	9,995	87.0	11,226	18.1	41.2
1981	1,598	13.0	11,950	87.0	13,548	18.6	43.1
1982	1,620	11.1	13,938	88.9	15,558	18.1	45.0
1983	1,731	10.9	15,185	89.1	16,916	18.2	45.8
1984[b]	1,738.4	9.4	16,453.7	90.4	18,192.1	18.5	46.8
1985[b]	1,777.7	9.5	16,681.7	90.5	18,669.4	17.4	46.1
1986[b]	2,001.9	10.3	17,490.2	89.7	19,492.1	17.3	45.9

[a] Fiscal year nearest to December 31 of year named. [b] Estimates taken from CANSIM data of *Local Government Finance.*

Sources: Statistics Canada, *Provincial Government Finance (Economic Classification)* and CANSIM, *Local Government Finance.*

Table 17.12 Provincial Governments: Transfers to Other Governments
and Hospitals, National Accounts Basis, 1947-86

Year[a]	Transfers to Local Governments				Transfers to hospitals
	To school corporations	Other	Total	Percent of local expenditures	
	millions of dollars			*percent*	*millions of dollars*
1947	67	34	101	16.8	—
1948	86	43	129	18.4	—
1949	107	50	157	19.6	—
1950	118	53	171	19.0	—
1951	131	66	197	17.9	—
1952	146	69	215	16.5	—
1953	157	85	242	18.6	—
1954	177	82	259	17.3	—
1955	224	103	327	19.2	—
1956	254	108	362	19.0	—
1957	301	151	452	21.5	—
1958	358	187	545	23.7	—
1959	415	207	622	23.9	—
1960	467	247	714	25.5	—
1961	547	294	841	28.0	694
1962	749	314	1,063	31.3	782
1963	808	340	1,148	31.0	836
1964	870	419	1,289	33.1	953
1965	963	477	1,440	32.0	1,120
1966	1,181	579	1,760	33.8	1,281
1967	1,397	628	2,025	34.9	1,521
1968	1,573	689	2,262	35.3	1,750
1969	1,804	697	2,501	34.7	1,994
1970	2,274	824	3,098	38.2	2,308
1971	2,504	986	3,490	39.7	2,509
1972	2,751	1,160	3,911	41.2	2,912
1973	3,010	1,378	4,388	41.4	3,152
1974	3,442	1,714	5,156	41.6	3,976
1975	4,220	2,340	6,560	44.9	4,780
1976	4,697	2,466	7,163	42.6	5,633
1977	5,885	2,960	8,845	47.0	6,355
1978	5,855	3,221	9,076	44.3	6,643
1979	6,284	4,781	11,065	50.1	7,304
1980	7,305	3,721	11,026	44.1	8,486
1981	8,360	4,528	12,888	45.4	9,608
1982	9,951	5,100	15,051	47.5	11,530
1983	10,686	5,194	15,880	47.7	12,548
1984	10,606	5,404	16,010	45.7	13,493
1985	11,887	5,698	17,585	47.8	14,224
1986	12,339	6,089	18,428	47.5	14,595

Source: Statistics Canada, *National Income and Expenditure Accounts*; CANSIM.

General Purpose Transfers

Federal Government: General Purpose Transfers

Statutory Subsidies

The oldest of any Canadian transfers are those undertaken to be paid to the provinces by the federal government at the time they entered Confederation. It was essential to replace the revenues lost to the provinces through repeal of pre-Confederation tariffs and duties, but a certain element of political persuasion was no doubt also present. From time to time there were revisions of the "terms of union" on various grounds, extending even to the 1949 terms on which Newfoundland entered Confederation. In the total of general purpose grants now exceeding $6 billion these so-called "statutory subsidies" are today only a tiny part—a mere $36 million.

Equalization Payments

This is the largest element in general purpose transfers, accounting for 90 to 95 percent of the total in recent years. Briefly, the present objective of the payments is to ensure that the yield of provincial taxes and related revenue sources reflect not the actual tax rates and tax capacity of the province but a broader notional average base and tax rate. Where the actual (or potential) provincial yield is below the notional yields a grant is paid to make up the difference. Where the provincial yield exceeds the notional yield no grant is paid. As this is an innovation of the last 20 years it requires some detailed explanation.

Origin of Equalization

The roots of the present complex and extensive system lie in the basis of compensation under the immediate postwar tax rental agreements previously described. An explanation of the basis of this compensation was deferred to this point, where it properly falls. Briefly, while the wartime tax agreements payments were primarily direct compensation for the taxes being given up, under the 1947-51 agreements there were two main options open to the provinces, only one of which included any element of provincial taxation. (A third option applied only to one province). The basis of the two principal options was a per capita figure, $12.75 in one and $15.00 in the other. (It was disagreement over the amount of this per capita figure that was the ostensible reason for Ontario's refusal to enter into the arrangements).

Annual payments were made through adjustments of the resulting provincial base for increases in average growth in the three years preceding the years of payment in the population of the province and in the per capita gross national product. In total, payments rose under the agreements from $59 million in 1948 to $97 million in 1952, including payments to Newfoundland for the last four years.

The significant point for these beginnings is the absence of any serious attempt to balance the position of agreeing and non-agreeing provinces.

The former received payments for 1947-51 based mainly on accelerated per capita figures while the latter were left free room for their own taxes through credits against federal taxes at levels established by that government. There was no particular attempt to ensure a balance between the two positions.

The 1952-57 Agreements

The federal offer for renewal of the agreements presented two options: (1) basically a 50 percent increase in the minimums under the previous agreement or (2) an alternative based on actual yields in the province at standard rates for the three tax sources involved—personal and corporate income tax and death taxes. For this purpose the personal income tax calculation would be retained at 5 percent but the corporate tax would be raised; by negotiation with Ontario it was increased from 5 percent to 8½ percent. This alternative was obviously designed to achieve a more balanced position for Ontario and Quebec in relation to the other provinces.

A significant change in the adjustment formula, which finally clinched the deal with the agreeing provinces and possibly influenced Ontario as well, was the federal offer to calculate annual payments using the population and per capita GNP increase of the single year preceding the payment year rather than the average of the previous three years. The former system meant that revenues had lagged far behind expenditure in a dynamic period, and the provinces wanted greater currency. The increased emphasis on tax yields established a closer balance between the alternatives, and was sufficiently attractive to Ontario to sign an agreement for the 1952-57 period. Payments under the agreements rose from $335 million in 1952 to $389 million in 1956, exclusive of additional payments to Newfoundland.

The 1957-62 Arrangements

The 1957 fiscal arrangements broke with the past in abandoning a per capita basis of payment and resting compensation solely on the basis of the yield of standard taxes in a province. The significant new development was that these revenues would be "equalized" to a basis higher than the actual yield to the province. Equalization was to be an answer to the argument of the non-agreeing provinces, principally Quebec, that the alternative between autonomous taxation and a deal with the federal government was biased financially in favour of the latter. As a result of consultation with the provinces more intensive than any since the 1946-47 Reconstruction Conference, the federal government announced that it would seek in its proposals for the 1957-61 period to remove any pressure for conformity and to ensure equality of treatment whether the provinces levied their own taxes or continued to leave them in suspense. For the agreeing provinces the former per capita bases of compensation, now outmoded, would be replaced by an unconditional grant based on the yield of the three main taxes at standard rates. More importantly, the grant would be on an equalized basis; i.e., it would be sufficient to bring the yield of standard rates of tax to the yield of those rates in the two highest provinces. Grants would be paid whether or not the province levied its own taxes, but would be subject to a deduction for the self-levied revenue. The standard rates would be: personal income tax, 10 percent of federal rates; corporate tax, 9 percent of corporate profits; succession duties, 50 percent of federal rates. This was an improvement over the basis on which Ontario had entered an agreement in 1952, which called for a 5 percent rate for personal income tax and an 8½ percent corporate rate. The precedent for the 10 percent personal income tax rate was a credit in this amount granted Quebec taxpayers when that province introduced a personal income tax in 1954.

In addition to the basic unconditional payment, which would be calculated each year on data for that year, there were guarantees of minima below which the payment would not be allowed to fall. The former adjustment to increase the tax yields has since been known as "equalization," and the guarantees as "stabilization."

In the outcome payments were made to eight provinces under new tax rental agreements made up of (1) the yield of standard rates; and (2) an additional grant to bring yields to the equalized level. Although the formula called for stabilization grants no province qualified. Ontario re-imposed its corporate tax, but continued to have the federal government collect its personal income tax. As one of the two highest provinces it received no equalization payments. British Columbia was the other high province, but as it fell below the average of the top two—Ontario and British Columbia—it received some equalization. In 1958 the standard rate for personal income tax was raised to 13 percent, of benefit to all provinces. Special short-term grants were also instituted during this period for the maritime provinces and Newfoundland. Quebec continued to levy its own taxes, and qualified for equalization.

Unconditional payments to the provinces for statutory subsidies, tax rentals, and equalization rose from $372 million in 1957 to $534 million in 1961. Of this equalization was approximately 36 percent in each year.

The 1962-67 Arrangements

Although equalization had broadened the scope of the previous arrangements they were still tax rental agreements, under which eight provinces had undertaken not to impose certain taxes in return for compensation from the federal government. These were to be the last arrangements in that mould. From 1962 the scene shifted to the reverse situation; the provinces were placed in a position where they were forced to impose taxes to preserve their financial position. This came about by adoption of the tax collection system. In place of payments based on a share of federal taxes the federal government undertook to collect taxes for a province on personal and corporate incomes at any rate the province might choose, as long as its legislation was uniform with the federal act. These collections were turned over to the provinces, but in a separate calculation additional payments were made to equalize them to the yield of standard tax rates applied to a national base. The standard rate for personal income tax was raised from 10 to 16 percent at the outset to be accelerated to 26 percent by 1967, with subsequent increases. The notional standard base for equalization was changed by the Diefenbaker government from the two highest provinces to the average of all provinces, but in 1964 a re-elected Liberal government restored the two-highest-provinces base. In 1962 provincial natural resources revenue was added to the base calculation (to reduce or eliminate equalization payments to provinces receiving substantial resource revenues, principally Alberta and Saskatchewan) at 50 percent of a three-year average. Additional guarantees were given both for the preservation of former equalization rights and for stabilization.

As provincial revenues from the three main tax sources were no longer paid under a tax rental contract but as collections under provincial legislation, they were excluded from statistics of future unconditional federal payments (although the financial effect was unchanged). For this reason these transfers dropped from $534 million in 1961 to $269 million in 1962, but by 1966 had risen to $456 million. Equalization became a more prominent factor in the payment, rising from 54 percent in 1961 to 78 percent in 1962 and 81 percent in 1966. Under the post-tax rental system equalization was to assume first place, and has remained the principal element in the general purpose payments.

The New Equalization

The introduction in 1962 of natural resource revenues as a new element was the beginning of an evolution toward a completely different role for equalization. From its original purpose of balancing the position of agreeing and non-agreeing provinces it developed into a broadly based measure of great economic and political significance for equating the yield of the revenue systems of all provinces, now so vital that it was enshrined in the constitution. Although the exact considerations that moved the federal government in this direction in the mid-sixties are not clear, the idea was not without precedent. The concept of a grant system to equalize fiscal potential was inherent in proposals advanced at various times over the previous half century, as, for example, those of the Rowell Sirois Commission. It had frequently been supported by the Maritime and western provinces, and had been put forward by some of these provinces in federal-provincial conferences in 1963. There was precedent in the ad hoc Atlantic provinces grants, and the Atlantic provinces, Manitoba and Saskatchewan had argued for a generalized and permanent system that would extend to more taxes and equalize yields to the level of the highest province. This approach of course did not always meet with warm approval from the more affluent provinces, which regarded money so spent as lost to the cause of reducing federal tax rates to give them more tax room.

The die was cast for the new approach in 1967 with the extension of equalization to include most major provincial revenue sources—16 in all. With this expansion the process of calculation also became much more complex. As some elements of the process remained constant the following description from *The National Finances* of the initial 1967-72 computation will give a helpful beginning.

For each of the revenue sources, a base was chosen to represent, as closely as possible, the actual base of that revenue source. Total revenue for all provinces from that source was then divided by the nationwide base to arrive at a "national average provincial revenue rate"—that is, the rate that, when applied to the base, would yield the revenue shown for that source. This rate was then applied to the base in a particular province and the resultant "tax" was divided by the provincial population to obtain the per capita yield of the "tax" at the national average rate. The difference between this per capita yield and the national average per capita yield, multiplied by the province's population, represented the equalization due the province with respect to that revenue source. Total equalization for each province represented the sum of the equalization amounts, both positive and negative, calculated for each revenue source. The calculation could also be worked out directly from percentage shares developed in the 1972 formula. The difference between the province's percentage share of population and its percentage share of the base was applied to the national revenue from that base to arrive at the equalization factor from that base. Thus a province with a relatively small income tax base—that is, low basic federal tax per capita—received equalization entitlements with respect to personal income. For most provinces receiving equalization, using national averages and aggregates minimized the effect of changing tax rates on equalization payments, since the larger provinces had a greater weight in establishing the national average.

Each province was guaranteed an equalization payment as high as its equalization and stabilization payments for the final year of the former agreements (1966-67). Special transitional arrangements were made for Saskatchewan, which appeared likely to lose its equalization payment abruptly under the new formula. Nova Scotia, New Brunswick, and Newfoundland were each guaranteed an additional equalization payment of $10.5 million, and Prince Edward Island $3.5 million, the equivalent of the payments under the Atlantic Provinces Additional Grants which were not continued.[17.6]

The system as adopted in 1967 employed national average tax bases and national average tax rates for 16 individual taxes. Under it total payments rose from $456 million in 1966 to $1,149 million in 1971. Of the latter amount 91 percent was for equalization.

The 1972-77 Arrangements

The same basic formula was continued, with some additions and changes in the taxes involved. At the outset three new sources were included to extend the total to 19; in 1973 a significant addition was municipal taxes imposed for local school purposes. The element of oil and natural gas revenues,

---

[17.6]Canadian Tax Foundation, *The National Finances, 1986-87* (Toronto: the foundation, 1987), 16:5.

inflated by OPEC actions, was reduced to revenue from basic sources by excluding the increase resulting from price rises. "Basic" petroleum revenues were fully equalized; "additional" revenues were equalized only to the extent of one-third. These changes brought the total of sources being equalized to 23.

A new form of payment was added during this period. As a price of provincial acceptance of the major tax reforms of 1972 the federal government guaranteed that no province would receive less revenue than it would have under the previous system. Total general transfers rose from $1,149 million in 1971 to $3,146 million in 1976. Of the latter amount $2,169 million (66 percent) was equalization and $943 million (29 percent) was revenue guarantee.

The 1977-82 Arrangements

At the outset the list of sources for equalization was extended to 29. But natural resource revenues were restricted to one-half and their equalization could not exceed one-third of total equalization for all sources. However, further rises in oil revenues over-ran these restrictions and with the prospect that even Ontario would become a recipient province, further restraints were introduced (mainly reduction in revenues from sale of Crown leases). As a final bar to Ontario it was ruled that no province with a per capita income higher than the national average could receive equalization. The full revenue guarantee, originally enacted for five years, expired during this period. A further limited guarantee for personal income tax revenue produced a small payment in only one year. Total payments rose from $3,146 million in 1976 to $3,662 million in 1981. Of the latter amount 99 percent was for equalization.

1982-87

A House of Commons Task Force, in its Report, *Fiscal Federalism in Canada*. (August 1981) approved of equalization, but recommended that property taxes for municipal purposes be added to the list and some unspecified further adjustments be made to limit the effect of resource revenues. A paper tabled with the budget in November 1981 proposed that municipal property tax and natural resource revenues be added to the formula, and that the yield of taxes in Ontario be the standard for equalization rather than the national average. An overall limitation however was that the rise in total payments each year would be restricted to the increase in GNP. In subsequent negotiations the equalization yield was set as the average for Quebec, Ontario, Manitoba, Saskatchewan, and British Columbia. The exclusion of Alberta from this formula avoided the problem of equalizing the other provinces to the Alberta level of revenues from oil. There were refinements in the new formula and further guarantees were given for an easy transition from the previous system. As well, in 1985-86 supplementary equalization payments were given to six provinces and Manitoba also received a substantial payment under the guarantee provision.

No payments had been made under the stabilization provision until 1983-84, when British Columbia entered a request and received payments both in that and the following year.

Other Federal General Purpose Transfers

Other transfers are for a variety of unrelated purposes. One of the oldest is a payment to the provinces of a share of the federal income tax paid by public utilities engaged in the generation or distribution, or both, of electrical energy, gas, or steam. During World War II the provinces saw the federal 100 percent excess profits tax on electric power and other utilities as an invasion of their right to natural resources revenue. The trend had been strongly to nationalization of utility companies, and the fact that they could be taken over mainly at the expense of the federal government was a considerable inducement. To remove this temptation the federal government offered to pay to the provinces over 90 percent, later increased to 95 percent, of its tax revenues from these companies. These payments continue today and have amounted to nearly $300 million annually.

Grants to municipalities in lieu of taxes on its real properties have also been paid since the early 1950s. There had previously been ad hoc arrangements with cities, like Ottawa, with heavy concentrations of government property, but the legislation of 1949 established a general system for the whole country. This was revised to a more comprehensive basis in 1980. In recent years these grants have amounted to nearly $300 million, most of it to municipalities.

In 1977 a long-standing issue of uncertainty and dispute was cleared up with legislation authorizing reciprocal agreements between federal and provincial governments to clarify liability for payment of consumption taxes. In 1982 the legislation was extended to include licences for off-road vehicles. In recent years federal payments have been in the $250 million area. Other payments have included amounts to Nova Scotia under the offshore oil and gas agreement with that province.

Table 17.13 sums up payments under the main federal general purpose transfer programs from 1947 to 1986.

Provincial Governments: General Purpose Transfers

All provinces make revenue supporting grants to their municipalities. Although of considerably less importance than transfers for specific expenditure, such as those for education, they are nonetheless an important element in support of general operations.

These grants fall into two classes: a grant in lieu of local property taxes on provincial properties, and a more general grant in support of local services. The former, although far from uniform, in practice takes the same general shape—a proportion varying from 100 percent to a much lower percentage of the real property tax that would otherwise be payable, with a great variety of exemptions and special arrangements. The general payments vary materially from province to province, and involve factors such as population, households, road mileage, density, policing, size and type of municipality, tax potential and tax effort, equalized assessment, a share of general or specific provincial taxes, etc. In 1979-80 Alberta favoured its municipalities with grants sufficient to retire most of their debt, and have relieved them of other burdens through grants and remissions.

The relative importance of the two types of grant in recent years is indicated by table 17.14, giving the latest figures available at the time of writing.

Specific Purpose Transfers

Under this rather unedifying title lies much of the substance of the twentieth century Canadian state. It is through the use of the superior money power of senior levels of government that politicians have implemented their own concepts of the ideal society and impressed on the citizens the unquestionable merits of a particular brand of politics. It has been propounded by some political scientists that the primary reason for sponsorship of social programs by central governments was to be able to exert a direct influence on citizens otherwise remote from the national sphere. Pragmatically, a transfer of funds between levels of government has been the easiest solution to the imbalance between revenue powers and expenditure responsibilities in the Canadian federation where massive amounts of money for new programs are involved. As we have seen, the transfers have taken many forms: by 1987 their management had become one of the principal functions of government, and their complexity and massive cost had put them beyond the understanding of all but a few experts. This is mostly true of grants in fulfilment of the grand social designs of the mid-twentieth century, with programs that will be examined in detail later. For the present we are mainly concerned with placing these programs in the context of intergovernmental grants in the postwar period.

Federal Government: Specific Purpose Transfers

Federal aid for specific provincial and local purposes is by no means a recent phenomenon. The federal government gave grants as long ago as 1900 for formation of 4-H clubs; in 1909 for railway grade crossings; in 1913 for agricultural instruction; in 1918 for employment offices; in 1919 for highway construction, combatting venereal disease, technical education, and collection of vital statistics. There followed a series of grants in aid of local bridge and wharf construction, to be succeeded in 1927 by the largest of the pre-World War II programs, the joint means-tested old age pension. During the Great Depression there were several federal programs to assist with relief and unemployment, and in 1936 joint pensions were instituted for blind persons; lesser grants for wharves and bridges continued to be popular. 1939 brought a further venture in the educational area with grants for youth training, to be superseded in 1942 by the Vocational Training Coordination Act. New programs in 1943 provided grants for national

Table 17.13 Federal Government: General Purpose Transfers to Provinces and Municipalities, 1947-86

Year[a]	Statutory subsidies	Equalization	Revenue guarantee	Reciprocal taxation	PUITTA[b]	Municipal grants[c]	Other[d]	Total
					millions of dollars			
1947	17.1	—	—	—	2.9	—	—	20.0
1948	17.1	—	—	—	3.7	—	—	20.8
1949	25.7	—	—	—	1.4	.4	—	27.5
1950	25.2	—	—	—	4.6	1.4	—	31.2
1951	26.6	—	—	—	3.7	2.0	—	32.3
1952	25.8	—	—	—	4.4	2.5	—	32.7
1953	24.9	—	—	—	6.8	3.4	—	35.1
1954	24.3	—	—	—	7.3	3.4	—	35.0
1955	23.4	—	—	—	7.9	7.2	—	38.5
1956	22.8	—	—	—	6.6	9.7	—	39.1
1957	22.0	136.0	—	—	7.4	17.5	—	182.9
1958	35.2	168.4	—	—	8.7	21.9	—	234.2
1959	28.7	208.0	—	—	4.8	22.6	—	264.1
1960	28.7	214.0	—	—	4.2	24.6	—	271.5
1961	31.5	189.7	—	—	6.4	24.9	—	252.5
1962	31.5	211.6	—	—	10.0	29.4	—	315.5
1963	31.6	202.4	—	—	8.9	31.7	—	274.6
1964	31.6	261.6	—	—	9.7	36.2	—	339.1
1965	31.6	310.0	—	—	6.4	37.1	—	385.1
1966	31.6	370.5	—	—	6.0	38.4	—	446.5
1967	31.7	547.6	—	—	6.7	40.8	—	628.6
1968	31.7	566.1	—	—	20.8	44.3	—	662.9
1969	31.8	683.3	—	—	23.6	49.5	—	788.2
1970	31.8	899.2	—	—	23.9	52.2	—	1,007.1
1971	33.8	1,049.6	—	—	24.3	55.4	—	1,163.1
1972	33.7	1,176.8	—	—	80.0	61.8	—	1,372.3
1973	33.8	1,500.1	42.6	—	25.9	62.7	—	1,665.1
1974	33.8	1,795.0	475.2	—	26.7	68.2	—	2,408.9

1975.	33.8	460.5	—	31.8	76.0	—	2,558.6
1976.	33.8	943.1	—	38.5	88.5	—	3,273.4
1977.	34.0	600.4	46.7	45.9	117.0	—	3,365.2
1978.	34.0	121.6	100.4	81.8	130.8	—	3,101.0
1979.	34.1	72.1	105.3	66.3	127.6	—	3,715.0
1980.	34.1	—	107.3	64.3	153.7	—	3,669.1
1981.	35.6	—	131.9	78.9	165.7	—	4,039.3
1982.	35.8	—	157.4	141.9	214.0	87.0	5,903.5
1983.	35.7	—	198.7	180.7	228.7	−101.6	5,891.6
1984.	35.8	—	209.3	291.2	274.9	−85.6	6,120.8
1985.	35.8	—	242.8	299.1	237.9	−229.1	5,962.3
1986.	35.9	—	263.3	290.0	283.7	−239.6	6,024.8

a Fiscal years nearest December 31 of year named. b Public Utilities Income Tax Transfer Act. c Mainly payments in lieu of property tax. d Various additional payments under short-term programs, less a deduction from Quebec for recovery of youth allowances.

Sources: Canadian Tax Foundation: Perry, Background of Current Fiscal Problems, p. 64; The National Finances.

Table 17.14   Provincial Governments: General Purpose Transfers to Local Governments, 1967-84

Year[a]	Grants in lieu of taxes[b]	General grants	Total
	millions of dollars		
1967	12.0	246.1	258.1
1968	23.3	266.3	289.6
1969	20.3	303.8	324.1
1970	14.5	311.6	326.2
1971	18.0	332.0	350.0
1972	23.0	391.6	414.6
1973	26.4	581.6	608.1
1974	36.0	695.5	731.5
1975	25.4	867.6	893.0
1976	27.4	1,039.4	1,066.8
1977	37.4	1,076.9	1,114.3
1978	39.9	1,341.7	1,381.6
1979	37.0	1,479.7	2,516.7
1980	222.7	1,008.5	1,231.1
1981	257.4	1,341.0	1,598.4
1982	296.7	1,334.0	1,630.7
1983	322.4	1,415.9	1,738.3
1984	312.5	1,465.4	1,777.9

[a]Fiscal year nearest December 31 of year named. [b]Excludes government-owned enterprises.

Source: Statistics Canada, *Provincial Government Finance.*

physical fitness and for lime production. Education again emerged in 1945, with federal grants for vocational schools, and in 1946 with grants for foremanship and supervisory training. Meanwhile a variety of grants for local highway and bridge construction and other infrastructure developments were given.

Postwar Developments

Many of these programs were of short duration, and most had expired at the outset of the postwar period. The joint old age pensions and the blind persons allowance were the only functioning measures of any significance, although federal assistance for vocational training had been temporarily renewed in 1946. As mentioned, the federal government offered a new program of social measures at the Reconstruction Conference in 1945-46, and their rejection left them in abeyance. The following is a brief outline of subsequent developments, with emphasis mainly on financial aspects involving intergovernmental grants.

Health

In 1948 the federal government introduced a program of grants for general health expenditures. These included 50 percent grants for hospital construction and cancer control and outright grants for a long list of other expenditures, including professional training, mental health, tuberculosis control, venereal disease control, public health research, general public health, health surveys, medical rehabilitation, and crippled children. To these were added grants for child and maternal health and laboratory and radiological services in 1953. The program continued for 24 years and was finally withdrawn in March 1972, by which time some $878 million had been distributed in federal grants. The largest part of the expenditure was for hospital construction.

Hospital Insurance

In 1958 the federal government, following a lead set by four provincial governments, introduced a national program of insurance for hospital care, to be effective from July 1, 1958. Under agreements with the provinces the federal government undertook to pay approximately one-half the provincial cost of providing specified hospital and diagnostic services under provincially-administered hospital plans for both in-patients and out-patients. (The actual formula adopted by the federal government was the sum of two amounts of 25 percent, one being the per capita national cost of in-patient services and the other being the same per capita cost but for the recipient province, less the per capita charges made by the province to patients (if any), times the number of persons eligible for the service). There was no limit to the amount of the payment to any province, and no conditions as to how the province would finance its share of the cost.

Grants for hospital insurance rapidly became the highest of the federal transfer payments, and remain such in 1988. (See table 17.15).

Medical Insurance

In 1968 the federal government announced a plan for joint federal-provincial health insurance, commonly known as medicare. For a provincial plan meeting the conditions of comprehensiveness of scope, universal coverage, public administration, and portability the federal government would pay approximately half the annual cost (calculated as one-half the per capita national cost of providing insured services times the average number of insured persons in the province). From January 1, 1971, all provinces had plans in place, and medicare payments rapidly rose to approximately half the level of hospital insurance payments (about $1 billion for medicare as against $2 billion for hospital insurance in 1976).

Extended Health Care

In 1977 the federal government offered additional grants to cover health services not embraced in the existing programs. These included nursing home intermediate care, lower level residential care for adults, health aspects of home care, and ambulatory health services not covered by the existing agreements. The new program absorbed grants for nursing home care begun in 1974 and replaced some expenditures under the Canada Assistance Plan. First, payment was made at $20 per capita, later years being accelerated for growth in GNP per capita. From an initial outlay of $460 million the cost of this program rapidly escalated to $1 billion in 1986-87.

Other Health Programs

Other minor health programs for which grants were paid included the Health Resources Fund in 1966, health training facilities and resources in 1967, family planning services in 1970, and health care for Indian communities in 1978.

Established Programs Financing—Health

In 1977 a change in the federal financing of health programs was introduced. Mention was made earlier of the procedure of replacing or supplementing direct cash payments with reductions or abatements in federal taxes in favour of the provinces, a plan first introduced in 1960 to allow Quebec to "contract-out" of federal programs. It had also been used in the 1967-72 period for federal support for post-secondary education, when existing per capita grants were replaced in part by the yield of 4 points of personal income tax and 1 point of corporate income tax.

Established Programs Financing, 1976

This method was adopted after 1976, in combination with cash payments, for financing the federal contributions for the health programs and post-secondary education, regarded by this time as "established." A new wrinkle was introduced, however. Previously under the tax "abatement" procedure the federal government calculated the equalized value of a designated part of its taxes and paid the resulting amount to the province as a share of its aid to a program. Under the tax transfer system adopted after 1976 the federal government reduced its taxes by a designated amount to give tax room for provincial increases and offset the value of that reduction against the payment it would otherwise make. In the result, the province was compelled to levy a similar tax to maintain its position.

Under the new arrangement the 4 point personal income tax transfer for post-secondary education was increased to 13.5 percent. (As a percentage of the reduced federal tax the 4 percent personal income tax credit was raised to 4.357 percent to be equivalent, and 9.143 percent was added to produce a 13.5 percent transfer). Along with the previous 1 point for corporate income tax, the annual equalized yield of these taxes was calculated as part of the transfer to the province.

Other changes were made concurrently. There had been differences in the per capita cash payments previously received by the provinces, and these were eliminated by phasing in a common national average for all. A change from past practice was the tying of future annual cash payments to growth in the GNP per capita, a feature still in effect. Transitional and levelling payments were included to protect provinces in the change to the new basis.

In effect, after 1976 federal support for provincial hospital insurance and medicare became a combination of cash payments and tax transfers, and remains so today. Further changes in the relationship between these two elements were significant, however.

EPF 1982-87

In 1982 the cash and tax transfer elements of the program were assimilated; this involved bringing the per capita cash payments and tax credits together in a per capita amount that was the same for all provinces. (The previous levelling had applied only to the cash payments). A 1976 base was established for each province representing the combined national average per capita federal contribution under both cash payments and tax credits, and annual payments were this base amount accelerated by the average increase in national per capita GNP in the three years preceding the year of payment times the population of the province. This calculation established a global entitlement for the EPF programs, and without the tax transfers would be the amount paid in cash. However, the equalized value of the tax transfers was deducted, and the cash payment to the province for the two health programs and post-secondary education was the balance remaining after this deduction.

In effect, under the system a grant based on actual expenditures for health care—a true conditional transfer—had been replaced by an annual amount that reflected health expenditures only in the 1976 base per capita allocation, and then only roughly. The amount transferred each year is not related in any other way to actual provincial health expenditure of the year, nor is there any requirement that it be so related. Furthermore there was not even any requirement that the base ratio of health to post-secondary educational expenditures be maintained. In effect the EPF transfers had become "block grants," to be spent in the discretion of the province, presumably at least within the EPF program areas. This result was to have consequences that had to be faced by the federal authorities, a subject for later exploration.

Later Developments

In the revised formula the acceleration based on GNP has become the crucial controllable element governing growth, and federal efforts at restraint have been concentrated on its manipulation. In 1983 and 1984 increases in payments for post-secondary education were limited to 6 and 5 percent respectively, but in 1985 additional payments made up the shortfall. Under legislation governing the 1987-91 arrangements the escalation for GNP increases will be limited to the excess over 2 percent. These restrictions have brought strong protests from provincial premiers, with renewal of long-standing complaints that the federal government lures the provinces into programs with substantial initial financing and later leaves them to carry the main load.

It should be emphasized that the so-called established programs financing applies only to the three programs cited above. Another very heavy program, the Canada Assistance Act, is not part of the EPF program.

Some Estimates of Cost

The ceding of tax room in lieu of direct cash grants has created a problem for the presentation of the budgetary effect of the EPF programs. Undoubtedly the reduction in federal revenues resulting from the transfer of 13.5 points of personal income tax and 1 point of corporate income tax when introduced in 1976 had the same effect on the budget as the corresponding amount of expenditure increase; and is still having that effect, one which can be measured annually. And undoubtedly this was the deal made with and accepted by the provinces. But this arrangement, made fourteen years ago, is now almost a historic curiosity, and seems to be nearly irrelevant to 1988 conditions. For one, the impact of the tax transfers has long since been absorbed in reduced federal tax revenues, and their retention in the EPF formula only gives the federal government some credit, or possibly some solace, for past benevolences, at the cost of a much simplified procedure. For another, the cash payments are the only concrete and relevant aspect of EPF today, and one would think that a system of acceleration of those transfers from a recent base would serve the same purpose as the present cumbersome arrangements. In fact, under the clutter this is nearly the present system. While in the pre-EPF arrangements the grants were directly related to a sharable cost of provincial health services, as stated above, under the EPF they became essentially a block grant calculated as a per capita amount for 1975-76 accelerated by the increase in a three-year moving average of GNP per capita. As the same formula is used for determining federal grants for post-secondary education an arbitrary allocation must be used to determine the two proportions based on their accidental relationship in 1975-76. And in the end the whole calculation is fictitious because there is no requirement that the province spend the funds on either health or education (but with the enormous pressure on these two services it is almost inevitable that the money is so spent, although not specifically on the assumed allocation between the two). Where we speak therefore of health or education transfers it must be recalled that the calculation is purely an arbitrary one based on formulae having no more than a very remote relationship to the function. As such it could easily be replaced by something much more realistic and understandable. At any rate, however they are determined, it is only the cash payments that have a direct effect on federal government expenditures, and only the cash payments are taken into account in the following review of federal government expenditures on EPF programs.

For health, as a percent of total federal expenditures cash payments rose from about 1 percent of total federal expenditure in 1958 to a peak of 7.9 percent in 1972, and have since dropped to 5.7 percent in 1986. As a percent of total major federal transfers to other governments cash payments for health were 47 percent in 1963, fell to 29 percent in 1967 as other new programs were introduced, rose sharply to 39 percent in 1972, fell to 32 percent in 1977, and have been in the 32-35 percent range since. In short, cash payments for health now count for 6-7 percent of total federal expenditure and about one-third of transfers to other governments.

See table 17.15 for federal health transfers for 1958 to 1987.

Education

Education in Canada, as aforementioned, is clearly and indisputably a provincial responsibility. There have been efforts over many years to have the federal government intervene more directly, but there is no reason to suppose from past attitudes that it would welcome a change in present arrangements—rather the reverse.

The federal government has some limited direct responsibilities, such as the education of native peoples under its jurisdiction. Some 100,000 veterans attended government-supported university courses after World War II and there are schools and colleges for current members of the armed services and their children. Its most direct contact with broader areas of education has been in matters related to the economy and in higher education. Here intervention has taken many forms over a long period of years, commencing, as mentioned, with grants for "agricultural instruction" as long ago as 1913. Following World War I there were grants to provinces for technical education, and by periodic extensions some type of vocational training grants were extended intermittently through World War II. They were followed by grants under the Vocational Training Co-ordination Act, 1944; assistance to vocational schools, 1945; foremanship and supervisory training, 1946; training for unemployed, 1948; training for disabled, 1949; vocational correspondence courses, 1950.

There were many other programs that would qualify as grants for education (e.g. grants for medical education under the 1949 health plan, grants for university research by various federal bodies, etc.). However, the most ambitious federal-provincial joint programs were the Technical and Vocational Training Assistance Act (1961 to 1967), university grants (1951 to 1966), and grants for post-secondary education (1967 to date).

Vocational Training

The Technical and Vocational Training Assistance Act of 1960 greatly expanded the existing programs in an effort to ease unemployment among unskilled workers. Emphasis was on training of technicians and technologists, and for some programs grants were in excess of 50 percent. Much of the expenditure was for training facilities. There had been capital assistance grants from 1945; these were continued under the new legislation, at a 75 percent rate for expenditures made prior to April 1963. Grants were also given for occupational training under shared-cost programs prior to 1967, but in that year the federal government assumed the full cost of adult job training, except in Alberta, under the Adult Occupational Training Act. Under this legislation it continued its program for payments of 75 percent of the capital cost of training facilities, at an outlay by 1972 of $695 million.

Table 17.15 Federal Government: Cash Payments and Tax Transfers to Provinces, Health Programs, 1958-87[a]

Year[b]	Cash payments			Tax transfers[d]	Total transfers	Cash payments as percent of	
	Insured health services[c]	Extended health care	Total			Major transfers to governments[e]	Total federal expenditure[e]
	millions of dollars					percent	
1958	54.7	—	54.7	—	54.7	10.9	0.9
1959	150.6	—	150.6	—	150.6	30.1	2.5
1960	188.9	—	188.9	—	188.9	31.5	2.3
1961	283.2	—	283.2	—	283.2	42.5	3.8
1962	335.8	—	335.8	—	335.8	43.4	4.4
1963	391.3	—	391.3	—	391.3	47.2	4.7
1964	433.0	—	433.0	—	433.0	45.4	5.1
1965	354.5	—	354.5	—	354.4	40.4	4.1
1966	383.7	—	383.7	—	383.7	36.4	3.9
1967	435.1	—	435.1	—	435.1	28.9	3.9
1968	583.3	—	583.3	—	583.3	31.4	4.7
1969	805.9	—	805.9	—	805.9	35.3	5.8
1970	1,088.6	—	1,088.6	—	1,088.6	36.1	7.0
1971	1,399.0	—	1,399.0	—	1,399.0	38.2	7.7
1972	1,648.7	—	1,648.7	—	1,648.7	39.3	7.9
1973	1,754.4	—	1,754.4	—	1,754.4	37.3	7.2
1974	2,121.1	—	2,121.1	—	2,121.1	35.6	6.8
1975	2,548.5	—	2,548.5	—	2,548.5	36.7	6.8
1976	3,008.2	—	3,008.2	—	3,008.2	35.4	7.4
1977	2,350.4	464.5	2,814.9	1,834.7	4,649.6	32.5	6.3
1978	2,968.1	520.3	3,488.4	1,978.5	5,466.9	36.0	7.0
1979	3,270.7	582.2	3,852.9	2,153.6	6,006.5	35.9	7.2

Year							
1980	3,473.1	640.4	4,113.5	2,495.0	6,608.5	35.0	6.6
1981	3,856.9	711.0	4,567.9	2,778.5	7,364.4	33.2	6.1
1982	3,465.4	815.0	4,280.4	3,602.6	7,883.0	29.3	4.8
1983	4,624.2	939.5	5,563.7	3,556.6	9,120.3	32.2	5.7
1984	4,114.6	1,009.1	6,123.7	3,779.6	9,903.3	32.0	5.6
1985	5,310.1	1,074.8	6,384.8	4,418.5	10,803.3	33.0	5.7
1986	4,412.9	1,139.5	6,652.4	4,349.0	11,001.4	33.5	5.7
1987	5,666.8	1,210.1	6,876.9	5,347.0	12,223.9	na	5.5

[a]Estimates only from 1977 onward. [b]Fiscal year ended nearest December 31 of the year named. [c]Hospital insurance and medicare. [d]Allocated on Treasury Board ratio of 68 percent for health services. [e]Based on federal government expenditure data from Table A.4, Part 1, and 1988 Fiscal Plan.

Source: Canadian Tax Foundation, *The National Finances*, and table 17.10.

Grants under these and earlier programs amounted to $813.3 million in 1962-67, and nearly a further $700 million was spent from 1967 to 1972, when the legislation expired (see table 17.10).

University Grants

Commencing in 1951 the federal government gave grants to provinces in support of universities. These were conditional but required no matching funds from the province. Paid as a per capita grant based on the provincial population, the rate started at 50 cents in 1951, rose to $1.00 in 1957, and to $1.50 in 1958, where it remained until 1966. Payments averaged $36 million in the last five years of the program.

Post-Secondary Education

In 1967 the per capita university grants were replaced by tax abatements of 4 percentage points of personal income tax and 1 point of corporate income tax, both, as with most tax transfers, on an equalized yield basis. This followed the tax transfer procedure adopted for opting out, and was the first major step towards the EPF type of aid—i.e., grants with no conditions attached. In addition to these tax value transfers some element of the previous system survived in a payment of 50 percent of post-secondary educational operating expenses (minimum $15 per capita) accelerated at the national rate of growth for such expenses.

The changes in established programs financing (health and post-secondary education) in 1976 have already been set forth in detail. Anyone wishing a further very helpful exposition of the basic elements in the formula for education may consult an official publication, *Federal and Provincial Support to Post-secondary Education in Canada, A Report to Parliament*, 1985-86.[17.7] The essential results of the computation for education are given in table 17.16, with tax credit values allocated on the same basis as health grants.

The total cash cost of federal post-secondary education assistance grew from $19 million in 1961 to $2.4 billion in 1987. As a ratio of federal expenditure the cash transfer has remained fairly consistently in the 2 to 2.5 percent range. As a share of total grants to other governments education has recently been in the region of 12 percent.

Other Educational Programs

Grants have been made for various other purposes, including instruction and language assistance for immigrants, bilingualism, bilingualism in public administration, shared cost schools for Indians, and co-operative education.

[17.7] Canada, Secretary of State, *Federal and Provincial Support to Post-Secondary* Education in Canada. A Report to Parliament (Ottawa: Supply and Services, 1987).

Table 17.16 Federal Government: Cash Payments and Tax Transfers to Provinces, Post-Secondary Education, 1961-87[a]

Year[b]	Cash payments	Tax transfers[c]	Total	Cash Payments as percent of Federal transfers to governments[d]	Federal expenditure[d]
	millions of dollars			*percent*	
1961	19.4	—	19.4	2.9	0.3
1962	26.3	—	29.3	3.4	0.4
1963	26.8	—	26.8	3.2	0.3
1964	27.3	—	27.3	2.9	0.3
1965	27.7	—	27.7	3.2	0.3
1966	70.9	—	70.9	6.7	0.7
1967	108.0	227.6	335.6	7.1	1.0
1968	276.6	247.0	523.6	14.9	2.2
1969	301.4	307.0	608.4	13.2	2.1
1970	388.3	341.3	729.6	12.9	2.5
1971	450.4	398.5	848.9	12.3	2.5
1972	481.1	468.9	950.0	11.5	2.3
1973	485.1	581.1	1,066.2	10.4	2.0
1974	503.6	708.2	1,211.8	8.4	1.6
1975	535.0	955.4	1,490.4	7.7	1.4
1976	648.7	904.1	1,552.8	7.6	1.6
1977	1,001.0	1,059.0	2,136.0	11.6	2.2
1978	1,302.0	1,290.0	2,448.0	13.4	2.6
1979	1,494.0	1,371.0	2,796.0	13.9	2.2
1980	1,596.0	1,602.0	3,151.0	13.6	2.6
1981	1,625.0	1,819.0	3,548.0	11.8	2.2
1982	1,532.0	1,911.0	3,716.0	10.4	1.7
1983	2,065.0	1,951.0	3,979.0	11.8	2.1
1984	2,265.0	2,104.0	4,218.0	11.9	2.1
1985	2,278.0	2,237.0	4,525.0	11.8	2.0
1986	2,380.0	2,442.9	4,802.9	12.0	2.0
1987	2,366.0	2,687.1	5,053.1	na	1.9

[a]Estimates only from 1977 onward. [b]Fiscal year ended nearest December 31 of the year named. [c]Allocated on Treasury Board ratio of 32 percent for post-secondary education. [d]Budgetary.

Source: Canada, Department of Secretary of State, *Federal and Provincial Support to Post-Secondary Education in Canada*, A Report to Parliament, 1985-86, 163: Tables A4, Part 1, and 17.10.

Social Services

The principal programs are now federally supported, a predominant trend since the introduction of family allowances in 1945 and old age security pensions in 1952. Joint pensions for the blind were begun in 1937; in the early fifties these were revised and joint pensions for old age assistance, disabled persons assistance, and unemployment assistance were added. The federal government paid 75 percent of blind persons allowances and 50 percent of the other allowances; all were administered by the provinces.

Canada Assistance Plan

In 1966 a federal measure was introduced to consolidate these plans and extend federal assistance on a much broader basis than ever before, covering nearly all provincial social activities. The basic program is a 50 percent sharing of the province's expenditure in meeting "basic requirements" of recipients, defined to include food, shelter, clothing, fuel, utilities, household supplies, and personal requirements. Such recipients must be "in need," and a means test is provided by which this condition can be established. The range of programs that are eligible includes assistance to needy mothers and dependent children, homemaker services, home support and similar services for families in need. Other eligible programs include various aspects of child welfare, special employment projects, and the improvement of welfare services. As mentioned earlier, some CAP functions were transferred to thé extended health care program in 1977. In 1978 a bill was introduced by the short-lived conservative government to adopt a payment formula similar to the EPF system, but this was not implemented by the successor Liberal government. The cost-sharing basis remains in effect therefore for this major program; there is no ceiling on annual expenditures. With heavy unemployment and increased numbers of families requiring assistance, grants under CAP rose from $2.2 billion in 1979 to over $4 billion in 1987. See table 17.17 for 1967-87 data.

Other Social Assistance Programs

A variety of other programs have been the subject of federal grants over time. Many of these relate to Indians or other native peoples, such as those of 1961 (child care); 1965, (community development and social services); 1971, (winter projects); 1978, (tripartite services), etc. Other programs include grants for self-help for elderly groups under the New Horizons program, 1972; grants toward a guaranteed income experiment in Manitoba, 1973-74; grants for nursing home care, 1974 (later absorbed under Extended Health Care); grants for services for young offenders, 1974; grants for welfare information systems, 1975. There were also numerous other programs, many of temporary duration.

Transportation

Forty years ago it was not possible to cross Canada by automobile, or at least not safely and in comfort on hard-surfaced roads. To remedy this serious national shortcoming the federal government instituted the Trans-Canada Highway plan in 1950, with grants to provinces varying from 10 to 50 percent. By 1971 over $825 million had been spent in completing this project.

There were also numerous other joint highway projects, including roads to resources in 1958, a Gaspé highway in 1965, a trunk highway program for the Atlantic provinces in 1966, prairie highway strengthening and western northlands highways in 1974, and strengthening of the highway network in 1977. In addition various bridges, rail line extensions, ferry

Table 17.17 Federal Government Share of Canada Assistance Plan Payments,
1967-87

Year[a]	Total Payment	Year[a]	Total Payment
	$ million		$ million
1967	21.0	1978	1,986.6
1968	456.5	1979	2,179.0
1969	521.9	1980	2,430.0
1970	580.3	1981	2,806.0
1971	782.1	1982	3,243.4
1972	987.1	1983	4,165.1
1973	1,027.2	1984	3,287.6
1974	1,079.4	1985	3,635.3
1975	1,374.9	1986	3,867.1
1976	1,606.9	1987	4,001.4
1977	1,808.3		

[a] Fiscal year ending nearest December 31 of year named.

Sources: Study Team Report to the Task Force on Program Review, *Canada Assistance Plan* and Canadian Tax Foundation, *The National Finances*.

services, and other infrastructure projects were subsidized, along with purchase of rolling stock for commuter services, buses for inter-urban use, and ship construction.

Natural Resources

It is not unexpected that Canada's ample natural resources have required frequent attention from government. Joint action was almost essential, as jurisdiction was shared in many instances by the two authorities.

In the area of water resources alone over 40 joint projects are recorded. Many of these were studies of present and future use including, recently, environmental effects in the Great Lakes, St. Lawrence River, and the Hudson and James Bay. Others involved major construction projects, among the leading being flood assistance for the Red River at Winnipeg, 1950, and further construction of the Greater Winnipeg Floodway, 1962, and Red River Dyking in 1968 (in total exceeding $50 million); and the South Saskatchewan River project, 1958-67, (in total exceeding $112 million). Various other projects for conservation or flood and drainage control included those in the Humber Valley and Upper Thames rivers and the Halton, Metro Toronto, and southwest regions of Ontario; the Fraser River and Okanagan Valley in British Columbia; The Saskatchewan, Nelson and Assiniboine Rivers and the Qu'Appelle Valley in the Prairies, the Maritime Marshlands, and flooding in the city of Montreal.

Forestry has been the subject of many joint programs. These have included inventory taking, reforestation, access roads, fire prevention and protection measures, spruce budworm spraying, measures against jack-pine infestation, and the establishment of the Forest Engineering Research Institute in 1975.

. Other joint projects have related to fisheries and mineral industrial development. Closely connected with the latter have been studies related to use and conservation of non-renewable energy resources, including coal, uranium, oil sands, heavy oils, etc. and alternative power sources, including tidal power energy.

One of the main joint programs for agriculture was crop insurance introduced in 1959. Under agreements with the provinces the federal government paid 50 percent of administrative costs and 25 percent of premium costs. Under present arrangements the province assumes all administrative costs and the federal government pays 50 percent of premium costs. Other joint agricultural programs (apart from ARDA and related measures to be discussed in a moment) have been largely of an emergency nature to cope with real or threatened disasters; shortages of feed, outbreaks of rabies or other diseases, damage that reduced crops or prevented harvesting, including bad weather conditions, germ or bug infestation, predatory migratory birds, shortage of harvesting equipment at the time and place needed, etc. etc.—all have brought the provinces to Ottawa for emergency help.

Regional Programs

It is obvious that in a country as diverse and widespread as Canada few actions of the central government will not have some regional impact. This is true of most of the measures just discussed; whether by accident or design their effect would be felt in many regions of the country. There are joint programs, however, in which the impact on a region is the principal goal. Most of these were designed for agricultural or rural areas.

ARDA Agreements

Agreements covering joint projects for rehabilitation of rural areas and development of the rural economy were first instituted under the Agricultural Rehabilitation and Development Act, 1961. Agreements with all provinces provided for the sharing of costs related to improving land use, improving employment opportunities and conserving water and soil resources. The initial agreements were for three years, 1962-65.

In 1965 agreements were signed for another five years, but under new legislation, the Agricultural and Rural Development Act (ARDA) was passed in 1966. Their objective was broadened to include all rural occupations, not just agriculture. The previous objectives were also extended to include a much broadened intervention in rural economic life, with Rural Development Areas (principally areas of high poverty) being identified for intensive assistance. A Fund for Rural Economic Development (FRED) was also established to provide grants for major projects in special rural development areas. Under the Act comprehensive development agreements were entered into between the two levels of government, at first covering New Brunswick, Manitoba, Quebec, and Prince Edward Island. Other agreements were developed later. In general they covered forestry improvement, recreation, wild life projects, land improvement, primary fishing projects, and tourist attractions.

Grants were also available under the Maritime Marshland Rehabilitation Act. A Council on Rural Development was established to advise the Minister on all these activities. For the Atlantic provinces a closely related measure was the Fisheries Development Act, 1966, under which grants were given for improved mechanization and training in the fishing industries.

Department of Regional Economic Development (DREE)

In 1969 DREE was established to take over all the programs related to regional development. These included, as well as ARDA, FRED, and the Marshland legislation, the Area Development Agency (ADA), the Atlantic Development Board (ADB), the Prairie Farm Rehabilitation Act (PFRA), the Cape Breton Development Corporation, and minor other agencies. Some of these administered programs that were entirely federal, and involved capital grants, loans or tax exemptions for industrial expansion, such as the Area Development Program started in 1963 and the Regional Development Incentives Act of 1969.

Under the much broader powers given the new department, economic development agreements were much more comprehensive than was possible under the previous scattered administration. In 1970 agreements with seven provinces were in effect covering development plans for 22 special areas. These were succeeded in 1974 by general development agreements signed with nine provinces for a ten-year period. Projects included water and sewer systems, industrial parks, servicing of residential land, schools, roads and highways, in some cases at the full expense of the federal government. The original agreements were supplemented by subsidiary agreements, such as the early highway construction agreements with the Atlantic provinces. Subsidiary agreements to broaden the scope of the original agreements became general; by 1977 there were over 70. Thus amplified, the general development agreements became the primary instrument for carrying out DREE programs in cooperation with provincial governments. See chapter 11 of the 1977-78 edition of *The National Finances* for a list of subsidiary agreements.[17.8] Under several programs social welfare expenditures were also continued on a substantial scale, particularly under ARDA and FRED.

Department of Regional Industrial Expansion (DRIE)

1982 brought a reorganization of federal regional development programs to further concentrate planning, development, and execution. General policy-making was given to the Ministry of State for Economic Development (1978) and the former DREE and Department of Industry, Trade and Commerce administrative responsibilities were combined in a new Department of Regional Industrial Expansion. Much of the program continued as before, however, although the former DREE budget of $700-800 million rose to over $2 billion on the combined basis. Much of the money disbursed

---

[17.8] Canadian Tax Foundation, *The National Finances, 1977-78* (Toronto: the foundation, 1978, 144-45.

took the form of loans and grants for a variety of purposes—industrial development, productivity, tourism, small businesses—in all regions of Canada.

Intergovernmental grants continued to be channeled mainly through the general development agreements and subsidiary agreements under them. Originally signed in 1974 for ten years, these were destined to expire in 1984. Under the Conservative government's Industrial and Regional Development Program these have been succeeded by Economic and Regional Development Agreements for a five-year period. Under the deficit-cutting program some expenditures have been eliminated or reduced, but the Western Diversification Office and the Atlantic Canada Opportunities Agency were introduced in August 1987, to restore vitality to the programs and decentralize approval procedures.

A Mixed Bag

As an intergovernmental grants measure the regional development program has been difficult to track. The total regionally dedicated expenditures have been a mix on the one hand, of direct federal government grants and loans, mainly to businesses (and tax concessions earlier described) and, on the other, of joint programs in which the main outlays have been in the form of grants to provincial governments under programs such as ARDA, FRED, PFRA, and the general development agreements. Compared to estimated federal-provincial transfers approaching $25 billion in 1986 for equalization, health services, post-secondary education and CAP, the provincial grants element of the DRIE budget would appear to be approximately only $144 million. To this should be added the federal cost of the joint projects with Nova Scotia in the Cape Breton Development Corporation, $120 million, for a total of $264 million. As the total federal budget for DRIE and DEVCO are about $1.2 billion it is obvious that the main outlays—nearly 90 percent—are now in the form of direct grants and loans to businesses and others for industrial development.

A list of over 100 federal-provincial agreements in effect on October 1, 1985, issued by the Department, projects federal grants to the provinces at about $2.5 billion over a five-year period. These will go in approximately the following proportions; Newfoundland, 11 percent; Prince Edward Island, 4 percent; Nova Scotia, 12 percent; Quebec, 24 percent; Ontario, 5 percent; Manitoba, 12 percent; Saskatchewan, 7 percent; Alberta, 3 percent and British Columbia, 12 percent.

An an experiment in economic and social strategy for regional betterment it is obvious that the federal programs have fallen short of achieving anything like equality, as great differences in standards still exist, and there are wide divergences of view among economists and others as to the advisability of such ventures. Their adoption demonstrates the extent to which policies of the national government in Canada, under no matter what party, are directed to relieving the effect of the wide economic disparities that exist. And some of the results of the programs are more subtle than can be measured by economic indicia. The ease of communication on the excellent highways now found in many unexpected parts of Canada in itself serves in a very tangible way to promote both a regional and a national purpose.

Miscellaneous Other Federal Transfers

Other grants given over the years that fall in no particular category include: Quebec, maple production equipment, 1945-55; Quebec, Rimouski and Cabano fire claims, 1950-55; campgrounds and picnic areas, 1957-64; municipal winter works, 1958-70; cancellation of indebtedness under Municipal Development and Loan Act, 1964-69; Centennial Commission grants, 1965-70; disaster relief assistance, 1972-73; P.E.I. centennial projects, 1972-73; metric conversion, 1976-77, and others.

Provincial Governments: Specific Purpose Transfers

Provincial specific purpose grants to local governments are dominated by education, health, roads and highways, and social services. Table 17.18 gives the total of such grants for the period 1967 to 1985 under the main headings where available. In this period they increased seven-fold.

Education

By far the largest specific purpose transfers are in support of local education, accounting for nearly 70 percent of the total in recent years. On average, as shown in table 17.19, provinces pay more than two-thirds of municipal costs for primary and secondary education; in the Atlantic provinces and Quebec all or nearly all of the cost is borne by the province. Grants are based on a variety of formulae, most recognizing either comparative costs or comparative resources, or frequently both. Some grants fill the gap between the cost of a foundation educational program and the yield of a standard property tax rate applied to an equalized assessment; others provide a per capita payment, while another has shared the yield of specified provincial taxes on an agreed basis. All take some account of the nature of the school and the courses offered, and recognition of capital expenditures, special courses, busing, text books, etc. is equally varied. There will be an opportunity to look more closely at these arrangements in a later more detailed section on education.

Health

Payments under this heading are exclusive of grants for hospital insurance and medicare, as these do not form part of provincial-municipal financing.

Health services have come under increasing provincial control in recent years. Health units established in local areas and financed by the provincial government are becoming common in most provinces. Of $23.5 billion spent in the provinces on health in 1983 only $2.2 billion, or 9 percent, was spent by local governments, and 80 percent of this was covered by provincial grants. Of these grants most (88 percent) were in Ontario, Saskatchewan, and Alberta, where some health activities not covered by hospital

Table 17.18 Provincial Governments: Specific Purpose Transfers to Municipalities, 1967-84

Year[a]	Education	Health	Transportation and communication	Social services	Environment	Housing	Other[b]	Total specific purpose transfers
				millions of dollars				
1967	1,516	23	179	121	—	—	70	1,909
1968	1,605	34	185	141	—	5	43	2,013
1969	1,906	39c	196	124	—	7	49	2,321
1970	2,265	30c	218	174	14	19	86	2,806
1971	2,624	34c	301	267	22	20	98	3,366
1972	2,800	37	298	247	38	31	99	3,550
1973	3,051	41	350	234	51	31	177	3,935
1974	3,609	63	460	231	76	22	292	4,753
1975	4,333	76	457	216	103	50	531	5,766
1976	4,979	88	631	216	101	65	335	6,415
1977	5,724	101	782	379	107	66	390	7,549
1978	5,923	115	820	372	148	83	409	7,878
1979	6,383	147	915	418	205	59	522	8,649
1980	7,279	335	1,015	524	314	87	509	8,995
1981	8,591	334	1,206	623	457	94	645	11,950
1982	9,222	1,167	1,416	797	480	196	660	13,938
1983	11,091	569	1,119	901	449	257	799	15,185
1984d	11,007	1,922	818	845	350	13	1,494	16,454

[a]Fiscal year nearest December 31 of year named. [b]Includes protection of persons and property, natural resources and industry, recreation and culture, regional planning and development, and miscellaneous. [c]Excludes hospital grants in the original published data of 1968, $1,730 million; 1969; $2,053 million; 1970, $2,320 million; also excluded in later years. [d]Data available only from *Local Government Finance*; previous breakout by economic classification discontinued in *Provincial Government Finance*.

Source: Statistics Canada, *Provincial Government Finance, Economic Classification*; and *Local Government Finance*, 1984.

Table 17.19   Education: Provincial Grants as a Percent of Total Provincial Specific Purpose Transfers and as a Percent of Municipal Education Costs, 1967-84

Year[a]	Education transfers as a percent of total provincial specific purpose transfers	Education transfers as a percent of municipal education expenditure
	percent	
1967..........................	79.4	54.1
1968..........................	79.8	52.4
1969..........................		
1970..........................	78.5	56.8
1971..........................	71.1	60.0
1972..........................	66.4	58.1
1973..........................	68.8	61.2
1974..........................	70.4	64.3
1975..........................	71.2	65.4
1976..........................	72.1	63.4
1977..........................	72.0	64.6
1978..........................	68.3	61.3
1979..........................	64.8	62.2
1980..........................	68.5	65.8
1981..........................	68.4	65.4
1982..........................	68.3	69.6
1983..........................	73.0	70.1
1984..........................	66.9	67.8

[a]Fiscal year ending nearest December 31 of year named.

Sources: Table 17.18 and Canadian Tax Foundation, *Provincial Finances* and *Provincial and Municipal Finances*.

insurance and medicare are carried on at the local level either on a joint or subsidized basis.

Transportation and Communications

The general arrangement in Canada is that roads within settled and organized areas are the responsibility of the local government and highways connecting urban areas come under the province. An important exception to this is the frequent case where highways traverse a municipality, when the province will bear the whole cost or give a substantial subsidy. Costs of some expensive structures, such as bridges, will also be shared by the province under some conditions.

Provinces also subsidize both the capital and current operating costs of urban transit systems, a fact of which passengers are usually advised by notices prominently posted in vehicles. Provincial grants in this area are of limited importance; as one of the primary municipal functions, local road construction is financed primarily from own sources. Of $3.6 billion spent by local governments in 1981 only 25 percent came from provincial grants.

Social Services

In contrast to the tradition of almost complete local responsibility for the "dependent poor" municipal social services expenditure is now a minor item in most provinces. Because of developments having their origin in the Great Depression the main social services are now provided by the provincial government, including welfare assistance for those in need, for the disabled, single mothers with dependent children, child welfare, senior citizens, special care homes, etc. Ontario is a conspicuous exception, with general welfare assistance, special assistance, children's aid societies, day care, and homes for the aged run by municipal or non-profit organizations with substantial subsidies from the province. Some elements of local responsibility also exist in Nova Scotia, Manitoba, Alberta, and British Columbia, but in the total these are not significant.

Of a total of $15.3 billion spent in all provinces in 1983 only $1.3 billion was spent by local governments, and of this $0.5 billion came from the provinces—over 80 percent of that in Ontario. Grants to local governments were less than 5 percent of total social service costs, and most of these were in Ontario.

Other Grants

Grants of growing importance in recent years include assistance with environmental programs, housing, recreation and culture, and industrial, commercial and tourist development. Selective programs not included here were the subsidization in some provinces of interest rates on municipal debt during the period of extremely high rates.

Subsidies

Somewhat similar to transfer payments but under a separate heading are subsidies paid by the federal and provincial governments for a wide variety of purposes. These reached a not inconsiderable total of nearly $11 billion in 1984, a figure swollen by the extraordinary payments under the National Energy Program, which have since declined.

The majority of payments, but not all, are directed to an economic objective, a prominent exception, for example, being the federal subsidy for the Canadian Broadcasting Corporation. Agricultural and railway subsidies are among the longest standing. Table 17.20 gives some details of federal expenditures and totals for provincial subsidies. In all the federal government has some 172 main programs, some with several sub-programs. Expenditures under many of these appear in the "Other" column of table 17.20; they include programs that offer cash payments, subsidized interest rates, guarantee of loans, credits, exemptions or refunds under the tax laws, travel assistance, research and development grants, support from specialized government agencies, etc. While the main objective of most of these is regional economic stimulus, a wide variety of other purposes is also served, including dance, music and theatre. The largest and most active federal category covers industry, trade and commerce, under which the main

Table 17.20 Federal and Provincial Governments: Expenditure on Subsidies, 1967-86

| | Federal | | | | | | | Provincial | Grand |
Year[a]	Agriculture	Railways	CBC	Oil imports	Job training	Other	Total[b]	total	total
	millions of dollars								
1967........	180	124	132	—	—	83	519	118	637
1968........	219	110	142	—	—	51	522	119	641
1969........	245	96	157	—	—	57	555	146	701
1970........	295	83	166	—	—	45	589	167	756
1971........	233	67	175	—	—	38	513	259	772
1972........	228	85	198	—	32	85	596	288	884
1973........	268	145	246	—	37	79	738	350	1,088
1974........	471	183	258	886	25	237	2,060	559	2,619
1975........	534	435	346	1,692	52	124	3,183	675	3,858
1976........	443	333	361	1,054	54	153	2,398	946	3,344
1977........	388	298	385	922	70	159	2,222	1,098	3,320
1978........	511	371	448	644	82	245	2,301	1,226	3,527
1979........	610	286	491	1,134	92	612	3,225	1,580	4,805
1980........	375	245	516	2,969	93	1,325	5,523	1,829	7,352
1981........	593	326	606	3,779	117	1,064	6,485	2,209	8,094
1982........	355	480	709	1,744	76	2,279	5,643	2,583	8,226
1983........	401	426	706	642	71	3,437	5,683	2,944	8,627
1984........	760	734	781	741	169	4,307	7,492	3,460	10,952
1985[c]......	1,225	632	811	455	117	3,120	6,368	4,532	10,900
1986[c]......	1,688	831	822	3	19	1,431	4,794	4,757	9,551

[a]Calendar year. [b]Includes payments under Petroleum Compensation Revolving Fund as follows (in millions of dollars); 1978, 9; 1979, 296; 1980, 993; 1981, 689; 1982, 1,298; 1983, 1,585; 1984, 2,484; 1985, 1,483; 1986, 8. 1984 also includes $615 million under the Western Grain Transportation Act. [c]Data on a revised basis.

Source: Statistics Canada, *National Income and Expenditure Accounts.*

program is that for Industrial and Regional Development. More localized programs include the Western Transportation Industrial Development Program, the Atlantic Enterprise Program, and Enterprise Cape Breton. Closely related are measures to encourage exports, including financing, information and promotional services. Other programs include Energy, Mines and Resources, agriculture, fishing and navigation, and housing; in the cultural area, programs in the arts, cinema and publishing provide grants and other forms of assistance for many activities; miscellaneous programs include assistance in medical, scientific and social research, various forms of special assistance for universities, etc.

Most of the provinces have similar but less ambitious programs, designed mainly to assist with regional economic development.

The National Debt

Massive government deficits and the growing cost of debt to finance them have been a frequent subject of this book. But one of the oddities of Canadian government finance is the lack of any authoritative estimate of the total of the debt itself. There are reliable figures for debt at the three levels of government but because of intergovernmental transactions these are not additive without some double-counting. Based on what evidence is available one can venture a crude estimate that the 1987 gross debt was about $450 billion, more or less. If this figure, used here only for demonstration purposes, has validity it would give a ratio to 1987 GNP of about 85 percent, which would compare with a ratio of about 45 percent in 1975, just before governments began to plunge into severe deficits. The corresponding, and statistically much more valid calculation for federal debt alone, is an increase from a 1975 ratio of 35 percent to a 1987 ratio of 60 percent. As federal government debt is the largest element in the total the increase in its ratio alone is indicative of the massive and growing size of government borrowings.

The above figures are for gross debt, disregarding the fact that a considerable portion of debt is created in order to lend or invest funds in government or business enterprises, and therefore is offset by assets. Comparisons based on gross debt can therefore be misleading. Later tables demonstrate the importance of these offsetting assets in the total.

Federal Debt

Details of federal debt are given in tables 17.21 to 17.23. In the four decades covered, net debt rose from $12.7 billion in 1946-47 to $246.1 billion in 1986-87. In relation to GNP the net debt percentage declined from 106.6 percent in 1946-47 to a low of 16.8 percent in 1974-75, but with the increases in deficits that began in the following year rose steadily to 51.8 percent in 1986-87. Like other forms of financing the nature of federal debt has changed in the postwar period. Where prior to 1939 most of it would have been in bonds, in 1987 only 47 percent was in that form; 34 percent was in treasury bills and 19 percent was in Canada Savings Bonds.

The lessened term of the debt—particularly that in treasury bills—has permitted the government to take advantage of short-term changes in interest rates. Nonetheless interest costs have soared as an element in the federal budget in the last decade. Interest on gross debt rose from a low point of 10.4 percent in 1974-75 to 22.9 percent in 1986-87. The corresponding figure for net interest costs (outgoing interest less interest earned by the government on assets) rose from 4.6 percent to 19.3 percent. Tables 17.21 to 17.23 give further details.

Provincial-Local-Hospital Debt

Because of the close relationship between provincial, municipal, and hospital debt financing their operations are frequently combined. And because at this level of government debt is more frequently used to finance tangible investments or ancillary enterprises, as table 17.24 indicates borrowings are offset by assets, to a much greater extent than at the federal, both financial and non-financial.

Table 17.25 gives an analysis of provincial debt for several years since 1980. It reveals clearly the importance of borrowings from the Canada Pension Fund and provincial pension funds in the total. Of $82.6 billion of provincial market and non-market borrowing outstanding in 1984, $35.7 billion, or 43 percent, was from this source. (Apparently a permanent loan; when the CPP appeared to be running out of money rather than call in some of the provincial borrowings revenues were increased by raising the contribution rates; see chapter 25). Another feature of provincial borrowing in recent years has been reliance on foreign sources for funds. Of the total indebtedness outstanding in 1985, $21.2 billion, or one quarter, was from abroad. The other substantial source, domestic market issues, at $12.1 billion, accounted for 15 percent.

Further details of provincial and municipal debt may be found in the Tax Foundation's *Provincial and Municipal Finances*, 1987.

Table 17.21 Federal Government: Public Debt, Selected Years, 1946-47 to 1986-87

Year	Gross public debt	Net recorded assets	Net public debt		GNP/GDP
				(per cent of GNP*)	(millions of dollars)
	millions of dollars				
1946-47	16,849	4,180	12,669	106.6	11,885
1951-52	15,940	5,544	10,396	48.0	21,640
1956-57	16,491	5,045	11,446	35.7	32,058
1957-58	16,805	5,163	11,642	34.7	33,513
1958-59	18,681	6,162	12,519	36.0	34,777
1959-60	19,409	6,290	13,119	35.6	36,846
1960-61	20,120	6,472	13,648	35.6	38,359
1961-62	21,906	7,310	14,596	35.7	40,886
1962-63	23,321	7,892	15,429	34.7	44,408
1963-64	25,127	8,529	16,598	34.8	47,678
1964-65	26,204	9,291	16,913	32.4	52,191
1965-66	26,802	10,192	16,610	28.9	57,523
1966-67	28,225	11,428	16,797	26.1	64,388
1967-68	29,810	12,302	17,508	25.4	69,064
1968-69	32,020	14,112	17,908	23.7	75,418
1969-70	33,260	15,684	17,576	21.2	83,026
1970-71	37,114	18,758	18,356	20.6	89,116
1971-72	41,169	21,271	19,898	20.5	97,290
1972-73	44,693	23,120	21,573	19.9	108,629
1973-74	47,542	23,970	23,572	18.5	127,372
1974-75	52,866	27,285	25,581	16.8	152,111
1975-76	59,612	28,294	31,318	18.3	171,540
1976-77	67,323	29,708	37,615	19.0	197,924
1977-78	79,879	31,838	48,041	22.0	217,879
1978-79	96,957	36,299	60,658	25.1	241,604
1979-80	104,780	32,621	72,159	26.1	276,096
1980-81	120,446	34,765	85,681	27.6	309,891
1981-82	137,573	37,020	100,553	28.2	355,994
1982-83	166,203	37,834	128,369	34.3	374,442
1983-84	199,497	38,729	160,768	39.6	405,717
1984-85	237,112	38,020	199,092	44.7	445,604
1985-86	269,286	35,790	233,496	48.7	479,446
1986-87	302,744	38,643	264,101	51.8	509,898

Note: Figures for GNP and GDP relate to the corresponding calendar year.

*For 1926-27 to 1960-61 inclusive, figures are expressed as a percentage of GNP.

Source: Public Accounts of Canada adjusted to reflect accounting changes. Canada, Department of Finance, Budget Papers, "The Fiscal Plan," February 10, 1988, 96.

Table 17.22 Federal Government: Public Debt Charges in Comparative Terms, 1966-67 to 1986-87

Year	Gross public debt charges as a percentage of			Net public debt charges as a percentage of		
	GDP*	Budgetary revenues	Budgetary expenditures	GDP*	Budgetary revenues	Budgetary expenditures
1946-47	3.9	15.5	18.0	3.4	13.2	15.4
1951-52	2.4	12.5	13.7	1.8	9.6	10.5
1956-57	1.6	9.1	9.7	0.9	5.4	5.7
1957-58	1.6	10.0	9.6	0.9	5.8	5.6
1958-59	1.8	12.3	10.5	1.1	7.5	6.4
1959-60	2.1	13.2	11.9	1.4	8.7	7.9
1960-61	2.1	12.5	11.5	1.3	7.9	7.3
1961-62	2.0	12.9	11.2	1.3	8.1	7.1
1962-63	2.1	13.7	12.2	1.4	9.1	8.0
1963-64	2.1	14.0	12.0	1.3	8.8	7.6
1964-65	2.0	12.8	12.3	1.2	7.6	7.3
1965-66	1.9	12.4	12.8	1.2	7.5	7.8
1966-67	1.8	12.1	11.9	1.0	6.8	6.7
1967-68	1.9	12.1	11.3	1.0	6.3	5.9
1968-69	1.9	12.3	11.9	1.0	6.4	6.2
1969-70	2.0	11.9	12.1	1.0	5.8	6.0
1970-71	2.1	12.7	12.1	1.0	6.0	5.7
1971-72	2.2	12.8	11.7	1.0	5.9	5.4
1972-73	2.1	12.0	11.1	1.0	5.4	5.0
1973-74	2.0	11.5	10.5	0.9	4.9	4.5
1974-75	2.1	11.1	10.4	0.9	4.9	4.6
1975-76	2.3	12.6	10.6	1.1	6.0	5.1
1976-77	2.4	13.7	11.6	1.2	6.7	5.7
1977-78	2.5	16.0	12.3	1.3	8.5	6.5
1978-79	2.9	19.1	14.2	1.6	10.8	8.0
1979-80	3.1	20.3	15.9	1.8	11.6	9.1
1980-81	3.4	21.9	17.1	2.0	13.0	10.2
1981-82	4.2	25.2	20.2	2.8	16.7	13.4
1982-83	4.5	27.8	19.1	3.3	20.2	13.9
1983-84	4.5	28.2	18.7	3.4	21.3	14.2
1984-85	5.0	31.7	20.6	4.1	25.7	16.7
1985-86	5.3	33.1	22.9	4.5	28.2	19.5
1986-87	5.2	31.1	22.9	4.4	26.1	19.3

*For 1926-27 to 1960-61 inclusive, figures are expressed as a percentage of GNP.

Source: Public Accounts of Canada adjusted to reflect accounting changes. Canada, Department of Finance, Budget Papers, "The Fiscal Plan," February 10, 1988, 95.

Table 17.23 Federal Government: Gross Public Debt, 1961-62 to 1986-87

Unmatured debt—held by outside parties

(millions of dollars)

	Marketable bonds*			Treasury bills	Canada Savings Bonds*	Less government's own holdings	Total	Superannuation accounts	Interest and debt accounts	Other liabilities	Gross public debt
	Domestic	Foreign	Total								
1961-62	10,838	287	11,125	1,885	4,055	−95	16,970	2,291	275	2,370	21,906
1962-63	10,802	568	11,370	2,165	4,582	−32	18,085	2,562	293	2,381	23,321
1963-64	11,075	533	11,608	2,230	5,092	−99	18,831	3,447	321	2,528	25,127
1964-65	10,899	533	11,432	2,140	5,552	−61	19,063	4,150	339	2,652	26,204
1965-66	10,745	528	11,273	2,150	5,733	−81	19,075	4,489	391	2,847	26,802
1966-67	10,018	523	11,541	2,310	6,017	−200	19,668	4,890	427	3,240	28,225
1967-68	11,573	318	11,891	2,480	6,096	−49	20,418	5,350	499	3,543	29,810
1968-69	12,294	600	12,894	2,840	6,169	−47	21,856	5,883	581	3,700	32,020
1969-70	12,279	605	12,884	2,895	6,579	−107	22,251	6,503	600	3,906	33,260
1970-71	13,021	495	13,516	3,735	7,804	−60	24,995	7,200	839	4,080	37,114
1971-72	13,385	493	13,878	3,830	9,712	−67	27,353	7,934	1,158	4,724	41,169
1972-73	13,423	491	13,914	4,920	10,989	−60	29,133	8,792	1,506	5,262	44,693
1973-74	13,592	415	14,007	4,905	10,406	−64	29,254	9,794	1,801	6,693	47,542
1974-75	14,311	365	14,676	5,630	12,915	−77	33,144	11,054	2,257	6,411	52,866
1975-76	15,281	337	15,618	6,495	15,517	−87	37,543	12,557	2,923	6,589	59,612
1976-77	17,748	335	18,083	8,255	16,304	−89	42,553	14,212	3,619	6,939	67,323
1977-78	21,182	1,190	22,372	11,295	18,011	−98	51,580	16,101	4,523	7,675	79,879
1978-79	26,532	7,376	33,908	13,535	19,247	−146	66,544	18,056	4,014	8,343	96,957
1979-80	32,947	4,860	37,807	16,325	18,081	−305	71,908	20,021	3,976	8,875	104,780
1980-81	40,849	4,794	45,643	21,770	15,812	−223	83,002	22,329	4,162	10,953	120,446
1981-82	43,493	5,428	48,921	19,375	24,978	−261	93,013	25,343	6,095	13,122	137,573
1982-83	48,377	6,405	54,782	29,125	32,641	−157	116,391	28,826	7,710	13,276	166,203
1983-84	57,036	6,106	63,142	41,700	38,204	−334	142,712	32,688	8,622	15,475	199,497
1984-85	69,438	9,077	78,515	52,300	41,960	−261	172,514	36,990	9,418	18,190	237,112
1985-86	81,067	13,810	94,877	61,950	44,245	−288	200,784	41,670	9,084	17,748	269,286
1986-87	94,426	12,010	106,436	76,950	44,309	−880	226,815	46,665	9,065	20,199	302,744

*Including government's holdings of its own debt.

Source: Public Accounts of Canada adjusted to reflect accounting changes. Canada, Department of Finance, Budget Papers, "The Fiscal Plan," February 10, 1988, 86.

Table 17.24 Provincial-Local-Hospital Government Assets and Liabilities, National Accounts Basis, 1961-86

Year	Financial Liabilities	Financial Assets	Net debt	Non-financial assets	Assets less liabilities	Financial Liabilities	Financial Assets	Net debt	Non-financial assets	Assets less liabilities
	(billions of dollars)					(percentage of GDP)				
1961	10.8	7.2	3.6	16.4	12.7	26.4	17.5	8.9	40.0	31.1
1962	11.7	7.8	3.9	17.9	14.0	26.3	17.5	8.8	40.3	31.5
1963	12.6	8.3	4.4	20.0	15.6	26.5	17.3	9.2	41.9	32.7
1964	13.8	9.0	4.8	21.8	16.9	26.4	17.2	9.3	41.7	32.4
1965	15.1	9.8	5.3	25.2	19.9	26.3	17.0	9.3	43.8	34.6
1966	17.3	11.1	6.2	28.8	22.5	26.9	17.2	9.7	44.7	35.0
1967	19.8	12.2	7.6	31.2	23.6	28.7	17.7	11.0	45.2	34.1
1968	22.1	13.8	8.3	33.1	24.8	29.3	18.3	11.0	43.9	32.9
1969	24.3	16.0	8.3	36.7	28.4	29.3	19.3	10.0	44.2	34.2
1970	27.0	18.3	8.7	40.7	31.9	30.3	20.5	9.8	45.6	35.9
1971	29.6	19.9	9.7	46.2	36.5	30.4	20.5	10.0	47.5	37.5
1972	32.8	21.6	11.2	51.1	39.9	30.2	19.9	10.3	47.0	36.7
1973	36.4	24.5	11.9	58.4	46.5	28.6	19.3	9.3	45.9	36.5
1974	41.1	28.5	12.7	74.5	61.8	27.1	18.7	8.3	49.0	40.6
1975	47.7	31.3	16.4	86.9	70.6	27.8	18.2	9.6	50.7	41.1
1976	53.7	35.3	18.4	97.0	78.6	27.2	17.9	9.3	49.0	39.7
1977	62.2	41.7	20.4	108.5	88.0	28.5	19.2	9.4	49.8	40.4
1978	69.9	49.6	20.3	120.1	99.8	28.9	20.5	8.4	49.7	41.3
1979	75.5	56.2	19.3	135.9	116.6	27.3	20.4	7.0	49.2	42.2
1980	84.0	66.1	18.0	154.4	136.5	27.1	21.3	5.8	49.8	44.0
1981	97.9	82.2	15.7	180.4	164.7	27.5	23.1	4.4	50.7	46.3
1982	114.3	90.3	24.0	198.9	174.9	30.5	24.1	6.4	53.1	46.7
1983	121.8	96.9	24.9	211.2	186.3	30.0	23.9	6.1	52.1	45.9
1984	134.4	107.8	26.6	222.2	195.6	30.2	24.2	6.0	49.9	43.9
1985	146.6	113.9	32.7	238.5	205.8	30.6	23.8	6.8	49.7	42.9
1986	170.5	126.9	43.6	259.3	215.7	33.4	24.9	8.6	50.8	42.3

Source: Statistics Canada, *National Balance Sheet Accounts*, annual, cat. 13-214. Canada, Department of Finance, Budget Papers, "The Fiscal Plan," February 10, 1988, 102.

Table 17.25   All Provinces: Outstanding Market and Non-Market Bond Issues by Provincial Governments, Selected Years[a], 1979 to 1984

	1979	1982[b]	1983[b]	1984[b]
	millions of dollars			
Market issues:				
Domestic	6,945.5	9,328.5	11,386.7	12,058.3
Foreign				
United States	6,989.4	9,259.6	9,881.7	12,846.4
Europe	843.8	1,521.9	1,882.9	2,238.8
Other..........................	464.5	693.8	887.9	1,020.2
International	1,157.8	3,544.4	4,044.2	5,124.5
Total foreign	9,455.4	15,019.6	16,696.7	21,229.9
Total market	16,400.9	24,348.2	28,083.4	33,288.2
Non-market issues to:				
Provincial governments	1,336.3	4,025.8	4,165.6	3,992.8
Own government enterprises	2,403.5	5,393.4	6,075.2	6,585.6
Provincial pension plans..............	5,158.0	7,228.8	8,005.7	9,510.6
Canada pension plan investment fund ...	14,892.4	21,597.1	23,934.2	26,167.3
Other[c]............................	707.8	1,665.1	2,216.9	3,050.0
Total non-market	24,498.0	39,910.1	44,397.5	49,306.4
Total bond issues...................	40,898.8	64,258.3	72,480.9	82,594.5

[a] Fiscal year ended nearest December 31 of year named. [b] Preliminary. [c] Includes savings bonds: 1979, $636.0 million; 1982, $986.7 million; 1983, $1,938.9 million; 1984, $2,670.5 million.

Source: Statistics Canada, *Provincial Government Finance*, Catalogue no. 68-209.

Bibliography, chapters 15 to 17

Bird, Richard M. *Financing Canadian Government: A Quantitative Overview.* Financing Canadian Federation no. 1. Toronto: Canadian Tax Foundation, 1979.

———. ed. *Fiscal Dimensions of Canadian Federalism.* Financing Canadian Federation no. 4: Toronto, Canadian Tax Foundation, 1980.

———. *Federal Finance in Comparative Perspective.* Financing Canadian Federation no. 6. Toronto: Canadian Tax Foundation, 1986.

———. *The Growth of Public Employment in Canada.* (Richard M. Bird in collaboration with Meyer W. Bucovetsky and David W. Foot.) *Public Sector Employment in Canada*, vol. 3. Toronto: Institute for Research in Public Policy, 1979.

———. "Tax Harmonization and Federal Finance: A Perspective on Recent Canadian Discussion." (September 1984) 10 *Canadian Public Policy*, 253-66.

Boadway, Robin W. *Intergovernmental Transfers in Canada.* Financing Canadian Federation no. 2. Toronto: Canadian Tax Foundation, 1980.

———. and Flatters, F. *Equalization in a Federal State: An Economic Analysis.* Ottawa: Department of Supply and Services, 1982.

Brady, Alexander L. *Democracy in the Dominions.* 2nd ed. Toronto: University of Toronto Press, 1952.

Breton, A., and Scott, A. *The Economic Constitution of Federal States.* Toronto: University of Toronto Press, 1978.

Breton, A. *The Design of Federations.* Montreal: Institute for Research in Public Policy, 1980.

Bryce, Robert B. *Maturing in Hard Times.* Public Administration Series. Toronto: The Institute of Public Administration of Canada, 1986.

Burns, R.M. *The Acceptable Mean; The Tax Rental Agreements 1941-1962.* Financing Canadian Federation, no. 3. Toronto: Canadian Tax Foundation, 1980.

Canada, Department of Finance. *Fiscal Arrangements in the Eighties—Proposals of the Government of Canada.* Ottawa: 1981.

———. *Federalism and Decentralization: Where do we stand?* Ottawa: 1981.

———. Parliamentary Task Force on Federal-Provincial Fiscal Arrangements. *Fiscal Federalism in Canada.* Ottawa: 1981.

———. *Report of the Royal Commission on Dominion-Provincial Relations.* Ottawa: 1940.

———. *Report of the Royal Commission on Taxation.* Ottawa: 1966.

———. *Report of the Royal Commission on the Economic Union and Development Prospects for Canada.* Ottawa: 1985.

———. Secretary of State. *Federal and Provincial Support to Post-Secondary Education in Canada.* A Report to Parliament. Ottawa: 1987.

———. Task Force on Canadian Unity. *A Future Together.* Ottawa: 1979.

Carmichael, Edward A. New Stresses on Confederation. Diverging Regional Economies. *Observation no. 28.* Toronto: C.D. Howe Institute, 1986.

Canadian Foundation for Economic Education. *Federal Provincial Relations.* Government and the Economy Series. Toronto: the Foundation, 1979.

Canadian Tax Foundation. *The National Finances.* Toronto: the Foundation, annual.

Carter, George E. *Canadian Conditional Grants since World War II.* Toronto: Canadian Tax Foundation, 1971.

Clark, Douglas H. *Fiscal Need and Revenue Equalization Grants.* Toronto: Canadian Tax Foundation, 1969.

Courchene, Thomas J. *Refinancing the Canadian Federation: A Survey of the 1977 Fiscal Arrangements Act.* Montreal: C.D. Howe Institute, 1979.

_____. *Economic Management and the Division of Powers.* Collected Research Studies of the Royal Commission on the Economic Union and Development Prospects for Canada, no. 67. Toronto: University of Toronto Press, 1986.

_____. *Regional Adjustment. The Transfer System and Canadian Federalism.* Research Report, 7903. London: University of Western Ontario, Department of Economics, 1979.

Economic Council of Canada. *Living Together.* Ottawa: 1977.

_____. *Financing Confederation: today and tomorrow.* Ottawa: 1982.

Forget, Claude. "The Harmonization of Social Policy." In Mark Krasnick, research coordinator, *Fiscal Federalism.* Collected Research Studies of the Royal Commission on the Economic Union and Development Prospects for Canada, no. 65. Toronto: University of Toronto Press, 1986.

Goodman, Wolfe D. *The New Provincial Succession Duty System: An Examination of the Succession Duty Acts of the Atlantic Provinces, Manitoba and Saskatchewan.* Canadian Tax Paper no. 56. Toronto: Canadian Tax Foundation, 1972.

Hartle, Douglas G. *The Expenditure Budget Process in the Government of Canada.* Tax Paper no. 60. Toronto: Canadian Tax Foundation, 1978.

_____. *The Expenditure Budget Process of the Government of Canada: A Public Choice—Rent-Seeking Perspective.* Canadian Tax Paper no. 81. Toronto: Canadian Tax Foundation, 1988.

Lamontagne, M. *Le federalisme canadien.* Quebec: Presses de l'Université Laval, 1954.

Laskin, Bora. "Reflections on the Canadian Constitution After the First Century." September 1967) *Canadian Bar Review,* 395-408.

La Forest G.V. *The Allocation of the Taxing Power Under the Canadian Constitution.* Second ed. Tax Paper no. 65. Toronto: Canadian Tax Foundation, 1981.

Lynn, James H. *Federal-Provincial Fiscal Relations.* Studies of the Royal Commission on Taxation, no. 23. Ottawa: 1967.

MacEachen, Hon. Allan J. Minister of Finance. *Federal-Provincial Arrangements in the Eighties.* (Submission to the Task Force on Federal Provincial Arrangements). Ottawa: 1981.

_____. *Fiscal Arrangements in the Eighties.* Budget Paper, November 12, 1981. Ottawa: 1981.

Moore, A.M., Perry, J.H., and Beach, D.I. *The Financing of Canadian Federation, the First Hundred Years.* Toronto: Canadian Tax Foundation, 1966.

Ontario. Budget Paper B. *Federal-Provincial Fiscal Reforms.* Toronto: 1977.

Ontario Economic Council. *Intergovernmental Relations, Issues and Alternatives 1977.* Toronto: the Council, 1977.

Perry, David B. "The Federal-Provincial Fiscal Arrangements for 1982-87." (January-February 1983) 31 *Canadian Tax Journal*, 30-47.

Perry, J. Harvey. *Taxes, Tariffs and Subsidies. A History of Canadian Fiscal Development*. Toronto: University of Toronto Press, 1955.

_____. *Taxation in Canada*. 4th ed. Toronto: Canadian Tax Foundation, 1984.

_____. *Background of Current Fiscal Problems*. Canadian Tax Paper no. 68. Toronto: Canadian Tax Foundation, 1982.

Quebec. Royal Commission of Enquiry on Constitutional Problems. *Report*. Quebec City: 1956.

Reuber, Grant L. *Canada's Political Economy: Part II. Economics of Confederation*. Toronto: McGraw-Hill Ryerson, 1980.

Safarian, A.E. *Canadian Federalism and Economic Integration*. Ottawa: 1974.

Simeon, Richard. *Federal-Provincial Diplomacy: the Making of Recent Policy in Canada*. Toronto: University of Toronto Press, 1972.

_____. ed. *Confrontation and Collaboration—Intergovernmental Relations in Canada Today*. Toronto: Institute of Public Administration of Canada, 1979.

_____. "Considerations on Centralization and Decentralization." (Fall 1986) 29 *Canadian Public Administration*, 445-61.

_____. "Division of Powers and Public Policy." In Mark Krasnick, Norrie, Kenneth, and Simeon, Richard research coordinators, *Federalism and the Economic Union*. Collected Research Studies of the Royal Commission on the Economic Union and Development Prospects for Canada, vol. 61. Toronto: The University of Toronto Press, 1985.

Smiley, Donald V. *Conditional Grants and Canadian Federalism*. Toronto: Canadian Tax Foundation, 1963.

_____. *The Federal Condition in Canada*. Toronto: McGraw-Hill Ryerson Limited, 1987.

_____. *Canada in Question: Federalism in the Eighties*. 3rd ed. Toronto: McGraw-Hill Ryerson Limited, 1980.

_____. and Watts, Ronald L. "Intrastate Federalism." In Peter Aucoin, research coordinator, *Representative Institutions*. Collected Research Studies of the Royal Commission on the Economic Union and Development Prospects for Canada, vol. 39. Toronto: University of Toronto Press, 1985.

Smith, E.H. "Allocating to the Provinces the Tax Income of Corporations." (September-October 1976) 24 *Canadian Tax Journal*, 543.

Thirsk, Wayne R. "Fiscal Harmonization in the United States, Australia, West Germany, Switzerland and the EEC." In *Federalism and the Canadian Economic Union*. Toronto: Ontario Economic Council, 1983.

Trebilcock, M.J., Prichard, J.R.S., Courchene, T.J., and Whalley, John. *Federalism and the Canadian Economic Union*. Toronto: Ontario Economic Council, 1983.

Vielleux, Gerard. *Les relations intergouvermentales au Canada, 1867-1967*. Quebec: Les Presses de l'Université du Quebec, 1971.

Whalley, John, and Trela, Irene. *Regional Aspects of Confederation*. Collected Research Studies of the Royal Commission on the Economic Union and Development Prospects for Canada, vol. 68. Toronto: University of Toronto Press, 1985.

Wheare, K.C. *Federal Government*. 4th ed. London: Oxford University Press, 1963.

18
Provincial Profiles—Newfoundland to British Columbia

The foregoing is a revealing analysis of nation-wide trends in postwar government finances and will serve as an introduction to consideration of individual provinces. What follows will be a mere sketch of 40 years of development, as there is material enough alone in the some 400 provincial budget speeches of this period for a book the size of the present, apart from hundreds of reports, studies, surveys and reviews. Information has been drawn primarily from summaries such as the Tax Foundation's *Provincial Finances* and *Provincial and Municipal Finances* and various reports of Statistics Canada. A central area of provincial responsibility—education— will be covered in somewhat more detail later, but the immediate purpose is to give a general impression of the postwar period.

Postwar Resumption of an Active Provincial Role

With the end of World War II the provinces began to resume their normal role as key members of the Canadian governmental system. For over a decade and a half they had been forced to take a secondary position under the harsh and stultifying regimen of the Great Depression and the over-whelming priorities of the war. This long period of constraint had left large gaps in physical facilities and shortages of personnel to perform their accus-tomed roles. The economic collapse of the thirties brought budgets of unprecedented stringency, and during the war, although the economy was active, by tacit agreement all provincial and local functions not related to its prosecution were kept to a minimum—in actuality, labour and material shortages gave no option. Public buildings, schools, hospitals, libraries, highways, roads, water systems, sanitary plants, etc. became run down or inadequate. Public service staffs in nearly every category were stripped to meet the needs of wartime. The provinces and municipalities therefore emerged from the war in 1945 with an enormous backlog of expenditures. Their dilemma stemmed from the fact that they had stripped their revenue sources in nearly every category to give priority to the wartime financing of the national government.

The need to restore provincial and municipal services to normal levels came much faster than anyone had foreseen. The rapid revival of the civilian economy and the unprecedented increase in population have been mentioned. Indicia more directly related to provincial activities were the doubling of motor vehicle registrations between 1947 and 1954, and another doubling between 1954 and 1964. The age of the expensive super-highway had arrived. Equally indicative was a doubling in school enrolment between 1951 and 1961, and a further 40 percent increase between 1961 and 1971.

The provinces might have coped comfortably with these developments had there not also been new and expensive programs for hospitals and social services. A revolution of expectations was also thrusting on them several new responsibilities—community planning, environmental control, cultural and recreational facilities, child care, financial aid for industrial development, stimulus for savings and investment, and greatly enhanced assistance for municipalities bursting their territorial and fiscal limits. The latter presented acute and unprecedented problems as local government structures designed initially for fairly tightly knit moderate sized relatively homogeneous cities and towns were recast to cope with the flood of new city dwellers. People of all ages, languages, and creeds sprawled over urban areas at distances that at one time would have represented a day's travel and which now is expected to be traversed in thirty minutes. In this area it is expected that all municipal services will be provided cheaply and efficiently and with due regard to differences of language, creed, colour, and sexual orientation.

As we have seen, and will see further, all this activity presented a massive bill to be paid. The federal government gradually relaxed its monopoly of the tax system, although with some reluctance, as its new economic creed called for dominance over the main taxes, and the renewal of defence expenditure following the Korean war tied its hands. The tax rental agreements assured it of a leading position in tax policy-making, which was maintained under the tax collection agreements. Even though the latter were designed to encourage provincial autonomy they simultaneously ensured federal control over the main terms of the personal and corporate income taxes and, along with various social programs, produced a regular and substantial flow of funds to the provinces.

A direct effect of the federal dominance was that in time the personal income tax became the main provincial source, as it had for the federal government, embodying after 1971 all the changes in the federal basic statute arising from tax reform, including a capital gains tax. The revenue equalization payments program, which brought the yield of this and other taxes to a standard level, was a revolutionary step, and for the weaker provinces yielded funds far beyond those obtainable from their own resources. This was particularly true of the personal income tax, where provincial levels are most disparate. Today the equalization payments represent the largest source of revenue in several provinces.

For additional revenues the provinces have relied heavily on consumption taxes, primarily the retail sales tax. By fairly steady increases in rates, most provinces have reached levels three or four times those at the outset. Motor fuels, tobacco, and liquor have also had the constant attention of provincial fiscal authorities, particularly in the last decade. Corporate taxation has been a relatively stable or declining source, although generally rates have moved upward, particularly since the 1981 recession.

With the virtual exhaustion of the governmental bag of economic tricks in the last decade the provinces, like the federal government, began to seek a livelier private sector, first through stimulation of consumer expenditure and then more directly by the use of various incentives for businesses, and in particular small businesses. These have included special reduced corporate rates or complete exemption for fixed periods, tax credits for capital expenditure and research and development, and other devices, generally after the federal models. Credits and exemptions for equity investment have also become common, including flow-through for shareholders. A trend in all provinces has been toward relief of the weight of municipal property tax through a variety of programs. These have generally taken the form of direct grants or refundable credits against income tax for homeowners and in some cases renters. Home ownership has also been encouraged by grants for first-time owners. In all provinces there have been major revisions of provincial-municipal financial arrangements, frequently involving the establishment of provincial-wide standards of property tax assessment and collection, in many instances involving provincial assumption of these responsibilities.

Following the federal precedent, all provinces eventually dropped their succession duties and gift taxes. Some taxes, such as the corporate capital tax and the insurance premiums tax, were either re-introduced or newly enacted. Generally the provincial pattern of innovation has been lacklustre, as a few tax sources have been exploited with higher rates year after year with monotonous and imitative regularity, a reflection of the narrow limits of scope for provincial initiatives.

The petroleum trauma of the seventies and eighties brought massive and complex and frequently competitive changes in taxation and royalty systems, including those of governments actually having oil and those that counted on OPEC prices to render viable their hitherto uneconomic resources. The details of these changes are being passed over here as they are too complex for capsule treatment. The massive inflow of revenue brought dramatic changes in oil-rich provinces, particularly Alberta and to a lesser extent Saskatchewan, and the subsequent collapse of prices has been calamitous, although both these provinces had wisely put aside a part of their revenues in a survival fund.

On the expenditure side it is timely again to remind the reader that the main changes at all levels of government have arisen from the launching of new programs, particularly in health, social welfare, and education. This has been accompanied by a massive shift between levels of government in the financing of these functions, a shift that in general has reflected the locus of fiscal authority. The federal government has employed its undoubtedly stronger revenue resources to assume or assist with functions most of which are constitutionally the undoubted responsibility of the provinces. Provinces for their part have been forced by the strong trends to urbanization and the concentration of much of their population in urban areas to drastically revise their support for all municipal functions, and in most cases to create new structures for municipal government. It is unfortunate to have to record that these otherwise apparently constructive developments have taken place in a general environment of fiscal imbalance, with deficits and growing debt the general experience at all levels of government. One would conclude from this that Canadian governments have found it an extremely costly business to assume long-range commitments for social and other programs based on an economy that is so heavily dependent on uncertain world markets for the sale of much of its output. At the same time possibly this instability is in itself the best reason for having adopted these programs, although the cost has been high.

This brief background introduces the up-dated profile of the provinces and municipalities that emerged in 1986.

The 1986 Profile

Revenues

In 1986 provincial gross general revenues were estimated to total $106 billion. The largest sources were expected to be personal income tax ($23.7 billion or 22.3 percent); transfers from the federal government ($21.6 billion or 20.3 percent); general sales tax ($12.9 billion or 12.2 percent); followed by return on investment ($11.0 billion or 10.4 percent). These four sources accounted for 65 percent of the total. The balance came from natural resources revenue ($5.4 billion or 5.1 percent); corporate income tax ($4.5 billion or 4.2 percent); health insurance permiums ($4.0 billion or 3.8 percent); motive fuel taxes ($3.4 billion or 3.2 percent); miscellaneous sources ($19.6 billion or 18.5 percent). The misleading influence of visibility is clearly demonstrated in the fact that the government liquor outlet, a prominent provincial symbol in most communities, contributed only about 3 percent of total revenues. Practically anonymous are the provincial personal income tax, which appears in nine provinces only as an add-on to the federal tax, and transfers from the federal government, together making up over 40 percent of the total.

Expenditures

In 1986 provincial gross expenditures were estimated at $112 billion. Of this total over $68 billion was expected to be for health, education, and social services, including grants from the federal government for these programs. They were respectively 25 percent, 19 percent, and 16 percent of the total—61 percent in all. Although this trinity had grown from a mere $24 billion a decade earlier, as a proportion they had in fact declined slightly from 63 percent in 1976. But the comparison with *three* decades before was the most revealing; then they accounted for only 45 percent, highways and roads having the top priority. Debt charges were the largest remaining item in 1986 ($12.3 billion or 11 percent), followed by resource conservation and industrial development ($6.9 billion or 5.8 percent), general services ($6.5 billion or 5.8 percent), transportation and communications ($6.3 billion or 5.6 percent); the balance was protection of persons and property, general purpose grants, and other ($11.5 billion or 10.3 percent).

The role of the "big-three" social expenditures—health, education and social services—accounting for over 60 percent of the total, is pre-eminent.

Deficits

Deficits of provincial governments have been growing rapidly over recent years. Following several years of overall surpluses (not shared by all provinces), in 1982 provincial budgets suffered an unprecedented shortfall of $5½ billion, some 6.5 percent of expenditure. Deficits on this general scale have persisted since: $4.5 billion in 1983; $3.3 billion in 1984; $5.0 billion in 1985, and an estimated $5.8 billion in 1986. Although higher in amount, the 1986 deficit at 5.2 percent of expenditures was a slight improvement over earlier peak years.

Total deficits in the five years 1982 to 1986 have exceeded $24 billion. Inevitably the result has been a marked increase in provincial debt. Between 1980 and 1986 (latest figures) unmatured provincial debt rose from $47.5 billion to $98.6 billion, an increase of 107 percent. Not all debt of course is the result of deficits, as many capital expenditures are automatically financed through borrowings. But in the last five years deficits have been the dominant factor.

Municipal Governments

Revenues

In 1986 municipal revenues were estimated to amount to $42.4 billion. Of this total $20.0 billion was expected to be grants from the federal and provincial governments (mainly the provincial) and $15.7 billion revenue from real property and related taxes; these two sources together were estimated to produce $35.7 billion, or 84 percent of the total. The largest other source, sales of goods and services, at $4.3 billion, made up most of the balance, accounting for 10.2 percent of the total. Privileges, licences and permits, return on investment, and other minor sources accounted for the rest.

Expenditures

In 1986 municipal expenditures were estimated at $44.1 billion. The main expenditures were for education, ($17.9 billion, or 40.6 percent); transportation and communications, ($4.3 billion or 9.8 percent); protection of persons and property, ($3.7 billion or 8.4 percent); environment, ($3.5 billion or 7.9 percent); debt charges ($3.3 billion or 7.5 percent); general services ($2.5 billion or 5.7 percent); recreation and culture, ($2.8 billion or 6.3 percent); health, ($2.6 billion or 5.9 percent); and social welfare ($1.6 billion or 3.6 percent). Other outlays included resource conservation and industrial development, housing, regional development, and other, ($1.8 billion or 4.1 percent).

Despite substantial marginal changes the basic pattern of municipal expenditures has not changed materially over a long period of years. In 1956 there were four main municipal functions—education, policing, road building, and general services—which then accounted for 71 percent of expenditures; in 1986 these were still the same basic services, and they accounted for

65 percent, not a great change in three decades. The changing order was reflected mainly in the emergence of new headings such as recreation and culture and environment, accounting for over 13 percent of the total. These were not even recorded in 1956. Municipal debt of course has increased substantially; between 1980 and 1986 it rose from $20.7 billion to $26.4 billion, an increase of 27 percent.

Historical Data

In the appendix to this chapter there are tables giving data on provincial and municipal finances for the whole postwar period.

Political Profiles

The programs and philosophies of political parties elected to power at the provincial level have a profound influence on financial management, as has been frequently demonstrated in Canada. Party labels are no longer a reliable indication in this regard, however, as performance is frequently the reverse of what might have been expected. For what it is worth the following is the record of the political labels of provincial governments in the postwar period.

Party	Term	Leader
Newfoundland		
Liberal	1949-72	Smallwood
Conservative	1972-79	Moores
Conservative	1979-	Peckford
Prince Edward Island		
Liberal	1943-52	Jones
Liberal	1952-59	Matheson
Conservative	1959-66	Shaw
Liberal	1966-79	Campbell
Conservative	1979-82	MacLean
Conservative	1982-86	Gee
Liberal	1986-	Ghiz
Nova Scotia		
Liberal	1945-54	Macdonald
Liberal	1954	Connolly
Liberal	1954-56	Hicks
Conservative	1956-67	Stanfield
Conservative	1967-70	Smith
Liberal	1970-78	Regan
Conservative	1978-	Buchanan
New Brunswick		
Liberal	1940-52	McNair
Conservative	1952-60	Fleming
Liberal	1960-70	Robichaud
Conservative	1970-87	Hatfield
Liberal	1987-	McKenna

Quebec
Union-nationale	1944-59	Duplessis
Union-nationale	1959-60	Sauve
Union-nationale	1960	Barrette
Liberal	1960-66	Lesage
Union-nationale	1966-68	Johnson
Union-nationale	1968-70	Bertrand
Liberal	1970-76	Bourassa
Parti quebecois	1976-85	Levesque
Liberal	1985-	Bourassa

Ontario
Conservative	1949-61	Frost
Conservative	1961-71	Robarts
Conservative	1971-85	Davis
Conservative	1985	Miller
Liberal	1985-	Peterson

Manitoba
Liberal	1948-58	Campbell
Conservative	1958-67	Roblin
Conservative	1967-69	Weir
N.D.P.	1969-77	Schreyer
Conservative	1977-81	Lyon
N.D.P.	1981-88	Pawley
Conservative	1988-	Filmon

Saskatchewan
C.C.F.	1944-61	Douglas
C.C.F.-N.D.P.	1961-64	Lloyd
Liberal	1964-71	Thatcher
N.D.P.	1971-82	Blakeney
Conservative	1982-	Devine

Alberta
Social Credit	1943-68	Manning
Liberal	1968-71	Strom
Conservative	1971-85	Lougheed
Conservative	1985-	Getty

British Columbia
Coalition	1947-52	Johnson
Social Credit	1952-72	Bennett (W.A.C.)
N.D.P.	1972-75	Barrett
Social Credit	1975-86	Bennett (W.R.)
Social Credit	1986-	Vander Zalm

Newfoundland

With virtually the status of a British colony prior to becoming a Canadian province in 1949 Newfoundland had much catching up to do. It emerged from a period of wartime affluence with an accumulated surplus which, following union with Canada in 1949, was increased as a result of federal assumption of provincial debt and the receipt of immediate grants and transitional grants spread over a twelve-year period. At the same time it also negotiated a tax rental agreement with the federal government, to its advantage. Union of course meant giving up tariff revenues, but the province replaced these in 1950 with a retail sales tax at 2 percent. Taxes along general provincial lines were gradually imposed, and provincial activities already established, including provincial hospital and medical services, in time qualified for federal grants.

The government's main concern was to raise Newfoundland's standard of living closer to the level of the other provinces, and an active program to stimulate the economy was launched. The Union surplus was put into a special fund to be used as far as possible for economic and social development. Several small industries were subsidized, and roads, schools, and fishery facilities were improved. The surplus disappeared fairly quickly. The province began to borrow and also adopted some imaginative steps to obtain outside help. In 1952 the Newfoundland and Labrador Corporation was set up to fund economic expansion. In 1954 the British Newfoundland Corporation was established to develop the power potential of Hamilton River Grand Falls in Labrador, which was ultimately done by the seventies.

The terms of Union had provided for review of its financial aspects after eight years, and a Royal Commission appointed by the federal government recommended additional funding of $8 million for the five years 1957-61. The province also received $7.5 million for the four years 1958-61 as its share of an annual grant of $25 million given the Atlantic provinces by the federal government. Following this period the province shared some of the general buoyancy of the Canadian economy, but not enough to avoid tax increases. These were fairly regular in the seventies and eighties, as the province strove to improve its standards of education, social programs, roads, municipal services, and so on. While there were iron ore resources on Belle Isle and one of the world's largest paper plants at Corner Brook, the basic economy was heavily dependent on fishing.

At Union the majority of the population lived in small fishing villages on the sea, largely inacessible by any other means but boat. Some of these outports have been consolidated, but they are still the home of much of the population. Many Newfoundlanders are directly dependent for their livelihood on inshore fishing, a source largely unchanged and frequently either unreliable or unrewarding. Offshore fishing however has been improved by the introduction of trawlers and freezing plants. The status of fishing has been a constant cause of concern for both the provincial and federal governments, the latter providing assistance in many ways, including granting eligibility for unemployment insurance for both fishermen and their wives.

The hope of the provincial government has been for an industrial base that would decrease the dependence on fishing and give the economy a lift-off. The Churchill Falls power development in Labrador, the unsuccessful oil refinery at Come-by-Chance, the recent oil discoveries, and the various industries financed by the government were all to be part of this base. But for a variety of reasons none have produced the answer. Forestry and mining provide some employment, but have failed to lift the economy to high

Table 18.1   Newfoundland: General Profile

	Year[a]	Province	All Canada	Province as percent of all Canada
Population (000)	1987	568	25,625	2.2
Gross Domestic Product ($ billion)	1986	6.8	506.5	1.3
G.D.P. per capita ($)	1986	11,937	20,030	59.6
Personal Income ($ billion)	1986	6.6	432.5	1.5
P.I. per capita ($)	1986	11,620	17,060	68.1
Unemployment rate (%)...............	1987	18.6	8.9	209.0
Provincial government: revenue ($ billion).........................	1986	2.5	202.5[b]	1.2
Provincial government: expenditure ($ billion).........................	1986	2.5	234.1[b]	1.1
Basic personal income tax rate (%)[c]	1988	60.0	46.5-60[d]	—
General corporate tax rate (%)	1988	16.0	14-17[d]	—
Retail sales tax rate	1988	12.0	6-12[d]	—

[a] Calendar year or fiscal year ending nearest to December 31 of year named. [b] All governments. [c] Percent of federal tax, except in Quebec. [d] Lowest and highest rate for all provinces.

Sources: Statistics Canada, *Canadian Economic Observer*; CANSIM; Department of Finance, *Quarterly Economic Review*; Canadian Tax Foundation, *Provincial and Municipal Finances*.

levels, nor have the Labrador power developments brought the province the expected returns. The promising oil discoveries off the Newfoundland coast are on hold for the foreseeable future, although their ultimate development was assured with the Hibernia agreement of July 1988.

Much more could be told of the Newfoundland experience; in fact the number of royal commissions, inquiries, studies, and reports on Newfoundland make it one of the best documented parts of the federation. The story is self-evident from the accompanying tables. Despite strenuous and imaginative efforts, it is apparent that the province has yet to find its goal of independent affluence. Its unemployment rate is among the highest and its per capita personal income among the lowest in Canada. However, by dint of raising taxes to levels beyond those of most other provinces, and much beyond the tax room left by the federal government, its dependence on Ottawa had been reduced to just over half in 1972, and to just below half by 1986. From 18 percent of revenues in 1952 provincial tax yields moved up to 37 percent in 1986. Natural resource revenue has been only 1 to 2 percent of the total.

On the expenditure side the share met by the province from its own revenues has increased from 32 percent in 1952 to 55 percent in 1986. Of individual expenditures education costs have increased most dramatically. At one time the province was offering free education at the provincial university in St. John's but fiscal pressure forced it to modify this. Although education is organized under 35 local boards for which municipalities have authority to raise local revenues, the province supplies most of the funding. Health, entirely a provincial function at union, has remained a high but fairly constant ratio of expenditure. Social services costs declined

Table 18.2   Newfoundland Finances: The Eighties

Year[a]	Revenue	Expenditure	Deficit
	millions of dollars		
1980	1,482.7	1,636.9	− 154.2
1981	1,632.3	1,701.2	− 68.9
1982	1,758.2	1,973.4	− 215.2
1983	1,948.2	2,233.5	− 285.3
1984	2,075.2	2,264.6	− 189.4
1985	2,318.8	2,461.6	− 142.8
1986	2,485.6	2,617.0	− 131.4
1987	2,597.0	2,895.7	− 298.7
1988	2,652.1	2,901.5	− 249.5

[a] Fiscal year ended nearest December 31 of year named.

Source: Statistics Canada, CANSIM; Budget speech, 1988.

Table 18.3   Province of Newfoundland, Revenue, Consolidated Finances Basis, Selected Years, 1952-86[a]

Source	1952	1962	1972	1982	1986
	millions of dollars				
Taxes	6.5	30.9	150.4	688.4	918.4
Natural resource revenue	0.8	1.5	5.8	30.7	34.2
Privileges, licences and permits	1.8	6.0	6.4	20.6	25.9
Liquor sales and regulation	2.8	5.0	20.9	61.4	76.3
Other revenue	1.2	0.9	41.7	112.9	266.2
Transfers from other governments[b]	22.5	66.2	246.6	844.2	1,164.6
Total	35.6	110.5	471.8	1,758.2	2,485.6
Own source revenue	13.1	44.3	225.2	914.0	1,321.0
Surplus or deficit	2.8	− 24.7	− 58.0	− 215.3	− 131.4
	percent of total revenue				
Taxes	18.3	28.0	31.9	39.1	36.9
Natural resource revenue	2.2	1.4	1.2	1.7	1.4
Privileges, licences and permits	5.1	5.4	1.3	1.2	1.1
Liquor sales and regulation	7.9	4.5	4.4	3.5	3.1
Other revenue	3.3	0.8	8.9	6.5	10.7
Transfers from other governments[b]	63.2	59.9	52.3	48.0	46.8
Total	100.0	100.0	100.0	100.0	100.0
Own source revenue	36.8	40.2	47.7	52.0	53.2

[a] Fiscal years nearest December 31 of the year named. [b] Includes both general and specific purpose transfers.

Source: Statistics Canada, *Historical Review; Financial Statistics of Governments of Canada*, 1952-62; *Provincial Government Finance*, 1972; and CANSIM.

Table 18.4   Province of Newfoundland, Expenditure, Consolidated Finances Basis, Selected Years, 1952-86[a]

	1952	1962	1972	1982	1986
	millions of dollars				
General services	1.7	5.9	21.0	91.3	139.2
Health......................	7.6	29.3	102.4	418.7	532.4
Social services	6.2	18.8	59.3	218.6	255.9
Education...................	6.1	40.3	144.0	478.2	578.2
Transportation and communications	6.1	22.7	70.4	148.9	204.6
Natural resources and industrial development	1.4	3.7	43.7	81.5	121.0
Charges on debt..............	0.8	6.4	56.2	300.2	494.1
Transfers to other governments[b]	0.3	1.8	3.8	30.3	42.5
Other.......................	2.6	6.3	29.0	205.8	249.1
Total.......................	32.8	135.2	529.8	1,973.4	2,617.0
Offsets:					
Specific purpose transfers	9.6	52.1	119.5	276.4	428.4
General purpose transfers	12.9	14.1	127.1	567.7	736.2
Own expenditure	10.4	69.0	283.1	1,129.4	1,452.4
	percent of total expenditure				
General services	5.2	4.4	4.0	4.6	5.3
Health......................	23.2	21.7	19.4	21.2	20.3
Social services	18.9	13.9	11.2	11.2	10.0
Education...................	18.6	29.8	27.2	24.2	22.1
Transportation and communications	19.6	16.8	13.3	7.5	7.8
Natural resources and industrial development	4.3	2.7	8.3	4.1	4.6
Charges on debt..............	2.4	4.7	10.6	15.2	18.9
Transfers to other governments[c]	0.9	1.3	0.7	1.5	1.6
Other.......................	7.9	4.7	5.3	10.5	9.4
Total.......................	100.0	100.0	100.0	100.0	100.0
Own expenditure	31.7	51.0	53.4	57.2	55.5

[a]Fiscal years nearest December 31 of year named. [b]General purpose transfers only; grants toward individual functions are included in the amount shown for that function.

Source: Statistics Canada, *Historical Review*; *Financial Statistics of Governments of Canada*, 1952-62; *Provincial Government Finance*, 1972; and CANSIM.

sharply, due no doubt to the federal income maintenance programs and the extension of unemployment insurance to fishermen.

The relatively limited role of municipalities is indicated by the minor transfers to them—1.6 percent of total expenditure. Deficits have been a regular feature of the provincial budget for many years, with a resulting debt that is high by any standard. As a percent of the total, debt charges rose from 2.4 percent in 1952 to nearly 19 percent in 1986, by far the largest increase in any part of the budget.

Footnote to Provincial Diaries

A provincial diary similar to the following diary for Newfoundland has been prepared for each province. They deal mainly with the content of annual provincial budgets to 1967, employing whatever budgets were on file (there are some gaps) and from then on using summaries given in Canadian Tax Foundation publications. These are largely summaries of sumaries and leave much to be desired as a record of provincial fiscal changes, and must be used with caution. The figures for budget forecasts are particularly suspect, as they represent a variety of changing concepts in effect over this long period, and are of value only as a general indication of the direction in which the province was moving at any particular time. Some uniformity has been achieved by combining current and capital figures throughout, where possible, in the current fashion, but there are other problems as well. For a consistent time series the revised Statistics Canada data should be used, and even this presents many problems over a 40-year period.

The diaries represent hundreds of hours of effort, and have been prepared with considerable care. They are most valuable as an index to dates of budgets and certain related documents that are also mentioned, and as a rough guide to annual tax changes rather than as a complete compendium of significant provincial fiscal developments; they should be used as a supplement to other parts of the book.

Newfoundland Diary

1949: November 30—Budget. This budget was largely devoted to a review of the position following Union with Canada. Main emphasis was on the need to develop the province. A tax rental agreement had been completed. The surplus fund was $40 million, which would be drawn on for the 1949-50 deficit.

1950: April 26—Budget. A sales tax was introduced as a Social Security Assessment. A report was given on the use of the surplus fund. The deficit would be met from the fund.

1951: May 9—Budget. A further report on the surplus fund. No new taxes.

1952: April 30—Budget. A further extensive explanation of the way the surplus fund was being used for economic and social development. A bond issue would be made to sustain the fund. The tax rental agreement was being renewed for a further five years. The Newfoundland and Labrador Corporation was created to assist with economic development.

1953: April 29—Budget. A detailed account of economic progress and improved roads, hospitals, and schools.

1954: May 31—Budget. Reported that on current account there had been 12 surpluses in the past 14 pre-union and union years; but the surplus fund was down to $2.7 million. British Newfoundland Corporation (BRINCO) established to survey power sources at Hamilton Falls in Labrador. Royal commissions on forestry, on agriculture and Terms of Union were appointed.

1955: April 18—Budget. No tax changes were announced. Major capital expenditures to be mainly for road and highway construction. Budget forecast, 1955-56: revenue, $38.8 million; expenditure, $38.4 million; surplus, $477,000.

1956: April 11—Budget. No tax changes. The Minister of Finance reviewed the improvement in the incomes of Newfoundlanders over the seven years since Confederation, and tabled a summary of the province's expenditure on capital account since Confederation. Of the total of $510.2 million, the largest share ($139.0 million) had been spent on the mining industry, the second largest ($110.0 million) on house construction, followed by $88.0 million on motor vehicles, $42.0 million on the pulp and paper industry, and $35.0 million on new industrial plants. Budget forecast, 1956-57: revenue, $42.8 million; expenditure, $42.6 million; surplus, $181,000.

1957: May 22—Budget. No tax changes. Budget forecast, 1957-58: revenue, $49.0 million; expenditure, $48.0 million; surplus, $79,000.

_____. Report of South Coast Commission.

1958: August 28—Budget. No tax changes. The delay by the federal government in tabling the Report of the McNair Royal Commission was responsible for the late tabling of the 1958 budget. The Minister of Finance expressed his disappointment with the recommendations of the Report and his satisfaction that the federal government had declined to act immediately on the recommendations. Recession-generated unemployment and increased need for capital expenditures and social assistance had resulted in a deficit of $2.3 million on 1957-58 operations, instead of the anticipated surplus. The Minister forecast a $25.0 million increase in revenue for the current year, $13.6 million of which would be the award recommended by the McNair Commission, established in accordance with the terms of the union agreement. Capital expenditures were estimated at $22.4 million. Budget forecast, 1958-59: revenue, $74.1; expenditure, $59.3 million; surplus, $14.8 million.

_____. May 31—Report, Federal Royal Commission on Newfoundland Finances (McNair Commission).

1959: June 25—Budget. No tax changes. The province had not yet received from the federal government the $13.6 million payment for 1958-59; preliminary figures (including receipt of the $13.6 million) indicated a surplus of $12.0 million on current account for 1958-59, and capital expenditures of $21.2 million. Budget forecast, 1959-60: revenue, $71.6 million; expenditure, $67.5 million; surplus, $4.0 million. Capital expenditures, $20.9 million.

1960: June 22—Budget. The Minister of Finance reviewed the 10-year forecast that had been made of the province's future spending and decried the paucity of the grants expected to come from the federal government: $8.0 million under the Term 29 award and $7.5 million under the Atlantic Provinces Adjustment Grants. The 1959-60 current account surplus of $5.0 million and $10.0 million raised from a bond issue were used to finance capital account spending. Tax increases announced by the minister included a 2¢ per gallon raise in gasoline taxes to 19¢, and an increase to 5 percent in the general sales tax, but food was to be exempted. Budget forecast, 1960-61: revenue, $80.7 million; expenditure, $77.0 million; surplus on current account $4.0 million. Capital expenditures were estimated at $21.0 million.

1961: February 22—Budget. No tax changes were announced. Preliminary figures for 1960-61 indicated a surplus on current account of approximately $3.0 million; capital expenditures of $22.5 million, and a bond issue of $10.0 million. Newfoundland's direct debt stood at $65.5 million and indirect (contingent) debt, $20.0 million. Budget forecast 1961-62: revenue, $82.1 million; expenditure, $80.6 million; surplus on current account, $1.6 million; capital expenditures, $15.2 million.

1963: May 30—Budget. No tax changes announced. A surplus on current account of $1.1 million (preliminary) was applied against capital expenditures in 1962-63. Budget forecast, 1963-64: revenue, $100.0 million; expenditure, $99.9 million; surplus on current account, $61,000; gross capital expenditure, $34.8 million.

1964: May 19—Budget. Taxes on tobacco and the price of beer, liquor and wine were increased. The current account surplus for 1963-64 of $61,000 was offset against gross capital expenditures of $41.6 million. Budget forecast, 1964-65: revenue, $116.0 million; expenditure, $111.0 million; surplus on current account, $5.0 million; capital expenditures, $46.5 million. The Minister of Finance gave some details of expenditures in Newfoundland over the 15 years since Confederation: provincial expenditures on roads, $215.2 million and on health, $199.3 million; spending by private interests on mineral exploration, $68.2 million.

1965: March 8—Budget. No tax changes were announced; first-year students at Memorial University were to receive free tuition. The estimated surplus on current account for 1964-65 of $6.0 million was applied against capital expenditure of $23.0 million. Budget forecast, 1965-66: revenue, $130.4 million; expenditure, $128.7 million; current account surplus, $1.7 million; capital expenditures, $49.8 million.

1966: February 16—Budget. No tax changes were announced. As of September 1, 1965 the province began to pay allowances to fifth-year students at Memorial University; as of September 1, 1966 the allowance was to be extended to fourth-year students as well. The expected deficit of $20.5 million on current and capital account was to be financed through loans. Budget forecast, 1966-67: revenue, $176.1 million; expenditure, $204.1 million; deficit, $28.0 million.

_____. Report, Royal Commission on Health.

1967: March 15—Budget. Effective April 1, the sales tax was raised from 5 to 6 percent, the corporation income tax from 10 to 11 percent and the gasoline tax from 19 to 20 cents per gallon. Budget forecast, 1967-68: revenue, $289 million; expenditure, $245 million; surplus, $43.8 million.

_____. Report, Royal Commission on Education and Youth.

1968: March 29—Budget. The sales tax was raised from 6 to 7 percent and the corporation tax from 11 to 12 percent. Tobacco taxes and liquor prices were also raised. The previously granted free tuition at Memorial University was restricted and cash living allowances were limited. Budget forecast, 1968-69: revenue, $271.5 million; expenditure, $317.5 million; deficit, $46 million.

1969: April 15—Budget. Tax increases included raises in the corporation tax from 12 to 13 percent and in the personal income tax from 28 to 33 percent of the federal tax, with broadening of the sales tax to cover transient accommodation and various services. Budget forecast, 1969-70: revenue, $209.5 million; expenditure, $259.6 million; deficit, $51.1 million.

1970: April 23—Budget. No tax changes were made. Budget forecast 1970-71 (revised basis): revenue, $237 million; expenditure, $293 million; deficit, $60 million.

1971: April 28—Budget. No tax changes were made. Budget forecast, 1971-72: revenues, $410 million; expenditure, $508 million; deficit, $98 million.

1972: Tax on tobacco products doubled. Assistance to students to be reduced and parent subsidy eliminated. Budget forecast, 1972-73: revenue, $439 million; expenditure, $590 million; deficit, $151 million.

1973: March 30—Budget. No tax changes were made. Budget forecast, 1973-74: revenue, $496 million; expenditure, $619 million; deficit, $123 million.

1974: April 10—Budget. The sales tax was increased from 7 to 8 percent and the personal income tax from 36 to 40 percent of the federal tax. The province was taking a controlling interest in the Churchill Falls (Labrador) Corporation to develop the Lower Churchill River and was assisting in the financing of oil refineries at Come-by-Chance. The government had entered into a ten-year agreement with the Department of Regional Economic Expansion. Changes were made in student loans and grants. Budget forecast, 1974-75: revenue, $619 million; expenditure, $753 million; deficit, $133 million.

1975: March 12—Budget. Capital expenditures would be emphasized. Tax changes were limited to revision in mining taxation following report of a royal commission. Budget forecast, 1975-76: revenue, $760 million; expenditure, $926 million; deficit, $165 million.

_____: November 24—Second Budget. In view of worsening financial and economic conditions a second budget was introduced to increase taxes, defer capital projects, freeze government employment, and reduce borrowing.

1976: March 26—Budget. The corporate income tax was increased from 13 to 14 percent and the gasoline tax from 25 to 27 cents per gallon. Expenditure cuts affected hospitals, schools, highway maintenance, and provincial government employment. Budget forecast, 1976-77: revenue, $889 million; expenditure, $1,005 million; deficit, $116 million.

1977: April 28—Budget. The personal income tax rate was set at 58 percent of the federal tax; tobacco taxes and the insurance premiums tax were increased; minor changes were made in sales tax exemptions; new taxes were imposed on cable television and mobile homes. Expenditure cuts included dropping the first-time home owner's grant and certain educational allowances, restricting new school and hospital construction, and closing a linerboard factory. A reformed local property tax was to be introduced. The provincial government at this stage was looking forward to better times with exploitation of its offshore oil resources. Budget forecast, 1977-78: revenue, $1,017 million; expenditure, $1,112 million; deficit, $95 million.

1978: March 17—Budget. In a reversal from most recent budgets, the 1978 version presented a "Blueprint for Development" with emphasis on capital spending. The elements of the program involved improved facilities or new capital expenditure for the fisheries, hydro-electric power, oil and gas, and general industrial development, all directed to increasing gross provincial product and reducing unemployment, a constant problem in Newfoundland. Revenue measures included daily hospital charges, a treatment fee under the children's dental plan, and tax increases. The latter included an increase in the sales tax from 10 to 11 percent (except that during 1978 under the federal offer of compensation, the rate was reduced by 3 points from April to October): an increase from 10 to 11 percent in the insurance premiums tax and in tobacco taxes. A lower rate of corporate tax for small corporations was introduced. A theme current in this budget was the province's conviction that it had made a poor deal in selling electricity from Churchill Falls to Quebec and urged a new agreement. Budget forecast, 1978-79: revenue, $1,132 million; expenditure, $1,216 million; deficit, $84 million.

1979: July 19—Budget. Current capital expenditures were proceeding, with emphasis on hydro-electric development for industrial use. Additional amounts were being spent on local education. A new grant for first-time home buyers was introduced. Taxes were increased on cigarettes and insurance premiums and new taxes were levied on aviation fuel and advertising. Passenger car registration charges were increased. Budget forecast, 1979-80: revenue, $1,277 million; expenditure, $1,396 million; deficit, $119 million. million.

1980: March 28—Budget. At this stage the minister was speaking with satisfaction of developments in the Hibernia oil discovery and the agreement that had been reached for division of its production, which it was thought would begin in five to seven years and probably last for 15 years. Unfortunately the oil refinery at Come-by-Chance had been forced into bankruptcy. Spending increases in the coming fiscal year would largely be for schools and hospitals and social assistance, including subsidized drugs for needy seniors. Municipal grants were being overhauled. Tax increases included a raise in the corporation tax from 14 to 15 percent, a raise in tobacco taxes and increases in various licences. Budget forecast, 1980-81: revenue, $1,340 million; expenditure, $1,538 million; deficit, $131 million.

_____. Report, Newfoundland Study by Economic Council of Canada.

1981: April 14—Budget. This budget reviewed the federal-provincial stalemate on control over oil resources, and reaffirmed that the province would spend no further money on oil exploration until the ownership of the resources was settled by the Supreme Court. Despite a dismal economic performance in 1980 and dull prospects ahead the budget increased spending in several areas, mainly for social assistance. The major revenue changes were increases in the tobacco and gasoline taxes and in motor vehicle and natural resource licences. Budget forecast, 1981-82: revenue, $1,572 million; expenditure, $1,708 million; deficit, $136 million.

1982: May 27—Budget. Following the recession the budget attempted to give some stimulus through increased capital expenditure but also raised taxes to reduce the deficit. The recently revised federal-provincial transfer formula would produce lower payments than expected, a complaint that became general in provincial budgets of this period. The main tax changes were an increase to 60 percent of the federal personal income tax, a one point rise in the corporate tax to 16 percent (the reduced rate remaining at 12 percent), a paid-up capital tax for banks and trust companies, increases in tobacco taxes, motor and business licences and in liquor revenues. Under the sales tax a preferred rate of 8 percent was given for construction materials, and exemptions were given on a selective basis for capital expenditures by small businesses. Budget forecast, 1982-83: revenue, $1,794 million; expenditure, $1,956 million; deficit, $162 million.

_____: November 19—Economic Statement. In view of a deteriorating fiscal position the minister introduced a range of fairly severe tax increases in November. The sales tax was increased from 11 to 12 percent, well above other provinces, exemptions were withdrawn for adult clothing and footwear, heating fuel for commercial purposes other than manufacturing, and low-cost meals; there were also increases in taxes on tobacco, gasoline, property insurance premiums, and in corporation fees.

1983: March 17—Budget. Strict budgeting continued in 1983, with restrictions on educational expenditures. Taxes were increased on marine fuels for specified uses and fees raised for provincial licences and permits. Budget forecast, 1983-84: revenue, $1,902 million; expenditure, $2,097 million; deficit, $195 million.

1984: March 20—Budget. Stringent budgeting continued, with freezes for salaries and pensions; a per diem hospital charge was withdrawn and replaced by higher charges for semi-private and private rooms. Increased fees were to be charged for college and vocational education and children's dental care. The sales tax was removed from manufacturing equipment and the small business corporate tax was reduced to 10 percent from 12 percent. Budget forecast, 1984-85: revenue, $1,993 million; expenditure, $2,202 million; deficit, $209 million.

1985: February 11—the Atlantic Accord. By this time the province, to its great satisfaction, had concluded the Atlantic Accord with the newly elected Conservative national government giving it basically the same right to collect resource revenues from ocean oil resources as the other provinces had for land resources. It also included a five-year development fund of which

75 percent would be provided by the federal government. There would also be guaranteed interim protection of equalization payments to offset the reduction due to inclusion of oil revenues. Unfortunately oil prices were falling to a level where the Hibernia oil discoveries were ceasing to be economic, so that the prospect of revenues from this quarter was put off to the indefinite future.

_____. May 16—Budget. This was a hold-the-line budget. Tax changes were minimal. Some minor exemptions from sales tax were given, but no major tax changes were made. Budget forecast, 1985-86: revenue, $2,260 million; expenditure, $2,492 million; deficit, $232 million.

1986: March 25—Budget. With some economic recovery the budget outlook was improving. Spending was increased for education, health, social services, job creation, and municipalities, with principal emphasis on capital outlays. Tax changes included removal of the special sales tax rates on building materials and insurance premiums. Both were made subject to the regular rate. Various fees and charges were increased. Budget forecast, 1986-87: revenue, $2,296 million; expenditure, $2,574; deficit, $279 million.

1987: April 2—Budget. As the province reached completion of four decades as a part of Canada, the Minister of Finance reviewed its progress and found the rate of its rise to national average standards had been discouragingly slow. It had approached the federal government for additional short- and long-term assistance without success. The recession of recent years had forced the province to curtail its expenditures and increase its taxes to the point where there was little room left for further action. Reduced federal payments under the EPF system would make matters even more difficult for the future.

Under the 1987 budget steps continued to be directed toward economic stimulus. These included measures to stimulate general industrial and commercial activity, the inshore fisheries, worker training, and help for small business. A community college system was to be instituted in 1987. Otherwise capital expenditures were fixed at present levels for three years. Tax changes were minimal. The insurance and corporate capital taxes were raised. Some fees and charges were increased and liquor prices went up. Budget forecast, 1987-88: revenue, $2,441 million; expenditure, $2,794 million; deficit, $353 million.

1988: March 29—Budget. A provincial stock saving plan was announced; liquor prices and licences and fees to be increased; the province approved of the federal income tax reforms; it did not increase its own income tax rates. The province remained committed and determined to eliminate its current account deficit over the next few years. Budget forecast, 1988-89: revenue, $2.7 billion; expenditure, $2.9 billion; deficit on combined account, $249.5 million.

Prince Edward Island

To most visitors the Island has the appearance of a pleasant and inviting parkland. However, it is one of Canada's original provinces, with a long

Table 18.5 Prince Edward Island: General Profile

	Year[a]	Province	All Canada	Province as percent of all Canada
Population (000)	1987	127	25,625	0.5
Gross Domestic Product ($ billion)	1986	1.5	506.5	0.3
G.D.P. per capita ($)	1986	11,611	20,030	58.0
Personal Income ($ billion)	1986	1.5	432.5	0.3
P.I. per capita ($)	1986	12,071	17,060	70.8
Unemployment rate (%)..............	1987	13.3	8.9	150.0
Provincial government: revenue ($ billion)........................	1986	0.5	202.5[b]	0.2
Provincial government: expenditure ($ billion)........................	1986	0.5	234.1[b]	0.2
Basic personal income tax rate (%)[c]	1988	56.0	46.5-60[d]	—
General corporate tax rate (%)	1988	15.0	14-17[d]	—
Retail sales tax rate	1988	10.0	6-12[d]	—

See table 18.1 for footnotes and sources.

and interesting history. Economically it is heavily dependent on the sea and on agriculture, its lobsters and potatoes being prized throughout Canada. But like other Atlantic provinces it is far from able, despite relatively high tax rates, to meet the cost of government without substantial assistance from the federal government.

On the revenue side, the province's own sources amounted to approximately one-half the total for much of the period since 1962, but in 1986 were estimated to rise to nearly 54 percent. Tax revenues reached their highest proportion in 1986 at 37 percent. Grants from the federal government dropped from 56 percent of the total in 1952 to 46 percent in 1986. Natural resources revenue is virtually non-existent.

On the expenditure side a dramatic increase in education costs from 14 to 24 percent of the total reflects the assumption by the province from the municipalities of most of the cost of primary and secondary education. Provincial grants cover the cost of basic foundation progams for grades 1 to 12; over 95 percent of local educational expense has been assumed by the province under this arrangement. Additional taxes may be imposed by the municipality for supplementary education. Post-secondary education development and financing in Prince Edward Island, Nova Scotia and New Brunswick are under the control of the Maritime Provinces Higher Education Commission. As a share of the total, both health and social services have risen sharply since 1952, but transportation has dropped. Prince Edward Island has not suffered deficits as frequently as the other Atlantic provinces, and the share of the budget going for debt charges rose only from 8.3 percent in 1952 to 11.5 percent in 1986. Transfers to municipalities are a minor element—less than 1 percent.

Table 18.6 Prince Edward Island Finances: The Eighties

Year[a]	Revenue	Expenditure	Deficit
	millions of dollars		
1980.....................	326.1	343.4	− 17.3
1981.....................	373.8	368.2	+ 5.6
1982.....................	398.3	422.2	− 23.9
1983.....................	442.1	434.6	+ 7.5
1984.....................	458.0	462.2	− 4.2
1985.....................	468.1	483.1	− 15.0
1986.....................	520.2	538.2	− 18.0
1987.....................	563.9	574.6	− 10.7
1988.....................	581.8	593.8	− 12.1

See table 18.2 for footnote and sources.

Table 18.7 Province of Prince Edward Island, Revenue, Consolidated Finances Basis, Selected Years, 1952-86[a]

Source	1952	1962	1972	1982	1986
	millions of dollars				
Taxes.......................	1.7	8.9	34.6	124.6	194.8
Natural resource revenue	—	—	0.4	0.3	0.5
Privileges, licences and permits ...	0.6	1.0	2.1	3.9	4.0
Liquor sales and regulation	0.9	1.4	3.5	7.8	8.9
Other revenue	0.6	1.3	16.5	62.1	71.1
Transfers from other governments[b]	4.8	13.5	57.1	199.6	240.9
Total.......................	8.6	26.1	114.0	398.3	520.2
Own source revenue	3.8	12.6	56.9	198.7	279.3
Surplus or deficit.............	0.2	− 3.3	1.7	− 25.5	− 18.0
	percent of total revenue				
Taxes.......................	19.8	34.1	30.4	31.2	37.4
Natural resource revenue	—	—	0.3	0.1	0.2
Privileges, licences and permits ...	7.0	3.8	1.8	1.0	0.9
Liquor sales and regulation	10.4	5.4	3.0	2.0	1.7
Other revenue	7.0	5.0	14.3	15.6	13.5
Transfers from other governments[b]	55.8	51.7	50.2	50.1	46.3
Total.......................	100.0	100.0	100.0	100.0	100.0
Own source revenue	44.2	48.3	49.8	49.9	53.7

See table 18.3 for footnotes and sources.

Prince Edward Island Diary

1950: March 14—Budget. No tax changes were announced. Preliminary figures for 1949-50 indicated a deficit of $1.8 million, including a provision for the sinking fund. Provincial debt at March 31, 1950 was forecast at $14.2 million. Budget forecast, 1950-51: revenue, $7.0 million; expenditure, $8.7 million; deficit, $1.6 million, including a sinking fund provision of $492,000. The federal government was expected to provide $4.0 million of the province's revenue.

Table 18.8 Province of Prince Edward Island, Expenditure,
Consolidated Finances Basis, Selected Years, 1952-86[a]

	1952	1962	1972	1982	1986
	millions of dollars				
General services................	0.4	1.1	9.2	26.9	38.8
Health.......................	1.3	5.8	20.8	84.9	110.0
Social services	0.5	2.6	10.6	49.1	55.9
Education....................	1.2	5.8	29.0	101.1	120.5
Transportation and					
communications.............	3.4	9.3	15.1	54.0	55.4
Natural resources and industrial					
development	0.4	1.2	10.3	35.7	63.7
Charges on debt...............	0.7	2.0	8.6	45.2	62.9
Transfers to other govern-					
ments[b]	0.1	0.5	0.5	3.0	4.0
Other.......................	0.4	1.1	8.2	22.2	26.9
Total.......................	8.4	29.4	112.3	422.1	538.2
Offsets:					
Specific purpose transfers	1.5	10.2	30.9	72.0	94.0
General purpose transfers	3.3	3.3	26.2	127.6	146.9
Own expenditures	3.6	15.9	55.2	222.5	297.3
	percent of total expenditure				
General services...............	4.7	3.8	8.2	6.4	7.2
Health.......................	15.5	19.7	18.5	20.1	20.5
Social services	6.0	8.8	9.4	11.6	10.4
Education....................	14.3	19.7	25.8	24.0	22.4
Transportation and					
communications.............	40.5	31.6	13.4	12.8	10.3
Natural resources and industrial					
development	4.8	4.1	9.2	8.5	11.9
Charges on debt...............	8.3	6.8	7.6	10.7	11.5
Transfers to other govern-					
ments[c]	1.2	1.7	0.5	0.7	0.7
Other.......................	4.7	3.8	7.4	5.2	5.1
Total.......................	100.0	100.0	100.0	100.0	100.0
Own expenditure	42.9	54.1	49.2	52.7	55.2

See table 18.4 for footnotes and sources.

1951: March 26—Budget. No tax changes. The preliminary deficit for 1950-51 was $2.0 million, including a sinking fund payment of $529,000. Budget forecast, 1951-52: revenue, $7.5 million; expenditure, $9.3 million; deficit, $1.9 million, including sinking fund provisions of $523,000. Provincial sources were expected to supply 39 percent of general account revenue and the federal government, 61 percent.

1952: March 31—Budget. No tax changes. Interim figures showed a deficit of $2.6 million for 1951-52, including a sinking fund provision of $569,000; debt was forecast at $17.6 million. Budget forecast, 1952-53: revenue, $7.9 million; expenditure, $9.7 million; deficit, $1.9 million, including a sinking fund provision of $583,000. Payments under the 1952 tax rental agreements were expected to total $3.9 million, or 89 percent of federal government ordinary account transfers of $4.3 million.

1953: March 26—Budget. No tax changes. Interim figures for 1952-53 showed a deficit of $552,000, including a sinking fund provision of $608,000. Budget forecast, 1953-54: revenue, $8.4 million; expenditure, $9.7 million; surplus, excluding provision for sinking fund, $56,141.

1954: March 30—Budget. Preliminary figures forecast a surplus of $70,000 for 1953-54, excluding the provision for debt retirement. Budget forecast, 1954-55: revenue, $9.1 million; expenditure, $10.1 million; deficit, $986,000.

1955: March 7—Budget. No tax changes. 1954-55 preliminary results indicated a surplus of $359,000 and net debt of $17.7 million at March 31, 1955. Budget forecast, 1955-56: revenue, $9.3 million; expenditure, $10.5 million; deficit, $1.2 million. Federal government transfers under the tax rental agreement were expected to total $3.7 million and for shared-cost programs, $525,000. Revenue from provincial taxes and other sources was estimated at $3.9 million; the gasoline tax was expected to raise $1.6 million of this. The main items of expenditure were expected to be: health and welfare, $2.0 million; education, debt charges, and transportation roughly $1.3 million each.

1956: March 13—Budget. No tax changes. The Minister of Finance reported an estimated deficit for 1955-56 of $2.3 million, bringing net debt to $20.1 million. Budget forecast, 1956-57: revenue, $11.3 million; expenditure, $12.4 million; deficit, $1.1 million. Transfers from the federal government ($6.3 million) made up 56 percent of the province's total revenue forecast, $4.1 million of which was estimated to be tax rental payments.

1957: March 26—Budget. The tax on gasoline was increased by 3¢ to 16¢ per gallon. The Minister reported an expected deficit of $1.8 million on 1956-57 operations and a net debt of $22.1 million at March 31. Budget forecast, 1957-58: revenue, $13.2 million; expenditure, $15.0 million; deficit, $1.8 million.

1958: April 8—Budget. During 1957 the province had started to levy a 2 percent tax on insurance permiums (formerly a federal tax). No new tax changes were announced. The Minister of Finance forecast net debt of $23.6 million at March 31, 1958, resulting from the expected deficit of $2.0 million for 1957-58. The province had been informed that it had been overpaid by $1.1 million under the 1952 Tax Rental Agreements because of population miscalculations; repayment of $228,000 per year would be necessary over a five-year period. Budget forecast, 1958-59: revenue, $15.2 million; expenditure, $15.3 million; deficit, $156,000. The Minister expressed his disappointment that the new federal-provincial arrangements had not taken up the Island's plea for higher payments based on need but remained hopeful of a more realistic plan in the future based on actual requirements, linked to tax potential.

1959: March 10—Budget. The Minister of Finance announced that premiums for the new hospital insurance program would be levied at $2.00 per month per single person, and $4.00 per family. He forecast a deficit of $2.0 million for 1958-59 and net debt of $25.3 million at March 31, 1959. Budget forecast, 1959-60: revenue, $18.2 million; expenditure, $18.7 million; deficit, $557,000. A new expenditure item of $1.5 million was included to cover the cost of the hospital insurance plan.

1960: March 30—Budget. The Minister of Finance announced that a retail sales tax would be levied at 4 percent. The recently elected Conservative government found an anticipated deficit of $5.5 million on 1959-60 operations had brought P.E.I.'s outstanding debt to $31.0 million. The new government felt it would be preferable to find new sources of revenue rather than curtail provincial programs. Budget forecast, 1960-61: revenue, $21.8 million; expenditure, $21.9 million; an almost balanced budget.

1961: March 7—Budget. The report of an outside accounting firm on the province's accounting and budgetary system recommended alterations in the accounting system. From the higher revenues generated in the 1960-61 fiscal year, outstanding debt was reduced by $71,000. Net funded debt at March 31, 1961 stood at $27.3 million. Budget forecast, 1961-62: revenue, $22.2 million; expenditure, $23.2 million; deficit, $1.0 million. Receipts from the federal government were expected to provide 56 percent of total revenues, of which 40 percent was payable through the tax-sharing arrangement. Education and health were expected to take 13 percent each of total spending, followed by debt charges at 12 percent, and welfare at 9 percent.

1962: March 20—Budget. No tax changes were announced. A small deficit of $22,000 for 1961-62 resulted in estimated net funded debt outstanding at March 31, 1962 of $25.0 million. Budget forecast, 1962-63: revenue, $27.0 million; expenditure, $28.0 million; deficit, $1.0 million, including debt retirement payments.

1963: April 16—Budget. The Minister of Finance announced increases in the general sales tax from 4 percent to 5 percent and the tax on gasoline by 2¢ to 18¢ per gallon. Interim figures showed a deficit of $2.5 million on 1962-63 operations, resulting in unfunded debt of $25.2 million at March 31, 1963. Budget forecast, 1963-64; revenue, $27.3 million; expenditure, $29.1 million; deficit, $1.8 million.

1964: March 5—Budget. No tax changes. A deficit of $3.1 million for 1963-64 was expected to result in net funded debt of $29.0 million at March 31, 1964. Budget forecast, 1964-65: revenue, $28.4 million; expenditure, $31.0 million; deficit, $2.6 million. Payments under the federal-provincial fiscal arrangements were estimated to provide $6.1 million of total federal transfers of $14.8 million; current expenditures on debt retirement were forecast at $3.3 million, health at $6.0 million, and education at $3.6 million.

1965: March 11—Budget. No tax changes. The forecast deficit for 1964-65 of $3.1 million was expected to be added to net funded debt. Budget forecast, 1965-66: revenue, $32.6 million; expenditure, $40.0 million; deficit, $7.4 million.

1966: March 24—Budget. No tax changes. The deficit forecast for 1965-66 totalled $6.0 million. Budget forecast, 1966-67: revenue, $37.1 million; expenditure, $44.5 million; deficit, $7.4 million.

1967: April 25—Budget. A Liberal government had replaced the Conservatives on July 28, 1966. The new Minister of Finance found that "the province had been living beyond its means" and provincial debt had risen to an estimated $61.0 million as of March 31, 1967. Preliminary figures for 1966-67 showed a deficit of $0.9 million. The minister expressed his dilemma in judging just where to cut expenditure: if shared-cost program spending were reduced, federal transfers would also be reduced; health, welfare, education, and agriculture programs costs were high but the government was providing services the public has grown to expect; public debt charges were high because debt was high. He reiterated the plea that federal transfers be based on need and size. No tax changes were announced. Budget forecast, 1967-68: revenue, $47.1 million; expenditure, $49.9 million; deficit, $2.8 million. Federal transfers were expected to provide 65 percent of total revenue, including $2.9 million under the tax collection arrangements, $14.1 million in equalization, and $7.9 in shared-cost transfers. Education was expected to take by far the largest share of the budget, at 25 percent, followed by health at 20 percent, welfare 14 percent, and debt charges at 13 percent.

_____. White Paper on Economic Planning and Development.

1968: March 19—Budget. Gasoline and tobacco taxes were raised; the sales tax was extended to transient accommodation, laundry and dry-cleaning, repairs to personal property, and books and lubricants. Budget forecast, 1968-69: revenue, $54 million; expenditure, $55.1 million; deficit, $1.1 million.

1969: April 15—Budget. The sales tax was increased from 5 to 7 percent; no other changes were made. Budget forecast, 1969-70: revenue, $65.4 million; expenditure, $69.6 million; deficit, $4.1 million.

1970: March 25—Budget. No tax changes were made. Budget forecast, 1970-71: revenue, $77.9 million; expenditure, $78.7 million; deficit, $0.8 million.

_____. Provincial-Municipal Fiscal Study. (Touche Ross).

1971: March 18—Budget. Provincial sales tax increased from 7 to 8 percent and personal income tax was raised from 28 to 33 percent of federal tax. Budget forecast, 1971-72: revenue, $91.6 million; expenditure, $94.5 million; deficit, $2.9 million.

1972: March 16—Budget. No tax changes were made. Budget forecast, 1972-73: revenue, $105.0 million; expenditure, $214.0 million; deficit, $4.0 million.

1973: February 8—Budget. Succession duties and gift tax would be terminated at March 31, 1974; the sales tax exemption for children's clothing and footwear was extended and children's free dental care proposed. The province intended to give increased grants to municipalities or direct grants to homeowners. Budget forecast, 1973-74: revenue, $120.6 million; expenditure, $122.0 million; deficit, $1.4 million.

1974: April 2—Budget. A substantial number of household goods were exempted from sales tax; a subsidy would be given to offset increasing costs of electric power and the provincial property tax was reduced. A supplement was to be paid to the federal family allowance and various development programs would go forward under the recent agreement with the federal government. Budget forecast, 1974-75: revenue, $147.6 million; expenditure, $147.1 million; a small surplus was forecast.

1975: May 13—Budget. With lower tax revenues due to reduced equalization payments (because other provinces were lowering their taxes!) the Minister felt it necessary to raise the tax on cigarettes. No other changes were made. Budget forecast, 1975-76: revenue, $178.8 million; expenditure, $181.7 million; deficit, $8.8 million.

1976: March 23—Budget. Continuing deficits and uncertainty over federal equalization payments led to a rigorous budget. Ceilings or reductions were imposed on many expenditures and the electricity subsidy was discontinued. Exemptions for energy saving equipment and materials were granted under the sales tax; liquor establishments would be required to collect a 10 percent tax on each drink. Budget forecast, 1976-77: revenue, $196.5 million; expenditure, $198.5 million; deficit, $2.1 million.

1977: March 30—Budget. This was to be a job creation budget, with an increase in capital expenditures. The Northumberland Strait electric cable would reduce the province's dependence on petroleum-generated electricity, along with a home insulation program. Other expenditures related to municipalities, education, welfare, and senior citizen housing. The only tax change set the personal income tax at 50 percent of the federal tax. Liquor prices were raised. Budget forecast, 1977-78: revenue, $225.8 million; expenditure, $231.8 million; deficit, $6.0 million.

1978: March 28—Budget. Poor economic performance in 1977 and reduced federal payments had produced a larger deficit than anticipated. Expenditure in the new year would emphasize agriculture, fisheries, forestry, and industrial development. Tax changes increased the sales tax exemption for meals and deferred property taxes for needy senior citizens. Incentives would be offered to encourage research on the Island. Budget forecast, 1978-79: revenue, $249.3 million; expenditure $256.0 million; deficit, $6.7 million.

1979: July 10—Budget. A new government elected in April presented the 1979 budget. Studies were underway in many areas and action was delayed for the meantime. Minor tax changes included a new tax on aviation fuel and an increase in the tobacco tax. Budget forecast, 1979-80: revenue, $277.6 million; expenditure, $281.8 million; deficit, $4.2 million.

1980: February 28—Budget. Some major tax increases were introduced; the sales tax was raised from 8 to 9 percent and some exemptions were withdrawn, the personal income tax rate went from 50 to 52.5 percent of the federal tax, the gasoline tax was increased and was to be indexed in the future; the provincial property tax was reduced. The expenditure program included a new municipal grants structure, aid for resource-based industries, energy, and roads. Budget forecast, 1980-81: revenue, $316.0 million; expenditure, $326.2 million; deficit, $10.2 million.

1981: March 21—Budget. Another rigorous budget brought further tax increases. The sales tax was raised from 9 to 10 percent and long-distance telephone calls made taxable, the provincial liquor tax was raised from 10 percent to 25 percent, the motor fuels tax was increased, and various corporate and other business fees were raised. There would be some increases in provincial programs but hiring of staff was frozen. Budget forecast, 1981-82: revenue, $361.2 million; expenditure, $369.6 million; deficit, $8.4 million.

1982: March 25—Budget. In the wake of the recession there was little room for any change. Most of the minister's revenue concerns were about federal-provincial payments. Budget forecast, 1982-83: revenue, $386.6 million; expenditure, $401.5 million; deficit, $14.6 million.

1983: April 14—Budget. The only increase in this budget was in the cigarette tax. Expenditure were to be concentrated in job creation; some social programs were to be cut. Budget forecast, 1983-84: revenue, $397.1 million; expenditure, $415.5 million; deficit, $18.2 million.

1984: April 10—Budget. No taxes were changed. Expenditures would concentrate on the capital side. Budget forecast, 1984-85: revenue, $434.9 million; expenditure, $444.8 million; deficit, $9.8 million.

1985: March 5—Budget. A reduction in motor fuels tax was the only tax change. Much was counted on from the transfer of the head office of the Department of Veterans Affairs to the Island and the regional economic agreement just signed with the federal government. Forecast, 1985-86: revenue, $468.1 million; expenditure, $483.1 million; deficit, $15.0 million.

1986: June 26—Budget. A new government (Liberal) had been elected and presented its first budget. It undertook increased spending on agriculture, energy, forestry, health and social services. These included enrichment of the child dental care program, pharmacare for senior citizens, and assistance for municipal governments. The government planned on a Commission on Government Expenditure to review all programs. The personal income tax rate was raised from 52.5 percent to 55 percent, the corporate income tax was set at 15 percent for large companies, and the tobacco taxes were increased. Budget forecast, 1986-87: revenue, $491.7 million; expenditure, $513.0 million; deficit, $21.2 million.

1987: March 24—Budget. The province moved closer to the goal of a reduced current account deficit without tax increases or severe expenditure cuts. Property tax payable by non-residents would be increased. Budget forecast, 1987-88: revenue, $528.2 million; expenditure, $538.7 million; deficit, $10.5 million.

1988: April 5—Budget. The personal income tax rate was raised from 55 to 57 percent and a surtax of 10 percent levied on personal income tax payable over $12,500; a 1.5 percent corporation capital tax levied on banks and financial institutions; exemptions broadened under the retail sales tax; and tobacco taxes raised. Cut-back in federal transfer programs had obliged the province to borrow funds to cover certain expenditures. The Commission on Government Expenditures appointed last year had not yet released its final report and the minister reiterated his determination to achieve a 1987-88 was projected at $19 million. Budget forecast, 1988-89: revenue, $581.8 million; expenditure, $593.8 million; combined deficit, $12.1 million.

Nova Scotia

Nova Scotia was one of the original members of Confederation and the most populous of the Maritime provinces. Its capital city, Halifax, is the commercial and financial centre not only for the province but to some extent for the whole Atlantic area. Today the province has an organized local structure of 3 cities, 39 towns, 25 villages and 24 rural municipalities, the apparatus of a relatively mature society. Like the other Atlantic provinces it suffers from chronic economic problems. Some of these are deeply-rooted in history. As population moved westward in the 19th century the Atlantic coastal regions lost the dominance they had enjoyed as the first and closest point of entry from Europe and the source of some of its natural produce. There is also the oft-repeated fact that the abundant forestry resources which enabled the region to build excellent wooden sailing craft could not save it from the inroads of the steel steam-driven ships that appeared in the mid-19th century. While the area has a varied economy nothing since has provided the same economic momentum.

In Nova Scotia agriculture, fishing, forestry, and mining have all been important. The coal deposits in Cape Breton for decades have been the base of a steel industry, the fortunes of which have periodically fluctuated but which has survived in recent years with the support of the federal and provincial governments. Military and naval establishments make a valued contribution to the economy. Halifax is the base for the North Atlantic NATO naval command and a marine construction centre.

Offshore petroleum exploration has been sufficiently encouraging to bring about an accord with the federal government for assistance and clarification of status, although findings so far apparently have been limited to natural gas. Like all other Atlantic provinces government plays a central role, with heavy support from the federal treasury. In Nova Scotia, the most independent of the Atlantic provinces, own-source revenues in most years have been above 55 percent and in 1986 were estimated to be over 60 percent. Transfers from the federal government dropped below 40 percent in 1986, a sign both of provincial tax levels and tightened federal purse strings. The share of expenditure being met by the provincial government has correspondingly increased—in the last five years to two-thirds or more. The bulk of the expenditures are under the familiar headings of health, education, social services, and charges on debt. In general Nova Scotia has followed the traditional pattern of shared responsibility for local services.

Table 18.9   Nova Scotia: General Profile

	Year[a]	Province	All Canada	Province as percent of all Canada
Population (000)	1987	879	25,625	3.4
Gross Domestic Product ($ billion)	1986	12.6	506.5	2.5
G.D.P. per capita ($)	1986	14,404	20,030	71.9
Personal Income ($ billion)	1986	12.1	432.5	2.8
P.I. per capita ($)	1986	13,899	17,060	81.5
Unemployment rate (%)................	1987	12.5	8.9	140.4
Provincial government: revenue ($ billion).........................	1986	3.1	202.5[b]	1.5
Provincial government: expenditure ($ billion).........................	1986	3.5	234.1[b]	1.5
Basic personal income tax rate (%)[c]	1988	56.5	46.5-60[d]	—
General corporate tax rate (%)	1988	15.0	14-17[d]	—
Retail sales tax rate	1988	10.0	6-12[d]	—

See table 18.1 for footnotes and sources.

Table 18.10   Nova Scotia Finances: The Eighties

Year[a]	Revenue	Expenditure	Deficit
	millions of dollars		
1980.....................	1,898.6	2,041.9	− 143.3
1981.....................	2,178.8	2,597.8	− 419.0
1982.....................	2,333.5	2,729.6	− 396.1
1983.....................	2,598.8	2,942.9	− 344.1
1984.....................	2,809.7	3,238.1	− 428.4
1985.....................	2,945.2	3,342.2	− 397.0
1986.....................	3,141.9	3,527.2	− 385.3
1987.....................	3,328.4	3,738.8	− 410.4
1988.....................	3,473.7	3,879.8	− 406.0

See table 18.2 for footnotes and sources.

About 40 percent of local education costs are met by the municipalities; they also bear a share of welfare costs. As with other provinces, for many years the financial record has been one of deficits and growing debt.

Nova Scotia Diary

1948: Estimates. No tax changes announced. Budget forecast for year ending November 30, 1948: revenue, $30.1 million; expenditure, $27.5 million; surplus, $2.6 million before providing for sinking fund payment of $1.3 million.

1949: March 31—Budget. The Minister of Finance announced that the collection of a highway poll tax in municipalities would be discontinued and a tax reduction of 3¢ per gallon of gasoline used on farms and in the lumbering and fishing industries. Budget forecast for year ending November 30, 1949: revenue, $34.5 million; expenditure, $34.6 million; surplus, $0.5 million after sinking fund provision.

Table 18.11 Province of Nova Scotia, Revenue, Consolidated Finances Basis, Selected Years, 1952-86[a]

Source	1952	1962	1972	1982	1986
	millions of dollars				
Taxes........................	9.9	53.1	249.4	933.1	1,438.5
Natural resource revenue	1.3	1.4	2.4	7.6	11.9
Privileges, licences and permits ...	4.3	7.2	16.8	39.3	46.8
Liquor sales and regulation	9.5	13.1	32.6	86.2	111.6
Other revenue	4.3	7.3	63.4	266.1	318.7
Transfers from other governments[b]	23.7	66.0	264.1	1,001.2	1,214.4
Total........................	52.9	148.1	628.7	2,333.5	3,141.9
Own source revenue	29.2	82.1	364.6	1,332.6	1,927.5
Surplus or deficit..............	0.1	0.8	−9.6	−395.7	−385.3
	percent of total revenue				
Taxes........................	18.7	35.9	39.7	40.0	45.7
Natural resource revenue	2.4	1.0	0.4	0.3	0.4
Privileges, licences and permits ...	8.2	4.8	2.7	1.7	1.6
Liquor sales and regulation	18.0	8.8	5.2	3.7	3.6
Other revenue	8.1	4.9	10.2	11.4	10.1
Transfers from other governments[b]	44.6	44.6	42.0	42.9	38.6
Total........................	100.0	100.0	100.0	100.0	100.0
Own source revenue	55.4	55.4	58.0	57.1	61.3

See table 18.3 for footnotes and sources.

1950: April 17—Budget. No tax changes. The Minister warned that because revenue was levelling off and expenditures were rising, study would be given to the idea of levying a direct sales tax. Public debt at November 30, 1949 amounted to $141.0 million. Budget forecast for 16-month period ending March 31, 1951: revenue, $47.7 million; expenditure, $49.5 million; deficit, $1.8 million.

1951: March 8—Budget. The Minister proposed levying a retail turnover tax but was awaiting an amendment to the BNA Act to allow him to do so. Budget forecast, 1951-52: revenue, $40.7 million; expenditure, $41.7 million; deficit on ordinary account: $1.0 million.

_____: June 12—Revised budget. Lacking the consent of all provinces, the necessary amendments to the BNA Act could not be made to allow Nova Scotia to levy a retail turnover tax; the Minister of Finance announced budget cuts, and tax increases of 2¢ a gallon on gasoline, of amusement taxes, and prices charged for liquor. The federal government had recently increased the rate of its manufacturer's sales tax from 8 to 10 percent and the minister felt he could not impose a retail sales tax this year.

1952: March 7—Budget. No tax changes. Budget forecast, 1952-53: revenue, $45.4 million; expenditure, $44.9 million; surplus on ordinary account, $0.5 million.

Table 18.12 Province of Nova Scotia, Expenditure, Consolidated Finances Basis, Selected Years, 1952-86[a]

	1952	1962	1972	1982	1986
	millions of dollars				
General services	1.4	5.5	26.4	86.1	147.7
Health	7.6	37.8	159.4	671.7	939.7
Social services	4.3	13.1	52.1	273.5	353.2
Education	11.7	32.8	159.2	662.2	756.9
Transportation and communications	14.7	30.3	74.1	181.6	177.1
Natural resources and industrial development	2.5	5.1	29.1	179.6	228.4
Charges on debt	6.8	14.9	72.2	374.7	614.2
Transfers to other governments[b]	0.9	1.3	3.9	58.5	52.4
Other	2.9	6.7	61.9	241.6	257.6
Total	52.8	147.3	638.3	2,729.5	3,527.2
Offsets:					
Specific purpose transfers	4.7	42.3	139.6	364.9	561.1
General purpose transfers	19.0	23.8	124.5	635.3	653.3
Own expenditure	29.1	81.4	374.2	1,729.3	2,312.8
	percent of total expenditure				
General services	2.6	3.7	4.1	3.2	4.2
Health	14.4	25.6	25.0	24.6	26.7
Social services	8.1	8.9	8.2	10.0	10.0
Education	22.1	22.2	25.0	24.2	21.5
Transportation and communications	27.8	20.5	11.6	6.7	5.0
Natural resources and industrial development	4.8	3.5	4.5	6.6	6.5
Charges on debt	12.9	10.1	11.3	13.7	17.4
Transfers to other governments[b]	1.7	0.8	0.6	2.1	1.5
Other	5.6	4.7	9.7	8.9	7.2
Total	100.0	100.0	100.0	100.0	100.0
Own expenditure	55.1	55.3	58.6	63.3	65.6

See table 18.4 for footnotes and sources.

1953: February 13—Budget. Tax levied on income derived from gypsum mining operations. Budget forecast, 1953-54: revenue, $47.4 million; expenditure, $57.4 million, including loan expenditures of $10.5 million; deficit, $10.0 million.

1954: March 9—Budget. No tax changes. Budget forecast on current account, 1954-55: revenue, $50.7 million; expenditure, $50.4 million; surplus after sinking fund provisions, $0.3 million. Gross funded debt at March 31, 1954 was $203.3 million.

1955: Budget. 2¢ tax increase to 17¢ per gallon of gasoline; increases in hunting licences and price charged for beer.

1956: March 19—Budget. No tax changes. Budget forecast on current account, 1956-57: revenue, $59.5 million; expenditure, $59.5 million; surplus after sinking fund provisions, $62,000.

1957: March 21—Budget. 2 percent tax levied on premiums of insurance companies.

1958: April 9—Budget. No tax changes immediately. The hospital services program was expected to cost the province $6.0 million in 1959, plus construction; a retail sales tax (hospital tax) was to be levied to help finance the program. Budget forecast excluding the hospital program for 1958-59: revenue, $73.6 million; expenditure, $67.6 million; surplus before sinking fund provisions of $5.9 million, $6.0 million on current account.

1959: March 5—Budget. The retail sales tax (hospital tax) went into effect at 3 percent on January 1, 1959. No other tax changes. Budget forecast, 1959-60: revenue, $82.9 million; expenditure $76.2 million; surplus of $6.7 million before sinking fund provisions of $6.7 million.

1960: Budget. No tax changes. Budget forecast, 1960-61: revenue, $93.0 million; expenditure, $93.0 million; surplus, $87,000.

1961: Budget. Increases were announced in the sales tax to 5 percent and gasoline tax, by 2¢ to 19¢ a gallon. Expenditures were forecast at $93.7 million.

1962: March 12—Budget. No tax changes. Budget forecast on current account for 1962-63: revenue, $108.0 million; expenditure, $100.4 million; surplus, $7.7 million.

1963: March 5—Budget. No tax changes. Budget forecast, 1963-64: revenue $116.7 million, after transfer of $1.0 million from hospital reserves; expenditure, $108.8 million; surplus of $7.9 million on ordinary account transferred to sinking fund. Touche, Ross, chartered accountants of Montreal, were appointed to study provincial-municipal taxation, municipal expenditures, and provincial grants to municipalities.

1964: February 19—Budget. No tax changes. Budget forecast on ordinary account, 1964-65: revenue, $127.1 million including transfer from hospital reserve account, $400,000; expenditure, $118.6 million; surplus transferred to sinking fund, $8.5 million.

1965: Budget. No tax changes. Budget forecast, 1965-66: revenue, $140.0 million; expenditure, $130.8 million; surplus, $9.2 million on ordinary account transferred to sinking fund.

1966: March 1—Budget. No tax changes. Budget forecast, 1966-67: revenue, $162.8 million; expenditure, $154.3 million; surplus on ordinary account, $8.5 million transferred to sinking fund.

1967: February 27—Budget. No tax changes. Budget forecast, 1967-68: revenue, $215.2 million; expenditure, $207.1 million; surplus on ordinary account, $8.1 million transferred to sinking fund.

1968: March 8—Budget. No tax changes were announced. New legislation would be required if medicare were introduced. Budget forecast, 1967-68: revenue, $215 million; expenditure, $250 million; deficit, $35 million.

1969: March 6—Budget. The sales tax rate was raised from 5 to 7 percent and the base was expanded to include motor vehicles and parts, residential electric power, and telephone service other than long-distance calls (already taxed); tobacco and motor fuel taxes were increased and auto licence fees were raised. Prices of beer, wine, and spirits sold through government stores were increased. Preliminary figures for 1969-70: revenue, $398 million; expenditure, $423 million; deficit, $25 million.

_____. Report, House of Assembly, a Select Committee on Sources of Revenue.

1970: March 16—Budget. No tax changes were made. Budget forecast, 1970-71: revenue, $435 million; expenditure, $465 million; deficit, $30 million.

_____. Report, Provincial Municipal Fact Finding Committee.

1971: March 16—Budget. The municipal poll tax would be abolished with compensation; home ownership incentive grants would be introduced. Budget forecast, 1971-72: revenue, $480 Million; expenditure, $527 million, deficit, $47 million.

1972: March 29—Budget. Liquor prices were increased and transient accommodation made subject to sales tax. Previously the personal income tax had been increased from 30.5 to 38.5 percent of the federal tax for 1972 and a new gift tax and succession duties had been enacted to replace the repealed federal tax. Budget forecast, 1972-73: revenue, $434 million; expenditure, $477 million; deficit, $53 million.

1973: February 23—Budget. The province would repeal its succession duties and gift tax as of March 31, 1974. Free dental care for children up to age 5 and free prescription drugs for senior citizens were announced, as well as extension of the exemption for children's clothing and footwear. Property owners would be assisted either through higher grants to municipalities or grants to homeowners.

1974: June 14—Budget. No tax changes were proposed. Municipal taxpayers were rebated 25 percent of their property tax and increased grants were given for local purposes. Several new programs were being undertaken under the Regional Economic Expansion agreement. Budget forecast, 1974-75: revenue, $828 million; expenditure, $869 million; deficit; $41 million.

_____. June: the Report of the Graham Royal Commission on Education, Public Service and Provincial-Municipal Relations recommended that the province assume full responsibility for education, health, social services, housing and the administration of justice. The report also recommended that a new municipal system be adopted.

1975: March 4—Budget. No tax changes were announced. Some stimulus was coming from projects under the General Development Agreement. The province was continuing study of the Graham report, but appeared to be moving in the direction of assuming the operating costs for education. Budget forecast, 1975-76: revenue, $929 million; expenditure, $980 million; deficit, $51 million.

1976: March 19—Budget. With a lagging economy the government had imposed restraints on expenditures in the previous autumn. These set the keynote for the 1976 budget. Expenditure increases were limited, and tax increases were made, including a raise in the sales tax from 7 to 8 percent and in the corporation tax from 10 to 12 percent. Increases were also made in the taxes on tobacco, long distance telephone calls, insurance premiums, motor vehicle and other licences and permits. Budget forecast, 1976-77: revenue, $1,128 million; expenditure, $1,186 million; deficit, $59 million.

1977: March 29—Budget. Like most other provinces Nova Scotia was attempting to stimulate the economy in its budget of this period. Funds were being allocated for job creation and for capital expenditures, with help from the General Development Agreement. A major development was the final takeover by the province of resident taxpayers' sharable education costs. Tax increases were made to reduce the deficit. These included a rise in the personal income tax to 52.5 percent of the federal tax, an increase in the tobacco taxes, and a rise in the prices of wine and liquor. Budget forecast, 1977-78: revenue, $1,272 million; expenditure, $1,354 million; deficit, $83.2 million.

1978: March 3—Budget. In a flagging economy a capital expenditure program and aid to resource industries were the main features of the budget. Under the federal offer the sales tax was reduced from 8 to 5 percent from April to October and a temporary surtax was introduced to pick up the reduction under federal taxation in this period. No other tax changes were made. Budget forecast, 1978-79: revenue, $1,413 million; expenditure, $1,523 million; deficit, $110 million.

1979: April 6—Budget. A new government presented an interim budget with few changes. The provincial economy had performed well in the previous year and there was little room for further stimulus. A current problem was the financing of the Cape Breton steel company, SYSCO, with unexpected calls for additional grants. There had also been heavy costs for a program to subsidize electric power rates. Increases were made in the tobacco taxes and prices for liquor, wine, and beer. Budget forecast, 1979-80: revenue, $1,535 million; expenditure, $1,668 million; deficit, $133 million.

1980: April 2—Budget. Expenditure programs were to be concentrated on helping resource industries—agriculture, mines, energy, tourism, and development. Grants would be paid to municipalities for water and sewer services. The province would attempt to reduce its dependence on off-shore oil for electricity production, which was 84 percent, against the national average of 44 percent. Coal mines and a tidalwave project might help in this direction. Nova Scotia was expecting to share in Atlantic offshore petroleum production, and at this session replaced its legislation with the Petroleum Resources Act. A Nova Scotia Heritage Fund was created after the model of the Alberta and Saskatchewan funds to hold future resource revenues. Tax increases included a rise in the general corporate tax to 13 percent, with a lower rate for small business of 10 percent. Minor changes were made in the retail sales tax exemptions. Budget forecast, 1980-81: revenue, $1,750 million; expenditure, $1,935 million; deficit, $184 million.

1981: April 10—Budget. This budget brought a considerably higher deficit to assist the economy. Both current and capital expenditures were expected to increase substantially as existing programs were enriched in education, vocational training, research, and health. The electricity rate freeze was continued, at provincial expense. Loans were provided for small businesses and an agreement had been made with the federal government for modernizing the SYSCO steel plant. The province was depending heavily on federal payments and no tax increases were made. Budget forecast, 1981-82: revenue, $1,919 million; expenditure, $2,303 million; deficit, $385 million.

1982: April 30—Budget. A budget of expenditure restraints and tax increases. Nearly all taxes were raised; the personal income tax rate went from 52.5 to 56.5 percent of the federal tax, the sales tax was increased from 8 to 10 percent, the general corporation tax rate rose from 13 to 15 percent and there were increases in the gasoline taxes, the tobacco taxes, the insurance premiums tax, in motor vehicle licence fees, business licences and fees, and liquor prices. A 4 percent rate was introduced for machinery and equipment previously free or fully taxable and long distance calls were made taxable at 10 percent. This assault on the taxpayers was intended only to reduce the deficit otherwise expected. Budget forecast, 1982-83: revenue, $2,322 million; expenditure, $2,651 million; deficit, $329 million.

1983: April 18—Budget. Expenditures continued to be concentrated on economic stimulation. The budget deplored the federal government's decision to cut back transfers to the provinces. The one tax change brought cable television charges under the amusement tax. Budget forecast, 1983-84: revenue, $2,389 million; expenditure, $2,838 million; deficit, $449 million.

1984: March 23—Budget. Attention was being addressed increasingly to reducing the deficit, with main emphasis on the current account. Capital expenditure would be increased to provide further economic stimulus. Modest tax changes included an increase in the tobacco taxes. A credit against corporate tax was granted for research and development expenditure and exemption from sales tax for equipment for this purpose. Budget forecast, 1984-85: revenue, $2,635 million; expenditure, $3,098 million; deficit, $463 million.

1985: April 19—Budget. Attention would be concentrated further on reducing the deficit. Spending would be restrained and taxes increased. The tobacco tax was again increased and the sales tax extended to expensive clothing and labour charges for repairs to tangible personal property. Budget forecast, 1985-86: revenue, $2,768 million; expenditure, $3,170 million; deficit, $402 million.

1986: April 18—Budget. Like most provinces Nova Scotia was struggling to achieve a more balanced budget and at the same time continue to offer stimulus to the economy. The 1986 budget showed spending restraints, with two tax changes for revenue, a capital tax on banks, trust and loan companies and an increase in the tobacco taxes. Other changes—tax incentives for a stock savings plan and a two-year tax holiday for newly incorporated small businesses—followed the recommendations of a Task Force on Taxes, as did the capital tax. Budget forecast, 1986-87: revenue, $2,962 million; expenditure, $3,404 million; deficit, $442 million.

_____. August 26—Canada-Nova Scotia Offshore Petroleum Resources Accord. This agreement with the federal government clarified outstanding issues of ownership and control of offshore oil resources, so far limited to findings of natural gas.

1987: April 19—Budget. Expenditure restraints were tightened as the province launched a three-year program to reduce its deficit. Sales tax exemptions for clothing and footwear were narrowed and the tobacco tax was increased. Budget forecast, 1987-88: revenue, $3,144 million; expenditure, $3,570 million; deficit, $426 million.

1988: April 15—Budget. No tax changes. Budget forecast, 1988-89: revenue, $3.5 billion; expenditure, $3.9 billion; deficit, $406.0 million.

New Brunswick

As one of the four original provinces that united in 1867 to become Canada, New Brunswick has now had 120 years of provincial status. In many respects therefore like Nova Scotia it is a mature society, with six cities, 24 towns and 84 villages, and a well-developed educational system and social apparatus. Its main and constant problem over the years have been economic, largely of the same origin as those of Nova Scotia. Fishing of course has been a long-time on-again-off-again income source which, with application of modern technology and business management, has been more stable in recent years. The forest has provided an industrial base both for lumber and paper manufacture, and base metal mines have been a fairly reliable natural resource. Neither however has provided income and employment for the whole population and there are depressed regions in the province.

While New Brunswick governments generally have been on the conservative side they have been in the vanguard in revising local educational financing. All expenditures of local elementary and secondary education are now paid by the province, with administration left to local boards of trustees. The province also carries out all aspects of the construction and financing of school buildings. The same approach has been taken to social assistance payments which are administered and paid for by the province.

Financially the province in recent years has been maintaining independent revenues in the range of 54 to 57 percent of total revenues. In 1986 it was marginally lower than its close neighbour, Nova Scotia, 57 percent compared with 61 percent. Their tax rates were roughly comparable (corporate tax, the same; personal income tax, N.B. 56.5 percent, N.S. 58 percent; sales tax, N.B. 11 percent, N.S. 10 percent) and the difference was due to a moderately higher amount of transfers from the federal government for New Brunswick.

Table 18.13   New Brunswick: General Profile

	Year[a]	Province	All Canada	Province as percent of all Canada
Population (000)	1987	712	25,625	2.8
Gross Domestic Product ($ billion)	1986	9.8	506.5	1.9
G.D.P. per capita ($)	1986	13,841	20,030	69.1
Personal Income ($ billion)	1986	9.2	432.5	2.1
P.I. per capita ($)	1986	12,878	17,060	75.5
Unemployment rate (%)..............	1987	13.2	8.9	148.3
Provincial government: revenue ($ billion)........................	1986	2.9	202.5[b]	1.4
Provincial government: expenditure ($ billion)........................	1986	3.1	234.1[b]	1.3
Basic personal income tax rate (%)[c]	1988	60.0	46.5-60[d]	—
General corporate tax rate (%)	1988	16.0	14-17[d]	—
Retail sales tax rate	1988	11.0	6-12[d]	—

See table 18.1 for footnotes and sources.

Table 18.14   New Brunswick Finances: The Eighties

Year[a]	Revenue	Expenditure	Deficit
	millions of dollars		
1980......................	1,604.6	1,687.0	− 82.4
1981......................	1,817.9	1,959.0	− 141.1
1982......................	2,010.6	2,392.2	− 381.6
1983......................	2,291.7	2,534.1	− 242.4
1984......................	2,501.8	2,738.4	− 236.6
1985......................	2,753.0	2,946.5	− 193.5
1986......................	2,855.6	3,075.4	− 219.8
1987......................	3,123.0	3,338.8	− 215.8
1988......................	3,304.4	3,595.6	− 291.2

See table 18.2 for footnotes and sources.

On the expenditure side New Brunswick has met between 55 and 63 percent by its own efforts over recent decades. In 1986 it expected to meet 60 percent compared to 65 percent for Nova Scotia. Again the higher amount of federal transfers to New Brunswick explains the difference.

Comparisons of individual expenditures show revealing contrasts. In 1986 the estimate was that New Brunswick spent 21 percent of its budget on health; Nova Scotia nearly 27 percent. On the other hand New Brunswick's social service expenditures were over 14 percent, compared with 10 percent for Nova Scotia. New Brunswick's debt charges were 13 percent; Nova Scotia's 17 percent. Despite the different systems for financing education in the two provinces the share going to this heading differed by less than 1 percent. Deficits and growing debt in New Brunswick are in the familiar provincial pattern.

Table 18.15   Province of New Brunswick, Revenue, Consolidated Finances
Basis, Selected Years, 1952-86[a]

Source	1952	1962	1972	1982	1986
	millions of dollars				
Taxes........................	16.2	39.7	232.5	799.0	1,298.1
Natural resource revenue	3.2	3.6	6.0	15.9	27.6
Privileges, licences and permits ...	3.4	6.0	14.8	30.2	45.4
Liquor sales and regulation	6.4	9.8	23.7	60.4	79.3
Other revenue	2.8	6.3	40.8	178.2	184.0
Transfers from other govern-ments[b]	20.7	56.4	244.8	926.9	1,221.2
Total	52.7	121.8	562.6	2,010.6	2,855.6
Own source revenue	32.0	65.4	317.8	1,083.7	1,634.4
Surplus or deficit	1.7	− 10.8	− 22.8	− 381.7	− 219.8
	percent of total revenue				
Taxes........................	30.7	32.6	41.4	39.8	45.4
Natural resource revenue	6.0	3.0	1.1	0.8	1.0
Privileges, licences and permits ...	6.5	4.9	2.6	1.5	1.6
Liquor sales and regulation	12.1	8.0	4.2	3.0	2.8
Other revenue	5.4	5.2	7.3	8.8	6.4
Transfers from other govern-ments[b]	39.3	46.3	43.4	46.1	42.8
Total	100.0	100.0	100.0	100.0	100.0
Own source revenue	60.7	53.7	56.6	53.9	57.2

See table 18.3 for footnotes and sources.

New Brunswick Diary

1947: March 20—Budget. No tax changes were announced. The secretary-treasurer reported that the surplus of $2.3 million for the year ending October 31, 1946 had been the largest recorded so far in the province's history. Budget forecast, 1947: revenue, $20.9 million; expenditure, $18.0 million; surplus, $2.9 million.

1948: March 16—Budget. No tax changes. The 1947 surplus on current account had been $6.3 million, capital expenditures totalled $12.0 million, and net debt increased by $2.9 million. Budget forecast, 1948: revenue, $23.8 million; expenditure, $23.5 million; surplus, $0.2 million.

1949: March 23—Budget. No tax changes. The surplus on current account for 1948 was $2.0 million and net debt increased by $10.3 million. Budget forecast, 1949: revenue, $26.1 million; expenditure, $26.0 million; surplus, $0.1 million.

1950: March 29—Budget. The Secretary-Treasurer announced that it would be necessary to impose a retail sales tax at 4 percent. While the 1949 surplus had amounted to $1.9 million, total net debt outstanding had risen to $108.0 million. Budget forecast, 1950: revenue, $28.9 million; expenditure, $28.8 million; surplus, on current account, $0.1 million.

Table 18.16   Province of New Brunswick, Expenditure, Consolidated Finances Basis, Selected Years, 1952-86[a]

	1952	1962	1972	1982	1986
	millions of dollars				
General services	1.4	4.1	29.1	109.6	194.1
Health	7.0	35.2	126.8	551.1	658.7
Social services	4.2	11.6	56.1	313.2	447.2
Education	8.4	20.6	168.2	569.6	687.1
Transportation and communications	15.4	31.5	70.6	208.1	238.4
Natural resources and industrial development	3.9	6.1	38.0	127.1	114.5
Charges on debt	7.3	12.0	42.5	247.4	407.6
Transfers to other governments[b]	2.2	6.6	—	94.5	117.6
Other	1.2	4.9	54.1	171.7	210.2
Total	51.0	132.6	585.4	2,392.3	3,075.4
Offsets:					
Specific purpose transfers	5.5	39.5	127.8	357.4	528.5
General purpose transfers	15.2	16.9	117.0	569.5	692.7
Own expenditure	30.3	76.2	340.6	1,465.4	1,854.2
	percent of total expenditure				
General services	2.7	3.1	5.0	4.6	6.4
Health	13.7	26.5	21.7	23.0	21.4
Social services	8.2	8.7	9.6	13.1	14.5
Education	16.4	15.5	28.7	23.8	22.3
Transportation and communications	30.2	23.8	12.1	8.7	7.7
Natural resources and industrial development	7.6	4.6	6.5	5.3	3.7
Charges on debt	14.3	9.0	7.3	10.3	13.2
Transfers to other governments[b]	4.3	5.0	—	3.9	3.8
Other	2.6	3.8	9.1	7.3	7.0
Total	100.0	100.0	100.0	100.0	100.0
Own expenditure	55.1	55.3	61.7	63.3	60.3

See table 18.4 for footnotes and sources.

1951: April 3—Budget. No tax changes. The fiscal year ending had been changed to March 31. Budget forecast for the period October 31, 1950 to March 31, 1951: revenue, $16.7 million; expenditure, $16.6 million; surplus, $0.9 million. Total net debt at October 31, 1950 was $115.8 million. Budget forecast, 1951-52: revenue, $46.4 million; expenditure, $46.1 million; surplus, $0.3 million.

1952: March 31—Budget. No tax changes. Interim figures for the 17-month period ending March 31, 1952 showed an estimated net debt of $116.1 million. Budget forecast, 1952-53: revenue, $46.5 million; expenditure, $45.2 million; surplus, $1.3 million on current account.

1953: February 24—Budget. Taxes on tobacco were raised and collection shifted to the wholesaler level. The recently elected Conservative Secretary Treasurer described the New Brunswick financial situation as being on the "brink of financial disaster," and stated that it would require Herculian efforts to straighten it out. The new government planned to improve the province's credit position and stimulate economic expansion. Budget forecast, 1953-54: revenue, $49.3 million; expenditure, $49.2 million; surplus on current account, $0.1 million.

1954: March 9—Budget. The sales tax was reduced to 3 percent and exemptions widened to include drainage tile. The tax on gasoline was raised to 15¢ per gallon, including the levy for winter roads. Budget forecast, 1954-55: revenue, $51.2 million; expenditure, $51.2 million; surplus, $0.1 million.

1955: March 1—Budget. No tax changes. Fiscal year 1954-55 was described as a year of continued financial improvement. Budget forecast, 1955-56: revenue, $53.7 million; expenditure, $53.7 million; surplus, $38,000 on current account. For the first time since the tax rental agreements had been in effect the province expected to receive less money from Ottawa than in the previous year, mainly because of the drop in the GNP for 1954.

1956: February 29—Budget. No tax changes. The Secretary-Treasurer reported that 1955 had been an outstandingly good year for the province as a whole. Preliminary figures indicated a surplus on current account for 1955-56 of $85,000 and net debt of $108.8 million. Budget forecast, 1956-57: revenue, $57.9 million; expenditure, $57.9 million; surplus, $57,000.

1957: March 13—Budget. The only tax change was the transfer to the provincial government from the federal of the 2 percent tax on insurance premiums. The provincial treasurer repeated his assertion that the unrealistic percentage formula of the federal-provincial arrangements was unfair to the Atlantic provinces. The provincial tax base was too narrow to cope with the increasing demands upon the provincial budget. Budget forecast, 1957-58: revenue, $64.3 million; expenditure, $64.2 million; surplus, $62,000.

1958: April 10—Budget. No tax changes. The treasurer commented that the payment of $7.5 million to New Brunswick under the Atlantic Provinces Adjustment Grants would help avert a potential crisis in the province's finances. Budget forecast, 1958-59: revenue, $73.4 million; expenditure, $73.2 million; surplus, $186,000 on current account. Net capital expenditures, $6.8 million.

1959: March 13—Budget. The treasurer announced that the new hospital insurance plan would be financed by premiums; no other tax changes. Budget forecast, 1959-60: revenue, $74.9 million; expenditure, $74.8 million; surplus, $46,000.

1960: March 9—Budget. Footwear was exempted from the provincial sales tax. The treasurer revealed that the province's net public debt had been held to $106.4 million at March 31, 1959. Budget forecast, 1960-61: revenue,

$83.6 million; expenditure, $83.4 million; surplus on current account, $169,000. Net capital expenditures, $7.0 million.

1961: March 8—Budget. Effective April 1, 1961 the gasoline tax was raised by 3¢ a gallon to 18¢ and the winter roads tax eliminated; prices charged for alcoholic beverages and some government services were raised. The new Liberal Minister of Finance announced that the downturn in economic conditions had resulted in lower than expected returns from the income taxes and payments from the federal government. Preliminary figures showed a deficit on current account of $6.5 million for 1960-61. The treasurer had incorporated the hospital care program into the budgetary framework and financing was to be made from current revenues. Budget forecast, 1961-62: revenue, $102.5 million; expenditure, $102.5 million; surplus, $15,000.

1962: March 6—Budget. No tax changes. Preliminary figures indicated a deficit of $6.2 million for 1961-62: Budget forecast, 1962-63: revenue, $108.6 million; expenditure, $112.5 million; deficit, $3.9 million.

1963: March 5—Budget. No tax changes. A Royal Commission on Higher Education had made a complete inventory of the province's university and college facilities and had recommended that additional resources be provided to improve educational facilitites for both English- and French-speaking students. Budget forecast, 1963-64: revenue, $117.1 million; expenditure, $123.3 million; deficit, $6.2 million on current account.

1964: January—Report of the Royal Commission on Finance and Municipal Taxation was received; its main recommendations are (1) real property assessment and tax collection be taken over by the province; (2) responsibility for elementary-secondary education be transferred to the province; (3) the rate of the sales tax be raised to 5 percent from 3 percent.

_____. March 3—Budget. No tax changes. The Minister of Finance expressed his satisfaction at the return of equalizing payments under the federal-provincial arrangements to the level of the top two provinces. The 1964-65 equalization payment was estimated at $22.1 million, compared to $15.9 million for the previous year. Budget forecast, 1964-65: revenue, $129.6 million; expenditure, $129.3 million; surplus on current account, $300,000.

1965: March 5—Budget. 1964 had been a record year for New Brunswick in terms of economic growth and the treasurer looked forward to an even higher level of economic activity. No tax changes were announced. Preliminary figures indicated a surplus on current account of $2 million for 1964-65. Canada Pension Plan funds had been loaned to the province in proportion to the contributions made by residents of New Brunswick. Budget forecast, 1965-66: revenue, $145.9 million; expenditure, $145.5 million; surplus on current account, $478,000; estimated net capital outlays, $18.2 million.

1966: April 12—Budget. No tax changes. The Minister of Finance forecast a continuance of the prosperity experienced in the province over the past few years. He compared favourably New Brunswick's direct debt of $326 million at March 31, 1964 with the direct debt of its neighbour, Nova

Scotia. The budget outlined the province's achievements in facilitating econominc development and plans for the coming year under the Program for Equal Opportunity. Budget forecast, 1966-67: revenue, $190.9 million; expenditure, $201.9 million; deficit on combined current and capital account, $11.0 million.

_____. November 15—Budget, Program for Equal Opportunity. Effective January 1, 1967 the new social services and education (sales) tax was raised to 6 percent from 3 percent, and a real property tax levy was set at $1.50 per $100 of assessment at market value. The launching of the new program meant the takeover by the province of full responsibility for assessment, education, health, welfare, and justice, at an estimated cost for the then current year of $21.8 million. Revenue from the new taxes was estimated at $14.1 million.

1967: April 11—Budget. No tax changes. Budget forecast, 1967-68: revenue, $300.8 million; expenditure, $313.6 million; deficit, $12.8 million.

1968: March 19—Budget. The sales tax was extended to include transient accommodation and long distance telephone calls, and gasoline tax and motor vehicle licences were increased. Budget forecast, 1968-69: revenue, $309 million; expenditure, $322 million; deficit, $13 million.

1969: March 18—Budget. The personal income tax rate was increased to 38 percent of the federal tax, the sales tax was raised from 6 to 8 percent and extended to include some services, the tobacco and gasoline taxes were raised, and the price of alcohol increased. Budget forecast, 1969-70: revenue, $366 million; expenditure, $376 million; deficit, $10 million.

1970: March 10—Budget. An increase in mining tax and minor increases in fees were made. The budget announced that no premiums would be levied for medicare about to come into effect. Budget forecast, 1970-71: revenue, $432 million; expenditure, $449 million; deficit, $18 million.

1971: March 16—Budget. The sole tax change was a new tax on aircraft fuel. Public works programs would be undertaken to reduce unemployment. Budget forecast, 1971-72: revenue, $481 million; expenditure, $513 million; deficit, $31 million.

1972: April 5—Budget. No tax changes were announced. Budget forecast, 1972-73: revenue, $541 million; expenditure, $589 million; deficit, $48 million.

1973: March 20—Budget. Succession duties and gift taxes were to be abolished at the end of the year and for farmers and fishermen immediately. A program of property tax credits would be studied. Budget forecast, 1973-74: revenue, $630 million; expenditure, $666 million; deficit, $36 million.

1974: March 15—Budget. Minor changes were made in sales tax exemptions; a credit for homeowners and renters was given as a result of the study previously announced. Economic development was to be aided by the general development agreement with the federal government. Provincial-municipal financial arrangements were being restructured as the result of recommendations of a 1972 task force and welfare payments were revised. Budget forecast, 1974-75: revenue, $752 million; expenditure, $794 million; deficit, $42 million.

1975: March 21—Budget. New programs were to be introduced, including pharmacare. Money for social assistance and housing would be increased. The federal grants would assist in economic development. Tax changes promised in a 1974 election were implemented, including a reduction in the personal income tax, beginning of the removal of the provincial property tax on owner-occupied residences over a four-year period, and removal of the sales tax from laundry and dry cleaning. A fundamental study of the province's revenue structure was being made. Budget forecast, 1975-76: revenue, $907 million; expenditure, $981 million; deficit, $74 million.

1976: March 16—Budget. A hold-the-line budget, aimed at reducing the deficit. No tax changes were made and no new programs were announced. A budget paper dealt with the province's economic and financial difficulties. Budget forecast, 1976-77: revenue, $1,046 million; expenditure, $1,129 million; deficit, $83 million.

_____. New Brunswick Economic Report.

1977: March 15—Budget. Provincial government economic spending would go forward under the DREE grants but current account spending would be restrained. A five-year program of personal income tax reductions was commenced, to result in a 5.5 percent reduction by 1979. The general corporation tax rate was raised to 12 percent from 10 percent, and the small business rate was cut to 9 percent. Real property taxes were reduced, a tax of 5 percent on the gross receipts of communication companies was proposed, along with increases in mining and forestry charges. Budget forecast, 1977-78: revenue, $1,191 million; expenditure, $1,279 million; deficit, $88 million.

1978: April 4—Budget. Restraint continued to be the order of the day, but with past programs being held. Economic development would depend heavily on the general development and subsidiary agreements. The planned personal income tax reductions would come into effect for 1978 and 1979 and the sales tax would be reduced by 3 points for six months following the budget under the federal offer. There were also minor changes affecting building materials and mobile homes. Tobacco taxes were increased, provincial property taxes were eliminated from owner-occupied homes in cities, towns and villages, the tenant's tax grant was abolished, and a new grant proposed for first time home-owners. Liquor prices would be higher. Budget forecast, 1978-79: revenue, $1,302 million; expenditure, $1,397 million; deficit, $95 million.

1979: March 29—Budget. Restraint continued, with several tax increases, including those on tobacco, diesel fuel, and insurance premiums. Motor vehicle charges were raised and user charges for hospital patients were introduced, with lower or reduced fees for seniors and welfare cases. Under the business property tax a reduction was given for small businesses. Minor changes were made in the sales tax. Budget forecast, 1979-80: revenue, $1,442 million; expenditure, $1,533 million; deficit, $91 million.

1980: March 25—Budget. Results for the previous year had been better than forecast, and restraints were relaxed. There was to be an increase in both capital and social expenditures. The hospital charges of the previous year were rescinded, and minor extensions of exemptions under the sales tax were made. Budget forecast, 1980-81: revenue, $1,604 million; expenditures, $1,732 million; deficit, $124 million.

1981: April 7—Budget. With the recession a more expansive budget was introduced, with a deficit on ordinary account. To help with revenues the general corporate income tax rate was increased from 12 to 14 percent, with the small business rate remaining at 9 percent; motor fuel taxes were changed to ad valorem rates to be adjusted quarterly; the tobacco taxes were also changed to ad valorem rates and increased. Budget forecast, 1981-82: revenue, $1,771 million; expenditure, $1,963 million; deficit, $182 million.

1982: May 4—Budget. In the aftermath of the recession this was an expansionary budget, with substantial increases in both ordinary and capital expenditures. Like most recipient governments the minister expressed discontent with current efforts of the federal government to reduce its transfers to the provinces. The main tax increase was removal of the reduction in the personal income tax to increase the rate by 5.5 percent to 55.5 percent of the federal tax. The sales tax was extended to railway rolling stock, but minor exemptions were given for other goods. The reduction in the business tax rate for small businesses was extended to a wider group and a reduction in property assessment for the needy was increased. Budget forecast, 1982-83: revenue, $2,013 million; expenditure, $2,435 million; deficit, $422 million.

1983: May 6—Budget. The previous year had been disastrous for both the economy and the budget, with the deficit substantially exceeding the forecast. The time had come therefore to strive for a budget closer to balance. Expenditure reductions included a salary freeze for civil servants, deferral of an increase in social payments, and freezing of grants to municipalities. Revenue increases included charges for out-patient hospital services, an increase in the personal income tax to 58 percent of the federal tax, a raise in the sales tax from 8 to 10 percent with a corresponding change in the tax on certain services to personal property, increases in the tobacco and gasoline taxes, and an increase in the property tax on owner-occupied homes. A new tax on transfers of real property was proposed. Budget forecast, 1983-84: revenue, $2,223 million; expenditure, $2,615 million; deficit, $392 million.

1984: April 17—Budget. Although attempting to give some stimulus to the economy this was essentially another budget directed to more balanced results. As with most other provinces and the federal government, the limits of government action appeared to be approaching, and the ball was being put in the court of the business community—particularly the small business community. The most pronounced step in this direction was the complete exemption of small businesses from the corporation income tax. However, the general rate was increased from 14 to 15 percent and the mining tax rate was raised to produce more revenue. A complete review of the provincial tax system was underway. Budget forecast, 1984-85: revenue, $2,454 million; expenditure, $2,760 million; deficit, $306 million.

1985: May 31—Budget. While the economy had improved restraint was essential to reach a balance on operating account in the near future. There would be an expansion in development expenditures under the economic development subagreements which should sustain the economy, but other outlays would be controlled. Restraint measures affected medicines for senior citizens, student assistance, and civil service wages. Revenue increases included a raise in the sales tax from 10 to 11 percent, higher fees for motor vehicle licences, and withdrawal of tax-free motor fuel for municipalities. The tax exemption for small businesses was replaced by a 5 percent rate; the increase in the mining tax was withdrawn. Budget forecast, 1985-86: revenue, $2,667 million; expenditure, $2,886 million; deficit, $218 million.

1986: April 22—Budget. Some new initiatives were to be taken in education and health care, and further assistance given to agiculture, housing, job training, and employment programs. As the main cooperative programs with the federal government had expired not as much money would be available for economic development. The user fees for hospitals would be dropped to conform with the Canada Health Act. Tax changes affected the property tax, under which a direct grant against the property tax bill would replace a special exemption for low income property owners; a licensing fee would be imposed on amusement devices. Budget forecast, 1986-87: revenue, $2,844 million; expenditure, $3,127 million; deficit, $283 million.

1987: April 28—Budget. Restraint continued, although programs for education, health, social assistance, and infrastructure received some enrichment. The budget dwelt at some length on the decline in expected revenues under the revised federal equalization formulas, and urged higher payments and interest-free loans for poor provinces. The only tax increase was in the paid-up capital taxes on banks and trust and loan companies. Budget forecast, 1987-88: revenue, $2,985 million; expenditure, $3,407 million; deficit, $422 million.

1988: April 6—Budget. The personal income tax rate was increased from 58 to 60 percent of basic federal tax; the corporate income tax was raised from 15 to 16 percent; the corporation capital tax on banks, trust, and loan companies was increased from 2 to 3 percent; tobacco products were made subject to the retail sales tax; gasoline and fuel taxes were increased from 8.3¢ to 9.3¢ per litre; seniors were to be eligible for a property tax deduction of up to $200, and motor vehicle licence fees were raised for 1989. The new Liberal government's first budget set out its pay-as-you-go policy with its stated intention of not encumbering future generations with today's costs. The budget reflects the new government's objective of getting the economy going through development and training programs. Among the restraint measures taken to decrease costs were the elimination of the civil legal aid program and the restriction of senior prescription drug assistance to those seniors in receipt of GIS. Budget forecast, 1988-89: revenue, $3.3 billion; expenditure, $3.6 billion; deficit, $291.2 million.

Quebec

Postwar developments in this 400-year-old French North American enclave were truly revolutionary, with massive social, political, and economic changes. In turn these had profound fiscal repercussions, both for the province and the federal government. A more detailed discussion of this province is therefore required.

Political and Social Upheavals

In the long period from 1936 to 1959 with one break the province had been under the dominance of the Union nationale party and Premier Duplessis. The main objective of government in this era was to protect Quebec's distinctive cultural and social institutions and structure, prominent among them the French language and the Catholic church. Autonomy was strongly supported by French-speaking intellectuals during this period but, with a few exceptions, in a passive way. Relations with the federal government were marked primarily by a "just leave us alone" attitude, with no attempt made to benefit in any way from programs in which Quebec did not participate.

The election of a Liberal government with an entirely different approach in 1960 under Premier Lesage began what has since been called "the quiet revolution." The essence of this revolution was the adoption of positive and specific policies to advance the French Canadian interest in every avenue. Central to the program was the introduction of measures to allow French Canadians to penetrate the economic structure of the province, a program

Table 18.17   Quebec: General Profile

	Year[a]	Province	All Canada	Province as percent of all Canada
Population (000)	1987	6,593	25,625	25.7
Gross Domestic Product ($ billion)	1986	119.4	506.5	23.6
G.D.P. per capita ($)	1986	18,262	20,030	91.2
Personal Income ($ billion)	1986	105.5	432.5	24.4
P.I. per capita ($)	1986	16,138	17,060	94.6
Unemployment rate (%)	1987	10.3	8.9	115.7
Provincial government: revenue ($ billion)	1986	32.2	202.5[b]	15.9
Provincial government: expenditure ($ billion)	1986	32.3	234.1[b]	13.8
Basic personal income tax rate (%)[c]	1988	—	46.5-60[d]	—
General corporate tax rate (%)	1988	13.94	14-17[d]	—
Retail sales tax rate	1988	9.0	6-12[d]	—

See table 18.1 for footnotes and sources.

in which government, as the only instrument wholly amenable to the influence of the French-speaking majority, would play a leading role.

The main steps to this end were the creation of government dominated spheres, such as the nationalization of Hydro-Quebec in 1962, the massive government sponsored power developments in northern Quebec and on James Bay, the acquisition of steel mills to form provincially-owned SIDBEC, the establishment of Société générale de financement (SGF) to provide financing for Quebec enterprises, and in 1965 the creation of the Caisse de dépôt et placement du Québec, an organization funded with the revenues from the Quebec Pension Plan, in time to become a major influence in Canadian capital markets. These and other economic measures were paralleled by equally aggressive steps in other spheres, such as the creation of the first provincial Department of Education and the assumption of control over education from the Catholic church, the adoption of new social programs, and other measures indicative of a shift of power from past institutions to the state. It was part of the plan that a modernized government staffed by a French-Canadian technocracy would also be brought into being.

The subsequent Quebec political history can be briefly told. The Lesage regime was replaced between 1966 and 1970 by Union nationale governments (Johnson, 1966-68; Bertrand, 1968-70). A Liberal government was then re-elected (Bourassa, 1970-76) to be replaced by the Parti quebecois (Levesque, 1976-85). In an election in 1985 the Liberals were again returned to power (Bourassa), and were the government at the time of writing.

The quiet revolution and the massive changes it precipitated brought into question all aspects of relations with the federal government. The principal political issue was the continuing status of Quebec within the Canadian federation. At the outset this did not emerge as a specific question, as the "quiet revolution" approach was primarily an insistence on autonomy in individual areas of government such as social legislation and education. It also involved a strong rejection of any move to amend the Constitution, and particularly the patriation of the right of amendment, which it was feared would weaken Quebec's status. However, the issue of independence was frequently and openly mooted among French Canadian intellectuals, and emerged as a concrete objective with the election of the Parti quebecois, dedicated to separation from Canada. But when this government put the question to the Quebec people through a plebiscite in May 1980, it was rejected by 59.5 percent of the voters. This and other developments began a lessening of federal-Quebec tension. A buoyant Quebec economy, in which French Canadian MBAs and entrepreneurs are finding a leading role, and the achievement of an accord between Quebec, Ottawa, and the other provinces, (the Meech Lake Agreement) to heal the Constitutional breach that has existed since 1972, are strong evidence of a new approach.

The Fiscal Consequences

The general attitude of Quebec on federal-provincial fiscal matters will by now be apparent from other parts of this book. The long-term and persistently pursued objective has been to secure sources of revenue adequate for provincial needs and as far as possible independent of the federal government. Even the partial achievement of this goal has exerted a profound influence on the federal taxing and transfer arrangements, many of which owe their past and present form to the need to accommodate Quebec. The first evidence of this influence was the abstention of Quebec from the tax rental and subsequent arrangements from 1947 on. This was a legitimate exercise in provincial autonomy, and was partially followed as well by Ontario. It was, however, largely a negative exercise. Prior to 1960 Premier Duplessis had simply taken a "count-Quebec-out" attitude regarding federal offers of tax agreements and money grants, without regard to the financial consequences of Ontario.

The government began to take a new approach in 1959, one that in time was to have profound significance for all governments. It negotiated with the federal government the University Finance Agreement, the first of the opting-out arrangements. Under it the federal government undertook to drop its corporate income tax rate by 1 point on Quebec corporations, thus assuring the province of an amount equivalent to that offered under the university grants system. After 1960 the successor Liberal government in Quebec adopted opting-out as a fixed policy; it negotiated for tax transfers in lieu of grants under all the large programs—education, health, and social welfare. This led the federal government to adopt its interim established program financing legislation of 1964 in which this option was opened to all provinces and ultimately to the comprehensive tax transfer legislation of 1976. The adoption by Quebec of its own version of the Canada Pension Plan in 1966 was also typical of its independent stand.

The influence of Quebec in initiating what ultimately became the federal equalization scheme for tax transfers was also significant. It had been argued by Quebec, as was earlier mentioned, that the financial balance under the tax rental and later arrangements was in favour of the agreeing provinces and against the provinces that remained out. This was not taken very seriously by the federal government for some years, but under Prime Minister Louis St. Laurent the position was not only recognized but was fundamentally changed by the revenue equalization program, now extended to all tax transfers and all provinces.[18.1] These tax equalization transfers to all provinces now (1986-87) amount to over $5.8 billion a year. Quebec of course is included in the provinces receiving these billions in cash.

The Fiscal Experience

The accompanying tables and diary give more details of the Quebec financial experience. In 35 years both revenue and expenditure have increased nearly one hundred-fold. By dint of high levels of rates tax revenues are about the same share of the budget as in 1952. Transfers from the federal

---

[18.1] See Robert B. Bryce, *Maturing in Hard Times.* Public Administration Series (Ottawa: The Institute of Public Administration of Canada, 1987), ch. 11.

government have varied, but have been in the 20 percent range for much of the period. The massive expenditure increases, as elsewhere, have been in health, social services, education, and debt charges. Like all provinces Quebec has been under constant budget pressure in recent years, heightened in its case by the transition the province has undergone in the last two decades.

Table 18.18 Quebec Finances: The Eighties

Year[a]	Revenue	Expenditure	Deficit
	millions of dollars		
1980	18,189.0	18,879.9	− 690.9
1981	21,602.6	21,808.6	− 206.0
1982	23,733.5	24,609.3	− 875.8
1983	26,250.0	27,045.2	− 795.2
1984	27,576.1	28,632.3	− 1,056.2
1985	30,375.8	31,555.9	− 1,180.1
1986	32,167.4	32,322.2	− 154.8
1987	34,424.9	34,484.2	− 59.3
1988	29,334.0	30,934.0	− 1,600.0

See table 18.2 for footnotes and sources.

Table 18.19 Province of Quebec, Revenue, Consolidated Finances Basis, Selected Years, 1952-86[a]

Source	1952	1962	1972	1982	1986
	millions of dollars				
Taxes	188.7	596.8	3,663.2	14,325.8	19,694.0
Natural resource revenue	25.5	35.6	84.5	115.3	148.0
Privileges, licences and permits	37.9	78.0	127.1	681.6	898.8
Liquor sales and regulation	33.8	62.0	146.0	341.3	474.5
Other revenue	0.6	16.0	453.8	3,054.8	4,366.5
Transfers from other governments[b]	28.3	306.7	1,259.5	5,214.7	6,585.4
Total	314.8	1,095.2	5,734.2	23,733.5	32,167.4
Own source revenue	286.5	788.4	4,474.0	18,518.8	25,582.0
Surplus or deficit	− 27.8	− 87.4	− 123.3	− 875.8	− 154.8
	percent of total revenue				
Taxes	60.0	54.5	63.9	60.2	61.1
Natural resource revenue	8.1	3.3	1.5	0.5	0.5
Privileges, licences and permits	12.1	7.1	2.2	2.9	2.8
Liquor sales and regulation	10.7	5.7	2.5	1.4	1.5
Other revenue	0.1	1.4	7.9	13.1	13.7
Transfers from other governments[b]	9.0	28.0	22.0	21.9	20.4
Total	100.0	100.0	100.0	100.0	100.0
Own source revenue	91.0	72.0	78.0	78.0	79.5

See table 18.3 for footnotes and sources.

Table 18.20 Province of Quebec, Expenditure, Consolidated Finances Basis, Selected Years, 1952-86[a]

	1952	1962	1972	1982	1986
	millions of dollars				
General services	13.0	46.9	256.1	1,771.9	2,202.6
Health	46.3	224.6	1,486.0	5,102.1	6,315.8
Social services	38.9	184.6	843.9	5,138.5	7,961.5
Education	54.5	296.8	1,393.0	6,029.0	6,945.0
Transportation and communications	108.8	180.4	549.8	1,683.7	1,381.9
Natural resources and industrial development	31.5	71.4	226.6	877.7	1,319.0
Charges on debt	14.8	37.4	286.7	2,433.7	3,057.2
Transfers to other governments[b]	1.6	6.3	197.2	262.5	271.6
Other	33.2	134.2	371.6	1,310.2	2,867.6
Total	342.6	1,182.6	5,610.9	24,609.3	32,322.2
Offsets:					
Specific purpose transfers	20.3	220.8	539.5	2,302.8	3,919.2
General purpose transfers	8.0	85.9	720.0	2,911.9	2,666.2
Own expenditure	314.2	875.9	4,351.4	19,394.6	25,736.8
	percent of total expenditure				
General services	3.8	4.0	4.6	7.2	6.8
Health	13.5	19.0	26.5	20.7	19.6
Social services	11.4	15.6	15.0	20.9	24.7
Education	15.9	25.1	24.8	24.5	21.5
Transportation and communications	31.8	15.3	9.8	6.8	4.3
Natural resources and industrial development	9.2	6.0	4.0	3.5	4.1
Charges on debt	4.3	3.2	5.1	9.9	9.5
Transfers to other governments[c]	0.5	0.5	3.5	1.1	0.8
Other	9.6	11.3	6.7	5.4	8.7
Total	100.0	100.0	100.0	100.0	100.0
Own expenditure	91.7	74.0	77.6	78.8	79.6

See table 18.4 for footnotes and sources.

Quebec Diary

1947: March 25—Budget. Preliminary figures for the fiscal year ended March 31, 1947 showed a surplus of $1.1 million on combined current and capital account, and net debt at March 31, 1947 was $291.3 million. The treasurer reminded the legislative assembly that only the province had jurisdiction over education and compared the $38.69 per capita cost of education to the province of Quebec taxpayer to taxpayers in cities in North America. Typical costs in Canadian cities were: Victoria, $12.47; Toronto, $17.19; and Saint John, N.B., $25.42. The treasurer rejoiced to announce that the 1942 taxation agreements with the federal government would terminate the following Monday. Under the new agreements Quebec had decided to re-establish its corporation income tax at 7 percent of profits but was not taxing the income of individuals. It was re-establishing its gasoline tax at 3¢ per gallon. Budget forecast, 1947-48: revenue, $147.4 million; expenditure, $137.9 million; surplus on combined account, $9.6 million.

1948: February 27—Budget. No tax changes. The overall surplus for the fiscal year ended March 31, 1948 was expected to be $1.6 million and net debt about $277.0 million. Budget forecast, 1948-49: revenue, $142.4 million; expenditure, $142.0 million; surplus on combined account, $421,000.

1949: February 24—Budget. No tax changes. The projected surplus on ordinary account for 1948-49 of $40.8 million was expected to be offset by capital expenditures of $66.5 million. Budget forecast, 1949-50: revenue, $176.7 million; expenditure, $176.5 million; surplus on combined account, $200,000. The highest share of expenditures was alloted to roads and highways, at 21 percent of the total; health, 15 percent; social welfare and youth, 11 percent; and education, roughly 10 percent.

1950: March 16—Budget. No tax changes. The current account surplus forecast for fiscal year 1949-50 of $31.1 million was partially offset by capital expenditures of $23.5 million; net debt at March 31, 1950 was forecast at $280.0 million. The treasurer explained that part of education expenditures were financed from the Education Fund, which derived its revenue from half the provincial sales tax of 2 percent, contributions from certain hydro companies, stumpage dues on certain forest industries, tax on the paid-up capital of companies refining petroleum, and telephone companies with capital over $1 million. For 1950-51 these revenues, about $19.5 million, were included in total provincial revenue estimates. Budget forecast, 1950-51: revenue, $201.3 million; expenditure, $200.6 million; surplus on combined account, $735,000.

1951 March 1—Budget. No tax changes. The 1950-51 fiscal year was expected to end with a surplus on combined account of $2.4 million and net debt of $274 million. In reviewing the previous year the treasurer commented on the calamitous fires at Rimouski and Cabano in May which had aroused the sympathy of all Canadians—who had contributed the funds to rebuild the communities. Intense continuing economic development in Quebec had necessitated higher and higher expenditures by the government in all areas. Budget forecast, 1951-52: revenue, $237.8 million; expenditure, $236.7 million; overall surplus, $1.0 million. Of total revenue, 22 percent (or $54.0 million) was expected to come from taxes on corporations, 16 percent ($37.5 million) from gasoline taxes, and 13.5 percent ($32.1 million) from the sales tax. Roads and highways continued to be the most costly provincial expenditure, taking 22 percent of the budget, followed by health at 13 percent, education at 11 percent, and welfare and youth, 10 percent.

1952: January 9—Budget. No tax changes. 1951-52 ended with an expected overall surplus of $1.2 million and net debt of $256 million. The Minister of Finance commented that increasing industrialization of the province called for more emphasis in education on the technical and practical sciences rather than relying totally on cultural traditions. The new railway line from Sept-Iles to Labrador, expected to be completed in 1953, would facilitate the transportation of iron ore from the mines there. Budget forecast, 1952-53: revenue, $262.7 million; expenditure, $260.8 million; overall surplus, $1.9 million.

1953: February 5—Budget. No tax changes. Preliminary figures showed a surplus on ordinary account of $42.2 million for 1952-53 and capital expenditures of $81.1 million; net debt was expected to total $337.7 million at March 31, 1953. Budget forecast, 1953-54: revenue, $288.5 million; expenditure, $286.9 million; overall surplus $1.6 million.

1954: February 12—Budget. A personal income tax was levied, for a period of three years, at rates ranging from 2.3 percent to 13.0 percent. The surplus of $36.4 million on ordinary account for 1953-54 was expected to be offset by capital expenditures of $60.1 million. Receipts of an estimated $22.0 million for 1954-55 from the new personal income tax were to be used to fund universities. The Minister of Finance stressed the need for the province to have exclusive jurisdiction over education to ensure the future of the French race in Quebec. Budget forecast, 1954-55: revenue, $323.0 million; expenditure, $321.2 million; surplus on combined account, $1.8 million.

1955: February 3—Budget. No tax changes. Quebec experienced a continuing growth in its economy although the year was not quite as buoyant for Canada as a whole. The surplus on ordinary account of $38.6 million was expected to be offset by capital expenditures of $64.6 million during 1954-55. Budget forecast, 1955-56: revenue, $331.9 million; expenditure, $331.2 million; surplus on combined account, $656,000. Taxes on corporations were expected to provide 20 percent of revenue, followed by gasoline taxes at 18 percent, the general sales tax at 13 percent; liquor revenue, 10 percent, and the provincial personal income tax, and natural resource revenue, each 8 percent. Roads and highways continued to be the province's most expensive function, taking an estimated 19 percent of the budget, followed by health at 18 percent, education at 14, and social welfare and youth, at 9 percent.

1956: February 3—Budget. No tax changes. Preliminary figures for 1955-56 showed a surplus on combined account of $75,000 and net debenture debt at March 31, 1955 was $368.4 million. Budget forecast, 1956-57: revenue, $374.3 million; expenditure, $374.1 million; surplus on combined account, $165,000.

————. Report of the Royal Commission of Inquiry on Constitutional Problems (Tremblay Commission). As regards taxation, the Commission found that the federal government looked at Canada as a whole, but it (the Commission) felt that taxes on incomes should belong to the government on which cultural and social responsibility was incumbent. The provinces could reduce taxes on individual incomes to allow room for the federal government; it found the principles of fiscal equalization of revenues of all provinces acceptable. The Commission made a 10-year projection of Quebec's revenue and expenditure and stressed that the province would need to make a choice between running financial deficits or failing to meet the requirements of its constituents.

1957: February 7—Budget. The corporation income tax was raised to 9 percent from 7. Interim figures showed a surplus for 1956-57 of $70.0 million, and capital expenditures of $85.3 million. The Minister of Finance commented that the nation's economic activity showed signs of uneasiness. The Union nationale government stood firm in its resistance to federal grants for universities rather than surrendering its autonomy over education in the province. Budget forecast, 1957-58: revenue, $473.3 million; expenditure, $471.5 million; surplus on combined account, $1.9 million.

1958: February 7—Budget. No tax changes. 1957 had continued to be a period of economic expansion. The surplus on combined account for 1957-58 was forecast at $1.3 million. The province had accepted from the federal government an equalization payment of $36.0 million. Budget forecast, 1958-59: revenue, $506.9 million; expenditure, $506.5 million; surplus on combined account, $406,000. Taxes on corporations were expected to provide 19 percent of total revenue, the gasoline tax, 17 percent, sales tax, 12 percent, the federal government, 9 percent, and revenue from the individual income tax, 8 percent. Roads and highways were the most costly function, expected to take 18 percent of the budget, followed by education at 17 percent, social welfare and youth 16 percent, and health 13 percent.

1959: February 20—Budget. No tax changes. 1958 saw a continuation of burgeoning expansion in the province. A surplus on combined account of $389,000 was forecast for 1958-59. Budget forecast, 1959-60: revenue, $541.9 million; expenditure, $548.9 million; deficit on combined account, $7.0 million.

_____. December 10—Budget. No tax changes. The Minister of Finance commented sadly on the death of Premier Duplessis in September and congratulated the province on the abilities of the new Premier. 1959-60 had turned out to be a year of economic prosperity for the province; interim figures showed a surplus on combined account of $839,000. Budget forecast, 1960-61: revenue, $617.8 million; expenditure, $617.3 million; surplus on combined account, $500,000.

1960: December 22—Amendments to the Corporation Tax Act and the Provincial Income Tax Act. A Liberal government had replaced the Union nationale in the election of June 22, 1960. Quebec's income taxes were brought into line with the federal and Ontario legislation, the rate was raised by 2 percent on corporate profits to 12 percent; personal income tax exemptions were lowered, and a surtax levied on non-Canadian investment income; 1 percent of Quebec's corporate rate related to the extra room vacated by the federal government in lieu of the province receiving direct grants for universities.

1961: April 14—Budget. The provincial sales tax rate was raised to 4 percent; the tax on fuel oil was repealed; meals of up to $1.00 were exempted;

and the tax on alcoholic beverages was raised. The new Premier and Minister of Finance revealed that actual results showed a deficit of $503,147 for fiscal year 1959-60 and a projected deficit of $113.6 million for 1960-61. The net funded debt of the province was $306.0 million and total net debt after deducting sinking funds was $182.8 million at March 31, 1960. The minister explained that there had been a slackening of the economy over the last several years in Canada but the momentary decline was not too alarming because the province's economy was in a stage of long-term expansion. The new hospital insurance program had raised projected health costs for 1961-62. Budget forecast, 1961-62: revenue, $686.5 million; expenditure, $793.7 million; deficit on combined account, $107.3 million. Taxes on corporations were expected to provide 21 percent of total revenue, gasoline tax 15 percent, personal income tax 11 percent, the sales tax and the federal government, 10 percent each. Spending on roads was expected to remain the most costly charge on the budget, taking an estimated 19 percent, followed by education at 18 percent, health at 16 percent, and family and social welfare 13 percent.

1962: April 12—Budget. The tax on diesel fuel was raised; the "mileage" tax on bus companies and small trucking companies was repealed. The Minister explained that substantial economic recovery, particularly in Quebec, was responsible for higher revenues than originally estimated. Preliminary results showed a surplus of $22.3 million on ordinary account, offset by capital expenditures of $105.5 million and an extraordinary expenditure item of $27.0 million for investment in universities. Budget forecast, 1962-63: revenue, $809.1 million; expenditure, $953.0 million; deficit on combined account, $143.9 million before payment of $40.0 million for financing of university investment.

1963: April 5—Budget. An increase in motor fuel taxes of 2¢ per gallon of gasoline to 15¢ and 21¢ per gallon of diesel fuel; a new tax of 10 percent of profits from forestry operations, deductible from federal and provincial corporation taxes; an increase in tax exemptions for children under the personal income tax. Premier Lesage expressed his desire to see the end of joint federal-provincial programs and repeated his requests for a higher percentage of the income and inheritance taxes levied by the federal government. Preliminary figures for 1962-63 showed a surplus of $17.9 million on ordinary account, offset by capital expenditures of $130.7 million and extraordinary expenditures of $30.0 million for university investment. Budget forecast, 1963-64: revenue, $899.2 million; expenditure, $1,045 million; deficit on joint account, $146.0 million before extraordinary expenditure on university investment, $40.0 million.

1964: March—First Interim Report of the Royal Commission on Taxation (Belanger Commission) recommended a uniform 6 percent rate of sales tax throughout the province.

_____. April 24—Budget. A uniform provincial sales tax of 6 percent replaced the 4 percent provincial sales tax and the 2 percent optional municipal tax—proceeds from 2 percent to go to municipalities and schools; increased sales tax on liquor to 6 percent; increased pari-mutuel betting tax;

increased exemptions under succession duties. Preliminary figures for 1963-64 showed a surplus on ordinary account of $25.2 million offset by capital expenditures of $160.6 million and extraordinary university financing of $33.0 million. Budget forecast, 1964-65: revenue, $1,050.4 million; expenditure, $1,229.4 million; deficit on combined account, $179.0 million before extraordinary expenditures: $35.0 million for university investment and $7.0 for Expo '67.

1965: April 8—Budget. A new tax was levied at 6 percent on hotel and similar accommodation, along with long distance telephone, telegraph, and other telecommunication services billed in the province; gasoline and diesel fuel taxes were raised by 1¢ to 16¢ per gallon of gasoline and 22¢ per gallon of diesel fuel; tobacco taxes were increased to 12 percent; the tax on meals was increased to 6 percent; the 2½ percent entertainment tax surcharge was dropped and the remaining 10 percent entertainment tax was left entirely to the municipalities; the distribution formula was changed for the portion of the sales tax allocated to municipalities. (The latter item was suggested in the second interim report of the Belanger Commission). Preliminary figures for 1964-65 showed a surplus on ordinary account of $35.7 million, capital expenditures of $206.8 million, university investment financing, $36.0 million, and Expo '67 expenditure, $9.3 million; net funded debt was estimated at $1,061.6 million at March 31, 1965.

Budget forecast, 1965-66: revenue, $1,552.6 million; expenditure, $2,054.6 million; deficit, $502.0 million on combined account, plus $35.0 for university investment and $4.6 million for Expo '67 expenditure. Of total revenue, 21 percent was expected to be derived from the retail sales tax, 19 percent from the personal income tax, 15 percent from federal government transfers, 16 percent from the gasoline tax, and 11 percent from corporation taxes. Health was estimated to take 20 percent of the total provincial budget, education 19 percent, roads 13 percent, and family and social services, 11 percent.

1966: January—Report of the Royal Commission on Taxation issued.

_____. March 31—Budget. Wider exemptions enacted for succession duties. Budget forecast, 1966-67: revenue $2,304.7 million; expenditure, $2,063.2 million; plus university investment financing, $25.0 million; surplus, $216.6 million.

1967: March 16—Budget. Sales tax increased from 6 to 8 percent. Income tax exemption for children abolished and replaced by provincial family allowance. Budget forecast, 1967-68: revenue, $2,303 million; expenditure, $2,440 million; deficit, $136 million.

1968: March 27—Budget. An austerity budget provided a 6 percent personal income surtax for 1968 and 1969 for upper incomes, raised taxes on gasoline, tobacco and corporate capital. Motor vehicle fees and liquor prices were also raised. Budget forecast, 1968-69: revenue, $2,689 million; expenditure, $2,957 million; deficit, $268 million.

1969: April 29—Budget. 1968 and 1969 temporary 6 percent surtax on personal income tax extended to 1970. Succession duty exemption increased.

Medicare plan to be introduced by July 1970. Budget forecast, 1969-70: revenue, $2,958 million; expenditure, $3,113 million; deficit, $155 million.

1970: March 31—Budget. No tax increases, but revisions of various existing programs were to be undertaken by a newly elected provincial government. Budget forecast, 1970-71: revenue, $3,469 million; expenditure, $3,614 million; deficit, $145 million.

1971: March 25—No tax changes; revisions announced in previous budget not yet made. Substantially increased investments in various Quebec Crown corporations. Budget forecast, 1971-72: revenue, $4,245 million; expenditure, $4,516 million; deficit, $271 million.

1972: April 18—Budget. Stock transfer tax and sales tax on industrial equipment abolished. Substantial reliefs in succession duties, with announced intention of ultimate complete removal. Income tax revised to harmonize with reformed federal act, including imposition of capital gains tax. Provincial share of education costs increased. Budget forecast, 1972-73: revenue, $4,231 million; expenditure, $4,614 million; deficit, $383 million.

1973: March 29—Budget. Exemptions for lower income taxpayers increased and corresponding exemptions or concessions given from health insurance contributions. Succession duties reduced by 20 percent and concessions given farmers under capital gains tax. Special two-year depreciation given for industrial machinery used in Quebec. Basis of grants to municipalities changed from sales tax revenue to per capita payment. Budget forecast, 1973-74: revenue, $4,841 million; expenditure, $5,119 million; deficit, $278 million.

1974: March 28—Budget. Further substantial increases in exemptions were given for lower incomes. Family allowances (provincial and federal) to be exempt from income tax. Province announced it would not follow federal indexation. Investment incentives and accelerated depreciation for anti-pollution equipment extended. Further 20 percent reduction in succession duty rates. Mining tax to be reviewed; province to increase its expenditure on mining and oil exploration and on steel production. Municipal grants increased. Budget forecast, 1974-75: revenue, $5,865 million; expenditure, $6,140 million; deficit, $275 million.

1975: April 17—Budget. Personal income tax exemptions further increased. Corporate tax concessions extended for two years and accelerated depreciation allowances extended indefinitely. Mining taxation revised. Succession duties reduced a further 20 percent. Motor registration fees increased. Further assistance for education financing. Budget forecast, 1975-76: revenue, $7,925 million; expenditure, $8,290 million; deficit, $365 million. (This deficit forecast was wide of the mark; in fact it turned out to be $873 million).

————. Report, Fiscal Aid for Municipalities.

1976: May 11—Budget. Major projects at the time were the James Bay power development, the Olympics, and Mirabel airport, all having financial and economic implications, although most were not reflected in the standard budget. This was however a busy budget. A new tax on transfers of immovable property to non-residents was introduced. Succession duty rates were reduced by another 20 percent. The tax status of investment corporations, funds, and NROs was revised. The tax on cigarettes was doubled (to help pay the Olympic deficit), and medicare premiums were raised. The sales tax exemption for production machinery was limited. Real property taxes were further relieved and a partial refund of school taxes was provided for the elderly. Budget forecast, 1976-77: revenue, $9,415 million; expenditure, $10,045 million; deficit, $630 million.

1977: April 12—Budget. Sales tax exemption for children's clothing and footwear was withdrawn and a new exemption was given for production tools. A 10 percent tax on meals and 2 percent tax on "air time" for advertising were introduced. Charges for drivers' permits were increased. Municipal taxing powers were extended. No further reduction in succession duties. Budget forecast, 1977-78: revenue, $10.9 billion; expenditure, $11.5 billion; deficit, $640 million.

1978: April 18—Budget. Personal income tax exemptions were raised. Rates for lowest incomes were reduced and those for higher incomes substantially increased. The dividend tax credit was harmonized with the federal credit; rules were established for charging business automobile expenses. A tax indexation rate for personal exemptions would be announced for each year in the future; the rate for 1979 would be 6 percent. The personal contribution for health care was abolished and replaced by a payroll tax for employers. Sales tax was removed from selected items (in an unsuccessful attempt to qualify for the federal compensation offer for a general sales tax reduction; the matter was later resolved through a federal credit against its income tax for Quebec residents). The taxes on tobacco products were increased. Succession duties and gift tax were radically revised to reduce their scope and weight but were not completely repealed. Further reforms were introduced for municipal real property taxation. Budget forecast, 1978-79: revenue, $12.3 billion; expenditure, $13.4 billion; deficit, $1.1 billion.

1979: March 27—Budget. Personal deductions under the income tax were indexed by 12.5 percent, and child care expenses and allowable pension contributions were increased. Individuals would be allowed a deduction from income for purchase of shares of qualifying Quebec companies. Exemption from sales tax extended for textiles, clothing, and footwear. Paid-up capital tax introduced. All government departments and agencies to pay all consumer taxes levied by province. Province assumed full standardized education costs and school property tax abolished. Other major changes in provincial-municipal arrangements were made. Budget forecast, 1979-80: revenue, $13.5 billion; expenditure, $15 billion; deficit, $1.5 billion.

1980: March 25—Budget. Personal income tax rates were reduced by 1.5 percent for 1980, and personal exemptions were indexed by 7.5 percent for 1981. Other changes included allowance of salary of working spouse, special deduction for petroleum exploration, inclusion of benefits under loans at less than market rate. The general corporate tax rate was increased to 13 percent from 12 percent and the insurance premiums tax went up. Succession duty exemptions and exemptions under sales tax were increased. The tax on tobacco products converted to ad valorem rates and increased. Budget forecast, 1980-81: revenue, $14.9 billion; expenditure, $17.2 billion; deficit, $2.3 billion.

1981: March 10—Budget. Personal income tax rates reduction increased from 3 to 5 percent and exemptions would be indexed by 7.5 percent from January 1, 1982; the child care deduction was changed. Reductions were made in tax on corporations for 1981, 1982, and 1983. The payroll tax on employers for health insurance was increased from 1.5 percent to 3 percent. Paid-up capital tax and tobacco tax were also increased. Budget forecast, 1981-82: revenue, $17.5 billion; expenditure, $19.0 billion; deficit, $1.5 billion.

_____. November 17—Supplementary Budget. This emergency budget doubled the gasoline tax, revised alcohol taxation, and cancelled the additional reduction in personal income tax provided in the spring budget. Even with this additional revenue the actual deficit at $2.9 billion was nearly twice that originally expected.

1982: May 25—Budget. In a tight budget the sales tax was increased from 8 to 9 percent to March 31, 1983, tobacco taxes and the pari-mutuel betting tax were increased, and liquor margins were raised. For 1983 personal income tax exemptions were indexed by 7.5 percent, and RHOSP liquidation rules were relaxed. The most drastic action was the freezing of civil service salaries and the reversal of increases already paid from the previous June. Budget forecast, 1982-83: revenue, $19.7 billion; expenditure, $22.7 billion; deficit, $3.0 billion.

1983: May 10—Budget. The increase to 9 percent in the retail sales tax was continued indefinitely. Personal income tax exemptions would be indexed by 5 percent, and RHOSP terms were further relaxed. Several changes for economic stimulus were introduced under the corporate income tax. Succession duty exemptions were further increased. A White Paper on Reform of the Taxation of Individuals was promised for later, to be implemented at the next session. Budget forecast, 1983-84: revenue, $21.1 billion; expenditure, $24.3 billion; deficit, $3.2 billion.

1984: May 22—Budget. Minor tax changes only were made. The tobacco tax was increased, succession duties and gift tax were further relieved, and highway tolls would be phased out over an 18-month period. The gasoline tax had been reduced from 40 to 30 percent in the previous November. The promised White Paper was not yet available but would be made public as soon as possible. Budget forecast for 1984-85: revenue, $22.5 billion; expenditure, $25.6 billion; deficit, $3.2 billion.

_____. White Paper on Personal Income Tax and Transfer Systems.

1985: April 23—Budget. Several changes in personal income tax based on the reform paper and later discussion were introduced. Many of these affected deductions and exemptions, generally to grant further relief. Particular emphasis was given to reducing the rates on middle and higher incomes, which were thought to be out of line with other provinces. Most of the previous economic incentive features were retained, some with broader scope.[18.2] The Quebec law would be amended as in past years to adopt, sometimes in revised form, the changes then being made in the federal law. The $500,000 lifetime capital gains exemption was adopted only in part; a form of minimum tax would be imposed by Quebec.

The final step was taken in this budget in the abolition of succession duties. Other changes included an increase in the tobacco tax, inclusion of selected items in the sales tax, revision of the mining tax, and exemption of profits of an international financial centre operating in Montreal.

_____. December 18—Minibudget. The newly elected Liberal government presented some changes in an interim budget shortly after assuming power. These included acceleration of the income tax reduction of the previous government, revisions in the capital gains exemption and the minimum tax, and reduction in the gasoline tax to 20 percent in designated areas. Budget forecast, 1985-86: revenue, $24.1 billion; expenditure, $27.2 billion; deficit, $3.2 billion.

1986: May 1—Budget. The corporation taxes, including the paid-up capital tax and the payroll tax, would be subject to a surtax of 7.25 percent. Under the sales tax the exemption for natural gas and heating oil would be limited to non-industrial use. Under the personal income tax the $1,000 exemptions for pension and interest and dividend income would be reduced by 50 percent unless the taxpayer was genuinely retired. The modified ad valorem tax for motor fuels and tobacco products would be replaced by specific per item charges. Other changes included adoption of the full federal capital gains exemption, reduction of the dividend tax credit, and dropping of the inventory deduction. Budget forecast, 1986-87: revenue, $25.6 billion; expenditure, $28.5 billion; deficit, $2.9 billion.

1987: April 30—Budget. The principal tax changes gave additional incentives under the corporate and personal income tax for research expenditures and reduced the income tax on low and middle income taxpayers. As in previous years there would be sales of Crown companies to provide revenues. Budget forecast, 1987-88: revenue, $27.7 billion; expenditure, $30.1 billion; deficit, $2.4 billion.

1988: May 12—Budget. Reform of the income tax system was announced to begin with the 1988 taxation year, to take full effect for 1989. For 1988 personal income tax rates range over five income brackets from 16 percent on taxable income up to $7,000 to 26 percent on taxable income over $50,000; subsidies designed to encourage an increase in the province's birth rate were introduced of $500 for each of the first two children and $3,000 for a third and subsequent children; family allowances exempted from personal income tax; first home buyers eligible to receive seven-year loan guarantees of $7,000; day care spaces to be doubled over seven years; amendments

---

[18.2] For further details see, Canadian Tax Foundation, Tax Memo No. 70 (Toronto: the foundation, 1986), 157-62.

made to the Quebec Stock Savings Plan; accelerated depreciation allowed on new machinery and equipment for manufacturing and new computer equipment; deductions increased for investment in the film industry; gradual abolition over five years of the special tax on oil refineries with interim investment tax credit allowed. The province enjoyed exceptional economic growth in 1987 and it was anticipated that economic expansion would continue. Reform of the income tax system was expected to increase Quebec's competitiveness and enable the province to attract new investment. Budget forecast, 1988-89: revenue, $29.3 billion; expenditure, $30.9 billion; deficit, $1.6 billion.

Ontario

The statistics for Ontario tell much of its story. As the most highly industrialized and affluent of the provinces it accounts for 36 percent of the population, has a personal income per capita 10 percent higher than the national average, an unemployment rate 2-3 points lower, and levies taxes at rates considerably below the highest. Its capital city, Toronto, in recent years has achieved international status as a metropolitan region and a commercial, financial, and cultural centre, and its other cities, including the national capital, Ottawa, have grown proportionately. But the rural areas of the province are well established and bring an important balance to the life of the province.

The influence of the provincial government, while tending to the conservative, has been strong on many national issues. The main impulse for Confederation came from its politicians jointly with their colleagues from Quebec, and the National Policy of 1879 was largely the creation of Ontario-oriented ministers. It is not surprising therefore that Ontario's Liberal government has stubbornly opposed the concept of free trade with the United States, even though the Liberal party has traditionally been a

Table 18.21   Ontario: General Profile

	Year[a]	Province	All Canada	Province as percent of all Canada
Population (000)	1987	9,271	25,625	36.2
Gross Domestic Product ($ billion)	1986	204.4	506.5	40.4
G.D.P. per capita ($)	1986	22,431	20,030	112,0
Personal Income ($ billion)	1986	172.1	432.5	39.8
P.I. per capita ($)	1986	18,882	17,060	110.7
Unemployment rate (%)...............	1987	6.1	8.9	68.5
Provincial government: revenue ($ billion)........................	1986	32.6	202.5[b]	16.1
Provincial government: expenditure ($ billion)........................	1986	32.7	234.1[b]	14.4
Basic personal income tax rate (%)[c]	1988	51.0	46.5-60[d]	—
General corporate tax rate (%)	1988	15.5	14-17[d]	—
Retail sales tax rate	1988	8.0	6-12[d]	—

See table 18.1 for footnotes and sources.

free trade or low tariff exponent. In many areas other provinces have tended to accept Ontario legislation as a model, although recently this has been less prevalent than in the past.

With the oldest and best organized municipal structure of any province the government has left more functions on a shared basis than in most other jurisdictions. Pre-secondary education, for example, is still the primary responsibility of a locally elected board of trustees, with authority to set its own budget costs, to be met by the local municipal authority. The province supports functions by grants based on ordinary and extraordinary expenditure, employing an equalized mill rate as a base measure. The province also provides the main base of longer time social welfare through its family benefits program but municipalities are left to administer several short term programs, with subsidization from the province.

As in other provinces rapid urban growth has presented a challenge for adaptation of the traditional municipal structure. Several cities and their satellite communities have been brought together under metropolitan governments, with some principal functions carried out on a common basis. For larger areas containing mixed urban and rural populations regional middle-ground administrations have been created.

Fiscally the province is among the least dependent on Ottawa, its own-source revenues having reached 85 percent of the total in 1986. In Ontario's case of course the other 15 percent was a considerable amount of money—$4.8 billion. The familiar big four—health, education, social services, and debt charges—accounted for 77 percent of its expenditures in that year. Deficits have been the end result of budgets for some time.

The Ontario governmental story has been told frequently in research papers of the Ontario Economic Council and in Budget Papers tabled with the annual budget speech. These are commended to the reader wishing further information on the province.

Ontario Diary

1947: March 11—Budget. Premier Frost announced that the province would not impose a personal income tax in the fiscal year beginning April 1, 1947 nor would it expect to receive a payment in lieu of such tax from the federal government. The provincial tax on corporate profits was set at 7 percent; the provincial gasoline tax was raised to 11¢ a gallon, exempting gasoline used by farmers, fishermen, and manufacturers; the mining tax was raised to 6-9 percent with no deduction for federal taxes. Fiscal year ended March 31, 1947 was expected to show a surplus of $454,000 on ordinary account and capital expenditure of $20.5 million. At March 31, 1947 net debt was $493.4 million and contingent liabilities, $116.5 million. Budget forecast, 1947-48: revenue, $182.7 million; expenditure, $225.2 million; deficit on combined account, $42.4 million.

1948: April 2—Budget. A tax on amusements (hospitals tax) was levied at 20 percent. Preliminary data forecast a deficit on combined current and capital account of $17.7 million for 1947-48. Budget forecast, 1948-49:

Table 18.22 Ontario Finances: The Eighties

Year[a]	Revenue	Expenditure	Deficit
		millions of dollars	
1980	17,335.7	18,168.6	− 832.9
1981	19,732.7	20,861.6	− 1,128.9
1982	21,532.5	23,932.4	− 2,399.9
1983	23,713.3	26,135.5	− 2,422.2
1984	26,667.0	28,239.2	− 1,572.2
1985	29,550.9	32,081.8	− 2,530.9
1986	32,620.5	33,692.4	− 1,071.9
1987	35,314.3	35,854.3	− 540.0
1988	32,501.0	34,884.0	− 2,383.0

See table 18.2 for footnote and sources.

Table 18.23 Province of Ontario, Revenue, Consolidated Finances Basis, Selected Years, 1952-86[a]

Source	1952	1962	1972	1982	1986
			millions of dollars		
Taxes	128.8	856.8	4,039.0	14,708.5	22,987.9
Natural resource revenue	25.0	43.5	63.0	131.1	288.0
Privileges, licences and permits	44.5	107.7	206.1	387.4	575.7
Liquor sales and regulation	47.6	89.6	256.1	743.0	986.4
Other revenue	8.4	27.6	567.7	2,310.1	2,977.0
Transfers from other governments[b]	148.3	320.5	1,227.7	3,252.4	4,805.5
Total	402.6	1,445.7	6,359.6	21,532.5	32,620.5
Own source revenue	254.3	1,125.2	5,131.9	18,280.1	27,815.0
Surplus or deficit	− 7.6	− 77.1	− 344.5	− 2,399.9	− 1,071.9
			percent of total revenue		
Taxes	32.0	59.3	63.5	68.2	70.5
Natural resource revenue	6.2	3.0	1.0	0.5	0.9
Privileges, licences and permits	11.8	7.5	3.2	1.9	1.8
Liquor sales and regulation	7.4	6.2	4.0	3.5	3.0
Other revenue	5.8	1.8	8.9	10.8	9.1
Transfers from other governments	36.8	22.2	19.4	15.1	14.7
Total	100.0	100.0	100.0	100.0	100.0
Own source revenue	63.2	77.8	80.6	84.9	85.3

See table 18.3 for footnotes and sources.

revenue, $206.5 million; expenditure, $257.3 million; deficit on combined account, $50.9 million.

1949: March 4—Budget. The 2 percent tax on athletic contests was dropped; the formula for allocation of taxable income under the corporation income tax was aligned with that of the federal and other provincial governments; exemptions under succession duties were widened. Interim figures for 1948-49 showed an expected $57.5 million deficit on combined

Table 18.24 Province of Ontario, Expenditure, Consolidated Finances Basis, Selected Years, 1952-86[a]

	1952	1962	1972	1982	1986
	millions of dollars				
General services	9.5	39.1	288.0	1,014.4	1,433.0
Health	67.5	380.2	2,033.3	6,930.3	10,459.0
Social services	26.8	91.9	568.1	3,554.4	4,946.3
Education	79.9	487.8	1,948.3	4,825.8	6,434.8
Transportation and communications	124.7	261.1	572.8	1,532.4	1,747.4
Natural resources and industrial development	22.4	45.5	181.6	875.6	1,159.4
Charges on debt	32.9	85.9	449.2	2,470.6	4,200.0
Transfers to other governments[b]	3.4	40.2	92.1	654.8	817.2
Other	43.1	91.1	570.7	2,074.1	2,495.3
Total	410.2	1,522.8	6,704.1	23,932.4	33,692.4
Offsets:					
Specific purpose transfers	24.5	318.7	1,177.4	3,203.9	4,669.3
General purpose transfers	123.8	1.8	50.3	48.5	136.2
Own expenditure	261.9	1,202.3	5,476.4	20,680.0	28,886.9
	percent of total expenditure				
General services	2.3	2.6	4.3	4.2	4.3
Health	16.5	25.0	30.3	29.0	31.1
Social services	6.5	6.0	8.5	14.9	14.7
Education	19.5	32.0	29.0	20.2	19.1
Transportation and communications	30.4	17.1	8.5	6.4	5.2
Natural resources and industrial development	5.4	3.0	2.7	3.7	3.4
Charges on debt	8.0	5.6	6.7	10.3	12.5
Transfers to other governments[b]	0.8	2.7	1.4	2.7	2.4
Other	10.6	6.0	8.6	8.6	7.3
Total	100.0	100.0	100.0	100.0	100.0
Own expenditure	63.9	79.0	81.7	86.1	85.6

See table 18.4 for footnotes and sources.

accounts. Budget forecast, 1949-50: revenue, $231.0 million; expenditure, $316.7 million; deficit on combined account, $85.6 million.

1950: March 17—Budget. A racing commission was established to regulate tracks and a tax of 12½ percent levied on wagers under the pari-mutuel system; exemptions were widened under the hospitals tax on amusements and the rate lowered to 15 percent; a tax was levied on logging operations similar to the mining tax. Interim results for 1949-50 indicated a deficit on combined account of $78.8 million. Budget forecast, 1950-51: revenue, $270.6 million; expenditure, $353.4 million; deficit on combined account, $82.8 million.

1951: March 6—Budget. The hospital tax on amusements was reduced to 12.5 percent; rates under the pari-mutuel betting tax were adjusted downward. Preliminary figures for 1950-51 showed a combined account deficit of $66.9 million. Budget forecast, 1951-52: revenue, $300.5 million; expenditure, $382.8 million; combined account deficit, $82.3 million.

1952: March 20—Budget. The pari-mutuel betting tax was again adjusted and rates reduced downward. Interim results for 1951-52: deficit on combined account, $185.3 million. Budget forecast, 1952-53: revenue, $310.8 million; expenditure, $413.6 million; deficit on combined account, $102.8 million.

1953: March 12—Budget. As a result of suspension of Ontario corporation income taxes under the 1952-56 tax rental agreements, capital and place of business taxes were removed; exemptions widened under succession duties; race tracks tax reduced to 8 percent; mortgage tax removed. Preliminary figures for 1952-53 registered a $162.9 million deficit on combined current and capital accounts. Budget forecast, 1953-54: revenue, $356.9 million; expenditure, $460.8 million; deficit on combined account, $103.9 million.

1954: March 11—Budget. No tax changes. Interim figures for 1953-54 showed a surplus on ordinary account of $1.0 million before providing for capital disbursements of $219.6 million. Budget forecast, 1954-55: revenue, $379.1 million; expenditure, $509.8 million; deficit on combined account, $130.8 million.

1955: March 10—Budget. The amusement tax was lowered to 10 percent and the initial exemption was raised to 25¢. Interim results showed a surplus on ordinary account for 1954-55 of $704,000 before providing for net capital expenditures of $115.5 million. Budget forecast: 1955-56: revenue, $393.6 million; expenditure, $569.0 million; deficit on combined account, $175.4 million.

1956: March 1—Budget. The race tracks tax on pari-mutuel was lowered to 6 percent; motor vehicle registration fees had been raised as of January 1, 1956. The treasurer discussed proposals for the forthcoming tax-sharing agreements and the unemployment insurance system. Interim results for 1955-56 showed a deficit on combined account of $98.4 million. Budget forecast, 1956-57: revenue, $446.0 million; expenditure, $648.0 million; deficit, $201.9 million.

1957: February 21—Budget. A new corporation tax at 11 percent of profits was introduced. The special business taxes on capital and places of business were reinstated; an insurance premium tax of 2 percent was levied and royalty taxes under the Mining Tax Act; the base on which logging tax was levied was widened; gasoline and diesel fuel taxes were raised by 2¢ per gallon of gasoline to 13¢; also raised were the fire marshal's tax and licence fees for brewers. The personal income tax continued to be levied by the federal government, the province sharing in federal receipts from the tax in Ontario. The treasurer discussed the hospital insurance program which was expected to be in force by 1959 and expressed Ontario's dissatisfaction with the terms of the federal-provincial tax-sharing arrangements. Interim figures for 1956-57 showed a deficit on combined account of $245.8 million. Budget forecast, 1957-58: revenue, $575.6 million; expenditure, $709.0 million; deficit, $133.4 million.

1958: February 26—Budget. Effective January 1, 1958 the provincial share of the personal income tax was increased to 13 percent. The treasurer announced an estimated surplus on ordinary account for 1957-58 of $547,000, to be offset by capital expenditures of $215.7 million. Budget forecast, 1958-59: revenue, $630.7 million; expenditure, $932.9 million; deficit, $302.3 million.

1959: February 25—Budget. Hospital insurance premiums were: $2.10 single and $4.20 married. Succession duties reduced and Corporations Tax Act amended to bring it into line with federal law. Preliminary results, 1958-59: deficit on combined account, $255.1 million. Budget forecast, 1959-60: revenue, $679.9 million; expenditure, $990.0 million; deficit, $310.1 million.

1960: February 25—Budget. No tax changes. Preliminary results, 1959-60: deficit on combined account, $224.5 million. Budget forecast, 1960-61: revenue, $782.3 million; expenditure, $1,006.6 million; deficit, $224.2 million.

1961: March 9—Budget. Retail sales tax of 3 percent imposed as of September 1. Interim figures forecast a deficit on combined account for 1960-61 of $115.3 million. Budget forecast, 1961-62: revenue, $815.3 million; expenditure, $995.3 million; deficit, $180.0 million.

1962: March 1—Budget. Amendments were made to the sales tax, the corporate income tax, and the amusements tax. The treasurer estimated a deficit for 1961-62 of $145.9 million. Budget forecast, 1962-63: revenue, $1,020.9 million; expediture, $1,219.6 million; deficit, $214.5 million.

1963: February 7—Budget. Exemptions widened under succession duties; minor adjustments to the sales tax; tax credits allowed for logging tax against corporation taxes; personal income tax for 1963 under the new fiscal arrangements set at 17 percent for 1963. The treasurer estimated the deficit for 1962-63 at $103.4 million. Budget forecast, 1963-64: revenue, $1,043.4 million; expenditure, $1,250.7 million; deficit, $207.3 million.

1964: February 12—Budget. Gasoline tax increased by 2¢ to 15¢ per gallon; duties on inheritances raised to 75 percent in line with the federal withdrawal; corporations tax amended to conform to federal act; and increased exemptions under the amusements tax. The treasurer forecast a deficit for 1963-64 of $111.4 million, and net capital debt of $1,397.8 million at March 31, 1964. He announced that the Ontario Committee on Taxation was carrying out research into each tax and revenue source, the financial obligations of the province and its municipalities, and into intergovernmental financial relations generally. Budget forecast, 1964-65: revenue, $1,123.3 million; expenditure, $1,372.7 million; deficit, $249.4 million.

1965: February 10—Budget. Personal income tax set at 21 percent of federal tax for 1965 in line with the federal withdrawal; corporate income tax and succession duties legislation amended; tobacco exempted from general sales tax and taxed under special tobacco tax. The treasurer forecast a deficit of $77.5 million for 1964-65 and outstanding net capital debt of $1,423.9 million at March 31, 1965. Budget forecast, 1965-66: revenue, $1,293.4 million; expenditure, $1,573.8 million; deficit, $280.4 million.

1966: February 9—Budget. Sales tax raised to 5 percent and base expanded; gasoline tax raised to 16¢ a gallon; tobacco tax, land transfer tax, and liquor prices raised; personal income tax raised in line with the federal abatement to 24 percent of federal tax for 1966; succession duties exemptions widened. Voluntary medical services insurance plan inaugurated as of April 1, 1966, with assistance for the needy. Excess contributions by Ontario residents to Canada Pension Plan, from January 1, 1966, to be made available to province in form of loans. Preliminary figures for 1965-66 forecast a deficit of $443.4 million and net capital debt of $1,464.4 million. Budget forecast, 1966-67: revenue, $1,847.3 million; expenditure, $2,322.8 million; deficit, $475.5 million.

1967: February 14—Budget. No new taxes or tax increases. Budget forecast, 1967-68: revenue, $2,031 million; expenditure, $2,793 million; deficit, $163 million.

_____. Report, Ontario Taxation Committee.

1968: March 12—Budget. Taxes on gasoline, tobacco and pari-mutuel betting were increased, along with motor vehicle registration fees and hospital insurance premiums. Budget forecast, 1968-69: revenue, $2.5 billion; expenditure, $2.8 billion; deficit, $215 million.

1969: March 4—Budget. Minor tax increases. Budget forecast, 1969-70: revenue, $2,998 million; expenditure, $2,996 million; surplus, $1.9 million.

_____. Insurance Plan (OHSIP) covering hospital and medical services offered on voluntary basis.

1970: March 31—Budget. Minor tax changes. Budget forecast, 1970-71: revenue, $3,739 million; expenditure, $3,728 million; surplus, $11.3 million

1971: April 26—Budget. Minor changes in succession duties; increased support for local education. Budget forecast, 1971-72: revenue, $4,586 million; expenditure, $5,001 million; deficit, $415 million.

1972: April 17—Budget. Taxes on cigarettes, gasoline, and alcohol increased. Property tax credit plan to replace basic shelter grant. Grants to local governments and school boards increased. Government hospital and medical insurance consolidated under Ontario Hospital Insurance Plan (OHIP) with single payment covering both types of insurance. Budget forecast, 1972-73: revenue, $4,454 million; expenditure, $5,051 million; deficit, $597 million.

1973: April 13—Budget. Sales tax increased from 5 percent to 7 percent. Additional grants given for local governments under "resource equalization grants" and support for local education increased. Budget forecast, 1973-74: revenue, $6,802 million; expenditure, $7,269 million; deficit, $467 million.

1974: April 9—Budget. Land speculation tax introduced. Corporation tax changes for mining industry. Flow through proposed for investment in venture investment corporations. Succession duties reduced. Further assistance granted for municipalities and local transport. Guaranteed Annual Income System (GAINS) introduced for needy elderly, blind, and disabled and property tax credit doubled. Property Tax Stabilization Program introduced. Budget forecast, 1974-75: revenue, $7,716 million; expenditure, $8,343 million; deficit, $627 million.

————. Report, Municipal Tax Reform.

1975: April 7—Budget. Sales tax reduced from 7 to 5 percent to December 1976. Production and processing machinery exempt under certain conditions. Succession duties reduced. Cars purchased July to December exempt from tax. Budget forecast, 1975-76: revenue, $8.8 billion; expenditure, $10.1 billion; deficit, $1.3 billion.

1976: April 6—Budget. Small business tax credit replaced with reduced corporate tax rate. Venture investment corporations to proceed; taxes increased on insurance premiums, tobacco, and alcohol. OHIP charge raised. Commission to consider property tax reform. Budget forecast, 1976-77: revenue, $10.8 billion; expenditure, $11.8 billion; deficit, $1 billion.

1977: April 19—Budget. Increases announced for personal income tax, paid-up capital tax, tobacco taxes, and motor vehicle charges. Relief granted under succession duties, gift tax, and land transfer tax. Budget forecast, 1977-78: revenue, $12 billion; expenditure, $13 billion; deficit, $1.0 billion.

————. Report, Provincial-Municipal Grants Reform Committee.

1978: March 7—Budget. Sales tax rate reduced from 7 to 4 percent to October under federal offer. Tobacco taxes increased. Mining taxes revised. Budget forecast, 1978-79: revenue, $12.9 billion; expenditure, $14.4 billion; deficit, $1.5 billion.

1979: April 10—Budget. Effective April 10 succession duties and gift tax were repealed. Corporate tax rates were increased to 10 percent (small businesses); 13 percent (manufacturing and processing), and 14 percent (all other). Small Business Development Corporation replaced venture investment legislation. Taxes on gasoline and tobacco and OHIP charges increased. Budget forecast, 1979-80: revenue, $13.4 billion; expenditure, $15.1 billion; deficit, $1.7 billion.

1980: April 22—Budget. Increased grants to Old Age Security and GAINS recipients. Property tax credits for those over 65 and grants to pensioners for sales tax introduced. Further incentives for business investment and mining exploration introduced. Minor reliefs were given under sales tax and paid-up capital tax. Budget forecast, 1980-81: revenue, $15.3 billion; expenditure, $16.7 billion; deficit, $1.4 billion.

1981: May 19—Budget. Personal income tax and OHIP rates increased. Taxes on motor fuels, tobacco, and alcohol converted to ad valorem rates, with quarterly adjustment for inflation. Budget forecast, 1981-82: revenue, $17.5 billion; expenditure, $19.0 billion; deficit, $1.5 billion.

1982: May 13—Budget. Sales tax extended to many goods and services previously exempt, for substantial increase in revenue. Concessions under corporation income tax widened to include two years accelerated depreciation for machinery and equipment, two-year small business tax holiday, retention of full year depreciation for first year, and inventory adjustment allowance. Charges for motor vehicle licences, OHIP, tobacco, and alcohol raised. Government and Economic Council to study separate personal income tax for Ontario. Budget forecast, 1982-83: revenue, $19.5 billion; expenditure, $22.3 billion; deficit, $2.8 billion.

1983: May 10—Budget. Social service maintenance tax imposed as personal income surtax. Corporation tax rates increased by 1 point, but small business holiday extended for another year. Exemption from sales tax granted for purchases of new furniture and household appliances in a given period, and exemption for machinery and equipment extended. Tobacco taxes and OHIP charge increased. Budget forecast, 1983-84: revenue, $20.9 billion; expenditure, $24.3 billion; deficit, $3.4 billion. Government opts not to levy a separate personal income tax.

_____. Report, *Separate Income Tax for Ontario*. Ontario Economic Council.

1984: May 15—Budget. Minor tax changes. OHIP premiums raised. General tax holiday for small business replaced by three-year holiday for new small business. Budget forecast, 1984-85: revenue, $23.5 billion; expenditure, $26.4 billion; deficit, $2.9 billion.

1985: October 24—Budget. Personal income tax increased and 3 percent surtax levied on higher incomes. General corporate tax rate increased by 0.5 percent, but small business rate left at 10 percent. Ad valorem rates on tobacco and gasoline replaced by specific taxes. Motor and alcohol charges increased. Budget forecast, 1985-86: revenue, $28.8 billion; expenditure, $31.6 billion; deficit, $2.7 billion.

1986: May 13—Budget. Personal income tax surtax made permanent. Tobacco taxes increased. Ontario will not tax capital gains exempted by the federal government. Several programs were given more funding. Budget forecast, 1986-87: revenue, $28.5 billion; expenditure, $31.0 billion; deficit, $2.6 billion.

1987: May 20—Budget. Property tax credit (maximum) increased from $500 to $600. Sales tax exempt amount for prepared meals increased from $2 to $4. Relief from property tax on farm lands raised from 60 percent to 100 percent. Three-year exempt period for new mines introduced. Post-secondary education and several other programs received additional funding. Budget forecast, 1987-88: revenue, $32.3 billion; expenditure, $34.3 billion; deficit, $2.1 billion.

1988: April 20—Budget. The retail sales tax was raised from 7 to 8 percent; the personal income tax rate raised from 50 percent of the basic federal tax to 51 percent for 1988 and 52 percent for 1989, and the surtax raised to 10 percent of tax paid over $10,000; amendments made to property and sales tax credits; Ontario home ownership savings plan introduced; amendments made to paid-up capital tax; depletion allowances for mining profits to be phased out over five years and replaced with resource allowance; the three-year tax holiday for new corporations to be phased out; cost adjustment rates for new manufacturing and processing machinery and equipment for use in Ontario to be phased in: 10 percent for 1989 purchases and 15 percent after 1989; superallowance deduction equal to 25 percent of qualifying R & D expenditures (35 percent for small business) introduced; gasoline and fuel taxes increased to 9.3¢ per litre; tobacco taxes increased to 3.83¢ per cigarette; liquor prices raised. The treasurer presented what he termed "a fiscally responsible budget" incorporating expenditure controls and introducing revenue measures essential to achieving the government's objective of redressing the funding imbalances inherited from the past. Budget forecast, 1988-89: revenue, $32.5 billion; expenditure, $34.9 billion; deficit, $2,383.0 million.

Manitoba

Manitoba enjoys the distinction of being roughly at the geographical centre of Canada, and in many ways shows mid-point characteristics. Historically the gateway to the west, with the commercial and financial functions of an entrepôt, this status gradually declined as the population moved westward to new provinces. As its economy is heavily involved in agriculture its interests are much those of the two other western provinces (weather, markets, transportation, prices, etc.) Its natural resources have not been as rewarding as those of Alberta and Saskatchewan, but base metals, along with ample hydro-electric power, have been an aid to economic development. Winnipeg is a rapidly growing metropolitan area with an industrial base, and with the more efficient communication of recent years has some advantages in its central location. However, it is not closely integrated with the Ontario-Quebec industrial complex.

Politically the province has only been on the fringe of the more radical trends exhibited in the farther western provinces, but in the last decade has had two NDP governments. Even these governments however do not appear to have drastically altered Manitoba's traditional conservatism, which emerged in the re-election of a minority Conservative government in an election in April 1988.

In fiscal terms the province has followed very much the general provincial pattern. It accepted the tax-rental agreements and other joint programs offered by the federal government, with resulting fairly heavy dependence on revenues from that source. The tighter federal control over payments since 1976, and particularly since 1982, have reduced this source significantly, to the distress of the provincial treasurer. For its own-source revenues the province has followed the general pattern of heavy reliance on the personal income tax, increased retail sales tax rates, and almost annual raises over a long period in taxes on gasoline, tobacco, and alcohol. There were changes in corporate taxation, but on the whole, with the exception of some experimentation with a new form of mining taxation (finally abandoned) the province was less inclined to favour the use of tax incentives than

Table 18.25 Manitoba: General Profile

	Year[a]	Province	All Canada	Province as percent of all Canada
Population (000)	1987	1,079	25,625	4.2
Gross Domestic Product ($ billion)	1986	19.1	506.5	3.8
G.D.P. per capita ($)	1986	17,829	20,030	89.0
Personal Income ($ billion)	1986	16.9	432.5	3.9
P.I. per capita ($)	1986	15,807	17,060	92.7
Unemployment rate (%)	1987	7.4	8.9	83.1
Provincial government: revenue ($ billion)	1986	4.3	202.5[b]	2.1
Provincial government: expenditure ($ billion)	1986	4.8	234.1[b]	2.0
Basic personal income tax rate (%)[c]	1988	54.0	46.5-60[d]	—
General corporate tax rate (%)	1988	17.0	14-17[d]	—
Retail sales tax rate	1988	7.0	6-12[d]	—

See table 18.1 for footnotes and sources.

Table 18.26 Manitoba Finances: The Eighties

Year[a]	Revenue	Expenditure	Deficit
	millions of dollars		
1980........................	2,283.8	2,396.0	− 112.2
1981........................	2,690.5	2,938.2	− 247.7
1982........................	3,038.6	3,457.2	− 418.6
1983........................	3,507.8	4,032.9	− 525.1
1984........................	3,747.1	4,171.9	− 424.8
1985........................	3,953.0	4,467.3	− 514.3
1986........................	4,336.0	4,817.1	− 481.1
1987........................	5,005.5	5,191.4	− 185.9
1988........................	4,226.7	4,556.7	− 334.1

See table 18.2 for footnotes and sources.

was common in some other provinces. There is enough petroleum in Manitoba that the province enjoyed a brief boost from this source in the seventies, and although natural resource revenues are still several times those of a decade ago they are less than 2 percent of total revenues.

Expenditures have increased in the familiar pattern of health, education, social services, debt charges, etc. The results have also been in a familiar pattern—almost continuous deficits for many years.

Manitoba Diary

1947: March 27—Budget. Gasoline tax raised to 9¢ per gallon as of March 31, when the federal government vacated this area; provincial tax of 5 percent on corporation income under the Dominion-Manitoba tax agreement, 1947, was to be repealed if the federal government levied this tax. The provincial treasurer forecast a surplus on ordinary account for the year ended April 30, 1946 of $4.7 million and gross public debt at April 30 of $4.3

Table 18.27   Province of Manitoba, Revenue, Consolidated Finances Basis, Selected Years, 1952-86ª

Source	1952	1962	1972	1982	1986
	millions of dollars				
Taxes........................	8.8	76.7	407.2	1,488.5	2,193.8
Natural resource revenue	2.7	4.7	12.4	38.0	82.4
Privileges, licences and permits ...	6.7	13.2	18.1	34.3	37.8
Liquor sales and regulation	8.5	15.4	37.6	119.6	148.9
Other revenue	5.6	15.1	88.8	435.7	653.2
Transfers from other governments[b]	32.9	55.4	273.7	922.5	1,219.9
Total........................	65.2	180.5	837.8	3,038.6	4,336.0
Own source revenue	32.3	125.1	564.1	2,116.1	3,116.1
Surplus or deficit	13.5	−71.3	33.5	−418.6	−481.1
	percent of total revenue				
Taxes........................	13.5	42.5	48.6	49.0	50.7
Natural resource revenue	4.1	2.6	1.5	1.3	1.9
Privileges, licences and permits ...	10.3	7.3	2.2	1.1	0.8
Liquor sales and regulation	13.0	8.5	4.5	3.9	3.5
Other revenue	8.6	8.4	10.5	14.3	15.1
Transfers from other governments[b]	50.5	30.7	32.7	30.4	28.0
Total........................	100.0	100.0	100.0	100.0	100.0
Own source revenue	49.5	69.3	67.3	69.7	71.9

See table 18.3 for footnotes and sources.

million. Budget forecast for fiscal year ending March 31, 1948: revenue, $29.5 million; expenditure, $29.4 million; surplus on ordinary account, $90,000.

1948: April 9—Budget. Tax levied on mining income; tax on amusements increased to 25 percent on admissions of 25¢ and over. The treasurer commented on the uncertainties of the financial positions of the seven provinces agreeing to the 1945 Dominion-provincial proposals, and the reflected uneasiness of provincial-municipal relations. Interim figures for 1947-48 estimated a surplus on ordinary account of $4.1 million: Budget forecast, 1948-49: revenue $33.8 million; expenditure, $33.7 million; surplus on ordinary account, $114,000.

1949: March 28—Budget. The province assumed the former municipal levy for old age and blind pensions. The federal government agreed to provide grants to the provinces for certain health and social services. The treasurer tabled preliminary figures for 1948-49 which indicated a surplus on ordinary account of $2.2 million. Budget forecast, 1949-50: revenue, $36.5 million; expenditure, $36.5 million; surplus on ordinary account, $51,000; capital expenditure, $25.0 million.

1950: April 4—Budget. No tax changes. Estimated surplus for 1949-50, $2.9 million on ordinary account. Budget forecast, 1950-51: revenue, $39.4

Table 18.28 Province of Manitoba, Expenditure, Consolidated Finances
Basis, Selected Years, 1952-86[a]

	1952	1962	1972	1982	1986
		millions of dollars			
General services	2.1	4.4	24.0	118.3	264.3
Health.......................	8.1	53.1	213.5	916.9	1,163.0
Social services	4.7	20.7	90.6	452.6	634.1
Education....................	9.4	41.7	203.3	746.2	937.5
Transportation and communications	13.7	29.7	68.7	185.6	189.9
Natural resources and industrial development	4.5	14.7	48.9	169.2	196.0
Charges on debt..............	4.8	17.7	53.7	472.4	857.2
Transfers to other governments[b]	0.1	3.8	16.2	94.0	107.0
Other.......................	4.3	10.6	85.5	302.0	468.1
Total.......................	51.7	196.4	804.3	3,457.2	4,817.1
Offsets:					
Specific purpose transfers	5.8	36.3	179.1	438.4	688.5
General purpose transfers	27.1	19.1	94.6	484.1	531.4
Own expenditure	18.8	141.0	530.6	2,534.7	3,597.2
		percent of total expenditure			
General services	4.1	2.2	3.0	3.4	5.5
Health.......................	15.6	27.0	26.5	26.5	24.2
Social services	9.1	10.5	11.2	13.1	13.2
Education....................	18.1	21.2	25.2	21.6	19.5
Transportation and communications	26.4	15.1	8.5	5.4	3.9
Natural resources and industrial development	8.7	7.5	6.1	4.9	4.1
Charges on debt..............	9.3	9.0	6.7	13.6	17.8
Transfers to other governments[b]	0.2	1.9	2.0	2.7	2.2
Other.......................	8.5	5.6	10.8	8.8	9.6
Total.......................	100.0	100.0	100.0	100.0	100.0
Own expenditure	36.4	71.9	66.0	73.3	74.6

See table 18.4 for footnotes and sources.

million; expenditure, $39.2 million; surplus on ordinary account, $297,000; capital expenditures, $29.5 million.

_____. November 7—Budget. The disasters caused by the Red River Valley Flood of May-June 1950 occasioned total spending of approximately $42 million for alleviating hardship, rehabilitating housing, roads and other facilities. Federal assistance was expected to total $12.5 million. Discussions with the federal government were initiated for the construction of the Red River Valley (Greater Winnipeg) Floodway.

1952: March 24—Budget. Provincial 5 percent tax on corporate income eliminated. The surplus for 1950-51, after flood expenditure of $3.0 million, was $1.8 million on ordinary account; gross public debt at March

31, $136.0 million. Interim figures for 1951-52 reported a surplus on ordinary account of $1.8 million, after flood expenditures of $3.6 million. Budget forecast, 1952-53: revenue, $49.6 million; expenditure, $49.1 million; surplus on ordinary account, $489,000; capital expenditures, $22.5 million.

1953: April 8—Budget. Amusement tax lowered to 17.5 percent from 25. The estimated surplus on ordinary account for 1952-53 was $420,000 and gross public debt at March 31, 1953 stood at $181.9 million. Budget forecast, 1953-54: revenue, $55.0 million; expenditure, $54.4 million; surplus on ordinary account, $531,000; capital expenditures, $24.0 million.

1954: March 17—Budget. Tax imposed on production from oil wells. Surplus on ordinary account for 1953-54 expected to total $33.5 million and gross public debt, including contingent liabilities, at March 31, 1954, $185.6 million. Budget forecast, 1954-55: revenue, $57.3 million; expenditure, $56.9 million; surplus on ordinary account, $439,000.

1955: March 23—Budget. No tax changes. Estimated surplus for 1954-55 on ordinary account was $299,000. Budget forecast, 1955-56: revenue, $58.5 million; expenditure, $58.3 million; surplus on ordinary account, $156,000; capital outlays, $20.0 million.

1956: March 28. Tax on amusements lowered; tax on gasoline and motive fuel increased to 11¢ per gallon of gasoline. Estimated surplus for 1955-56 on current account of $310,000. Budget forecast, 1956-57: revenue, $65.0 million; expenditure, $64.6 million; surplus on current account, $443,000; capital expenditure, $30.5 million; funds for utilities, $25.5 million.

1957: March 25—Budget. Increases in exemptions under the amusement tax. Surplus for 1956-57 was estimated at $301,000 on ordinary account. Budget forecast, 1957-58: revenue, $76.9 million; expenditure, $76.8 million; surplus on ordinary account, $137,000; capital expenditures on highways, $7.0 million; advaces to utilities, $52.0 million.

1958: March 26—Budget. Increases in exemptions under the amusement tax. Preliminary figures showed a nominal surplus of $1,000 on ordinary account for 1957-58. Budget forecast, 1958-59: revenue, $81.1 million; expenditure, $81.0 million; surplus on ordinary account, $41,000.

1964: Report, Manitoba Royal Commission on Local Government Organization and Finance.

1966: Domestic heating fuel exempted from tax on fuel. Preliminary figures showed a nominal surplus on current account of $239,000 for 1965-66 after a transfer of $10.5 million from the revenue surplus account. Budget forecast, 1966-67: revenue, $298.2 million; expenditure, $298.0 million; surplus on current account, $169,000.

1967: February 6—Budget. Sales tax introduced at 5 percent, as Manitoba Education Tax. Exemptions included food, machinery used in manufacture of tangible property, and many other items. Budget forecast, 1967-68: revenue, $353 million; expenditure, $355 million; deficit, $2 million.

1968: April 8—Budget. No tax changes. Budget forecast, 1968-69: revenue, $378 million; expenditure, $377 million; modest surplus.

1969: April 10—Budget. No tax changes. Budget forecast, 1968-69: revenue, $379 million; expenditure, $378 million (current account only); modest surplus expected.

1970: April 30—Budget. No tax changes. Budget forecast, 1970-71: revenue, $449 million; expenditure, $443 million (current account only); modest surplus expected.

1971: May 13—Budget. No tax changes. Budget forecast, 1971-72: revenue, $498 million; expenditure, $509 million; deficit, $11 million.

1972: April 6—Budget. Taxes on tobacco products were raised, the sales tax exemption for production equipment was ended, a mining property acreage tax was levied, and an income-tested credit against personal income tax was allowed for education taxes to replace a previous school tax reduction program. Budget forecast, 1972-73: revenue, $573 million; expenditure, $568 million; surplus, $5 million.

1973: March 27—Budget. The budget announced complete removal of the health insurance premium. It also announced subsidization of purchase of prescription drugs for seniors and an increase in the income-tested allowance for education and property taxes. The province also undertook in future to pay over to municipalities 5 percent of its personal and corporate income tax revenue. Budget forecast, 1973-74: revenue, $695 million; expenditure, $687 million; surplus, $8 million.

1974: March 21—Budget. The major item in this budget was a proposal for several new forms of taxation on mining activity in the province, with an interim increase in the existing royalty. Other tax changes included a reduction in gasoline tax, removal of amusement taxes (except the pari-mutuel betting tax) and a credit for inflation against personal income tax. Substantial expenditure increases were planned to index social benefits, extend pharmacare, provide day-care centres, improve medical facilities, etc. The government would also contribute 25 percent of the cost of a joint guaranteed income experiment in the province. Budget forecast, 1974-75: revenue, $838 million; expenditure, $912 million; deficit, $76 million.

1975: April 24—Budget. A new system of grants for municipalities was forecast, with promises of full examination of alternatives; for 1976 municipalities would be given the revenue from 2 percentage points of personal income tax and 1 percentage point of corporate tax. The 2 percent income-limited inflation credit was raised to 3 percent; the gasoline tax was increased; succession duty exemptions were raised; changes were made in natural resource levies following federal action. Budget forecast, 1975-76: revenue, $1,021 million; expenditure, $996 million; surplus, $25 million.

1976: April 13—Budget. An inflation surtax on higher income was introduced. The credit against personal income tax for property taxes was increased; the corporate income tax was increased from 13 percent to 15 percent to December 31, 1978, and a corporation capital tax was introduced; rates were increased on gasoline, tobacco, and motor vehicle licences and liquor prices were raised. Municipalities were authorized to levy "growth taxes" on certain sales and services and on land transfers. Budget forecast, 1976-77: revenue, $1,164 million; expenditure, $1,264 million; deficit, $100 million.

1977: April 22—Budget. The budget set the personal income tax rate at 56 percent of the federal rate, increased the tax credit for home-owners, and raised succession duty and gift tax exemptions. Budget forecast, 1977-78: revenue, $1,158 million; expenditure, $1,180 million, deficit, $22 million.

1978: April 10—Budget. The personal income tax rate was dropped from 56 percent to 54 percent for 1978, the surtax was repealed for 1979, and the property tax credit was increased. The 2 percent additional corporate tax increase was extended indefinitely for a general rate of 15 percent, but the small business rate was reduced from 13 percent to 11 percent. Under the federal offer the sales tax was reduced from 5 percent to 2 percent from April to September, but the tobacco tax was increased. Provincial succession duties and gift tax were repealed. A ratio for sharing tax revenues with municipalities was established for the 54 percent rate. Budget forecast, 1979-80: revenue, $1,556 million; expenditure, $1,670 million; deficit, $114 million.

1979: May 15—Budget. Minimal tax changes were made, a single rate mining royalty replaced the previous graduated rates and other taxes on industrial minerals were terminated. Sales tax exemptions were extended. A White Paper would be submitted on reform of tax relief and income support programs. A large unknown for the future was the cost of the flood damage at Winnipeg. Budget forecast, 1979-80: revenue, $1,711 million; expenditure, $1,833 million, deficit, $123 million.

1980: May 13—Budget. A tax credit for political contributions was introduced and the property tax credit was raised. Further exemptions from sales tax were given, and specific rates were enacted to replace ad valorem taxes on gasoline. Tobacco taxes were raised. A general review of property tax assessment was being made and changes would follow. In the meantime the budget presented a White Paper on the tax credit system and related income assistance programs. Budget forecast, 1980-81: revenue, $1,883 million; expenditure, $2,022 million; deficit, $140 million.

1981: April 14—Budget. Tax changes were minimal. A further raise was made in the property tax credit, the capital tax on banks and trust and loan companies was increased. Once again tobacco taxes and liquor markups were raised. A new provincial program was proposed to provide for provincial property taxes in support of education. (The opposite approach to Quebec, which at this point was removing such taxes). Budget forecast, 1981-82: revenue, $2,161 million; expenditure, $2,381 million; deficit, $220 million.

1982: May 11—Budget. A surtax on higher income was levied under the personal income tax. Under the corporate tax the rate for small business was reduced from 11 percent to 10 percent. The capital tax on banks was increased from 0.9 percent to 2 percent, and the insurance premiums tax was raised from 2 percent to 3 percent on general insurance. A payroll tax of 1.5 percent was introduced to provide revenues for health and post-secondary education. Tobacco taxes and taxes on some forms of motor fuel were increased. Budget forecast, 1982-83: revenue, $2,495 million; expenditure, $2,830 million; deficit, $335 million.

1983: February 28—Budget. Like most other provinces Manitoba was having a difficult time coping with the results of the recession and with reduced payments from the federal government under its decelerating equalization and other payments. Tax increases were therefore common. The 1983 budget increased the sales tax from 5 percent to 6 percent, the tax levied on "package" liquor from 10 percent to 12 percent, the corporate income tax from 15 percent to 16 percent (small business rates remaining at 10 percent), and the gasoline and tobacco taxes. The temporary increase in the capital tax on banks was extended for another year. Professor Barber of the University of Manitoba was making a survey of provincial budget and other statements. Budget forecast, 1983-84: revenue, $2,749 million; expenditure, $3,327 million; deficit, $579 million.

1984: April 24—Budget. Further increases were made on tobacco products and on diesel fuel. The bank capital tax was extended for another year. An investment tax credit was introduced for production machinery and equipment installed by December 1985. The exemption limit for the payroll tax was raised. Budget forecast, 1984-85: revenue, $2,969 million; expenditure, $3,458 million; deficit, $489 million.

1985: March 21—Budget. More increases were introduced for the gasoline and tobacco taxes. The manufacturing investment tax credit was extended for another year. The budget speech appealed for a program of reform for the federal income tax and for a review of federal transfer payments to the provinces. Budget forecast, 1985-86: revenue, $3,713 million; expenditure, $4,184 million; deficit, $471 million.

1986: May 22—Budget. The tax rate on large corporations was increased from 16 to 17 percent, the capital tax was raised from 0.2 percent to 0.3 percent, with special higher rates for banks and trust companies; the tobacco tax was increased, and additional fuels made subject to the motive fuel tax. Charges for drivers' licences and motor vehicle registration were increased. Budget forecast, 1986-87: revenue, $3,380; expenditure, $3,870 million; deficit, $489 million.

1987: March 16—Budget. This was a budget of both tax increases and continuing assistance for agriculture, small business, senior homeowners, and users of hydro power. The Minister argued for more stable payments from Ottawa and general tax reform. His tax changes included an increase from 6 to 7 percent in the sales tax and its extension to tobacco products and other items, a flat tax of 2 percent on net income of individuals, with low incomes spared, an increase to 2.25 percent in the payroll tax and increases in the taxes on corporate capital, tobacco, motor fuels and land transfers. Budget forecast, 1987-88: revenue, $3,773 million; expenditure, $4,188 million; deficit, $415 million.

1988: February 26—Budget. The personal income tax was amended to conform to the reformed federal structure; a labour sponsored investment fund introduced; surtax increased on leaded gasoline and tax on locomotive and aviation fuel increased; tobacco taxes raised; mining taxation reformed; and farm school tax assistance program extended for one year. The budget continued the government's commitment to matching economic and social progress with fiscal improvement. Budget forecast, 1988-89: revenue, $4.2 billion; expenditure, $4.6 billion; deficit, $334.1 million.

_____: March 8—The government was defeated on a confidence motion on the budget; in the election of April 26 the Conservatives took power.

_____: August 8—Budget. The new Minister of Finance's budget forecast a deficit of $195.9 million for 1988-89. Increased revenue from higher federal equalization payments and from the mining industry was expected to lower the deficit from the original projection. Budget forecast, 1988-89: revenue, $4,364.6 million; expenditure, $4,560.5 million.

Saskatchewan

Saskatchewan has been noted for three-quarters of a century as one of the world's great food baskets. Its wheat fields have produced lavishly and agriculture has survived through many tribulations and much change. In more recent years it has joined its neighbour Alberta as a producer of oil, and its potash and uranium resources have brought it good returns.

Perhaps even more distinctive however has been its role as the progenitor of radical political parties. There have been radical political organizations in other provinces, but none can claim the record of the socialist-oriented CCF (Cooperative Commonwealth Federation) and the NDP (the New Democratic Party, successor to the CCF) in having the reins of provincial government for three-quarters of the time since first elected in 1944. The development of government in the province has been profoundly influenced by the instability related to dependence on world markets for its agriculture and mineral resources, and the insistence despite this instability—or perhaps because of it—on providing the best possible life for its residents through government programs and institutions. Granted that this attitude is not entirely foreign to other provinces, but the difference with Saskatchewan has been more than a matter of degree; it has been ready to break new ground long before others.

In the postwar period its ready receptivity of the federal social proposals at the 1945-46 Reconstruction Conference was characteristic. In the health area 30 years before in 1916 its rural municipalities had been authorized to employ doctors to provide community health services, and in 1945, even before the conference, the Saskatchewan legislature had passed a bill authorizing provincial health insurance. When the federal proposal was rejected the province immediately proceeded with its own hospital insurance scheme, 10 years before there was federal legislation. Similarly in 1962 the province introduced health insurance, six years before federal legislation and several years before most of the other provinces acted. The province has been active in other areas, and other instances could be given of its willingness to move forward rapidly on social legislation. It has also done much

Table 18.29   Saskatchewan: General Profile

	Year[a]	Province	All Canada	Province as percent of all Canada
Population (000)	1987	1,014	25,625	4.0
Gross Domestic Product ($ billion)	1986	17.2	506.5	3.4
G.D.P. per capita ($)	1986	17,021	20,030	85.0
Personal Income ($ billion)	1986	15.9	432.5	3.7
P.I. per capita ($)	1986	15,766	17,060	98.3
Unemployment rate (%)..............	1987	7.3	8.9	82.2
Provincial government: revenue ($ billion)........................	1986	4.3	202.5[b]	2.1
Provincial government: expenditure ($ billion)........................	1986	4.8	234.1[b]	2.0
Basic personal income tax rate (%)[c]	1988	50.0	46.5-60[d]	—
General corporate tax rate (%)	1988	17.0	14-17[d]	—
Retail sales tax rate	1988	7.0	6-12[d]	—

See table 18.1 for footnotes and sources.

for both the financing and organization of education and municipal government.

In economic matters the socialist influence was not especially apparent. One reason for this was the extent to which government already dominated economic life; the wheat crop was marketed by a federal government agency and as likely as not carried by a government-owned railway; the majority of natural resources were owned by the provincial government and all the conditions for the development, extraction, and sale of these resources were set by the province or its agencies. Under these conditions the main economic activities left little room for socialist exercises. This appeared mainly in the establishment of government-owned corporations to carry out economically-oriented functions, although whether there were more of these than in other provinces would be difficult to say.

Even on the fiscal side there has been little to differentiate the province from the others. The pattern is much the same; growing reliance on the personal income tax and the retail sales tax (although western provincial rates are lower than eastern), and almost annual increases in tobacco and liquor revenues. During one affluent period the province repealed its gasoline tax but with harder times from declining prices for oil, potash, and wheat the tax has been restored to help an ailing budget. The provincial budget was deeply mired in deficit in 1987 and draconian measures were being taken to achieve some improvement. Although less dependent on the federal government than at earlier periods the province complains bitterly in its straitened circumstances of recent reductions in federal grants. In this it was not alone.

Saskatchewan Diary

1947: March 6—Budget. The provincial gasoline tax was raised by 2¢ to 10¢ per gallon (the federal government had just vacated this field), and the

Table 18.30   Saskatchewan Finances: The Eighties

Year[a]	Revenue	Expenditure	Deficit
		millions of dollars	
1980.....................	2,833.1	2,635.5	+ 196.6
1981.....................	3,139.6	3,038.3	+ 101.3
1982.....................	3,306.0	3,601.5	− 295.5
1983.....................	3,613.4	3,855.0	− 241.6
1984.....................	3,731.9	4,261.6	− 529.7
1985.....................	3,907.1	4,476.3	− 569.2
1986.....................	4,293.5	4,763.7	− 470.2
1987.....................	4,152.5	4,897.2	− 744.7
1988.....................	3,607.7	3,935.9	− 312.8

See table 18.2 for footnotes and sources.

Table 18.31   Province of Saskatchewan, Revenue, Consolidated Finances Basis, Selected Years, 1952-86[a]

Source	1952	1962	1972	1982	1986
			millions of dollars		
Taxes........................	35.7	107.0	268.5	1,314.8	1,687.7
Natural resource revenue	6.7	28.0	46.7	570.3	643.3
Privileges, licences and permits ...	5.8	10.2	17.4	47.2	64.3
Liquor sales and regulation	11.0	14.5	18.1	114.4	245.6
Other revenue	7.8	37.8	104.9	596.4	971.1
Transfers from other governments[b]	33.4	68.6	273.8	662.9	681.5
Total........................	100.4	266.1	729.4	3,306.0	4,293.5
Own source revenue	67.0	197.5	455.1	2,643.1	3,612.0
Surplus or deficit..............	11.0	22.3	31.6	− 295.5	− 470.2
			percent of total revenue		
Taxes........................	35.5	40.2	36.8	39.7	39.3
Natural resource revenue	6.7	10.5	6.4	17.3	15.0
Privileges, licences and permits ...	5.8	3.9	2.4	1.5	1.5
Liquor sales and regulation	10.9	6.2	2.5	3.4	5.8
Other revenue	7.8	14.2	14.4	18.1	22.6
Transfers from other governments[b]	33.3	25.8	37.5	20.0	15.8
Total........................	100.0	100.0	100.0	100.0	100.0
Own source revenue	66.7	74.2	62.4	80.0	84.1

See table 18.3 for footnotes and sources.

province was prepared to add another 2¢ on behalf of municipalities if they desired it; exemptions under the general sales tax (education tax) were widened. Saskatchewan ended fiscal year 1945-46 with a surplus on current account of $491,000; net debt at December 31, 1946 was $187.7 million. The budget made no preliminary estimates of 1946-47 results. The province was cancelling $21.8 million in advances to municipalities from 1935-37 for seed grain. Budget forecast: 1947-48: revenue, $45.6 million; expenditure, $45.6 million; surplus on current account, $20,000.

Table 18.32 Province of Saskatchewan, Expenditure, Consolidated Finances Basis, Selected Years, 1952-86[a]

	1952	1962	1972	1982	1986
	millions of dollars				
General services	4.2	8.0	27.0	246.0	316.6
Health	29.1	70.1	182.7	882.8	1,232.0
Social services	7.7	24.3	80.3	548.8	499.9
Education	12.3	51.8	164.6	558.5	726.1
Transportation and communications	19.2	31.0	82.0	201.9	216.4
Natural resources and industrial development	6.6	14.8	89.9	312.1	429.1
Charges on debt	6.0	23.8	43.3	482.4	848.0
Transfers to other governments[b]	0.1	0.3	—	102.5	115.7
Other	4.2	19.7	28.0	266.5	379.9
Total	89.4	243.8	697.8	3,601.5	4,763.7
Offsets:					
Specific purpose transfers	7.1	39.7	136.1	475.2	669.2
General purpose transfers	26.3	28.8	137.7	187.7	12.3
Own expenditure	56.0	175.3	424.0	2,938.6	4,082.2
	percent of total expenditure				
General services	4.7	3.3	3.9	6.8	6.6
Health	32.6	28.7	26.1	24.5	25.9
Social services	8.6	10.0	11.5	15.3	10.5
Education	13.8	21.2	23.5	15.5	15.3
Transportation and communications	21.5	12.7	11.7	5.6	4.5
Natural resources and industrial development	7.4	6.1	12.9	8.7	9.0
Charges on debt	6.7	9.8	6.2	13.4	17.8
Transfers to other governments[b]	0.1	0.1	—	2.8	2.4
Other	4.6	8.1	4.2	7.4	8.0
Total	100.0	100.0	100.0	100.0	100.0
Own expenditure	62.6	71.9	60.7	81.6	85.7

See table 18.4 for footnotes and sources.

1948: February 26—Budget. No tax changes. The 11-month period ending March 31, 1947 showed a surplus on current account of $121,000. Budget forecast, 1948-49: revenue and expenditure, $52.2 million each; surplus on current account, $17,000.

1949: March 2—Budget. No tax changes. The surplus on current account for 1947-48 was $1.5 million. Budget forecast, 1949-50: current account revenue and expenditure, net of federal subsidies, $49.1 million each; surplus on current account, $10,000. The treasurer pointed out that the hospital tax (maximum charge $20 per year per family) did not pay the province's cost of the program, estimated at $1.4 million for 1947-48.

1950: March 8—Budget. The education tax replaced by a 3 percent education and hospitalization tax, two-thirds of receipts to be used for education and the balance for hospitalization costs. Continued prosperity was reflected in the financial affairs of all three levels of government. The public accounts for 1948-49 showed a surplus on current account of $1.0 million. Budget forecast, 1950-51: revenue, $55.1 million; expenditure, $55.0 million; surplus on current account, $33,000; capital expenditures, $18.0 million.

1951: February 21—Budget. No tax changes. The treasurer reported a surplus of $254,000 on current account for 1949-50; net debt at December 31, 1950 was $147.9 million. Budget forecast, 1951-52: revenue, $58.2 million; expenditure, $58.0 million; surplus on current account, $244,000.

1952: February 27—Budget. No tax changes. The treasurer commented that although 1951 had been "an extremely varied and even difficult" year for some of the province's farmers, the overall result had been extremely favourable. The recorded surplus on current account for 1950-51 was $263,000; net debt at the end of 1950 was $151.6 million. Budget forecast, 1952-53: revenue and expenditure, both $65.9 million; surplus on current account, $49,000.

1953: March 4—Budget. Gasoline tax raised by 1¢ to 11¢ per gallon; the public revenue tax was abolished. The recorded surplus on current account for 1951 was $119,000; liquor board profits of $9.5 million were not taken into revenue but were used for debt retirement. Net debt of the province at December 31, 1952 was $97.8 million and contingent liabilities, $65.2 million. Budget forecast, 1952-53: revenue, $70.5 million; expenditure, $70.4 million; surplus on current account, $90,000; capital expenditures, $17.3 million.

1954: March 3—Budget. No tax changes. The surplus on revenue account for 1952-53 was recorded at $4.7 million, plus $10.2 million in liquor profits. Budget forecast, 1954-55: revenue, $78.4 million; expenditure, $78.1 million; surplus on revenue account, $296,000; capital expenditures, $21.4 million. The treasurer pointed out that any windfall profit from the sale of exploration and production rights on Crown lands was not placed in general revenues but added to the School Lands Fund.

1955: March 2—Budget. No tax changes. The treasurer noted that 1954 was the first year that the economy of the country had suffered a downturn since the end of the war. In Saskatchewan the farmers had suffered a crop failure because of poor weather and a rust infestation. For 1953-54 the net surplus on combined revenue and capital account had been $4.2 million; direct and indirect debt at December 31, 1954 totalled $179.8 million, including $100.0 million in contingent liabilities. Budget forecast, 1955-56: revenue and expenditure, $80.0 million each; surplus on revenue account, $21,000; capital expenditures, $19.8 million.

1956: March 5—Budget. No tax changes. 1955 had brought an early end to the recession of the previous year but the recovery had not extended to the farm sector. The treasurer outlined federal proposals for revising federal-provincial tax sharing and for a national hospital insurance plan. The surplus on revenue account for 1954-55 was recorded at $4.5 million; liquor profits of $10.2 million had been used for capital expenditures. Budget forecast, 1956-57: revenue, $87.2 million; expenditure, $87.1 million; surplus, $25,000 on revenue account; capital expenditures, $20.2 million.

1957: March 6—Budget. Revision upward of the royalty schedule on production from oil and gas leases on Crown land; 2 percent tax on insurance premiums taken over from the federal government; tax on gasoline raised by 1¢ to 12¢ a gallon and registration fees raised for large commercial vehicles; farm fuels exempted from sales tax. Saskatchewan farms had produced a bumper crop in 1956 but the cost-price relationship in western agriculture continued to worsen. Fortunately prosperity had returned to the provincial economy as a whole. The province raised its share to 75 percent of municipal social aid costs after it had accepted the federal sharing offer under the unemployment assistance agreement. Federal-provincial discussion continued on tax sharing and the province voiced its dissatisfaction with the federal offer. The 1955-56 revenue account surplus had been $37,000 and further liquor profits of $9.1 million were used for capital financing. Direct and indirect debt at December 31, 1956 totalled $222.5 million. Budget forecast, 1957-58: revenue, $119.9 million; expenditure, $116.2 million; revenue account surplus, $3.6 million; non-budgetary requirements, $60.0 million.

1958: February 28—Budget. No tax changes. The surplus on revenue account for 1956-57 was reported to be $6.0 million, plus liquor profits of $11.0 million that were applied to capital expenditures; net direct and indirect debt totalled $278.2 million on December 31, 1957. Budget forecast, 1958-59: revenue, $131.5 million; expenditure, $130.0 million; surplus on current account, $1.5 million; non-budgetary requirements, $78.0 million.

1959: February 27—Budget. No tax changes. The treasurer remarked on the paradox of creeping inflation that was threatening the economy along with the severe recession which had finally ended in the second half of 1958. Budgetary accounts for 1957-58 showed a surplus of $13.2 million; debt at December 31, 1958 stood at $333.2 million, including loans on behalf of Crown corporation of $272.9 million. Budget forecast, 1959-60: revenue, $133.3 million; expenditure, $133.2 million; surplus on budgetary account, $80,000; net non-budgetary expenditure, $5.9 million. Federal reimbursement of provincial costs under the hospital insurance agreement which Saskatchewan signed on July 1, 1958 was expected to total $13.3 million.

1960: February 26—Budget. No tax changes. Surplus on budgetary account of $3.2 million for 1958-59; total direct and indirect debt at December 31, 1959: $344.7 million. Budget forecast, 1960-61: revenue, $148.9 million; expenditure, $148.6 million; surplus on budgetary account, $286,000; non-budgetary requirements, $6.2 million.

1961: February 27—Budget. Motor fuel taxes raised to 14¢ per gallon of gasoline and 17¢ per gallon of diesel fuel; alcohol prices increased. Public Accounts for 1959-60 reported a surplus on budgetary account of $2.8

million. Budget forecast, 1961-62: revenue, $144.7 million; expenditure, $147.4 million; budgetary deficit, $2.8 million. Payments under the tax sharing arrangements of $38.0 million for 1961-62 were expected to be slightly lower than for the previous fiscal year and oil revenues were also expected to drop.

1962: March 9—Budget. Under the new federal-provincial arrangements Saskatchewan levied its own income taxes: personal income tax at 22 percent for 1962 and corporation income tax at 10 percent (the 6 percent and 1 percent surcharges earmarked for financing the Saskatchewan medical insurance plan slated to start July 1—along with 1½ percent of the 2 percent increase in the sales tax to 5 percent). The deficit for 1961-62 was estimated at about $4.0 million. Budget forecast, 1962-63: revenue, $171.8 million; expenditure, $174.2 million; deficit, $2.4 million.

1963: March 1—Budget. No tax changes except to conform to federal-provincial tax sharing arrangements. The budgetary surplus estimated for 1962-63 was more than $5.0 million. The treasurer announced that the province had decided to appoint its own Saskatchewan Royal Commission on Taxation to cooperate with the federal commission in making a comprehensive study of taxation at all three levels of government in the province. Budget forecast, 1963-64: revenue, $184.3 million; expenditure, $187.8 million; deficit, $3.5 million; non-budgetary requirements, $7.2 million.

1964: February 21—Budget. No tax changes were announced. The treasurer pronounced that 1963 had been a very good year for Saskatchewan that had resulted in an estimated budgetary surplus of about $7.5 million for 1963-64. Budgetary forecast, 1964-65: revenue, $214.8 million; expenditure, $214.4 million; surplus, $444,000; non-budgetary requirements, $5.3 million. The retail sales tax was expected to be the main source of revenue, providing an estimated 21 percent of budgetary revenue, followed by the gasoline tax at 14 percent, natural resource revenues from petroleum and natural gas, 12 percent, the federal equalization payment, 11 percent, and the personal income tax, 9 percent. Health and education both were expected to be the most costly functions, each taking an estimated 27 percent of the total budget, followed by highways and roads, 16 percent, and social welfare, 9 percent.

1965: February 19—Budget. The retail sales tax rate was lowered to 4 percent and exemptions broadened; new tobacco tax of 10 percent; a $1,000 sales tax exemption for newly-weds for furniture and household appliances during first year of marriage; exemption from mineral levy for farmers; other minor tax adjustments mainly for farmers; new mines coming into operation in the province after December 24, 1964 were subjected to a new rate of royalties ranging from 5 to 9 percent. The treasurer forecast a budgetary surplus of $5.5 million for 1964-65 and predicted that Saskatchewan was on the verge of rapidly expanding industrial development. Budget forecast, 1965-66: revenue, $221.0 million; expenditure, $220.8 million; surplus, $250,000; non-budgetary requirements, $4.4 million.

_____. July—Saskatchewan Royal Commission on Taxation (Johnson Report) recommended that responsibility for education and social services be shifted to the province from the local governments and improved revenues be obtained from existing provincial sources.

1966: February 25—Budget. 1¢ increase in gasoline tax to 15¢; 1 percent reduction in personal income tax surcharge; sales tax extended to soaps and cleaning materials and more agriculture products exempted; direct grants for home owners announced. The budgetary surplus for 1965-66 was expected to be $6 million. Budget forecast, 1966-67: revenue, $268.8 million; expenditure, $268.5 million; surplus, $291,000: non-budgetary requirements, $13.3 million.

1967: February 17—Budget. No tax increases or changes. Budget forecast, 1967-68: revenue, $303 million; expenditure, $303 million.

1968: March 1—Budget. Tax increases included sales tax from 4 to 5 percent, taxes on gasoline, tobacco, transient accommodation, and pari-mutuel betting. Motor fees were raised and a charge levied for hospital and medical care. Budget forecast, 1968-69: revenue, $339 million; expenditure, $338 million; small surplus expected.

1969: February 18—Budget. Increase in mining acreage tax. Legislation was to be introduced to rebate 75 percent of the federal estate tax paid on Saskatchewan estates. Budget forecast, 1969-70: revenue, $365 million; expenditure, $365 million.

1970: March 2—Budget. Tax increases announced for gasoline and provincial personal income tax (1 percent to 34 percent). The home-owner's grant increased from $50 to $60 and a $500 grant was given for new homes built. Budget forecast, 1970-71: revenue, $395 million; expenditure, $405 million; deficit, $10 million.

1971: February 26—Budget. No tax changes. Pollution Authority created. The home-owner's grant was increased and the new home grant extended. Budget forecast, 1971-72: revenue, $451 million; expenditure, $451 million.

1972: March 10—Budget. Changes were made in gift tax and succession duties and the sales tax exemption for meals was raised. Natural resource charges were to be increased. Various measures for social and environmental ends were introduced. Budget forecast, 1972-73: revenue, $514 million; expenditure, $513 million; surplus, $1 million.

1973: February 9—Budget. The personal income tax was increased from 37 percent to 40 percent of the federal tax and the corporation tax raised to 12 percent from 11 percent. The cigarette tax was increased and further raises in natural resource charges were to come. School grants were raised, and programs were introduced to encourage farmers to improve their farms and stay on the land. Budget forecast, 1973-74: revenue, $724 million; expenditure, $723 million; surplus, $1 million.

1974: March 8—Budget. Most fiscal changes took place outside the budget in 1974. Soaring petroleum and agricultural prices were swelling provincial revenues and government announcements reflected the change. Gasoline taxes were cut by roughly a third, taxes on oil and gas producers were raised, assistance to local governments was increased, property owners were given further assistance with improvements, and a "family income payment" for low income families with children was to be given. Other programs included the first phase of dental care for children and expanded grants for day-care and community service centres. The budget foresaw a loss of revenue from the recently introduced federal indexation. Budget forecast, 1974-75: revenue, $901 million; expenditure, $899 million; surplus, $2 million.

1975: March 14—Budget. A flat $100 reduction for personal income tax was given. A royalty tax rebate would be given for royalties not deductible under the federal income tax. Succession duty exemptions were increased. Property improvement grants were raised. Budget forecast, 1975-76: revenue, $1,144; expenditure, $1,141; surplus, $3 million.

1976: March 24—Budget. An anti-inflation budget was introduced to contain expenditures and increase revenues. A surtax was imposed on higher incomes, gasoline and tobacco taxes were raised. A lump-sum tax exemption for gift tax was given. The province was creating an Energy and Resource Development Fund from annual transfers from oil and gas revenues. Budget forecast, 1976-77: revenue, $1,330 million; expenditure, $1,328 million; surplus, $2 million.

1977: March 10—Budget. Under the personal income tax the flat tax cut was increased to $120 and the general rate was set at 58.5 percent. The general corporate income tax was raised from 12 percent to 14 percent; succession duties and gift taxes were abolished, effective January 1, 1977. The budget outlined several ways in which the province would lose revenue under the 1976 federal transfer revisions. Details were not given, but a deficit was expected for the 1977-78 year. It appears to have finally been about $40 million.

1978: March 17—Budget. In face of a slowing economy, the budget reduced personal income tax from 58.5 percent of the federal tax to 53.0 percent, raised the flat tax credit but with a vanishing formula, and gave an additional tax credit for children. Under the corporate tax it reduced the low rate from 12 percent to 11 percent and under the sales tax increased the tax on alcohol from 5 percent to 10 percent; the federal offer was also implemented for a 2 percent reduction for six months. Tobacco taxes were increased. Property improvement grants were raised. At this period the Energy and Resource Development Fund was renamed the Heritage Fund, to receive all provincial revenues from natural resources. Expenditures would be made from the fund for assistance with energy supply exploration and development and environmental protection, particularly for uranium. Transfers were also to be made from the fund to the Consolidated Fund, and the Heritage Fund stood outside the regular budget and received about one-third of provincial revenues. Budget forecast, 1978-79: revenue, $2,091 million; expenditure, $2,043 million; surplus, $54 million.

1979: March 8—Budget. Minor tax changes included an increase in the tobacco tax and relief from capital gains tax on farm sales. The property improvement grant was extended to renters and converted for senior citizens into a special school tax rebate. Allowances under the Family Income Plan were also increased. Budget forecast, 1979-80: revenue, $1,994 million; expenditure, $1,926; surplus, $68 million.

1980: March 31—Budget. Under the income tax a new tax credit for seniors was given and the tax credit for children was raised (both vanishing); the 10 percent surtax was extended to 1980. For corporations a capital tax was introduced, and under the sales tax exemptions for farm equipment were extended. Tobacco tax rates were increased. During this period the province, following a court case which had invalidated a main element in potash taxation, had negotiated new royalty arrangements with the potash companies. The details of these arrangements are explained in other Tax Foundation publications. Budget forecast, 1980-81: revenue, $2,279 million; expenditure, $2,128 million; surplus, $150 million. Of this revenue an estimated 28 percent was from natural resources.

1981: March 5—Budget. The personal income tax rate was reduced to 51 percent and the surtax on higher incomes was increased from 10 percent to 12 percent. The small business corporation tax was reduced to 10 percent from 11 percent, the general rate remaining at 14 percent. Tobacco taxes were increased. The budget expressed concern over the National Energy Policy and the fact that Saskatchewan would no longer qualify for equalization grants under the prospective amendments in the formula. Budget forecast, 1981-82: revenue, $2,748 million; expenditure, $2,432 million; surplus, $315 million.

1982: March 18—Budget. The position of the 1982 budget is confused by the intervention of an election and a change in government on April 26 before the proposals could be enacted into law. Some of the changes were adopted by the new government, including an exemption from sales tax for children's clothing and footwear, an increase in the tobacco taxes, higher amounts under the property improvement grants, the senior citizen's school tax rebate program, and the renter's property tax rebate. A new shelter allowance for senior citizens whose shelter costs exceeded 25 percent of their income was also introduced. In fulfilment of an election promise the new government removed the provincial tax on gasoline from May 9.

————. November 24—Second Budget. This budget confirmed further study of motor fuel taxation, removed the capital tax from all insurance corporations, but increased the insurance premiums tax from 2 to 3 percent and further increased the tax on tobacco products. An interesting development of this period was the replacement of an income tax levied on freehold oil and gas producers with a production tax similar to the Crown royalty on government land following the 1982 amendment to the Constitution giving the provinces power to impose such forms of tax. Budget forecast, 1982-83: in view of the broken presentation of tax and other changes during the year no accurate forecast is available. The November budget projected a deficit of $220 million for the year after the changes in that budget.

1983: March 29—Budget. The budget announced a number of programs for economic stimulation. A previous restriction preventing transfer of no more than 80 percent of Heritage Fund annual revenues would be removed. Tobacco taxes were increased and the remaining tax on diesel fuel for locomotives was raised. Budget forecast, 1983-84: revenue, $2,808 million; expenditure, $3,125 million; deficit, $317 million. (Heritage Fund revenues, well over $300 million only two years before, were expected to barely exceed $100 million, and a hoped-for dividend of $50 million from Crown corporations had not materialized).

1984: March 21—Budget. This budget followed the path of several other provinces in adopting stimulative tax changes. These included a venture capital tax credit, complete exemption from corporate tax for small manufacturing firms and a livestock investment tax credit. Farmers were given relief by exemption from school taxes for their home quarter-section, and exemption from sales tax for their electricity, a relief that applied as well to general residential use. Tax increases included a raise in the general corporate income tax from 14 to 16 percent, an increase in the tax on fuels used by railway locomotives and aircraft and, inevitably, an increase in tobacco taxes. Budget forecast, 1984-85: revenue, $3,012 million; expenditure, $3,279 million; deficit, $267 million.

_____. May: A local Government Finance Commission was appointed to study the financing of municipalities, school divisions, libraries, and hospital boards.

1985: April 10—Budget. The personal income tax rate was reduced to 50 percent, and a flat rate tax of 1 percent was applied to net income. The 12 percent surtax was continued for higher incomes; taxes on lower incomes were reduced. The senior citizen's tax credit was replaced by a cash grant, geared to income, on application. The corporation capital tax for banks was increased to 2 percent; used vehicles were made subject to sales tax and tobacco taxes were increased. Budget forecast, 1985-86: revenue, $4,077 million; expenditure, $4,302 million; deficit, $225 million.

_____. Proposals in the Report of the Local Government Finance Commission were followed in changes made at this time. This included abolition of the property improvement grant, the renter's property tax rebate, and the senior citizen's school tax rebate. The funds saved in this way would be allocated directly to education.

1986: March 26—Budget. The sales tax was removed from clothing, footwear, and yard goods costing less than $300. Newly incorporated small businesses were to be exempt from corporate tax for two years. A 20 percent tax credit was granted for investment in a labour-sponsored capital investment fund, and it was proposed that an investment tax credit be given for purchase of shares in a company having 25 percent or more of its wage bill in the province. The livestock investment credit was renewed for three years and a new credit was provided for livestock facilities. The general corporate income tax was raised from 16 to 17 percent, and the corporate capital tax and tobacco taxes were also raised. Budget forecast, 1986-87: revenue, $3,359 million; expenditure, $3,748 million; deficit, $389 million.

1987: June 27—Budget. Saskatchewan finances were becoming grim. The budget reported that in place of a deficit of $389 million forecast for the previous year it was now estimated to have been $1,235 million. There would therefore have to be both expenditure reductions and revenue increases. Among the former were: eliminating 2,000 civil service positions, amalgamating several agencies, deferring capital projects, freezing salaries for two years, introducing a minimum deductible under the drug plan, and limiting child dental care. Many other programs were frozen or reduced. Tax increases included: raising the sales tax from 5 to 7 percent, reintroducing the motor fuel tax at 7 cents per litre, raising the flat personal income tax from 1 percent to 1½ percent and increasing the capital tax on trust and loan companies, and the tobacco tax. Budget forecast, 1987-88: revenue, $3,203 million; expenditure, $3,780 million; deficit, $577 million. Revenue of the Heritage Fund was estimated at $58 million.

1988: March 31—Budget. Flat tax on personal income raised to 2 percent from 1.5 percent; corporate income tax lowered to 15 percent from 17 percent; tax holiday extended for new small businesses; tax reduction for small manufacturing and processing businesses to be eliminated as of January 1, 1989; venture capital tax credit program to be introduced; corporation capital tax extended to federal Crown corporations and their subsidiaries; and a 2 percent corporation capital tax surcharge levied on large resource corporations; tobacco taxes increased; resource royalties reduced by 1 percent; funds to be made available to local governments to persuade them to reduce or eliminate their taxes on business. The minister announced that the province had achieved the first objective as set out in the 1987 economic and financial report of reducing the deficit—to an estimated $588 million for 1987-88. Further efficiency measures within government were to be required to reach the fiscal target set for 1988-89. Budget forecast, 1988-89: revenue, (including the Heritage Fund, $50.2 million), $3.6 billion; expenditure (including the Heritage Fund, $43.8 million), $3.9 billion; deficit, $328.2 million.

Alberta

Alberta, originally mainly a cattle and wheat producing province, has been distinguished for some years by the happy possession of very substantial oil and gas reserves. Starting from the modest Turner Valley discoveries of the early twenties the provincial heritage blossomed in 1947 with the discovery of the Leduc field. There have been other somewhat less dramatic discoveries since, and for two decades, although agriculture remained a major factor in the economy, prices and markets for oil have been as potent an influence on the prosperity of the province as those for wheat and cattle. During the seventies and early eighties as much as 40 percent of provincial revenues came from oil in some years, and the billions of dollars that came from this source gave it financial strength beyond that of any other province.

Despite the fact that from the mid-thirties until 1968 the province was under the radically oriented Social Credit party it has been very conservatively governed. There was little attempt to adopt the fundamental Social Credit ideas, although the province did establish virtually its own banking

Table 18.33   Alberta: General Profile

	Year[a]	Province	All Canada	Province as percent of all Canada
Population (000)	1987	2,380	25,625	9.3
Gross Domestic Product ($ billion)	1986	58.3	506.5	11.5
G.D.P. per capita ($)	1986	24,533	20,030	122.5
Personal Income ($ billion)	1986	42.2	432.5	9.8
P.I. per capita ($)	1986	17,776	17,060	104.1
Unemployment rate (%)...............	1987	9.6	8.9	107.9
Provincial government: revenue ($ billion).........................	1986	11.5	202.5[b]	5.7
Provincial government: expenditure ($ billion)........................	1986	14.3	234.1[b]	6.1
Basic personal income tax rate (%)[c]	1988	46.5	46.5-60[d]	—
General corporate tax rate (%)	1988	15.0	14-17[d]	—
Retail sales tax rate	1988	—	6-12[d]	—

See table 18.1 for footnotes and sources.

system in the Alberta savings branches, which still exists. Conservative party governments in power since 1971 employed a prudent approach to financing that has served the province well in coping with the billions of dollars that poured in from its resources. Indicative of this is the repayment of not only the province's debts but also the debts of its municipalities, hospitals, universities, and similar public organizations. Much of the provincial infrastructure—roads, highways, schools, hospitals, urban transportation, etc.—was modernized. Social programs were upgraded, but with main emphasis on assisting the aged and needy. It is typical, however, that Alberta was one of the most reluctant provinces in adopting government-run hospital and medical insurance, and is one of only three provinces that still levies a specific charge for these services, a charge which is frequently increased.

Alberta is the only province without a sales tax and it levies the lowest personal and corporate income tax rates in Canada. For a long period it had no gasoline tax, restoring it only in 1987. Like Saskatchewan, it has set aside a share of its natural revenues in a Heritage Fund which at the latest report held $12.7 billion of assets, despite withdrawals for budget support in recent years. The province is finding this a very helpful resource in the recent period of declining oil revenues, although it is determined that the whole amount will not be dissipated on constantly growing budgets. With this objective in mind the province has recently introduced some tax increases, although these are far short of the measures adopted by its neighbour, Saskatchewan.

Alberta Diary

1947: March 7—Budget. The province abolished its social service tax to allow its municipalities full use of this field. The treasurer designated his budget as a "transition" budget designed for the postwar adjustment

Table 18.34 Alberta Finances: The Eighties

Year[a]	Revenue	Expenditure	Deficit
	millions of dollars		
1980	10,145.2	7,047.8	+3,097.4
1981	11,687.9	9,959.9	+2,728.0
1982	12,955.2	12,461.9	+493.3
1983	13,484.0	12,362.8	+1,121.2
1984	14,534.3	12,449.2	+2,085.1
1985	14,355.4	13,784.2	+571.2
1986	11,470.2	14,341.4	-2,871.2
1987	12,775.8	13,766.8	-991.0
1988	10,254.3	10,925.1	-670.8

See table 18.2 for footnotes and sources.

Table 18.35 Province of Alberta, Revenue, Consolidated Finances Basis, Selected Years, 1952-86[a]

Source	1952	1962	1972	1982	1986
	millions of dollars				
Taxes	18.1	89.5	527.4	3,006.0	3,141.2
Natural resource revenue	63.7	129.9	351.9	5,256.7	2,700.0
Privileges, licences and permits	10.0	19.3	32.7	76.9	107.9
Liquor sales and regulation	15.0	25.7	72.2	239.2	318.1
Other revenue	7.4	28.5	174.2	3,249.2	3,510.4
Transfers from other governments[b]	41.3	91.7	295.5	1,127.2	1,692.8
Total	155.5	384.6	1,453.9	12,955.2	11,470.2
Own source revenue	114.2	292.9	1,154.4	11,828.0	9,777.4
Surplus or deficit	40.9	11.6	-24.4	493.3	-2,871.2
	percent of total revenue				
Taxes	11.6	23.3	36.4	23.2	27.3
Natural resource revenue	41.0	33.8	24.3	40.5	23.5
Privileges, licences and permits	6.4	5.0	2.3	0.6	0.9
Liquor sales and regulation	9.6	6.7	5.0	1.8	2.8
Other revenue	4.8	7.4	11.7	25.0	30.7
Transfers from other governments[b]	26.6	23.8	20.3	8.9	14.8
Total	100.0	100.0	100.0	100.0	100.0
Own source revenue	73.4	76.2	79.7	91.3	85.2

See table 18.3 for footnotes and sources.

period. Public Accounts for 1945-46 showed a surplus on combined ordinary and capital account of $10.3 million and preliminary figures showed a moderate surplus for the 1946-47 fiscal year. The province had reduced its outstanding funded and unfunded debt to $144.6 million at December 31, 1946. Budget forecast, 1947-48: revenue, $46.4 million; expenditure, $45.6 million; surplus, $844,000 before debt retirement.

1948: March 5—Budget. No tax changes. Interim figures projected a surplus of $5.9 million before debt retirement for 1947-48. Budget forecast,

Table 18.36   **Province of Alberta, Expenditure, Consolidated Finances Basis, Selected Years, 1952-86**[a]

	1952	1962	1972	1982	1986
	millions of dollars				
General services	5.2	8.7	74.2	598.1	1,002.6
Health	17.8	80.4	387.1	2,616.3	3,414.7
Social services	7.8	35.1	158.7	1,088.5	1,486.1
Education	17.4	124.6	436.9	2,079.1	2,640.2
Transportation and communications	39.0	59.5	97.3	1,020.4	896.6
Natural resources and industrial development	11.0	21.4	70.1	2,783.9	2,349.9
Charges on debt	2.6	0.7	92.5	529.3	724.8
Transfers to other governments[b]	6.5	16.9	45.9	221.9	228.0
Other	7.3	25.7	115.6	1,524.4	1,598.5
Total	114.6	373.0	1,478.3	12,461.9	14,341.4
Offsets:					
Specific purpose transfers	7.8	67.5	272.6	891.2	1,474.5
General purpose transfers	33.5	24.2	22.9	236.0	218.3
Own expenditure	73.3	281.3	1,182.8	11,334.7	12,648.6
	percent of total expenditure				
General services	4.5	2.3	5.0	4.8	7.0
Health	15.5	21.5	26.2	21.2	23.8
Social services	6.8	9.4	10.7	8.7	10.4
Education	15.1	33.4	29.5	16.6	18.4
Transportation and communications	33.9	15.9	6.6	8.2	6.3
Natural resources and industrial development	9.6	5.7	4.7	22.2	16.5
Charges on debt	2.3	0.2	6.3	4.2	5.0
Transfers to other governments[b]	5.6	4.5	3.1	1.8	1.6
Other	6.7	7.1	7.9	12.3	11.0
Total	100.0	100.0	100.0	100.0	100.0
Own expenditure	64.0	75.4	80.0	91.0	88.2

See table 18.4 for footnotes and sources.

1948-49: revenue, $47.0 million; expenditure, $53.0 million; deficit before debt retirement, $6.0 million. The treasurer pointed out that over one-third of the province's revenue was received in the form of a grant from the federal government under the interim tax transfer agreement.

————. Report of the Royal Commission on Taxation.

1949: March 4—Budget. No tax changes. To implement some of the recommendations of the Royal Commission on Taxation the province discontinued its practice of charging local governments for 10 percent of the costs of old age and blind pensions and reduced to 20 percent from 25 percent its charge on them for mothers' allowances; the province assumed from the local governments 60 percent of the costs of needy and child welfare services, and provided grants to local governments for roads,up to 25 percent of the cost of assessment services, and special grants to municipal districts for schools. The treasurer reiterated his dissatisfaction with the country's monetary system and his advocation of the need to supplement the earned income of the Canadian people through consumer dividends. He commented on the importance of the development of Alberta's oil resources to the economy of both the province and the country as a whole. Because oil revenue represented depletion of the province's natural resources, he felt it should be used only for capital purposes. Interim figures for 1948-49 suggested an overall surplus for the year. Budget forecast, 1949-50: revenue, $64.2 million; expenditure, $66.3 million; deficit $2.1 million.

1950: March 3—Budget. No tax changes. The province improved its grants to local governments to assist with the costs of education and debt. The treasurer pointed out that revenue from natural resources exceeded revenue from taxes. Interim figures indicated a surplus for 1949-50. Budget forecast, 1950-51: revenue, $77.2 million; expenditure, $74.4 million; surplus, $2.8 million before debt retirement.

1951: March 5—Budget. A reduced, simpler form of car licensing was introduced; trade registration fees replaced annual business and trade licences; 1¢ tax removed from fuel used on farms and for industrial purposes; regular gasoline tax raised by 1¢ to 10¢ a gallon—4¢ of the tax to be diverted to local governments. Interim figures estimated a surplus of $20 million for fiscal year 1950-51. Budget forecast, 1951-52: revenue, $94.2 million; expenditure, $91.4 million; surplus $2.8 million.

1952: March 7—Budget. No tax changes. A new school assistance program for local governments was introduced; 50 percent of receipts from the gasoline and fuel oil taxes replaced the 4 percent share of gasoline tax transfer to local governments. Preliminary figures indicated a surplus of $3.5 million for 1951-52. Budget forecast, 1952-53: revenue, $116.9 million; expenditure, $116.6 million; surplus, $279,000.

1953: March 6—Budget. No tax changes. A new municipal act was to be designed to improve transfers to local governments as well as providing better access to loan funds. Interim figures showed an expected surplus for 1952-53 of $22.0 million. Budget forecast, 1953-54: revenue, $138.4 million; expenditure, $138.0 million; surplus, $410,000.

1954: March 5—Budget. No tax changes. Budget forecast, 1954-55: revenue, $157.3 million; expenditure, $156.9 million; surplus, $366,000. Natural resources were expected to provide 40 percent of total revenue, the tax transfer from the federal government, 22 percent; fuel taxes and car licences, 19 percent. Highways and roads were expected to take 36 percent of the total budget, education 15 percent, health 14 percent, and welfare 6 percent.

1955: March 4—Budget. No tax changes. Budget forecast, 1955-56: revenue, $177.4 million; expenditure, $180.0 million; deficit, $2.5 million.

1956: February 24—Budget. The unearned increment tax was repealed. The treasurer forecast an overall deficit of $5.0 million for the fiscal year ending

March 31, 1956. Budget forecast, 1956-57: revenue, $208.8 million; expenditure, $192.5 million; surplus $16.2 million.

1957: March 1—Budget. The province took over a tax of 2 percent of insurance premiums formerly levied by the federal government; entertainment tax on admissions of 60¢ and under abolished. Budget forecast, 1957-58: revenue, $252.6 million; expenditure, $214.0 million; surplus, $38.7 million. The treasurer announced a budgetary expenditure provision of $11.0 million to be distributed to Canadian residents over 21 years of age who had been resident in Alberta for five years, in the form of a dividend from one-third of net royalties from oil and gas produced in the province.

1958: Budget. No tax changes. The treasurer announced that the new hospital scheme would go into effect on April 1; local governments were to be assessed a levy of about 3 mills of taxation to cover their share of the program. Budget forecast, 1958-59: revenue, $263.7 million; expenditure, $258.1 million; surplus, $5.6 million.

1959: Budget. The amusement tax on theatre admissions was repealed; the levy on municipal councils to cover their share of the operating and capital costs of the Alberta Hospitalization Benefits Act was set at 4 mills on an equalized assessment basis. Budget forecast, 1958-59: revenue, $361.3 million; expenditure, $304.7 million; deficit, $43.4 million.

1960: Budget. No tax changes. Budget forecast, 1960-61: revenue, $328.6 million; expenditure, $328.6 million; surplus, $12,000.

1961: Budget. No tax changes announced in budget. Later in the year motor fuel taxes were increased by 2¢ a gallon to 12¢ on gasoline and 14¢ on diesel fuel. Budget forecast: revenue, $323.4 million; expenditure, $336.7 million; deficit, $13.3 million.

1962: Budget. Liquor prices raised. Interim figures projected a deficit of $20.0 million for 1961-62. Budget forecast, 1962-63: revenue, $355.0 million; expenditure, $354.9 million; surplus, $61,000.

1963: Budget. No tax changes. The treasurer predicted that the 1962-63 fiscal year would end with a small budget surplus. Budget forecast, 1963-64: revenue, $373.8 million; expenditure, $373.8 million; surplus, $25,000. The province was considering introduction of a medicare program for residents in need of financial assistance.

1964: Budget. No tax changes. An examination of provincial revenues and expenditures was being carried out by a 12-member committee. Budget forecast, 1964-65: revenue, $411.8 million; expenditure, $414.5 million; deficit, $2.7 million.

1965: March 3—Budget. No tax changes. Interim figures projected a surplus of over $30 million for 1964-65. Budget forecast, 1965-66: revenue, $471.1 million; expenditure, $493.8 million; deficit, $22.6 million.

1966: March 4—Budget. No tax changes. The surplus for 1964-65 was reported in the public accounts at $79.1 million and the estimated surplus for 1965-66 was expected to be over $35.0 million. A home owner's tax discount plan was to go into effect on April 1, discounting property taxes by up to $50. Budget forecast, 1966-67: revenue, $613.1 million; expenditure, $682.0 million; deficit, $68.8 million.

_____. Report, Alberta Expenditure and Revenue Study Committee.

1967: March—Budget. No new taxes were proposed. The province would rebate 75 percent of provincial succession duties on the estates of Alberta residents. Budget forecast, 1967-68: revenue, $767 million; expenditure, $834 million; deficit, $67 million. At this point one-third of revenues were from natural resources.

1968: March 1—Budget. Charges were increased on motor fuels and motor vehicle licences. The provincial treasurer thought the province should be introducing "more substantial new forms of taxation" for the future. Budget forecast, 1968-69: revenue, $823 million; expenditure, $893 million; deficit, $70 million.

1969: February 28—Budget. The personal income tax was increased from 28 percent to 33 percent and the corporation income tax from 10 percent to 11 percent. A tax on tobacco products was introduced and the gasoline tax was increased. Budget forecast, 1969-70: revenue, $966 million; expenditure, $1,000 million; deficit, $34 million.

1970: February 13—Budget. No tax changes were announced, but with introduction of medicare in mid-summer a premium would be charged. Budget forecast, 1970-71: revenue, $963 million; expenditure, $1,092 million; deficit, $129 million.

1971: February 26—Budget. No tax changes were announced. New authorities for environmental control and hospital administration were set up. Municipal grants were capped. Budget forecast, 1971-72: revenue, $1,040 million; expenditure, $1,027 million; deficit, $167 million.

1972: March 17—Budget. No tax changes were proposed. A refund of education tax was provided for property-owning senior citizens and an annual shelter grant was provided for senior citizen renters. Budget forecast, 1972-73: revenue, $1,129 million; expenditure, $1,330 million; deficit, $201 million.

1973: March 2—Budget. No tax changes were announced. Municipalities were assisted through provincial assumption of a greater share of health and social assistance costs and by increases in grants. Refunds and credits for seniors, renters, and home-owners were increased. Increased grants would be given in the following year for education and universitites, agriculture, highways and streets, mass transportation, and housing. Petroleum charges would be revised. Budget forecast, 1973-74: revenue, $1,387 million; expenditure, $1,313 million; surplus, $74 million.

1974: March 22—Budget. Provincial finances changed dramatically with the 1973 OPEC rise in oil prices and Alberta budgets began to be dominated by revisions in oil royalties and charges and oil exploration and production incentives which are too complex for this brief summary; they are well described in other sources. The new prosperity affected many other aspects of government, however. In 1974 the gasoline tax was reduced, a natural gas rebate was given users, the provincial education tax was repealed, and with it the tax credits formerly given to seniors; social allowances were increased, health charge exemptions were extended, and transportation outlays were increased. Budget forecast, 1974-75: revenue, $1,934 million; expenditure, $1,915 million; surplus, $19 million. (These figures were not indicative of the province's real financial position. The province's revenue from incremental oil royalties and its share of the oil export tax was being paid into the newly established Heritage Savings Trust Fund. The amount deposited in the fund in respect of the 1974-75 fiscal year was estimated at $819 million. A table at the end of this section gives the transactions of the fund).

1975: February 7 and May 30—Budget. An election intervened before the February budget was passed but a basically similar budget was adopted in May. The income tax was reduced from 36 percent to 26 percent of the federal tax and low income taxpayers were given a substantial reduction. Provincial taxes on certain royalties were refunded and a royalty tax credit was given for others. Expenditures under several programs were increased. Budget forecast, 1975-76: revenue, $2,574 million; expenditure, $2,535 million; surplus, $39 million. (In addition an estimated $646 million was paid into the Heritage Fund).

1976: March 19—Budget. In view of an annual average increase of 23 percent in expenditures over the last five years a restraint program to hold expenditure increases to 11 percent was in effect, but no tax increases were made in this budget. In future 30 percent of resource revenues, or some $570 million, would be allocated to the Heritage Fund, giving a total of over $2 billion at March 31, 1977. Budget forecast, 1976-77: revenue, $2,930 million; expenditure, $2,961 million; deficit, $31 million.

1977: March 11—Budget. Restraint policy continued. The main expenditure increase related to general grants to municipalities and grants to subsidize consumer gas costs and municipal borrowing interest rates. The personal income tax rate was set at 38.5 percent, the low income exemption extended, and a credit granted for each dependent. Budget forecast, 1977-78: revenue, $4,312 million; expenditure, $3,329 million; surplus $983 million. (A change in reporting accounts for the marked increase in surplus over previous years. Revenues include the amounts to be allocated to the Heritage Fund, whereas previously they were excluded. The forecast after deducting an estimated $734 million transfer to the Fund and other expenditures was a deficit of $40 million).

1978: March 17—Budget. The provincial tax on gasoline and diesel oil was removed. Low income reliefs and grants for senior citizen renters were raised. Extra funds were provided mainly for capital expenditures on housing, hospitals, post-secondary schools, roads and highways. Budget forecast, 1978-79: revenue, $4,836 million; expenditure, $4,056 million; surplus, $780 million. A transfer to the fund of $1,046 million was forecast for this year. (Fund transactions as reported from year to year give an unreliable indication of its status; as mentioned earlier a separate statement of the history of the Fund is given later to clarify the matter).

1979: March 14—1979. The main item of this budget was the municipal debt reduction program. Under it $1.0 billion was appropriated to allow municipalities to pay off debt of $760 million and to make cash grants to centres where debt was less than $500 per capita. The renter assistance credit program was also enriched. The 11 percent small corporation tax was reduced to 5 percent for the smallest corporations. Budget forecast, 1979-80: revenue, $5,255 million; expenditure, including municipal debt retirement, $5,629 million; deficit, $374 million. In addition $1,184 million was transferred to the Heritage Fund.

1980: April 2—Budget. This budget introduced the Alberta Business Incentive Tax System, under which the province assumed control of the taxation of corporations from January 1, 1981. Under it the existing tax structure would remain unchanged, but interested parties were invited to submit proposals for tax incentives in the interim. It was reported that under the local debt retirement plan $648 million had gone to cancel debt and $383 million had been paid in grants. In the fall an amount of $1.1 billion would be set aside to partially fund provincially administered pension plans. Another $340 million would be used to retire hospital debt. Health insurance premiums were increased by $1 per month for single persons and $2 per month for families. Budget forecast, 1980-81: revenue, $7,158 million; expenditure, $6,849 million; surplus, $309 million.

1981: April 14—Budget. With declining oil activity and the onset of recession the expected surplus of the previous year had become a deficit of $746 million. The 1981 budget was therefore conservative. Tax changes were minor as the government was still considering proposals for tax incentives under its corporate income tax. Health care premiums were increased. Budget forecast, 1981-82: revenue, $6,367 million; expenditure, $6,703 million; deficit, $336 million. (It was expected that by March, 1982 the Heritage Fund would have assets of $10.9 billion).

1982: March 18—Budget. In a counter-recession budget provincial expenditures were slated to increase by 25 percent. Tax changes mainly affected the oil industry, generally to lighten tax and royalty burdens. Tax credits for rental investment (MURBS) were continued and enriched. Otherwise business tax incentives had been limited (inevitably) to aiding the oil industry. The provincial treasurer gave warnings of future declines in oil revenues and cited examples of tax increases that might have to be made. Budget forecast, 1982-83: revenue, $6,520 million; expenditure, $8,969 million; deficit, $2,449 million. (In this year the transfer to the Fund was expected to be $1,618 million; in fact was probably about $1.3 billion. As an offset $860 million of the Fund's interest revenue (50 percent) was transferred to the ordinary budget. At this stage along with the share of resource revenues, the Fund was earning interest revenues estimated at $1,345 million for 1982-83).

1983: March 30—Budget. Revenue measures to stem the growing deficit dominated this budget. In addition to increases in tobacco taxes, raises in hospital insurance premiums, and introduction of per diem hospital charges, major measures included a reduction from 30 to 15 percent in the share of resource revenue going to the Heritage Fund and an increase to 100 percent in the Heritage Fund interest revenues being transferred to the general budget. Liquor Board prices were also increased. The precarious position of the budget is evident in retrospect in the assumption (an uncertain one) that oil prices would be $29-30 per barrel in the coming year. Budget forecast, 1983-84: revenue, $8,391 million; expenditure, $10,015 million; deficit, $867 billion. (The Heritage Fund was estimated to have $13 billion in assets at the end of the year).

1984: March 27—Budget. No tax changes were announced in the budget but later in October the personal income tax rate was increased from 38.5 percent to 43.5 percent of the federal tax. Other changes in corporate taxation were announced in October (see below). An extensive capital program, including beginning facilities for the 1987 winter Olympics, would go forward in the coming year. To increase revenues 100 percent of the Fund's interest receipts would be taken into the budget rather than the planned 50 percent. Budget forecast, 1984-85: revenue, $9,680 million; expenditure, $9,938 million; deficit, $258 million.

1985: March 25—Budget. On April 1, a tax incentive program for manufacturing and processing income of Alberta companies would come into effect. This included a five-year holiday for small companies, and a reduction to 5 percent in the rate on this part of the income of large companies. Companies eligible for the federal tax credit would qualify for the provincial. On non-eligible income the rate would remain at 11 percent. The most substantial change in the province's outlook came with the virtual end of the National Energy Program in 1985, the withdrawal of federal oil and gas price controls, and of the federal special taxes on the oil industry. In 1985 the Premier announced a small business stock investment incentive plan similar to that of several other provinces. No other taxes were changed, although minor increases were made in some charges. Budget forecast, 1985-86: revenue, $14.3 billion; expenditure, $13.3 billion; surplus, $951 million.

1986: April 10—Budget. The budget announced on April 10 was nullified by a provincial election in May. A new budget was introduced in June by the same government which followed closely on the previous one. With declining oil revenues a substantial deficit was expected. No tax changes were made. A new system for financing hospital and university building was introduced in the form of the Alberta Capital Fund. Budget forecast, 1986-87: revenue, $8,638 million; expenditure, $11,134 million; deficit, $2,496 million.

1987: March 20—Budget. Falling prices for oil and wheat were depressing the provincial economy. The budget estimates were based on oil at $18 per barrel by the end of 1987 (as it turned out an optimistic expectation). To reduce the deficit all transfers to the Heritage Fund would cease, all resource revenues would go into the budget, expenditures would be curtailed, and taxes increased. There would be a 16 percent reduction in all but major programs and government staff would be reduced. Health insurance premiums would be raised. Tax increases included a raise in the personal income tax from 43.5 to 46.5 percent of the federal tax, with a surtax of 8 percent for upper incomes for 1986 and an additional flat tax of 1 percent of taxable incomes for 1987. Taxes on tobacco products were raised and a tax

Table 18.37 Alberta Heritage Savings Trust Fund,[a] 1976-86

Fiscal year[b]	Transfers of non-renewable resource revenues[c]	Net income on fund investments	Total income of fund	Funds transferred to budget[d]	Spent on non-income earning capital projects	Total outgo from fund	Financial assets at end of year
			millions of dollars				
1976-77	620	88	708	—	36	36	2,182
1977-78	931	194	1,125	—	87	87	3,521
1978-79	1,060	294	1,353	—	132	132	4,450
1979-80	1,332	343	1,675	—	478	478	5,686
1980-81	1,444	724	2,168	—	227	227	7,618
1981-82	1,434	1,007	2,441	—	349	349	9,700
1982-83	1,370	1,482	2,852	866	296	1,162	11,397
1983-84	719	1,467	2,186	1,469	330	1,799	11,776
1984-85	737	1,575	2,312	1,575	228	1,803	12,274
1985-86	685	1,667	2,352	1,667	240	1,907	12,716
1986-87	216	1,445	1,661	1,445	227	1,672	12,745[e]
Total	10,548	10,286	20,834	7,022	2,630	9,652	

[a]Created by the Alberta legislature in May, 1976. [b]Year ended March 31. [c]30 percent of such revenue from 1976-77 to 1982-83; 15 percent from 1983-84 to 1986-87; no transfer to be made in 1987-88. [d]50 percent transferred to general revenue in 1981-82 and 100 percent from 1983-84 to 1986-87. [e]Details of financial assets at March 31, 1987 in millions of dollars:

Alberta Investment Division[f]	7,847
Capital Investment Division	200
Energy Investment Division	9
Canada Energy Investment Division[g]	1,857
Commercial Investment Division	233
Cash and Marketable Securities and other Assets	2,599
Total	12,745

[f]Mainly loans to provincial Crown corporations—telephones housing, municipal and agriculture. [g]Loans to other provinces.

on gasoline restored. The general corporate rate was increased to 15 percent. The renter assistance program was dropped. Budget forecast, 1987-88: revenue, $9.0 billion; expenditure, (including expenditure under Alberta Capital Fund), $11.1 billion; deficit, $2.1 billion.

1988: March 24—Budget. The flat rate tax on personal income was cut by one-half to 0.5 percent and the natural gas rebate program for primary agricultural producers was extended to March 31, 1991. The provincial treasurer reported that the economy was growing again and Alberta's future was looking brighter. Budget forecast, 1988-89: revenue, $10.3 billion; expenditure, $11.1 billion; deficit, $896.2 million.

British Columbia

As Canada's westernmost presence on the Pacific Ocean British Columbia has always played a unique role. The building of a railway over three thousand miles long through spectacular mountain ranges to link it with the other provinces was the most massive and visible symbol of the new country's existence a century ago, and maintaining connections has since been a continuing physical and cultural priority. The Pacific environment—more typical of California than of any other part of Canada—the mountainous terrain and rich natural resources have given the province its own separate and distinct character. The emergence of Vancouver as a financial and industrial centre and host of the spectacularly successful Expo 86 has been a sign of coming of age for the whole province.

Despite growing affluence, heavy dependence on the ever changing fortunes of natural resources gives the provincial economy an unstable base. Like several other parts of Canada, a buoyant economy depends on a high level of exports at profitable prices. British Columbia's heavily forested valleys and mountains have provided ample supplies of wood for export in a variety of forms (from lumber to paper) and this is now the principal resource industry. Mining has also been important; for a long time gold, but currently coal, base metals and petroleum products, particularly natural gas, predominate. The province enjoyed some of the fruits of the OPEC price rise, but not nearly to the extent of its neighbour, Alberta.

Politics, except for a short period in the seventies, have been dominated by the Social Credit party since 1952. Even less attempt was made to implement the fundamental propositions of this group than in Alberta, where at least the province did establish its own bank. Possibly the most concrete evidence was the reluctance to have the province use taxpayers' money for payment of interest on debt, an objective that was achieved by borrowing through a variety of Crown corporations or special funds that were set up outside the regular accounts. Even this practice has been abandoned in recent years, and the province now borrows in its own name.

This conservatism was not evident in other areas of policy, however. Like Saskatchewan, British Columbia preceded most other provinces by a decade in introducing hospital insurance in 1949 and was one of the first provinces to accept the federal offer on medicare in 1968. In other social

Table 18.38 British Columbia: General Profile

	Year[a]	Province	All Canada	Province as percent of all Canada
Population (000)	1987	2,926	25,625	11.4
Gross Domestic Product ($ billion)	1986	56.5	506.5	11.2
G.D.P. per capita ($)	1986	19,556	20,030	97.6
Personal Income ($ billion)	1986	48.8	432.5	11.3
P.I. per capita ($)	1986	16,896	17,060	99.4
Unemployment rate (%).............	1987	12.0	8.9	134.8
Provincial government: revenue ($ billion)........................	1986	10.8	202.5[b]	5.3
Provincial government: expenditure ($ billion)........................	1986	11.7	234.1[b]	5.0
Basic personal income tax rate (%)[c]	1988	51.5	46.5-60[d]	—
General corporate tax rate (%)	1988	14.0	14-17[d]	—
Retail sales tax rate	1988	6.0	6-12[d]	—

See table 18.1 for footnotes and sources.

Table 18.39 British Columbia Finances: The Eighties

Year[a]	Revenue	Expenditure	Deficit
	millions of dollars		
1980......................	6,817.4	6,838.2	− 20.8
1981......................	8,055.0	8,014.7	40.3
1982......................	8,738.8	9,853.0	− 1,069.2
1983......................	9,628.8	10,558.8	− 930.0
1984......................	10,122.0	10,959.0	− 837.0
1985......................	10,325.2	10,948.5	− 623.3
1986......................	10,843.1	11,718.6	− 875.5
1987......................	11,839.3	12,722.9	− 883.6
1988......................	11,440.0	11,835.0	− 395.0

See table 18.2 for footnotes and sources.

areas the province was innovative in assisting with home ownership, aging, and other social problems. The terrain poses unique handicaps to communication, and the province has been aggressive in overcoming these with highways, railways, ferries, and other means.

Except for its reluctance to incur provincial direct debt the fiscal picture in British Columbia is much like that of other provinces. The personal income tax is the principal tax source, followed by sales tax, motor fuels, corporation income tax, and in British Columbia medicare premiums. Natural resource revenues, while high, were only 6.5 percent of total revenue in 1986. Transfers from the federal government were 17 percent in that year.

The principal outlays are for health, social services, education, transportation and public debt charges, the familiar provincial list.

Table 18.40   Province of British Columbia, Revenue, Consolidated
Finances Basis, Selected Years, 1952-86[a]

Source	1952	1962	1972	1982	1986
	millions of dollars				
Taxes	72.7	227.2	1,015.8	5,595.6	6,426.9
Natural resource revenue	25.9	67.2	215.2	596.2	706.3
Privileges, licences and permits	12.0	24.8	52.1	124.7	137.6
Liquor sales and regulation	20.9	31.5	97.4	347.7	456.8
Other revenue	9.8	13.1	183.7	906.4	1,262.5
Transfers from other governments[b]	58.4	84.3	314.6	1,213.2	1,853.0
Total	199.7	448.1	1,878.8	8,783.8	10,843.1
Own source revenue	141.3	363.8	1,564.2	7,570.6	8,990.1
Surplus or deficit	16.5	7.0	127.5	−1,069.2	−875.5
	percent of total revenue				
Taxes	36.4	50.7	54.1	63.8	59.1
Natural resource revenue	13.0	15.0	11.4	6.8	6.5
Privileges, licences and permits	6.0	5.5	2.8	1.4	1.3
Liquor sales and regulation	10.5	7.0	5.2	4.0	4.2
Other revenue	4.8	3.0	9.8	10.3	11.9
Transfers from other governments[b]	29.3	18.8	16.7	13.7	17.0
Total	100.0	100.0	100.0	100.0	100.0
Own source revenue	70.7	81.2	83.2	86.2	82.9

See table 18.3 for footnotes and sources.

British Columbia Diary

1947: January 20—Report, Provincial Municipal Relations (Goldenberg) in British Columbia.

_____. February 26—Budget. Interim figures for the year ending March 31, 1946 showed a revenue surplus of $8.1 million. The Minister of Finance reported that net provincial debt at December 31, 1946 totalled $132.6 million. Budget forecast, 1947-48: revenue, $58.9 million; expenditure, $58.8 million; surplus, $108,000.

1948: March 17—Budget. A retail sales tax of 3 percent was levied and amusement tax and timber royalties were increased. Budget forecast, 1948-49: revenue, $77.6 million; expenditure, $77.5 million; surplus on revenue account, $166,000. One-third of receipts from the sales tax was to be transferred to the municipalities.

1949: February 25—Budget. No tax changes. Net debt at December 31, 1948 was reported at $127.6 million. Budget forecast, 1949-50: revenue, $93.0 million; expenditure, $92.3 million; surplus on revenue account, $672,000.

1950: February 28—Budget. No tax changes. Net debt at December 31, 1949 totalled $146.1 million. The Minister of Finance made reference to the

Table 18.41 Province of British Columbia, Expenditure, Consolidated Finances Basis, Selected Years, 1952-86[a]

	1952	1962	1972	1982	1986
	millions of dollars				
General services	8.9	17.7	97.3	669.6	667.6
Health	45.0	94.7	476.0	2,743.2	3,332.3
Social services	16.9	51.0	210.9	1,608.2	1,901.6
Education	27.9	93.2	355.3	2,158.1	2,057.6
Transportation and communications	35.7	96.4	230.3	824.1	833.0
Natural resources and industrial development	15.4	27.7	98.3	505.0	796.1
Charges on debt	9.7	1.0	35.8	348.3	1,002.1
Transfers to other governments[b]	13.9	12.8	54.9	108.5	105.9
Other	9.8	46.6	192.5	888.0	1,022.4
Total	183.2	441.1	1,751.3	9,853.0	11,718.6
Offsets:					
Specific purpose transfers	10.1	79.8	308.0	1,204.0	1,821.1
General purpose transfers	48.3	4.5	6.6	9.2	31.9
Own expenditure	124.8	356.8	1,436.7	8,639.8	9,865.6
	percent of total expenditure				
General services	4.8	4.0	5.5	6.8	5.7
Health	24.5	21.5	27.1	27.9	28.4
Social services	9.2	11.6	12.0	16.3	16.2
Education	15.2	21.2	20.2	22.0	17.6
Transportation and communications	19.5	21.9	13.1	8.3	7.1
Natural resources and industrial development	8.4	6.3	5.6	5.1	6.8
Charges on debt	5.3	0.2	2.4	3.5	8.6
Transfers to other governments[b]	7.6	2.9	3.2	1.1	0.9
Other	5.5	10.4	10.9	9.0	8.7
Total	100.0	100.0	100.0	100.0	100.0
Own expenditure	68.1	80.9	82.0	87.7	84.2

See table 18.4 for footnotes and sources.

hospital insurance fund "that was inaugurated some fifteen months ago," and reported a deficit of $4.6 million in the fund that had to be taken care of from general revenues. Social assistance recipients received free hospitalization financed from the retail sales tax. Budget forecast, 1950-51: revenue, $105.8 million; expenditure, $105.6 million; surplus, $237,000.

1951: March 13—Budget. Hospital insurance premiums were increased. The hospital insurance fund incurred a further deficit in 1950-51. The finance minister warned that too high a proportion of the province's budget was being used to fund social assistance, welfare, and education and that far too little attention was being paid to productive services such as the development of agriculture, mining, forestry and fishing industries, and the building up of highways, bridges, ferries and other means of communication. A study was in process by a firm of management engineers of departmental management and administrative affairs. Also up for discussion were the new federal tax-sharing proposals. Budget forecast, 1951-52: revenue, $118.5 million; expenditure, $118.3 million; surplus, $234,000.

1952: March 4—Budget. No tax changes. Budget forecast, 1952-53: revenue, $142.0 million; expenditure, $141.9 million, including $6.5 million in capital costs; surplus on revenue account, $82,000.

1953: February 18—Budget. Hospitalization premiums reduced; tax on income of mining operations raised to 10 percent from 4 with a higher level of exempt income; tax of 10 percent imposed on net profit of logging operations (such taxes to be deductible in calculating federal tax); higher exemptions under meals tax; reduction in motor vehicle licence fees; real property assessment to be equalized throughout the province; changes to be made in the system of financing education; sharing of retail sales tax receipts with local governments to be replaced by direct grants. Budget forecast, 1953-54: revenue, $167.1 million; expenditure, $143.5 million; surplus on revenue account, $23.6 million; capital expenditures, $35.3 million.

1954: March 8—Budget. Retail sales tax raised to 5 percent and hospital insurance premiums abolished; reduction in basic rate of the amusement tax; reduction in registration fees for motor vehicles; special tax on liquor sales cancelled. Net debt at December 31, 1953 was reported to be $154.9 million. Budget forecast, 1954-55: revenue, $193.9 million; expenditure, $143.1 million; surplus on revenue account, $50.8 million; hospital insurance expenditures, $28.9 million; capital expenditures, $33.3 million.

1955: February 4—Budget. Adjustments made to provincial property tax in unorganized and other areas, coincident with equalization of assessment for education taxation; provincial grant structure to municipalities revised. Net debt at December 31, 1954 totalled $139.4 million, plus guaranteed debt of $117.5 million. Budget forecast: revenue, $194.5 million; expenditure, $151.3 million; surplus on current account, $43.3 million; hospital insurance service expenditure, $28.9 million; capital expenditure, $31.7 million.

_____. March 7—Budget Supplement. Adjustments made to provincial property taxation in unorganized areas. Budget forecast, 1955-56: unchanged.

1956: February 1—Budget. Amusement tax reduced; minor amendments to the assessment equalization act, the meals tax, and oil and gas taxation. At December 31, 1955 net debt totalled $125.9 million and guaranteed debt, $138.7 million. Budget forecast, 1956-57: revenue, $224.5 million; expenditure, $167.6 million; surplus on current account, $56.9 million; hospital insurance expenditures, $30.4 million; capital expenditure, $60.3 million.

1957: February 22—Budget. 2 percent tax levied on the premium income of insurance companies (formerly levied by the federal government); basis for taxing mining and logging profits brought into line with federal tax; grant payable to home-owners to alleviate property taxation. Net debt at December 31, 1956 had been reduced to $114.2 million and total guaranteed debt increased to $223.5 million. The Premier reviewed developments in the federal-provincial tax-sharing arrangements. Budget forecast, 1957-58: revenue, $262.3 million; expenditure, $208.5 million; surplus on revenue account, $53.8 million; capital expenditures, $58.0 million.

1958: February 7—Budget. No tax changes. Net direct public debt at December 31, 1957 had been reduced to $57.1 million and total guarantees increased to $360.4 million. The Premier again expressed his dissatisfaction with federal proposals for revised tax-sharing arrangements; he endorsed the federal principle of a fully comprehensive national hospital insurance program, and was happy with the new federal cost-sharing winter works program. Budget forecast, 1958-59: revenue, $267.5 million; expenditure, $215.9 million; surplus on current account, $51.6 million; capital expenditure (net), $56.2 million.

1959: February 6—Budget. No tax changes. At December 31, 1958 net public debt had been reduced to $27.0 million and guaranteed debt increased to $449.9 million. Budget forecast, 1959-60: revenue, $287.8 million; expenditure, $230.9 million; surplus on current account, $56.9 million; net capital expenditure, $57.2 million.

1960: February 12—Budget. No tax changes. At December 31, 1959 the province's gross direct debt of $96.6 million was entirely offset by investments; guaranteed debt totalled $543.2 million. Budget forecast, 1960-61: revenue, $306.8 million; expenditure, $331.1 million; deficit, $24.3 million.

1961: February 10—Budget. Tax on gasoline and diesel fuel increased by 3¢ to 13¢ per gallon of gasoline. At December 31, 1960 gross direct debt totalled $91.3 million and guaranteed debt, $601.5 million. Budget forecast: revenue, $326.1 million; expenditure, $340.0 million; deficit, $13.9 million.

1962: February 9—Budget. Provincial personal and corporate income taxes levied as of January 1, 1962 to comply with federal-provincial arrangements; tax on amusements lowered to 5 percent from 10 percent and initial exemption raised to 75¢; school textbooks exempted from the retail sales tax. At December 31, 1961 guaranteed debt totalled $1.3 billion. Budget forecast, 1962-63: revenue, $336.0 million; expenditure, $356.1 million; deficit, $20.1 million. Of total forecast revenue, 22 percent was expected to be derived from the new personal and corporate income taxes, 26 percent from the retail sales tax, 13 percent from gasoline taxes, and 17 percent from natural resources.

1963: February 8—Budget. Provincial succession duties levied with credits allowed for one-half of federal estate tax paid; 5 percent amusement tax on theatre admissions and entrance to sporting events abolished; logging taxes allowed as an offset against corporate income taxes. The Premier estimated that there would be a surplus of $4.0 million for 1962-63. Budget forecast, 1963-64: revenue, $372.9 million; expenditure $372.7 million; surplus, $0.2 million.

1964: February 7—Budget. Bridge, highway, and tunnel tolls eliminated; electric power and gas rates reduced; home-owner grant increased. The Premier announced that the province would provide up to one-quarter of the capital for the proposed Bank of British Columbia. Guaranteed debt at

December 31, 1963 totalled $1.4 billion. Budget forecast, 1964-65: revenue, $396.0 million; expenditure, $395.6 million; surplus, $0.4 million.

1965: February 5—Budget. Electric power and gas rates reduction forecast; exemptions increased under succession duties; home-owner's grant raised. The Premier announced a new program to share medical insurance premiums for low-income families and singles. Budget forecast, 1965-66: revenue, $447.2 million; expenditure, $446.0 million; surplus, $1.2 million.

1966: February 11—Budget. The 5 percent retail sales tax was removed from meals, magazines, perodicals, and newspapers; from candies and soft drinks, children's clothing and footwear, and school supplies; the property tax was removed from community halls in unorganized areas; home-owner's grant increased; the provincial share of medical premiums of low-income taxpayers was raised. At December 31, 1965 guaranteed debt outstanding totalled $1.5 billion. Budget forecast, 1966-67: revenue, $659.8 million; expenditure, $657.3 million; surplus, $2.5 million.

1967: February 3—Budget. No new taxes or tax increases were introduced. A new program of grants for first-time home buyers and an increase in the provincial home-owner's grant were announced. Budget forecast, 1967-68: revenue, $740 million; expenditure, $739 million; small surplus expected.

1968: February 9—Budget. Increases were announced in the grants for home-owners and first-time home buyers. Tax changes were limited to adjustments in the forestry and mining charges. Budget forecast, 1968-69: revenue, $867 million; expenditure, $866 million; small surplus expected.

1969: February 7—Budget. Special funds would be set aside out of surpluses for various social and economic purposes. Increases were made in grants for home owners, first-time home buyers and municipalities. As an alternative to a grant first-time home buyers could obtain a low rate second mortgage. No tax changes were made. Budget forecast, 1969-70: revenue, $867 million; expenditure, $866 million; small surplus expected.

1970: February 6—Budget. The sole tax change was an increase in exemptions under succession duties. Increased grants were given to home owners, old age pensioners, welfare cases, nursing and boarding homes, and municipalities. Budget forecast, 1970-71: revenue, $1,166 million; expenditure, $1,166 million; small surplus expected.

1971: February 5—Budget. The gasoline tax was increased and new taxes levied on tobacco and hotel and motel accommodation. Another increase was made in the home-owner's grant. A fund would be set up to help with addiction problems, and money would be provided to several agencies for capital expenditures. Budget forecast, 1971-72: revenue, $1,301 million; expenditure, $1,301 million; a small surplus was expected.

1972: February 4—Budget. Succession duty exemptions were raised and a gift tax was imposed. New and increased grants were given for several purposes under special funds. Budget forecast, 1972-73: revenue, $1,453 million; expenditure, $1,452 million; a small surplus was expected.

1973: February 9—Budget. The corporation income tax was increased from

10 to 12 percent and a new tax on paid-up capital of corporations was imposed. Petroleum royalties were increased 30 percent. As in past years the home-owner's grant was increased and the per capita grant to municipalities was raised. Studies were being made of educational and health systems of the province. Budget forecast, 1973-74: revenue, $1,722 million; expenditure, $1,719 million, surplus, $3 million.

1974: February 11—Budget. A new NDP government brought down a budget with limited changes, but other measures were introduced later. An entirely new basis for mineral taxation was enacted; in June a reduction in premiums under the new provincially run automobile insurance plan was given in lieu of a reduction in gasoline tax; local governments' grants were increased, all home owners would receive a grant towards school tax, and the local government share of welfare costs was reduced. Free prescription drugs were provided for seniors, some property taxes could be deferred, and a grant was introduced for renters, higher in amount for seniors. Expenditure projects were mainly for resources and transportation. Various special funds were set up or supplemented. Budget forecast, 1974-75: revenue, $2,178 million; expenditure, $2,173 million; surplus, $5.0 million.

1975: February 28—Budget. The corporation income tax was increased from 12 to 13 percent but reduced to 10 percent for small business, and the gasoline tax was increased by 2 cents per gallon. A credit against income tax was granted for low-income renters. Budget forecast, 1975-76: revenue, $3,223 million; expenditure, $3,223 million (excluding special fund expenditures); a small surplus was expected.

1976: March 29—Budget. An election changed the government; with a revised appraisal of the previous government's budgets and a declining economy, a deficit in excess of $500 million was forecast. To cope with this situation several reductions in expenditure and increases in revenue were made. The latter included an increase in personal income tax from 30.5 percent of the federal tax to 32.5 percent; an increase in the general corporate tax from 13 to 15 percent and the small business rate from 10 percent to 12 percent; an increase in the sales tax from 5 to 7 percent; a rise in the tobacco taxes, and a 50 percent increase in medical insurance premiums. The additional daily hospital stay charge was raised and liquor licence fees were increased. Budget forecast, 1976-77: revenue, $3,587 million; expenditure, $3,615 million; deficit, $28 million.

1977: January 24—Budget. The principal tax change in this budget was the abolition of succession duties and gift tax. The personal income tax rate was increased to 46 percent to take up the additional room given under the 1976 federal-provincial arrangements. Very substantial borrowings were being made throughout this period to finance B.C. Crown corporations, the medium through which the province did much of its financing. Budget forecast, 1977-78: revenue, $3,830 million; expenditure, $3,830 million.

1978: April 10—Budget. In fairly buoyant conditions but with unacceptable levels of unemployment a budget with several changes was presented. The main feature of the year was the 2 percent reduction in sales tax under the federal offer of compensation for a fixed period, although the B.C. reduction was indefinite. Exemptions for small business machinery purchases were given as well. The exemptions under the paid-up capital tax were raised. The tobacco taxes and liquor retail mark-ups were increased, and the pari-mutuel betting tax reduced. Grants were raised for senior home owners and renters and for first-time home buyers. Substantial increases were made in payments to municipalities. Budget forecast, 1978-79: revenue, $4,394 million; expenditure, $4,280 million; surplus, $117 million.

1979: April 2 and June 8—Budgets. A budget was introduced in April and following an intervening election was re-introduced in June. Its main tax features were a 2 point reduction in personal income tax to 44 percent and a proposal to increase the dividend tax credit by 5 points for B.C. companies if the federal government agreed (it did not agree). The sales tax rate, already reduced to 5 percent, was further reduced to 4 percent, except for liquor purchases, which remained at 7 percent. Exemptions and rates for small companies under the capital tax were eased. The renter's tax credit and the home owner's grant were raised. The province proposed to introduce an allowance for small business venture capital investments and had already announced the lauching of the B.C. Resources Investment Corporation. In this and previous years there were substantial amendments to the mining and forestry legislation and taxes. Budget forecast, 1979-80: revenue, $4,567 million; expenditure, $4,567 million.

1980: March 11—Budget. The small business corporation rate was reduced from 12 to 10 percent. Legislation would soon be introduced for tax credits for investment in small business venture capital corporations. Higher rates of sales tax were introduced for heavy-gas-consuming cars and exemptions were granted for certain fuels used in homes. Rates of corporation capital tax were increased for banks and trust companies. Further amendments were made in mining taxation. Home-owner grants for seniors were raised; medical plan premiums were also increased, and in future would be indexed to inflation. Budget forecast, 1980-81: revenue, $5,800 million; expenditure, $5,450 million; surplus, $250 million.

1981: March 9—Budget. Falling resource revenues had presented the prospect of a deficit. Substantial tax increases were therefore made, including a 10 percent surtax on upper income level income taxes; an increase from 15 percent to 16 percent in the general corporation tax, with a reduction in the small business rate to 8 percent; an increase in the sales tax from 4 to 6 percent; a switch to ad valorem gasoline tax with an increase in rates and an increase in tobacco taxes and the hotel room tax. In keeping with a policy that medical insurance premiums should cover 35 percent of medical insurance costs notice was given of an increase in future premiums. In this budget the minister urged the federal government to adopt a more flexible attitude toward provincial requests for special features in the income tax law, no doubt as a reaction to the denial of the additional dividend tax credit the province wanted to give. He also wanted some protection against unexpected losses of revenue from federal changes in tax base over which the province had no control. The province has not yet acted on a threat to withdraw from the collection agreement if these requests were not granted. The budget included background papers on a variety of subjects. Budget forecast, 1981-82: revenue, $6,636 million; expenditure, $6,454 million; surplus, $182 million.

————. Report, School Taxation, Minister of Finance.

1982: April 5—Budget. This budget presented a revised accounting system in which spending from various special funds was included in the total. An intention was given to set up a resource revenue stabilization fund to counter extreme fluctuations in these revenues, provincial assistance for local school financing was substantially revised, and a program to relieve municipalities of their 10 percent share of social welfare costs over the coming two years was introduced. Tax changes were minimal; the paid-up capital tax on banks was raised, additional farm items were exempted from sales tax, and some fuels were exempted from the gasoline tax. The minister again registered his dissatisfaction with the terms of the federal-provincial collection agreements; several additional papers were presented with this budget. Budget forecast, 1982-83: revenue, $7,301 million; expenditure, $7,688 million; deficit, $358 million. (Figures for the deficits of the two previous years on the revised basis of this budget were $257 million for 1980-81 and $279 million for 1981-82).

1983: July 7—Budget. With continuing economic decline severe budget restraints were being imposed. These included ceilings on departmental expenditures, reductions of staff, pay scales related to productivity, and abandonment of such long standing programs as the personal income tax credits for renters and the first-home buyer's grant. Tax rates were also increased; the sales tax was raised to 7 percent, tobacco and provincial property taxes went up, and the hospital co-insurance fee was raised. A notable feature of the budget was a plan to reform the basis of property tax in the municipalities, which was set out in an Appendix to the budget. Budget forecast, 1983-84: revenue, $6,842 million; expenditure, $8,445 million; deficit, $1,603 million. For this and the prior year the government for the first time in many years had borrowed for government requirements, most previous borrowing having been for Crown corporations.

1984: February 20—Budget. The restraint program would continue. Grants for students, for the elderly, needy, and for municipalities would depend on growth in provincial revenues. In future 70 percent of resource revenues would go to the resource revenue fund and 30 percent to meet ordinary expenses. Revenue would be lost by the requirement to withdraw the co-insurance daily hospital charge under the new Canada Health Act. Tax changes included an additional 4 percent surtax on all personal income taxes, a "health care maintenance tax" at 8 percent, an increase in the hotel room tax, and the minimum property tax. Minor additional exemptions were given under the sales tax. Budget forecast, 1985-85: revenue, $7,719 million; expenditure, $7,920 million; deficit, $201 million. British Columbia had the distinction at this point of receiving the first payment to any province under the revenue stabilization feature of the federal-provincial agreements, $174 million.

1985: March 14—Budget. The 1985 budget was designed to give some encouragement to businesses in the province. A refundable tax credit was given for employment in small businesses; a venture capital tax credit was given for equity investment in venture capital corporations for financing small businesses; special tax reliefs were provided for businesses being established in special enterprise zones; Vancouver would become an international financial centre; critical industries would be given special attention, and the capital tax would be phased out for all companies but out-of-province banks. Further sales tax exemptions were given for agricultural cost items and for minor other business costs. The insurance premiums tax was increased and inevitably the tobacco taxes as well. The coming Expo in Vancouver had a minor reflection even in the tax legislation—both the Expo 86 site and the rapid transit were exempted from property tax. A much more significant permanent change was the exemption of machinery and equipment from property tax for school tax purposes, to be spread over three years. Property taxes on commercial and industrial property were also being reduced. Budget forecast, 1985-86: revenue, $10.1 billion; expenditure, $10.8 billion; deficit, $693 million.

1986: March 20—Budget. Expo 1986 and improving exports were bringing a better outlook to the province. Funds had been set up for Excellence in Education and for Health Improvement which it was confident would help provide the necessary level of funding in these two areas. Forestry and other resource industries were beginning to pick up. Expenditure restraints were still in effect however for the the general budget. Tax changes were mainly downward: the corporation income tax was reduced to 15 percent for 1987 and to 14 percent for 1988. The small business capital investment program was extended and minor changes were made in the insurance premium tax and other lesser taxes. Budget forecast, 1986-87: revenue, $8,768 million; expenditure, $9,643 million; deficit, $875 million.

1987: March 19—Budget. Lacking the stimulus of Expo 1986 the province expected slower economic activity. A long strike in the forestry industry had also slackened the economic pace. Revenue shortages had resulted in a larger than expected deficit in the previous year, and the budget introduced several measures to reduce the deficit. The surtaxes on personal income taxes were eliminated as of January 1, 1987 and the basic rate increased from 44 percent to 51.5 percent of the basic federal tax; the corporate income tax was increased from 8 to 11 percent; land registration fees were replaced by a two-rate property tax; the tax on leaded motor fuel was increased by 2 cents a litre; the sales tax rate was reduced to 6 percent. Budget forecast, 1987-88: revenue, $9,370 million; expenditure, $10,220 million; deficit, $850 million, to be financed by direct borrowing.

1988: March 24—Budget. The general corporate income tax rate was reduced to 14 percent from 15 percent and the rate on small business reduced to 9 percent from 11 percent; the retail sales tax on liquor raised to 10 percent from 6 percent; the tobacco tax raised to the equivalent of $1.13 per pack of 25 cigarettes; exemptions raised under the hotel room tax; gasoline tax raised to 22.5 percent from 20 percent; tax on vehicle insurance premiums raised; medical services plan premiums raised; mining taxes reduced; provincial property taxes raised; business licences and other fees raised. The Minister repeated the goals of his government's long-range plan: elimination of the current account deficit, reduction of accumulated debt, and stabilization of revenues. Budget forecast, 1988-89: revenue, $11.4 billion, expenditure, $11.8 billion; deficit, $395.0 million.

Table 18.42   All Governments: Revenue by Level of Government, Including and Excluding Intergovernmental Transfers, National Accounts Basis, 1947-86

Year[a]	Federal	Provincial		Local		Hospitals		Pension plans	Total[b]
		Incl. grants	Excl. grants	Incl. grants	Excl. grants	Incl. grants	Excl. grants		
				billions of dollars					
1947	2.8	0.9	0.7	0.6	0.5	—	—	—	4.0
1948	2.7	1.0	0.8	0.7	0.5	—	—	—	4.1
1949	2.7	1.1	0.9	0.7	0.6	—	—	—	4.2
1950	3.0	1.2	1.0	0.8	0.6	—	—	—	4.6
1951	4.2	1.4	1.0	0.9	0.7	—	—	—	6.1
1952	4.7	1.5	1.2	1.1	0.9	—	—	—	6.7
1953	4.8	1.6	1.1	1.2	0.9	—	—	—	6.9
1954	4.6	1.7	1.2	1.3	1.0	—	—	—	6.8
1955	5.0	1.8	1.4	1.4	1.1	—	—	—	7.5
1956	5.7	2.1	1.6	1.6	1.2	—	—	—	8.5
1957	5.7	2.4	1.9	1.8	1.4	—	—	—	8.9
1958	5.4	2.6	2.0	2.1	1.5	—	—	—	8.9
1959	6.1	3.1	2.2	2.3	1.7	—	—	—	10.0
1960	6.5	3.3	2.3	2.6	1.9	—	—	—	10.7
1961	6.8	3.7	2.3	2.9	2.0	0.8	—	—	11.4
1962	7.0	4.4	2.6	3.2	2.1	0.8	—	—	12.5
1963	7.3	4.8	3.3	3.5	2.3	0.9	—	—	13.3
1964	8.4	5.4	4.2	3.7	2.4	1.0	0.1	—	15.0
1965	9.1	6.3	4.9	4.2	2.6	1.2	0.1	—	16.8
1966	10.0	7.4	5.8	4.8	3.0	1.4	0.1	0.7	19.5
1967	10.9	8.7	6.8	5.4	3.3	1.6	0.1	0.9	22.0
1968	12.2	10.3	8.0	6.0	3.7	1.9	0.1	1.0	25.0
1969	14.5	12.0	9.3	6.7	4.1	2.1	0.1	1.2	29.1

Year									
1970	15.5	13.9	10.5	7.6	4.4	2.4	0.1	1.3	32.0
1971	17.2	16.0	11.7	8.3	4.7	2.7	0.1	1.5	35.3
1972	19.6	17.7	13.3	9.3	5.2	3.1	0.1	1.7	39.8
1973	22.8	20.6	15.9	10.1	5.6	3.3	0.2	1.9	46.3
1974	30.0	26.1	20.0	11.6	6.2	4.2	0.2	2.3	58.8
1975	31.7	29.8	22.3	14.0	7.3	5.0	0.2	2.8	64.2
1976	35.3	34.3	26.0	16.1	8.7	5.9	0.3	3.3	73.5
1977	36.5	40.7	31.1	19.0	9.8	6.7	0.3	3.7	81.3
1978	38.4	46.3	35.7	20.3	10.9	7.0	0.3	4.2	89.5
1979	43.6	52.3	40.8	23.5	12.1	7.7	0.4	4.9	101.7
1980	50.6	58.9	46.2	24.8	13.3	8.6	0.4	5.7	116.3
1981	65.0	68.5	54.6	28.2	15.0	10.2	0.6	6.5	141.6
1982	66.0	76.1	60.4	31.7	16.3	12.2	0.7	7.8	151.3
1983	69.6	83.8	66.5	33.7	17.3	13.3	0.7	8.0	162.1
1984	76.7	92.5	72.9	35.5	18.4	14.2	0.8	9.0	177.8
1985	83.7	98.6	77.2	37.9	19.4	15.2	0.9	9.9	191.1
1986	91.4	101.0	80.2	40.0	21.1	15.3	1.0	10.7	204.4

Note: Figures for 1981-86 on 1981 preliminary national accounts basis.

[a]Calendar year. [b]Excludes grants.

Sources: Canada, Department of Finance, *Economic Review*, April 1985; Statistics Canada, *National Income and Expenditure Accounts*, Fourth Quarter, 1986.

Table 18.43   Provincial Governments: Revenue by Type, National Accounts Basis, 1947-86

Year[a]	Direct taxes		Indirect taxes	Total taxes	Transfers from persons	Invest-ment income	Transfers from govern-ment	Capital consumption allowances	Total
	Persons	Corpo-rations							
					billions of dollars				
1947	0.1	0.1	0.4	0.6	—	0.1	0.2	—	0.9
1948	0.1	0.1	0.4	0.6	—	0.1	0.2	0.1	1.0
1949	0.1	0.1	0.5	0.7	—	0.1	0.2	0.1	1.1
1950	0.1	0.1	0.5	0.7	0.1	0.1	0.3	0.1	1.2
1951	0.2	0.2	0.6	0.9	0.1	0.1	0.3	0.1	1.4
1952	0.1	0.1	0.6	0.8	0.1	0.1	0.4	0.1	1.5
1953	0.1	0.1	0.7	0.9	—	0.2	0.4	0.1	1.6
1954	0.2	0.1	0.7	1.0	0.1	0.2	0.4	0.1	1.7
1955	0.2	0.1	0.8	1.1	—	0.1	0.5	0.1	1.8
1956	0.2	0.1	0.9	1.2	0.1	0.2	0.5	0.1	2.1
1957	0.2	0.2	1.0	1.4	0.1	0.2	0.5	0.1	2.4
1958	0.2	0.2	1.0	1.4	0.1	0.2	0.7	0.1	2.6
1959	0.3	0.3	1.1	1.7	0.2	0.3	0.9	0.1	3.1
1960	0.3	0.3	1.1	1.7	0.2	0.3	1.0	0.1	3.3
1961	0.3	0.3	1.3	1.9	0.2	0.3	1.1	0.2	3.7
1962	0.6	0.4	1.6	2.6	0.2	0.3	1.1	0.2	4.4
1963	0.7	0.5	1.7	2.9	0.2	0.4	1.1	0.2	4.8
1964	0.8	0.5	2.0	3.3	0.3	0.4	1.2	0.2	5.4
1965	1.1	0.5	2.3	3.9	0.3	0.5	1.4	0.2	6.3
1966	1.4	0.6	2.6	4.6	0.3	0.5	1.6	0.3	7.4
1967	1.9	0.6	3.0	5.5	0.4	0.6	2.0	0.3	8.7
1968	2.2	0.7	3.4	6.3	0.5	0.7	2.3	0.3	10.3
1969	2.5	0.8	3.9	7.2	0.8	0.9	2.7	0.4	12.0

Year									
1970	3.1	0.8	4.2	8.1	1.0	1.0	3.4	0.4	13.9
1971	3.6	0.9	4.6	9.1	1.0	1.2	4.3	0.4	16.0
1972	4.2	1.0	5.3	10.5	1.0	1.4	4.4	0.5	17.7
1973	4.9	1.4	6.2	12.5	1.0	1.8	4.7	0.6	20.6
1974	6.1	2.0	7.2	15.3	1.0	2.9	6.1	0.8	26.1
1975	6.9	2.1	7.5	16.5	1.0	3.7	7.6	1.0	29.8
1976	8.1	2.1	9.1	19.3	1.3	4.4	8.4	1.0	34.3
1977	11.1	2.1	10.0	23.2	1.5	5.2	9.7	1.1	40.7
1978	13.0	2.5	10.4	25.9	1.8	6.7	10.6	1.3	46.3
1979	13.8	3.2	11.9	28.1	2.1	8.4	11.5	1.4	52.3
1980	15.5	3.7	13.0	32.2	2.2	10.1	12.6	1.7	58.9
1981	19.7	3.5	15.3	38.5	2.5	11.7	14.0	1.9	68.5
1982	22.2	2.5	17.9	42.6	2.8	13.0	15.6	2.1	76.1
1983	23.5	2.8	20.3	46.6	3.2	14.5	17.3	2.2	83.8
1984	25.8	3.7	22.5	52.0	3.3	15.1	19.6	2.5	92.5
1985	26.7	3.9	24.6	56.8	3.4	15.9	21.4	2.7	98.6
1986	29.7	3.7	26.8	60.2	3.5	13.6	20.8	2.9	101.0

Note: Figures for 1981-86 on 1981 preliminary revised national accounts basis.

aCalendar year.

Sources: Same as table 18-42.

Table 18.44   Provincial Governments: Revenue by Type, National Accounts Basis, Percent of Total, Selected Years, 1947-86

Year[a]	Direct taxes		Indirect taxes	Total taxes	Transfers from persons	Investment income	Transfers from government	Capital consumption allowances	Total
	Persons	Corporations							
					percent				
1947	11.1	11.1	44.4	66.6	—	16.2	22.2	—	100.0
1953	6.3	6.3	43.7	56.3	—	12.5	25.0	6.2	100.0
1955	11.1	5.6	44.5	61.2	—	5.6	27.8	5.4	100.0
1960	9.1	9.1	33.3	51.5	6.0	9.2	30.3	3.0	100.0
1965	17.5	8.0	36.5	62.0	4.8	8.0	22.2	3.0	100.0
1970	22.2	5.8	30.2	58.2	7.2	7.2	24.4	3.0	100.0
1975	23.2	7.1	25.2	55.5	3.4	12.4	25.5	3.2	100.0
1980	26.4	6.3	22.1	54.8	3.7	17.2	21.4	2.9	100.0
1981	28.8	5.1	22.3	56.2	3.6	17.1	20.4	2.7	100.0
1982	29.1	3.3	23.5	55.9	3.7	17.1	20.5	2.8	100.0
1983	28.1	3.3	24.3	55.7	3.8	17.3	20.6	2.6	100.0
1984	27.9	4.0	24.3	56.2	3.6	16.3	21.2	2.7	100.0
1985	27.1	4.0	24.9	56.0	3.4	16.1	21.7	2.8	100.0
1986	29.4	3.7	26.5	59.6	3.4	13.5	20.6	2.9	100.0

Based on table 18.43.

Table 18.45   All Governments: Expenditure by Level of Government as Percent of Gross National Product, Excluding Intergovernmental Grants, National Accounts Basis, 1947-86

Year[a]	Federal	Provincial	Local	Hospitals	Pension plans[b]	Total
			percent			
1947	14.1	5.2	4.4	—	—	23.7
1948	11.6	5.8	4.5	—	—	21.9
1949	11.9	5.9	4.8	—	—	22.6
1950	11.4	5.9	4.9	—	—	22.2
1951	13.4	5.6	5.1	—	—	24.1
1952	16.7	4.9	5.3	—	—	26.9
1953	16.3	4.7	5.4	—	—	26.4
1954	16.2	5.4	5.8	—	—	27.4
1955	14.3	5.2	5.8	—	—	26.3
1956	14.3	5.6	5.9	—	—	25.5
1957	14.6	5.7	6.3	—	—	26.6
1958	15.8	6.0	6.6	—	—	28.4
1959	15.2	6.8	7.1	—	—	28.8
1960	15.0	7.3	7.3	—	—	29.7
1961	15.4	6.1	7.3	2.0	—	30.8
1962	14.9	6.1	7.8	2.0	—	30.8
1963	13.9	6.3	8.0	2.0	—	30.2
1964	13.5	6.4	7.6	2.1	—	29.6
1965	12.9	6.8	8.1	2.1	—	29.9
1966	13.1	7.3	8.3	2.3	—	30.9
1967	13.5	8.3	8.6	2.4	—	32.9
1968	13.6	8.7	8.8	2.6	—	33.7
1969	13.4	9.0	8.9	2.6	0.1	34.1
1970	13.8	10.2	9.4	2.8	0.2	36.4
1971	13.8	11.1	9.3	2.8	0.2	37.3
1972	14.8	11.0	8.9	2.8	0.3	37.8
1973	14.3	10.7	8.5	2.7	0.3	36.5
1974	15.4	11.1	8.3	2.8	0.4	37.9
1975	16.8	12.1	8.8	3.0	0.5	41.3
1976	15.7	12.0	8.7	2.9	0.6	40.0
1977	16.1	12.5	8.9	2.9	0.7	41.1
1978	16.4	12.8	8.8	2.9	0.8	41.7
1979	15.5	12.9	8.3	2.7	0.8	40.2
1980	16.2	13.5	8.3	2.8	0.9	41.8
1981	16.9	13.7	8.2	2.9	1.0	42.6
1982	19.5	15.2	8.7	3.2	1.1	47.7
1983	19.6	15.6	8.4	3.2	1.2	47.9
1984	20.3	15.4	8.1	3.0	1.3	48.2
1985	20.4	15.4	7.9	3.0	1.5	48.2
1986	19.5	15.5	7.9	3.0	1.6	47.5

Note: Figures for 1981-86 on 1981 preliminary revised national accounts basis.

[a] Calendar year. [b] Canada and Quebec Pension Plans.

Sources: Canadian Tax Foundation, *The National Finances*; Canada, Department of Finance, *Economic Review*, April 1985 and National *Income and Expenditure Accounts*, Fourth Quarter, 1986.

Table 18.46 Provincial Governments: Revenue, Expenditure, and Balances, National Accounts Basis, 1947-86, Dollar Figures in Billions

Year[a]	Revenue $	% of GNP	Expenditure $	% of GNP	Surplus or deficit			
					Including intergovernmental transfers $	% of GNP	Excluding intergovernmental transfers $	% of GNP
	$	%	$	%	$	%	$	%
1947	0.9	6.7	0.8	5.9	0.1	0.1	—	—
1948	1.0	6.5	1.0	6.5	—	—	—	—
1949	1.1	6.5	1.1	6.5	-0.1	-0.1	-0.1	-0.6
1950	1.2	6.6	1.2	6.5	—	—	-0.1	-0.5
1951	1.4	6.5	1.4	6.5	—	—	-0.1	-0.5
1952	1.5	6.1	1.4	5.7	0.1	—	-0.1	-0.4
1953	1.6	6.2	1.5	5.8	0.1	—	-0.1	-0.4
1954	1.7	6.6	1.6	6.2	—	—	-0.1	-0.4
1955	1.8	6.5	1.8	6.4	—	—	-0.1	-0.4
1956	2.1	6.5	2.1	6.5	—	—	-0.2	-0.6
1957	2.4	7.2	2.4	7.2	—	—	-0.1	-0.3
1958	2.6	7.5	2.7	7.8	-0.1	—	-0.2	-0.6
1959	3.1	8.4	3.1	8.4	—	—	-0.3	-0.8
1960	3.3	8.7	3.5	9.2	-0.2	—	-0.5	-1.3
1961	3.7	9.3	3.9	9.8	-0.3	-0.1	0.1	0.3
1962	4.4	10.2	4.5	10.5	-0.1	—	0.7	1.6
1963	4.8	10.4	4.9	10.7	-0.1	—	0.8	1.7
1964	5.4	10.7	5.5	10.9	-0.1	—	0.9	1.8
1965	6.3	11.4	6.3	11.4	—	—	1.2	2.2
1966	7.4	11.9	7.5	12.2	-0.2	—	1.3	2.1
1967	8.7	13.2	9.1	13.7	-0.3	—	1.3	2.0
1968	10.3	14.2	10.3	14.2	-0.1	—	1.6	2.2
1969	12.0	15.0	11.7	14.6	0.3	—	2.1	2.6

1970	13.9	16.2	14.1	16.5	−0.2	—	1.8	2.1
1971	16.0	17.0	16.5	17.5	−0.5	0.1	1.2	1.3
1972	17.7	16.8	18.4	17.5	−0.7	0.1	1.7	1.6
1973	20.6	16.7	20.7	16.8	−0.1	—	2.7	2.2
1974	26.1	17.7	25.4	17.2	0.7	0.1	3.7	2.5
1975	29.8	18.0	31.6	19.1	−1.8	1.1	2.1	1.3
1976	34.3	17.9	35.9	18.7	−1.5	0.8	2.9	1.5
1977	40.7	19.4	41.5	19.7	−0.7	0.3	4.8	2.3
1978	46.3	19.9	45.5	19.6	0.7	0.3	5.9	2.5
1979	52.3	19.8	52.4	19.8	−0.1	—	6.7	2.5
1980	58.9	19.8	59.5	20.0	−0.7	0.2	6.0	2.0
1981	68.5	19.9	69.6	20.2	−1.1	0.3	7.5	2.2
1982	76.1	21.0	81.5	22.5	−5.4	1.5	5.4	1.5
1983	83.8	21.3	89.8	22.8	−6.1	1.5	5.2	1.3
1984	92.5	21.5	96.0	22.3	−3.5	0.8	6.9	1.6
1985	98.6	21.4	103.6	22.4	−4.9	0.9	5.9	1.3
1986	101.0	20.7	109.3	22.4	−8.2	1.7	4.4	0.9

Note: Figures for 1981-86 on 1981 preliminary revised national accounts basis.

aCalendar year.

Sources: Same as table 18-42.

Table 18.47   Provincial Governments: Main Categories of Expenditure, National Accounts Basis, 1947-86

Year[a]	Goods and services	Transfers to persons	Interest on debt	Subsidies	Capital assistance	Transfers to other govern-ments[b]	Capital formation	Total	Deficit or surplus
				billions of dollars					
1947	0.3	0.2	0.1	—	—	0.1	0.1	0.8	0.1
1948	0.3	0.3	0.1	—	—	0.1	0.2	1.0	—
1949	0.4	0.3	0.1	—	—	0.2	0.2	1.1	-0.1
1950	0.4	0.4	0.1	—	—	0.2	0.2	1.2	—
1951	0.5	0.4	0.1	—	—	0.2	0.2	1.4	—
1952	0.5	0.3	0.1	—	—	0.2	0.3	1.4	0.1
1953	0.5	0.4	0.1	—	—	0.2	0.3	1.5	0.1
1954	0.5	0.4	0.1	—	—	0.3	0.3	1.6	0.1
1955	0.6	0.4	0.1	—	—	0.3	0.4	1.8	—
1956	0.7	0.5	0.1	—	—	0.5	0.5	2.1	—
1957	0.7	0.5	0.1	—	—	0.5	0.5	2.4	—
1958	0.8	0.7	0.1	—	—	0.5	0.5	2.7	-0.1
1959	0.9	0.9	0.1	—	—	0.6	0.6	3.1	—
1960	1.0	1.1	0.1	—	—	0.7	0.6	3.5	-0.2
1961	1.0	0.6	0.2	—	—	1.5	0.5	3.9	-0.3
1962	1.1	0.7	0.2	—	—	1.8	0.6	4.5	-0.1
1963	1.2	0.8	0.2	—	—	2.0	0.7	4.9	-0.1
1964	1.3	0.8	0.2	0.1	—	2.2	0.8	5.5	-0.1
1965	1.5	1.0	0.3	0.1	—	2.5	0.9	6.3	—
1966	1.9	1.2	0.3	0.1	—	3.0	1.0	7.5	-0.2
1967	2.3	1.6	0.4	0.1	—	3.5	1.0	9.1	-0.3
1968	2.7	2.0	0.5	0.1	—	4.0	1.0	10.3	-0.1
1969	3.0	2.4	0.6	0.1	—	4.5	1.0	11.7	0.3

1970	4.1	2.6	0.8	0.2	—	5.4	1.0	14.1	−0.2
1971	4.7	3.1	0.9	0.3	0.1	6.0	1.4	16.5	−0.5
1972	5.3	3.2	1.1	0.3	0.1	6.8	1.6	18.4	−0.7
1973	6.1	3.6	1.4	0.4	0.1	7.5	1.6	20.7	−0.1
1974	7.5	4.5	1.5	0.6	0.1	9.1	2.1	25.4	0.7
1975	9.6	5.5	1.8	0.7	0.2	11.4	2.4	31.6	−1.8
1976	10.8	6.6	2.3	0.9	0.2	12.8	2.2	35.9	−1.5
1977	12.4	7.5	2.7	1.1	0.2	15.2	2.4	41.5	−0.1
1978	14.0	8.4	3.4	1.2	0.2	15.7	2.7	45.5	0.7
1979	16.1	9.4	3.8	1.6	0.2	18.4	2.9	52.4	−0.1
1980	18.8	11.4	4.7	1.8	0.3	19.3	3.2	59.5	−0.7
1981	21.9	12.6	6.2	2.5	0.3	22.5	3.7	69.6	−1.1
1982	24.6	14.8	7.8	3.0	0.6	26.6	4.1	81.5	−5.4
1983	27.4	16.4	9.0	3.8	1.1	28.4	3.7	89.8	−6.1
1984	29.3	17.6	10.4	4.3	0.8	30.0	3.7	96.0	−3.5
1985	30.8	19.1	11.7	4.7	0.9	32.3	4.1	103.6	−4.9
1986	33.3	20.4	12.3	4.9	1.1	33.4	3.9	109.3	−8.2

Note: Figures for 1981-86 on 1981 preliminary revised national accounts basis.

aCalendar year. bIncludes transfers to hospitals.

Sources: Same at table 18.42.

Table 18.48 Provincial Governments: Main Categories of Expenditure as Percent of Total,
National Accounts Basis, Selected Years, 1947-86

Year[a]	Goods and services	Transfer to persons	Interest on debt	Subsidies	Capital assistance	Transfers to other govern- ments	Capital formation	Total
				percent				
1947	27.5	25.0	12.5	—	—	12.5	12.5	100.0
1953	33.3	26.7	6.7	—	—	13.3	20.0	100.0
1955	33.4	22.2	5.6	—	—	16.7	22.1	100.0
1960	28.6	31.4	2.9	—	—	20.0	17.1	100.0
1965	25.4	15.9	4.8	—	—	39.7	14.2	100.0
1970	29.1	18.4	5.7	1.4	—	38.3	7.1	100.0
1975	30.4	17.4	5.7	2.2	0.6	36.1	7.6	100.0
1977	29.9	18.1	6.5	2.7	0.5	36.5	5.8	100.0
1979	30.8	17.9	7.3	3.0	0.4	35.1	5.5	100.0
1980	31.6	19.2	7.9	3.0	0.5	32.4	5.4	100.0
1981	31.4	18.1	8.9	3.6	0.4	32.3	5.3	100.0
1982	30.2	18.2	9.6	3.7	0.7	32.6	5.0	100.0
1983	30.5	18.3	10.0	4.2	1.2	31.6	4.2	100.0
1984	30.5	18.3	10.8	4.5	0.8	31.3	3.8	100.0
1985	29.7	18.4	11.3	4.5	0.9	31.2	4.0	100.0
1986	30.4	18.6	11.3	4.5	1.0	30.6	3.6	100.0

Based on table 18.47.

Table 18.49   Provincial Governments: Expenditure by Function, Consolidated Finances Basis, 1952-86

Year[a]	Genl. govt.	Prot. of persons and prop.	Trans and Comm.	Health	Social services	Educ.	Nat. res.	Debt charges	General purpose transfers	Other	Total
					billions of dollars						
1952	0.1	0.1	0.4	0.2	0.1	0.2	0.1	0.1	—	—	1.3
1953	0.1	0.1	0.4	0.3	0.1	0.2	0.1	0.1	—	—	1.4
1954	0.1	0.1	0.4	0.3	0.2	0.3	0.1	0.1	—	—	1.5
1955	0.1	0.1	0.5	0.3	0.2	0.3	0.1	0.1	—	—	1.7
1956	0.1	0.1	0.6	0.3	0.2	0.4	0.1	0.1	—	0.1	2.0
1957	0.1	0.1	0.6	0.4	0.2	0.5	0.1	0.2	0.1	—	2.3
1958	0.1	0.1	0.7	0.4	0.3	0.5	0.1	0.2	0.1	0.1	2.6
1959	0.1	0.1	0.8	0.7	0.3	0.7	0.1	0.2	0.1	—	3.1
1960	0.1	0.1	0.8	0.7	0.4	0.7	0.2	0.2	0.1	0.1	3.4
1961	0.1	0.1	0.7	1.0	0.4	0.9	0.2	0.2	0.1	0.1	3.8
1962	0.1	0.2	0.8	1.1	0.5	1.2	0.2	0.2	0.1	—	4.4
1963	0.2	0.2	0.8	1.2	0.5	1.2	0.2	0.2	0.2	0.1	4.8
1964	0.2	0.2	0.9	1.3	0.5	1.4	0.3	0.3	0.2	0.1	5.4
1965	0.3	0.2	1.1	1.5	0.8	1.6	0.2	0.3	0.2	0.4	6.6
1966	0.4	0.3	1.3	1.8	0.9	2.0	0.2	0.3	0.2	0.5	7.9
1967	0.4	0.3	1.3	2.2	1.1	2.7	0.2	0.4	0.3	0.5	9.3
1968	0.5	0.4	1.3	2.6	1.2	3.0	0.3	0.6	0.3	0.6	10.6
1969	0.5	0.5	1.4	3.2	1.3	3.5	0.3	0.7	0.3	0.8	12.5
1970	0.7	0.5	1.5	4.0	1.6	4.1	0.3	0.8	0.3	1.0	14.9
1971	0.8	0.6	1.7	4.6	1.9	4.6	0.4	0.9	0.4	1.3	17.3
1972	0.9	0.7	1.8	5.2	2.1	5.0	0.4	1.1	0.4	1.4	19.1
1973	1.1	0.8	2.1	5.8	2.8	5.5	0.4	1.4	0.6	1.6	22.0
1974	1.7	1.1	2.6	7.1	3.7	6.6	0.6	1.6	0.7	2.3	28.0

(Table 18.49 continued on next page.)

Table 18.49 Continued

billions of dollars

Year[a]	Genl. govt.	Prot. of persons and prop.	Trans and Comm.	Health	Social services	Educ.	Nat. res.	Debt charges	General purpose transfers	Other	Total
1975	1.7	1.2	2.9	8.6	4.7	8.0	2.0	1.7	1.0	2.4	34.2
1976	2.2	1.4	3.0	9.7	5.6	9.2	2.4	2.0	1.1	2.3	38.9
1977	2.6	1.5	3.3	10.6	6.4	10.3	2.8	2.2	1.1	2.6	43.4
1978	2.8	1.6	3.6	11.6	7.1	10.9	3.5	2.8	1.4	3.1	48.4
1979	3.4	1.8	4.0	12.9	8.0	11.9	4.1	3.1	2.5	3.3	55.0
1980	3.4	2.0	4.5	15.2	9.6	13.6	4.8	4.8	1.2	4.0	62.1
1981	3.8	2.4	5.2	18.1	10.8	16.0	4.5	5.9	1.6	4.5	72.8
1982	4.3	2.6	6.1	21.0	13.3	18.3	6.0	7.7	1.6	5.2	86.1
1983	5.0	2.8	5.9	23.0	14.9	19.5	6.0	8.4	1.7	5.6	92.8
1984	5.5	3.1	6.0	24.6	14.7	19.7	6.3	9.7	1.8	5.2	97.6
1985	6.1	3.4	6.6	26.0	17.1	21.8	6.4	11.1	2.0	5.9	106.4
1986	6.5	3.5	6.3	28.1	18.5	21.8	6.9	12.3	1.9	6.1	111.9

Note: Years prior to 1965 not exactly comparable with later years.

[a]Fiscal year nearest December 31 of the year named. [b]Specific purpose transfers are included in the function involved.

Source: Statistics Canada, *Historical Review Financial Statistics of Governments of Canada*, 1952-62; CANSIM; *Historical Statistics of Canada*.

Table 18.50 Local Governments: Revenue, Expenditure, and Balances, National Accounts Basis, 1947-86

Year[a]	Revenue[b]	% of GNP	Expenditure[b]	% of GNP	Surplus or deficit[c]	% of GNP	Surplus or deficit excluding government transfers[c]	% of GNP
	$ bill.	%	$ bill.	%	$ bill.	%	$ bill.	%
1947............	0.6	4.4	0.6	4.4	—	—	-0.1	-0.7
1948............	0.7	4.5	0.7	4.5	—	—	-0.2	-1.3
1949............	0.7	4.2	0.8	4.7	-0.1	-0.6	-0.2	-1.2
1950............	0.8	4.3	0.9	4.9	-0.1	-0.5	-0.3	-1.6
1951............	0.9	4.2	1.1	5.1	-0.2	-0.9	-0.3	-1.4
1952............	1.1	4.5	1.3	5.3	-0.2	-0.8	-0.4	-1.6
1953............	1.2	4.7	1.3	5.0	-0.2	-0.8	-0.4	-1.6
1954............	1.3	5.0	1.5	5.8	-0.3	-1.2	-0.5	-1.9
1955............	1.4	4.9	1.7	6.0	-0.3	-1.0	-0.6	-2.1
1956............	1.6	5.0	1.9	5.9	-0.3	-0.9	-0.7	-2.2
1957............	1.8	5.4	2.1	6.3	-0.3	-0.9	-0.8	-2.4
1958............	2.1	6.0	2.3	6.6	-0.3	-0.9	-0.8	-2.3
1959............	2.3	6.0	2.6	7.1	-0.2	-0.5	-0.9	-2.4
1960............	2.6	6.8	2.8	7.3	-0.2	-0.5	-1.0	-2.6
1961............	2.9	7.3	3.0	7.6	-0.1	-0.3	-1.0	-2.5
1962............	3.2	7.5	3.4	7.9	-0.1	-0.2	-1.2	-2.7
1963............	3.5	7.6	3.7	8.0	-0.2	-0.4	-1.4	-3.0
1964............	3.7	7.4	3.9	7.8	-0.1	-0.1	-1.5	-3.0
1965............	4.2	7.6	4.5	8.2	-0.3	-0.5	-1.9	-3.4
1966............	4.8	7.8	5.2	8.4	-0.3	-0.5	-2.1	-3.4
1967............	5.4	8.1	5.8	8.7	-0.3	-0.5	-2.4	-3.6
1968............	6.0	8.3	6.4	8.8	-0.4	-0.6	-2.7	-3.7
1969............	6.7	8.4	7.2	9.0	-0.5	-0.6	-3.0	-3.8

(Table 18.50 continued on next page.)

Table 18.50   Continued

Year[a]	Revenue[b]	% of GNP	Expenditure[b]	% of GNP	Surplus or deficit[c]	% of GNP	Surplus or deficit excluding government transfers[c]	% of GNP
	$ bill.	%	$ bill.	%	$ bill.	%	$ bill.	%
1970	7.6	8.9	8.1	9.5	−0.5	−0.6	−3.6	−4.2
1971	8.3	8.8	8.8	9.3	−0.5	−0.5	−4.1	−4.3
1972	9.3	8.8	9.5	9.0	−0.2	−0.2	−4.2	−4.0
1973	10.1	8.2	10.6	8.6	−0.5	−0.4	−4.9	−4.0
1974	11.6	7.9	12.4	8.4	−0.8	−0.5	−6.1	−4.1
1975	14.0	8.5	14.6	8.8	−0.6	−0.4	−7.2	−4.4
1976	16.0	8.3	16.8	8.8	−0.8	−0.4	−8.0	−4.2
1977	19.0	9.0	18.8	8.9	−0.2	0.1	−9.0	−4.3
1978	20.3	8.7	20.5	8.8	−0.2	−0.2	−9.5	−4.1
1979	23.5	8.9	22.1	8.4	1.4	0.5	−9.8	−3.7
1980	24.8	8.3	25.0	8.4	−0.2	−0.1	−11.5	−3.9
1981	28.2	8.2	28.4	8.2	−0.2	−0.1	−13.3	−3.3
1982	31.8	8.8	31.7	8.8	0.1	—	−15.4	−4.3
1983	33.7	8.6	33.3	8.5	0.4	0.1	−15.8	−4.0
1984	35.5	8.3	35.0	8.1	0.5	0.1	−16.4	−3.8
1985	37.9	8.2	36.8	8.0	1.1	0.2	−17.1	−3.7
1986	40.0	8.2	38.8	7.9	1.2	0.2	−17.7	−3.6

Note: Figures for 1981-86 on 1981 preliminary revised national accounts basis.
[a] Calendar year. [b] Includes intergovernmental transfers. [c] Includes intergovernmental transfers. [d] Excludes intergovernmental transfers.
Sources: Same as table 18.42.

Table 18.51 Local Governments: Main Categories of Expenditure, National Accounts Basis, 1947-86

Year[a]	Goods and services	Transfer to persons	Subsidies	Interest on debt	Transfers to other govts.	Gross capital formation	Total	Deficit or surplus
				billions of dollars				
1947	0.4	—	—	—	—	0.2	0.6	—
1948	0.5	—	—	—	—	0.2	0.7	− 0.1
1949	0.6	—	—	—	—	0.2	0.8	− 0.1
1950	0.6	—	—	—	—	0.2	0.9	− 0.1
1951	0.7	—	—	—	—	0.3	1.1	− 0.2
1952	0.8	—	—	—	—	0.4	1.3	− 0.2
1953	0.9	—	—	0.1	—	0.3	1.3	− 0.2
1954	1.0	—	—	0.1	—	0.4	1.5	—
1955	1.1	—	—	0.1	—	0.5	1.7	− 0.3
1956	1.2	—	—	0.1	—	0.5	1.9	− 0.3
1957	1.4	—	—	0.1	—	0.6	2.1	− 0.3
1958	1.5	0.1	—	0.1	—	0.6	2.3	− 0.3
1959	1.7	0.1	—	0.2	—	0.6	2.6	− 0.2
1960	1.9	0.1	—	0.2	—	0.6	2.8	− 0.2
1961	2.0	0.1	—	0.2	—	0.7	3.0	− 0.1
1962	2.2	0.1	—	0.3	—	0.8	3.4	− 0.1
1963	2.4	0.1	—	0.3	—	0.9	3.7	− 0.2
1964	2.6	0.1	—	0.3	—	0.8	3.9	− 0.1
1965	3.0	0.1	—	0.3	—	1.1	4.5	− 0.4
1966	3.4	0.1	—	0.4	0.1	1.2	5.2	− 0.3
1967	3.9	0.1	—	0.4	0.1	1.3	5.8	− 0.3
1968	4.4	0.1	—	0.5	0.1	1.3	6.4	− 0.4
1969	5.1	0.1	—	0.5	0.1	1.3	7.2	− 0.5

(Table 18.51 continued on next page.)

Table 18.51   Continued

Year[a]	Goods and services	Transfer to persons	Subsidies	Interest on debt	Transfers to other govts.	Gross capital formation	Total	Deficit or surplus
				billions of dollars				
1970	5.8	0.2	—	0.6	0.1	1.4	8.1	−0.5
1971	6.3	0.3	—	0.7	0.1	1.6	8.8	−0.5
1972	6.8	0.2	—	0.7	0.1	1.6	9.5	−0.2
1973	7.8	0.3	—	0.8	0.1	1.7	10.6	−0.5
1974	9.1	0.2	—	0.9	0.1	2.2	12.4	−0.8
1975	10.8	0.3	—	0.9	0.1	2.5	14.6	−0.6
1976	12.6	0.3	—	1.2	0.1	2.7	16.8	−0.8
1977	14.1	0.3	—	1.4	0.1	2.9	18.8	−0.2
1978	15.5	0.3	—	1.7	0.1	2.9	20.5	−0.2
1979	16.6	0.3	—	1.8	0.1	3.2	22.1	1.4
1980	18.8	0.4	—	2.0	0.1	3.7	25.0	−0.2
1981	21.0	0.5	0.4	2.2	0.2	4.1	28.4	−0.2
1982	23.5	0.6	0.5	2.5	0.1	4.5	31.7	0.1
1983	24.7	0.8	0.5	2.8	0.2	4.3	33.3	0.4
1984	26.2	0.8	0.6	3.0	0.2	4.2	35.0	0.5
1985	27.5	0.9	0.6	3.2	0.2	4.4	36.8	1.1
1986	29.0	1.0	0.6	3.5	0.2	4.5	38.8	1.2

Note: Figures for 1981-86 on 1981 preliminary revised national accounts basis.

[a] Calendar year.

Sources: Same as table 18.42.

Table 18.52 Local Governments: Main Categories of Expenditure as Percent of Total, National Accounts Basis, Selected Years

Year[a]	Goods and services	Transfer to persons	Subsidies	Interest on debt	Transfers to other govts.	Gross capital formation	Total
				percent			
1947	66.7	—	—	—	—	33.3	100.0
1953	69.2	—	—	—	—	23.1	100.0
1955	64.7	—	—	—	—	29.4	100.0
1960	67.8	3.6	—	7.2	—	21.4	100.0
1965	66.7	2.3	—	6.6	—	24.4	100.0
1970	71.6	2.5	—	7.4	1.2	17.3	100.0
1975	74.0	2.1	—	6.2	0.7	17.0	100.0
1980	75.2	1.6	—	8.0	0.4	14.8	100.0
1981	74.0	1.8	1.4	7.7	0.7	14.4	100.0
1982	74.1	1.9	1.6	7.9	0.3	14.2	100.0
1983	74.1	2.4	1.6	8.4	0.6	12.9	100.0
1984	74.9	2.3	1.6	8.6	0.6	12.0	100.0
1985	74.8	2.4	1.6	8.7	0.6	11.9	100.0
1986	74.8	2.5	1.6	9.0	0.5	11.6	100.0

Based on table 18.51.

Table 18.53 Local Governments: Gross Expenditure by Function, Consolidated Finances Basis, 1952-86

Year[a]	Genl. govt.	Prot. of persons and prop.	Trans. and comm.	Health	Social services	Educ.	Environ.	Rec. and cult.	Debt charges	Other	Total
						billions of dollars					
1952	0.1	0.1	0.2	0.1	—	0.3	—	—	0.1	0.1	1.0
1953	0.1	0.1	0.2	0.1	—	0.4	—	—	0.1	0.1	1.1
1954	0.1	0.1	0.2	0.1	—	0.4	—	—	0.1	0.3	1.3
1955	0.1	0.1	0.3	0.1	—	0.5	—	—	0.2	0.2	1.4
1956	0.1	0.2	0.3	0.1	0.1	0.5	—	—	0.1	0.2	1.6
1957	0.1	0.2	0.4	0.1	0.1	0.6	—	—	0.1	0.2	1.8
1958	0.1	0.2	0.4	0.1	0.1	0.6	—	—	0.1	0.3	1.9
1959	0.1	0.2	0.4	0.1	0.1	0.7	—	—	0.2	0.4	2.2
1960	0.1	0.2	0.5	0.1	0.1	0.8	—	—	0.2	0.4	2.4
1961	0.1	0.3	0.5	0.1	0.1	0.8	—	—	0.2	0.4	2.5
1962	0.2	0.3	0.5	0.1	0.1	1.0	—	—	0.2	0.4	2.8
1963	0.2	0.3	0.5	0.1	0.1	1.0	—	—	0.2	0.5	2.9
1964	0.2	0.3	0.5	0.1	0.1	1.0	—	—	0.2	0.6	3.0
1965	0.2	0.4	0.6	0.2	0.1	1.8	—	0.1	0.3	0.8	4.5
1966	0.2	0.4	0.7	0.3	0.1	2.3	—	0.2	0.4	0.8	5.4
1967	0.3	0.4	0.6	0.3	0.1	2.8	—	0.2	0.4	0.9	6.0
1968	0.3	0.5	0.8	0.3	0.2	3.2	—	0.2	0.5	0.8	6.8
1969	0.3	0.5	0.9	0.4	0.2	3.7	—	0.3	0.5	0.7	7.5
1970	0.3	0.6	0.9	0.5	0.3	4.0	—	0.3	0.6	0.8	8.3
1971	0.3	0.6	1.1	0.5	0.4	4.4	—	0.4	0.7	1.0	9.4
1972	0.4	0.8	1.2	0.5	0.4	4.6	—	0.5	0.7	1.2	10.3
1973	0.5	0.9	1.3	0.5	0.5	4.7	—	0.7	0.8	1.3	11.2
1974	0.6	1.0	1.7	0.6	0.5	5.6	—	0.9	0.8	1.6	13.3

1975	0.7	1.2	1.9	0.7	0.5	6.8	1.4	1.0	0.9	0.9	16.0
1976	0.8	1.4	2.1	0.8	0.5	7.8	1.7	1.1	1.2	1.1	18.5
1977	0.9	1.6	2.4	0.9	0.6	9.0	1.8	1.3	1.4	1.1	21.0
1978	1.1	1.7	2.7	1.1	0.7	9.7	2.0	1.4	1.7	1.0	23.1
1979	1.2	1.8	2.8	1.2	0.8	10.5	2.0	1.5	1.8	1.0	24.6
1980	1.5	2.1	3.3	1.4	0.8	11.6	2.4	1.8	2.0	1.2	28.1
1981	1.7	2.5	3.6	1.7	0.9	13.4	2.6	2.0	2.2	1.4	32.0
1982	2.0	2.8	3.9	2.0	1.1	14.6	2.7	2.1	2.6	1.6	35.4
1983	2.1	3.0	3.8	2.0	1.3	15.9	2.9	2.3	2.8	1.6	37.7
1984	2.3	3.2	4.0	2.2	1.4	16.7	3.0	2.4	3.0	1.6	39.8
1985	2.5	3.5	4.1	2.4	1.6	17.4	3.2	2.5	3.1	1.8	42.1

Note: Years prior to 1965 not exactly comparable with later years.

a Fiscal year ended nearest December 31 of year named.

Source: Statistics Canada, Historical Review, Financial Statistics of Government in Canada 1952-62; Local Government Finance; CANSIM; Historical Statistics of Canada.

Table 18.54 Hospital Revenue and Expenditure, National Accounts Basis, 1961-86

Year[a]	Revenue			Expenditure			
	Transfers from government	Capital consumption allowances	Total[b]	Goods and services	Interest on debt	Capital formation	Total
				billions of dollars			
1961	0.7	—	0.8	0.6	—	0.2	0.8
1962	0.8	—	0.8	0.7	—	0.2	0.9
1963	0.9	0.1	0.9	0.8	—	0.2	1.0
1964	1.0	0.1	1.0	0.9	—	0.2	1.1
1965	1.1	0.1	1.2	1.0	—	0.2	1.2
1966	1.3	0.1	1.4	1.2	—	0.2	1.4
1967	1.5	0.1	1.6	1.4	—	0.2	1.6
1968	1.8	0.1	1.9	1.6	—	0.2	1.9
1969	2.0	0.1	2.1	1.9	—	0.2	2.1
1970	2.3	0.1	2.4	2.1	—	0.2	2.4
1971	2.5	0.1	2.7	2.4	—	0.2	2.7
1972	2.9	0.1	3.1	2.7	—	0.2	2.9
1973	3.2	0.1	3.3	3.0	—	0.3	3.3
1974	4.0	0.2	4.2	3.8	—	0.3	4.1
1975	4.8	0.2	5.0	4.6	0.1	0.3	4.9
1976	5.7	0.2	5.9	5.2	0.1	0.3	5.6
1977	6.4	0.2	6.7	5.6	0.1	0.3	6.0
1978	6.7	0.3	7.0	6.2	0.1	0.4	6.6
1979	7.3	0.3	7.7	6.8	0.1	0.4	7.2
1980	8.2	0.3	8.6	7.9	0.1	0.5	8.5
1981	9.6	0.4	10.2	9.4	0.1	0.6	10.1
1982	11.5	0.5	12.2	10.7	0.1	0.7	11.5
1983	12.5	0.6	13.3	11.4	0.1	0.9	12.4
1984	13.4	0.6	14.1	12.0	0.1	0.8	13.0
1985	14.3	0.7	15.2	12.7	0.1	0.8	13.6
1986	15.0	0.7	16.0	13.7	0.1	0.8	14.6

Note: Figures for 1981-86 on 1981 preliminary revised national accounts basis.

[a] Calendar year. [b] Includes minor other revenue.

Sources: Same as table 18.42.

Part 5

The Social Revolution

19
The Canadian Background

Government has made many changes in relations with its citizens in the postwar period, but none have been more radical than in social policy. Hardships once left to be met unaided by the citizen as a private matter are now the concern of government. Help has been given in many ways, most involving the transfer of financial resources through taxation and social services. Grants, pensions, and free or subsidized services have been furnished to temper the trials of old age, retirement, unemployment, family raising, and illness. Expenditures on these programs now constitute the largest category of government outlays, over one-third in 1987.

What is behind this phenomenon? Why, in the four decades since 1945, despite heavy burdens of debt accumulated during the Great Depression and World War II, did Canada launch social programs of an unprecedented scale and expense, collectively known as the Welfare State.

The Welfare State

While the welfare state may appear to be of recent origin, its roots lie many decades deep, buried in the upheavals of the last century that resulted in a complete transformation of social and economic systems. Among the many explanations of this phenomenon that of the Royal Commission on the Economic Union and Development Prospects for Canada (Macdonald Commission) seems particularly appropriate and timely. The Commissioners said:

> The new economic and industrial order left people particularly vulnerable to the loss of earnings of the primary breadwinner during periods of unemployment, illness, disability and old age. At the same time, traditional social institutions, such as the family, the church and the local community, were less and less able to cope with Canadians' social needs. The traditions of private charity, which were an important part of the small, stable and closely knit communities in rural areas and small towns, eroded steadily in the face of a mobile and increasingly urban population. The intense economic and social dislocation of the 1930s graphically demonstrated the inadequacies of the traditional welfare mechanisms and the need for a more comprehensive system of social security . . . The pressures for social reform thus flowed, in the first instance, from economic development . . . The twentieth century witnessed a growing acceptance of the legitimacy of social security and, more generally, a deepening belief in the importance of a wider set of social rights which would complement the legal and political rights already established. In the period that followed the Second World War, these ideas were reinforced by the spread of

economic theories that were much more compatible with significant income redistribution than earlier orthodoxies had been . . . During the first half of the twentieth century, support for the welfare state grew steadily. Intellectuals, social reformers and the developing profession of social work often led the way in documenting the severity of social problems and outlining blueprints for their solution. The emergence of left-wing political protest in the form of the Co-Operative Commonwealth Federation (CCF) generated a third force in Canadian politics that was strongly dedicated to social change. Organized labour, which grew rapidly after the mid-1930s, also became a consistent champion of expansion of the welfare state. In addition to these external pressures, reformist elements developed within the major political parties and in part of the senior civil service. Moreover, established political leaders were clearly sensitive to the broad current of public support for social spending.[19.1]

King and Leacock

Because of their unique and influential position in Canada the roles of two prominent Canadians are of interest. These were Mackenzie King and Stephen Leacock. Writing in the immediate aftermath of World War I both expressed strong belief that a better world would emerge from the shock and horror of this tragic event. Plainly indignant with the shortcomings of Canadian social policy, which had changed little in a century, they urged the adoption of new programs, many of which were already in effect in other countries of the British Empire. King, later to become one of Canada's longest serving and most influential prime ministers, set forth his own agenda for a new society in his *Industry and Humanity*,[19.2] published in 1918. In this book he wrote forcefully of the industrial and social distress he had witnessed in his career as a social worker and labour expert and presented a strong appeal for what he called "A National Minimum of Health and Well-Being For All" and set forth a program for realizing this objective. It is tempting to speculate, in view of his later dominant role in the Liberal party, that much of the ultimate welfare state in Canada was simply the implementation of King's 1918 proposals—a view incidentally accepted by Bruce Hutchison in his biography of King, *The Incredible Canadian*.[19.3]

Leacock, in a long essay published in 1920, the "Unsolved Riddle of Social Justice," wrote with equal force of his conviction that radical changes needed to be made. Many associate his name only with humorous writing, but the following excerpt shows another side of this world-renowned author. "Unemployment," he wrote,

---

[19.1] Canada, *Report of the Royal Commission on the Economic Union and Development Prospects for Canada* (Macdonald Commission), Vol. 2 (Ottawa: Department of Supply and Services, 1985), 545.

[19.2] W.L. Mackenzie King, *Industry and Humanity*, 1918, Social History of Canada Series (Toronto: University of Toronto Press, 1973).

[19.3] Bruce Hutchison, *The Incredible Canadian*, A Candid Portrait of Mackenzie King (Don Mills: Longmans Canada, 1970).

in the case of the willing and able becomes henceforth a social crime. Every democratic government must henceforth take as the starting point of its industrial policy, that there shall be no such thing as able bodied men and women "out of work", looking for occupation and unable to find it. Work must either be found or must be provided by the state itself . . . in one form or another, the economic loss involved in illness and infirmity must be shifted from the shoulders of the individual to those of society at large . . . Put in plainest prose, then, we are saying that the government of every country ought to supply work and pay for the unemployed, maintenance for the infirm and aged, and education and opportunity for the children. These are vast tasks, and they involve, of course, a financial burden not dreamed of before the war.[19.4]

Neither man was to live to see more than a small venture into the world for which they pleaded; Leacock died in 1944 and King in 1950, both having witnessed the distress of the Great Depression and World War II. They were not alone of course in the views they held, nor had they been the first to hold them. But by the time of their death their views had become much more widely accepted, and events were about to move.

Post World War II

The scene—the aftermath of another world war. In the quarter century interim there has been a decade of relative prosperity, followed by a decade of the Great Depression, with economic collapse and misery on a world scale, to be succeeded by five years of another world conflict—World War II. There were a few landmarks in social policy during the quarter century. In 1927 a joint federal-provincial old age pension had been started, under a government led by King. The depression had forced a closer integration of governmental resources for providing relief for the unemployed 25 percent of the work force and for the victims of agricultural crop failures, with the federal government finally assuming principal financial responsibility. Efforts of a Conservative government to introduce broad-scale social measures in 1935 under the Employment and Social Insurance Act had been thrown out by the courts as beyond federal powers. In 1941, with the consent of the provinces, the federal government introduced a contributory plan of unemployment insurance, and in 1945 family allowances were started (both incidentally under governments led by King). These were instalments on a welfare program, but were far short of the objectives of new political parties that emerged during the depression—the CCF and Social Credit—which, combined with increasingly aggressive unions, were promoting much more advanced ideas. Business organizations were becoming more accustomed to activist government following the role assumed at all levels during the depression and war. Plans for comprehensive social security programs had been advanced in the Beveridge Report for Britain

---

[19.4]Stephen Leacock, "The Unresolved Riddle of Social Justice," in *The Social Criticism of Stephen Leacock*, Social History of Canada Series (Toronto: University of Toronto Press, 1973), 28.

and the Marsh Report for Canada. Intensive work had been carried out by committees of officials in Ottawa and the provincial governments for new programs. The stage had been set for action. From these beginnings were to develop programs which by the early eighties were accounting for 38 percent of total government expenditure.

The Canadian Social Security Programs

In addition to the general ethos of the time there were some distinctively Canadian influences which shaped the form of the actual measures.

The Federal System

The imbalance of powers in Canada, under which the provinces have most of the authority in the social area and the federal government has the main revenue sources, has been the cause of considerable confusion between means and objectives. There has been a continual need to reconcile the aims of the federal government with the frequently widely divergent views of the provinces, at least one of which, Quebec, desires exclusive control over social programs for its own citizens. Constant bargaining and compromise have accompanied every step, a condition that has seldom led to neat and clear-cut solutions.

The Provincial Contribution

The federal milieu nonetheless has had its positive side. In several areas provincial initiatives produced systems and practices that were influential in the design of national plans. This was particularly true of hospital and medicare insurance and the Canada Pension Plan, all joint projects. Some provinces have adopted plans for supplementing income of low-income workers, and useful innovations have been made in recent years in provincial and local social services.

Making it Canadian

A certain raggedness has resulted from the degree of improvisation required to suit the experience of other countries to Canadian conditions. Neither the United States nor the United Kingdom, frequently looked to by Canada for guidance, were of much help, as they were following widely divergent paths. Since Canada came fairly late to social legislation there were numerous models in other countries, but none could simply be translated into Canadian terms without massive revision. Canada proceeded, therefore, very much on its own, with a good deal of pragmatic adjustment in the process.

Step-by-Step Approach

The incremental step-by-step approach followed in Canada, while it had some notable advantages, lacked the cohesion that would have resulted from a strong overall guiding philosophy. This is the nature of the democratic process: it is productive of obscure objectives and frequently clumsy means of achieving them.

Indexation

A comprehensive attempt has been made to maintain the value of most parts of the social program in the face of substantial inflation. In the 1973-74 to 1984-85 period indexation added $35 billion to the cost of four programs—OAS, GIS, Spouses' Allowances, and Family Allowances— which otherwise would have amounted to $64 billion, an enhancement of over 50 percent. The bulk of this was for OAS. The present government has discovered to its chagrin that in the case of Old Age Security the indexation that was originally intended only as an act of reason in the face of excessive inflation has become enshrined as an unchangable obligation, in confirmation of the worst forebodings of critics of the welfare state. An adjustment of indexation for certain other programs has been effected, but also against great public resistance.

The Role of the Private Sector

Private sector initiatives have been significant in the social service area. Perhaps the most notable example is the path-breaking role played in the health insurance field by insurance companies, Blue Cross, and similar organizations. The experience they provided was invaluable, but perhaps their most important contribution was in educating the public in the advantages of prepayment for hospital and medical services, an essential prelude to introduction of state-sponsored plans.

The Bottomless Purse

As the history of individual programs reveals, cost estimates presented at the time of their introduction were grossly below ultimate results. But despite this recurring experience new programs and additions to existing programs continued to be introduced. One federal Minister of Finance, the Hon. Mitchell Sharp, was concerned enough to hold off implementation of medicare for a year in the late sixties, but this had no apparent effect as an example for later programs. Despite strong inflationary pressures and growing budget deficits, in the next decade several billions in costs were added through the expansion of Unemployment Insurance, the enrichment of Family Allowances, the introduction of Extended Health Care in 1976 and the Child Tax Credit in 1979. As well, the most extravagant method of indexation—adjustment for the full extent of inflation—was adopted. Ironically, at the same time efforts were being made to control expenditures through consultation with the provinces, by periodic ceilings on indexation, and by adoption of the Established Programs method of financing. One gets the feeling of a rudderless ship steaming ahead at full speed.

Universality

The final criterion of the Canadian program, and the one that has shaped it most conspicuously throughout, is that national measures must be universal. This deeply ingrained sentiment originated in distaste for the procedures used to determine eligibility under selective means-tested programs. It has also been argued that two-level programs—full members and means-tested members—are socially demoralizing. And of course universality has required that programs be governmental. The vast hospital and health insurance program could have been developed through private organizations, with subsidized premiums for low-income groups, if the pressure for universality, particularly from the unions and the NDP had not been so strong. It is not unlikely of course that sponsors of universality in government measures see advantages in eliminating the profit margin required by private enterprise and, as well, the possibility of spreading costs across all incomes through taxation. On the other hand there is a willingness to sacrifice the principle of universality in some circumstances; the Guaranteed Income Supplement, which is an income-tested payment, has met no opposition.

The Actual Programs

There are various ways of categorizing social programs. The chapters which follow have no particular pattern, but deal with the major pieces in the order of their apparent interest and significance at the present time. The headings are:

> Health
> Unemployment Insurance
> Pensions
> > Pensions for Older Citizens
> > Wage-related Government Pensions
> > Private Sector Pensions
> Supplementary Assistance
> Family Income
> The Problem of Poverty

Course of Events

The following is a bare calendar of the main social security events over the total period. As priority is being given in this study to national programs the main emphasis is on federal initiatives. More detailed accounts of these developments are given in later chapters.

The War and Inter-war Period

1919. Following World War I, to assist the provinces with preventive health measures, the federal government gave grants in aid of venereal disease control. These were continued almost throughout the period up to and including World War II.

1927. The federal and provincial governments launched a means-tested Old Age Pension of $20 a month. This was continued, with periodic increases in rate, until 1952, when it was succeeded by Old Age Security.

1935. The federal Parliament passed the Employment and Social Insurance Act giving the government broad powers to introduce social legislation. In the following year the Act was found beyond federal constitutional powers by the Privy Council.

1941. The federal government introduced an Unemployment Insurance Plan, based on employer-employee contributions with federal subsidization.

1943. Marsh Report on Social Security. Dr. Marsh's proposals, representing a comprehensive attack on poverty and insecurity, were based on a broad scheme of social insurance buttressed by family allowances, a national health scheme, and a large-scale national employment program.

1945-1960

1945. The Family Allowances Act was passed by Parliament to provide payment of allowances for children under 16 by the federal government.

____. At the Federal-Provincial Conference on Reconstruction the federal government advanced proposals for contributory old age pensions and a joint health insurance program. With the collapse of the conference none of these proposals was adopted.

1947. Saskatchewan introduced a provincial hospital insurance plan, the first in Canada.

1948. The federal government introduced grants for provincial health services, including hospital construction, which survived until the seventies.

1949. British Columbia introduced a provincial hospital insurance plan.

1951. Federal Old Age Security Act was passed authorizing pensions from January 1, 1952 to persons aged 70 and older without a means test. Revenue from designated taxes was earmarked for OAS.

____. The Old Age Assistance Act was passed to share with provinces from 1952 the cost of income-tested pensions for persons aged 65-69.

1952. Blind Persons Act passed, for similar pensions.

1954. Disabled Persons Act passed for pensions on similar basis.

1956. The federal Hospital Insurance and Diagnostic Services Act was passed to introduce joint federal-provincial hospital insurance. All provinces had plans in effect by 1959.

1957. Ontario appointed the Portable Pensions Committee to recommend changes in provincial laws governing pensions.

1961-1970

1961. The federal government appointed a Royal Commission on Health Services (the Hall Commission), which issued a report in 1964.

____. A Committee of Enquiry (the Gill Committee) was appointed to examine unemployment insurance, and reported in the following year.

1962. Saskatchewan introduced medical care insurance.

1963. Ontario passed the Pension Benefits Act.

1964. British Columbia introduced medical care insurance.

1965. The Old Age Security Act was amended to extend eligibility to persons aged 65 by steps over a five-year period.

1966. The federal Parliament passed the Medical Care Act, providing for a joint federal-provincial system of medical insurance to be effective from July 1968. Provinces entered over the following two years, the last, New Brunswick, in January 1971.

____. The Canada Assistance Plan was passed to extend the scope of federal grants for social services previously provided under legislation passed in 1952.

1967. The wage-related Canada Pension Plan, based on employer-employee contributions, came into effect.

____. Quebec enacted the Quebec Pension Plan, in terms similar to the Canada Pension Plan.

____. The Guaranteed Income Supplement was introduced as an income-tested addition to Old Age Security.

1968. The federal government launched a joint consultation with the provinces on the status of the Canadian constitution.

1969. At a federal-provincial conference the federal government presented a document on Income Security and Social Services as a working paper for clarification of the respective roles of the two levels of government in the social assistance field.

1970-1988

1971. Substantial changes were made in Unemployment Insurance.

1972. The special earmarked taxes for Old Age Security were repealed and henceforth payments were made from general revenues.

1973. A joint federal-provincial review of social security programs commenced. The Minister of National Health and Welfare issued a Working Paper on Social Security in Canada as a basis for discussion.

1974. Family allowances were substantially increased and the basis of payment changed.

1975. The spouses' allowances for spouses aged 60 to 64 was introduced as part of Old Age Security.

1977. The Established Programs Financing Act was enacted to substitute block transfers for shared-cost grants toward post-secondary education and health insurance.

____. The Extended Health Care Act was passed to provide additional health services.

1979. The federal Child Tax Credit was introduced.

1982. The Federal-Provincial Fiscal Arrangements Act was passed to establish a basis of federal transfers for health and post-secondary education for the next five years.

1984. The Canada Health Act was passed to replace existing federal health statutes.

1985. A Commission of Inquiry on Unemployment Insurance was appointed.

_____. A federal consultation paper on Child and Elderly Benefits was issued.

_____. The federal budget of May 23 proposed future changes for child benefits, tax treatment of private pension plans, and indexation under federal government programs.

1988. Federal child care program proposed but not implemented.

Counting the Cost

Accurate and recent information on social expenditures is difficult to obtain. There are several sources and each seems to have its own basis for compilation. The most authoritative information is published by Statistics Canada, as part of its *Consolidated Government Finance* series. The data in Table 19.1 covering the period 1965-66 to 1981-82 are from this source, supplemented by more recent figures from Statistics Canada's CANSIM.

Total health and welfare expenditures of all governments increased from $5.3 billion in 1966-67 to an estimated $92.1 billion in 1987-88, nearly an 18-fold rise. As a share of total government expenditure, this represented an increase from slightly over one-quarter to over one-third. The most significant comparison is the proportion of gross national product devoted to this outlay. The ratio may appear to be lower than concern over the subject would indicate, but each one percent of GNP represents today over $5 billion. The rise has been from 8.6 percent in 1966-67 to 17.1 percent in 1987-88, approximately 50 percent.

Table 19.1   All Governments: Canadian Social Expenditures, 1966-67 to 1987-88

Fiscal year	Health	Social welfare	Total health and social welfare	Total government expenditure	Social expenditures as a percent of Total expenditure	Social expenditures as a percent of Gross national product[a]
		millions of dollars			*percent*	
1966-67	1,995	3,330	5,325	19,318	27.6	8.6
1967-68	2,325	3,944	6,269	22,123	28.3	9.2
1968-69	2,712	4,463	7,175	24,802	28.9	9.7
1969-70	3,474	4,893	8,367	27,995	29.9	10.2
1970-71	4,262	5,808	10,070	31,484	32.0	11.5
1971-72	4,886	6,968	11,854	36,327	32.6	12.4
1972-73	5,478	8,819	14,297	41,009	34.9	13.3
1973-74	6,069	10,620	16,689	47,013	35.5	13.3
1974-75	7,357	13,387	20,744	59,298	35.0	13.8
1975-76	8,961	16,248	25,209	71,810	35.1	14.9
1976-77	10,140	18,447	28,587	80,584	35.5	14.7
1977-78	10,995	20,736	31,731	90,996	34.9	14.9
1978-79	12,039	22,685	34,724	100,436	34.6	14.7
1979-80	13,442	24,839	38,281	112,223	34.7	14.2
1980-81	15,702	29,379	45,081	132,536	34.1	14.9
1981-82	18,800	32,968	51,768	153,545	33.7	15.0
1982-83	21,672	41,852	63,524	179,578	34.8	17.6
1983-84	24,154	47,072	71,226	194,228	36.7	18.1
1984-85	26,130	50,757	76,887	211,715	36.3	17.8
1985-86	27,845	53,592	81,437	224,598	36.3	17.5
1986-87	29,953	57,452	87,405	234,085	37.3	17.7
1987-88	32,150	59,948	92,098	244,101	37.7	17.1

[a]Gross national product for year ending in fiscal year.

Source: Statistics Canada, *Consolidated Government Finance* and CANSIM.

Bibliography, chapter 19

Banting, K.G. *The Welfare State and Canadian Federalism*. Montreal: McGill-Queen's University Press, 1982.

———. "State and Society: Canada in Comparative Perspective." In Keith Banting, research coordinator, *State and Society in a Modern Era*. Collected Research Studies of the Royal Commission on the Economic Union and Development Prospects for Canada. Toronto: University of Toronto Press, 1985.

———. "Universality and the Development of the Welfare State." In Green, Alan, and Olewiler, Nancy, eds. *Report of the Forum on Universality and Social Policies in the 1990s*. Kingston, Ontario: Queen's University, John Deutsch Institute for the Study of Economic Policy, 1985.

Beveridge, Sir William. *Social Insurance and Allied Services*. H.M.S.O.cmd. 6404, 1942.

Burbidge, John. *Social Security for Canada: An Economic Appraisal*. Canadian Tax Paper no. 79. Toronto: Canadian Tax Foundation, 1987.

Business Council on National Issues. *Social Policy Reform and the National Agenda*. Ottawa: the Council, 1986.

Canada. *Income Security and Social Services*. Working Paper on the Constitution. Ottawa, 1969.

———. Department of National Health and Welfare. *Income Security for Canadians*. Ottawa: 1970.

———. Minister of National Health and Welfare. Working Paper on Social Security in Canada. Ottawa: 1973.

———. Minister of Reconstruction. *Employment and Income*. Ottawa: 1945.

———. Royal Commission on Dominion Provincial Relations. *Report*. Ottawa: 1940.

———. Royal Commission on Economic Union and Development Prospects for Canada. *Report*, vol. 2. Ottawa: 1985, chaps. 19 and 20, and Conclusions and Recommendations.

———. Statistics Canada. *Social Security (National Programs)*. Ottawa: 1976, and 1978.

———. *Working Paper on Social Security in Canada*. Ottawa: 1973.

Canadian Council on Social Development. *Social Policies for Canada*. Canadian Welfare Council (previous name of Canadian Council on Social Development) Ottawa: the Council, 1969.

———. *Social Security for Canada*. Ottawa: the Council, 1958 and 1973.

———. *Social Policies for the Eighties*. Ottawa: the Council, 1981.

———. "Proposals for short term reform." Ottawa: (Winter 1988) 12 *Perception*, 5-10.

———. "Social Development: A Progress Report." (Spring 1988) *Perception*, Special Issue.

———. "Towards Social Reform-WIN: Work and Income in the Nineties." (Fall 1986) *Social Development Overview*, 1-16.

Clark, R.M. *Economic Security for the Aged in the United States and Canada*. Ottawa: Department of National Health and Welfare, 1959. (mimeographed).

Collins, Kevin. "Three Decades of Social Security in Canada." (January-February 1976) 51 *Canadian Welfare*, 5-9.

Courchene, Thomas J. *Social Policy in the 1990s; Agenda for Reform*. Policy Study no. 3. Toronto: C.D. Howe Institute, 1987.

Courchene, Thomas J., Conklin, David W., and Cook, G.C.A. eds. *Ottawa and the Provinces: The Distribution of Money and Power*. Toronto: Ontario Economic Council, 1985.

Flora, Peter, and Heidenheimer, H.J. eds. *The Development of Welfare States in Europe and America*. London: Transaction Books, 1984.

Grauer, A.E. *Public Assistance and Social Insurance*. Royal Commission on Dominion Provincial Relations. Appendix 6. Ottawa: Queen's Printer, 1940.

Handleman, Stephen. "Raising the axe again to cut the welfare tree." *The Toronto Star*, June 8, 1985.

Heclo, Hugh. "Towards a New Welfare State." In *The Development of Welfare States in Europe and America*. London: Transaction Books, 1984.

Hunsley, Terry. "A Warming Climate for Reform." (June 1986) 5 *Policy Options*, 9-13.

Kent, Tom. *Towards a Philosophy of Social Security*. Paper presented to the Study Conference on National Problems. Kingston: September, 1960.

King, W.L. Mackenzie. *Industry and Humanity, 1918*. Social History of Canada Series. Toronto: University of Toronto Press, 1973.

Laidler, David. "Approaches to Economic Well-Being." In David Laidler, research coordinator, *Economic Ideas and Social Issues*. Collected Research Studies of the Royal Commission on the Economic Union and Development Prospects for Canada, vol. 26. Toronto: University of Toronto Press, 1985.

Lalonde, Mark. Address. In *Report of Proceedings of the Twenty-Fifth Tax Conference*, 1973 Conference Report. Toronto: Canadian Tax Foundation, 1974.

Leacock, Stephen. "The Unsolved Riddle of Social Justice." In *The Social Criticism of Stephen Leacock*. Social History of Canada Series. Toronto: University of Toronto Press, 1973.

Marsh, L. *Social Security for Canada (1943)*. Report. Reprint. Toronto: University of Toronto Press, 1975.

Meech Lake Accord, The. (September 1988) *Canadian Public Policy*. 14 Supplement.

National Council on Welfare. *Statement on Social Security*. Ottawa: the Council, 1971.

Ontario Economic Council. *Social Security, Issues and Alternatives*, 1976. Toronto: the Council, 1976.

Pinker, Robert. *The Idea of Welfare*. London: Heinemann Educational Books Ltd. 1979.

Quebec. *Income Security*. Report of the Commission of Enquiry on Health and Social Welfare (Castonguay-Nepveu Report). Quebec: 1971.

_____. Ministere des Finances. *White Paper on the Personal Tax and Transfer Systems*. Introductory Paper. Quebec: 1984.

Reisman, D.A., and Richard Titmuss. *Welfare and Society*. London: Heinemann Educational Books Ltd., 1977.

United Kingdom. *Reform of Social Security*. London: Her Majesty's Stationery Office, 1985.

United Nations. International Labor Organization. *Into the 21st Century: The Development of Social Security*. Geneva: The Organization, 1983.

United States. Natural Resources Planning Board. *Security, Work and Relief Policies*. Washington: the Board, 1942.

Vaillancourt, Francois. "Income Distribution and Economic Security in Canada." In Francois Vaillancourt, research coordinator, *Income Distribution and Economic Security in Canada*. Collected Research Studies of the Royal Commission on the Economic Union and Development Prospects for Canada, vol. 1. Toronto: University of Toronto Press, 1985.

"The Withering of Europe's Welfare States." *The Economist*, October 16, 1982, 67.

Health

20
Hospital Insurance—the First Step

One of the most dramatic symbols of the welfare state has been the transfer of health care for the Canadian mass of the population from an almost exclusively private and personal matter to one primarily of public financing and administration. A massive project, one of the most ambitious ever undertaken in Canada—hospital and medical health care—is now the largest single expenditure of Canadian governments. The effects of this revolution have been profound and have dramatically altered the lives of millions of Canadians to a degree that only those whose life-span encompasses pre-medicare days can fully appreciate.

Whatever shortcomings the public approach may have, and there are several, at least it is generally conceded that it has relieved individual Canadians of the often catastrophic financial consequences of illness. In this respect lower income and older Canadians have especially benefited. The assumption by the state of virtually the full cost of medical care is an instance of the income redistribution implicit in all welfare policies.

The term "health insurance," which is used frequently in the present and later chapters, has some obvious shortcomings. Health cannot be insured, otherwise we would all be constantly healthy. Nor do the publicly-operated plans in Canada meet insurance principles such as the setting of premiums to reflect the risk experience of the person or group involved. A more accurate term is "prepayment of medical care expenses," but this too has shortcomings. Many recipients of health care in fact meet only a small part of its cost through prepayment. However, given its generality of use we will employ the term "health insurance" most frequently. "Private health insurance" and "public health insurance" will be used to distinguish between private and public programs of organized financial prepayment, the former through the Blue Cross type of plan, plans of professional medical organizations, and insurance companies, and the latter through governments or governmental agencies. This distinction is highly relevant in view of the struggle between the two for dominance.

Role of Governments

The effect of the distribution of powers on the social security program has already been emphasized; nowhere are the consequences more apparent than in the area of health care. Jurisdiction over health matters is clearly within provincial competence, and is a right which they have jealously guarded and exercised. The existing public insurance plans in Canada are provincial measures, financed and managed according to provincial priorities, over which the federal government exercises some tutelage by virtue of footing a substantial share of the cost. The federal government achieved its objective of national programs by offering financial assistance to the provinces in three steps: first, the granting from 1948 on of substantial funds for hospital construction and other public health activities; second, the enactment of the Hospital Insurance and Diagnostic Services Act in 1958, to assist in the financing of provincial hospital insurance; and third, the enactment of the Medical Care Act in 1968, to assist in the financing of provincial health care insurance. The offer of federal money for these programs was more than any province could resist, and all accepted, some more willingly than others. The result has been the national health care plan, which most Canadians regard with some pride and satisfaction.

The Beginnings

There were signs of concern over the financial hazards of ill health in our earliest history. The *Report of the Royal Commission on Health Services* records such instances as a contract for medical services between 17 men and their families and a master surgeon in Ville-Marie (Montreal) in 1665; an offer by St. Joseph's Hospital, in Victoria, B.C., to provide doctors' visits, hospital admission, and medicines for $1 per month; and a medical check-off for employees of a Glace Bay colliery as early as 1883 to cover medical and hospital treatment. Later, other mining companies, including Hollinger Consolidated Gold Mines and Consolidated Mining and Smelting, adopted this model. There were isolated instances of hospitals offering medical and hospital treatment on a prepayment basis, such as the Medicine Hat General Hospital in 1889 and the Hotel Dieu in Chatham, New Brunswick. The Report commented that "These scattered examples, developed around the turn of the century, were clearly the forerunners of our present prepayment system."

The Western Provinces

The three prairie provinces and British Columbia evidenced interest in prepaid public health programs long before most of the rest of the country. Their experience is unique—and enlightening.

Saskatchewan

The hard years of early settlement on the prairies gave birth to some of the first government-inspired moves toward prepaid public health care. The Saskatchewan rural municipalities led the way. Under the Union Hospitals Act of 1916 local municipalities were authorized to set up hospitals to serve their common needs—in effect, a municipal prepayment hospital care program which some municipalities financed through land taxes levied on their residents. Similar although more limited programs were set up under Alberta legislation in the same period.

Concurrently in Saskatchewan the Municipal Doctors system appeared. It began with the initiative taken in 1914 by one municipality paying the salary of the town's only doctor, who was about to leave. There followed an amendment in 1916 to the Rural Municipalities Act to authorize rural municipalities to levy land taxes for this purpose, a right soon extended to other municipalities. Under the Municipal and Medical Hospital Services Act of 1939 the taxing right was extended to include a personal tax not exceeding $50 per family. By 1948, the peak year, 107 municipalities, 59 villages, and 14 towns were employing 180 doctors either on a part- or full-time basis. It is recognized that despite serious shortcomings the Municipal Doctors system ensured that thousands of rural residents of Saskatchewan had access to rudimentary medical services that isolation and cash shortages would otherwise have put beyond their reach. This background also explains Saskatchewan's implementation of provincial hospital insurance in 1947 and medical care insurance in 1962, both long before federal assistance became available.

British Columbia

British Columbia also evidenced an interest in health insurance as long ago as World War I, although at a provincial rather than municipal level. In 1919 the province appointed a royal commission to study the subject, but no action was taken. Constant discussion in the Legislature finally resulted in the appointment of a second royal commission in 1929 which, in its 1932 report, recommended a system of compulsory health insurance. To implement this proposal a Health Insurance Commission was appointed, legislation was drafted, a plebiscite was held, with affirmative results, but just before the plan was to come into effect in 1937, it was dropped because of continuing opposition. There followed the establishment of the doctor-sponsored Medical Services Associated in 1940, which filled the need for a prepayment plan for some years. It was consistent with this background that British Columbia, like Saskatchewan, introduced a hospital insurance program in 1949 and medical care insurance in 1965, in both instances before federal legislation had been passed.

Alberta

The Alberta legislature showed passing interest in health insurance, but with minimal results. A legislative inquiry reported in 1929 that public health services needed improvement. A commission was appointed in 1932 to report on prepaid medical insurance, a proposal which it supported in a 1934 report. In 1935 a comprehensive health insurance act was passed, but was not brought into effect. Further acts were passed in 1942 and 1946, but were either repealed or allowed to lapse. A modest Maternity Health Care system was introduced in 1944, and in 1949 subsidies were paid to assist with municipal hospital care programs. In 1963 the Alberta Medical Plan was introduced to subsidize membership of low income persons in Medical Services (Alberta) Incorporated. No further public action was taken until the federal plans became available.

Manitoba

Manitoba evidenced some interest in prepaid services but little action was taken. In the early years of the depression a legislative committee proposed extension of the limited municipal doctors plan and consideration of health insurance for urban areas but little seems to have resulted from these proposals. In 1945 the Legislature passed the Health Services Act which provided for several major health care developments, including prepaid physicians' services and hospital insurance, but only minor parts of this program were implemented.

Other Provinces

Interest in government-sponsored programs was limited almost completely to provinces west of Ontario. In 1935 Newfoundland established its Cottage Hospital and Medical Care Plan, mainly for outport residents, but of course it was not yet a part of Canada. In 1935 Ontario initiated free home and office physicians' services for persons receiving public assistance, a considerable proportion of the population during the Great Depression, a precedent followed by the western provinces and Nova Scotia. In 1942 Quebec appointed a commission on hospital services, which recommended a system of health insurance. A Health Insurance Commission, established in 1943, was abolished in 1945 on a change in government.

Private Prepaid Plans

This was the era of private hospital and health insurance in the central and eastern provinces, and for the meantime public prepaid care programs were put aside. Indeed, despite interest in public plans in western Canada, private plans were also successfully established there.

The private plans originated mainly with provincial hospital associations and physicians' organizations and with insurance companies. A survey made by the Canadian Medical Association in 1934 revealed that there were already 27 hospital-sponsored prepayment plans in operation in six provinces. The Edmonton Group Hospitalization Plan, involving all four hospitals, and the plan of the two hospitals in Kingston, Ontario were cited as path-breaking efforts. From these beginnings programs of broader scope developed. The most familiar of these is the Blue Cross, which is still in operation. The first Canadian Blue Cross plan was authorized for Winnipeg in 1938; enrolment was soon extended to the whole province under the Manitoba Blue Cross. This successful initiative was followed in most other provinces: Ontario in 1941, Quebec in 1942, and the Maritimes and British Columbia in 1943 and 1944. The sponsorship of Blue Cross varied from province to province; usually hospital associations or community social groups were involved, and much of the organizational work was voluntary. The Ontario Hospital Association Blue Cross had the largest membership —over 2.3 million by 1958, representing 39 percent of the province's population. It was typical of the volunteer operation of this program that the author organized a group in the federal Department of Finance where he was employed during the 1940s, and thousands of others were doing the same in their places of employment. On the whole it was a very satisfactory exercise in self-help. Coverage was for basic public ward hospital care and in-hospital treatment.

Professionally Sponsored Medical Care Plans

A counterpart non-governmental development in prepaid medical care was the growth of plans sponsored by the medical profession in several provinces. Starting in 1939 with models in Windsor, Ontario and Regina, Saskatchewan, a province-wide plan was introduced in British Columbia in 1940 and by 1948 there were similar plans in Manitoba, Ontario, Alberta, and Nova Scotia. The Blue Cross added medical benefits in Quebec, Ontario, and the Maritimes. Although coverage was far from universal, by 1961 nearly five million members were enrolled in these plans, again a remarkable record.

Commercial Insurance

Several companies offered various forms of medical insurance coverage. The majority of members were enrolled through groups in their places of employment, but individual contracts were also sold. A survey made by the Royal Commission on Health Services showed that over 4.6 million Canadians were covered by commercial insurance.

The Drive for Universality

Allowing for some overlapping of membership it seems clear that by 1960 at least 9 million Canadians, of a total population of approximately 18½ million, were covered for prepaid medical care of one form or another. For a substantially voluntary, i.e. non-governmental, movement this was an impressive showing. However, in the social and political climate of the fifties and sixties the lack of universality was a fatal weakness. Supporters of public programs (the unions, the CCF party, and gradually the federal Liberals) argued that only under compulsory government plans could coverage be provided for all, including the poor and the handicapped. Supporters of the private approach (the Conservative party, the medical establishment, the insurance companies, and some provincial premiers) countered that it was not necessary to erect an elaborate government bureaucracy and rob medical practitioners of their professional standing to achieve this end; it could easily be reached by having government subsidize the membership of lower income persons. The counter-argument, passionately advanced by egalitarian proponents, was that this would reduce a substantial element in society to the status of second-class membership by requiring submission to a means test for eligibility, a device fast becoming unpopular.

For over two decades following the end of the war and during the gestation period of the health insurance programs the controversy between these two opposing positions went on whenever the issue arose. Events moved slowly, but in retrospect it seems almost inevitable that the ultimate result was to be prepaid hospital and medical care programs for all Canadians under government-sponsored programs. The provincial governments remained key players, but the new element, and the one that eventually led to adoption of a universal national health program, was the intervention of the federal government.

Limited Federal Response

Until the 1940s, the federal government's interest in health concerns appears to have been intermittent and limited largely to its constitutional responsibilities. A Department of Health had been established in 1919; in 1928 this became the Department of Pensions and National Health, and in 1944 the Department of National Health and Welfare. Much of the activity of the Department related to interprovincial and international drug, disease, and similar matters, including the administration of food, drugs, narcotics, and patent medicine legislation, quarantine, international health, and venereal disease control. It had become involved in the latter in 1919 with a grants program to provincial governments to aid preventive work during the rampant spread of venereal disease following World War I. The grants had been paid until 1932-33, when they were discontinued, except for a minor amount in aid of the distribution of medicines.

Renewed concern over a revival of venereal disease in World War II led to resumption of grants in 1943-44; they were merged with other general health grants in 1948. (In the light of present concern over AIDS this activity has more than passing interest.) Another program in tune with current thought was passage of the National Fitness Act in 1943, under which grants were paid to the provinces in aid of efforts to improve general physical health.

With main responsibility for health matters in provincial hands communications between levels of government was essential. A useful medium was the Dominion Council of Health, consisting of the Chief Medical Officer of Health of each province, a scientific adviser, four lay members and the Deputy Minister of National Health, who acted as Chairman. The Council was helpful in a coordinating role, and played an active part later in the development of federal-provincial insurance programs; its existence did not alter the fact, however, that the main burden of health needs of the day fell almost exclusively on the provincial and municipal governments.

In 1943 total health expenditures of all governments amounted to $11.2 million. Of this the federal government accounted for only $1.1 million, of which over one-third was for the fitness and venereal diseases grants. The balance, or $10.1 million, was spent by provincial and local governments. In addition the heavy expense of mental institutions and tuberculosis sanitoriums fell on the provinces. (Incidentally, the *daily* expenditure on health in 1985 by Canadian governments was approximately $76 million).

Federal Interest in Health Insurance

The Liberal party is said to have adopted health insurance as a part of its platform in 1919, but there was no evidence of further interest for a decade. In 1928 the House of Commons asked the Standing Committee on Industrial and International Relations to investigate unemployment, sickness, and disability insurance, and the committee recommended in the following year that a study be made of a national health program. The next significant parliamentary action was the passage of the Employment and Social Insurance Act in 1935, the main feature of an election platform that the depression-ridden Conservative government hoped would return it to power in the election of 1936. The Act established an Administrative Commission to develop various forms of social insurance for enactment by the government, including health insurance; it succeeded neither in winning the election nor in surviving an appeal to the Supreme Court and the Privy Council, both bodies holding it beyond the powers of the federal Parliament. (The judicial decisions were as significant as the failed legislation, as they established the guidelines for later federal social measures).

The issue of health insurance regained momentum through the recommendations of the 1940 Report of the Royal Commission on Dominion-Provincial Relations, which suggested that the federal government was in the best position to finance a health insurance plan. From 1941 forward health insurance was a regular feature of the federal health agenda, particularly in meetings of the Dominion Council of Health whose members were receptive to studying insurance proposals. The Minister of Pensions and National Health gave formal status to health insurance studies by the appointment of an Advisory Committee on Health Insurance in February 1942, later known as the Heagerty Committee after its chairman, the Director of Public Health Services in the Department. These efforts were greatly encouraged by the adoption by the Canadian Medical Association in January 1943 of a resolution approving health insurance in principle.

Events appeared to be moving forward rapidly in 1943 and 1944. A Select Committee on Social Security of the House of Commons was appointed by the government with a mandate to develop "a comprehensive national scheme of social insurance . . . which will constitute a charter of social security for the whole of Canada." Primarily it was expected to investigate a national system of health insurance and a more generous plan of old age pensions. We will examine the old age pensions issue later. The committee held extensive hearings on a report and a draft bill on health insurance prepared by the Advisory Committee. These produced an unprecedented interest in health insurance; 32 groups appeared, represented by 117 witnesses. Not all witnesses favoured health insurance, but on the basis of a strong majority support the Committee in its report to the House of Commons in July approved the proposal in principle. The Committee later held further hearings which resulted in modifications of the details of the plan. Its final recommendation was that the bill to implement the proposals be submitted to a Dominion-Provincial Conference.

The government committed itself in the Throne Speech opening the 1944 session to programs for both national health insurance and old age security. In order to sound out provincial reaction to its health insurance proposals it held a meeting of Ministers of Health in Ottawa in May 1944, the result of which was their approval in principle. Rather than hold a special meeting of First Ministers on this subject it was decided to add health insurance to the agenda of a postwar Conference on Reconstruction planned for August 1945.

Reconstruction Conference

The Reconstruction Conference of 1945 represented a bold attempt by the federal government to establish some permanent ground rules for governmental relations in the postwar period. In essence, its proposals would have left the federal government with the main powers that it had exercised during the war, particularly in fiscal and economic matters. In a paper on Employment and Income presented to Parliament earlier in the year it adopted Keynesian economic policies without reservation, and the government was convinced that it must continue to have exclusive control over the main tax sources to implement this pledge. The Wartime Tax Agreements were to expire in 1947, and the principal purpose of the conference therefore was to persuade the provinces to renew these or similar agreements. A complementary objective was to expand the program of social measures that would also play an essential part in the new postwar role of government. In 1945 these included old age pensions (1927), unemployment insurance (1940), and family allowances (1945). Health insurance and better old age pensions were to be next on the agenda.

The Conference discussions were almost exclusively devoted to a series of ten "Green Books" presented by the federal government. These contained a comprehensive review of many areas of postwar Canada requiring government action; the author can still recall his own incredulity on first receiving a set. Having then been in government for the decade that spanned the final years of the Depression and the daily trauma of wartime crises, he knew full well that the small group of ministers and officials who had carried this crushing burden were verging on complete exhaustion; in fact in some cases were ill. The end of hostilities had renewed flagging energies, but the group was bone weary, and faced no surcease to their efforts. The coming of peace simply brought a range of new and equally urgent issues. The comprehensive material presented to the conference was therefore a remarkable tribute to the resilience and dedication of this small group.

In the end the hopes that were held for the conference were disappointed. The federal government had misjudged the mood of the central provinces, which far from being willing to accept continued federal control over the tax and fiscal system, only wished for the immediate and full restoration of their former powers. Intervening discussions and formal renewal of the August conference in April 1946, brought ultimate failure, with none of the objectives accomplished. The later partial success of the federal government in achieving its tax objectives is another story. But it is the fate of the health proposals that concerns us here.

The 1945 Health Insurance Proposal

The draft proposal presented to the conference was very much an interim version, the result of revisions in the Advisory Committee draft from provincial input, committee hearings and some high-level reworking by senior federal officials. The full text as presented to the conference is given in an appendix to this chapter. Briefly, it contemplated an initial program of planning and organizational grants to enable the provinces to prepare for introduction of the health plan within a reasonable time. This would be done in two stages. Stage 1 would cover general practitioner service, hospital care, and visitor nursing service. Under a second stage, specialist care, dental service, pharmaceutical and laboratory services would be introduced. The first phase, when fully operative, was expected to cost $115 million a year, of which the federal government would contribute about two-thirds. Cost for the total final program was estimated at $250 million, of which the federal government would also contribute about two-thirds. In addition, and quite apart from the health insurance program, the federal government over a period of years would pay for health grants, estimated at $13.6 million. (This was the direct genesis of the later program, and covered almost identical areas). Finally, the federal government would give low interest loans for the construction of hospitals.

These were regarded as radical proposals at the time, and were seminal for later developments. However, in typical Canadian fashion, nothing worked out quite as planned. The main attention at the conference was absorbed by the crucial issue of dividing up peacetime fiscal resources, and little time was given to other proposals. Not surprisingly the most extensive comment was submitted by Saskatchewan, then on the eve of launching its own hospital care plan. In a thoughtful presentation it made 19 proposals, some of which influenced later developments. Ontario and one or two other provinces cautioned that their health facilities were already over-burdened and would require expansion before additional services were assumed. Timing therefore was far from the original design. It would be 20 years before a health insurance plan was finally implemented, and it would be preceded by a hospital insurance program, which in turn had been preceded by a national hospital construction program, in which assistance took the form of outright grants rather than low-interest loans. And dental services never have been introduced on a national basis; this has been left to the initiative of the provinces.

Financial Implications

The current most pressing concern, the financial implications, received astonishingly little attention in 1945, and one gathers that few foresaw the course of subsequent events. Federal financial officials had been able to exert some restraining influence in the conceptual stages of the measures, initially through the Economic Advisory Committee chaired by the Deputy Minister of Finance, and later (November 1943) by the appointment of a committee of officials on health insurance financing. This committee worked closely with the federal-provincial committee of health officials and influenced the financing proposals that were finally approved by the House Special Committee on Social Insurance. There is no indication, however, that they were motivated by other than ordinary caution in approaching a new policy of government.

At this remove it is difficult to bring the health care expenditures of this period into focus. In effect what was being proposed was that substantially all expenditures on health be transferred from the private purse to the public budget; therefore it was total health expenditures that were relevant for this purpose. The data available at the time of the conference related to 1943, when total Canadian health expenditures were less than $300 million. Of this, $250 million was being spent by the public, and it was this amount that would be added to government budgets. A slightly more realistic set of data, less affected by wartime conditions, is that for 1947. By that time health expenditures had risen to $345 million, of which the public was spending about $275 million.

On a per capita basis total expenditure was in the $21-$23 level; as a ratio of GNP it was at the 2.6-2.7 percent level. Moving ahead to current times the degree of change over four decades is almost beyond comprehension. The figure that compares with the $345 million for 1947 is an estimated $39.8 billion for 1985. The per capita cost is $1,568, and the ratio to GNP has increased over three times to 8.6-8.8 percent. Obviously expenditures of this magnitude were unforeseen in 1945.

Under the 1945 proposals the federal government estimated that $100 million of the additional costs would fall on the provinces and $150 million on the federal budget. It was thought that these expenditures would be financed on a contributory basis, the favoured approach in Ottawa at this period. The Advisory Committee had proposed that the provinces levy a per capita tax of $12 to meet their costs, and it appears to have intended that a similar levy, though higher in amount, would be imposed by the federal government. These proposals were abandoned in advance of the Reconstruction Conference, along with the Committee's proposed model act for provincial enactment, and no specific suggestions for financing were put forward. The federal government's thinking was that it would simply undertake to pay a maximum of 60 percent of forecast expenditures, and leave the problem of financing the rest to the provinces. It apparently had in mind a "social security tax," based on income, to cover its share. Unfortunately the provinces, in the absence of any other proposal for provincial financing, addressed themselves to the Advisory Committee's abandoned per capita tax, on which the Premier of Ontario poured scorn as a "poll tax." Saskatchewan raised doubts because it felt that the dual taxes would not be accepted by the public. This was where the whole issue of public health insurance and its financing was left following the break-up of the conference in April 1946. It would be another quarter-century before all the pieces would come together.

Saskatchewan Goes Ahead

The long experience of Saskatchewan with local public health programs made it a natural candidate for adopting comprehensive provincial measures independently of federal initiatives. The CCF party in opposition had pressed for health insurance, and the incumbent Liberal government had appointed a Select Special Committee on Social Security and Health Services to hold hearings in 1943. This committee was re-appointed in February 1944; upon receipt of a copy of the bill prepared by the Heagerty

Committee, it recommended that the province prepare for the introduction of the federal program. With uncharacteristic haste, within a matter of weeks the government had introduced "A Bill Respecting Health Insurance" and Royal Assent was given on April 1, 1944. This was to have been the winning plank in a platform for an election on June 15, but the government was defeated, and the CCF party came to power with a substantial majority. The new government took immediate steps to implement its strong commitment to health insurance. With a view to the long term, it appointed a Planning Staff. For specific advice on immediate steps, it appointed a one-man Health Commission, to be assisted by a corps of medical and administrative experts. As an interim token of its intentions it adopted a full medical care insurance program for all persons receiving social assistance.

Following a recommendation in the report of the Health Commissioner a permanent five-member Health Services Planning Commission was appointed in 1945 to draw up specific proposals. The Commission gave first priority to the state of hospital services in the province, and proposed adoption of the Hospital Services Plan, under which in return for payment of a compulsory monthly premium all citizens in the province would be given free hospital care at standard ward level. Extensive discussions were held with all groups concerned. Little opposition was encountered and legislation was introduced and passed at the Spring session of the legislature in 1946. The plan became operative on January 1, 1947.

It is acknowledged that Saskatchewan performed a unique and valuable service for the later introduction of general hospital insurance in the other provinces; it had done so at considerable expense to the provincial treasury, as no federal contributions were available until 1954. Professor Malcolm Taylor, in his epical volume, *Health Insurance and Canadian Public Policy*, stated: "All of Canada benefitted from the Saskatchewan experience. From its inception until the Quebec Hospital Plan came into effect in 1961, no provincial government failed to send its officials to Regina to learn at first hand how the programs operated, and what policies and procedures could be adapted to their home provinces."[20.1]

British Columbia Follows

British Columbia followed quickly upon the Saskatchewan action. Under the Hospital Insurance Service Act of 1948 it established a compulsory system of insurance along much the same lines. The plan was snarled for a period in the administrative difficulties of collecting premiums, but these were finally overcome in 1952. Premiums were replaced by an increase in the provincial sales tax from 3 to 5 percent.

[20.1] M.G. Taylor, *Health Insurance and Canadian Public Policy: The Seven Decisions that Created the Canadian Health Insurance System* (Montreal: McGill-Queen's University Press, 1978), 104.

Alberta Goes Part Way

By 1950 Alberta had introduced a hospital insurance plan for maternity cases and for recipients of social assistance. In that year it added to these a plan under which municipalities were authorized to enter into a contract with hospitals to provide ward care for all ratepayers and their dependants. Not all municipalities entered into the arrangement so coverage was not universal, an estimated one-quarter of residents being excluded.

Federal Health and Hospital Construction Grants

While much of the enthusiasm for health measures had been cooled by the outcome of the Reconstruction Conference, the hope of making some progress had not been abandoned in Ottawa. A new Minister of Health and Welfare, the Hon. Paul Martin, persuaded the Prime Minister, then on the verge of retirement, that the government should at least proceed with the medical services and hospital building grants, as these would prepare the way for later more comprehensive measures. Both forms of assistance had been offered in the 1945 proposals, and subsequent experience had underlined their importance. In particular the rapid acceleration of demand for hospital services under the Blue Cross and similar plans had revealed a shortage of hospital beds and given higher priority to the construction of additional facilities.

The Prime Minister announced the national health grants program in May 1948. It included an annual amount of $13 million for matching grants for hospital construction (in place of the low-interest loans previously proposed) and annual grants for general health services, totalling nearly $17 million, as follows: general public health, $4.4 million; mental health, $4.0 million; tuberculosis control, $3.0 million; cancer control, $3.5 million; crippled children, $500,000; professional training, $500,000; venereal disease control, $275,000; public health research, $100,000, the latter to be increased over five years to $500,000; $645,000 for health survey grants, to be used partly to prepare for health insurance. No special taxes or tax increases were announced for these expenditures; they were to be paid from the general budget. The Prime Minister stated that the measures represented "the first stages in the development of a comprehensive health insurance plan for all Canada."

No time limitation was specified but the results of the plan were to be appraised at the end of five years. The hospital construction matching grants were $1,000 for active treatment beds and $1,500 for chronic beds, with an objective of 46,000 beds in total over the first five years. This objective was achieved, but a bed shortage remained in 1953 and the grants were therefore continued. The total annual commitment was cut in half, to $6.7 million. Bed shortages remained throughout the fifties and sixties, but in gradually diminishing numbers. In 1958 the grants were increased to $2,000 for each type of bed, and hospitals continued to be built. The program was finally terminated on March 31, 1970. By this time some $325 million had been paid out and over 130,000 new beds provided, of which 87,100 were active care, 24,600 were mental, 13,200 were chronic-convalescent and 5,300 were for tuberculosis.

In 1953 three additional types of health grant were introduced: child and maternal care, ($500,000 rising to $2.0 million); laboratory and radiological services, ($4.3 million rising to $7.0 million); medical rehabilitation, ($1 million). Further changes were made following the introduction of hospital insurance in 1960. Some grants were discontinued and others were merged, but those for general health care, mental health, and professional training were increased, and henceforth accounted for two-thirds of the total. Other grants continued throughout were those for tuberculosis, cancer control, public health research, medical rehabilitation, crippled children, and child and maternal health.

With the introduction of medicare the program was phased out over a three-year period ending March 31, 1972, except for the public health research grant and the grant for professional training. In recent years grants under the remnants of the program have amounted to $15-$25 million a year. To 1972, when the main program was terminated, including the value of an opting-out tax credit for Quebec, approximately $1 billion was expended under it. Since most grants had to be met by an equal provincial expenditure the total outlay was at least double this amount. In fact, as all provinces did not claim their full entitlement, the amount actually spent on the selected services was probably even greater. The investment of this money had two results: (1) it improved general health services and treatment in several individual areas—mental, tuberculosis, cancer, etc., (2) it supplied Canada's need for additional hospitals. Between 1948 and 1970, when the hospital grants program was terminated, the number of hospitals reported by Statistics Canada increased from 774 to 1,170, a growth of 50 percent. General bed capacity rose from 110,000 to 198,000. These figures were not precisely classified, however, and recent data gives more accurate information by category of bed. In 1987 there were 176,000 beds in operating hospitals, and another 150,000 beds in 4,000 approved residential facilities for the aged. There has been a shift in the nature of hospital bed accommodation from acute to long-term care. In 1950 there were 5.4 acute care beds per thousand of population; these had fallen to 4.8 per 1,000 in the seventies. In the same period long-term care beds rose from 1.1 to 2.2 per thousand of population.

Federally Sponsored Hospital Insurance

With programs in place that would meet the needs of "free" hospital care the federal government thought more seriously of implementing at least this element of its 1945 health proposals. Its approach was cautious, and with good reason. In 1952 the additional cost of Old Age Security had just been assumed and almost concurrently participation in the Korean War had necessitated heavy additional defence expenditures. As a result the budget was in deficit, and expensive new social programs were not welcomed by the Minister of Finance. Further, the new Prime Minister, the Hon. Louis St. Laurent, was of the view that it would be inadvisable to launch a hospital insurance program until more hospital facilities were actually in place. This was still not the case in the early fifties.

Furthermore a consensus had not yet developed in Ottawa on the nature of the federal government's role in the delicate negotiation of this massive joint social program, the largest up to that time. The vehicle would have to be an agreement between the levels of government, as constitutional authority clearly lay with the provinces. But there were widely divergent views among governments on the nature of the possible arrangements. For the federal authorities a central issue was the degree to which it could insist that certain requirements be met as a condition of receiving the federal grant. There were the closely related questions of just what the federal grant would be and how the additional expenditure would be met in the federal budget. The model bill produced by the Advisory Committee in the 1940s, which envisaged close federal restrictions on many aspects of provincial plans, had been abandoned. Furthermore the unsatisfactory experience of attempting to devise a contributory system of revenues for the Old Age Security plan launched in 1952 had not offered much encouragement for this avenue of financing. With these and other issues unresolved the federal authorities were inclined to treat a new large-scale social program rather gingerly in the early fifties.

Nonetheless pressure for action on the health front was building. The Saskatchewan and British Columbia plans were now in operation as precedents. Ontario, after an extensive inquiry by Professor Malcolm Taylor, made the decision to go the public route for health insurance, and pressed the federal government to reactivate its 1945 commitments. A study of sickness expenditures released by The Dominion Bureau of Statistics in 1953 gave new insights into the widespread incidence of illness and the uneven economic burden of health costs. The labour unions, both through their central organizations and with the support of the CCF Members of Parliament, after introduction of Old Age Security in 1952, turned their attention increasingly to health insurance as the next target. At federal-provincial conferences in 1950 and 1955 the subject received further attention, despite the strongly negative position of the federal government at the 1950 conference. During this period the study resources of the Department of Health and Welfare were strengthened, and the departmental attitude remained aggressive. A Division of Health Insurance Studies was established in 1947, and under an able staff new data were collected and analyzed, a process in which the provinces actively participated.

Following an election in 1953 the federal government undertook a general review of the possible future federal role in social policy; while the cost of the Korean war and Old Age Security ruled out implementation of the full health insurance program, something less expensive began to seem feasible. Hospital beds were now becoming available, and hospital insurance therefore was the next logical step.

The Hospital Insurance and Diagnostic Services Act

At the insistence of several of the provinces, most particularly Ontario which had advanced its plans for hospital insurance almost to the point of execution, the federal government reluctantly included "health and welfare services" in the agenda of a federal-provincial conference in October 1955. In his opening remarks the federal Prime Minister left it to the provinces to establish some priorities among alternate health programs as a guide to future action, but made it a clear that federal participation would require the agreement of a substantial majority of provincial governments representing a substantial majority of the Canadian people. It would not be justified in imposing federal taxation for the benefit of a minority of the population. A wide variety of responses emerged, and a continuing committee of federal and provincial Ministers of Health and Finance was appointed to sort them out. At a meeting of the committee early in 1956 the federal Minister of Health and Welfare set forth the position of his government. Subject to the overriding condition of majority coverage, it would pay a share of the cost of provincial plans for hospital and diagnostic services; the federal share would be the sum obtained by multiplying the number of insured persons in the province by two per capita figures; (1) 25 percent of the average per capita cost of hospital services in Canada as a whole, and (2) 25 percent of the average per capita costs in the province itself. No contribution would be made in respect of mental hospitals or tuberculosis sanatoria or toward administrative costs.

There followed a long delay before a sufficient number of provinces responded. A year later only three provinces—British Columbia, Alberta and Saskatchewan—had accepted. There was some public opposition to the plan, but the crucial factor was acceptance by the required number of provinces, which had been identified as six. The acceptance of either Ontario or Quebec was thought to be essential. After long negotiations with Ontario an agreeement was achieved, and with the required number thus assured, in March and April 1957, Parliament passed the Hospital Insurance and Diagnostic Services Act. On the finally determined date of commencement, July 1, 1958, five provinces—Newfoundland, Manitoba, Saskatchewan, Alberta, and British Columbia—had plans in operation under the program. On January 1, 1959 Nova Scotia, New Brunswick, and Ontario followed; Prince Edward Island commenced on October 1, 1959 and Quebec on January 1, 1961. Thus was achieved at least one of the goals for comprehensive medicine—universal access to hospital care.

As the first major step toward our present comprehensive and expensive health program it is relevant to check financial expectations at this stage. It is clear that the apparent indifference to health insurance costs evidenced at the 1945 conference had been replaced by a much more lively concern by the end of the fifties. The federal budget had been in deficit for three of the preceding four years, reaching a high point in 1958-59, when it exceeded 10 percent of expenditures. The federal Ministers of Finance had anticipated a postwar expenditure level of $2 to $2.5 billion, but between 1949 and 1959 outlays had risen from $2.2 billion to $6.5 billion, an increase to which defence spending, higher social security costs, and inflation had contributed. In the same period provincial expenditures had approximately tripled, with heavy new demands for schools, highways, municipal expansion, and social services. The economy had shown acute and unpredictable changes during the fifties, and was ending the period with a slump. The mood was therefore much more cautious than a decade before, and availability of funds was becoming the main influence in timing.

In addition a good deal more knowledge and research had replaced the guesswork of a decade before. At a practical level there was the experience of Saskatchewan and British Columbia with their provincially-sponsored hospital insurance programs. The data-gathering and research activities of the federal Department of Health and Welfare, in cooperation with other federal agencies and the provincial governments, had immensely extended this knowledge base, and much of this had been sobering in financial terms. The federal government had presented the 1955 Federal-Provincial Conference with much improved estimates of the costs of various elements of a comprehensive health services program. Compared to the $250 million or so estimated in 1945 the total had been raised to $620 million a decade later. As expenditure of all governments in 1955 was approximately $7.5 billion, adoption of the total program would mean an increase of about 8 percent, a chilling prospect for government treasury officials. A hospital insurance program, estimated at $312 million, would cost less than half this amount, undoubtedly a factor that weighed heavily in its favour. With the federal government paying half, most provinces would find the burden tolerable.

The problem of squeezing hospital insurance costs into already strained budgets was met in various ways. Several provinces simply absorbed the additional costs into the general budget, but some levied special taxes or premiums. The latter included Nova Scotia (sales tax), Ontario (premiums), Manitoba, (special taxes on personal and corporate income), Saskatchewan (half sales tax revenue), and Alberta (a special property tax). British Columbia continued to devote a portion of its sales tax to hospital insurance. At the outset Ontario, Manitoba, Saskatchewan, and Alberta charged monthly premiums; British Columbia, Alberta, Saskatchewan, and Manitoba also imposed a daily patient charge, usually at a nominal rate. In most provinces these revenues fell short of meeting the whole provincial cost of the hospital insurance plan, necessitating substantial allocations from the general budget. We will return to subsequent aspects of financing later.

The introduction of hospital insurance had been accomplished with relatively amicable accord among governments and, despite some opposition, with general public support. It gave no portent of the tumultuous events that were to follow in the next decade with the implementation of medical care insurance.

21
Health Insurance

It is one of the enigmas of Canadian social history that the federal government, having very reluctantly presided over the introduction of hospital insurance in the fifties, against all expectations appeared as the sponsor of a comprehensive national medical insurance program during the sixties. It was not for lack of other concerns that it came to occupy this role. The unpredictable vagaries of the economy, serious problems with the balance of payments, GATT tariff negotiations, budget deficits, tax policy, inflation, separatism in Quebec, the centenary of Confederation, choosing a national flag, and dozens of other issues were of equal concern. Nonetheless by the end of the sixties a plan that covered all Canadians was in place, despite acrimonious controversy and active hostility from several influential elements of society, both governmental and non-governmental.

Saskatchewan Leads the Way—Again

In his extensive study of events leading to the introduction of health insurance in Canada, *Health Insurance and Canadian Public Policy*, Professor Taylor lists seven stages: 1) The 1945 Health Insurance Proposals. 2) The Saskatchewan Hospital Services Act. 3) Ontario Hospital Insurance. 4) The National Hospital Insurance Program. 5) The Saskatchewan Medical Care Program. 6) The National Medicare Program. 7) Quebec Medicare. Of these seven stages the province of Saskatchewan accounts for two, a not exaggerated index of its role in the total process. The first four of the phases have been covered; we turn to the second appearance of this western province on the medical stage. The story is a long and dramatic one, and requires over 90 pages in the telling in the Taylor study. It will be greatly curtailed here.

Saskatchewan's experience with prepaid municipal medical and hospital programs, the studies made in the 1940s leading to the passage of the Health Services Act in 1944, the adoption of a complete medical care program for recipients of social assistance in 1945, and province-wide hospital insurance in 1947 are hallmarks of an intense interest in health services. The provincial socialist government under the CCF party had sustained this interest in comprehensive medical insurance, and the Health Services Planning Commission, appointed in 1945, and its Advisory Committee had continued to explore possible plans. Early steps were taken to expand existing municipal plans to provincial health regions, resulting in the establishment of two demonstration regions in Swift Current and Health Region No. 1. This action was significant mainly in precipitating the issues that would create increasingly tense relations between the medical profession and the government for the next decade. Namely, these were: the method of payment (fee for services, per capita or salary); the centre of authority (an officially appointed commission or an independent professionally-oriented body); and the adoption of regionalization as a basic pattern.

During the decade 1945-55 no concrete steps were taken by the government toward health insurance. A Health Survey Commission appointed in 1949 recommended in its 1951 report adoption of a health insurance program based on existing organizations and facilities, a recommendation interpreted by the Saskatchewan medical profession as excluding a state-sponsored plan. This was the most recent position adopted by the Canadian Medical Association in 1949, and in the light of this policy the proposal aroused little opposition. As the fifties progressed the medical profession became more confident of its ability to head off government interference. Professionally-sponsored medical service plans in Saskatoon (Medical Services, Inc.) and Regina (Group Medical Services) had increased enrolments to a total of over 300,000 by 1959, and were being promoted as a viable alternative to a compulsory state plan. At the insistence of the Saskatchewan College of Physicians and Surgeons professional members were appointed to the Hospital Services Planning Commission in 1955. The College began to give vigorous support for the approach then being adopted by the non-governmental elements of the health business—the provision of prepaid health services through multiple insurers with enrolment of lower income persons being subsidized, in whole or in part, by government.

In retrospect, an ultimate collision between government and the medical profession was inevitable. The government was pledged to a plan of universal medical care, and delayed its implementation mainly because of lack of money. The subsidy from the federal government for hospital insurance would offset about 45 percent of its expenditures under that heading, and along with additional revenues from other sources implementation began to seem feasible. It was growing weary of the delaying tactics of the medical profession in implementing its regional proposals, and reduced support in an election in 1956 convinced it that new initiatives were needed. It therefore reactivated its internal planning processes in 1959 with an Interdepartmental Committee to draw up legislation and financing proposals. The news of its decision to proceed with a medical care insurance program was announced on the radio by the Premier in December 1959, and given formally in the Throne Speech at the opening of the 1960 session. The date of commencement was to be July 1, 1961.

Subsequent events made medical history. The full details of the tense and trying period that followed can hardly be recounted here. The aroused and angry Saskatchewan medical profession fought the measure by every means at its command, with the support of the Canadian profession as a whole. It finally threatened strike action as the effective date approached, and did withdraw its services for 23 days following July 1, 1961, an action that attracted international attention and gave rise to a heated controversy over the responsibility of doctors to stay on the job. The intervention of an English medical expert acting as a moderator and the granting of some relatively minor concessions by the government finally broke the impasse. The plan came into effect immediately in late July, but the government was not forgiven for the emotional trauma of a year and a half of public turmoil. It was defeated in the next election.

To finance the plan from its own resources Saskatchewan was forced to find approximately $25 million; its total current expenditure at this time was in the neighbourhood of $125 million, so that the new burden meant an increase of about 20 percent. At the same time taxpayers were being relieved of personal health expenditures of considerably more than this amount. The additional revenues were found from an increase in the retail sales tax from 3 to 5 percent, (about 50 percent); increases in personal and corporate income tax (about 22 percent) and an annual premium of $12 per individual and $24 per family (about 28 percent). At the outset the plan paid 85 percent of the College schedule of fees, and did not provide for out-patient services, which were added later.

National Medicare Program

The environment of the 1960s which led to the rounding out of Canada's social welfare structure was clearly unique. Since medical insurance was one of its principal emanations it may fittingly be reviewed here.

The Political Circumstances

The decade following 1957 was chequered with elections, minority governments, and swift political turnabouts. Following a 22-year period of Liberal dominance (1935-1957), during which the party was led by Prime Ministers Mackenzie King and Louis St. Laurent, in 1957 a minority Conservative government was elected under Prime Minister John Diefenbaker. In a 1958 election the Conservatives were returned with a substantial majority, but were again reduced to minority status in an election in June 1962. In April 1963, the Liberals were returned to power under Prime Minister Lester Pearson, but also with a minority. The Pearson government continued in power after an election in 1965 with a minority, but in 1968 the Liberals were re-elected under Prime Minister Pierre Trudeau with a substantial majority, only to slip back into a minority position from 1972 to 1974. Returned with a majority in the latter year, except for the short-lived government under Prime Minister Joseph Clark in 1979 the Liberals were in power for another decade. They were replaced in 1984 by a Conservative government with a substantial majority under Prime Minister Brian Mulroney.

This long period of political instability, particularly that of the 1957-68 decade, wrought a massive change in Canadian politics. Constant minority government changed policy-making time horizons from the distant prospects of the next election to survival on that day. Minority governments remained in power with the consent of one of the opposition groups—for most of this period the NDP—and paid the price by sponsoring programs acceptable to that party.

These trying and uncertain conditions attracted to politics an exceptional breed of aggressive, well educated and highly motivated young men and women. The sixties of course marked a watershed of change. (What parent of teen-agers during this period needs to be reminded?) All institutions and customs were being challenged. The postwar pledge for renewal and betterment was only partly met, and a new and less tradition-bound generation was strongly supportive of further measures. Canadian social programs fell short of those in many other countries, and the government was being frequently reminded of that fact by the unions and their political allies.

Money from the generally buoyant economy of the sixties was rolling into the federal treasury, and pleas of Ministers of Finance for caution were taken lightly. Without tax increases—indeed even with substantial shifting of tax sources to the provinces—federal revenues increased from $6.5 billion in 1960 to $15.5 billion in 1970. But expenditures increased even more, with the result that from 1954 to 1969 with the exception of one year the budget was in deficit throughout, in some years substantially in deficit. As this was a period of intensive economic activity when the federal budget should have been showing Keynesian surpluses the role of the Minister of Finance was not a happy one; but social policy marched forward nonetheless.

The Royal Commission on Health Services

The Report of the Royal Commission on Health Services undoubtedly acted as a catalyst for health insurance. The Commission was appointed by Prime Minister Diefenbaker, largely at the instance of the Canadian Medical Association, under the chairmanship of a trusted friend and former colleague, Mr. Justice Emmett Hall, Chief Justice of Saskatchewan. The inquiry of seven members became operative mid-1961 and released its report in June 1964, having conducted extensive hearings and studies over a three-year period. The Report, among many other recommendations, came down unanimously and forcefully in favour of federal-provincial cooperation "to assist the provinces to introduce and operate comprehensive, universal provincial programs of personal health services." Such services were to include "medical services, dental services for children, expectant mothers, and public assistance recipients, prescription drug services, optical services for children and public assistance recipients, prosthetic services, and home care services." There was no equivocation about this language —the Commission firmly supported programs introduced and operated by the provinces; in short, government-sponsored health insurance programs.

This outcome posed a problem for the federal government. At a Policy Conference at Queen's University in 1962 the Liberals had adopted health insurance as an objective, and in the 1962 and 1963 campaigns, in which they were elected, they had promised action. The commitment therefore was firm, but its implementation would not be easy. The accelerating costs of social programs already in effect—hospital insurance, family allowances, and old age security—were making finance officials wary of taking on additional measures, and there were many other equally pressing demands. Commitments of this magnitude would require substantial increases in taxation, a concern that found frequent echo in Cabinet discussions.

For the private sector the prospect was completely disconcerting in view of the strong trend over the past decade in its favour. Except for the Saskatchewan move the main developments had been almost exclusively toward prepayment through private plans. So strong indeed had this trend been that the Canadian Medical Association (CMA) had proposed the appointment of the Commission in the confident expectation that it would favour further action in this direction. As previously mentioned, in the decade 1955-65 there had been a marked increase in enrolments under Blue Cross and similar organizations, and in insurance company plans, with a total enrolment of over 10 million. A national organization, the Trans-Canada Medical Services, had been established to coordinate the activities of the former, and the latter had joined forces under the Canadian Health Insurance Association (CHIA). In 1960 these organizations formed the Canadian Conference on Health Care to support common objectives. In a common front with the Canadian Medical Association they adopted and strongly supported the approach of maintaining multiple suppliers of medical services, with government-paid enrolment for recipients of social assistance and government subsidization of premiums for lower income individuals. The test for subsidization would be the level of the income tax exemptions. This proposal was made in the briefs of the CMA and the CHIA to the Commission, and it was also advanced by at least 35 different groups of witnesses in its hearings. The Commission's recommendation for a government dominated plan was therefore a shocking miscarriage of the total strategy. It created frustration and anger among the private groups, and a firm resolve to oppose the recommendation by every means possible.

Several provincial governments were equally upset. At least three of them—Ontario, Alberta and British Columbia—had either adopted the CMA/CHIA approach or were in the process of doing so. Alberta had led the way in 1963, with passage of legislation authorizing the provincial government to subsidize the cost of medical insurance with approved carriers for low income individuals. Some thirty companies qualified under the plan and within a year 1.1 million of the total Alberta population of 1.3 million were insured, of whom 150,000 were subsidized. It was estimated however that more than twice this number were eligible for subsidy, and had not come forward. The amount of subsidy was based on the previous year's income, with no further test of means.

Between 1963 and 1966 the Ontario government developed legislation which after several revisions created the Ontario Medical Services Insurance Plan. Under it the provincial government, after experimenting with insurance through other agencies, established its own organization to insure individuals in need of assistance. In 1966 nearly 600,000 individuals were enrolled. Along with 6.2 million under other plans this gave coverage of about 95 percent in Ontario.

In British Columbia a similar process had been followed, leading to the eventual establishment of the B.C. Medical Plan, a government agency to provide medical assistance for those unable to afford their own premiums.

In these three provinces, which accounted for a substantial part of the total Canadian population, the bulk of the people, by government decision, were being left to arrange their medical prepayments through the private sector. The Royal Commission's recommendation for state-sponsored compulsory health insurance in the face of provincial moves away from this approach was deeply resented in the provinces involved, and strengthened resistance to federal programs that altered provincial priorities through the offer of financial assistance and required compliance with federally-conceived rules and regulations.

In the midst of these very unpropitious circumstances the federal government nonetheless made the decision to proceed with health insurance. The Royal Commission had proposed the convening of a federal-provincial conference to discuss health services, and in the Throne Speech opening the 1965 parliamentary session, the government announced its intention to hold such a conference. At the conference held in July the federal government set forth its own terms for action. Its conditions would be much less restrictive than those that had governed hospital insurance; there would be no required minimum of accepting provinces, and the operation of the plans would be almost entirely under provincial control.

There were however four broad requirements to be met by the provinces: (1) all services provided by general practitioners and specialists must be covered; (2) the plan must be universal; (3) the plan must be provincially administered; and (4) benefits must be fully transferable between provinces. The federal contribution would be a per capita payment for provincial residents enrolled in the plan equal to one-half of the national per capita cost, with no account being taken of actual provincial costs and with no ceiling on sharable expenditures. Use of the national per capita expenditure would aid the provinces that spent less than the national average by raising their grant to a level higher than their actual expenditure.

Reaction to this proposal was delayed. No particular umbrage appears to have been taken to it at the conference, but in following weeks opposition was frequently and violently expressed by some provoked provincial leaders, particularly at the conference of provincial premiers in August, as well as by private spokesmen.

The Medical Care Act

Despite this resistance the government persisted in its decision to submit legislation to Parliament at the 1966 session for a plan to come into effect on July 1, 1967, the centennial of Confederation. This decision was not unopposed in Cabinet, the Minister of Finance pleading caution in view of deficit prospects and threats of inflation. During passage of the Bill a concession was made to his appeal by postponement of the effective date by one year to July 1968. The debate on the bill had traumatic moments which must be passed over here; in December 1966 it received final reading in the House (177 for: 2 opposed) and in the Senate, and was immediately given Royal Assent. The federal Minister of Finance continued to argue for a further postponement of the effective date, with the support of some of the provincial premiers. However, no further changes were made, and in practice a solution was found by the provincial governments in postponing their own dates of inception. Only two provinces, Saskatchewan and British Columbia, qualified by July 1, 1968; in April 1969, Newfoundland, Nova Scotia and Manitoba commenced, followed by Alberta (July 1, 1969); Ontario, (October 1, 1969); Quebec (November 1, 1970); Prince Edward Island (December 1, 1970); and New Brunswick (January 1, 1971). The Northwest Territories began on April 1, 1971 and the Yukon a year later.

This episode left much bad feeling among certain provinces. Ontario was outspoken in its resentment. Its normally moderate premier, John Robarts, who had devoted himself to alleviating federal-provincial stress through his Confederation of Tomorrow Conference held in 1965, as well as in other ways, said: "Medicare is a glowing example of a Machiavellian scheme that is in my humble opinion one of the greatest political frauds that has been perpetrated on the people of this country." This sense of grievance was further inflamed by the action of the federal government in pre-empting much of the room for tax increases in its budgets of 1969 and 1970, including the imposition starting in 1969 of a "social development" tax of 2 percent of taxable income, with a ceiling of $120.

The Quebec Episode

The position of Quebec deserves special mention. Its entrance to the plan in November 1970—one of the last provinces to enter—was the culmination of a traumatic period reminiscent of the Saskatchewan experience. The tension was even further exacerbated by the public turmoil of very troubled times, including the kidnapping of a foreign diplomat, the murder of a cabinet minister, and the declaration of a state of "apprehended insurrection" by the federal government, and with hundreds of arrests of Quebec citizens.

Quebec governments had flirted with the idea of state medicine for some time. In the 1940s a Commission on Health Insurance had recommended a plan, a Health Insurance Commission had been appointed by one government to carry out the proposal and two years later had been abolished by another government. It had entered the Hospital Insurance Plan in 1961, and in 1966, following presentation of the federal proposal for health insurance, had appointed the Commission on Health and Social Services (Castonguay-Nepveu Commission) to consider the whole range of social measures in the province. In its first report in 1967 the Commission recommended adoption of "a complete and universal health insurance plan" for Quebec. In the light of strong public support for the proposal the government announced its intention to move toward a universal plan in the Throne Speech of the 1968 session, the target date to be July 1, 1970. This was further supported by the announcement in the 1969 Budget Speech that a universal plan would be introduced.

Two conflicts were to impede implementation. The first was the continuing struggle of Quebec to free itself from financial dependence on Ottawa by obtaining more room to impose its own taxes. This drive had already resulted in the enactment of the Established Programs (Interim Arrangements) Act, 1965, under which any province could "opt out" of five main programs (category I) in return for additional tax room under the personal income tax (totalling 20 points). There was also a list of five lesser programs (category II) for which it could continue to receive the equivalent of the amount payable under the program. Quebec was the sole province to opt out, taking the whole category I list, of which hospital insurance accounted for a 14-point tax abatement and health grants for 1 point. From 1965 forward therefore the cost to the federal government of an extensive list of programs would include the tax revenues specifically surrendered to Quebec in lieu of direct payments. In time this was to be the pattern for all programs for all provinces, and its adoption under pressure from Quebec was therefore a portent of the future.

As the Quebec budget was substantially in deficit at this time the additional $90 million forecast for health insurance by the Castonguay Commission was a formidable deterrent. Initially Quebec pressed the federal government to turn over to it the revenue to be collected from Quebec residents under its "social development" tax, but failing in this it simply gave a pledge to continue its efforts to obtain additional funds from the federal government, and proceeded to establish the Quebec Health Insurance Board to develop a specific program.

In March 1970, a Health Insurance Act was introduced into the legislature and given unanimous first reading. Finances were to come from a 0.8 percent personal income tax and a 0.8 percent tax on payrolls of employers. However, before final passage a new government was elected. The legislation was reintroduced substantially unchanged, except for one feature; the first bill had allowed for opting out of the plan by medical practitioners but under the new legislation a ceiling of 3 percent was imposed as a limit on this privilege.

"Opting-out" almost instantly became a source of heated confrontation with the medical profession. The original privilege had been strongly opposed by a coalition of unions, teachers, and farmers, and in attempting to meet this criticism the government resorted to the device of the ceiling, which in turn created a storm among the doctors, or more particularly among the specialists, as the general practitioners appeared to accept it. The original opting-out clause had allowed for reimbursement of the patient by the health plan, but as the conflict with the specialists heightened this clause was withdrawn; effectually therefore opting out was eliminated. The confrontation between the government and the specialists was long and bitter, and led, as in Saskatchewan, to a withdrawal of services. Legislation was passed to end the strike, which the specialists resisted, but the political crisis of October 1970 and the threat of possible mass violence during this period was the occasion for a general return to duty by the medical profession. The Quebec health insurance plan came into operation the following month.

22
Financing Health Care

By 1971 the main elements of the health care program were in place. From this time forward attention was centred on the financing of the massive expenditures involved.

First, two complementary additions to the program should be mentioned —the Health Resources Fund and Extended Health Care. Under the former the federal government undertook to pay 50 percent of the cost of provincial projects for "the acquisition, construction, and renovation of health training facilities and research institutions" incurred between January 1966 and December 1980, to a total contribution of $500 million. Projects included medical schools, teaching hospitals, and schools of dentistry, nursing, and pharmacy. Under the program over $425 million was contributed to provincial use.

The Extended Health Care program was introduced in 1977 to provide services not previously covered under the hospital insurance agreements or else provided under non-medical programs, including nursing home intermediate care, lower level residential care for adults, and the operation of ambulatory health services. Expenditures started at the $500-$600 million level but by 1985-86 were estimated at $1.1 billion, representing a substantial addition to the health budget.

The Total Health Bill

The financial consequences of Canada's preoccupation with health care make a fascinating saga. Statistics Canada estimates that as a nation in 1985 we spent over $39 billion; forty years ago, in 1945, the comparable figure was $250 million. The per capita expenditure then was about $21; in 1985 it was $1,568, seventy-five times as much. Surprisingly, the share of gross national product going to health care has risen much less dramatically than these comparisons would suggest. From about 2½ percent in 1945 the ratio has hovered around 8.5 percent in recent years, less than four times the former level.

Several factors accounted for this rise. An approximate doubling in population over the four decades was partly responsible, but other factors must also have been present to produce an increase in per capita costs. There was an inevitable catching up in the period after the war, when medical services for civilians were minimal. The rapid growth of private hospital and medical plans described earlier accelerated the use of health services in the years to 1960, and indeed represented a breaking-in period for later government measures. Introduction of national universal hospital insurance and medicare further broadened access and stimulated use of all health services. Medical science made great advances over the four decades, and new cures for many illnesses became common, with a consequent rise in the demand for their treatment. Finally, there was the effect of inflation. Measured even by the consumer price index, costs increased five-fold from the decade of the forties to the eighties, and health costs no doubt increased proportionately more. In 1945 prices, the 1985 per capita cost drops from $1,568 to about $315, a figure that gives a more accurate comparison with the $21 of 40 years ago. Even so this represents a rise of some 15 times, a not inconsiderable increase in the real consumption of health services.

Table 22.1 gives health care totals and related comparisons for selected years since 1945. These data are from official sources, but may not be consistent throughout; it serves well enough to indicate general trends.

Table 22.1 Canada: Total Health Care Expenditures, Selected Years, 1945-85

Year	Total health expenditures	Government health expenditures[a]	Government share of total	Percent of GNP Total health	Percent of GNP Government health
	$ million			percent	
1945	250	68	26.4	2.2	0.6
1948	389	154	39.6	2.5	1.2
1950	503	232	46.1	2.7	1.2
1958	1,145	535	46.6	3.3	1.5
1959	1,290	732	56.7	3.5	2.0
1960	2,138	841	39.3	5.5	2.2
1961	2,371	1,032	43.5	5.9	2.6
1962	2,557	1,153	45.1	5.9	2.7
1967	4,317	2,298	53.2	6.4	3.4
1969	5,496	3,474	63.2	6.7	4.2
1970	6,245	4,145	66.4	7.1	4.7
1971	7,108	4,886	68.7	7.4	5.1
1972	7,775	5,478	70.5	7.3	5.1
1973	8,703	6,069	69.7	6.9	4.8
1974	10,227	7,357	71.9	6.8	4.9
1975	12,239	8,961	73.2	7.2	5.3
1976	14,088	10,141	72.0	7.3	5.2
1977	15,494	10,995	71.0	7.3	5.2
1978	17,252	12,039	69.8	7.3	5.1
1979	19,430	13,442	69.2	7.2	5.0
1980	22,719	15,702	69.1	7.5	5.2
1981	26,643	18,801	70.6	7.7	5.5
1982	31,173	21,672	69.5	8.6	6.0
1983	34,697	24,154	69.6	8.8	6.1
1984	34,420[b]	26,130	75.9	8.7	6.0
1985	39,793[b]	27,845	70.0	8.6	6.0

[a]For fiscal year ending in calendar year named. [b]Preliminary.

Sources: *Historical Statistics of Canada*; Department of National Health and Welfare, *National Health Expenditures in Canada 1975-1985*; Statistics Canada, Consolidated Government Finance and CANSIM; Bank of Canada *Review*.

Government Expenditures

The rise in government expenditures of course reflects the introduction of new programs which gradually replaced private health expenditure with public. The first minor rise came after 1948, with the health services and hospital construction grants. Following introduction of hospital insurance in 1958, government expenditures rose rapidly, passing the billion dollar level for the first time in 1961, and accounting for 44 percent of total health costs as compared with 26 percent in 1945. Despite the absence of new programs expenditures doubled to over $2 billion by 1967, and the government share moved to over 50 percent. With medicare, which became fully effective early in the seventies, outlays rose rapidly, rising from $4.9 billion in 1971 to $10 billion in 1976, then to $11 billion in 1977 after the Established Programs system of financing and the introduction of Extended Health Care, reaching $28 billion in 1985. The ratio to GNP rose from 0.6 percent in 1945 to 2.7 percent in 1962 and to 5.1 percent in 1971 and seemed to have stabilized around 5 percent during the seventies. However in the early eighties it moved up to 6 percent, and has remained there for four successive years. This last rise was unexpected, and experts are still puzzled by it. The government share of the total expenditure has remained, with minor variations, at 70 percent since 1971, a remarkable consistency in view of other major shifts and changes during the last decade and a half.

The main element of government spending is undoubtedly hospital care. Of some $27 billion (plus or minus) of government expenditure on health programs in 1985 it is estimated that, based on data for earlier years, over $16 billion, or 60 percent went for this purpose. Medical care expenditures are estimated at $8 billion, or 30 percent of the total. It is the predominance of hospital expenditures that has led governments to concentrate their expenditure control efforts on this aspect of the health services program. And it is not the building of the hospitals as such that is the big expense, costly as that may be today; it is the expense of running them. In general only 6 percent of the total spent on hospitals is for capital; the remaining 94 percent is for running costs.

The Federal Share

Until 1975 the federal contribution was determined as a share of provincial expenditures for both hospital insurance and medicare. This system was revised from 1976 onward.

Hospital Insurance

It will be recalled that for hospital insurance the contribution was determined by multiplying the covered population of the province by two per capita amounts (1) 25 percent of the national per capita government expenditure on the prescribed services, and (2) 25 percent of the provincial per capita expenditure on the same services. This produced payments which overall amounted to half the provincial costs in total, but initially varied between an estimated share of 72 percent of Newfoundland expenditure to

45 percent for British Columbia, with the provinces from Quebec east being above 50 percent and those from Ontario west being below. These ratios changed drastically over the period of the program as the quality and cost of services changed, with less sharp extremes between the high and low ends.

The original estimate of total cost of the hospital insurance program was $365 million, of which the federal share, one-half, would be $182.5 million. In actuality costs rapidly exceeded this amount. By 1962 federal costs were over $300 million, by 1966 had reached $400 million, in 1968 passed $450 million, and really took off in the seventies. By 1971 they had soared to over $850 million, to $950 million in 1972, and to over $2 billion in 1976. To these amounts must be added the value of the tax credits granted to Quebec in lieu of cash payments, which in the middle seventies were $400-600 million a year, and rising. Obviously governments had taken a rather large lion by the tail with hospital insurance. Some increases in costs was allowed for with growing population, inflation, and increasing use, but nothing like the rise in two decades from $365 million to over $4 billion was contemplated.

Medicare

Much the same surprise lay in store for the authorities in introducing medicare. The Hall Commission had estimated that in 1971 the full health care program that it visualized would cost about $4.6 billion, whereas by that year total expenditures were nearly $7 billion. The Commission prepared its estimates seven or eight years beforehand, and could not have foreseen the acceleration of costs in the late sixties resulting from inflation and increased usage. The Minister of National Health and Welfare estimated that if Medicare had been in full effect for all provinces in 1967 the cost would have been $680 million, $340 million for each level of government. Actual payments rose only gradually with delays in implementation, and the first full annual federal contribution was not made until 1971-72, in the amount of $575 million. This was about 70 percent more than had been estimated for 1967, only five years before. By 1975 the federal cost had risen to nearly $800 million, and in 1976 to over $950 million.

Interim Restraints

The rapid escalation of costs in the late sixties and early seventies alarmed all governments, as there seemed to be no limit to the upsurge. There was an increase in excess of 100 percent between 1967 and 1971, and another over-100 percent rise between 1971 and 1975. At a conference in 1971 the federal health authorities broached the possibility of abandoning the shared-cost approach, as it lacked a ceiling and was completely unrelated to economic conditions. They favoured an alternative that would provide the provinces with sufficient funds to meet normal growth but would exert some discipline on expansion. In the following years, far from slowing down, there were increases in hospital beds, in services, and in physicians' incomes far beyond expectations. As an interim restraining measure the federal government announced in the 1975 budget that the growth in the per capita contribution for Medicare would be limited to 13 percent in 1976, 10.5 percent in 1977, and 8.5 percent in later years. Only the restrictions on the first two years were finally applied, and along with population growth gave ceilings of 14.5 percent and 12 percent. In 1975, after intensive study of the causes of the increase, the Ontario government imposed restrictions on the number of physicians entering practice and on the number of hospital beds in service. Other provinces were also considering ways of containing the growth.

Established Programs Financing Act

A general reference was made earlier to the adoption of the EPF basis for financing federal educational and health grants. This is now examined in greater detail in connection with health grants. The Federal-Provincial Fiscal Arrangements and Established Programs Financing Act, passed in 1977, established a new basis for federal financing of hospital insurance, medicare, and extended health care, as well as post-secondary education. Commencing on April 1, 1977, transfers would henceforth be a combination of cash payments and tax transfers. A special arrangement was adopted for extended health care (see below). For the three main programs (hospital insurance, medicare, and post-secondary education) cash payments were to be established as 50 percent of average per capita contributions for 1975-76, plus $7.63. (The amount of $7.63 represented the cash value of a revenue guarantee paid to the provinces since 1972 in compensation for the possible effects of tax reform on their revenues. In practice it was calculated as the yield of 1 point of the personal income tax, and lumped in with payments under Established Programs through an increase in a previous 12.5 percent tax transfer to 13.5 percent). This calculation gave a per capita amount which, increased by the rise in per capita GNP over the past three years and multiplied by the population of the province, gave the amount of the cash grant for the three programs. The variation between provinces in the health grants under the old arrangement was to be eliminated by bringing all provinces to a common per capita figure over a five-year period. The tax transfers were to be the amount of revenue in the year of payment from 1 percent of corporate taxable income and 13.5 percent of federal basic personal income tax in the province. Quebec would continue to receive as well the value of the tax transfer it had opted for in lieu of the cash payment for hospital insurance. Transitional grants were made to ease the various adjustments under the new arrangements.

The Extended Health Care program was excluded from the Established Programs plan and was set as a payment of $20 per capita, escalated for growth in GNP, to cover home care, community health programs, ambulatory health services, nursing homes, and other extended health care. As some of these services had been financed under the Canada Assistance Plan that function was relieved of a corresponding expenditure.

In 1981 the whole transfer program underwent a thorough review by a House of Commons Task Force. Following the recommendations in its report, *Fiscal Federalism in Canada*, changes were made in the established programs arrangements. These were first proposed in the November 1981 budget, to come into effect on April 1, 1982, but with delays in enactment, some parts were held over until the following year. A principal financial change was the elimination of the guaranteed revenue payment of 1 percent of personal income tax, which would have exceeded $1 billion if continued over the five-year renewal period. This was accomplished by establishing a uniform basic entitlement for all the established programs, equal to population multiplied by the national average federal contribution in 1976, escalated for changes in GNP, per capita, as under the previous Act. The value of the tax transfers, and associated equalization, was then deducted to arrive at the cash payment to be provided by the operating federal departments.

The tax transfers and the cash payments would be designated specifically for the three programs in the federal accounts, but the provinces would be free, as before, to make their own allocation between programs. Despite extensive consultation on the development of national standards for post-secondary education and health services nothing came of this exercise, except perhaps the holdback provisions of the Canada Health Act.

In practice under the new arrangement the value of the tax transfer is first established for each program and an additional cash payment then calculated sufficient to bring the total contribution up to the province's entitlement for that program. As the allocation of tax revenues between individual programs must be done on an arbitrary basis, since they are not earmarked in any specific way, it is clear that except for the grounding of the basic contribution in the increasingly remote year of 1976 the federal transfers for health programs under the present arrangements have only a tenuous connection with current provincial health expenditures.

In 1983 the statute covering these arrangements was revised and renamed the Federal-Provincial Fiscal Arrangements and Federal Post-Secondary Education and Health Contributions Act, 1977, possibly more precise but hardly a memorable contribution to legislative nomenclature. A temporary objective of the new statute was to impose limits to growth in transfers for education to 6 percent in 1983-84 and 5 percent in 1984-85, but these did not apply to the hospital insurance and medicare transfers.

Federal EPF Health Transfers

The nature of the federal system of grants for health under EPF was explored fully in chapter 17 and need not be repeated here. Table 17.5 in that chapter gives historical statistics of federal cash and tax transfers for the years 1958 to 1987.

Federal Charges

No special taxes or charges have been imposed by the federal government to finance its share except for the short-lived Social Development Tax, levied in 1969 and 1970 at 2 percent of personal income with ceilings. The $6.9 billion of cash expenditure in 1987 is equivalent to about 20 percent of the 1986 federal revenue from the personal income tax.

The Provincial Role

The provincial role is the predominant one in health care. The provinces have constitutional power over the field and make the rules under which most of the key participants operate. They pay the bills under the hospital and medicare insurance programs for services performed for their citizens by the thousands (or the millions) and their expenditures account for the bulk of health care costs in Canada. Much of this expenditure is met from the general revenues of the province, but the federal contribution and revenues from premiums and earmarked taxes supply the necessary additional funds. Actual expenditures usually outrun forecasts, so that additional funds are constantly having to be appropriated. Provincial gross outlays (with no deduction for the federal contribution or other revenues) over the past decade and a half are shown in table 22.2.

Over the decade and a half expenditures have risen by more than four times but have maintained a fairly consistent share of the total budget at around one-quarter. The relationship to GNP was in the neighbourhood of 5 percent until 1982, when it rose almost to 6 percent. It has since fallen back moderately.

How the Provinces Financed Health Care

With approximately half their revenue for health expenditures originally coming from the federal government the provinces were left with a sizable burden, which they met in a variety of ways. Some have throughout met the whole cost of the two main programs from general revenues. These are Newfoundland, Prince Edward Island, and New Brunswick (where an election was fought with the financing of hospital care as a central issue). Others imposed special charges or taxes to meet part of the cost, with exemptions or subsidized rates for lower income persons and in some cases for the elderly. The following is a list of the measures taken by these provinces to find additional revenues. Technically a charge should be included only where the revenues were specifically earmarked for health purposes, but this list is given more broadly to demonstrate the financial steps taken to tap additional revenue sources to meet the new expenditure.

Nova Scotia imposed a 3 percent retail sales tax (Hospital Tax) in 1959 and increased the rate to 7 percent in 1969 on introduction of medicare; the revenue is earmarked for health programs.

Quebec increased its corporation tax by 2 percentage points and lowered its personal income tax exemptions on introduction of hospital insurance, but did not earmark revenues for that purpose; in 1973 it introduced a payroll tax on employers, employees, and self-employed, which since 1978 has applied only to employers. Quebec for a period also levied a minimum daily charge for hospital stay.

Ontario has charged a monthly premium throughout. Commencing at $3.25 for single and $6.50 for family membership for hospital insurance, these rates have been increased periodically and for 1985 reached $29.75 and $59.50 respectively, including both hospital insurance and medicare

Table 22.2   Provincial Governments: Gross Health Expenditures, 1974-87

Year[a]	Provincial health expenditures	Health expenditure as a percent of GNP	Health as a percent of provincial expenditure
	$ million	*%*	*%*
1974.....................	7,054	4.8	25.3
1975.....................	8,608	5.2	25.2
1976.....................	9,739	5.1	25.1
1977.....................	10,580	5.0	24.4
1978.....................	11,609	5.0	24.0
1979.....................	12,891	4.9	23.5
1980.....................	15,160	5.1	24.4
1981.....................	18,072	5.3	24.9
1982.....................	20,998	5.9	24.4
1983.....................	22,972	5.9	24.7
1984.....................	24,431	5.7	24.9
1985.....................	26,208	5.6	24.4
1986.....................	28,271	5.7	25.2
1987.....................	30,514	5.7	25.7

Source: Statistics Canada, CANSIM, Bank of Canada *Review*.

[a]Fiscal year ended nearest December 31 of year named.

coverage. Fees were frozen in 1985 and had not been increased to 1988. Alternative forms of financing had been considered from time to time but no changes had been made.

Manitoba. The yield of 1 percent of corporate income tax and a 5 percent addition to personal income tax were labelled Hospital Service Tax but proceeds were not earmarked. In addition monthly premiums were levied until 1973, when they were withdrawn. From 1973 to 1982 full costs were met from general revenues, but in that year a payroll tax was introduced to provide revenues for health and education costs. It was levied at a 1.5 percent rate in 1985, and increased to 2.25 percent on April 1, 1987.

Saskatchewan levies a 5 percent retail sales tax (Education and Health Tax) with one-half the proceeds earmarked for health services. Monthly premiums were charged until 1974, when they were abolished.

Alberta initially authorized municipalities to levy a 4 mill property tax for health services, which was repealed in 1970. Premiums were introduced in 1969 with the enactment of the Alberta Health Care Insurance Plan, and are still in effect. A daily charge was also levied for hospital stay in the past.

British Columbia initially attempted to collect premiums for hospital insurance but in 1954 substituted an increase in sales tax from 3 percent to 5 percent. Premiums were reintroduced in 1965 for the provincial medical care plan, and are still being collected (as of May 1988 at monthly rates ranging from $29 to $42). In 1984 a 4 percent surtax on provincial personal income tax was enacted as a health care maintenance tax, the rate increasing to 8 percent for 1985. The province also made a daily bed charge for hospital stay in the past.

To sum up: as a result of the trend away from earmarked financing only three provinces, Ontario, Alberta, and British Columbia, now collect premiums. These provinces contain over one-half the national population. Obtaining revenues in this way has been accepted from the beginning, and does not conflict with any federal rules. Premium revenue is substantial, amounting in 1984-85 to almost $2.1 billion, approximately 8.5 percent of total provincial health expenditures and about 14.3 percent of the expenditures of the provinces collecting them.

Of the $24.4 billion total provincial expenditure on health in 1984, approximately $10.0 billion was met by transfers from the federal government and $3.5 billion from hospital and medicare premiums and taxes, leaving $10.9 billion, or about 45 percent, to be raised from other sources.

The Canada Health Act

In 1984 a new statute, the Canada Health Act, was passed to replace the existing measures under which federal grants had been paid—the Hospital Insurance and Diagnostic Services Act, the Medical Care Act, and the Extended Health Care Act. A main purpose was to establish more precise conditions to be met by provincial plans to qualify for federal aid. There had been growing discontent in Ottawa with the extent to which universality was being infringed upon by extra-billing of patients by doctors or special hospital charges in several provinces.

A second report in 1981 by Mr. Justice Emmett Hall, appointed as a Special Commissioner to review the state of health care services, declared that extra-billing was contrary to the intent of the health programs and should be banned. The issue of reasonable compensation for physicians should be settled by binding arbitration. In 1983 the Minister of National Health and Welfare issued a position paper re-affirming the federal commitment to universal access, a prelude to passage of the Canada Health Act in 1984, which enacted a dollar for dollar holdback for extra billing and for hospital charges.

Provincial Impact of the Canada Health Act

For the provinces the main impact of the Canada Health Act was financial. It would penalize a province through a holdback equivalent to the revenue the province received from user charges (usually daily room charges) and for an estimate of the income its doctors received from extra billing (charges in excess of those approved for the plan of the province). The user charges presented little problem. They were modest, both in amount and revenue yield, and fully under the control of the province. Imposed mainly by British Columbia, Alberta, and New Brunswick, their removal was not a troublesome issue. Extra billing was quite a different matter. It required direct intervention in doctor-patient relations, always a delicate issue for a government. In some provinces this step had already been taken; for some time extra billing had been outlawed directly, or else patients of extra-billing doctors received no reimbursement at all, in British Columbia, Saskatchewan, Manitoba, and Quebec. In the Atlantic provinces it was not an issue; although there were no legal prohibitions, doctors did not extra-bill. This left Alberta and Ontario as the provinces principally affected by the ban. Alberta introduced legislation to forbid the practice, which was of course opposed by the medical associations but was passed by the legislature.

The Ontario Debacle

1986 turned out to be the year of the doctors' rebellion in Ontario, an unhappy event from which none of the protagonists emerged with much credit. An almost year-long battle between the medical profession and the provincial government began with the introduction in December 1985 of legislation to ban extra billing by doctors under OHIP. The practice had been allowed by the province without restrictions, and was particularly common among specialists. Ontario would suffer a holdback of over $50 million a year, which had already affected payments over a six months' period, if the practice was allowed to continue. Though the law provided that withheld funds would be accumulated and paid over if the province conformed before April 1, 1987, for a cash-hungry provincial treasury the loss of $4 million a month was not to be taken lightly. The government had also promised in its election campaign of the previous fall that the extra billing privilege would be ended, a move which appeared to have public support. The provincial Minister of Health had attempted for some months to negotiate an amicable settlement with the medical associations, but without success. The province therefore finally felt it had no option but to introduce legislation.

The doctors reacted immediately—and violently. The legislation was attacked as infringing on the civil rights of doctors, the fine of $10,000 was assailed as treating doctors more severely than many criminals, it was denied that any patient suffered through extra billing, interference of this kind was just the thin edge of autocratic dominance by the provincial government, etc. In mid-January it was announced that the legislation would be challenged in the courts, but this would not be possible until it was passed.

There followed weeks of angry statements and exhibitions on the part of the doctors. At various times there were reports of possible compromises with the government, but these appeared to be going nowhere. In April a province-wide strike had been authorized by the Ontario Medical Association; in early May an estimated 3,000 doctors and their supporters rallied at a protest meeting at the provincial legislature, and on this occasion their leader spoke of having only one more meeting with the government before calling a strike; later in May the provincial government confirmed its intention of proceeding with the legislation; on May 23 the Association announced that doctors would strike on the following Thursday and Friday; the success of this strike led to threats of a longer strike; meanwhile the legislature was proceeding with examination of Bill 94, the Health Care Accessibility Act, which in fact had been made even tighter than the original draft. There appeared to be no communication whatever between government and the doctors, and the request of the doctors for a mediator had been refused.

The Doctors Strike

At this point the doctors apparently felt that a longer strike would break the impasse, and began a withdrawal of service on June 12. It is difficult to gauge the effect of the strike, as hospital emergency facilities were kept open and it is doubtful if any serious medical problem went unattended. Major operations were probably postponed, and in general the public delayed attention to medical concerns that otherwise would have meant a visit to a doctor. A great deal of public inconvenience resulted, and as the strike went on for days and weeks there was a growing "plague on both your houses" impatience, to the credit of neither of the contenders.

The Law is Passed; the Strike Continues

On June 20 the government became impatient with delays in passage of Bill 94 and evoked a seldom used time limiting procedure to end the debate. After an all night session the law was passed on June 21. It might have been expected that since the doctors were striking to avoid this result they would have given up at this point; in the following week there was some talk of ending the strike—then a couple of weeks old—if the government would submit the bill immediately for a test of its constitutionality, but this did not turn out to be feasible. The Premier made conciliatory offers of reasonable treatment for the doctors, but these were rejected; there appeared to be no grounds for compromise.

After the Strike

The strike in fact went on until the weekend of July 5, by which time it had lasted 25 days, two days longer than the Saskatchewan doctors' strike of 1962 (a symbolic act?). Following the strike the Medical Association appears to have encouraged the doctors not to return to "business as usual," in effect to charge for services previously given free, to be less available, etc. It also proceeded with the appeal of Bill 94 before the Supreme Court of Ontario. In late July there were some minor rotating strikes, but in August it was announced that these would be ended. In their place there would be "public information days" in which doctors would explain the results of Bill 94. Their insistence that they were fighting for their professional freedom in their opposition to the Bill did not appear to have been convincing to all the public. Two years later, in mid-1988, the Ontario doctors' strike is a distant memory. The resounding victory of the government that had engineered Bill 94 in an election in the fall of 1986 must have given the doctors some second thoughts about the success of their opposition, and no doubt reviews of the fee schedules have compensated for some of the financial losses from the ban on extra billing. Some doctors appear to have adopted charges for services previously given free (telephone consultations, etc.) but on the whole the practitioners appear to be back to "business as usual." Whether this is true at the policy making level is not clear, although the 1988 Ontario budget mentioned a joint task force with the Ontario Medical Association to study and make recommendations regarding the factors influencing the increasing use of medical services and how they are provided, an obviously salutory development in this contentious area.

Other Provinces

1986 was a year of unrest among doctors. Saskatchewan doctors, whose predecessors had introduced the strike as a medical weapon in 1962, held rotating strikes before settling a new contract in June. While there was no strike in Alberta there was a prolonged impasse with the government over extra billing, finally settled in August. In British Columbia, where there had been no extra billing, the situation was exacerbated by submission of a government bill that would allow the medical plan to determine where a doctor would practice and establish regional quotas for patients, and court challenges to this legislation were underway. A nine-month impasse over a new contract was finally settled in August. A similar but, for the doctors, an even more restrictive situation threatened in Quebec. There the government had proposed legislation that would allow it to regulate the number of doctors in each specialty and in each medical institution, to force young doctors to practise for at least four years in remote areas and to limit doctors' incomes.

Government Concern Over Rising Costs

Federal Inquiries of the Eighties

The influential role of the second Emmett Hall report (1981) has been mentioned. Two other official federal exercises also reviewed the health programs and passed judgment on them. These were the Macdonald Royal Commission and the Nielsen Task Force team on Health and Sports. The latter was the most complete. It made general proposals for a revised basis of relations between the federal and provincial governments and also examined the causes of rising costs and possible means of controlling them.

The General Scheme of the Nielsen Task Force[22.1]

The Task Force appeared to have three main objectives—establish a leadership role in health matters for the federal government to ensure that standards were maintained; broaden interest in health beyond the present preoccupation with medical services; return to an approximate 50-50 sharing of costs under a formula that would give the provinces more financial autonomy.

The Task Force fully accepted that the five existing criteria, namely, accessibility, universality, comprehensiveness, portability, and public

---

[22.1] Canada, *Improved Program Delivery, Health and Sports*. A Study Team Report to the Task Force on Program Review (Ottawa: Department of Supply and Services, 1985).

administration, were essential to the program. They felt that the criteria must not only be retained but that the federal government had an obligation to monitor the system to ensure that they were observed. This end could be achieved under federal-provincial agreements that would "define more precisely the national standards criteria of health insurance services to be provided by the provinces; and provide a mechanism to monitor and ensure that standards are, in fact, met." The Task Force preferred close study, publicity, and consultation for this purpose rather than a financial penalty. It envisaged a leadership role for the federal Minister of National Health and Welfare in the promotion of better health standards for Canadians and a reduced dependence on "sickness treatment" now characteristic of the medical program.

By contrast the provinces should be given much much greater financial autonomy. The Task Force recommended "a substantial portion of EPF to become unconditional in form, unrelated to health and post-secondary education. To the extent possible, the cash portion of the EPF package would be converted into additional income tax room for the provinces." Its objective in putting forward these proposals was to "reduce the level of friction between the two senior levels of government on matters of finance and jurisdictions and to permit for positive collaboration on the issues facing our health care system."

The Practical Issues

In addition to the launching of a concerted program to arouse interest in broad measures for a healthier lifestyle the Task Force saw the following as major issues in the health program.

The Elderly. It projected that nearly 15 percent of the population would be 65 + by 2006 and that this would create an enormous demand for hospital beds because of the lengthy stays involved; in 1980-81 the average hospital stay was 12 days, while that of patients 65 and over was 25.8 days. In 1980-81 elderly patients accounted for 48 percent of hospital patient days. These trends would be even stronger as the proportion of elderly over 85 increased. The solutions favoured in Task Force studies were essentially the development of lower-cost services for the care of the elderly, including services for day care, respite care, home nursing care, and improved nursing homes.

Technology. The rapid introduction of new technology has been costly and has raised an expectation among patients that almost any medical problem can be overcome. It has also given rise to a variety of problems: has the value of the technology been adequately demonstrated? would it replace existing procedures or become an add-on? how would staff be trained in its use and in what numbers? was there any plan for avoiding duplicate investment in a region? where equipment was scarce and demand heavy how are rationing decisions made? The studies before the Task Force favoured greater coordination of assessment of new technologies, closer coordination of use between areas, and closer supervision over application in daily use.

Manpower. The issue of the number and distribution of physicians has been of increasing concern. The efforts of the nursing profession to achieve complete baccalaureate status, of various groups to obtain a fee-for-services payment basis, and an exclusive "scope of practice" status have important implications for manpower and remuneration.

Studies made by the federal and provincial governments indicate a projected 12 percent surplus, or nearly 6,000 physicians, by the year 2000. The recommendations are for reduced entry of foreign trained physicians and for lower output from Canadian medical school. Some provinces have shortages in remote areas and in certain specialties, but in general are beginning to take steps to reduce supply or control doctors' incomes. The surplus of doctors is felt to contribute to the growing costs of medical programs as marginal doctors are compelled to prescribe extra medical services for their patients in order to bolster their incomes.

Utilization. At present individuals expect the latest and most expensive services and there are no constraints in the system to discourage this attitude. In addition doctors are strongly motivated to maximize income and communities to seek the best facilities for their residents. Some provinces are attempting to moderate demand and rationalize entry into various services, but without marked success.

The Task Force also made an extensive review of the health services provided by the federal government and made recommendations in several areas.

Macdonald Commission Study

A much shorter effort, the Macdonald Commission study, compared Canadian health expenditures with those of other countries and found them lower than most. The difference between Canada and the United States was particularly marked; in 1982 the percentage of GNP spent on health was in excess of 10 percent in the U.S. and approximately 2 percentage points lower in Canada. The study covered the by now familiar grounds of the effect of the aging of the population (by 2006 the 65 + group will account for 50 percent of hospital services costs) and the likely increase in costs from new technology. The study concludes with the proposition that having abandoned any economic criteria for the measurement of health services most of the decisions to be made are social decisions which will be implemented through the political process, a much more delicate and sensitive means than the economic system. A now familiar warning is also given that "many factors influencing health are quite unrelated to the health services sector. There is, in fact, a low correlation between the health status of a society and its expenditures on health care (Fuchs, 1975). Other factors such as personal lifestyles, environment, and heredity appear to have a greater influence on health; thus, policies designed to improve the health of Canadians must go beyond the health services sector."[22.2]

[22.2]Gilles Grenier, "Health Care Costs in Canada: Past and Future Trends," in Francois Vaillancourt, research coordinator, *Income Distribution and Economic Security in Canada.* Collected Research Studies of the Royal Commission on Economic Union and Development Prospects for Canada, vol. 1 (Toronto: University of Toronto Press, 1985), 277.

Provincial Views

The concern for growing medical costs that began only shortly after medicare had been introduced in the early seventies remains a constant theme of provincial budgets, now heightened by the federal trimming of EPF grants. The story in every province is a long record of studies and inquiries with resulting actions to stem the flow.

The most recent budgets, those of 1988, give evidence that harrassed provincial treasurers are still grappling with this massive and intractible issue. The following are typical instances. In a budget which showed 33 percent of total expenditure going for health the Minister of Finance and Corporate Affairs of British Columbia announced an increase in hospital premiums and urged that "Health care practitioners must provide cost effective care."

In Alberta the Provincial Treasurer announced the establishment of the Premier's Commission on Future Health Care for Albertans, to study the issues and options for health care and report by December 31, 1989. Alberta spends 26 percent of its budget on health.

Nova Scotia, which spends 27 percent of its budget on health, also announced the appointment of a Royal Commission on Health Care, to review costs of health care and make recommendations.

The Minister of Finance in New Brunswick stated that "We must plan our service growth in these fields within the range of what we can afford," and proceeded to eliminate subsidized drugs for seniors not on Guaranteed Income Supplement.

Ontario had experienced a temporary period of uncertainty following the election in 1985 of a government that had promised to abolish the health care premium. The Premier himself had suggested that the income tax might be extended to apply to health benefits to obtain alternative revenues, but this appeared to have been reconsidered when it was pointed out that this would require doubling the existing income tax rates. But provincial health care premiums had been frozen at their 1984 level, and growth in costs of health insurance had been financed from general revenues, mainly the sales and other commodity taxes.

The 1988 Ontario budget, as a means of public education, contained a seven-page budget paper on Health Care, showing that in 1988-89 33 percent of the total provincial expenditure would go for health. The share of provincial health and educational expenditure met by the federal government under EPF grants had dropped from 51.8 percent in 1979-80 to 39.3 percent in 1987-88. With rates of health premiums frozen at 1984 levels revenues from this source as a percent of total health care costs had fallen from 19.0 percent in 1984-85 to 14.9 percent in 1987-88. The provincial budget therefore was carrying a substantially increased share of the total.

Various studies had been made by committees and task forces, including a review headed by Dr. John Evans in 1977, but no marked changes in the financial structure had resulted. Steps appear to be underway toward greater concentration of health care at the community level, and one

Table 22.3   Provincial Governments: Hospital and Medical Services Annual Premiums, Selected Years, 1962-88

Year	P.E.I. S	P.E.I. F	Ont. S	Ont. F	Man. S	Man. F	Sask. S	Sask. F	Alta. S	Alta. F	B.C. S	B.C. F
						dollars						
1962	24	48	25	50	24	48	36	72	—	—	—	—
1964	—	—	39	78	24	48	26	52	—	—	—	—
1967	—	—	99	198	24	48	36	72	76	152	60	120-150
1969	—	—	137	274-309	102	204	36	72	69	138	60	120-150
1971	—	—	137	274-309	50	100	36	72	69	138	60	120-150
1973	—	—	132	264	—	—	36	—	69	138	60	120-150
1975	—	—	132	264	—	—	—	—	69	138	60	120-150
1976	—	—	192	384	—	—	—	—	85	169	60	120-150
1977	—	—	192	384	—	—	—	—	92	184	90	180-225
1978	—	—	228	456	—	—	—	—	92	184	90	180-225
1979	—	—	240	480	—	—	—	—	104	208	90	180-225
1980	—	—	240	480	—	—	—	—	114	228	102	204-225
1981	—	—	276	552	—	—	—	—	114	228	138	276-345
1982	—	—	324	648	—	—	—	—	168	336	180	336-384
1983	—	—	340	680	—	—	—	—	168	336	180	336-384
1984	—	—	357	714	—	—	—	—	168	336	192	360-408
1985	—	—	357	714	—	—	—	—	168	336	204	384-432
1986	—	—	357	714	—	—	—	—	168	336	204	384-432
1987	—	—	357	714	—	—	—	—	216	432	204	384-432
1988	—	—	357	714	—	—	—	—	216	432	204	384-432

S Single. F. Family.

Note: In addition in Saskatchewan, Alberta, and British Columbia at various times there were daily charges for hospital stay. Quebec has used payroll taxes on employers and a direct charge on self-employed for revenues.

Source: Canadian Tax Foundation, *Provincial Finances* and *Provincial and Municipal Finances*.

assumes that the province gives full support to the federal ban on advertising of tobacco products, as one of its task forces had urged reduction in tobacco use as a health measure. The idea of illness prevention rather than illness treatment was becoming attractive to all provincial authorities. The 1988 Budget Paper was mainly a historical review, but gave as the objective: "New ways must be found to control rising health care costs without sacrificing the quality of care." Various studies were underway toward this objective, obviously one which would not be achieved without stepping on some toes—perhaps the beneficiaries this time.

Retrospective—1988

It would be fascinating to continue pursuit of the odyssey of health insurance, as it is probably the most sensitive of the elements in the whole social security structure, and a constant source of conflict and tension, both between governments and between governments and governed. This overly long story must be terminated, however, with only a few brief words.

The vast and expensive phenomenon of health care has given rise to much thoughtful reflection by economists, social scientists, medical experts, and others. They ask such questions as: was it really necessary to set up such an elaborate governmental structure to achieve the objective of universality that might have been reached under private plans with a little more imagination? Was it wise to give such emphasis to hospitalization in health care with the early grants program for hospital construction? Were hospitals given too much freedom in the services they could provide? Have doctors been allowed too much discretion in prescribing those services for their patients? Should a basis other than fee for services have been adopted for doctor remuneration? Has the emphasis on treatment of illness in the Canadian program, and the vast amount of money that is now committed to that end, been to the detriment of more positive preventive programs? Would not more attention to health problems arising from working conditions, environment, or lifestyle—diet, alcoholism, drug addiction, etc.—be a wise investment? Are community health centres a useful innovation for this purpose? Will the system be able to cope with the rising number of older persons whose hospital stays are longer and more demanding than those of younger people? Is universality and first dollar coverage really essential for fair treatment of all citizens, or are they unnecessary extravagances? What values will be sacrificed in other areas of social concern if a continually rising share of GNP must be devoted to health care? With these and other penetrating questions unanswered we leave our review of the fascinating subject of how best, in the words of the Canada Health Act, "to protect, promote and restore the physical and mental well-being of residents of Canada."

Appendix
Health

The 1945 Proposals[22.3]

The following is the text of the detailed health proposals.

Proposals of the Federal Government

The specific proposals which the federal government wishes to put forward at this time for consideration by the Conference include:

(a) Grant for Planning and Organization;
(b) Health Insurance;
(c) Health Grants;
(d) Financial Assistance in the Construction of Hospitals.

It is believed that none of these proposals involves in itself any change in the constitutional jurisdiction or responsibility of federal or provincial governments under the British North America Act.

(a) Planning and Organization Grant

As a preliminary step towards the establishment of health insurance, the federal government proposes to make available to the provincial governments grants for planning and organization so that each provincial government may as soon as possible establish a full-time planning staff to prepare for and organize health insurance benefits within the province, and make provision for the training of necessary personnel. This grant will be available as part of an agreement under which the provincial governments undertake to complete the preliminary preparations within 18 months, and, before the expiration of that time, to submit provincial health insurance programmes to the federal government. The amount of the grant offered comes to a total of $620,000, divided among the provinces on the basis of $5,000 each, plus five cents per person according to the distribution of population at the time of the 1941 Census. The apportionment of this grant by provinces is shown in the table on page 672.

(b) Health Insurance Proposal

The federal government's health insurance proposal is designed to put provincial governments in a financial position to develop and administer a comprehensive health insurance programme worked out by progressive stages on an agreed basis. To this end the various

---

[22.3] Canada, *Dominion-Provincial Conference (1945)*. Dominion and Provincial Submissions (Ottawa: King's Printer, 1946), 89-94.

health benefits which the federal government would be prepared to assist in providing have been classified (see table below) and a procedure suggested for a wide degree of flexibility in each province in introducing them.

The proposed federal government's contributions to the cost of each benefit under the health insurance plan as it is brought into effect in each province or in any area within a province is

(i) a basic grant of one-fifth of the *estimated* cost of each service as shown on the table which follows (as from time to time revised by agreement), and

(ii) one-half the additional *actual* cost incurred by each provincial government of providing each benefit, provided that the total federal contribution does not exceed the amount stated in the table for each service, or a maximum of $12.96 per person, when the complete programme is in operation.

The table below shows the basis of the federal government's contribution to the provincial governments for health insurance in respect of each of the suggested benefits.

In order to get the plan started, for the next three years the cost of each benefit will be taken to the amounts shown in the table. These figures will be replaced after each three years by the actual average cost of giving each benefit.

The provinces may introduce the benefits by stages and may establish any benefit for the whole or any part of the province. For example, a province may secure assistance in providing nursing assistance in rural areas of part of the province. The federal government would then contribute as above to the cost of this service, for all the people in the area served. This arrangement would allow each province to institute the benefits for which it feels the most pressing need and to develop complete health insurance services through those stages which appear to be most expedient for the province concerned.

In order to ensure early provision of basic services, a provincial government entering the plan would agree to furnish general practitioner services, hospital care and visiting nursing services within two years of its entering upon the plan.

The table of benefits with the figures at which the cost of each will be set until replaced after three years by the average actual cost of each service follows:

The per capita cost of the general practitioner services, hospital care and visiting nursing services, grouped together as the First Stage, will be approximately $10.20 for the country as a whole on the basis of the cost shown in the table. For this, the federal government would provide a basic grant of one-fifth, or $2.04 per capita. In addition it would share equally all additional actual costs up to the estimated total cost. The federal contribution in respect to these three services

Basis of Federal Contributions for Health Insurance
(Dollars per capita)

Service Provided	Estimated Average Cost of Service[1]	% of Total Cost	Basic Dominion Grant (20% of total est.)	Maximum Additional Dominion Grant (50% of additional actual cost to maximum)
	$	%	$	%
First Stage				
General practitioner service	6.00	28	1.20	2.40
Hospital care	3.60	17	0.72	1.44
Visiting nursing service	0.60	3	0.12	0.24
Total First Stage	10.20	48	2.04	4.08
Later Stages				
Other medical services (consultant, specialist and surgical	3.50	16	0.70	1.40
Other nursing services (including private duty)	1.15	5	0.23	0.46
Dental care..................	3.60	16	0.72	1.44
Pharmaceutical (drugs, serums and surgical appliances)........	2.55	12	0.51	1.02
Laboratory services (blood tests, X-rays, etc.)	0.60	3	0.12	0.24
	21.60	100	4.32	8.64

[1] Estimated cost to be revised on basis of actual costs after three years.

would consequently be made up of the basic grant of $2.04 plus an additional amount up to $4.08 per capita, or a total of $6.12. Again, on the figures shown in the table and on the assumption that the benefits provided in the First Stage were extended to all of Canada, the cost to the federal government for the First Stage would be $70 million and about $45 million for the provincial governments.

A province's participation in the plan would begin

(1) Upon a province making use of the proposed Planning and Organization Grant within eighteen months and presenting a plan, satisfactory to the Governor-in-Council, describing the existing services and benefits in the province and the stages by which benefits will be provided and the full health insurance plan put into effect;

(2) Upon a province within the same period of eighteen months making an agreement with the federal government to provide the initial benefits for the First Stage of general practitioner services, hospital care and visiting nursing services within two years of the signing of the agreement. The agreement should further provide

for the carrying into effect of the total health insurance programme over a term of years, for a registration fee to be paid by or on behalf of every person, who has attained his sixteenth birthday and whose normal place of residence is in the province or area where benefits are provided, for a registration, accounting and reporting system, for the cost of administration within the province to be paid out of money provided by the provincial government, and such other provisions and conditions as may be agreed to between the provincial government and the federal government.

A complete health insurance service for all the people of Canada must obviously take a number of years to introduce. The cost to the federal and provincial governments would depend on the health benefits provided at any given time. For the full health insurance programme when finally realized the total cost, for the population shown in the 1941 Census and for benefits as shown in the table above, would be $250 million per annum. On this basis the federal government's share would be $150 million and the provincial government's share $100 million.

On the same assumption the payments by the federal government for the various stages are shown on the following table:

These proposals are being made by the federal government as the most realistic method by which to realize, as soon as possible, the ultimate goal of a complete system of health insurance on a nationwide basis. The provision of separate stages and the various alternatives left open to the provincial governments have been adopted in order to make the scheme more flexible and practicable, and not with any idea of limiting the total scope. It is hoped that in this way the needs and circumstances of all the provinces can be adequately met, and the greatest possible degree of progress achieved.

(c) Health Grants

Previous references have indicated the wide variations in the provision of public health measures in the provinces. The object of public health grants is to ensure a more nearly standard quality and quantity of public health services throughout Canada at a higher level.

Vital statistics, the control of communicable disease, the control of water pollution, industrial hygiene, tuberculosis control, venereal disease control, laboratory services, maternal and child hygiene, nutrition, mental health, public health research and the training of technical personnel, are all matters of much more than provincial interest, and freely cut across provincial boundaries and affect all the population of Canada. In the field of health perhaps more than in any other field, every part of Canada has a definite relationship to and interdependence with every other part. We can't effectively fight separate wars in public health.

Cost to the Federal Government of Initial Benefits Under Health Insurance
First Stage
(In thousands of dollars)

Province	General practitioner service	Hospital care	Visiting nursing service	Total
Prince Edward Island	342	206	34	582
Nova Scotia	2,081	1,248	208	3,537
New Brunswick	1,646	988	165	2,799
Quebec	11,995	7,197	1,199	20,391
Ontario	13,636	8,181	1,363	23,180
Manitoba	2,627	1,576	263	4,466
Saskatchewan	3,256	1,935	323	5,514
Alberta	2,866	1,720	287	4,873
British Columbia	2,944	1,767	294	5,005
Total cost to federal government ..	41,393	24,818	4,136	70,347

Cost to the Federal Government of other Benefits Under Health Insurance
Later Stages
(thousands of dollars)

Province	Other medical service	Other nursing service	Dental care	Pharmacists	Laboratory service	Total
Prince Edward Island ..	200	66	205	145	34	650
Nova Scotia	1,214	399	1,249	884	208	3,954
New Brunswick	960	316	988	700	165	3,129
Quebec	6,997	2,299	7,197	5,098	1,199	22,790
Ontario	7,954	2,614	8,181	5,795	1,363	25,907
Manitoba	1,532	503	1,576	1,117	263	4,991
Saskatchewan	1,882	618	1,935	1,371	323	6,129
Alberta	1,672	549	1,720	1,218	287	5,446
British Columbia	1,718	564	1,767	1,251	294	5,594
Total cost to federal government	24,129	7,928	24,818	17,579	4,136	78,590

There are good reasons why the provision of the public health grants should not await the inauguration of the health insurance plan. The return from the armed services of trained personnel will largely take place within the next eighteen months. It is important that the services of the best people should be obtained for this public health work before they are dispersed—perhaps to other countries. It is important also that a solid base of public health services should be laid down on which can be built the health insurance plan. The Government is therefore giving consideration to providing a series of grants on the following basis without waiting for the inauguration of health insurance.

(1) General Public Health Grant—A General Public Health Grant of 35¢ per capita annually on the basis of the population at the latest Census of Canada, to be made available to assist the provincial

governments in the development of general public health services
as described in the First and Third Schedules to the Draft Health
Insurance Bill; provided that a province and its local governments
shall continue to expend on these public health services amounts
exclusive of the grant, at least as great as those spent previously.

(2) Tuberculosis Grant—A Tuberculosis Grant not to exceed
$3,000,000 annually to be made available to assist the provincial
governments in providing free treatment for persons suffering
from tuberculosis and to be distributed as follows:—

   (i) 50 percent on the basis of population as enumerated at the
   latest Census of Canada; and

   (ii) 50 percent according to the number of new cases of venereal
   disease reported in the previous calendar year as certified by
   the Dominion Statistician.

but the grant to a province not to exceed one-quarter of the total
monies, exclusive of capital expenditures, expended by the provincial government and its local governments during the previous
fiscal year for the prevention of tuberculosis and treatment of all
persons suffering from tuberculosis.

(3) Mental Health Grant—A Mental Health Grant not to exceed
$4,000,000 annually to be made available to assist the provincial
governments in the prevention of mental illness, in providing free
treatment for all persons suffering from mental illness and for
mental defectives. The Grant to be distributed according to
the per capita distribution of the population as enumerated at the
latest Census of Canada, but the grant to a province not to exceed
one-fifth of the total monies, exclusive of capital expenditures,
expended by the provincial government and its local governments
during the previous fiscal year for the prevention of mental illness
and treatment of all persons suffering from mental illness and for
mental defectives.

(4) Venereal Disease Grant—A Venereal Disease Grant not to exceed
$500,000 annually to be made available to assist the provincial
governments in the prevention and free treatment of venereal
disease, and to be distributed as follows:

   (i) 50 percent on the basis of population as enumerated at the
   latest Census of Canada; and

   (ii) 50 percent according to the number of new cases of venereal
   disease reported in the previous calendar year as certified by
   the Dominion Statistician.

The federal government would match the expenditure of each
province up to the limit of each province's share of the grant. The
grant proposed here would be in substitution for the existing grant
for venereal disease.

(5) Crippled Children Grant—A Crippled Children Grant not to
exceed $500,000 annually to be made available to assist the pro-

vincial governments in meeting the urgent need of an extensive programme for the prevention and treatment of crippling conditions in children, and to be distributed on the basis of the population as enumerated at the latest Census of Canada, or on such other method of distribution as may be arrived at by the federal government after consultation with the Dominion Council of Health.

(6) Professional Training—An item not to exceed an amount of $250,000 annually for professional training of personnel in the field of public health to assist the provincial governments in embarking upon an expanded programme of public health services.

(7) Public Health Research—An item not to exceed $100,000 annually for Public Health Research to encourage public health research and to assist the provincial governments in meeting emergent conditions.

(8) Civilian Blind—An amount to be determined annually to be made available to permit the pension age for blind persons to be lowered from 40 to 21 years of age and to provide for treatment of the blind who will benefit therefrom, and of persons suffering from conditions which might lead to blindness, the cost to be financed on the basis of 50 percent by the federal government and 50 per cent by the provincial governments.

General Conditions—The grants to be conditional upon the Governor in Council being satisfied after consultation with the Dominion Council of Health that the provisions and administration of the general public health services and special services are such as would secure the effective and satisfactory use of the grants to extend and improve these services throughout the province.

Estimated Cost—The maximum cost of these grants to the federal government, on the assumption that they are made full use of by the provinces, and their distribution to the provincial governments would be as follows:—

(d) Financial Assistance in the Construction of Hospitals

It is recognized that the provision of complete health insurance services would require a considerable extension in hospital facilities throughout the country. Much of this expansion would be required even for the first stage specified. It is also recognized that this expansion would be desirable quite aside from health insurance in order to provide the proper facilities for treatment and research.

To make a hospital extension program less burdensome to the provincial governments and to local communities, it is proposed that the federal government should provide loans to the provincial governments entering health insurance agreements, and through provincial governments to municipalities and other organizations, for necessary expansion of hospital facilities, at a rate of interest equal to or only

**Estimated Cost and Distribution of Planning and Organization Grant
and Health Grants
(In thousands of dollars)**

Provinces	Planning and Organization Grant	(1) General Public Health	(2) Tuberculosis Grant	(3) Mental Health Grant	(4) Venereal Disease Grant
	$	$	$	$	$
Prince Edward Island ...	9.8	33.3	25.5	33.0	2.5
Nova Scotia............	33.9	203.3	178.5	200.6	27.0
New Brunswick.........	27.9	160.1	132.0	158.7	20.0
Quebec...............	171.6	1,166.2	1,107.0	1,156.2	143.5
Ontario	194.4	1,325.7	765.0	1,314.3	167.0
Manitoba.............	41.5	255.4	184.5	253.2	32.0
Saskatchewan	49.8	313.6	180.0	310.9	29.5
Alberta	44.8	278.7	178.5	276.3	31.5
British Columbia	45.9	286.3	249.0	283.8	46.5
Total cost to the federal government .	619.6	4,022.6	3,000.0	3,987.0	499.5

Provinces	(5) Crippled Children Grant	(6) Professional Training	(7) Public Health Research	(8) Civilian Blind	Total for Health Grants 1 to 8
	$	$	$	$	$
Prince Edward Island ...	4.2	....	....	19.5	118.0
Nova Scotia............	25.0	....	....	114.0	748.4
New Brunswick.........	19.8	....	....	136.4	627.0
Quebec...............	144.4	....	....	452.1	4,169.4
Ontario	164.2	....	....	284.0	4,020.2
Manitoba.............	31.6	....	....	60.2	816.9
Saskatchewan	38.8	....	....	64.0	936.8
Alberta	34.5	....	....	47.9	847.4
British Columbia	35.4	....	....	65.8	966.8
Total cost to the federal government .	497.9	250.0	100.0	1,243.9	13,600.9*

*Does not include Planning and Organization Grant, which is non-recurring but does include $350 thousand to be spent by Dominion on Professional Training and Public Health Research.

slightly above the cost of such loans to the Dominion, and that the interest and amortization would be payable out of the hospital care benefit under the Health Insurance Grant, or out of the Tuberculosis Grant or the Mental Health Grant, as the case may be.

Summary

The National Health Program includes proposals for Health Insurance to provide health services to individuals, Health Grants to assist and extend public health and preventive medicine, a grant for Organization and Planning, and provision for low-interest loans for the construction of hospitals. The federal government is developing its own health services so that in its own field it will be fully prepared to discharge its constitutional responsibilities. In order also to assist the provincial governments in their fields the federal government will be prepared to make its staff available in a consultative capacity and to consider providing the staff and equipment necessary for doing those things which the provincial governments agree are capable of being done most effectively by the federal government.

The National Health Program also contemplates the construction of a National Laboratory as a post-war development project, the extension of health services to the Civil Service, the application of proper health and sanitation standards for the federal government buildings, the development of the National Fitness program, the provision of consultative services for departments of the federal government, and a very great increase, wherever possible, in all fields of cooperation between the federal and provincial governments, so as to press forward the best possible health programme for the people of Canada.

Bibliography, chapters 20 to 22

Badgley, R.F., and Smith, R.D. *User Charges for Health Services*. Toronto: Ontario Council of Health, 1979.

_____, and Wolfe, S. *Doctors' Strike: Medical Care and Conflict in Saskatchewan*. Toronto: MacMillan, 1967.

Bird, R.M., and Fraser, R.D. *Commentaries on the Hall Report*. Toronto: Ontario Economic Council, 1981.

British Columbia. Hospital Insurance Inquiry Board. *Report*. Victoria: 1951.

Brown, M.C. *The Financing of Personal Health Care Services in New Zealand, Canada and Australia*. Research Monograph no. 20. Canberra: The Australian National University, 1977.

_____. *National Health Insurance in Canada and Australia*. Canberra: The Australian National University, 1983.

_____. "The Implications of Established Program Finance for National Health Insurance." (Summer 1980) VI *Canadian Public Policy*, 521-32.

Bryden, M.H. "Financing Provincial Hospital Insurance." (January-February 1961) *Canadian Tax Journal*, 38-40.

Boulet, J.A., and Grenier, G. *Health Expenditures in Canada and the Impact of Demographic Changes on Future Government Health Insurance Expenditures*. Discussion Paper no. 123. Economic Council of Canada. Ottawa: the Council, 1978.

Canada. Advisory Committee on Health Insurance. *Report*. Ottawa: 1943.

_____. Department of National Health and Welfare. *National Health Expenditures in Canada*. Ottawa: Statistics Canada, occasional.

_____. *The Community Health Centre in Canada*. Report of the Community Health Centre Project to the Conference of Health Ministers. Ottawa: 1972.

_____. *Review of Health Services in Canada*. Ottawa: 1974.

_____. *A New Perspective on the Health of Canadians*. Ottawa: 1975.

_____. *Estimates, Part III. Expenditure Plan*. Ottawa: annual.

_____. *National Health Expenditures in Canada, 1960-1975*. Ottawa: 1979.

_____. *National Health Expenditures in Canada, 1970 to 1982*. Ottawa: 1984.

_____. Dominion-Provincial Conference on Reconstruction. *Proposals of the Government of Canada*. Ottawa: 1945.

_____. Dominion-Provincial Conference on Reconstruction. Reference Paper. *Health, Welfare and Labour*. Ottawa: 1945.

_____. Dominion-Provincial Conference (1945). Dominion and Provincial Submissions and Plenary Conference Discussions. Ottawa: 1946.

_____. Economic Advisory Committee. *Report*. 1943. (Mackenzie King Papers). Ottawa: 1943.

_____. House of Commons. Special Committee on Social Security. *Minutes of Proceedings and Evidence*. Ottawa: 1943.

_____. House of Commons. Special Committee on Estimates. *Proceedings No. 1-5*. Ottawa: 1956.

————. House of Commons. Standing Committee on National Health and Welfare Respecting Consideration of the Health Care System of Canada and its Funding. *Fifth Report*. Ottawa: 1988.

————. *Preserving Universal Medicare*. Ottawa 1983.

————. Royal Commission on Health Services. *Report*. Ottawa: 1964.

————. Statistics Canada. *A Prognosis for Hospitals: The Effects of Population Change on the Need for Hospital Space*. Cat. no. 83-520E. Ottawa: Statistics Canada, 1979.

————. Statistics Canada. *Consolidated Government Finance*. Cat. no 68-202. Ottawa: Statistics Canada, annual.

————. Statistics Canada. *Historical Statistics of Canada*, 2nd ed. Cat. no. CS 11-516E. Ottawa: 1983.

————. Statistics Canada. *Perspectives on Health*. Cat. no. 82-540E. Ottawa: Statistics Canada, 1983.

Canadian Council for Social Development. *Better Health Care for Canadians*. Ottawa: The Council, 1962.

————. *Health Services for Canada*. Ottawa: the Council, 1965.

————. *The Challenge of Health Care for Canadians*. Ottawa, the Council, 1979.

————. *The Role of Local Government in the Provision of Health and Social Services in Canada*. Ottawa: the Council, 1987.

Canadian Tax Foundation. "Health and Priorities;" "Health Care Estimates." (July-August 1964) XII *Canadian Tax Journal*, 223-29.

————. "Health Plan Costs—Continued." (July-August 1965) XIII *Canadian Tax Journal*, 269-75.

————. *The National Finances*. Toronto: the Foundation, annual.

————. *Provincial and Municipal Finances*. Toronto: the Foundation, annual.

Canadian Medical Association. *Health: A Need for Redirection. A Task Force on the Allocation of Health Care Resources*. Ottawa: the Association, 1984.

Comanor, W.S. *National Health Insurance in Ontario; the Effects of a Policy of Cost Control*. Washington, D.C.: American Enterprise Institute for Public Policy Research, 1980.

Cassidy, H.M. *Public Health and Welfare Reorganization in Canada*. Toronto: Ryerson, 1945.

Castonguay, Claude. *New Distribution Program for Social and Health Services in Quebec*. Address to the 62nd Annual Meeting of the Canadian Public Health Association. Toronto: April 22, 1971.

Culyer, A.J. *Measuring Health: Lessons for Ontario*. Toronto: Ontario Economic Council, 1978.

Denton, F.T., and Spencer, B.G. "Population Aging and Future Health Costs in Canada." (December 1984). X:4 *Canadian Public Policy*, 155-63.

Economic Council of Canada. *Fifth Annual Review*. Ottawa: Queen's Printer, 1968.

Enterline, P.E. "The Distribution of Medical Services before and after 'free medical care'—the Quebec Experience (1973)." 289 *New England Journal of Medicine*, 1174-78.

Evans, R.G., and Stoddart, G.L. eds. *Medicair at Maturity*. Calgary: University of Calgary Press, 1986.

Evans, R.G. "Hang Together, or Hang Separately: The Viability of a Universal Care System in an Aging Society." (June 1987) 13 *Canadian Public Policy*, 165-80.

_____. *Strained Mercy: The Economics of Canadian Health Care*. Toronto: Butterworths. 1984.

"Extra Billing Row Growing." *The Financial Post*, August 3, 1985.

Feeney, D., and Stoddard, G. "Towards Inproved Health Technology in Canada." (September 1988) 14 *Canadian Public Policy*, 254-65.

Grenier, Gilles. "Health Care Costs in Canada: Past and Future Trends."In Francois Vaillancourt, research coordinator, *Income Distribution and Economic Security in Canada*. Collected Research Studies of the Royal Commission on the Economic Union and Development Prospects for Canada, vol. 1. Toronto: University of Toronto Press, 1985.

Gross, H. John, and Schwenger, Cope W. *Health Care Costs for the Elderly in Ontario. 1976-2026*. Toronto: Ontario Economic Council, 1981.

Hall, E.M. *Canada's National-Provincial Health Program for the 1980's: A Commitment for Renewal*. Ottawa: Department of National Health and Welfare, 1980.

_____. "Health Service Costs." (September-October 1964) XII *Canadian Tax Journal*, 364-72.

Lougheed, W. Associates. *Underwriting Canadian Health; An Economic View of Welfare Programs*. The Canadian Chamber of Commerce and the Canadian Life Insurance Officers Association. Toronto: 1957.

Manga, Pran. *The Political Economy of Extra-Billing*. Ottawa: Canadian Council on Social Development, 1983.

Marsh, L.C. *Report on Social Security for Canada*. Ottawa: 1943.

Maxwell, R.S. *Health and Wealth; An International Study of Health-Care Spending*. Lexington, Mass.: D.C. Heath & Co., 1981.

National Council of Welfare. *Medicare: The Public Goal and Private Practice*. Ottawa: 1982.

OECD, *Financing and Delivering Health Care: A Comparative Analysis of OECD Countries*. Paris: OECD, 1987.

Ontario. The Health Planning Task Force. *Report*. Toronto: 1984.

_____. The Special Program Review. *Report*. Toronto: 1975.

Ontario Economic Council. *Issues and Alternatives-1976. Health*. Toronto: the Council, 1976.

_____. *Issues and Alternatives: Update, 1979*. Toronto: the Council.

Ontario Health Review Panel. *Towards a Shared Direction for Health in Ontario*. Report of the Ontario Health Review Panel. Toronto: 1987.

Perry, D.B. "The Cost of Medicare." (May-June 1968) 16 *Canadian Tax Journal*, 198-201.

_____. "The Financing of Medicare." (July-August 1968) 16 *Canadian Tax Journal*, 87-89.

Quebec. *Report of the Commission of Enquiry on Health and Social Welfare* (Castonguay-Nepveu Commission). Quebec: 1971.

Saskatchewan. Health Survey Committee. *Report*. Regina: 1951.

Shillington, H. *The Road to Medicare in Canada*. Toronto: Del Graphics, 1972.

Stevenson, M.H., and Williams, A.P. "Physicians and Medicare: Professional Ideology and Canadian Health Care Policy." (September 1985) 11:3 *Canadian Public Policy*, 504-21.

Stoddard, Greg L. "Rationalizing the Health Care System." In Courchene, Thomas J., Conklin, David W., and Cook, Gail A. eds. *Ottawa and the Provinces, The Distribution of Money and Power*, vol. 2. Toronto: Ontario Economic Council, 1985.

Taylor, M.G. *Financial Aspects of Health Insurance.* Toronto: Canadian Tax Foundation, 1957.

———. "Financing Health Insurance-What Lies Ahead?" In *Report of Proceedings of the Eleventh Tax Conference*, 1958 Conference Report. Toronto: The Canadian Tax Foundation, 1958, 21.

———. *Health insurance and Canadian Public Policy*: The Seven Decisions that Created the Canadian Health Insurance System. Montreal: McGill-Queen's University Press, 1978.

———. *The Administration of Health Insurance in Canada.* Toronto: Oxford University Press, 1956.

Taylor, M.G., Stevenson, H.M., and Williams, A.P. *Medical Perspective on Canadian Medicare.* Montreal: the Institute for Research in Public Policy. 1986.

Waller, G.R., and Manga, P. "The Development of Health Policy in Canada." In *Politics of Canadian Public Policy.* Toronto: University of Toronto Press, 1983.

Wilkins, R., and Adams, O. *Healthfulness of Life.* Montreal: The Institute for Research in Public Policy, 1984.

York, G. *The High Price of Health.* Toronto: James Lorimer & Co. 1987.

Unemployment Insurance

23
Unemployment Insurance

One of the most distressing features of the mid-eighties economy is the failure of employment to keep pace with the otherwise reasonably satisfactory recovery. Canada is not alone in this problem, as many other countries are equally plagued. For the individual, prolonged unemployment can be emotionally and financially disastrous. For society it presents a dilemma for which there are no quick or easy solutions. Social programs are not designed for the long-term support of 8-10 percent of the labour force. To cope in some sort of way the existing measures must be adapted to the emergency, and in the process can be overloaded for periods far beyond their design capacity. And so it has been with unemployment insurance in Canada.

Origins of the Plan

Unemployment insurance was established as a federal program under the Unemployment Insurance Act passed in 1940 in recognition of the fact that the historic provincial-municipal relief system was a hopelessly inadequate instrument for dealing with unemployment on a national scale. By this time under Keynesian influence the federal government was beginning to accept more responsibility for economic stability, and an effective unemployment insurance program was an essential element. Both the National Employment Commission in 1937 and the Royal Commission on Dominion-Provincial Relations in 1940 had pressed for federal assumption of responsibility for the "employable unemployed," and the federal government had been willing to accept this recommendation as part of the rearrangement of powers recommended by the Royal Commission. Although conferences with the provinces failed in this purpose, the federal government was determined nonetheless to proceed with a program of unemployment insurance. Implementation of its proposal required the consent of the provinces for constitutional reasons; this being obtained, the necessary amendment to the British North America Act was passed by the United Kingdom Parliament and Canadian legislation followed in 1940. The plan commenced operation in 1941.

Despite its origin in the long years of the Great Depression it is clear that the measure was intended, as the insurance principle implied, as a means of bridging the normally short gap between having one job and finding another. It was not designed to be a long-term income support program. Its present use therefore is at cross purposes with this intention.

Some Basic Characteristics

While there have been numerous changes in the plan in the quarter-century since 1940 some basic elements have remained intact. For one, the program has operated throughout as a separate account with its own revenues and expenditures, until recently, as a fund outside the general budget. For another, it has been supported by contributions from three sources—employees, employers, and the federal government. The first two elements, although changed substantially from time to time, have been relatively stable; by contrast the contribution of the federal government has shifted radically with changing concepts of its appropriate role. A basic requirement, although not maintained with complete consistency, is that in the ordinary case the receipt of benefits must be preceded by the making of contributions and have some relation to the amount of those contributions. However this principle has operated without regard to the experience rating of the industry and has been subject to some marked departures for special situations.

Coverage

All persons in employment are subject to the Act except for named exclusions. In the 1940 legislation the exclusions were workers in agriculture, forestry, fishing, hunting, trapping, transportation by air and water, stevedoring, domestic service, teaching, non-profit hospitals and charitable institutions, the armed forces, police, federal civil servants, provincial civil servants unless the province agreed, and municipal employees certified as permanent. In addition casual and part-time employees were excluded and employees earning more than $2,000 a year. Coverage was gradually extended by regulation over the first decade to include workers in air and water transportation, stevedoring, lumbering and logging, professional nursing, public utilities, hospitals and optionally charitable institutions. Further extensions prior to 1971 included parts of the agricultural and forestry industries, fishermen, barbers, hairdressers, taxi and bus drivers.

The government appointed a committee of inquiry in 1961, known after its chairman as the Gill Committee, to study several aspects of the plan. The committee's report made recommendations for substantial changes, but these were not acted on immediately. An interdepartmental committee was appointed in 1966 to review the Gill and other proposals, and in turn its recommendations were reviewed by a project team which issued a report in 1968. This activity was the prelude to government presentation of a White Paper in June 1970, followed by enactment of the Unemployment Insurance Act of 1971, given Royal Assent in June 1971. Coverage under the new Act was almost universal. Some large exempt groups, such as teachers and civil servants, over one million in all, were brought in. The excluded workers after 1971 were mainly those who could control their own employment, recipients of Canada or Quebec Pension benefits, persons over 70, and certain classes of casual workers. Changes were also made in the exclusions on an income basis. The original earnings exclusion of $2,000 set in 1941 was increased to $2,400 in 1943, $3,120 in 1948, $4,800 in 1950, $5,460 in 1959, and $7,800 in 1968. The 1971 legislation removed the exclusion entirely, so that all employees at any level of salary were covered. However an annual amount was retained as the maximum insurable salary, and by indexation based on the annual increase in wage and salary levels this had reached $565 a week by 1988. There has also been a floor for minimum insurable earnings. Eligibility depends on earning over 20 percent of maximum insurable earnings; workers receiving time-calculated earnings must have worked for 15 hours per week. Minimum eligible earnings rose from $30 in 1972 to $113 in 1988.

Between 1972 and 1987 the labour force increased from 8.9 million to 13.1 million, and the insured population from 7.8 million to 11.9 million. Insurance coverage has therefore averaged 89 to 90 percent of the labour force. The main non-employed exclusions, (i.e. members of the labour force other than employees) roughly a million in all, are self-employed, proprietors, and unpaid family workers.

One of the most contentious extensions of coverage has been the inclusion of self-employed fishermen from 1955, and later their wives. This move was challenged by the Gill Committee as an attempt to use the insurance mechanism as a welfare measure to cope with a specific problem of a long-term character, and not the provision of assistance during temporary periods of unemployment. The White Paper of 1971 proposed that a fishing income stabilization scheme replace insurance coverage, but to 1988 no such scheme had been adopted. In the meantime the federal government is financing 90 percent of fishermen's benefits, as premiums from the industry cover 10 percent or less of the pay-out.

Equally contentious among experts has been the extension of "off-season" benefits, in addition to regular benefits, without payment of additional premiums. This was started in 1946, the "off-season" then being designated as January 1 to March 31. There followed a phase in which Supplementary Benefits succeeded to Seasonal Benefits, but since 1955 the program has officially provided for Seasonal Benefits. Beginning in 1957-58 the seasonal benefit period was extended to five-and-a-half months, but has been varied at other times.

The regularity and predictability of seasonal unemployment in Canada in such industries as construction, forestry, and agriculture and the granting of extra benefits without additional charge has been a constant source of dissatisfaction to experts and representatives of other more stable industries. The Gill Committee in 1962 stated that this had been the most common source of its complaints. The Committee opposed the introduction of Experience Rating (premium charges that reflect the actual benefit experience of each industry), but this principle was recommended in modified form by the 1968 Study Group, was further modified in the 1970 White Paper and embodied in the 1971 Act. However no regulations were adopted to implement the authority granted, and following the Report of the 1977 Comprehensive Review it was repealed. A Task Force of 1981 again reviewed Experience Rating and rejected it. This negative experience has not deterred economists from continuing to express their dissatisfaction with this break with the insurance principle and the need to keep the scheme from being cluttered by measures which they see as income transference devices. Apparently the depth of this concern has failed to impress the officials, and even less the politicians, who no doubt view with considerable distaste the thought of imposing the highest premiums on the least stable industries.

Entitlements and Benefits

There have been some standard tests for eligibility throughout, such as being legitimately unemployed and capable of and available for work (the exceptions being sickness and pregnancy eligibility introduced in 1972). There have also been penalties for "voluntary quits" and other self-imposed absences. The attendance at a course or training school recommended by the Commission has frequently also been a pre-condition. Usually also there has been a requirement that following a period of drawing benefits from the fund a minimum repayment into the fund must be made. Employees receiving benefits have been allowed to earn limited amounts of income without losing their eligibility—up to 50 percent under the 1941 system, reduced to 25 percent under the 1971 regime.

Leaving these matters aside, the main condition for eligibility has been the making of contributions to the fund on the basis of which a corresponding benefit is earned. We will concentrate on this fundamental aspect to avoid undue complications.

In the 1940 Act the main requirement was payment of the premium on at least 180 days of work in the previous two years. Benefits were earned at the rate of one day for each five days of contribution made in the last five years, with a penalty of one day for each three days of benefit in the last three years. Benefits could be received for a minimum of 6 weeks to a maximum of 51 weeks. A waiting period was required, which started at nine days, (plus one non-compensable day). This was reduced to eight days in 1950, to five days in 1952 and set at six days after 1955. In 1971 it was increased to two weeks, where it has remained.

The original daily basis of tallying was replaced by a weekly basis in the 1955 legislation, and the eligibility test for benefits was considerably relaxed. In place of a minimum payment in each of 180 days, the new requirement was for a payment in each of 30 weeks in the preceding two years, of which at least eight were required to be in the year just past. At the same time the basic minimum benefit, previously six weeks, was increased to 15 weeks. The maximum benefit was lowered from 51 weeks to 36 weeks, but was raised again to 52 weeks in 1959.

The eligibility provisions were made extremely complicated in the 1971 Act. The basic change was the creation of two classes of beneficiaries—(1) workers with a minor attachment to the work force, and (2) workers with a major attachment. The former was composed of workers having eight but less than twenty weeks of employment in their qualifying period; the latter were workers having more than twenty weeks of such employment. Following the two weeks waiting period the "minors" were entitled to up to eight weeks of initial benefits, while the "majors" were entitled to up to fifteen weeks. (In both cases part of the initial benefit was paid as an "advance" of initial benefit). If the worker was still unemployed at the end of the initial period of benefits, that period could be "re-established" and further benefits paid.

In addition, a new concept of "extended benefits" was introduced, which varied with the national rate of unemployment. A minor beneficiary who was still unemployed after receiving eight weeks of initial benefits and a further series of payments under re-established initial benefits could receive "extended benefits" for a further eight weeks if the national unemployment rate was over 5 percent, for four weeks if the rate was between 4 and 5 percent but none if the rate was below 4 percent. Major claimants were similarly treated. For both categories a further series of extended benefits was paid if the regional rate of unemployment exceeded the national rate, the additional period varying with excesses of 1, 2 and 3 percent. For example, when the regional rate was more than 3 percent higher than the national rate, the extension was for 18 weeks. Other new benefits for major claimants included unemployment because of illness or pregnancy (under closely defined conditions); a lump-sum severance payment equal to three weeks benefits was also provided for major claimants on reaching 70 years of age or receiving a Canada or Quebec Pension Plan payment.

Major changes were made in this complex system in 1976 and 1977. In 1976 the payment of an advance on initial benefits was abandoned. In 1977 the remaining payment phases were reduced from five to three.

The Present System

The three phases of the present system are the initial phase, the labour force extended phase, and the regional extended phase. (1) The initial phase pays up to 25 weeks of benefits based on the number of weeks worked in insurable employment. (2) The labour force extended benefits phase provides additional benefits up to a maximum of 13 weeks based on the number of weeks worked over 26; (3) The third phase provides an extended benefit based on the regional unemployment rate. The scale gives an additional two weeks of benefit for each 0.5 percent of unemployment above 4 percent, to a maximum of 32 weeks for a regional rate of 11.5 percent and over. Benefits based on a national unemployment rate were dropped. The total available period of benefits is 50 weeks in any 52 week period, for which a claimant can qualify depending on the unemployment rate in the district in which he lives, with as low as 10 weeks of contribution.

These changes in benefits were accompanied by tougher entitlement requirements. From 1979 on, 16 to 20 weeks of insurable employment were required for new benefits for workers who had received substantial benefits in the previous 52 weeks; 20 weeks of contributions were required for new entrants and re-entrants.

Changes during the seventies deprived retiring employees of a perk that was becoming fairly general—the practice of applying for unemployment insurance immediately on retirement. This pleasant supplement to retirement income was eliminated by an amendment which cut off eligibility for persons at age 65. Retirees henceforth would be given the three weeks lump-sum payment previously mentioned.

Contributions, Benefits, and Operating Results

The many and complex changes in the financial aspects of the plan make it almost impossible to give a satisfactory overview. Some very approximate indications must suffice, the presentation being divided between the pre-1971 and post-1971 regimes.

Much of the information in the following text has been reduced to tables which appear later. See table 23.1 for data on the 1941-71 period, and table 23.2 for the post-1971 period.

1941-71
Contributions

As was previously mentioned, revenues throughout have come from premiums paid by employers and employees and from amounts contributed by the federal government. In the pre-1971 period about 70 percent of revenues came from the private sector and about 30 percent from the government. Until 1972 the employer-employee contributions were required by law to represent equal aggregate contributions to the fund. Actual premiums were based on schedules of insurable earnings of eligible workers, at first measured on a daily basis and later on a weekly. The 1940 schedules set out differing amounts of premiums to be paid on specified wage scales, but the employer and employee schedules differed in detail to reflect concepts of appropriate slopes of progression held by officials of the day. The scales were set to ensure that lower wage workers paid a lower premium in relation to their benefits than higher income workers. The problems of maintaining this very delicate balance in periods of rapidly changing wage levels became too complex, and in 1950 uniform scales for employee and employer contributions were adopted. The effort to maintain highest benefit ratios for lowest paid workers continued until the 1971 Act was passed, when both premiums and benefits were established as a uniform percentage applicable to insurable earnings at all levels.

Under the pre-1972 plan the government contribution was calculated as 20 percent of the combined employer-employee revenues. Administrative expenses were paid by the government, and it also paid the amount required from it as an employer. In practice government was responsible for a fairly stable share of 25 to 30 percent of revenues over the period. It also funded special features, such as the coverage of self-employed fishermen.

Benefits

Until 1968 benefits increased only modestly. The maximum benefit, payable to a person with dependants, increased from $14.40 in 1941 to $36.00 weekly commencing in 1959. In July 1968 the $36.00 went to $53.00, and in January 1971, to $58.00. These increases reflected in part the extension of coverage to higher salary levels; as a result they are misleading as an indication of the change in the general level of benefits. Table 23.1 gives rates of contributions and benefits for the 1941-71 period at main points of change. This fragmentary information is based on best available sources, but is not intended to give more than a rough idea of developments in the two sides of the equation.

Operating Results

Higher wage and salary levels, lower levels of unemployment and a fairly tight rein on benefits produced a substantial and growing surplus. By the early fifties, when annual revenues were about $200 million, the accumulated surplus had reached more than $900 million, and interest revenues on this reserve were substantial. A wave of unemployment between 1958 and 1962 wiped out much of this, but it accumulated rapidly in the late sixties and again reached nearly the half billion dollar mark by 1971.

Post-1971

As previously outlined, the post-1971 plan was in many respects a more generous model than its predecessor. A sharp reduction in the qualifying period, a major increase in coverage and standard benefits, the introduction of extended and regional benefits, and the inclusion of sickness and pregnancy benefits all added up to a greatly expanded program, the cost of which turned out to be at least double the official forecasts. The heavy unemployment of the late seventies and early eighties greatly exacerbated the financial impact.

Contributions

Under the new Act employee contributions were to be set from year to year as a uniform percentage of insurable earnings, and the employer contribution was to be 1.4 times the employees' contribution. The actual rates of premium are given in table 23.2. Financing was to continue to be on a shared basis with the federal government, but on entirely new terms. Broadly, the standard costs of the plan would fall entirely on the private sector, and the extra costs would be met by the government. At the outset under the new Act standard costs to be met by employer-employee contributions included all the costs attributable to an unemployment rate of 4 percent, all special benefits (e.g. sickness and pregnancy) and costs of administration. However this share increased substantially over the period as a result of a government policy to shift an increasing load and ultimately the total burden of unemployment insurance to the private sector. This development was inherent in the replacement of the former Unemployment Insurance Fund with the Unemployment Insurance Account, to which the surplus of the old fund was transferred in 1971. While provision was made for obtaining advances from the Minister of Finance for temporary periods, the Account was not expected to run either a surplus or a deficit. In short, except for short-term situations, the account was to be self-financing. The changes over the last decade to bring about this result have been gradual but still painful. Originally under the 1971 Act the government share was to be the cost of benefits attributable to an unemployment rate over 4 percent, all extended benefits and all benefits paid to claimant trainees and to self-employed fishermen and their wives. Changes were first made in the determination of the base for payment of extended benefits. In 1976 the 4 percent level, above which the government had previously met benefit costs, was replaced by an eight-year moving average of the unemployment rate. This meant an immediate increase in the threshold to 5.6 percent in 1976, with the cost of the additional 1.6 percent falling on the private sector. With some further intermediate steps, by 1980 the benefit based on a national unemployment level had been abandoned and replaced by a labour force extended benefit, under which additional benefits were based on weeks of insurable employment over 26 weeks. The full cost of this extended benefit is charged to the private side. Similarly the funds used from 1977 for job creation, training and work-sharing projects were from the privately financed side of the Account, as were the related costs of the Canada Employment and Immigration Commission and the Department of Employment and Immigration after 1980. The government has continued to pay the extended benefits based on regional employment rates and the cost of benefits for fishermen and their wives.

Benefits

As with contributions, benefits were established on a uniform percentage basis of insurable earnings. This began as 75 percent for claimants with dependants and 66.6 percent for other claimants. The dependant rate was dropped in 1975 and a general rate of 60 percent was adopted in 1979. It is difficult to compare these single rates with the ranges given in table 23.1 for pre-1971 percentages, but one estimate is that the pre-1971 average benefits-to-earnings ratio was 43 percent. The increase in this ratio to 66.6 to 75 percent and later 60 percent, combined with the raise in maximum weekly benefits from $53 to $100, explains much of the unexpected increase in costs under the new act.

Operating Results

Operating results were considerably different under the new Act from experience under the 1941 Act. Where the preceding legislation had ended with a surplus, the successor act by 1985 had run a deficit of about $5 billion. Undoubtedly the new measure was more generous, and economic conditions were hardly comparable. The fifties and sixties included some of the most prosperous years in Canadian history; the late seventies and eighties had years of recession that were comparable with the Great Depression. For the entire period of 14 years (1972-85) there were many areas of the country where the regional unemployment rate was above the threshold that triggered the extended benefits. National unemployment rates were more than 11 percent in 1982, 1983, and 1984, and even higher, and were unprecedented since the Great Depression.

The effect of the government's efforts to shift the unemployment insurance burden to the private sector are evident from the data in table 23.2. Between 1972 and 1987 there is a more than fourteen-fold increase in employer-employee contributions and a less than three-fold increase in those of the government. The greater part of the government's contribution now goes for the cost of regional extended benefits and benefits paid to fishermen. Substantial rate increases have been made when the private sector share was showing a deficit, as in 1974 (40 percent), 1981, (33 percent) and 1983, (39 percent). The latest increase substantially balanced the private share account for 1987, but still left an accumulated deficit from past years of over $4.4 billion. This has been provided through temporary advances from the Minister of Finance, which it is apparently intended will be liquidated gradually in the future.

Tax and Related Changes

As part of the tax reform process, since that year unemployment insurance premiums have been deductible (converted to a tax credit under the 1988 tax reform), and benefits have been taxable. In addition to regular income tax, starting in 1979 there has also been a special levy of 30 percent of unemployment insurance benefits in excess of threshold amounts. The threshold started at $20,690 in 1979, and was indexed to $38,610 for 1986.

A further step designed to reduce unemployment insurance benefits was the requirement that pension income of a retiree be offset against unemployment insurance benefits commencing January 1, 1986. The result was the reduction of benefits to nominal amounts.

Premiums are now collected by the Department of National Revenue as a part of its regular tax collection process.

The Future

It will not be surprising to report, in view of the past history of reviews and studies, that the Minister of Finance of the Conservative government announced in his first budget speech of November 1984, that a study would be made of options for change in the unemployment insurance program. These would be set forth in a discussion paper to be made public in 1985. However, in lieu of this it was announced in July 1985, that a Commission of Inquiry would hold public hearings and report to the government by March 31, 1986, a deadline later advanced to June 1986.

The nature of the issues to be faced is fairly apparent from the earlier text. The liberality of the post-1971 program has been a constant concern of labour market experts, employers, and the federal treasury. There was a strong view among economists that the post-1971 plan had directly affected work efforts, or, more specifically, on the inclination to go onto insurance rather than to seek employment. The results of six Canadian studies have been summarized as follows: "The published studies have tended to indicate that UI has increased the unemployment rate in Canada, that the 1971 liberalization of the Act has served to increase the unemployment rate beyond what it would otherwise have been, and that the 1979 tightening up had the opposite effect."[23.1] The six studies mentioned are reviewed in the Boadway and Kitchen work for any reader wishing to follow this aspect further. Economists have generally been opposed to the use of an insurance-based measure for income transference purposes, mainly because this use loaded costs onto employers and employees which should be a charge on the general budget, and imposed a special burden on small and weaker employers. Furthermore the levy of a uniform charge on all industries, no matter what their experience with lay-offs or seasonal unemployment, is wholly inconsistent with any actuarially sound insurance scheme.

None of these issues was new; the government had before it the views of several official inquiries, including the report of the Committee of Inquiry into the Unemployment Insurance Act, (Gill Committee) 1962; Report of the Study for Updating the Unemployment Insurance Programme (1968); Unemployment Insurance in the 1980's, Task Force Report (1981); the Macdonald Royal Commission Report of October 1985, and the Report of the Commission of Inquiry on Unemployment appointed by the government in July 1985, to report by March 1986 (the Forget Commission; final report, December 1986). As well there are several other official sources and dozens of privately authored studies, including that by Kesselman for the Canadian Tax Foundation, which was invaluable for the preparation of this chapter.

The Macdonald Commission

In view of the extensive public interest in the report of the Macdonald Commission its views on unemployment insurance should be recorded (October 1985). While agreeing that the program has been of great help to many Canadians and has also assisted economic recovery by providing automatic stabilization during a slump, the Commission, like other critics, was opposed to its use for income redistribution. It also reported the following defects: it contributes to an increase in the duration of unemployment; it increases the volume of temporary lay-offs; it reinforces the concentration on temporary or unstable jobs in high-unemployment and low-wage regions; it provides too generous a subsidy to Canadians whose labour-force behaviour is characterized by repeated unstable employment.

The Commission proposed several changes to overcome these weaknesses. The most familiar of these was experience rating of premiums, to which the Commission gave first priority. It also recommended:

• reducing the benefit rate to 50 percent of insurable earnings (from the existing 60 percent);

• increasing the entrance requirement to 15-20 weeks of insured work in the preceding year (in place of the existing 10 weeks);

[23.1] Robin W. Boadway and Harry M. Kitchen, *Canadian Tax Policy*, 2nd ed., Canadian Tax Paper no. 76 (Toronto: Canadian Tax Foundation, 1984), 320.

• establishing a ratio of two or three weeks as qualification for one week of benefits (in place of 8 weeks for a maximum period of 44 weeks of payments);

• eliminating the extended benefit period based on regional unemployment rates.

The Commission gave an estimate that at April 1985 rates of unemployment these changes would probably result in savings of at least $4 billion. [23.2]

The Forget Commission

The latest review of unemployment insurance is that of the Forget Commission (December 1986). Its recommendations are well summarized in the following excerpt from the Canadian Tax Foundation's *National Finances* for 1986-87.

The Commission's recommendations call for a complete restructuring of the existing unemployment insurance and income support systems. The report observed that the unemployment insurance system now has two main functions: providing temporary assistance to workers who are between jobs and providing income supplementation in cases of long-term unemployment. It concluded that the present system is not appropriate for this latter function because benefits are based on past earnings, not need. It suggested that the unemployment insurance program return to its basic role of providing temporary assistance during periods of unemployment and that other programs be developed to provide the income supplementation functions.

The specific recommendations of the commission can be divided into three major, but interconnected, areas—restructuring the unemployment insurance program, replacing the income supplementation aspect of the current unemployment insurance system, and administrative/organizational changes to improve delivery of the unemployment insurance program.

The report recommended that the existing unemployment insurance program be phased out gradually and replaced by a program that includes:

1) a standard entrance requirement of 350 hours of insurable earnings,

2) annualization of benefits—basing benefits on the average weekly insurable earnings in the 52 weeks prior to unemployment,

3) benefits equal to two-thirds of insurable earnings, and

4) benefits payable for a maximum of 50 weeks after a two week waiting period.

[23.2] Canada, *Report of the Royal Commission on the Economic Union and Development Prospects for Canada*, vol. 2 (Ottawa: Department of Supply and Services, 1985), 815.

The commission suggested that the job creation programs currently funded through the program be replaced with longer term employment programs that are operated independently of the unemployment insurance system. It also recommended that extended benefits to individuals on approved training courses be eliminated and that such individuals receive benefits only for the period of their regular entitlement.

Once the reformed unemployment insurance system was in place, the report suggested that the benefits and administrative costs of the program be financed entirely from employee and employer premium contributions.

The report recommended that the regionally extended benefits phase of the current unemployment insurance system should be phased out and replaced over a four- to five-year period with an earnings supplementation program. The earnings supplementation program would provide assistance, based on total family income, to individuals who participate in the labour force but have inadequate incomes. These supplements would be reduced as other income rose, but at a rate low enough to encourage work incentives. The commission's earnings supplement program differs from a guaranteed annual income in that it would be based on past earnings. The report recognized that such a program would require federal-provincial agreements and would have to be coordinated with other federal and provincial social security programs.

The report also recommended that the special benefits paid to fishermen be phased out over a five-year period and be replaced with an income supplement plan based on need. This income supplement plan should have resources at least equal to those currently available to fishermen through the unemployment insurance program.[23.3]

The report was obviously in the let's-get-back-to-basics category, with proposals for stripping the system of its social support elements and replacing these with income supplementation programs for those below the poverty level. Along with the fairly radical recommendations for changes in the system itself the package was probably more than the government wanted at this time. Even more awkward for the government was the strong minority report submitted by the two union members of the Commission, which rejected the main recommendations not only in detail but in principle. The report, the most comprehensive of the studies made so far, was therefore badly flawed for government acceptance by this serious division within the Commission. Furthermore, it would appear that unemployment insurance is a subject as fraught with controversy within the government as outside.

[23.3] *The National Finances, 1986-87* (Toronto: Canadian Tax Foundation, 1987), 8:19-20.

Government Reaction to Reports

No serious public attention was given to either the Macdonald or the Forget recommendations, and a diligent search of budget speeches and papers and similar policy statements fails to reveal any discussion of the subject since 1985, a curious omission in a government that has typically buried every problem in a mountain of pro and con documentation. As it was simply announced that no changes would be made in the scheme, one must assume that this is an issue on which the government has not been able to bridge wide differences of view within its own ranks. As a result the unemployment insurance scheme remains substantially unchanged from its 1985 pre-report form, and at mid-1988 gives every appearance of remaining that way. As table 23.2 reveals the government continues to spend $2.5 to $2.8 billion for extended coverage, fishermen, etc., a not inconsiderable sum. However the fund itself has moved into a surplus position ($1.5 billion in 1987) and the government's past advances are being liquidated, a process that will continue with reducing unemployment. The financial crisis therefore seems to have passed, a fact reflected in the announcement in November of an increase in the maximum benefit and a reduction in premiums for 1989.

Related Programs

While the main interest here has been in the unemployment insurance program because of its central role there are many other programs that deserve at least brief mention. Principal among these is the program for unemployment relief, generally directed toward individuals and families not qualified under other programs. The federal government had become deeply involved with the provinces in giving aid to the unemployed starting with the Great Depression, and had continued this practice on an ad hoc basis after. In 1955 it proposed a formula at a federal-provincial conference that would regularize its position. It offered to assume one-half the cost of relief where numbers of recipients exceeded .45 percent of the provincial population. Recipients of any other form of federal payment would be excluded.

In 1956 Parliament passed the Unemployment Assistance Act, which authorized the government to enter into agreements with provincial governments for this purpose. Agreements were concluded with all provinces in the following two years. The character of the program was drastically modified in 1957, when the .45 percent threshold was withdrawn under provincial pressure. Federal expenditure had been about $8 million in the first two years of the program, and it rose to a $40 million level almost immediately, the combined result of removal of the threshold and the entrance of late provinces. In view of the buoyant economic conditions of the 1960s growth under the program was surprising. Federal expenditure rose to $143 million by fiscal year 1966-67, and it was estimated that there were on average some 790,000 monthly recipients. The plan ceased to operate as such in 1966 when it was supplanted by the Canada Assistance Plan (see later).

There have been innumerable direct aid measures designed to relieve unemployment. Some have been directed to creating temporary employment, such as winter works and local initiative programs, some have been aimed at regional unemployment while others have offered means of improving job skills and increasing labour mobility. Details of the current phase of these programs may be found in the 1987-88 version of *The National Finances*, chapters 8 and 10.

Table 23.1 Unemployment Insurance: Some Contribution and Benefit Rates, 1941-71

| Year | Contributions[a] | | Benefits | | |
	On min. weekly earnings	On max. weekly earnings	On min. weekly earnings	On max. weekly earnings	Benefits as a percent of earnings[b]
	$	$	$	$	%
1941					
Single	.33	.63	4.08	12.24	63 to 38
With Dependant	.33	.63	4.80	14.40	74 to 45
1955 (Sept.)					
Single	.48	1.08	6.00	17.10	75 to 30
With Dependant	.48	1.08	7.50	24.00	86 to 42
1955 (Oct.)					
Single	.32	1.20	9.00	23.00	50 to 39
With Dependant	.32	1.20	12.00	30.0	67 to 50
1959					
Single	.20	1.88	6.00	27.00	67 to 36
With Dependant	.20	1.88	8.00	36.00	89 to 48
1968 (June)					
Single	.20	2.80	16.00	42.00	64 to 44
With Dependant	.20	2.80	21.00	53.00	84 to 56
1971 (June)					
Single	.40	2.80	13.00	46.00	52 to 34
With Dependant	.40	2.80	17.00	58.00	68 to 42
1971 (Aug.)					
Single	.40	3.30	20.00	100.00	66⅓
With Dependant	.40	3.30	20.00	100.00	75

[a] Includes both employer and employee contributions. [b] Benefits related to mid-point of earnings range; the larger percentages relate to the minimum benefits.

Source: Statistics Canada, Social Security (National Programs) 1978, and Jonathan Kesselman, *Financing Canadian Unemployment Insurance*, Canadian Tax Paper no. 73.

Table 23.2 Unemployment Insurance Fund: Unemployment Rate, Contributions, and Financial Results, Calendar Years 1972-87

Year	Unemployment rate	Maximum benefit[a]	Employer contribution	Employee contribution	Private[b] contribution	Private[c] benefits	Surplus or deficit	Government contribution[d]
	percent		*dollars*		*millions of dollars*			
1972	6.2	100	1.25	.90	711	1,991	(388)	980
1973	5.5	107	1.40	1.00	928	2,161	(350)	917
1974	5.3	113	1.96	1.40	1,545	2,305	85	875
1975	6.9	123	1.96	1.40	1,953	3,334	321	1,707
1976	7.1	133	2.31	1.65	2,476	3,529	301	1,356
1977	8.1	147	2.10	1.50	2,551	4,124	210	1,788
1978	8.4	160	2.10	1.50	2,838	4,762	327	2,255
1979	7.5	159	1.89	1.35	2,812	4,192	(91)	1,295
1980	7.5	174	1.89	1.35	3,125	4,811	(656)	1,037
1981	7.6	189	2.52	1.80	4,716	4,665	(331)	909
1982	11.0	210	2.31	1.65	4,793	8,345	(2,728)	1,675
1983	11.9	231	3.22	2.30	7,017	9,920	(1,457)	2,680
1984	11.3	255	3.22	2.30	7,627	9,698	(692)	2,740
1985	10.5	276	3.29	2.35	8,753	9,939	101	2,722
1986	9.6	297	3.29	2.35	9,616	10,186	653	2,623
1987e	8.9	318	3.29	2.35	10,439	10,317	1,525	2,817

[a]Single person. [b]Employer-employee premiums. [c]Total benefit payments, excluding fishermen. Fishermen's benefits in 1986 totalled $207.5 million. [d]The government's contribution in 1986 was made up of: 94.0 percent regional benefits, 4.3 percent training benefits, and 1.7 percent job creation benefit. Fishermen's benefits, $191.1 million, are excluded from total government contribution shown.

Sources: 1972-81: Jonathan R. Kesselman, *Financing Canadian Unemployment Insurance*, 62, Canadian Tax Paper no. 73; 1982-87: Public Accoun Statistics Canada, *Canadian Economic Observer*; Bank of Canada *Review*; Estimates, 1988-89, Part III.

Table 23.3 Unemployment Insurance Benefits: Some General Comparisons, Selected Years, 1951-86

Year	Monthly average number of beneficiaries	Percent of the labour force	Yearly benefits paid[a]	Benefits as a percent of GNP	Benefits as a percent of personal income
	thousands	%	*$ million*	%	%
1951	—	—	76	0.4	0.4
1961	481[b]	7.5	494	1.2	1.6
1966	314[b]	4.2	295	0.5	0.6
1971	603[b]	7.0	891	1.0	1.2
1972	804[b]	9.0	1,872	1.7	2.2
1973	828[b]	8.9	2,004	1.6	2.1
1974	828[b]	8.6	2,116	1.4	1.8
1975	1,049[b]	10.5	3,130	1.9	2.3
1976	701	6.9	3,332	1.7	2.1
1977	750	7.1	3,900	1.8	2.3
1978	803	7.4	4,508	1.9	2.4
1979	713	6.3	3,947	1.5	1.8
1980	703	6.1	4,332	1.4	1.8
1981	720	6.0	4,757	1.4	1.6
1982	1,138	9.5	8,455	2.3	2.7
1983	1,248	10.2	10,063	2.6	2.9
1984	1,194	9.6	9,859	2.3	2.6
1985	1,145	9.1	10,118	2.2	2.5
1986	1,095	8.5	10,394	2.1	2.4

[a] Includes benefits for fishermen. [b] Claimants. Number of beneficiaries not available.

Sources: Public Accounts; Statistics Canada, *Social Security National Programs*; *Canadian Statistical Review*; *Canadian Economic Observer*; Department of Finance, *Economic* Review; Bank of Canada *Review*.

Bibliography, chapter 23

Boadway, Robin W., and Kitchen, Harry, M. *Canadian Tax Policy*. 2nd. ed. Canadian Tax Paper no. 76. Toronto: Canadian Tax Foundation, 1984.

Cairns, J.P. "Unemployment Insurance in Canada: the Problem of Conflicting Principles." (May 1962) 28 *Canadian Journal of Economics and Political Science*, 262-68.

Canada. Committee of Inquiry into the Unemployment Insurance Act. *Report*. Ernest C. Gill, Chairman. Ottawa: 1962.

_____. Commission on Unemployment Insurance. C. Forget, Chairman. *Report on Unemployment Insurance*. Ottawa: 1986.

_____. Department of Employment and Immigration. *Annual Reports*. Ottawa: 1978-1982.

_____. *Labour Market Developments in the 1980s*. Task Force Report. Ottawa: 1981.

_____. *Unemployment Insurance in the 1980s*. Task Force Report. Ottawa: 1981.

_____. Department of Finance. *The Fiscal Plan*. Budget Paper. Ottawa: April 19, 1983.

_____. Department of Labour. *The Labour Gazette*. Ottawa.

_____. Department of Manpower and Immigration. *Unemployment Insurance Plan in the 70's*. (White Paper). Ottawa: 1970.

_____. House of Commons. Standing Committee on Labour, Employment, and Immigration. *Minutes of Proceedings and Evidence*, 1986 and 1987.

_____. Statistics Canada. *Historical Labour Force Statistics: Actual Data, Seasonal Factors, Seasonally Adjusted Data, 1982*. Ottawa: 1983.

_____. National Employment Commission. *Final Report*. Ottawa 1937.

_____. The Royal Commission on Dominion Provincial Relations. *Report*. Ottawa: 1940.

_____. The Royal Commission on the Economic Union and Development Prospects for Canada. *Report*, vol. 2. Ottawa: 1985.

_____. Unemployment Insurance Commission. *Report*. Ottawa: annual.

_____. *Report of the Comprehensive Review of the Unemployment Insurance Program in Canada*. Ottawa: 1977.

_____. *Report on Sickness and Maternity Benefits*. Prepared by William M. Mercer, Ltd. Ottawa: 1971.

_____. *Report of the Study for Updating the Unemployment Insurance Programme*. Ottawa: 1968, vols. 1-4.

Canadian Tax Foundation. *The National Finances*. Toronto: annual.

CCH Canadian Limited. *Canadian Unemployment Insurance Legislation*. Don Mills, Ont.: CCH Canadian, misc. editions.

Canadian Welfare Council. *Unemployment Insurance in the 70's*. Staff Submission to the House of Commons Standing Committee on Labour, Manpower and Immigration. Ottawa: 1970.

Cloutier, J.E. *The Distribution of Benefits and Costs of Social Security in Canada,*

1971-1975. Discussion Paper no. 108. Ottawa: Economic Council of Canada, 1978.

Cloutier J.E., and Smith, A.M.M. *The Evaluation of an Alternative Unemployment Insurance Plan.* Discussion Paper no. 159. Ottawa: Economic Council of Canada, 1980.

Cousineau, J.-M. "Le rapport Forget et l'economie politique de l'assurance-chomage." (March 1988) 14 1 *Canadian Public Policy*, 1-6.

Dingledine, G.A. *Chronology of Response: The Evolution of Unemployment Insurance from 1940 to 1980.* Employment and Immigration Canada. Ottawa: 1981.

Economic Council of Canada. *Fifteenth Annual Review.* Ottawa: 1978.

_____. *Policies and Constraints.* Nineteenth Annual Review. Ottawa: 1982.

Grauer, A.E. *Public Assistance and Social Insurance.* Royal Commission on Dominion Provincial Relations. Appendix 6. Ottawa: 1940.

Green, Christopher, and Cousineau, Jean-Michel. *Unemployment Insurance in Canada. The Impact of Unemployment Insurance.* Study prepared for the Economic Council of Canada. Ottawa: 1976.

Hum, D.P.J. *Unemployment Insurance and Work Effort: Issues, Evidence and Policy Directions.* Discussion Paper Series. Toronto: Ontario Economic Council, 1981.

Kaliski, S.F. "Unemployment and Unemployment Insurance: Testing Some Corollaries." (November 1976), 9 *Canadian Journal of Economics*, 705-12.

_____. "Some Aspects of the Nature and Duration of Unemployment in Canada." In *Issues in Canadian Policy (II).* Proceedings of a Conference, edited by R.G. Wirick and D.D. Purvis. Kingston: Queen's University, Institute for Economic Research, 1979.

Kapsalis, C. *Equity Aspects of the Unemployment Insurance Program in Canada.* Discussion Paper no. 116. Ottawa: Economic Council of Canada, 1978.

_____. "Unemployment Insurance: Insurance or Welfare? A Comment." (Autumn 1979) 5 *Canadian Public Policy*, 553-59.

Kesselman, J.R. "Pitfalls of Selectivity in Income Security Programs." (Fall 1980) *Canadian Taxation*, 154-63.

_____. *Financing Canadian Unemployment Insurance.* Canadian Tax Paper no. 73. Toronto: Canadian Tax Foundation, 1983.

_____. "Comprehensive Income Security for Canadian Workers." In Francois Vaillancourt, research coordinator, *Income Distribution and Economic Security in Canada.* Collected Research Studies of the Royal Commission on the Economic Union and Development Prospects for Canada, vol. 1. Toronto: University of Toronto Press, 1985.

Osberg, Lars. "Unemployment Insurance in Canada: A Review of the Recent Amendments." (Spring 1979) 5 *Canadian Public Policy*, 223-35.

Pal, Leslie, A. "Revision and Retreat: Canadian Unemployment Insurance, 1971-1981." In Ismael, Jacqueline, S. *Canadian Social Welfare Policy: Federal and Provincial Dimensions.* Kingston and Montreal: McGill-Queen's University Press and the Institute of Public Administration of Canada, 1985.

_____. "Sense and Sensibility: Comments on Forget." (March 1988) 14 *Canadian Public Policy*, 7-14.

_____. "The Finance View: The Case of Unemployment Insurance, 1970-78." (July-August 1985) 33 *Canadian Tax Journal*, 786-801.

Shaw, R.P. "The Burden of Unemployment in Canada." (June 1985) XI *Canadian Public Policy*, 143-60.

Pensions

24
Pensions for Older Citizens

The proportion of the population living to be 65 and over has increased dramatically. Improvements in medical science in the last 25 years have ended many diseases once fatal and, along with better and more generally available medical services, have increased life expectancy. A declining birth rate has also meant that on average the older population has become a larger proportion of the total. Since 1961 the ratio of persons aged 65 and over has increased from 7.6 percent to over 9 percent, a jump of nearly 20 percent. By the end of the century it is estimated that over 65s will be 11.2 percent of the total, a further increase of 24 percent. In 1985 some 2.3 million of the total of 25 million were in this category; the estimate for 2001 is 3.4 million of a total of 29-30 million. Shifts of population on this scale will have—are already having—profound effects on many aspects of living. The declining numbers of the young has reduced student enrolments, and schools are being closed as a result. By contrast the increase in the older population has brought added strain on community resources such as medical and hospital services and retirement facilities. The impact on government programs to provide or supplement the incomes of the elderly has also been marked. We will look at these programs in this section.

The Programs

Canada's income measures for the elderly in 1987 include, at the federal level, a universal non-contributory pension payable to persons at age 65, (Old Age Security, which includes a Guaranteed Annual Income Supplement and a Spouses' Allowance), and a wage-related pension on a contributory basis, also payable at age 65 (Canada Pension Plan, which includes benefits for survivors and orphans and for disability). At the provincial level they include the Quebec Pension Plan (in lieu of the CPP) and in some provinces supplements to federal programs. We deal with Old Age Security in the present chapter and the Canada Pension Plan in the next.

Income Support for the Elderly

The main programs of income support for the elderly are federal and are the outcome of developments over a period of three-quarters of a century. The stages of this history are marked by (1) the Old Age Pensions Act of 1927; (2) the Old Age Security Act of 1951, and (3) the Guaranteed Income Supplement introduced in 1967. We must begin, however, with a self-help measure introduced before World War I—the Government Annuities Plan.

Government Annuities

Several countries had introduced government social programs in the years immediately preceding World War I. Most of these were in Europe, including the United Kingdom, but by 1908 New Zealand and Australia had programs providing several kinds of benefits. These European and Commonwealth developments produced agitation in Canada for comparable action, led mainly by trade unions, but the federal government of the day rejected the principle of public pensions in favour of individually accumulated savings. Annuities were available from insurance companies but, in order to provide a less expensive instrument, the government introduced its own annuity. Among other advantages administrative expenses were absorbed by the government, and later when an income tax was introduced government annuity proceeds were exempted. The amount of annuity that could be purchased was limited (the maximum reached was $5,000) and proceeds could only be withdrawn as an annuity. Conditions under which the program operated varied with the philosophy of the government in power. Under some regimes terms were improved and sales promotion was encouraged; under others the program was neglected or even discouraged. However it survived until the sixties when both the Glassco and Porter Commissions recommended that, in view of the introduction of a universal old age pension in 1952, the government need no longer feel obliged to maintain the measure. In 1967 promotional activity ceased, and the branch now only services outstanding contracts.

Undoubtedly some persons were enabled or encouraged to make provision for their years of retirement under the plan, but it had not been the answer to the growing problem of mass dependency among elderly workers employed in low-level jobs which had neither carried a pension nor paid them enough to accumulate their own savings.

Old Age Pensions Act, 1927

Agitation for some form of public pension plan resumed both inside and outside Parliament following World War I and became more strident as the decade progressed. Opinion among supporters was divided between a contributory and a publicly funded basis, but there was agreement among a small but active group that some form of public pension plan was essential. In the tortuous political climate of the twenties the question of assistance for the dependent elderly gradually emerged as an issue at the major party level, and is said to have been a determining factor in bringing the Liberals to power in 1926. In any event it was the Liberal government that legislated the first old age pensions plan in 1927.

The federal program took the form of an offer to pay 50 percent of the cost of pensions provided by a province to its residents over 70 years of age. This form was dictated by doubts regarding the constitutional powers of the federal government to act directly and also by the belief that the provinces would have had more administrative experience with this type of program. Agreements setting forth operating details would be entered into with each province. Provinces would be given ten years' notice of termination of the plan to avoid being left with sole responsibility.

Ontario and the western provinces implemented the plan within the next two years. The maritime provinces, either because of leaner budgets or political difficulties, or both, (the country was in the grips of the depression by this time) came in slowly in succeeding years, New Brunswick, the last, delaying until 1936. Quebec, giving early signs of its by now customary misgivings over social programs requiring cooperation with the federal government, also delayed implementation until 1936.

The amount of the pension was $20 a month at the outset (roughly $150 in 1985 values), of which the federal government paid 50 percent. In 1931 a newly elected federal government increased its share to 75 percent. Although most provinces paid supplements the basic pension remained unchanged until 1943, when the federal government unilaterally announced an increase to $25 a month. With postwar inflation, pressure for increases brought a further raise to $30 per month in 1947 and to $40 in 1949. Several provinces continued to pay supplements throughout in addition to their share of these increases.

Means Test

This bare outline leaves untouched the most contentious feature of the 1927 plan, which in the long run contributed substantially to its demise. This was the use of a means test as a device for determining eligibility. This test was based mainly on a calculation of income from other sources. At the outset the pensioner was allowed $125 a year of outside income without loss of pension; for each dollar of such income in excess of $125 a corresponding deduction was made in the pension. When outside income exceeded $365 a year ($1 per day) the pensioner was no longer eligible. This full offsetting of other income was a discouragement to self help, both before and after retirement.

On the whole the device was probably consistent with values of the times and was no doubt made more palatable by the desperate situation in which many people found themselves as a result of the depression. Nonetheless it did involve the indignity of close inquiry into personal circumstances. Even more objectionable were some of the enforcement features. For example, adult children were expected to maintain their parents and, eventually, when attempts to enforce parents' maintenance legislation failed to achieve this result, the parents were assumed to have received benefits from their children for calculation of their pension, whether actually received or not. The income value of assets (most commonly a home) was taken into account in calculating outside income under rules determined by the pension authorities. This could be avoided by turning over interest in the asset to the government. The authorities had power to recover the value of pensions from the estates of pensioners after death. These and other means test rules were left to the provinces to apply, and there is evidence that even under the admonitions of the federal Department of Finance, which eventually administered the plan for the federal government, the vigour with which they responded was considerably mixed. Data cited by Bryden in his extensive study (on which much of this chapter is based) makes this conclusion fairly obvious. Strict enforcement only increased the unpopularity of the measure.

Old Age Security

Agitation for an improved pension continued throughout World War II in union and political circles. There was growing dissatisfaction with the eligibility date of 70 years. Most workers retired at age 65 and, as employer pension plans were still in their infancy, they frequently faced immediate hardship. The amount of the old age pension, $25 per month at the end of the war, was considered inadequate, particularly as inflation quickly appeared. The increases of 1947 and 1949 (raising the level to $40 by the latter date) had barely offset continuing price rises. The unpopularity of the means test has already been mentioned.

While agreement was emerging on remedying some of these features there was wide division of opinion on the method of financing a non-means-test plan. It was the means test which held down costs, and it was estimated that a new plan would more than double outlays. Financing proposals, largely reflecting political coloration, ranged from simply throwing the whole burden onto the general budget to be financed from general tax revenues to financing solely by contributory charges, unemployment insurance being the model for the latter proposal. There were various combinations for these possibilities, all somewhat confused, as Bryden points out, since widely different meanings were given the same term by different advocates.

Political parties had been developing their own platforms on postwar social policy (elections did not stop for the war) and a limited amount of informal and unpublicized research on postwar social policy had been going forward within the federal government. The trend of thought was moving toward a more comprehensive approach, stimulated by the Beveridge Report and by legislation, such as New Zealand Social Security Act. The Liberal party, then led by Mackenzie King, had established a House of Commons committees in 1943 and 1944 with a mandate to develop "a comprehensive national scheme of social insurance . . . which will constitute a charter of social security for the whole of Canada."[24.1] The 1944 Speech from the Throne promised a national system of health insurance and a more generous plan of old age pensions, on a contributory basis.

In the meantime the Family Allowances Act was passed, with payments to commence in 1945. Further proposals were embodied in the Green Book on Social Security presented to the Reconstruction Conference in 1945, emphasis then being placed on health insurance, assistance for the employable unemployed not covered by unemployment insurance, and on improv-

---

[24.1] K. Bryden, *Old Age Pensions and Policy-Making in Canada* (Montreal: McGill-Queen's University Press, 1974), 113.

ing old age assistance. Upon the rejection of its proposals the federal government put them aside, but only temporarily.

The unions and the CCF had intensified their campaigns for universal old age pensions and health insurance, all to be provided at federal expense. In its 1948 convention the Liberal party committed itself to introducing old age insurance on a contributory basis and, as a sequel, in the 1950 session of Parliament a Joint Committee of the Senate and House of Commons on Old Age Security was appointed. After extensive public hearings the Committee submitted a report recommending (1) a universal old age pension of $40 per month at age 70; (2) a means-test pension for ages 65 to 69, also at $40 per month. The main and most costly change in this proposal was the abandonment of the means test for pensions 70 and over, and the committee made it clear that in its view this action would mean that revenues could not be drawn from the general budget. A contributory system would be necessary to act as a brake on future pension increases. This was essential "not only because of the importance of this in raising the total money required, but also because of the importance of establishing a close association in the mind of the individual between his contribution to the cost of the ultimate benefit he is to receive." It thought a method of financing involving contributions from employers, employees, and the government might be considered, after the pattern of unemployment insurance.

The government now found itself with a proposal from an all-party committee of both houses that in form was fully consistent with its own policies. It would be pleased to implement this proposal except for one very relevant question—how to pay for it. Its own policy statements for some time had favoured a contributory basis, but when put to the test of practice real difficulties were encountered. The Privy Council judgment in 1936 on the Social and Health Insurance Act had established that the federal government could not exercise its taxing powers to enter an area of provincial jurisiction. This principle had been recognized in the 1940 amendment to the British North America Act that had authorized the federal government to establish unemployment insurance, and would apply equally for a contributory old age security plan. There was therefore a constitutional barrier to this route.

However, it was the administrative problem of collecting a charge that proved most formidable. Previous thought had been in terms of the unemployment insurance precedent, but this was applied only to employed people, a group easily identified and accessible through employers. For old age security an additional two to three million persons, such as self-employed proprietors, professional people, farmers, etc., would be required to contribute. At the time many of these were not subject to income tax, so that obtaining a payment from them would be a new and separate operation, requiring administrative procedures never before employed by the federal government. (It is an interesting commentary on the improvement in administrative practices that 15 years later the self-employed were brought into the Canada Pension Plan to pay their own contribution with very little trouble).

The new program would be quite costly, and the means of financing received close public attention. The cost to the federal government was estimated to be about $350 million as compared with $100 million under the old program, a net increase of $250 million (in 1987 values the equivalent of over one and one-half billion dollars). The total federal budget in 1950 was $2.9 billion, so that an increase of about 8 percent was involved. Furthermore the personal income tax in 1950 yielded $652 million; an increase of about 40 percent would therefore have been necessary to finance the full cost by that route. An unexpected and complicating factor was the Korean war, which had commenced during the period when these decisions were being made, and had required sharp increases in defence expenditure.

The revival of defence spending caused the Canadian Tax Foundation, hitherto non-commital on public issues, to label the proposed pension plan as improvident and misdirected, and to argue that its introduction should be postponed until after the Korean War.

Despite these formidable obstacles the government decided to proceed, and in 1951 Parliament passed the Old Age Security Act. It authorized the payment, at the expense of the federal government, of pensions of $40 per month to all persons age 70 or over, without means test, to commence in January 1952. Eligibility would depend on residence in Canada for at least 20 years immediately preceding the date of application. A companion measure, the Old Age Assistance Act, was passed—in effect to extend the former means-tested pensions under the Old Age Pensions Act to persons aged 65 to 69, who of course were not eligible for old age security. Costs were to be shared 50-50 with the provinces. The Blind Persons Act was also passed to provide means-tested pensions of $40 per month for blind persons 21 years of age or over, 75 percent of the cost to be assumed by the federal government. (Basically this was the continuation of a feature of the Old Age Pension plan that had been started in 1938).

With the commencement of Old Age Security on January 1, 1952, pension cheques began going out to 643,000 recipients, more than double the 308,000 eligible in the last mailing for the Old Age Pension.

Earmarked Taxes

The government, still intent on having identifiable revenue sources for financing old age security, but forced to give up on the direct contribution route, settled for the second best solution by imposing taxes the yield of which would be earmarked for a separate fund. The hope was to stem the desire of the public for heavy pension increases by establishing that higher benefits would require higher taxes. The formula commenced with the now historic "2-2-2" structure; an additional 2 percent rate of sales tax, an additional 2 percent of corporation income tax, and an additional 2 percent of personal income tax, the latter to a maximum of $60 per annum. Subsequent increases in these rates were required as pensions rose. In 1959 the rates were raised to 3 percent, with the personal income tax maximum going to $90. In 1964 the personal income tax alone was raised to 4 percent (maximum $120). These special earmarked taxes were abandoned in 1972, although the fund was maintained for another four years with revenues from the last rates being entered on an estimated basis, for the information of the public, a largely wasted effort. Since 1972 the cost of old security payments has in actuality been a charge on general revenues.

Quite significant developments took place in the plan during the sixties and seventies. These included marked increases in the amount of the pension to compensate for inflation, reduction of the eligibility age from 70 to 65, and introduction of the Guaranteed Income Supplement and the Spouses' Allowance.

Increases in Basic Pension

Principal increases in the basic pension over the period of three decades since introduction are given in table 24.1. Further details may be found in the social welfare chapter of the Foundation's annual publication, *The National Finances*.

Initially ad hoc increases were given as seemed fitting to the government, which brought the original $40 to $75 per month by 1967. From that time on most increases have been related to an official index. From 1968 to 1971 there was an adjustment for rises in the pensions index, (an index compiled for this use) but not to exceed 2 percent per annum. In 1971 the basic pension was stabilized at $80 per month, without further indexation, but in 1973 there was a single increase to $100 per month, and henceforth the amount was indexed quarterly. As part of a government austerity program a ceiling of 6 percent was imposed for indexation in 1983 and approximately 5 percent in 1984, (changes continued to be made on a quarterly basis, a practice still followed). In the 1985 budget it was announced that further adjustments would be made only for the excess of inflation beyond 3 percent per annum, a move later abandoned in the face of violent public protest. Indexation is now therefore made for the full amount of inflation, or 4.4 percent in 1987. As a result of this long incremental process the $40 pension of 1952 (current value about $250) stood at $310.66 for January 1988.

Extension to Age 65

Extension of coverage to age 65 was enacted in 1965. Each year for five years an additional year was included, so that by 1970 all persons upon reaching their 65th birthday were eligible. Having served its purpose the Old Age Assistance Act was then repealed, with any further aid falling under the Canada Assistance Plan. OAS residence requirements have also been relaxed over the years. At present the basic requirement is ten years of residence prior to application, and provision is made for absence from the country, both during the qualifying and receiving period.

The Guaranteed Income Supplement

The Guaranteed Income Supplement was introduced in 1967. Its original objective was to add to the other income of a pensioner an amount that would produce a total income of $105 per month. A statement of income must be filed annually for eligibility for GIS. The maximum amount receivable has been raised several times. The original maximum in 1967 was $30, which, along with the OAS payment of $75, gave the then guaranteed monthly amount of $105. By 1985 the maximum GIS had increased to an amount exceeding $325, higher in fact than the basic pension by reason of some ad hoc increases and by the exemption of GIS from the constraints on indexation in 1983 and 1984. By 1988 the combined amount receivable was $680 for an individual pensioner. The total for a married couple —$1,102 in 1988—is reduced to slightly under double that for a single person. Over half the recipients of OAS also qualify for some payment under the GIS (see table 24.1).

Spouse's Allowance

In 1975 a pension was provided for the spouse aged 60 to 64 of a recipient of an old age security pension. The amount of the pension is set at one-half the maximum basic plus GIS pension for a couple aged over 65. By offsetting other income a spouse ceases to be eligible for the allowance in 1988 when family income exceeds $17,250. Starting in 1979 the allowance was payable to a spouse aged 60 to 64 after the death of the main pensioner, and in 1985 it also became payable to widows and widowers whether or not the deceased spouse had been a pensioner (provided of course that the other requirements for eligibility were met.) The spouses' allowance had therefore become a pension for all impoverished widows and widowers aged 60 to 64, a development incidentally that had not escaped the attention of unmarried men and women in this status.

The Financial Cost

By 1988 the combined cost of the basic pension, the guaranteed income supplement, and the spouses' allowance was about $14.5 billion. There were over 2.8 million recipients of the basic pension, i.e. over 99 percent of persons aged 65 and over. Approximately one-half of these were also receiving the GIS, and some 160,000 additional persons were receiving the spouses' allowance. By 1990 an additional 400,000 persons are forecast to qualify for the basic pension.

The financial history of the growing outlay is given in table 24.3. Naturally the financial prospects for the future are of growing concern to the federal government. An indication of this was the step proposed in the May 1985 budget of limiting indexation for the main plans to the excess over 3 percent for 1986, a proposal which the government was forced to abandon. This action followed the issuance in January 1985, of a Consultation Paper on Child and Elderly Benefits. The statement contained the declaration that, "After careful consideration, the government has decided not to put forward a consultation option for the reform of elderly benefits . . . In the government's view no change is required in the Old Age

Security/Guaranteed Income Supplement payment system."[24.2] The statement invited comments "regarding the age exemption and the pension income deduction" under the income tax. The consultation paper went before the House Standing Committee on Health, Welfare and Social Affairs which, in April, reported itself in agreement with the government's position that no changes were needed in Old Age Security. These activities pre-dated the May budget speech and did not reflect the de-indexation proposal it made. Had it not been for this proposal Old Age Security would have been quiescent. Principal attention had been focussed on massive proposed changes in the tax treatment of private pension plans and in revision of child benefits under Family Allowances and the income tax. Both these matters are dealt with in later chapters; first we consider a different type of government retirement pension—the contributory, wage-related Canada Pension Plan.

[24.2] Canada, Department of National Health and Welfare, *Child and Elderly Benefits.* Consultation Paper (Ottawa: the Department, 1985), 10 and 11.

Table 24.1   Maximum Monthly Pension Under Old Age Security Act, Selected Years, 1952-88

Date effective	Basic pension	Guaranteed income supplement	Maximum pension[a]
		dollars	
1/1/52.............	40.00	—	40.00
1/7/57.............	46.00	—	46.00
1/11/57.............	55.00	—	55.00
1/6/62.............	65.00	—	65.00
1/10/63.............	75.00	—	75.00
1/1/67.............	75.00	30.00	105.00
1/1/68.............	76.50	30.60	107.10
1/1/69.............	78.00	31.20	109.20
1/1/70.............	79.58	31.83	111.41
1/4/71.............	80.00	55.00 (95.00)	135.00 (255.00)
1/1/72.............	82.88	67.12 (119.24)	150.00 (285.00)
1/4/73.............	100.00	70.14 (124.60)	170.14 (324.60)
1/1/74.............	108.14	75.88 (134.74)	183.49 (351.02)
1/1/75.............	120.06	84.21 (149.58)	204.27 (389.70)
1/1/76.............	132.90	93.22 (165.56)	226.12 (431.36)
1/1/77.............	141.34	99.13 (176.06)	240.47 (458.74)
1/1/78.............	153.44	107.62 (191.12)	261.06 (498.00)
1/1/79.............	167.21	137.28 (228.30)	304.49 (562.72)
1/1/80.............	182.42	149.76 (249.04)	332.18 (613.88)
1/1/81.............	202.14	202.94 (312.94)	405.08 (717.22)
1/1/82.............	227.73	228.63 (352.54)	456.36 (808.00)
1/1/83.............	251.12	252.10 (388.74)	503.22 (890.98)
1/1/84.............	263.78	265.60 (409.72)	529.38 (937.28)
1/1/85.............	273.80	325.41 (423.86)	599.21 (971.46)
1/1/86.............	285.20	338.95 (441.50)	624.15 (1,011.90)
1/1/87.............	297.37	353.41 (460.34)	650.78 (1,055.08)
1/1/88.............	310.66	369.21 (480.94)	679.87 (1,102.26)

[a] Amounts in brackets are those payable to a married couple.

Source: *The National Finances*, 1987-88.

Table 24.2   Old Age Security Taxes, 1952-71

	Sales tax	Corporation income tax	Personal income tax
		percent	
1952-59......................	2	2	2 (max. $60)
1959-64......................	3	3	3 (max. $90)
1964-69......................	3	3	3 (max. $120)
1969-71......................	3	3	4 (max. $240)
1972-......................	all taxes repealed; embodied in general rates		

Table 24.3 Old Age Security, Recipients and Payments, Selected Years 1977-87[a]

Fiscal year	Recipients as of March			Payments			
	OAS	GIS	Spouses	OAS	GIS	Spouses	Total
	number			*millions of dollars*			
1977	2,075,247	1,136,445	73,835	3,668.6	1,077.6	115.0	4,861.2
1979	2,236,049	1,190,579	81,024	4,680.9	1,495.0	146.2	6,322.1
1980	2,302,841	1,245,188	85,179	5,322.1	1,918.1	177.7	7,417.8
1981	2,368,569	1,256,813	87,103	6,104.6	2,241.9	202.8	8,585.3
1982	2,425,685	1,250,852	87,524	7,005.3	2,416.3	221.5	9,643.0
1983	2,490,881	1,246,119	87,890	7,649.0	2,524.5	232.9	10,406.3
1984	2,569,488	1,296,545	93,114	8,215.9	2,952.9	248.8	11,417.6
1985	2,652,234	1,329,886	142,302	8,857.7	3,319.4	347.8	12,524.8
1986	2,748,504	1,345,391	125,188[b]	9,520.0	3,451.4	473.2	13,444.7
1987	2,800,000	1,400,000	160,000	10,321.0	3,678.0	498.0	14,593.0

[a]Estimates. [b]For April.

Sources: *The National Finances, 1987-88.*

Bibliography, chapter 24

Ascah, L. "Recent Pension Reports in Canada: A Survey." (December 1984) 10 *Canadian Public Policy*, 415-428.

Asimakopulos, A. "Financing Canada's Public Pensions—Who Pays?" (June 1984) 10 *Canadian Public Policy*, 156-66.

_____. *The Nature of Public Pension Plans: Intergenerational Equity, Funding and Saving*. Ottawa: Economic Council of Canada, 1980.

Boadway, R.W. and Kitchen, H.M. *Canadian Tax Policy*. 2nd. ed. Canadian Tax paper no. 76. Toronto: Canadian Tax Foundation, 1984.

Bryden, K. *Old Age Pensions and Policy-Making in Canada*. Montreal: McGill-Queen's University Press, 1974.

Canada. Advisory Council on the Status of Women. Discussion Paper. *Pension Reform for Women*. Ottawa: the Council, 1981.

_____. Department of Finance. Budget Papers. *Building Better Pensions for Canadians*. Ottawa: February 1984.

_____. Budget Papers. *Action Plan for Pension Reform*. Ottawa: February 1984.

_____. Budget Papers. *Securing Economic Renewal*. Ottawa: May 1985.

_____. Department of National Health and Welfare. National Pensions Conference, 1981. *Summary of Submissions*. Ottawa: 1982.

_____. *Working Paper on Social Security in Canada*. Ottawa: 1973.

_____. *Social Security in Canada*. Ottawa: 1974.

_____. Consultation Paper. *Child and Elderly Benefits*. Ottawa: 1985.

_____. Report. *Old Age Security*. Ottawa: annual.

_____. Report. *The Guaranteed Income Supplement*. Ottawa: annual.

_____. House of Commons. Parliamentary Task Force on Pension Reform. *Report*. Ottawa: 1983.

_____. House of Commons. Report of the Auditor General. *Public Pension Management*. Ottawa: 1985.

_____. *Income Security and Social Services*. Working Paper on the Constitution. Ottawa: 1969.

_____. Joint Committee of the Senate and House of Commons on Old Age Security. *Minutes of Proceedings and Evidence* (no. 1-31) and *Report*. Ottawa: 1950.

_____. National Advisory Council on Aging. *The Economic Impact of Canada's Retirement Income System*. Ottawa: the Council, 1983.

_____. Royal Commission on the Taxation of Annuities and Family Corporations. *Report*. Ottawa: 1945.

_____. Senate. Special Committee on Retirement Age Policies. *Retirement Without Tears*. Ottawa: 1979.

_____. Statistics Canada. *Pension Plans in Canada*. Cat. no. 74-401. Ottawa: annual.

_____. Statistics Canada. *Social Security (National Programs)*. Cat. no. 86-201. 1978.

_____. Task Force on Retirement Income Policy. *The Retirement Income System in Canada: Problems and Alternatives for Reform*. Ottawa: 1980.

Canadian Council on Social Development. *How Much Choice? Retirement Policies in Canada*. Ottawa: the Council, 1975.

_____. *Statement on Retirement Policies*. Ottawa: the Council, 1976.

Canadian Life Insurance Officers Association. *Memorandum on Old Age Security*. Toronto: the Association, 1958.

Canadian Tax Foundation. "The Critical Question of Old Age Pensions." (January-February 1951) I:1 *Tax Bulletin*. 15-16.

_____. "Financing Old Age Pensions." (September-October 1951) I:5 *Tax Bulletin*, 119-23.

_____. *The National Finances*. Toronto: the Foundation, annual.

C.D. Howe Institute. *Pensions and the Economic Security of the Elderly*. Policy Commentary no. 2. Montreal: the Institute, 1981.

Clark, R.M. *Economic Security for the Aged in the United States and Canada* (mimeographed).Ottawa: Department of National Health and Welfare, 1959.

_____. "Old Age Security." In *Report of Proceedings of Fourteenth Tax Conference*, 1960 Conference Report. Toronto: Canadian Tax Foundation, 1961, 117-22.

Collins, Kevin. *Women and Pensions*. Ottawa: The Canadian Council on Social Development, 1978.

Coward, L.E. *Mercer Handbook of Canadian Pension and Welfare Plans*. Don Mills, Ontario: CCH Canadian, various years.

_____. *Pensions in Canada*. Don Mills, Ontario: CCH Canadian, 1964.

Douglas, M. *Financing Old Age Pensions: A Personal View*. Toronto: Canadian Tax Foundation, 1951.

Economic Council Of Canada. *One in Three—Pensions for Canadians to 2030*. Ottawa: 1979.

Financial Executives Institute of Canada. Conference Proceedings. *Probing the Pension Issue*. Toronto: the Institute, 1981.

Hougham, George. *The Clark Report*. Ottawa: Canadian Welfare Council, 1959.

Kernaghan, K. "Politics, Public Administration and Canada's Aging Population." (Winter 1982) VIII: *Canadian Public Policy*, 69-79.

Marsh, L. Report. *Social Security for Canada (1943)*. Toronto: University of Toronto Press, 1975.

MacGregor, D.C. *The Proposed Old Age Pension*. Canadian Tax Papers no. 4. Toronto: Canadian Tax Foundation, 1951.

Mendelson, M. *Universal or Selective? the Debate on Reforming Income Security in Canada*. Toronto: Ontario Economic Council, 1981.

Ontario Economic Council. *Pensions Today and Tomorrow*. Toronto: the Council, 1983.

Organization for Economic Cooperation and Development. *Old Age Pension Schemes*. Paris: OECD, 1977.

_____. "Old Age Pensions: Level, Adjustment and Coverage." (1973) *OECD Observer*, 19-24.

Perry, Harvey. "Financing Old Age Security." (November 1959) 35 *Canadian Welfare*, 254-58.

Pesando, J.E., and Rea, S.A. Jr. *Private and Public Pensions in Canada—An Economic Analysis*. Toronto: University of Toronto Press, 1977.

Price Waterhouse. *Pension Reform*. Toronto: Price Waterhouse, 1984.

Provinces:

British Columbia. *Developing a Pension Policy for the Future*. Victoria: Ministry of Provincial Secretary and Government Services, 1982.

Nova Scotia. *Report*. Nova Scotia Royal Commission on Pensions. 1983.

Ontario. Royal Commission on the Status of Pensions in Ontario. *Report*. Toronto: 1980.

_____. Select Committee of the Ontario Legislature on Pensions. *Report*. Toronto: 1982.

_____. *Ontario Proposals for Pension Reform: Adapting to Social and Economic Transformation*. Toronto: 1984.

Quebec. *Financial Security for the Elderly in the Report*. Quebec City: Confirentes, 1977.

_____. *Action Now for Tomorrow on Retirement Income Security*. Quebec City: 1985.

_____. Pension Board. *Report*. Quebec City: the Board, annual.

Queen's University. *Industrial Retirement Plans in Canada*. Kingston: Industrial Relations Sector, 1938.

"Report on Pensions and Benefits," *The Globe and Mail*, August 16, 1985.

Stone, L.O., and MacLean, M.J. *Future Income Prospects for Canada's Senior Citizens*. Montreal: Institute for Research on Public Policy, 1979.

Torrey, B.B., and Thompson, C.J. *International Comparison of Pension Systems*. Washington: President's Commission on Pension Policy, 1980.

Trudeau, P.E. *Income Security and Social Services*. Ottawa: Queen's Printer, 1969.

25
Wage-Related Government Pensions

Attention among pension advocates turned for a decade to improving the terms of the universal plan that took effect under the 1951 legislation. The principal objectives were reduction of the eligibility age from 70 to 65 and increasing the amount of the pension above $40 per month. The target amount rose with inflation to $75 and finally to $100, and, as the previous section has demonstrated, in time all these changes came to pass.

An approach of long standing to which a great deal of lip service had been devoted was the introduction of a contributory pension plan. Old Age Security had been conceived as contributory, but in practice the government had been forced to settle for earmarked taxes. The OAS was obviously directed mainly to the relief of low income elderly people, but there remained the millions of employed wage earners who would find their life savings and their company pensions, if any existed at all, quite inadequate to maintain a reasonable standard of living following retirement. Late vesting of pension rights and lack of portability were unpopular features of the limited number of private pension plans then established. Once the OAS became established, it became apparent that there was still a gap in public coverage in Canada, a gap that received increasing attention from political parties in the fifties.

Apart from its obvious political appeal, an advantage foreseen by governments was the lessening of pressure for raises in the OAS. There were precedents in other countries; the United Kingdom and Sweden, for example, in 1959 added contributory plans to their basic non-contributory schemes; since 1935 there had also been the example of the U.S. social security system, mainly financed on a contributory basis. The gap of course might have been filled, or partially filled, with tax and other incentives for private pensions and annuities, but this was not the spirit of the times.

The proposal began to take concrete form during the Diefenbaker regime (1957-63), particularly following completion of a study in 1959 of the United States program by R.M. Clark. In his report, *Economic Security for the Aged in the United States and Canada*, Professor Clark demonstrated that the U.S. system was not transferable to Canada. Although he carefully avoided making recommendations, as his terms of reference did not call for them, in an analysis of the pros and cons of a wage-related government plan for Canada, he appeared to lean toward the proposal. For example: "I have come to the conclusion that many Canadian employees would be willing to contribute more to a government pension program with benefits above the minimum than to the existing type of flat rate benefit program."[25.1] In any

---

[25.1] R.M. Clark, *Economic Security for the Aged in the United States and Canada* (Ottawa: Department of National Health and Welfare, 1959), 654 (mimeographed).

event his report usefully clarified many of the questions that would be faced in Canada.

There were a wide range of subsidiary issues, on which opinions varied. These included the possibility of extending coverage and providing survivorship and disability benefits—an especially prickly subject. One of the results of their inclusion, according to the legal authorities, would be that the 1951 amendment to the BNA Act that gave the federal government powers to legislate for old age pensions would be inadequate, and a further amendment would be required.

The Diefenbaker government started the wheels turning in 1962 by proposing a plan to the provinces for consideration. All provinces but Quebec and Ontario agreed; the latter two had definite and different ideas as to future developments in the pension area. As it turned out the Liberals returned to power in 1963 and it was left to Prime Minister Pearson to settle the delicate issues at stake. This was to take place between 1963 and 1966, in a busy period which also saw the introduction of the Guaranteed Income Supplement, the Canada Assistance Plan, and substantial increases in Old Age Security. Progress was slow, partly because of the need to achieve agreement with the two key provinces, Quebec and Ontario, and partly because the detailed shaping of a plan turned out to be far more complex than had been anticipated. The Liberal government's first move to meet its election commitment to early action was the introduction in June 1963 in the House of Commons of a resolution, followed by a further explanatory statement a month later. These brought generally unfavourable reactions from all sides, particularly from the two largest provinces. Quebec's difficulties were predictable. It wished to handle this sensitive matter itself, and only wanted the federal government to exclude Quebec from its plan. Furthermore the Quebec government's own studies appeared to have advanced beyond the federal and there were several features of the federal plan to which it took exception. It proposed therefore to proceed on its own, asking only that the federal government not impede its progress. Ontario, on the other hand, was not in sympathy with a public pension at this stage. Its own efforts, following study by a committee, had been directed to improving the terms of private pension plans as an alternative to further state action. The result had been passage of the Pension Benefits Act in 1963. In retrospect it appears that Ontario was running counter to the mood of the times. The sixties evidenced more social concern and produced more government social legislation than any other period in Canadian history, including health insurance, the Canada Pension Plan, the Canada Assistance Plan, the Guaranteed Income Supplement, and more generous Old Age Security benefits. As a realistic footnote to this scenario it should be conceded that political parties were not unaware of the credit to be gained by reasonable acquiescence in this trend, nor were government treasurers unmindful of financial resources that would pour into their coffers, at least temporarily, through such devices as the Canada Pension Plan.

The details of the negotiations which produced a final accord between the provinces and Ottawa are too extensive to cover here. The issues raised by Quebec in particular were quite fundamental, and had to do with such questions as coverage, the period of transition for early entrants, sharing of funds, earnings ceilings, basic exemptions, employee and employer contribution rates, qualifying age, rate of benefits, indexation, and related relevant and important questions. They are well described in Bryden's study if the reader wishes further details. The notable accomplishment, for which both sides are given credit, was the series of compromises negotiated between the federal and Quebec governments. The result was an integration so complete that Quebec's separate plan has operated virtually in tandem with the federal plan without difficulty, and there has been close continuing cooperation to maintain this result. Ontario also compromised on several issues to achieve a final conclusion. Without the two largest provinces, the plan would not have proceeded; their agreement was crucial. It appears in perspective that the conclusion of this phase was well received by most elements of the community, with the undoubted exception of the life insurance companies, which protested with considerable justification that the state had invaded a major area of their business.

The Canada Pension Plan

The plan came into operation in January 1967. Its general scheme was to provide an income-related pension to all persons (with some stated exceptions), whether employed or self-employed, at age 70, and benefits to the survivors and dependants of such persons. Pensions would be paid from a fund supported by contributions from employers and employees. The fund was to be self-supporting; the initial surplus in the fund, after deduction of administrative costs, would be loaned to the provinces. The Quebec Pension Plan was identical to the federal plan in all important respects. At the outset it was necessary to adopt transitional measures to gradually bring retired persons aged 65 to 69 under coverage. This was done by reducing the eligible age by one year at a time until age 65 was reached in 1970. From that time forward all employed and self-employed persons, with the exception of certain excluded categories, such as employees in highly seasonal industries, between the ages of 18 and 64 would be required to contribute. All retired contributors aged 65 and over would be eligible for benefits, both for themselves and, under specified conditions, for their dependants. Non-retired persons may continue to contribute to age 70.

Basic Benefits and Contributions

The details of the benefit computations are quite complicated, and need not be detailed here. The following concepts are essential to even a broad understanding.

Pensionable Earnings

This concept is central to the main calculations. It refers to a bracket of earnings that provides both a floor and a ceiling for contribution and benefit calculations. The bracket principle was established in 1967, when the range was between $600 and $5,000. The exemption and the maximum have been indexed in various ways since 1967 and by 1988 had reached a lower limit of $2,600 and a maximum of $26,500. (Indexation is described later). The lesser amount is exempt from contribution and is not counted in any calculation of benefits. The higher amount sets the ceiling for earnings to be included, and is known as the maximum pensionable earnings. The lesser amount is deducted from the maximum to determine the actual amount of pensionable earnings subject to contribution. The maximum also plays a part in the computation of the retirement benefit.

Contributions

This is essentially a euphemism for a payroll tax levied on both the employer and employee at equal rates. It is based on the amount of "pensionable earnings" in the year as just defined. If they fall below the exemption no contribution is payable, and if any has been deducted it is refunded. No contribution is payable on "pensionable earnings" above the maximum. The rate since inception of the plan has been 3.6 percent, one-half (1.8 percent) payable by the employer and one-half (1.8 percent) by the employee. On the basis of maximum pensionable earnings of $26,500 in 1988 the maximum amount payable by each was $478.00. Self-employed persons must pay the total amount.

Retirement Benefits

The short explanation of the retirement benefit is that it is 25 percent of average pensionable earnings. However, in practice, the calculation becomes rather complex. It is explained in the following words: "For each year after age 18 (or the beginning of the plan in 1966), an individual calculates the ratio of his earnings to the maximum pensionable earnings for that year. The ratio has a value of 1 if earnings exceed maximum pensionable earnings. The average ratio for the entire contribution period is then calculated for the individual by simply averaging the ratios obtained for all years in the period. This lifetime average ratio of earnings to maximum pensionable earnings is multiplied by the average of maximum pensionable earnings for his last three years of employment to arrive at average pensionable earnings. The pension paid is then 25 percent of the average pensionable earnings thus calculated."[25.2] Fortunately a retiree is spared this complex calculation in most offices, (at least such was the experience of the present author) but those independent persons who wish to verify the calculation may do so if they have the necessary information.

Supplementary Benefits

Supplementary benefits are also paid in the form of death benefits, pensions for the surviving spouse, and benefits for orphans. The death benefit is paid in a lump sum, and is the lesser of one-half the annual retirement benefit at

---

[25.2] Boadway and Kitchen, supra footnote 23.1, at 297-98.

the time of death or 10 percent of that year's maximum pensionable earnings. Spouses of deceased pensioners receive a survivor pension if they are over 34 years of age, are supporting dependent children, or are disabled. The surviving spouse's pension is based in part on a flat amount and in part on the pension of the deceased spouse, is larger for ages over 45, and less for younger spouses. Pensions for surviving spouses that became payable before age 65 can continue beyond that age.

Orphan's pensions are a flat amount paid to orphan children of a deceased pensioner under the age of 18 and unmarried, or payable to age 25 if attending school.

Disability pensions, introduced in 1970, are paid at the full amount of a retirement pension for persons over 65, and at a reduced amount for persons under 65, provided they have contributed for at least five of the ten prior years.

Indexation

Indexation has been granted for all aspects of the CPP since inflation became significant. Both the contribution base (exemption and maximum pensionable earnings) and the benefits payable were indexed in accordance with the Pensions Index, a specially computed index which mainly reflected increases in the Consumer Price Index. However the maximum increase was limited to 2 percent per year under this index until 1974, when the full annual average increase to October 31 in the previous year was substituted. A special step was taken in 1974 to bring the level of the maximum pensionable earnings into line with the level of average industrial earnings. The maximum was increased by 12.5 percent per year, which achieved the purpose in 1981. Since then the maximum has increased at the same rate as average industrial earnings. The effect of this can be seen in the doubling of the maximum retirement benefit from $122 to $244 between 1975 and 1980, and the subsequent substantial annual increases. It should perhaps be emphasized that this step has only been applied to raise the maximum pension for calculation purposes. Once established the indexation is based on the annual change in the consumer price index in the previous year, the system instituted in 1974.

Table 25.1 gives the contributions and the benefits payable under various features of the Canada Pension Plan over a selected range of years. The effect of indexation is fully apparent.

Basis of Financing

Financing the pension could have gone the way of either pay-as-you-go or of funding. The former would have involved matching charges with outlays in a general way on the model of unemployment insurance or the Canada Pension Plan. The latter method, in its most rigorous application, would have meant building up a capital amount the return from which would be sufficient to meet outlays without invading the principal amount. In typical Canadian fashion we adopted neither. In principle, the plan is funded; by

Table 25.1 Canada Pension Plan: Monthly Contributions and Benefits for Selected Years from Inception of Program

Effective date	Exempt earnings	Yearly maximum pensionable earnings	Maximum contributions,[a] employers and employees	Retirement	Spouse under 65	Orphan[b]	Disability
				dollars			
1/1/66	600	5,000	79.20	—	—	—	—
1/1/70	600	5,300	84.60	43.33	67.16	26.53	92.88[c]
1/1/75	700	7,400	120.60	122.50	88.31	37.27	139.35
1/1/80	1,300	13,100	212.40	244.44	148.92	57.25	240.58
1/1/82	1,600	16,500	268.20	307.65	186.17	70.68	301.42
1/1/83	1,800	18,500	300.60	345.15	208.03	78.60	337.46
1/1/84	2,000	20,800	338.40	387.50	229.18	83.87	374.50
1/1/85	2,300	23,400	379.80	435.42	250.84	87.56	414.13
1/1/86	2,500	25,800	419.40	486.11	273.35	91.06	455.64
1/1/87	2,500	25,900	444.60	521.52	290.36	94.79	634.09
1/1/88	2,600	26,500	478.00	543.06	302.61	98.96	660.94

[a]Since self-employed persons contributed both as employer and employee, their contribution is double the amount shown. [b]Reduced by one-half for each orphan in excess of four. [c]Effective February 1970.

Source: *The National Finances, 1987-88.*

1985 a reserve of $31 billion had been accumulated as revenues from contributions in the early years far exceeded outlays for benefits. Revenues were still exceeding outlays in 1985, and the actuarial forecast was that this would continue until the fund reached a peak of $45.3 billion in 1993, after which it would start to decline. It was forecast that the fund would be virtually depleted by 2003. To avoid this result income and outgo would have to be brought into balance. The expectation of pensions anticipated for the plan, would have meant only one thing—an increase in contributions, and that increase, to be effective, would need to be made well in advance of the demise of the fund.

The Canada Pension Plan Advisory Committee in a report issued in March 1985, proposed that the 3.6 percent contribution rate be maintained until 1994, and that for the long-run the fund then be stabilized at a level that would meet two years of benefits and administrative expenses. This could be accomplished by increasing the contribution rate in the following year to 3.97 percent, and hence gradually to 10.76 percent by 2030. It warned however that any future changes in benefits should be costed and provided for in the contribution structure.

To make any changes in the plan the government would have to start discussions with the provinces in the near future, as two-thirds (seven) of them, representing two-thirds of the population, would have to agree to any changes. Quebec had already announced in April 1985, that it was undertaking a complete review of its retirement income programs, including both the Quebec Pension Plan and private plans. Quebec's stated position was that "the financial security of retirees should be based more on insurance programs such as the Quebec Pension Plan, than on assistance programs." It foresaw that increases in contributions would be necessary to avoid depletion of the fund, and proposed that these begin in 1987 at a rate of 0.4 percent, and continue to 1994. As for the future of QPP, it favoured adoption of the 1977 Cofirentes[+] report, which would raise the replacement rate on the first half of the pension from its present 25 percent to 50 percent, while leaving the rate on the other half at 25 percent. The considerable increase in contributions required for this change should be spread over five to 10 years. It did not favour the inclusion of "homemakers" in the QPP, as this would "considerably alter the nature of the plan." Full public discussion and close consultation with the federal government was promised before enactment of any of these changes.

In September 1985, the federal government made known its own proposals in a consultation paper—*The Canada Pension Plan: Keeping it Financially Healthy*. The paper pointed out that the original projections in 1964 were that the fund would remain liquid at the commencing rate for twenty years, but would probably require increases in contributions after that time to avoid a future deficit. The twenty years were over and, as predicted, the end of the fund was foreseeable. The annual deficit forecast for 1994 would continue to grow each year until it had exhausted the fund in 2003. Factors contributing to the projected deficit were the "aging" of the population and the fact that a larger proportion of retirees were qualifying for full pensions. To postpone action until the fund was exhausted would require an immediate doubling, or more, in contributions to keep it solvent on a "pay-as-you-go basis," and, in the meantime, would also require repayment of some $45 billion borrowed from the fund by the provinces. The paper favoured increased contributions as of 1987, but was not specific as to the amount. It stated:

> To meet the objective of putting the CPP on a firm financial footing for the future in the fairest and least disruptive way, it has been suggested that gradual increases in the contribution rate take effect each year, until the present rate of 3.6 percent reaches approximately 11 percent some time in the next 50 to 75 years. Suggestions as to the size of the annual contribution rate increases have typically ranged from 0.1 to 0.2 of a percentage point.

As described by the Foundation's *The National Finances*, legislation to revise the Plan passed in 1986 had the following effect:

> 1) The annual contribution rate will be increased to 0.2 per cent per year for the first five years and by 0.15 per cent per year for the following 20 years. This will increase the current contribution rate of 3.6 per cent to 7.6 per cent by the year 2011. The equal split between employer and employee contributions will be maintained.
>
> 2) The retirement age at which CPP benefits can be received has been made more flexible. At the option of the contributor, CPP retirement benefits can begin at any age between 60 and 70 with appropriate actuarial adjustments.
>
> 3) Procedures have been introduced to provide a federal-provincial review of the adequacy of the CPP financing at five-year intervals.[25.3]

It was estimated that this formula would ensure solvency of the fund for the foreseeable future. No mention was made in the Act of the government's pre-election promise to bring housewives into the plan. In November 1985, the federal Minister of National Health and Welfare stated that this proposal was still on the government's agenda, and would soon be broached with the provinces. Early reaction from provincial authorities was lukewarm, and nothing had been done to 1988.

Investing the Fund

With billions of dollars available to be shared, the use of the accumulated fund had been the subject of sharp negotiation in 1964-65. In the end the federal government agreed to lend the provinces the full amount of additions to the fund each year, subject to the retention of an amount to cover administrative expenses. The CPP Investment Fund purchased securities of an individual province in proportion to the revenues that originated in that province each year. The reserves are thus now composed of provincial government securities that would have to be redeemed to meet annual

---

[25.3] *The National Finances*, supra footnote 23.3, at 8:10.

deficits if they ever occurred. Every province would cheerfully avoid such an event, and would promptly agree to higher contribution rates.

In most provinces the CPP funds (on which interest must be paid) have replaced borrowings that otherwise would have been obtained from the market. In Quebec, however, the monies, along with other similar savings fund proceeds, have gone into a separate organization, the Caisse de Depôt et Placement du Québec. Conceived by Jacques Parizeau, a former Minister of Finance in the Levesque government, the Caisse was designed not only to make Quebec independent of the usual financial sources but as well to promote Quebec economic interests in every way. To 1985, $20 billion of funds had been made available to the Caisse which were used to finance Quebec enterprises and acquire substantial holdings in some 100 existing companies, valued at over $6 billion. As a result the Caisse is said to be one of the largest operators in Canadian stock markets.

Table 25.2 gives the amount of securities of individual provinces held by the Canada Pension Plan Fund at March 31, 1987, and Table 25.3 gives further details of the Plan.

The Canada Pension Plan was to be the last of the large government-sponsored pension programs. In the grim budgetary outlook of the last decade governments have been seeking ways of inducing the private sector to share in the load.

Table 25.2 Provincial and Federal Securities Purchased by the Canada Pension Plan Investment Fund for Fiscal Years Ending March 31, 1966 to 1987

Securities of	1966 to 1984	1985	1986	1987
	millions of dollars			
Newfoundland	522.9	47.1	50.6	60.0
Prince Edward Island	109.0	10.5	9.0	13.5
Nova Scotia	992.5	85.8	91.8	109.6
New Brunswick	752.0	67.1	46.1	75.5
Quebec[a]	104.5	5.4	5.8	6.9
Ontario	13,500.5	1,133.2	1,213.5	351.3
Manitoba	1,439.6	119.3	126.0	150.0
Saskatchewan	1,135.7	104.3	112.5	133.7
Alberta	2,747.8	305.4	332.3	398.7
British Columbia	3,811.2	355.0	185.4	226.0
Yukon	—	—	—	0.6
Canada	188.7	16.7	240.0	1,352.3
Total	25,304.7	2,249.7	2,412.8	2,877.7

[a]Amounts available to Quebec relate only to the contribution of some federal employees of that province (for example, armed forces personnel and RCMP officers).

Source: *The National Finances*, 1987-88.

Table 25.3 Number of Pensioners and Revenue and Expenditure of the Canada Pension Plan Account for Selected Fiscal Years Ending March 31, 1967 to 1988

Year	Number of recipients[a]	Revenue		Total	Expenditure		Net increase in account	Funds transferred to CPP investment fund	Cumulative operating balance
		Total contributions	Other[b]		Benefit payments	Administrative expenses			
	thousands	millions of dollars							
1967	3	587.2	12.7	599.9	0.1	8.4	591.5	580.7	65.4
1970	160	745.6	143.9	889.6	47.3	17.7	824.5	809.8	99.6
1975	631	1,238.8	518.6	1,757.4	399.0	29.9	1,328.6	1,284.9	280.5
1980	1,213	2,367.5	1,289.0	3,656.5	1,635.1	58.4	1,963.0	1,868.1	722.4
1982	1,413	3,281.9	1,585.0	5,132.2	2,455.6	76.4	2,600.3	2,447.8	1,024.9
1983	1,520	3,446.4	2,235.9	5,682.2	3,035.8	85.5	2,560.9	2,413.2	1,172.6
1984	1,624	3,715.9	2,533.7	6,249.7	3,656.8	89.0	2,503.9	2,369.2	1,307.3
1985	1,723	3,879.5	2,888.3	6,767.8	4,223.3	100.0	2,444.5	2,249.2	1,502.6
1986	1,847	4,495.1	3,161.6	7,656.7	4,887.1	111.2	2,658.4	2,412.8	1,773.0
1987	2,107[c]	4,975.7	3,403.9	8,379.6	5,721.3	140.4	2,517.9	2,877.8	1,978.4
1988[d]	2,200	5,430.0	3,509.0	9,598.0	7,010.0	122.2	2,465.8	2,276.0	2,159.0

[a] As of March 31 of year. [b] Largely interest on investment fund. [c] As of April 30, 1987. [d] Estimates, part III.

Source: *The National Finances, 1987-88.*

Bibliography, chapter 25

Bryden, K. *Old Age Pensions and Policy Making in Canada*. Montreal: McGill-Queen's University Press, 1974.

Canada. Advisory Committee on Canada Pension Plan. A Report to the Minister of National Health and Welfare on the Funding Principles of the Canada Pension Plan. Ottawa: 1976.

_____. Majority and Minority Reports. *Indexation of Benefits*. Ottawa: 1980.

_____. *Review of the Objectives of the CPP*. Ottawa: 1978.

_____. *The Rate of Return on the Investment Fund of the Canada Pension Plan*. Ottawa: 1975.

_____. Department of National Health and Welfare. *Canada Pension Plan*. Ottawa: annual.

_____. *The Canada Pension Plan: Keeping it Financially Healthy*. Ottawa: 1985.

_____. Senate and House of Commons. Special Joint Committee of the Senate and House of Commons on Bill C-136 (Canada Pension Plan). *Minutes and Proceedings of Evidence*. Ottawa 1964.

_____. Task Force on Retirement Income Policy. *The Retirement Income System in Canada: Problems and Alternatives for Reform*. Ottawa: 1980.

Clark, R.M. *Economic Security for the Aged in the United States and Canada*. (mimeographed). Ottawa: Department of National Health and Welfare, 1959.

Province of Ontario. Ministry of the Treasury, Economics and Intergovernmental Affairs. *Review of the Issues in Financing the Canada Pension Plan*. Toronto: 1973 and 1976.

_____. Royal Commission on the Status of Pensions in Ontario. Toronto: 1981.

26
Private Sector Pensions

In the pension area interest has turned full circle and attention is shifting back to the private sector and the individual saver. The federal government had originally feared the consequences of attempting to meet expectations for retirement income through public plans, and had introduced a subsidized annuity to encourage private savings. In the fifties and sixties this cautious attitude was abandoned and government plans multiplied. But by the seventies and eighties it was becoming painfully apparent that the ship of state could founder under the load of providing retirement income for all. New ways of fostering private savings were therefore being advanced.

In broad terms, private pension savings fall into two categories: (1) private savings outside the employment relationship, and (2) employer-employee pension plans.

The upsurge in recent years in private non-employment savings has been truly astonishing. The tax measures for independent savers (RRSP, etc.) have become everyman's (and woman's) tax shelter. Millions of dollars are spent by banks, trust, and insurance companies just in advertising to promote their individual plans, reaching a peak as the end of February approaches, and billions of dollars go into them annually. Thousands of individuals in all walks of life are now more savings conscious than ever before, and are fully familiar with the latest moves in interest rates.

Equally remarkable has been the preoccupation with employer pension plans. In the last decade there has been an outpouring of reports and studies on defects in the present arrangements and means for making them fairer and more attractive. A list of only the major studies from 1977 to 1984 includes fifteen substantial works, several of them reports of royal commissions, task forces, or legislative committees (see the reference list). The federal government sponsored a National Pensions Conference in Ottawa in 1981, and the Conservative government produced volumes of material even in its first year in office. There have also been countless studies and conferences in the private sector, now focused through a permanent organization, the Canada Pension Association. Action by the Liberal government to give effect to some of the many proposals that emerged from all this study appeared to be imminent in 1984 but did not occur following its defeat in a fall election. The cause was taken up vigorously by the successor Conservatives, with specific proposals put forward in the May 1985 budget, and later legislation for implementation.

The Key Element—Taxation

A crucial element in the success of retirement savings plans of any type is their treatment under the income tax. Although constitutional power over pensions lies with the provinces, the federal government through its income tax policies has influenced changes far beyond its direct competence.

Background

Historically, jurisdiction over pensions was hardly an issue until World War II. Data is scanty, but it appears that in 1918 there were 172 plans and in 1936, 600. The floodgates parted during the war, and widened further during the 1950s. In 1946 the number of plans had risen to 3,000; by 1960 there were nearly 9,000.

This growth had taken place during a period when almost the only supervision over the incorporation and operation of these plans was that exercised by the federal Department of National Revenue incidental to its administration of the income tax. The author recalls clearly the genuine concern of the wartime Minister of Finance, the Hon. J.L. Ilsley, with the potentially serious implications of this situation, and the many meetings that were held with hard-pressed tax administration officials saddled with an enormous responsibility arising only from their task of collecting the income tax. Pension funds and plans were becoming the repository of billions of dollars of savings of Canadian workers, most of whom no doubt assumed that federal "approval" carried some sort of guarantee of solvency. In fact the sole reason for the federal intervention, and the only one for which it had constitutional authority, was to determine that the amounts contributed by employers and employees were legitimate deductions for income tax purposes. This was a very strong weapon, since it carried the threat of disallowance, which would have meant the end of the road for any plan. At the same time, however, the granting of approval required that the tax administration develop standards in aspects of pension plans which it had been advised were matters falling within provincial jurisdiction, except for industries under federal regulation.

In practice this situation was controllable until thousands of new plans were introduced in the forties and fifties. There were only minor legislative changes on pensions over the first three decades of income tax. In 1917 there was little problem in allowing the employer's contribution as a business expense for the few pension plans then in existence. In 1919 a special provision was enacted to provide a deduction for the employee contribution, no limit being stated. These arrangements remained unchanged until 1936 when the government, no doubt as an austerity move, enacted a specific maximum of $300 a year for the employee deduction. Early in World War II the employer's contribution was limited to 5 percent of total remuneration but not more than $300 per employee. Following the Report of the Ives Commission in 1945 the maximum limits on both employer and employee deductions were raised to $900. By this time both employer and employee contributions for past service were also being allowed.

This type of limitation was fully within the federal powers, and caused no problem. The crunch came with such questions of detail as terms of vesting, rules for eligibility, calculation of the final pension, and similar matters. Finding answers for these questions within the limited federal powers became urgent in the face of the thousands of applications filed during World War II.

The government adopted a bold front by appearing to strengthen its powers under the Income Tax Act. In 1942, for example, the condition was made for the first time that the pension plan must be "approved by the Minister for the purposes of this paragraph." This was elaborated in 1945 with the substitution of the words "approved by the Minister in respect of its constitution and operations for the year." Apparently these words were regarded as too strong a show of authority, and in the 1948 general revision of the Act the wording was reduced to the simple requirement that the fund or plan be "approved." To amplify this scanty law and give more specific guidance, in 1950 the Tax Department issued the so-called "pension blue book"—Statement of Principles and Rules Respecting Pension Plans for the Purposes of the Income Tax Act. For example, the requirement on the crucial matter of vesting was that it take place after 20 years of contribution and on reaching the age of 50. The blue book was replaced in 1959 by Information Bulletin No. 14, which no longer contained a requirement on vesting, then recognized as beyond federal powers.

The Provinces Move In

There is still a voluminous amount of federal regulation governing many essential aspects of pension plans, and without income tax registration a plan could not succeed. But until the provinces began to exercise their authority several crucial aspects of pension plans were left unsupervised. The provincial initiative was led by Ontario in 1963 with passage of its Pension Standards Act, to the great relief of the federal authorities. It is now a requirement for federal income tax purposes that where a province has pension legislation an application must first be approved by the appropriate provincial body. The federal government also has its own Pension Standards Act, but this applies only to industries under its jurisdiction.

Employer-Employee Pension Plan Developments

The Ontario government's initiative started a process of reform that is not yet complete. The province has a natural interest in employer-employee pension plans because of its heavy industrial and commercial population, and has given this neglected area high priority for two decades. In 1957 it appointed the Portable Pension Plans Committee which, in its 1961 report, made recommendations far beyond the issue of portability. It found that there were several shortcomings in the existing regime, such as: the limited number of plans in existence; low membership in existing plans due to restrictions on entry; failure of a high proportion of members to ever receive a pension for which they had contributed due to vesting requirements and non-portability; absence of regular supervision and inspection (except for the income tax requirements and the supervision of plans with life insurance companies—about one-third of the total); the limited opportunity for older workers to enrol; and the reluctance of employers to employ older workers who might be eligible to join a plan.

The Ontario government went some way in dealing with these issues in the Pension Benefits Act that was passed in 1963, to come into effect on January 1, 1965. The Act at first required that pension plans be compulsory, but this was withdrawn in 1964 in view of the imminent enactment of the Canada Pension Plan. The legislation established the requirements for a standard pension plan, among them vesting after 10 years of employment and after reaching the age of 45. In the prevailing chaotic condition this was a notable contribution and was adopted by nearly every other pension jurisdiction in Canada. Provision was also made for portability of a pension right to another plan. A Pension Commission was established to register and supervise plans in the province, and to ensure that the statute was carried out.

These measures dealt with several of the more pressing problems of the early sixties, but rapidly changing social expectations and the phenomenal growth in number of plans (from 8,920 in 1960 to 14,586 in 1980) brought new issues and revived old ones. Ontario responded to this development with the appointment in 1978 of a Royal Commission on the Status of Pensions in Ontario. Its ten volume report, issued in 1981, has been the source of much of Ontario's thinking on pensions. Its proposals were refined through hearings by a select legislative committee, which reported in 1982, and by official consideration. Final views were presented in a statement of the then Treasurer of Ontario in 1984—*Ontario Proposals For Pension Reform*. This statement made proposals for OAS, GIS and GAINS (the latter a limited guaranteed income scheme for Ontario citizens); extensive proposals for the CPP; proposals for further substantial changes for employer pensions (inflation protection, vesting after five years, portability rights, mandatory eligibility at age 30, fairer treatment of women, and several other matters); and proposals for individual-based pension arrangements, with improvement in tax assistance.

Many of these proposals no doubt would have been superseded or revised following the federal budget of May 1985, but their fate was uncertain in view of the change in government in Ontario in June 1985. By its earlier actions and studies Ontario had given the lead for well considered improvements by all governments in the terms for private pension plans, and the new government supported this by amendments to pension legislation in 1986.

Federal Initiatives

Federal interest in retirement programs had been almost continuous; constant attention was required for the Canada Pension Plan, the OAS, the GIS, and the income tax treatment of both employer and self-employed savings plans. However it was not until the late seventies that issues under private pension plans began to receive close attention. In 1979 a report was issued by a federal Task Force on Retirement Income Policy—*The Retirement Income System in Canada: Problems and Alternative Policies for Reform*. In 1981 the federal government hosted a National Pensions Conference in Ottawa, with representatives from all elements. In 1982 specific federal proposals for revision were put forward in *Better Pensions For Canadians*, issued jointly by the Minister of Finance and the Minister of National Health and Welfare. This was followed in the February 1984 budget with more detailed proposals for change, supported by two studies —*Building Better Pensions for Canadians* and *Action Plan for Pension Reform*. These proposals fell by the wayside when the Liberal government was defeated in the September 1984 election, but the successor Conservative government subsequently adapted the inherited mass of studies and proposals to its own philosophy. The budget of May 1985 advanced definitive amendments, apparently acceptable to the provinces, which were approved as part of the tax enactments passed later in the 1985 session, some to be effective 1986 and others later. We will look at these and later developments in a moment.

First, however, note must be taken of a proposal that surely offered the "final" and ultimate solution for Canadian retirement income problems. It appeared in the February 1984 budget paper, *Building Better Pensions for Canadians*, Chapter 3. Its basic design was summarized as follows: "For each individual a target pension—or maximum tax assisted pension—is first established on the basis of his or her earnings history. The savings required to produce the pension are then determined. Next, actual retirement savings, in the form of both *defined benefit* pension accruals and past contributions to *money purchase* plans, are subtracted to give the remaining deduction entitlement for the taxation year." In short, name your own plan, based on your career earnings expectations, and contributions required to realize it will be tax deductible. A major flaw was that it would only be possible to start the new system in 1985, since the earnings history for individuals would not be available for earlier years. The other major drawback was that the government that proposed it was defeated before implementation. It would have been interesting to follow its fate.

May 1985 Budget Proposals

The Minister of Finance did not attempt anything as ambitious as this in his May 1985 budget but his proposals were fairly sweeping nonetheless. The Minister could speak only for employees of federally regulated industries, which include banking, interprovincial transportation, radio and television broadcasting, and federal Crown corporations—about one million pensioners of the four-and-a-half million total. He gave the assurance, however, that there had been close consultation and cooperation with the provinces, and he was confident that "similar provincial legislation will be proposed where necessary to ensure a high degree of uniformity in pension plan standards across the country." Indicative of this cooperation is the fact that the objectives for private pension reform announced by Quebec in April, a month before, in its *Policy for Retirement Income Security*, were almost identical with those in the federal budget (although the Quebec proposals appear not to have been implemented through legislation).

The main budget proposals were as follows:

Vesting—after two years.

Portability—all vested benefits will be portable, with several choices for retransfers, including transfer to a new savings instrument, or a locked-in RRSP.

Minimum Employer Contribution—on retirement or changing jobs, employers must establish that they have contributed at least 50 percent of the pension being realized by the employee, and must make up any deficit below that proportion, or else contributions must be made according to a formula that will produce this result.

Non-vested contributions—must be returned, with interest, to the employee on leaving.

Accessibility—plans must cover both full- and part-time workers, the former after at least two years of service and the latter after having earnings with the employer in two consecutive years of more than 35 percent of the average industrial wage.

Early Retirement—there would be a right of early retirement at age 55 or over, with an actuarial adjustment in the size of the pension, whether or not provided by the plan.

Improvements for Women—survivor pensions will no longer be terminated on remarriage, and benefits will continue for the surviving spouse of a deceased retired pensioner at 60 percent of the amount otherwise payable. On marriage breakdown pension rights will be split equally to reflect the pension earned during the period of the marriage. Finally, following the Report of the Advisory Committee on Equal Pension Benefits, equal pensions will be required to be paid to men and women retiring in identical circumstances.

Inflation Protection—indexation will not be mandatory at this time, but the government requests voluntary cooperation in industries under its jurisdiction and will monitor the response to this appeal.

Information Disclosure—the plans must provide its members with annual statements of benefits earned and of accumulated contributions.

Representation—members may have representatives on the employer's pension committee if they wish.

Tax Treatment—the tax treatment of defined benefit and money purchase pension plans will be revised to remove discrimination in favour of the former. The discrimination has arisen because the joint employer-employee tax deductible contribution permitted for the defined benefit plan has been determined by a formula which permitted a total deduction, and a much greater pension, than that allowed for money purchase plans. The former are frequently the pensions of corporate and government employees, while the latter are mainly those of self-employed savers. It was proposed to remove the discrimination over the next five years by staged increases in the allowable deduction that would bring the money purchase plans to the same basis as the defined benefit plans. A new element of flexibility would be introduced with an allowance for individuals to contribute up to $15,500 to defined benefit plans, but the total limit on tax deductible employee contributions would be reduced from 20 percent of earnings to 18 percent.

Indexation—maximum contributions and pension benefit limits would be indexed to the average industrial wage, starting in 1991.

This ambitious program when announced was generally well received by pension experts, and there appeared to be a sense of relief that after many years of intensive effort there was good prospect that changes would finally be made.

Federal Legislation

The general changes for pension plan eligibility were implemented under the Pension Benefits Standards Act in 1986. Schedules for the increase in the deductible contribution were issued in October 1986, in general implementing the proposal for a short run up to a maximum of $15,500 by 1990. However, as part of the 1987 tax reform package the schedule for money purchase plans was revised to postpone any change to 1989, and then to rise more slowly to reach $15,500 in 1994, thenceforth to be indexed to average wages. It is noteworthy that pension contributions were retained as income deductions under the tax reform, although nearly all other personal deductions were converted to tax credits.

Provincial Legislation

Most provinces enacted legislation to follow in varying degrees the pattern of the federal proposals. In the crucial area of vesting some were adopting a five-year term (Alberta); others five years leading to two years (Manitoba); others two years (Ontario, New Brunswick, Nova Scotia.) Quebec and New-foundland appear to have stayed with the 10-year-age 45 rule. The new terms generally would apply only to pensions relating to earnings of a future period, commencing variously on January 1, 1987 to 1990. Several provinces adopted the 50 percent rule, portability to a locked-in RRSP, if not to another employer, and other features. Ontario, as the lead province, was the most comprehensive in its changes.

Late arising and contentious issues were the ownership of surpluses in pension plans and indexation of benefits. Most provinces legislated on the former, a variety of treatments being formulated, generally in favour of plan members rather than employers. Ontario was conspicuous in also adopting a plan for indexation. Following a recommendation of its Task Force on Inflation Protection for Employment Pension Plans (January 1988), the Ontario Pension Benefits Act provided for a form of indexation related to earnings of a future period. At mid-1988 formal steps had still to be taken to implement this measure, the report of the Task Force still being under consideration. Unless the author has missed it following a diligent search there is no evidence of action in Quebec to legislate on private pensions, despite the proposals made in the 1985 paper, *Policy on Retirement Income Security*.

Self-Saver Plans: the RRSP

One must go to the origins of the self-saver movement in the immediate postwar years for the background of the surprising developments that have since taken place.

The income tax amendments that opened the floodgates for the self-saver after 1956 were adopted in response to the appeals of a very limited group of taxpayers. Professional associations, such as the Canadian Medical Association, the Dominion Association of Chartered Accountants, and the Canadian Bar Association had been urging for some years that as members of professional partnerships they had been suffering discrimination in the denial of tax-deductible contributions to a pension plan. The denial arose from the fact, among other reasons, that professional persons generally are not allowed to incorporate. Had they been, they would have been able to put themselves in the status of employees and thereby meet the requirement of the law: that to be tax deductible an employee's pension contribution must be "actually retained by his employer in connection with an employee's superanuation fund or pension plan." This seems like a legal quibble, but the requirement was insisted upon by the administration as an essential barrier to fraudulent tax claims. Another cause of the denial was that the appeals fell on relatively deaf ears. Ministers of Finance of the day were themselves mainly members of the legal profession, and failed to be impressed by the lack of evidence that their former colleagues were suffering any great hardship in their careers under the law as it stood.

Despite rebuffs the professions continued their agitation, a cause which the author found himself drawn into by virtue of his position at that time as Director of the Canadian Tax Foundation—then, as now, sponsored by the Canadian accounting and legal professions. He ensured that opportunity was given for airing this issue at the annual conferences, and made occasional contributions through speeches and articles, usually in an attempt to advance a balanced view of the case and to defuse the "discrimination" issue, which he regarded as a loser.

In the budget of 1957 the issue was finally conceded. At this remove it is not clear what precisely tipped the scale. There was a new Minister of Finance who may have taken a different approach, or perhaps everyone just became tired of hearing about the subject, as sometimes happens. In any event the budget proposed an amendment to allow a deduction for contributions to a retirement instrument that was to be called a Registered Retirement Savings Plan. This specific allowance was to be the lesser of $2,500 or 10 percent of income, annually paid into a plan under a contract with either an annuity issuing firm or a trust company after its registration with the Income Tax Department. The proceeds of the plan were to be withdrawn as an annuity at age 65 or later, but not beyond the age of 71.

The accumulation in the plan was in theory locked-in, but could be withdrawn at the expense of full taxation, with a 25 percent tax to be withheld at the time of withdrawal. In this event the plan would be deregistered, and could no longer be used. There was no provision to begin with for participation by employees already members of a pension plan. This change, along with many others, was to come later.

A panel that discussed the new proposals at the 1957 Annual Tax Foundation Conference included representatives of both insurance and trust companies, who frankly admitted that they had no idea of how the public would respond to the new scheme. The most perceptive comment was made by the representative of the Taxation Department, John Forsyth, who said, regarding the future: "The first thing is that tax deferment is going to be a basic part of future planned savings. Just as a pension plan is the basis of savings for employees, so will a registered savings scheme be the basis for future well planned savings." He ended by agreeing that there would no doubt be future changes in the legislation. "Of one thing you may be sure, it will be an interesting development."[26.1]

From the perspective of 1988 these words have a prophetic quality. Income tax data for 1985, the latest year available, record personal contributions to RRSPs by 2,892,892 taxpayers in the amount of $6.7 billion, an amount which incidentally exceeded the $4.9 billion of personal contributions to registered employer pension plans. Insurance policies that have a savings content have been eligible, and thousands have been registered. Under arrangements with the trust companies, which must administer the plans, the large savings institutions, including the banks, have mounted powerful drives to obtain their share of these tax deductible deposits. Competition has been intense, with each institution vying to offer the most attractive package. The author freely concedes that as one fairly close to the origins of the self-saver tax relief, subsequent events have had an air of unreality. It is almost certain that the extent to which the RRSP has become the tax haven for the average citizen, was not foreseen by any of those involved in its original conception. As John Forsyth forecast at the 1957 Conference, it has been an interesting experience indeed.

Income Tax Treatment

Over the years the deductible annual contribution has been raised to reach $7,500 in 1987, to $8,500 in 1988 and thence by annual increases to $15,500 in 1991. However, as part of the 1987 tax reform this rise was extended to reach $15,500 only by 1995, a stretch-out of an additional four years, as with registered pension plans. In a further announcement in August 1988 the raise to $8,500 for 1988 was postponed a year, but the schedule was to be maintained by a double jump to $10,500 in 1990 to reach $15,500 in 1995, in each year within the limit of 18 percent of income. Even this modified tax benevolence will undoubtedly make the RRSP an even more popular tax shelter than in the past.

[26.1] John S. Forsyth, "What's to do About Self-Employed Pension Plans?" in *Report of the Eleventh Tax Conference* (Toronto: Canadian Tax Foundation, 1957), 75.

Bibliography, chapter 26

Canada. Department of Finance. *Better Pensions for Canadians*. Budget Paper. Ottawa: February 1984.

_____. *Securing Economic Renewal*. Budget Paper. Ottawa: May 23, 1985.

Canada. Statistics Canada. *Pension Plans in Canada*. Cat. no. 74-401. Ottawa: annual.

Common, F.B., Dickinson, F.G., and Morrison, K.J. "Pensions for the Self-Employed." In *Report of Proceedings of the Tenth Tax Conference*, November 12-13, 1956. Toronto: Canadian Tax Foundation, 1957, 189.

Forsyth, J.S., Coate, F., and Lawson, F.R. "What to do About Self-Employed Pension Plans?" In *Report of Proceedings of the Eleventh Annual Tax Conference*, November 11-12, 1957. Toronto: Canadian Tax Foundation, 1958, 74.

Perry, J.H. "Discrimination? Tax Treatment of the Self-Saver." (November-December 1954) XII *Canadian Tax Journal*, 351-58.

Pesando, J.E. *Issues Regarding the Reform of Canada's Private Pension System*. Ottawa: Department of Supply and Services, 1983.

_____. and Rea, S.A. Jr. *Private and Public Pensions in Canada: An Economic Analysis*. Toronto: University of Toronto Press, 1977.

Price Waterhouse. *Pension Reform*. Toronto: Price Waterhouse, 1984.

Province of Alberta. *Proposals for Improving the Effectiveness of the Private Sector Pension Systems of Alberta*. Edmonton: 1984.

Province of Manitoba. Pension Commission of Manitoba. *Proposals for Amendments to the Pension Benefits Act*. Winnipeg: 1983.

Province of Nova Scotia. Nova Scotia Royal Commission on Pensions. *Report*. Halifax: 1983.

Province of Ontario. Committee on Portable Pensions. *Summary Report*. Toronto: February 1961.

_____. Committee on Portable Pensions. Second Report. Toronto: August 1961.

_____. Royal Commission on the Status of Pensions in Ontario. Toronto: 1980.

_____. Select Committee of the Ontario Legislature on Pensions. *Report*. Toronto: 1982.

_____. *Ontario Proposals for Pension Reform: Adapting to Social and Economic Transformation*. Toronto: 1984.

Family Income

27
Family Income

Family Allowances

Family allowances—the payment to families of an amount for each child (the "baby bonus" in the vernacular)—was the second substantial social program to be introduced by the federal government following unemployment insurance. Its introduction in 1945, as an exclusively federal program, was the outcome of study within government during the war of the problem of income maintenance under peacetime conditions. A payment to families had much to offer for this purpose. In lower income families the arrival of each child brings increased financial needs but not added income to meet them. Child payments would not only give income support for families but would put money where it would be immediately spent, a desirable result under the Keynesian prescription for economic prosperity.

The family allowance idea was not new, but appears to have become attractive to governments in the immediate postwar period. There had been industrial plans in France, usually based on a single industry or even a single business, as long ago as 1858, which were generalized under laws passed in 1932. In 1946 in a social system reorganization family allowances became universal. Belgium had an elementary plan from 1922, and Germany also had paid family allowances for some years. They had been recommended for Great Britain in the Beveridge Report of 1942, and were introduced in 1946. Plans were also implemented in the Scandinavian countries: Sweden in 1948 and Denmark in 1949. Most other countries have since followed, with a wide variety of types in use.

The concept is not without its critics. The primary fault is said to be its effect in increasing the birth rate, particularly in low income families. Another is that such gratuitous cash payments tend to stultify work effort on the part of the worker. A third is that if financed by a payroll tax (as it was in some European countries) its effect is to burden small business and depress wage levels. Some economists have worried about their stimulus to consumption during inflationary periods. It is also argued that if the plan is universal, as many are, allowances are paid to families that do not need them. Supporters argue that this type of income maintenance is easier to administer than any other (such as the guaranteed income or negative income tax), it has less effect on work incentive than other proposals, it fills an obvious gap in the general structure of social security systems, it brings no stigma to the recipient families, and today brings important marginal assistance to the single or separated parent. Finally it is argued that the few hundred dollars it brings to the family is unlikely to have much effect on attitudes toward work or child-bearing.

The Canadian Plan

Under the Family Allowances Act of 1944 cash payments commenced in July 1945. The main requirement for eligibility until January 1974, was that the child be "under sixteen." Payments were made for all children (under some plans the first child is excluded) with rates that varied with age. Until August 1957, there were four brackets, as follows:

0-5 years of age—$5 per month
6-9 years of age—$6 per month
10-12 years of age—$7 per month
13-15 years of age—$8 per month.

At the outset reductions were made in the payment for children beyond the fourth. This was dropped after March 1949. In September 1957, the brackets were reduced to two, as follows:

0-9 years of age—$6 per month
9-15 years of age—$8 per month.

This change gave an extra dollar per month for children 0-5 years and 10-12 years of age, with some increases in total outlays. By contrast with other elements in the social services structure these were the only significant alterations in the first twenty-eight years of the family allowances plan. Although payments under several other programs had been indexed for inflation in the late sixties, nothing of this sort was done for family allowances until 1973, when several drastic changes were made, to be described shortly.

As illustrated by table 27.1, between 1946 and 1972 the number of families receiving allowances approximately doubled (from 1,593,000 to 3,110,000) as had the number of children for whom they were paid (from 3,633,000 to 6,757,000). The proportion of the population represented by these children increased moderately (from 28.9 percent to 33.9 percent). The monthly average payment per child rose only from $5.95 to $6.75 and the average payment per family only from $13.62 to $14.66, despite an inflation of over 100 percent between these two years. Even this limited increase rose mainly from the change in brackets in 1957. Total payments went from $245 million in 1946-47 to $548 million in 1972-73, somewhat more than doubling. As a result of rising incomes and inflation the importance of the allowances in family income dropped drastically—from just over 5 percent in the forties to less than 1.4 percent in 1972. In two or three provinces additional allowances were paid as supplements for the federal payment.

Youth Allowances

To fill the gap in ages 16 and 17 for disabled children and children attending school, the federal government introduced the Youth Allowance Plan in 1964. It paid a flat $10 per month for eligible children in all provinces except Quebec, which had its own Schooling Allowance. Quebec opted out of the federal scheme for tax points under the Federal-Provincial Fiscal Revisions

Act, 1964. A plan of family assistance was also adopted in 1962 to provide for newly arrived immigrants in the year of waiting for family allowances eligibility. The number of children qualifying for these allowances, including the Quebec Schooling Allowance, rose from about 560,000 in 1965 to over 700,000 in 1973, the cost rising from $38 million in 1965 to about $70 million in 1973.

The 1973 Changes

The review process started in the late sixties ultimately resulted in very drastic renovation of the family allowances plan, although the process was to require several years.

The proposals that began the revisions were presented in the 1970 study, *Income Security for Canadians*,[27.1] and touched all aspects of the income maintenance system. The paper expressed dissatisfaction with the existing family allowances plan as a means of relieving poverty; the payments were too low and did not direct enough help to lower incomes. It was estimated that in 1971 only 24 percent of payments would go to families with incomes under $5,000—the bulk of the money went to middle or higher income families. It would be disastrously expensive to increase the existing allowance to an amount that would be significant for lower income families because it would have to be paid to all families; an entirely new approach was therefore needed.

It was proposed that the existing family and youth allowances be replaced by the Family Income Security Plan (FISP). Its essence was that for families with incomes over $10,000 allowances would be abolished. For incomes below that amount an allowance would be paid, not on the basis of the age of the child, as formerly, but geared to the income level of the family. A schedule of payments was proposed that declined from $16 a month per child for a family with an income of $4,500 or less, by $500 intervals, to $5 per child where income was between $9,501 and $10,000. Above $10,000 it was zero. For the lowest incomes the monthly cash payment would be increased by approximately 100 percent; for incomes over $10,000 it would be reduced by 100 percent. If satisfactory arrangements could be made with Quebec the Youth Allowance would be incorporated into FISP and would cease to be paid as such. It was estimated that FISP would cost about $660 million for family allowances alone, and an extra $100 million if the Youth Allowance were incorporated with it. The cost of the existing programs was about $560 million in 1969-70; there would therefore be an increase of up to $200 million under FISP. However, a part of the proposal was that family allowances would become taxable (they had previously been exempt) and revenue from this source was estimated at $100 million.

[27.1] Canada, Department of Finance, *Income Security for Canadians*. (Ottawa: 1970).

FISP Abandoned—the 1973 Alternative

The FISP proposal was greeted with shock and dismay by several million parents, particularly by the 70 percent whose allowances were to be cut off. Protests poured into Ottawa by mail, phone, and delegation, and it quickly became apparent that the concept of universality was not to be lightly tampered with. A special committee of the Canadian Council on Social Development proposed an alternative plan involving retention of the principle of universality and continued grading by age of the child, but with a substantial special tax applying to the allowance over a threshold level that would substantially reduce the benefit for higher incomes. The income tax exemption for children under 18 would also be removed. Some of these features appeared in the plan later adopted. Other groups put forward alternatives; few supported FISP in its original form.

The plan finally adopted was presented in the so-called Orange Paper— *Working Paper on Social Security in Canada*—put forward in 1973 by a later Minister of National Health and Welfare. The specific proposal for family allowances was that they "should be increased from their present average of $7.21 per child to an average of $20.00 per child, and be made taxable (included in the income of the parent claiming the child as a dependant). Further, that the level of the allowances should be reviewed from time to time in the light of changes in the consumer price index." A supplementary proposal was that at the wish of a province the allowance for its recipient children could be varied to suit its particular needs or philosophy. No estimate was given in the Working Paper for the cost of the proposals.

As an interim step toward implementation an across-the-board increase to $12 for all children was introduced in October 1973. The full plan came into effect in January 1974, following passage of the Family Allowances Act, 1973. It adopted an allowance of $20 per month for all children, without age differentiation, brought all children under 18 under the plan, abolished the Youth Allowance, provided for indexation at the beginning of each year based on the increase in the consumer price index in the 12 months ended the previous October 31, made the family allowance taxable as ordinary income, and provided for provincial variation at the wish of the province.

The financial impact of the new plan was immediate—and drastic. In lieu of the comparable total of about $615 million estimated for the existing programs for 1973-74 the actual payment, at almost $950 million, was more than 50 percent higher. But this only included three months at the new rates. For 1974-75, with the full program in effect and the $20 allowance indexed to $22.08, the cost soared to $1,824 million, 3½ times the level of three years before. As part of an austerity measure indexation was dropped for 1976, but the cost still rose to $1,957 million. By 1977-78 the individual payment was $25.68 and the total reached $2,122 million, four times the level of 1972-73. With the end of the Youth Allowance the tax credit granted Quebec for opting out was retained in order to avoid revision of the provincial rate structure but an amount equivalent to the abatements was recovered from other payments to Quebec.

The Refundable Child Tax Credit

1979 brought a further remarkable change in the federal child benefit program. Its principal feature was an additional flat tax credit per child of $200 per year, ($16.66 per month) which was payable in full to persons below the tax exempt level and claimable as a credit against tax by taxable persons. For income taxpayers the credit itself was gradually eliminated by a recovery tax above a threshold amount. The tax credit and the tax recovery were related to income of the previous year, so that they could be calculated in the return filed in the following spring. The recovery was $5 for each $100 over the threshold, and the threshold, initially set at $18,000, was to be indexed.

Concurrently with the introduction of the tax credit, the family allowance was cut back to $20. However, all the main elements of the new plan—the family allowance, the tax credit, and the recovery threshold—were to rise with the consumer price index. This was not done consistently or completely. There were ceilings on indexation in 1983 and 1984 and the threshold was frozen for three years at its 1983 level, but was reduced for 1986-88. The annual amounts of the allowance, the tax credit and the threshold are given below.

	Family allowance	Child tax credit	Threshold
		dollars	
1978	308.16	200	18,000
1979	240.00	218	19,620
1980	261.60	238	21,380
1981	287.52	293	23,470
1982	322.92	343[a]	26,330
1983	342.24	343	26,330
1984	359.40	367	26,330
1985	375.24	384	26,330
1986	378.96	454	23,500
1987	383.16	489	23,760
1988	388.56	559[b]	24,090

[a] A one-time increase of $50 was given in 1982, but the amount was frozen for the following year. [b] Raised in December 1987 from 524.

The tax credit approach had several obvious advantages. It concentrated benefits in the lower incomes, while retaining the principle of universality; it avoided a conflict with the provinces in the personal income tax, as it left unchanged the basic federal tax on which the provincial supplements are calculated; it obscured the very substantial additional amounts flowing to families, as the whole operation is carried out by the Department of National Revenue and appears as a reduction in taxation—not as an expenditure. Not that the amount of the tax loss has deliberately been concealed. It is published annually in the Taxation Statistics of the taxation department, and for the years available in 1988 were as follows, in millions of dollars: 1979, 933; 1980, 1,013; 1981, 1,069; 1982, 1,513; 1983, 1,446; 1984, 1,494; 1985, 1,484. Thus to the recent cost of the basic allowances, $2.5 billion in 1985, there must be added another $1.5 billion for the child credit, making a total of $4.0 billion. This is approximately seven times the expenditure of 1972-73 ($554 million), only a decade before.

The Future

In January 1985, the federal government issued a consultation paper, *Child and Elderly Benefits*. This was considered by the House of Commons Committee on Health, Welfare and Social Affairs, and on the basis of the report of that committee and other input the future of child benefits was spelled out in the budget of May 23, 1985, with details in the Budget Paper, *Securing Economic Renewal*. Essentially three lines of action were proposed: (1) continuation of family allowances as now structured, with indexation for increases in excess of 3 percent; (2) increase in the child tax credit by predetermined amounts to $454 in respect of 1986, $489 in respect of 1987, and $524 in respect of 1988 (in each case payable in the following year) with indexation beyond 1988 for increases in the CPI in excess of 3 percentage points; (3) a phased reduction in the child allowance under the income tax from the existing $710 to $560 in 1987, and $470 in 1988, with a further reduction in 1989 to bring it to the current value of the family allowance. Following that time it would be indexed for increases in CPI in excess of 3 percentage points.

In support of these proposals it was argued, once again, that they would shift benefits from higher to lower income families, with little additional cost to the government. The estimates were $15 million in 1985-86 and $40 million in 1986-87. This nominal cost no doubt reflected the saving from elimination of indexation for the first 3 points of inflation, a proposal immediately strongly opposed by welfare and child organizations. The National Council of Welfare presented a detailed analysis of the proposals in *Giving and Taking: the May 1985 Budget and the Poor*, which expressed strong dissatisfaction with the proposals and advanced alternatives.

The plan outlined by the Minister was substantially implemented in following years, but three major developments also took place in relation to children.

Sales tax credit. In 1986 a refundable sales tax credit was introduced in the amount of $25 per child (and $50 per adult) for families having an income below $15,000. In 1988 this was increased to $35 per child aged 18 or under ($70 per adult), and the threshold was raised to $16,000, beyond which the credit would be reduced by 5 percent of the excess.

Advanced payment of child tax credit. Commencing in November 1986, a prepayment of $300 of the child tax credit usually paid in the following year was introduced.

1987 tax reform. Under the tax reform proposals of 1987 the former deduction for the dependent child was converted to a tax credit of $65. It was explained that as the former income deduction was slated to be reduced to the level of the family allowance in 1989 this was the equivalent calculation for 1988 expressed as a tax credit of 17 percent of the estimated family allowance for that year.

Child Care

The new and growing state supported family expense was for child care—care of the child while both parents are away at work. The federal government announced a new program in 1987 for this purpose, to cost $6.4 billion over a seven-year period.

Income Tax. The previous maximum allowance for child care expense would be increased from $2,000 to $4,000 for children aged six and under and for those not having receipted child care expenses a supplement to the child tax credit of $100 in 1988 and $200 thereafter would be paid. This was estimated to cost $2.3 billion under the plan.

Child Care Facilities. In addition it was announced that a seven-year program of grants would be paid the provinces to double the number of day care units to 400,000. This would cost the federal government $4 billion, with additional expense for the provinces. A further $100 million would be provided for research and development of child care models.

This legislation was on the agenda for the summer and fall 1988 session of Parliament. With the attention being given concurrently to abortion laws children born and unborn were occupying an unprecedented share of the time of the national legislature. The legislation failed to be passed before the November election, and in any event appeared to satisfy no one.

Canada Assistance Plan

During the Great Depression the federal government assumed a substantial share of provincial and local expenditures on relief, but with the war and full employment these programs had expired. However, in the early fifties Parliament enacted programs of grants to share provincial assistance for special groups. Under the Blind Persons Act, the Disabled Persons Act, and the Old Age Assistance Act the government was authorized to enter into agreements with the provinces for cost-sharing of means-tested payments to eligible persons. For the aged and disabled the share was 50 percent; for the blind 75 percent. All provinces and the Yukon and Northwest Territories entered into agreements. Initial payments were $40 per month, rose to $46 in 1957, and later in the same year to $55, to $65 in 1962, and to $75 in most provinces in 1963 and 1964. In several provinces supplements were paid at the expense of the province. In fiscal year 1965 federal expenditures under these three programs were about $70 million. Outlays under a companion program, the Unemployment Assistance Act, mentioned previously in relation to unemployment insurance, were another $100 million.

In 1966, following consultation with the provinces, the federal government greatly expanded its participation in provincial and local social services and assistance through a new measure, the Canada Assistance Plan, generally known as CAP. In place of the categories covered by the old legis-

Table 27.1 Family Allowances from the Beginning

Total[a]	Number of families[a]	Percent of total	Number of children[a]	Total payments	Average monthly payment		Percent of family income
					Per child	Per family	
	(000)	%	(000)	$ million	$	$	%
1945-46[b]	1,406	—	3,299	172.6	—	—	—
1946-47	1,593	52.4	3,633	245.1	5.95	13.62	—
1947-48	1,670	54.1	3,755	263.2	5.92	13.31	—
1948-49	1,729	54.3	3,889	270.9	5.89	13.25	—
1949-50	1,852	54.3	4,202	297.5	6.01	13.64	—
1950-51	1,910	58.1	4,367	309.5	6.00	13.72	4.6
1951-52	1,967	57.6	4,530	320.5	6.00	13.82	—
1952-53	2,041	58.7	4,729	334.2	6.02	13.94	—
1953-54	2,117	58.9	4,942	350.1	6.03	14.08	4.1
1954-55	2,195	59.6	5,169	366.5	6.03	14.20	—
1955-56[b]	2,263	61.1	5,377	382.5	6.04	14.35	—
1956-57	2,327	60.4	5,571	397.5	6.05	14.49	3.7
1957-58	2,407	60.9	5,796	437.9	6.68	16.08	3.9
1958-59	2,493	61.7	6,035	474.8	6.67	16.15	3.9
1959-60	2,551	61.7	6,220	491.2	6.67	16.27	—
1960-61	2,603	62.7	6,397	506.2	6.68	16.42	3.7
1961-62	2,649	62.5	6,562	520.8	6.69	16.58	—
1962-63	2,681	62.1	6,660	531.6	6.69	16.63	3.4
1963-64	2,711	61.6	6,736	538.3	6.71	16.67	—
1964-65	2,747	61.7	6,817	545.8	6.72	16.68	3.1
1965-66	2,786	61.5	6,865	551.7	6.73	16.59	—
1966-67	2,834	61.5	6,883	555.8	6.76	16.42	2.6
1967-68	2,888	61.5	6,901	558.8	6.77	16.19	—
1968-69	2,937	61.1	6,883	560.2	6.80	15.93	2.1
1969-70	2,978	60.7	6,865	560.0	6.80	15.68	—

Year							
1970-71	3,024	59.6	6,824	557.9	6.81	15.37	1.8
1971-72	3,063	59.4	6,783	554.4	6.79	15.04	1.6
1972-73	3,110	59.6	6,757	548.6	6.75	14.66	1.4
1973-74	3,344	62.2	7,249	946.2	20.00	43.74	3.5
1974-75	3,446	61.7	7,344	1,824.0	22.08	47.70	3.5
1975-76	3,510	61.2	7,312	1,957.5	22.08	46.50	2.9
1976-77	3,561	61.1	7,244	1,979.9	23.89	49.31	2.9
1977-78	3,595	60.8	7,139	2,122.4	25.68	52.06	2.8
1978-79	3,611	60.3	7,001	2,093.0	20.00	39.45	2.0
1979-80	3,631	59.8	6,916	1,725.8	21.80	41.89	1.8
1980-81	3,645	57.8	6,826	1,850.9	23.96	45.08	1.8
1981-82	3,642	56.7	6,733	2,019.5	26.91	50.78	1.8
1982-83	3,642	55.8	6,672	2,230.6	28.52	53.00	1.8
1983-84	3,637	54.9	6,622	2,326.6	29.95	55.07	1.8
1984-85	3,635	54.0	6,585	2,416.0	31.27	57.16	..
1985-86	3,645	..	6,585	2,500.6	21.58	57.88	..
1986-87	3,659	..	6,592	2,534.4	31.93	58.22	..
1987-88	3,666	..	6,597	2,562.0	32.38	59.05	..

.. not available. a As at March. b Partial year.

Source: Statistics Canada, Social Security (National Programs).

lation it substituted a general and comprehensive program that would meet all classes of need not already covered by other legislation.

Federal-provincial agreements were authorized for grants of 50 percent of the cost of programs to meet "basic requirements" of recipients, an expression defined to include food, shelter, clothing, utilities, household supplies and personal requirements. Need continued to be used as a criterion for assistance, but the previous income (means) test was replaced by an assessment of the particular needs of each recipient.

Federal assistance was extended through the provinces to some 200,000 needy mothers and dependent children not previously covered, to some 50,000 children in the care of child welfare agencies, and to homes for the aged, nursing homes, homes for unmarried mothers, hostels for transients, and child care institutions. A special contribution was given toward assistance to Indians on reserves or in Indian communities. In 1975 CAP was extended to cover programs for young offenders and for needy persons in provinces with universal home care programs.

Not all the existing programs came to an end with the enactment of CAP. Some provinces, for example, continued with old age assistance for persons over 65 and not yet 70 until the age limit under Old Age Security was dropped to 65. Minor amounts also continued to be paid to blind and disabled persons for some years. Quebec opted out of coverage under the Act, and in its place receives the yield of 5 percentage points of personal income tax.

Federal contributions under CAP in its first full year, 1967-68, were $225 million. To this must be added the $120 million cost of the opting-out tax transfer to Quebec, for a total of $345 million. However, in the unemployment-ridden era of the eighties, with even middle-class families receiving local relief after exhaustion of their unemployment insurance benefits, payments to the provinces soared to the billions.

The Estimates for 1987-88 provided for payments of $4,192 million, to which must be added $488 million for the tax transfer to Quebec, or a total of $4.7 billion. And the prospect was that this level would persist for some years.

Bibliography, chapter 27

Canada. Department of Finance. Budget Papers: *Securing Economic Renewal.* Ottawa: May 23, 1985.

_____. Department of National Health and Welfare. Consultation Paper. *Child and Elderly Benefits.* Ottawa: 1985.

_____. *Income Security and Social Services.* Ottawa: 1969.

_____. *Family Income Security Plan.* Ottawa: 1972.

_____. *Working Paper on Social Security in Canada.* Ottawa: 1973.

_____. House of Commons. *Family Allowances Act, 1945.* Ottawa: 1945.

_____. Special Committee on Child Care. *Report.* Ottawa: March 1987.

Canadian Council on Social Development. Special Income Security Issue. (Winter 1985) *Overview,* 2.

Ismael, Jacqueline, ed. *Canadian Social Welfare Policy: Federal and Provincial Dimensions.* Institute of Public Administration of Canada. Toronto: McGill-Queen's University Press, 1985.

Kapsalis, Constantine. "In Defence of Family Allowances." (Winter 1980) *Canadian Public Policy,* 107-09.

"MPs tackle bill on family benefits." *The Toronto Star,* September 14, 1985.

Province of Quebec. Ministry of Family and Social Welfare. *Guidelines for a New Quebec Family Allowance Policy.* Quebec: 1969.

_____. Ministere des Finances. White Paper on the Personal Tax and Transfer Systems. Quebec City: 1984.

_____. Ministere des Finances. *1985-86 Budget Speech.* Quebec City: April 23, 1985.

Sayeed, Adil. "Choosing Between Tax Credits and Exemptions for Dependent Children." (September-October 1985) 33 *Canadian Tax Journal,* 975-82.

28
The Problem of Poverty

Finally, and inescapably, there is the problem of poverty. Despite the enormous effort and expenditure represented by the programs described in the previous pages a substantial proportion of the Canadian population lives in poverty. This fact has attracted much attention and it will be possible to deal here only with the bare essentials of an extremely complex and emotionally charged subject. The analysis will be divided into four main areas —income distribution; poverty lines; the poor, and anti-poverty programs.

Income Distribution

The problem stems, of course, from the fact that there are differences in income at different social levels in Canada, a phenomenon which is found in every country. If incomes were equal the concept of poverty (comparative well-being) would not exist within a society (although a whole society could be in poverty compared to other societies). Income distribution is therefore at the root of most social issues.

Putting aside several entangling questions involved in its computation the basic pattern of income distribution in Canada is quite clear. Statistics Canada has compiled data for over 30 years, and from this an astonishingly unchanging pattern emerges. This data is usually employed to show the percentage of the total income of households going to each "quintile," or each 20 percent of households, ranging from the lowest to the highest. Table 28.1 shows the results for selected years from 1951 to 1986. The bottom quintile, or the poorest 20 percent, has consistently had around 4.0-4.5 percent of total income, while the highest quintile, the best off 20 percent, has consistently had around 41-43 percent, or 10 times the share of the lowest quintile. Even the share of the bottom two quintiles taken together (40 percent of households) is consistently only 15 percent, while the share of the bottom three quintiles (60 percent of households) at around 33 percent is less than the 42 percent received by the top quintile.

In the above compilation "household" includes all income receiving units in the country, with a division made between families and unattached individuals. The term "household income" can be taken to represent total personal income in Canada. Since this compilation includes all the social payments described in earlier chapters one can only conclude that economic and social forces produce the "rich get richer and the poor get poorer" syndrome, and that if the social measures now in place had not been adopted the distribution would have been even more uneven than it has been.

Two further aspects of this general data are worthy of mention.

Table 28.1   Household Income by Quintile Shares 1951-86

	Bottom	Second	Middle	Fourth	Top	Total
			percent			
1951............	4.4	11.2	18.3	23.3	42.8	100.0
1954............	4.4	12.0	17.8	24.0	41.8	100.0
1957............	4.2	11.9	18.0	24.5	41.4	100.0
1959............	4.4	11.9	18.0	24.1	41.6	100.0
1961............	4.2	11.9	18.3	24.5	41.1	100.0
1965............	4.4	11.8	18.0	24.5	41.4	100.0
1967............	4.2	11.4	17.8	24.6	42.0	100.0
1969............	4.2	11.0	17.6	24.5	42.6	100.0
1971............	3.6	10.6	17.6	24.9	42.3	100.0
1972............	3.8	10.6	17.8	25.0	42.9	100.0
1973............	3.9	10.7	17.6	25.1	42.7	100.0
1974............	4.0	10.9	17.7	24.9	42.5	100.0
1975............	4.0	10.6	17.6	25.1	42.6	100.0
1976............	4.3	10.7	17.4	24.7	42.9	100.0
1977............	3.8	10.7	17.9	25.6	42.0	100.0
1978............	4.1	10.4	17.6	25.2	42.7	100.0
1979............	4.2	10.6	17.6	25.3	42.3	100.0
1980............	4.1	10.5	17.6	25.3	42.5	100.0
1981............	4.6	10.9	17.6	25.0	41.8	100.0
1982............	4.5	10.7	17.3	25.0	42.5	100.0
1983............	4.4	10.3	17.1	25.0	43.2	100.0
1984............	4.5	10.3	17.1	25.0	43.0	100.0
1985............	4.7	10.4	17.0	25.0	43.0	100.0
1986............	5.0	10.0	17.0	25.0	43.0	100.0

Source: Statistics Canada, *Income Distributions by Size in Canada, Canada Year Book.*

The Upper Quintile

It might be assumed that the top quintile, with its 41-43 percent of income, represents the millionaire class of Canada. On the contrary the magic realm was entered at relatively modest levels of household income in various years: levels which two income earners in a family would generally surpass.

Lower limit of top quintile

	dollars			dollars
1965	8,344		1977	25,594
1967	9,468		1979	30,400
1969	11,111		1981	38,107
1971	12,941		1983	43,770
1973	15,943		1985	47,914
1975	20,598		1986	50,380

Source: See table 28.1.

The Gini Coefficient

The Gini Coefficient is a means of measuring the extent by which actual income distribution deviates from equal distribution. A zero coefficient would indicate complete uniformity and a co-efficient of 1 would mean the opposite. A lower number indicates a greater approach to equal distribution. The coefficient by itself means very little to any one but an expert in income distribution series, but is useful for making comparisons, for example between different years in the same country or between individual countries. In this respect some of the data given in a study—*Income Distribution and Security in Canada*—published by the Macdonald Commission is interesting. The Gini coefficients for Canada for 1951-81 are given as: 1951, 0.390; 1961, 0.368; 1971, 0.400; and 1981, 0.377. This irregular pattern shows a generally downward move to the extent that the last year, 1981, was lower than the first. However, more recent compilations by Statistics Canada show a reversal, with coefficients of 0.384 for 1982, 0.394 for 1983, 0.390 for 1984 and 0.389 for 1985. No doubt this rise to levels markedly higher than 1981 was the result of heavy unemployment and reduced annual wage increases.[28.1] Another interesting recent comparison is given for the United Kingdom, Canada, and the United States, with Gini coefficients for 1979 respectively of 0.375, 0.387 and 0.400.

Gini coefficients can only be compiled when income distribution becomes available, and the timing has long lags. The OECD in 1976 published a study of "Income Distribution in OECD Countries," and although much of the material is now over a decade old it is nonetheless still of interest. The Gini coefficients for economic families, in order of closest approach to equality, were as follows:

	Year	Rank	Gini
Australia	1966-67	1	0.313
Japan	1969	2	0.335
United Kingdom	1973	3	0.344
Sweden	1972	4	0.346
Norway	1970	5	0.354
Canada	1969	6	0.382
Netherlands	1967	7	0.385
West Germany	1973	8	0.396
United States	1972	9	0.404
France	1970	10	0.416

There are some surprises in this ordering; one would have assumed, for example, that the dedication to income equality in the Scandinavian countries would have put them closer to the top. One might also have expected that the United States, with its generally higher level of total income, would be higher in the scale. Minor differences may not be significant, and undoubtedly there have been changes in more recent years. As pointed out by the author of the Macdonald Commission study previously mentioned, several factors can affect a long-term calculation, such as changes in the data (for example, in Canada farm families were not included until 1965); changes in the composition of the population (changing proportions of the young, the old and unattached individuals over a period affect the income

---

[28.1] Statistics Canada, *Income After Tax Distributions by Size in Canada* (cat. no. 13.206), 1983.

distribution); changes in labour participation (female participation rose markedly over recent years, with considerable effect on both family and individual income), and changes in transfer payments (in Canada many new programs came into effect in the sixties and seventies). However, the data does establish that unequal income distribution is a universal phenomenon; there is no Gini coefficient for the Soviet Union, but a recently issued survey, based on such information as is available, suggests that income distribution is not greatly different there than in the capitalist countries.

Poverty Lines

From the information on income distribution there has emerged the concept of a "poverty line," an income level below which a family or individual would be deemed to be living in poverty. The determination of such a line involves very subjective judgments. There are two main contending philosophies—one, that the line should be at or near the amount required to provide the bare essentials of life, (food, clothing, shelter, and meagre extras) and the other, that it should bear a relationship to the general standard of living of the community and provide for more than a minimum existence. There are models of both approaches in Canada.

Social Assistance

While not described as poverty lines, the family budget levels established for provincial and municipal social assistance allow for the essentials of food, shelter, and clothing at minimal levels, and for very little else. The CCSD (Canadian Council on Social Development) National Task Force on the Definition and Measurement of Poverty surveyed long-term provincial rates for 1983 and produced average nation-wide figures of $3,956 for a single person and $9,860 for a family of four. These were half or less than the levels determined under the alternative methods for that year.

Statistics Canada Low Income Cut-offs

A compilation issued annually by Statistics Canada stands part way between the two extremes. Its starting point of the calculation is the proportion of income actually spent by the average Canadian family on food, clothing, and shelter as reported in its Annual Survey of Consumer Finance. Statistics Canada determines a proportion roughly related to this broad average that in its view indicates a poverty condition. In recent years, with the average general expenditure at 38.5 percent, it has assumed that any family that is spending more than 58.5 percent of its income on food, clothing, and shelter is in "straitened circumstances." By determining from its survey the income level at which this occurs it establishes an amount which it calls the "low income cut-off."

Data is published annually for five categories of residential area—rural and four sizes of urban population, the results most frequently used being those for families and individuals in urban centres of 500,000 and over.

The Canadian Council on Social Development

Since 1973 CCSD has supported a poverty line related to the general level of income without reference to actual living expenditures. This approach reflects the philosophy that the poor should share in the rising standard of living of the society, and that this is best reflected by the general level of income. The base of the CCSD poverty line is 50 percent of the average income for a family of three, with adjustments to produce counterparts for units of other sizes. Following the study by its Task Force, CCSD issued a report—*Not Enough, the Meaning and Measurement of Poverty in Canada* —in which it re-affirmed its adherence to a poverty line "based on 50 percent of the national average family income" with variation for the size of family as in the past, but with the addition in the future of "adjustments to the national poverty standard to account for the extra costs associated with disabilities. . ."

The Senate

The Special Senate Committee on Poverty issued a report in 1971 proposing adoption of a poverty line that would provide a reasonable standard of living for a family of four, as determined by the Committee, with a formula for adjustment for units of other sizes and provision for annual revisions to reflect changes in the average standard of living. The Committee proposed extension to families in excess of four, the limit then used for the Statistics Canada cut-off lines. For most categories the Senate lines are close to 50 percent of general average expenditures. Annual revisions of the Senate data are issued as an appendix to the Senate debates, under the authority of Senator David Croll, the Chairman of the Committee that produced the Poverty Report.

The Formulae Applied

The results obtained under the three main approaches—Statistics Canada, the Canadian Council on Social Development, and the Senate Committee on Poverty—are given in the following tables. The Economic Council of Canada and the National Council on Welfare have also issued estimates, but the following will be sufficient to demonstrate the purpose and results of such compilations.

As the figures presented were culled from sources that are under almost constant revision it is impossible to be certain that they are completely comparable, but they are sufficiently accurate for present purposes.

Poverty Lines Compared

Despite the different bases of calculation with some exceptions the cut-off lines for poverty are within the same general areas. It is fairly clear that on the basis of these measurements in 1986 a single unattached person required upward of $11,000 a year and a family of four over $25,000 a year for the bare necessities under these measurements. Actual incomes under existing social support programs are far below these levels.

Table 28.2   Low Income Cut-offs, Selected Years, 1976-86

	Statistics Canada[a]		CCSD		Senate	
Year	Single person	Four persons	Single person	Four persons	Single person	Four persons
			dollars			
1976	4,117	9,054	4,076	9,500	4,660	10,860
1978	4,844	10,654	4,800	11,200	5,300	12,390
1980	5,822	12,807	6,849	15,981	6,610	15,440
1981	8,045	16,361	7,610	17,760	7,370	17,210
1982	8,914	18,129	8,244	19,236	7,940	18,530
1983	9,429	19,175	8,688	20,272	8,540	19,940
1984	9,839	20,010	8,963	20,914	8,850	20,650
1985	10,233	20,812	9,411	21,960	9,330	21,770
1986	10,651	21,663	10,089	23,541	9,930	23,180

[a] Urban areas 500,000 and over; 1976-80, 1969 base; 1981-86 1978 base.

Sources: Statistics Canada, *Income Distributions by Size in Canada*; Canadian Council on Social Development, *Factbook on Poverty* (various dates) and unpublished sources; Senate, Appendix to Senate Debates, usually in December.

Degrees of Poverty

Table 28.3 gives some general data on degrees of poverty among unattached individuals and families. The rate among the former is in general at least three times that of the latter. It is encouraging that the ratio for both under all three measurements has declined in 1985 and 1986 from the levels reached in 1983 and 1984.

Limitations of Formulae

Obviously the use of measures of this kind as the basis for statements of the number of Canadians "living in poverty" must be hedged with some reservations as to the nature of the computation. While there is no doubt about the existence of the poverty trap some experts question the completeness of present data on income at the lower levels; doubts are also raised as to the permanence of the conditions portrayed, as many individuals experience short periods of low income at the beginning of their career or during it, and will be counted in the lower quintile, although there for only a temporary period. For those who look only to the income distribution as a test it is sufficient proof of continuing poverty that the quintile relationship has not changed in many years. At the same time the Statistics Canada basis shows a considerable reduction in poverty over the last three decades. This has resulted from the fact that as the real income of society has increased the share required to purchase basic essentials has declined, a fact reflected in the reduction of the Statistics Canada cut-off line from 70 percent or more spent on essentials to the 58 percent used today. This has reduced the percentage of families falling below the poverty cut-off from 28 percent in 1961 to 12 percent in 1986. This sort of change in poverty conditions has come about by virtue of a general rise in real incomes of the society without any appreciable difference in income distribution. And there are those that

Table 28.3   Degree of Poverty, Selected Years, 1979-86

Year	Statistics Canada[a]			CCSD		Senate		
	Total	In-dividuals	Families	In-dividuals	Families	Total	In-dividuals	Families
1979.....	15.7	40.3	13.1	41.2	21.7	24.7	40.5	23.0
1980.....	15.1	39.6	12.2	41.4	21.2	na	40.2	21.9
1981.....	14.7	37.8	12.0	38.7	20.6	na	na	na
1982.....	16.1	37.4	13.2	38.4	20.9	na	na	na
1983.....	17.1	41.3	14.0	41.6	22.0	23.4	40.3	21.8
1984.....	17.8	38.4	15.0	37.4	22.1	23.9	37.8	22.3
1985.....	15.9	36.6	13.1	36.5	20.6	22.8	35.9	21.1
1986.....	14.9	34.3	12.3	36.7	21.2	22.4	35.4	20.9

[a] 1978 base.

Sources: Same as table 28.2.

would argue that a very strong protection against poverty is the maintenance or increase in the real value of incomes, which means the increase in economic productivity and the avoidance of inflation.

From another approach, that of the CCSD and the Senate, it is argued that as general incomes rise poverty lines should rise also, which means in effect that there is always likely to be a gap to fill to keep abreast of the line. This also has its supporters, on the basis that poverty is a condition relative to the general income level of the community, and that those in poverty should share in a rise in that level. We later examine various specific programs proposed for ending the undoubted poverty that exists in society, no matter how it is measured. Perhaps the greatest cause for reservation regarding them is that no Canadian government, after at least a quarter century of lip-service, has adopted any of the comprehensive anti-poverty programs.

The Individual Poor

As part of its annual report on income distribution Statistics Canada compiles special data on the characteristics of low income Canadians, such as the relationship of poverty to family membership, unattached status, age, sex, marriage, employment, education, regional location, etc. These factors may not be the cause of poverty but the fact that some or all may be closely related is a clue of some importance. The following is a necessarily brief survey of this data.

The Last Eight Years

Statistics Canada adopted a new base for its poverty lines in 1978, and there is now sufficient consistent data available from the following year to provide some reliable results. The main features are shown in table 28.4. In the overall category there was a moderate decline in poverty from 15.7 percent in 1979 to 14.9 percent in 1986, although the rate climbed to 17.3 percent in 1984 and dropped sharply in the following two years. For the family category the same general pattern is shown.

Table 28.4 Percent of Poverty in Main Categories, 1979-86

	1979	1980	1981	1982	1983	1984	1985	1986
				percent				
All Canada	15.7	15.1	14.7	16.1	17.1	17.3	16.0	14.9
All families	13.1	12.2	12.0	13.2	14.0	14.5	13.3	12.3
By age of head								
24 and under	20.5	21.1	22.7	28.4	34.7	30.1	32.0	30.2
65 and over	21.9	14.2	14.5	11.0	11.1	11.4	10.0	9.5
By sex of head								
Males under 65	8.5	8.1	8.3	9.7	10.4	10.9	9.5	9.1
Females under 65	43.9	45.6	40.5	44.7	47.1	46.1	46.7	42.0
Males over 65	21.8	13.3	12.9	9.4	10.4	10.1	9.1	8.7
Females over 65	22.2	21.2	24.7	23.2	17.0	21.4	16.5	16.5
All unattached individuals	40.3	39.6	37.8	37.4	41.3	37.8	36.8	34.3
By age								
24 and under	37.2	42.1	37.4	42.7	49.3	47.1	48.0	47.7
65 and over	66.3	61.5	58.6	56.0	57.5	49.6	45.8	42.7
By sex								
Males under 65	25.8	24.6	24.5	29.2	32.1	30.1	30.0	28.8
Females under 65	35.0	36.7	34.6	31.7	37.4	37.4	36.3	33.9
Males over 65	58.6	51.9	48.4	43.6	48.0	43.1	33.7	31.9
Females over 65	68.8	65.4	62.2	60.1	60.6	51.7	51.0	46.1

Source: Statistics Canada, *Income Distribution by Size in Canada*, 1986.

Much more striking was the increase in the ratio of poverty for the young and the reduction for the old. For heads of families aged 24 and under, the poverty ratio rose from 20.5 percent in 1979 to 30.2 percent in 1986, while that for ages 65 and over declined from 21.9 percent to 9.5 percent. The same trend is apparent in data for unattached individuals, showing a rise from 37.3 percent to 47.7 percent for age 24 and under and a drop from 66.3 percent to 42.7 percent for ages 65 and over.

The heavy incidence of poverty among females—called by CCSD "the feminization of poverty"—is also apparent in this data. At 42.0 percent in 1986, there was nearly five times the degree of poverty among female heads of families under 65 as there was among corresponding male heads (9.5 percent), and neither had changed greatly over the period. After a temporary upsurge in 1983, by 1986 both were back to about their 1979 levels.

Similarly the incidence of poverty among unattached individuals is higher among females at all ages than among males.

In nearly every category data for 1986 showed a sharp drop from 1985, striking evidence of the impact of the economic recovery enjoyed by Canada in that period. No doubt 1987 and 1988 will show further declines.

A Closer Look at 1986

Table 28.5 gives more detailed information for 1986, with a clearer demarcation between families and unattached individuals.

Table 28.5 Canada: Status of Various Categories of Families and Unattached Individuals Having Incomes Below Statistics Canada Poverty Lines, 1986

	Families	Unattached individuals
	percent	
All Canada	12.3	34.3
By province or region		
Atlantic	15.8	38.6
Quebec	15.3	44.6
Ontario	8.7	28.3
Prairies	12.9	31.3
British Columbia	13.3	33.0
By size of area		
500,000 and over	12.3	35.3
Rural	12.2	30.4
By age		
70 years and over	9.9	44.9
65 and under	12.8	31.2
24 and under	30.2	47.7
By sex and age		
Males under 65	9.1	28.8
Males 65 and over	8.7	31.9
Females under 65	42.0	33.9
Females 65 and over	16.5	46.1
By marital status of head		
Single	39.0	32.3
Married	9.1	34.0
Other	30.8	36.9
By employment status of head		
In labour force	10.3	25.2
Not in labour force	27.8	64.4
Full-time worker	4.7	9.0
Part-time worker	23.7	49.1
By education		
0-8 years	16.7	53.5
Some high school—no post-secondary	14.4	34.4
Some post-secondary	11.2	33.3
Post-secondary certificate or diploma	7.2	25.4
University degree	4.2	15.8
By family characteristics		
Married couples only	8.1	—
Married couples with single children	9.6	—
Lone parent families		
Male head	16.4	—
Female head	44.1	—

Source: Statistics Canada, *Income Distribution by Size in Canada*, 1986.

Families and Unattached Individuals

The overall poverty ratios of 12.3 percent for families and 34.3 percent for unattached individuals gives a general indication of the relative standing of the two categories under all headings. Apart from the likelihood of having more wage earners, the family unit appears to have economic advantages over separate status.

Regional Poverty. As might have been expected, family poverty was highest in the Atlantic region and lowest in Ontario. A surprising statistic is the high level of poverty among unattached individuals in Quebec—44.6 percent.

Size of Area. Family poverty levels were about the same in metropolitan regions as they were in the rural, just over 12 percent. The rate for individuals was slightly higher in large centres.

Age. For those 70 and over families appear to be a strength. Only 9.9 percent of such family members were in poverty, compared with 44.9 percent of comparable unattached individuals. The "young" aspect of poverty shows in the relatively high ratios for ages 24 and under—30.2 percent in families and 47.7 percent for individuals. Nearly half the young Canadians living outside families are in poverty conditions, a fact that explains much about current youth behaviour.

Sex and Age. The striking contrast here was between males and females. Where families headed by males under 65 had among the lowest levels of poverty (under 9 percent) those headed by comparable females had among the highest, at 42.0 percent.

Marital Status. The low ratio of 9.1 percent of poverty in families with a married head (or heads) is further evidence of the economic strength of the traditional form of family, while the high ratio (39.0 percent) for families with a single parent is striking proof of the struggle now faced by many young mothers attempting to make it on their own.

Employment. The ratios here are indicative of the advantages of a family head holding a steady job. Among full-time workers who were heads of families, the poverty ratio was at its lowest point—4.7 percent. Among unattached individuals not in the labour force (for a great variety of reasons), the poverty ratio was 64.4 percent.

Much has been made of the fact that, despite the apparently comfortable position of some of the employed poor a very substantial proportion of the total—up to one-half—is employed at wages below the poverty line. As will be seen later, this aspect of poverty has received a great deal of attention, as it runs counter to the accepted dictum that the cause of poverty is unwillingness to work.

Education. Here the data is about what would be expected; the lowest ratios were for family members, and poverty was less likely as the degree of education rose. Nonetheless it is surprising that there was 4.2 percent of poverty among family members with a university degree. For unattached individuals over one-half those with up to eight years of education were below the poverty line; the ratio declined with more education, but it is still disconcerting that 15.8 percent of unattached individuals with a university degree was living in poverty.

Family Characteristics. Here again the data forcefully illustrates the uphill climb of the single female mother attempting to raise a family. Where less than 10 percent of married couples with or without children and 16.4 percent of lone male parents were below the poverty line, for lone female heads of families the ratio was 44.1 percent, approaching one-half.

Poor Families and Others

Where the previous data has illustrated the relationship of families and individuals below the poverty line some comparisons can also be made between those below the poverty line and families not in poverty. These are set forth in table 28.6. The non-poor families have characteristics which explain much of their status, all in striking contrast to the poverty families. Among heads of families 79 percent are males under 65 and only 6 percent are females of that age; 90 percent of heads of families are married; 80 percent are in the labour force; 69 percent work 49-52 weeks a year; 72 percent had had no unemployment (although 13 percent had); 15 percent were university educated and 76 percent were property owners. In one respect however there was little difference between the two groups, that is in size of family. Whereas it might be expected that poor families would be larger than non-poor, in fact it is not so. Families are almost identical in size.

Overview

There are other analyses that could be made, but sufficient has been said to illustrate that families tend to cope better in meeting their needs than individuals on their own; that females, either as heads of families or as unattached individuals, suffer particular disadvantages; that age is a difficult period, particularly for unattached women, although their position has improved markedly in recent years; that many of the employed are working for wages below the poverty level; that the position of the family heads aged 24 and younger deteriorated over the 1979-86 period; that education appears to have a relationship to poverty. This is quite apart from the obvious connections with the general state of the economy, with regional differences in employment and incomes, etc.

A personal aside from one who has experienced the events of the 1950-80 years and agonized through some of its parental problems (and how few parents escaped!). The income issues of this period seem to be to some unmeasurable but quite real extent the product of a social transition, the full extent of which even by the mid-1980s was not yet clear. I remember quite well as a child that when my mother's parents reached the age where they needed daily help they moved in with our family for some time and later went on to live out their days with another of their children. There was nothing exceptional about this. It was simply taken for granted that this was in the natural order. Similarly, although children took employment after completing their education, they normally continued to live with their family until they married and set up their own home. Usually they raised their own children as a married couple, (although there were exceptions) and as advancing age required, the cycle was repeated.

Table 28.6   Some Features Distinguishing Poor Families from Others, 1986

	Low income families	Other families
	percent	
Sex and age of head		
Males under 65.............................	58	79
Males 65 and over	9	13
Females under 65............................	34	6
Females 65 and over	32	1
Marital status of head		
Single	10	2
Married....................................	64	90
Other......................................	27	8
Size of family		
Two persons................................	40	39
Three persons..............................	25	22
Four persons	20	25
Five or more persons.........................	15	14
Employment status of head		
In labour force.............................	58	80
Employees.................................	45	71
Not in labour force	42	20
Time worked		
None......................................	45	17
49-52 weeks	27	69
Full-time worker	24	67
Did not work	45	17
Unemployment		
no one unemployed........................	60	72
some unemployment.......................	31	13
Education		
Post-secondary	7	12
University certificate or diploma................	5	15
Ownership of property	40	76

Source: Statistics Canada, *Income Distribution by Size in Canada*, 1986.

While this traditional system no doubt survives in some areas it is no longer the accepted order. Elderly parents are now expected to survive on their own resources, and are seldom welcome as permanent residents in a child's home, where they would interfere financially and functionally with the daily ministration of a standard of living that requires the joint earning efforts of husband and wife (or friend and partner) to sustain. By the same token children escape this home as early as possible for the freedom of a "pad" of their own, frequently even before they have completed their education. Marriage is less frequently the normal goal of a relationship, and living together arrangements are easily ended. As a result it is no longer a dire social error for a young female to bear and raise a child out of wedlock; this occurs with great frequency, unfortunately, with the mother a teen-ager. The scene therefore is completely changed; the fragmentation of the family, which once held its members together and supported them through their trials, has meant that individuals are now either required or choose voluntarily to find their own succor. The result is that elderly persons, particularly women, now need not only income but housing; teen'age children require ample assistance with education costs, and young females have become single heads of families, which they are attempting to raise on inadequate incomes.

The conclusion from this observation is that some part of the present need for large-scale social programs is the result not of income distribution but of choices voluntarily taken by the families and individuals involved. There are, of course some pluses in the greater social freedom and breaking of past shackles that have resulted. But as a society we are suffering the fairly massive diseconomies of living in small independent households, many of them headed by females with insecure and frequently inadequate income, and with growing dependency on the state.

Anti-Poverty Programs

Interest in the development of a comprehensive measure to overcome poverty as a social problem in one stroke has been a phenomenon of the postwar period. The various schemes advanced fall into two main groupings: (1) guaranteed annual income programs, such as the negative income tax and (2) extension of existing programs to cover more of the poverty gap, demogrants (grants paid universally without eligibility tests) being the favoured device. As much of Canada's anti-poverty program has taken the latter form, and has already been described, the following is devoted mainly to the first type.

Guaranteed Annual Income Plans

Plans that would finally and effectively cope with poverty grew out of disillusionment in the sixties with the programs that had been put in place. It had been confidently expected that these measures, bolstered by the buoyant economy of the period, would effectively reduce the ranks of the poor. But this did not happen or at least not to the extent expected. Income distribution had remained almost unchanged, and poverty measures still showed substantial numbers falling below poverty lines. There was a growing conviction that, while it had been of benefit to many, the welfare state had missed a major target—those most in need. This should not have been surprising, since under universality all were receiving the same treatment, and three-quarters of recipients were above poverty lines. In short, the universal measures had not been designed to give any greater aid to the poor than to any other category. More direct and positive steps were therefore needed to reach these people.

This new attitude was expressed in the words of an academic of the day, Robert Theobald, when participating in a panel of distinguished economists at the National Symposium on Guaranteed Income held in Washington in December 1966: "The first area of agreement is that the initial step on the way to eliminate poverty is to supply money rather than moral uplift, cultural refinements, extended education, retraining programs, or make-work jobs. In addition, it is agreed that the prime criterion for the distribution of funds should be the poverty of the individual rather than whether Congress is willing to pass legislation protecting the income rights of any special group the individual is presumed to be in . . . There is another area of agreement which is crucial; funds should be provided as an absolute right and the size of grants should be determined on the basis of objective criteria rather than on the whims and prejudices of the bureaucrat."[28.2] In the cynical and financially hard-pressed mood of the eighties these words echo with a somewhat hollow resonance, and would not pass entirely unchallenged. Nonetheless much of the intervening development has reflected this approach in some degree.

GAI—Not Simple

In practice the details of guaranteed income measures are quite complex; decisions must be made no matter which individual plan is chosen. Since the payment is intended to cover a shortage of income, what definition of income will be used? As it is intended to cover a poverty gap, how is the gap to be measured? Is it the intention to fill the gap fully or partly? Will the payment be in addition to existing programs, or will it replace some or all of them? If some are to be replaced, which ones? Is the receipt of earnings or other income to be taken into account as an offset against the payment? If so, to what extent? How is the payment to be treated under the regular income tax? What accompanying changes in features of the income tax would be desirable under the system? Many of these questions of course have already been encountered, and it will not be necessary to review them fully again.

Negative Income Tax

One of the most popular versions of the guaranteed income plan was the negative income tax, which had many supporters throughout the world. The proposals of a group of U.S. academics, its most enthusiastic proponents in the 1960s, will serve to give the essentials of its original form. There were various plans named after their authors—the Lampman Plan, the Swartz Plan, the Theobald Plan, the Tobin Plan, the Friedman Plan, and others. Many of these had little in common except that assistance by means of money payments would be given the poor with incomes below either the income tax exemption level or a selected poverty line, and these would be juxtaposed with other income when and if received. Whether or not these payments would replace or supplement existing measures seemed to vary with authors; also, the manner in which duplication of payments and other income would be removed varied considerably. Indeed, so vague were the details of the negative income tax that almost any scheme that had a rela-

---

[28.2] Robert Theobald, "The Guaranteed Income: What and Why," paper prepared for The National Symposium on Guaranteed Income, December 9, 1966 (Washington: U.S. Chamber of Commerce), 4.

tionship to the tax system and involved the making of a comprehensive payment was given that label.

Perhaps the most distinctive version of the NIT, and one that most clearly justifies the name, was that proposed by Professor Milton Friedman. Friedman espoused the NIT in his *Capitalism and Freedom*, published in 1962 and saw it as an inexpensive substitute for nearly all existing welfare programs. His plan simply turned the income tax upside down. In place of positive taxable income—income which exceeds the exemptions—there would be "negative taxable income," the amount by which income fell below the exemptions. To this amount there would be applied an appropriate tax rate (Friedman seemed to favour 50 percent) to establish an allowance that would be paid to the taxpayer by the government. In effect the government's payment under the Friedman plan would not exceed a fraction (say 50 percent) of the taxpayer's unused personal income tax exemptions. Since any other income would reduce the unused amount of the exemption, and therefore the amount of the payment from the government, Friedman felt that a 50 percent rate would serve without introducing a disincentive for efforts to escape from poverty by earning outside income. Since the Friedman calculation depended entirely on there being a shortfall of income below the exemption limits, payments automatically phased out at the exemption level.

This version of the NIT is somewhat more spartan than that proposed by Professor James Tobin in the seminar earlier mentioned. He described his plan as follows: "Under the proposal, the IRS would provide an extended schedule which would tell you, in case your income and family size do not qualify you to pay tax, how much the federal government owes you. . . For a family which had literally earned no income on its own, the schedule would specify a certain government payment. This can be regarded as the income guarantee—the amount a family would receive in the worst of circumstances. As family income increased, the government payment or income supplement would decline. But not—and this is the important point I wish to stress—dollar for dollar. Instead the supplement would decline by only a fraction of every dollar of additional family income. A fraction of ⅓, for example, would mean the same as a 33% marginal income tax bracket—you keep for yourself two-thirds of each extra dollar you earn. At some income level the government would cease to pay supplements altogether, and families with incomes above this breakeven point would pay taxes."[28.3] Professor Tobin was more mindful of practical realities than some of his colleagues, such as how the family would feed and clothe itself currently. "How would the system operate? By a simple declaration to the Internal Revenue Service a family could begin to receive payments monthly, or twice monthly, at the rate to which it expects to be entitled. Later in the year, the family's circumstances might change; for example, a man might obtain a job and begin paying withholding tax. The next April 15 would be

---

[28.3] James Tobin, "Income Guarantees and Incentives," paper prepared for The National Symposium on Guaranteed Income, ibid., at 13.

a day of general reckoning. The upshot might be that the government owes the "taxpayer" money, or the other way round."[28.4]

In Canada there was also an outpouring of academic proposals in the mid-sixties—the Smith Formula, the Cutt Formula, the Crowley-Dodge Formula, the Deutsch-Green Formula, and others—each with some variation of the basic theme. One of the more detailed examinations of various types of plan was that made by the authors of "A Comparative Analysis of Alternative Income Support Programs in Canada." Their definition of a Negative Income Tax was reasonably clear:

> A NIT program design has three basic variables: a guaranteed minimum level of income paid in the event of zero income from other sources; a "tax" rate or allowance—reduction rate, at which government payments or allowances are reduced for each one-dollar increment in before-allowance income; and a break-even level of earned income at which the allowance payment from the government is reduced to zero . . . In effect, there is a *basic allowance* or income guarantee which the eligible individual or family unit may claim from the government *if there is zero income from other sources*. There is also an *offsetting tax* which every recipient of the allowance must pay on his other income. The *net benefit* to the recipient is the basic allowance less the offsetting tax. While the regular or positive income tax allows the government to share in a family's earnings when those earnings exceed a minimum that depends on the number and magnitude of allowable deductions, the negative income tax obliges the government to provide benefits and thus to share in any *shortfalls of family income* similarly, if not necessarily identically, calculated . . . All NIT schemes are income-tested, and are thus defined as *selective* as distinct from *universal* schemes, which are not income-tested.[28.5]

While "unfelicitously" named (Professor Tobin's description) the negative income tax was said to have several advantages. For the recipient it avoided the embarrassment of applying to a public office and suffering the humiliation of the means test process; it simply required filing an income tax return. Thus it also employed an administrative system already in place, the income tax machinery. The ideological break with the current practice of reducing social assistance by one dollar for each one dollar of other earnings was profoundly significant. Also, as the reduction for other income could be allowed for in advance it avoided the problem of collecting overpayments later. Finally, as its U.S. supporters were fully aware, as part of the income tax system its policies and procedures would be in federal rather than state hands, a distinct advantage for universal adoption.

[28.4] Ibid.

[28.5] James Cutt, John Tysall, and Leigh Bailey, "A Comparative Analysis of Alternative Income Support Programs in Canada," Tax Essay (January-February 1972) 20 *Canadian Tax Journal*, 74-106.

The Canadian Interest

Canadian interest in social programs accelerated in the sixties with growing attention to poverty. Credit is given to Tom Kent, then a Liberal party "brain truster" for urging a switch from the then favoured universal grant approach to "more precisely effective measures," in a paper presented to the Study Conference on National Programs in Kingston in 1960. The influence of this policy conference was evident throughout the next decade in many ways. In the income security area, for example, it no doubt motivated the income-tested Guaranteed Income Supplement introduced in 1967. The subject of poverty was receiving much direct attention. In its Annual Review of 1968 the Economic Council of Canada dealt with the issue at some length, and returned to it again periodically. Statistics Canada estimates of poverty lines and shortfalls from them were appearing regularly, a new element in the scene. The subject was discussed at a Federal-Provincial Conference on Poverty and Opportunity held in Ottawa in December, 1965. At this conference support for guaranteed income plans was given by several provinces, and the federal government was left to bring forward ideas for further study. In 1968 the Senate appointed a Special Committee to investigate poverty, which after extensive hearings issued a report in 1971 urging adoption of a guaranteed annual income. Several Canadian political leaders, among them Conservative leader Robert Stanfield, Ontario Premier John Robarts, and British Columbia Premier W.A.C. Bennett were espousing the general proposition. Newspapers were finding the subject good but sometimes confusing copy. Headlines were a medley of "Support Grows for Plan to Fight Poverty"; "A Guaranteed Income May Be the 'Only Solution' to the Welfare Jungle"; "Guaranteed Income Project May Be Accepted—But Will it Solve the Welfare Problem?"; "Canada Gains in the War on Poverty" and, for contrast, "20 Years of 'Progress' Leave Canada's Poor Just As Far Behind."

In 1970 The Federal Minister of National Health and Welfare issued a White Paper, "Income Security for Canadians," which virtually rejected universality, including general guaranteed income plans, in favour of an "income security policy which will have the effect of assisting the people in greatest need . . . Selective payments based on income should be made, where possible, in place of universal payments which disregard the actual income of the recipient. . . . The best approach . . . does not lie in the direction of dismantling the system in favour of one, overall guaranteed income program."[28.6] It forecasts that in the future the guaranteed income technique would be used mainly for people not in the labour force, such as the old and the disabled, and would also be used to convert the family allowance to a selective program.

Efforts to apply this principle quickly ran aground, however. A bill introduced in 1971 to gradually phase out family allowances at incomes above $10,000 was held over, and re-introduced later in the year as the

---

[28.6] Canada, Department of National Health and Welfare, *Income Security for Canadians* (Ottawa: the department, 1970), 1-2.

Family Income Security Plan, again with allowances that were reduced by a percentage as family income rose, ultimately ceasing. This proposal was greeted with a storm of protest from parents of children whose allowances were being dropped, and the measure was not adopted.

A landmark at the provincial level was the publication in 1971 of the Report of the Quebec Commission of Inquiry on Health and Social Welfare, the Castonguay-Nepveu Report. It proposed a guaranteed annual income plan, to be called the General Social Allowance Plan. It had the unique feature of two sets of payment systems, to be chosen at the option of the recipient. Payments were to be made to raise income to the level of current poverty lines (as adjusted). Stage I payments up to $2,000 would be subject to reduction for one-third of outside income and above $2,000 the reduction would be 55 percent. Stage II payments, which would be considerably higher than the Stage I level, would be subject to full offset or outside income. The assumption was that Stage I would apply to those in employment but having inadequate incomes, while Stage II would best suit those without other income. The Commission also proposed payment of a family allowance for children in addition to the child part of the social allowance and retention of the social insurance programs, but restricted to protection against emergency or unexpected reductions of income. The integrated approach was lauded by several experts, and contrasted favourably with the piecemeal approach of the federal government. In 1973 the Quebec government introduced substantial increases in family allowances as a step toward a guaranteed income plan for that province.

A Nuffield Conference sponsored by the Canadian Council on Social Development and attended by some forty experts from all over the world was held in 1972. The conclusion regarding an overall comprehensive annual income payment that would replace all other social income was much the same as that of the federal White Paper on Income Security. As the Executive Director of CCSD recorded in his summary, "The major lesson of the seminar was, in my view, that we cannot achieve the goal of an adequate guaranteed income at one fell swoop or through one measure alone."[28.7] There could be better integration of programs, but it would require the continuation of several programs to meet the needs of the poor. The Council however continued to support the principle of the guaranteed annual income in the report of a task force in 1973, periodic policy statements, studies and conferences over the decade, the last major commitment being the Report of the Task Force of 1983 on *Definitions of Poverty*. The National Council on Welfare, an advisory body to the Minister of National Health and Welfare, has also strongly supported the concept in periodic statements.

[28.7] Reuben Baetz, "The Nuffield Canadian Seminar and After: A Personal View," in *Guaranteed Annual Income: An Integrated Approach*, proceedings of the Nuffield Canadian Seminar held at Ste-Adele, Quebec, April 12-14, 1972, organized by The Canadian Council on Social Development (Ottawa: The Council, 1973), 39.

The Federal Provincial Review

The Working Paper on Social Security in Canada, issued by a new Minister of National Health and Welfare in 1973, dealt in general terms with the main problems in employment and income maintenance. It was issued as the prelude to a joint federal-provincial review of the whole existing social security apparatus that was to take place over the following two or three years. Its specific proposals were limited; one of these was a plan for continuing family allowances at a higher level on a universal basis, but subject for the first time to income tax. It also invited public discussion and proposals for "income supplementation for the working poor," a challenge accepted by several organizations.

An interesting outcome of the attention to the latter subject was the launching of a joint federal-provincial experiment with the negative income tax in Dauphin, Manitoba commencing in 1975. There were several similar experiments underway in the United States, and one in New Jersey had been completed. There are several sources of information on the results of the Manitoba experiment, which was concluded in 1978.

Despite the commitment to a federal-provincial review program the provinces and federal government went ahead with their individual programs. Some of the provinces—notably Saskatchewan, Alberta, and British Columbia—launched measures in 1974 designed primarily to supplement the incomes of the working poor, Saskatchewan's being the most generous. Ontario also launched a program, although addressed to elderly, blind and disabled persons. The federal government ultimately assisted in these programs under the Canada Assistance Act. Meanwhile over the decade the federal government in 1971 made drastic changes in unemployment insurance, in 1974 substantially increased family allowances, in 1975 introduced the spouses' allowance as a part of old age security, and in 1979 instituted the child tax credit. The measures that aided families and the elderly were vaguely consistent with the 1973 working paper, but the closest approach to an income-tested program was the gradual encirclement of the insurance and social payments within the tax system, either through the income tax or special taxes or both. It began to appear in fact that this had become a fixed formula with the federal government. Universality would be maintained, but benefit for upper incomes would be curtailed through taxation. From the mid-seventies there was little indication that a negative income tax was on the federal agenda, despite arguments of Welfare Minister Marc Lalonde that the poor were suffering hardship from the levels of inflation then prevalent. The budget was beginning to sink farther into deficit with each year, and other programs were given greater priority. Most of the payments were indexed to compensate for inflation, however, which at least substantially maintained their value.

Macdonald Commission Proposal

With thoughts of guaranteed annual income having become almost dormant on the Canadian agenda of the mid-eighties, the recommendation of the Macdonald Royal Commission in 1985 for adoption of a radically revised system of social welfare in Canada to this end came as a surprise. The Commission's proposal was bold, forthright, and controversial. The report and related studies were full and detailed, and scant justice can be done to them here. The following is the barest outline.

The Commission criticized the present system as being ineffective (many Canadians live in poverty); complex (too many programs and too many people administering them); creates work disincentives (benefits paid too long, recovery rate of 100 percent too high); inequitable (more benefit goes to high income families than to low); the sustainability of the system is questionable. "In sum", it said, "these considerations suggest that our Canadian income-security system is badly flawed. This is hardly surprising. Its provisions were constructed piecemeal, in combination with sometimes uncoordinated adjustments to Canada's personal income tax. The amalgam may have been partially suitable for the Canadian society of 1950, but it is much less appropriate for that of the later 1980s. The issue is not whether reform is necessary, but rather, how deep and rapid that reform must be."[28.8] (Royal Commissions apparently feel compelled, in order that their recommendations will have some impact, to speak in this authoritarian language!)

What specifically did the Commission propose? "Commissioners believe that the provision of a Universal Income Security Program with a universally available income guarantee, subject to reduction at a relatively low 'tax-back' rate, constitutes the most appropriate foundation for Canada's income security programs. We therefore recommend that the USIP replace existing federal tax and transfer programs including:

—GIS
—Family Allowances
—Child Tax Credits
—Married Exemptions
—Child Exemptions
—The Federal Share of CAP Social Assistance Programs
—Federal Social Housing Programs."

The one substantial program not affected by these proposals was to be Old Age Security.

The Commission proposed two stages for implementing its program: "In the first stage, . . . the Family Allowance, Child Tax Credit, and Child Tax Exemption progams would be eliminated, to be replaced with a single, large, Family Allowance-type payment or a larger tax credit, payable monthly. For the year 1985, an amount of $1000 annually would likely be in the appropriate range . . . The tax-back structure on the enlarged child benefit would have to be somewhat different from the system used for the current child tax credit. . . The social assistance benefits covered by the

---

[28.8] Supra, footnote 19.1, at 783.

Canada Assistance Plan should also be changed in structure, to permit the application of a lower tax-back rate . . ."[28.9] The tax-back rate proposed for the new child benefit was 25 percent to apply where family income exceeded $26,000 to eliminate any benefit for families in the $35,000 range; a 50 percent tax-back rate was proposed for social assistance payments. Except for the elimination of the income tax exemption for children the first stage mainly involved substituting one demogrant for the family allowance and the child tax credit.

The second stage was more radical: "At the second stage of program reform, all relevant exemptions should be eliminated from the tax system; the federal government would discontinue payment of its portion of social assistance; and the GIS would be incorporated into the system. The federal government or the federal and provincial governments in co-operation would institute the Universal Income Security Program, and provincial governments would provide social assistance top-ups, where necessary, for Canadians with little or no employment income."[28.10]

The Commission also proposed radical changes in Unemployment Insurance and the introduction of a Transitional Adjustment Assistance Program to ease temporary employment problems, which have been discussed earlier.

The new element in the income security package is the Universal Income Security Plan. The Commission opted for a relatively low guaranteed income and a much lower tax-back rate than normally contemplated—20 percent. It offered two options, with the suggestion that many others were available. "In Option A, the personal income-tax exemption would also be eliminated, and changes would be made to programs as listed above. Based on mid-1984 figures, a guaranteed income of $3825 per annum for each adult and for the first child in a single-parent family, and $765 for any other child can then be provided for all Canadians, without incurring extra costs. In Option B, the personal income-tax exemption is left in place, which means that the guaranteed income would drop to $2750 per adult (and for the first child in a single-parent family) and $750 per child."[28.11] The transfer between levels of income is substantial. Under option A two-earner/two children families with earned annual incomes below $30,000 would gain. Families earning over $40,000 annually would lose to a maximum of $3800. Under either option families in the working poor range would gain substantially—$5000 to $7000 under option A and $4000 to $5000 under Option B.

The Commission emphasized that one of its main concerns was that total spending in the social security area not be reduced as a result of its proposals; some of these would improve provincial finances, and it argued for close federal-provincial cooperation to ensure that some or all of this money

[28.9] Ibid., at 801-02.

[28.10] Ibid., at 802.

[28.11] Ibid., at 796.

be devoted to social welfare. It also gave a solemn warning of an "immutable fact: it is not possible to provide higher benefits at the bottom of the income scale without reducing net incomes at the middle and higher levels."

Renewal of Interest in General Programs

The Commission's proposals appear in retrospect to have coincided with a renewal of interest in general programs for income maintenance, as several studies have been issued and programs proposed in recent years. The Report of the federal Commission of Inquiry on Unemployment Insurance (1986) proposed an income maintenance program in lieu of some aspects of unemployment insurance. At the provincial levels relevant reports included the Quebec White Paper on *The Personal Income Tax and Transfer System*, (Quebec, Ministère des Finances, 1984), the Newfoundland Royal Commission on Employment and Unemployment, *Building on our Strengths* (St. John's, Queen's Printer, 1986); Ontario's *Transitions* (Report of the Social Assistance Review Committee, September 1988).

Non-governmental publications include *Social Policy in the 1990s*, Policy Study No. 3, C.D. Howe Institute, Thomas J. Courchene; *WIN: Work and Income in the Nineties*, Canadian Council on Social Development, 1986; *Social Security in Canada: An Economic Appraisal*, Canadian Tax Foundation, Canadian Tax Paper No. 79, John Burbidge; *Social Policy Reform and the National Agenda*, Business Council on National Issues, (Ottawa, 1986). It was even rumoured that the guaranteed annual income might raise its head as an issue in the 1988 federal election, but this did not transpire. At least there would now be greater comprehension of the issues at stake than in the beginnings of a quarter century ago.

A Final Word on Integrating Tax and Benefits Systems

Most proposals for reform of the income maintenance programs involve integrating them with the personal income tax. The apparent logic of making one system serve two purposes is appealing, but it is far more difficult than would be expected. Some of the problems have been touched on in earlier pages; they were convincingly summarized in an article in the *Canadian Tax Journal* by Derek P.J. Hum, based on his experience with the Canadian NIT experiment in Manitoba, Mincom.

INTEGRATION OF DESIGN
Because a negative income tax is actually a refundable income-tested tax credit, many observers conclude that a NIT system consists in nothing more than an extension of the tax rate schedule to the "negative income" zone. This infatuation with symmetry gives rise to two types of technical design problems. First, complications arise whenever the level of exemptions, E, granted under the PIT does not correspond to the breakeven level, B, of the NIT. Second, there are problems when the income tax rate, t, of the lowest income bracket under the PIT does not merge smoothly with the NIT offset rate, r. Thus the

design integration problem centres on the fact that breakeven levels and exemptions do not match ($E \neq B$) and that NIT and PIT tax rates are unequal ($t \neq r$) at the point where tax units switch from one tax regime to the other (the notch effect).

It is highly unlikely that there is any simple design solution to these difficulties. The fundamental aims of the NIT and PIT portions of an integrated system differ too widely. The PIT objective is to enhance tax revenues, and this will be accomplished by a design that has a low value for E and a high (average) value for t. The alleviation of income poverty, on the other hand, dictates a NIT design with high G levels. To minimize work disincentives, the marginal income tax rate r should be as low as possible, and certainly no greater than t. But a generous G and low r combination will result in a high value for B, the breakeven threshold. Given the existing patterns of income distribution in Canada, and given a value of G socially determined by reference to some reasonable notion of poverty-line income, it is unimaginable that taxes and transfers can be integrated with E equal to B and t equal to r at the notch.[28.12]

INTEGRATION OF THE TAX BASE

. . .

The conflict that will arise from any attempt to integrate the PIT and a NIT through a common tax base may now be stated simply. The objective of the PIT is to raise revenues. Given this objective, ability to pay is one appropriate principle for determining the tax base. Wealth might reasonably be excluded from the base on the grounds of economic efficiency (to avoid distorting saving decisions) and equity (to avoid double taxation of income, once when received and again when saved). Income alone, broadly defined, is an acceptable tax base for the purpose of raising revenue.

The objectives of a NIT are different. They involve the maintenance of a certain level of consumption for tax units, and hence degree of need is a more important consideration than ability to pay. Equity and political reasons dictate the inclusion of wealth in the tax base. Economic efficiency considerations usually focus on labour supply rather than on savings.[28.13]

INTEGRATION OF THE TAX UNIT

The individual has always been the tax unit for the personal income tax. On the other hand, the family is the customary unit for many transfer proposals . . .

[28.12] Derek P.J. Hum, "On Integrating Taxes and Transfers, (May-June 1988) 36 *Canadian Tax Journal* 671-90, at 671.

[28.13] Ibid., at 685.

Mincome affords a glimpse of the range and complexity of the administrative arrangements that arise when the family is the tax unit. These arrangements have been documented and discussed elsewhere. The problems faced by Mincome included income determination, the treatment of inkind benefits, the treatment of the changes in family status that arose when individuals left or joined family units on a permanent or a temporary basis, and the treatment of common-law relationships. Obviously, family arrangements can take many forms, as can understandings within a family about the sharing of income and expenses. Hence the essential question in the present context is this: Would the integration of transfers and taxes across family units reduce unintended transfers or revenue losses by enough to justify the increased administrative complexity that integration would require? Any amount of regulation is possible, but with what violence to the goal of simplicity?[28.14]

SUMMING UP

Society's view of government's appropriate treatment of its citizens, or of citizens' reciprocal obligation to the state, is one thing when the state is "taking," quite a different thing when the state is "giving." Because of this profound and fundamental ambivalence, there can never be complete integration of social transfers with the personal income tax.

The current re-examination of the Carter report in the context of the debate on tax reform is appropriate, since the report represents an earlier systematic view of Canada's tax system. Equally well-timed is the resurgence of attention to social security reform occasioned by such inquiries as the Forget commission and by the Macdonald commission's forthright plea for a guaranteed income system. The mere contemplation of an integrated PIT/NIT system serves as a salutary reminder that taxes and transfers cannot be viewed as conceptually distinct elements of public policy.[28.15]

[28.14] Ibid., at 687-88.

[28.15] Ibid., at 690.

Bibliography, chapter 28

Adams, I. Cameron, W., Hill, B., and Penz, P. *The Real Poverty Report*. Edmonton: M.G. Hurtig, 1971.

Canada, Department of Finance, *Analysis of Federal Tax Expenditures for Individuals*. Ottawa: 1981.

_____. *Integration of Social Program Payments into the Income Tax System*. A discussion paper on the feasibility of integration. Ottawa: 1978.

_____. Department of National Health and Welfare. *The Measurement of Poverty*. Ottawa: 1969.

_____. *Income Security for Canadians*. Ottawa: 1970.

_____. *Characteristics of the Working Poor in Canada*. Ottawa: 1976.

_____. *The Distribution of Income in Canada: Concepts, Measures and Issues*. Ottawa: 1977.

_____. *Proceedings of War on Poverty Conference*. Ottawa: 1965.

_____. Minister of National Health and Welfare. Working Paper on Social Security in Canada. Ottawa: 1973.

_____. Senate. Report of the Special Committee on Poverty. *Poverty in Canada*. Ottawa: 1971.

_____. Statistics Canada. *Income Distribution by Size in Canada (including Statistics on Low Income)*. Ottawa: annual.

Canadian Chamber of Commerce. *Submission* on the Working Paper on Social Security in Canada. Montreal: the Association, 1974.

Canadian Council on Social Development. Nuffield Canadian Seminar. *Guaranteed Annual Income: An Integrated Approach*. Ottawa: the Council, 1973.

_____. *Income Supplementation for the Working Poor*. Ottawa: the Council, 1974.

_____. *Not Enough: the Meaning of Poverty in Canada*. Report of the CCSD National Task Force on the Definition and Measurement of Poverty in Canada. Ottawa: the Council, 1984.

_____. *Women in Need; a Source Book*. Ottawa: the Council, 1976.

_____. "Toward Social Reform. WIN: Work and Income in the Nineties." (Fall 1986) *Overview*. 1-4.

Canadian Federation of Independent Business. "3 options Open on Negative Income Tax." (April 1974) 23 *Mandate*.

Caskie, Donald M. *Canadian Fact Book on Poverty, 1979*. Ottawa: Canadian Council on Social Development, 1979.

Courchene, Thomas J. "How Canada Practises Economic Discrimination Against the Poor." (November-December 1971) XLVII *Social Service Review (Canada)*, 216-31.

Crowley, R.W. and Dodge, D.A. "Cost of the Guaranteed Annual Income." (November-December 1969) 17 *Canadian Tax Journal*, 395-408.

Cutt, J. "A Guaranteed Income—Next Step in the Evolution of Welfare Policy?" (June 1966) XLII *Social Service Review (Canada)*, 216-31.

Cutt, J., Tysall, J., Bailey, L. "A Comparative Analysis of Alternative Income Support Programs in Canada." (January-February 1972) 20:1 *Canadian Tax Journal*, 74-100.

Deutsch, A., and Green, C. "Income Security for Canadians: A Review Article." (January-February 1971) 19 *Canadian Tax Journal*, 8-18.

Economic Council of Canada. *Fifth Annual Review*. Ottawa: 1968.

———. *Sixth Annual Review*. Ottawa: 1969.

———. *In Short Supply: Jobs and Skills in the 1980s*. Ottawa: 1982.

Gillespie, W. Irwin. *In Search of Robin Hood*. The Effect of Federal Budgetary Policies During the 1970s on the Distribution of Income in Canada. Montreal: C.D. Howe Institute, 1978.

Green, C. *Negative Taxes and the Poverty Problem*. Washington, D.C.: The Brookings Institution, 1967.

Gunderson, M. *Economics of Poverty and Income Distribution*. Toronto: Butterworths, 1983.

Harp, J., and Hofley, J.R. eds. *Poverty in Canada*. Scarborough, Ont.: Prentice Hall, 1971.

Henderson, D.W., and Rowley, J.C.R. *The Distribution and Evolution of Family Incomes, 1965-1973*. Discussion Paper no. 91. Economic Council of Canada. Ottawa: 1977.

Hill, Karen. "A core income program for Canada." (September-October 1986) 10 *Perception*. 12-13.

Hindle, C. "Negative Income Tax and the Poverty Problem in Ontario." (March-April 1971) 19 *Canadian Tax Journal*, 116-23.

Hum, D.P. *Federalism and the Poor*. A Review of the Canada Assistance Plan. Toronto: Ontario Economic Council, 1983.

———. Canada's Admistrative Experience with Negative Income Taxatation." (Spring 1981) 3 *Canadian Taxation*, 2-16.

———. "Negative Income Tax Experiments: A Descriptive Survey with Special Reference to Work Incentives." In *Reflections on Canadian Incomes*. Ottawa: Economic Council of Canada, 1980.

———. "Macdonald's Guaranteed Annual Income: There has to be a Broader Focus." *The Financial Post*, September 28, 1985.

Hum, D., Laub M., and Powell, B. *The Objectives and Design of the Manitoba Basic Annual Income Experiment*. Technical Report no. 1. Winnipeg: Mincome Manitoba, 1979.

Kakwani, N. *Issues in the Measurement of Poverty*. Kingston: Institute for Economic Research, Queen's University, 1979.

Kesselman, Jonathon, R. "Pitfalls of Selectivity in Income Security Programs." (Fall 1980) 2 *Canadian Taxation*, 154-63.

Lithwick, N.H. *Urban Poverty*. Research monograph no. 1. Ottawa: Central Mortgage and Housing. Ottawa: 1971.

Marsh, Leonard. "GAI: A New Look at Welfare Policy?" (November-December 1973) 49 *Canadian Welfare*, 4-6.

Manitoba Pool Elevators. *Poverty in Canada*. Winnipeg: 1965.

National Council of Welfare. *Jobs and Poverty*: A Report on Canada's Working Poor. Ottawa: 1977.

———. Guide to the Guaranteed Income. Ottawa: 1976.

_____. *Poverty Lines*: Estimates by the National Council of Welfare. Ottawa: annual.

_____. *Statement on Social Security*. Ottawa: 1971.

_____. *The Working Poor; People and Programs*: A Statistical Profile. Ottawa: 1981.

_____. *Giving and Taking: The May 1985 Budget and the Poor*. Ottawa: 1985.

Okner, Benjamin A. *Transfer Payments: Their Distribution and Role in Reducing Poverty*; and *Alternatives for Transferring Income to the Poor: The Family Assistance Plan and Universal Income Supplements*. Reprint 254. Washington: D.C. The Brookings Institution, 1973.

Pechman, Joseph A., and Timpane, Michael, eds. *Work Incentives and Income Guarantees: The New Jersey Negative Income Tax Experiment*. Washington: Brookings Institution, 1975.

Podoluk, J.R. *Income of Canadians, 1961*. Census Monogram. Ottawa: Queen's Printer, 1968.

Prager, C.A.L. "Poverty in North America: Losing Ground." (March 1988) 14 *Canadian Public Policy*, 52-65.

Province of Ontario. The Social Assistance Review Committee. *Report*. Toronto: 1988.

Provine of Quebec. Commission of Enquiry on Health and Social Welfare, Income Security. Quebec: 1971.

Reuber, Grant L. "The Impact of Government Policies on the Distribution of Income in Canada; A Review." (Spring 1979) 4 *Canadian Public Policy*, 505-529.

Ross, D. *Canadian Fact Book on Poverty*. Ottawa: Canadian Council on Social Development. Ottawa: 1975 and 1983.

_____. "Core income would encourage socially profitable activities." (May-August 1987) *Perception*, 46-50.

Royal Commission on the Economic Union and Development Prospects for Canada, vol. 2. Toronto: The University of Toronto Press. Chaps. 19, 20; and Conclusions and Recommendations, 769-827.

Rolph, E.R. "The Case for a Negative Income Tax Device." VI (February 1967) *Industrial Relations*, 121-65.

Rhys-Williams, Lady Juliet. *Something to Look Forward to: a Suggestion for a New Social Contract*. London: Macdonald and Co., 1943.

Smith, D.B. "A Simplified Approach to Social Welfare." (May-June 1965) 13 *Canadian Tax Journal*, 260-65.

United States. Congress. *Guaranteed Minimum Income Programs Used by Governments of Selected Countries*. Material Prepared For the Joint Economic Committee. Washington, D.C.: 1968.

"What are we waiting for?" *The Economist*, October 14, 1972, 81-83.

29
Education: The Troubled Agenda

We have encountered education in various contexts without yet having a comprehensive picture of the total phenomenon. That it merits further attention is unquestioned. In the twentieth century the world has placed its hopes in education as the road to a better life. But the pursuit of this unanimously supported goal has been the universal source of controversy over goals and methods. As these words are being written its future role has emerged as a leading issue in the 1988 U.S. elections, and in Canada the subject is always high on the public agenda, if for no other reason than that of the language to be used. The subject is therefore vital—and inexhaustible.

The Canadian Postwar Challenge

Two issues dominated Canada's postwar educational experience. First, the unprecedented flood of children to be educated—the postwar baby boom. This bulge not only created immediate problems but affected programs over the whole period as it moved forward through education channels. The second and equally influential issue was the goal of achieving a higher standard of education at all levels. This goal reflected both a change in attitudes towards education as an element in the social structure and an urgent need to cope with a knowledge and technological explosion that was rapidly outdating the existing information base as well the people employed in using it.

Some random data will illustrate the scale of the response to this double challenge. The share of GNP devoted to education climbed from a nominal 2.5 percent in 1950 to a record level of 9 percent in 1970, with a subsequent decline to the current 7 percent. As a proportion of government expenditure education costs more than doubled between 1950 and 1970, rising from 10 percent to 20-22 percent, with a subsequent decline to around 12 percent. The teacher population rose from 89,000 in 1950 to 334,000 in 1987, an increase of 270 percent compared to a rise of only 83 percent in the total population. The proportion of students in the 5-17 age group attending elementary and secondary schools rose from 81 percent in 1951 to 98 percent in recent years, and for students in the 18-24 age group the proportion in post-secondary education rose from 6 percent in 1951 to over 25 percent in 1987. See also table 29.1, in which education expenditures are related to various socio-economic indicators. A later section also gives further quantitative evidence of this upheaval.

Educational Philosophy; Changing Concepts

As for the philosophical aspects of the phenomenon, a daunting mass of material has been produced over the four decades; educationists are inevi-

Table 29.1   Education Expenditures[a]: Relation to Various Socio-Economic
Indicators, Selected Years, 1950-86

Year	Personal income	Gross national product	Total population	Labour force	Full-time students
	percent			*dollars per capita*	
1950	3.1	2.4	32	—	166
1955	3.9	2.9	53	148	244
1959	5.2	4.0	84	236	355
1960	5.8	4.4	95	266	389
1961	6.4	4.9	106	296	419
1962	7.3	5.5	128	359	492
1963	7.3	5.5	134	377	503
1964	7.8	5.7	150	417	548
1965	8.3	6.1	173	476	622
1966	9.0	6.7	208	560	734
1967	9.9	7.6	247	653	857
1968	10.4	8.0	279	730	948
1969	10.6	8.2	312	803	1,060
1970	11.5	9.0	360	914	1,207
1971	11.3	8.9	388	968	1,312
1972	10.4	8.2	398	975	1,371
1973	9.8	7.8	434	1,032	1,542
1974	9.5	7.5	495	1,148	1,773
1975	9.5	7.8	570	1,298	2,093
1976	9.7	7.9	657	1,479	2,468
1977	10.0	8.2	740	1,639	2,856
1978	9.5	7.8	773	1,668	3,073
1979	9.3	7.6	841	1,779	3,439
1980	9.1	7.5	923	1,917	3,859
1981	8.8	7.5	1,042	2,130	4,445
1982	8.9	7.9	1,148	2,362	4,949
1983	9.1	7.8	1,227	2,508	5,318
1984	8.8	7.6	1,270	2,574	5,570
1985	8.4	7.3	1,337	2,682	5,920
1986	8.4	7.4	1,418	2,819	6,362

[a] For all governments in Canada. As calculated by the Education, Culture and Tourism Division of Statistics Canada.

Sources: *Historical Statistics of Canada*; Statistics Canada, *Educational Statistics*; *Education in Canada*, 1986; and *Advance Statistics of Education*.

tably fairly literate, and tend to take their role quite seriously. Governments have also contributed to the accumulation through a constant stream of reports and studies. It will only be possible here to give the most superficial view of some of the main lines of thought. Everyone at all involved in education would agree that its main goal is the betterment of the human condition, a goal as old as the Greek philosophers. But the Greek philosophers had strong differences of view on how this goal was to be reached, and in this respect little has changed.

In the older conservative view education was a process of giving the individual enough basic training to operate in society—the three Rs. This could be done at lowest cost through a relatively simple basic curriculum with success determined by periodic examinations. In Canada this approach fitted the needs not only of a frontier economy, with its one-room one-teacher arrangement, but was the general pattern before World War II for most schools, even in large cities. (It was the curriculum under which the author attended high school in Toronto, for example). The vigorous post-war move toward consolidation of isolated small rural schools into larger centralized units to which children are bused substantially removed the last physical vestiges of this system; it still has recurrent support, however, particularly among parents and employers who believe that as a minimum all high school graduates should be able to read and write, by no means the general case now.

One school of educationists had been advocating the new approach before World War II and support was revived on return of peace. The basis of this approach was that education should be freed from its existing rigid confines and become a more liberating process for the students, one designed to stimulate interest and adapt to individual capacities and personalities. This would best serve society by producing more imaginative and flexible citizens better adapted to coping with the changes then foreseen. Although in their millions each student could not be given individual attention, at least broad groupings could be established with appropriate courses for each category. This became a strong influence on education methods and curriculum during the fifties and sixties, and probably reached its zenith in the in the Hall-Dennis report in Ontario.

It turned out that there were serious flaws in the over-enthusiastic adoption of this approach, however. The conduct of the daily life of the country required the services of a considerable number of skilled workers, and the new education methods were not producing them. A reaction among employers developed when this shortage became so pronounced that it was necessary to bring in skilled workers from other countries at a time when there was unemployment in Canada. Employers argued that the young were not being prepared to make a useful contribution to the life of the country, and that the education system was at fault.

To remedy this defect increasing attention began to be paid to technical and practical instruction at the high school level, the place where at least there were already so-called manual training courses. In some provinces high school students, after a preliminary year or two of general study, were streamed into different courses, one directed to preparation for university and others to training for the workforce. While this system had advantages it was only a partial step and was succeeded by the establishment of separate vocational schools, a move given strong impetus after 1960 by federal support for training facilities. The launching of the community colleges in Ontario and the CEGEPs in Quebec in the late sixties was the final and conclusive evidence of the strength of this innovation, which has remained strong ever since. Part of the appeal of the community colleges was that they opened a path to higher levels of education for non-academic students, a path that previously had been available only to students headed for university. An incidental benefit therefore was a marked reduction in the drop-out rate at the end of high school.

A different shock was given education by the unexpected Soviet launching of the Sputnik space rocket in 1957. Coming at the height of the cold war this event aroused the western world to sudden concern over the state of its research and the supply of scientists being produced by the universities. President Kennedy's appeal to the U.S. Congress for massive support for education was symbolic of the reaction in that country. In Canada to meet the crisis, as it was then regarded, in 1960 for the first time the federal government offered support to the provinces for university education, and from this beginning there has been some form of federal support for the university level ever since. The knowledge and technological revolution has reinforced the need for highly trained personnel in many categories, and support for post-secondary education has been a prime cause of government over the last two decades, although stringent budgets and the pressure of other demands has forced a lessening of financial support.

There were other strong and sometimes conflicting trends in education. For one, there was a growing view that the education system had a role to play in the use of leisure time, which had been markedly increased by the arrival of labour-saving devices unheard of a decade before, both in the home and the factory. Educationists saw this as an opportunity to advance the role of the schools in providing both cultural and recreational activities, and as a result a good deal more art and music appreciation came into the curriculum. School sports facilities also became more open and accessible for after-hours use or else special facilities were provided.

Another powerful influence came from the generation now looked on as the "flower children," the teen-agers of the sixties, who saw the education system as a powerful instrument for levelling class distinctions. They vigorously argued that a freer and more open system would reduce class barriers by allowing those at the bottom of the economic scale to move upward. This in turn would break what appeared to be the monopoly of the upper classes in gaining admission to the professions and corporate executive ranks. Concrete expression of these views usually took the form of demonstrations in universities and elsewhere for a stronger student role in policy-making and administration. Parades or sit-ins became common, but the most drastic step in Canada was the destruction of student computer records at Sir George Williams University in Montreal. This was all very low-key compared to the widespread violent opposition to the Vietnam war in the United States, and in most universities had the result of gaining recognition for student membership on most governing bodies and a good deal more democracy in the conduct of university affairs, on the whole a beneficial result. Quite obviously the grand goal of eliminating class distinctions has not been achieved, but the society of the eighties is certainly drastically changed from that of the immediate postwar years.

The Bloom Fades

Much of the almost constant ferment of the fifties and sixties had been aided—or tolerated—by governments enjoying relative affluence under conditions of economic well-being. Even in troubled periods governments were willing to give education priority; for example, the federal government programs for university and vocational grants were introduced in the not very buoyant conditions of 1960. But by the seventies this receptive atmosphere had ended and education entered a period of slump, the result of several factors. The most telling was the end of the pressure from the baby-boomers; in 1970 elementary-secondary enrolment reached a peak of 5.9 million, and began to decline immediately, dropping by over 700,000 during the seventies. This decline left many schools and teachers redundant and, incidentally, produced a strong new union movement to save as many teachers' jobs as possible.

In post-secondary education enrolment continued to increase but at a rate far below the level of the boom years of the sixties. Between 1960 and 1969 the average annual growth had been about 17 percent; in the seventies it was 3 percent. The slow-up in the seventies was a result of a reduction in the university age population and, as well, of a certain disillusionment with the value of more education when holders of Ph.D. degrees, for no cause of their own, were either unemployed or working at mediocre jobs. This skepticism was apparently also shared by corporations and governments and contributed to a weakening of support. In the case of governments the removal of any conditions for counterpart expenditure for grants received after 1976 under the EPF system was no doubt also a contributing factor. However it was mainly the unhappy combination of inflation, unemployment, and lagging economic growth that left governments little alternative but to move education to a lower priority. Education expenditure continued to rise but other expenditures more closely related to the problems of the times rose faster. As a result education fell from 20-22 percent of budgets to 12 percent, where it remained in 1987. Interest in post-secondary education has revived in the mid-eighties with economic recovery; over 25 percent of the 18-24 age group was attending either college or university in 1987, a new high. With this revival, these institutions are pressing increasingly for relief from financial stringency.

Despite the slowing up, the total annual bill for education was estimated at nearly $38 billion for 1987. Of this the government share was to be about $34.8 billion, a not inconsiderable sum and still the third largest in the trio of social services, health and education. And there seems to be a renewed support for education as an essential element in a well-rounded and satisfying life, and one which calls for constant renewal and enrichment over a lifetime. Its scope now extends from pre-school classes for 3-5 year-olds through the normal educational ages of 5-24 to part-time courses for the elderly retired. In all, with their teachers, these "students" account for over a third of the population. No phenomenon engaging such widespread attention will be long off the public agenda.

Questions and controversies will remain, as in the past. Is it true that many high school graduates are unable to read, much less to write? If so, in this audio-visual dominated age does it really matter? What is the effect of family break-up on child education? How far can the schools fill the gap left by the lack of a full and satisfying family life? What skills are needed in an increasingly robotized industry? Can our universities compete with foreign institutions in producing graduates capable of coping with the flood of new knowledge in every realm of thought? What will be the effect of new methods of communication on the school as an institution if Toffler's *Third Wave* projections arrive? Will it be possible to overcome resistance to radical change in the future in time to maintain standing? How will education be paid for in the future, particularly at the university level, where it is now exhorbitant? Will current financial stringency result in permanent loss to our institutions of higher learning? And of course in Canada there is the eternal and apparently insoluble controversy over the language of education in our multi-racial society. These and many more questions will face education in Canada in the future—to some degree are being faced today.

A Statistical Retrospective

Battles of the Bulge

The first of the postwar challenges for the education system was the "veterans' bulge." Under the Veterans Rehabilitation Act the federal government had undertaken to provide vocational or university education for veterans of World War II. As a temporary but large scale task this was fulfilled through whatever facilities were available, sometimes using even the provisional barracks in which the veterans had received their military training or abandoned munitions plants (e.g. Ajax in Toronto). The result was to increase full-time university enrolment from 40,000 in 1944-45 to 64,000 in 1945-46 (an increase of more than 50 percent). There was a further rise to 80,000 in 1946-47 and to 83,000 in 1947-48. As veterans left the universities, enrolment declined to 63,000 in 1952-53, the low figure for the postwar period.

The Baby Boom

As mentioned, Canada's birthrate accelerated at a rate not only unprecedented for Canada but for industrialized countries. As a result in the early fifties there were twice as many school-age children to be crowded into elementary schools as there were in 1945. This growth continued apace during the sixties and peaked in the early seventies, by which time the baby boom had passed the high school level.

Table 29.2 gives the available data. It is interesting that the decline in the number of children aged 5-17 stabilized in the mid-eighties, as the children of the baby-boomers began to reach the education level. The post-secondary population was fairly stable for the decade of the seventies, but has been declining since 1981, according to available data.

Table 29.2   Canada, School-age Population, Selected Years, 1951-87

Year	Total population[a]	Population aged 5-17		Population aged 18-24		Population aged 5-24	
		Number[a]	Percent of total	Number[a]	Percent of total	Number[a]	Percent of total
			percent		percent		percent
1951	14.0	3.2	22.9	1.5	10.7	4.7	33.6
1955	15.7	3.8	24.2	1.6	10.2	6.7	34.4
1958	17.1	4.3	25.1	1.6	9.4	5.9	34.5
1960	17.9	4.7	26.2	1.7	9.5	6.3	35.2
1961	18.2	4.8	26.4	1.7	9.3	6.5	35.7
1962	18.6	5.0	26.9	1.8	9.6	6.8	36.6
1963	18.9	5.1	27.0	1.8	9.5	6.9	36.5
1964	19.3	5.3	27.5	1.9	9.8	7.2	37.3
1965	19.6	5.4	27.5	2.0	10.2	7.4	37.8
1966	20.0	5.5	27.5	2.2	11.0	7.7	38.5
1967	20.4	5.6	27.5	2.3	11.3	7.9	38.7
1968	20.7	5.7	27.5	2.4	11.6	8.1	39.1
1969	21.0	5.8	27.6	2.6	12.4	8.4	40.0
1970	21.3	5.8	27.2	2.6	12.2	8.5	40.0
1971	21.6	5.9	27.3	2.7	12.5	8.6	39.8
1972	21.8	5.8	26.6	2.7	12.4	8.5	39.0
1973	22.0	5.8	26.4	2.8	12.7	8.6	39.1
1974	22.4	5.7	25.4	2.9	13.0	8.6	38.4
1975	22.7	5.7	25.1	3.0	13.2	8.7	38.3
1976	23.0	5.6	25.6	3.1	13.5	8.6	37.4
1977	23.3	5.5	23.6	3.1	13.3	8.6	36.9
1978	23.5	5.4	23.0	3.2	13.6	8.6	36.6
1979	23.7	5.3	22.4	3.3	13.9	8.5	35.9
1980	24.0	5.2	21.7	3.3	13.8	8.5	35.4
1981	24.4	5.1	20.9	3.4	13.9	8.5	35.8
1982	24.6	5.0	20.3	3.4	13.8	8.4	34.1
1983	24.8	4.9	19.8	3.4	13.7	8.3	33.5
1984	25.0	4.9	19.6	3.3	13.2	8.2	32.8
1985	25.2	5.0	19.8	3.2	12.7	8.2	32.5
1986	25.4	5.0	19.7	3.2	12.6	8.2	32.3
1987	25.7	5.1	19.8	3.1	12.1	8.2	31.9

[a] Population figures in millions.

Source: Statistics Canada, *Population Projections for Canada and the Provinces*, 1976-2001.

School Enrolment

The dramatic increase in school-age population had startling effects on school enrolment. To illustrate: the evidence is that in 1947 elementary-secondary schools had 2.0 million students enrolled; just over a decade later in 1959 the schools were accommodating twice this number, 4.0 million; approximately another decade later in 1970 enrolment had reached 5.9 million. Educating nearly six million students in a two-million-student system was an enormous undertaking in terms of accommodation, teaching staff, and expenditures—which on the whole was successfully accomplished.

Table 29.3   Canada, Total Population and Total Full-Time School Enrolment, Selected Years, 1951-87

Year[a]	Population	School enrolment[b]	Percent of total population	Percent of population aged 5-24[c]
	million	*million*	*percent*	*percent*
1951.................	14.0	2.7	19.3	58.1
1955.................	15.7	3.4	21.6	63.4
1958.................	17.1	4.0	23.3	66.3
1959.................	17.5	4.2	24.0	67.5
1960.................	17.9	4.4	24.6	69.0
1961.................	18.2	4.6	25.3	70.1
1962.................	18.6	4.8	25.9	71.1
1963.................	18.6	5.0	26.9	72.0
1964.................	19.3	5.2	26.9	72.6
1965.................	19.6	5.5	28.1	73.5
1966.................	20.0	5.7	28.5	73.7
1967.................	20.4	5.9	28.9	74.0
1968.................	20.7	6.1	29.5	75.2
1969.................	21.0	6.3	30.0	74.6
1970.................	21.3	6.4	30.0	75.2
1971.................	21.6	6.4	29.6	74.3
1972.................	21.8	6.3	28.9	74.0
1973.................	22.0	6.3	28.6	72.9
1974.................	22.4	6.2	27.6	72.4
1975.................	22.7	6.2	27.3	71.6
1976.................	23.0	6.1	26.5	70.8
1977.................	23.3	6.0	25.8	69.8
1978.................	23.5	5.9	25.1	69.0
1979.................	23.7	5.8	24.5	67.9
1980.................	24.0	5.8	24.0	67.7
1981.................	24.4	5.7	23.3	67.7
1982.................	24.7	5.7	23.1	68.2
1983.................	24.8	5.7	23.0	68.9
1984.................	25.0	5.7	22.8	69.2
1985.................	25.2	5.7	22.6	69.6
1986.................	25.4	5.7	22.4	70.0
1987.................	25.7	5.7	22.2	69.7

[a]School year beginning in year shown for enrolment; mid-point of calendar year for population. [b]Excludes trade schools, private business colleges and apprenticeship programs. [c]Percent of population aged 5-24 in full-time school enrolment.

Sources: *Historical Statistics of Canada*; and Statistics Canada, *Advance Statistics of Education*; *Population Projections for Canada and the Provinces*, 1976-2001.

Tables 29.3 to 29.6 give a closer look at school enrolment. The percentage of the total population in full-time attendance at school rose from 19 percent in 1951 to a high of 30 percent by 1970. Including part-time school enrolment, at least one person in three in the Canadian population was attending school in 1970.

Table 29.4   Canada, Enrolment in Elementary-Secondary and Post-secondary Schools, in Total and as a Percent of Relevant Population, Selected Years, 1951-87

Year[a]	Enrolment Elementary-Secondary				Enrolment Post-secondary		
	Total enrolment	Total	Percent of total	Percent of population aged 5-17	Total	Percent of total	Percent of population aged 18-24
	thousands		*percent*		*thousand*	*percent*	
1951	2,716	2,625	96.7	82.9	91	3.3	6.0
1955	3,397	3,291	96.9	86.7	106	3.1	6.8
1958	3,964	3,827	96.5	88.4	137	3.5	8.3
1959	4,157	4,009	96.4	89.2	148	3.6	8.9
1960	4,368	4,204	96.3	86.5	163	3.7	9.8
1961	4,595	4,413	96.0	87.6	182	4.0	10.8
1962	4,809	4,613	95.9	89.3	197	4.1	11.2
1963	5,036	4,805	95.6	90.7	220	4.4	12.0
1964	5,241	4,997	95.3	91.7	244	4.7	12.6
1965	5,475	5,201	95.0	93.2	274	5.0	13.4
1966	5,667	5,356	94.5	94.3	311	5.5	14.2
1967	5,870	5,517	94.0	94.3	353	6.0	15.4
1968	6,093	5,698	93.5	95.9	395	6.5	16.8
1969	6,262	5,825	93.0	98.0	437	7.0	17.0
1970	6,364	5,886	92.5	99.1	476	7.5	20.1
1971	6,364	5,867	92.2	97.8	497	7.8	20.6
1972	6,330	5,817	91.9	97.8	513	8.1	20.8
1973	6,257	5,723	91.5	97.6	534	8.5	21.0
1974	6,232	5,674	91.1	97.7	558	8.9	21.3
1975	6,187	5,595	90.4	97.8	592	9.6	21.8
1976	6,116	5,514	90.1	97.4	603	9.9	21.8
1977	6,026	5,411	89.8	97.2	616	10.2	21.7
1978	5,912	5,294	89.5	97.4	618	10.5	21.2
1979	5,808	5,185	89.3	98.1	624	10.7	21.0
1980	5,750	5,106	88.8	98.7	643	11.2	19.4
1981	5,706	5,030	88.2	99.1	675	11.8	20.1
1982	5,716	4,994	87.2	99.8	722	12.6	21.3
1983	5,742	4,975	86.6	100.0	767	13.4	22.6
1984	5,729	4,946	86.3	100.0	783	13.7	23.2
1985	5,718	4,928	86.2	99.4	790	13.8	24.1
1986	5,733	4,941	86.2	98.3	792	13.8	25.0
1987	5,757	4,962	86.2	97.3	795	13.9	25.9

[a] Academic year beginning in year given.

Sources: *Historical Statistics of Canada*; Statistics Canada, *Decade of Educational Finance*, 1960-69 and 1970-71 to 1979-80; *Education in Canada*, 1986; *Advance Statistics of Education*; and *Population Projections for Canada and the Provinces*, 1976-2001.

The proportion of the population of school age (5-24) in full time attendance rose from 58 percent in 1951 to 75 percent in 1970, a remarkable record. Both ratios have since declined from their 1970 peaks.

Table 29.5   Education: Full-time Post-secondary Enrolment by University and Community College, Selected Years, 1945-87

| Year[a] | Enrolment | | University Enrolment | | | | Community College enrolment | |
	Total	Percent of pop-ulation	Under-graduate	Graduate	Total	Percent of total	Total	Percent of total
	thousand	*percent*		*thousand*		*percent*	*thousand*	*percent*
1945........	—	—	61.8	2.9	64.7	—	—	—
1950........	—	—	64.0	4.6	68.6	67.4	—	—
1955........	106.0	0.7	69.3	3.4	72.7	68.6	33.3	31.4
1958........	137.4	0.8	90.4	4.6	95.0	69.1	42.4	30.9
1959........	148.2	0.8	96.7	5.2	101.9	68.7	46.3	31.3
1960........	163.1	0.9	107.2	6.5	113.7	69.7	49.4	30.3
1961........	182.0	1.0	121.3	7.3	128.6	70.7	53.4	29.3
1962........	196.7	1.1	132.7	8.4	141.1	71.7	55.6	28.3
1963........	220.1	1.1	146.8	11.1	158.0	71.7	62.2	28.3
1964........	243.6	1.2	163.8	13.8	177.6	72.8	66.0	27.2
1965........	273.6	1.2	187.0	17.2	204.2	74.6	69.4	25.4
1966........	310.5	1.6	210.6	19.7	230.3	74.2	80.2	25.8
1967........	352.9	1.7	229.3	24.2	253.5	71.9	99.4	28.1
1968........	395.3	1.9	239.7	26.1	265.8	67.2	129.5	32.8
1969........	436.9	2.0	263.9	30.2	294.1	67.3	142.7	32.7
1970........	475.5	2.2	276.3	33.2	309.5	65.1	166.1	34.9
1971........	496.8	2.3	287.1	35.9	323.0	65.0	173.8	35.0
1972........	513.4	2.4	284.9	37.5	322.4	62.8	191.0	37.2
1973........	533.6	2.4	295.0	37.1	332.1	62.2	201.5	37.8
1974........	558.2	2.5	309.5	37.8	347.4	62.4	210.8	37.6
1975........	592.0	2.6	331.0	39.9	370.9	62.6	221.6	37.4
1976........	603.7	2.6	335.9	40.6	376.5	62.4	227.2	37.6
1977........	615.9	2.6	333.5	40.7	374.2	60.8	241.7	39.2
1978........	616.0	2.6	326.8	41.2	368.0	59.7	248.0	40.4
1979........	622.9	2.6	329.9	41.4	371.4	59.6	251.5	40.4
1980........	643.4	2.7	337.9	44.6	382.6	59.5	260.8	40.6
1981........	675.3	2.8	354.7	47.2	401.9	59.5	273.4	40.4
1982........	722.0	2.9	376.2	50.2	426.4	59.7	295.6	40.9
1983........	766.7	3.1	397.4	53.2	450.5	58.8	316.2	41.2
1984........	782.8	3.1	406.3	54.9	461.2	58.9	321.6	41.1
1985........	789.8	3.1	412.5	54.9	467.3	59.2	322.5	40.8
1986........	791.7	3.1	414.4	56.4	470.8	59.5	320.9	40.5
1987........	795.4	3.1	417.2	57.6	474.8	59.7	320.6	40.3

See table 29.4 for footnote and sources.

Table 29.4 gives an analysis of the distribution of enrolment between elementary-secondary and post-secondary categories. Obviously the elementary-secondary, normally ten times or more than the post-secondary, is the main influence on the total. However, a growing post-secondary enrolment has gradually reduced the elementary-secondary share from nearly 97 percent of the total to 86 percent. While the actual number of elementary-secondary enrolments has declined since 1970 by over 900,000

**Table 29.6   Education: Full-time University Enrolment, Percent of
Graduate and Undergraduate Students, Selected Years, 1945-87**

Year	Undergraduate	Graduate	Total
		percent	
1945	95.5	4.5	100.0
1950	93.3	6.7	100.0
1955	95.3	4.7	100.0
1958	95.2	4.8	100.0
1959	94.9	5.1	100.0
1960	94.3	5.7	100.0
1961	94.3	5.7	100.0
1962	94.0	6.0	100.0
1963	92.9	7.1	100.0
1964	92.2	7.8	100.0
1965	91.6	8.4	100.0
1966	91.4	8.6	100.0
1967	90.5	9.5	100.0
1968	90.1	9.9	100.0
1969	89.7	10.3	100.0
1970	89.3	10.7	100.0
1971	88.9	11.1	100.0
1972	88.4	11.6	100.0
1973	88.9	11.1	100.0
1974	89.1	10.9	100.0
1975	89.2	10.8	100.0
1976	89.2	10.8	100.0
1977	89.1	10.9	100.0
1978	88.8	11.2	100.0
1979	88.8	11.2	100.0
1980	88.3	11.7	100.0
1981	88.3	11.7	100.0
1982	88.2	11.8	100.0
1983	88.2	11.8	100.0
1984	88.1	11.9	100.0
1985	88.3	11.7	100.0
1986	88.0	12.0	100.0
1987	87.9	12.1	100.0

Sources: *Historical Statistics of Canada*; Statistics Canada, *Advance Statistics of Education.*

students, the attendance of 5-17 year-olds at school has held at the 98-99 percent mark.

The most striking change, and the strongest evidence of the rising standards of education in Canada, came in post-secondary enrolment. In 1951 3.3 percent of the population was attending such institutions—universities and colleges. By 1987 the proportion had risen to nearly 14 percent. Even more significant was the enrolment of students in the relevant age group, 18-24. From 6 percent in 1951 this rose to over 25 percent in 1987. In the latter year nearly 800,000 students were forecast to be enrolled: 475,000 in universities and 320,000 in community colleges. This marked increase in post-secondary enrolment is among the most significant in Canadian educational history. Equally notable was the fact that in 1950 only 20 percent of university enrolment was female; in 1987 it was forecast to be over 40 percent.

Further evidence of the rising standards of university education is the growing proportion of graduate students (tables 29.5-29.6). In 1945 they made up 4.5 percent of university enrolment; for 1987 they are estimated at 12 percent. Again the female share of this category has doubled—from 15 percent to over 30 percent.

Table 29.5 also gives evidence of the effect of the introduction of community colleges as a new element at the post-secondary level. By 1987 there were expected to be 320,000 students attending such schools compared to 33,000 in 1955.

The Teachers

Between 1950 and 1987 the number of Canadian teachers rose from 89,000 to 334,000, an increase of 272 percent, a growth greater than the 211 percent increase in student enrolment. A reduction in classroom load accounts for much of the difference in growth. The total number of elementary-secondary teachers rose annually from 1950 to 1977, peaking at 285,000 in the latter year, some seven years after the peak in student enrolment. Since then there has been a moderate decline, reaching a low of 272,000 in 1984. The following three years have shown a modest growth to 273,000 in 1987. As a proportion of the total teaching complement they dropped from 93 percent to 82 percent.

The number of post-secondary teachers has risen throughout, showing a five-fold gain from 12,000 in 1960 to 61,000 in 1987, further evidence of the growing emphasis on advanced education. In 1987 they were 18 percent of the teaching complement compared to 7 percent in 1960. (Table 29.7 gives data for 1960).

Some information on salary levels at the elementary-secondary level is also available for the 1960-85 period. The average rose from $4,247 per annum in 1960 to $38,000 in 1985. As a proportion of elementary-secondary expenditures these salaries ranged between a low of 55.1 percent in 1965-66 and a high of 62.5 percent in 1977, averaging around 52 percent over the period; clearly there are quite heavy expenses in the school system other than the salaries of teachers.

Schools and Classrooms

The long-term trend has been toward a substantial reduction in the number of elementary-secondary schools, reflecting mainly the replacement of small rural units with larger centralized facilities to which the children are bused. The result was a drop from 27,373 schools in 1960 to 15,533 in 1987, a decline of over 40 percent. This drop was accompanied by a more than doubling of enrolment per school until 1970, but since that time there appears to have been a stabilization of the average size at just over 300. This

Table 29.7 Education: Full-time Teachers in Elementary-Secondary and Post-Secondary Schools, 1960-87

Year[a]	Elementary-secondary					Post-secondary	
	Total	Number	Percent of total	Average salary[bc] of teachers	Salaries as a percent of elementary-secondary expenditure[b]	Number	Percent of total
	thousands		%	*dollars*	%	*thousands*	%
1960	165	153	92.7	4,247	55.3	12	7.3
1961	176	163	92.6	4,414	55.6	13	7.4
1962	188	174	92.6	4,522	55.5	14	7.4
1963	197	181	91.9	4,722	56.4	16	8.1
1964	209	192	91.9	4,954	56.6	17	8.1
1965	217	197	90.8	5,215	55.1	20	9.2
1966	234	211	90.2	5,567	55.1	23	9.8
1967	257	231	89.9	6,524	57.4	26	10.1
1968	274	245	89.4	6,495	58.4	29	10.6
1969	290	257	88.6	7,124	59.7	33	11.4
1970	299	262	87.6	7,688	59.3	37	12.4
1971	305	263	86.2	8,525	59.8	42	13.8
1972	309	265	85.8	10,436	59.6	44	14.2
1973	309	264	85.4	11,397	58.3	45	14.6
1974	310	264	85.2	12,760	58.8	46	14.8
1975	330	281	85.2	14,619	59.0	49	14.8
1976	335	285	85.1	17,358	61.3	50	14.9
1977	336	285	84.6	19,134	62.5	52	15.4
1978	334	281	84.1	20,506	61.9	53	15.9
1979	333	278	83.6	22,468	61.4	55	16.4
1980	332	276	83.1	24,877	60.3	56	16.9
1981	334	278	83.1	28,766	60.5	57	16.9
1982	334	276	82.6	32,268	61.0	58	17.4
1983	333	274	82.5	35,124	60.7	58	17.5
1984	330	272	82.2	36,113[d]	60.3	59	17.8
1985	331	272	82.2	38,000[d]	60.5	59	17.8
1986	333	272	81.7	na	na	60	18.0
1987	334	273	81.7	na	na	61	18.3

[a] Academic year beginning in year given. [b] Data for Quebec excluded for all years; Ontario for 1969-71; Saskatchewan, 1965; P.E.I., 1973; the territories, before 1972. [c] Salary, including fringe benefits. [d] Estimate.

Sources: *Historical Statistics of Canada*; Statistics Canada, *Decade of Educational Finance*, 1960-69 and 1970-71 to 1979-80; *Advance Statistics of Education*.

pattern is also apparent in the average number of teachers per school, which rose from 6 in 1960 to 18 in the late 1970s, and has remained relatively unchanged since. One goal appears to have survived throughout these radical changes—reduction in the pupil-teacher-ratio. The available data show a continuous reduction from 26.5 in 1960 to the 17-18 level in the eighties, a

Table 29.8 Number of Schools, Elementary-Secondary and Post-secondary, Average Enrolment, Teachers per School, and Pupil-Teacher Ratio, Selected Years, 1960-87

Year	Elementary-Secondary Schools				Post-secondary		
	Number of schools	Pupils per school	Teachers per school	Pupil teacher ratio	Community colleges	Universities	Total
1960	27,373	154	6	26.5	—	—	—
1961	26,868	164	6	26.1	—	—	—
1962	26,264	176	7	25.7	—	—	—
1963	25,806	186	7	25.3	—	—	—
1964	25,214	198	8	25.2	—	—	—
1965	23,359	222	9	24.8	—	—	—
1966	21,773	246	10	24.8	—	—	—
1967	20.042	275	11	23.8	—	—	—
1968	19,006	300	13	22.6	—	—	—
1969	17,946	325	15	22.0	—	—	—
1970	17,432	338	16	20.8	159	67	226
1971	16,335	359	16	20.7	170	67	237
1972	16,186	359	16	20.3	176	70	246
1973	16,027	357	16	20.1	183	70	253
1974	15,141	374	17	19.4	186	71	257
1975	15,121	369	18	18.9	189	66	258
1976	15,227	362	19	18.3	189	65	252
1977	15,365	352	17	18.0	187	66	256
1978	15,442	343	18	17.9	186	65	251
1979	15,429	336	18	17.6	189	66	256
1980	15,581	328	18	18.5	195	65	260
1981	15,634	322	18	18.1	197	68	265
1982	15,670	318	18	18.2	196	66	262
1983	15,643	318	18	18.3	197	66	263
1984	15,574	317	18	18.2	200	67	267
1985	15,634	316	17	18.2	198	68	266
1986	15,627	316	17	18.2	198	68	266
1987	15,533	319	17	18.2	198	68	266

Source: *Historical Statistics of Canada*; Statistics Canada, *Decade of Educational Finance, 1960-69* and *1970-71 to 1979-80*; *Advance Statistics of Education.*

remarkable accomplishment in the face of rising school enrolment. Universities enjoyed their massive growth during the sixties, when existing institutions were expanded and several new campuses appeared. In 1945 there were 27 degree granting bodies; in 1969 there were 40. Some of these, like the University of Toronto, included several member universities, which produced the higher figures given in table 29.8.

With the seventies growth dropped off, although post-secondary enrolment continued to increase. The new emphasis in several provinces was on the so-called community colleges, degree-granting institutions giving major emphasis to the technical subjects and operated on a more economical scale, offering both day-time classes and part-time study to thousands in the evenings. Launched in most provinces in the late sixties (in Quebec known as CEGEPs), by 1987 they numbered 198 in all.

Education Expenditures

Expenditure on education has been ranked in this study as one of the original big three, along with social services and health. Certainly the 86-times increase from $438 million in 1950 to a projected $37.8 billion in 1987 continues to qualify it for this standing.

Most of this expenditure is made by government under the Canadian system. As shown by table 29.9, government regularly accounts for 89-90 percent of the total, with a peak of 93 percent in the mid-seventies. The non-governmental tenth is covered by fees and other revenues, with fees usually accounting for slightly more than half, and thus for 5-6 percent at the most of total expenditure. They are of course a larger proportion of the total at the post-secondary level, where they are a more customary feature.

Government Expenditure

In Canada the provinces have primary responsibility for education and meet by far the largest proportion of its costs. But as we have seen billions of dollars in grants are shuttled around between levels of government for education (as well as other purposes) and weighing the outcome of this process varies with the accounting system being followed. The data used in earlier tables of government expenditure allocated outlays to the level of government where the actual expenditure was made, which for much of education is the local school board. An alternative system allocates the expenditure to the level of government appropriating the funds (making the grants) which gives an entirely different allocation. The detailed data used so far in the sector is from the Education Division of Statistics Canada, which has chosen to adopt the latter system, although with modifications. We have therefore carried on with this data, but with the notice that the allocation and total of education expenditure varies considerably from that given in earlier tables in this book.

On this basis, as shown in Table 29.10 in recent years the federal government has met 9.5 to 10 percent of the total, the provinces 65-68 percent, and the municipalities 16-17 percent. In 1950 the sharing was 5.1 percent federal, 44.1 percent provincial, and 50.8 percent municipal. The marked change, therefore, as pointed out earlier, has been the assumption by the senior levels of government of a greater share of costs, and in particular a massive shift from the municipalities to the provinces has taken place. This has allowed the municipalities to reduce their reliance on the municipal property tax for education revenues, particularly in provinces east of Ontario. In Ontario the property tax is still a major source of education revenue, and as well is used in most of the western provinces.

While government education expenditures have continued to rise in each year of the postwar period the pace has slackened in the last decade. In the decade 1950-59 the annual average increase was 3.3 percent. In the 1960-74

Table 29.9 Education: Expenditures^a by Government and Other Sources, Selected Years, 1950-87

Year^b	Federal^c	Percent of total	Provincial	Percent of total	Municipal	Percent of total	All governments	Percent of total	Other^d	Percent of total	Total
	$	%	$	%	$	%	$	%	$	%	$
1950	20	4.7	173	39.4	199	45.4	393	89.5	47	10.5	439
1955	57	6.9	343	41.3	343	41.4	743	89.6	86	10.4	829
1959	119	8.1	613	41.5	583	39.5	1,315	89.1	160	10.9	1,475
1960	132	7.7	729	42.8	653	38.3	1,514	88.8	192	11.2	1,706
1961	161	8.3	852	44.2	691	35.8	1,705	88.3	226	11.7	1,931
1962	355	14.9	1,031	43.6	739	31.1	2,131	89.6	247	10.4	2,378
1963	298	11.7	1,122	44.2	826	32.5	2,246	88.4	295	11.6	2,541
1964	290	10.0	1,328	46.0	915	31.7	2,533	87.7	357	12.3	2,890
1965	369	10.9	1,588	46.7	1,031	30.5	2,993	88.1	407	11.9	3,400
1966	539	13.0	1,985	47.8	1,155	27.8	3,679	88.6	475	11.4	4,155
1967	627	12.5	2,597	51.6	1,312	26.1	4,535	90.2	490	9.8	5,025
1968	658	11.3	3,141	54.4	1,478	25.6	5,276	91.3	500	8.7	5,777
1969	736	11.2	3,572	54.5	1,677	25.6	5,986	91.3	569	8.7	6,555
1970	930	12.1	4,316	56.2	1,719	22.4	6,965	90.7	710	9.3	7,676
1971	923	11.1	4,967	59.4	1,720	20.6	7,612	91.1	747	8.9	8,359
1972	944	10.9	5,252	60.5	1,785	20.6	7,981	92.0	694	8.0	8,675
1973	985	10.3	5,943	62.1	1,871	19.5	8,799	91.9	777	8.1	9,577
1974	1,051	9.5	7,023	63.5	2,079	18.8	10,153	91.8	907	8.2	11,060
1975	1,204	9.3	8,416	65.0	2,356	18.2	11,976	92.5	971	7.5	12,947
1976	1,359	9.0	9,874	65.4	2,838	18.8	14,071	93.2	1,027	6.8	15,098
1977	1,549	9.0	11,377	65.1	3,098	18.0	16,244	93.1	1,188	6.9	17,212
1978	1,617	8.9	11,881	65.4	3,415	18.8	16,913	93.1	1,254	6.9	18,167
1979	1,658	8.3	13,124	65.7	3,695	18.5	18,477	92.5	1,498	7.5	19,975
1980	1,886	8.5	14,711	66.3	3,861	17.4	20,458	92.2	1,731	7.8	22,189
1981	2,156	8.5	16,965	66.9	4,286	16.9	23,407	92.3	1,953	7.7	25,360
1982	2,489	8.8	19,348	68.4	4,300	15.2	26,137	92.4	2,150	7.6	28,287
1983	2,748	9.0	20,734	67.9	4,733	15.5	28,215	92.4	2,320	7.6	30,535
1984	2,936	9.2	21,222	66.5	5,074	15.9	29,232	91.6	2,680	8.4	31,912

1985	3,247	9.6	22,281	65.7	5,481	16.2	31,009	91.5	2,885	8.5	33,896
1986	3,676	10.1	23,731	65.5	5,947	16.4	33,354	92.0	2,921	8.0	36,276
1987	3,585	9.5	24,812	65.6	6,382	16.9	34,779	92.0	3,041	8.0	37,819

[a]Dollar figures in millions. [b]Fiscal year ending nearest to December 31 of year shown. [c]Excluding federal transfers to the provinces for universities and French language courses, which are included in provincial expenditures. [d]Fees and other revenues. In recent years the two sources have been divided in a ratio of about 4 to 3.

Sources: *Historical Statistics of Canada*; Statistics Canada, *Decade of Educational Finance*, 1960-69 and 1970-71 to 1979-80; *Education in Canada*, 1986; and *Advance Statistics of Education*.

Table 29.10   Education: Expenditure by Level of Government,
Percentage Distribution, Selected Years, 1950-87

Year	Federal	Provincial	Municipal	Total
		percent		
1950................	5.1	44.1	50.8	100.0
1955................	7.6	46.2	46.2	100.0
1960................	9.0	46.6	44.4	100.0
1965................	12.3	53.2	34.5	100.0
1970................	13.3	62.0	24.7	100.0
1975................	10.0	70.3	19.7	100.0
1980................	9.2	71.9	18.9	100.0
1985................	10.5	71.8	17.7	100.0
1986................	11.0	71.2	17.8	100.0
1987................	10.3	71.4	18.3	100.0

Based on table 29.8.

period it was about 4.5 percent; in the decade ending in 1987 it had fallen to around 2 percent. As previously stated, in terms of share of total government expenditure education peaked at 20-22 percent in the early seventies and has been declining ever since, reaching the 12 percent level in the mid-eighties.

Post-secondary Costs

The growing emphasis on post-secondary education drastically shifted the pattern of education expenditure over the period. From an approximate 15 percent of total costs in 1950, post-secondary education rose to nearly double that proportion at 28 percent by the late sixties and has remained in that neighbourhood since. While university expenditure rose in every post-war year its share of the total peaked at 23-24 percent in the late sixties and declined to 20 percent in later years. Concurrently the share of non-university (community college) costs rose from 2.7 percent to over 8 percent.

The financial consequences of this growing emphasis on post-secondary education becomes more apparent in table 29.12, which compares the per student cost of elementary-secondary and post-secondary education, the latter being a multiple of several times the former. This multiple was over six times in 1955, but growing enrolment in post-secondary institutions has spread costs over a larger mass and the multiple has declined sharply. Still at $12,868 per student in 1986, it cost three to four times as much to educate a post-secondary student as an elementary-secondary student ($4,685), a rather impressive evidence of cost differential.

Although not included in post-secondary costs, outlays on vocational education have also contributed to rising costs beyond the elementary-secondary level. They had risen from 3 percent of the total in 1950 to 7.6 percent in 1987.

Capital Costs

As buildings are a prominent feature of educational institutions and many new structures have been built in the last 40 years it is relevant to inquire as to the financial aspect of this development. Table 29.13 gives a partial answer.

For public schools capital costs rose consistently from 1950 in dollar expenditure but declined after the early sixties as a percent of total operating costs. When the degree of inflation is taken into account the increase from $72 million in 1960 to $520 million in 1985 in fact represents a decline in real terms. Debt costs related to capital expenditure rose sharply from $158 million in 1960 to $1,014 million in 1985. Debt costs are included as capital expenditure in the official tabulation.

It is not surprising, with several completely new university complexes erected and equipped in the hectic sixties, that capital costs for universities reached a high of 36.5 percent of total operating costs in 1964 and were above 30 percent in every year, 1963-67. Capital costs have since declined sharply, and were down to the 6 percent level in the late 1970s. In 1988 there were increasing complaints from universities that facilities were overcrowded and equipment was worn out or outdated.

Provincial-Municipal Arrangements

In the beginning phases of Canadian development, education of the young was almost exclusively left to the local community. The churches were the first to undertake the task in many communities, not only in Quebec but in other regions as well. The desire for non-sectarian education grew as population became more mixed and training needs broadened, and some of the earliest forms of support by higher governments were in aid of secularization. This process usually included establishing a local school board, hiring a teacher, and providing accommodation for classes, initially in a small one-room school-house. Revenues came from a tax on property and from provincial grants.

As communities grew into cities with mature economic and cultural bases provincial governments became more concerned with the quality of educational programs. In time, in the words of one authority, financial grants "were designed by the central authorities to enforce the adoption of practices considered necessary and to encourage localities to improve or extend their educational services in approved ways. These grants were almost always dependent upon the employment of a certificated teacher, sometimes on the achievement of teachers, and often on the salaries paid to teachers; on total or school population, or the number of teachers on the roll; or on the length of the school year. Grants were used to enforce the use of authorized textbooks, to set up school libraries, or to ensure the introduction of new subjects such as manual training, art, agriculture, or new services such as medical inspection."[29.1]

[29.1] K. Grant Crawford, *Provincial School Grants, 1941 to 1961*, Canadian Tax Papers no. 26 (Toronto: Canadian Tax Foundation, 1962), 5-6.

Table 29.11　Education: Total Expenditure[a] by Educational Level, Selected Years, 1950-87

| Year[b] | Total | Elementary-secondary | Percent of total | Post-secondary | | | | | | Vocational | Percent of total |
				Non-university	Percent of total	University	Percent of total	Total	Percent of total		
	$	$	%	$	%	$	%	$	%	$	%
1950	439	359	81.7	12	2.7	55	12.5	67	15.3	13	3.0
1955	829	674	81.3	31	3.7	104	12.5	135	16.3	19	2.3
1959	1,475	1,162	78.8	47	3.2	229	15.5	276	18.7	37	2.5
1960	1,706	1,328	77.9	58	3.4	273	16.0	331	19.4	47	2.7
1961	1,931	1,499	77.7	58	3.0	311	16.1	369	19.1	62	3.2
1962	2,378	1,809	76.1	74	3.1	379	15.9	452	19.0	117	4.9
1963	2,541	1,879	74.0	82	3.2	461	18.2	544	21.5	118	4.6
1964	2,890	2,066	71.5	93	3.2	597	20.7	690	23.9	133	4.6
1965	3,410	2,411	70.9	99	2.9	737	21.7	835	24.6	153	4.5
1966	4,155	2,791	67.2	125	3.0	992	23.9	1,117	26.9	248	5.9
1967	5,025	2,230	64.3	200	4.0	1,243	24.7	1,443	28.7	352	7.0
1968	5,777	3,775	65.3	251	4.4	1,360	23.5	1,611	27.9	391	6.8
1969	6,624	4,281	65.0	347	4.2	1,604	24.1	1,950	28.1	392	6.7
1970	7,676	4,880	63.6	430	5.6	1,791	23.3	2,221	28.3	575	7.5
1971	8,350	5,389	64.5	530	6.5	1,865	22.3	2,395	28.8	566	6.7
1972	8,669	5,625	64.8	573	6.8	1,868	21.5	2,441	28.3	603	6.9
1973	8,635	6,313	65.3	657	7.0	2,030	21.2	2,686	28.2	636	6.5
1974	11,049	7,191	65.0	792	7.3	2,372	21.4	3,164	28.7	693	6.3
1975	12,926	8,348	64.6	976	7.5	2,760	21.4	3,736	28.9	842	6.5
1976	15,049	10,033	66.7	1,085	7.2	2,977	19.8	4,061	27.0	955	6.3
1977	17,364	11,650	67.1	1,266	7.3	3,378	19.4	4,644	26.7	1,070	6.2
1978	18,455	12,261	66.4	1,496	8.1	3,625	19.7	5,121	27.8	1,074	5.8
1979	20,247	13,518	66.8	1,611	8.0	3,949	19.5	5,560	27.5	1,168	5.7

1980	22,189	65.8	1,850	8.3	4,438	19.8	6,288	28.1	1,332	6.1
1981	25,360	65.9	2,093	8.3	4,981	19.6	7,074	27.9	1,582	6.2
1982	28,287	65.5	2,188	7.7	5,704	20.2	7,842	28.0	1,863	6.5
1983	30,535	65.7	2,393	7.8	6,043	19.8	8,436	27.5	2,040	6.7
1984	31,912	65.1	2,532	7.9	6,473	20.3	9,005	28.2	2,128	6.7
1985	33,896	64.5	2,644	7.8	6,985	20.6	9,629	28.4	2,401	7.1
1986	36,276	63.8	2,812	7.8	7,353	20.2	10,166	28.0	2,961	8.2
1987	37,819	64.3	2,963	7.8	7,687	20.3	10,650	28.1	2,834	7.6

[a]Dollar figures in millions. [b]Fiscal year nearest December 31 in year named.

Sources: *Historical Statistics of Canada*; Statistics Canada, *Decade of Education Finance*, 1960-69 and 1970-71 to 1979-80 and *Advance Statistics of Education*.

Table 29.12   Education: Per Student Costs, Elementary-Secondary
and Post-secondary Levels, Selected Years, 1955-86

Year	Elementary-secondary costs per student	Post-secondary costs per student	Post-secondary as multiple of elementary-secondary
	dollars		
1955	109	657	6.02
1959	290	1,865	6.43
1960	316	2,031	6.43
1961	347	2,027	5.84
1962	401	2,143	5.34
1963	398	2,472	6.21
1964	420	2,840	6.76
1965	470	3,058	6.50
1966	527	3,603	6.84
1967	592	4,088	6.91
1968	670	4,078	6.09
1969	731	4,462	6.10
1970	888	4,666	5.25
1971	953	4,819	5.06
1972	1,004	4,758	4.74
1973	1,131	5,034	4.45
1974	1,267	5.670	4.48
1975	1,492	6,311	4.23
1976	1,820	6,735	3.70
1977	2,153	7,539	3.50
1978	2,316	8,286	3.58
1979	2,607	8,910	3.42
1980	2,853	9,779	3.43
1981	3,321	10,480	3.16
1982	3,711	10,861	2.93
1983	4,032	10,999	2.73
1984	4,201	11,501	2.74
1985	4,426	12,235	2.76
1986	4,685	12,868	2.75

Sources: Canada, *Decade of Education Finance*, 1960-69 and 1970-71 to 1979-80; *Education in Canada*, 1986; and *Advance Statistics of Education*.

The subsequent trend was away from the conditional grant to encourage specific educational purposes toward a new objective, "the equalization of educational opportunity. The principle of making the grant vary inversely to the value of assessable land was introduced in the North West Territories in 1901 and was adopted by the provinces of Saskatchewan and Alberta when they were formed out of these territories in 1905. Ontario made the grants partly dependent on the amount of the assessment in 1907, but it was not until the 1930's that the principle of equalization became fully accepted as a major basis for the distribution of grants."[29.2] This authority described the trend subsequent to 1940 as reflecting the "democratic principle that

---

[29.2] Ibid., at 6.

Table 29.13 Education: Operating and Capital Expenditures, Public Schools and Universities, Selected Years, 1950-85

Year	Public schools[b]					Universities			
	Operating costs	Capital costs	Debt costs	Total costs	Capital as percent of total	Operating costs	Capital costs	Total costs	Capital as percent of total
	millions of dollars				percent	millions of dollars			percent
1950	261	n.a.	47[c]	308	15.3	41	12	55	21.8
1955	475	n.a.	101[c]	576	17.5	84	16	104	15.4
1959	799	n.a.	200[c]	999	20.0	150	69	229	30.1
1960	902	72	158	1,132	20.3	183	80	273	29.3
1961	1,010	78	178	1,266	20.2	211	85	311	27.3
1962	1,126	93	191	1,410	20.2	244	112	379	29.6
1963	1,266	92	209	1,567	19.2	290	146	461	31.7
1964	1,460	82	230	1,772	17.6	345	218	597	36.5
1965	1,681	84	245	2,010	16.4	433	252	737	34.2
1966	1,930	75	269	2,274	15.1	582	324	992	32.7
1967	2,280	88	304	2,672	14.7	749	378	1,243	30.4
1968	2,731	87	352	3,170	13.8	897	336	1,360	24.7
1969	3,180	61	398	3,639	12.6	1,084	356	1,604	22.2
1970	3,597	64	426	4,087	12.0	1,224	392	1,791	21.9
1971	3,919	77	450	4,446	11.8	1,366	315	1,865	16.9
1972	4,194	102	523	4,819	13.8	1,434	239	1,907	12.5
1973	4,726	119	509	5,354	11.7	1,578	161	2,026	7.9
1974	5,382	129	547	6,058	11.2	1,837	189	2,373	8.0
1975	6,455	167	582	7,204	10.4	2,168	236	2,787	8.5
1976	7,712	129	630	8,471	9.0	2,449	156	2,987	5.2
1977	8,723	132	664	9,519	8.4	2,746	207	3,382	6.1
1978	9,400	149	662	10,211	7.9	2,976	233	3,635	6.4
1979	10,310	162	703	11,175	7.7	3,240	252	3,951	6.4
1980	11,356	277	736	12,369	8.2	3,665	293	4,438	6.6
1981	12,918	367	784	14,069	8.2	4,172	305	4,981	6.1
1982	14,528	419	842	15,789	8.0	4,738	392	5,704	6.9
1983	15,364	483	957	16,804	8.6	5,073	402	6,043	6.7
1984	16,150	486	1,083	17,719	8.9	5,379	369	6,518	5.7
1985	16,880	520	1,014	18,414	8.3	5,720	440	7,035	6.3

[a] Academic year beginning in year named. [b] School boards. Does not include private schools. [c] Capital and debt costs combined.

Sources: *Historical Statistics of Canada* and Statistics, Canada: *Decade of Education Finance*, 1960-69 and 1970-71 to 1979-80; CANSIM data.

each child and person, regardless of his economic status, accident of birth or residence in one part of the country or another, is entitled to equal opportunity to develop his abilities and talents and to become an effective member of our Canadian society."[29.3]

These words from 1962 were prophetic, as the theme of equalization of costs and opportunities has run strongly through all subsequent provincial developments. It was probably the main motivation leading to the assumption by the provinces of New Brunswick and Prince Edward Island of all costs of education. It no doubt also explains the adoption in other provinces of much greater shares of local costs under increasingly complicated formulae usually employing equalized property assessments and foundation programs with equalized components. There will not be space here to trace the course of these developments over the past forty years, as in detail they are extremely complicated, but the following brief descriptions of the present system in each province will serve to give a general impression of the current status. These summaries are based on a publication of the Council of Ministers of Education, *The Financing of Elementary and Secondary Education in Canada*, December 1986. In this volatile field changes may have been made since this material was published.

British Columbia

Provincial grants are made toward a Sharable Operating Budget for each school district, a basic 55 percent being paid first, with possible additional grants toward the remaining 45 percent. The latter are based on a provincial equalization formula. A home-owner grant is also paid by the province, but directly to residents. The province obtains its revenue for grants from general sources, provincial non-residential property tax, and miscellaneous shared sources. Amounts not covered by the province in the sharable budget and allowable additions to the sharable budget must be covered by the municipality from residential property tax and miscellaneous sources.

The study gives the following breakdown of 1985-86 revenues and expenditures of B.C. school districts, in percentages of the total: revenues— grants, 41.8; non-residential property tax, 30.4; home-owners' grant, 14.8; residential tax, 9.0; miscellaneous revenues, 4.1; expenditures—sharable operating budget, 88.1; debt service, 9.1; all additions, 1.9; non-sharable capital, 0.9.

Alberta

Revenues of local school authorities come from the provincial School Foundation Program Fund, other provincial grants, supplementary requisitions from municipalities, and miscellaneous revenues. Grants under the foundation program cover basic revenues. Grants under the foundation program cover basic instruction, transportation, administration and debt service support. Other provincial grants are for special education. Supple-

---

[29.3] Ibid.

mentary requisitions are required to pay the amount not covered by grants, and are dispersed on the basis of equalized assessments. Local school board revenue sources in 1985 were estimated to originate as follows, in percentages: provincial foundation grant, 44.1; requisitions from municipalities, 30.8; other provincial grants, 11.4; local provincially set foundation grants, 7.7; miscellaneous revenues, 6.0. A home-owners' rebate of about 3 percent of school revenues is accounted as part of the education revenue budget.

On the assumption that the municipal requisitions are met from property tax revenues it would appear that approximately 31 percent of education expenditures are supported from this source. However, in addition the province, like British Columbia, collects a property tax on non-commercial property for education.

Saskatchewan

The province establishes financial need for each school division on the basis of recognized need and recognized revenue, the former determined by applying standardized rates to school enrolment, transportation, administration, etc., and the latter employing an equalized assessment and a standard mill rate. The difference is paid to the school district as a grant which normally covers about 50 percent of education costs in the province. The balance is met through local property taxation. Special grants are given from the Educational Development Fund and under the program for Learning Resources and Efficiency.

Manitoba

The existing Support of Education Program, introduced in 1985, has four main grants: Categorical Support; Block Support; Equalization Support, and Capital Support. Under these various programs revenues in 1985 were as follows, in percentages: provincial grants, 74.2; municipalities, 21.5; other, including federal government, Indian bands, and private, 3.3. To meet a share of its costs under the Support of Education Program the government levies a tax on farm, residential, and commercial properties, which in 1985 paid about one-third of the cost of the program.

Ontario

After several experiments Ontario in 1985 adopted a system in which most of the elements were brought to an equalized basis. Under the Mill Rate Equalization Plan the objective is to give all school boards the same per student revenues through a combination of local property tax and provincial grants. The provincial grant makes up the difference between the school board's so-called recognized expenditure and a uniform mill rate applied to an equalized assessment. Recognized expenditure is the school board's actual operating expenditure, but with a per pupil ceiling. In 1985 the province funded 46.5 percent of school board expenditure and 53.5 percent was met from local taxation.

Quebec

The Quebec program represents a substantial revision introduced in 1980-81, when a system based on approval of actual expenditures was replaced with one in which factors for specified types of outlay were established, to be revised periodically for inflation and the evolution of student enrolment. In 1980-81 a standardized property tax previously levied by local school boards was also surrendered to the municipalities and replaced by provincial grants. School boards may still levy a supplementary property tax within limits set by law.

The provincial grants for operating expenditures are based on predetermined rules under three categories: Basic Allocations, Supplementary Allocations, and Specific Allocations. The bases for each of these categories are too involved to be explained here. Furthermore new arrangements for 1986-87 were forecast in the study, involving further changes in the allocation system. In 1985-86 Quebec elementary-secondary revenues were as follows in percentages: general grants, 73.5; debt assistance grants, 7.6; transportation grants, 6.4; property tax, 4.3; other, 8.1.

New Brunswick

The provincial government pays the full cost of operating budgets of local school boards. Various standards are applied to determine funding under the main headings of expenditure.

Nova Scotia

Since 1981 school board financing has been through a combination of provincial grants and property taxation. The former are composed of global grants and specific purpose grants, with enrolment being a heavily weighted factor in the determination of the global amounts. The property tax for education is levied at a uniform rate set by the province and applied to a uniform assessment of all property. On average, 80 percent or more of funding comes from the province.

Prince Edward Island

Since 1972 a former school tax on property levied by municipalities has been combined with the normal property tax and responsibility for elementary and secondary school costs assumed by the province. Support is given on the basis of a foundation program in which various factors are weighted.

Newfoundland

Local education costs are paid mostly by the province. Teachers' salaries and benefits are paid directly by the Department of Education (75 percent of total costs), and provincial grants cover a substantial part of the balance. Municipalities are expected to levy local taxation for education, but in practice revenue from this source is very limited.

Overview

A pattern appears to have developed for provinces east of Ontario that is quite different from that of Ontario and the western provinces. In Quebec and the Atlantic provinces provincial governments have assumed financial responsibility for local education ranging from 75 to 100 percent; in the other provinces a substantial share of the burden has been left with local or district bodies. In the general case the share of costs assumed by the province through grants and other assistance appears to be in the range of 50-60 percent, although in some circumstances it can be higher. There is no obvious explanation for this divergence although it likely has its origin in local success in the use of the property tax, the only significant source available for local revenues.

Some Landmarks

The following is a brief catalogue of the studies and reports of Committees and Commissions that were influential in bringing about some of the main changes of the postwar period.

Provincial Reports and Related Studies

1945. British Columbia. *Report of the Royal Commission of Inquiry into Educational Finance* (Cameron Report).

1947. British Columbia. *Report of Inquiry into Performance of Municipal Functions* (Goldenberg Report).

1950. Ontario. *Report of Royal Commission on Education* (Hope Report), Toronto.

1951. Manitoba. *Report of Committee on Provincial Municipal Relations.*

1954. Nova Scotia. *Report of the Royal Commission on Public School Finance in Nova Scotia.*

1955. New Brunswick. *Report of the Royal Commission on Financing of Schools.*

1956. Saskatchewan. *Report of the Royal Commission on Agricultural and Rural Life.*

_____. Quebec. *Report of the Royal Commission of Inquiry on Constitutional Problems.*

1959. Manitoba. *Final Report of the Royal Commission on Education.*

_____. Alberta. *Report of the Royal Commission on Education in Alberta.*

1960. British Columbia. *Report of the Royal Commission on Education.* (Chant Report).

_____. Prince Edward Island. *Report of the Commission on Educational Finance and Related Problems of Administration.*

1962. K. Grant Crawford. *Provincial School Grants, 1941-1961.* Canadian Tax Foundation, Tax Paper no. 26.

_____. British Columbia. *Higher Education in British Columbia and a Plan for the Future.* John B. Macdonald, University of British Columbia, Vancouver.

1963. Quebec. *Report of the Royal Commission of Inquiry on Education in the Province of Quebec* (the Parent Report).

_____. New Brunswick. *Report of the Royal Commission on Finance and Municipal Taxation in New Brunswick.*

_____. Saskatchewan. Department of Education. *A Plan for the Reorganization of Instruction in Saskatchewan Schools.*

_____. Ontario. Committee of Presidents of Provincially Assisted Universities and Colleges of Ontario, *Post-Secondary Education in Ontario, 1962-1970.*

1966. Ontario Department of Education, Colleges of Applied Arts and Technology, *Basic Documents.* 1966.

_____. Ontario. Department of Education. *Report of the Minister's Committee on the Training of Elementary School Teachers,* 1966.

1967-68. Newfoundland. *Report of the Royal Commission on Education and Youth.*

1968. Ontario. *Living and Learning.* The Report of the Provincial Committee on Aims and Objectives of Education in the Schools of Ontario. (Hall-Dennis Report).

1972. Alberta. *Education Alberta. A Choice of Futures* (Worth Report).

1973. Ontario. *The Learning Society.* Report of the Commission on Post-secondary Education in Ontario.

_____. Manitoba. *Report of the Task Force on Post-secondary Education in Manitoba* (Oliver Report).

_____. Manitoba. *The Secondary School: Report.* Core Committee on the Reorganization of the Secondary School.

_____. New Brunswick. *Education Tomorrow* (MacLeod-Pinet Report). New Brunswick Committee on Educational Planning.

1972-75. Ontario. Committee on the Costs of Education, *Interim Reports.*

1974. Nova Scotia. *Report of the Royal Commission on Education, Public Services and Provincial-Municipal Relations* (the Graham Report).

1976. Ontario. Ontario Economic Council. *Education Issues and Alternatives.*

1981. Nova Scotia. Report of the Commission on Public Education Finance.

_____. Ontario. *Report of the Secondary Education Review Project.* Ministry of Education.

1982. Alberta. Minister's Task force on School Finance, *Financing Schooling in Alberta.* Alberta Education.

1983. Manitoba. *Report of the Education Finance Review*, Manitoba Department of Education.

1984. Alberta. Minister's Advisory Committee, *Review of Secondary Programs*, Minister of Education.

———. Alberta. *Directions: The Final Report*. Minister's Advisory Committee on Instruction and Curriculum Review.

———. British Columbia. *New Financial Management System*, Ministry of Education, Victoria.

1985. Alberta. *Secondary Education in Alberta: Policy Statement*.

———. British Columbia. Provincial School Review Committee. *Let's Talk About Schools*. Vols. I to V. Ministry of Education.

———. Ontario. *The Report of the Commission on the Financing of Elementary and Secondary Education in Ontario*.

———. Ontario. *Report of the Commission on the Future Development of the Universities of Ontario*.

Federal and Other General Documents

1951. Federal. *Report of the Royal Commission on National Development in the Arts, Letters and Sciences*, Ottawa, Queen's Printer.

1958. Addresses and Proceedings of the Canadian Conference on Education, Ottawa. Mutual Press.

1962. *Report of the Second Canadian Conference on Education*, University of Toronto Press, Toronto.

1965. Association of Universities and Colleges of Canada, *Financing Higher Education in Canada*, University of Toronto Press, Toronto.

1969. John B. Macdonald et al, *The Role of the Federal Government in Support of Research in Canadian Universities*, Ottawa, Queen's Printer.

1971. Economic Council of Canada. *Design for Decision-Making*. Ottawa: Information Canada.

1973. Economic Council of Canada, Education Committee, *Outlook Paper*, the Council.

1976. OECD. *Reviews of National Policies on Education: Canada*. Paris: Organization for Economic Co-operation and Development.

———. Hodgson, Ernest D., *Federal Intervention in Public Education*. Toronto: Canadian Education Association.

1985. Federal. *Report of the Royal Commission on the Economic Union and Development Prospects for Canada*.

———. Council of Ministers of Education. *Principles for Interaction: Federal-Provincial Relations and Post-Secondary Education in Canada*.

_____. Council of Ministers of Education. *Changing Economic Circumstances: The Challenge for Postsecondary Education and Manpower Training.*

_____. *One in Every Five: A Survey of Adult Education in Canada.* Statistics Canada and Department of Secretary of State of Canada.

1987. Federal. *Federal and Provincial Support to Post-Secondary Education in Canada.* Department of the Secretary of State of Canada.

Bibliography, chapter 29

Aaron, Henry J. *Politics and the Professors: the Great Society in Perspective*. Washington, D.C.: The Brookings Institution, 1978.

Breneman, David W. *Strategies for the 1980s*. Reprint Series. Washington, D.C.: The Brookings Institution, 1982.

Brown, Wilfred J. *Education Finance in Canada*. Ottawa: Canadian Teachers' Federation, 1981.

_____. *The Financing of Elementary and Secondary Education in Canada*. Toronto: Council of Ministers of Education, Canada, 1986.

_____. *New Goals, New Paths: The Search for a Rationale for the Financing of Education in Canada*. Parts 1 and 2. Ottawa: The Canadian Teachers' Federation, 1973.

Business Council on National Issues. *Social Policy Reform and the National Agenda*. Ottawa: the Council, 1986.

Canada. Department of the Secretary of State. *Support to Education by the Government of Canada*. Ottawa: 1983.

_____. *Federal and Provincial Support to Post-Secondary Education in Canada*. Ottawa: 1987.

_____. Statistics Canada. *Advance Statistics of Education in Canada*. Ottawa: annual.

_____. *Education in Canada*. Ottawa: annual.

_____. *Financial Statistics of Education*. Ottawa: annual.

_____. *Historical Compendium of Education Statistics: From Confederation to 1975*. Ottawa: 1978.

_____. *Historical Statistics of Canada*. 2nd ed. F.H. Leacy, Editor. Ottawa: 1983.

_____. Royal Commission on Economic Union and Development Prospects for Canada. *Report*. vol. 2. Ottawa: 1985.

Canadian Chamber of Commerce. *Policy Declaration on Education, 1962-63*. Toronto: the Association, 1962.

Canadian Education Association. *Education in Transition: A Capsule Review, 1960-1975*. Toronto: the Association, 1975.

_____. *An Overview of Canadian Education*. 3rd ed. Toronto: the Association. 1984.

Canadian Tax Foundation. *The National Finances*. Toronto: the Foundation, annual.

_____. *Provincial and Municipal Finances*. Toronto: the Foundation, annual.

Canadian Teachers' Federation. *Current Thinking on the Relationship Between Education and Economic Growth*. Information no. 64. Ottawa: the Federation, 1963.

Channon, G.L., and Brown W.J. *Education, A Continuing Priority*. Ottawa: Canadian Teachers' Federation, 1978.

Crawford, K. Grant. *Provincial School Grants 1941 to 1961*. Toronto: Canadian Tax Foundation, 1962.

Conklin, David W., and Courchene, Thomas J. eds. *Ontario Universities: Access, Operations and Funding*. Toronto: Ontario Economic Council, 1985.

Croskery, George G., and Nason, Gerald, eds. Addresses and Proceedings of the Canadian Conference on Education, February 16-20, 1958. Ottawa: Mutual Press, 1958.

Economic Council of Canada. Staff Study Number 25. Ottawa: 1968.

Forget, Claude E. "Education Policy in Canada: the Urgent Issues." *Commentary*. Toronto: C.D. Howe Institute, January 1985.

Gayfer, Margaret. *An Overview of Canadian Education*. Toronto: the Canadian Education Association, 1974.

_____. *An Overview of Canadian Education*. 2nd ed. Toronto: the Canadian Education Association, 1978.

Graham, John F. "Financing Elementary and Secondary Education." In Barbara Jamieson, ed. *Governing Nova Scotia—Policies and Priorities and the 1984-85 Budget*. Halifax: Dalhousie University, 1985.

Hall, Oswald and Carlton, Richard. *Basic Skills at School and Work*. Toronto: Ontario Economic Council, 1977.

Henchey, Norman. *Education for the 21st Century: Canadian Imperatives*. Ottawa: Canadian Teachers' Federation, 1983.

Hennessey, P.H., "The Three R's and Survival." (December 10, 1962) *The Bulletin of the Ontario Secondary School Teachers Federation*, 479-512.

"Horse and Buggy Education." *The Globe and Mail*, August 26, 1983.

James, F. Cyril. "What Kind of Education Does Canada Want?" (March 31, 1959) *The Bulletin of the Ontario Secondary School Teachers Federation*, 79-104.

Johnson, A.W. *Giving Greater Point and Purpose to the Federal Financing of Post-Secondary Education and Research in Canada*. Secretary of State of Canada. Ottawa: 1985.

Johnson, Henry, F. *A Brief History of Canadian Education*. Toronto: McGraw-Hill Company of Canada Ltd., 1968.

Lawr, Douglas, and Gidney, Robert, *Educating Canadians*. A Documentary History of Public Education Updated. 2nd ed. Toronto: Van Nostrand, Reinhold, 1983.

Lawson, Stephen B. *The Price of Quality*. The Public Finance of Elementary and Secondary Education in Canada. Toronto: The Canadian Education Association, 1987.

Livingston, D.W., Hart, D.J., and MacLean, L.D. *Public Attitudes Towards Education in Ontario*. Toronto: Ontario Institute for Studies in Education, 1982.

MacDonald, H. Ian. "Higher Education in Countries with Federal Systems of Government. Financial Effects of Federalism: National and Local Governments." Paper presented to the Association of Commonwealth Universities Congress. Vancouver: 1978.

_____. "Federal Involvement in Post-Secondary Education." *Education Canada: Federal-Provincial Relations*. Toronto: 1981.

"The money squeeze on universities." *MacLean's*, April 25, 1988, 44-45.

Neatby, Hilda. *So Little for the Mind*. Toronto: Clarke, Irwin & Co., 1953.

Noordeh, A. ed. *Reforming the Financing Arrangements for Post-Secondary Education in Canada*. Toronto: Ontario Economic Council, 1985.

Ontario Economic Council. *Education Issues and Alternatives*. Toronto: the Council, 1976.

OECD. *Canada: Reviews of National Policies for Education*. Paris: 1976.

Perry, David B. "The Escalating Cost of Education." (September-October 1983) 31 *Canadian Tax Journal*, 879-80.

Perry, J, Harvey. "Education Grows Older." (September 1979) 2 *Report*, 7-9.

_____. "What Level of Education can the Canadian Economy Support?" *Report*. Second Conference on Education. Toronto: University of Toronto Press, 1962.

Phillips, Charles E. *The Development of Education in Canada*. Toronto: W.J. Gage and Co. 1957.

Phimmister, Z.S. "Keeping Pace with Modern Problems." (February 1957) *Argus*, 39-61.

Price, Fred. W. ed. The Second Canadian Conference on Education March 4-8, 1962. *A Report*. Toronto: University of Toronto Press, 1962.

Robinson, F.G. *Canadian Education, 1955, An Evaluative Essay*. Ottawa: Canadian Council for Research in Education, 1965.

Symons, Thomas H.B. *To Know Ourselves*. The Report of the Commission on Canadian Studies. Ottawa: the Association of Universities and Colleges of Canada, 1975-83.

Rivers, F.S. "Education, 1930-1980: Fifty Years of Crisis." (September 1964) *Canadian Education and Research Digest*, 169-82.

St. John, J. Bascom. "Crisis in Canadian Education." (January-February 1958) *Canadian School Journal*, 5-7.

Stevenson, H.A. and Wilson, J.D. eds. *Precepts, Policy and Process; Perspectives on Contemporary Canadian Education*. London: Alexander, Blake, 1977.

Stewart, F.K. *Education in Canada Today*. Toronto: W.J. Gage and Co. Ltd. 1956.

_____. "Government Aid and Control of Education in Canada." (June 1961) *Current History*, 353-60.

Studies in the Economics of Education. Ottawa: Economics and Research Branch, Department of Labour, 1965.

University of Manitoba. *Issues in Higher Education*. Monograms in Education. Winnipeg: the University, 1979.

Wesenthal, M. *The Threat of Increasing Number and Costs in Post-Secondary Education* Ottawa: Dominion Bureau of Statistics, 1969.

Wilkinson, B.W. "Elementary and Secondary Education Policy in Canada: A Survey." 12 *Canadian Public Policy*, 535-72, 1986.

Wilson, J. Donald, ed. *Canadian Education in the 1980s*. Calgary: Detselig Enterprises, 1981.

Wilson, J. Donald, Stamp, Robert M., and Audet, Louis-Philippe. *Canadian Education: A History*. Scarborough, Ont.: Prentice-Hall of Canada, 1979.

Part 6
Mainly International

Tariffs and Trade

Prologue
Some Facts About Canadian Trade

In the closing years of the twentieth century Canadians are once again deeply involved in a debate on their trade relations with the rest of the world. For Canada this debate is crucial—and inescapable. For over four centuries Canada's growth has relied heavily on its ability to sell the rest of the world its furs, fish, lumber, wheat, and minerals. In the beginning these were in their raw state, but with industrial development, manufactured and processed products have become a larger element. Every community in the country therefore is deeply affected by the state of world trade and Canada's share in it. Inevitably there are wide and clashing differences of opinion on the best approach to success, arising both from the regional diversity of the economy and the growing competition against traditional Canadian products in world markets. The questions are by no means solely economic; where the future welfare of the country is at stake emotions deep-rooted in issues of national sovereignty and regional antagonisms quickly enter the debate.

A full understanding of the ramifications of foreign trade for Canada would require a review of two or three centuries of history. Current events fall within a shorter span, but must be seen in the perspective of actions which began at least 50 years ago. This will be the purpose of the three following chapters. They are followed by three chapters reviewing more recent developments. But first, a brief introduction to the basic facts regarding Canada's present trade with the rest of the world.

Share of Gross Domestic Product

On the basis of data for 1980, at just in excess of one-quarter of its GNP Canada's dependence on foreign trade was third among 12 leading industrial countries. It was exceeded only by Belgium/Luxembourg (53.4 percent) and Netherlands (44.1 percent), and was followed closely by West Germany (23.6 percent) and United Kingdom (22.0 percent) but far outranked France (17.1 percent), Japan (12.4 percent), and United States (8.4 percent).[1] The fact that the Canadian dependence on exports was twice that of the Japan, popularly regarded as the leader among world's traders, is probably realized by few Canadians, and is a tribute to the visibility of Japanese imports in the world's consumer markets.

---

[1] Jock A. Finlayson, "Canada, Congress and U.S. Foreign Economic Policy," in *The Politics of Canada's Economic Relationship with the United States.* Volume 29 of the studies for the Macdonald Commission (Toronto: University of Toronto Press, 1985).

Canada's Trading Partners

The long-term trend of export trade has been away from Europe and increasingly towards the United States. In 1900, for example, 55 percent of exports went to Europe, mainly to Britain, while 38 percent went to the U.S. By contrast, in 1987 the European share was 7.4 percent, and the U.S. share was 77 percent. Japan, which in 1900 represented 0.1 percent of exports, in 1987 had risen to 5.4 percent, now Canada's third most important market.

For imports the United States provided 60 percent in 1900, and in no period since then has the ratio fallen below that level. From the 1920s in fact it has been in the area of 70 percent, and was frequently higher, standing at 69 percent in 1987. A feature of the last quarter century has been the origination of 10-15 percent of imports in developing countries.[2]

Canada's Exports

Total merchandise exports in 1987 were $126 billion, representing a wide range of goods. Table 1 gives for selected years 1960-1987 the percentage distribution of exports between the main commodity groups. The main commodities within these groups, accounting for about three-quarters of the total, are wheat; crude petroleum, natural gas, coal and coal products; lumber, wood pulp and newsprint; ores and concentrates, iron, steel and alloys and non-metallic minerals; chemicals; automobiles and parts; aircraft and parts; communications and electronic equipment, industrial machinery and other equipment and tools.

The decline in the role of food exports and the increase in the share of manufactured goods are notable features of the last quarter century. A substantial share of the latter increase is attributable to the exports of autos and parts under the 1965 Automobile Agreement with the U.S. These were 2.2 percent of total trade in 1964; 25.5 percent in 1987. As well, many exports which involve advanced manufacturing processes in Canada, such as newsprint, are included in other categories since they require further production to become "final" products, such as newspapers.

Canada's Imports

The import picture is relatively simple. Canada has always depended heavily on imports of manufactured goods, and despite a developing industrial structure this remains the position today. Of total imports of $115.1 billion in 1987, 68 percent were in the fully manufactured category. The heaviest imports were transportation and communication equipment (40.8 percent), industrial machinery (8.4 percent), other equipment and tools (8.2 percent), and other consumer goods (11.0 percent). Included in these groups are

---

[2]Michael C. Webb and Mark W. Zacher, "Canadian Export Trade in a Changing International Environment," in *Canada and the International Political/Economic Environment*. Volume 28 of the studies for the Macdonald Commission (Toronto: University of Toronto Press, 1985).

Prologue   Table 1   Merchandise Exports—Main Commodity Groups,
Selected Years, 1960 to 1987

Year	Food, beverages and tobacco	Inedible crude materials	Inedible fabricated materials	Finished manufactured goods
	percentage			
1960.................	18.8	21.1	51.9	7.8
1965.................	20.0	20.7	43.7	15.3
1970.................	11.4	18.8	35.8	33.8
1975.................	12.7	24.5	30.4	32.2
1980.................	11.1	19.8	39.4	29.4
1981.................	11.6	18.7	37.6	31.2
1982.................	11.7	17.5	33.0	33.9
1983.................	11.1	15.8	33.1	36.7
1984.................	9.2	15.4	31.9	40.0
1985.................	7.9	16.5	31.7	43.1
1986.................	8.1	12.9	30.5	45.8
1987.................	8.2	12.4	32.7	43.2

Source: Statistics Canada.

motor vehicles and parts, communications and related equipment, agricultural machinery, office equipment, clothing, books, and photo supplies. A closely related industrial category, accounting for 18.2 percent of imports, is fabricated materials, inedible. (Tariff designers seem to have a preoccupation with how imports will sit with the human tummy). This category includes textiles and materials, plastics and synthetic rubber, petroleum products, and metal and metal alloys. Two smaller categories make up the balance: food, feed, beverages and tobacco, (5.8 percent) and crude materials, inedible, (6.5 percent).

Some aspects of the trade picture would surprise the average consumer, who probably visualizes imports in terms of liquors, meats, fresh fruits and vegetables, coffee, cocoa, tea, and similar household items. In fact in 1987 the amount spent on communications and electronic equipment (computers, etc.) at $9.8 million was nearly 25 percent more than that spent on the former items; the amount spent on automobiles and parts was four times the food category. The heavy emphasis on imports of manufactured goods means that Canada runs a heavy deficit in these products, fortunately offset by a surplus in other trade sufficient to produce an overall favourable trade balance, amounting to $11.0 billion in 1987.

Origin of Imports

The proportion of imports from the United States—about three-quarters—reflects the close economic relations evidenced by export trade. The remainder comes from Japan, the European Economic Community, Commonwealth countries, and some of the developing countries. There are several sensitive issues in this area; for example, imports of automobiles, clothing and footwear, to be explored later.

30
The GATT Experience—The Rounds

The most influential element in restoring world commerce to an orderly basis in the postwar period has been the General Agreement on Tariffs and Trade (GATT). Born of the economic folly of extreme protectionism during the depression and the disastrous effects of World War II the GATT, with some shortcomings, continues to exert a profound influence on trade between nations.

Economic theory supports maximum trade between countries as the route to world-wide economic development. The optimum allocation of resources (the golden grail of economists) will be achieved when each country is doing what it does best and is trading its goods for the goods of other countries which are also engaged in their most efficient activities. It follows that in order not to impede this process the channels of international trade should be as free of obstructions as possible.

Unfortunately economic principles and the international behaviour of sovereign states frequently are in conflict. It is accepted as the right—indeed the duty—of a state to resist, with force if necessary, any action of another state that seriously threatens its well-being. In the economic area this includes sheltering its industries from the inroads of "unfair foreign competition" by tariffs or other barriers to trade. Resort to such protection has been the basis of long-term trade policy for some notably successful economies, such as the United States. By contrast the United Kingdom enjoyed its most opulent economic development in the half century following 1848 under virtually free trade conditions.

Economic theory and national interest had their most shattering confrontation during the Great Depression, when all countries adopted "beggar-thy-neighbour" trade policies, with devastating results. The unprecedented economic collapse slashed Canada's trade by 50 percent between 1929 and 1931, an experience shared by many other countries. The Depression was prolonged and deepened as trading nations resorted to every possible form of protective trade barrier designed to close their markets to foreign goods. The United States tariff, already at high levels, was raised by 50 percent or more under the Hawley-Smoot changes of 1930. In retaliation under the Ottawa-Commonwealth Agreements in 1932 tariffs of Commonwealth countries were also raised by approximately 50 percent. European countries replicated these actions, in an effort to save as much of the home market as possible for their own producers. Tariffs, quotas, and exchange controls all contributed to the strangulation of the exchange of goods on world markets.

The lessons of this disastrous experience were clear. Left to their own counsels countries adopt measures to protect themselves which in the end are self-defeating. The leading trading nations in the thirties were convinced that the world's trade channels must be freed of the depression-born obstructions and steps must be taken to prevent the recurrence of this unhappy experience in the future. The accomplishment of this objective has been one of the great enterprises of the postwar period. The principal instrument used for this purpose has been the General Agreement on Tariffs and Trade (GATT).

Creation of GATT

It is generally recognised that the GATT originated in the conviction of the Roosevelt administration, elected in 1933, that the restoration of international trade flows would make a major contribution toward ending the Depression. This goal could be most easily and quickly achieved by tariff-reducing treaties between countries. But the Administration had first to obtain from the Congress broad authority to carry out this purpose. In this Cordell Hull, the U.S. Secretary of State, played a leading role, and persuaded the Congress to pass the Reciprocal Trade Agreements Act of 1934. This legislation marked an historic turning point in U.S. tariff policy, under which tariff rates had been maintained at high protectionist levels, with few breaks, since the early 1860s. It gave the Administration authority to enter into tariff agreements to reduce rates by 50 percent from the level of the Tariff Act of 1930.

Canada was among the first to respond to the opportunity presented by the legislation. Following up an initiative that had been taken by R.B. Bennett's government, the newly elected W.L. Mackenzie King, on returning to office in October 1935, gave high priority to the conclusion of an agreement with the United States. By keeping its provisions simple a treaty was negotiated by Hull and King in a few weeks, late in 1935, the first in the seventy years since the termination of the Reciprocity Treaty in 1866. In 1938, in what amounted almost to triangular negotiations, important new agreements were entered into between the United States, Canada, and the United Kingdom. In the opinion of one of the leading participants this series provided the model for later multilateral rounds under the GATT.[30.1]

World War II interrupted further treaty-making, but did not deter the United States from promoting its long-range goal of freeing up international trade. At its insistence the Atlantic Charter of 1941 contained a commitment to a multilateral non-discriminatory postwar trade system. Countries receiving aid under Lend-lease were required to pledge themselves to eliminate "all forms of discriminatory treatment in international commerce, and to the reduction of tariffs and other trade barriers . . ." The theme was pursued at meetings of trading countries in London and Washington in 1943 and 1944, in which Canadian representatives took an active part. In December 1945, after the end of active hostilities, the United States quickly took the initiative by issuing to the leading trading nations of the world a document known as "A Proposal for Expansion of World

---

[30.1] Dana Wilgress, *Memoirs* (Toronto: Ryerson Press, 1967).

Trade and Employment." The proposal was that under the aegis of the United Nations a permanent body should be established to be known as the International Trade Organization. Its charter would provide a code for the conduct of commercial policy, commodity policy, restrictive business practices, employment, and development. With the United Kingdom giving support, the United Nations appointed a Preparatory Committee to draft a charter.

This draft was published by the United Nations in late 1946, and after further revisions during 1947 it was submitted to a large World Trade Conference held in Havana, Cuba in the following winter. The conference adopted the proposal (which thus became known as the Havana Charter) and recommended it for implementation by world governments. However adoption became a virtual deadletter when the U.S. Congress itself refused enactment. Other governments also found its provisions too restrictive, particularly in the light of the more activist role that was being foreseen for government following the war. This result disappointed sponsors of the Charter but was not fatal to the main objective. As an interim measure to permit negotiation of treaties prior to adoption of the Charter a Conference in Geneva in 1947 borrowed the more acceptable (and probably more workable) of its provisions and embodied them in a document to be known as the General Agreement on Tariffs and Trade. This Agreement, commonly referred to as GATT, became the centrepiece of postwar trade negotiations.

The Agreement

Much has been written about the document itself, which by the 1980s has become quite complex. The following brief description will be sufficient for present purposes.

The General Agreement itself consists of thirty-eight Articles, divided into four Parts. Part I contains the first two Articles, which set out the basic most-favoured-nation (MFN) rules and govern the application of the tariff rates established under GATT negotiations; these Articles can only be amended by unanimous agreement of all members. Part II contains twenty-one Articles governing the use of particular trade-policy measures and practices. The Part-II Articles can be amended by a two-thirds vote, but amendments are effective only to members that accept them. Part III, with thirteen Articles, deals mainly with procedural matters. Part IV contains three new Articles which were added in the mid-1960s to deal with the special trade interests of developing countries.[30.2]

The main terms are set out in some of the early Articles. Article I states that all provisions of the agreements negotiated between individual countries will apply on a non-discriminatory and most-favoured-nation basis to

---

all other countries. Numerous exceptions have been granted to this rule—for example, to continue tariff concessions in existence in 1939, to allow countries to form customs unions, to make special rules for trade in textile products, for limited discrimination for balance of payments purposes, and for other purposes. Other major provisions guarantee treatment no less favourable than national treatment for imports, establish the basis for customs valuation, prohibit quantitative restrictions on imports (with several exceptions), deal with the use of subsidies, countervailing duties, and dumping duties, and cover safeguards, state trading, and disputes settlement.

The significance of these and other related provisions will become clearer in later pages as specific examples of GATT activities are reviewed. At this point it is sufficient to say that the Agreement is considerably more than an instrument for achieving multilateral reductions in tariffs. Many of the commercial principles and rules that were to be in the Charter have since had their counterpart in the Agreement. In effect it has become a form of commercial code, capable of elaboration and expansion to meet unforeseen demands. In addition to the negotiation of tariff changes this process of elaboration has taken place at conferences which came to be known as Rounds. There had been seven of these to 1986.

The Rounds—Some Governing Conditions

Breaking With History

The most impressive aspect of the whole postwar realignment of international trade, in which GATT has played a central role, is that for many countries it forced the abandonment of historic policies of very long standing. The turnabout in Canada's relations with the United States and the United Kingdom are dramatic examples. For three-quarters of a century Canada and the United States faced each other across highly protective tariff walls in which there were openings only for materials, produce, or equipment—entrance of which happened to serve the national objectives of the receiving country. Through the trade agreements of 1935 and 1938 and the following seven GATT rounds both countries have travelled a long way from the historic policies. The two economies are by no means completely open to each other, but they are more open than at any time in the past century. Changes in Canada's relations with the United Kingdom have been equally dramatic. From 1846 onward the United Kingdom followed virtually a free trade policy, leaving the Commonwealth countries to fend for themselves. Canada attempted to maintain the trade connection by instituting the British Preferential Tariff in 1898, which in time offered reduced rates for imports from all Commonwealth countries. The Commonwealth preference system provided the basis for the Ottawa Agreements of 1932, when the United Kingdom abandoned free trade for high tariffs against non-Empire countries. Until the mid-forties Canada's trade was about equally divided between the United Kingdom and the United States, but this balance has rapidly shifted to a one-quarter:three-quarters ratio in favour of the United States. While the U.K. market is still important to Canada the traditional close relationship has greatly altered, particularly since the accession of the United Kingdom to the Common Market.

The Difficult United States Congress

The United States was the dominant power following World War II. Its Marshall Plan for Europe had established it as the benefactor and guide of the war-torn countries, and it directed massive efforts to achieving economic and political union in Europe as quickly as possible. Despite this, one of the main uncertainties in all the GATT rounds was the role that the United States would play. The main U.S. actor, the President, could only negotiate under authority given him by the Congress, and Congressional cooperation was grudging and unpredictable. The Reciprocal Trade Agreements Act expired in 1944 and a successor Act gave the President authority to reduce rates by 50 percent from the 1945 level. This authority was used to negotiate the opening agreements under GATT, but was then renewed for only one year at a time. Despite repeated requests from the President for more negotiating room he continued to be limited to 50 percent of the 1945 rates. By the early 1950s some U.S. rates had been reduced by 75 percent from the 1930 level, and the room for further drops was virtually exhausted. This uncertainty over the actions of the U.S. Congress prevailed throughout the postwar period. And so dominant was the position of the United States that the nature and length of the authority given would determine the pattern of negotiations during the round for all other countries. Small wonder that as the countries of the trading world regained economic momentum and greater independence they were frequently restive with the delays and frustrations caused by the United States Congress.

European Common Market

The birth of the Common Market in 1959 was a momentous event for Europe and for the GATT. During the 15 years following the end of World War II European countries had repaired their physical plant and with the encouragement of the United States were slowly moving toward a more unified political and economic system. The Organization for European Economic Cooperation (a loose grouping largely required for administration of the Marshall and similar joint programs) was succeeded in 1957 by the OECD, the Organization for Economic Development. The OECD had much broader objectives and included Canada and the United States as members.

The first step toward industrial integration in Europe was the formation of the European Steel and Coal Community. This included six countries— France, West Germany, Italy, and the Benelux countries—Belgium, the Netherlands and Luxembourg. There followed the proposal in 1955 that the common market in steel and coal be extended to all economic activity; specifically, that a customs union be established for external trade, that all barriers to internal trade be removed, and that among the six there be harmonization of taxation, freedom of movement of labour and capital, a common agricultural policy, and various other policies and institutions for collective action.

The United Kingdom and the remaining European countries made a counter-proposal for a less ambitious Free Trade Area, of which the Common Market could be a part. This proposal was rejected, and in March 1957, the six countries signed the Treaty of Rome, to create the European Economic Community, (EEC or the Common Market). The process of internal tariff reduction began on January 1, 1958, and was to be completed over the following decade. Simultaneously the external tariffs were being brought to a common base, taken as the arithmetical average of their individual customs duties in 1957.

Under a treaty signed in 1959 the other European countries—Austria, Denmark, Norway, Portugal, Sweden, Switzerland, and the United Kingdom—formed the European Free Trade Area (EFTA), under which they agreed to eliminate tariff barriers among themselves, but they would retain their own external tariffs against others. The process of tariff adjustment began in 1960, and was completed in 1966. A feature common to both EEC and EFTA is that tariff reductions applied only to industrial goods; tariffs on agricultural products were excluded. In both areas there was an immediate and phenomenal increase in trade. This was aided as well by the return to external convertibility of the main European currencies in 1958.

The EEC has become the largest trading area in the world. Its advent exerted a profound influence on trade relations and tariff negotiations under the GATT. It also set the pattern for many other free-trade areas, most of which were formed in the early sixties.

The New Industrial Countries

The rise of new industrial powers, such as Japan, Taiwan, South Korea and Hong Kong, had not been contemplated in the planning stages of GATT. In fact in 1947 Japan was catalogued among the less developed countries. The ability of these economies to produce manufactured goods of excellent quality at low prices precipitated some of the most controversial issues in the history of GATT, even in that citadel of capitalist enterprise, the automobile industry.

The Less Developed Countries

The accession to the United Nations Assembly of dozens of former colonies on achieving the status of sovereign powers has brought an entirely new influence to bear on GATT negotiations. The founding group was a fairly close-knit collection of industrialized capitalist countries intent mainly on trading with each other on the most favourable possible basis. The aggressive demands of new members of United Nations for a place in the international trading sphere, and for much help in other ways, has introduced unforeseen strains and stresses.

The Administrative Challenge

The actual conduct of a round of negotiations posed a massive administrative task. In principle each country attended in order to bargain with every other country, and the GATT secretariat theoretically was required to schedule meetings between up to one hundred countries. In fact the process started by obtaining from each country a list of the items on which it wished to negotiate and those on which it did not, and then providing all the other countries with those lists. In practice therefore not all countries needed to negotiate with every other country, so that the numbers were greatly reduced. In addition the non-discrimination and most-favoured-nation principles, by automatically extending all rate changes to all other countries, also eliminated many negotiations that otherwise would have been necessary.

Another administrative problem was communications between the home country and the negotiating team. In Canada, as an example, the agencies needing to be kept in very close touch included the federal cabinet and several federal departments and bureaus, any provincial government that had interests at stake, and various trade and industry associations. In addition there were the media and the general public. Several methods were followed for serving all these interests, and some were more successful than others. Communications during the Tokyo Round were regarded as the most satisfactory so far.[30.3]

World Monetary Crises

The recurrent monetary crises of the postwar period were extremely disruptive for international trade. Canada, for example, engaged in negotiating its first GATT agreements at Geneva in 1947 at a time when, because of a foreign exchange crisis, it was imposing additional taxes and quota restrictions on imported products under the Emergency Foreign Exchange Conservation Act.

A full recounting of international trade developments in the postwar years would therefore include the efforts to establish a systematic process for dealing with monetary issues through the International Monetary Fund and other organizations. As Wynne Plumptre said in his *Three Decades of Decision*, "It is useless to establish international rules governing (for example) tariffs or dumping duties or import restrictions if countries remain free to juggle their exchange rates or to impose restrictions on the release of foreign exchange to pay for imports."[30.4] The truth of this statement is fully acknowledged, but the monetary side must be passed over here in the interests of the main study.

[30.3] Gilbert R. Winham, "Bureaucratic Politics and Canadian Trade Negotiation" (Winter 1979-80) *International Journal*, 64-89.

[30.4] A.F.W. Plumptre, *Three Decades of Decision* (Toronto: McClelland and Stewart Ltd., 1977), 38.

The Human Factor

GATT rounds have made the reputation of several country representatives. The Canadian government has always enlisted some of its most experienced and talented minds for these tough bargaining sessions, and veteran negotiators have confirmed their reputations and young men have made theirs at these meetings. The uniqueness of the experience and the high stakes at issue have created a brotherhood among those who experienced it. This is particularly true of survivors of the early rounds. A good deal of nostalgia is involved; nothing has been as good since. See for example the reflections of Sidney Golt, a former member of the British team.[30.5]

GATT as an Institution

Although less exalted than the IMF and the World Bank, which were blessed with a more august paternity, from its fairly humble origins the GATT developed a full-time permanent structure over the last quarter century. This includes the usual United Nations complement of a building of its own in Geneva and a staff of over three hundred. For major policy purposes, meetings are held of ministers of the trading countries. The key senior committees are the Council of Representatives, the Committee of Contracting Parties, and the Consultative Group of Eighteen. In addition numerous special committees or councils have been established, such as the Balance of Payments Committee, the Trade and Development Committee, and the Committee on Safeguards. There are also many committees and panels that monitor, study, or enforce special provisions of the General Agreement or supplementary arrangements. The latter have become increasingly important with the new procedures for adjudication of non-tariff barriers following the Tokyo Round.

Making It Work—The Seven Rounds

Of the seven rounds of GATT five are named after a city and two after individuals, the latter both American. The situs names appears to have reflected diplomacy rather than locale, as all the effective work of GATT is centred in Geneva, where the main office and secretariat are located and the principal meetings are held. The rounds were as follows: Geneva, Switzerland, 1947; Annecy, France, 1949; Torquay, England, 1950-51; Geneva, 1955-56; Dillon, 1961-62; Kennedy, 1964-67; Tokyo, 1973-79. A rough measure of the expanding scale of these sessions is given by the number of contracting parties at the rounds—23 in 1947; 99 in 1979. In addition some 30 developing countries qualify without formal membership pending final decision as to their commercial policy. Some of the Eastern bloc countries (Czechoslovakia, Hungary, Poland, and Romania) have joined GATT but neither Russia nor China, both members of United Nations, have done so.

[30.5] Sidney Golt, *The GATT Negotiations, 1973-75: A Guide to the Issues* (London: British-North American Committee, 1974), 1-2.

The first five agreements, except for their multilateral application, were much in the style of prewar item-by-item trade negotiations. A new general approach involving a reduction measured by an overall percentage was adopted for the Kennedy Round and followed in the Tokyo Round. Details of individual rounds follow.

Geneva, 1947

Following preparations and negotiations extending over a two-year period agreements were signed between 23 countries on October 30, 1947. This event was described at the time as the most comprehensive and far-reaching step ever taken between the world's trading nations. Almost one-half of total world imports was affected. The agreement was for a term of three years, but subject to extension beyond that time with a right of termination on six months' notice. The effective date for the changes was January 1, 1948; Canada and a few other countries achieved this but most straggled in over the following months. Each country's commitments are listed in a separate schedule. Canada's list was in Schedule V. It contained 1,050 items or sub-items, of which 590 provided reductions below existing rates and 460 bound or consolidated rates. Canada obtained concessions from other countries on wheat, wheat flour, coarse grains, cattle, seed potatoes, turnips, seeds, apples, berries, dairy products, eggs, cheese, butter, miscellaneous other agricultural products, liquors, cod fillets and other fishery products, lumber, base metals, non-metallic minerals, chemicals, and certain manufactured goods. Canadian authorities appear to have been well pleased with the agreement, and expressed satisfaction with the substantial increase in exports, which was largely attributed to the GATT arrangements.

Annecy, 1949

As an interim step between meetings on the main agreement a session was held at Annecy, France in 1949 for negotiations with a group of countries that had not signed up in 1947. Eleven countries accepted invitations to attend and ten completed negotiations and became signatories. Among the new members were Denmark, Finland, Greece, Italy and Sweden, a significant expansion of the group. Canada carried on extensive negotiations with both old and new members and gained further concessions. The revised list with the United States included certain bars and forgings, wood and paper products, butter, Oka cheese, hides and leather manufactures, granite and limestone, and other minor products. In general these changes came into effect on January 1, 1950.

During this period Canada continued its restrictions on imports under the Emergency Foreign Exchange Conservation Act of November 1947. These were being retained, according to the official explanation, until foreign exchange reserves had reached a level where the country could "face the future with confidence." The quotas imposed under the Act were increased in the March 1949 budget, and were gradually withdrawn in following years.

Torquay, England, 1950-51

The conference at Torquay was held in anticipation of the approaching expiry of the original agreement on January 1, 1951. There were high expectations throughout the Western world for further concessions from the United States, then its main source of growth. The Canadian Minister of Finance expressed such hopes in his Budget Speech of March 1950: "I believe that in the present conditions of unbalanced world trade, the success of the Torquay Conference will depend largely on the leadership given by the United States. If the United States is prepared to make significant tariff reductions, I am confident that these coming trade talks will make an important contribution to the restoration of a saner trading world." He went on to give the assurance that "We in Canada are not unmindful of our own responsibility, and I can say that we will take the opportunity to consider appropriate adjustments in our customs tariff which should contribute to a better balance in our trade with the United States, the sterling area and Western Europe."

The results accomplished at Torquay hardly met these high expectations. Negotiations followed the general pattern of previous meetings and tariff changes were made, but the notable feature of the round was the addition of several new members. These were Austria, Korea, Peru, the Phillipines, Turkey, and West Germany. The last was a strategic addition, as a result of which some changes of importance to Germany were made by the United States, which were automatically extended to all other signatories under the multilateral principle. The addition of further commodities in negotiations as a result of expansion of the membership substantially extended the scope of the agreement.

Geneva Round, 1955-56

This was a routine round required by the accession of Japan to the GATT. As additional countries joined the GATT it became necessary to negotiate new agreements covering conditions of trade with them. United States' authority was strictly limited by this stage, and gave little chance for further negotiations.

The Dillon Round, 1960-62

As it was the first round of negotiations following the formation in 1959 of the European Economic Community, probably more was expected of this meeting than actually transpired. A conference was held in Geneva between September 1960 and July 1962, in two phases. The first, completed by May 1961, was devoted to renegotiating previously established tariff rates, chiefly for Benelux and Germany, which required adjustment as a result of adoption of the Common External Tariff by the EEC countries in 1959. The second phase—known as the Dillon Round—took the traditional form of a GATT conference devoted to negotiation of tariff changes, in this instance between 28 countries. Concessions were granted on 4,000 items representing more than $5 billion in world trade. The Canadian Minister of Trade and

Commerce was pleased to report that Canada had received provisional assurances of access to the new EEC for fisheries products, wood and wood products, base metals, minerals and chemicals, and miscellaneous other products totalling nearly $250 million of Canadian trade. He also had been assured of access for Canadian wheat and other agricultural items pending development by the EEC of its agricultural policy. While these assurances were welcome to Canada, its main concern was for continuing access to the British market, at this time beclouded by United Kingdom membership in the EFTA and by the imminent possibility of its admission to the Common Market.

The Minister of Finance, in his budget speech of June 1961, reflected this strong concern in the following statement: "Moreover, the historic right of commonwealth free access to the United Kingdom market for agricultural products, industrial material and most manufactured goods is the keystone of the commonwealth trading system. Not only for economic reasons, but for political as well, we would not wish to see this system abandoned."

Following the Dillon Round observers began to feel that the scope for further negotiations was quite limited. At this point Sidney Golt saw little hope. "By the end of the 'Dillon Round' in 1962, the process was beginning to run out of steam; indeed had gone a long way on this road." A new dramatic act on the part of the United States government was needed to give a fresh start.

The Kennedy Round, 1964-67

A newly elected Democratic President, John F. Kennedy, provided the momentum by persuading the Congress to pass the Trade Expansion Act of 1962. He argued for power to come to grips with the newly formed Common Market and stressed the necessity for maintaining close economic relations with Europe in order to strengthen the Atlantic Community. A new approach, and authority to implement it, would be required for this goal.

The Trade Expansion Act passed by the Congress appeared to fill the bill. The general basis for negotiation under the Act was a reduction of 50 percent across the board from current tariff levels, to be phased in over a five-year period. But there were other provisions of a much more radical character. Where the combined U.S. and EEC exports of a commodity group were 80 percent or more of free-world total trade in that commodity (the dominant supplier) tariff cuts of up to 100 percent could be made. U.S. tariff rates of less than 5 percent could be eliminated entirely. Tariffs on tropical agricultural and forest products could be completely eliminated if EEC would reciprocate. It was also part of the U.S. approach to urge negotiations on non-tariff barriers and agricultural products.

American hopes rode heavily on the "dominant supplier" proposal. In this they suffered early disappointment. Harry Johnson, a well-qualified observer, explained the outcome as follows: "The dominant supplier authority was, however, predicated on the expectation that Britain would be admitted to membership in the Common Market, as the 'Grand Design' of

President Kennedy's policy towards Europe intended her to be. France's rejection of Britain's application for membership in the Common Market knocked the lynch-pin out of the Trade Expansion Act, by reducing the eligible commodity groups from perhaps twenty-five to two (depending on the interpretation)—vegetable oils and aircraft, neither of which offers scope for a vast liberalization of trade . . . The United States was therefore obliged to embark on the Kennedy Round on the basis of the 50 percent general authority for tariff cutting.''[30.6]

Even this disappointment was not the end. To quote Johnson again:

At the beginning of the preparations for the Kennedy Round early in 1963, the French pressed the view that the objective of negotiations should be, not an equal percentage reduction of tariff rates, but a rationalization of tariff structures around lower rates, "rationality" consisting of a low rate generally applicable to raw materials, a higher rate generally applicable to semi-manufactured goods, and a still higher rate generally applicable to finished manufactures . . . Subsequently, the French made issue of the fact that the U.S. tariff rates, though they average somewhat higher or lower than Common Market tariff rates depending on what average is used, vary substantially more from item to item, and claimed that equal percentage reductions in these rates would be unfair to the Common Market . . . the tariff disparity issue, however, soon shifted to concern about disparities between tariff rates levied by different countries on the same commodity, and a claim that the lower-tariff country should not have to cut its tariff by as much as the high-tariff country . . . A compromise formula was arrived at, according to which a disparity was defined as a tariff rate in one country more than double that in the other and above it by ten percentage points, and in case of such disparity the lower-tariff country is obliged to cut its tariff by only 25 percent.[30.7]

His conclusion was that "the main objective of the Trade Expansion Act—completely free trade in a large sector of industrial products between Europe and the United States—had been frustrated by the rejection of British entry into the Common Market, and the bargaining had instead been concerned with partial tariff reductions of the type achieved through previous rounds of GATT negotiations . . .''[30.8]

Despite these difficulties the Kennedy Round tariff changes were undoubtedly on a scale far larger than any previous round. Over 50 countries, including Japan, and 30 less developed countries, took part in the negotiations. The Canadian Minister of Trade and Commerce described these as the "largest trade negotiations ever in terms of participants, in terms of world trade coverage, and in terms of scope and depth of tariff

---

[30.6] Harry G. Johnson, *The World Economy at the Crossroads* (Montreal: Private Planning Association of Canada, 1965), 35.

[30.7] Ibid., at 35-36.

[30.8] Ibid., at 37.

reduction. Some $45 billion of world trade has been affected and major participating countries are making tariff cuts on 70 per cent of their dutiable industrial imports, of which some two-thirds will be reductions of 50 per cent or more.''

The agreements were formally signed on June 30, 1967, to be effective on January 1, 1968, with many of the changes being phased in over a period of four years. It is of incidental interest that although the main countries negotiated on the basis of an across-the-board percentage reduction, Canada excused itself from this procedure. The Minister of Finance explained in his Budget Speech of March 1964, that "Our trading partners have recognized that such a system would not be appropriate for countries such as Canada." This simple explanation leaves much to be clarified, but apparently was sufficient for the other GATT signatories. A more detailed study of the effect of the Kennedy Round on the Canadian tariff is given in a recent Economic Council discussion paper.[30.9]

An official Canadian release listed, along with "unprecedented and farreaching tariff reductions," a new Anti-Dumping code and special measures to reduce tariffs on goods from less developed countries without full reciprocity. Discussions of agricultural policy with the Common Market produced no results at this meeting. There will be further comment on all these matters later.

The Tokyo Round, 1973-79

The last, and from many perspectives the most precarious of the GATT rounds, was the seventh. Drastic changes in the international situation had taken place since the Kennedy Round. The United States had lost its dominant world role and had been forced to take emergency action in 1971 to cope with a growing balance of payments deficit. The Vietnam war had undermined American financial and spiritual resources. Inflation was becoming a world problem, and was to worsen as the decade of the seventies wore on. The sharp rise in oil prices in 1973 and again in 1978 threw the balance of world trade and payments, fragile enough beforehand, into chaos. The United Kingdom had finally gained admission to the Common Market (February 1973), and the EEC had become an even stronger, and in many ways more threatening, presence particularly for countries wishing to trade in agricultural products. Japan, closely followed by Taiwan, Korea, and Hong Kong, had assumed commanding positions in industrial production and trade. The less developed countries were strident in their demands for more concessions from the rest of the world, and through their dominance of the United Nations Assembly were using that organization to advance their cause. Protectionist sentiment was increasing in most countries, and was emerging mainly in the form of non-tariff barriers—quotas,

---

[30.9] John R. Baldwin and Paul K. Gorecki, *The Determinants of the Canadian Tariff Structure Before and After the Kennedy Round: 1966-70.* Discussion Paper No. 280 (Ottawa: Economic Council of Canada, 1985).

export financing aids, technical obstructions, and other forms of market influence.

With this background the likelihood of making any progress at all seemed very remote. However, at the end the longest of the GATT rounds (1973 to 1979), agreement was reached not only on substantial tariff concessions but as well some progress was made on several much more contentious issues.

To dispose first of the tariff changes. In the beginning the conference showed no progress at all. At an opening meeting of 99 ministers of trading countries in Tokyo in September 1973, a statement of intentions was drawn up and issued. But then almost nothing further happened for two years. The original plan was that a Trade Negotiating Committee would begin work in November 1973, and conclude by 1975, but several circumstances delayed this schedule. Neither of the main parties, the United States and the Common Market, was prepared to proceed immediately. The Market authorities had not yet agreed on an approach to the negotiations, and their deliberations were complicated by the recent accession of the United Kingdom to membership in the EEC. However a Directive was finally prepared and given to the EEC negotiators early in 1975. Meanwhile the United States Congress was undergoing its usual protracted process of passing President Nixon's Trade Reform Bill.

Introduced in 1973, it became law two years later. But this was not the end of the American troubles. In the uncertainties following the Watergate scandal the Ford Administration did not feel competent to undertake serious international negotiations, and these were left until a new Administration under President James Carter came to power in January 1977. By mid-year the new Administration had resumed proceedings under the Trade Reform legislation. As usual Congress had imposed an expiry date, which effectively required termination of negotiations by March 1979, less than two years away. During this lapse of over three and one-half years the secretariat and committees of GATT made what preparations were possible in the circumstances. The usual request and offer lists were submitted and substantial progress was made in developing positions on some of the larger non-tariff issues on the agenda. At meetings of the principal contracting parties a commitment to the original objectives of the round were reaffirmed, and an accelerated schedule drawn up.

The next step was to agree on a basis for the tariff negotiations—a "working hypothesis." The pressure for tariff harmonization had resumed in even more complex form. Both the American and Common Market original proposals involved higher percentage cuts for the highest rates, with a declining scale for lower rates, but a stalemate developed between the two sides on details. This was broken by adoption of a compromise formula suggested by the Swiss, under which the actual rate of reduction was estimated to be in the range of 35 to 45 percent.

After a delay of nearly five years, negotiations finally moved very quickly, and were substantially terminated by April 1979. Ninety-nine countries had taken part, including GATT and non-GATT members, representing nine-tenths of world exports. Tariff concessions on an unprecedented scale were adopted. Information issued by GATT gave the total trade affected by the agreements at $155 billion. Of a total of $141 billion of trade of developed countries under negotiation, $127 billion was in industrial products and $14 billion was in agricultural. It was estimated that the weighted average tariffs on industrial products would decline from 7.0 to 4.7 percent, or a reduction of tariff revenues of 34 percent. Significant reductions were also made for some agricultural products and for imports from less developed countries.

The Swiss formula was said to have achieved a substantial harmonizing effect, with considerable reduction in differences in national tariff levels.[30.10] Concessions were to be phased in over a period of eight years, commencing on January 1, 1980.

A Canadian official press release stated that "the results, from Canada's point of view, represent a significant step forward in dealing with non-tariff as well as tariff barriers . . . The average weighted depth of tariff cut on Canadian exports to the United States, the European Community and Japan taken together will be close to 40 percent. The average reduction in the Canadian tariff will be comparable . . . Of particular importance for Canada, a number of U.S. tariffs covering an important proportion of Canadian exports will be eliminated. Overall, well over 90 percent of current Canadian exports will enter at tariff rates of 5 percent or less and close to 80 percent will be duty free, taking account of trade under the Automotive Agreement . . . In the case of Canadian tariffs, the average rate of industrial imports will be reduced to between 9 and 10 percent . . . like other participants, Canada has made no reductions—or comparatively small reductions—in the level of Canadian tariffs on such items as textiles, clothing, footwear and ships."

The *Review of Canada's Trade Policy*, a 1983 publication of the Department of External Affairs, gave further details:

Once these reductions are fully implemented, tariffs on most manufactured goods in the EEC and Japan will be in the order of 5 to 7 percent, while raw materials will, with some exceptions, enter these markets free of duty or at low rates . . . for the United States, the average tariffs on manufactured goods will be in the area of 4 percent, although some products such as certain chemicals, textiles and footwear will continue to enter at much higher rates . . . Of particular importance for Canada, a number of US tariffs covering an important proportion of Canadian products such as paper products and machinery will be eliminated. Overall, well over 90 percent of current Canadian exports will be duty free, taking account of trade under the Automotive Agreement . . .

[30.10] Director-General, GATT, *The Tokyo Round of Multilateral Trade Negotiations: Supplementary Report* (Geneva: The Secretariat, 1980), 6.

On the agricultural side, important concessions were exchanged with Canada's major trading partners covering over $1 billion worth of Canadian exports. Of particular significance were the breadth and depth of the concessions obtained from the United States . . . Important foreign concessions were gained for certain fish products of benefit to both East Coast and West Coast producers, although these did not fully satisfy Canadian objectives. Finally, improved access has been obtained for Canadian whiskey in the United States, European and Japanese markets.[30.11]

An indication of the industries being spared tariff reductions was given in a U.S. study of reductions that fell short of those called for by the Swiss formula. A Background Paper prepared by the Congressional Budget Office of the U.S. Congress showed shortfalls by categories; in the United States, for example, these categories were textiles, apparel, leather products (especially footwear), and some stone, clay, and glass products. In the EEC only one minor category met the called-for reduction. The Swiss role appears to have been that of starter rather than pace-setter, but as such they still performed an essential role.[30.12]

At the Tokyo Round Canada proposed that negotiations be on a sectoral basis, but this was not accepted by the conference. However, some progress was made by Canada in applying this concept in its own negotiations. To quote the *Review*:

One of Canada's major objectives at the Tokyo Round of multilateral trade negotiations was the reduction of foreign trade barriers in resource-based products, specifically in the non-ferrous metals and forest product sectors. For this purpose Canada proposed sector negotiations aimed at eliminating or reducing to the greatest extent possible all the barriers that affect trade in the various forms of a particular resource product . . . Although many of our trading partners were not prepared to cut tariffs in these sectors to the extent proposed by Canada, a number of Canada's objectives for these sectors were achieved. The US tariff reductions in forest products, in effect, fully responded to the tariff-cutting component of the Canadian proposals. In addition, the USA made major concessions of importance to Canada which resulted in the reduction of tariff escalation on more highly processed non-ferrous metal products. In other major markets, the Tokyo Round resulted in some significant reductions in effective tariff protection accorded to processing activities, but left intact other trade barriers to upgrading of Canadian resources prior to export.[30.13]

[30.11] Canada, Department of External Affairs, *A Review of Canadian Trade Policy: A Background Document to Canadian Policy for the 1980s* (Ottawa: Department of Supply and Services, 1983), 8-9.

[30.12] Congress of the United States, *U.S. Trade Policy and the Tokyo Round of Multilateral Trade Negotiations* (Washington, D.C.: Congressional Budget Office, 1979), 12-14.

[30.13] Supra footnote 30.10, at 48-49.

Table 30.1   Canada's Tariff Levels, 1932-1985

Year	Ratio of duty collected to total imports		Ratio of duty collected to dutiable imports		Percent of imports free of duty	
	All countries	United States	All countries	United States	All countries	United States
	percent					
1932.............	19.4	—	30.0	—	35.1	36.6
1935.............	15.4	—	27.4	—	38.8	39.7
1940.............	13.6	13.0	23.9	20.3	43.0	35.9
1945.............	11.1	11.3	21.1	19.3	39.6	41.5
1950.............	8.8	9.2	17.1	16.3	48.1	43.6
1955.............	10.5	10.8	18.2	17.3	42.2	37.5
1960.............	9.7	10.2	17.7	17.2	44.4	40.4
1965.............	8.4	8.0	16.5	16.2	49.4	51.0
1970.............	6.4	5.2	15.2	14.4	57.6	63.8
1975.............	5.6	5.1	15.0	14.3	62.6	64.3
1976.............	5.5	5.2	15.0	14.6	63.3	64.2
1977.............	5.4	5.0	15.2	14.8	64.4	66.4
1978.............	5.1	4.5	14.4	14.2	64.6	67.9
1979.............	4.9	4.3	14.3	14.2	66.5	69.5
1980.............	4.4	4.0	13.8	13.6	68.1	70.2
1981.............	4.4	4.0	13.2	12.8	66.3	68.8
1982.............	4.4	4.1	13.0	12.2	66.1	70.0
1983.............	4.4	3.4	12.7	11.7	65.0	71.3
1984.............	4.1	3.1	11.9	10.8	65.5	71.3
1985.............	3.9	2.8	11.5	10.4	66.2	72.9

Source: *Historical Statistics of Canada*; Statistics Canada, catalogue 65-203.

The Tokyo Round made a huge dent in tariff levels. While there remained room for further cuts in strategic areas world tariffs were so reduced that some experts described them as now being only a nuisance. And this position had some official support. In the *Review* there appeared the following: "Successive rounds of tariff negotiations have reduced tariffs to such levels that for many sectors they are no longer major impediments to access to our industrialized trading partners' markets. Some sensitive areas, e.g., textiles, footwear and clothing, still enjoy relatively high tariff protection, but for many industrial goods the average tariffs of our major partners (the USA, the European Community, and Japan) are now or soon will be at levels where they can no longer be considered as a serious obstacle to the efficient development of the Canadian economy."[30.14] In short, the main obstacles to foreign trade now lie in other areas.

Effect on Canada's Tariff Levels

The overall impact of the GATT and other agreements on Canada's tariff levels has been substantial, as illustrated by Table 30.1. A common measure

[30.14] Ibid., at 153.

of tariff weight is the ratio of duties collected to total imports and to dutiable imports. Except for differences over time in the value and nature of imports the results are fairly accurate. Between 1932 and 1985 the ratio for total imports declined from a peak of 19.4 percent to 3.9 percent; on dutiable imports it dropped from 30 percent in 1932 to 11.5 percent in 1985. The corresponding ratio for imports from the United States showed an even greater decline, standing respectively at 2.8 percent for all imports and 10.4 percent for dutiable imports in 1985.

The ratio of duty to the value of dutiable imports must be treated with some caution; if, for example, only 5 percent of trade was dutiable and the rate on that trade was very high, say 50 percent, then the ratio given in that column would also be 50 percent and would be a completely misleading index of the general tariff weight imposed by the country concerned. An equally relevant index therefore is the proportion of the import trade that is completely free of duty. Here the change is quite remarkable. Over the half-century period for total imports the ratio rose from about one-third to two-thirds; nearly three-quarters of imports from the United States entered Canada free of duty in 1985. It is only on the one-quarter of dutiable U.S. imports therefore that tariff rates averaging around 10 percent were applied.

31
Non-tariff Barriers and Other Problems

Numerous policies and programs, other than tariffs, have a direct or indirect influence on foreign trade. Most of these fall under the general heading of non-tariff barriers, and include quotas, subsidies, voluntary export restraint agreements, and various technical and other restrictions that delay or inhibit trade. Many domestic programs now have an indirect bearing on foreign trade by subsidization of industries subject to foreign competition or creation of market conditions which make it difficult or impossible for foreign produced goods to compete.

That these issues still required attention—indeed have required constant and drastic attention for two decades—was completely contrary to the original GATT design. The Agreement was categorical in its condemnation of quotas and similar restrictions. Article XI stated that "no restrictions other than duties, taxes or other charges, whether made effective through quotas, import or export licenses or other measures, shall be instituted or maintained by any contracting party." Any existing non-tariff restrictions were to be immediately abolished. The one exception from this iron rule in the 1947 Agreement was permission to use quotas and similar non-tariff restrictions for balance of payment emergencies, and then for only the shortest possible period.

Textiles—the Near Nemesis

It was the inundation of cheap textiles, mainly from Japan, in the late fifites that forced countries to take whatever actions were necessary to save their own industries from being wiped out. All countries so affected adopted emergency measures, whether or not permitted under the GATT. Japan had joined GATT in 1955, but this did not prevent the other members from taking strong steps against Japanese textiles. Japan responded with the pragmatic solution of bilaterial agreements to reduce exports, no doubt with the encouragement of the countries involved. In the late fifties there were twenty such agreements, including one with Canada.

This initial reaction had all taken place outside the GATT, and represented a serious challenge to its basic premises. The alternatives open to GATT were to disregard the development and let it take its own course, with the possibility of a resurgence of uncontrolled protectionism, or to work out an accommodation for it. The latter course was chosen. Action began in 1960. An initial survey was made of the scale of the general problem, which revealed more than 800 uses of non-tariff barriers among GATT members (many of which of course were repetitions of the same type of restriction).

The main problem was to find a formula for regularizing these practices in the future under agreed GATT rules, the immediate issue being textiles.

The first step in this direction was the Decision on the Avoidance of Market Disruption in 1960. This was followed by the Short-Term Arrangement valid for one year following October 1, 1961. This in turn was succeeded by the Long-Term Arrangement Regarding International Trade in Cotton Textiles, which basically extended the previous agreement for the five years beginning October 1, 1962. These arrangements authorized the use of quotas and voluntary export restraint agreements, all under the general rubric of avoidance of market disruption. A final comprehensive document providing long-term arrangements, the Multifibre Arrangement, was adopted in 1973, effective January 1, 1974, for a period of four years.

Canada was among the countries that acted to protect its textile and clothing industries. It was feared that many of the approximately 190,000 jobs in these industries were threatened by low-cost imports, and various forms of protection were established. Tariffs were maintained on competing products at a fairly high level. Under the procedures established by GATT, Voluntary Export Restraint Agreements were entered into with 22 countries to guarantee them at least 37 percent of the Canadian market in return for accepting voluntary agreements. In fact under this regime between 1981 and 1984 the foreign share rose from 31 percent to 43 percent. These country agreements expired in 1985 and were renewed until 1987.

In the late sixties the federal government also took the decision that rationalization was overdue for the industry and to carry this out announced the Textile Policy and established the Textile Board to administer it. The essence of the policy was to provide constant surveillance over the problems of the industry, study the effects of imports, particularly as to the extent of their actual injury or threat of serious injury, to establish criteria for the granting of protection, to support rationalization in favour of the most competitive lines and to grant adjustment assistance, both for workers and for companies, where needed. The textile industry program for the eighties was announced by the government in June 1981. It involved the expenditure of $250 million on industry modernization over a five-year period and continuation of the limitations on textile imports. The Canadian Industrial Renewal Board was established in October 1981, charged with administration of government incentive programs for modernization and renewal of existing plants or alternatively to seek employment for laid-off staff where plants are closed.[31.1] However, the Canadian Industrial Renewal Program expired on March 31, 1986 and has not been renewed.

Despite this program there had been a steady decline in employment and the industry had argued for increased protection, favouring a global quota in place of the individual country restraint agreements. A task force was appointed to chart a future strategy for the industry but gave up in the face of differences of view among branches of the industry. In mid-1986 a policy statement was needed both for the coming trade negotiations and the expiry

---

[31.1]For further details see Caroline Pestieau, *The Canadian Textile Policy: A Sectoral Trade Adjustment Strategy* (Montreal: C.D. Howe Research Institute, 1976).

at the end of July of the GATT Multi-Fibre Arrangement. The policy had to reconcile differences between the textile industry, which favoured restrictions on textile imports, and the garment industry, which wanted free entry for materials but quotas for garments. An additional complication was that textiles came mainly from developed countries and garments from the newly developed world, so that quite different international trade relations were involved.

Some steps, although less dramatic, were taken for non-rubber footwear. To stem the flood of low cost imports a quota was imposed from December 1977 to November 1981 on leather and synthetic footwear; in December 1981 a quota was imposed for synthetic and canvas footwear and in July 1982 was re-imposed for leather shoes. In November 1985, the federal Minister of Trade announced that quotas would be dropped on men's, boys', children's and infants' shoes. Quotas on women's and children's shoes would be phased out over a three-year period.

The irony of this whole development is that simple and cheap forms of textiles, clothing and footwear are the very types of goods that have a logical place in the industry of a developing country. They are needed by the residents of those countries and can easily be produced in quantities sufficient for export. Yet they are also the very products which nearly every advanced country has found it necessary to restrict simply in order to avoid the chaos and distress of having whole industries wiped out. It should be said for Canada, and for several other countries as well, that programs to assist both the industries and their employees to adjust to these radically changed conditions are in place. At the same time it must be conceded that the instances in which countries have succeeded in making a full adjustment are rare.

Non-tariff Restrictions at the Tokyo Round

A distinctive feature of the Tokyo Round was the prolonged consideration given to most of the "non-tariff" issues. This reflected a fear that protectionist pressure was growing, and with tariffs reduced to nominal levels non-tariff restrictions were being imposed. The International Monetary Fund shared this view and expressed its concern in the publication of a study—The Growing Trend to Protectionism. IMF staff papers echoed the same theme. In preparation for the Round the GATT staff made a new survey and compiled a list running to 800 pages and covering 600 measures. These were classified under five headings: government participation in trade and restrictive practices; customs and administrative entry procedures; technical barriers to trade; specific limitations, such as quantitative restrictions, import licensing, export restraints, measures to regulate domestic prices, special charges on imports, and miscellaneous vexations such as prior deposits, border tax adjustments, discriminatory credit restrictions, etc. Almost ten years were devoted during the Tokyo Round to the negotiation or preparation for negotiation of these controversial issues. The main objective throughout was to establish procedures that would allow for consultation and adjudication in place of precipitate retaliatory action.

The elements of a formula developed for this purpose required reporting of a grievance to GATT, consultation with the offending party, an interval for reversal of the offending action, and compensatory action of an agreed kind if the offence was not eliminated. The Tokyo Round also achieved a good deal of clarification of previously vague terms and withdrawal of practices that had been long-standing irritants. The understandings so achieved were embodied in supplementary Agreements (also known as Codes), rather than amendments to the main document. These Codes related to Subsidies and Countervailing Duties, Anti-Dumping, Government Procurement, Customs Valuation, and Standards (technical barriers). Agreements were also negotiated on Import Licensing Procedures, Trade in Civil Aircraft, and Bovine Meat. A Framework for the Conduct of International Trade was also adopted. The following brief comments relate to some of the more significant of these Codes.

Subsidies

Government subsidies that have an influence on international trade can be of two general types—direct subsidies which allow exports to be sold at a lower price than otherwise, or indirect subsidies given for other purposes which have an influence on foreign trade. The former are usually easily identified, although some recent types, such as subsidized financing by government, are less apparent. It is the indirect types that raise the most difficult questions of motivation and definition. Governments now use grants for a wide assortment of social, regional, and economic purposes, and this practice has greatly complicated the identification of those that have an influence on international trade. In the view of some observers government assistance in a variety of forms has now become so prevalent that as an influence on international trade it has succeeded to the role once performed by tariffs.

The original Article of GATT dealing with subsidies (Article XVI) was not a blanket prohibition. It required notification to GATT of any subsidies likely to increase exports or decrease imports; it also provided that an injured party must have an opportunity to consult once serious prejudice had been established. However these general conditions were made more explicit in 1955 when Additional Provisions on Export Subsidies were added to Article XVI. Under these new clauses subsidies on non-primary products were prohibited if they resulted in reducing prices for export below domestic prices. Where this practice had caused, or was threatening to cause, material injury to an industry of another signatory to the Additional Provisions that signatory was entitled to impose countervailing duties on those imports equal to the margin of the subsidy. There was much discontent with this provision. A principal cause was the exclusion of agricultural products.

There was also general dissatisfaction with the automatic imposition of countervailing duties by the United States, without any test of material injury to a U.S. industry, against any manufactured product that had been subsidized in any way by a foreign government. Other shortcomings were that neither form of subsidy was defined in the Agreement, the determination of injury was left to the importing country, and not all members of GATT had signed the Additional Provisions.[31.2]

The issue of subsidies was therefore far from settled. In 1960 some further progress was made. A list of prohibited export subsidies was drawn up and a procedure established to be used by a country claiming "material injury" from subsidized imports from another country. Such a country must first attempt to obtain redress through GATT investigation and appeal procedures, and if its complaint was supported and no corrective action was taken that country was entitled to impose countervailing duties against the subsidized imports from the other country.

This is where the matter stood for a decade, but with growing unease. The OECD became sufficiently concerned that in 1974 it instituted an annual pledge among its members to avoid any further quantitative restraints on trade, a pledge which was adopted permanently in 1980. Concern arose over the general proliferation of grants and subsidies for industrial development and the continued refusal of the United States to cooperate in the rules the GATT signatories were attempting to formulate. The frequent resort to restrictions by the United States stemmed mainly from a legal requirement for the automatic imposition of a countervailing duty once it had been established that a bounty or grant had been provided toward the manufacture, production, or export of goods from a foreign country. This legislation had been on the books before the GATT was drawn up, and therefore was exempt from its requirements.

In 1972 it had been used against Canada in the form of countervailing duties on the import of Michelin tires produced in a subsidized plant in Nova Scotia. There were also other U.S. programs, described later.

The issue was inevitably on the agenda of the Tokyo Round. After much discussion, a general prohibition against the use of any form of subsidy, including domestic subsidies, to stimulate exports or impede imports was affirmed. The 1960 list of prohibited export subsidies was revised and a new list of prohibited domestic subsidies was added. The concept of material injury and the conditions for imposing countervailing duties were clarified. Provision was made for investigation by GATT and, if needed, hearings by a panel before action to impose countervailing duties was taken. The adherence by the United States to this agreement was a landmark of the Tokyo Round. Its legislation was amended to require the finding of injury to U.S. industry, and a new organization, the International Trade Commission, (of which Canadians recently have heard a great deal) was established for this purpose. This action ended the automatic application of countervailing duties, and all countervailing duties that had previously been imposed against Canada were removed as a result.

[31.2]See Caroline Pestieau, *Subsidies and Countervailing Duties: The Negotiating Issues* (Montreal: C.D. Howe Research Institute, 1976), 6-8.

Safeguards

A closely related aspect of GATT is the provision for safeguard action. Article XIX, Emergency Action on Imports of Particular Products, authorizes the use of restrictive measures to block or reduce imports that "cause or threaten serious injury to domestic producers." Before any measures are taken notice must be given the offending country and there must be consultation on the issue. The provision has been the source of much controversy and dissatisfaction in actual application, among other reasons because the rule of non-discrimination, lacking the absolution given for textiles, makes it impractical to act against individual offending countries. Article XIX was given much attention at the Tokyo Round, mainly with a view to revising its wording, but no agreement was reached. The article was left for further study by a committee.

Anti-Dumping Duties

As has been indicated, countervailing duties are the instrument used in the GATT to obtain compensation for injury from subsidized imports. The Agreement also allows protective action to be taken against dumping. Canada instituted its first "anti-dumping duties" as part of its Customs Act as long ago as 1904, and both the United States and the United Kingdom have had long experience in their use. It was inevitable therefore that this form of redress would come under GATT examination very early in its existence.

The most common feature of dumping is the unloading of unusual quantities of goods at prices well below the market price. A typical instance would be a surplus of a perishable fruit or vegetables that would be wasted if not sold. Domestic producers do not take kindly to having their product undersold, and would ask for protection. The dilemma for the authorities in reacting to such a request is that the level of price can seldom be used as the sole criterion of injury. To do so would require imposing defensive duties on all imports at lower than internal prices, and forever cutting off one's consumers from whatever bargains were available on the international market. The issue, therefore, is to determine what imports, based on some prescribed test, bring more injury than benefit to the importing country.

As described by Rodney de C. Grey,[31.3] the original Canadian system had three main characteristics:

1) It was a set of general rules of law.

2) It appeared to be automatic in its application once conditions of dumping had been determined.

3) It applied only when the dumped goods were "of a class or kind made or produced in Canada." The term "produced in Canada" from 1936

[31.3] Rodney de C. Grey, *The Development of the Canadian Anti-Dumping System* (Montreal: Private Planning Association of Canada, 1973), 15-17.

on meant production equal to 10 percent or more of normal Canadian consumption.

The complaint of other countries against this system was that it contained no specific requirement that the dumping had resulted in injury to a Canadian business. The Customs administration gave its decision, probably based largely on the quantity involved and the level of the import price in relation to the domestic price, and if the importer wished to appeal he did so through the ordinary courts. The courts would give a decision based on general rules of law, the relevance of which the importer frequently failed to appreciate. Or at least so went the complaint. Article VI of the GATT held that dumping is "to be condemned if it causes or threatens material injury to an established industry . . . or materially retards the establishment of a domestic industry." Both the U.S. and British systems involved the determination of "material injury" on a case-by-case basis. In the United States this was done by the independent Tariff Commission, and in Great Britain by the Anti-Dumping Division of the Board of Trade. Both countries pressed Canada to adopt similar systems.

For this reason and because the Canadian government itself had become dissatisfied with its deficiencies the decision was made to offer the existing system for negotiation in 1966 during the Kennedy Round, the subject then being on the agenda. From these deliberations there emerged a new Code in the form of an Agreement on the Implementation of Article VI. The Code gave much closer definition of most of the main concepts, retaining at the core the principle of "material injury" to an industry in the country of import. Canada, although employing different language, adopted the main lines of this new Code in the Anti-Dumping Act of 1968, and in the establishment of the Anti-Dumping Tribunal (renamed the Canadian Import Tribunal in 1984). The Canadian system has functioned much like the American since then, with the Customs officials determining the existence of dumping and the Tribunal ruling on the issue of material injury to a Canadian industry.

Canada has traditionally relied almost exclusively on its anti-dumping provisions and only recently have other powers been given under the Customs Act. The Department of Finance's 1980 paper—*Proposals on Import Policy*—suggested revisions of the system to increase its scope. Canadian recourse measures had not even taken advantage of GATT provisions, and had also fallen behind U.S. measures, which occasionally were being used against Canada. U.S. Trade Agreement Acts of the postwar period have opened several avenues for protective action. Prominent among these are the escape clause, the national security amendment, and the peril-point provision. Under the escape clause the President was authorized to eliminate or modify any tariff concession given under a trade agreement if it had resulted or threatened to result in serious injury to a domestic industry. The question of injury was to be established by the Tariff Commission. Of 134 investigations between 1947 and 1961 there had been findings of injury in 33 cases, and in respect of these the President had used the escape clause in only 15. Canada was particularly concerned at the time with action taken on alsike clover seed and lead and zinc. The national security amendment gave authority to the President to increase duties or apply quotas where imports were thought to be a threat to the national security of the United States.

It is difficult under conditions of the 1980s to fully appreciate the reasoning that resulted in the application of quotas to imports of foreign oil, including Canadian oil, under this provision. The theory apparently was that reliance on foreign oil supplies could be a threat to the ability of the United States to defend itself.

Under the peril-point provision the Tariff Board was required to determine in advance of negotiations the safe margin for reduction of tariffs of a particular industry before causing or threatening to cause serious damage to that industry. These limits were not binding on the President, but he was required to explain to Congress in writing if he exceeded them.[31.4]

Legislation based on the Department of Finance paper was passed in 1984, and gave Canada the advantage of action permitted under several GATT provisions.

Customs Valuation

GATT stipulates that customs valuations should be on "actual values," a term which in general means the value at which goods are invoiced between the supplier and the purchaser. In practice however there has existed a variety of different bases; Canada's base was the normal market price in the country of origin. On entering GATT members were allowed to continue with their past practices, but it was understood that at some time in the future a uniform method would have to be adopted. At the Tokyo Round full consideration was given to this issue, and a Code was drawn up for implementation in the near future.

The revised provisions re-affirmed, as the first and primary method, the invoice price of the goods being imported, subject to adjustment for commissions, brokerage fees, packaging costs, etc. However, four other methods were also listed, presumably for countries that were unable to make the changeover, which in practice would be quite complex. The Agreement covered many technical aspects in detail and established a committee to supervise its implementation. Canada undertook to conform to the uniform basis by January 1985, and the Tariff Board developed new tariff schedules that would produce the same revenue and impose the same burden of tariff as the existing basis. Legislation to implement these changes was passed late in the 1984 session. Upward changes required renegotiation with Canada's GATT partners.

Government Procurement

The original GATT rules excluded government purchases from the requirement of non-discrimination. Governments could purchase under any condi-

---

[31.4]See Howard S. Piquet, *The U.S. Trade Expansion Act of 1962* (Washington, D.C.: Canadian-American Committee, 1963), 4-5.

tions they wished, the most common discrimination of course being in favour of local or national suppliers. At the Tokyo Round an Agreement was negotiated to cover this area. It required non-discriminating purchase of products (services being excluded) where the value was over SDR 150,000, (an amount, depending on current foreign exchange values, of U.S. $170,000-190,000). Technical requirements for tendering and rules for dispute settlement were established and a Committee on Government Procurement set up to oversee implementation.

Technical Barriers to Trade—Import Licensing Procedures

Agreements were entered into to remove unnecessary barriers to trade through the adoption of international standards and the administration of import licensing procedures on as equitable and non-discriminatory a basis as possible. Both were directed to minimizing the restrictive effect of border requirements. It was agreed that all procedures should be as simple as possible and administered with maximum dispatch.

Developing Countries

GATT, dominated by the large industrial countries, came very slowly to recognize the special problems of the Developing (or Less Developed) Countries. It is basic to the GATT concept that all economies must engage in foreign trade to achieve maximum growth. The need of developing countries to finance a wide range of essential imports gives this concept a special meaning for them as they rely mainly on the export of agricultural products and unprocessed primary materials, supplemented by returns from tourist trade, to offset their imports. Despite concessions made for them the almost universal restriction on agricultural trade has been an impediment, and in non-agricultural areas the role of large multinational corporations is frequently crucial, and offers complex problems with which LDCs are seldom prepared to deal.

A handful of developing countries has been able to establish manufacturing industries, usually specializing in a narrow range of products, which have competed successfully in developed country markets. Hong Kong, South Korea, Mexico, Brazil, India, Singapore, Malaysia, Argentina, Pakistan, and Colombia have had varying degrees of success in this way. This trade has become crucial for several of these countries in meeting payments on their international indebtedness. But the importation of their manufactured goods has encountered strong resistance in most developed countries where long established national industries have been threatened by the reduced prices made possible by lower wage structures. GATT has been forced to depart from some of its fundamental principles to accommodate actions taken by industrial members in applying quotas and other restrictions on textiles, clothing, footwear, electrical appliances, automobiles, and miscellaneous other products. Japan of course was the first such country to encounter these restrictions, but has survived to become a world economic power.[31.5]

One of the first formal steps taken by GATT in recognition of the Less Developed Countries was the adoption of a statement of intentions following publication in 1958 of the findings of a special panel, known after its chairman as the "Haberler Report." This 1958 "Declaration on Promotion of the Trade of Less-Developed Countries" was followed by a much more substantive step in 1965 when a new section was added to the main Agreement—Part IV. Under it the Contracting Parties agreed, "except in cases where overriding considerations make it impossible, (a) to refrain from imposing new barriers on imports of special interest to the developing countries, (b) to grant high priority to the reduction of barriers to imports from these countries, and (c) to seek to reduce taxes that restrict their consumption."[31.6]

In the opinion of some authorities this new Part went some way toward meeting the complaints of the LDCs, but the LDCs failed to agree. These fine words were weighed and found wanting in the light of adoption of restrictions on cotton textiles in the 1960s and disappointment in the meagre Kennedy Round tariff cuts for LDC commodities. Disillusioned with GATT they turned to another avenue, the United Nations itself. By a majority vote the Assembly adopted a resolution in 1962 to establish the United Nations Conference on Trade and Development (UNCTAD). Although all the leading trade nations of the world were members UNCTAD increasingly became the voice of the less developed countries. A major tariff issue from this time on became the granting of concessions by the developed countries on a non-reciprocal basis. At a meeting of 121 countries in New Delhi in 1968 a resolution was unanimously adopted "in favour of the early establishment of a mutually acceptable system of generalized non-reciprocal and non-discriminatory preferences which would be beneficial to the developing countries."[31.7] At later meetings of UNCTAD the LDCs continued to press for a standstill on trade barriers and for preferential and non-reciprocal tariff reductions.

Reaction to these requests among the developed countries was mixed. Some had already moved in this direction. The United Kingdom continued to maintain and improve its British Preferential Rates, and this appears to have helped some of the former colonies in their access to the British market. The EEC countries had also given their present and former colonies access to GATT preferences through associate membership, generally on a basis which brought the advantages of GATT with few of the obligations. These arrangements were made first in 1963 with 18 former colonies under the Yaounde Convention, and were extended and formalized in the Lome

---

[31.5] See Caroline Pestieau and Jacques Henry, *Non-Tariff Barriers as a Problem in International Development* (Montreal: Private Planning Association of Canada, 1972), 7.

[31.6] Ibid., at 41.

[31.7] Ibid., at 49.

Convention of 1975, under which the EEC countries granted duty-free entry to the principal products of 46 African, Caribbean and Pacific countries. However many other developed countries were apprehensive of the results that might follow from these substantial trade concessions, and wished to proceed very cautiously in granting them.

The OECD played the role of intermediator at this point by developing some general principles and elements for a workable system. This outline was adopted by the second session of UNCTAD in 1968. Further discussion within both OECD and GATT culminated in a waiver of Article 1 of the General Agreement, the non-discrimination clause. Once this hurdle had been cleared individual countries quickly passed legislation to grant preferences of their own choosing. The first move was made by the EEC in 1971, and the United States complied in 1976. By 1981 twenty OECD countries and as well most of the Eastern European countries had implemented what has come to be known as the Generalized System of Preferences.

Canada implemented the system in 1974, and since then the Customs Tariff has included a special schedule of rates for this purpose. The general basis for the rates has been one-half the most-favoured-nation rates or the lowest offered to other countries. However because the major sensitive Canadian areas have been protected there is a question as to how much advantage has been given. A study issued by the Economic Council of Canada concludes that, based on models constructed by its two authors, "The impact of the Canadian preferential tariffs for LDC imports (a reduction of one-third with some goods excluded) is absolutely miniscule for global imports, causing them to increase by one-tenth of one per cent. Neither is it of large benefit to the LDCs themselves, whose exports to Canada are augmented by a mere 1 per cent."[31.8] This study preceded the successful marketing of the Hyundai cars, which benefited considerably from the lower GSP tariff rate on imports from Korea.

At the Tokyo Round pressure from the LDCs brought further attention. In keeping with the official title of the round—Multilateral Trade Negotiations—all countries, whether or not members of GATT, had been invited to attend and many developing countries were there. On their behalf special attention was given to Tropical products, Non-tariff measures, Agriculture, and the Framework for the Conduct of World Trade. The report of the Director-General on the conference emphasized the benefit to the developing countries of the various Codes previously described, particularly those that "reduce the scope for arbitrary use of non-tariff measures in a number of areas and provide a mechanism for consultation . . ." It also listed as major accomplishments "the provision of a legal basis for the Generalized System of Preferences, for preferential trade relations among developing countries, and for other forms of special and differential treatment for

---

[31.8] Vittorio Corbo and Oli Havrylyshyn, *Canada's Trade Relations with Developing Countries*, study prepared for the Economic Council of Canada (Ottawa: Department of Supply and Services, 1980), 77.

these countries, including special treatment for the least-developed among them."[31.9]

On tropical products 2900 tariffs concessions were granted; some concessions, although much less significant, were granted on manufactured products. Tariff "escalation," an oblique term referring to the imposition of higher rates of duty on goods of more advanced manufacture, continues to be a feature of customs schedules that operates against the LDCs. However on some of the items under the preferential schedules these are overridden by the granting of free entry.

One concession favouring the developing countries was to be excused from a commitment given by developed countries that they will not use export subsidies for industrial products. However, they are adjured not to use such subsidies in a way that will cause "serious prejudice" to the industry of another country, and, if used, to remove or reduce them as soon as possible. Concessions were also made for the special needs of developing countries under technical requirements for import, customs valuation, government procurement, import licensing procedures, and provision of information.

In the area of quotas and other restrictions on the more advanced of the countries there was little change. The older economies are still cautious and fearful about relaxing restrictions, recalling the explosive force with which Japan, Taiwan, Hong Kong, Korea, and other low-cost Asiatic countries flooded their home markets with manufactured goods. Apart from the concessions on the use of subsidies the LDCs were given little further relief from quotas and similar restrictions during the Tokyo Round. The developing countries have continued active promotion of their case from other platforms, in particular the United Nations. A mark of their success was the official adoption by the United Nations Assembly of the Declaration on the Establishment of a New International Economic Order in May 1974. Under the Declaration all agreeing states acknowledged the sovereignty of every state over its own resources. This was followed in December 1974 by the charter of Economic Rights and Duties of States, the purpose of which was to define "the national and international economic responsibilities of nations so as to promote a more equitable division of global wealth."

These declarations have become the focus of proposals by the LDCs for increased aid, for establishment of buffer stocks to stabilize prices and supplies of LDC products, and for the free entry of these products into the markets of developed countries at maintained prices. At conferences in recent years attention has been centered on the pricing and financing of buffer stocks of LDC commodities in a way that will maintain export income. This has evolved into a proposal for a Common Fund—a sort of international banking arrangement to assist LDCs with their trade problems using funds supplied by the developed countries. Although some developed

---

[31.9]Director-General, GATT, *The Tokyo Round of Multilateral Trade Negotiations: Report, 1979* (Geneva: The Secretariat, 1979), 154.

countries have shown a limited enthusiasm for the proposal most have grave reservations. The depressed economic conditions of the late seventies and early eighties and the apparently ever-escalating demands of the LDCs have given this idea a low priority with most developed countries.[31.10]

An exercise in the same general category is the proposed adoption of a code to govern the actions of multinational enterprises (MNEs) in international trade and investment. The OECD adopted a declaration in June 1976, establishing some elementary guidelines for the conduct of MNEs. This has been both revised and extended. The United Nations, through the Economic and Social Council, has been studying a draft code over a period of years, but no agreed text had emerged by 1986.[31.11]

Agricultural Trade Under GATT

Authorities agree that the sector in which GATT has accomplished least is trade in agricultural products. In the words of Stone: "From the start, the GATT rules were less strict for agricultural products than for other products; even so, restrictions and distortions in this area of trade have spread far beyond the bounds permitted by the special dispensations from the normal GATT rules. Barriers and trade-distorting measures by governments in this area of trade include virtually the entire range of non-tariff barriers, export subsidies and tariffs . . . it has been the agricultural policies of the European Economic Community (EEC), the United States (USA) and Japan, affecting trade in temperate zone products, which have raised the most serious issues and have chiefly blocked efforts to liberalize world agricultural trade."[31.12]

From the beginning exceptions were made for agriculture under the Agreement, largely at the insistence of the United States, which has retained several agricultural support programs introduced during the Great Depression. These concessions included the right to impose quantitative restrictions on imports of agricultural and fisheries products and to subsidize export of agricultural and primary products, both features of the U.S. agricultural program. Quantitative barriers have been imposed by the United States on dairy products, meat, and sugar; anti-dumping and countervailing duties have been applied to several specific products and generally high tariff rates are levied on processed food. Canada too has protected its agriculture through a variety of devices. The Canadian Wheat Board, the Canadian Dairy Commission, and other agencies control imports by outright prohibition (butter, fluid milk, margarine) or by quota

---

[31.10]E. Hugh Roach, *The Commodity Question, Towards a Common Fund—Rhetoric or Reality?* Behind the Headlines, XXXVI no. 6. (Toronto: Canadian Institute of International Affairs, 1978).

[31.11]J.G. Crean, *The International Community and the Multinational Enterprise: Response and Regulation.* Behind the Headlines, XL no. 3 (Toronto: Canadian Institute of International Affairs, 1982).

[31.12]Frank Stone, *Canada, the GATT and the International Trade System* (Montreal: The Institute for Research in Public Policy, 1984), 155.

(cheese, eggs, turkeys, chickens). Seasonal duties are regularly applied to protect home-grown produce and high tariffs are levied against foreign processed food. Japan maintains high tariffs or quotas on foreign fruits, vegetables, processed foods, and livestock and dairy products. However, by far the most comprehensive system of agricultural support is that of the EEC.

The Common Agricultural Program (CAP)

Improvement in the condition of agriculture was given a high priority in the Treaty of Rome which established the EEC in 1958. Negotiations resulted in the adoption of the Common Agricultural Policy in 1962. Its objectives were to create a unified market with common prices, protection from imports, and financing through a Community body, all designed to make the EEC as self-sufficient as possible in farm products. The principal device used for market influence is setting official prices. As explained in the February 1985 *Quarterly Review of the National Westminster Bank*:

> The key to this system of official prices is the annual target price which represents an objective rather than a guaranteed price and is fixed for each commodity in the 'zone of greatest deficit.' For cereals this is Duisburg in West Germany. Below the target price and directly linked to it is the threshold price which represents the lowest price at which imports can cross the Community's frontier without undermining the target price. The difference between these two is accounted for by transport and storage costs. When the lowest import price is below the threshold price, a levy, representing the difference, is chargeable. Thus, each day variable import levies are calculated in Brussels so as to ensure complete protection for Community farmers . . . Furthermore, under the CAP, provision is made for intervention buying. Thus, the Community guarantees to support the market by a system of intervention prices at which farmers can sell their produce to the Intervention Boards in the event of low market prices. Intervention does not apply in all sectors and details vary from commodity to commodity although generally, the intervention price is 10 to 20 per cent below the target price . . . The price supporting mechanism is completed by export refunds, or restitutions as they are known, which subsidize Community exports when world prices are lower than EEC prices (as is usually the case!). An export restitution thereby enables Community farmers to sell at the world price. An export levy applies when world prices are higher than Community prices.[31.13]

In total the CAP program has been successful to the point of embarrassment. In many agricultural products the community is now self-sufficient—in many it has exportable surpluses. Agricultural products fell from 29 percent of total imports in 1973 to 15 percent in 1982. Of great relevance to

---

[31.13]Michael J. Roarty, "The EEC Common Agricultural Policy and its Effects on Less-Developed Countries" (February 1985) *National Westminster Bank Quarterly Review*, 3-4.

Canada, for example, is the reduction in the United Kingdom's dependence on imports of temperate food products from 29 percent in 1973 to 25 percent today. There have been dramatic increases in output of cereals and sugar, and there have been enormous accumulations of other products—a lake of wine and a mountain of butter are typically cited. The accession of Greece in 1981 and of Spain and Portugal in 1986 have certainly not eased the wine problem. The growing of wheat under these ideal conditions is said to have created a new millionaire class in some EEC countries.

The agricultural program has required massive financial support, particularly for export subsidies, and accounts for a large part of the EEC budget. There have been violent differences among countries on this massive expense, and attempts have been made to curtail support for some of the more abundant products. These have produced violent reactions from the farmers affected, so that change has been limited.

The variable import levy and the export subsidies are the features which draw strongest protest from countries outside the Community. In effect an additional tariff is imposed where imported goods of certain categories are priced below the Community price. In addition the subsidized pricing of exports has been injurious for world trade, particularly for the LDCs. Products massively over-produced in Europe have been sold on world markets in competition with the output of less developed countries, to their detriment. Between 1972 and 1982 the share of world agricultural trade of developed countries increased from 66 percent to 71 percent, with a corresponding decline in the share of LDCs. Sugar is an outstanding example. The EEC converted a 5 percent net import in 1974 to a net export of 13 percent in 1982, with a resulting sugar glut and low prices on world markets for a product which has been a staple export for many developing countries. For Canada the principal concern is with the recent loss of several smaller markets through subsidization of wheat sales and the 20 percent decline in wheat prices in 1986 to the lowest level in seven years as a result of price-cutting by the U.S. and the EEC. The Canadian government announced a higher domestic price for wheat for the new crop year, but this does not necessarily affect export prices. In the international competition for subsidization Canada is a small—and losing—player. For 1987 Canada's support was estimated at 85 cents per bushel, while the U.S. support was estimated at $2.92 and the EEC $3.13 per bushel. The higher Canadian domestic price was expected to add 6½ cents to the price of a loaf of bread, to the consternation of consumer groups and smaller bakeries.

The U.S. and the EEC have been at logger-heads on agricultural policy at several GATT rounds, culminating in a crucial confrontation at the Tokyo round. The United States has pressed for a more liberal regime, without indicating willingness to give up any of its own programs, and the EEC has argued the need to protect its own farmers. President Reagan raised the issue at the Meeting of Seven in Tokyo in May 1986, and the U.S. Secretary of Commerce has lately voiced a further protest; the current irritant at that time was the prospect of a loss of $1 billion annual sale of U.S. agricultural products in Spain. Under an accord reached early in July 1986, the U.S.

agreed to suspend planned retaliatory action against EEC tariffs for six months in return for compensation to U.S. farmers to remove an irritating impediment to GATT preparations. Undoubtedly agricultural trade will be a prime issue in the forthcoming round.

What Lies Ahead for GATT?

In the economic slump of the late seventies and early eighties there were signs of back-slipping in world trade conditions. In a publication issued in 1978, *The Rise of Protectionism*,[31.14] the IMF expressed its concern, citing the record of actions to impede trade and restrict imports in the United States, Canada, and the EEC. These had risen respectively to 16, 37, and 41 in 1977 from an average of 5 in 1971. Another study by the IMF issued in 1985 tabulated countervailing actions taken in the 2½ years from July 1982 to December 1984, which showed that of 42 impositions of definitive duties, 37 were by the United States. Other data indicated that as tariff rates decreased there had been an increasing resort to non-tariff barriers, with the U.S. leading the way.

Supporters of GATT are determined that it will continue to play a central role in international trade. In 1979 a work program for the eighties was established, and in 1980 various new functions that developed from the Tokyo Round were put in motion. At a top-level meeting of the Ministers of Contracting Parties in November 1982, it was agreed that "the multilateral trading system, of which the General Agreement is the legal foundation, is seriously endangered. In the current crisis of the world economy . . . protectionist pressures on governments have multiplied, disregard of GATT disciplines has increased . . . The Contracting Parties are resolved to overcome these threats to the system." Further: "They are therefore determined to create, through concerted action, a renewed consensus in support of the GATT system, so as to restore and reinforce confidence in its capacity to provide a stable and predictable trading environment and respond to new challenges." The Contracting Parties reaffirmed their commitment to abide by the GATT obligations, to preserve it as a functioning system, and to use it as a continuing forum of negotiation. Pledges were given for more regard for developing and less-developed countries, to bring agriculture more fully into GATT, to liberalize trade in textiles, and to conclude an agreement on the use of safeguards and on other worthy objectives.[31.15]

A work program was assigned to the staff and committees on a long list of subjects in support of these commitments. In its 1983 Annual Report the IMF lauded this initiative, and placed the onus squarely on the shoulders of the developed countries: "Because of the severe external constraints facing many of the developing countries, the possibility of achieving significant reductions in trade restrictions will depend to a large extent on the leader-

---

[31.14]Barham Nowzad, *The Rise of Protectionism*, IMF Pamphlet Series no. 24 (Washington, D.C.: International Monetary Fund, 1978).

[31.15]GATT, *GATT Activities in 1982* (Geneva: The Secretariat, 1983).

ship provided by the industrial countries."[31.16] An early result of this new resolve was the issuance of a report from a GATT study committee in 1984 which recommended the abolition of all restraints on trade in fibres and textiles, although nothing very significant appears to have resulted from this recommendation. In 1985 the GATT Secretariat issued an urgent plea for resolution of the growing problems facing the trade system in the statement, *Trade Policies for a Better Future: Proposals for Action*.

During the summer and fall of 1985 influential groups were attempting to initiate a GATT round. In June representatives of 21 industrial and developing nations met in Stockholm in an effort to persuade reluctant GATT members to negotiate soon. It appeared that the New Industrial Countries and the LDCs are least anxious for a meeting, apparently fearing that it will be to their disadvantage. In particular Brazil, India, and Egypt are said to fear that their service industries will be exposed to much greater competition under a new GATT round. The insistence of the U.S. that services be included has strengthened this fear.

In July a smaller group, composed of the Trade Ministers of Canada, the United States, Japan, and the EEC, met in Canada to discuss tactics and issues for a new GATT round. No official announcements were made but some revealing indications emerged: Canada's Trade Minister, for example, issued a statement that set out Canada's objectives for the next GATT round. The same group met in the United States in January 1986 for further discussion of GATT issues.

At the request of the United States a top-level three-day meeting of 90 contracting members of GATT was held in Geneva in October 1985. Discussion nearly foundered on an open split between the industrial and less developed countries mainly on the issue of inclusion of services. Pressure, amounting almost to threats of isolation, were made by the U.S. and EEC delegates against the veto being exercised by these countries; a final compromise involved delaying a decision until the GATT annual meeting a month later, apparently leaving developing nations some power of veto over the future agenda. The official statement following the meeting said: "A preparatory process on the proposed new round of multilateral trade negotiations has now been initiated."

At the Ministerial meeting in November 1985, a firm decision was made on a new round. It was agreed that an agenda would be established by July 1986, and that negotiations would commence in September. This agreement was confirmed at the Tokyo Meeting of Seven in May 1986, with the undertaking that Ministers of Finance would meet in September to begin preparations. This decision appeared to have been generally well received by trading countries, including Canada. Data on declining growth of world trade and increasing trends to protectionism were signs that disturbed GATT supporters and clearly indicated the need for a global scale review. It did bring

---

[31.16] International Monetary Fund, *Annual Report 1983* (Washington, D.C.: the Chairman, 1983), 63.

into question the value of separate negotiations between Canada and the United States, as one of the strongest arguments in their support had been the remoteness of a GATT round. However both governments proceeded with preparations for bilateral negotiations, although it was not at all clear what effect the forthcoming GATT round would have on the objectives for Canada-U.S. trade relations.

One immediate result for Canada is that troubles with the EEC are now to be on the table. These involve several issues: Canadian efforts to curtail imports of wine, cheese, footwear, and beef, and EEC quotas on Canadian newsprint, blueberries, and other products. The higher mark-up imposed by provincial liquor authorities on imported wines is a long-standing grievance with European wine producers. The accession to the EEC of Greece in 1981 and of Spain and Portugal in 1986 would also require trade adjustments with the EEC.

GATT in Retrospect, 1986

The GATT record is a mixed one. The central role it played in restoring world trade after the chaos of the Great Depression and World War II is unquestioned. The several rounds have been a constant challenge to the trading countries of the world to adhere to the high promises made at the outset. There have been some notable shortcomings, but in the light of the enormous odds against success its record has been a remarkable one. But each round has presented a more complex agenda than the previous one, and it was one of the accidents of history that the Tokyo Round finally achieved some success. Increasingly trade negotiations are dominated by large trading blocs—the United States and the EEC in particular—and individual countries with one or two exceptions (West Germany or Japan) have less hope of advancing their own interests, and must rely mainly on the most-favoured-nation principle for tariff and other concessions. Another conspicuous disadvantage of the GATT process is its cumbersome operating procedures and the difficulties of making changes in GATT rules. The principle of reciprocity also militates against the raising of many crucial matters in GATT negotiations as countries are not always willing to make concessions or extend restrictions which must be applied to all other members. World trade conditions have changed so rapidly that GATT rules are frequently outdated by the time a new round has been arranged. Issues now penetrate far beyond the simple early questions of tariff rate and related and visible restrictions, reaching into the basic principles of a country's economic and social philosophy. The role of governmental subsidies, frequently mentioned in early pages, is a classical—and for Canada a crucially important—issue. These of course are developed country hazards in the GATT processes. Beyond them lies a whole range of matters of equal concern to the less developed countries.

Undoubtedly, from the frequency with which it has been mentioned, the U.S. GATT agenda will give high priority to the development of multinational rules for international trade in services. The former U.S. representative, William Brock, first raised the issue in 1982; it was formally presented to GATT in the following year in a U.S. document—*U.S. National Study on Trade in Services*—and the present Trade Representative, Clayton Yeutter, has mentioned it frequently. The proposal has been resisted by developing countries which fear loss of initiative in the establishment of indigenous service industries, and has been one of the main causes of the delay in the launching of a new GATT round. There are wide differences of view among experts on the possibility of reaching a consensus, or even on what form the arrangements should take, given the present volatile nature of the technology and conflicts between international requirements in such areas as information flows and legitimate concerns for national sovereignty.

The eighth GATT round will be a test for the organization's ability to survive. It has surmounted some previous unlikely looking prospects and it will be interesting to follow its fate with the latest round. A particular issue will arise from the Soviet indication that it might ask for observer status, a position already granted to China. Initial reaction indicated that the request would probably be refused on the grounds that GATT is an arrangement between free market economies and would not be able to accommodate a state-run economy as large as the Russian.

32
Meanwhile Back in Canada: Other Major Developments

The Canada-U.S. Auto Agreement, 1965

By far the most dramatic of the moves outside GATT, the main subject to this point, was the Canada-United States Agreement Concerning Automotive Products—the Auto Agreement. The agreement originated in Canadian concern for the growing deficit in automobiles and parts in Canada-United States trade. The tariff in particular prevented concentration of production in one place; plants on each side of the border were duplicating the same processes. The industry therefore was a natural candidate for rationalization.

Canada started the process of examination by appointing Professor Vincent Bladen, a distinguished Canadian economist, to study the situation and make recommendations for change. His report on the problems of the Canadian automotive industry was issued in 1961.[32.1] Principal recommendations were that in order to remove one disadvantage faced by the Canadian industry a federal excise tax of 7½ percent be repealed. This was done in 1961. He also recommended integration of the parts and automobile industry by free entry between the two countries. A tentative move in this direction was first taken by Canada in the granting of duty remissions on parts imported into Canada for use in production in Canada. This move was not popular in Washington, but it did bring the issue to the fore. General Motors, Ford, and Chrysler were helpful in support of free trade to aid cross-the-border rationalization. Following some tough negotiations an agreement between the two federal governments was announced in 1965.

The main purpose of the agreement was to provide free trade in automobiles and automobile parts. Some conditions were made by each country. The United States, cautious about use of the open channel by countries other than Canada, stipulated that completed autos must have a North American content of at least 50 percent. Canada for its part was more concerned to ensure substantial continuing manufacturing in Canada. Its concessions were granted to a "Canadian manufacturer," and to qualify for this status at least 75 percent of its production must be Canadian production for each model and in each model year, or the percentage in the 1964 model year, if higher. Canada also stipulated that the Canadian content of Canadian manufactured vehicles must not be less than the dollar value of the content in 1964. Supplementary to this agreement, Canadian

---

[32.1] Canada, *Report of the Royal Commission on the Automobile Industry* (Ottawa: Queen's Printer, 1961).

manufacturers gave undertakings to increase the Canadian value-added in future years.

It is generally agreed that the industry has become more efficient under the agreement, having taken advantage of opportunities to rationalize production. However, the pact is in or out of grace with the balance of trade under it. Until the early seventies the balance was in Canada's favour, and the U.S. administration was beginning to talk of a revision. One U.S. report in 1971 said that "the Agreement has thus far fallen well short of the goal of free automotive trade and the consequent benefits which would flow from optimum patterns of investment, production, and trade in a unified market. The reason for the failure so far to achieve these results lies in the unwillingness of the Canadian Government to allow the expiration of arrangements which were viewed by U.S. officials as transitional at the time the Agreement was reached . . . The U.S. Government has been contending since 1969—without success—that these transitional restrictions should be eliminated . . . Furthermore, many Canadians have interpreted the Agreement to mean that Canada is entitled to a share of North American automotive production equal to Canadian consumption and have argued for a retention of safeguards until that goal is reached."[32.2]

The Commission urged that all remaining barriers to the import of American cars into Canada be removed. However with a favourable U.S. balance under the agreement for the next nine years little more was heard of its shortcomings. One contentious issue arose in the late seventies over grants offered by Canadian governments to encourage U.S. producers to expand in Canada, an issue which Simon Reisman, one of the original negotiators of the Agreement, was appointed as a Royal Commission to investigate in 1978.[32.3] Although nothing was done following his report the question of the role of government was to become an increasingly contentious general issue between the two countries.

These problems, all related to a reasonably healthy international industry, took second place from 1980 onward to those of an industry in deep trouble. The decline in the world economy, the threat of gasoline shortages, and the market invasion of Japanese cars made deep cuts in North American production and sales. To counter the flood of Japanese cars, quotas were introduced but there were also thoughts of introducing American content requirements. However sales of American cars rebounded following 1983 and with the aid of massive government loans and guarantees the industry was restored to health. In early 1985 U.S. quotas on imports of Japanese cars were lifted.

In Canada, the 1982 report of the federal Task Force on the Canadian Motor Vehicle and Automotive Parts Industry, *An Automotive Strategy for*

[32.2] Commission on International Trade and Investment Policy, *United States International Economic Policy in an Interdependent World*. Papers submitted to the Commission and published in conjunction with the Commission Report to the President (Washington, D.C.: the Commission, 1971), 228-29.

[32.3] See David Leyton-Brown, "The Mug's Game: Automotive Investment Incentives in Canada and the United States" (Winter 1979-80) *International Journal*, 170-84.

Canada, recommended a domestic content requirement for all cars sold in Canada—a suggestion not adopted by the Liberal government. The greater production from 1982 onward of some models in Canada swung the balance under the Auto Agreement heavily in Canada's favour; 1985 in fact was a record year for the automobile industry in Canada. No changes have been made in the Agreement, but it is unlikely that its future would be any less contentious than its past.[32.4] Its status under the free-trade negotiations was by no means certain.

Canada retained quotas on Japanese cars in 1985, but in place of the previous numerical limit (170,000) the ceiling was set as 18 percent of the Canadian market. Foreign producers, principally Japanese, were bowing to government pressure for investment in Canada, and in 1985 both Toyota and Honda let contracts for Canadian plants. The Korean producer, Hyundai, was considering similar action.

The Minister of International Trade announced late in June that new arrangements governing automobile imports would be finalized in a few weeks. Part of the coming arrangements involved an increase in the tariff on Hyundai cars, then free, to two-thirds of the level for Japanese and European cars, on January 1, 1987.

The Emergency Foreign Exchange Conservation Act

During World War II Canada imposed quotas and other restraints on imports to reduce consumer spending and conserve non-sterling exchange under the Foreign Exchange Conservation Act. This legislation was repealed following the war, but much the same program was reintroduced in November 1947, through the medium of a radio address by the Minister of Finance, to save dollars. This program included high domestic excise taxes on goods having a substantial import content and quotas or prohibitions on specific items imported from dollar countries, and was extremely unpopular. Housewives, starved for new electrical appliances after the long drought of the Great Depression and the war, could not understand why they were now being deprived of them. Many marginal items had been swept in that were not important in the main picture and only caused unnecessary confusion and hardship. Because it had been introduced under extraordinary powers revisions could be made by order-in-council, and these were frequent. Legislation was enacted in March 1948, (The Emergency Foreign Exchange Conservation Act) to give validity to the taxes and duties still in effect, but these were all withdrawn on July 31, 1948. Some quotas were retained following this date, but were gradually eliminated.

The Tariff Structure

For some decades the tariff had contained three schedules—the General, the Most-Favoured-Nation, and the British Preferential. In the seventies two

---

[32.4]Carl E. Beigie and James Stewart, "The Leading Case of Autos" (March 1984) *Policy Options*, 12-18.

more were added—one for the United Kingdom and Ireland, and another for the General Preferential Tariff. The former was introduced when the United Kingdom joined the EEC and no longer qualified for British Preferential rates. The latter met Canada's commitment to give preferred treatment to developing countries.

The Most-Favoured-Nation schedule is by far the most important, as it applies to all countries with which Canada has an agreement, including all GATT members. The General tariff is least significant, as it applies to only a few countries that are not covered by the other schedules, such as Oman, Libya, Albania, and North Korea. The BP rates are for imports from certain Commonwealth countries, of which only Australia and New Zealand are assured the rates by treaty. The United Kingdom and Ireland rates applied until the Tokyo Round reductions were fully implemented in 1987, after which MFN rates applied. The GPT rates are calculated as the lower of the BP rate or the MFN rate less one-third. The schedule was first enacted for a period of ten years and has recently been renewed for another ten years, to June 30, 1994. Specific rates (by weight, number, etc.) were still employed, mainly for agricultural and textile products, but these have been replaced by ad valorem rates under the new valuation basis.

The saw-toothed profile of the Canadian tariff—low rates on many ingredients and high rates on finished products—contrasts sharply with the commonly flatter profile of tariffs of European countries and has complicated the task of finding equivalent and "harmonized" trade-offs in tariff negotiations. It has also made even more complex the measurement of its weight, already an exercise for which there is a variety of competing methods.[32.5] The External Affairs *Review* attempted to summarize some of its main features as follows: "Actual duty levels vary greatly. A large number of products now enter duty free under all but the General tariff, including tropical products, a range of producer goods, and many goods not made in Canada. On the other hand, a range of sensitive consumer goods such as clothing and footwear are protected by tariffs as high as 25 percent. The average incidence of the tariff on all imports is now between 4 and 5 percent, and the average rate on dutiable goods is currently between 12 and 13 percent."[32.6]

Significant structural changes lay ahead for the tariff. As mentioned earlier, Canada changed its basis for customs valuation effective January 1, 1985 to conform with GATT requirements. A far more ambitious program is the complete recasting of the classification of goods for customs tariff and trade statistics purposes in the form of the Harmonized System. Preparation for this change had already involved years of study and consultation, but the project was sufficiently advanced that the Minister of Finance announced in his February 1986 budget speech that Canada would adopt the system on January 1, 1988, provided that the United States, Japan, and the European Communities were prepared to take similar action at the same

---

[32.5] Supra footnote 31.9, at 117-27.

[32.6] Supra footnote 30.11, at 129.

time. In the meantime as agreed with the United States at the Tokyo round the effect of the "made or not made in Canada" classification has been studied by the Tariff Board and changes made to meet the U.S. request that specific product descriptions be substituted to clarify this omnibus category where possible. These very substantial changes in the basic tariff structure was accompanied by a massive turnover of procedures to computer technology,[32.7] then well under way.

Anti-Dumping and Safeguarding

As discussed earlier Canada historically has relied heavily on its anti-dumping law to deal with injury-causing imports. The first anti-dumping provisions were enacted in 1904, and a general power to impose countervailing duties dates back to the early thirties. In addition since 1977 section 7 of the Customs Act has given specific authority to impose countervailing duties on subsidized imports as provided under the GATT. Findings of material injury are left to the Canadian Import Tribunal, but the imposition of duties is reserved for the Governor-in-Council. In general, it has not been necessary for the Governor-in Council to act, settlements usually having been made by consultation.

Safeguarding against real or threatened injury from causes other than dumping or subsidization may take one or all of several forms. These include a surtax on imports for 180 days under section 8 of the Customs Tariff, renewable with the consent of Parliament. There is authority under section 5 of the Export and Imports Permits Act for the Governor-in-Council to impose quotas if the Textile and Clothing Board or the Canadian Import Tribunal find that imports are causing or threatening to cause serious injury to Canadian producers. Imports of fresh, frozen, or chilled beef or veal may be restricted for the same reason. A power now apparently used frequently for commercial purposes is given under the Export and Import Permits Act, 1947. It has been employed to require licences for the import of eggs, chickens, and turkeys in support of the Farm Products Marketing Agencies Act and to fluid milk and dairy products, including cheese, under the Agricultural Stabilization Act. Global quotas on textiles, clothing, and footwear have also been provided under this Act, along with restrictions in several other areas.

Canada's use of safeguarding measures is summed up in the *Review*, as follows: "Temporary and emergency surtaxes have been imposed on bicycles, polyester filament yarn, men's and boys' shirts, and certain sensitive horticultural products. Quotas (both global and country-specific) have been applied on a range of textile, clothing and footwear products, as well as cattle, beef and veal. A special valuation provision was applied to imports of turkeys in the mid-sixties. Discussions with Japan have led to that country exercising self-restraint in the export of automobiles, a measure

---

[32.7] For further details on administration see J. Harvey Perry, *Taxation in Canada*, Tax Paper No. 68 (Toronto: Canadian Tax Foundation, 1984), 213-27.

analogous to safeguard action, as it did in the late 1950s and early 1960s regarding exports of non-textile, low-cost consumer products such as stainless steel flatwear.''[32.8]

As mentioned earlier, the apparatus of recourse administration was overhauled with the passage of the Bill C-8 at the 1984 session of Parliament. This concluded a phase that had started with the issuance of the paper, *Proposals on Import Policy*, by the Department of Finance in 1980. The purpose of the legislation, as explained by officials before a parliamentary committee, was to make Canada's anti-dumping and countervail legislation more effective, and to take full advantage of its rights under GATT. The bill replaced the countervail provisions of the Customs Tariff with new parallel procedures for anti-dumping and countervail cases. It also provides a formula under the Customs Act that will trigger safeguarding measures. The former Anti-dumping Tribunal was replaced by the Canadian Import Tribunal, which was empowered to make recommendations to the Minister of Finance for the imposition of the recourse measures provided under the Act.[32.9]

Duty Remissions

A feature of the tariff that has come into very active use in recent years is the power to remit duties under the Financial Administration Act when "it is deemed to be in the public interest." Remissions are given for a variety of purposes. An example is the Machinery Program introduced in 1968, under which remissions of duty are given for imports of machinery not made in Canada, while full protection is given for Canadian manufacturers. More recent examples given in the *Review* are "the various remission programmes which have been established for companies engaged in automotive production and similar schemes established to assist Canadian manufacturers of other goods (e.g., front-end loaders) in rationalizing their production with affiliated companies in foreign countries."[32.10] A system which offers facilities very similar to free trade zones is also available under the Inward Processing Remission Order, 1979. As explained in the *Review*, "The Inward Processing Remission Order allows companies to manufacture 'in bond' for export production without the necessity of tying up funds in customs duty on imported components pending export of the finished product." Canada also has an array of "temporary tariff items" which provide duty-free entry for components and materials used in Canadian manufacturing.[32.11] For further information see "Checklist" in the *Canadian Tax Journal*, which lists remission orders in each issue.

[32.8]Supra footnote 30.11, at 137-38.

[32.9]Canada, Standing Senate Committee on Banking, Trade and Commerce, *Proceedings*, Issue no. 14, June 28, 1984 (Ottawa: Department of Supply and Services, 1984).

[32.10]Supra footnote 30.11, at 131.

[32.11]Ibid., at 132.

Budget Changes

There were also the normal annual changes through the budget. Many of these arose from references to the Tariff Board, a separate agency to which the Minister of Finance referred problems for study and recommendation. A reference can involve only one item or several, and frequently requires a review of all the tariffs affecting a whole industry. Consistent with long-standing policy many changes gave relief for producer items, particularly for those imported by primary industries. Many changes were simply required to keep the tariff in pace with new products and technology, such as plastics and electronics. Latterly reliefs were given for consumer products to offset inflation.

The following is a summary of the tariff content of budgets from 1947 to 1986. References are brief, as it is impossible to get into the minutiae of nearly four decades of tariff changes. GATT changes were usually provided under special legislation, but some were made through the annual budget.

March 1947. Special wartime changes and rates under the War Exchange Conservation Act were repealed and prewar regular and British Preferential rates were restored.

May 1948. Free entry was granted for the United Kingdom cotton and rayon piece goods and many other United Kingdom items were given free entry or reduced rates to assist in postwar industrial recovery.

March 1949. A 25 percent increase was given in quotas for consumer goods under the Emergency Foreign Exchange Conservation Act.

March 1950. Minor tariff changes were made.

April 1951. Tariffs on synthetic resins and plastics were revised following a Tariff Board study. Reductions in cost items were made for agriculture, mining, and fishing.

April 1952. Four Tariff Board reports dealt with plastic, glass, iron and steel shot and grit, and free entry for architects' and engineers' plans. Several changes gave relief on mining industry imports.

February 1953. Further minor changes were made, mainly by exempting cost items for agriculture.

April 1954. A mass of revisions were made to over 50 items. A quotation from this budget gives a notion of the quixotic mix in a typical customs cocktail. "The duty is being eliminated on machinery and apparatus, including tubing of a class or kind not made in Canada, for the operation of potash and rock salt mines. A former drawback item is being re-established to provide a drawback of 99 percent of the duty paid on fire clay for fire brick used by basic producers of iron and steel. Duty free entry is provided for materials and parts used in construction and repair of railway signal systems . . . Some of the principal items on which the tariff has been substantially reduced include automatic controls for certain sterilizing processes, tear gas ammunition for use of law enforcement authorities, and impregnated jute fabric used by nurserymen."

April 1955. Further amendments to the fast changing plastic items were made. More reliefs for farm costs were given and (post-Korean war) relief was granted from duties for a stated value of gifts imported by returning armed forces personnel.

April 1956. Agricultural machinery parts were declared exempt; a tariff on potatoes was being considered. Tariff Board membership was increased from 3 to 5 with a heavier program.

March 1957. Several major studies were before the Tariff Board, including iron and steel, pipes and tubes, chemicals and footwear. Trade discussions with Australia were being planned as the existing agreement had not been amended for 25 years.

June 1958. Revisions in the Customs Act were proposed to allow Canada to deal with a flood of low-cost primary textiles. Major revisions in the iron and steel tariffs were proposed following Tariff Board reports. (These and all subsequent changes affecting rates bound under the GATT were preceded by negotiations with the other relevant members of the GATT). Other adjustments affected woolen fabrics, zinc and zinc products, plastics, and lumber. The government was watching rubber footwear imports and planned to discuss fruit and vegetable imports with the United States. An increase in the tourist exemption was granted for absences exceeding two weeks, the beginning of the present system.

April 1959. Textiles remained a concern, with all schedules under study by the Tariff Board. No changes were made yet in rubber footwear. Fluorospar was under study. Fruit and vegetable tariffs in future would vary with the season—lower in off-season and higher in on-. The status of six items of machinery was clarified; also that of computers.

March 1960. Major revisions of textile and clothing schedules were made following extensive study by the Tariff Board, generally in the direction of increased protection.

December 1960. A short budget gave a summary of tariff revisions of 1958 to 1960. The Minister, the Hon. Donald Fleming, said: "My 1958 budget introduced a comprehensive revision of the iron and steel sector of the tariff; the 1959 budget dealt with fruit and vegetables; and the 1960 budget dealt with the bulk of the textile schedule. Among them, these three budgets involved the amendment of some 400 items in the Canadian tariff."

June 1961. Textiles continued to hold attention. The new rates and schedules had been negotiated with other GATT signatories and were ready to be passed by Parliament. Voluntary Restraint Agreements had been negotiated with Japan and Hong Kong for restriction of textile imports. Miscellaneous changes were made in several tariff schedules.

April 1962. Further changes in textile schedules were being negotiated. From June 1962, an import surcharge was levied on textile imports under Customs Act powers.

June 1963. The last of the Tariff Board reports on textiles was implemented.

March 1964. Only minor changes were made pending conclusion of the Kennedy Round.

April 1965. Kennedy Round was not yet completed and no major changes were made. Import surcharges on textiles had been in effect at this point for nine months, and the Minister was not considering removing them.

June 1967. Kennedy Round changes had been settled but not yet made public. Among minor changes was granting of import of margarine under special permit, the first break in the outright prohibition of use in Canada. Other changes removed some machinery from the free category.

October 1968. Major changes in plastics and chemicals were made following the Kennedy Round. To comply with a GATT undertaking to revise anti-dumping law the government issued a White Paper for study.

Based on public comment it introduced a Resolution on an Anti-Dumping Code, which was referred to a parliamentary committee for study.

June 1969. Minor changes were made, including reliefs for printing equipment and certain apparatus for engineering, etc.

June 1971. Rates for feedstocks for petrochemicals were reduced and those for polyethylene slightly increased. Kennedy Round machinery tariff was being reviewed for possible extension of free entry to further items of a class not made in Canada. Heavy oil (used by pulp and paper companies and others) was granted two years free entry.

May 1972. A Resolution was introduced to authorize the General Preference System for developing countries. An increase was made in rates on knit goods following a United Kingdom increase in the British Preferential rates on cotton goods.

February 1973. As an anti-inflationary move a list of consumer goods was given reduced rates for one year.

May 1974. Reduced rate consumer goods list was extended to December 31, 1974.

November 1974. Reduced rate consumer goods list extended to June 30, 1976, but shortened. Tourist exemptions were increased—the 48-hour exemption was raised from $25 to $50 and 12-day from $100 to $150. Changes were made for aircraft and engines not made in Canada. Duty-free shops were to be allowed at border points as well as airports.

May 1976. The reduced rate consumer goods list was extended to June 1978, with some deletions. Some machinery items were removed from British Preferential schedule and raised to Most-Favoured-Nation schedule. Further concessions were made under General Preferential System.

April 1978. Reduced rate consumer list was extended to June 30, 1979, with some further deletions. Other changes related to parts for lighting fixtures, fatty alcohols, aircraft and engines, and minor other items. Again some U.K. imports were transferred from the British Preferential schedule to MFN rates with withdrawal of British Preferential rates by the United Kingdom.

December 1979. The short-lived Conservative budget made no mention of renewal of the consumer goods list, which had expired on June 30. It proposed issuance of a White Paper on new GATT anti-dumping and countervailing duty procedures, but with defeat of the government this and other proposals were not implemented.

October 1980. Changes affected goods imported by institutions established for scientific, religious, educational, and similar purposes; changes also affected antiques, collectibles, and amateur radio and other equipment.

November 1981. Further additions were made to the General Preference System following study by the Tariff Board with special rates for less developed countries (LLDCs). Tokyo round reductions were being implemented throughout the tariff schedules.

June 1982. No further tariff changes were proposed, as those in the previous budget had not been implemented. The metric system was implemented for tariff schedules. A Trade Agreement with New Zealand was authorized. Changes affecting dental material, products for disabled persons, and other minor items were proposed. Final legislation was not passed until December 1982.

April 1983. Further reductions were made in GPS rates and the system was extended for a further ten years to June 30, 1994. Tourist allowances were raised, the quarterly from $50 to $100 and the annual from $150 to $300. Miscellaneous other changes were made.

February 1984. Amendments to the Customs Act were proposed to implement the new basis of customs valuation required by the GATT, but were not immediately enacted because of the calling of an election. The same fate met amendments to the Customs Tariff to implement Canada's GATT undertakings, which included free entry of civilian aircraft and parts under the Agreement on Trade in Civil Aircraft, and an increase in the duty on some items to maintain the same level of tariff protection as had prevailed before the change to the GATT basis of valuation as recommended by the Tariff Board. Other proposed amendments affected goods made/not made in Canada and also increased the allowable value of gifts sent from abroad to $40 from $25. Legislation to implement these proposals was passed at a new session under the new Conservative government late in 1984.

May 1985. Tariffs on automobiles and parts from developing countries were revised; changes were made to further reduce the goods in the "made/not made in Canada" category following Tariff Board recommendations; the $100 exemption for tourist imports would be available for any number of absences during the year of at least 48 hours duration; several other miscellaneous changes were made.

February 1986. A duty-free import plan was announced for imports from over 20 islands in the Caribbean (CARIBCAN) effective June 15, 1986, excluding textiles, clothing, footwear, luggage, handbags, and similar goods; Canada would adopt the Harmonized Commodity Description and Coding System on January 1, 1988, provided the United States, Japan and the European Communities also do so at the same time; further "made/not made in Canada" items were defined; Canadian tourists would be able to claim the $300 exemption for goods shipped from any country (previously this right was restricted to shipments from beyond North American continental limits); duties were removed from large size off-highway tires, backhoes and power shovels for mining, articles for guide dogs for the blind, and miscellaneous other goods.

33
Pre-1984 Tariff Policy

It would be appropriate now to attempt to review the position of Canadian tariff policy after the intensive changes under GATT and as a result of other developments. To distinguish the longer term background from policy under the Conservative government, which will be reviewed later, a somewhat artificial division is made at the year 1984.

To synopsize: it is clear that historically the Canadian tariff, as an encouragement for basic industries, has granted free entry or low rates for cost items of agriculture, mining, forestry, manufacturing, etc. This treatment was extended to machinery and equipment not made in Canada. As a counterpart, protection has been given to manufacturing through high tariffs on final products. The system has been altered materially by the multilateral rate reductions negotiated under the GATT. Tokyo Round changes when completely implemented will reduce the general tariff level to its lowest point in a century. Some sensitive industries will continue to have high protection through a variety of devices; in this respect Canada has the company of most other countries.

Canada has been deeply committed to the GATT, and few countries have been more scrupulous in meeting their undertakings both in word and spirit. But the approach to major change has been cautious, and the objective of Canada's international trade policy—to the extent that it can be separately identified—has remained much as it has been for decades. The fairly consistent objective has been to gain access to the large markets of advanced industrial countries for Canadian primary products (lumber, newsprint, pulp, wheat, minerals, etc.) in return for modest concessions under the Canadian tariff for entry of products of other countries. Much of the trade in manufactured or semi-processed goods is between corporations in the same category of business (automobiles and parts for U.S. automobile companies, newsprint for press publishers, copper and other base metals for final product producers, etc.) Despite increasing emphasis on manufactured products, even in the eighties the well-being of large segments of the Canadian economy depends mainly on the export of materials to supply the industries of developed countries and food to feed the world's masses. Some of the most crucial tariff issues still relate to this aspect of the economy—for example, in 1986 lumber and fish exports to the United States.

The engulfing revolution in the character of world trade in the late twentieth century has caught Canada largely unprepared. The old foundations on which Canadian trade was built are rapidly crumbling. The so-called smoke-stack industries of other countries, particularly those of the United States, which were a prime market for many of Canada's exports, are declining. New technologies and radically different materials are demanding innovative approaches and the abandonment of outdated methods—sometimes the abandonment of whole industries or communities. Canadian monopolies or semi-monopolies (such as nickel) have been undermined by discoveries in other countries or the development of competitive materials. Some markets for agricultural products have disappeared with improvement of local sources of supply, or else access has been reduced by restrictive policies. Canada has been left on the outside of vast and increasingly self-sustaining market areas, such as the EEC, as it is not a member of any of these blocs. The flood of low-cost textiles, footwear, automobiles, and electronic equipment from Pacific-rim countries has posed a threat to important Canadian industries. The energy crises and the economic recession of the late seventies and early eighties have added materially to Canada's (and the world's) dilemma, although a fortuitous result of the reduced value of the Canadian dollar has been very substantial trade surpluses.

These are the conditions facing Canada in the last years of the twentieth century. The solution for many of the current problems of course goes far beyond the issues of tariff and trade policy. Even in this area however there is no agreement on solutions and the search for a policy goes on in increasingly intensive public debate. The elements of the pre-1984 debate are examined briefly in the following pages.

The Free Trade Lure

Reciprocal free trade with the United States has been the phantom hope of many Canadians for a century. The prosperity associated with the 1854 treaty kept free-trade sentiment alive in some older parts of Canada. Despite the adoption of the high-tariff National Policy, sentiment for Reciprocity remained strong enough that in 1911 it was the issue in a national election. Later it became, and has largely still remained, the battle-cry of the exporting provinces west of Ontario.

Possibly this condition was—and still is—inevitable. The U.S. market undoubtedly has a magnetic attraction. Its proximity, wealth, and familiarity of language and customs gives it a natural affinity for Canadians. Business ties through multinational corporate relations are close, and tariff and other arrangements have facilitated these connections. It is perhaps not surprising therefore that the thought of obtaining full free access to this market has received rather constant attention in Canada in recent years, particularly as the recession of the early eighties lingered and alternative choices were limited.

The issue raises much heated debate, and is highly controversial. On the Canadian side it has brought forth mixed and controversial expressions from politicians, officials, economists, businessmen, editorial writers, trade associations, and others. The United States reaction in recent years has been one of mild and tolerant interest, with assurances being given that if Canadians can come to an agreement on a proposal it will receive serious consideration in Washington. We will look further into more recent developments later; in the meantime a review of the traditional positions of influential elements in Canada in the past will serve as an instructive guide to possible future developments.

The National Government

GATT has made it easier to track the trade policies of the world's trading nations because it has forced them to keep this subject under almost constant review. Furthermore, the occasions for making these policies known have come with increasing frequency. For Canada a study of past policy statements leads to some interesting conclusions. With some rare exceptions, regardless of party, there has not been much talk in the last half century in favour of full, complete, and untrammeled free trade with any other country, including the United States. The policy has been that trade concessions would be negotiated on a reciprocal basis among a balanced group of countries where there appeared to be an equality of benefit and the benefits would be shared fairly among Canadians. Tribute paid to the beneficial results of freer trade could generally be read as rather thinly veiled appeals for freer access for Canadian goods to the large markets of the world; and always it was implied that the bargaining for access to the Canadian market would be tough and restricted, and a long way from an open door.

The 1957 Report of the Royal Commission on Canada's Economic Prospects fairly reflected the prevailing skepticism on free trade in the following words: "In view of what has been said in the preceding paragraphs, broad reciprocity with the United States, in the opinion of the Commission, cannot now or in the foreseeable future be regarded as a practical proposition. This does not mean, however, that we should eliminate completely any thought of reciprocal arrangements of more limited scope with the United States, or with other countries, which may be consistent with Canada's international obligations."[33.1] In short the federal government should try to maintain a balanced trade relationship with its main trading partners.

In practice, as trade with the United States began to assume greater importance, official efforts to maintain and diversify trade with other countries were intensified. This motivated the strongly expressed opposition to the United Kingdom's entry into the EEC, which would deprive Canada of a century of access to its markets. This policy was made specific in 1970 in the government's White Paper—*Foreign Policy for Canadians*—which gave high priority to achieving closer relations with EEC countries. In 1972 a policy statement from the Secretary of State for Foreign Affairs listed three options: maintain existing relations with the United States, move closer to the United States, or "strengthen the Canadian economy and other aspects of our national life and in the process to reduce the present Canadian vulnerability." The statement favoured the "third option," which the Economic Council interpreted as opposition to "forces tending to bring Canada into a north-south continental economic system."

[33.1] Canada, Royal Commission on Canada's Economic Prospects, *Final Report* (Ottawa: Queen's Printer, 1958), 445.

A 1973 report of the Canadian Standing Senate Committee on Foreign Affairs commented on the declining Canadian share of trade with EEC and recommended "A more vigorous and concentrated effort . . . to penetrate the sophisticated Community consumer markets with Canadian manufactured and semi-finished exports."[32.2]

Clearly the federal government through the sixties and early seventies was attempting to hold a balance in Canada's trade relations. No doubt some changes in trade trends resulted from this policy, but they were not dramatic. Trade with the United Kingdom faced increasing obstacles as that country drew further into the Common Market, while economic ties with the United States continued to strengthen.

It was a Liberal government that negotiated the Canada-U.S. Automobile Agreement in 1965, and during the 1968 to 1984 term of the Liberal party further selective agreements of this kind became an objective. Thus at the time of defeat of this government in 1984 all the evidence pointed to so-called sectoral free trade. We will examine later the departure from this policy by the successor Conservative government.

The Department of External Affairs *Review*, issued by the Liberal government, reflected prevailing skepticism on general free trade. The balance of arguments is weighed, and the conclusion is negative. "The free-trade option has been a contentious issue throughout Canada's history, due less to economic considerations than to issues of sovereignty and self-determination. The evidence to date of the need to proceed is not convincing, nor does a call for free trade command broad support. Most assessments tend to highlight the economic advantages for Canada without taking full account of the costs or consequences both political and economic. It remains, however, an option and may garner broader support at some time in the future if changed circumstances lead to different attitudes."[33.3] Not surprisingly, the *Review* favoured free trade limited to a sectoral basis.

The Canadian Senate

The Canadian Senate is in a position to issue policy statements on almost any subject, and frequently does so. On trade it has favoured reduction of any barriers that are restrictive. The statement issued by the Senate Standing Committee on Foreign Affairs in 1972 on opening channels with the EEC was in this spirit. In 1978 the same Committee issued a report favouring study of free trade with the United States, and in a further report in 1982, *Canada's Trade Relations with the United States*, the Committee advocated a comprehensive and preferential free trade agreement between the two countries as a means of getting "a handle on U.S. non-tariff barriers." The Senators in both countries seemed to be moving along parallel paths at this point. Under the U.S. Trade Agreements Act of 1979 the Presi-

---

[33.2] Canada, Parliament, Senate Standing Committee on Foreign Affairs, *Canadian Relations with the European Community* (Ottawa: Information Canada, 1973), 38.

[33.3] Supra footnote 30.11, at 212.

dent was required to report to Congress on the possibilities of free trade agreements between countries "in the northern portion of the Western Hemisphere." The President did so duly report, but gave no commitments or even promises of further study of the idea.[33.4]

Economic Council of Canada

The Council expressed the economist's creed on trade issues in its First Annual Review (1964), and with some intrusions of pragmatism has adhered to it throughout: economies will be strongest if exposed to the rigorous discipline of international competition. In 1964 it said: "We wish to emphasize that Canada must continue to be highly interdependent with the world economy, and that deliberate policies calculated to create a more insulated and isolated economy will not, and cannot, point the way towards an alternative route to high economic performance in this country."[33.5] This credo has been frequently repeated in later reviews. The Third Annual Review (1966), for example, specifically urged the benefits of foreign trade, as follows: "In this context, Canada has clearly reached a stage in its progress towards economic maturity which warrants a much closer look at the possible contributions which freer trade could make to productivity growth in various sectors of the economy."[33.6]

The Seventh Annual Review (1970) addressed the issue of free trade directly. It said: "Many economists believe that free trade with the United States would raise Canadian productivity and average real living standards substantially . . . But any such arrangement in today's world would involve far-reaching political, social and cultural, as well as economic, considerations . . . If Canada were to pursue this path, adequate adjustment programs must be available . . ."[33.7]

In 1975 the Council issued its 200 page report, *Looking Outward*, one of the most comprehensive studies of the whole spectrum of arguments on trade policy. In principle it gives unqualified endorsement of the economist's classical argument for free trade. "We believe that Canada could prosper in a totally free trade situation, provided the adjustment was eased by means of appropriate transitional arrangements. A move towards free trade entails a transformation of the existing pattern of production to one with greater competitive viability. There is no reason to suppose that a viable economy is not available to Canada, which has immense resources of all kinds—raw materials, capital, labour—and a sophisticated and advanced social system well-equipped to cope with change . . . Thus we have

---

[33.4] Canada, Parliament, Senate Standing Committee on Foreign Affairs, *Canada's Trade Relations with the United States* (Ottawa: Department of Supply and Services, 1982).

[33.5] Canada, Economic Council of Canada, *Economic Goals for Canada to 1970* First Annual Review (Ottawa: Queen's Printer, 1964), 204.

[33.6] Canada, Economic Council of Canada, *Prices, Productivity and Employment* Third Annual Review (Ottawa: Queen's Printer, 1966), 29.

[33.7] Canada, Economic Council of Canada, *Patterns of Growth* Seventh Annual Review (Ottawa: Queen's Printer, 1970), 85-86.

suggested that a free trade policy is not only feasible for Canada but it is the best guarantee of its national interests."[33.8]

The Report's 23 recommendations are too lengthy to list here. Their general purport is that "the Canadian government actively explore the conditions under which Canada might join an open-ended free trade area with other interested countries. To this end, discussions should be held initially with the United States, the EEC, and Japan, with a view to establishing, before the end of the decade, an arrangement under which the barriers to trade in industrial products might be eliminated over a ten-year period—in accordance with an agreed method and schedule."[33.9] Other recommendations dealt with the need for adjustment programs and a variety of other issues, but free trade was the main theme.

In its Fourteenth Annual Review (1977) the Council reaffirmed its faith that "during a period of relative buoyancy, the economy as a whole should be able to absorb or offset transitional employment problems created by the move to freer trade."[33.10] However, it conceded that in the late seventies the times were not right. Many essential conditions were not then present. The matter would have to wait.

Ontario Economic Council

The Ontario Economic Council joined the debate in May 1984, with the publication of a study, *Trade, Industrial Policy and Canadian Manufacturing*.[33.11] The two authors, professors from Queen's University and the University of Western Ontario, said that the results of their studies of the benefits of free trade with the United States were "quite startling," projected as lower Canadian prices, higher Canadian incomes and increases of 20 to 25 percent in Canadian productivity. Losses of industries that would suffer would be offset by benefits of those that gained, it was claimed.

The Academic Contribution

The free trade versus tariffs debate has been a part of classical economics for over a century, and many distinguished economists have engaged in it. Adam Smith and David Ricardo were among the first of the English economists to argue against tariffs. In Canada the long list of economists who have contributed to the debate in recent years includes C.L. Barber, A. Breton, Carl E. Beigie, R.E. Caves, D.J. Daly, S. Globerman, H.E. English, D.J. Fowler, H.G. Johnson, A. Raynauld, G. Reuber, A.E.

[33.8] Canada, Economic Council of Canada, *Looking Outward: A New Trade Strategy for Canada* (Ottawa: Information Canada, 1975), 185.

[33.9] Ibid., at 188.

[33.10] Canada, Economic Council of Canada, *Into the 1980s* Fourteenth Annual Review (Ottawa: Department of Supply and Services, 1977), 42.

[33.11] Richard G. Harris with David Cox, *Trade, Industrial Policy, and Canadian Manufacturing* (Toronto: Ontario Economic Council, 1984).

Safarian, Arthur J.R. Smith, B.W. Wilkinson, P. Wonnacott, R.J. Wonnacott, and several others.

The majority of Canadian academic economists (not surprisingly) adhere to the classical economic position. Competition in an open market will result in the most efficient use of economic resources. Tariffs and other barriers inhibit competition and produce weak and unenterprising industries. In the limited Canadian market manufacturers have been destined to low productivity because of short runs and over-diversification. The high tariff forced foreign companies to set up subsidiaries in Canada that were small-scale versions of their home plants, and these were inefficient for the same reasons. Reciprocal free trade, with increased competition and greater access to foreign markets, particularly in the United States, would be the solution for these problems.

Economic reports, journals, and books provide a mass of writings on the issues, and it will only be possible to pull together a few threads of the argument, starting from the late sixties. In 1966 Prof. J.H. Dales published a series of eight essays (many of which had appeared previously) under the title *The Protective Tariff in Canada's Development.* Professor Dales examined the National Policy from the viewpoint of its contribution to Canadian economic development, and concluded that it has been "a dismal failure."[33.12] A more elaborate presentation of the free trade position came with the publication in 1967 by the Wonnacotts of their *Free Trade Between the United States and Canada: The Potential Economic Effects.*[33.13] This was later supported by other writings, including *Canada's Trade Options,* (1975) and "On the Employment Effects of Free Trade with the United States" (1986) by Ronald J. Wonnacott.[33.14]

A useful non-technical exchange among several leading economists appeared in the October 1982 supplement of *Canadian Public Policy,* an issue devoted solely to Canada-United States Trade and Policy Issues. Here the Wonnacotts restated their original arguments and dealt with the criticisms of it during the 15 years following 1967.

The Wonnacott position (and that of other like-minded economists) is that access to the U.S. market would be enormously beneficial for Canada. To quote: "Because of economies of scale in many lines of manufacturing, Canada would reap substantial benefits from a bilateral free trade arrangement. As we specialized to service the North American rather than the Canadian market, the increased volume would bring lower costs. As a result, the potential gains to Canada would not be confined to the relatively small triangular gains estimated for other countries on the assumption of

---

[33.12] J.H. Dales, *The Protective Tariff in Canada's Development* (Toronto: University of Toronto Press, 1966), 44.

[33.13] P. Wonnacott and R.J. Wonnacott, *Free Trade Between the United States and Canada, the Potential Economic Effects* (Cambridge, Mass.: Harvard University Press, 1967).

[33.14] Ronald J. Wonnacott, *Canada's Trade Options* (Ottawa: Economic Council of Canada, 1975) *and* "On the Employment Effects of Free Trade with the United States" (March 1986) XII no. 1 *Canadian Public Policy,* 258.

constant or rising costs. In fact our estimate (1967:300) was that the potential benefit would be as high as 7-10.5 per cent of GNP."[33.15] Direct benefits would come from increased specialization within industries and within plants. Wages would rise to U.S. levels in the Ontario and Quebec industrial regions, while prices would drop. Canadians would benefit from removal of Canadian tariffs, which are said to be paid not by U.S. exporters but by Canadian buyers.

The Wonnacott propositions of course failed to receive unanimous acceptance from fellow economists. One of the main criticisms was against their simplicity. For example, Wilkinson said: "In my judgment there is no single solution to the difficulties which plague Canadian manufacturing. Productivity differences which exist between Canada and the United States in many sectors will not be easily eliminated by free trade, any more than the productivity differences among varying parts of Canada have been readily eliminated over the past 115 years of confederation."[33.16] Other reservations were that conditions of perfect competition had been assumed, an unlikely possibility; that the effect on certain sectors of Canadian industry would be devastating, and that rationalization should precede rather than follow free trade; that large multinational corporations would simply close their Canadian plants and concentrate production in the United States once there was free access to the Canadian market; that multilateral free trade with all the main markets would be preferable to exclusive concentration on the United States; that in any event the Tokyo Round had achieved much of the free trade objective. Some economists added that Canada would soon lose its political independence once it became economically dependent on the United States.

These and other positions were put forward with considerable vigour, and were answered with equal spirit by the Wonnacotts. Obviously an extensive exposition would be required to do full justice to all participants; enough has been given to indicate the essentials of the academic debate, which have not changed materially since. The economists have performed a useful service in bringing into focus some of the aspects of an issue (in particular that of productivity) that traditionally have been mainly debated on the political platform. However, rather than giving the trade policy debate a new political dimension this intervention ironically appeared to have had little effect in the 1984 election campaign, where neither trade nor tariffs were an issue, even though much of the economic future of the country depends on its foreign trade.

The Business Community

Traditionally there has been a variety of tariff views among businessmen, depending largely on their particular interest in the economy. For exporters

---

[33.15] Paul Wonnacott and Ronald J. Wonnacott, "Free Trade Between the United States and Canada: Fifteen Years Later" (October 1982) XIII Supplement *Canadian Public Policy*, 412-27 at 412-13.

[33.16] Bruce W. Wilkinson, "Canada-U.S. Free Trade and Some Options" (October 1982), VII Supplement *Canadian Public Policy*, 428-39, at 437.

the freer the access to foreign markets the better, with the reservation that the price for access to some markets may be too high. Importers are also generally in favour of lower tariffs as a means of increasing the volume of their own business and lowering prices to consumers. The strongest opposition to removing tariff protection has historically come from manufacturers. The Canadian Manufacturers Association, founded in 1874, has vigorously supported tariff protection for more than a century, and has argued that the presence of many industries in Canada is proof of its value. The Association looked on with dismay as tariff walls were dismantled under the GATT, and its members were particularly upset by the Tokyo Round. A statement issued during the negotiations said in part that while Canadian manufacturers were in favour of world wide free trade, they had "serious misgivings about what they perceive to be a single minded pursuit of tariff reduction initiatives aimed at lower consumer prices, with little regard for the question of whence will come the employment income to finance consumers' purchases when companies were forced to give up their manufacturing activities in favour of importing their products."[33.17] The statement deplored the dropping of the previous anti-dumping provisions following the Kennedy Round as this had resulted in "exposure of the peculiarly vulnerable Canadian market to predatory dumping from U.S.A. and abroad."

One of the notable changes in the early 1980s has been the moderation of the general opposition of the business community to comprehensive tariff negotiations; in fact some influential bodies have given support to the need for a new commercial policy. The strongest opposition has come from protected industries—textiles, clothing, footwear, furniture, and assorted other lines. More of this later.

Canadian Labour

Canadian labour has been consistently protectionist in its policies. A spokesman during the Tokyo round is quoted as saying that "we used to preach the gospel that we could survive in the world of total free trade. We have now concluded free trade won't work." The Canadian Labour Congress policy statement during the Tokyo round called for greater attention to jobs and employment in the negotiations, stressing the precarious position of the textile industries. It also urged that more attention be devoted to non-tariff barriers, as these had succeeded to tariffs as a means of restricting trade. As will be seen later, labour has changed little in its opposition to prospects of forthcoming negotiations with the United States.

The Liberal Compromise

As a point of departure for the new approach of the Conservative government the policy of the Liberal government in recent years should be recorded. In its simplest terms it could be described as a free trade policy

---

[33.17] Canadian Manufacturers Association, *Agenda for Action*: A Position Paper of the Canadian Manufacturers Association (Toronto: the Association, 1977).

applied on a selective basis. It envisioned the selection of individual sectors of the two economies for cross-the-border rationalization of tariffs and other conditions in selected industries after the model of the automobile agreement. The Liberal government had made the case for sectoral negotiation at the Tokyo round, but had failed to win support. Canada saw it as an opportunity to clear obstructions at all levels of a vertically integrated industry, with the objective of raising it to world-class standards. The case of base metals was prominent in Canadian minds as an example, and a rich prospect was foreseen for this industry if all phases from raw materials to fully fabricated products could be relieved of tariffs and other impediments. The advantage would be to give the United States the assurance of supplies of raw materials and at the same time allow Canada to increase its local processing. The United States did not actively oppose the idea in the Tokyo round, but looked on it as a less desirable alternative than further general tariff reductions.

Subsequent developments showed that the door was not closed to the sectoral approach in Washington. The Trade Act of the early seventies included a Sectoral Negotiations Objective, and in its report on the bill the Senate Committee on Finance listed five industries for which it felt the sectoral method would be particularly appropriate. Official negotiations were carried on with Washington during 1984, but with inconclusive results, and elections in both countries forced postponement of the talks. The sectoral approach did not survive under the newly elected Conservative government, but there were other issues that did not go away. Rodney de C. Grey set out his list of items for Canada-U.S. negotiation in the 1980s in his *Trade Policy for the 1980s, An Agenda for Canada-U.S. Relations*, which included:

• government procurement (too much is excluded under the present abstention agreement, in particular items in which Canada has some capability, such as mass transit and electricity generating and distribution equipment);

• U.S. safeguarding action (Canada was likely to be unfairly swept in with other countries in U.S. measures);

• anti-dumping and countervail action (Canada is vulnerable because Canadian businesses rely on exports for survival to a much greater extent than American, and government assistance more frequently appears to be in aid of export trade, and therefore subject to countervail in the U.S.);

• customs valuation (the new base for Canada could cause problems if it required renegotiating higher rates of duty to compensate for a reduced base);

• difficulties in the pricing of transactions between related firms, estimated to represent 60 per cent or more of Canada-U.S. trade, and of imports where there is one Canadian importer, and for "end of the line goods";

• lower rates of duty for petrochemicals (a Canadian objective for the Tokyo round on which no progress was made);

• no doubt extensive revisions to the Automobile Agreement to cope with the fact that Canada is now an international market for auto parts as foreign producers are setting up their own plants;

• taxation (a better understanding about U.S. measures such as DISC and various incentives under Canadian tax law).[33.18]

Some of these issues have since been resolved, but most have remained, in some instances in greater strength.

The Conservative Alternative

As neither trade nor tariffs were prominent issues in the 1984 campaign it is remarkable that within a year of the election of the new Conservative government the country was deep in a debate on the possibility of free (or freer?) trade with the United States, a situation unprecedented in decades. What brought about this dramatic change?

Obviously a principal need was to achieve some finality in the unfinished Liberal negotiations with Washington. These could either be dropped or extended. The Conservatives chose not only to carry on but to widen the scope to a much more comprehensive basis, one that has since been given the label of "free trade," although whether or not this was the original intention is somewhat obscure. Lacking the perspective of future historians one can only advance the following tentative explanations for this turn of events: (1) the need to ensure access to markets in the United States by forestalling a growing threat of protectionism there; (2) a desire to move forward with trade policy in the absence of any immediate prospects for a GATT negotiating round; (3) a more continentalist approach by the new government, as evidenced in relaxation of the conditions for foreign investment in Canada, in the removal of measures favouring national petroleum firms, and in Canada-U.S. defence arrangements; (4) the Canadian political environment, which called for the new government to produce its own trade policy to replace the Liberal sectoral tariff plan; (5) pressure from the governments of the Atlantic and western provinces and British Columbia for assured access to the U.S. market for their products; (6) the continuing problem of regaining momentum for the Canadian economy, which, although reviving, was not growing at a rate sufficient to reduce unemployment to acceptable levels. This last was the continuing concern of economists, and found its most influential expression in the *Report of the Royal Commission on the Economic Union and Development Prospects for Canada* (the Macdonald Commission) issued in September 1985.

[33.18] Rodney de C. Grey, *Trade Policy in the 1980s: An Agenda for Canadian-U.S. Relations* (Montreal: C.D. Howe Institute, 1981).

34
Post-1984 Tariff Policy

The launching of negotiations for a Canada-U.S. trade agreement in 1986 was the culmination of events in both countries extending over the preceding year and a half. The following pages track these developments, and conclude with a review of the public debate which accompanied them in Canada.

Canadian Developments
Sectoral Free Trade

In October, following the Liberal election defeat, the press was reporting that already sectoral trade was losing favour. Liberal negotiations in Washington on four industries had reached a stalemate, and the Canadian Export Association was supporting a renewed round of multilateral agreements at GATT. The government had not declared its policy at this point.

November 4, 1984 Budget Speech

The Minister of Finance broached the tariff issue in a budget paper, *A New Direction for Canada*, as follows: "The government will examine, as a matter of priority, and in close consultation with the provinces and the private sector, all avenues to secure and enhance market access. This will include a careful analysis of options for bilateral trade liberalization with the United States in the light of various private sector proposals, as well as preparations for and opportunities provided by multilateral trade negotiations." Several questions were listed for consideration, among which the following two are of special interest: "Are there complementary or alternative approaches to sectoral trade liberalization which should be considered?" and "How would Canadian firms and regions adjust to the changed trade flows in a Canada/U.S. free trade arrangement?" At this point tariff policy options were still open.

Minister of International Trade Statement

The budget itself dealt mainly with the revision of export financing programs, and promised an early statement on trade policy. A discussion Paper, *How to Secure and Enhance Canadian Access to Export Markets*, was issued by the Minister for International Trade in January 1985. This was the strongest positive indication of government policy up to this point. It reviewed the various options open to the government and came down strongly in favour of a drive for the U.S. market through a broad measure of tariff reduction. The objective, it said, must be "A comprehensive agreement, which provided for the removal of tariffs and non-tariff barriers on substantially all bilateral trade," and the sooner realized the better.[34.1] It conceded that there were several complex issues for settlement, including transitional measures, government subsidization policies, excluded categories, non-tariff barriers, trade in agriculture products and services, and export quotas and taxes. While the paper was designed to elicit discussion, for the media it had all the earmarks of a policy statement; from that time forward "comprehensive agreement" was translated as "free trade," despite official efforts to discount that interpretation.

St. Patrick's Day Summit Meeting

The cause of trade negotiation moved forward dramatically at the meeting between Prime Minister Mulroney and President Reagan in Quebec City in March 1985. Agreement was reached for early action on several outstanding trade issues, and in developing "a bilateral mechanism to chart all possible ways to reduce and eliminate existing barriers to trade." The Canadian Minister for International Trade, James Kelleher, and the then U.S. Trade Representative, William Brock, were asked to take on this assignment and report within six months.

Discussion Paper—Competitiveness and Security

This paper was issued by the Secretary of State for External Affairs as a contribution to a forthcoming Parliamentary review of the two main international issues of the day, trade and defence. For trade the primary objective was expanded access to the U.S. market. "Trade with the United States dwarfs our trade with any other country . . . Protectionist pressures are strong in the United States and could result in new restrictions on the entry of our goods into the American market . . . For almost every export sector of the Canadian economy except grains, secure and enhanced access to the U.S. market is very important. Efforts to achieve it proceed both multilaterally and bilaterally . . . But multilateral rules, although necessary, may no longer be a sufficient means of managing our most important trade relationship. Canadians are now asking whether, in our own interests, we should consider complementing the multilateral approach by negotiating a special, bilateral trade arrangement with the United States . . . A new Canada-U.S. trade regime, incorporating expanded mutual trade obligations, could provide a stable, long-term solution to Canada's vital objectives of secure export market access and enhanced international competitiveness."[34.2] The study presents four options for achieving this result—The Current Approach, A Framework Agreement, Sectoral or Functional Agreements, and a Comprehensive Trade Agreement, with no indication of government preference.

[34.1] Canada, Minister for International Trade, *How to Secure and Enhance Canadian Access to Export Markets*, Discussion Paper (Ottawa: Department of External Affairs, 1985), 26.

[34.2] Canada, Department of External Affairs, *Competitiveness and Security* (Ottawa: Minister of Supply and Services, 1985), 30-31.

Canada must also continue to give full support to GATT. "Canada supports the initiation of a new round of multilateral trade negotiations in the GATT which will offer the opportunity to revitalize the system of rules, to address new and emerging issues such as trade in services, and to restore confidence and predictability to international trade. A new trade round would demonstrate international commitment to the multilateral trading system; the fact of negotiations would, in itself, be a valuable weapon in the battle against protectionism."[34.3]

The paper took a less positive stand on issues than that of the Minister for International Trade, rather posing questions on which the public should express an opinion in the forthcoming parliamentary review.

Prime Minister Non-committal

At a news conference in Ottawa late in June the Prime Minister observed that the Canadian people were about evenly divided on the issue of free trade with the U.S., as was the federal Cabinet. He conceded that whatever decision the government made, it would be unpopular with an important element of the economy.

Parliamentary Review

Before Parliament rose for the 1985 summer recess it appointed a Joint Special Committee on International Relations composed of 17 members of the Senate and House of Commons representing all parties. The Committee was asked to sound out and report on public opinion regarding Canada's defence role and its future tariff and trade relations. The media translated this assignment as "Star Wars" and "free trade," although in fact considerably more was involved.

The Committee spent a month, commencing in Halifax on July 15, in hearings across the country. It heard dozens of witnesses from business, academia, and social, political, and economic organizations. It was exposed to the full spectrum of views, ranging from the opinion of some economists that Canada had no feasible alternative to a broad and comprehensive removal of trade barriers with the United States, the results of which were asserted to be beneficial, to expressions of grave concern for Canada's economy, culture, and political sovereignty under "free" or "freer" trade.

The report of the Committee, issued in late August, proposed different priorities than those in governmental statements, the obvious influence of its opposition members. For the almost unreserved commitment to comprehensive bilateral negotiations with the United States there was substituted, as first priority, the promotion of a new round of multilateral trade negotiations. "A successful and timely round of multilateral trade negotiations would be the most satisfactory means of dealing with Canada's trade problems." However, the Committee agreed that a new GATT round could hardly be completed before 1990, and that the status quo with the United

---

[34.3] Ibid., at 30-34.

States was unsatisfactory. Trade talks should be initiated with the U.S. in the meantime in order to deal with near-term problems, but not as a substitute for multilateral trade negotiations. These talks should address such matters as non-tariff trade barriers, the effect of governmental subsidies, and the clarification of jurisdictional authority. Before entering into any other negotiations the government should study the effect of changes in Canada's trading arrangements on a wide range of industries, and should negotiate exclusions for Canadian cultural institutions and businesses, social policies, the agricultural sector, and the auto pact. Transitional provisions should phase in some changes over a long period (maximum ten years) and there should be adjustment programs for industries and their employees seriously affected by tariff and other changes. Nowhere did the Committee give endorsement to a comprehensive trade agreement with the U.S. In interviews with the press after release of the report there were wide differences of view between government and opposition members as to its basic thrust, specifically as to whether it had advanced or hindered the cause of "free" trade.

Prime Minister's Reaction

When questioned in Vancouver on the report on the day following its release, the Prime Minister stated that, although he had not read it in full, he said he was encouraged by the information he had been given regarding it. When asked for his views on the possibility of free trade with the United States he said he had "never favoured absolute free trade with that country." The Prime Minister was responding to rumblings of concern then beginning to emanate from the Ontario government. He confirmed that the Cabinet would be making a decision on trade negotiations later in September.

Report of the Macdonald Royal Commission

The Report of the Royal Commission on the Economic Union and Development Prospects for Canada, isued in early September, was in sharp contrast to the Parliamentary Committee's middle-of-the-road position. Its Chairman, the Hon. Donald Macdonald, a former Liberal Minister of Finance and distinguished lawyer, had earlier signalled his own conversion to free trade in a speech in New York, and the Commission's report gave unreserved support for the concept. In long and closely reasoned chapters in the main report, supported by voluminous special studies running to hundreds of pages, the Commission presented the fairly familiar economic arguments for removal of impediments to international exchange of goods, with transitional adjustments for affected industries. These have largely been presented in earlier text, and will not be repeated here. (Several of the economists previously cited were in fact either members of the Commission or authors of special studies). The "free" trade theme of the report (although even here the wording is alternatively "free" or "freer") was probably persuasive beyond the expectations of the Commission.

The appearance of the report in the month the Cabinet was scheduled to make its policy decision and the strength of its arguments no doubt moved the government toward comprehensive trade negotiations with the United States. At least the enthusiastic Chairman of the Commission was convinced of this; he told a group in November that "The Prime Minister has taken my advice and he's now opened negotiations with the United States."

Federal Trade Advisory Committee

In mid-September the federal government established a committee of some 20 to 30 representatives of business, labour, culture, and academia to advise and assist it in its trade and tariff negotiations. The Chairman was Walter Light, former chairman of Northern Telecom. The Committee was to be supported by the strong official network within the government that had been compiling studies and information for several months.

Kelleher Report

The Canadian Minister for Trade on September 26 presented to the Prime Minister a report recommending negotiations with the United States to secure better trading conditions and rules therefor. This report resulted from the six months' joint Canada-U.S. ministerial study launched at the Quebec Summit.

Prime Minister to President

On September 26 Prime Minister Mulroney announced that he had advised President Reagan in a telephone call that Canada was prepared to enter into trade negotiations with the United States. This was a necessary preliminary because under U.S. laws the President must first notify the Senate Finance Committee and the House Ways and Means Committee of his intention to negotiate, and these committees have 60 days in which to register consent or opposition. With favourable support, notice of intention to negotiate is published in the Federal Register, and 90 days thereafter formalization of a treaty may commence. The process had only begun with these preliminaries, however, and final negotiation would occupy three years.

Reisman Appointment

In mid-November Simon Reisman, a former Deputy Minister of Finance and a prime negotiator of the Auto Pact, was appointed as Canada's representative to conduct both preliminary discussions and actual negotiations with the United States representatives. Reisman was known as a convinced supporter of freer trade arrangements with Canada's principal market.

Parliamentary Debate

Throughout the fall the Opposition took every opportunity to harass the government on its trade policy formulation. The object of attack was "free" trade, which the government was alleged to have adopted as its goal (although it had carefully avoided saying so). The NDP party, reflecting strongly held union views, was opposed to any relaxation on Canada's part. The Liberal party attacked the government for lack of preparation for the negotiations, for being potentially easy prey for U.S. blandishments, and for assorted other shortcomings.

On the government side comments were restrained, but ministers periodically gave assurances as to favourite aspects of Canadian life that would not be "on the table," including the social security program, marketing boards, Canadian cultural institutions, etc. etc. Some ministers, in particular the Minister of Trade, were actively promoting the forthcoming trade moves in a series of speeches across the country.

1986 Budget Speech

The Minister of Finance returned to the trade issue in his February 1986 budget speech. He said: "This government has invited the government of the United States to enter into negotiations toward a more secure and enhanced bilateral trade relationship. Similarly, preparations are under way for Canada's active participation in the next round of multilateral trade negotiations to commence this Fall. I am strongly encouraged by the positive response of Canadian business and industry to the trade challenge this government has initiated. This response shows that Canadians do not shrink from fair competition . . . I cannot overstate the importance to Canada of ensuring that foreign markets remain open to Canadian exports and that Canadian companies take maximum advantage of markets abroad."[34.4] In the same budget speech he announced CARIBCAN, a plan to allow free-duty entry of imports after June 15, 1986, from over 20 Commonwealth islands in the Caribbean. Textiles, clothing, footwear, and miscellaneous other goods would not qualify.

The Prentice-Hall Case

A cloud over U.S.-Canada relations in 1985 arose from the refusal of the Canadian government to approve the sale of a Prentice-Hall Canadian subsidiary to a giant U.S. conglomerate, Gulf and Western. The reason given was that the transaction might affect Canadian cultural interests unfavourably, a position that confused, perplexed, and angered the U.S. government, and revealed once again the depth of difference in approach between the two countries. Clearly for the United States the flag follows investment, a position that has led to confrontations in many countries. The issue was resolved just prior to the Prime Minister's visit to Washington in March when the federal cabinet gave its approval.

[34.4]Canada, The Budget Speech, *Securing Economic Renewal* (Ottawa: February 26, 1986), 18.

Mulroney-Reagan Meeting

In a somewhat less harmonious atmosphere than prevailed a year earlier the two government leaders met in Washington on March 19 and 20. In an agenda dominated mainly by issues over acid rain some attention was given to defence and trade. A new five-year NORAD agreement was signed, and it appeared that assurance was given Mr. Mulroney by Administration and Congressional leaders that all necessary steps were being taken to facilitate the bilateral trade negotiations, despite the apparent preoccupation in Washington with Nicaragua and the budget deficit.

Warning to Canadians

In a speech in Montreal in March the Chairman of the U.S. International Trade Commission warned Canadians again of the grave concern of the U.S. authorities with the extent of government subsidization of economic activity in Canada, and forecast that this issue was certain to be a fundamental one in forthcoming trade negotiations. After mid-June 1986 a new voice would be heard, as Susan Liebeler replaced Paula Stern as chairman.

Canadians Cooling on Free Trade

Periodic polls on the question of free trade had shown a decline in support over the year to February 1986, from about three-quarters in favour to slightly more than one-half. In the prevailing uncertainty as to the government's objectives and the extent to which these would be realized it was not surprising that public conviction on the issue was less than complete.

The April Shock

The near demise of the fast-track process for the Canada-U.S. negotiations with the threatened rebellion of the U.S. Senate Finance Committee in mid-April shocked both Ottawa and Washington and sent negotiators scurrying through the halls of the Congress. For a week it was uncertain whether the negotiations were on or off. However the split vote in the Committee the following week ended the problem, to everyone's intense relief.

The Canadian Negotiating Apparatus

Over the spring months, under Trade Minister Kelleher and Trade Negotiator Reisman, a strong team of staff and committees was created as back-up for the negotiations. A staff of some 85 experts was assembled; an assistant appointed to Mr. Reisman and other senior positions were filled; chairmen for 15 committees representing individual economic sectors were appointed; and the advisory group under Walter Light was expanded from 25 to 40 members, including labour, business, and academic members. This structure should serve not only for the U.S.-Canada negotiations but for the GATT round as well.

The Office of Trade Negotiations issued a video cassette and an information kit for MPs and Senators dealing with aspects of the trade negotiations.

Opening Meeting Announced

On April 30 the Trade Minister informed a parliamentary committee that the first meeting with the United States representatives would take place in Ottawa on May 21-22. He explained that the meeting would be preparatory, and not a negotiating session per se; it was unlikely that substantial issues would be on the agenda until the summer.

Tokyo Summit

The meeting of first ministers of seven major industrial countries in Tokyo early in May confirmed that preparation for international trade negotiations would go forward at a meeting of ministers of finance in September. The issue of agricultural policy was discussed and in the closing statement concern was expressed about the surpluses that existed as a result of domestic subsidies and market protection. Canada's main interest was in wheat, since its market was rapidly being decimated by the intense competition between the United States and the EEC. Prime Minister Mulroney took a strategic step on the eve of his departure for the conference by proposing an increase in the domestic price of wheat following August 1. Agricultural policy will no doubt be a prime and contentious item on the agenda for the GATT, with the likelihood that results will be little different than on previous occasions.

Canadian Corn Farmers Strike Back

It was reported in early May that Canada's 35,000 corn farmers were preparing to file a complaint under Canadian law against imports of subsidized U.S. corn. It is stated that some 68 direct and indirect U.S. subsidies have been identified. As this would be the first action taken under Canadian countervail legislation it was welcomed by trade lawyers as an initiative that, in the light of frequent U.S. resort to this practice, was long overdue.

Busy Canadian Negotiator

The normally ebullient Simon Reisman made several comments in the week before the first meeting which cast some light on his own view of the negotiations. He would try to inform the U.S. negotiators on the basic nature of Canada, as they were no doubt in need of such education. The first meeting would probably be devoted mainly to housekeeping matters involved in the conduct of the actual meetings. It would probably require at least 10 years for both sides to fully implement all the consequences of a free trade agreement. Both sides would have to make substantial concessions if a deal was to be reached. But government social programs would not be in issue.

Negotiations Commence

On May 21 and 22 principal negotiators, Messrs. Reisman and Murphy and supporting staff (seven members on the Canadian team) met in Ottawa for the first discussions. Housekeeping details were the main business; as described by Mr. Reisman these were "the shape of the table, who is going to be at the table, when we meet, where we meet, what our framework is for negotiations, how we're going to relate to the media and the press." Nonetheless it appeared from statements made at the conclusion of the meeting that social programs, such as medicare and unemployment insurance, would not be in issue at the outset and would be kept "off the table" if at all possible. It was agreed to meet again in Washington on June 17.

Studies Released

Co-incident with the opening meetings the Department of External Affairs released some 26 government-sponsored studies on the effects of free trade. These were done mainly by independent outside organizations, gave a great variety of results, and were being quoted by the media as suited their individual policy positions. The mass of material available following this addition was now far beyond the absorptive powers of most of the citizens of Canada.

May Shocks

In a pattern that may become painfully familiar, Washington delivered two shocks to the already tense Canadian psyche on May 23, immediately following the opening meeting.

Cedar Shakes and Shingles

Following a ruling of the International Trade Commission, the President announced that a tariff of 35 percent would be imposed from June 6 on imports of western red cedar shingles and shakes from Canada. The tariff would apply over a five-year period; 35 percent for the first 30 months, 20 percent for the next two years, and 8 percent for the last six months. Some $250 million of Canadian exports and the jobs of several hundred workers were involved.

In the face of total Canadian lumber exports of over $3 billion to the United States and the extreme pressure exerted on the President to take some action this might not have seemed a matter of earth-shaking consequence to the U.S. Administration. However, the move was regarded as a shattering blow by the Canadian Parliament and lumbering industry. It was roundly condemned by Prime Minister Mulroney in the House of Commons and precipitated a lively debate among aroused members, with demands that the free trade talks be abandoned. Admittedly the timing was shocking, coming as it did at the very outset of the bilateral negotiations and combined in the same week with the decision of the U.S. lumber coalition to petition for a 27 percent tariff against Canadian softwood lumber. It gave good grounds for legitimate concern over U.S. intentions for their trade relations with Canada. The President's move was greeted with delight by the U.S. lumber industry as a fully warranted fulfilment of a presidential promise made earlier, which of course did not enhance its acceptability in Canada.

Canadian "Retaliation"

The Canadian government reacted to the "shingles and shakes" move in a manner that could hardly be described as poised. It first demanded compensation for its effects on the Canadian industry, a right given under GATT, but since lumber was not covered in the Agreement this request was firmly refused. Following a week-end of consideration by the Cabinet the Minister of Finance on June 3 announced retaliatory tariffs to match the U.S. move, both in timing (June 6) and amount of revenue (about $80 million). The new duties were comprised of (1) 5 percent on computer parts and semi-conductors; (2) 20 percent on books and some special periodicals, and (3) increased tariffs on oatmeal, tea, diesel engines, Christmas trees and cider. This action caused no particular concern in Washington, except to bring forth denials that the U.S. had started a trade war. It generally failed to please any one in Canada, (as usual) and indeed caused deep concern in the fragile Canadian book publishing industry that it might jeopardize an exemption which permitted the printing in Canada of U.S. authored books for sale in the United States. The more ironic results of the whole episode were: (1) Canadians learned that the new tariff was mainly a tax on them, which would considerably raise, for example, the price of books imported from the U.S.; and (2) the U.S. industry was reported to have found that after retail prices for shakes and shingles were raised by the amount of the tariff demand for them had dropped off. The red cedar shingles problem incidentally has a long history in Canada-U.S. relations. Forty years ago there was violent protest from the U.S. industry for concessions granted under GATT.

The Congressional Trade Bill

The second shock was the passage on May 23 by the Democratic dominated House of Representatives of Bill H.R. 4800, a comprehensive protectionist measure aimed primarily against Japan, Taiwan and West Germany but having potential effects for Canada as well. Much of the debate leading to passage dwelt on "unfair" subsidization of exports by foreign governments, and the measure would make obligatory the imposition of tariffs against imports from such countries, or from countries that had an excessive trade surplus with the United States. Imports of lumber, fish, and potatoes from Canada were mentioned in the debate.

The Senate would also be required to pass the legislation but probably would not consider it until summer. The President objected strenuously to passage of the Bill by the House and stated flatly that he would veto the measure, as he did its predecessor the previous December. In the meantime it remained an unpleasant shadow over Canada-U.S. trade relations, which were beclouded enough already.

Objectives Clarifying

It was becoming clear that an essential objective of Canadian negotiations with the United States would be either abandonment or moderation of the use of countervailing measures against Canadian imports. Trade Minister

Kelleher told a legislative committee on April 30 that "Contingency protection has got to be the essence of the protection we are seeking;" that is, protection against the application of U.S. anti-dumping, countervail, and safeguard restrictions against Canadian products. Simon Reisman was quoted as saying that the issue of the countervailing duties was crucial, and without concessions in that area an agreement would be meaningless. At a University of Ottawa conference on Canada-U.S. Trade Negotiations Donald Macdonald said that a treaty without protection from countervailing duties was not worth entering into. Other Canadian voices were echoing the same theme.

Equally, however, U.S. voices were stating flatly that any such hoped for concessions would never be accepted by the U.S. Congress. It should also be said on behalf of the United States that their employment of countervailing duties, levied after due inquiry, is fully consistent with the GATT rules, particularly where there is evidence of government subsidization of exports by the foreign country, an especially heinous offence in U.S. eyes and one against which they have long waged battle. It had in fact been one of the main accomplishments of the Tokyo GATT round to have the United States establish a review procedure prior to use of countervailing duties in place of previous arbitrary impositions. Canada has the same power, but Canadians have not chosen to exercise it, except for the corn episode just mentioned. The Canadian protest has been directed not against the legality of the procedure but the conditions under which it has been evoked and the frequency of its use.

The Canadian Trade Debate

The general influences that have given trade negotiations some urgency at the present time were reviewed earlier. These are mainly economic, admittedly of great importance, but not the stuff of the excited public debate that went on in all parts of Canada on a day-to-day basis in 1985, and which promised to continue through later years. There was nothing comparable during the GATT negotiations, and when one considers how little there is left to negotiate in the tariff area following the seven GATT rounds, clearly the central issue is not the "general" level of tariffs. This has not therefore been the traditional "high tariff" versus "low tariff" debate. There must be other influences to explain the current interest.

Undoubtedly the prospect of direct trade negotiations with the U.S. has an immediacy and a relevance that has been absent from the GATT rounds. The rounds took place in distant parts of the world, involved dealings between up to 100 countries on obscure issues the exact relevance of which was only clear to experts, and not always even to them. Direct meetings between the Canadian and U.S. governments therefore have much greater reality than GATT rounds. The issues emerge much more clearly, and their relevance for Canada-U.S. trade is fairly evident. The bias toward the emotionally charged issue of "free" trade has also been influential. For some people, "free" trade can only be interpreted as meaning the disappearance of present measures of protection, and is easily translated into loss of jobs in certain Canadian industries. This general sensitivity is vastly heightened by the shortage of alternative employment, and might in fact not be present at all if the economy were as dynamic as it was during the sixties. For others it spells the removal of real or threatened barriers to existing exports to U.S. markets and the possibility of opening new avenues, thus assuring jobs and incomes.

Not all Issues Are Economic

Since Canada undoubtedly might have become part of the United States at any time in the last 200 years it must be assumed that there was quite strong resolve against this step. Indeed much of Canada's history is written in terms of maintaining an arm's length relationship with its powerful southern neighbour, much of the time at great cost to itself. There was nervousness about abandoning this long cherished policy, particularly in the vital area of trade relations, where there would be no turning back once committed. (These concerns were expressed by Simon Reisman in a panel discussion at the Brookings Institution in 1984).[34.5] Even though economic issues dominate the present debate, there is an underlying sense that deeper matters are at stake—a sense which tradition-steeped Americans fully understand.

The Media

This concern was the stuff of active public debate in Canada on the eve of the negotiations. Its influence was most clearly evident in the media. The subject has provided a field day for the press with unlimited possibilities for journalistic initiative. The Ontario press was most active. The *Toronto Star*, true to its pro-Canada tradition, has had very little favourable to say, in its almost daily attention, to what it labelled from the beginning as "free trade." Other daily papers, the financial press, and magazines also gave the subject regular and informative coverage. On television and radio there were frequent panel discussions. A curious turn in the coverage appeared in mid-summer of 1985, in headlines that said "Bloom is fading fast for free trade," and "The surge toward free trade has abated." By September free trade had become very much a lively issue, following the full endorsation given by the Macdonald Commission. Making some allowance for editorial bias, a dedicated follower of media coverage would be reasonably well informed of the issues in the trade debate despite a certain note of fantasy introduced by the assumption in some of the media treatment that the government had absolute certainty of its ultimate objectives and a press reaction verging on hysteria to U.S. proceedings against lumber in May.

[34.5] Simon Reisman, "Canada-United States Free Trade" Paper in *U.S.-Canadian Economic Relations, Next Steps?* (Washington, D.C.: The Brookings Institution, 1984), 35-51.

The Business Community

It is difficult to generalize on business opinion because of the diversity of interests involved. The general associations appeared to be in favour of negotiating on a comprehensive scale, but not prepared to support full free trade. In an appearance before the Ontario Select Committee on Economic Affairs, the President of the Canadian Manufacturers Association said: "I'd like to make it clear that we are not talking about free trade, but freer trade, or what we call enhancement of trade." The Association favoured an early round of GATT negotiations, and had several reservations about the Canada-U.S. negotiations. The Business Council on National Issues established a Trade Task Force and pressed the federal government for early negotiation of new trade arrangements. The Canadian Chamber of Commerce appeared to give similar support. The Export Association reported in May that only 6 percent of its members opposed free trade, but that a long phasing-in period would be essential.

These views were by no means unanimous, however. The Automobile Parts Manufacturers Association of Canada was opposed to "rushing into" free trade. The Canadian Federation of Agriculture was opposed to having agricultural products "on the table" as Canadian farmers could lose a great deal and gain little in free trade negotiations, which could mean the end of subsidy and orderly marketing programs. The Ontario Federation of Agriculture took the same position. The Ontario Truckers Association feared the loss of thousands of jobs under a free trade agreement. The Canadian Pulp and Paper Association foresaw problems for production of special forms of paper if existing protection were removed. And obviously the other Canadian industries now receiving protection—textiles, clothing, furniture, footwear, etc.—were strongly opposed.

With the increasing attention paid to subsidization in Washington it follows that almost every business in Canada receiving assistance from government was nervous about the implications of free trade for their position. Similarly the growing use of service facilities in the United States by Canadian firms (data processing, for example) elicited arguments from Canadian providers of similar services for some form of restriction.

Provincial Governments

Provincial governments have played an important role in setting the tone for negotiations. At the first federal-provincial Conference of First Ministers held by the Mulroney government in Regina in February 1985, the matter was raised and freely discussed. At this time several of the provinces, led by western premiers, pressed the federal ministers to negotiate for free trade. Ontario held out, reserving opinion. The western premiers continued to promote free trade, and at their own annual meeting issued a statement favouring a "comprehensive common market arrangement," a proposal going far beyond the free trade concept. This embarrassed the NDP Premier of Manitoba, one of the four premiers present at the meeting, and that province was forced to state that its support was limited only to freer trade.

An unusual step was taken in August, when it was announced that the premiers of Nova Scotia, Quebec, Alberta, and British Columbia would meet regularly with a committee of the U.S. National Governors' Association in an effort to ease trade issues.

From August on the position of Ontario largely dominated the provincial approach to trade negotiations. At the annual conference of provincial premiers in St. John's, Newfoundland in mid-August the newly elected Liberal premier of Ontario refused to join his nine colleagues in a statement in support of free trade. He countered accusations of stubborn adherence to traditional Ontario positions with the statement that under free trade Ontario would lose 300,000 jobs. He was prepared to explore freer trade possibilities, but not at this expense. And this declaration was followed by an open assault on the federal government. Ontario preceded its attendance at a federal-provincial Conference of First Ministers in late November by release of an elaborate study which detailed the expected job loss from free trade. Among some 53 vulnerable industries it listed leather, shoes, gloves, handbags, carpets and rugs, hosiery, clothing, commercial printing, publishing, metal stamping, heating equipment, commercial refrigeration and ship-building, electrical appliances, pharmaceuticals, paint and varnish, soap and cleaning compounds, chemicals, jewellery and silverware, sporting goods, toys and signs. In releasing the studies Premier Peterson hinted at what would turn out to be his main play at the conference—the provinces should have a role in the negotiations. In a heated exchange with Prime Minister Mulroney at the conference Peterson succeeded in achieving his objective, as was confirmed in a communique issued at the conclusion of the conference.

Within a week, in early December, there was controversy as to just what had been agreed to, Premier Peterson claiming that the provinces had been given the right to veto any federal move they did not like, and the federal authorities rejecting this interpretation as going far beyond the intention. The issue was not aired again in a public meeting, but there were reports of consultations between federal and provincial representatives to settle on a working arrangement. Premier Peterson of Ontario and his officials continued to insist on a prominent role for Ontario in the negotiations, and Prime Minister Mulroney promised a meeting with the Premiers in late April or early May. In the week before the opening meeting, the provinces delegated Premier Don Getty of Alberta to confer with the Prime Minister on their behalf and a meeting of federal and provincial Ministers was set for June 2. At this meeting it was agreed that first ministers would meet with Prime Minister Mulroney every three months during negotiations and that the provinces would have the right of veto at their conclusion. This appeared to satisfy the ministers, although a question arose later over an alleged understanding that provincial trade ministers would meet monthly with the federal Secretary of State for External Affairs. At the working level, negotiations appeared to have been left to Simon Reisman, and in mid-May following a conference with provincial trade ministers he reported that progress had been made towards a better understanding. An intriguing note was introduced in this area with the appointment of Jake Warren, a distinguished public figure and a former federal official, to represent the province of Quebec in their negotiations.

The Academics

The academic position has been set out previously. The impression given in appearances by many economists before various inquiries and in speeches, reports, and articles was that the basic classical position in favour of free access to markets and full exposure of industries to foreign competition had been sharpened in debate, although somewhat modified by the reality of what one economist described as the U.S. "warren of escape clauses, injury clauses, 'Buy America' provisions, countervail and anti-dumping legislation" that constituted a "legislative minefield that stands in the way of secure access." The fundamental conflict in the accepted role of government in the two countries that was vividly outlined in the Congressional bills and decisions of the Trade Commission on alleged export subsidization also forced some rethinking of positions. Focus on the specifics of trade negotiations with the U.S. therefore had a salutary influence, and while it did not dampen the enthusiasm of free trade proponents it did introduce a healthy note of realism into the discussion.

Further than this one dare not go, as the record of economists' contributions to various public inquiries is mountainous, the material and studies of the Macdonald Royal Commission and the 26 studies released by the government surpassing in volume any previous Canadian treatment of trade and tariff issues. Appearances before the touring federal parliamentary inquiry, the Ontario Select Committee on Economic Affairs, and attendance at various conferences over the winter and spring produced a volume of academic comment too substantial to detail here.

Labour and the NDP

Canada's unions and the closely affiliated New Democratic Party (NDP) have consistently and unreservedly opposed free trade with the United States. At its Annual Meeting in June 1985, the NDP unanimously voted against it. The Canadian Labour Congress (CLC) President, when issuing a CLC policy statement later in the month, said that free trade with the U.S. would be a disaster. The annual convention of the Ontario Federation of Labour in November voted opposition to free trade negotiations. In December, following a split in union leaders over the issue, the CLC informed the government that it would not be accepting the invitation to take part in the previously mentioned private Advisory Committee on Trade. In December the Canadian Centre on Policy Alternatives, a union-sponsored think-tank, issued a study demonstrating that thousands of Canadians would lose their jobs through free trade. In January 1986, at a union-sponsored conference in Ottawa, "Dialogue 86," free trade was attacked by many speakers as a sell-out. All these pressures came to a head in bitter and unrelenting opposition voiced at the Annual Conference of the Canadian Labour Congress in May in Toronto.

Research Organizations

The trade issue received the attention of the customary research organizations. The C.D. Howe Institute, heavily drawn on previously in this work, in 1985 issued two further studies, in general favouring free trade. Other studies were published by the Economic Council of Canada, the Institute for Research in Public Policy, the Canadian Institute of International Affairs, and the Ontario Economic Council. This material was an important addition to the debate, although somewhat overshadowed by the massive efforts of the Macdonald Commission and the federal government.

United States Developments

Meanwhile events had been moving in the United States in a mixed climate. At the highest official level—President to Prime Minister—a much more cordial atmosphere prevailed under the Mulroney government. There had been an obvious strain in relations between Pierre Trudeau and Ronald Reagan (a greater contrast in personalities could hardly be imagined), and Washington had been deeply offended by recent Canadian policies, particularly the screening of foreign investment under the FIRA and the nationalistic tone of the National Energy Program. The new Canadian leader, Brian Mulroney, as the former president of a large U.S.-owned Canadian corporation, was well tuned to U.S. sensitivities, and was personally warmly disposed to President Reagan, a feeling that was reciprocated. Furthermore he had undertaken to pull the teeth of both the investment and review agency and the National Energy Policy, which he quickly proceeded to do.

The more relaxed personal relationship was evident in many ways, most prominently in the so-called St. Patrick's Day Summit in March 1985 and the U.S. financial press welcome for the other measures. Typically, of course, the initial warmth of the new relationship cooled somewhat in the following year as the two countries occasionally offended or disappointed each other, but this was to be expected. Canadian and U.S. interests are frequently at odds, but the underlying wish is to achieve compromise if at all possible.

By contrast the non-political atmosphere had become increasingly hostile toward selected Canadian industries. U.S. businesses were loud in their protest against allegedly unfair competition from imported carbon steel, lumber, fish, hogs, iron and steel pipes and tubes, etc. and were including Canada among the culprits—and in at least one major instance, softwood lumber, as the principal culprit. This climate engendered heated appearances before Congressional Committees and the International Trade Commission and produced a docket of over 300 Congressional bills. A growing U.S. trade deficit further inflamed an already tense situation. A sense of urgency in Canada for trade negotiations reflected as much a fear of loss of existing U.S. concessions or erection of new barriers as a desire to achieve substantial new arrangements.

Sectoral Free Trade

As a carry-over from the previous summer's talks with Liberal government negotiators hearings were commenced in Washington in January 1985, by the Trade Representatives Office and by the International Trade Commission on the possibility of free trade in 10 industrial sectors. These hearings attracted little public attention. At this point trade with Canada, as one headline said, was on the back burner. There was more interest in Canadian fiscal and monetary policy, in investment flows and provincial purchasing policies. The limited expressions of view on free trade at this stage were skeptical. Company executives felt that it might well lead to the closing of Canadian subsidiaries and concentration of production in the United States. Martin Feldstein, late economic advisor to the President, was quoted as saying that the time was not favourable for achieving further access to the U.S. market.

St. Patrick's Day Summit

As the meeting in March between the President and the Prime Minister approached there was evidence, as one Canadian headline said, that "U.S. is warming to the idea of free trade with us." One sign was the recent conclusion of a free trade agreement with Israel. Another was the public position taken by William Brock, the U.S. Trade Representative at the time, that the U.S. was not only concerned with the economic aspects of trade agreements but was also looking for opportunities to negotiate sweeping agreements for trade liberalization as an example to the increasingly protectionist trading countries of the world. The media were beginning to speculate that the mid-March meeting with the Canadian Prime Minister could start the process. The outcome of that meeting has already been given; at Quebec the enthusiastic William Brock declared his support for a free trade agreement, but the U.S. was being careful to leave the initiative to Canada.

Further and Conflicting Signals

Intermittent reports of policy development in Washington were conflicting. The influential Paula Stern, Chairman of the U.S. International Trade Commission, in a speech in July in Toronto, said that the benefits Canada would derive from a comprehensive free trade agreement with the U.S. were obvious, but she was not clear what advantages there would be for the United States. There would have to be equal benefits for the proposal to gain a fair hearing—a fundamental point that did not appear to have occurred to anyone else up to this time. Other reports mentioned that traditional free trade business groups in the United States were muting their voices because of the effects of imports on some of their members. As the Congressional elections approached there were increasing threats from Congress to enact protectionist legislation if the President did not act. The President in turn stated that he would veto any measure of this kind. On a visit to Toronto in mid-September the U.S. Secretary of Commerce gave assurance that there was more interest in freer trade in the United States than in protectionism. He warned, however, that negotiations would be tough in a Canada-U.S. treaty, citing that by 1987, 80 percent of Canada's imports into the United States would enter duty free, while only 65 percent of U.S. goods would have the same position in entering Canada. Furthermore average tariffs on the U.S. goods entering Canada were 9 to 10 percent, while Canadian goods entering the U.S. bore average rates of only 4 percent.

In late September, a few days before word was expected from Prime Minister Mulroney, the President told a business group that he was willing to enter into bilateral trade treaties with other countries if no significant progress was made toward a new GATT round, clearly the top priority of the U.S. Administration. A few days later the Administration announced the arrangement with four trading partners to force down the value of the U.S. dollar as a means of reducing the trade deficit. Within a few days the President sent a message to Congress promising intensification of investigations of trade restrictive practices of Japan, South Korea, and Brazil and stronger measures against dumping. He also requested funds for export financing and authority to enter into multilateral trade negotiations. He made it amply clear that he would veto protectionist legislation. On September 25 Trade Representative Yeutter delivered to the President his version of the report requested at the March meeting in Quebec. It took particular aim at Canadian government subsidies, "Buy Canadian" policies, the Canadian system of patents and copyrights, and obstacles to U.S. investment in Canada.

New Voices

During the summer of 1985 William Brock was succeeded as U.S. Trade Representative by Clayton Yeutter. The new incumbent, aided by his staff, began almost immediately to give his own imprint to the future Canadian negotiations. He was frequently quoted as favouring the most comprehensive possible agenda, with "everything on the table." A deputy, William Merkin, who dealt with Canada, had stated at a Trade Conference in the previous April, that there was no chance of the Congress waiving countervail and anti-dumping duties under a Canadian trade treaty. Speaking in Detroit in October, he reaffirmed that Canada could expect no special favours in trade negotiations, and later in Montreal said that Yeutter "wants to see everything on the table going in, whether it's manufacturing or agriculture."

Another fresh voice was that of the recently appointed U.S. Ambassador to Canada, Thomas Niles, who succeeded Paul Robinson in September 1985. In interviews before his arrival he gave strong support to the principle of free trade, and urged that Canada and the U.S. get down to serious negotiations quickly. He regarded this as one of the principal concerns of his new position. In a statement in October he assured Canadians that neither their social nor welfare programs would be at stake in the negotiations.

A third new participant was Peter O. Murphy, a career U.S. trade official, who was appointed late in the year to act for the U.S. under Mr. Yeutter's direction as negotiator in dealing with Simon Reisman, his Canadian counterpart. Mr. Murphy, formerly in the U.S. GATT representation office in Geneva and well versed in tariff negotiations, now represented the United States on the opposite side of the table to Mr. Reisman.

President Uses Veto

In December the President vetoed legislation passed by Congress that would have given added protection to textiles, apparel, shoes and copper. This led to a promise to the AFL-CIO Executive Council by House Speaker O'Neill in February 1986, of "veto-proof" legislation following the November 1986 Congressional elections.

President Acts on Canadian Negotiations

In mid-December, approximately 2½ months after the message sent by Prime Minister Mulroney in late September, the President took the formal step of requesting authority from the Congress to enter into so-called "fast-track" trade negotiations with Canada. The Congress had 60 working days to consider the request, and many other subjects of greater priority on its plate. Two committees—the Sub-committee on Trade of the Ways and Means Committee and the Senate Finance Committee—would probably have until some time in April to reject the request; if no action were taken it would automatically be granted.

Senate Threatens to Rebel

The unhappy state of the Senate Committee has been mentioned. The 20-member committee met in the week of April 14th to vote on the President's request, as the period of 60 days was about to expire. The so-called "fast-track" procedure was introduced some years ago to speed Congressional action on forthcoming trade negotiations. Once implemented it allows the President to proceed without further Congressional intervention, although the final treaty must be submitted to both Houses either for rejection or adoption in whole. At the meeting of the committee at which a vote was to be taken it appeared that 13 of the members would oppose, apparently as an expression of strong discontent with lack of administrative action against Canadian lumber imports. In view of this prospect the vote was postponed for a week, when by virtue of a 10-10 split the request was granted. The intervening week had been devoted to intense lobbying by U.S. and Canadian officials and by businessmen from both sides of the border, which saved the day for the trade negotiations.

Apparently the committee was required to renew the fast-track procedure by January 1988, when it expired, and would have an opportunity to refuse to do so. Also, the final treaty had to be approved by a majority vote in both the Senate and the House, and its fate would be uncertain even at that stage.

The Tokyo Summit

President Reagan left for the Tokyo Summit meeting in late April asserting that he would urge participants to work toward the reduction of tariffs, quotas, subsidies, and other barriers to trade in agricultural products. As earlier indicated the concluding statement of the meeting paid lip-service to this subject.

Yeutter Lists Objectives

In an appearance before the Senate Finance Committee in late April Trade Ambassador Yeutter listed issues that had been urged on the administration for negotiation with Canada. These included tariffs, government procurement, non-tariff barriers, investment, trade in services (trucking, information, and computer services, insurance and advertising), intellectual property (drug patents), and government subsidies.

Congressional Activities

Meanwhile Congress continued its own preoccupation with trade matters. In a speech to the annual conference of the American Textile Manufacturers Institute in April Senate majority leader Robert Dole promised further Congressional action against imports of foreign clothing. House representatives also promised that the Textile and Apparel Trade Enforcement Act, which the President had vetoed in December 1985, would be reintroduced in August in an attempt to overcome the veto.

Early in May the House Ways and Means Committee approved a sweeping trade bill that would impose quotas on many foreign imports and would transfer administration of some measures from the President to the Trade Representative. As earlier related, this measure was passed by the House of Representatives in late May, but had also to pass the Senate and was likely to be vetoed by the President.

Sharpening Issues

At later public conferences in both Canada and the United States U.S. panel members attempted to deflate Canadian expectations of concessions from the United States. There were flat denials that any relief whatever would be granted on an exclusive basis for Canada, that no relief was likely to be given for industries receiving government subsidies, that "cultural sovereignty" and other sensitive Canadian subjects would have to be "on the table," including broadcasting, publishing, and cultural industries, that bargaining would be very tough, etc. etc. Peter Murphy, the U.S. negotiator, contributed to this scene by stating in interviews in Washington in the week before the first meeting that the Canadian welfare programs, the Auto Pact, many provincial practices and procedures, and all other objectionable matters would be "on the table." Further confusion arose when Thomas Niles, the U.S. Ambassador to Canada, later denied publicly that the welfare programs in either country would be in issue. And a senior Canadian cabinet minister had the last word in suggesting to Mr. Murphy that if this was to be his attitude he would be well advised to catch the next plane back to Geneva. Much of this was no doubt pre-bargaining manoeuvring, but certainly left the impression that traditional U.S. benevolence toward Canadian sensitivities had faltered, if not disappeared.

Some Specific Cases

Fortunately the general decline in the value of the U.S. dollar and the drop in petroleum prices was beginning to ease the U.S. trade deficit in early 1986, following the record high of nearly $150 billion in 1985. However, this had not materially affected the Canada-U.S. dollar relationship. For many Canadian exports the price advantage was as great as it had ever been, so that specific grievances of several individual U.S. industries had not been removed. Some of the invading Canadian products had been dealt with, but there remained major areas of dissatisfaction.

Softwood Lumber

The most difficult of all the Canada-U.S. trade problems in recent years, and the one raising the most fundamental issues, has been the successful marketing of Canadian softwood lumber in the United States. In recent years the Canadian share of the U.S. market rose from about 20 percent to over 30 percent. Exports in 1984 were $3.2 billion, a major factor in the British Columbia economy, where unemployment ran in excess of 15 percent. Canadian producers attributed their success to the competitive pricing advantage under a low-valued Canadian dollar, but the U.S. northwestern lumber interests thought differently. They argued that the Canadian companies had the advantage of much lower lumber costs under stumpage rates set by provincial governments, and that this amounted to a government subsidy, against which a countervailing duty should be imposed. The Canadian industry replied that U.S. wood prices are higher because timber limits are privately owned there and cutting rights are acquired at auction and are therefore higher and that in any event this was not as significant a differential as the exchange rate. Furthermore the U.S. concessions had been given in return for Canadian actions in GATT rounds.

The U.S. interests made their case before the International Trade Commission in 1982, but the Commission ruled that there was no present legislation under which the level of government natural resource charges could be deemed to represent a subsidy.

In the following year in ruling on this issue the U.S. Department of Commerce had held that the Canadian charges did not represent a subsidy. Several bills were introduced into the Congress to support the lumbermen's position in 1984 and 1985. None of these created more concern for Canada than that of Congressman Sam Gibbons, Chairman of the influential House Subcommittee on Trade of the Ways and Means Committee, whose bill, among other things, attempted to define government subsidies to include stumpage fees on government-owned land; the bill's measurement of the subsidy was the extent to which Canadian stumpage fees fell short of U.S. stumpages. In practice this concept could have produced duties of 30 to 60 percent on lumber imports from Canada. In principle, the Gibbons bill basically brought into question all government programs not specifically directed to export assistance but which indirectly might have this result. (In a trading country such as Canada, what actions of government, no matter how remote from them, do not have some effect on exports?) If this concept were accepted as U.S. trade negotiation policy, it would have devastating consequences not only for Canada but for nearly every other country.

Other bills presented in 1985 by an increasingly aggressive Congress were designed to reduce the Canadian share of the U.S. market to 20 percent by imposing quotas or charges on imports. In June a Congressional Committee held hearings on Bills presented in 1985; they were opposed by representatives of the Canadian forestry industries and the U.S. Administration, the latter arguing that the Gibbons bill was contrary to GATT agreements and if adopted would open a Pandora's box in international trade. Concurrently the International Trade Commission was again holding hearings on the request of the lumbermen for protection against "subsidized" Canadian imports.

During the summer Canada's Trade Minister said that he would like to have the lumber issue settled before starting on treaty negotiations, and at his confirmation hearings in June the new U.S. Trade Representative, Clayton Yeutter, gave his own view that no progress would be made toward negotiations while the issue was outstanding. In late September Trade Minister Kelleher took the unusual step of writing to Congressman Sam Gibbons asking that he withdraw his trade bill. Yet time moved on without a settlement. In October the Trade Commission, in response to a second lumber industry petition, ruled, as it had in 1982, that there was no basis in existing law for the case being made.

These and other hearings brought to Washington Canadian business and government representatives (including the Premier of British Columbia) in unprecedented numbers, and gave many their first experience of Washington lobbying.[34.6] There was evidence in November that the issue had surfaced in Washington at a top policy level when the Administration decided to ask Canada for immediate high-level talks to find a solution, and U.S. Trade Representative Clayton Yeutter had communicated this message to International Trade Minister James Kelleher. Congressional pressure was directed at having Canada "rethink their stumpage pricing policies." If realized, this objective would upset arrangements (largely provincial) which were generally the result of a century or more of negotiations and experience that had little to do with selling lumber in the U.S. market in 1986. There had been no settlement early in 1986, but monthly meetings were begun between specially appointed trade authorities for the two countries, and members of Congress were expressing satisfaction that the U.S. Admin-

---

[34.6] For subsequent organized efforts see the statement of the Minister of State (Forestry) Commons *Debates*, May 13, 1986.

istration was finally "getting tough" with the Canadians over lumber. The Prime Minister was said to have been given a firm warning of possible impending action during his March visit to Washington, but nothing further happened over the following month, much to the discontent of members of Congress. This delay no doubt was mainly responsible for the threatened rebellion of the Senate Finance Committee in mid-April. Although negotiations had continued it was fairly clear that the Canadian government was not prepared to settle this major issue prior to the opening of trade talks; the federal Forestry Minister stated publicly that Canada should not budge in its position.

The Canadian lumber industry offered some help to its U.S. counterparts but this was unwanted. Meanwhile pressure from the U.S. lumber industries continued to build in Washington. In early May the President wrote to the Chairman of the Senate Finance Committee to assure him that if current Canada-U.S. negotiations failed to settle the issue he would "take such action as may be necessary to resolve this problem consistent with U.S. law." Nonetheless a coalition of U.S. lumber companies declared its intention of filing a new appeal with the International Trade Commission, apparently this time with greater expectations of success, but in mid-May was persuaded to withhold this action for one week in view of a Canadian proposal that the two governments appoint high level envoys to settle the dispute. When this idea fell through the coalition filed a petition for a 27 percent countervail against Canadian softwood lumber, on which a hearing was held on June 10. The Commission had until July 3 to determine whether material injury had been suffered by the industry. The Commission reached a positive judgment on this question, and the case was to be considered by the U.S. Department of Commerce to determine whether the injury resulted from the granting of a subsidy, an issue which depended on an interpretation of a provision of the 1930 Tariff Act. This process might extend to late summer or early fall before the results were known. Canadian representatives appeared before the Commission hearing, and met in June to consider what further steps to take.

Obviously the lumber question is a grievous issue on both sides of the border, and unfortunately a settlement that would appease both countries seems highly unlikely. Although it is by far the largest issue in the forestry area there are others as well. There were almost no tariff restrictions on entry of other forestry products into the U.S., but Canadian tariffs on several forms of paper were at protective levels. The Canadian industry valued this protection; the U.S. producers wanted it removed.

Steel

The low estate of the steel industry has been an extremely delicate problem in the United States in recent years. A flood of imports from new low cost producers in several countries had devastated the U.S. industry, much of it badly in need of modernization. Canada's exports of carbon steel, the crucial product, were $1.3 billion in 1984 and some 2,000 jobs were at stake, so that the matter was not trivial. Canada had made no special drive on the

U.S. market and while it was agreed by the U.S. authorities that it was a "fair trader" there was always the possibility that it might be caught up in restrictions imposed on other countries. The issue reached a fever pitch on the eve of the U.S. election in 1984, when Canadians feared a politically-motivated protectionist program. A headline in the *Toronto Star* of September 12 asked: "Will the U.S. election decide fate of Canada's steel exports?"

The U.S. steel companies approached both the Congress and the Trade Commission for help, asking that foreign imports be limited to 15 percent of the market, about half the existing 33 percent. A Democrat-sponsored trade protection measure was before Congress for months, and was finally passed in October. For steel its terms were an anti-climax, as the President had already announced a program. This had been prompted partly by Congressional pressure and partly by the success the steel companies had enjoyed with the Trade Commission. During the summer the Commission had given favourable rulings on two appeals and, after hearings and studies, recommended to the President that he impose both quotas and tariffs on imported steel for a five-year period to allow the U.S. mills time to modernize. In September the President rejected this advice, announcing that the Administration would rely on other measures available to it, mainly voluntary export restraint agreements. Such an agreement had been negotiated with the EEC previously, and in due course similar understandings were developed with Japan and 13 developing countries, with the objective of restricting foreign imports to 18-20 percent of the U.S. market.

Canada was the only significant U.S. supplier that was not asked to enter into a restraining agreement, but it was understood that Canada's share was to be reduced to 3 percent, and Canadian imports were being monitored. This informal action did not preclude request for a restraining agreement if the objective was not achieved. In June the President complained that Canada was among countries whose exports to U.S. were "well above traditional levels." In August 1985, Canada was included on a list of countries that had increased their U.S. steel exports, a further indication of dissatisfaction in Washington. In November there were reports of steel shipments arriving in the U.S. from countries having no steel industry, regarded in Washington as a blatant and fraudulent attempt to evade the steel import quotas. Where the steel issue would ultimately come to rest was difficult to tell on the eve of the Canada-U.S. trade negotiations.

A move not necessarily related to the negotiations was taken on June 3 when anti-dumping duties were imposed on Canadian steel products for use in oil and gas wells sold in the U.S. by three Canadian companies. A revealing aspect of the case was the imposition of a countervail duty, in addition to the anti-dumping duty, on the IPSCO company of Regina in respect of a subsidy it had received from the federal and provincial governments as long ago as 1979-81 to expand its capacity. Although the penalty imposed was minor, its imposition was an additional instance of the growing U.S. concern over government subsidies of any kind no matter when received.

Pork Meat and Hogs

In a pattern becoming familiar, Canadian hog producers were subjected in 1985 to a countervailing duty on processed pork and a special 4.4 cents per pound tariff on live swine, on the grounds that Canadian pork exports were subsidized by government. Following appearances before the Trade Commission by pork interests from both Canada and the U.S., in June the Commission lifted the duty on processed pork but left the charge on live swine. The Canadian Minister of Trade challenged this act as probably contrary to GATT.

Atlantic Fish

In June 1985, the International Trade Commission ruled that salted cod from Canada was being sold in the United States at less than fair value, and recommended that a duty of 20.75 percent be imposed. On an appeal in May 1986, it ruled that conditions had not changed and the duty should be continued. In 1985 it also heard arguments from New England fishermen that Canadian fish exports benefitted from 80 different government subsidies, and countervailing duties should apply. As is now customary the issues were battled out by representatives from both sides of the border, with very little light thrown on the general question of ineligible subsidies. The Commission was able to satisfy itself on this score, however; in a ruling early in January 1986, it held that 12 federal programs and 19 provincial programs assisted Canadian exports. It recommended a 6.85 percent duty on Canadian imports of cod, haddock, sole, and other groundfish.

Other Imports

The above are the major trade items on which action had been taken by the United States to 1986. Clearly the lead given by Representative Gibbons on the issue of government subsidies was influential in attacking successful Canadian imports. In addition a long list of other commodities was either under study or had been subject to action by the Commission, including iron and steel pipes and tubes, softwood shingles, sugar and products containing sugar, rock salt, raspberries, specialty steel products, etc. We return later to subsequent developments in these and other areas.

35
Trade Update: Mid-1988

The Free Trade Negotiations

After the opening meeting in May 1986 discussions between Simon Reisman for Canada and Peter Murphy for the United States, and their accompanying experts, followed at more or less regular monthly intervals in alternating locations in the two countries. These were usually Washington and Ottawa, but on occasion other sites were chosen. While the early pace was fairly relaxed both sides were fully aware of the October 3, 1987 deadline for the first step to "fast-track" congressional treatment. As months passed pressure became more intense.

What actually transpired at these meetings, over twenty in all, will only be known when either Murphy or Reisman or some of their staff write their memoirs or official papers become available. The burden of short press interviews at the conclusion of each meeting was that progress was being made but that many difficult problems remained. The media made the most of these brief insights, and with the support of other leads there was frequent conjecture on the central issues. In the jargon of the negotiations this became a question of whether or not a certain matter was "on the table." At various times almost every aspect of Canadian life was reported to be "on the table," a media ploy that had the desired result of at least eliciting a statement, usually a denial, from someone close to the process.

One matter that was clearly on the table from the Canadian side was the growing use by the United States of countervailing duties against Canadian imports, the most recent and devastating instance being the softwood lumber case. Apparently Canada's first objective was to be excluded from the countervailing practice, a proposal which, if seriously made, was justifiably rejected by the Americans. Canada had, after all, accepted this method under the GATT agreements where government subsidies were involved. Clearly subsidies from government have been a Canadian way of life—granted that their effect on exports is not always clear. As a second best Canada argued strenuously for a separate dispute settlement mechanism that would develop a new set of trade rules and give binding decisions on trade issues between Canada and the United States, thus avoiding existing U.S. trade laws and appeal processes. This proposal almost ended the possibility of an agreement, and survived in attenuated form in the final draft (see later).

Other delicate and difficult issues acknowledged to be under debate at various times were Canadian restrictions on foreign investment, the Canada-U.S. Auto Pact, cultural industries, energy, and government procurement. The veil was drawn on what little was being said about proceedings with the announcement by Simon Reisman in July, 1987 that with the approach of the negotiations to some of the more crucial issues it would no longer be possible to keep the media informed. But a month later, rather than a black-out, at the conclusion of a meeting in Cornwall, Ontario, said to be a crunch round, Reisman told the media in apparent frustration that if any further progress was to be made the heads of state of the two countries would have to become involved. It was assumed from this that the negotiators had failed to reach agreement on several major issues, a supposition verified by later events. No doubt this partly reflected preoccupation of the U.S. trade officials with preparations for the GATT round and current U.S. confrontations with the EEC over agricultural subsidies. Nor were relations with Canada at their best at this juncture. The imposition of tariffs by the U.S. on Canadian softwood lumber and potash and friction over steel imports were not regarded in Canada as the actions of a friendly neighbour. And in the background there was the ever present threat of new and tough provisions of a trade bill being drafted by a joint committee of Congress, described as being a nightmare for Canada and other U.S. trading partners. Perhaps it was fortunate that the main attention of Congress became distracted by the Iran-Contra affair at this stage and that the U.S. balance of trade appeared finally to be improving. Trade issues temporarily became secondary.

Canada Withdraws

The exact course of events that preceded the action is not clear, although the statement at the end of the Cornwall meeting might have been a portent. On September 23 Simon Reisman walked out of a negotiating meeting in Washington and declared that negotiations were ended. He was reported to have blamed the United States for intransigence on the key issue of a joint trade tribunal to issue binding decisions. Pat Carney, the Canadian International Trade Minister, also accused the United States of raising last minute difficulties on some issues that it had been agreed were not on the table—such as Canada's regional and cultural subsidies. It was of course to be expected that the United States' officials had their version of where the intransigence lay, with charges of renewal of argument on matters which they regarded as settled. As a healing gesture on the day of Reisman's departure Clayton Yeutter issued a statement affirming U.S. willingness to continue negotiations. In the House of Commons on the following day the Prime Minister supported Mr. Reisman's action, but also left the door open for resumption of negotiations.

With two weeks left to the final date for drafting an agreement outline to submit to the Congress under the "fast-track" system and many major issues still unsettled, urgent action was needed. At this point a senior group of cabinet level negotiators took over. On the Canadian side it included Pat Carney, Michael Wilson, the Minister of Finance, and Derek Burney, the Prime Minister's chief of staff. On the U.S. side the central figure was Treasury Secretary James Baker, with whom Wilson had previously arranged to confer just at this time in preparation for a Monetary Fund meeting. On Thursday, September 24, the two met in Washington as previously arranged, and spent some time on resumption of trade negotiations. As a sequel, on the following Sunday, September 27, Mr. Baker was given a letter setting out Canadian conditions for a resumption. This led to a 7½ hour session the following day, Monday, September 28, between the Canadian group and Secretary Baker and Clayton Yeutter. Pat Carney told the media that much progress had been made at the meeting and Mr. Baker issued a statement confirming that the United States was willing to resume negotiations.

In the following week the federal inner Cabinet met to consider further steps. The Canadian group went off to Washington again but after a short and apparently discouraging meeting with Treasury Secretary Baker and Clayton Yeutter on Thursday, October 1, they returned home empty-handed. Such was the despondency at this point that it was reported from Ottawa that the free trade deal with the United States was dead. But in the evening of the same day Secretary Baker telephoned a proposal for a tribunal on trade problems which, although not meeting all Canada's requests, was thought to be workable. As a result the high level Canadian group returned to Washington the next day and plunged back into negotiations. By October 3, the last day—after 27 hours of intensive work with Baker, Yeutter and a battery of experts—an outline of a treaty was completed only a short time before midnight. Prime Minister Mulroney and the Cabinet were informed of the conclusion of the negotiations and letters signed by President Reagan were dispatched to the two houses of Congress before midnight officially informing them that he would be entering into a free trade agreement with Canada, all that was required at this stage to meet the "fast-track" deadline. Both Murphy and Reisman were involved in the final negotiations and appeared to be pleased with the outcome.

On Monday, October 5, the summary text of the tentative agreement appeared in the press, and the great trade debate sprang to life on all sides, finally with some substance in place of rumour. As the details of the final agreement will be examined later the headings of the outline will be sufficient at this stage. They were Agriculture, Alcoholic Beverages, Energy, Automotive Industry, Services, Financial Services, Investment, Intellectual Property, Culture, Customs, Government Procurement, Personnel Movements, General Elimination of Import and Export Restrictions, Standards, Import Safeguards, Dispute Settlement, and Subsidies and Dumping.

Subsequent Developments

At this point the timetable was dominated by the coming expiry of the President's fast-track authority on January 2, 1988. The President was required to give notice of his intention to enter into an agreement with Canada 90 days before this date, and this had been met on October 3. Having fulfilled the first condition, the next need was to produce the full agreement in 90 days and submit it to Congress by midnight of January 2. Although much of the legal and technical work had already been completed the outline had still to be fleshed out into a full-scale document that would cover all matters in detail and be signed by the President and the Prime Minister. This would require establishing clearly just what had been agreed to in the two-day marathon that had produced the outline. There were further deadlines even beyond this; each country would have to introduce legislation making the changes in its laws called for by the agreement, allow time for committee hearings and legislative debate, and obtain passage by the end of 1988, a truly challenging race to the finish.

The achievement of the full version of the agreement was not without friction. Discussions between the two countries were resumed, and this was left to the original negotiators, Reisman and Murphy, aided by a battery of lawyers. Early in December it appeared from remarks by Reisman that in his view some terms of the agreement were being re-negotiated, but the Prime Minister denied this, and Clayton Yeutter echoed the same denial from Washington. Canadian ministers were following developments closely, and appeared prepared to travel to Washington again if necessary. The press listed issues that were said to be under pressure from the United States, but these were settled without further high level travel.

An Agreement is Completed

As attention had been focused on the January 2 date the issuance of a final version of the agreement on December 11 came as a surprise. The Prime Minister took advantage of the event to make a dramatic presentation to Parliament of the printed text of the 218-page document that embodied the agreements between the two countries. His speech of introduction received a standing ovation from his own party, but opposition members were prompt to register deep distress over the move and to call for an immediate election to obtain the views of the country. This opposition did not deter the Prime Minister. He signed the agreement in Ottawa and the President signed at his ranch in California on January 2, 1988.

The Main Terms of the Agreement

It will not be possible here to give more than a brief view of the contents of the agreement; it was in any event well covered in many other sources. The document opens with a preamble, the gist of which is that the two countries wish to improve their trade relations and for this purpose, "consistent with Article XXIV of the General Agreement on Tariffs and Trade, hereby establish a free-trade area." Some definitional sections follow as a prelude to the main purpose of the agreement, the removal of tariffs, and other barriers to trade between the two countries.

Tariffs

For removal of tariffs three groupings are established. Tariffs will be removed on January 1, 1989 for a group of products recognized as ready to compete; for another group requiring a longer period to be ready to compete tariffs will be removed over a five-year period following January 1, 1989; for yet another group, requiring a significant period for adjustment to free trade, tariffs will be removed over the ten years following January 1, 1989. This latter group includes most agricultural goods, textiles and apparel, softwood plywood, railcars, steel, appliances, and tires, and indicates the most sensitive areas. Over the term of the agreement certain other trade features will be eliminated, including customs user fees, duty drawbacks, duty waivers or remissions and import and export restrictions, the latter with some exceptions. The Harmonized System was to be the basis for tariff changes, which are contained in a fat appendix to the Agreement.

Trade Barriers

National treatment of imported goods, already established under GATT, is re-affirmed. Technical barriers to trade will be kept to a minimum. Where domestic producers are caused serious injury by the reduction in tariffs, earlier rates or most-favoured nation rates may be restored for a maximum of three years, but not to extend beyond 1998. Each country also agreed to exempt the other country from measures taken to restrict trade with a third country or countries for emergency reasons. Both countries will be allowed to continue their prohibition against export of logs.

Agriculture

The longest chapter of the Agreement (Seven) dealt with the controversial issue of agricultural subsidies. It commenced with the statement that "The Parties agree that their primary goal with respect to agricultural subsidies is to achieve, on a global basis, the elimination of all subsidies which distort agricultural trade, and the Parties agree to work together to achieve this goal, including through multilateral trade negotiations such as the Uruguay Round." There followed designated treatment for a few products, but the main bulk of the chapter arose from a commitment by Canada to lift restrictions on imports of U.S. wheat, barley, and oats when U.S. subsidization of these products falls to or below the Canadian level of subsidization. Elaborate schedules listed the programs of subsidization in each country and the formulae to be used in calculating their comparative levels. A Working Group was even established to consult annually on the making of these calculations. The whole is a fascinating exercise in the identification of specific subsidies in a large economic area of the two economies; in Canada some 17 programs are listed.

Wine and Spirits

A chapter dealing with wine and spirits follows. In addition to the removal of tariffs the chapter ruled out any discrimination against U.S. products. Differential mark-ups on spirits were to be eliminated immediately and those on wines over a six-year period. This was regarded as the death knell for Ontario and B.C. grape growers and wineries. Beer and malt beverages were specifically excluded from the treaty.

Investment

In the delicate field of foreign investment Canada undertook to grant treatment no less favourable than that granted its own nationals but would retain its foreign investment review process, with liberalized terms. It agreed specifically to raise its existing threshold of $5 million for review of foreign investments to $150 million in four steps by 1992. Ceilings for indirect investment were to be raised and all restrictions dropped after 1992. Performance requirements, such as Canadian ownership, minimum expenditures in a locality or region were to be prohibited, but certain other requirements, such as expenditure on research and development, were to be allowed. Existing arrangements were unchanged for oil, gas and uranium, and the ownership of the communications and transportation industries. Existing preferential treatment for maritime shipping in each country was to be retained.

Energy

In the basic area of energy each country retained its right to control imports in an emergency, but agreed that it would not take direct action to reduce the ratio of its exports to the other country below that of the previous 36 months. This is not to be interpreted as an undertaking that the ratio will be maintained—each country will have to compete in the market as under normal circumstances. It was a commitment that the ratio would not be changed by government action.

Government Procurement

For government procurement the main change was a lowering of the threshold for open bidding for federal contracts from the present GATT limit of $171,000 U.S. to $25,000, with some forms of purchases omitted.

Services

For the first time this agreement covered services. This was almost inevitable in view of the U.S. threat to boycott the GATT round if services were not to be on the agenda. A distinction was made between general services and banking and finance services. The former, which are to be subject to no barriers by either country, were listed in detail as "covered" services, being services for agriculture and forestry, mining, construction, distribution, insurance, real estate, commercial, and other; the last included the very important item of computer services. The largest group is commercial services. Any service not detailed in these lists of course remains open for discriminatory treatment.

For financial services the trade was one-sided. The U.S. had little to offer as ownership of investment companies, now open to banks in Canada, was still barred in the U.S. by the Glass-Steagall Act, and much of the restrictive legislation on branching and foreign ownership was state legislation, and therefore beyond the agreement. In return for almost nothing Canada removed for U.S. banks and financial institutions the main impediments to ownership and operation that had become a main element of Canadian banking law. It also made the same concessions regarding U.S. federally incorporated trust, investment, insurance, and loan companies.

Auto Pact

The 1965 Auto Pact several times was said not to be on the table but in the end some concessions had to be made by Canada, although the main body of the agreement, including the vital performance commitments, remained intact. The changes included withdrawal of all tariffs on cars and parts imported from the U.S. in the next ten years, a feature that had not been previously included. Canadian restrictions on the import of used cars would also be removed over the next five years. Much of the rest was directed to denying newly arrived foreign, and particularly Asian, companies from taking advantage of the pact unless they met the condition of a 50 percent North American content by their 1989 models. Otherwise the provisions of the pact would be restricted to companies currently eligible, as listed in the agreement (some 150 names). Duty remission on export of parts from Canada would be eliminated in 1989.

Cultural Industries

The dreaded effect of the agreement for Canadian cultural industries was put to rest by a special clause excluding them from its terms. Apart from a reduction in postage on U.S. periodicals to give them the same rate as Canadian no other changes of significance appear to have been made.

Disputes Settlement

On the nearly fatal issue of disputes settlement the agreement set out two mechanisms: one will be employed for settling disputes under the terms of the agreement; the other will deal with the now familiar cases of anti-dumping measures and countervailing duties, which are not affected otherwise by the agreement.

For the first set of problems a new Canada-U.S. Trade Commission will be established. In relation to the agreement the commission was empowered "to resolve disputes . . . oversee its further elaboration and to consider any other matter that may affect its operation." The commission will be composed of equal numbers of members, with at least one cabinet minister from each country. Under the treaty each country agreed to inform the other of any major changes in its policy or practices that would affect the agreement and if, following consultation, a difference of view existed as to the acceptability of the change, either of the countries or both might ask that the issue be referred to the Trade Commission. The commission was empowered to deal with the matter itself, but was directed to establish a roster of experts for panels to which the dispute might be referred. Once a verdict was arrived at, if either country did not follow it the other could take retaliatory action, usually by the imposition under GATT rules of countervailing duties.

The second procedure would be used where one country amended its anti-dumping or countervailing duty laws or imposed countervailing duties against the other. Cases were to be considered by bi-national panels having equal representation from each country and, as under the present GATT appeal system, a decision would be given as to the propriety of the actions in the light of the situation of the country and the rules of GATT. The findings of a panel were to be final, and if the offending country did not change or withdraw its action the other country might take offsetting steps. To facilitate this procedure a Secretariat was to be established having an office and staff in both Ottawa and Washington.

The system based on secretariat and panels would last for five years, with a possible extension for two years. A clear indication of the origin of most of the problems in this area was given by inclusion of a separate section, one of the most crucial of the whole agreement. It provided for the establishment of a Working Party with directions to "(a) seek to develop more effective rules and disciplines concerning the use of government subsidies; (b) seek to develop a substitute system of rules for dealing with unfair pricing and government subsidization." Each party undertook to ensure that this process went forward, and the secretariat was directed to do everything possible to assist with it. In the end the results of this exercise could bring about more fundamental changes in the policies of the two governments than any other provision of the agreement. It will be fascinating to observe the success of this effort to terminate long-standing and deeply ingrained attitudes toward the role of government in the economy, the subject of much of this book.

Selling the Deal

The signing of the agreement was the signal for release of a barrage of promotional material from the Departments of External Affairs and Finance and the International Trade Office in Ottawa. This took the form mainly of press releases and pamphlets, for which press runs were in the millions. In this fervent campaign an Economic Assessment issued by the Department of Finance supplied some much needed realism. The opposition parties complained bitterly that appropriations they were asked to pass to support this publicity were really part of the government's platform for re-election, and not properly chargeable to the public purse. Various public relations experts were reported from time to time to be in charge of this campaign for the government, but the campaign never quite succeeded in achieving a comprehensive role at this early stage.

In Parliament

The free trade issue was only one of several that made the 1988 session among the most controversial in years. Also demanding urgent attention was legislation on refugees, child care, abortion, tax reform, privatization, financial institutions, the Meech Lake Accord, etc. And the prospect was for an election in the near future, the result of which could easily hinge on decisions in any one of these areas. Despite this long list free trade appeared to be a top priority and one that seemed most likely to be a main election issue.

The 1987 Committee Hearings

The House of Commons Standing Committee on External Affairs and International Trade provided a platform for expression of wide ranging public views on the free trade outline in hearings that started in October immediately after its release. The record of its 36 sessions, at which some 240 individuals or groups appeared (Minutes 29 to 65), is probably as good a source of every shade of opinion as is available, although some views may have changed subsequently when the full text appeared. The committee report, issued in December, also served as strong evidence of the deep cleavage between the government and the opposition parties. The majority report, following a lengthy review of the tentative agreement and the hearing evidence, concluded that, "on balance, it is a good agreement for Canada." The two opposition parties made separate and vigorous dissents from the majority report, in general rejecting both the hurried manner in which the hearings had been conducted and more importantly the contents of the draft treaty. On March 16 Parliament allowed itself a day to debate a general motion on the issue of free trade, in which the leaders of all three parties participated. The government had no difficulty in winning the subsequent vote, 160-58.

The Government

The government prepared itself for the undoubtedly long and wearing process of guiding the agreement and the supporting legislation through Parliament by appointing the scrappy and articulate John Crosbie as Minister for International Trade in March. The first parliamentary action taken by the new minister was the introduction on May 23 of Bill C-130, An Act to implement the Free Trade Agreement between Canada and the United States of America. The Act paid little attention to the agreement, except to say, in Section 7, that "the agreement is hereby approved." The main purpose of the legislation was to provide interim appeal procedures until a new Canadian International Trade Tribunal was established (to replace the Canadian Import Tribunal, the Tariff Board, and the Textile and Clothing Board) and to amend some 27 statutes to implement agreement undertakings. It is significant that for textiles, one of the more exposed of Canadian industries, special provision was made for appeals by that industry against injury from imports.

With action by the opposition to use every possible tactic for delaying passage of the bill the government in mid-June was threatening to keep Parliament in session all summer if necessary. With planned committee hearings on the bill and tardy passage by a Senate poised to be difficult, the timetable for passage of the legislation by the end of the year was expected to be very tight.

The Official Opposition

The opposition leader, John Turner, was unremitting in his attack on the free trade proposals. At this early stage, his position seemed to be that he was not opposed to freer trade but he would not have tried to achieve it by the route of an omnibus agreement which in his view held the threat of affecting many other aspects of Canadian life as well as trade. He frequently urged the Prime Minister to abandon his program, particularly at crucial stages when the outcome was in doubt. He also frequently demanded that the Conservatives hold an election on the free trade issue before concluding a final agreement. If elected he promised that the Liberal party would "tear up" the agreement, a feat which it soon became apparent from its bulk would be at least a physical impossibility.

It appeared that the leader's position was not always acceptable to his Parliamentary group, as there were rumours of dissent on this subject as well as the Meech Lake Accord. Differences in view were not limited to Liberal members of Parliament; former Liberal cabinet members, most of them one-time colleagues of Turner, were emerging on opposite sides of the debate. Donald Macdonald, the Chairman of the Royal Commission on Economic Union and a former Liberal cabinet minister, obviously fully supported the idea. On the other hand Eric Kierans and Edgar Benson spoke out against it. There probably is no "Liberal" view on trade policy today as there was at one time, although shades of some former Trudeau policies were appearing in proposals that Canada should be seeking a broadening of world markets rather than concentrating on the United States. A brochure issued by the party following signing of the trade agreement said: "A very simple and basic rule of business tells us that you do not sell all your products to just one buyer." A more formal statement of the Liberal position was issued on June 13, under the title, *Expanded Choices*. This manifesto was followed by others as the time for the expected election approached.

The New Democrats

The other opposition party, the New Democrats, at this stage, went far beyond the Liberals in the violence of their opposition to free trade. In keeping with their close association with the Canadian unions the party on every occasion advanced the long list of fatal consequences that would befall Canada under a free trade deal, including the loss of Canadian culture, sovereignty, social programs, and jobs. The call for cessation of negotiations was constant, and obviously wasted on the government. In their policy statement following the signing the NDP listed a whole range of options the government could follow which in their view would produce much greater economic benefit than the trade deal. Their proposals included lowering interest rates, exploiting Canada's energy resources for Canadian benefit, encouraging local economic development, spending more money on research and development, extending trade with much broader horizons than the United States, etc. The report conceded that the NDP approach was interventionist, hardly a revelation.

The Polls

Clearly all efforts of the parties were now focused on the election which the government would normally hold four years after its coming to power (although the Constitution allows five years). The issues were involved enough to make this a crucial contest, but the polls on party standing were not adding much light. At mid-summer 1988 the Liberals were leading but the Conservatives were emerging from the cellar, where they had been for months, to displace the NDP in second place. Under these conditions almost any outcome was possible.

The Provinces

The federal government met its commitment to keep the provinces informed in two ways. Provincial ministers of trade, or their counterparts, met at frequent intervals with the Canadian negotiating team. Higher priority was given regular meetings of First Ministers with the Prime Minister. Following an initial meeting in June 1986, the First Ministers met with the Prime Minister every quarter. The opportunity for public utterances was not left unexploited by those attending these meetings and in time the relative provincial positions on free trade became fairly clear. After some wavering on the part of others three provinces finally emerged in early 1988 as being opposed—Ontario, Manitoba, and Prince Edward Island. Among the others, the western provinces in particular were enthusiastically in support. Attitudes of course reflected the balance of gains and losses expected for each jurisdiction.

The Ontario opposition had some element of surprise, as one of the province's most vibrant industries, the automobile plants, owed much to the free trade aspects of the Auto Pact. By the same token it was fear of losing some of these benefits that no doubt motivated much of the opposition. Historically the National Policy had been largely the brain-child of leaders from Ontario in the federal government, and had been the primary instrument for creating the manufacturing base of that province. In this sense Ontario had most to lose from free trade, even though it had gained much from it in the past, not only from the Auto Pact but, for example, in free entry of newsprint, agricultural implements, and other products into the U.S. market.

The position of the other two provinces was also fairly clear. Prince Edward Island feared a loss of its markets for lobster and potatoes under an agreement; the government of Manitoba was formed by the NDP party at the time and was following the policy of strict opposition adopted by the national organization. But in March 1988, the Manitoba NDP government was defeated in an election, and the successor government switched to the yes side. This left only massive Ontario and tiny Prince Edward Island in opposition.

The attitude of Quebec is of special interest. From a position of non-commitment in early 1987, by August of that year Premier Bourassa had moved to full support of free trade, and later expressed satisfaction with the October draft treaty. He also received support in his stand from fellow economist Jacques Parizeau, leader of the Parti quebecois, in an appearance in September 1987, before a committee of the Quebec National Assembly.

In the end it was Ontario that represented the official opposition outside Parliament. In August Premier Peterson announced an election for September 10, 1987 and made it clear that free trade would be the principal issue. The Premier's Liberal party swept to a commanding victory in the election, a result which appeared to justify his opposition. From this time on he became the champion of provincial rights, threatening to veto the agreement if it appeared to be infringing on them in any way. Apparently he and some of the other premiers had assumed that because they were being consulted they would have the right of approval, but the federal government quickly disabused them of this idea. He was told by the Prime Minister in October that the provinces had no legal rights in the matter and that the federal government had at least 97 percent of the power it needed to enter into the trade agreement. Premier Peterson then threatened to take the matter to the courts, and continued to express dissatisfaction after the signing of the agreement on January 2, 1988. International Trade Minister Crosbie re-affirmed this view of federal powers in introducing Bill C-130 on May 23. A legal opinion prepared by the Attorney General of Ontario took issue with this position, and the Premier promised a court challenge at least on the issue of the right of the federal government to force the provinces to give up their discriminatory pricing of foreign wines and liquors.

At mid-1988 it was not clear what steps Ontario might take; in any event the province would have to wait until the federal legislation had become law before challenging it. Incidentally, the lack of full consent of the provinces to the deal was frequently raised by U.S. members of Congress opposed to it, with the assertion that support should be withheld until this consent was forthcoming. It continued to be raised intermittently, and was even mentioned by Peter Murphy in June as a possible handicap to its passage in the U.S. The view appeared to be, however, that President Reagan would not permit this shortcoming to withhold his final approval of the Agreement after passage by Congress.

The Canadian Public Debate

We return later to a further look at the course of events in the U.S. What of the public debate in Canada?

The public at large, despite considerable media attention, only slowly took an interest in the free trade issue. Polls in 1986 and early 1987 showed not more than 2-3 percent familiarity with it. There were reasons for this. At the outset the federal government had played a low key role; after much stalling and many inconclusive statements it clearly adopted free trade late in 1985, even then making no special effort to sell the idea to the public. Public apathy slowly changed as a result of growing media attention, increasing political pressure in Parliament, and the primacy of the issue in the 1987 Ontario election. Polls in 1988 were showing that 40-50 percent of respondents felt that free trade was the most important issue facing the country. Polls to sound out support or opposition had registered wavering allegiance to one side or the other, but the early 1988 polls seemed to be registering an increase in the affirmative view.

The Contending Sides

The main positive support came from business and consumer groups and from academic and research organizations known to support free trade principles. The business community established the Canadian Alliance for Trade and Job Opportunities as its main voice in the free trade debate, co-chaired by Donald Macdonald and former Alberta Premier Peter Lougheed. Both men had been actively promoting free trade in public appearances not only in Canada but in the U.S. as well. The Business Council on National Issues, Canadian Chamber of Commerce, Canadian Manufacturers' Association, Canadian Exporters' Association, and Canadian Federation of Independent Business also endorsed free trade, as had the Canadian Consumers' Association on behalf of consumers. Many individual businesses declared their support as well. A new light on business views on the effect of free trade came from a survey published in early June, 1988. It was found that fewer than 12 percent of either Canadian or U.S. companies were expecting to relocate or close branches or plants in Canada, a fear that had been one of the main arguments advanced by those opposed to removal of Canadian tariff barriers. Prominent among the non-business organizations favouring free trade were the Economic Council of Canada and the C.D. Howe Institute, both with long records of support. The Council made forecasts of the increases in employment that free trade would produce, an invitation for the production of job loss figures by free trade opponents, and one that was warmly accepted. The government had also enlisted academic help. Professor John Crispo of the University of Toronto was given the mission of promoting free trade at every opportunity.

Opposing groups formed a loose federation known as the Pro-Canada Network, financed in part by the trade unions—the strongest and most consistent element of opposition. The unions were adamant and unrelenting in their efforts, and saw closer trade association with the United States as the end of an independent Canada; indeed, the end of the trade union movement. Unfortunately the union point of view has been clothed in such rhetoric and emotion that it is difficult to assess its real point.

Fear of loss of jobs is understandable but the Armageddon foreseen for the whole Canadian nation is not. But the battle was carried on without reservation. At the annual meeting of the Canadian Labour Congress in May 1988, the President, Shirley Carr, promised that Canadian labour would be put on a war footing to defeat free trade as the future of Canada was at stake. This would be achieved mainly by organizing the union forces of the country to ensure the defeat of the Conservative government in the next election. In this fight they would have the full support of their political associates in Parliament, the NDP party.

Almost equally strong were the recognized nationalist groups, whose purpose has always and clearly been to oppose closer relations with the U.S. The leader of the best known current organization in this field, the Council of Canadians, was Mel Hurtig, an Edmonton publisher. Like the union movement the Council was relying on an election in 1988 to bring the downfall of the Conservative government and an end to the free trade threat.

Scattered opposition had been registered during the course of the negotiations from groups fearing damage to an individual industry or a facet of Canadian life. The alcoholic beverage industries feared for loss of position in Canada from foreign competition; the beer industry's concerns were recognized; those of the wine and liquor industries were not. Much emotion was expended on fears for Canadian culture, but in the end the threat did not materialize. There was deep concern for possible radical changes in the Auto Pact, but the revisions actually foreseen do not appear to have disturbed the Canadian industry unduly.

In listing opposing forces one should not overlook the *Toronto Star*. True to its long held opposition to closer proximity to the U.S., the *Star* employed its vast resources and excellent staff not only in covering every minute aspect of the free trade debate but in unremittingly opposing the free trade deal. As a result of this pre-occupation, editorial policy aside, the *Star* has proven to be an unfailing source of information, to the great satisfaction of myself and no doubt other authors.

The Economists

From the earlier review it is clear that Canadian economists had much to do with the original doubts about the benefits of the National Policy and with stimulating interest in free trade with the United States, and they were not loathe to participate in the debate of the 1980s. There had been some critical re-examination of the original assumptions on which the high expectations of benefits were based (now encompassed in the word "models") and pluses had been written down somewhat as a result. Nonetheless it was true that the majority of economists continued to favour free trade, with the reservations that are customary to the profession. Among many statements few were more balanced or more cogently expressed than that of Professor William G. Watson, Department of Economics, McGill University. In an exchange with Professor Tim Hazledine in *Canadian Public Policy*, he rebutted the main accusations against the position of economists in the following words:

On the Grounds of Debate

> Perhaps the real point, then, is simply that the proponents of free trade should be more humble in trying to persuade people of the correctness of their case. I will not argue against humility. But the favour should be returned. Because our understanding of the links between economics, culture, and national identity are even less reliable than our models of (by comparison) quite simple economic interactions, there is even greater room for self-doubt on the other side of the argument. I happily concede that there is at least the possibility of a threat to Canadian identity if the proposed Canada-US free trade agreement goes through (though 1) I don't think it is a large threat and 2) steps can be taken and have been taken to minimize it, such as keeping culture off the table). But, for their part, will the opponents of free trade not admit the possibility that Canada's permanently imperilled

but also apparently quite durable cultural identity will *not* be greatly damaged? They seem very reluctant to do so. And will they also describe the precise causal mechanisms by which Canadian society will be put at risk? And explain how it is that despite 40 years of liberalized Canada-US trade, we now seem both more secure in and more jealous of our separateness? As Holmes himself tells us in *The Sign of Four*: 'The emotional qualities are antagonistic to clear reasoning . . .'[35.1]

On the Search for a Perfect Model

I would be the last to argue that such work should not go forward. On the other hand, I hold out much less hope for its reconciliatory power than Hazledine seems to do. Large models—large questions, really—involve too many parameters, most of which have to be estimated with precision if the model is to provide useful results. Yet estimating parameters is a notoriously tricky business: the data are almost always suspect, while the choice of econometric technique is invariably open to question and invariably crucial. Multiply this problem several dozen-fold and it becomes clear that a model capable of commanding a consensus of economists is unlikely to be available soon. In the meantime, commercial policy must continue to be made. . . .

But the fact that the computer models rely on assumptions which have not been, and probably cannot be, fully vetted does not mean economists need be wholly meek in their support for free trade. A great deal of evidence justifies much boldness on their part: We *know* most people who seek protection do so mainly for their own good. We *know* governments do many things that are wasteful, often in full knowledge that there are better ways to achieve what they claim to be their objectives. We *know* optimal tariffs are hard to calculate. We *know* tariff schedules are almost entirely discretionary, and therefore constitute an ideal mechanism for political manipulation. We *know* small, open economies are particularly ill-suited to pursuing optimal tariffs. We *know* trade leads to inter- and intra-industry specialization. We *know* specialization increases productivity. We *know* past trade liberalizations have been accompanied by rising living standards. We *know* the best way to secure liberalization is to get politicians out of trade policy. We *know* most of the world's trade deals allow ample room for domestic social and regional policies. Finally, we *know* that many of the social programs that are alleged to play such an important role in maintaining and expressing our distinct identity were themselves put into place during a period of Canada-US trade liberalization. It is for reasons such as these, and not because a numerical general-equilibrium model produces a large gains-from-trade number, that most Canadian economists probably do support at least the concept of Canada-US free trade.[35.2]

[35.1] William G. Watson, "The Case of the Disputed Benefit: A Reply to Tim Hazledine" (June 1988) *Canadian Public Policy*, 214-22, at 218-19.

[35.2] Ibid.

Some Remaining Issues

Obviously the most crucial of the unsettled issues is the matter of government subsidies. In the international sphere subsidies in agriculture have become the target of bitter confrontations in the GATT round, and Canada will be prominently involved in this debate. But the whole field of subsidization has been opened for study in the free trade agreement, and the result will be to bring into stark contrast the widely different philosophies of the two countries, and Canada will be challenged to defend its many programs as not increasing the export capacity of Canadian companies. Equally clear will be the fact that many of the U.S. programs at both state and federal levels are subject to the same scrutiny. It is not difficult to understand the reasoning of the negotiators in holding this issue over for the future; there would have been an interminable delay otherwise in settling the main Agreement. But whether this ploy would work with the Congressional Committees was another matter, and not at all certain in June 1988.

Trade and United States

Prelude: A Personal Reflection

The author, having some time ago reached the age of spending winters in Florida, each year in the period 1985 to 1988 has undergone the emotional trauma of making the adjustment from the growing public tension and the increasingly turbulent output of the Canadian media on free trade to the absolute blank wall on the subject in the United States. He can recall only one or two occasions in that four-year period when the excellent local paper, said to be owned by the New York Times, even mentioned trade between Canada and the United States, and then only briefly in connection with a visit of one head of state to the other. Otherwise silence; pages and pages of coverage of the minutest aspect of anything involving the Iran-Contra affair, Nicaragua, Israel, Lebanon, Russia, Panama—the short list of high priority political subjects in which the U.S. media seem constantly to be entrapped. For a trade treaty with Canada, the United States' largest trading partner, nothing, or practically nothing.

The more contentious cases, such as softwood lumber, attracted some attention to trade relations with Canada but this was very limited. What is more relevant, however, is that such cases revealed a different United States than the one we had dealt with before. This was a new America, one that had its back to the wall on trade issues. Gone was the benevolence toward Canada that had led to its exemption from U.S. measures—as for example in the early seventies under the U.S. balance of payments program.

Times have changed. Canada has developed economically to a much higher level than two decades ago, while the United States has lost its preeminent position in the world. And personal diplomacy, such as existed between Prime Minister King and President Roosevelt, has been supplanted by laws, rules, and appeal boards. This non-personal environment has been produced either by adherence to GATT rules or by an increasingly aggressive and assertive Congress. The apparently warm personal relationship between the two 1988 heads of government was threatened throughout by the growing protectionist mood of that body, and one of the strongest arguments of the Canadian government for a free trade agreement has been to shield Canada from the drastic trade legislation being developed in Congressional committees.

United States—Not the Evil Empire

Despite this new environment the author's impression is that Canada is high on the American friendly list. It seems to him that in the free trade agreement the U.S. has attempted, in the turmoil of many other preoccupations and at the request of Canada, to achieve a more rational form of trade link between itself and its largest trading partner. It is easy to lose focus on events of this magnitude, and to over-exaggerate their importance. Earlier Canadian treaties, negotiated through GATT in faraway countries, increased the free trade element of our trade from about 38 percent to 75 percent, and substantial reductions in tariffs were also made. None of this attracted much attention in Canada, even though its results were very material.

Tariffs of course are not the whole story. Under the free trade agreement the veil was being drawn on areas that were previously spared, and more than trade was involved in the proposed deal. But it was not more than would be faced in the upcoming GATT negotiations, in which Canada was simultaneously involved.

A Time for Review

Perhaps the most salutary aspect of the process for Canada has been the need to reappraise economic support policies that have been felt essential for at least a century, but have been relied on even more heavily in the post-war period. Clearly an activist Keynesian role for the state has dominated in this period, to the extent that most Canadians would find its abandonment unthinkable. The symbol of this dominance is now the government subsidy, and we will have to do some hard thinking to determine what its future role should be. The free trade argument has at least forced us to face up to this issue.

Fate of Bill C-130

In Canada, the House of Commons gave third reading to Bill C-130, the free trade implementation act, on August 31, but on instructions from the Liberal party leader the Liberal-dominated Senate refused to consider the legislation until after an election. The election was called to take place on November 21.

Washington Developments

In the approximately two years since preparation of the early part of this chapter (June 1986) the Washington side of the Canada-U.S. trade picture can be summarized in two parts: (1) the battle between Congress and the President over protectionist trade legislation that inferentially would have affected Canada, and (2) specific issues related to cedar shakes and shingles, softwood lumber, steel, potash, etc. A conditioning element in all these issues was the growing U.S. trade deficit.

The U.S. Trade Deficit

For reasons too complex to go into here, since 1975 the United States has suffered a continuously growing annual trade deficit. The last trade surplus was in 1975, and each year since has shown a larger shortfall, reaching an all-time high in 1987. There was some improvement with a cheaper dollar in the early months of 1988, but the deficit is still substantial. The following are the annual balances from 1976 to 1987. (There are several balance figures; the following are for the Trade Balance, with all years showing deficits).

Table 35.1   U.S. Trade Deficits, 1976-87

billions of dollars

1976	− 5.9	1980	− 24.2	1984	− 122.4
1977	− 26.3	1981	− 27.6	1985	− 133.6
1978	− 23.4	1982	− 31.8	1986	− 156.2
1979	− 27.6	1983	− 57.6	1987	− 171.2

Source: U.S. *Federal Reserve Bulletin.*

Congressional Protectionism

These large and growing trade deficits were understandably greeted with consternation by Congress, particularly as they were accompanied by a flood of cheap imports which caused large-scale unemployment among Congressional voters. In their view the easiest way to correct this problem was to keep out the imports that were doing the damage (steel, softwood lumber, textiles, etc.) and the mood therefore was becoming increasingly protectionist. As early as the spring of 1986 only a tie in the voting in the Senate Finance Committee enabled the President to proceed with negotiation of a free trade treaty with Canada. With control of the Senate going to the Democrats in the fall election, in addition to their prior control over the House, the President's influence in the Congress began to weaken, and he was forced to use his veto powers to kill protectionist legislation. A report from Washington in July 1986, mentioned that 782 international trade bills were before Congress. Of these 134 were aimed at Canada, and 70 of these had protectionist features. In August 1986 the President had been forced to veto a bill to establish textile quotas.

More alarming was a massive omnibus trade bill being concocted in the Congress. A version was introduced during 1986 which died at the end of the session when the Senate failed to act on it. A similar bill was reintroduced in the 1987 session and passed by the House in May with a substantial majority. A feature of the bill of particular concern to Canada was a broadening of the definition of a subsidy which would have caught many Canadian assistance programs. In a similar mood of belligerence in July the Senate passed its own highly protectionist measure, despite threats of veto by the President. This measure, after being reconciled with the House bill, was passed again by each arm of the legislature in April 1988, and was almost immediately vetoed by the President. The attempt to achieve a majority of two-thirds to overcome the veto failed in the Senate, so that the bill died on the legislative agenda. Nonetheless the development was disturbing for Canada, as there were fears that the free trade agreement might be caught in the crossfire between President and Congress, and that some of the ideas that the Congressional committees had failed to have adopted in their own legislation might re-appear in the legislation on the agreement. (A later and modified version of this measure again was vetoed, but there was sufficient support for it in Congress to overcome the veto, and the President reluctantly signed it).

Free Trade in Congress

The congressional committees had begun to examine the agreement early in 1988, and the results were hardly reassuring. In February a group of 20 senators had written the President demanding that the agreement be re-opened, mainly on the basis that it was injurious to U.S. natural resources in that it failed to eliminate Canadian subsidies to these industries. Concurrently the House Committee was taking strong exception to a Canadian plan to grant duty-free importation of textiles from other countries to assist the Canadian clothing industries. The U.S. textile industry exerted a good deal of clout in Congress, and the Textile Caucus could have stopped the Agreement. At this stage Michigan car parts manufacturers also renewed long standing objections to the Auto Pact. Trade Representative Clayton Yeutter and Treasury Secretary Baker were doing their best as witnesses before these committees to put out anti-free-trade fires. Their main message was that if Congress started to tinker with the agreement it would collapse. U.S. businessmen formed an organization in its support and also spoke out in favour of the agreement. Nonetheless the committees continued to obstruct progress. The Senate Finance Committee, for example, inserted a clause that would have required withholding formal approval of the agreement until all ten provinces had accepted it in the knowledge that this was not likely to happen. As mentioned, observers assumed that the President would overlook this clause, as he wished the free trade agreement to be a part of his legacy.

A nearly final version of the agreement approved by the Senate Committee included size restrictions on imported Canadian lobsters, restraints on potato imports, and delay in reduction of tariffs on wood imports because of a dispute over wood standards. The Canadian government officially protested against these changes and warned that counteraction would be taken if they went ahead. Apparently these and other aspects of the legislation being drafted in the committees, and in particular the definition of subsidies, continued to concern the Canadian government, and Derek Burney, the Prime Minister's chief of staff, was sent to Washington a sufficient number of times to protest new developments that the Chairman of the Senate Finance Committee stated that "If they keep sending Derek Burney down here to renegotiate, they are going to delay things to a point where finally we're not going to have an agreement."

As time moved on relentlessly to mid-1988, legislative processes in both countries moved forward at a sluggish pace. The pressure in the United States was to have Congress approve final legislation before a summer recess, after which all attention would be on the November elections. There were reports from Washington of various issues that were still outstanding, with official assurances that these would all be resolved shortly. This is where matters stood in Washington in mid-June 1988, with final passage of the free trade agreement very much in the air. (In fact the House passed the implementing bill in August and the Senate in September, with Presidential signature following on September 28). With the return of the Conservative government in Canada following an election dominated by the free trade issue, the Commons and Senate passed matching legislation late in 1988, and the Agreement came into effect on January 1, 1989.

Special Trade Issues

We turn now to some special trade issues that had been very much in the public eye over this period.

Cedar Shakes and Shingles

On May 23, 1986, the President had approved a 35 percent duty on imports of cedar shakes and shingles, and the Canadian government, in retaliation, on June 6, had imposed duties on books, computer parts, Christmas trees, and other minor products. This action only demonstrated, as has been often stated by international trade economists, that in the case of many goods Canadians are price receivers, not price setters. The price of all these goods, and particularly of books, simply rose by the amount of the duty, mainly to the detriment of Canadian sellers and the public rather than American exporters. In the budget of February 18, 1987, these duties were withdrawn. The Minister justified this action by the additional strength that had been given the industry through tighter restrictions on the export of cedar logs and bolts, which forced U.S. mills to rely on more expensive U.S. logs.

The whole issue was a portent of what was to follow on softwood lumber. It aroused assertions from Canadian industry leaders that the main reason for Canada's competitive edge was not government subsidization but greater efficiency in more modern Canadian mills and of course the cheap Canadian dollar.

Softwood Lumber

As last reported, in July 1986, the International Trade Commission issued a finding that the U.S. softwood industry had suffered material injury from Canadian imports, and the matter was referred to the Department of Commerce to decide whether the cause of the injury was government subsidization and if so what response should be made. The U.S. Coalition for Fair Lumber Imports had argued that the charges made for timber by Canadian governments were too low and represented a subsidy. The Coalition had asked for a 27 percent duty to offset the alleged subsidy; this was later raised to 32 percent. A ruling was expected from the Department of Commerce on October 9, or not later than October 16.

During the interim Canadian interests were consulting on what steps might be taken to influence the outcome. In a surprising about-face British Columbia announced that it was prepared to review its stumpage charges but this would take some time. In September, on behalf of Premier Vander Zalm, Canadian International Trade Minister Pat Carney asked for a delay in the ruling to enable the province to complete its study. The B.C. study was greeted with satisfaction by Clayton Yeutter but the request for more time was strongly opposed by the U.S. lumber coalition. Shortly after the Commerce Department denied the request for an extension.

In Canada discussions of alternative offers were continued at official and business levels, and the possibility most frequently mentioned was a provincial tax on lumber to increase export prices. This took formal shape in a "one-time" offer made in Washington on October 1 by Pat Carney on behalf of four Canadian provinces—Ontario, B.C., Alberta, and Quebec—in effect to increase the price of their lumber by 10 percent through higher stumpage charges. On October 3 this offer, when presented by the Commerce Department, was rejected by the Lumber Coalition as inadequate; as a gesture to leave open the possibility of a last minute compromise, on October 8 the Secretary of Commerce postponed his ruling another week.

When it was given on October 16 it called for a duty of 15 percent on imports of Canadian softwood lumber. This reversal of the position the Department had taken in 1983 was said to be on the basis of new information and changed conditions. As this trade represented nearly $4 billion of Canadian exports and employment of 50-60,000, this was a serious blow for Canada, although there were mixed reactions among lumber executives as to the possible effect. The most disturbing aspect of the decision of course was the breadth of the interpretation of what constituted a government subsidy to an export industry, since tax credits and other general forms of assistance had been included. Some experts felt that if the concept was to be broadened to this degree there was not much left among government programs that would not be included, whether or not the measure was intended as assistance to an export industry.

But all was not final as yet. The October ruling did not take effect until December 30, thus leaving another two and a half months for producing further compromise proposals. In addition there was a lapse until the Commission confirmed its ruling that injury had been suffered by the U.S. industry. Pat Carney promised to take advantage of this time to fight the decision through any means. At this point the Canadian media and opposition politicians were flailing the government for having botched the negotiations and urging that Canada "strike back" by every means. It was also asserted in many quarters that the free trade negotiations should be dropped immediately. In this same period the Congress imposed an import surcharge on all imports into the United States (nominal in amount) and Canada levied an import duty of $1 per bushel against U.S. feed corn imports—neither of these being gestures designed to smooth troubled waters at this juncture. Canada asked the President to veto the import charge, which would cost its exporters some $200 million, but he was unable to do so because it was included in a general budget measure. Along with the $550 million cost of the lumber import duty some three-quarters of a billion dollars was involved in the two measures.

The Canadian government first decided to contest the lumber finding through legal channels in the U.S. and through GATT appeal procedures. On further consideration it abandoned this route and decided to continue with the search for a negotiated settlement. The end result, after weeks of meetings and negotiation, in which provincial authorities were also involved, was an eleventh hour deal on December 30th, 1986 with the U.S. Department of Commerce and the Lumber Coalition for Canada to impose a 15 percent duty on exports of softwood lumber to the U.S. This was essentially the offer that had been made earlier, but with a higher price tag. Its timing enabled the Commerce Department to drop its finding against the Canadian lumber industry, due to be made only a few hours away, which was one of the main objectives of the Canadian approach. Had the concept of subsidies used in the finding been allowed to come into effect any number of U.S. industries would have been invited to make similar appeals. The deal also had the advantage for strapped provincial governments for promising to produce about $600 million in revenue.

There was some consternation in Canada among sovereignty-sensitive individuals that the deal was an invasion of Canada's rights; more realistic was the realization of its effect on employment in wood-cutting provinces. The concern for sovereignty related to the condition that the tax could only be reduced as stumpages were increased and that the U.S. would have to be given detailed reports on the lumber trade in each province to police this condition. This was thought to give the United States control over the exercise of Canadian rights, a somewhat questionable view, as the Canadian provinces could do nothing very much in the situation even if they wished.

The unpopularity of the agreement both in the industry and among Canadian politicians no doubt had some bearing on the long delay in passage of the enabling legislation, which was not enacted until July. There had been wrangling over the meaning of some of the clauses and these finally had been clarified. The delay allowed some companies to postpone payment of the tax, but National Revenue claimed that most were up to date. An unfavourable result of the delay was that the Lumber Coalition would not agree to any revision of the agreement until the legislation was passed, and as it turned out there was basis for a new understanding. In the meantime a committee of forestry ministers had failed to come up with an administrative device that would allow the provinces to take over collection of the tax, and it began to appear that the federal government might be saddled with it for all time. This became a much less urgent matter when it was possible to amend the agreement. As a result of reductions in its stumpage charges exports from British Columbia were relieved from the tax; on the grounds that most forest lands were privately owned in the Atlantic provinces, exports from that area were also exempted. This left exports from Quebec, Ontario, and Alberta subject to the agreement, a considerably shrunken operation.

Knotty Plywood

While in the wood environment it might be appropriate to add a note on a problem involving knotty plywood under the free trade agreement. Canada has standards governing the use of plywood with knotholes which exclude the American low-grade plywood because the holes are too big. CMHC refused to allow the use of this plywood in homes it financed, and was required under the agreement to reconsider its policy. Having done so it did not change its mind; the U.S. plywood could still not be used. The agreement called for review by a joint panel of experts in this event, with the right to delay tariff reductions by the U.S. on Canadian plywood until a common standard was achieved. Such a panel, composed of officials from both countries, was appointed in 1988, and was at work on the development of appropriate tests—a business that could take months. Furthermore, affronted members of Congress from plywood-producing states were threatening to hold up approval of the agreement until Canada accepted the U.S. product. The Canadian producers were said to be less concerned about the effect of the treaty than they were about the competitive advantage the cheap U.S. plywood would gain abroad if it could be sold as now having the approval of the Canadian housing authorities.

Problems in the lumber area seem to be especially tangled, but they are relatively managable compared to those in agriculture.

Agriculture

Their large farm sectors inevitably produce constant problems between Canada and the U.S. Canada's array of marketing boards and import control systems has few exact counterparts in the United States, but government subsidies and other schemes are just as common there as in Canada. Recent signs of friction include a Canadian per bushel duty on imports of U.S. feed corn (first imposed in 1986 at $1.10 per bushel and reduced to 46¢ in February 1988) and confirmation by the International Trade Commission of countervailing duties on Canadian hogs on the ground of government subsidization. There were also U.S. duties on fish and threatened duties on potash, an agricultural fertilizer, that caused Canadian concern. The threat to potash however was removed in January 1988 with the agreement of eight Canadian producers to maintain higher export prices over the following five years.

Agricultural Subsidies

These issues were overshadowed by the battle that was soon to be joined over general agricultural subsidies. There had been smouldering discontent over competition from heavily subsidized grain, sugar, and other products at GATT rounds, but this had been buried. Opposition even to discussion of the issue at any time was particularly strong from the EEC, whose agricultural policies have been explained previously. But by 1988 the issue was very much in the open, and was being reviewed with more heat by the month.

The United States, through actions in the last two years apparently designed to force the issue, seems to have provided the spark. It precipitated a confrontation in 1986 with an offer to the Soviet Union of heavily subsidized wheat, which, if accepted, would have substantially replaced Canada as a source of Soviet supplies. This action met violent opposition from Canada and Australia, then both sources of Soviet supplies, and resulted in a meeting in Cairns, Australia of 14 agricultural countries which became known as the Cairns Group. The group demanded the immediate end to all agricultural subsidies, and has since been expressing strongest opposition on every occasion to their continuation. In the end the Soviet continued to buy wheat from Canada, but the subsidy issue did not die. The United States had defended its offer of subsidized wheat on the ground that if it did not do so other countries with subsidized exports would steal all its markets. This was a zero sum game in which there were no winners and which only led to destructive and futile competition.

This issue was brought to a head by President Reagan in July 1987 in a special appeal for worldwide elimination of all agricultural subsidies, tariffs, and trade barriers by the year 2000. Forestry and fish products would be included. The statement made concrete a growing world sense that some action had to be taken. In May, 24 OECD countries had signed an agreement calling for "a progressive reduction of assistance to and protection of agriculture," supported by a statement of principles that should govern. At a summit meeting of the Big Seven countries in June 1988, a declaration was issued in favour of major reforms in agricultural trade, and a similar declaration was issued at Toronto, Canada after the June 1988 summit meeting.

The EEC Financial Crisis

Apart from their effect in disrupting international trade all countries of course were concerned with the growing share of their budgets going for farm support. This was particularly true of the EEC. In the face of a deficit of $6 billion in its 1987 budget of $41 billion, Margaret Thatcher had insisted on a review of the massive expenditure on agriculture before giving Britain's approval. Community officials had considered, and abandoned under U.S. protest, a tax on imported fats and vegetable oils as a means of raising revenues. A decision was taken at a meeting in July to at least freeze farm price levels. Facing possible bankruptcy, and with Britain refusing to assist without some action on farm subsidies, the impasse persisted into

1988, by which time Britain had been joined in dissent by the Netherlands and Belgium.

Canada's Position

Prime Minister Mulroney had fully supported the President's objectives even though, as often ironically happens, low wheat prices and a drought in the western provinces were forcing his government to give further assistance to hard-pressed farmers in that region. With farm payments of various kinds exceeding $5 billion the prospect of budget relief was an attractive one. During a trip to Europe in May 1988, he frequently berated the EEC for its level of farm support, but was pulled up short by an EEC official with the charge that Canada was almost as great an offender; as a percentage of farm income (a measurement not often used in Canada) Canadian subsidies amounted to 46 percent as against 49 percent for the EEC. Canadian officials had to concede the correctness of the data; but they might have spared the Prime Minister his embarrassment. It is worth mentioning that the attempt to define farm subsidies affecting trade in wheat, oats, and barley in the Canada-U.S. free trade agreement is probably a pathbreaking exercise of its type in an official trade document. And it would have been much less complicated if the subsidies were being ended rather than held to a level determined by complex formulae. It stands as an example of the sort of compilation that would eventually be necessary if universal action were to be taken on agricultural subsidies.

Such subsidies of course are only one side of the general question of the role of government in the economy, an issue that goes deep into national attitudes and policies and inevitably raises sharp conflicts of philosophy. As national barriers dissolve in a shrinking world such conflicts will extend to many other areas, with increasing clashes between the theoretical and the pragmatic.

Steel

Concern over the virtual collapse of the once powerful U.S. steel industry brought steel imports under close watch. Quotas were set for most countries, but Canada was omitted on its undertaking to provide no more than 3 percent of total U.S. consumption. Much of the problem over the 1986-88 period related to policing this agreement. In August 1986, Clayton Yeutter by letter accused Canada of breaking its agreement, to which the newly appointed Pat Carney had replied that Canada would be "prudent" in its steel exports to the U.S. As Canada's exports continued to exceed its agreed limit, despite assurances from Canadian steel mills that they were doing everything possible to control the flow, warnings continued to be given by Washington. The U.S. authorities were not appeased by the Canadian explanation that the excess seemed to be from brokers who customarily handled steel from any source, domestic or foreign, and were beyond the control of the Canadian mills. A bill was introduced in the U.S. Senate in September 1986 to cut the Canadian share to 2.4 percent of U.S. demand, as against the actual share of 3.3 percent at the time. While the legislation did not pass, it prompted yet another statement from Clayton Yeutter that a quota might be established. In time the exercise became a monthly numbers game, with frequent wide differences in each side's figures and constant debate as to what they meant. To end the argument Canada introduced a monitoring process in June 1987, under which a licence was required to export steel to the United States. It was thought that this would bring an end to the data debate, but it was not conclusive.

1987 saw a rapid increase in Canadian exports, accounting for some 4 percent of U.S. consumption, well above the agreed limit. As a result there were renewed demands for a Canadian quota from the U.S. steel industry. In May 1988, in an appearance before the Senate Finance Committee hearings on free trade, the steel industry gave conditional endorsement of the agreement but argued for a voluntary quota for Canada. This position was supported by the 36 members of the Senate steel caucus. No action was taken by the administration, possibly because the industry appeared to be operating near full capacity with the aid of new and more efficient casting technology.

The Canadian steel industry, incidentally, had declared its full support for the free trade agreement.

The Auto Pact

The changes in the Auto Pact have been covered earlier. These grew primarily from U.S. dissatisfaction with the use of its duty-free privileges by foreign makers, particularly of Asian origin, to obtain duty-free access to the American market. Under the revised arrangements the original terms will apply only to the companies that have already qualified, but any new company will be eligible only if it has achieved a 50 percent North American content for its 1989 model year. Canada will give up its rebate of customs duties on imported parts originally designed to encourage foreign companies to assemble in Canada, will remove tariffs on U.S. cars over a period, and lift its restrictions on import of used cars. These terms would allow at least one Japanese firm with an established plant to come under the agreement without change in its production; others with plants in course of construction interpret the 1989 model limit as a barrier they could not surmount and one that might debar them indefinitely.

The Bank of Canada provided a useful analysis of recent experience under the Auto Pact in its monthly *Review* of July 1987. On the crucial issue of the balance of advantage under the agreement its calculations showed that Canada in the years 1982 to 1986 had favourable balances in the range of $4.1 to $6.4 billion, far exceeding anything previously experienced by either country. That, if for no other reason, meant the Auto Pact was slated for review under the free trade deal.

Textiles

Textile issues have continued to be of major concern, with developed countries acting to protect their own industries by quota agreements permitted under the Multi-Fiber Arrangement. The arrangement, first negotiated in 1974 and twice extended, was to expire in July 1986. With 53 countries signing, it was renewed for another five years. At this time Canada had agreements with 30 countries, but was dissatisfied with the results. Low cost imports had risen at an average rate of about 11 percent a year in the early eighties, rising by 26 percent in 1983 and 15 percent in 1984. As a result the domestic industry's share of the Canadian market had fallen from 69 percent in 1981 to 57 percent in 1985. Following the renewal of the arrangement the government announced a new program designed to curtail imports further. New agreements would be negotiated with much curtailed quotas for countries like Hong Kong, Taiwan, and South Korea, but poorer, less developed countries would be given greater consideration.

As free trade became more of a reality firms began to position themselves for the more open market, after loss of the protection of tariffs in the 20 percent range. One of the most audacious of these steps was the attempt of a Canadian textile producer, Domtex, to take over one of the largest U.S. firms, Burlington Mills, to strengthen its position in the more competitive free trade world. This coup did not materialize. A plan announced by the government to assist Canadian textile manufacturers by remission of duties on imports from countries other than the U.S. ran into opposition from both Canadian manufacturers and the U.S. Congress. The plan, proposed by the government in November 1987, roused fears in the Canadian textile manufacturing industry of a flood of cheap imports of fabric from many countries; the U.S. Congressional members from textile areas accused Canada of using a back-door method of frustrating U.S. benefits under the treaty. (Canada in fact had until June 30, 1988 to introduce performance-based remission programs, to be effective for 10 years, under the free trade agreement. It had also apparently been forced at the last minute of the negotiations in Washington in October to accept a quota on imports into the United States of Canadian clothing made from foreign textiles).

In early 1988, after final signing of the treaty, one of the many risks to its adoption by Congress was the threat of the American Textile Manufacturers Institute to oppose its passage unless Canada withdrew its duty remission plan. In February a committee of the National Governor's Association approved the free trade deal but with the reservation that the Canadian government must withdraw its duty remission program on textiles. International Trade Minister Carney rejected this pressure, and said that Canada would go ahead with its program.

True to this position on March 22, 1988 the Minister of Finance announced a program of combined tariff reductions and duty remissions, which were made official by order in council in June. The orders will extend from January 1, 1989 to December 31, 1997. The Minister also announced that the new Canadian International Trade Tribunal would be asked, when established, to recommend ways of bringing Canada's textile tariffs in line with those of other industrial countries. Obviously textiles promise to continue as one of the livelier of the trade issues.

Adjustment Programs

The Economic Council of Canada had issued a report in March 1988 giving the results of its study of past programs and recommending principles to be followed in the future. However, the textile adjustment program was the only major program of this type announced by the government for the free trade regime.

General Agreement Revisited

In September 1986, the eighth round of GATT commenced. The mood of the times was not propitious. A trade war between the U.S. and the EEC had just been called off by a last minute compromise. There had been competition in the sale of heavily subsidized grain in foreign markets, which appears to have culminated in the imposition by Spain of higher tariffs on U.S. corn and sorghum. Provoked by this action the U.S. had threatened restrictions on the importation of wine, beer, and some foods from EEC. A six months' truce eased the feud, but left tension. A preparatory committee had struggled for six months to agree on an agenda, and reports of its meetings were punctuated with threats of one group or another to walk out if any of their most cherished practices were to be "on the table." There was said to be strong opposition by the EEC to having agriculture even listed, and services were rejected by other countries. But the draft agenda agreed to in July (known as W47 or the Swiss-Colombian text) included most of the troublesome issues, with scheduling of changes over long periods.

The mood of pessimism was reflected in the annual GATT report issued early in September 1986, particularly over the degree to which trade had become "managed." It said: "The danger in the present situation is that policies centred on subsidies and discriminatory quantitative restrictions, whose bankruptcy is evident from the experience in these three sectors, will continue to spread to other parts of the economy." The three sectors mentioned were agriculture, textiles, and clothing. If these trends continued the GATT, once the source of such high hopes, would become meaningless. There would have to be a return to first objectives, with a broadening of the scope of the agreement and strengthened powers of enforcement for the GATT organization. The battle over agricultural sales and subsidies continued to dominate preparations. As noted earlier, at a meeting of 14 agricultural exporting countries in Australia in August a belligerent group produced a resolution that subsidies be discontinued immediately, a proposal which Canada rejected, choosing to stand by the W47 proposals. A higher level quadrilateral meeting, a six months' regular event between U.S., Canada, Japan, and the EEC in the week before the GATT round was devoted mainly to agriculture and failed to achieve any agreement on the future of subsidies. In a fairly rough exchange of views it mainly confirmed the wide gap between the U.S. and the EEC on this subject.

The Uruguay Round

The opening session of the current GATT round took place in September 1986, in Punta del Este, Uruguay. Some 74 countries were gathered for a week to consider a final agenda for what is now labelled the Uruguay Round. The U.S. delegation came prepared with an agenda which included four essential items: freeing up agricultural trade, services, and investment, and reducing production of bogus look-alike goods. Trade Representative Clayton Yeutter had said in a speech in the previous week that omission of any of these four items would lead to U.S. withdrawal from the talks; a fifth item, strengthening of GATT dispute settlement procedures, was also supported, but not to the extent of these four. Exactly what transpired at this opening session can only be judged by its results; at the end of the week it was announced that the objectives of the full round would include a phasing out of agricultural subsidies and inclusion of services in the agenda. This was described as the basis for achieving a dynamic structure for international commerce into the 21st century, a result that could hardly have been predicted only a week before. Apparently compromises by the French assisted in the subsidy concessions and by Brazil and India for inclusion of services.

This of course was only the beginning, although a favourable one; reports of harsh differences arising even in December of the same year in the planning of the full round reflected continuing doubts and reservations. And the friction between the U.S. and the EEC had not eased. The original truce had provided that the EEC would give compensation for the loss of trade with Spain for U.S. farmers, but as differences arose over the amount to be paid both sides proposed to impose duties against the other. In the end cooler judgments prevailed, and a compromise was reached. The U.S. had also had a problem with Japan flooding its market with computer chips, despite a 1986 agreement, and had imposed a countervailing duty in April 1987. This duty was reduced in June as a concession to Japan. Based on the experience of previous rounds it will be five years or more before any final conclusions are reached, and at any point in time the results will be completely unpredictable. In meantime meetings will go on in Geneva or occasionally elsewhere (14 working groups have been established; a full meeting was scheduled for Montreal for December of 1988), and events will be influenced by Summit meetings of the seven countries, by meetings of the OECD, and by events such as the new Japan-U.S. trade treaty announced on June 21, 1988. The increase in the number of single interest groups in the GATT round (e.g. The Cairns Group of agricultural countries) has added a further complication to an already badly mixed format. Events will go forward rapidly at some stages, and barely move at others. Little progress was made at the Montreal meeting which bogged down in a confrontation between the U.S. and the EEC over agricultural subsidies. A further meeting was scheduled for April 1989. Observers will need patience.

Canada and GATT

It is a new experience for Canada to be charged with an offence under the GATT. In June 1987, the United States complained to GATT that Canada was engaging in unfair trade practices in restricting the export of herring and salmon from the West coast. The "guilty" decision of a GATT panel also struck a blow at the favourite Canadian provincial practice of discriminating against foreign wine and beer in their mark-up and pricing. This was acknowledged by the federal government and discussions were started both with EEC and Canadian provinces to achieve a compromise. It appeared that the EEC was not interested in a compromise, so that the matter was left with the federal government and the provinces to settle. In the event that Canada does not settle it invites retaliation under the GATT.

The same issue arose of course under the free trade agreement, and was one of the more contentious questions, particularly with the province of Ontario.

The New Tariff

Before leaving this endless story of foreign trade and its grave importance for Canada it should be recorded that on January 1, 1988, the new Harmonized System came into effect for imports into Canada. This was a considerable accomplishment, as it required recasting 3,200 items of the existing tariff, some of them going back to the last century. This will greatly simplify tariff administration and customs compliance.

Bibliography, chapters 30 to 35

Bank of Montreal. "Canada and the Kennedy Round." *Business Review*, July 31, 1967.

Barber, C.L. "Canadian Tariff Policy." (Nov. 1955) XXI, *Canadian Journal of Economics and Political Science*, 523-24.

Beigie, Carl E. *The Canada-U.S. Automotive Agreement: An Evaluation*. Montreal: Canadian American Committee, 1970.

Beigie, Carl E., and Stewart, James. "The Leading Case of Autos." (March 1984) *Policy Options*, 12-18.

Bergsten, Fred C. *Completing the GATT: Towards New International Rules to Govern Export Controls*. Washington, D.C.: British-North American Committee, 1974.

Bergsten, Fred C., and Cline, William R. *Trade Policy in the 1980's*. Washington, D.C.: Institute for International Economics, 1982.

Biggs, Margaret A. *Canada and the Third World/The Challenge: Adjust or Protect?* Ottawa: The North-South Institute, 1980.

Brean, Donald J.S. *International Issues in Taxation: The Canadian Perspective*, Canadian Tax Paper no. 75. Toronto: Canadian Tax Foundation, 1984.

British-North American Committee. *Prospective Changes in the World Trade and Monetary Systems—A Comment and Policy Statement*. Montreal: the Committee, 1972.

Britton, J.N.A. "Locational Perspectives on Free Trade for Canada." (Winter 1978) *Canadian Public Policy*, 4-19.

Brock, William E. "Interview on International Trade." (Spring 1984) 3 *The Brookings Review*, 26-31.

Bryce, Robert B. "Basic Issues in Postwar International Relations." (March 1942) 32 *American Economic Review*, Supplement, 165-81.

C.D. Howe Institute. "Closing A Trade Deal: The Provinces' Role." *Commentary, no. 11*. Toronto: the Institute, 1986.

_____. *Policy Harmonization: the Effects of a Canadian-American Free Trade Area*. Toronto: the Institute, 1986.

Canada. Department of External Affairs. *Canada's International Relations*. Ottawa: 1986.

_____. *Canada-U.S. Free Trade Agreement. The Regions*. Ottawa: 1988.

_____. *Canadian Trade Policy for the 1980s: A Discussion Paper*. Ottawa: 1983.

_____. *A Review of Canadian Trade Policy: A Background Document to Canadian Policy for the 1980s*. Ottawa: 1983.

_____. *An Overview*. Studies in Canadian Export Opportunities in the U.S. Market. Ottawa: 1988.

_____. *Series on TRADE*: Securing Canada's Future; the Canada-U.S. Free Trade Agreement; including individual publications on Agriculture, Canadian Consumers, Energy, Fisheries, Forest Product Sector, Minerals and Metals, Women, and Synopsis of the Agreement. Ottawa: 1988.

_____. *Summary of Canada's Bilateral Restraint Arrangements—Textiles and Clothing*. Ottawa: 1982.

_____. Text of the Free Trade Agreement. December 1987. Ottawa: 1987.

_____. *The World Our Market: Canada, GATT and the Uruguay Round*. Ottawa: 1988.

_____. Department of Finance. Annual Budget Speeches. Ottawa: the Department.

_____. The Canada-U.S. Free Trade Agreement. *An Economic Assessment*. Ottawa: 1987.

_____. *A New Direction for Canada. An Agenda for Economic Renewal*. Budget paper. Ottawa: 1984.

_____. *Proposals on Import Policy: A Discussion Paper Proposing Changes to Canadian Import Legislation*. Ottawa: 1980.

_____. Department of Industry, Trade and Commerce. *Canada's Trade Performance 1960-77, Volume I: General Developments*. Ottawa: 1978.

_____. Department of Regional Expansion. *The Canada-U.S. Free Trade Agreement and Industry*. Ottawa: 1988.

_____. House of Commons. Bill C-130. An Act to Implement the Free Trade Agreement between Canada and the United States. Introduced on May 24; passed by House on August 31, 1988.

_____. Standing Committee on External Affairs and International Trade. *Report: The Canada-United States Free Trade Agreement*. Ottawa: 1987.

_____. Mulroney, The Rt. Honourable Brian. Statement to the House of Commons September 25, 1986. Ottawa: House of Commons Debates, 1st Session, 33rd Parliament, 7055-56.

_____. Royal Commission on Canada's Economic Prospects. *Canadian Commercial Policy*. Ottawa: 1957.

_____. Royal Commission on the Automobile Industry. *Report*. Ottawa: 1961.

_____. Royal Commission on Canada's Economic Prospects. *Final Report* Ottawa: 1958.

_____. Royal Commission on the Economic Union and Development Prospects for Canada. *Report*, vol. 1, Part 2, chaps. 5 and 6; and Conclusions and Recommendations Ottawa: 1985.

_____. Royal Commission on the Economic Union and Development Prospects for Canada. Stairs, Denis, and Winham, Gilbert R., research coordinators, *Canada and the International Political/Economic Environment*. Vols. 28-30, of Collected Research Studies of the Royal Commission. Toronto: University of Toronto Press, 1985.

_____. Royal Commission on the Economic Union and Development Prospects for Canada. Whalley, John, research coordinator, *International Trade*. Vols. 9-14, of Collected Research Studies of the Royal Commission. Toronto: University of Toronto Press, 1985.

_____. Royal Commission on the Economic Union and Development Prospects for Canada. Whalley, John, research coordinator with Hill, Roderick. *Canada-United States Free Trade*. Vol. 11. Collected Research Studies of the Royal Commission. Toronto: University of Toronto Press, 1985.

_____. Senate. Standing Committee on Foreign Affairs, Canada-United States Relations. *III: Canada's Trade Relations with the United States*. Ottawa: 1982.

_____. *Canadian Relations with the European Community*. Ottawa: 1973.

_____. Special Joint Committee of the Senate and of the House of Commons on Canada's International Relations. *Interim Report to Parliament*. Ottawa: 1985.

_____. Trade Negotiations Office. Special Release. *Canada-U.S. Trade Negotiations—A Chronology*. October 5, 1987. One of four documents issued in a press kit entitled *Trade-Securing Canada's Future*. Ottawa: 1987.

Canadian-American Committee. *Bilateral Relations in an Uncertain World Context: Canada-U.S. Relations in 1978*. A Staff Report. Montreal: the Committee, 1978.

_____. *Changes in Trade Restrictions Between Canada and the United States*. Washington, D.C.: the Committee, 1960.

_____. *A New Trade Strategy for Canada and the United States. A Statement*. Washington, D.C.: the Committee, 1966.

_____. *A Possible Plan for a Canada-U.S. Free Trade Area*. A Staff Report and Committee Statement. Washington, D.C.: the Committee, 1965.

_____. *A Time of Difficult Transitions: Canada-U.S. Relations in 1976*. A Staff Report. Montreal: the Committee, 1976.

_____. *Towards a More Realistic Appraisal of the Automotive Agreement. A Statement*. Washington, D.C.: the Committee, 1970.

Canadian Export Association. *Canada's Approach to the GATT Negotiations*. Montreal: the Association, 1973.

Canadian Foundation for Economic Education. "The Canada-U.S. Free Trade Agreement: Background, Overview and Perspectives." *Economic Bulletin 2*. Toronto: the Foundation, 1988.

Canadian Institute of International Affairs. "Canadian Foreign Policy: Comments on the Green Papers." *Behind the Headlines*. Toronto: the Institute, 1985.

Canadian Labour Congress. Presentation to the House of Commons Committee on External Affairs and International Trade. Ottawa: the Congress.

Canadian Manufacturers Association. *Competing in the Global Village, Self Help is the Best Help*. Toronto: the Association, 1982.

_____. *Tariff Policy for Canada*. Business and Government in Canada. Toronto: the Association, 1969, chapter 29.

Cape, Edward M. *Canada's Role in Britain's Trade*. Montreal: Private Planning Association of Canada, 1965.

Carmichael, Edward A. "Confronting Global Challenges." *Policy Review and Outlook, 1987*. Toronto: C.D. Howe Institute, 1986.

Caves, Richard E., and Jones, Ronald W. *World Trade and Payments: An Introduction*, 2nd ed. Toronto: Little Brown, 1977.

Clark, M.G. *Canada and World Trade*. Staff Study no. 7. Ottawa: Economic Council of Canada, 1966.

Corbo, Vittorio, and Havrylyshyn, Oli. *Canada's Trade Relations with Developing Countries*. A study prepared for the Economic Council of Canada. Ottawa: 1980.

Cornell, Peter. *Understanding Canada's International Trade Policy*. Toronto: Canadian Foundation for Economic Education, 1980.

Council of Canadians. Presentation to the House of Commons Committee on External Affairs and International Trade. The Council, 1987.

Courchene, Thomas J. *The Free Trade Agreement: Reflections of a Market Nationalist*. London: Department of Economics, University of Western

Ontario, 1988.

Crandall, Robert W. *Steel Imports: Dumping or Competition?* Reprint. General Series 381. Washington D.C.: Brookings Institution, 1982.

Creen, John G. "The Coming Negotiations under GATT." (June 1973) *Behind the Headlines*. Toronto: The Canadian Institute of International Affairs, 1973.

_____. "The International Community and the Multinational Enterprise: Response and Regulation." (December 1982) *Behind the Headlines*. Toronto: Canadian Institute of International Affairs, 1982.

Crispo, John, ed. *Free Trade: The Real Story*. Toronto: Gage Educational Publications, 1988.

Crosbie, The Honourable John. Statement on Introduction of Bill C-130, Canada-U.S. Free Trade Implementation Act. House of Commons Debates, May 24, 1988.

Dales, J.H. *The Protective Tariff in Canada's Development*. Toronto: University of Toronto Press, 1966.

Dauphin, Roma. *The Impact of Free Trade in Canada*. Study prepared for the Economic Council of Canada. Ottawa: 1978.

Deutsch, John J. "Tariffs, Subsidies and Agriculture." (1957) 5(2) *Canadian Journal of Agricultural Economics*, 38-49.

Dobson, Wendy. "Exports to Developing Countries." (July 1979) no. 20, *H.R.I. Observations*.

Eastman, Harry C. and Stychold, Stephen. *The Tariff and Competition in Canada*. Toronto: MacMillan, 1967.

Economic Council of Canada. Annual Reviews. Ottawa.

_____. *Effective Protection in the Canadian Economy*, Special Study no. 9. Ottawa: 1968.

_____. *The Bottom Line: Technology, Trade and Income Growth*. Ottawa: 1983.

_____. *Looking Outward: A New Trade Strategy for Canada*. Ottawa: 1975.

_____. *Venturing Forth. An Assessment of the Canada-U.S. Trade Agreement*. Ottawa: 1988.

Elliott, G.A. *Tariff Procedures and Trade Barriers: A Study of Indirect Protection in Canada and the United States*. Toronto: University of Toronto Press, 1955.

English, H.E. *Canada in a Wider Economic Community*. Toronto: University of Toronto Press, 1972.

Fischer, Lewis A. *Canadian Agriculture and the World Food Problem*. Montreal: C.D. Howe Research Institute, 1976.

_____. "The Common Agricultural Policy of the EC: Its Impact on Canadian Agriculture." (September 1979) *Journal of European Integration*, 29-50.

GATT. *Basic Instruments and Selected Documents, Volume 4*. Geneva: The Secretariat, 1969.

_____. Director-General. *The Tokyo Round of Multilateral Trade Negotiations: Report* (1979) and *Supplementary Report* (1980). Geneva: The Secretariat.

_____. *GATT Activities*. Geneva: the Secretariat, annual.

_____. *GATT: What It Is, What It Does*. Geneva: The Secretariat, 1982.

_____. *Text of the General Agreement*. Geneva: 1986.

Gilmour, J. "Industrialization and Technological Backwardness: The Canadian Dilemma." (Winter 1978) *Canadian Public Policy*, 20-33.

Globerman, Steven. "Canadian Science Policy and Technological Sovereignty."

(Winter 1978) *Canadian Public Policy*, 34-45.

Golt, Sidney. *The GATT Negotiations, 1973-75: A Guide to the Issues*. London: British-North American Committee, 1974.

———. *The GATT Negotiations 1973-79: The Closing Stage*. London: British-North American Committee, 1978.

———. *Trade Issues in the Mid 1980's*. London: British-North American Committee, 1982.

Graham, W.C. "Governmental Procurement Policies: GATT, the EEC and the United States." In *Federalism and the Canadian Economic Union*. Papers presented at a Conference held at the University of Western Ontario Law School, December 1981. Toronto: Ontario Economic Council, 1983.

Grey, Rodney de C. *The Development of the Canadian Anti-Dumping System*. Montreal: Private Planning Association of Canada, 1973.

———. "Some Issues in Canada-U.S. Trade Relations." (VIII Supplement 1982) *Canadian Public Policy*, 451-57.

———. *Trade Policy in the 1980s: An Agenda for Canadian-U.S. Relations*. Montreal: C.D. Howe Institute, 1981.

———. *United States Trade Policy Legislation: A Canadian View*. Montreal: The Institute for Research in Public Policy, 1982.

Grover, Glenn, ed. *Free Trade and Social Policy*. Ottawa: Canadian Council on Social Development, 1988.

Gupta, K.R. *A Study of the General Agreement on Tariffs and Trade*. Delhi: S. Chand, 1967.

Hazledine, T. "Not So Elementary." (June 1988) 14 *Canadian Public Policy*, 204-13.

Hazledine, T., and Wigington, I. "Canadian Auto Policy." (December 1987) 13 *Canadian Public Policy*, 490-501.

Higgins, Benjamin, and Jean. *Canada's Trade Policy in the Second Decade*. Montreal: The Private Planning Association of Canada, 1970.

Jenkins, Glenn P. *Costs and Consequences of the New Protectionism: The Case of the Canadian Clothing Industry*. Ottawa: North-South Institute, 1980.

Johnson, Harry G. *Aspects of the Theory of Tariffs*. Cambridge, Mass.: Harvard University Press, 1972.

———. "Canadian-American Economic Integration: A Time for Decision." (August 1966) *Journal of Canadian Studies*, 31-36.

———. *International Economic Questions Facing Britain, the United States, and Canada in the 70's*. London: British-North American Committee, 1970.

———. *U.S. Economic Policy Towards the Developing Countries*. Reprint 149. Washington, D.C.: The Brookings Institution, 1968.

———. *The World Economy at the Crossroads*. Montreal: Private Planning Association of Canada, 1964.

Krause, Lawrence B. *The International Economic System and the Multilateral Corporation*. Reprint 250. Washington, D.C.: The Brookings Institution, 1972.

Lazar, Fred. *The New Protectionism: Non-Tariff Barriers and Their Effect on Canada*. Toronto: James Lorimer in Association with the Canadian Institute for Economic Policy, 1981.

League of Nations. *Commercial Policy in the Interwar Period: International Proposals and National Policies*. Geneva: The Secretariat, 1942.

Lee, Sperry and Webly, Simon. *Multinational Corporations in Developed Countries: A Review of Recent Research and Policy Thinking*. Washington, D.C.: British-North American Committee, 1973.

Lipsey, Richard G. "The Canada-U.S. Free Trade Agreement and the Great Free Trade Debate." *Trade Monitor no. 1*. Toronto: C.D. Howe Institute, 1987.

Lipsey, Richard G., and Dobson, Wendy, eds. *Shaping Comparative Advantage*. Toronto: C.D. Howe Institute, 1987.

Lipsey, Richard G., and Smith, Murray G. *Taking the Initiative: Canada's Trade Options in a Turbulent World*. Toronto: C.D. Howe Institute, 1985.

Lipsey, Richard G., and York, Robert C. *Evaluating the Free Trade Deal: a Guided Tour through the Canada U.S. Agreement*. Toronto: C.D. Howe Institute, 1988.

Leyton-Brown, David. "The Mug's Game: Automotive investment Incentives in Canada and the United States." (Winter 1979-80) XXXV *International Journal*, 170-84.

Leyton-Brown, David, and Gold, Marc. *Trade-offs on Free Trade: the Canada-United States Free Trade Agreement*. Toronto: Carswell, 1988.

MacBean, Alasdair. *A Positive Approach to the International Economic Order Part I: Trade and Structural Adjustment*. London: British-North American Committee, 1978.

Marsh, John S. *British Entry to the European Community—Implications for British and North American Agriculture*, together with a statement by the Committee. London: British-North American Committee, 1971.

Matthews, Roy A. "Canada and Economic Unions." (1959) 14.3 *International Journal*, 190-201.

_____. "Challenge of the Third World: A Threat to Canadian Industry and Workers?" (no. 4, 1981) *Behind the Headlines*. Toronto: Canadian Institute of International Affairs, 1981.

_____. *Industrial Viability in a Free-Trade Economy*. Toronto: University of Toronto Press, 1971.

Melvin, James R., and Wilkinson, Bruce W. *Effective Protection in the Canadian Economy*. Special Study no. 9. Ottawa: Economic Council of Canada, Queen's Printer, 1968.

Miles, Caroline M. "After the Kennedy Round." (January 1968) 44(1) *International Affairs*, 14-25.

Morici, Peter. *Canada-United States Trade and Economic Interdependence*. In *Canada-U.S. Prospects*, a series sponsored by the C.D. Howe Research Institute. Toronto: C.D. Howe Research Institute, (Canada) and National Planning Association (U.S.A.), 1980.

Nowzad, Barham. *The Rise of Protectionism*. IMF Pamphlet Series no. 24. Washington, D.C.: International Monetary Fund, 1978.

Office of Official Publications of the European Communities. *The Agricultural Policy of the European Community*. 2nd ed. Luxembourg: the Office, 1979.

Ontario, Ministry of Industry, Trade and Technology. *Assessment of Direct Employment Effects of Freer Trade for Ontario's Manufacturing Industries*. Background paper for the Annual First Ministers' Conference. Halifax, November 28-29, 1985. Toronto: 1985.

_____. Finance Committee. *Report on Free Trade*. Toronto: 1988.

Organization for Economic Co-operation and Development. *The Generalized*

System of Preferences. Review of the First Decade. Paris: the Organization, 1983.

Pearson, Charles, and Salembier, Gerry. *Trade, Employment and Adjustment.* Montreal: the Institute for Research on Public Policy, 1983.

Perry, J.H. "Canada and the GATT."(September-October 1954) *Canadian Tax Journal,* 272-79.

_____. *Taxes, Tariffs and Subsidies.* Toronto: University of Toronto Press, 1954.

Pestieau, Caroline. *The Canadian Textile Policy: A Sectoral Trade Adjustment Strategy.* Montreal: C.D. Howe Research Institute, 1976.

_____. *The Sector Approach to Trade Negotiations: Canadian and U.S. Interests.* Montreal: C.D. Howe Research Institute, 1976.

_____. *Subsidies and Countervailing Duties: The Negotiating Issues.* Montreal: C.D. Howe Research Institute, 1976.

Pestieau, Caroline, and Henry, Jacques. *Non-Tariff Barriers as a Problem in International Development.* Montreal: Private Planning Association of Canada, 1972.

Piquet, Howard S. *The U.S. Trade Expansion Act of 1962.* Washington, D.C.: Canadian-American Committee, 1963.

Plumptre, A.F.W. *Three Decades of Decision.* Toronto: McClelland and Stewart Ltd., 1977.

Price, Victoria Curzon. *Free Trade Areas, the European Experience: What Lessons for Canadian-U.S. Trade Liberaliziation?* Toronto: C.D. Howe Institute, 1987.

Rabbior, Gary. *Export Canada. Opportunities and Challenges in the World Economy.* Toronto: Canadian Foundation for Economic Education, 1984.

Reisman, Simon. "Canada-United States Free Trade." Paper presented at Conference on U.S.-Canada Economic Relations. Washington, D.C.: The Brookings Institution, April 1984.

_____. "Let's get it straight." *The Globe and Mail,* October 4, 1988.

Reuber, Grant. *Canada's Interest in the Trade Problems of Less-Developed Countries.* Montreal: Canadian Trade Committee, The Private Planning Association of Canada, 1964.

Richards, A.E. "GATT Negotiations, Geneva 1947, Annecy 1949 and Torquay 1950-51." (August 1953) 23(4) *Economic Analyst,* 77-79.

Roach, E. Hugh. "The Commodity Question—Towards a Common Fund—Rhetoric or Reality?" (no. 6, 1978) *Behind the Headlines.* The Canadian Institute of International Affairs.

Roarty, M.J. "The EEC Common Agricultural Policy and its Effects on Less-Developed Countries." *National Westminster Bank Quarterly Review,* February 1985.

Safarian, A.E. "The Canada-U.S. Free Trade Agreement and Foreign Direct Investment." *Trade Monitor* no. 3. Toronto: C.D. Howe Institute, 1988.

_____. *Governments and Multinationals: Policies in the Developed Countries.* Washington, D.C.: British-North American Committee, 1983.

Sarna, A.J. "The Evolving International Trade Environment." (no. 6, 1984) *Behind the Headlines.* Toronto: Canadian Institute of International Affairs, 1984.

Saunders, R.S. "Continentalism and Economic Nationalism in the Manufacturing Sector: Seeking Middle Ground." (1983) Supplement *Canadian Public Policy,* 463-79.

Sharp, Mitchell. "Introduction." In Philip E. Urin, ed. *East West Trade.* Toronto: Canadian Institute of International Affairs, 1966, pp xiii-xvi.

Sinclair, Sol. *The Common Agricultural Policy of the E.E.C. and its Implications for Canada's Exports.* Montreal: Private Planning Association of Canada, 1964.

Slater, David W. "Canada in the Kennedy Round." (Autumn 1967) *Canadian Banker*, 7.

Slayton, P. *The Tariff Board*: A Study for the Law Reform Commission of Canada. Ottawa: Law Reform Commission, 1981.

Smith, Arthur J.R. "Canada's Policy Problem." In *Canada and the New International Economy.* Toronto: University of Toronto Press, 1961.

Southworth, Constant, and Buchanan, W.W. *Changes in Trade Restrictions Between Canada and the United States.* Montreal: Private Planning Association of Canada, 1960.

Stegemann, K. *Canadian Non-Tariff Barriers to Trade.* Montreal: Private Planning Association of Canada, 1973.

_____. "Special Import Measures Legislation." (Autumn 1982) *Canadian Public Policy*, 573-85.

Stern, Robert M., Trezise, Philip H., and Walley, John. eds. *Perspectives on a U.S. Canadian Free Trade Agreement.* Based on a Conference jointly sponsored by the Institute of Public Policy Studies at the University of Michigan and the Centre for the Study of International Economic Relations at the University of Western Ontario. Washington, D.C.: the Brookings Institution, 1987.

Stone, Frank. *Canada, the GATT and the International Trade System.* Montreal: The Institute for Research in Public Policy, 1984.

"Talking Free Trade with the pact man." *The Financial Times of Canada*, July 25-31, 1988.

United States. Commission on International Trade and Investment Policy. *United States International Economic Policy in an Interdependent World.* Papers submitted to the Commission and published in conjunction with the Commission's Report to the President. Washington, D.C.: 1971.

_____. Congress. *U.S. Trade Policy and the Tokyo Round of Multilateral Trade Negotiations.* Washington, D.C.: Congressional Budget Office, 1979.

_____. *The Effects of the Tokyo Round of Multilateral Trade Negotiations on the U.S. Economy: An Updated View.* Washington, D.C.: Congressional Budget Office, 1979.

Warley, T.K. *Agriculture in an Interdependent World: U.S. and Canadian Perspectives.* Montreal: Canadian-American Committee, 1977.

Watson, W.G. "Canada-U.S. Free Trade: Why Now?" (September 1987) 13 *Canadian Public Policy*, 337-49.

_____. "The Case of the Disputed Benefit: A Reply to Tim Hazledine." (June 1988) 14 *Canadian Public Policy*, 214-21.

Wilgress, Dana. *Memoirs.* Toronto: Ryerson Press, 1967.

_____. *Canada's Approach to Trade Negotiations.* Montreal: Private Planning Association of Canada, 1963.

Wilkinson, B.W. *Canada in the Changing World Economy. Canada-U.S. Prospects*, a series sponsored by the C.D. Howe Research Institute (Canada) and the National Planning Association (U.S.A). Toronto: C.D. Howe Research Institute, 1980.

_____. *Canada's International Trade: An Analysis of Recent Trends.* Montreal: Private Planning Association of Canada, 1968.

_____. "Canada-U.S. Free Trade and Some Options." 1982 (Supplement). *Canadian Public Policy*, 428-39.

_____. "Canada-United States Free-Trade: the current debate." (Winter 1986-87) *International Journal*, 199-218.

Williams, J.R. *Resources, Tariffs and Trade: Ontario's Stake.* Toronto: University of Toronto Press, 1976.

Winham, Gilbert R. "Bureaucratic Politics and Canadian Trade Negotiations." (Winter 1978-79) *International Journal*, 64-90.

Wonnacott P. and Wonnacott, R.J. *Free Trade Between the United States and Canada, the Potential Economic Effects.* Cambridge, Mass.: Harvard University Press, 1967.

_____. "Free Trade Between United States and Canada: Fifteen Years Later." (Supplement 1982) *Canadian Public Policy*, 412-27.

_____. *U.S. Canada Free Trade: The Potential Impact on the Canadian Economy.* Montreal: Canadian-American Committee. 1968.

Wonnacott, Paul. "The Canada-U.S. Free Trade Agreement and the Auto Pact." *Trade Monitor no. 2.* Toronto: C.D. Howe Institute, 1988.

_____. *The United States and Canada: The Quest for Free Trade.* Washington, D.C.: Institute for International Economics, 1987.

Wonnacott, Ronald J. *Canada's Trade Options.* Ottawa: Economic Council of Canada, 1975.

_____. "On the Employment Effects of Free Trade with the United States." (March 1986) *Canadian Public Policy*, 258.

Young, John H. *Canadian Commercial Policy*, Royal Commission on Canada's Economic Prospects. Ottawa: Queen's Printer, 1957.

Defence—The Continuing Dilemma

Prologue
Defence—The Continuing Dilemma

Canada has shared in most major wars of the last century, the Vietnam conflict excepted. These wars have been dealt with as they arose. The mobilization of men and weapons followed the outbreak of hostilities, and the wind-down to peacetime conditions came very rapidly after hostilities ceased. The defence forces dwindled, defence weapons were neglected, and armed conflict was forgotten until the next emergency arose.

This approach to war-making was possible when arms were simple and training of fighting men in their use was elementary. Under the British regime hastily trained Canadian militia supplemented the Imperial troops, its members only recently having left the implements of farm or town for the musket and cannon. With Confederation Canada became responsible for its own defence, and before World War I maintained a modest military establishment. This was expanded exponentially after 1914 but once again shrank to nominal size after the war and remained so until 1939, when a new war loomed ahead. World War II weaponry, particularly in the air, was more complex to produce and required more specialized training to operate, but it was still feasible for newly inducted recruits to reach a level of competence in a short time.

Since the end of World War II the nature of war has changed completely. Three new and unhappy events are responsible—the arrival of the atomic and later the nuclear age, the development of the long-range missile, and the need to maintain preparedness in the world dominated by the two superpowers, Russia and the United States. In these conditions the role of a middle power has been perplexing and controversial. For Canada the near —and friendly—proximity of one of these powers adds enormously to the complications. The United States in its own interests must take defence measures, and many of these by their nature provide a defence shield for Canada as well. And Canada is inevitably involved in these measures, as many of them depend on our cooperation to be effective. Should Canada simply rely on the indirect benefits of U.S. efforts and limit its own expenditures to a minimum? Or, in keeping with its past record of major participation in world wars, and its almost inevitable fate, because of its geographical position, as a protagonist in a Russia-U.S. conflict, should it push its defence to the limit of its resources? In a world now held in the frightening balance of nuclear terror, what should Canada's position be on the distribution and use of nuclear arms?

Canada's answer to the dilemma has been to commit itself to the role of a participant, the practical fulfillment of which has varied over the last three decades as conditions have changed. In principle, through close ties with the United States and membership in the North Atlantic Treaty Organization (NATO), it has elected to maintain a permanent defence establishment capable of offering a reasonable deterrence toward a hostile nation. This is a far different peacetime program than formerly followed, and one in which Canadians instinctively do not feel comfortable.

There has been no agreement on preparations to fill this role, and steps that have been taken have been criticized as being either (1) too much, or (2) too little. Proponents of the former view argue that the United States must take measures in its own interest that will provide sufficient defence for the whole continent, and that any contribution Canada can make is trivial by comparison; the latter reason that Canada must make a responsible effort to maintain a defence establishment if it is to have any influence on massive international decisions that will inevitably affect its interests. This view has prevailed, but the search for a middle path (in which Canada of course is not alone) has been pursued without much conviction and with indecisive results. Compared to a peak expenditure of 35 percent of GNP during World War II Canada's current levels are around 2 percent, and place it second last among NATO members, outranking only Luxembourg.

Surveys of the media show that the one defence issue that arouses any public interest is the employment of nuclear weaponry by the Canadian forces or even the testing of nuclear capable Cruise missiles in Canada.[1] While the decision against nuclear arms taken at least 15 years ago has profoundly affected Canada's defence program, the residual of problems remaining since then has demonstrated that it is far from being the only issue in defence policy. How much is to be spent on defence? What is the relative role for each service? Where are forces to be located? What equipment is to be employed? What defence industry should be sustained in Canada? What should Canada's role be in cooperating with other nations? Finally, and crucially, is there a place for a Canadian-made indigenous defence policy?

The following pages do not attempt to propound answers for these questions, a task far beyond the capacities of the present author. Rather they describe in non-technical terms the actual course of Canada's postwar defence program in an effort to give some background for understanding future developments. This is a sufficiently formidable task as the subject is massive, complex and volatile. Chapters 36 to 39 review developments to 1986. Chapter 40 brings the narrative up to 1988.

---

[1] Don Munton, "Public Opinion and the Media in Canada from Cold War to Détente to New Cold War," (Winter 1983-84) *International Journal*. 171-213; and T.A. Keenleyside, B.E. Burton and W.S. Soderlund, "The Press and Foreign Policy: Canadian Newspaper Coverage of Relations with the United States," October-December, 1982 (Winter, 1985-86) *International Journal* 189-220.

36
Defence Policy

The average citizen, based on observation of well patrolled entrances to defence establishments, is justified in regarding all matters military as hidden from public view. In fact the policies and practices of the national defence program are normally a well documented aspect of the federal government. Much information must remain secret, but a White Paper or similar document dealing with existing and future policies and programs has in the past been frequently presented to Parliament, and further information has been given by officials before parliamentary committees and in official publications. As a result the basis of defence policy is better documented than many other aspects of government, although there was a serious lack in the delay of a policy statement by the Conservative government, finally delivered in 1987. These key statements are essential to an understanding of the shifting phases of Canadian defence policy.

Policy in the Making

Rebuilding the Forces

Following the end of World War II the forces had almost been completely demobilized and expenditures had been drastically reduced. Although Canada had been a founding member of NATO in 1949 and had passed Mutual Aid legislation in 1950 the country was completely unprepared for participation in the Korean War, which started in 1951. A new approach to defence had to be quickly adopted, and a three-year program, to cost about $5 billion, was announced by the Minister of National Defence on February 5, 1951, and was later elaborated in *Canada's Defence Programme, 1951-52*. There were to be three objectives for postwar defence, as follows:

"(1) The immediate defence of Canada and North America from direct attack;

(2) implementation of any undertakings made by Canada under the Charter of the United Nations, or under the North Atlantic Treaty or other agreement for collective security;

(3) the organization to build up our strength in the event of a total war."[36.1]

These objectives were further confirmed and amplified in subsequent annual statements, and by 1954 it was being reported that the original program, which had mainly been along World War II conventional lines, had been substantially effected at a cost of $5.2 billion. However a new and ominous note began to appear in *Canada's Defence Programme, 1955-56*.

[36.1] Canada, Minister of National Defence, *Canada's Defence Program, 1951-52* (Ottawa: Queen's Printer, 1951), 6.

"During the past year the United States has made considerable progress in the production of atomic and thermonuclear weapons. The U.S.S.R., after carrying out hydrogen bomb tests, has indicated that production of a stockpile of nuclear bombs is underway . . . It is now clear that a single thermonuclear bomb can be made large enough to destroy a major city and all its inhabitants by direct effect of blast and heat . . . For North America, the possibility appears for the first time of an attack that could cripple the military and industrial potential of Canada and the United States . . . It becomes all the more important, therefore, that we spare no effort progressively to reduce international tension and eventually to eliminate war. At the same time we must ensure that together with our allies we have sufficient military strength to deter any potential aggressor."[36.2] Cooperation with the United States and NATO therefore was even more essential than hitherto.

Canada's Defence Programme, 1956-57, contained a revealing statement indicative of the approach to nuclear warfare in the pre-missile era. It postulated that the primary objective of preventing a third world war "requires that there must be a powerful strategic bomber force, backed by the means to ensure that this force can be immediately effective under any circumstances, and supported by the forces-in-being required to blunt an attack by a would be aggressor for long enough to permit the West's retaliatory forces to carry out their role. This combination of forces constitutes the best possible deterrent under present conditions."[36.3] The bombers would be from a strategic air force of the United States, augmented by that of Great Britain. It was assumed at this time that thermonuclear weapons dropped from heavy bombers would be used both for the attack and reprisal, in retrospect an incredibly naïve attitude in view of the heavily populated areas in which nuclear armaments were planned for use.

In *Report on National Defence*, 1957, Canada again expressed its continued unreserved support for NATO defence plans. "Canada's defence policy is meaningful only when related to NATO strategy and planning." The primary element of NATO forces is "retaliatory striking power, provided by the U.S. Strategic Air Command with nuclear weapons produced in that country . . ." But other elements were also crucial, and in these Canada would play an essential role. "With growing Soviet construction of nuclear submarines the NATO anti-submarine force has become of crucial importance . . . The primary role of the Royal Canadian Navy has for some years been anti-submarine warfare in all its aspects."[36.4] As for the air force, first priority was given to its role in sounding an early warning and in providing deterrence and interception. The total NATO concept was extolled as providing countries like Canada with the chance to give constructive help

---

36.2 Canada, Minister of National Defence, *Canada's Defence Program, 1955-56* (Ottawa: Queen's Printer, 1955), 4.

36.3 Canada, Minister of National Defence, *Canada's Defence Program, 1956-57* (Ottawa: Queen's Printer, 1956), 3.

36.4 Canada, Minister of National Defence, *Report on National Defence, 1957-58* (Ottawa: Queen's Printer, 1957).

without being required to build up complete and balanced forces. The prevailing conception of nuclear warfare was again evident in the assumption that the effective engagement of forces would take place following a nuclear exchange; paramount emphasis was given to the duties to be performed by the forces after the nuclear battle had been fought.

The Missile Age

A major shift of policy came abruptly in the late fifties with the development of long range missiles to carry nuclear warheads. One immediate effect was to completely alter Canada's role in early detection. Existing systems relied heavily on radar deployed in "lines" in Northern Canada. These were designed to identify long-range bombers, and would now be useless for missiles, which required a different technique. But the lines would still be needed, since they would have to be maintained against the original bomber threat.

The new technology, along with the mass production of the nuclear bomb, affected all aspects of defence and drastically reduced the number of countries whose voice would be heard in defence decisions. The heavy reliance on research and on costly and rapidly changing technology excluded all but the most highly industrialized countries from direct participation. Increasingly the main weapons of war were under the control of the two great powers, Russia and the United States. As a result the agencies for development of combined strategies between these countries and their allies, such as NATO and NORAD for the West, assumed an even more crucial role as centres of communication and planning. The Minister of National Defence made this very clear in the following statement in 1959: "The requirements deemed necessary for defence today will almost certainly be outmoded a few years from now. This, of course, is not solely a Canadian problem; it is a problem facing every country today. In our endeavours to solve it we should be ready and willing to consult with our partners in Europe and on the North American continent . . . By co-operating with our allies we are able to have an integrated, balanced force among all the allies rather than attempting to have a balanced force within each nation. It has been obvious for some time that no country can stand alone or can plan its defence in isolation." And again: "While the increased range of offensive weapons equipped with nuclear warheads brings the North American Continent within the target range in any future war, it is realized that the defence of this area cannot be considered in isolation."[36.5]

Nuclear Policy Challenged

By this time Canada had adopted a limited nuclear role, and this step was challenged in 1960 by a parliamentary committee that was suspicious of everything connected with it. In particular the committee questioned the stationing of nuclear-armed Bomarc missiles in Canada in place of intercep-

---

[36.5] Canada, Minister of National Defence, *Defence 1959* (Ottawa: Queen's Printer, 1959).

tor aircraft, the latest development in U.S.-Canadian cooperation. The committee sat for over two months and heard some 600 pages of evidence from the Minister and his officials. The Minister dealt very bluntly with the concerns of the members over Canada's collective commitments. He said: "No nation can afford a unilateral defence. Our defence expenditures are not providing complete protection but in combination with others, they are contributing to the overall effectiveness of an insurance against possible agression."[36.6] In an age of nuclear missiles the staggering costs had to be shared among many countries to be bearable. Nonetheless growing opposition to nuclear arms was a portent of developments in the next decade.

Policy was supplemented slightly in 1961 with two objectives: first, to maintain peace by preventing a third global war; and second, to prevent subjection to a foreign power, both objectives that could best be achieved by international co-operation. The Minister of Defence revealed at this time that three of the weapons in Canada's armaments had "nuclear capacity"—the Honest John surface-to-surface guided missile, the Bomarc anti-aircraft missile and the CF-104 aircraft.

This was the period of the Berlin crisis, and a program was launched to expand the armed forces. However, the aggressive mood did not last. Internationally there began the so-called "era of appeasement," to which Canada quickly adapted. The next year, after the Berlin crisis had passed, the government was feeling a financial pinch and as part of an austerity program cut back growth in defence expenditures. The nuclear issue continued to simmer. In reply to a question in the House Prime Minister Diefenbaker stated his view that "in the event that nuclear war was launched, nuclear weapons should be placed in the possession of Canadians."[36.7]

1963 was a year for a further in-depth review of defence policy by Parliament prior to the issuance of a new White Paper. A Special Committee on Defence was established in June to study defence and foreign policy, and issued an *Interim Report* in December, which, among other matters, recommended that integration of the services be studied, that projections be made of future defence spending, that Canada remain a member of NATO and maintain forces in Europe, that Canada remain a partner in NORAD, that Canada continue peace-keeping missions and that "Canadian defence policy should be Canadian policy in the sense that it should get its inspiration and content from Canadian sources in contact with the outside world."[36.8] This last plea was to continue to be made by defence specialists for two decades.

[36.6] Canada, Minister of National Defence, *Memorandum for the Special Committee on Defence Expenditure* (Ottawa: Queen's Printer, 1960).

[36.7] Canada, House of Commons, *Debates*, 4th Parliament, 5th Session, (February 26, 1962), 1250.

[36.8] Canada, House of Commons. Special Committee on Matters Relating to Defence, *Interim Report* (Ottawa: Queen's Printer, 1963.

Nuclear Armament Formally Accepted

In August 1963, Canada entered into a formal agreement with the United States to equip its forces in Canada and Europe with nuclear weapons. Nuclear devices for this purpose would be stored by the United States, but firing would be a joint responsibility. The Bomarc weapons would have nuclear warheads by the end of 1963 but the other systems would take longer to equip.

1964 White Paper

A White Paper on Defence issued in March 1964, presented a somewhat revised defence policy for the future, but was mainly notable for its proposed organizational changes. The main goals would continue to be three in number, namely: "to preserve the peace by supporting collective defence measures to deter military aggression; to support Canadian foreign policy including that arising out of our participation in international organizations and to provide for the protection and surveillance of our territory, our air space and our coastal waters." Major expenditures should be made in the next five years to re-equip the army for greater air mobility, to acquire tactical aircraft and improve maritime anti-submarine capability.

Some of the more significant proposals involved organization. Prominent among these was the plan to integrate the three services into one force, a task in which the Department would be engaged for some years. An important immediate step was taken in 1964 with the combining of the Ottawa headquarters of the three services. In 1965 a single system of recruiting went into effect and the process of integration of field commands was begun. In the following year the first steps were taken toward integration of reserve forces. Other changes were to follow rapidly (to be reviewed later). These changes were ultimately to be given statutory sanction under the Canadian Forces Reorganization Act, 1967.

The White Paper also stated that defence activities in the future would be grouped under specific programs covering all arms of the services, such as force structures, weapon systems, logistic arrangements, and so on, in order to ensure an integration of both functions and organizations.[36.9]

Nuclear Arms Rejected—Forces "Domesticated"

1969 marked a sharp turn in Canadian defence policy. The Trudeau government elected in 1968 began early to implement its own approach. One firm break with the past was the abandonment of any nuclear role for Canada after 1972; another was the decision to cut by one-half the Canadian armed forces maintained in Europe. Canadian forces both in Europe and Canada would be re-organized to achieve greater mobility, with more extensive use of light and mobile land equipment, helicopters, and smaller and faster

---

[36.9]Canada, Minister of National Defence *White Paper on Defence* (Ottawa: Queen's Printer, 1964).

naval vessels. More attention would be paid to Arctic surveillance, not only for military purposes but for the protection of Canada's sovereignty and for seabed and pollution control in northern waters. More attention would also be given to the assistance of civilian authorities in emergencies.

These specific objectives were restated in the 1970-71 *Estimates* with the following general policy declaration:

By military capabilities

(1) to preserve sovereignty over and ensure security within the territorial limits of Canada and to supplement the civil authorities and contribute to national development;

(2) to enhance the security of Canada by contributing to collective measures for the prevention of war: (a) through cooperation with the United States in North America defence activities and (b) through collective defence activities in Europe and the North Atlantic area; and

(3) to promote the resolution of international disputes by contributing peacekeeping activities in cooperation with other members of the international community.[36.10]

The 1971 White Paper

The new focus was given definitive statement in the White Paper on defence —*Defence in the 70s*—issued in August 1971. Along with the Defence Structure Review in 1975 this represents the policy that was to be in effect until the Conservative White Paper was issued in 1987. It therefore deserves detailed attention. A useful summary of the two documents was given by John Gellner in a 1985 publication of the Canadian Institute of International Affairs.

As set out in the 1971 white paper on defence the roles—the actual words used were 'the major areas of activity'—were as follows:

1 the surveillance of Canadian territory and coastlines, that is, the protection of Canadian sovereignty;

2 the defence of North America in co-operation with United States forces;

3 the fulfilment of such NATO commitments as may be agreed upon;

4 the performance of such international peacekeeping roles as Canada might from time to time assume.

In 1975, the Defence Structure Review, which could be viewed as the second phase of the study that led to the 1971 white paper, identified fifteen specific objectives within the four roles:

1 to ensure an adequate overall capability for surveillance of Canadian territory, airspace and sea approaches;

[36.10] Canada, *Main Estimates for the Fiscal Year Ending March 31, 1971* (Ottawa: Queen's Printer, 1970), 14-14.

2 to enforce, through military involvement, respect for and compliance with Canadian territorial and jurisdictional authority;

3 to provide aid to civil law enforcement agencies on request, in execution of their constitutional responsibilities;

4 to promote Canadian unity and identity;

5 to support emergency relief and search and rescue; and

6 to foster economic growth, social justice, a high quality of life, and the preservation of an harmonious national environment.

Under role 2:

7 to deny the advantage of surprise in armed attack on North America;

8 to contribute to the protection of land-based United States retaliatory capability against neutralization; and

9 to provide response to other military threats to North America.

Under role 3:

10 to prevent or contain armed attack against the NATO area (Europe, the north Atlantic and North America);

11 to sustain the confidence of the United States and of other allies, and

12 to ensure that applied policies include provisions for Canada's security interests.

Under role 4:

13 to avoid great power confrontation in local conflicts;

14 to prevent the outbreak of hostilities in other areas of tension; and

15 to provide military training for foreign personnel under Military Assistance Programs in Canada and abroad.[36.11]

This position was a far move from the early sixties, when the paramount Canadian military commitment was deterrence of an enemy through NATO and international cooperation, with no concern for Canadian domestic interests and no reservations on the use of nuclear weapons.

The Financial Constraints

Many of the 1971 objectives are as valid today as a decade ago, and undoubtedly will survive in some form in the future. Others will no doubt be added to reflect changed conditions resulting from new technology and a more aggressive approach to defence. However, before leaving the policy area, and admittedly anticipating the next sections on Policy in Practice,

---

[36.11] John Gellner, *The Defence of Canada: Requirements, Capabilities, and the National Will*. Behind the Headlines, XLII no. 3 (Toronto: Canadian Institute of International Affairs, 1985), 5-6.

one point must be made, because it has coloured all policy implementation; the greatest weakness of any Canadian defence policy is not its objectives, although these are complex enough, but the parsimony with which it is administered. Nowhere has this been more evident than in outlays for equipment. For two decades equipment programs were initiated mainly in response to emergencies or when it became painfully clear that the Canadian force could hardly perform *any* defence role with existing worn-out and obsolete armaments. In a world of inflationary price rises and costly new technology Canada's equipment budget had been kept at a starvation level. After the initial spending under the Korean War program defence was frozen in 1964 for five years at $1.5 billion and for a further three years in 1969 at about $1.8 billion. As a result an ever-rising share of the total went for the higher pay and accommodation required to attract recruits into the peacetime military, until the equipment share had fallen to 8 percent by the early seventies. It was the lament of many experts that Canada had allowed its defence equipment to fall so far behind requirements that a massive outlay would be needed to make even a beginning in restoring it to standing. Fortunately the start made in 1973 to recover lost ground will remedy much of the shortage if continued for sufficient time. The ceiling of $2 billion was broken in 1973, and current totals are at least four times that level. But, as we will see later, budget stringency is still a governing condition, and, although budget appropriations are being increased, finances will determine the overall commitment, no matter what the policy adopted.

Policies in Practice

The actual implementation of policies in the postwar Canadian defence program has been closely related to three principal conditions—the philosophy of the party in power, prevailing world tensions, and the state of the federal budget.

The first consideration may be easily disposed of. It is generally true that no Canadian national government has shown more than a lukewarm interest in defence in the postwar years. Canada has responded when called on for assistance in international crisis, and has met these obligations in an unstinting way. But there has been no joy in the call to arms. Canadian governments generally do not prepare happily for the warpath, and in this they no doubt reflect the sentiments of the vast majority of Canadians. The abandonment of nuclear armament was popular, and today the slightest threat of location of nuclear weapons in Canada even during a period of imminent hostilities, or the testing of unarmed Cruise missiles, makes alarm bells ring, in Parliament and elsewhere.

The other two influences—world tensions and the state of the budget—played their role intermittently, although the latter was a pervasive and dominant influence.

1951-60. In the rude awakening of the Korean War in 1951 the Minister of National Defence announced a three-year build-up program, costing about $5 billion, to increase the armed forces strength by 80 percent, reconstruct military facilities all over Canada, and renew and modernize equipment. Both air and land forces would be sent to Europe to operate under NATO. This program, as modified from time to time, was substantially carried out over the fifties, and provided Canada with regular forces of 120,000 (compared with 47,000 in 1950), a naval fleet of about 50 ships, and an air force and army with much improved equipment. It also financed substantial contributions to Mutual Aid and the first stages of the northern warning lines. For several years capital expenditures (equipment and construction) exceeded 50 percent of the total, a ratio that as mentioned was to decline to 8 percent by the early 1970s.

1961. Grave international tension arose during the Berlin Crisis, when the Russians cut off land access to Berlin and the city had to be supplied by a massive Allied airlift. In the uncertainty of the outcome of this episode the Prime Minister announced that after consultation with NATO allies the strength of Canadian forces would be raised from 120,000 to 135,000 and additional funds provided for equipment and for civil defence. The airlift defeated the embargo and it was abandoned after some weeks.

1962. Tension was further heightened in 1962 by the abortive Soviet attempt to mount missile bases in Cuba. The crisis was acute but short-lived, and did not override Canadian budget problems. The government's accounts were showing the fourth consecutive and largest deficit of the postwar period, and the Minister of Finance was slashing expenditures. As part of a general austerity program substantial cuts were made in defence expenditures, involving reduction of the strength of the armed forces, disbandonment of some units in Europe, and other measures.

1963. With a continuing substantial deficit, further reductions in forces' strength and in planned equipment purchases were announced. The strength of reserve forces was to be reduced from 51,000 to 30,000. Despite the austerity program armed forces' strength reached its postwar peak in the early sixties and there was concern as to the control over future growth. The government created a Special Committee on Defence in Parliament to consider the whole question of Canada's future defence role.

1964. The 1964 White Paper on Defence announced the plan to integrate the three services into one force. It was expected that this move would streamline operations and cut down overhead. The savings on manpower and overhead would be spent on purchasing modern equipment. Integration was to be completed by 1967, and was expected to produce economies that would ease the federal budget, still in deficit in 1964. As mentioned, a ceiling of $1.5 billion was adopted for the following five years.

1965. With the restoration of the budget to somewhat greater health the armed forces were granted $1.5 billion to spend on re-equipment over a five-year period. All aspects of the services would benefit. Meanwhile integration was progressing, and was expected to be completed in 1970.

1969. Hard times arrived again for defence. Following a brief period of three years in which the federal budget moved closer to balance, it plunged into deep deficit again in 1968 and 1969 and all aspects of government came under review. Defence was not spared. In September 1969, it was announced that for a further three years beginning with 1969-70 the budget of the Department of National Defence would be frozen, this time at $1.8 billion. The re-equipment program, which had reached about three-quarters completion by 1968-69, was not renewed and would have to be completed under the ceiling. Also, the forces' strength was to be reduced by 16,000 to 82,000 by 1972. This would be a cut of 35 percent from a peak of 126,000 in 1962. The Canadian force of 10,000 in Europe would be cut in half, to 5,000. For the future there would be more emphasis on highly mobile forces, employing helicopters and lighter land and sea equipment. Arctic surveillance was to be extended.

1971. The 1971 White Paper on Defence indicated that the 1969 freeze would be lifted one year earlier than planned, that is, by fiscal year 1972-73, but that an increase of only 1 percent would be permitted during that year. Total defence expenditure, which included outlays other than those of the Defence Department, in fact had reached about $2 billion by fiscal year 1973, and remained above that figure thereafter.

1973. In October 1973, a five-year modernization plan was proposed, to begin in 1974. Expenditures would rise by 7 percent a year starting from a base of $2.1 billion, but in order to provide more funds for equipment the strength of the forces was to be reduced to 78,000.

1975. The Minister announced that the defence authorities were again engaged in a complete review of the tasks that should be performed by the defence services, the personnel and equipment that would be required, and the funds that would be needed. Re-equipment, as the result of earlier orders, began to be evident in delivery of new long-range patrol aircraft and new or modernized tanks. The effect of inflation was specifically countered by the concession that defence capital expenditures would be allowed to rise sufficiently to offset inflation in 1976-77 and would be assured of an increase of 12 percent in real terms in the following five years. Continuing efforts were being made to reduce fixed costs.

Force numbers were being held at 78,000 and plans were being made to close several installations, although they were deferred because of high unemployment.

1977. By this time the five-year re-equipment program had been extended to 15 years, and a systematic plan was being developed for maintaining all arms in up-to-date condition. Substantial orders were being issued, and studies were being conducted to determine the best planes, tanks, weapon systems, etc. for Canada's needs. Forces' strength would be increased from the level of 78,000 to 83,000 over the next few years. A commitment was given as a member of NATO to achieve real growth in defence spending of 3 percent per year in 1979 and later.

1979 and 1980. Austerity cut defence spending once again. A reduction of $150 million in planned outlays was to be made over the following two years. Total annual expenditure by this time exceeded $4 billion.

1981 to 1986. The renewal program was gathering momentum by this time and was expected to cost $15 billion during the eighties. Annual defence expenditure rose steadily, reaching $9.6 billion in fiscal 1985-86. See later for subsequent developments.

Personnel

Targets for strength of the armed forces shifted frequently over the postwar period. From a low point of 35,000 in March 1948, numbers were rapidly increased to over 112,000 at March 31, 1954 for the Korean War, and were maintained in the 115,000 to 120,000 range over the following decade. From a temporary peak of 126,000 at March 31, 1962, reached in response to the Berlin and Cuban crises, numbers fell steadily to under 100,000 by 1970, and continued to decline to a low point of 78,000 to 80,000 in the 1975 to 1978 period, a drop of one-third from the 1962 peak. There was a moderate rise in the following four years under a program adopted in 1977 to increase strength, and by 1985 total forces had regained a level of about 83,000. The 1986-87 *Estimates* authorized additional personnel to bring the total to about 84,500. The distribution of the forces in selected earlier years is shown in Table 36.1.

Table 36.1   Canadian Armed Forces Strength, Selected Years, 1962-83

Fiscal years ending March 31	Navy	Army	Air Force	Canadian Armed Forces	Total
1962	21,500	51,855	53,119	—	126,474
1969	18,291	37,445	42,604	—	98,340
1972	15,388	32,212	37,333	—	84,933
1976	7,599	18,295	21,943	31,901	79,738
1978	6,501	15,500	18,700	40,436	81,137
1979	5,952	14,212	17,209	43,218	80,591
1980	5,437	13,032	15,771	46,058	80,299
1981	4,943	11,832	14,284	49,802	80,861
1982	4,543	10,671	12,992	54,652	82,858
1983	4,188	9,899	12,089	56,729	82,905

Source: Canada Year Book, 1985.

Efforts were being concentrated on reducing civilian personnel employed in various non-combattant jobs. Their numbers had tended to grow during the fifties, reaching a peak of 57,000 in 1958. There followed a gradual decline during the sixties and seventies, dropping to 37,872 in 1975-76. The decline continued during the eighties, to 36,708 in 1984-85; 35,587 in 1985-86; and 34,525 in 1986-87, as authorized in the 1986-87 *Estimates*.

The combined numbers for forces and civilian personnel showed a steady increase from about 60,000 in 1948 to 150,000 during the Korean War, rising thereafter to a peak of 180,000 in 1962. The decline from that peak was continuous and at times rapid, numbers dropping to 135,000 by 1970 and to 110,000-115,000 for most of the seventies. By 1985 there had been a slight rise to 120,000. (Figures are all approximate, as methods of counting varied from period to period).

These numbers take on greater meaning when related to figures for the total labour force. From a high of 14.2 percent during World War II (1944), the ratio declined to slightly under 2 percent in the fifties, to about 1.5 percent during the sixties, then gradually dropped in the early eighties to 1 percent or less. Comparative data issued for NATO members for 1985 shows Canada at 1 percent as second last in this regard, followed only by Luxembourg. Although ratios for the main countries were not strikingly large, being respectively for the U.S., Germany, and the U.K. 2.9, 2.4, and 2.0 percent, they were double or more those for Canada.

A variable quantity in the forces complement is the reserve element. Each arm maintains part-time forces of men and women, for the most part civilians or former members of the forces, who enter into training programs in the evening during the inclement months of the year and more extensive activities during the summer. While not trained to the level of professionals they achieve familiarity with procedures, weapons, vehicles, communications systems, etc., and are closer to combat-readiness than raw recruits. Reserve strength varies with international tension and budget stringency, showing a downward trend in the last two decades. During the fifties numbers exceeded 50,000 in most years, and were hastily increased to nearly 90,000 in 1962.

They fell rapidly to 30,000 in the late sixties and to below 20,000 during most of the seventies. In the early eighties a postwar low of 16,000 was reached. The significance of the reserve forces is that they are expected to take over the defence of Canada as soon as units of the regular forces are withdrawn to a scene of battle, wherever that may be.

Some related aspects of defence personnel policies during the postwar period are of interest.

(1) *Pay and Allowances*: sharp increases in levels of pay for the peacetime forces were required to attract recruits. Pension terms were made particularly liberal in order to ensure that force members retired before age reduced their effectiveness. In 1966, during one of the periodic campaigns to increase enlistment, a cash bonus was offered to non-commissioned officers and men who signed up for further service. Pilots were also offered the chance to sign for permanent commissions rather than for the customary three- to five-year terms.

(2) *Married Quarters and Schools*: the permanent force encouraged the enlistment of married personnel by building much improved living accommodation and providing schools and teachers. The isolation of many defence installations, not only in Canada but overseas, and the likelihood of periodic transfers, necessitated both these developments.

(3) *Female Employment*: plans for recruitment of females were announced in 1951, and by 1954, 6,400 women had enlisted. By 1984 this figure had risen modestly to 6,900. Women were being employed for a lengthening list of duties, but none had yet reached the eminence of one

female member of the U.S. Marine Corps, who was appointed to the rank of General in February 1985.

(4) *French Language Recruiting*: in 1978 it was announced as government policy that a target of 28 percent had been set for representation in the armed forces of members speaking the French language.

Equipment

It is far beyond the limits of this brief study to catalogue in detail the hundreds of types of equipment that the armed forces have acquired and abandoned in the postwar era, but a few notable items may be mentioned.

Home Grown Products

Canada emerged from World War II with capacity and experience in the production of aircraft, tanks, ships, weapons, mobile equipment, and sundry related defence items. This capacity has been used in the postwar years to produce defence material both for Canada and its allies, particularly the United States. Much of this production has been based on proven designs, principally of U.S. origin. However, it has also led Canada into experiments with some designs of its own. The latter have met with varying degrees of success. One of the best known, and possibly the most advanced technologically, was the Arrow fighter aircraft (CF-105) on which development work had commenced in 1952. Intended for use against long-range enemy bombers in the World War II pattern, the Arrow was developed to the point of test flying, to the great satisfaction of proponents of a Canadian aircraft industry. But on the eve of starting manufacture the government announced, on February 20, 1959, that it would not go into production. The reason given was that the Arrow had been outmoded before it even came into being, as the inter-continental missile had completely altered defence strategy. Although this possibility had been foreseen by some air strategists, consternation was general among enthusiasts for Canadian-produced aircraft, and many still regard the death of this apparently well-designed but untimely Canadian plane as one of the most traumatic episodes in Canadian military history. Some critics, foreseeing a return to weapons of conventional warfare, continue to lament this move even today.

Somewhat less notable were the experiments with a mobile troop carrier known as the Bobcat and a hydrofoil water craft named the Bras d'Or. After trials extending over many years and a good deal of expense both were shelved as not proven. Many Canadian innovations or adaptations met a better fate, as for example the Canadian class destroyers built for the Maritime forces in Canadian shipyards, and some of the equipment mounted in these ships.

The Main Tools of War

A major purpose of the postwar initial equipment program announced in 1951 was to substitute up-to-date items of American design for the assorted types inherited from World War II.

Air

In the early fifties the air force relied mainly on the F-86 Sabre jet fighter, (one of the best planes of its type at the time) and the CF-100 all weather fighter. Assorted other planes were used for training, surveillance and transport; of over 2,800 aircraft in use in 1954 there were 21 different types. Although the Sabre was very efficient it was becoming obsolete, and following a $1 billion re-equipment program was replaced by the CF-104, a new single seater U.S. jet fighter. In 1961 the CF-100s in use for interception in Canada began to be replaced by the American designed supersonic F-101B Voodoo interceptor. By 1963 it was also planned to replace the faithful Harvard, used since mid-World War II as a training plane, with a new training jet, the CL-46. In the mid-sixties, re-equipment concentrated on providing new planes for air transport and search and rescue, including the C-130 Hercules and the Buffalo medium transport plane. The CF-5, a new tactical close ground support plane, made its appearance in the sixties, and along with the CF-104 in Europe and the CF-101B Voodoo in Canada, provided the main elements of the air force striking power. Improved versions of the CF-101 were supplied to some of the Canadian squadrons in 1972.

For Maritime surveillance air squadrons were maintained on each coast, with main reliance on the Argus plane. It was announced in 1972 that the anti-submarine emphasis in this service would be given less prominence in favour of more general duties, and that as existing equipment wore out it would be replaced by aircraft more suitable for this altered role. A major move was made in 1976, with the announcement of a contract with Lockheed Aircraft Corporation for the purchase, at a cost of about $1 billion, of 18 long-range patrol aircraft, the Aurora, to replace 26 Argus, delivery to begin in 1980. This was the first multi-million dollar purchase, average cost being $21.2 million per plane. In addition another $125 million was to be spent on spare parts. One reason for the explosion in costs for aircraft—indeed of all military apparatus—was high-tech electronic equipment, increasingly complex and expensive. An extensive program of renewal of helicopters used for surveillance and rescue was also launched at this time.

A dramatic and long awaited step was taken in April 1980, with the announcement of a contract for 138 F-18 fighter aircraft, at a cost of approximately $5 billion. These would replace the outdated air force workhorses—the CF-104 Starfighter, the F-101 Voodoo and, to some extent, the CF-5. Forty-four planes were delivered by March 1985, and further deliveries brought the total to 65 by September 1985. The total was expected to reach 102 by March 1987. Another $64 million was being spent on replacing the outer wing of the CC-130 Hercules aircraft; $211 million was to be paid in coming years for 12 Canadian Challenger aircraft and $98 million for 6 Dash 8 planes. Also $341 million had been approved for acquiring a stock of air-to-air missiles. Many of these outlays of course were spread over several years.

The 1986 strength of the Air Force was 39 Regular Force squadrons and seven Air Reserve squadrons; 34 of the former under the Commander, Air

Command, and the remaining five under the Commander, Canadian Forces Europe.

Maritime

At the end of World War II Canada had a navy of 200 ships. This number dropped to 58 in the early fifties. The destroyer was the largest of these, and at various times eight different destroyers were involved in the Korean War. In the initial 1951 build-up the navy was cast in an anti-submarine role, and its equipment was so geared. It was to be increased to 100 ships of various sizes, and the *Estimates* provided for the purchase of new escort vessels, minesweepers and gate vessels. Periodic strength figures were issued, and combat numbers showed a rapid increase. In a four-year period ending in 1956, 25 new fighting ships and 26 auxiliary ships were added and 32 ships were modernized. New destroyers were of the St. Laurent class; three were added to the fleet in 1956 and another ten were under construction. The largest of the Navy's ships—the light aircraft carrier Bonaventure—was commissioned in 1957. A statement of combat strength in 1957 listed a total of 47 vessels, including 1 aircraft carrier, 7 destroyers, 11 tribal class destroyers, 18 frigates and 10 minesweepers. The 7 destroyers were of the Canadian-designed St. Laurent class. In the immediately following years they were to be joined by another 13 destroyers of the Restigouche class, the building of which was the main navy outlay in the early sixties. These destroyers were supplemented by the lighter Mackenzie and Annapolis classes, and the Algonquin and Tribal class destroyer escorts. Other expenditures were directed mainly to submarine detection and destruction equipment.

In 1962 the proposed purchase of eight general purpose frigates of advanced design was announced. These were to have anti-submarine capability, guided missile systems and gun armament. They were to have cost about $240 million, but the plan was reconsidered when projected costs had mounted to $400-500 million in the following year. The project appears to have been abandoned in favour of a more widely diversified list in 1965-66, including the purchase of 4 helicopter-carrying destroyers, at an average cost of $35 million, 2 support ships at $18 million each, improvement of 7 Restigouche class destroyers, 1 conventional submarine, 12 Sea King helicopters, (part of a complete order of 41), a major refitting of the Bonaventure, and several outlays of lesser importance. A general refitting expense at this time was the provision of ship-board helicopter landing facilities, the installation of advanced sonar submarine detection equipment, and Canadian Sea Sparrow surface-to-air missiles for destroyers and other combat vessels.

In 1969 the outmoded aircraft carrier, Bonaventure, was taken out of service, and its squadron of Tracker aircraft was given different duties until 1973, when it would be disbanded. Four new anti-submarine destroyers were under contruction. By the fall of 1970 the combat strength was 9 helicopter-carrying destroyers, 11 destroyer escorts, 4 submarines and 3 operational support ships. Experiments were being conducted with the hydrofoil vessel, later terminated.

In the early years of the seventies the Maritime re-equipment program concentrated mainly on up-dating existing materiel rather than on purchase of new types. One exception was a submersible diver lock-out submarine, specially equipped for Arctic and continental shelf surveillance. At this time delay and rising expense in the construction of four helicopter-carrying destroyers begun in 1968 were causing concern. Still not completed four years later, their estimated cost had risen from $220 million to $252 million, or an average of $63 million apiece, by far the most expensive single pieces of equipment ever purchased for defence to that time. A special review committee recommended procedures for ensuring more realistic estimates for the future and closer cooperation between government and contractors during production. The four ships were finally delivered and commissioned during 1972 and 1973. At this point eleven months of tuning and trial-running lay ahead, the expense of which was to come under the $252 million cost.

Studies were being made during this period on future requirements for naval equipment, with increasing attention being paid to the Arctic. Pending a re-equipment program annual expenditures mainly went for upgrading existing ships, usually for the installation of newly developed technology—a perpetual problem—and for improvement of capital facilities.

The Maritime Command shared substantially in the post-1977 refitting exercise. Three main programs were covered: (1) $5.3 billion for 6 patrol frigates, delivery to start late in 1989; (2) $134 million for the Destroyer Life Extension program to refurbish 16 of 19 destroyers, involving complete updating of 10 of the 16, and improvement in sea-worthiness for the remaining 6. The program was expected to be completed in 1987. (3) $42 million for submarine operational update. In addition, $23 million was approved for Tribal Class update, but no contract had been awarded, and $112 million had been approved for testing and acquisition of sonar equipment for the six new frigates and two destroyers.

The decision to order the six new frigates was announced in December, 1977, following an extensive study of Maritime requirements. An undated and unattributed memorandum, apparently official, explained that "A fleet of 24 vessels was accepted as the requirement to meet Canada's commitment to collective defence." The government announced its decision to order the new frigates in December 1977, and it was explained that "These new frigates will replace the oldest of the present fleet of steam driven destroyers, the ST. LAURENT class, which were originally designed for 20 to 25 years service . . . Between 1989 and 1999 the remainder of the steam driven destroyers of the RESTIGOUCHE, MACKENZIE and ANNAPOLIS classes will reach the end of their economical life and they in turn will have to be withdrawn from service." Actual contracts were not awarded until July 1983; three ships were to be built in St. John, N.B., and three in the province of Quebec.

Land

Land equipment has been required for troops stationed in Europe as well as Canada. It has taken the more or less familiar form of vehicles for the movement of personnel and artillery and armoured vehicles for combat. In the latter category the British Centurion tank was used in the early postwar army, and in the former a variety of tracked vehicles and light trucks. Artillery has become more sophisticated with advanced electronic aiming systems, and automatic rifles, machine guns and rockets have greatly increased the fire power of ground troops. The 105mm howitzer and the Honest John rocket were favoured land weapons in the early sixties. The French SS-11 anti-tank rocket had been selected for army use, and in 1966 a new Swedish anti-tank weapon was acquired. The best equipped of the Canadian land forces were those located in Europe. The brigade there had reconnaissance and transport helicopters, anti-tank guided missiles, Carl Gustav medium anti-tank weapons, Centurion tanks, bridge layer tanks, surveillance equipment, armoured personnel carriers, 155mm howitzers and 81mm mortars.

The Centurion tank was given improved firepower during the early sixties and improved rifles and machine guns were acquired. On the basis of experimental use an order for 480 of the amphibious armoured troop carrier, the Bobcat, was given in 1963. But this order was cancelled in the following year because of failure of the Bobcat, after ten years of development, to meet requirements during trials. In its place 500 U.S. M113 armoured troop carriers were ordered. In 1967 orders were given for full-track armoured vehicles to replace the aging Mk.1 Ferret scout cars, and for 800 new Mk. 38A2 utility trucks, which are air-portable and air-droppable. Acquisition of new technology for communications, weapons control, etc. went ahead steadily in succeeding years.

The re-equipment for the Mobile Command has included $312 million for Medium Logistic Vehicles (128 Leopard tanks to replace Centurion tanks); $67 million for 1¼ ton trucks; $115 million for 2,500 new ¼ ton trucks; approval of $137 million to be spent on 700 7- to 9-ton trucks; $37 million for armoured personnel carriers and $28 million for armoured engineering vehicles. New artillery was purchased and existing artillery renovated; $352 million was approved for a long-range program to replace small arms, and another $540 million to acquire an inventory of ammunition. Some of these projects were completed or almost so; others were only commencing.

It is interesting that the rather abstruse question of equipment for the army has attracted the attention of at least some of the press in Canada. A 1986 article in the *Toronto Star* listed, as acquisitions of the last decade: 128 Leopard tanks, 513 General Purpose Armoured Vehicles, 100 BV-206 All Terrain Carriers, 2600 ILTIS Canadian Light Trucks, 213 AN PPS-15A battlefield radar, Blowpipe Anti-Low-Level Aircraft Missiles and anti-tank missiles. the considerable quantities of weaponry and transport vehicles acquired over the postwar period were also listed (mortars, anti-tank weapons of various kinds, howitzers, armoured personnel carriers, command and reconnaissance vehicles and trucks) but it is not known to what extent this equipment is still in service.[36.12]

Retrospect on Costs

Although cost information for individual items of equipment is not very reliable, the following then-and-now comparisons are based on reasonably accurate sources. For example, the Sabre jet fighter was purchased by the air force in the fifties for $400,000 and the CF-100 for about $750,000. The 1986 fighter, the CF-18 Hornet, of which Canada bought 138, cost $4.9 billion, or an average of $35 million. In the 1960s the navy was buying destroyers for about $35 million. The cost of six new patrol frigates will be $4-5 billion. In the early 1950s a Centurion tank cost $125-150,000; the last order of Leopard tanks averaged $1.5 million.

Capital Expenditure

The largest part of the capital expenditure allocated over time has been for the equipment just discussed. for 1986-87 the *Estimates* provided $617 million for ships, $632 million for aircraft and engines, and $86 million for military equipment and vehicles. In addition there were other quite important items. In the 1986-87 *Estimates* the following amounts were provided for these: construction and acquisition of land, buildings and works, mainly for buildings of various types, training areas and facilities, hospitals, control towers, etc., $158 million; armaments, (including the first stage of the small arms replacement program previously mentioned) $165 million; ammunition and bombs, (including the first stage of ammunition replacement program) $347 million; electronic communications equipment; $327 million. Another $122 million was listed for miscellaneous technical equipment and $126 million for development, the latter being mainly for advanced high-tech equipment.

The objective under the re-equipment program started in 1974 had been to raise the share of capital expenditures in the defence budget from the approximately 8 percent level of the early seventies to at least 25 percent. The new Conservative Minister of Finance in his *Agenda for Economic Renewal* presented to Parliament on November 8, 1984, took satisfaction from the expectation that by the mid-1980s the ratio would be about 26 percent. This was the approximate percentage for the 1986-87 estimated expenditures.

Status of Major Programs

The *Estimates* for 1986-87, Part III, give the following information for the 1986 status of the main capital expenditure programs.

36.12Ron Lowman, "Who Will Defend Us on Our Home Turf?" (*The Toronto Star*, May 24, 1986).

Table 36.2   Details of Major Capital Projects, 1986-87

	Currently estimated total cost	1985-86 forecast expenditure	Estimates 1986-87	Future years requirements
	$ million			
Canadian patrol frigates............	5,254	1,025	624	3,604
Submarine operational update.......	42	38	0.4	4
Destroyer life extension	134	100	14	20
1¼ ton trucks	67	65	0.5	1.3
Medium logistic vehicles............	313	298	15	—
Military operation support trucks	115	74	15	26
Armoured personnel carriers	37	21	10	6
Long-range patrol aircraft	1,168	1,156	2.6	9.4
CF-18 fighter aircraft	4,942	3,723	672	547
Challenger aircraft	211	182	12	17
Dash 8 aircraft....................	98	37	39	22
CC-130 Hercules replacement	64	59	4	1
Small arms replacement	352	60	57	235
Ammunition replacement, land......	540	—	165	375
CF-18 air-to-air missiles	341	87	81	173

Source: 1986-87 Estimates, Part III.

37
The Forces

Organization

Drastic changes in the organization of the defence services followed the adoption of integration as announced in the White Paper of March 1964. The government had decided that the unification of the existing three forces into a single body would improve efficiency and reduce costs, and planned to have the process completed by 1967.

Some earlier steps had produced effective results. In 1952 the tri-service Regular Officer Training Plan had been adopted, under which career officers with the necessary academic background were given courses that were co-ordinated under a joint directorate at Headquarters. In 1958 the chaplain and recruiting services had been integrated, and in 1959 the Canadian Forces Medical Service had been established in place of previous individual service units. The Minister of National Defence had been given authority under an amendment passed in 1959 to unify any of the branches of the forces at any time. The 1964 announcement therefore represented the culmination of a process that had already been initiated.

To implement full integration the first step taken was to bring together the former Army, Navy and Air Force Headquarters at Ottawa in a unified Canadian Forces Headquarters. The immediate result was the establishment of data processing programs to relate military functions and missions with financial, personnel, and equipment resources, resulting in a saving of 30 percent of staff. The same process continued for construction, engineering, communications, and some further steps for recruiting.

The 11 existing field commands of the three services underwent consolidation in a series of moves. The first was to create six functional commands that would be responsible for all services within their jurisdiction. These were Mobile Command, Maritime Command, Air Defence Command, Training Command, and Materiel Command. A seventh command, Reserve and Survival Organization, was charged with administration of reserve forces and related matters. Canada was divided into six military districts, and five of the Command Headquarters were given regional as well as functional duties. In the early seventies a common walking-out uniform was adopted for all services, one of the most contentious—and in the view of some—the most demoralizing aspects of intergration.

Changes were introduced with experience. In 1968 the Materiel Command was eliminated and the function was transferred to Headquarters. In 1970 Militia and Air Reserves became the responsibility of individual commands. An integrated Supply and Management Program was completed in 1971, reducing supply depots from 14 to 5. In 1975 a single new Air Command replaced the former Air Defence and Air Transportation Commands, and became responsible for all airmen in the armed forces. For operations purposes airmen were assigned to the Mobile and Maritime Commands and to NORAD. At the same time training activities were transferred to respective commands, and the Training Command was eliminated. A new Canadian Forces Training System was developed to recruit and train men in areas common to all services. In 1976 the Department of National Defence was made responsible for coordinating all search and rescue activities on both coasts.

The structure under National Defence Headquarters in 1986 was made up of five commands—Maritime (Atlantic and Pacific Regions), Mobile, Air, Communications, and Canadian Forces Europe, augmented by the Canadian Forces Training System and the Northern Region. The main activities under these Commands are Maritime Forces, Land Forces in Canada, Air Forces in Canada, Canadian Forces in Europe, Communications Services, Personnel Support, Materiel Support, Policy Direction and Management Services, and various geographic/regional responsibilities.

The Minister of National Defence is charged with carrying out Canada's defence policies. In this he is aided by his senior advisers in the department, the Deputy Minister of Defence and the Chief of the Defence Staff. The former is responsible for the functioning of the department as an administrative unit and, as he is the alter ego of the Minister, holds a somewhat senior position. The latter is responsible for the planning, preparation, and conduct of military operations. Many functions of the department are co-headed by the Deputy Minister and the Staff Chief, and both have under them senior officials either as Vice or Deputy Chiefs or as Assistant Deputy Ministers.

Defence of North America

Maritime Command (1986)

Although Maritime Command is destined ultimately to total dedication to NATO in the meantime its duties relate primarily to North American defence. In 1986 the Command accounted for 15 percent of total personnel strength and 19 percent of defence spending. It consisted of a force of 4 DDH 280 class destroyers, 19 frigates, 3 submarines, 3 support ships and one diving support vessel. In addition there were smaller vessels for training and harbour and fleet support. Patrol aircraft and anti-submarine helicopters also act under the control of the Maritime Command.

The Commander Maritime Command, with headquarters in Halifax, Nova Scotia, commands all surface and sub-surface forces and exercises operational control over the maritime aircraft of Air Command on the Atlantic and Pacific oceans. The navy and associated maritime air forces are structured mainly to defend, along with the United States of America and NATO allies, the ocean approaches to North America and the reinforcement and resupply routes across the Atlantic to Europe. They also have the responsibility in ocean areas assigned to Canada to detect submarines threatening North America with ballistic or Cruise missiles.

In addition to its NATO commitments Maritime Command carries out extensive surveillance on both shores and in the Arctic for territorial control and other reasons. Long-range surveillance planes, light vessels and submarines are used for this purpose. Incidentally, Canada slipped almost accidentally into ownership of submarines. Its acquaintance started with the loan early in the sixties of a U.S. Navy submarine for training purposes on the west coast. This was replaced by an Oberon class submarine purchased by Canada about mid-decade. Orders for another two similar submarines were given at the same time, and with the addition of one further ship by the outset of the 1970s there were four in all. Three of these are still part of the combat strength, and although outdated, are being refitted under the big overhaul of the 1980s. As later explained, submarines play a leading and contentious role in the 1987 White Paper proposals.

Mobile Command (1986)

(Land forces in Canada)—accounted for 20 percent of forces personnel and 15 percent of defence expenditures. Under Mobile command there are Brigade Groups at Valcartier, Quebec, and Calgary, Alberta and a special Service Force at Petawawa, Ontario. Each unit is equipped with artillery, armour, infantry, engineers, signals and service support units. Mobile Command is also responsible for five bases throughout Canada and for a combat training centre at Gagetown. Commander Mobile Command, with Headquarters at St. Hubert, Quebec, commands all land forces in Canada as well as 10 Tactical Air Group, which provides light and medium air transport and 4 squadrons of tactical helicopters. From these forces Canada provides units for United Nations peacekeeping, but its main commitment was to bring the existing Brigade Group in Germany to combat strength and to provide a Transportable Brigade Group for the defence of North Norway in the event of hostilities. These units are being trained for combat in Arctic conditions.

A smattering of information gleaned from official sources (although not vouched for as completely accurate) gives a glimpse of the evolution of Canada's oldest service, the army, to its present position.

From the early fifties its structure has remained fairly consistently as a mobile striking force and four infantry brigades, three of which have been located in Canada. Total strength averaged 50,000 during the fifties and 40,000 during the sixties, all located in Canada except for 5,000-6,000 in Europe and a few hundred others on peacekeeping missions. Originally two of the brigade groups located in Canada were committed for transfer to Europe in the event of hostilities; these brigades also supplied men for rotation of the existing NATO brigade. The third brigade was originally designated as a defence of Canada unit, but in the mid-sixties was converted into a special air-transportable force of 3,500 men trained and equipped to carry out military tasks anywhere in the world. It was to be equipped as well as the NATO brigade and would have special capabilities for the Arctic, including parachuting and reconnaissance skiing.

As Canada is a part of the Canada-United States region of NATO Canadian ground forces must work under common strategy with U.S. forces. This requires exchange of information and conduct of exercises and trials to improve planning and organization. A particular duty of the Canadian forces has been training personnel for combat in Arctic conditions.

Under integration, land forces have increasingly taken to the air. On its establishment Mobile Command was given the 1st and 3rd Canadian Infantry Brigade groups, the special service force and tactical air units. Within a year it included in Canada two air transportable brigades, one airborne regiment, and one tactical air group, along with one mechanized brigade. Its European forces included one mechanized brigade group in Germany and two air-transportable brigades committed to the mobile force in Europe. With further development it emerged in a pattern that survived for many years, composed of three air-transportable combat groups, a tactical air group and a Canadian airborne regiment capable of parachute operations. Combat groups have included unfantry battalions, a light armoured regiment and supporting services. Helicopters are in extensive use for surveillance by Mobile Command units. Arctic concerns have received increasing attention in training and command; Northern Regional Headquarters were established at Yellowknife, Northwest Territories.

Air Command (1986)

(Air forces in Canada)—accounted for 27 percent of defence personnel and 28 percent of defence expenditure. Air Command is divided into six functional air groups reporting to a headquarters in Winnipeg, Manitoba. The Fighter Group was established in 1982 to replace the Air Defence Group, with Headquarters in North Bay, Ontario. It brings under common control the new CF-18s, two CF-5 squadrons and all other fighter groups in Canada.

The various groups within Air Command are Air Transport Group, headquartered at Trenton, Ontario; Maritime Air Group, headquartered at Halifax, Nova Scotia; 10 Tactical Air Group, St. Hubert, Quebec (mainly offering helicopter support for units of Mobile Command); 14 Training Group (training in trades and in flying); Air Reserve Group.

In addition to training and exercises that continue to stress cooperation with NORAD in the defence of Canada and joint exercises with Norwegian forces the air force is frequently engaged in search and rescue exercises and in airlift of supplies to Arctic outposts and to peacekeeping units overseas.

NORAD

The North American Air Defence Command was formed by agreement between Canada and the United States to coordinate efforts to warn and defend against air attack of North America. Based on strategic thought at the time of its origination in 1957 it was designed to protect against long-range heavy bombers under arrangements that have been renewed by specific agreement from time to time. The principal means for this purpose were (1) radar lines across northern Canada; (2) interceptor fighter planes stationed at strategic points, and (3) for a temporary period, ground-to-air Bomarc missiles located in Canada. The combined annual costs of NORAD operations in Canada were in the neighbourhood of $260 million in the early eighties, of which the United States paid $80 million. Approximately 10,000 Canadian armed personnel are involved.

Warning Lines

Heavy reliance was placed on radar warning lines from the beginning. These took the form of the distant Early Warning Line (DEW line) located at the northern limits of the continent and the Pinetree line, extending from Newfoundland to British Columbia roughly along the U.S.-Canada border. (A Mid-Canada line, constructed by Canada at a cost of over $200 million in the early fifties, covered the area between the two other lines, roughly along the 50th parallel. It was gradually phased out from 1963 onward as improvements were made in the other radar stations.) The lines give information on aircraft movements directly to NORAD headquarters in Colorado Springs, Colorado. Improvements have been made by the use of computerized equipment, by establishing area centres at North Bay and Edmonton in Canada, and by the installation of new technology in the Pinetree line as announced in 1978. Arrangements for constructing, maintaining, and manning the lines have varied over the quarter century of their existence. In general the DEW line has been a U.S. responsibility, and the U.S. has also shared in the costs of the Pinetree line.

The aging of both the DEW and Pinetree lines led to the joint U.S.-Canada announcement of March 1985, that the former would be replaced and the latter abandoned at a total cost of $7 billion. The new north warning line will be able to identify missiles as well as aircraft, and will greatly enhance surveillance over the northern approaches. Canada's share of the total cost is to be $850 million, and full control over operations will be in Canada's hands on completion.

Supplementary to the North American lines the U.S. has constructed a missile detection line with stations in Greenland and England, in which Canada is not involved.

Intercepter Aircraft

Canada has supplied intercepter aircraft manned by Canadian crews and stationed at strategic locations throughout the country. These were equipped for many years with CF-101 Voodoo fighters, which are being replaced with 36 of the new CF-18 fighters. Canada's commitment under the current five-year agreement signed in February 1986, is to provide three squadrons of CF-101 aircraft, 24 surveillance radar stations, two satellite tracking stations and participation in the operation of DEW and Pinetree radar installations. During 1986 first steps were to be taken to begin implementation of the new northern warning system, including closure of some Pinetree radar locations, with others to follow in 1987 and 1988. A project manager was appointed at Defence headquarters to cooperate in the program.

Bomarc Missiles

At Canada's request in the late sixties two stations manned with ground-to-air Bomarc missiles were located in Canada by the United States. These stations, located at North Bay, Ontario and La Macaza, Quebec, were constructed and manned by Canada, but became the centre of heated controversy because the Bomarc missile was equipped with a nuclear warhead. The arrival of the inter-continental missile, which largely outdated the installations, and the adoption of a non-nuclear policy by the federal government led to the phasing out of the Bomarc missile in 1972.

Foreign Commitments

NATO

The North Atlantic Treaty Organization (NATO) came into being with the signature of the North Atlantic Treaty by 12 nations in 1949. With the later addition of three others it became a permanent organization of 15 countries devoted to the joint defence of the European continent and the countries on the rim of the North Atlantic. Canada's contribution has taken the form of training of aircrew for European forces, transfers of surplus equipment, stationing of land and air forces in Europe, and maintenance of air and sea forces for patrol of the Atlantic. Training of aircrew began in 1950. The first navigators and pilots, 77 in all, graduated in 1951. By the time the program was terminated in 1958 some 5,500 aircrew had been trained under it.

Transfers of equipment came under the Mutual Aid program. Following World War II Canada had surplus equipment in several categories and resources to produce additional supplies very quickly. Transfers included 300 Sabre jets for the United Kingdom, 150 Sabre jets for NATO forces, minesweepers for France, and armaments, ammunition, radios and radio sets, military vehicles, and assorted other equipment. Between 1950 and 1970, when the program was substantially completed, equipment and other transfers totalling $2 billion had been made under mutual aid, largely at the expense of Canada.

Land and air forces were stationed in Europe promptly in the early fifties, amounting respectively to one brigade group and 12 air squadrons, or about 12,000 men in all. In 1953 the 1st Canadian Infantry Division was formed, with headquarters and two brigades stationed in Canada and the other in Europe. This remained the basic organization for several years along with periodic upgrading of equipment and changes in role as suited NATO strategy and equipment capabilities. The number of air squadrons was reduced to eight in 1964 and to six in 1967. Four of the six at this time were strike-attack fighters equipped with nuclear and conventional armament. The remaining two were reconnaissance squadrons.

A basic change came in the early seventies. In 1969 the Minister of Defence announced that by 1972 European land forces would be reduced to a mechanized battle group of 2,800 men in place of the previous 5,000 and that European forces would give up their nuclear role. Following 1972, land forces would be concentrated in southern Germany and would be reorganized as a light air mobile force. Support elements in Canada would be maintained, and forces allocated to Canadian defence would take part in NATO exercises and would be available in time of emergency. Commitments to maintain special forces for NATO in Canada would be somewhat reduced, but maritime cooperation would continue. With the abandonment of nuclear arms, air strength would also be reduced by three squadrons. Total strength in Europe would then be about 5,000 men.

Major equipment renewals have been made with the purchase of new Leopard tanks for the land forces and the substitution of the F-18 fighter planes for CF-104 planes stationed in Europe.

Part III of the 1986-87 *Estimates* described Canadian Forces in Europe in 1986 as consisting of: 4 Canadian Mechanized Brigade Group and 1 Canadian Air Group, located at two bases in southwest Germany—Lahr and Baden-Soellingen. The Canadian Air Group had three squadrons, of which one was being given CF-18 fighters as they become available. The other two squadrons were equipped with CF-104 Starfighters. Personnel totalled about 5,900, but was being increased by 1,220 during 1986. The following forces in Canada have been designated for deployment with the European Forces in time of crisis: Canadian Air Sea Transportable Brigade Group; Allied Command Europe Mobile Force (Land); Allied Command Europe Mobile Force (Air); two rapid reactor squadrons, and other augmentation and reinforcement units.

Maritime Command. As previously stated, Canada's naval activities have been closely linked with NATO Allied Commander, Atlantic, and a substantial number of ships and aircraft would automatically come under that Command on the outbreak of hostilities. Canadian headquarters control forces operating in a sub-area of the Atlantic, and Canadian officers share in other duties. Early emphasis was on Canada's convoy duty undertaken in previous wars, but an anti-submarine role has been added in view of the massive Russian building program. While other duties have been introduced for the Canadian navy these remain its basic roles.

Other Commitments. Canada's other commitments to NATO in Europe included a share of a $2.5 billion continuous warning system across Western Europe, continuing substantial contributions towards NATO infrastructure and various other outlays, including minor amounts of mutual aid.

Money and Defence

As a result of the firm control over expenditures defence has not been a major outlay in postwar government spending. In the 39 years 1947-1985 the total slightly exceeded $100 billion, the equivalent of about two years of current federal expenditure on health and social security. This was 5.4 percent of total government expenditure, 10.5 percent of federal expenditure, and averaged 3.0 percent of Gross National Product over the 39 years.

For 26 of the 39 years defence outlays did not exceed $2 billion annually, although with the revival of the defence program during the fifties outlays rose to 35-40 percent of the federal budget for several years. They first exceeded $2 billion in 1973, approximately doubled to $4.2 billion by 1979 and more than doubled to $9.6 billion by 1985. As price levels increased by 1½ times between 1973 and 1985 the "real" element of this growth was less than appeared, although by previous standards it was substantial. This growth followed from the re-equipment program commenced in 1973, and the commitment to NATO to achieve an annual increase of 3 percent in excess of inflation from 1979 on. Even so, defence expenditures have been in the neighbourhood of only 2 percent of GNP since 1971, as compared with ratios 50 to 200 percent higher in many NATO countries.

The Conservative government's 1985 paper—*Competitiveness and Security*—had the following to say regarding this record: "We emerged from the Second World War a major military power, with an army of half a million soldiers, a navy of 200 ships and an airforce comparable to that of Britain. After the war, we set a definite upper limit on our military capability when we ruled ourselves out of the nuclear club, and in the mid-1960s our conventional military power began a steady decline—in respect of both personnel and equipment".[37.1]

Table 37.1 gives data on Canadian defence expenditures for the full period 1947-1985. These data are prepared as part of the National Accounts, and vary slightly from the budgetary figures.

[37.1] Canada, Department of External Affairs, *Competitiveness and Security* (Ottawa: Department of Supply and Services, 1985), 26.

Table 37.1 Defence Expenditures: 1947-85

Calendar year	National defence expenditure	As percent of federal government expenditure	As percent of total government expenditure	As percent of gross national product
	$ billion	*percent*		
1947	0.2	11.9	7.0	1.7
1948	0.2	12.1	7.0	1.5
1949	0.4	16.3	9.4	2.1
1950	0.5	20.8	12.1	2.7
1951	1.2	36.2	22.1	5.3
1952	1.8	40.1	27.3	7.3
1953	1.9	40.9	28.0	7.4
1954	1.7	37.1	24.4	6.7
1955	1.8	36.6	23.5	6.2
1956	1.8	35.3	21.9	5.6
1957	1.8	32.6	19.8	5.3
1958	1.7	26.9	16.7	3.4
1959	1.6	24.1	14.6	4.2
1960	1.5	22.9	13.6	4.0
1961	1.6	22.4	13.2	4.1
1962	1.7	22.4	12.7	3.9
1963	1.6	20.7	11.3	3.4
1964	1.6	19.8	10.6	3.2
1965	1.6	18.2	9.4	2.8
1966	1.7	17.5	8.9	2.8
1967	1.8	16.4	8.3	2.7
1968	1.8	14.7	7.4	2.5
1969	1.8	13.4	6.6	2.3
1970	1.9	12.2	6.0	2.2
1971	1.9	11.1	5.5	2.0
1972	2.0	9.7	4.9	1.9
1973	2.2	9.7	4.8	1.8
1974	2.5	8.8	4.6	1.7
1975	2.8	7.8	45.1	1.7
1976	3.2	8.3	4.2	1.7
1977	3.7	8.4	4.3	1.8
1978	4.1	8.3	4.2	1.8
1979	4.2	7.9	3.9	1.6
1980	4.8	7.9	3.9	1.6
1981	5.6	7.8	3.8	1.7
1982	6.8	7.9	4.0	1.7
1983	7.2	7.6	3.5	1.9
1984	8.2	7.6	4.0	1.9
1985	9.4	8.2	4.2	2.0

Source: Based on Economic Review, Department of Finance, April, 1985; Fourth Quarter, 1985, National Income and Expenditure Accounts.

38
Related Activities

Production and Purchasing

As a carry-over from the World War II Department of Munitions and Supply the Department of Defence Production was established in 1951 as the sole purchasing agent for defence supplies. The Department operated through offices in Canada, the United States, and Europe, and served not only the Department of Defence but other federal agencies as well. Its Minister also supervised five Crown companies—Canadian Arsenals, Canadian Commercial Corporation, Crown Assets Disposal, Polymer, and Defence Construction. The latter corporation was responsible for all construction at defence installations.

The main function of the Department was the negotiation of contracts for equipment to meet requirements of the armed forces. In the 17 years of its operation (1951-1968) the value of these contracts exceeded $13 billion. In its initial period the Department financed much of the capital equipment required to fill defence orders, retaining ownership of the assets. Later contractors were encouraged to provide their own financing, with the incentive of accelerated depreciation for tax purposes.

The Department also had the responsibility of ensuring that Canadian industry was maintaining an efficient defence capacity. To this end the Defence Industry Productivity Program was established in 1959. Assistance was given under this program in the form of grants for development, modernization, and tooling, and in other ways. This function was taken over by the new Department of Industry in 1963. Another role the Department undertook was the creation of a contingency supply centre that would be activated in a time of emergency—the Emergency Supply Planning Branch. The Department also acted to ensure that contracts were obtained from other countries for the Canadian defence industry. During World War II defence-sharing arrangements had developed between the Allies, and for the United States these had been perpetuated in the Statement of Principles of Economic Cooperation of 1950. A ministerial committee on joint defence agreements developed general policies for sharing defence production; accelerating costs and more complex dealings resulted in specific arrangements in 1959. Under the new arrangements Canadian manufacturers had the opportunity to tender on U.S. contracts. The Department also aided Canadian companies in research and development of defence materiel of importance to other governments, with an eye to export business. This function was assumed by the Department of Industry in 1967. These several activities, in particular defence production-sharing, brought contracts valued at several hundred million dollars to Canada.

Defence Production ceased to exist as a separate organization in 1968. The Report of the Royal Commission on Government Organization (1962) had recommended that a central purchasing agency replace the wide variety of individual arrangements then in effect. As a transitional measure the Canadian Government Purchasing Service had been established, and some procedural improvements in defence purchasing had been implemented. In 1968 the Department of Supply and Services was set up to bring together not only the purchasing function but many others as well. Defence purchasing has since been carried on by a division of that Department.

Defence Research

Throughout the postwar period research was carried on by the Defence Research Board. The Board not only cooperated closely with counterpart organizations in other countries but developed new products through its own efforts.

The designated functions of the Board were (1) to advise the Minister and the forces on scientific and technological matters relating to national defence; (2) to assist the forces in assessing, evaluating, and developing equipment and in solving technological and operational problems; (3) to maintain a knowledge of domestic and foreign research related to defence matters; and (4) to encourage and support basic research of defence interest in the Canadian scientific community and industry.

The Board carried out its work in eight research establishments throughout Canada, with a staff exceeding 2,500 at most times and a budget usually in the $50-75 million range. Some of the areas in which it specialized were detection and tracking of submarines, defence against missiles, exploration of the upper atmosphere, communications, electronics, defence against chemical, biological, and atomic weapons, biosciences, and operational research. The latter included many aspects of the design of ships, aircraft, vehicles, detection devices, ammunition, weapons, safety equipment, training devices, even clothing, and general stores. In the haste of postwar technological development new subjects would undoubtedly appear frequently on the research agenda. During the sixties the Board designed and built satellites; the first, the Alouette I, was launched by the U.S. Air Force in 1962, followed by Alouette II in 1965. Three other satellites, Isis A, B, and C, were launched in following years. This program was carried out in cooperation with NASA (National Aeronautics and Space Administration) although the satellites were produced in Canada.

Research in universities and defence industries was sponsored through six research fellowships and grants to industry toward specific projects. There could be 150 to 200 of these in effect at any one time, most of them related to electronics and physics, propulsion and power sources, aeronautics and materiel research. In 1975 the Defence Research Board was terminated, and since then research has been coordinated through the Department of National Defence, the National Research Council and other departments.

Survival Program

A minor but important aspect of the defence program has been the steps taken to encourage attention to the safety and survival of non-combattants during a war. Minor amounts for this purpose were provided beginning in 1951-52. These started at about $1 million and rose to over $7 million at the end of that decade. Grants were made by the Department of National Health and Welfare to provinces and municipalities for projects that would assist in emergencies.

A much more serious effort began in 1959, reflecting the arrival of the nuclear age, through a plan announced by the Prime Minister. Under it the federal government assumed more authority, increased its grant share to provinces to 75 percent, and established primary responsibility in the Department of National Defence, with specific functions allocated to the Departments of Justice and National Health and Welfare. An Emergency Measures Organization was set up in the Privy Council Office to ensure that plans were coordinated. The Organization operated under a Cabinet Committee chaired by the Minister of National Defence.

In the uncertain period of transition to the ballistic missile age the impossibility of mass evacuation of large cities, on which previous plans were based, was recognized, and attention was paid to underground shelters. Studies established that the cost of blast-proof large-scale shelters was prohibitive, and the solution then favoured, although without much enthusiasm, was the low-cost shelter that would give protection from fall-out. At a practical level specific new assignments were given. The Health and Welfare Department was made responsible for maintenance of medical and hospital services, assistance for provincial shelter and feeding services, and for training of civil defence operations at the Civil Defence College at Arnprior, Ontario; the Royal Canadian Mounted Police were to preserve law and order and some aspects of traffic control; most other responsibilities were left with the Department of National Defence, with assistance from other departments and agencies. A major role for National Defence was warning of attacks, reporting on fall-out conditions, controlling rescue and other operations in bombed areas, and ensuring communications. The army established a national survival attack warning system in 1959 for this purpose. The Emergency Measures Organization (EMO), under the control of the Privy Council, was responsible for coordination of all federal civil defence measures.

In this area, as in others, the Berlin Crisis stimulated further action. In 1961 Project Bridge was adopted, essentially to provide safe underground emergency shelters for senior federal, provincial, and military personnel to continue operations in the event of attack. At the same time the army established emergency national and provincial headquarters, and it was announced that 100,000 personnel would be given special six-week courses in national survival. (In fact 70,003 people completed the course, a considerable accomplishment, even though falling short of the target.) National Health and Welfare stockpiled essential medical supplies, the EMO established an Essential Records Program to safeguard records essential to emergency operations, and various other steps were taken.

This activity, although short-lived as the emergency soon passed, meant a rise in expenditures; from a level of $4.4 million in 1959-60 they rose to over $10 million in 1963-64, of which about $4 million was paid in grants to the provinces.

In 1963 the EMO was transferred from Privy Council to the Minister of Defence Production. At this juncture a White Paper on Defence stated, in connection with the civil defence program, that a number of civil defence policy matters could not be resolved until it had been decided whether or not to "deploy or not to deploy an anti-ICBM system." By this time some 17 departments and agencies were involved, with heaviest responsibility still resting with Defence and Health and Welfare. At a meeting in 1965 it was decided to give more emphasis to work connected with peace-time disasters such as floods, fires, explosions, and air crashes. Progress reports at this time indicated that regional emergency headquarters had been established by six provinces, emergency shelters had been built near Ottawa for government officials, 40,000 people had been trained in emergency planning, medical supplies had been stockpiled and many municipalities had purchased fire-fighting equipment.

From 1968-69 civil defence activities took a less prominent role and more emphasis was given to preparation by planning. The Emergency Measures Organization was succeeded by Emergency Planning Canada, with authority once again back in the Cabinet under the President of the Privy Council. An Assistant Secretary to the Cabinet heads the actual organization which, for administrative purposes, is attached to the Department of National Defence. Ottawa headquarters are divided between plans and operations. The former is responsible for coordination of federal agencies and for conducting courses at the Arnprior centre. The latter acts through 11 regional offices, each with a regional director, to coordinate plans with provinces and municipalities. It also provides the Privy Council with status reports on each region, and maintains a public information division and an administrative division. Emergency Planning Canada is also charged with sponsoring interest in emergency planning, generally assisting provinces and municipalities with grants for projects, and coordinating Canadian plans with those of the United States and NATO. Its expenditures were estimated at about $13 million for 1984-85; roughly $7 million for operating costs and $6 million for grants and contributions.

United Nations International Stability Programs

Canada has participated in United Nations "peacekeeping missions" almost from the first ventures of this kind. In the fifties it furnished a unit of 950 soldiers and airmen for the Emergency Force located in Egypt. In July 1960, 300 officers and men were stationed in the Congo, and in 1964 some 1,150 troops were sent to Cyprus; other assistance included observers for duty in Korea, Kashmir, Palestine, Yemen, Vietnam, Cambodia and

Laos. In 1985 a substantial force was still maintained in Cyprus, other lesser groups were located in Israel and in the Golan Heights. In 1988 a contingent was sent to assist with supervision of suspension of hostilities in the Iran-Iraq War. Although costs of these operations are shared by the United Nations the Canadian share can still be substantial. An infantry battalion, specially trained and equipped for this service, is maintained in Canada. The Canadian government has declared that it will engage in these missions in the future only if there is some prospect of a successful outcome.

Search and Rescue

While Search and Rescue activities have been provided by the defence services for some years they have been given sharper focus since 1976, when an interdepartmental committee was formed. This committee, chaired by a senior officer from the Department of National Defence, represents half a dozen departments or agencies concerned with the subject. All plans and procedures are coordinated through this committee.

Actual operations stem from four Rescue Coordination Centres located in Halifax, N.S., Trenton, Ont., Edmonton, Alta., and Victoria, B.C. The Canadian Coast Guard has sub-centres at St. John's, Nfld. and Quebec City. The main centres, except for Edmonton, are manned jointly by Canadian Forces and Coast Guard personnel, and have at their disposal aircraft, helicopters, surface vessels, and hovercraft, and can draw on the Canadian Forces and the Department of Fisheries and Oceans for additional equipment and assistance. Other agencies of government, such as the RCMP, assist when it is feasible to do so.

Over 10,000 incidents required action by the Centres in 1982, of which about 80 percent were marine cases. Several hundreds of these were responses to radio beacon alarms, of which the official report states that most were false alarms. Since 1978 most helicopters in the program have undergone a complete overhaul.

Two other aspects of Search and Rescue deserve mention. One is the important role played by volunteer helpers, particularly through the Civil Air Search and Rescue Association. The other is the cooperation of Canada with France, the United States, and Soviet Russia in an international search and rescue program based on the use of meteorological satellites. Norway and the United Kingdom have also expressed interest in joining. The program was in its experimental phase in 1985, and probably would not be completed for another two years.

39
Defence under the Conservative Government

The preceding pages presented Canada's defence program as it stood at approximately mid-summer, 1984. The Conservative government elected in September 1984, came to power with a strong commitment to an increased defence effort, and undoubtedly has given the subject higher priority than previous governments.

Higher Priority for Defence

New Uniforms

One of its earliest acts was to announce that distinctive walking out uniforms for the three main services would replace the common green uniform adopted under integration. This was a popular step, as the morale of the forces was said to have been undermined by the previous move.

Additional Troops in Europe

In March 1985, there came the announcement that an additional 1200 troops would be sent to Europe to bring the strength to 7100.

Northern Warning System

A major and dramatic event was the agreement signed by President Reagan and Prime Minister Mulroney at a so-called St. Patrick's day Summit at Quebec City for a new northern warning system of state of the art design to replace the DEW line. The project, including related measures, would cost a total of $7 billion, of which Canada's share would be $840 million. This would include dismantling the Pinetree Line, with compensation to communities that will suffer from this action.

F-18 Hornet Deliveries

With substantial deliveries on the order of F-18 Hornet fighter planes, Defence officials were urging that the government exercise its option to order an additional 10 to 20 of this aircraft. The government decided against this recommendation, and allowed the option to lapse.

New Defence Ministers

The appointment of a new Minister, Erik Nielsen, gave the Defence Department added clout in the battle for funds. The original minister, having embarrassed the government by some innocent-appearing night life on a visit to Europe, resigned from the office. Erik Nielsen, his successor, was also Deputy Prime Minister and therefore a person of considerable authority in the new government. He had served in the air force in World War II and was closely in tune with the military, so that Defence officials greeted his appointment with unconcealed satisfaction. However, the heavy responsibilities carried by Mr. Nielsen in the conduct of a review of the main functions of government allowed him only limited time for defence, and his load was relieved by the appointment in 1985 of an Associate Minister, Harvie André, who appeared to have taken effective steps to share authority. Neither minister had given any hint of future defence policy, except to indicate that reserve forces in Canada should be strengthened. In 1986 a new minister, Perrin Beatty, succeeded to the post of Minister of National Defence.

Parliament

Parliament has shown an active concern for defence in postwar years, and this interest was sustained in the 1980s. Recent Committee reports included those of the Sub-Committee on National Defence of the Senate Standing Committee on Foreign Affairs on *Manpower in Canada's Armed Forces* (1982) and on *Canada's Maritime Defence* (1983). In 1985 there appeared reports from the Special Committee of the Senate on National Defence on *Canada's Territorial Air Defence* and an Interim Report of a Senate and House of Commons Special Joint Committee on Canada's International Relations *Pertaining to Bilateral Trade with the United States* and *Canada's Participation in Research in the Strategic Defence Initiative*. In February 1986, a Report was issued by the House of Commons Standing Committee on External Affairs and National Defence on NORAD. Most of these reports were preceded by extensive public hearings, in some cases in localities throughout the country.

Concern with SDI

Following announcement of the agreement for a new Northern Warning Line the Commons cross-examined the government closely on any possible link between the new system and President Reagan's Strategic Defence Initiative project. This concern was somewhat relieved when the Prime Minister announced in September 1985, that Canada would not cooperate officially, but that any private Canadian firm would be free to enter into contracts for research or production. But Parliament continued to be agitated on this issue for some time.

Secretary of State for External Affairs

To raise public understanding of issues in both international trade and defence and prepare the way for a forthcoming Parliamentary inquiry the Secretary of State for External Affairs issued a substantial publication in May 1985 entitled *Competitiveness and Security: Directions for Canada's International Relations*. Designed rather to raise questions than give answers, the defence aspect of the paper was quickly reduced by the media to the question of Canada's participation in President Reagan's Strategic Defence Initiative project, by then labelled as Star Wars. However, as the following quotations demonstrate, the paper raised most of the general issues in defence, many of them familiar.

> The most direct threat to Canadian security derives from the Soviet Union's military capabilities and antipathy to our values, and from the consequent distrust and competition between East and West . . . There are also indirect threats to our security. There is always a risk of turmoil in Eastern Europe or in a Third World region producing a crisis which draws the superpowers into direct confrontation. At the same time, East/West rivalries are exacerbating Third World conflicts. And conflict in the Third world is being carried to North America and Europe by terrorist groups, some state-sponsored . . . we cannot afford to do all those things we would like to do and fiscal prudence is necessary. There is already a major discrepancy between the security tasks we have set for ourselves and the resources we have been prepared to devote to fulfilling these tasks effectively . . . We need to set priorities and in setting priorities, we need to put the emphasis on those issues where our interests and our capabilities coincide . . . The economics of security is, for all countries, a central factor. The cost of modern weapons systems is very high and our budget deficit is enormous.[39.1]

In listing defence priorities the following were selected:

> Nothing is more fundamental to statehood than the ability to exert control over sovereign territory. And nothing is more fundamental to a state's security than the ability to mount a defence against a potential aggressor. In earlier centuries, both these requirements could often be satisfied by national forces on their own. Today, however, no state, not even a superpower, can alone guarantee its security. As a consequence, alliances are necessary and national efforts need to be adapted to take account of alliance requirements. Control over our national territory, airspace and coastal waters is essential, both for the assertion of our sovereignty and for the preservation of our security. To be effective, control requires a surveillance and detection system able to provide a continuing picture of activities on land, in the air and at sea. Control also requires a capability to intercept aircraft and ships engaged in unauthorized or illegal activity—whether civilian intruders running narcotics or military intruders probing Canada's defences . . . a major upgrading of joint Canadian/American air defence warning facilities has become necessary.
>
> Europe remains the most critical military region in the world. It is where the line is drawn most graphically between East and West, and it is where the task of deterring aggression must start, and it is where

---

[39.1] Supra, footnote 37.1, at 37.

[39.2] Ibid., at 38-39.

we have stationed forces for 35 years as one component of our contribution to NATO and collective defence.

Maintaining deterrence in Europe, without undue reliance on nuclear weapons, requires that the conventional military imbalance in favour of the Warsaw Pact be rectified . . . New concepts of strategic defence raise important defence and arms control issues . . . In the future, Canada may need to take decisions on some of the diverse and sometimes contradictory strategic, arms control and technological interests at stake in strategic defence."

On the UN System and Multilateralism it said:

It is the UN's security role that most needs attention . . . A number of countries, some of them friends and allies, no longer attach the importance to the UN that they once did . . . We have in the past, and could again, make a solid contribution to the UN through peacekeeping . . . If, despite its problems, the UN is irreplaceable, what priority should we put on revitalizing it and what practical steps can be taken.

On regional conflicts:

In deciding whether and how we might want to respond to particular Third World conflicts, we need to determine how our interests are engaged (whether fundamentally or marginally), what means we have at our disposal and how much our responsibility to the international system requires. The underlying reality is that we cannot afford to make everything a priority."[39.3]

While many of the issues raised in *Competitiveness and Security* were familiar and far from dramatic the update was useful. The paper provided the basis for a coast to coast series of hearings by a Special Joint Committee of the House of Commons and Senate on International Relations in July and August 1985. In the Committee's Report, issued on August 23, detailed attention was given to the question of Canada's participation in the U.S. SDI project. The report gave a thorough and knowledgeable review of the state of air space technology and urged support of the fledgeling Canadian industry, but dodged the direct issue of official participation in SDI. It said: "The majority of the Committee is of the opinion that the government of Canada should remain fully committed to NATO and NORAD and should strive to fulfil our Alliance responsibilities. The majority of the Committee recommends that the government continue to support pragmatic defence-oriented research and development programs where those programs contribute to our ability to fulfil our military roles and responsibilities. Further, that the government continue to enter into joint defence research programs."[39.4] These rather nebulous recommendations seemed to point away from close involvement in SDI and toward independent Canadian

---

[39.3] Ibid., at 41.

[39.4] Canada, Senate and House of Commons Special Joint Committee on Canada's International Relations, *Minutes*, Issue no. 18, August 23, 1985 (Ottawa: Department of Supply and Services, 1985), 64-66.

research. In any event a month later the government announced its policy of non-involvement.

The Long Postponed White Paper

The exercises of the summer of 1985 were to have been the prelude to the issuance of a Green Paper on Defence, but with delays this was dropped in favour of a White Paper in 1986. As previously mentioned, the government in the meantime had dealt with the SDI issue, but as the review in the earlier chapters has shown this is only one of dozens of issues in the defence constellation. In June, the defence White Paper was still to be issued, despite frequent promises of early presentation. Press reports indicated that the new Associate Minister of Defence had given priority to this project, and a document was said to be well advanced and almost ready for release. In fact, it did not appear for another year and under another minister (see later).

Vox Populi

Unlike many other aspects of government—for example, social security—the input of the general public on defence is negligible. Popular attention is attracted almost solely by any nuclear issue, for which well-orchestrated "anti" demonstrations of thousands can appear on short notice. This sort of performance undoubtedly attracts attention to global issues, but produces little that is constructive as a guide for future Canadian defence policy. This role is left to defence specialists, a handful in Canada, but here the situation is the opposite to that with the anti-nuclear groups. While highly articulate and productive of much thought on defence, their public impact is very limited. John Gellner, one of Canada's most vocal defence specialists, deplores this situation: "What is lacking, on the one hand, is an understanding among a wider public of Canada's security requirements, and on the other hand, a readiness among the cognoscenti to engage in independent strategic thinking that would lead to national solutions to the problem."[39.5] However, despite this not unfamiliar predicament in a public policy issue, one can still find views of informed unofficial observers that throw light on the Canadian defence dilemma. Large books have been written on the Canadian situation (see reference lists) but conditions change so rapidly today that the most relevant comment is found in pamphlets, articles and press statements. The following sampling is by no means exhaustive, and certainly is not the stuff of which sophisticated defence policies are made. Nevertheless it has a touch of reality.

Defence Policy

This of course is the main issue; without a general policy all is improvisation. To review: the current policy is that set forth in the White Paper of 1971, supplemented by the Defence Structure Review of 1975. It calls for

[39.5] Supra footnote 36.11 at 1.

(1) surveillance of Canadian territory and coastline; (2) cooperation with the United States in the defence of North America; (3) meeting NATO commitments, and (4) performing international peacekeeping roles. The first two roles have involved mainly participation in deterrence (warning systems) against air attack, either by missile or air breathing craft, and maintenance of some air and ground defences in Canada. The third has been met by maintenance of an armed force in Europe, an additional force to be transported to Norway on short notice, and concentration of the Canadian Navy on convoy and anti-submarine preparations under NATO direction. The last has been met by frequent provision of small forces for surveillance in troubled areas. The essence of this policy was stated in the Defence *Estimates* for 1985-86, Part III, as follows: "Canada must, however, in the final analysis rely mainly upon the retaliatory capabilities of the strategic forces of the United States of America. For this reason, a substantial portion of Canada's defence effort has gone into assisting the United States of America in maintaining an adequate and credible capacity—the essence of deterrence."[39.6]

To the non-military layman this has at least the appearance of a defence policy. But for many defence specialists it is deficient in several ways, but principally in not being designed by Canadians and for Canadians. In John Gellner's view Canadian attitudes derive "from a military experience which has been that of fighting wars in succour of a leading power—and, as a rule, of gathering the means for such succour only after being called upon to do so . . . Canada still generally acts in accordance with strategic concepts—whether those of the United States or the North Atlantic Treaty Organization (NATO)—to the designing of which it has contributed little, if anything."[39.7] In his writings he cites instances of decisions accepted by Canada in the postwar period which in his view were "senseless" or counter to Canadian interests.[39.8] He is encouraged by the establishment within the Department of National Defence of a Combat Development Committee, particularly as in his view there is a trend toward increased reliance on conventional attack. He also commends the emphasis being placed on air doctrine by the Air Force and the work of the Strategic Analysis and Strategic Policy Planning Directorates of the Department. The Department has also funded chairs in the strategic studies at Canadian universities, a step long-since taken by the United States and one which is apparently attractive to Canadian students. Gellner appeals for a more candid approach to Canada's defence problems, and is certain that the public would accept the need for higher defence spending if it understood the magnitude of the tasks Canada has assumed (or should assume) and the inadequate preparations it has made for meeting them.

[39.6] Canada, *Estimates*, 1985-86, Part III (Ottawa: Department of Supply and Services, 1985), 13.

[39.7] Supra, footnote 36.1, at 1.

[39.8] John Gellner, "Strategic Analysis in Canada" (Summer, 1978) *International Journal*, 493-505.

Peter Newman, long a student of military affairs, in his *True North: Not Strong and Free*, argued that Canada was probably the only country in the world that did not have a plan for its own defence, and forcefully made the case for a Canadian-oriented defence policy. In his view, "The absence of any deep-rooted military tradition is probably the most important factor preventing any collective push for higher spending on national defence. There is also an absence of respect and interest towards the military on the part of both the public and many of our political leaders . . ."[39.9] He later hailed the appointment of Erik Neilsen as raising the status of defence to a top category as compared with the previous government. Mr. Newman particularly favoured the withdrawal of Canada's "toy contingent" from Europe and the creation of a Northern Command of NATO, with a rejuvenated army, navy and air force to protect Canada's northern flank.

V.L. Johnson, former commandant of the Defence College at Kingston, has argued against any Canadian commitments to NATO. Canada should either withdraw entirely or else return its forces to Canada and remain a member of NATO political bodies as France did in 1966.[39.10]

Jeffrey Simpson, of the Ottawa staff of *The Globe and Mail*, has urged a complete review of Canada's defence program on the grounds that Canada has assumed too many commitments and not provided enough money to meet them; consolidation is essential.[39.11]

Attention continues to turn to the northern approaches. An interview by Ron Lowman, *Toronto Star* Military Affairs writer, with Lt. Gen. C.H. Belzile, head of Mobile Command, starkly presents the problem of defending Canada from a Russian northern invasion with present resources. Actual forces in the north are 700 Inuit and Indian Rangers scattered in 37 settlements and armed with rifles only. Other commitments, such as simultaneously sending troops to Europe, would leave only 9,900 troops in Canada for all defence purposes.[39.12]

Val Sears, of the Ottawa staff of the *Toronto Star*, in an article peppered with scathing comments on present defence resources, speculated that proposals in the White Paper would include strengthening domestic forces by a greatly increased reserve establishment, the possibility of transferring European forces to Canada, or, alternatively, the possibility of locating the Norway force closer to Norway, heavier concentration on northern defence and greater access to independent information through a satellite for sole Canadian use.[39.13]

[39.9] Peter Newman, *True North: Not Strong and Free* (Markham, Ont.: Penguin Books of Canada Ltd., 1984), 25.

[39.10] L.V. Johnson, "Better Option than NATO for Canada?" *The Globe and Mail*, February 11, 1986.

[39.11] Jeffrey Simpson, "Offguard for Thee," *The Globe and Mail*, April 22, 1985.

[39.12] Supra, footnote 36.10.

[39.13] Val Sears, "Politics of Defence," *The Toronto Star*, May 24, 1986.

Equipment

The low state of Canada's defence equipment evokes the most unbridled critical comment and unlimited proposals for expenditure. Almost anything done or commenced in recent years, including the orders for 138 CF-18 Hornets and six frigates, is regarded as only a timid step towards filling the massive need. The new Northern Warning System, to which Canada's contribution is in the neighbourhood of $800 million, is accepted as filling an existing weakness in the detection system, but it far from meeting Canada's requirements for an adequate northern defence.

Some possible programs mooted from time to time, and listed in an article by Ron Lowman in the *Toronto Star*, include $700 million for an ice-breaker to patrol northern waters, $1 billion to replace the existing three outdated Oberon submarines, $1.5 to $2.5 billion for 30 to 50 new helicopters for the mid-1990s, $600 million for new automatic gun and missile systems for troops and air fields in Europe, new anti-aircraft guns to replace World War II models, $1 billion for a state of the art Tactical Command, Control and Communication Systems, and possible increases in the regular forces from the current 85,000.[39.14] Even this list would not meet all suggestions. A retired naval commander, Vice Admiral Fulton, has proposed the addition of three 10,000 to 15,000 ton ships each to carry eight Sea King-type helicopters for anti-submarine warfare. The price for the basic ships would be $350 to $400 million apiece, plus armaments and helicopters.[39.15] This proposal was rejected by his successor on the ground that what was expected of Canada was frigates for convoy escort.

An interesting counter-proposal to these suggestions for more equipment was put forward by Nils Orvik, Director of the Centre for International Relations at Queen's University, as follows:

With such limited resources we are supposed to pull up the slack of neglect and obsolescence, acquire many more aircraft and naval ships, keep our brigade in Europe in top shape and participate in the building of new northern bases! On top of that we should train northern experts in the technological skills they will need to fill the needs of a new North American defence force.

Rather than keep doling out little bits to the services, we should now face the problem frankly and squarely. Canada cannot at this point maintain a full-scale national defence force. As we can only do parts of it, we should be very careful in selecting the criteria on which the choice should be made.

The big bulk of Canadian taxpayers' money should go to functions which are more likely to raise our professional military status. This would mean the highest priority to jointly serviced education and

---

39.14 Ron Lowman, "Erik Nielsen: Rating his Juggling Acts," *The Toronto Star*, October 26, 1985.

39.15 Ron Lowman, "Frustrated Fulton Fires Broadside," *The Toronto Star*, May 19, 1985.

training programs. This would mean reversing the present trend where the bulk of defence money is being sucked up by the weapons and equipment purchases.

As to our equipment needs:

> We do not buy. We borrow or lease it . . . under a new restructured Lend-Lease arrangement with the United States.[39.16]

The equipment proposals, if all realized, along with existing commitments would bring total annual defence expenditure to $15 billion or so in the next few years. Outlays of this magnitude would have major implications for defence acquisition procedures and for Canada's defence production industries. The latter, in the view of some experts, have been allowed to deteriorate to a dangerous point. But the financial state of the budget will no doubt come first.

In the End Money Will Decide

The efforts of the federal government to reduce its substantial deficit will make finance the governing criterion in defence spending, as it largely has been in the past. Already there are signs of lessening commitment to the promises of much increased defence spending by the Conservative government. The Prime Minister has conceded that the defence progam will fall short of his wishes and expectations because of the government's serious financial position. Substantial increases have been made which have raised defence spending from $8.2 billion in 1984-85 to a projected $9.4 billion in 1985-86, but curtailment of the rate of further increases was announced in the February 1986 Budget Speech. The Minister of Finance stated that by planned reductions $285 million would be saved over the years 1986-87 and 1987-88. He proposed that on completion of the commitment given in 1979 by NATO countries to increase their "real" defence spending by 3 percent after inflation Canada would reduce its increase to 2.75 percent for 1986-87 and to 2 percent thereafter.

Even with these reductions the defence appropriations would rise to $9.9 billion in 1986-87 and to $10.5 billion in 1987-88. These are considerable amounts of money, but given that the Defence Department could easily find ways of productively spending two or three times those amounts the defence dilemma reappears. Within the amount of money that it chooses to spend what should Canada's defence role be? How far should it attempt to fill it by independent action? What resources should be devoted to cooperative effort with other countries? How much re-equipment is required to overcome past underspending? Has Canada exhausted other possible roles, as, for example, that of a middle power peacemaker? The White Paper will serve Canada magnificently if it gives well-reasoned answers to even some of these questions. We examine it in the following chapter.

[39.16]Nils Orvik, "Joint U.S.-Canada Defence Effort Advocated," *The Toronto Star*, May 19, 1985.

40
Defence Update: Mid-1988

The White Paper, 1987

By 1987 the issuance of the White Paper was becoming urgent. The Senate Subcommittee on National Defence issued a fourth report in 1986 dealing with military air transport, and in concluding its efforts strongly urged adoption of a revised defence policy. In his 1987 report the Auditor General made detailed recommendations for major revisions in the defence structure. In the meantime negotiations between the United States and the Soviet Union for withdrawal of medium-range missiles were moving toward a new strategic balance in Europe, a shift that would affect Canada's role in that area. A policy response from the government was overdue.

A new Minister of Defence, Perrin Beatty, was appointed on June 30, 1986 and immediately gave the White Paper top priority. As preparation he undertook further extensive consultations, both inside and outside government, visited most of Canada's 35 military bases, and proceeded with a wargame to test the feasibility of Canada's commitment to expedite troops and supplies to Norway. With final agreement of the Cabinet the White Paper was issued in June 1987, with the title, *Challenge and Commitment; A Defence Policy for Canada.*

Two main themes were predominant in the new policy; first, the need to close the "commitment-credibility" gap, the lack of resources to back up the various commitments made in the past both for support of allies and the defence of Canada, as spelled out in previous pages of this book. The other was the change in Canada's defence needs arising from new conditions that had emerged since the 1971 White Paper was issued. In this period Canada had developed strong interests in the Asia Pacific region; the submarine had emerged as a new strategic weapon for the launching of cruise missiles, and its ability to move around under the Arctic ice-cap had revealed Canada's incapacities in that area, even for surveillance in the interests of national sovereignty; the Warsaw Pact had achieved dominance over NATO in conventional armaments in Western Europe—3:1 in artillery and armed helicopters and 2:1 in main battle tanks and tactical aircraft—a dominance that would become crucial with the removal or reduction of medium-range nuclear weapons.

To meet these altered conditions the White Paper proposed: (1) clarification of Canada's defence objectives; (2) establishment of priorities between protection of national sovereignty, North American defence and international commitments; (3) determination of the appropriate level of defence expenditure, and (4) a revised allocation of financial and human resources to close the credibility gap.

As these are almost the inevitable elements of any Canadian defence posture much of the new policy represented a rearrangement of priorities, the notable feature of which was the prominence given the Arctic region and the role of the Maritime Forces. Based on these objectives the White Paper projected a program to be carried out over the next 15 years, with a full review every five years. In this sense it is a program to be completely filled by the end of the century.

The Financial Commitment

In the strained condition of the federal budget the funding of *any* program was a first consideration. This was clarified with a commitment to an annual increase over a 15-year period of 2 percent beyond inflation. Based on a gross expenditure of around $10 billion in 1987-88 this would represent an increase of $200 million per annum. An annual cabinet review was proprosed, the first result of which in December 1987, was the adoption of a five-year defence budget growing at an annual rate of 3 percent after inflation; the February 1988 budget speech made specific provision for a two-year program at a 3 percent growth rate, after inflation.

Specific Programs

Details of the new program began to unfold with the 1987-88 expenditure estimates. A broad indication of priorities is given in the allocation between capital goods (weapons and equipment), operating costs, and personnel. Compared to the low point of 8 percent for capital goods of the early seventies, capital goods will account for 26.5 percent; 43.7 percent will be for personnel, and 28.1 percent for operating costs.

Maritime Forces

A main objective of the new defence policy is to establish Canada's sovereignty over the Northwest Passage and the Arctic archipeligo through a modernized three-ocean navy. Forty-one percent of the capital budget will be allocated to the maritime forces to make a beginning in meeting this objective. The most costly and certainly the most controversial of the proposals is the acquisition of 10-12 nuclear-powered submarines to be delivered at the rate of one every two years over the next 25 years. Amounting in all to $7-8 billion, this program replaced a previously planned program for diesel-electric submarines, for which tenders had already been called. Along with a Polar 8 icebreaker these submarines are intended to give Canada a versatile means of at least policing its northern waters, which would require long-time submersion under the ice-cap. Canada's concern had been registered with the United States over travel by U.S. ships, and had produced an agreement in January 1988, that U.S. icebreakers and commercial vessels will ask Canadian permission before entering Canadian Arctic waters. This agreement however does not apply to movements by U.S. submarines.

The program also calls for construction of a further six frigates in addition to the original contract. (The first of the initial group was launched by the Prime Minister's wife in May 1988). Updating of the remaining tribal class destroyers will be undertaken, 51 new ship-borne helicopters and 10-12 new mine-sweepers and identification vessels will be acquired. Underwater sonar and other systems of identification will also be strengthened.

A further evidence of the new concentration on the Arctic was the announcement in February 1988, of the establishment of Northern Headquarters in the Northwest Territories by mid-1991.

NORAD

Progress is reported in the construction of the new Northern Warning System earlier undertaken jointly by Canada and the United States. Scheduled for completion by 1992, several phases have already been installed and are currently being tested. Canadian participation will be strengthened by the purchase of long-range patrol aircraft and modernization of the Tracker medium-range aircraft fleet.

Europe (NATO)

The White Paper pledged Canada's continued participation in NATO at the existing level but proposed several changes in arrangements. The undertaking to maintain a readily available troop contingent for transfer to Norway in the event of a European war would be abandoned, as the war game rehearsal had demonstrated that successful movement and supply of these forces, along with other obligations, would be highly unlikely. Instead Canadian forces in Europe would be strengthened and concentrated in one place in Germany in a division-sized unit of 10,000. Since 1986 European forces have been re-equipped with new small arms weapons, rifles and machine guns. Contracts have been let for improved low-level air defence units employing a range of anti-tank and anti-aircraft devices to be supplied over the next three years. The White Paper also proposed acquiring 250 main battle tanks for European forces at a probable cost exceeding $2 billion.

Air

The principal investment for the air forces has been the contract for 138 CF-18 Hornet fighter aircraft at a cost of nearly $5 billion. Of these 119 had been delivered by December 1987, and the total was expected to rise to 127 by March 1988. Problems of airframe fatigue and engine durability may considerably reduce the service life of the aircraft. The White Paper proposed the purchase of at least six long-range patrol aircraft to replace 18 CP Aurora patrol planes.

Personnel

As expected the White Paper proposed a greater role for reserve forces. This took the form of a proposal to increase primary and secondary reserve forces from about 42,000 to 90,000 in five years and to achieve closer integration with the regular forces, numbering about 85,000. Reserve force budgets would be increased to allow for acquiring minesweepers and transport aircraft for their use, and it was contemplated that they would be trained for specific wartime functions. (The author recalls having learned to shoot an antiquated 18 pounder cannon and do assorted other military chores as a reservist in World War II). Details of the structure and organization of the main defence commands are given in the Defence chapter, *The National Finances, 1987-88.*

International Peacekeeping

The White Paper committed Canada to continuing to provide up to 2,000 personnel for peacekeeping operations. At the time there were three groups in the Middle East at Jerusalem, Golan Heights, and the Sinai Desert—and a fourth on Cyprus, each forming part of a multinational contingent. A fifth contingent was sent to join in peacekeeping in the fall of 1988 following a truce in the Iran-Iraq war.

Defence and the Economy

Defence expenditure at approximately $10 billion a year is a relatively low item in government budgets in relation to the big three (or four) headings frequently mentioned in this book. At about 2 percent of GNP it represents a modest increase from the 1.6 percent level of the late seventies, and compares not very impressively with the average of 4 percent among NATO members. Nonetheless because of the substantial sums of money involved in individual programs and the lift that a large defence contract can give certain areas of the country they are eagerly sought after. All Canadian defence contracts call for a substantial Canadian content, and sometimes specify an expenditure of a designated amount, or share in a particular area; their local impact can therefore be quite significant. The contract for the first six frigates was given to a Canadian shipyard in Saint John, New Brunswick after intensive lobbying by other cities, and in December 1987, it was announced that the second six would be built by the same firm, to the great satisfaction of local owners and shipyard workers. Since the White Paper announcement of the submarine purchase there has been intensive lobbying for this contract, with competition mainly between Great Britain's Trafalgar class and France's Rubis class, whose builders have had the advantage of being able to demonstrate a working model. Three or four Canadian groups have also entered the competition, but without any track record of actual performance. The decision was to be announced in June 1988, but was finally put off until after the election.

Competition for servicing defence equipment has been equally keen. An instance that received wide public attention was the award of a maintenance contract for CF-18 aircraft to a Montreal firm in place of a Winnipeg company, with accompanying charges of political interference, etc.

Reception in Parliament

Parliamentary reception was mixed, as is customary. The opposition parties, as they are wont to do, queried most of the assumptions on which the policy was based, and reacted with alarm against the proposed nuclear-powered submarines. The Liberals had previously adopted a policy favouring a nuclear weapon-free zone, and particularly in the Arctic. They had little choice but to oppose nuclear-powered submarines in that region. The NDP advanced its stated party policy of opposition to continued membership in NATO and NORAD, both far removed from the basic assumptions of the White Paper.

On referral to the House of Commons Standing Committee on National Defence, hearings began in June 1987, and had not been completed nine months later. To April 1988 some 20 sittings had been devoted to the White Paper, mainly to examine officials, but with a sprinkling of outside witnesses.

Public Reaction

A NATO report issued in September 1987, found Canadians to be indifferent or ignorant of strategic defence issues. "Canadians in general manifest a certain detachment from security considerations," it said, "and particularly those with which NATO is concerned." The report thought this was due to the proximity of the American "nuclear umbrella" which it was felt would protect Canada. One would judge that the public reaction to the White Paper had been of about the same order, although the Minister expressed himself as being pleased with the response that he had identified. Serious comment however was left mainly to the professionals, and there was a good deal of it. This may be found in the columns of the papers and magazines that show an interest in this subject, as well as the publications of the Canadian Institute of International Affairs, the Canadian Institute of Strategic Studies, the Canadian Institute for International Peace and Security, and comments from centres for strategic studies at several Canadian universities. Finally, one may consult the Defence chapter of the Foundation's 1987-88 edition of *The National Finances*, the source of much of the information in this chapter.

As with Members of Parliament, the mention of nuclear powered submarines touched the keen public sensitivity to the very word "nuclear," and this became the main general point of interest in the White Paper. It also served particularly well the propaganda purposes of thousands of working mothers with vast expectations for government financed child care facilities, and produced indignant and shocked comparisons between the $6.5 billion to be spent on child care over seven years and the $7-8 billion to be spent on submarines over the next 25 years. However, as neither program had been approved by Parliament prior to its adjournment for the November election both were in suspense until the successful party picked up the threads in a new session. (As it turned out defence played a minor role in the election; at year-end no further action had been taken on the submarine contract).

Bibliography, chapters 36 to 40

Atkinson, M.M. and Nossal, K.R. "Bureaucratic Politics and the New Fighter Aircraft Decision." (Winter 1981) 24.4 *Canadian Public Administration*, 531-58.

Bagnall, James. "Beatty's Doctrine." Defence Special Report. *The Financial Post*, November 16, 1987.

"Battle of the subs." *MacLean's*, December 7, 1987.

Beatty, The Honourable Perrin. "Defence Industrial Preparedness." Address delivered to the Montreal Chamber of Commerce. Montreal: February 2, 1988.

Brewin, A. et al., "Defence in the 70's: Comments on the White Paper" 7-8 *Behind the Headlines*. Toronto: Canadian Institute of International Affairs, 1971.

_____. *Stand on Guard; the Search for a Canadian Defence Policy*. Toronto: McClelland and Stewart, 1965.

Burns, E.L.M. *Defence in the Nuclear Age; an Introduction for Canadians*. Toronto: Clarke, Irwin, 1976.

"Business armed and ready for defence dollars." *Financial Times of Canada*. June 8, 1987.

Business Council on National Issues. *Canada's Defence Policy: Capabilities Versus Commitments*. Ottawa: the Council, 1984.

Byers, R.B. "Canadian Security and Defence: The Legacy and the Challenges." (January 1986) *Adelphi*, 214.

_____. "The 1987 Defence White Paper: An Analysis." (Autumn 1987) 17 *Canadian Defence Quarterly*.

_____. *Canada and Maritime Defence: Past Problems, Future Prospects*. Occasional Paper no. 6. Research Program in Strategic Studies. York University. Toronto: the University, 1985.

Byers, R.B., Harme, J., and Lindsey, G.R. *Aerospace Defence: Canada's Future Role?* Wellesley Paper no. 9. Toronto: Canadian Institute of International Affairs, 1985.

Canada. Department of External Affairs. *The Department of National Defence*. Ottawa: 1984.

_____. *Competitiveness and Security: Directions for Canada's International Relations*. Ottawa: 1985.

_____. Department of National Defence. Army. *A Brief History of the Canada-United States Permanent Joint Board of Defence, 1940-1960*. Ottawa: 1961.

_____. *Canada's Defence: Information on Canada's Defence Achievements and Organization*. Ottawa: 1947.

_____. *Canada's Defence News Bulletin*. Ottawa: monthly.

_____. *Canada's Defence Programme, 1949-50*. Ottawa: 1949.

_____. *Canada's Defence Programme, 1955-56*. Ottawa: 1955.

_____. *Canada's Defence Programme, 1956-57*. Ottawa: 1956.

_____. *Challenge and Commitment. A Defence for Canada*. White Paper. Ottawa: June 1987.

_____. *Defence, 1959.* Ottawa: 1959.

_____. *Defence.* Ottawa: 1971.

_____. *Defence Research Board. The First Twenty-five Years.* Ottawa: 1972.

_____. *Memorandum* for the Special Committee on Defence Expenditure. Ottawa: 1960.

_____. *National Defence; Explanatory Material Relating to the 1961-62 Estimates.* Ottawa: 1961.

_____. *White Paper on Defence.* Ottawa: 1964.

_____. *White Paper on Defence.* Ottawa: 1971.

_____. House of Commons. *Minutes of Proceedings and Evidence of the Standing Committee on National Defence Respecting Consideration of the White Paper on National Defence.* Issues no. 13, 14, 16-23, 27-31, 36-39, commencing June 16, 1987. Ottawa: 1987.

_____. Special Committee on Defence. *Minutes of Proceedings and Evidence, 1963-1964-65.* Ottawa: 1963-65.

_____. Special Committee on Defence Expenditures. *Minutes of Proceedings and Evidence.* Ottawa: 1960.

_____. Standing Committee on External Affairs and National Defence. Defence Estimates; Minister's *Statement.* Ottawa: 1983.

_____. *Minutes of Proceedings and Evidence,* 1st Session, 1968-69. Ottawa: 1968.

_____. *Order of Reference Respecting NORAD. Minutes of Proceedings and Evidence.* Ottawa: 1985-1986

_____. *Report Respecting Maritime Force.* Tenth Report. Ottawa: 1970.

_____. *Report Respecting Canada-U.S. Relations.* Ottawa, 1970.

_____. Standing Committee on National Defence. *Minutes of Proceedings and Evidence,* 1966-68. Ottawa: 1966-68.

_____. First Report. *The Reserves.* Ottawa: June 1988.

_____. Second Report. *The Canadian Submarine Acquisition Project.* Ottawa: August 1988.

_____. Minister of National Defence. Statement on Three-year Build-up of Defence Forces. House of Commons *Debates.* February 5, 1951.

_____. Statement on Defence Policy. House of Commons *Debates.* October 15, 1974.

_____. Senate. Special Committee of the Senate on National Defence. *Canada's Territorial Air Defence.* Ottawa: 1985.

_____. Standing Committee on Foreign Affairs. *Canada's Maritime Defence.* Report of the Sub-Committee on National Defence. Ottawa: 1983.

_____. *Manpower in Canada's Armed Forces.* Report of the Sub-Committee on National Defence. Ottawa: 1983.

_____. Senate and House of Commons Special Joint Committee on Canada's International Relations. *Interim Report: Pertaining to Bilateral Trade with the United States and Canada's Participation in Research on the Strategic Defence Initiative.* Ottawa: 1985.

_____. Treasury Board. *Estimates, Part III.* Ottawa: annual.

"Canada will join three-nation force to defend Norway." *The Toronto Star,* June 25, 1988.

Canadian Association for Adult Education. *Canada's Defence Policy.* Toronto: the Association, 1960.

Canadian Broadcasting Corporation. *The Northern Front.* Toronto: C.B.C. Transcripts, 1985.

Canadian Institute of International Affairs. "Comments on the White Paper." *Behind the Headlines.* Toronto: the Institute, September 1987.

Canadian Institute for Strategic Studies. *Canadian Defence Policies for the Future.* Toronto: the Institute, 1980.

_____. *The Canadian Strategic Review.* Toronto: the Institute, 1982.

_____. *Guns and Butter: Defence and the Canadian Economy.* Toronto: the Institute, 1981.

_____. *NATO: A Thirty Year Appraisal.* Toronto: the Institute, 1980.

_____. *Parliament and Defence Policy; Preparedness or Procrastination.* Toronto: the Institute, 1982.

_____. *War in the Eighties: Men Against High Tech.* Toronto: the Institute, 1983.

Canadian Tax Foundation. *The National Finances.* Toronto: the Foundation, annual.

"Canadians ignore defence issues NATO study says." *The Toronto Star*, September 15, 1987.

Centre for International Relations. *Canadian Defence Policy; Selected Speeches and Documents, 1964-1981.* Kingston: Queen's University, 1982.

Conant, M.A. "A Perspective on Defence: the Canada-United States Compact." *Behind the Headlines.* Toronto: Canadian Institute of International Affairs, 1974.

Cowan, J.S. *See No Evil; A Study of the Chaos in Canadian Defence Policy.* Toronto: Annex Publications, 1965.

Cox, D. "Canadian Defence Policy, the Dilemmas of a Middle Power." *Behind the Headlines.* Toronto: Canadian Institute of International Affairs, 1968.

Cox, David. "Where will Ottawa find the money?" *The Globe and Mail*, March 18, 1988.

Crane, B. *An Introduction to Canadian Defence Policy.* Toronto: Canadian Institute of International Affairs, 1964.

Cuthbertson, B. *Canadian Military Independence in the Age of the Superpowers.* Toronto: Fitzhenry and Whiteside, 1977.

David, C. *Political and Military Issues Affecting Canadian Defence Policy.* Ottawa: Department of National Defence, 1981.

"Defence Special Report." *The Financial Post*, November 16, 1987.

"Defence Special Report." *The Financial Post*, August 22, 1988.

Dosé, D.C. *NORAD: A New Look.* National Security Series, Centre for International Relations. Kingston: Queen's University, 1983.

Dosman, Edgar J. "The Department of National Defence: The Steady Drummer." In Katherine A. Graham, ed. *How Ottawa Spends. 1988-89. The Conservatives Heading into the Stretch.* School of Public Administration. Ottawa: Carleton University, 1988.

Dow, J. *The Arrow.* Toronto: James Lorimer, 1979.

Dwyer, Gwynne. "Is it Time for the Break-up of NATO?" *The Toronto Star*, May 11, 1987.

Eayers, J. *Northern Approaches; Canada and the Search for Peace.* Toronto: MacMillan, 1961.

Eustace, M. *Canada's European Force, 1964-1971; Canada's Commitment to Europe.* National Security Series, Centre for International Relations. Kingston: Queen's University, 1982.

Foulkes, C. "Canadian Defence Policy in a Nuclear Age." *Behind the Headlines.* Toronto: Canadian Institute of International Affairs, 1961.

"French prepare pitch for $7 billion submarine contract." *The Toronto Star,* July 25, 1987.

"From Sea to Sea, Canada's Naval and Maritime Perspectives." *Financial Times of Canada,* July 20, 1987.

Galligan, C.G. *The Economic Impact of Canadian Defence Expenditures: Fiscal Year 1984-85 Update.* Centre for Studies in Defence Resource Management. Kingston: Royal Military College of Canada, 1986.

Gellner, John. "The Military Task: Sovereignty and Security, Surveillance and Control in the Far North." In Edgar J. Dosman, ed. *The Arctic in Question.* Oxford: Oxford University Press, 1976.

―――. "Problems of Canadian Defence." *Behind the Headlines.* Toronto: Candian Institute of International Affairs, 1958.

―――. Strategic Analysis in Canada. (1978) *International Journal,* 493-505.

―――. "The Defence of Canada: Requirements, Capabilities and National Will." *Behind the Headlines.* Toronto: Canadian Institute of International Affairs, 1985.

Goar, Carol. "Ottawa's nuclear-sub plan hits stormy seas." *The Toronto Star,* June 11, 1988.

Gray, C.S. *Canada's Maritime Forces.* Wellesley Paper no. 1. Toronto: Canadian Institute of International Affairs, 1973.

―――. *Canadian Defence Priorities: a Question of Relevance.* Toronto: Clarke, Irwin, 1972.

―――. Is the *Canadian Military Relevant?* Croton-on-the-Hudson, N.Y.:Hudson Institute, 1976.

Greer, H. "Defence Expenditures." In *Report of Proceedings of the Thirteenth Tax Conference.* Toronto: Canadian Tax Foundation, 1961, 109-22.

Gwyn, Richard. "What Canada ought to be saying to NATO." *The Toronto Star,* June 3, 1987.

Halstead, J.G.H. "Canada's Security in the 1980's: Options and Pitfalls." *Behind the Headlines.* Toronto: Canadian Institute of International Affairs, 1983.

Hinsley, F.H. "Peace and War in Modern Times." (Summer 1985) *International Journal,* 530-43.

Holmes, John, W., et al. *No Other Way.* Toronto: Canadian Institute of International Affairs, 1987.

―――. *Dyer Consequences: A Response to the TV Series "Defence of Canada."* Toronto: Canadian Institute of International Affairs, 1986.

"The home front in the submarine war." *The Financial Times of Canada,* May 9, 1988.

Kronenberg, V.J. *All Together Now: the Organization of the Department of National Defence in Canada 1964-1972.* Wellesley Paper no. 3. Toronto: Canadian Institute of International Affairs, 1973.

Leyton-Brown, David. "U.S. Reaction to the Defence White Paper." (July-August 1987) *International Perspective.*

Lindsey, G.R. *Research on War and Strategy in the Canadian Department of National Defence.* Ottawa: Department of National Defence, 1983.

Lowman, Ron. "Admiral hails 'flexibility' of nuclear subs." *The Toronto Star,* June 13, 1987.

_____. "Comparison Shopping for Subs." *The Toronto Star,* August 1, 1987.

_____. "Tough tanks sought to fill $2 billion bill." *The Toronto Star,* June 30, 1987.

_____. "Who will defend us on our home turf." *The Toronto Star,* May 24, 1986.

Malone, R.S. "The Muddle in Defence; Suggestions for a Sound Defence Policy." *Winnipeg Free Press,* 1969.

_____. "Organizing for Defence; Some Comments on the Government White Paper. *Winnipeg Free Press,* 1964.

McLin, J.B. *Canada's Changing Defence Policy, 1957-1963; Problems of a Middle Power in Alliance.* Baltimore: John Hopkins Press, 1967.

Middlemiss, Danford W. "Department of National Defence." In B. Doern, ed. *Spending Tax Dollars: Federal Expenditures, 1980-81.* School of Business Administration. Ottawa: Carleton University, 1980.

Minifie, J.M. *Peacemaker or Powder-Monkey: Canada's role in a revolutionary world.* Toronto: McClelland and Stewart, 1960.

Morton, D. *Canada and War: a Military and Political History.* Toronto: Butterworths, 1981.

Munton, D. "Public Opinion and the Media in Canada from the Cold War to Détente to New Cold War." (Winter 1983-84) *International Journal,* 171-213.

"New defence plan to cost well over $183 billion." *The Toronto Star,* June 6, 1987.

Newman, Peter C. "About face in defence strategy." *MacLean's,* January 12, 1987.

_____. "Guardians for the Far North." *MacLean's,* May 25, 1987.

_____. *True North: Not Strong and Free; Defending the Peaceable Kingdom in the Nuclear Age.* Markham, Ontario: Penguin Books of Canada, Ltd. 1984.

Orvik, N. *Canada's Northern Security: the Eastern Dimension.* Centre for International Studies, Kingston: Queen's University, 1982.

_____. "Joint U.S.-Canada Defence Effort Advocated." *The Toronto Star,* May 19, 1985.

_____. *NATO and the Northern Rim.* Centre for International Studies, Kingston: Queen's University, 1979.

Ottawa Forms Industry Group 17 member advisory committee to tackle technology base plan." *The Toronto Star,* October 7, 1987.

Porter, G. *In Retreat; the Canadian Forces in the Trudeau Years.* Ottawa: Deneau and Greenberg, 1978.

"Rebirth of the navy." *MacLean's,* May 30, 1988.

Reford, R. "Making Defence Policy in Canada." *Behind the Headlines.* Toronto: Canadian Institute of International Affairs, 1963.

"Retreating from Norway." *MacLean's,* February 23, 1987.

Ritchie, R.S. *NATO. The Economics of an Alliance.* Toronto: Canadian Institute of International Affairs. 1956.

Rosenblum, S. *Misguided Missiles: Canada, the Cruise and Star Wars.* Toronto: James Lorimer, 1985.

Stewart, L. *Canada's European Force, 1971-1980: a Defence Policy in Transition.*

National Security Series. Centre for International Relations, Kingston: Queen's University, 1980.

Simpson, Jeffrey. "Offguard for Thee." *The Globe and Mail*, April 22, 1985.

Solomon, Hyman. "Our armed forces impossibly stretched." *The Financial Post*, September 12, 1986.

Tarasofsky, A. *The Subsidization of Innovative Projects by the Government of Canada*: a Study Prepared for the Economic Council of Canada. Ottawa: 1984.

Taylor, A.M. "For Canada—Both Swords and Ploughshares: a Plea for an Integrated Defence and Foreign Policy for Canada." *Contemporary Affairs*, no. 30. Toronto: Canadian Institute of International Affairs, 1963.

Treddenick, J.M. *Peace, Security, and Economics*. Toronto: Ryerson Polytechnical Institute, 1985.

_____. "The Arms Race and Military Keynesianism." (1985) XI.I *Canadian Public Policy*, 77-92.

United States. Congress. House Committee on Armed Services. *Continental Air Defence*. Washington: U.S. Government Printing Office, 1981.

_____. Congressional Budget Office. *Defense Spending and the Economy*. Washington: the Office, 1983.

_____. *Resources for Defense: a Review of Key Issues for Fiscal Years 1982-86*. Washington: the Office, 1981.

_____. U.S. *Projected Forces; Requirements, Scenarios and Options*. Washington: the Office, 1978.

Viljoen, Tina, and Dwyer, Gwynne. *The Case for Canadian Neutrality; or the Only Good Holmes is a John Holmes*. Toronto: Canadian Institute of International Affairs, 1987.

Yost, W.J. *Industrial Mobilization in Canada*. Conference of Defence Associations. Ottawa: 1983.

International Taxation

41
International Taxation

Issues and Treaty Beginnings

Tariffs are centuries old, but the emergence of taxation as an international factor is almost entirely a phenomenon of the modern era. Undoubtedly even in ancient times "foreigners" were subject to special conscripts of some kind, but it was the more general adoption of the income tax in the twentieth century that contained the seeds of what soon was labelled "double taxation." The early income tax measures were seldom intentionally directed against non-residents. Most often they were simply caught in the trammels of laws enacted to apply to nationals. These accidental victims were mainly enterprisers whose physical presence in the taxing government's territory made them conspicuous targets. Typically their visits were periodical—travelling salesmen and the ships engaged in international trade were common cases. No doubt also a commercial office of a foreign firm would attract the attention of tax collectors. Double taxation, which in practice could be multiplied to triple or further dimensions, arose because each of the foreign jurisdictions wanted its share of tax and the home country overlapped all these levies with its own tax on the sum total of the incomes.

Measures were adopted to alleviate the more glaring cases by general consent among the few countries that had an income tax before World War I. But these devices proved inadequate for the drastically changed conditions following the war, when every major country was levying the tax at high rates.

After a pause, the re-opening of trade channels released a strong revival of commercial trade, for which the tax climate was totally unprepared. The expense, irritation, and discouragement of this impasse led to a resolve among all concerned to find a solution.

The search for international harmonization was launched early in the 1920s, and marks one of the turning points in the history of taxation. All subsequent events have underlined its crucial importance. The world has since become a global arena for a massive interplay of trade and investment, in which the multinational corporation is the favoured instrument and capital and enterprise cross national boundaries with incredible mobility. The income tax is now so complex and sophisticated an instrument that the search for "tax neutrality" among national systems is the full-time occupation of many tax practitioners and economists.[41.1] In this pursuit minor differences in treatment are conspicuous and major differences are crucial.

41.1 Donald J.S. Brean, *International Issues in Taxation: The Canadian Perspective*, Canadian Tax Paper no. 75 (Toronto: Canadian Tax Foundation, 1984).

The tax tail is certainly not wagging the trade and investment dog, but everyone is acutely conscious that the tail is a remarkably influential sector of the anatomy.

In the following pages we will follow the historical efforts of governments, international organizations, and world business to beat a way through the international tax jungle. Before commencing, however, two preliminary observations should be made. First, the ingredients of this complex subject are surprisingly simple. They resolve into two basic questions: How is a country to treat an economic activity carried on within its jurisdiction by "foreigners"? How is the native country of those "foreigners" to treat their returns from an economic activity carried on in another country? (Economic activity as used here includes investment, the use of copyrights or patents, etc.). Second, the solution to these innocent looking issues has been immensely complicated, indeed at times almost completely frustrated, by widely different and substantially opposed philosophies among nations. These differences have mainly reflected the position of the country as a creditor or a debtor and, more recently, as developed or undeveloped. It is not unusual that confrontations arise in world affairs from self-interest; it has been one of the major obstacles to the achievement of international tax harmony.

More of this later. We now follow from its inception the long course of events by which, despite its difficulties, the so-called problems of "double taxation" have been greatly reduced and in some cases eliminated. The description begins with the sort of steps a country could take largely on its own initiative, such as introducing tax credits for foreign taxes or exempting specific kinds of foreign income. We then move on to the inevitable (and perpetual) phase of international efforts to achieve solutions through numerous tax treaties between the principal countries of the world, usually under the umbrella of an international organization.

National Measures

The principal devices employed by individual countries are (1) the tax credit, and (2) the exemption of specific forms of income. It is significant that although the tax credit is today the device most often favoured, there are also elements of the exempting procedure in most tax systems. The modern income tax is a mixture of the two.

The tax credit removes double taxation by allowing the taxpayer who has borne tax on income originating in a foreign country to offset that tax against the tax imposed by the country of residence, usually up to the amount of the residence tax on the same income. It was the colonial powers of Europe that first inaugurated the method in a systematic way, with the Dutch probably leading. In 1893 the Netherlands first provided a tax credit to individuals, and in 1918 extended it to their companies. In 1906 Belgium introduced a relief for its companies. A significant experience was that of the United Kingdom which, in view of its long history with the income tax, was one of the first of the great powers to encounter the problem of imposing an income tax on taxpayers with substantial foreign income. Until 1916 it had recognized foreign taxes only by allowing them as a deduction from taxable income; but in 1916 it introduced a tax credit not exceeding 50 percent of its own tax for taxes imposed by a Commonwealth country. Other tax credits were negotiated by treaty until 1950, when the Finance Act was amended to increase the Commonwealth credit to 75 percent and to grant a 50 percent credit for income from any other source. A provision was also enacted at this time for a full credit to be made available in the future only under a treaty, but in 1953 this condition was removed and a full credit was extended irrespective of the existence of a treaty.

The United States, which had begun to tax incomes only in 1913, introduced its statutory tax credit in 1918. At first a full allowance was provided for any amount of tax paid abroad; in 1921 it was restricted to the amount of the U.S. tax on the same income. Canada followed in 1919. By section 8 of the old Income War Tax Act it granted a non-reciprocal credit for tax paid to "Great Britain or any of its self-governing colonies or dependencies for income tax in respect of income of the taxpayer derived from sources therein." It also granted a credit on a reciprocal basis for tax to any other foreign country "if such foreign country in imposing such tax allows a similar credit to persons in receipt of income derived from sources within Canada." The amount of the credit was to be limited to the "amount of the tax which would otherwise be payable under the provisions of this Act . . ." The measure remained substantially in this form until 1944, when the requirement for reciprocal treatment was withdrawn.

In 1944 Canada also enacted a general tax credit for the foreign income of Canadian corporations. Originally limited to foreign tax paid by a wholly owned subsidiary, in 1947 the ownership requirement was reduced to 50 percent. There followed in 1949 the enactment of section 28(1)(d) under which dividends were totally exempt from tax when received by a Canadian corporation having a 50 percent ownership. In 1951 the ownership requirement was reduced to 25 percent following a recommendation of the Advisory Committee on Overseas Investment. The remaining story of the increasingly complex Canadian provisions will be recounted later.

The alternative to the tax credit—the exemption of income of specific types or from specific sources—was a favourite device with certain European countries. In some countries full exemption was granted for foreign income received by a taxpayer, a system followed by France and Switzerland. This produced approximately the same result as a full tax credit; and with tax rates at nominal levels it was probably a tolerable alternative. One of the pitfalls of this approach, however, was that philosophically it carried the implication that the country of origin had a prior right to tax income earned within its boundaries, and in some countries, particularly the Latin-American, this was carried to the extreme of asserting a sole right to tax. Such a position came into direct conflict with the residence basis, under which the country of residence of the taxpayer asserts a right to tax the full income of its nationals, making whatever allowance for double taxation it may wish to provide in the interests of equity and neutrality.

Some other specific features of European taxation at this time were of interest. For example, France limited its taxation of industrial and commercial profits to those allocated to a permanent establishment in France, thus excluding from French tax profits allocated to an establishment abroad. This contained the seeds of a modern treaty rule. In the early twenties Italy, some of the central European countries, and the Swiss cantons adopted the French approach. The United Kingdom taxed only income remitted to that country by a company carrying on business in its jurisdiction if its seat of management and control was outside the country.

The Beginnings of International Tax Treaties

While the measures just described brought relief for some problems of overlapping taxation they were enacted within the structure of each country's own laws without regard for the corresponding provisions of the laws of other countries. Many of the basic and essential terms—residence, domicile, permanent establishment, profit computation, income allocation, taxes to be creditable—were subject to a variety of interpretations from country to country. No uniform principles were emerging which an international business could confidently expect would be applied in any specific situation. As a result, double and triple taxation of the same income was encountered regularly—or if not encountered was threatened—a situation almost equally undesirable. The urgent need therefore was for agreements between countries to establish uniform and reasonable definitions governing liability for tax. The international tax treaty became the accepted vehicle for this purpose.

Tax treaties were not unknown at this stage. The United Nations issued a compilation in 1951 that covered treaties commencing with 1843. But with few exceptions treaties entered into prior to World War I were for narrow specific purposes. As previously mentioned the taxation of travelling salesmen and shipping companies created early problems of double taxation, and many of the treaties dealt with these. A treaty between Germany and the Netherlands allocated the income of a company constructing a railway on the basis of track mileage in the two countries.

The first comprehensive treaty for the avoidance of double taxation of income was entered into in 1899 between Austria-Hungary and Prussia, and was followed by similar treaties between central European powers. This limited effort, while encouraging, hardly produced the sort of treaty that would serve as a model for all countries. Following the interruption of the war the search for such a model was taken up in earnest by the international groups mainly concerned.

The International Business Community

Business interest was focused through the International Chamber of Commerce (ICC) at this stage. At its first conference in 1920 the ICC adopted relief from double taxation as an issue of major concern. It urged that the new League of Nations take up the subject and also devoted considerable time and effort itself to it. As might be expected, the planning at this initial stage was on a grand—and hopeful—scale. The world's taxes were to be categorized on some logical basis that would satisfy all countries for all time. This led the experts of the day into some fairly theoretical exercises which in retrospect seem frustrating and unproductive, but which in fact were probably a necessary step in laying the ground-work for the ultimate development of some acceptable rules and practices. One of these logical-sounding ideas was developed by the Chamber's Double Taxation Committee. It postulated that taxes should be divided between "personal," based on status and total income, and "impersonal," being levied on specific types of income without regard to personal status. The former would be levied by the country of residence and the latter by the country of source. This approach was adopted by a conference at Stockholm in 1927, but was rejected by United States spokesmen as unrealistic, since the United States did not distinguish its taxes in this way.

The Committee produced other ideas from time to time. The most persistent of these was taxation entirely on the basis of residence. This proposal obviously favoured the wealthier income-receiving creditor countries, and was opposed by the debtor countries, such as Italy. As the League's proposals were developed they came before the Chamber, but failed to receive unanimous support. This process went on until the very eve of World War II; the Congress in Copenhagen in 1939 appeared to be no closer to an agreement than in previous meetings. The Chamber was to renew its quest following the war, finally achieving results through the draft OECD treaty.

The League of Nations

Meanwhile the Financial Committee of the League of Nations, at the request of the International Economic Conference of 1922, had been engaged in its own search for immutable principles. The first important step of the Committee was to call on the advice of four wise men of the day—prominent economists from Italy, the Netherlands, Great Britain and the United States. The last two were respectively Sir Josiah Stamp and E.R.A. Seligman, both renowned in the English-speaking world, and undoubtedly the others were equally well qualified in their own communities. Their report, produced in 1923, presented a thorough discussion of the issues. Its practical proposals were that income from tangible property be taxable at source and that income from intangibles be taxed by the country of residence. The two principles of source and residence could be reconciled by the use of tax credits, by income exemptions, by joint reduction of rates, or by the assignment of specific taxes to one jurisdiction or another, or by a mixture of these various devices.

While this learned exercise was still in progress the Financial Committee instituted another study of the administrative and practical aspects of double taxation, this time relying on a group of seven officials. This committee had both its membership and terms of reference enlarged, and at the conclusion of several meetings it produced not one model treaty but four, that dealt with income and property taxes, succession duties, administrative assistance, and judicial assistance. These were considered at a conference of 27 countries in 1928 in Geneva. While there was general satisfaction that considerable progress had been made, particularly in the clarification of definitions, the inevitable differences of philosophy appeared in the vital issue of the allocation of taxing powers.

In the result, the goal of a single model treaty for income tax was abandoned, and three income tax models that could be negotiated between individual countries were adopted. These were known as Drafts Ia, Ib and Ic. Draft Ia continued the distinction between personal and impersonal taxes, with specific allocation of taxing powers relative to the type of tax. The United States again opposed this proposal. Under Draft Ib, which the United States and the United Kingdom both supported, nearly all income would be taxed on a residence basis, except that the country of origin would have priority to tax income from immovable property, profits from industrial, commercial, and agricultural undertakings, and one or two other sources. Draft Ic provided that nearly all income would be taxed at the source.

Undeterred by this outcome the League appointed a permanent Fiscal Committee in 1929 and put it back to work. It would appear that the main accomplishment of the committee during the thirties was the clarification of the permanent establishment concept and income allocation rules for the taxation of industrial and commercial profits. More than a decade passed before the League offered another treaty to its members.

During this period a new element emerged in the adoption by several countries of a withholding tax on interest and dividends being paid to residents of other countries. This action immediately raised further instances of double taxation, particularly for countries having no general tax credit system. There was also the threat of sharp increases in rates; countries offering a tax credit, such as the United States and Canada, entered into an agreement in 1936 solely to fix the rate which each country would levy against the other. From this time forward the withholding tax became one of the prime items for negotiation in a treaty.

No doubt the more general use of the withholding tax was construed as giving support for the principle of taxation at the source, not an unwarranted assumption, particularly as the United States, one of the strongest of the creditor countries, had adopted it despite apparent earlier opposition. At any rate a new draft model treaty put forward by the Fiscal Committee at a regional meeting in Mexico City in 1940 leaned heavily toward source taxation. This emphasis was based on a study of treaties entered into over a period of two decades prior to the meeting, which showed a trend toward the 1928 Draft Ic. This was not a general meeting, and while it was attended by representatives of Canada and the United States the majority of those present were from Latin-American countries, and the results reflected their strong disposition toward source taxation. The Mexico City meeting was reconvened in 1943, again with Latin-American countries substantially in the majority, and a model treaty reflecting their views was adopted.

However a more balanced judgment emerged from a meeting in London in 1946. It was tactfully agreed that some progress had been made in Mexico City but that the tone of the model adopted reflected exclusively the views of those present. It was reported that the participants at the London meeting "held, on various points, different views from those which inspired the model conventions prepared in Mexico." Changes were made which restored the policies of the developed countries for the treatment of interest, dividends, royalties, annuities, and pensions. The meeting recommended that a group under the United Nations, then about to begin operations, review and consolidate the drafts and produce a version more generally acceptable. This was one of the last acts of the Fiscal Committee. In March 1946 it was terminated, to be succeeded in October by the Fiscal Commission of the United Nations.

Inter-war Treaties

Despite the uncertainty on a model treaty a considerable number of treaties were entered into between countries in the twenties and even during the Great Depression. In the twenties Germany and Italy negotiated with several other countries, and France entered into several agreements in the early thirties. By 1939 there were some sixty bilateral general conventions, and more than another three hundred dealing with taxation of shipping, air navigation, income of sales agents, death duties, and miscellaneous other issues. Of these, as previously mentioned, the greatest number were treaties dealing with taxation of shipping profits. A land-mark treaty of the period was the U.K.-Irish Free State treaty of 1926, which provided for complete exemption in the country of residence for income which had been taxed in the other country, a treaty so unique that it was not regarded as a model for anything.

The United States negotiated its first treaty in 1932, to come into effect in 1936. It was with France. Its second treaty—with Sweden—came into effect in 1940. Further U.S. treaties were entered into immediately following World War II, with Canada (1946), the Netherlands (1948), Denmark (1948), and a long list of other countries in subsequent years.

Canada also became more active during this period. Between 1929 and 1932 it entered into 11 agreements by exchange of notes on the taxation of shipping profits, these were followed in 1935 by an exchange of notes with the United Kingdom on the taxation of income arising from an agency, and in 1936 the previously mentioned exchange with the United States on the rate of withholding tax.

In 1938 by exchange of notes an arrangement was entered into with the Netherlands to avoid double taxation of income. Negotiations were started before the war on an income tax treaty with the United States and, after an interruption, these resulted in the first full-scale Canada-U.S. treaty, signed in 1942, to come into force on January 1, 1941. This was followed in 1944 by a comprehensive treaty on death duties. Canada's other main income tax treaty, that with the United Kingdom, came into effect in 1946.

Treaty negotiation generally terminated during the war, but resumed very actively upon its conclusion.

42
Postwar Treaty Developments

United Nations and the OECD

As in many other areas the immediate postwar period was one of intensive activity in international taxation. The income tax had become almost universal, and wartime peak rates were slow in coming down. Taxes on estates and successions (not to be studied in detail in this work) had multiplied, and postwar capital taxes were being imposed in several European countries to catch war profiteers. The resolve of many of the world's leaders to create international accord through institutions and agreements, as represented by the United Nations and all its satellite organizations, had its influence as well on international tax matters. The immediate revival of trade and investment following the war gave an urgency to international tax problems. A spate of tax treaties resulted.

The United Kingdom and the United States led the way, and as a result of their influence the new agreements differed in many respects from the old. According to a United Nations review in 1951:

> After World II, the United Kingdom and the United States spear-headed the movement for the conclusion of general tax agreements in pursuance of their efforts to promote foreign trade and investment. The United Kingdom obtained an almost complete coverage of the Commonwealth, concluding agreements with five Dominions and 36 dependencies. These Anglo-American agreements introduced new patterns for the control of international double taxation. Instead of the allocation of tax jurisdiction among the co-contracting Governments, the Anglo-American agreements use a combination of various tax relief methods, especially tax credit, reduction and exemption. The pivotal tax credit clause itself is firmly anchored in the unilateral relief legislation of those countries. Under it the country of residence (and in the case of the United States, the country of nationality) retain paramount taxing power over all the tax payer's income, foreign or domestic, subject, however, to the taxpayer's right to take credits against his home country's tax on account of taxes paid abroad on his foreign income. With this important relief assured to the taxpayer, all other provisions in the agreement are rather complementary . . . This system serves especially well for capital-exporting countries which want to eliminate tax deterrents to the foreign investment and trading activities of their residents and citizens yet, expecting no important *quid pro quo* from capital-importing co-contracting governments, wish to reserve full power to tax their residents or citizens. In order to limit the revenue loss imposed by this device on the home country, these agreements (especially those concluded by the United States)

often provide for a reduction in the tax imposed by the country of source on such typical foreign income items as dividends and royalties.[42.1]

A compilation made by the United Nations in 1951 showed that the United Kingdom in the previous five years had negotiated or renegotiated treaties with United States, Canada, Union of South Africa, Australia, New Zealand, Netherlands, Sweden, Israel, Burma, Denmark, Ceylon, France, and Norway. Treaties were also concluded with a long list of non-self-governing territories. A list of the United States treaties include most of the countries on the British list, and in addition Belgium, Ireland, Greece, and Switzerland. Canada by 1951 had income tax agreements with the United States, Great Britain, France, Sweden, and several of the Commonwealth countries, the latter through extension of the U.K. agreement. Negotiations were being carried on with another four countries, and would shortly result in agreements.

European countries had not been idle during this period. The prewar network had been extended, and with some exceptions included Austria, Belgium, Denmark, Finland, France, West Germany, Italy, Netherlands, Norway, Sweden, and Switzerland—the United Kingdom and United States also involved with most of these countries. The United Nations in 1951 recorded more than 300 tax agreements then in effect.

In 1954 Japan entered into its first general agreements, one for income tax and another for death duties. Not surprisingly these were negotiated with the United States. This step had been preceded in the previous year by Japanese enactment of a tax credit that would apply to both personal and corporate income.

The United Nations played an important role during this period, through the activities of the Fiscal Commission established under the Economic and Social Council. The role however was one somewhat different from that of the League. The UN made no further attempt to develop a model treaty, relying instead on the London Model of 1946 to provide a basis for negotiations. As a result many of its features appeared in the postwar agreements. The UN also pressed governments to negotiate treaties. In 1949 the Economic and Social Council put forward a resolution, sponsored by the Fiscal Commission, urging all member governments to enter into bilateral tax agreements.

The Commission compiled and published a record of new and existing treaties. Its International Tax Agreement series commenced in 1948 with an update of League of Nations records for the 1928 to 1936 period, and extended this to a historical record of all agreements entered into between 1843 and 1951. This role is still performed by the UN. In 1954 the Fiscal Commission and its Committee on International Tax Relations was termi-

---

42.1 United Nations, Department of Economic Affairs, Fiscal Division, *International Tax Agreements*, Vol. III, World Guide to International Tax Agreements, 1843-1951 (New York: United Nations, 1951), x-xi.

nated, but the UN continued to give assistance to developing countries through the technical assistance program. The author, for example, undertook a fiscal mission to Ghana in 1958 and many other fiscal experts were similarly engaged.

The OECD Model Convention

Despite the spreading network of tax treaties the developed countries continued to be dissatisfied with the lack of uniformity in the application of some of the central concepts. Disagreements among countries were still frustrating and time-consuming and frequently led to double taxation. At the urging of its members, the International Chamber of Commerce, at its Tokyo Congress in 1955 (in a move that must have been deja vu to at least some one present!), agreed by resolution to ask the Organization for European Economic Co-operation (OEEC) to study the possibilities of developing a model tax treaty, primarily in pursuit of that elusive goal—uniformity. The following year the OEEC established a Fiscal Committee to deal with technical fiscal questions, and instructed it to study and report on means for coping with current issues of double taxation.

In its first report on "The Elimination of Double Taxation" (1958) the Committee acknowledged the progress that had been made in the past, as a result of which "a great advance has been made in eliminating double taxation." However, it felt that much remained to be done.

A number of countries have not yet concluded Conventions between themselves or have concluded Conventions covering certain fields of taxation only. Cases of double taxation still therefore remain which are being rendered more difficult by the extension of taxation and more acute by the steadily increasing development of economic relations between Member countries and the increasing interdependence of their economies. These same factors, moreover, are continually giving rise to new cases for which solutions must be found. Bilateral Conventions cannot, in general, provide a solution in cases involving a third State . . . Another point is that as between the current bilateral Conventions, the rules to be applied for avoiding double taxation are still by no means uniform . . . It is a fact that in many cases the Conventions cannot be clearly interpreted and this makes them difficult to understand, except for experts . . . As a result it is impossible for a taxpayer to ascertain exactly what tax liabilities he incurs by engaging in economic activities in other countries.[42.2]

The Committee conceded that there were many other more rigid restraints on international trade and investment, but that there was no need to continue with those originating in taxation, as many of them could be removed by cooperation between OEEC members.[42.3] The Committee was optimistic

---

[42.2] Organization for European Economic Co-operation, *The Elimination of Double Taxation* Report of the Fiscal Committee of the O.E.E.C. (Paris: O.E.E.C., 1958), 10-12.
[42.3] Ibid.

that given time it would be able to develop a model treaty that would be acceptable to all OEEC members. In order to make its work as productive as possible it recommended that members adopt new proposals as they were accepted by the OEEC Council.

The operations of the Committee were crisp and efficient, a demonstration of the productivity that can be achieved by a group of knowledgeable experts working toward an agreed objective. There were of course some differences of view, but in general the OEEC members shared common purposes—certainly to a greater extent than the members of the League of Nations. Even so the Committee drew heavily on the experience under the League Models, particularly the 1943 Mexican and the 1946 London versions. It began by setting out its program of study in its 1958 report, listing four subjects being given immediate attention and another seven that would follow. The Committee was able to report that it had made such headway in dealing with the first four questions that already several countries involved in its work had implemented its proposals. In three following annual reports the committee put forward its recommendations as these were developed. By 1961 the content of 25 Articles had been settled, and taken together they formed the basis for a model agreement. In that year the OEEC was replaced by the Organization for European Economic Development (OECD) and the Fiscal Committee was continued under the new organization. In 1963 the OECD issued a document—*Draft Double Taxation Convention on Income and Capital*—bringing together all the previous draft Articles plus another six adopted in the interim. The Committee strongly urged the immediate adoption of its model treaty by all OECD members, reserving the right to continue to study some remaining unfinished aspects.

There is a massive body of literature on the draft, and only its main features need be mentioned here. Its 30 Articles dealt with the basis of liability, the nature of the taxes covered, the concept of fiscal domicile, the definition of permanent establishment, the taxation of income from immovable property, the computation of business profits, the treatment of shipping and air transport, the taxation of dividends, interest, royalties, and capital gains, the treatment of independent and dependent personal services, directors' fees, pensions, and fees of artistes and athletes, and the status of students and government employees. It contemplated two methods of eliminating double taxation—either by exemption or tax credit in the country of residence. A single Article dealt with taxation of capital. Final Articles covered non-discrimination, exchange of information, privileges of consular and diplomatic officials, territorial extension, coming into force, and termination. Every Article was supported by an explanatory Commentary, which greatly facilitated interpretation.

Canada reserved its position on several Articles, as did the United States. Canada could not accept the requirement that the treaty should apply to political subdivisions, since such an undertaking was beyond the constitutional competence of the federal government; it reserved its right to include as a permanent establishment a person who has a stock from which he regularly fills orders; reserved its right to levy a withholding tax on interest at a rate higher than the 10 percent provided in the model; it reserved the right to tax royalties and directors' fees at the source. Other Canadian reservations related to government employees' pensions, certain payments from an estate or trust, and differentiation on the basis of nationality.

The OECD draft is a milestone. From this time forward whether or not one agreed with all its provisions, one started with the 1963 draft. After more than four decades of uncertainty this was a remarkable accomplishment. It contributed materially to international trade and investment that a corporation would be taxed on its business operations in a foreign country only if it had a permanent establishment in that country, and only income directly related to the operations of that establishment would be taxed. The definitions of permanent establishment and the rules set forth for determining their profit were also of central importance. Limitations on withholding tax rates of 5 percent for dividends paid to another corporation that owned 25 percent or more of the paying corporation, 15 percent on other dividends, and of 10 percent on interest payments, also introduced some salutary guidelines. Under the draft, royalties would be entirely exempt from withholding tax at the source. In general remuneration for personal services was to be taxed in the country of residence of the person performing such services, but exceptions were made depending on the time spent in the source country, the degree of attachment to an establishment in that country, and other conditions. Shipping and airline profits would be taxed only in the country of residence of the corporation. The basic objective of removal of double taxation was to be accomplished by either of two methods: exemption from tax in the country of residence (but the foreign income could be included for determining the rates that would apply to other income), or the granting of a tax credit by the country of residence. Both these methods were to be found in practice in the fifties and sixties, and today the tax systems of most countries have mixed elements of both. The treaty provided for many other situations, but the above are the salient points.

The 1963 draft became the model for nearly all treaties entered into between industrialized countries in the following two decades. By the time of adoption of the final version in 1977 OECD members (which by then also included Australia, Finland, Japan, and New Zealand) had 179 bilateral conventions on income and capital taxes in effect among them. Of these 69 represented new treaties and 49 were revisions based on the 1963 Model. Many of these reflected further work of the OECD Committee, which had been designated the Committee on Fiscal Affairs in 1971. The Committee proposed several revisions in 1972 and 1974, and with some further changes the Council of OECD adopted a final draft in 1977 as an approved Model Convention to replace the 1963 version. The Committee had also produced a draft convention on international taxation of estates and inheritances in 1966, which does not appear to have been further revised.

The 1977 Model Convention, as explained in its introduction, was a refinement of the previous model rather than a complete overhaul. The report stated: "In essence, the new text does not differ appreciably from the previous one, as the object of the revision of the 1963 Draft Convention was not to question its principles and general structure . . . On a number of points, a wide measure of agreement has made it possible to introduce amplifications to or changes in the text of certain Articles. The essential part of the Committee's work, is, however, reflected in the Commentaries on the Articles which, in some cases, have been the subject of additions, clarifications or updatings."[42.4] The evidence of this is that while relatively minor changes were made to seven Articles, the number of pages of Commentary increased from 103 to 146 between the 1963 and 1977 versions.

Tax Treaties at the United Nations

If the 1963 OECD draft met the general support of the developed countries this could not be said for the developing nations. Few treaties had been signed with them, and the reason given was that the OECD draft had been drawn up to meet the common objectives of developed countries, which were not only different from those of developing countries but were sometimes antithetical to them. This had been admitted by the OECD Fiscal Committee in a 1965 report, *Fiscal Incentives for Private Investment in Developing Countries*. It said: "Existing treaties between industrialized countries sometimes require the country of residence to give up revenue. More often, however, it is the country of source which gives up revenue. Such a pattern may not be equally appropriate in treaties between developing and industrialized countries because income flows are largely from developing to industrialized countries and revenue sacrifice would be one-sided."[42.5]

This statement very accurately summed up the dissatisfaction of the developing countries at this juncture, and, as happened with the GATT arrangements, they looked to the United Nations as a platform from which to air their grievances. As a result, in 1967, by resolution of the Economic and Social Council, a committee was established as the Ad Hoc Group of Experts on Tax Treaties between Developed and Developing Countries. Some 15 countries were represented in the original Group, including Argentina, Chile, Ghana, India, Israel, Pakistan, Philippines, Sudan, Tunisia, and Turkey; the industrial members were France, West Germany, Japan, Netherlands, Sweden, Switzerland, United Kingdom, and United States. Its instructions were to explore "ways and means for facilitating the conclusion of tax treaties between developed and developing countries . . ."

The Group took the OECD draft as its working document, and its proposals were addressed to that model. In general they were designed to widen the tax net for developing countries by giving a greater emphasis to

---

42.4 Organization for Economic Co-operation and Development, *Model Double Taxation Convention on Income and on Capital* Report of the O.E.C.D. Committee on Fiscal Affairs (Paris: O.E.C.D., 1977), para. 11-12.

42.5 Organization for Economic Co-operation and Development, *Fiscal Incentives for Private Investment in Developing Countries* Report of the O.E.C.D. Fiscal Committee (Paris: O.E.C.D., 1965), 57.

source taxation. As an example, the permanent establishment definition was shortened to include a construction project having a life of six months, with the option of reducing this to three months, in place of twelve months under the OECD draft. The provision of services, the delivery of goods, purchase activity, and activities of independent agents (in some cases on an optional basis), were brought within the ambit of the permanent establishment concept. Countries other than the country of residence of the shipping firm were given a share of shipping profits. The Group was unable to accept the limitations on withholding tax rates for interest and dividends as set out in the OECD draft, but at the same time were unable to agree on alternative rates. They did agree however that both borrowing and lender countries should have the right to tax interest. Taxes on royalties should be shared between countries. Source taxation would also be permitted for insurance premiums, persons engaged in independent services, top-level managerial officers, and pension and social security benefits. Minor other changes were proposed; many others were considered and dropped.

The problems of the developing countries under the tax credit method for removal of double taxation received sympathetic consideration. It was agreed that their effect was to nullify tax incentives granted by developing countries to stimulate foreign investment. Under the tax credit system the benefit of tax reductions so granted went to the government of the investor's country (through a lowering of the foreign tax taken as a credit against the domestic tax) rather than the investor, whose total tax remained unchanged. The developing countries agreed that a method should be evolved under which a reduction given by a developing country through incentive or other programs should be for the benefit of the investor, not the government of the investor's country. The proposal of the developing countries was a system under which income would be taxed by the source country only, with no further taxation in the country of residence. This approach was not acceptable to the developed countries, and an alternative was proposed known as "tax sparing." Under it a tax credit is allowed to the investor by the country of residence at the rate that would have applied had there not been an incentive reduction. This solution has not received general approval among industrial countries, to the extent, for example, of being embodied in the OECD Convention. However Canada has adopted the philosophy it represents, and has implemented tax sparing in several recent treaties with developing countries.

After seven meetings and extensive consultations with other countries the Group produced a set of principles published in 1974 as Guidelines for Tax Treaties between Developed and Developing Countries, followed by a Manual for the Negotiation of Bilateral Tax Treaties between Developed and Developing Countries. In 1978 the Economic and Social Council requested the Group to pursue their work further and produce a Model Treaty with a deadline of one year. The Group considered a draft prepared by the UN staff and adopted it, with revisions, at a meeting late in 1979, which was published in 1980 as the United Nations Model Convention. The UN model appears to have had little influence as yet, although the U.S.

government has expressed itself as willing to accept most of its provisions.[42.6] Perhaps the most meaningful response has been that of Canada and several other countries in introducing the tax-sparing provision in its recent treaties with developing countries. There are also traces of a more sympathetic approach on Canada's part in other ways in recent treaties.

The U.S. Treasury Model Income Tax Convention

To complete this tour of the model treaties it is necessary to review one that the U.S. Treasury issued in 1977 for public examination. This produced much discussion, and resulted in the issuance of a revision in 1981. This in turn has precipitated further public discussion, and as yet no "final" version has been issued. As the basis for future U.S. treaties the model is of considerable importance. In its main outlines of course it closely resembles the OECD model, the Articles having almost identical headings and arrangement. There are some variations, however. As usual the U.S. retains its right to tax on a citizenship basis, including for ten years a former citizen whose loss of citizenship "had as one of its principal purposes the avoidance of income tax . . ." Certain U.S. taxes are excluded from the treaty, person is defined to include an estate, trust or partnership, the definition of residence includes citizenship and place of incorporation, but omits the OECD test of place of effective management and control for businesses (nowhere in the treaty is this favourite European test mentioned).

Permanent establishment includes a drilling rig or ship, business deductions include some additional items, such as research and development expenses, the apportionment basis for allocating profits is omitted, and the rental of films or tapes used for radio or television is included as a business. For dividends the 5 percent rate is granted where there is 10 percent ownership (25 percent under the OECD treaty); there are more restrictive rules for taxes on interest and there is no 10 percent rate ceiling. Royalties taxes are narrowed, taxation of capital gains is slightly broadened, there is no special Article dealing with directors' fees, and an exemption is introduced under the Artistes and Athletes Article. The treatment of certain forms of income, such as social security benefits, annuities, alimony, and child support payments is spelled out in detail.

The provision that has caused the greatest controversy, Article 16, Limitation of Benefits, is entirely new, and largely represents the efforts of the Congress to restrict the benefits of U.S. treaties to those for whom they were intended. One draft of the Article limited relief from taxation under the treaty for a resident person (excluding individuals) of another country to an entity owned to the extent of more than 75 percent by residents of that country. An additional requirement in effect was that the non-resident entity must operate for the main benefit of non-resident persons. Such was

---

[42.6] See Stanley S. Surrey, *United Nations Model Convention for Tax Treaties Between Developed and Developing Countries* (Amsterdam: International Bureau of Fiscal Documentation, 1980).

the furor raised by this draft that it was replaced by a later one of such complexity that it almost defies understanding. However, those who claim to have mastered it still complain bitterly against its motivation, and nothing has yet been settled, either on the Article or the model treaty, but some features of the model are said to be identifiable in recent U.S. conventions. Some appeared in the Canada-U.S. treaty of 1984, although by no means all of them.

43
Canadian Tax Reform: The Canadian Treaties

Tax treaty developments have been and continue to be of great concern to Canada. However, they are supplementary to the basic provisions of the tax law, which are the touchstone of the government's policy. Policies of course are not graven in marble, and change with evolving needs and objectives. A major review was conducted in the decade beginning in 1967, following the Report of the Royal Commission on Taxation. The Commission's mandate was to study the federal tax system in its entirety, including its international aspects. Although adopted in considerably modified form by the government, its proposals began a process that produced massive changes in the Canadian approach to international taxation. The pre-reform system may be briefly described.

Basis of Liability

Residence was the main test of liability. A resident was taxable on total world income, a non-resident on income originating in Canada. Personal residence depended on the indicia of more or less continuous presence, such as a home, a family, bank accounts, and so on. For corporations there were several tests, including place of management and control, place of incorporation, and place where business is carried on.

Canadian Source Income

Business: corporations resident in Canada, whether or not owned by non-residents, were taxable like any other Canadian corporation; non-residents carrying on business directly, usually through a branch, were taxed on income attributable to the business. In addition to the ordinary corporation tax Canada imposed a tax at 15 percent on after-tax profits of a branch.

Property income: a withholding tax of 15 percent was levied on dividends, interest, royalties, estate and trust income, and patronage dividends paid to non-residents. Some forms of such payments were given a reduced rate and interest on government bonds issued after April 1966 was exempt.

Employment income: in general was taxable in Canada, but short-term employment was exempt.

Foreign Source Income

Business income: income earned by a Canadian-owned foreign corporation was taxable when dividends were received in Canada. The amount of the dividends was grossed up to include direct taxes paid in the country of source and a credit was allowed against the Canadian tax, but not to exceed that tax. Income from direct business activity in a foreign country, (i.e. through a branch), was subject to Canadian tax when earned, whether or not paid to the Canadian owner. In this case a tax credit was allowed for the income tax paid to the foreign country, again not exceeding the Canadian tax payable on that income.

Property income: taxable on receipt by a Canadian resident, with a tax credit for a withholding tax or similar tax in the foreign country.

Employment income: taxable in the year earned by the Canadian resident, with a credit for tax paid to the foreign country on such income.

Like most countries, Canada limited its tax credit to the amount of Canadian tax payable on the income item involved.

The Commission's Appraisal

The Commission found these provisions consistent with the general standards of the time, particularly as they were closely adapted to the tax systems of Canada's principal trading partners—the United Kingdom and the United States. However, the Commission had developed some fairly rigorous general tests which it was applying to all elements of the federal tax structure, and by these standards they found some shortcomings. In its view certain provisions were inequitable between individual taxpayers, were lacking in neutrality because they distorted economic decisions, and were inefficient in that they frequently did not serve Canada's best interests. The Commission acknowledged that in areas as complex as the tax treatment of international trade and investment the ideal could be only very roughly approximated. But this would be sufficient, particularly since many other factors had much greater influence than taxation. In its view there were three provisions of the current law that were so questionable that it recommended complete repeal. These were (1) section 28(1)(d); (2) the foreign business corporation; and (3) the non-resident-owned investment corporation.

Section (28)(1)(d). The origins of this provision have been mentioned earlier. Prior to its introduction in 1949 a tax credit had been allowed to corporations for taxes paid abroad through a complex gross-up-and-credit procedure. As most foreign income originated in either the United Kingdom or the United States, and as their tax rates were as high as the Canadian rates the normal result was complete exemption for such income. Section (28)(1)(d) was enacted to provide a short-cut to this end. At first limited to dividends from a foreign company that was 50 percent or more Canadian owned, in 1951 on the recommendation of the Advisory committee on Overseas Investment, the ownership requirement was reduced to 25 percent.

Undoubtedly to the great surprise of its official authors this provision soon qualified Canada as a tax-haven country. It was one of the concessions that led to the listing of Canada as a country offering "favorable tax factors for international business" in a publication issued by the International

Program in Taxation at the Harvard Law School.[43.1] In this listing it found itself in the company of such well-known tax havens as Bermuda, Liberia, the Netherlands Antilles, Liechtenstein, Tangier, and Uruguay. A Canadian Tax Foundation publication by an independent author described the law as being "exceptionally favourable and generous as well as unique to the Canadian treatment of foreign income. No other capital exporting country offers comparable encouragement taxwise to its residents who have invested abroad or contemplate doing so, and provides for the unilateral relief from international multiple taxation in such an effective way."[43.2] The author of the present publication recalls having the tax manager of a large United States firm say to him at a tax conference: "Give me your Section 28(1)(d) and I won't ask for anything more."

Some of this enthusiasm was no doubt directed to the original purpose of the provision. But the Commission's research suggested that this was not a very high proportion. As it said rather laconically in its report,

> The tax minimization possibilities of the exemption privilege, in combination with the use of foreign tax havens, have not gone unnoticed. The provision can be used to reduce Canadian tax on income generated in Canada for the benefit of Canadians. By establishing companies in jurisdictions which impose little or no tax, Canadians can reduce their Canadian tax by engaging in a series of paper transactions which exploit the provisions of tax treaties in combination with section 28(1)(d) . . . There is also evidence that the provision has offered the possibility to use Canada itself as a tax haven for international business. Data compiled for us by the Taxation Division show that over a period of years a very substantial part of the dividends reported under this section has originated in jurisdictions imposing little or no tax, and that a very high proportion of these dividends has been received in Canada by holding companies not having a substantial Canadian economic interest but representing for the most part foreign ownership. Of a total of $1,500 million received by all Canadian corporations (including those that were owned by non-residents) in the five years from 1957 to 1961, only 10 per cent came from the United States and 4 per cent from the United Kingdom.[43.3]

This was enough evidence for the Commission. Something had gone seriously wrong with this innocent-seeming well-intentioned measure. It said: "The defects of the present section 28(1)(d) are obvious, and we therefore recommend its repeal."[43.4]

[43.1] William J. Gibbons, *Tax Factors in Basing International Business Abroad* (Cambridge: Harvard Law School, International Program in Taxation, 1957).

[43.2] Jean B. De la Giroday, *Canadian Taxation and Foreign Investment*. Canadian Tax Papers no. 9 (Toronto: Canadian Tax Foundation, 1955), 60.

[43.3] Canada, *Report of the Royal Commission on Taxation*, vol. 4 (Ottawa: Queen's Printer, 1967), 511.

[43.4] Ibid., at 512.

Foreign Business Corporations

Under a provision that dated from 1918 a category of companies having their assets and business located substantially outside Canada was granted complete exemption from corporate taxation. The exemption applied even though the corporation's main offices, with large administrative staffs, were located in Canada. It had been granted originally to allow several Canadian companies which owned and directed large utility systems in Mexico and Brazil to continue to operate from Canada without income tax. Its scope had gradually been broadened over the 40 years of its existence, and there were signs of growing abuse during the fifties, as resident companies pushed the provision to its limits and non-residents took advantage of the tax shelter it provided. The Harvard Law School publication earlier mentioned[43.5] stated that the majority of non-resident companies that were using Canada as a "tax base" country had qualified as foreign business corporations.

In the view of the Commission the "provisions were not only giving too much scope for tax avoidance by Canadians but were also attracting foreigners . . . thereby facilitating international tax avoidance on a grand scale. This occurred principally through purchases of goods in the United States and their sale in other countries under the protection of Canada's treaties."[43.6] Amendments to restrict the provision had only been partially successful. The law had been changed in 1959 to cut off creation of any further companies in this category, but existing companies still offered opportunities for abuse. The Commission therefore recommended complete repeal, to be staged over a period of five years.

Non-Resident-Owned Investment Corporations

From 1936, a Canadian resident company having 90 percent or more foreign ownership could restrict its Canadian tax to an annual charge of 15 percent. In order to qualify for this status its income had to be restricted to ownership or trading in bonds, shares, debentures, mortgages and similar investments, from the lending of money, from rents, hire of chattels, and similar remuneration, or from estates or trusts. Rents could not exceed 10 percent of its income and its principal business could not be banking. No further tax was payable on withdrawal of funds from Canada. The provision had very mixed results. For dividends the 15 percent tax merely anticipated the normal withholding tax, and offered no particular advantage. For other forms of income, such as rents and interest, it substituted a 15 percent rate for the higher corporate tax that would otherwise have applied. The Commission found very little evidence that the measure had met its objective of increasing investment in Canadian equities, but instead had provided a low tax instrument for the holding of Canadian interest-bearing debentures and rental property by non-residents. It thought this was permitting

---

[43.5]Supra, footnote 43.1.

[43.6]Supra, footnote 43.3, at 558.

foreign investors to avoid tax in their own countries without Canadian penalty, and that the provision should be repealed, in this case in stages over a ten-year period.

The subsequent reform of these three provisions marked the beginning of a period when Canada was to take a more cautious approach to such special international measures. Section 28(1)(d) survived only as part of a new and closely hedged treatment of dividends from foreign entities, the foreign-owned business corporation provision was repealed, and the non-resident-owned investment corporation was substantially revised. Some of the same trend was evident in the United States. In the sixties that country had its Western Hemisphere Trade Corporation, its China Trade Act Corporation, and various special provisions for income earned in Puerto Rico, Virgin Islands, Guam, and other U.S. possessions. During the sixties concern with the use of foreign tax havens for escaping tax resulted in the enactment of Sub-Part F of the Internal Revenue Code, a model for later Canadian action. In the Tax Reform Act of 1976 some of the special provisions were repealed or modified. Of course in the meantime (1971) the United States Congress had passed the Domestic International Sales Corporation (DISC) legislation, a measure giving marked incentives for foreign trade.

The Main Canadian Reform Changes

The details of the process of tax reform have already been described in chapter 13, and need not be repeated here. The general pace was painfully slow, and the international area crept forward at even slower progress. Nearly a decade went by between the commencement of the government's consideration of the foreign context and final implementation of the main changes. In order to allow time for logical sequence in the adoption of fairly radical new measures the effective date of some was set for 1974 and for others as late as 1976. The drafting of law and regulations proved to be of enormous complexity, and the result has been by far the most impenetrable body of tax legislation ever enacted in Canada. The following description of the new arrangements is a gross over-simplification, but gives enough detail to be reasonably accurate.

Foreign Income of Canadians

Business or investment income from a foreign corporation. Under the new dispensation the status of income from a foreign corporation depends on three factors: (1) the degree of ownership or control held by Canadians; (2) the nature of the business carried on, and (3) the existence (or absence) of a tax treaty between Canada and the country in which the foreign corporation is located.

(1) Degree of ownership. New categories of corporation were created called "foreign affiliate" and "controlled foreign affiliate" to reflect degrees of ownership. The former is a non-resident corporation in which a Canadian resident has an equity percentage of not less than 10 percent. The latter is a

foreign corporation in which a Canadian resident or a Canadian resident and a group of associates have control over the corporation.

(2) Nature of business carried on. The nature of the business carried on is relevant to the Canadian taxable status of income of the corporation. If the foreign affiliate's income is totally derived from carrying on an active business dividends from it are exempt from tax when received by a Canadian corporation. Where its income includes other than active business income (generally investment or property income), there are consequences for the Canadian owner which are described below.

(3) The existence of a tax treaty. A condition for the exemption of dividends under (2) above is inclusion of the name of the country of location of the affiliate in a "prescribed" list of countries with which Canada either has a tax treaty or is in the process of negotiating one.

It will be noted that in the simplest case falling within the above requirements, the receipt of dividends from an affiliate solely carrying on an active business in a country with which Canada has a tax treaty, the position is the same as under the repealed section 28(1)(d). Dividends are income of the Canadian company only on receipt, and are then exempt from tax. Much more complicated is the status of income of a foreign affiliate having passive income.

Passive income is generally all income that is not active business income, and includes dividends, interest, capital gains, royalties, rentals, etc. The law embraces all such income under the rubric of "foreign accrual property income" (FAPI). Where the foreign affiliate is not controlled dividends are taxable to a Canadian shareholder on receipt, but the amount to be included in income is reduced by a factor which compensates indirectly for taxation imposed in the country of source. The factor incorporates not only a withholding tax but, as well, the underlying business income tax imposed on the corporation by the foreign country, although recognition is granted through an income deduction rather than a tax credit. Any business income earned by a company also having passive income is exempt as described above.

Where the corporation is a "controlled foreign affiliate" the treatment of FAPI is different. Its purpose is to frustrate the use of the affiliate as a means of deferring tax through the accumulation of surpluses of investment and related income in the affiliate by owners having control over its actions. Each year the increment of FAPI over the previous year is taxable to the Canadian controlling shareholder or shareholders whether distributed or not, the amount allocated being in proportion to share ownership. A dividend so included is reduced by a factor representing foreign taxes as described above, a reduction which applies to individuals as well as corporations.

In order to conform to this regime the record-keeping requirements of foreign affiliates are formidable. They must maintain accounts which clearly identify their surpluses by origin, as this identification governs their taxable status. Their records must segregate exempt surplus (usually income from an active business), taxable surplus, (e.g. passive income), and pre-acquisition surplus. On actual distributions of passive income, previously taxed as a deemed distribution, credit must be taken for the pre-payment. A source of endless complexity in the law and regulations has been the necessity of extending to foreign affiliates the whole intricate legal apparatus governing reorganizations, amalgamations, terminations, capital gains, etc. to cover not only relations between foreign affiliates and their Canadian parents but between foreign affiliates and all other corporations.

The Tax Credit

Apart from the special provisions for income from foreign affiliates the tax credit remains the main Canadian device for alleviation of double taxation. A distinction is now made in the law between a business and a non-business income tax. The former is a tax levied on a business carried on by a taxpayer in a foreign country, the clearest instance being a tax on income of a branch. The most common form of non-business income tax is the withholding tax on dividends. A shareholder, whether corporation or individual, owning 10 percent or less of a foreign company is restricted to a tax credit for this type of tax. The benefit of the tax credit has been substantially improved by the allowance of a carry-over of unabsorbed amounts to other years in specific instances, as well as inclusion of taxes imposed by sub-governments in some circumstances.

Personal Service Income

Employment has increasingly taken on international dimensions, and Canada has adapted its laws to the greater mobility of taxpayers through measures which reduce instances of double taxation. Canadian income tax law for some time has exempted a minimum amount of personal income earned outside the country. In 1980 the exemption was established as 50 percent of employment income, to a maximum of $50,000, earned by a Canadian resident employed outside Canada for a period of more than six consecutive months. In 1984 this was increased to a credit of 80 percent of the tax on up to $100,000 of such income, following a recommendation of the Export Trade Development Board.

Foreign Income Originating in Canada

Tax changes for income of foreigners originating in Canada were much less dramatic. For business taxation the basic elements remained intact. Foreign-owned subsidiaries continue to be taxable in Canada basically in the same manner as other Canadian corporations. Withholding taxes continue to be imposed on dividends, interest, and similar payments going abroad and the tax on after-tax branch earnings continues to be imposed.

A notable feature was the increase in withholding tax from 15 to 25 percent and its extension to forms of payment previously exempt. This increase was intended to bring Canada up to the higher U.S. and U.K. levels, thus giving more bargaining power in treaty negotiations. It was the stated intention of the government to reduce this rate to 15 percent or less in treaties on a reciprocal basis. The 15 percent rate on non-resident investment corporations and on branch profits was also increased to 25 percent, to be negotiated downward in tax treaties. By statute, where a foreign corporation had a required degree of Canadian ownership, the withholding tax on dividends going abroad was 5 percentage points lower than the treaty rate. This provision was repealed in 1981.

Non-residents were required to pay tax on capital gains on dispositions of real property, business property, capital stock, trust assets, and partnership interests in Canada. Another feature affecting foreign-owned corporations was the provisions creating a "thin capitalized" corporation. Such a corporation was disallowed a deduction for interest payments to a foreign parent on indebtedness which exceeded three times its equity capital.

Canadian Tax Treaties

Tax treaties have come to play a crucial role under the post-reform arrangements. This central position became inevitable under the government's own reform measures. The Commission had found treaties a useful device and had proposed the addition of others to the dozen or so then in effect. Under the governmental measure, however, the effect of key elements of the new arrangements varied markedly with the absence or existence of a treaty. In this regard the government made its intentions known at an early stage. In the first governmental Proposals for Tax Reform, issued in 1969, the exemption of dividends from foreign affiliates was to be contingent on the conclusion of a tax treaty with the country of origin. Similarly any reduction in the new 25 percent rate of Canadian withholding tax would require the negotiation of a treaty. These proposals were carried through to the final legislation enacted in 1971, when the effective date of these and other key changes was delayed either to 1974 or 1976 to leave time for completion of as many treaty negotiations as possible.

Early treaty negotiations were divided about equally between developed and developing countries. The former included France, Belgium, Israel, Switzerland, Austria, Italy, Spain, Roumania, and the United Kingdom. During the same period new treaties were also completed with Pakistan, Singapore, The Phillipines, The Dominican Republic, Malaysia, Liberia, Korea, Indonesia, Jamaica, and Barbados. Succeeding countries included Australia, New Zealand, Bangladesh, Tunisia, United Republic of Cameroon, Sri Lanka, Kenya, Egypt, Ivory Coast, Sweden and Luxembourg. Several of the treaties in the latter group had been signed and were awaiting Parliamentary approval to become effective in 1983. This was not forthcoming and expectations of action in 1984 were overtaken by political events, including a national election. At the outset of 1985 a considerable list of signed treaties therefore remained in limbo.

Overall progress was reported from time to time by the Department of Finance. By June 1980, 24 treaties were in force, 31 were under negotiation, and 13 were signed but not yet in force. By March 1982, the standing was: 32 in force, 32 under negotiation (of which 25 were new), and three signed but not yet in force. The 1982 reckoning gives a potential total of 67, compared to about a dozen at the commencement of the exercise. A notable absence from the lists up to this time was any Latin American country, an omission that has since been rectified through treaties with several countries.

During the years when the federal government imposed an estate tax it entered into treaties for the avoidance of double taxation, but following its repeal in 1971 these were allowed to lapse. The foregoing description has therefore dealt mainly with income tax treaties, and in the interest of simplicity has used the term "treaty" to cover what are technically known as conventions, treaties, and agreements. There are legal differences between these forms, but they are not crucial to the general narrative of this work.

The prominent role of tax treaties under the new system has had its effect in many ways. Once an esoteric procedure conducted in private by a small group of officials, treaty negotiations have now become one of the most closely observed of governmental tax exercises. The Department of Finance announces in advance its intention to conduct negotiations with a country, and asks for public comment and suggestions. Interested parties have opportunity for discussion during the course of the negotiations. The signing of a treaty is usually a well publicized event, and copies are given wide circulation. Elaborate loose-leaf services are now available which give full details of treaties, with extensive commentary. The details of new and proposed treaties are given thorough examination at conferences of such organizations as the Canadian Tax Foundation and the Canadian branch of the International Fiscal Association. As a result treaty watching has become a full-time occupation for a very considerable number of tax practitioners.

The signing of a treaty, usually by the ministers of the respective governments, is just the first step in a protracted process. The treaty will not be effective until implemented by legislation, and before this is passed there are hearings of both House and Senate Committees. As a result the legislative process has become so protracted that it can occupy several years, especially as the same procedure normally must be duplicated in the other contracting country. Issues only remotely related are frequently introduced into the discussion of the implementing legislation. A striking example was the last Canada-United States treaty—an update of the 1942 treaty—which suffered a long delay because, among other reasons, a stand-off developed as a result of Canadian irritation with U.S. action to curtail convention spending in Canada and U.S. annoyance with Canadian measures that disallowed a tax deduction for Canadian advertising on U.S. border radio and TV stations. There were other causes for delay, but four years went by between signing and enactment, a delay sufficient to require signing of a protocol in 1983.

The record of the Canadian Parliament in many years has been a long trail of unfinished treaty business. The late seventies were probably the worst example; the list of unattended legislation at the end of sessions invariably included bills to implement tax treaties signed years before. The culmination of this delay was Bill S-2, given Royal Assent in December

1980, an omnibus measure to give ratification for a dozen outstanding treaties or revisions of treaties or agreements, several of which had been signed as long ago as 1976. Most had been before Parliament on two or three occasions without action being taken. Among the more important of these was a revision of the Canada-United Kingdom treaty of 1966, which had been signed in 1978. More recent experience has shown less delay, but it is quite evident that parliamentarians rank foreign tax treaties very low on their scale of priorities.

Revision by Regulation

An effort was made by the government to expedite revisions under powers it obtained from Parliament to keep treaties up to date by regulation. First introduced in the bill to implement treaties with France, Belgium, and Israel in 1976, the authorization has also appeared in subsequent legislation. However, Parliament has kept a close rein on its use. Action under it must be supported by resolution of a minimum number of members of the House and Senate, and must be followed by publication of the amendments in the Canada Gazette, so that in the end its contribution to speedier action has been doubtful.

Income Tax Conventions Interpretation Act

In 1983 the government submitted legislation to Parliament to overcome a decision of the Supreme Court in which it had held that the taxes to which a treaty applied and the laws that governed its implementation were those in effect at the time of signature. This was contrary to the interpretation given by Canada and most other countries in day to day administration, and was a most sensitive point, particularly where later changes had drastically altered the law, either for or against the interests of the taxpayer. The main purpose of the bill, entitled the Income Tax Conventions Interpretation Act, was simply to ensure that a treaty related to the current law, not the law in effect at the time of its implementation. The measure was not passed in 1983, and was re-introduced and passed in 1984.

Other Amendments

Other amendments affecting international taxation have been relatively few in recent years. In 1987 the Minister of Finance introduced an amendment to implement deferral provisions in some treaties where countries taxed proceeds of corporate reorganizations on different dates. No changes of substance have been introduced in treaties of the mid-eighties, and the 1987 tax reform process has left the basic Canadian tax arrangements unchanged. Treaties governing international treatment of social security payments were becoming common, and Canada had negotiated several of these. The federal legislation for tax-free international banking centres in Montreal and Vancouver was a new departure for Canada, but not unique in the international tax realm. Otherwise there has been little to mention.

Treaties: the Final Standing

One of the problems in keeping track of the score on Canada's treaties has been the dropping of a procedure adopted by the Department of Finance of listing treaties as soon as they had been signed. This practice delighted treaty-watchers, but had been found by the Department to relieve the other contracting government of any sense of urgency in completing its share of the deal. The listing on signature was therefore discontinued by Canada, and is now only made on final ratification. This leaves some problems for tax planning, as final dates are unpredictable. Furthermore, while a great many treaties are signed, it is difficult for even an avid treaty-watcher such as Alex McKie, Editor of Butterworth's *Canada's Tax Treaties*, to say exactly how many are operative. A McKie list of work in progress in September 1984 included 15 new treaties, 7 revised treaties and 3 protocols —25 in all, then under negotiation. A list in January 1988, recorded 19 announcements of negotiations, some of long standing, that had not yet borne fruit. Perhaps the most meaningful listing is the actual contents of the Canadian loose-leaf treaty services. A rough check at mid-1988 shows an average listing of 45-50 treaties.

The Withholding Tax

The central role of tax treaties in relation to withholding taxes must be emphasized. It has been made clear that such taxes are the product of long-standing and contentious differences in philosophy between taxation at the source and taxation on the basis of residence. One would have assumed, therefore, that after half a century or more there would be a clear separation between countries that as a matter of national policy imposed taxes at the source and those that did not. Such a result might at least have been expected to flow logically from the quite different economic interests of debtor and creditor countries.

In fact no such thing has happened. On the contrary withholding taxes have simply become a standard feature of most major tax systems. All jurisdictions levy withholding taxes on dividends, interest, and many other forms of payment leaving the country at rates from 15 to 35 percent or more. This general move was undoubtedly the result of competitive response to actions of other countries rather than adherence to a principle. It was also no doubt facilitated by the broad adoption of the tax credit system, which removed the sting of double taxation. And it was here that the tax treaties performed a major role. The threat of escalation of rates forced countries to achieve some form of constraint, and the tax treaty, with its opportunity for bargaining and compromise, became the favourite vehicle for this purpose. As a result, negotiations on withholding taxes became a central element in the treaty process. The rates suggested in the model treaties and the actual rates settled in current negotiations established some broad standards of reasonableness, around which rates tended to gravitate.

Canadian Experience

By the mid-eighties Canada had used the withholding tax for over half a century. It was first levied in 1934, at a 5 percent rate, and applied then only to interest and dividends. In 1944 the rate was raised to 15 percent, and in 1976 to 25 percent. Specific features of the statutory treatment of dividends, interest, and other payments are briefly described below.

Dividends

The postwar general rate was 15 percent, but a reduced rate of 5 percent was given for dividends of Canadian companies going abroad. This latter rate was repealed in 1960, following which such dividends were fully taxable at 15 percent. The tax on branch profits was introduced at this time at a 15 percent rate. In 1963 some of the previous special position for Canadian companies was restored through a reduction to 10 percent on dividends of a company having "a degree of Canadian ownership and control," this being defined first as 25 percent or more. It was proposed in the same budget that the rate on dividends from companies not in this position, as well as the rate on branch profits, be increased to 20 percent. Neither of these increases was enacted, so that the general rates remained at 15 percent. With tax reform the general rate went to 25 percent. The reduction of 5 percent for dividends from a company having a degree of Canadian ownership and control was retained until November 1981, after which time it could be obtained only through a tax treaty. A typical arrangement, for example, is that under the new Canada-U.S. Convention. On Canada's side the general rate of withholding tax is reduced to 15 percent, but the rate on dividends going to the U.S. is reduced to 10 percent where the Canadian company is at least 10 percent U.S.-owned. Similarly the standard U.S. withholding rate of 30 percent is reduced to 15 percent, and a reduced rate of 10 percent applies where the U.S. company is at least 10 percent Canadian-owned. (In 1986 the U.S. unilaterally removed its 30 percent rate from portfolio investment, a treatment even better than that provided under the treaty).

Interest

The treatment of interest has been equally varied but has changed more frequently through statutory amendments than treaty revisions. Postwar, until 1966, interest payments in general were subject to a rate of 15 percent. In that year a major step was taken with the exemption of interest on new direct or guaranteed issues of bonds of all three levels of government and their agencies. By periodic renewal this exemption has remained in effect since, and was renewed for another three years on its expiry in 1986. A further important change was the exclusion of interest on corporate bonds having a term of five years or more and a limit on early redemptions issued at arm's length to non-residents after June 25, 1975. This exemption was renewed periodically, and at mid-1988 was in effect for bonds issued before 1989, and had been extended to bonds convertible into shares. Other exempt interest payments include those on residential mortgages on real estate outside Canada, foreign currency chartered bank deposits of a non-resident, extended in 1986 to deposits of other Canadian deposit-receiving institutions, Canadian currency deposits at foreign offices, interest on an arm's length business loan from a foreign lender, and interest paid to an organization exempt from tax in the foreign country.

Other Payments

In contrast to this growing list of interest exclusions withholding has been broadened to cover many new forms of payment. In 1968 royalty payments for patents, trademarks or designs, for industrial, commercial, or scientific equipment or for "know-how" were made taxable. Tax reform added further items, including nearly all forms of pensions (OAS excluded), retiring allowances, death benefits, unemployment insurance, and payments from an RRSP or profit-sharing plan. For some of these the government was authorized to reduce the withholding rate, presumably where it had not been given a lower rate under a treaty. After 1976 Canada and Quebec Pension Plan payments were exempt. Alimony and child support payments, patronage dividends, RHOSP payments, annuity payments in general, and payments for the use in Canada of a motion picture film, TV film, and video tape were added during the seventies.

The Canada-U.S. tax convention illustrates some typical modifications of these provisions. On royalties, Canada has reduced its 15 percent rate to 10 percent and on alimony and child support payments to zero; United States has reduced its withholding tax on social security payments from 7.5 percent to zero. Several other examples could be cited.

Treaties After Seven Decades

The development of the modern tax treaty has been traced from its origins in the League of Nations' efforts of the twenties, and it is evident that the early goal of a universal model for all countries has not been realized. For developed countries the OECD model has served very well, and is the basis for most current treaties. For developing countries, the new members on the international stage, there are shortcomings in the OECD, but its acceptance as a starting point for a version more to their liking was an acknowledgement of the progress it represented over previous efforts. The OECD final draft sufficiently clarified enough of the main concepts that a major impediment to treaty making was removed, or at least greatly reduced. The fact that it failed to meet the aspirations of all countries of the world is not surprising.

The United Nations Model Convention has met some of the objectives of the developing countries, and its main need now appears to be its more general adoption by industrial countries in their negotiations with developing countries.

Other International Tax Developments

Canada's economic welfare depends so heavily on its ability to export that almost any significant tax change that stimulates internal economic growth or, for that matter, any major change in the taxes in one of its foreign markets—in particular the United States—can have some influence on its international standing. By this test a great many more measures would have to be included than can be contemplated here. However there are a few items that deserve mention.

The U.S. DISC Measure

A major U.S. innovation of the seventies deeply disturbed not only Canada but many other countries as well. This was the measure to stimulate U.S. exports, known as the Domestic International Sales Corporation (DISC) introduced in 1971. Complex in detail, its purpose was to allow corporations to hive off their export income in a separate domestic corporation and obtain a tax advantage by doing so. This advantage took the form of deferral of tax on a portion of the DISC income. From 1976 the deferral applied to half the excess of the DISC income over the average of its previous four years. The amount of income equal to the average and the remaining half of the excess was taxable to the shareholders of the corporation in that year whether distributed or not. In effect an amount equal to two-thirds of the base period gross receipts was taxable in the year and tax on the other one-third was deferred until distributed.

This measure was designed to encourage U.S. manufacturers to continue to produce in the United States, and also to offset incentives being offered by other industrial countries. Canada's response, made in 1973, was to give a reduction of 6 percent in the corporate rate applicable to manufacturing profits, a step which, unlike the DISC, is still in effect.

Foreign Sales Corporation

The DISC provision was repealed and replaced in 1984 by the Foreign Sales Corporation, which requires establishment of a corporation in an approved area outside the United States, the income of which is partially exempt under certain conditions. This is a much less attractive measure than the DISC and has not been taken up to the same extent.

Unitary Taxation

A move of an opposite character was the adoption by a dozen or so U.S. states during the seventies of so-called unitary taxation. The essence of this practice was that for purposes of state corporate income tax the income of a corporation included not only its income from U.S. sources but as well the profits of all subsidiaries in foreign countries. This of course was attacked by many critics, both from the U.S. and other countries, as being extraterritorial taxation and beyond the powers of the states. The federal Secretary of the Treasury opposed it and appointed a Working Group to consider a solution. In Washington it was urged that federal legislation be passed to outlaw the practice. Under pressure states began to repeal their laws, led by Florida and Massachusetts in 1985, and after the introduction of federal legislation other states followed. By 1986 California, one of the leading proponents, had given up. Passage of federal nullification legislation ended the measures of the remaining three states.

The U.S. Netherlands Antilles Tax Treaty

Among Canadian treaty-watchers a cause of considerable distress was the revision of the U.S. Netherlands Antilles tax treaty to remove a feature that had served to give a fairly unobstructed passage for income flowing to Canada from the United States. This distress was alleviated somewhat by the reduction in the U.S. withholding tax to 10 percent in the 1984 revision of the Canada-U.S. treaty.

Assistance for Canadian Media

One of the dilemmas Canada faces from the close and over-powering presence of the United States is the preservation of some semblance of a Canadian culture. This has been particularly difficult in the publishing business, since the exposed Canadian border serves as an outlet for U.S. marginal production of books and periodicals. The Canadian market, one-tenth or less the size of the American, is fragile enough without this competition. Much the same situation holds for radio and television, but with a slightly different twist. Heavily dependent on advertising revenues, U.S. across-the-border stations have encouraged Canadian businesses, many of which are U.S. subsidiaries, to address their advertising to Canadian consumers from the U.S. rather than the Canadian side of the border. This is very potent competition for Canadian stations in close range of broadcasters in cities like Buffalo, Detroit, and Seattle, particularly as they carry many programs that are popular with Canadian viewers. The Canadian approach to these situations was typically pragmatic. Both problems were tackled through the tax system.

After a great deal of agonizing the federal government, instinctively pledged to free and open dissemination of knowledge, introduced a measure in 1965 to disallow advertising expenditures in a non-Canadian publication or periodical where the advertising was addressed primarily to a market in Canada. This measure lost most of its teeth with the exemption of its two principal targets, *Time* and *Readers' Digest*, for nearly the next decade. In 1977 this exemption was removed. At the same time a non-Canadian publication was defined as one having more than 20 percent of its contents the same as a foreign publication.

1977 also marked the beginning of similar treatment for expenditures on advertising through foreign broadcasters. After September 21, these were non-deductible if the advertising was directed primarily to a Canadian market. In 1979 the Minister of Communications was able to report that a study conducted by his department indicated that the tax change had "achieved one of its principal objectives in redirecting Canadian advertising expenditures to Canadian broadcasters . . ."

Neither of these measures was received with great joy south of the border. Protests, official as well as non-official, were strenuous, and there were threats of retaliation. The issue no doubt arose during the Canada-U.S. free trade negotiations, with the result that a discriminatory postal rate for U.S. periodicals was modified. Otherwise the protective measures remained in place.

International Cooperation in Tax Compliance

In addition to the usual exchanges of information and the process of appeals to the "competent authority" provided in the tax treaties, tax authorities in Canada and the United States have cooperated through joint examination of the accounts of multinational corporations and in several other ways. There have been less friendly Canadian reactions to U.S. requests, as part of anti-drug traffic enforcement, for confidential information from Canadian banks on the accounts of U.S. citizens in branches of Canadian banks abroad.

Bibliography, chapters 41 to 43

Arnold, Brian J. *The Taxation of Controlled Foreign Corporations: An International Comparison.* Canadian Tax Paper no. 78. Toronto: Canadian Tax Foundation, 1986.

———. "The Taxation of Controlled Foreign Corporations: Defining and Designating Tax Havens." (May-June 1985) 33 *Canadian Tax Journal,* 445-89.

———. "An Analysis of the Amendments to the FAPI and Foreign Affiliate Rules." (March-April 1983) 31 *Canadian Tax Journal,* 183-206.

Bird, Richard M., and Brean, Donald J.S. "Canada-U.S. Tax Relations: Issues and Perspectives." Paper presented at the Second Annual Workshop on U.S.-Canada Relations at the University of Western Ontario, November 18-19, 1983.

Bloch, Henry S., and Ecker-Racz, Laszlo. "International Tax Problems," In *Proceedings of the Forty-Second Annual Conference of the National Tax Association,* September 19-22, 1949. Sacramento, Calif.: the Association, 1950, 135.

Brean, Donald J.S. "International Portfolio Capital: The Wedge of the Withholding Tax." In *Proceedings* of the Administrative Sciences Association of Canada. Vancouver, 1983.

———. *International Issues in Taxation: The Canadian Perspective.* Canadian Tax Paper no. 75. Toronto: Canadian Tax Foundation, 1984.

Broadhurst, David G. "Recent Developments Here and There in Taxing International Income." International Tax Planning feature (March-April 1979) 27 *Canadian Tax Journal,* 201-05.

———. "The All New 1983 Foreign Affiliate Regulations-Part I." International Tax Planning feature (November-December 1982) 30 *Canadian Tax Journal,* 891-98.

———. "The All New 1983 Foreign Affiliate Regulations, Part II." International Tax Planning feature (January-Feburary 1983) 312 *Canadian Tax Journal,* 61-68.

———. "Revised Foreign Affiliate Regulations." International Tax Planning feature (March-April 1985) 33 *Canadian Tax Journal,* 344-52.

Brown, Robert D. "Canada's Expanding Tax Treaty Network and the Channelling of International Investments." International Tax Planning feature (November-December 1977) 25 *Canadian Tax Journal,* 637-43.

———. "Canada-U.S. Tax Issues: The Tax Treaty, Unitary Taxation and the Future." International Tax Planning feature (May-June 1984) 32 *Canadian Tax Journal,* 547-71.

Burge, Marianne, and Brown, Robert D. "Negotiations for a New Tax Treaty Between Canada and the United States—A Long Story." International Tax Planning feature (January-February 1979), 27 *Canadian Tax Journal,* 94-104.

Canada, *Report of the Royal Commission on Taxation,* vol. 4 Ottawa: Queen's Printer, 1967.

Canadian Tax Journal. Checklist: International Section. Each Issue.

Carroll, Mitchell B. "History of Movement to Remove Tax Barriers to International Trade." In *Report of Symposium on Tax Barriers to Trade* conducted by the Tax Institute, December 2-3, 1940. Philadelphia: Tax Institute, 1941, 205.

Coulombe, Gerard. "Certain Policy Aspects of Canadian Tax Treaties." In *Report of Proceedings of the Twenty-eighth Tax Conference*, 1976 Conference Report. Toronto: Canadian Tax Foundation, 1977, 290-303.

Dancey, K.J., Friesen, R.A., and Timbrell, D.Y. *Canadian Taxation of Foreign Affiliates*, 3rd ed. Toronto: CCH Canadian, 1982.

De la Giroday, Jean B., *Canadian Taxation and Foreign Investment*. Canadian Tax Paper no. 9. (Toronto: Canadian Tax Foundation, 1955).

Donner, Arthur, and Kliman, Mel. "The Effect of Section 19.1 of the Income Tax Act on Television Advertising." (November-December 1984) 32 *Canadian Tax Journal*, 1084-95.

"The Dutch Shell Game." *Forbes Magazine*, December 3, 1984.

Ehrenzweig, Alberta A., and Koch, F.E. *Income Tax Treaties*. Chicago: Commerce Clearing House, Inc., 1950.

Frisch, Daniel J. *Issues in the Taxation of Foreign Source Income*. National Bureau of Economic Research, Working Paper no. 798. November 1981.

Gibson, R.C. "Imputation Tax Systems in France, Italy, West Germany and the United Kingdom: Wave of the Future." International Tax Planning feature (May-June 1979) 3 *Canadian Tax Journal*, 347-59.

Herndon, John Goodwin. *Relief from International Income Taxation: The Development of International Reciprocity for the Prevention of Double Income Taxation*. Chicago: Callaghan, 1932.

Histrop, Lindsay Ann. "Taxation of Canadian Resident Athletes and Artists Performing in the United States." (November-December 1984) 32 *Canadian Tax Journal*, 1060-83.

Kyrouz, M.E. "Foreign Tax Rates and Bases." (March 1975), 28 *National Tax Journal*, 61-80.

Lang, Walter. "The Avoidance of International Double Taxation of Income." (November-December 1958) 6 *Canadian Tax Journal*, 447-52.

Lanthier, Allan R. "Liquidation of Foreign Affiliates Under Subsection 88(3)." (March-April 1985) 33 *Canadian Tax Journal*, 245-68.

Lazerow, Herbert I. *The OECD Draft Influence on United States Income Tax Treaties*. Amsterdam: International Bureau of Fiscal Documentation, 1976.

League of Nations. *Report Presented by the Committee of Technical Experts on Double Taxation and Tax Evasion*. Geneva: the Secretariat, 1927.

_____. *Double Taxation and Fiscal Evasion: Collection of International Agreements and Internal Legal Provisions for the Prevention of Double Taxation and Fiscal Evasion*. Geneva: the Secretariat, 1928.

_____. *Report of the General Meeting of Government Experts on Double Taxation and Fiscal Evasion*. Geneva: the Secretariat, 1928.

_____. *Taxation of Foreign and National Enterprises*. (5 volumes). Geneva: the Secretariat, 1933.

_____. Fiscal Committee. *Report of Work of the Tenth Session of the Committee*. London, March 20-26, 1946.

Litvak, Isaiah A., and Maule, Christopher J. "Canadian Multinational Media Firms and Canada-United States Relations." *Behind the Headlines* no. 5. Toronto: Canadian Institute of International Affairs. 1982,

McDaniel, Paul R., and Ault, Hugh J. *Introduction to United States International Taxation*. The Netherlands: Kluwer, Deventer, 1977.

McKie, A.B. "Tax Implications of International Banking." (February 1981) 88 The *Canadian Banker and ICB Review*, 34-39.

———. "Expatax." (September-October 1988) The *Canadian Banker*, 40-43.

Messere, K.C. "Capital Gains and Related Taxation in OECD Countries." In *Report of Proceedings of the Thirty-Second Tax Conference*, 1980 Conference Report. Toronto: Canadian Tax Foundation, 1981, 505-24.

Morgan, Vivien. "Unitary Taxation Update." International Tax Planning feature (March-April 1985) 33 *Canadian Tax Journal*, 352-59.

Musgrave, P.B. "Multijurisdictional Business Taxation." In *Report of Proceedings of the Thirty-First Tax Conference*, 1979 Conference Report. Toronto: Canadian Tax Foundation, 1980, 445-51.

Mutti, John, and Grubert, Harry. "Disc and its Effects." In Robert Baldwin and Anne Kreuger eds. *The Structure and Evaluation of Trade Policy*. Chicago: University of Chicago Press, 1983.

Norr, Martin. "Jurisdiction to Tax and International Income." (March 1962) 17 *Tax Law Review*, 431-62.

Organization for Economic Co-operation and Development. *Draft Double Taxation Convention on Income and Capital*. Report of the OECD Fiscal Committee. Paris: O.E.C.D., 1963.

———. *Model Double Taxation Convention on Income and on Capital*. Report of the O.E.C.D. Committee of Fiscal Affairs. Paris: O.E.C.D., 1977.

Organization for European Economic Co-operation. *The Elimination of Double Taxation*. Report of the Fiscal Committee of the O.E.E.C., 1958.

———. *The Elimination of Double Taxation*. 2nd Report of the Fiscal Committee of the O.E.E.C. Paris: O.E.E.C., 1959.

———. *The Elimination of Double Taxation*. 3rd Report of the Fiscal Committee of the O.E.E.C. Paris: O.E.E.C., 1960.

———. *The Elimination of Double Taxation*. 4th Report of the Fiscal Committee of the O.E.E.C. Paris: O.E.E.C., 1961.

Robertson, John R. "The Use of Tax Evasion and Tax Avoidance by Multinational Companies: A Canadian View." (September-October 1977) 25 *Canadian Tax Journal*, 513-27.

Schwartz, Alan M. "Tax Free Reorganizations of Foreign Affiliates." (November-December 1984) 32 *Canadian Tax Journal*, 1039-59.

Stikeman, H.R. "Taxation Law 1923-1947." 26th *Canadian Bar Review*, 1948.

Surrey, Stanley S. *United Nations Model Convention For Tax Treaties Between Developed and Developing Countries*. Amsterdam: International Bureau of Fiscal Documentation, 1980.

United Nations. Department of Economic Affairs, Fiscal Division. *International Tax Agreements, vol. 1*. New York: U.N., 1948.

———. *International Tax Agreements, vol. II*. New York: U.N., 1951.

———. *International Tax Agreements, vol. III. World Guide to International Tax Agreements, 1843-1951*. New York: U.N., 1951.

———. *International Tax Agreements, vol. IV*. New York: U.N., 1954.

———. *International Tax Agreements, vol. V. World Guide to International Tax Agreements*. New York: U.N., 1954.

————. Fiscal and Financial Branch. *International Tax Agreements, vol. VI.* New York: U.N., 1956.

————. Department of Economic and Social Affairs. *International Tax Agreements, vol. VII.* New York: U.N., 1958.

————. *Tax Treaties Between Developed and Developing Countries.* New York: U.N., 1st Report, 1969; 2nd Report, 1970; 3rd Report, 1972; 4th Report, 1973; 5th Report, 1975; 6th Report, 1976.

————. *Guidelines for Tax Treaties Between Developed and Developing Countries.* (U.N. Sales no. E. 74. XVI, 5.) New York: U.N. 1974.

United States. Treasury Department. *Model Income Tax Treaty.* Washington: 1981.

Ward, David A. "Principles to be Applied in Interpreting Tax Treaties." (May-June 1977) 25 *Canadian Tax Journal,* 263-70.

Index